CREATED EQUAL

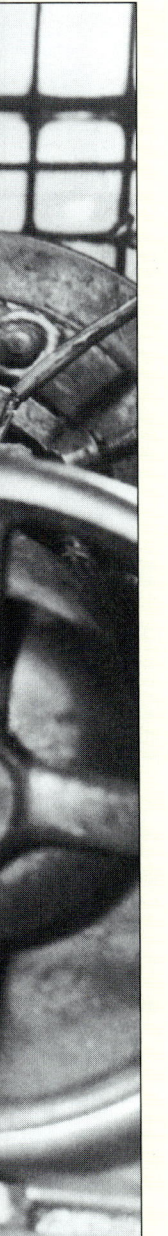

CREATED EQUAL

A SOCIAL AND POLITICAL HISTORY OF THE UNITED STATES

BRIEF SECOND EDITION

Jacqueline Jones
Brandeis University

Peter H. Wood
Duke University

Thomas Borstelmann
University of Nebraska

Elaine Tyler May
University of Minnesota

Vicki L. Ruiz
University of California, Irvine

PEARSON
Longman

New York San Francisco Boston
London Toronto Sydney Tokyo Singapore Madrid
Mexico City Munich Paris Cape Town Hong Kong Montreal

To our own teachers, who helped set us on the historian's path, and to our students, who help keep us there. You have touched our intellects, our hearts, and our lives.

A nuestros propios maestros, quienes nos ayudaron a seguir en el sendero de historiador, y a nuestros estudiantes que ayudan a mantenernos alli. Usted ha tocado nuestros intelectos, nuestros corazones, y nuestras vidas.

Executive Editor: Michael Boezi
Development Editor: Marion B. Castellucci
Assistant Development Manager: David Kear
Executive Marketing Manager: Sue Westmoreland
Supplements Editor: Brian Belardi
Production Manager: Ellen MacElree
Project Coordination, Text Design, and Electronic Page Makeup: Electronic Publishing Services Inc., NYC
Cover Design Manager: Wendy Ann Fredericks
Cover Designer: Base Art Co., Ltd.
Cover and frontispiece photos: ©SuperStock, Inc.
Photo Researcher: Photosearch, Inc.
Manufacturing Buyer: Lucy Hebard
Printer and Binder: Courier/Kendallville
Cover Printer: Coral Graphics

Credits for literary selections, selected maps and figures, and photos not credited on page appear on pages C-1 to C-4.

Library of Congress Cataloging-in-Publication Data
Created equal : a social and political history of the United States / Jacqueline Jones ... [et al.]. -- Brief 2nd ed.
    p. cm.
    Includes bibliographical references and index.
    ISBN-13: 978-0-321-42980-3 (Complete Edition)
    ISBN-10:   0-321-42980-X
1. United States--History. 2. United States--Social conditions. 3. United States--Politics and government. 4. Pluralism (Social sciences)--United States--History. 5. Minorities--United States--History. 6. Pluralism (Social sciences)--United States--History--Sources. 7. Minorities--United States--History--Sources.
E178.C86 2007
973--dc22

200610165

Copyright © 2008 by Pearson Education, Inc.

All rights reserved. No part of this publication may be reproduced, stored in a retrieval system, or transmitted, in any form or by any means, electronic, mechanical, photocopying, recording, or otherwise, without the prior written permission of the publisher. Printed in the United States.

Please visit our website at http://www.ablongman.com

ISBN-13: 978-0-321-42980-3 (Complete Edition)
ISBN-10:   0-321-42980-X
ISBN-13: 978-0-321-42981-0 (Volume I: To 1877)
ISBN-10:   0-321-42981-8
ISBN-13: 978-0-321-42979-7 (Volume II: From 1865)
ISBN-10:   0-321-42979-6

3 4 5 6 7 8 9 10—CRK—10 09 08 07

Brief Contents

Detailed Contents vi
Maps xvi
Figures and Tables xvii
Preface xviii
Meet the Authors xxv
Acknowledgments xxvii

PART ONE
North American Founders 2

1. First Founders 4
2. European Footholds in North America, 1600–1660 31
3. Controlling the Edges of the Continent, 1660–1715 55

PART TWO
A Century of Colonial Expansion to 1775 82

4. African Enslavement: The Terrible Transformation 84
5. An American Babel, 1713–1763 110
6. The Limits of Imperial Control, 1763–1775 137

PART THREE
The Unfinished Revolution, 1775–1803 162

7. Revolutionaries at War, 1775–1783 164
8. New Beginnings: The 1780s 191
9. Revolutionary Legacies, 1789–1803 216

PART FOUR
Expanding the Boundaries of Freedom and Slavery, 1803–1848 240

10. Defending and Expanding the New Nation, 1803–1818 242
11. Expanding Westward: Society and Politics in the "Age of the Common Man," 1819–1832 261
12. Peoples in Motion, 1832–1848 283

PART FIVE
Disunion and Reunion 308

13. The Crisis over Slavery, 1848–1860 310
14. "To Fight to Gain a Country": The Civil War 333
15. Consolidating a Triumphant Union, 1865–1877 356

PART SIX
The Emergence of Modern America, 1877–1900 380

16. Standardizing the Nation: Innovations in Technology, Business, and Culture, 1877–1890 382
17. Challenges to Government and Corporate Power, 1877–1890 403
18. Political and Cultural Conflict in a Decade of Depression and War: The 1890s 422

PART SEVEN
Reform at Home, Revolution Abroad, 1900–1929 444

19. The Promise and Perils of Progressive Reform, 1900–1912 446
20. War and Revolution, 1912–1920 466
21. The Promise of Consumer Culture: The 1920s 486

PART EIGHT
From Depression and War to World Power, 1929–1953 506

22. Hardship and Hope in the 1930s: The Great Depression 508
23. Global Conflict: World War II, 1937–1945 530
24. Cold War and Hot War, 1945–1953 550

PART NINE
The Cold War at Full Tide, 1953–1979 572

25. Domestic Dreams and Atomic Nightmares, 1953–1963 574
26. The Nation Divides: The Vietnam War and Social Conflict, 1964–1971 595
27. Reconsidering National Priorities, 1972–1979 615

PART TEN
Global Connections at Home and Abroad, 1979–2006 634

28. The Cold War Returns—and Ends, 1979–1991 636
29. Post–Cold War America, 1991–2000 655
30. A Global Nation for the New Millennium 676

Appendix A-1
Glossary G-0
Credits C-1
Index I-1

Detailed Contents

Maps xvi
Figures and Tables xvii
Preface xviii
Meet the Authors xxv
Acknowledgments xxvii

PART ONE
North American Founders 2

CHAPTER 1
First Founders 4

Ancient America 5
    The Question of Origins 5
    The Archaic World 6
    The Rise of Maize Agriculture 7

A Thousand Years of Change: 500 to 1500 8
    Valleys of the Sun: The Mesoamerican Empires 8
    The Anasazi: Chaco Canyon and Mesa Verde 10
    The Mississippians: Cahokia and Moundville 11

Linking the Continents 12
    Oceanic Travel: The Norse and the Chinese 13
    Portugal and the Beginnings of Globalization 13
    Looking for the Indies: Da Gama and Columbus 15
    In the Wake of Columbus: Competition and Exchange 16

Spain Enters the Americas 18
    The Devastation of the Indies 18
    The Spanish Conquest of the Aztec 19
    Magellan and Cortés Prompt New Searches 21
    Three New Views of North America 21

The Protestant Reformation Plays Out in America 23
    Reformation and Counter-Reformation in Europe 23
    Competing Powers Lay Claim to Florida 25
    The Background of English Expansion 27
    Lost Colony: The Roanoke Experience 27

Conclusion 28
Sites to Visit 29
For Further Reading 29

> ■ INTERPRETING HISTORY
> *"These Gods That We Worship Give Us Everything We Need"* 20

CHAPTER 2
European Footholds in North America, 1600–1660 31

Spain's Ocean-Spanning Reach 32
    Vizcaíno in California and Japan 32
    Oñate Creates a Spanish Foothold in the Southwest 33
    New Mexico Survives: New Flocks Among Old Pueblos 35
    Conversion and Rebellion in Spanish Florida 36

France and Holland: Overseas Competition for Spain 37
    The Founding of New France 37
    Competing for the Beaver Trade 38
    A Dutch Colony on the Hudson River 39
    "All Sorts of Nationalities": Diverse New Amsterdam 40

English Beginnings on the Atlantic Coast 41
    The Virginia Company and Jamestown 42
    "Starving Time" and Seeds of Representative Government 43
    Launching the Plymouth Colony 44

The Puritan Experiment 45
    Formation of the Massachusetts Bay Company 45
    "We Shall Be as a City upon a Hill" 46
    Dissenters: Roger Williams and Anne Hutchinson 48
    Expansion and Violence: The Pequot War 49

The Chesapeake Bay Colonies 50
    The Demise of the Virginia Company 50
    Maryland: The Catholic Refuge 51
    Tobacco Becomes a Way of Life 52

Conclusion 53
Sites to Visit 53
For Further Reading 54

> ■ INTERPRETING HISTORY
> *Anne Bradstreet: "The Tenth Muse, Lately Sprung Up in America"* 47

CHAPTER 3
Controlling the Edges of the Continent, 1660–1715 55

France and the American Interior 56
    The Rise of the Sun King 56
    Exploring the Mississippi Valley 57

King William's War in the Northeast 59
Founding the Louisiana Colony 60

The Spanish Empire on the Defensive 62
The Pueblo Revolt in New Mexico 62
Navajo and Spanish on the Southwestern Frontier 64
Borderland Conflict in Texas and Florida 65

England's American Empire Takes Shape 66
Monarchy Restored and Navigation Controlled 66
Dutch New Netherland Becomes New York 67
New Restoration Colonies: New Jersey, Pennsylvania, and Carolina 68

Bloodshed in the English Colonies: 1670–1690 70
Metacom's War in New England 70
Bacon's Rebellion in Virginia 71
The "Glorious Revolution" in England 73
The "Glorious Revolution" in America 73

Consequences of War and Growth: 1690–1715 75
Salem's Wartime Witch Hunt 75
The Uneven Costs of War 76
Storm Clouds in the South 77

Conclusion 78
Sites to Visit 80
For Further Reading 80

■ **INTERPRETING HISTORY**
"Marry or Do Not Marry" 61

PART TWO

A Century of Colonial Expansion to 1775 82

CHAPTER 4

African Enslavement: The Terrible Transformation 84

The Descent into Race Slavery 85
The Caribbean Precedent 85
Ominous Beginnings 86
Alternative Sources of Labor 87
The Fateful Transition 88

The Growth of Slave Labor Camps 88
Black Involvement in Bacon's Rebellion 89
The Rise of a Slaveholding Tidewater Elite 90
Closing the Vicious Circle in the Chesapeake 90

England Enters the Atlantic Slave Trade 91
The Slave Trade on the African Coast 91
The Middle Passage Experience 94
Saltwater Slaves Arrive in America 95

Survival in a Strange New Land 96
African Rice Growers in South Carolina 97

Patterns of Resistance 99
A Wave of Rebellion 100

The Transformation Completed 101
Voices of Dissent 101
Oglethorpe's Antislavery Experiment 104
The End of Equality in Georgia 105

Conclusion 107
Sites to Visit 108
For Further Reading 109

■ **INTERPRETING HISTORY**
"Releese Us out of This Cruell Bondegg" 103

CHAPTER 5

An American Babel, 1713–1763 110

New Cultures on the Western Plains 111
The Spread of the Horse 112
The Rise of the Comanche 113
The Expansion of the Sioux 113

Britain's Mainland Colonies: A New Abundance of People 115
Population Growth on the Home Front 116
"Packed Like Herrings": Arrivals from Abroad 116
Non-English Newcomers in the British Colonies 118

The Varied Economic Landscape 120
Sources of Gain in the Carolinas and Georgia 121
Chesapeake Bay's Tobacco Economy 123
New England Takes to the Sea 124
Economic Expansion in the Middle Colonies 125

Matters of Faith: The Great Awakening 125
Seeds of Religious Toleration 126
The Onset of the Great Awakening: Pietism and George Whitefield 127
"The Danger of an Unconverted Ministry" 128
The Consequences of the Great Awakening 129

The French Lose a North American Empire 129
Prospects and Problems Facing French Colonists 130
British Settlers Confront the Threat from France 131
An American Fight Becomes a Global Conflict 132
Quebec Taken and North America Refashioned 134

Conclusion 135
Sites to Visit 135
For Further Reading 136

■ **INTERPRETING HISTORY**
"Pastures Can Be Found Almost Everywhere": Joshua von Kocherthal Recruits Germans to Carolina 118

CHAPTER 6

The Limits of Imperial Control, 1763–1775   137

New Challenges to Spain's Expanded Empire   139
- Pacific Exploration, Hawaiian Contact   139
- The Russians Lay Claim to Alaska   140
- Spain Colonizes the California Coast   141

New Challenges to Britain's Expanded Empire   142
- Midwestern Lands and Pontiac's War for Indian Independence   143
- Grenville's Effort at Reform   144
- The Stamp Act Imposed   145
- The Stamp Act Resisted   145

"The Unconquerable Rage of the People"   148
- Power Corrupts: An English Framework for Revolution   148
- Americans Practice Vigilance and Restraint   149
- Rural Unrest: Tenant Farmers and Regulators   150

A Conspiracy of Corrupt Ministers?   152
- The Townshend Duties   152
- The Boston Massacre   153
- The *Gaspee* Affair   154

Launching a Revolution   155
- The Tempest over Tea   155
- The Intolerable Acts   156
- From Words to Action   157

Conclusion   159
Sites to Visit   160
For Further Reading   160

■ **INTERPRETING HISTORY**
"Squeezed and Oppressed": A 1768 Petition by 30 Regulators   151

PART THREE

The Unfinished Revolution, 1775–1803   162

CHAPTER 7

Revolutionaries at War, 1775–1783   164

"Things Are Now Come to That Crisis"   166
- The Second Continental Congress Takes Control   166
- "Liberty to Slaves"   167
- The Siege of Boston   168

Declaring Independence   168
- "Time to Part"   168
- The British Attack New York   169
- "Victory or Death": A Desperate Gamble Pays Off   172

The Struggle to Win French Support   174
- Breakdown in British Planning   174
- Saratoga Tips the Balance   176
- Forging an Alliance with France   176

Legitimate States, a Respectable Military   177
- The Articles of Confederation   178
- Creating State Constitutions   178
- Tensions in the Military Ranks   179
- Shaping a Diverse Army   180
- The War at Sea   181

The Long Road to Yorktown   182
- Indian Warfare and Frontier Outposts   182
- The Unpredictable War in the South   184
- The Final Campaign   186
- Winning the Peace   187

Conclusion   189
Sites to Visit   189
For Further Reading   190

■ **INTERPRETING HISTORY**
"Revoking Those Sacred Trusts Which Are Violated"   170

CHAPTER 8

New Beginnings: The 1780s   191

Beating Swords into Plowshares   193
- Will the Army Seize Control?   193
- The Society of the Cincinnati   195
- Renaming the Landscape   196
- An Independent Culture   196

Competing for Control of the Mississippi Valley   197
- Disputed Territory: The Old Southwest   198
- American Claims and Indian Resistance   199
- "We Are Now Masters": The Old Northwest   200
- The Northwest Ordinance of 1787   202

Debtor and Creditor, Taxpayer and Bondholder   203
- New Sources of Wealth   203
- "Tumults in New England"   205
- The Massachusetts Regulation   206

Drafting a New Constitution   207
- Philadelphia: A Gathering of Like-Minded Men   207
- Compromise and Consensus   208
- Questions of Representation   209
- Slavery: The Deepest Dilemma   210

Ratification and the Bill of Rights   211
- The Campaign for Ratification   211
- Dividing and Conquering the Anti-Federalists   212
- Adding a Bill of Rights   213

Conclusion   214

Sites to Visit 214
For Further Reading 215

> ■ INTERPRETING HISTORY
> *Demobilization: "Turned Adrift Like Old Worn-Out Horses"* 194

CHAPTER 9

Revolutionary Legacies, 1789–1803 216

Competing Political Visions in the New Nation 217
    Federalism and Democratic-Republicanism in Action 218
    Planting the Seeds of Industry 219
    The Whiskey Rebellion: A Tax Revolt in the Countryside 220
    Securing Peace Abroad, Suppressing Dissent at Home 220

People of Color: New Freedoms, New Struggles 223
    Blacks in the North 224
    Manumissions in the South 225

Continuity and Change in the West 226
    Indian Wars in the Great Lakes Region 227
    Indian Acculturation in the West 227
    Land Speculation and Slavery 228

Shifting Social Identities in the Post-Revolutionary Era 230
    Artisan-Politicians and the Plight of Post-Revolutionary Workers 231
    "Republican Mothers" and Other Well-Off Women 231
    A Loss of Political Influence: The Fate of Nonelite Women 233

The Election of 1800: Revolution or Reversal? 235
    The Enigmatic Thomas Jefferson 235
    Protecting and Expanding the National Interest: Jefferson's Administration to 1803 236

Conclusion 237
Sites to Visit 238
For Further Reading 238

> ■ INTERPRETING HISTORY
> *A Sailmaker Discusses "Means for the Preservation of Public Liberty" on the Fourth of July, 1797* 232

PART FOUR

Expanding the Boundaries of Freedom and Slavery, 1803–1848 240

CHAPTER 10

Defending and Expanding the New Nation, 1803–1818 242

The British Menace 244
    The Embargo of 1807 244
    On the Brink of War 245

The War of 1812 247
    Pushing North 247
    Fighting on Many Fronts 248
    An Uncertain Victory 250

The Era of "Good Feelings"? 251
    Praise and Respect for Veterans After the War 251
    A Thriving Economy 253
    Transformations in the Workplace 254
    The Market Revolution 254

The Rise of the Cotton Plantation Economy 255
    Regional Economies of the South 256
    Black Family Life and Labor 256
    Resistance to Slavery 258

Conclusion 259
Sites to Visit 259
For Further Reading 260

> ■ INTERPRETING HISTORY
> *Cherokee Women Petition Against Further Land Sales to Whites in 1817* 252

CHAPTER 11

Expanding Westward: Society and Politics in the "Age of the Common Man," 1819–1832 261

The Politics Behind Western Expansion 262
    The Missouri Compromise 263
    Ways West 264
    The Panic of 1819 and the Plight of Western Debtors 266
    The Monroe Doctrine 267
    Andrew Jackson's Rise to Power 268

Federal Authority and Its Opponents 269
    Judicial Federalism and the Limits of Law 270
    The "Tariff of Abominations" 271
    The "Monster Bank" 272

Real People in the "Age of the Common Man" 273
    Wards, Workers, and Warriors: Native Americans 273
    Slaves and Free People of Color 274
    The Legal and Economic Dependence of Women 276

Ties That Bound a Growing Population 278
    New Visions of Religious Faith 279
    Literate and Literary America 279

Conclusion 281
Sites to Visit 282
For Further Reading 282

■ **INTERPRETING HISTORY**
José Agustin de Escudero Describes New Mexico as a Land of Opportunity, 1827 276

CHAPTER 12

Peoples in Motion, 1832–1848   283

Mass Migrations   284
- Newcomers from Western Europe   285
- The Slave Trade   287
- Trails of Tears   287
- Migrants in the West   289
- New Places, New Identities   291

A Multitude of Voices in the National Political Arena   292
- Whigs, Workers, and the Panic of 1837   292
- Suppression of Antislavery Sentiment   293
- Nativists as a Political Force   295

Reform Impulses   297
- Public Education   297
- Alternative Visions of Social Life   299
- Networks of Reformers   299

The United States Extends Its Reach   300
- Global Trade   301
- The Lone Star Republic   301
- The Election of 1844   302
- War with Mexico   302

Conclusion   306

Sites to Visit   307

For Further Reading   307

■ **INTERPRETING HISTORY**
Senator John C. Calhoun Warns Against Incorporating Mexico into the United States   304

PART FIVE

Disunion and Reunion   308

CHAPTER 13

The Crisis over Slavery, 1848–1860   310

Regional Economies and Conflicts   311
- Native American Economies Transformed   312
- Land Conflicts in the Southwest   312
- Ethnic and Economic Diversity in the Midwest   313
- Regional Economies of the South   314
- A Free Labor Ideology in the North   315

Individualism vs Group Identity   316
- Putting into Practice Ideas of Social Inferiority   317
- "A Teeming Nation"—America in Literature   317
- Challenges to Individualism   319

The Paradox of Southern Political Power   321
- The Party System in Disarray   321
- The Compromise of 1850   322
- Expansionism and Political Upheaval   322
- The Republican Alliance   324

The Deepening Conflict over Slavery   325
- The Rising Tide of Violence   326
- The *Dred Scott* Decision   328
- The Lincoln-Douglas Debates   328
- Harpers Ferry and the Presidential Election of 1860   329

Conclusion   331

Sites to Visit   331

For Further Reading   332

■ **INTERPRETING HISTORY**
Professor Howe on the Subordination of Women   318

CHAPTER 14

"To Fight to Gain a Country": The Civil War   333

Mobilization for War, 1861–1862   335
- The Secession Impulse   335
- Preparing to Fight   337
- Barriers to Southern Mobilization   338
- Indians and Immigrants in the Service of the Confederacy   341

The Course of War, 1862–1864   341
- The Republicans' War   342
- The Ravages of War: The Summer of 1862   344
- The Emancipation Proclamation   345
- Persistent Obstacles to the Confederacy's Grand Strategy   345

The Other War: African American Struggles for Liberation   346
- Enemies Within the Confederacy   346
- The Ongoing Fight Against Prejudice in the North and South   347

Battle Fronts and Home Fronts in 1863   348
- Disaffection in the Confederacy   348
- The Tide Turns Against the South   349
- Civil Unrest in the North   350
- The Desperate South   350

The Prolonged Defeat of the Confederacy, 1864–1865   351
- White Men's "Hard War" Toward African Americans and Indians   351
- "Father Abraham"   352
- The Last Days of the Confederacy   352

Conclusion   354

Sites to Visit   354

For Further Reading   355

■ **INTERPRETING HISTORY**
A Virginia Slaveholder Objects to the Impressment of Slaves   338

CHAPTER 15
Consolidating a Triumphant Union, 1865–1877   356

The Struggle over the South   357
- Wartime Preludes to Postwar Policies   358
- Presidential Reconstruction, 1865–1867   358
- The Postbellum South's Labor Problem   363
- Building Free Communities   364
- Congressional Reconstruction: The Radicals' Plan   366

Claiming Territory for the Union   368
- Federal Military Campaigns Against Western Indians   368
- The Postwar Western Labor Problem   369
- Land Use in an Expanding Nation   371
- Buying Territory for the Union   372

The Republican Vision and Its Limits   373
- Postbellum Origins of the Woman Suffrage Movement   373
- Workers' Organizations   374
- Political Corruption and the Decline of Republican Idealism   376

Conclusion   378
Sites to Visit   378
For Further Reading   379

■ INTERPRETING HISTORY
A Southern Labor Contract   361

PART SIX
The Emergence of Modern America, 1877–1900   380

CHAPTER 16
Standardizing the Nation: Innovations in Technology, Business, and Culture, 1877–1890   382

The New Shape of Business   384
- New Systems and Machines—and Their Price   385
- Alterations in the Natural Environment   386
- Innovations in Financing and Organizing Business   387
- New Labor Supplies for a New Economy   389
- Efficient Machines, Efficient People   391

The Birth of a National Urban Culture   391
- Economic Sources of Urban Growth   392
- Building the Cities   393
- Local Government Gets Bigger   393

Thrills, Chills, and Bathtubs: The Emergence of Consumer Culture   394
- Shows as Spectacles   395
- Mass Merchandising as Spectacle   396

Defending the New Industrial Order   396
- The Contradictory Politics of Laissez-Faire   397
- Social Darwinism and the "Natural" State of Society   399

Conclusion   401
Sites to Visit   401
For Further Reading   401

■ INTERPRETING HISTORY
Andrew Carnegie and the "Gospel of Wealth"   400

CHAPTER 17
Challenges to Government and Corporate Power, 1877–1890   403

Resistance to Legal and Military Authority   404
- Chinese Lawsuits in California   405
- Blacks in the "New South"   406
- "Jim Crow" in the West   408
- The Ghost Dance on the High Plains   409

Revolt in the Workplace   411
- Trouble on the Farm   411
- Militancy in the Factories and Mines   412
- The Haymarket Bombing   414

Crosscurrents of Reform   416
- Transatlantic Networks of Reform   417
- The Goal of Indian Assimilation   417
- Women Reformers: "Beginning to Burst the Bonds"   419

Conclusion   420
Sites to Visit   420
For Further Reading   421

■ INTERPRETING HISTORY
"Albert Parsons's Plea for Anarchy"   415

CHAPTER 18
Political and Cultural Conflict in a Decade of Depression and War: The 1890s   422

Frontiers at Home, Lost and Found   423
- Claiming and Managing the Land   424
- The Tyranny of Racial Categories   425
- New Roles for Schools   427
- Connections Between Consciousness and Behavior   428

The Search for Alliances   429
- Class Conflict   429
- Demise of the Populists   432
- Barriers to a U.S. Workers' Political Movement   432
- Challenges to Traditional Gender Roles   433

American Imperialism   435
- Cultural Encounters with the Exotic   435
- Initial Imperialist Ventures   436

The Spanish-American-Cuban-Filipino War of 1898   437
Critics of Imperialism   440
Conclusion   441
Sites to Visit   442
For Further Reading   442

> ■ **INTERPRETING HISTORY**
> *Proceedings of the Congressional Committee on the Philippines*   440

PART SEVEN

Reform at Home, Revolution Abroad, 1900–1929   444

CHAPTER 19

The Promise and Perils of Progressive Reform, 1900–1912   446

Immigration: The Changing Face of the Nation   447
The Heartland: Land of Newcomers   449
The Southwest: Mexican Borderlands   449
Asian Immigration and the Impact of Exclusion   450
Newcomers from Southern and Eastern Europe   452

Work, Science, and Leisure   453
The Uses and Abuses of Science   453
Scientific Management and Mass Production   455
New Amusements   456
"Sex O'Clock in America"   456
Artists Respond to the New Era   457

Reformers and Radicals   458
Muckraking, Moral Reform, and Vice Crusades   458
Women's Suffrage   459
Radical Politics and the Labor Movement   460
Resistance to Racism   460

Expanding National Power   461
Theodore Roosevelt: The "Rough Rider" as President   461
Protecting and Preserving the Natural World   462
Expanding National Power Abroad   462
William Howard Taft: The One-Term Progressive   463

Conclusion   464
Sites to Visit   465
For Further Reading   465

> ■ **INTERPRETING HISTORY**
> *Defining Whiteness*   454

CHAPTER 20

War and Revolution, 1912–1920   466

A World in Upheaval   467
The Apex of European Conquest   467
Confronting Revolutions Abroad   468

Conflicts over Hierarchies at Home   470

The Great War and American Neutrality   471
"The One Great Nation at Peace"   472
Reform Priorities at Home   472
The Great Migration   474
Limits to American Neutrality   475

The United States Goes to War   475
The Logic of Belligerency   475
Mobilizing the Home Front   476
Ensuring Unity   477
The War in Europe   479

The Struggle to Win the Peace   480
Peacemaking and the Versailles Treaty   481
Waging Counterrevolution Abroad   482
The Red and Black Scares at Home   483

Conclusion   483
Sites to Visit   484
For Further Reading   484

> ■ **INTERPRETING HISTORY**
> *African American Women in the Great War*   478

CHAPTER 21

The Promise of Consumer Culture: The 1920s   486

The Business of Politics   487
Warren G. Harding: The Politics of Scandal   487
Calvin Coolidge: The Hands-Off President   488
Herbert Hoover: The Self-Made President   489

The Decline of Reform   489
Women's Rights After the Struggle for Suffrage   489
Prohibition: The Experiment That Failed   490
Reactionary Impulses   491
Marcus Garvey and the Persistence of Civil Rights Activism   492

Hollywood and Harlem: National Cultures in Black and White   493
Hollywood Comes of Age   493
The Harlem Renaissance   493
Radios and Autos: Transforming Leisure   495

Science on Trial   496
The Great Flood of 1927   496
The Triumph of Eugenics: *Buck v. Bell*   497
Science, Religion, and the Scopes Trial   498

Consumer Dreams and Nightmares   499
Marketing the Good Life   500
Writers and Critics   500
Poverty Amid Plenty   501
The Stock Market Crash   502

Conclusion   504
Sites to Visit   504

For Further Reading 505

■ **INTERPRETING HISTORY**
Mario Puzo, **The Fortunate Pilgrim** *503*

PART EIGHT

From Depression and War to World Power, 1929–1953 506

CHAPTER 22

Hardship and Hope in the 1930s: The Great Depression 508

The Great Depression 509
 Causes of the Crisis 509
 Surviving Hard Times 511
 Enduring Discrimination 512
 The Dust Bowl 512

Presidential Responses to the Depression 514
 Herbert Hoover: Tackling the Crisis 514
 Franklin Delano Roosevelt: The Pragmatist 515
 "Nothing to Fear but Fear Itself" 516

The New Deal 518
 The First Hundred Days 518
 Monumental Projects Transforming the Landscape 521
 Protest and Pressure from the Left and the Right 521
 The Second New Deal 522
 FDR's Second Term 524

A New Political Culture 526
 The Labor Movement 526
 The New Deal Coalition 527
 A New Americanism 527

Conclusion 528
Sites to Visit 529
For Further Reading 529

■ **INTERPRETING HISTORY**
Songs of the Great Depression *516*

CHAPTER 23

Global Conflict: World War II, 1937–1945 530

Mobilizing for War 531
 The Rise of Fascism 531
 Aggression in Europe and Asia 532
 The Great Debate: Americans Contemplate War 533

Pearl Harbor: The United States Enters the War 534
 December 7, 1941 534
 Japanese American Relocation 534
 Foreign Nationals in the United States 536
 Wartime Migrations 536

The Home Front 537
 Building Morale 538
 Home Front Workers, "Rosie the Riveter," and "Victory Girls" 538

Race and War 540
 The Holocaust 541
 Racial Tensions at Home 541
 Fighting for the "Double V" 543

Total War 543
 The War in Europe 544
 The War in the Pacific 545
 The End of the War 547

Conclusion 548
Sites to Visit 548
For Further Reading 549

■ **INTERPRETING HISTORY**
Zelda Webb Anderson "You Just Met One Who Does Not Know How to Cook" *542*

CHAPTER 24

Cold War and Hot War, 1945–1953 550

The Uncertainties of Victory 551
 Global Destruction 552
 Vacuums of Power 552
 Postwar Reconversion 553
 Contesting Racial Hierarchies 553
 Class Conflict 554

The Quest for Security 555
 Redefining National Security 555
 Conflict with the Soviet Union 555
 The Policy of Containment 556
 Colonialism and the Cold War 558
 The Impact of Nuclear Weapons 558

A Cold War Society 560
 Family Lives 560
 The Growth of the South and the West 561
 Harry Truman and the Limits of Liberal Reform 562
 The Cold War at Home 562
 Who Is a Loyal American? 563

The United States and Asia 565
 The Chinese Civil War 565
 The Creation of the National Security State 565
 At War in Korea 566

Conclusion 569
Sites to Visit 570
For Further Reading 570

■ **INTERPRETING HISTORY**
NSC-68 *567*

PART NINE
The Cold War at Full Tide, 1953–1979   572

CHAPTER 25
Domestic Dreams and Atomic Nightmares, 1953–1963   574

Cold War, Warm Hearth   575
- Consumer Spending and the Suburban Ideal   576
- Race, Class, and Domesticity   577
- Women: Back to the Future   578

The Civil Rights Movement   580
- *Brown v. Board of Education*   580
- White Resistance, Black Persistence   581
- Boycotts and Sit-Ins   581

The Eisenhower Years   583
- The Middle of the Road   583
- "What's Good for General Motors…"   584
- Eisenhower's Foreign Policy   584

Outsiders and Opposition   586
- Youth, Sex, and Rock 'n' Roll   587
- Rebellious Men   588
- Mobilizing for Peace and the Environment   589

The Kennedy Era   589
- Domestic Policy   591
- Foreign Policy   591
- A Year of Turning Points   592

Conclusion   593

Sites to Visit   594

For Further Reading   594

■ INTERPRETING HISTORY
Rachel Carson, Silent Spring   590

CHAPTER 26
The Nation Divides: The Vietnam War and Social Conflict, 1964–1971   595

Lyndon Johnson and the Apex of Liberalism   596
- The New President   596
- The Great Society: Fighting Poverty and Discrimination   597
- The Great Society: Improving the Quality of Life   598
- The Liberal Warren Court   599

Into War in Vietnam   599
- The Vietnamese Revolution and the United States   600
- Johnson's War   600
- Americans in Southeast Asia   601
- 1968: The Turning Point   602

The Movement   604
- From Civil Rights to Black Power   604
- The New Left and the Struggle Against the War   605
- Cultural Rebellion and the Counterculture   607
- Women's Liberation   608
- The Many Fronts of Liberation   609

The Conservative Response   610
- Backlashes   610
- The Turmoil of 1968 at Home   611
- The Nixon Administration   611
- Escalating and Deescalating in Vietnam   612

Conclusion   613

Sites to Visit   614

For Further Reading   614

■ INTERPRETING HISTORY
Martin Luther King Jr. and the Vietnam War   606

CHAPTER 27
Reconsidering National Priorities, 1972–1979   615

Twin Shocks: Détente and Watergate   616
- Triangular Diplomacy   616
- Scandal in the White House   617
- The Nation After Watergate   618

Discovering the Limits of the U.S. Economy   620
- The End of the Long Boom   620
- The Oil Embargo   621
- The Environmental Movement   622

Reshuffling Politics   623
- Congressional Power Reasserted   625
- "I Will Never Lie to You"   625
- Rise of a Peacemaker   626
- The War on Waste   627

Diffusing the Women's Movement   628
- The Meanings of Women's Liberation   628
- New Opportunities in Education, the Workplace, and Family Life   629
- Equality Under the Law   631
- Backlash   631

Conclusion   632

Sites to Visit   633

For Further Reading   633

■ INTERPRETING HISTORY
The Church Committee and CIA Covert Operations   624

PART TEN
Global Connections at Home and Abroad, 1979–2006   634

CHAPTER 28
The Cold War Returns—and Ends, 1979–1991   636

Anticommunism Revived   637
- Iran and Afghanistan   637

The Conservative Victory of 1980   638
Renewing the Cold War   639
Republican Rule at Home   640
"Reaganomics" and the Assault on Welfare   641
An Embattled Environment   642
A Society Divided   643
Cultural Conflict   645
The Rise of the Religious Right   645
Dissenters Push Back   647
The New Immigration   648
The End of the Cold War   649
From Cold War to Détente   649
The Iran-Contra Scandal   650
A Global Policeman?   651
Conclusion   653
Sites to Visit   653
For Further Reading   654

■ **INTERPRETING HISTORY**
Religion and Politics in the 1980s   646

CHAPTER 29
Post–Cold War America, 1991–2000   655
The Economy: Global and Domestic   656
The Post–Cold War Economy   657
The Widening Gap Between Rich and Poor   657
Labor Unions   659
Tolerance and Its Limits   659
"We Can All Get Along"   660
Values in Conflict   660
Courtroom Dramas   661
The Changing Face of Diversity   663
Violence and Danger   663
Domestic Terrorism   664
Kids Who Kill   664
A Healthy Nation?   665
The Clinton Presidency   666
Clinton: The New Democrat   666
Clinton's Domestic Agenda and the "Republican Revolution"   666
The Impeachment Crisis   667
The Nation and the World   668
Trade Agreements   668
Efforts at Peacemaking   669
Military Interventions and International Terrorism   670
The Contested Election of 2000   671
The Campaign, the Vote, and the Courts   672
The Aftermath   672
Legacies of Election 2000   673
Conclusion   674

Sites to Visit   674
For Further Reading   675

■ **INTERPRETING HISTORY**
Vermont Civil Union Law   662

CHAPTER 30
A Global Nation for the New Millennium   676
The George W. Bush Administration   677
The President and the War on Terrorism   678
Security and Politics at Home   678
The War in Iraq   679
The Election of 2004 and After   681
America's Place in a Global Economy   682
The Logic and Technology of Globalization   682
Free Trade and the Global Assembly Line   683
Who Benefits from Globalization?   684
The Stewardship of Natural Resources   685
Ecological Transformations in the Twentieth Century   685
Pollution   686
Environmentalism and Its Limitations   687
The Expansion of American Popular Culture Abroad   687
A Culture of Diversity and Entertainment   688
U.S. Influence Abroad Since the Cold War   688
Resistance to American Popular Culture   689
Identity in Contemporary America   691
Social Change and Abiding Discrimination   691
Still an Immigrant Society   692
Conclusion   693
Sites to Visit   694
For Further Reading   695

■ **INTERPRETING HISTORY**
The Slow Food Movement   690

Appendix   A-1
The Declaration of Independence   A-3
The Articles of Confederation   A-5
The Constitution of the United States of America   A-8
Amendments to the Constitution   A-13
Presidential Elections   A-17
Present Day United States   A-20
Present Day World   A-22

Glossary   G-0
Credits   C-1
Index   I-1

Maps

1.1 America Before Columbus   9
1.2 Opening New Ocean Pathways Around the Globe, 1420–1520   16
1.3 The Extent of European Exploration of North America by 1592   26
2.1 The Spanish Southwest in the Early Seventeenth Century   34
2.2 European and Native American Contact in the Northeast, 1600–1660   39
2.3 Cultures Meet on the Chesapeake   52
3.1 France in the American Interior, 1670–1720   58
3.2 Changes in the Southwest   63
3.3 Virginia and the Carolinas, c. 1710   79
4.1 Regions of the African Slave Trade in 1700   93
4.2 One Century in the Transatlantic Slave Trade (1700–1800): African Origins, European Carriers, American Destinations   96
4.3 Enslaved People Living in North America in 1750: Distribution by Colony, Percentage of Total Population   98
4.4 English-Spanish Competition and the Expansion of Slavery into Georgia   107
5.1 The Horse Frontier Meets the Gun Frontier, 1675–1750   114
5.2 Economic Regions of the British Colonies   122
5.3 The British Conquest of New France, 1754–1760   133
6.1 Spanish Exploration After 1760 and the Start of the California Missions   142
6.2 British North America, 1763–1766   147
6.3 British North America, April 1775   157
7.1 Britain at War: The Global Context, 1778–1783   166
7.2 The Revolutionary War in the North   175
7.3 The Revolutionary War in the West   183
7.4 The Revolutionary War in the South   185
8.1 The Spread of Smallpox Across North America, 1775–1782   192
8.2 Southern Land Debates After 1783   198
8.3 Settlers' Ohio, After 1785   203
9.1 The Northwest Territory   226
9.2 Western Land Claims of the States   229
10.1 Lewis and Clark   243
10.2 The Public Domain in 1810   246
10.3 The Northern Front, War of 1812   248
11.1 The Missouri Compromise   263
11.2 Principal Canals Built by 1860   264
11.3 Mexico's Far Northern Frontier in 1822   266
11.4 The Cherokee Nation After 1820   271
12.1 Western Trails   286
12.2 Indian Removal   288
12.3 The U.S.–Mexican War   303
13.1 Territorial Expansion in the Nineteenth Century   313
13.2 The Kansas-Nebraska Act, 1854   324
13.3 The Underground Railroad   327
14.1 Slavery in the United States, 1860   334
14.2 The Secession of Southern States, 1860–1861   336
14.3 Sherman's March to the Sea, 1864–1865   353
15.1 Radical Reconstruction   365
16.1 Agricultural Regions of the Midwest and Northeast   386
16.2 Population of Foreign-Born, by Region, 1880   390
17.1 Indian Lands Lost, 1850–1890   410
18.1 Indian Reservations, 1900   425
18.2 Manufacturing in the United States, 1900   430
18.3 The Spanish-American-Cuban-Filipino War of 1898   438
19.1 Foreign-Born Population, 1900   448
19.2 Areas Excluded from Immigration to the United States, 1882–1952   451
20.1 U.S. Interests and Interventions in the Caribbean Region, 1898–1939   469
20.2 World War I in Europe and the Western Front, 1918   479
20.3 Europe After World War I   481
21.1 The Mississippi River Flood of 1927   497
21.2 Americans on the Move, 1870s–1930s   501
22.1 Dust and Drought, 1931–1939   513
22.2 Areas Served by the Tennessee Valley Authority   519
23.1 The Internment of Japanese Americans During World War II   536
23.2 World War II in Europe   544
23.3 World War II in the Pacific   546
24.1 Europe Divided by the Cold War   557
24.2 The Korean War, 1950–1953   569
25.1 Major Events of the African American Civil Rights Movements, 1953–1963   582
25.2 Cold War Spheres of Influence, 1953–1963   586
26.1 Percentage of Population Living Below the Poverty Line, 1969 (by State)   598
26.2 The American War in Vietnam   603
27.1 Building Nuclear Power Plants   629
28.1 Trouble Spots in the Middle East, 1979–1993   639
28.2 The Soviet Bloc Dissolves   652
29.1 States With Large Numbers of Undocumented Immigrants, 1995   658
29.2 The Breakup of Former Yugoslavia   671
29.3 The Contested Election of 2000   673
Present Day United States   A-20
Present Day World   A-22

Figures and Tables

Figures

2.1 The Tough Choice to Start Over 49
4.1 Goods Traded in Africa 92
5.1 Comparison of Overall Population Structure by Gender and Age: British Mainland Colonies, 1760s, and United States, 2000 117
7.1 British Government Expenses on Armed Forces Throughout the World (in Millions of Pounds), 1775–1782 177
8.1 Concentration of Security Notes in the Hands of a Few: The Example of New Hampshire in 1785 206
19.1 Number of Immigrants Entering the United States, 1821–2000 450
21.1 Number of Immigrants and Countries of Origin, 1891–1920 and 1921–1940 492
21.2 Urban and Rural Population, 1890–1990 493
25.1 Marital Status of the U.S. Adult Population, 1900–2000 576
27.1 Imported Petroleum as Share of U.S. Petroleum Consumption 621
28.1 Unequal Distribution of Wealth and Income 644
29.1 Childhood Obesity Rates for Boys and Girls, Aged 6–17, 1960s and 1990s 665
30.1 Top Ten U.S. Trading Partners, 2005 685
30.2 Self-Described Religious Affiliation in the United States, 2000 691

Tables

9-1 The Election of 1796 222
9-2 The Election of 1800 235
10-1 The Election of 1804 244
10-2 The Election of 1808 245
10-3 The Election of 1812 247
10-4 The Election of 1816 251
11-1 The Election of 1820 267
11-2 The Election of 1824 268
11-3 The Election of 1828 269
11-4 The Election of 1832 272
12-1 The Election of 1836 292
12-2 The Election of 1840 295
12-3 The Election of 1844 302
13-1 The Election of 1848 321
13-2 The Election of 1852 322
13-3 The Election of 1856 325
13-4 The Election of 1860 330
14-1 The Election of 1864 352
15-1 The Election of 1868 367
15-2 Estimates of Railroad Crossties Used and Acres of Forest Cleared, 1870–1910 372
15-3 The Election of 1872 377
15-4 The Election of 1876 378
16-1 The Election of 1880 397
16-2 The Election of 1884 398
16-3 The Election of 1888 399
18-1 The Election of 1892 431
18-2 The Election of 1896 432
19-1 The Election of 1900 461
19-2 The Election of 1904 462
19-3 The Election of 1908 463
19-4 The Election of 1912 464
20-1 The Election of 1916 473
21-1 The Election of 1920 488
21-2 The Election of 1924 488
21-3 The Election of 1928 489
22-1 The Election of 1932 516
22-2 Key New Deal Legislation, 1933–1938 523
22-3 The Election of 1936 525
23-1 The Election of 1940 533
23-2 The Election of 1944 538
24-1 The Election of 1948 563
24-2 The Election of 1952 568
25-1 The Election of 1956 583
25-2 The Election of 1960 589
26-1 The Election of 1964 597
26-2 The Election of 1968 611
27-1 The Election of 1972 618
27-2 The Election of 1976 625
28-1 The Election of 1980 639
28-2 The Election of 1984 641
28-3 The Election of 1988 651
29-1 The Election of 1992 666
29-2 The Election of 1996 667
29-3 The Election of 2000 672
30-1 The Election of 2004 681

Preface

> *"We hold these truths to be self-evident: That all men are created equal; that they are endowed by their Creator with certain unalienable rights; that among these are life, liberty, and the pursuit of happiness. . . ."*

Ever since the Continental Congress approved the Declaration of Independence on July 4, 1776, the noble sentiments expressed in the document have inspired people in the United States and around the world. The Founding Fathers conceived of the new nation in what we today would consider narrow terms—as a political community of white men of property. Gradually, as the generations unfolded, diverse racial and ethnic groups, as well as women of all backgrounds, cited the Declaration in their struggle to achieve a more inclusive definition of American citizenship. American history is the story of various groups of men and women, all "created equal" in their common humanity, claiming an American identity for themselves.

In fact, American history consists of many stories—the story of territorial growth and expansion, the story of the rise of the middle class, the story of technological innovation and economic development, and the story of U.S. engagement with the wider world. *Created Equal* incorporates these traditional narratives into a new and fresh interpretation of American history, one that includes the stories of diverse groups of people and explores expanding notions of American identity. Not surprisingly, when we first published our overview, it took us more than a thousand pages to tell this dramatic story. But even as the first full-length edition of *Created Equal* rolled off the press, we knew that we wanted to tackle a shorter version. Our aim was not merely to lighten students' backpacks. Instead, we hoped to make this rich saga more accessible to a broad audience, so we published a brief edition several years ago. Since then we have revised the full edition, and we have now taken time to craft a second brief edition as well.

The Second Edition

This second brief edition of *Created Equal* retains and strengthens the basic structure of the original brief text—its organization, themes, and style. This edition covers key events during both administrations of President George W. Bush, adding new material in sections titled "The President and the War on Terrorism," "Security and Politics at Home," "The War in Iraq," and "The Election of 2004 and After." The second edition also includes substantial revisions that reflect the suggestions of the many instructors who used the first edition in their classrooms.

First-time users of the book told us that they appreciated the elements that make *Created Equal* unique. These elements include a strong chronological narrative emphasizing significant political developments throughout American history, the stories of individuals that enliven the narrative, and the intertwining of four themes: our rich social diversity, the changing natural environment, class and power relations, and ongoing globalization: the vital intersection of foreign and domestic affairs. We added new material related to all of these themes.

Several new features enhance the book's accessibility for students. At the request of instructors we have included an "Interpreting History" primary document feature in each chapter, and the new topics covered by these primary materials vary widely. For the eighteenth century, documents include a brochure recruiting German immigrants to Carolina (Chapter 5), a surprising Proclamation of Independence from 1776 (Chapter 7), and a candid discussion of demobilization by a Revolutionary War soldier (Chapter 8). Among the new texts for the nineteenth century are documents describing opportunities for sheep farming in New Mexico (Chapter 11), a Southern labor contract during Reconstruction (Chapter 15), and Congressional testimony regarding conduct of the 1898 War in the Philippines (Chapter 18). The new "Interpreting History" features for the twentieth century include songs of the Great Depression (Chapter 22), a provocative sermon by Martin Luther King Jr. concerning the Vietnam War (Chapter 26), and the views of two ministers on religion and politics in the 1980s (Chapter 28). We have added study questions with each document to encourage students to hone their critical thinking skills. Also, a glossary at the back of the book defines terms that are highlighted in the body of the text, providing a handy reference for students as they read.

Perhaps most important of all—since historical interpretation never stands still, and new research calls for deeper discussion—we have enlivened the narrative with fresh material in many chapters. Chapter 2, for example, concludes with a new section on dramatic changes in the early Chesapeake economy entitled "Tobacco Becomes a Way of Life," and Chapter 10 contains a new section on "The Market Revolution" of the early nineteenth century. The next five chapters (11-14) incorporate new material on such varied topics as the Erie Canal, the treatment of the insane, the role of immigrants in the Confederacy, and General Custer's defeat at the Little Big Horn. New opening vignettes concern industrialist Andrew Carnegie (Chapter 16) and the attacks of September 11, 2001 (Chapter 30).

Four Themes

We have chosen to highlight four significant themes that run throughout American history.

- **Diversity.** In considering the theme of diversity, we acknowledge that the formation of social identity is a central element of the American story. We examine how individual Americans have understood and identified themselves by gender, religion, region, income, race, and ethnicity, among other factors. Native Americans, African Americans, Spanish-speaking inhabitants of the Southwest, Chinese immigrants, members of the laboring classes, women of all groups—all of these people have played a major role in defining what it means to be an American. At the same time, diverse forms of identity are by no means fixed or static. For example, in the early twentieth century, a Russian immigrant garment worker on New York's Lower East Side might think of herself in any number of ways—as a Jew, an employee, a union member, a single woman, a resident of a thriving city—and these forms of identity might change over time, depending on the woman's circumstances.

- **Class and systems of power.** Socioeconomic class and power systems have shaped American society in profound ways, and an understanding of them is fundamental to understanding events in American history. Class and power structures take many forms. The institution of slavery denied people of African descent basic human freedoms. Class differences based on income and formal education mocked broader ideals of social equality. Some groups used the law to deny other groups the right to participate in the political system. Popular ideas related to alleged social differences and innate inferiority served to justify the treatment of certain groups as second-class citizens. U.S. military leaders launched military campaigns against vulnerable peoples within and outside the nation's borders. By the end of the nineteenth century, the United States boasted the largest and most comfortable middle class in the world—and yet the most substantial political and economic power was distributed among a relatively small contingent of white men. During the twentieth century, Americans dismantled the legal system of inequality that reduced blacks, women, and other groups to second-class citizenship. Nevertheless, a growing gap between the rich and poor continued to mock the notion of true equality.

- **Globalization.** The globalization of the United States' economy and society increased in recent decades. But as an immigrant nation and the modern world's superpower, America has long been engaged with the rest of the world. Since the earliest days of colonial settlement, Americans have traded goods, cultural practices, and ideas with peoples outside their borders. America's foreign and domestic relations have always been intertwined. After World War II, Americans' fears of communism and the Soviet Union exerted a profound effect upon the country's politics and society. In the wake of the terrorist attacks of September 11, 2001, all Americans were forced to confront the role of the United States in the larger world, with all the opportunities and dangers that role entailed.

- **Environment.** The role of the environment in American history has been significant. The physical landscape has profoundly shaped American society, and has in turn been shaped by it. The theme of the environment is key to understanding cultural, political, and economic developments. Many Native American groups shared a sense of oneness with the land; for them, the material and spiritual worlds were intimately related. In contrast, many European Americans saw the land as a means of making a living or making money, or as the source of valuable raw materials—in other words, as a thing to be bought, sold, and used. The vast richness of the American landscape has provoked violent conflict over the years, even as it has formed a key component in American wealth and power. We examine regional differences in all geographical areas—not just the eastern seaboard.

These four themes serve as the lenses through which we view the traditional narrative framework of American history. Readers of *Created Equal* will understand the major political developments that shaped the country's past, as well as the role of diverse groups in initiating and reacting to those developments. Chapter 13, for example, which focuses on the 1850s, includes a detailed account of the effects of the slavery crisis on Congress and the political party system, as well as a discussion of shifting group identities affecting Indians, Latinos, northern women, and enslaved and free blacks. Chapter 18, focusing on the 1890s, covers the rise of the Populist party and stirrings of American imperialism, as well as a discussion of barriers to a U.S. workers' political party and challenges to traditional gender roles. Thus, *Created Equal* builds upon the basic history that forms the foundation of most major textbooks and offers a rich and comprehensive look at the past by including the stories of all Americans.

Chronological Organization

One of the challenges in writing *Created Equal* has been to emphasize the way in which the four major themes come together and influence each other, affecting specific generations of Americans. Thus, the text is organized into ten parts, most of these covering a generation. Many textbooks organize discussions of immigrants, cities, the West, and foreign diplomacy (to name a few topics) into separate chapters that cover large time periods. In contrast, *Created Equal* integrates material related to a variety of topics within individual chapters. Although the text adheres to a chronological organization, it stresses coherent discussions of specific topics within that framework. This provides students with a richer understanding of events. Chapter 15, for example, which covers the dozen or so years after the end of the Civil War, deals with Reconstruction in the South, Indian wars on the High Plains, and the rise of the women's and labor movements, stressing the relationships among all these developments. To cite another example: many texts devote a chapter exclusively to America's post–World War II rise to global power; *Created Equal* integrates material related to that development in a series of six chapters that cover the period of 1945 to 2006. Each of these chapters illustrates the effects of dramatic world developments on American social relations and domestic policy on a decade-by-decade basis. This approach allows readers to appreciate the rich complexity of any particular time period and to understand that major events occur not in a vacuum, but in a larger social context.

Special Features

The book includes a number of features designed to make American history clear and engaging to the reader, and to encourage students to "do" history on their own. These features include:

- **Parts and timelines.** *Created Equal* consists of ten parts covering three chapters each. An opening section that lays out the basic themes of the period introduces each part. Each part opener also includes an illustrated timeline highlighting major events covered in the three chapters that follow.

- **Chapter introductory vignettes and conclusions.** Each chapter begins with a story that introduces the reader to groups and individuals representative of the themes developed in the chapter. Among the chapter introductory vignettes are the stories of a Norwegian immigrant woman in Wisconsin (Chapter 12), a group of runaway slaves accused of treason by Confederate authorities in wartime (Chapter 14), Spanish-speaking inhabitants of northern New Mexico struggling to retain their culture in the face of an onslaught of European American settlers (Chapter 17), and a Sioux Indian boy at a government boarding school (Chapter 18). At the end of each chapter, a concluding section sums up the chapter's themes and points the reader toward the next chapter.

- **Maps, charts, pullout quotes, and artifacts.** Illustrations—photographs, tables, pictures of objects from the time period, and figures—enhance the narrative. Large maps offer geographical detail and invite students to see the relationship between geography and history. Highlighted quotes help the reader grasp the chapter's major themes.

- **"Interpreting History."** Every chapter includes a boxed feature entitled "Interpreting History." Each full-page box consists of an intriguing primary document on a topic relevant to the chapter's themes. Through these documents, we hear the voices of a variety of Americans, such as an eighteenth-century Virginia slave, a council of Cherokee women, industrial titan Andrew Carnegie, and environmental activist Rachel Carson. We have added a brief introduction before each original text, and we have placed several questions at the end of the feature in order to guide study and prompt further discussion.

- **"Sites to Visit" and "For Further Reading."** At the end of each chapter is a list of "Sites to Visit," identifying sites on the World Wide Web relevant to the chapter and occasionally listing the location of important historical sites and landmarks as well. There is also a list of suggested works related to each section of the chapter. These features encourage students to follow up on major topics on their own—either on the computer or in the library.

- *New!* **MyHistoryLab Icons** Icons in the margins throughout the book identify additional materials on **MyHistoryLab.com**, Longman's premium Web site for U.S. history. Each icon indicates the type of resource—document, image, map, video, or audio—and is placed in context to relate directly to the chapter contents and themes.

- **Glossary.** The second edition includes a glossary of terms culled from the text and defined at the back of the book. Sample terms (out of several hundred) include pocket veto, aqueduct, canal locks, sit-down strike, antebellum, carpetbaggers, scalawags, vigilantes, and fatigue work. Glossary terms are highlighted in **boldface type** in the chapter text.

Combining Social and Political History

In designing this book, we have built upon a strong chronological foundation, emphasizing change over time. After all, it is important to understand events in their full contemporary context as they unfold. Within this logical and familiar chronological framework, the text offers a unique combination of social and political perspectives. *Created Equal* introduces students to recent scholarship in social history as well as providing a firm grounding in the traditional political narrative. In each period, from the distant past to the present day, we have interwoven the important political developments with the social and economic changes taking place throughout the country.

Along the way, we incorporate numerous groups and individuals who impelled, and experienced, the nation's most significant changes. Their stories, both familiar and unfamiliar, enliven the narrative and help to provide a more accurate, thorough, and compelling view of the American past. We hope that readers will gain an understanding of our country's social diversity but also learn about the power relations that have shaped our past—which groups have had influence and how they have maintained and wielded that influence. *Created Equal* tells the evolving saga of America in all its complexity. It is the story of a diverse and idealistic people—"created equal," yet struggling through generations to achieve true equality.

The Authors

Supplements For Qualified College Adopters

Instructor Supplements

- ***Instructor Resource Center*** This instructor-only resource allows you to browse and download book-specific instructor resources (see below) and to receive immediate access and instructions on installing course management content to your campus server. If you already have access to CourseCompass, you can log in to the IRC immediately using your existing login and password. Otherwise, please visit the Instructor Resource Center at www.ablongman.com/irc to register for access today.

- ***Instructor's Manual*** This book-specific supplement offers suggestions on how to generate lively class discussion and involve students in active learning, as well as a file of exam questions and lists of resources, including films, slides, photo collections, records, and audio cassettes. It was prepared by Yvonne Johnson of Central Missouri University and Nancy Zens of Central Oregon Community College. ISBN: 0-205-56251-5.

- ***Test Bank*** Prepared by David Rice of the University of Florida, this test bank contains more than 3,500 objective, conceptual, and essay questions. All questions are keyed to specific pages in *Created Equal*, Brief Edition. ISBN: 0-205-56248-5.

- ***TestGen-EQ Computerized Testing System*** This flexible, easy-to-master computerized test bank includes all of the items in the printed test bank. The software allows instructors to edit existing questions and to add their own items. Tests can be printed in several different formats and can include features such as graphs and tables. ISBN: 0-205-53007-9.

- ***Text-Specific Transparency Set*** A set of full-color transparencies showing maps from the comprehensive edition of *Created Equal*. The transparencies are available for download at www.ablongman.com/irc.

- ***PowerPoint Presentations*** These presentations prepared to accompany the comprehensive version of *Created Equal* may include key points and terms for a lecture on the chapter, as well as full-color slides of selected important maps, graphs, and charts within a particular chapter. The presentations are available for download at www.ablongman.com/irc.

- **History Digital Media Archive CD-ROM** This resource contains electronic images, interactive and static maps, and video clips. ISBN: 0-321-14976-9.

- **Visual Archives of American History, Updated Edition** Available on two CD-ROMs, this encyclopedic collection of instructor resources contains dozens of narrated vignettes and videos, as well as hundreds of photos and illustrations. ISBN: 0-321-18694-X.

- **Discovering American History Through Maps and Views Transparencies** This set of 140 full-color acetates contains an introduction to teaching history through maps and a detailed commentary on each transparency. Prepared by Gerald Danzer of the University of Illinois at Chicago, the collection includes pictorial maps, views, photos, urban plans, building diagrams, and works of art. The transparencies are available for download at www.ablongman.com/irc.

- **History Video Program** Qualified adopters are granted access to our list of over 250 videos for classroom use. Adopters can choose 1 video per 100 books that are ordered each semester (maximum of 3 for each adopter). Videos are available for virtually every topic of United States history.

- **Readers and Biographies—Available at Half Price!** Qualified adopters can choose from more than 100 half-priced options to supplement *Created Equal*, Brief Second Edition. From comprehensive readers and brief biographies to discounted Penguin books, Longman has a wide selection of products to broaden your students' history experience beyond the textbook. To learn more about this special offer, visit us at www.ablongman.com/historyvaluepacks.

Student Supplements

- **Voices of Created Equal** This collection of primary sources, tied to the table of contents of *Created Equal*, includes both classic and lesser-known documents describing the rich mosaic of American life from the pre-contact era to the present day. Ranging from letters, diary excerpts, stories, and novels, to speeches, court cases, and government reports, these sources tell the story of American history in the words of those who lived it. These titles are available at no additional cost when bundled with a *Created Equal* text. Volume I ISBN: 0-321-39591-3; Volume II ISBN: 0-321-39599-9.

- **Study Guide** Created by William Pelz of De Paul University, each volume includes chapter outlines, significant themes and highlights, a glossary, learning enrichment ideas, sample test questions, exercises for identification and interpretation, and geography exercises based on maps in the brief version of *Created Equal*. Volume I ISBN: 0-205-56249-3; Volume II ISBN: 0-205-56250-7.

- **Study Card for American History** Students are given a chronological context to understand important political, diplomatic, social, economical, cultural, and technological events in American history on this study card. This study card is available at no additional cost when valuepacked with a new book. ISBN: 0-321-29232-4.

- **Research Navigator™ Guide** This guidebook includes exercises and tips on how to use the Internet to further your study of American history. It also includes an access code for Research Navigator™—the easiest way for students to start a research assignment or research paper. Research Navigator™ is composed of three exclusive databases of credible and reliable source material including EBSCO's ContentSelect™ Academic Journal Database, *New York Times* Search by Subject Archive, and "Best of the Web" Link Library. This comprehensive site also includes a detailed help section. Also available on MyHistoryLab. ISBN: 0-205-40838-9.

- **Longman American History Atlas** A full-color reference tool and visual guide to American history that includes almost 100 maps and covers the full scope of history. The Atlas is $3.00 when bundled with a new book. ISBN: 0-321-00486-8.

- **Mapping American History, Third Edition** This two-volume workbook, written by Sharon Bollinger of El Paso Community College, presents the basic geography of the United States, helping students place the history of the United States into perspective. Available at no additional cost to qualified college adopters when bundled with a new book. Volume I ISBN: 0-321-47559-3; Volume II ISBN: 0-321-47560-7.

Supplements for Students and Instructors

- **MyHistoryLab** MyHistory Lab is a comprehensive collection of Longman's online multimedia resources. Instructive, intuitive, and interactive, MyHistoryLab allows both students and professors to be a few clicks away from a host of materials that support your American history survey course: primary sources; maps and illustrations; quizzes and review materials; and an electronic version of the textbook itself. MyHistoryLab gives students dozens of different avenues in which to learn, explore, and analyze the material outside of the classroom, no matter what type of learner they are. One-Semester Student Access Code Card ISBN: 0-205-53961-0; Two-Semester Student Access Code Card ISBN: 0-205-53956-4; Course Compass Student Access Code Card ISBN: 0-205-53960-2; BlackBoard WEB CT Student Access Code Card ISBN: 0-205-55039-8. Available for purchase at www.myhistorylab.com, or packaged at no additional charge with your textbook.

- **MyHistoryKit** MyHistoryKit for American history contains a sampling of Longman's premium history content from MHL. This Web site includes practice tests to challenge students' knowledge, learning objectives and chapter summaries introducing the major American history topics, flashcards for help with studying and remembering terms and events, Web links to assist in the research process, media and primary source activities (documents, maps, video and audio clips, and more), and Research Navigator™. Available for purchase at www.myhistorykit.com or packaged at no additional cost with your textbook.

- **American History Study Site** The American History Study Site is an open-access Web site that is designed to support all of Longman's American history survey titles. Organized by topic, this Web site includes practice tests to challenge students' knowledge, flashcards for help with studying and remembering terms and events, and Web links to assist in the research process.

Meet the Authors

Jacqueline Jones teaches American history at Brandeis University, where she is Harry S. Truman Professor. She was born in Christiana, Delaware, a small town of 400 people in the northern part of the state. The local public school was desegregated in 1955, when she was a third grader. That event, combined with the peculiar social etiquette of relations between blacks and whites in the town, sparked her interest in American history. She attended the University of Delaware in nearby Newark and went on to graduate school at the University of Wisconsin, Madison, where she received her Ph.D. in history. Her scholarly interests have evolved over time, focusing on American labor, and women's, African American, and southern history. In 1999 she received a MacArthur Fellowship. One of her biggest challenges has been to balance her responsibilities as teacher, historian, wife, and mother (of two daughters). She is currently working on a history of Savannah, Georgia, during the Civil War era (1854–1872). She is the author of several books, including *Soldiers of Light and Love: Northern Teachers and Georgia Blacks* (1980); *Labor of Love, Labor of Sorrow: Black Women, Work, and Family Since Slavery* (1985), which won the Bancroft Prize and was a finalist for a Pulitzer Prize; *The Dispossessed: America's Underclasses Since the Civil War* (1992); and *American Work: Four Centuries of Black and White Labor* (1998). In 2001 she completed a memoir that recounts her childhood in *Christiana: Creek Walking: Growing Up in Delaware in the 1950s.*

Peter H. Wood was born in St. Louis (before the famous arch was built). He recalls seeing Jackie Robinson play against the Cardinals, visiting the courthouse where the *Dred Scott* case originated, and traveling up the Mississippi to Hannibal, birthplace of Mark Twain. Summer work on the northern Great Lakes aroused his interest in Native American cultures, past and present. He studied at Harvard (B.A., 1964; Ph.D., 1972) and at Oxford, where he was a Rhodes Scholar (1964–1966). His pioneering book *Black Majority* (1974), concerning slavery in colonial South Carolina, won the Beveridge Prize of the American Historical Association. Since 1975 he has taught early American history at Duke University, where he also coached the women's lacrosse club for three years. The topics of his articles range from the French explorer LaSalle to Gerald Ford's pardon of Richard Nixon. In 1989 he coedited *Powhatan's Mantle: Indians in the Colonial Southeast.* His demographic essay in that volume (now in a new edition) provided the first clear picture of population change in the eighteenth-century South. His most recent books are *Strange New Land: Africans in Colonial America* (2003) and *Weathering the Storm: Inside Winslow Homer's "Gulf Stream"* (2004). Dr. Wood has served on the boards of the Highlander Center, Harvard University, Houston's Rothko Chapel, the Menil Foundation, and the Institute of Early American History and Culture in Williamsburg. He is married to colonial historian Elizabeth Fenn; his varied interests include archaeology, documentary film, and growing gourds. He keeps a baseball bat used by Ted Williams beside his desk.

Thomas ("Tim") Borstelmann, the son of a university psychologist, taught and coached at the elementary and high school levels in Washington state and Colorado before returning to graduate school. From 1991 to 2003, he taught American history at Cornell University while living in Syracuse, New York, before becoming the Elwood N. and Katherine Thompson Distinguished Professor of Modern World History at the University of Nebraska–Lincoln. He lives with his wife, a health care administrator, and two sons in Lincoln. An avid bicyclist, runner, swimmer, and cross-country skier, he earned his B.A. from Stanford University in 1980 and Ph.D. from Duke University in 1990. He became a historian to figure out the Cold War and American race relations, in part because he had grown up in the South. His first book, concerning American relations with southern Africa in the mid-twentieth century, won the Stuart L. Bernath Book Prize of the Society for Historians of Foreign Relations. His second book, *The Cold War and the Color Line,* appeared in 2001. His commitment to the classroom earned

him a major teaching award at Cornell, the Robert and Helen Appel Fellowship. He found writing *Created Equal* a natural complement to what he does in the classroom, trying to provide both telling details of the American past and the broad picture of how the United States has developed as it has. A specialist in U.S. foreign relations and modern world history, he is equally fascinated with domestic American politics and social change. He is currently working on a book about the United States and the world in the 1970s.

Elaine Tyler May grew up in the shadow of Hollywood, performing in neighborhood circuses with her friends. She went to high school before girls could play on sports teams, so she spent her after-school hours as a cheerleader and her summer days as a bodysurfing beach bum. Her passion for American history developed in college when she spent her junior year in Japan. The year was 1968. The Vietnam War was raging, along with turmoil at home. As an American in Asia, often called on to explain her nation's actions, she yearned for a deeper understanding of America's past and its place in the world. She returned home to study history at UCLA, where she earned her B.A., M.A., and Ph.D. She has taught at Princeton and Harvard Universities and since 1978 at the University of Minnesota. She has written four books examining the relationship between politics, public policy, and private life. Her widely acclaimed *Homeward Bound: American Families in the Cold War Era* was the first study to link the baby boom and suburbia to the politics of the Cold War. The *Chronicle of Higher Education* featured *Barren in the Promised Land: Childless Americans and the Pursuit of Happiness* as a pioneering study of the history of reproduction. *Lingua Franca* named her coedited volume *Here, There, and Everywhere: The Foreign Politics of American Popular Culture* a "Breakthrough Book." She served as president of the American Studies Association in 1996 and as Distinguished Fulbright Professor of American History in Dublin, Ireland, in 1997. She is married to historian Lary May and has three children, who have inherited their parents' passion for history.

Vicki L. Ruiz is a professor of history and Chicano/Latino studies at the University of California, Irvine. She is currently chair of the department of history. For her, history remains a grand adventure, one that she began at the kitchen table, listening to the stories of her mother and grandmother, and continued with the help of the local bookmobile. She read constantly as she sat on the dock, catching small fish ("grunts") to be used as bait on her father's fishing boat. As she grew older, she was promoted to working with her mother, selling tickets for the *Blue Sea II*. The first in her family to receive an advanced degree, she graduated from Gulf Coast Community College and Florida State University, then went on to earn a Ph.D. in history at Stanford in 1982, the fourth Mexican American woman to receive a doctorate in history. Her first book, *Cannery Women, Cannery Lives,* received an award from the National Women's Political Caucus, and her second, *From Out of the Shadows: Mexican Women in 20th-Century America,* was named a *Choice* Outstanding Academic Book of 1998 by the American Library Association. She is coeditor with Ellen Carol Dubois of *Unequal Sisters: A Multicultural Reader in U.S. Women's History.* She and Virginia Sánchez Korrol have also edited the three-volume *Latinas in the United States: A Historical Encyclopedia* and a recent anthology *Latina Legacies.* Ruiz and Sánchez Korrol were recognized by *Latina Magazine* as Latinas of the Year in Education for 2000 and in 2005 they received a "21 Leaders for the 21st Century" award by women's e-news network. In addition, she and Donna Gabaccia have completed the anthology *American Dreaming, Global Realities: Re-Thinking U.S. Immigration History.* Active in student mentorship projects, summer institutes for teachers, and public humanities programs, Dr. Ruiz served as an appointee to the National Council of the Humanities. A fellow in the Society of American Historians, she was elected to the national governing bodies of the American Historical Association, the Organization of American Historians, and the American Studies Association. Currently, she is immediate past president of both the Berkshire Conference of Women Historians and the Organization of American Historians. She is also the president-elect of the American Studies Association. The mother of two grown sons, she is married to Victor Becerra, urban planner and gourmet cook extraordinaire.

Acknowledgments

As authors, we could not have completed this project without the loving support of our families. We wish to thank Jeffrey Abramson, Lil Fenn, Lynn Borstelmann, Lary May, and Victor Becerra for their interest, forbearance, and encouragement over the course of several editions. Our own children have been a source of inspiration, as have our many students, past and present. We are grateful to scores of colleagues and friends who have helped shape this book, both directly and indirectly, in more ways than they know. Along the way, Matt Basso, Chad Cover, Eben Miller, Andrea Sachs, Mary Strunk, and Melissa Williams provided useful research and administrative assistance; their help was invaluable. Louis Balizet provided careful reading of several chapter drafts.

Our friends at Longman have continued their generous support and assistance for our efforts. We thank all the creative people associated with Longman (and there are many) who have had a hand in bringing this book to life. We are especially grateful to Michael Boezi and Marion Castellucci for their care and encouragement in bringing this edition to life. Former Development Manager Betty Slack improved the text in lasting ways; Executive Marketing Manager Sue Westmoreland and her great sales force have embraced the book with enthusiasm. We also acknowledge with gratitude the contributions of Managing Editor Val Zaborski, Production Manager Ellen MacElree, and Production Editor Scott Hitchcock and the staff at Electronic Publishing Services Inc. who put the finishing touches on this brief second edition and deftly guided it through the many phases of production.

Finally, we wish to express our deep gratitude to the following individuals who read and commented on the first brief edition. Their thoughtful criticism, advice, and suggestions have all helped improve the book: S. Carol Berg, *College of St. Benedict;* Roger Bromert, *Southwestern Oklahoma State University;* Charlotte Brooks, *State University of New York—Albany;* Eduardo Canedo, *Columbia University;* Nancy Carnevale, *Montclair State University;* John A. Collins, *Freed-Hardeman University;* Cole P. Dawson, *Warner Pacific College;* Barbara C. Fertig, *Armstrong Atlantic State University;* Van Forsyth, *Clark College;* Martin Hershock, *University of Michigan, Dearborn;* Richard Hughes, *Eastern Oregon University;* Kimberly Jensen, *Western Oregon University;* Cynthia M. Kennedy, *Clarion University of Pennsylvania;* Annette Laing, *Georgia Southern University;* Michael Lansing, *Augsburg College;* Carolyn J. Lawes, *Old Dominion University;* Sandy Moats, *University of Wisconsin—Parkside* ; Earl F. Mulderink, *Southern Utah University;* C. Samuel Nelson II, *Ridgewater College;* Jason C. Newman, *Cosumnes River College;* David R. Novak, *Purdue University;* Melissa Soto-Schwartz, *Cuyahoga Community College;* Deborah Syrdal, *Humboldt State University;* Michael M. Topp, *University of Texas, El Paso;* Sylvia Tyson, *Texas Lutheran University;* Mark D. Van Ells, *Queenborough Community College, CUNY;* David Voelker, *University of Wisconsin—Green Bay;* Charles Westmoreland, *University of Mississippi;* Julie Winch, *University of Massachusetts, Boston;* David Wolcott, *Miami University;* and Jason Young, *State University of New York, Buffalo*

This brief edition owes much to the many conscientious historians who reviewed the full-length edition of the textbook. For their insights and constructive critiques, we are indebted to the following reviewers.

Ken Adderley
Upper Iowa University

Leslie Alexander
Ohio State University

Marynita Anderson
Nassau Community College

John Andrew
Franklin and Marshall College

Abel Bartley
University of Akron

Donald Scott Barton
Central Carolina Technical College

Mia Bay
Rutgers University

Chris Bierwith
Treasure Valley Community College

Charles Bolton
University of Arkansas at Little Rock

Susan Burch
Gallaudet University

Tommy Bynum
Georgia Perimeter College

Robert B. Carey
Empire State College–SUNY

Todd Carney
Southern Oregon University

Kathleen Carter
Highpoint University

Jonathan Chu
University of Massachusetts

Barak Cook
University of Missouri

Amy E. Davis
University of California–Los Angeles

Judy DeMark
Northern Michigan University

James A. Denton
University of Colorado

Joseph A. Devine
Stephen F. Austin University

Margaret Dwight
North Carolina Agricultural and Technical University

Nancy Gabin
Purdue University

Lori Ginzberg
Pennsylvania State University

Gregory Goodwin
Bakersfield College

Amy S. Greenberg
Pennsylvania State University

Charlotte Haller
Worcester State College

Nadine Isitani Hata
El Camino College

James Hedtke
Cabrini College

Traci Hodgson
Chemeketa Community College

Rose Holz
University of Nebraska–Lincoln

Fred Hoxie
University of Illinois

Tera Hunter
Carnegie Mellon University

Creed Hyatt
Lehigh Carbon Community College

David Jaffe
City College of New York

Jeremy Johnson
Northwest College

Yvonne Johnson
Central Missouri State University

Kurt Keichtle
University of Wisconsin

Anne Klejment
University of St. Thomas

Dennis Kortheuer
California State University–Long Beach

Joel Kunze
Upper Iowa University

Joseph Laythe
Edinboro College of Pennsylvania

Chana Kai Lee
Indiana University

Dan Letwin
Pennsylvania State University

Gaylen Lewis
Bakersfield College

Kenneth Lipartito
Florida International University

Kyle Longley
Arizona State University

Edith L. Macdonald
University of Central Florida

Lorie Maltby
Henderson Community College

Sandra Mathews-Lamb
Nebraska Wesleyan University

Constance M. McGovern
Frostburg State University

Henry McKiven
University of South Alabama

James H. Merrell
Vassar College

Carl Moneyhan
University of Arkansas–Little Rock

Earl Mulderink
Southern Utah State University

Jason C. Newman
Consumnes River College

Steven Noll
University of Florida

Jim Norris
North Dakota State University

Elsa Nystrom
Kennesaw State University

Keith Pacholl
California State University–Fullerton

William Pelz
Elgin Community College

Melanie Perrault
University of Central Arkansas

Delores D. Petersen
Foothill College

Robert Pierce
Foothill College

Louis Potts
University of Missouri–Kansas City

Sarah Purcell
Central Michigan University

Niler Pyeatt
Wayland Baptist University

Steven Reschly
Truman State University

Arthur Robinson
Santa Rosa Junior College

Robert E. Rook
Fort Hays State University

Thomas J. Rowland
University of Wisconsin–Oshkosh

Steven Ruggles
University of Minnesota

Leonard J. Sadosky
Iowa State University

Rebecca Shoemaker
Indiana State University

Howard Shore
Columbia River High School

James Sidbury
University of Texas

Arwin D. Smallwood
Bradley University

Margaret Spratt
California University of Pennsylvania

Rachel Standish
Foothill College

Jon Stauff
St. Ambrose University

David Steigerwald
Ohio State University–Marion

Kay Stockbridge
Central Carolina Technical College

Daniel Thorp
Virginia Tech University

Michael M. Topp
University of Texas–El Paso

Clifford Trafzer
University of California–Riverside

Deborah Gray White
Rutgers University

Scott Wong
Williams College

Bill Woodward
Seattle Pacific University

Nancy Zens
Central Oregon Community College

David Zonderman
North Carolina State University

CREATED EQUAL

25,000 to 11,000 years ago
Low ocean levels expose land bridge linking Siberia to Alaska

14,000 years ago
Early Paleo-Indians inhabit sites in North and South America, including Monte Verde, Chile

13,900 to 12,900 years ago
Clovis hunters spread across North America

10,000 to 3,000 years ago
Archaic Indians flourish in diverse settings

4,200 to 2,700 years ago
Poverty Point culture exists in Louisiana

A.D. 300 to 900
Mayan culture flourishes in Mesoamerica

400
Polynesian explorers reach the Hawaiian Islands

500 to 600
Teotihuacan in central Mexico becomes one of the world's largest cities

900 to 1100
Anasazi culture centers in Chaco Canyon in Southwest

1000
Norse explorers establish a Vinland colony in Newfoundland

1100
Cahokia in Illinois becomes one focus of Mississippian culture

1250 to 1400
Mississippian culture reflected at Moundville in Alabama

1400
Aztec build capital at Tenochtitlán (site of modern Mexico City)

1405 to 1433
Chinese fleet of Admiral Zheng He reaches Indian Ocean and Africa's east coast

1418 to 1460
Prince Henry of Portugal sends ships to explore Africa's west coast

1492 First voyage of Columbus

1494 Treaty of Tordesillas arranges an equal division of the globe between competing overseas claims of Spain and Portugal

1497 to 1499 Vasco da Gama completes trading voyage from Portugal to India

1517 Martin Luther launches Protestant Reformation

1519 Cortés invades Mexico

PART ONE

North American Founders

W E SOMETIMES CALL THE FRAMERS OF THE U.S. CONSTITUTION America's Founding Fathers, using capital letters for emphasis. The men who met in Philadelphia in 1787 were indeed founders in a political sense, having drafted our enduring frame of government. But the 1780s seem recent in relation to most of North America's long human history. We must explore far back in time, long before the eighteenth century, to find the varied men and women who were the continent's first founders.

Two kinds of foundation builders emerge: the distant ancestors of today's Native Americans and newcomers from abroad who colonized North America in the sixteenth and seventeenth centuries.

Our earliest human ancestors evolved in Africa and then spread across the landmass of Eurasia. In the Southern Hemisphere, they managed to cross to Australia some 40,000 years ago, but evidence suggests that they reached the Americas from Asia much later, probably less than 20,000 years ago. These first human arrivals took advantage of the land bridge that joined Siberia to Alaska when Ice Age glaciers prompted a dramatic decline in sea levels. Roughly 14,000 years ago, these hunters apparently bypassed melting glaciers to reach the North American interior. They came on foot, but additional newcomers may have skirted the Pacific coast in small boats or even drifted across the South Pacific.

We still understand very little about these earliest Americans. What we do know is that they spread rapidly across North America over the next thousand years, and they continued to hunt mammoths and other large animals until these ancient species became extinct. Later, their descendants adapted to a wide range of different environments, learning to fish, hunt for smaller game, and gather berries. It has been 10,000 years since the extinction of the mammoths and 3,000 years since the early signs of agriculture in the Americas. By A.D. 500 complex societies were beginning to appear in equatorial America, and a succession of diverse and rich societies had arisen in the Americas by the time a second set of founders appeared around A.D. 1500.

Although Vikings from Scandinavia had preceded Christopher Columbus by five centuries, their small outpost on the coast of Newfoundland lasted only a few years. In contrast, when Columbus reached the West Indies and returned to Spain in 1492, his voyage launched a human and biological exchange between the Eastern and Western Hemispheres that has never ceased. Spanish and Portuguese ships initiated this exchange, but they were soon followed by vessels from England, France, and Holland. Half a century after Columbus's first voyage, Spanish overland expeditions had already pushed from Florida to Arkansas and from Mexico to Kansas. French explorers, hoping to find a Northwest Passage to Asia, had penetrated far up the St. Lawrence River in Canada.

Europeans brought new materials such as iron and new animals such as horses, cattle, and pigs. They also brought deadly diseases previously unknown in the Americas, such as measles and smallpox, which had a catastrophic impact on Native American societies. By 1565 Europeans had established their first lasting outpost in the North American continent, the town of St. Augustine in Spanish Florida. Two decades later the English tried, unsuccessfully, to plant a similar colony at Roanoke Island along the coast of what is now North Carolina.

In the first decades of the seventeenth century, permanent European settlements took hold at Quebec on the St. Lawrence River and at Santa Fe near the Rio Grande. A transatlantic outpost of English society appeared at Jamestown on Chesapeake Bay in 1607. Farther north, behind the sheltering hook of Cape Cod, other settlers formed additional coastal outposts and renamed the region New England.

Numbers were small at first, but these communities and others endured and expanded, often with crucial help from Native Americans who knew the keys to survival in their own domains. The gradual success of these European footholds prompted imitation and competition; colonizers clashed with each other and with longtime Indian inhabitants over control of the land and its resources. Disappointed in their early searches for easy mineral wealth, the new arrivals made do in various ways: cutting timber, catching fish, raising tobacco, or trading for furs. The French in particular, with aid once again from Native Americans, explored the interior of the continent. By 1700 they had laid claim to the entire Mississippi River valley and established a colony on the Gulf of Mexico.

Each new colonizing enterprise in the seventeenth century took on a distinctive life of its own—or, rather, numerous lives. First of all, there was the internal life of the community: who would be allowed to take part, how would participants govern themselves, and how would they subsist? In each instance, relations with the region's native inhabitants constituted a second unfolding story. Complicated ties to Europe—economic, religious, social, and political—made a third crucial narrative. Furthermore, relations between colonies and between the distant European powers that backed them had a determining influence, as when England took over the Dutch colony at New Netherland in the third quarter of the seventeenth century. Finally, there was the compelling drama of the newcomers' relationship to the environment itself. These founding generations labored to understand—or to subdue and exploit without fully understanding—the continent they had started to colonize.

1519 to 1522
Magellan's ship circumnavigates the globe and returns to Spain

1533 Pizarro overthrows Inca Empire in Peru

1534 to 1543
Expeditions of Cartier (Canada), de Soto (Southeast), and Coronado (Southwest) probe North America

1565 Spanish establish St. Augustine

1577 to 1580
Voyage of Drake challenges Spanish dominance in the Pacific

1585 to 1590
English attempt to establish Roanoke colony fails

1588 Spanish Armada fails in effort to invade England

1599 Spanish colonize New Mexico

1607 England's Virginia Company launches colony at Jamestown

1620 *Mayflower* passengers establish Plymouth Colony

1630 English Puritans found Massachusetts Bay Colony

1637 Pequot War in New England

1660 Restoration of monarchy in England under Charles II

1664 Charles II grants charter to his brother James, Duke of York, sanctioning the takeover of the Dutch New Netherland colony and the creation of New York

1675 to 1676
Metacom's War in New England

1676 Bacon's Rebellion in Virginia

1680 Pueblo Revolt in New Mexico

1681 Quaker William Penn receives charter for Pennsylvania

1682 La Salle explores the Mississippi River and claims Louisiana for France

1689 Dutch leader William of Orange and his wife Mary become joint English sovereigns in the Glorious Revolution, replacing King James II

1691 Witchcraft trials in Salem, Massachusetts

1699 Iberville begins colony in French Louisiana

1711 to 1715
Tuscarora Indians in North Carolina, and then the Yamasee in South Carolina, resist English colonial expansion

CHAPTER 1

First Founders

CHAPTER OUTLINE

Ancient America

A Thousand Years of Change: 500 to 1500

Linking the Continents

Spain Enters the Americas

The Protestant Reformation Plays Out in America

Conclusion

Sites to Visit

For Further Reading

One day in 1908, a cowboy named George McJunkin was checking fences on a cattle ranch near Folsom, New Mexico, when something strange caught his eye. McJunkin noticed several large bones protruding from the earth. Dismounting from his horse, he also spotted an old arrowhead, something common in these parts. But it was the bones beside it that seemed unusual. They were larger than cattle bones and buried under layers of dirt, so McJunkin decided to show them to others.

Nearly twenty years later, ancient-bones expert Jesse Figgins came to Folsom after seeing McJunkin's evidence. Soon Figgins unearthed an extensive bone bed containing the remains of twenty-three large Ice Age bison of a species that had been extinct for 10,000 years. He also uncovered a spear point, clearly fashioned by human hands, embedded between two bison ribs. Figgins's finds confirmed McJunkin's earlier discovery. The objects stirred first disbelief and then excitement, for they proved that human hunters had existed in North America 7,000 years earlier than scientists had supposed. The discovery of the thin projectile tips, named Folsom points after the site, sparked a revolution in North American archaeology.

■ In 1908 a discovery by African American cowboy George McJunkin started a revolution in American archaeology.

In 1908, the year of McJunkin's discovery, the nation still had a great deal to learn about the oldest chapters in American history. The United States had just commemorated the 300th anniversary of England's Jamestown settlement in Virginia, and across the country, U.S. citizens memorialized Anglo-American beginnings. Textbooks of the era paid scant attention to the earlier Spanish and French arrivals in North America and none at all to the Native American inhabitants who had preceded them by thousands of years.

In the century since George McJunkin picked up a prehistoric bison bone, all of that has changed. Scholars who explore and debate the long history of early North America have steadily learned more about the continent's first inhabitants. An expanding American history now stretches back in time far before the Jamestown settlement and reaches broadly from coast to coast. Its earliest roots lie with the indigenous inhabitants of the continent over many millennia. In addition, the foreigners who suddenly intruded into portions of the Native American world in the sixteenth century—speaking Spanish, French, and occasionally English—also represent a significant beginning. All these people now number, in different ways, among America's first founders.

Ancient America

The discoveries at Folsom more than doubled archaeologists' estimates of the time span that humans had lived in North America. Clearly, they had resided on the continent for at least 10,000 years.

After the Folsom find, collectors soon located additional evidence at nearby Clovis, New Mexico, 170 miles south of Folsom and close to the Texas border. In 1929 a teenager reported spotting large, well-chipped spearheads near Clovis. Three years later, amateur collectors located more in the same vicinity, this time beside the tooth of an extinct mammoth. These so-called Clovis points lay beneath a soil layer containing Folsom points, so they were clearly older than McJunkin's and Figgins's finds.

Since then, scientists have unearthed Clovis-like points throughout much of North America. According to the latest calculations, humans started creating these weapons roughly 13,900 years ago and ceased about 12,900 years ago. This means that people were hunting widely on the continent nearly 14,000 years ago. Archaeologists continue to push back and refine the estimated date for the appearance of the first people in the Americas. Recently, they have unearthed evidence suggesting the possible presence of pre-Clovis inhabitants.

The Question of Origins

Like all other peoples, the Native American societies whose ancestors have lived in America for at least 14,000 years retain rich and varied accounts of their own origins. No amount of scientific data can diminish or replace the powerful creation stories, in the Americas or elsewhere throughout the world, that have been passed down from distant ancestors and continue to serve an important cultural purpose. Nevertheless, modern researchers continue to compile evidence about the origin and migrations of the diverse peoples whom explorer Christopher Columbus mistakenly lumped together as "Indians" more than 500 years ago.

DOCUMENT
Iroquois Creation Story

Scientists have determined that it was scarcely 70,000 years ago when the most recent ancestors of modern humans moved from Africa to spread across the Eurasian landmass, the area comprising Europe and Asia. By 40,000 years ago some of these Stone Age hunter-gatherers had already reached Australia. Others lived on the steppes of central Asia and the frozen **tundra** of Siberia. They had perfected the tools they needed to survive in a cold climate: flint spear points for killing mammoths, reindeer, and the woolly rhinoceros; and bone needles to sew warm, waterproof clothes out of animal skin.

Over thousands of years, bands of these northern hunters migrated east across Siberia in search of game. Eventually they arrived at the region where the Bering Strait now separates Russia from Alaska. Between 25,000 and 11,000 years ago, cold conditions expanded arctic ice caps, trapping vast quantities of the earth's water in the form of huge **glaciers**. As a result, ocean levels sank by 300 feet—enough to expose a bridge of land 600 miles wide between Asia and America.

The Bering Land Bridge formed part of a frigid, windswept region known as Beringia. Small groups of people could have subsisted in this cold landscape by hunting mammoths

■ Archaeologists digging at Cactus Hill, Virginia, and several other sites have unearthed artifacts that suggest human habitation before the arrival of hunters using Clovis points. The foreground objects are laid out clockwise by apparent age, with the most recent at the top. Clovis-like spearheads appear in the second group. The third and fourth groups, taken from lower layers of soil, are thought to be older items, some reaching back well beyond 14,000 years. With the most primitive tools, it becomes difficult to separate implements made by humans from natural rock fragments.

and musk oxen until Ice Age glaciers receded about 14,000 years ago. As the climate warmed and the ocean rose again, some might have headed farther east onto higher ground in Alaska. If so, these newcomers would have been cut off permanently from Siberia as water once more submerged the land bridge. But the same warming process also eventually opened a pathway through the glaciers blanketing northern America.

Clovis Points

This ice-free corridor along the eastern slope of the Rocky Mountains could account for the sudden appearance of Clovis hunters across much of North America nearly 14,000 years ago. Small bands of people, armed with razor-sharp Clovis points, spread rapidly across the continent, destroying successive herds of large animals that had never faced human predators before. According to this theory, generations of hunters (known as **Paleo Indians**) could have migrated as far as the tip of South America within several thousand years.

In recent decades, three new developments have complicated the picture. At Cactus Hill, Virginia, and other sites, archaeologists have uncovered artifacts suggesting the presence of immediate predecessors to the Clovis people. In addition, a provocative discovery in South America—a campsite at Monte Verde, Chile, dating back more than 14,000 years—suggests to some that small groups may have used a coastal route around the North Pacific rim to reach the Americas by water. Meanwhile, genetic comparisons of different peoples, present and past, are yielding increasingly specific, if controversial, details about ancient migrations and interactions. Advances in understanding DNA—the genetic material that determines our physical make-up and transmits it to our offspring—may someday sharpen or change our awareness regarding the origins of the earliest Paleo-Indians.

Genetic comparisons of different peoples are yielding increasingly specific, if controversial, details about ancient migrations and interactions.

The Archaic World

Some 10,000 years ago, the Paleo-Indian period in North America gradually gave way to the **Archaic** period, which lasted for roughly 7,000 years. Major changes in wildlife played a large part in the transition. As the continent warmed further and the great glaciers receded north, more than 100 of America's largest species disappeared. These included mammoths, mastodons, horses, camels, and the great long-horned bison. Researchers debate whether these large animals were hunted to extinction, wiped out by disease, or destroyed by climate change.

Human groups had to adapt to the shifting conditions. They developed new methods of survival. Inhabitants turned to the smaller bison, similar to modern-day ones, that had managed to survive and flourish on the northern plains. Archaic-era hunters learned to drive herds over cliffs and use the remains for food, clothing, and tools. A weighted spear-throwing device, called an **atlatl**, let hunters bring down medium-sized game. Archaic peoples also devised nets, hooks, and snares for catching birds, fish, and small animals. By 4,000 years ago, they were even using duck decoys in the Great Basin of Utah and Nevada.

Though genetically similar, these far-flung bands of Archaic Indians developed diverse cultures as they adapted to very different landscapes and environments. Nothing illustrates this diversity more clearly than speech. A few early languages branched into numerous language families, then divided further into hundreds of separate tongues. Similar cultural variations emerged in everything from diet and shelter to folklore and spiritual beliefs.

The Rise of Maize Agriculture

One condition remained common to all the various Archaic American groups, despite their emerging regional differences: they all shared a lack of domesticated animals. Archaic Indians, like their Asian forebears, did possess dogs, and settlers in the Andes domesticated the llama over 5,000 years ago. But no mammal remaining in the Americas could readily be made to provide humans with milk, meat, hides, and hauling power.

Although their prospects for domesticating animals were severely limited, early Americans had many more options when it came to the domestication of plants. Humans managed to domesticate plants independently in five different areas around the world, and three of those regions were located in the Americas. First, across parts of South America, inhabitants learned to cultivate root crops of potatoes and manioc (also known as cassava, which yields a nutritious starch). Second, in **Mesoamerica** (modern-day Mexico and Central America), people gradually brought squash, beans, and maize (corn) under cultivation—three foods that complement one another effectively in dietary terms.

Maize agriculture became a crucial ingredient for the growth of complex societies in the Americas, but its development and diffusion took time. Unlike wheat, the Eurasian cereal crop which offered a high yield from the start, maize took thousands of years of cultivation in the Americas to evolve into an extremely productive food source. The differences between Mesoamerica and North America proved substantial when it came to mastering maize agriculture. Southwestern Indians in North America began growing thumb-sized ears of maize only about 3,000 years ago (at a time of increasing rainfall), well after the crop had taken hold in Mesoamerica. More than a thousand years later, maize reached eastern North America, where it adapted slowly to the cooler climate and shorter growing season.

In the east, a different agriculture had already taken hold, centered on other once-wild plants. This was the third zone where the independent domestication of plants occurred in the Americas. As early as 4,000 years ago, eastern Indians at dozens of Archaic sites were cultivating squash and sunflowers. These domesticated plants provided supplemental food sources for eastern communities that continued to subsist primarily by hunting and gathering until the arrival of maize agriculture in the eastern woodlands during the first millennium A.D.

About 3,000 years ago, as maize cultivation began in the Southwest and gardens of squash and sunflowers appeared in the Northeast, the first of several powerful Mesoamerican cultures—the Olmec—emerged in the lowlands along the southwestern edge of the Gulf of Mexico. Their name meant "those who live in the land of rubber," for they had learned how to turn the milky juice of several plants into an unusual elastic substance. The Olmec grew maize

> *Southwestern Indians in North America began growing thumb-sized ears of maize only about 3,000 years ago.*

and manioc in abundance, and their surplus of food supported a hierarchical society. They built large burial mounds and pyramids, revered the jaguar in their religion, developed a complex calendar, and played a distinctive game with a large ball of solid rubber. Since they traded widely with people across Mesoamerica, they passed on these cultural traits, which reappeared later in other societies in the region.

Olmec traders, traveling by coastal canoe, may even have encountered and influenced the Poverty Point culture that existed in northeast Louisiana 4,200 to 2,700 years ago. The Poverty Point culture, with a trade network on the lower Mississippi River and its tributaries, stands as a mysterious precursor to the mound-building societies of the Mississippi Valley that emerged much later. Remnants of these more extensive Mississippian cultures still existed when newcomers from Europe arrived to stay, around 1500. In many parts of North America, smaller and less stratified Archaic cultures remained intact well into the era of European colonization. To subsist, they combined hunting for a variety of animals with gathering and processing local plant foods.

A Thousand Years of Change: 500 to 1500

The millennium stretching from the fifth century to the explorations of Columbus in the fifteenth century witnessed dramatic and far-reaching changes in the separate world of the Americas. In the warm and temperate regions on both sides of the equator, empires rose and fell as maize agriculture and elaborate irrigation systems provided food surpluses, allowing the creation of cities and the emergence of hierarchical societies.

On the coast of Peru, the expansive Inca empire emerged in the 1400s, building on previous societies. Inca emperors, ruling from the capital at Cuzco, prompted the construction of a vast road system throughout the Peruvian Andes. Stonemasons built large storage facilities at provincial centers to hold food for garrisons of soldiers and to store tribute items such as gold and feathers destined for the capital. Until the empire's fall in the 1530s, officials leading pack trains of llamas ferried goods to and from Cuzco along mountainous roadways.

Similarly, Mesoamerica also saw a series of impressive civilizations—from the Maya to the Aztec—in the millennium spanning 500 to 1500 in the western calendar. Developments in North America in the same millennium were very different but bear enough resemblance to patterns in Mesoamerica to raise intriguing and still unanswerable questions. Did significant migrations northward from Mesoamerica ever take place? And if not, were there substantial trade links at times, allowing certain materials, techniques, ideas, and seeds to reach North American peoples? Or did the continent's distinctive societies, such as the Anasazi in the Southwest and the Cahokia mound builders on the Mississippi River, develop almost entirely independently?

Valleys of the Sun: The Mesoamerican Empires

Pre-Columbian Societies of the Americas

In Mesoamerica, the Maya and the Aztec established rich empires where worship of the sun was central to their religious beliefs. Mayan culture flourished between 300 and 900. The Maya controlled a domain stretching from the lowlands of the Yucatan peninsula to the highlands of what is now southern Mexico, Guatemala, Honduras, and El Salvador. They derived their elaborate calendar—a fifty-two-year cycle made up of twenty-day months—and many other aspects of their culture from the earlier Olmec, but they devised their own distinctive civilization. The Maya built huge stone temples and held ritual bloodletting ceremonies to appease their gods. Recently, researchers have deciphered the complex pictographs,

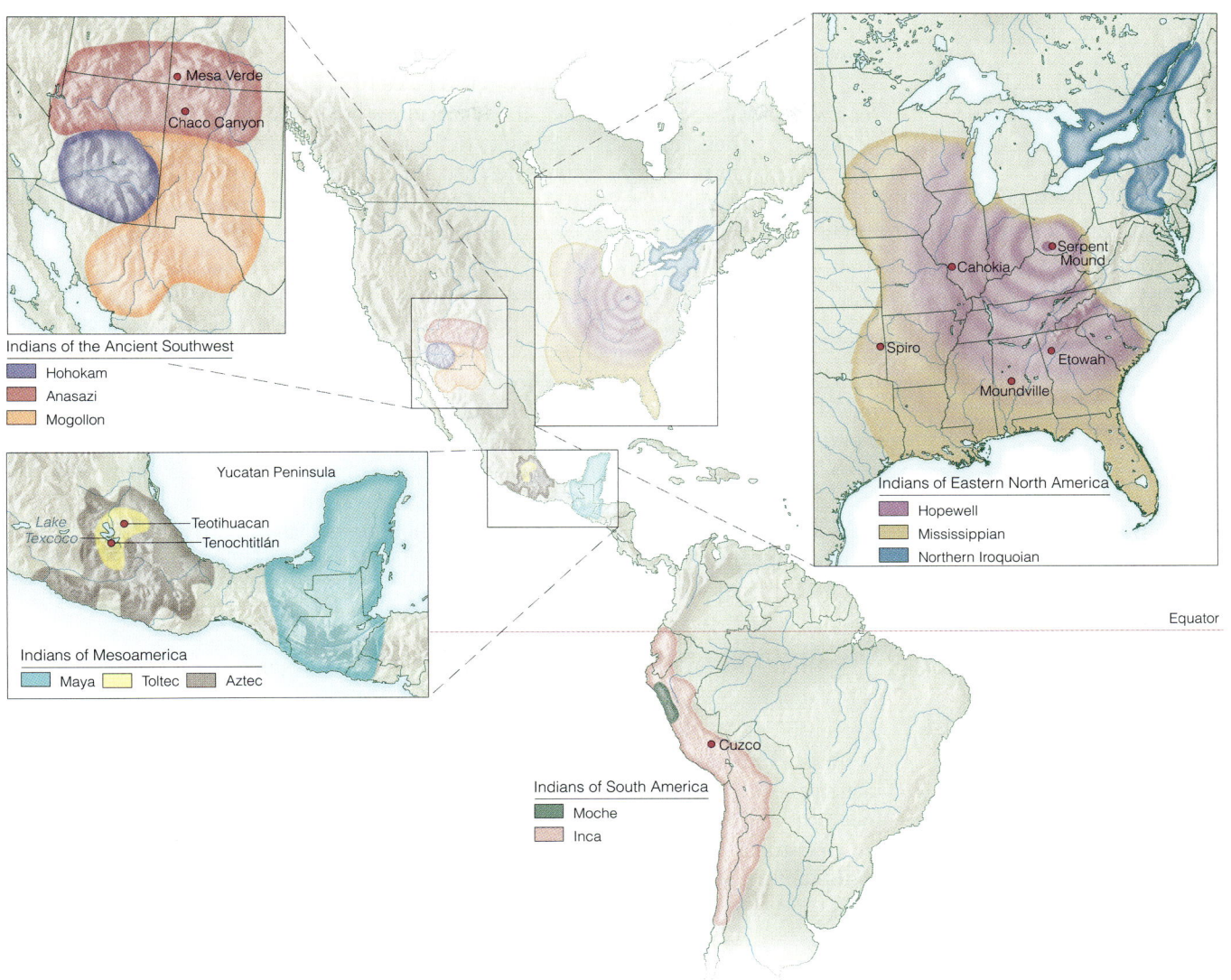

■ MAP 1.1
AMERICA BEFORE COLUMBUS   Distinctive cultures emerged in the Americas during the ten centuries before 1500. But debate continues over the extent of trade and travel networks at any given time.

or glyphs, that appear throughout Mayan art, yielding. New discoveries are pushing back the earliest dates for Mayan culture.

The Maya declined rapidly after 750, and dominance in Mesoamerica moved farther west, where great cities had arisen in central Mexico. The people who constructed the metropolis of Teotihuacan in the Mexican highlands remain an enigma. They appear to have traded with the Maya and perhaps with the Olmec before that. They laid out their immense city in a grid, dominated by the 200-foot Pyramid of the Sun. By 500, the city held more than 100,000 inhabitants, making it one of the largest in the world. But Teotihuacan's society declined fast, for unknown reasons, succeeded first by the Toltec and then by the Aztec.

The Aztec (or Mexica) had migrated to the central Valley of Mexico from the north in the twelfth century. Looked down upon at first by the local people, they swiftly rose to power through strategic alliances and military skill. According to legend, the Aztec's war god instructed their priests to locate the place where a great eagle perched on a cactus. They found such a spot, on a swampy island in Lake Texcoco. By the 1400s the Aztec had transformed the island into Tenochtitlán, an imposing urban center, located on the site of modern Mexico City.

The impressive city of Tenochtitlán, surrounded by Lake Texcoco and linked to shore by causeways, became the Aztec capital. Its architecture imitated the ruined temple city of Teotihuacan, which lay 35 miles to the north. The Aztec also adopted many other features of the cultures they had displaced. They used the cyclical fifty-two-year Mesoamerican calendar, and they worshipped the great god Quetzalcoatl, the plumed serpent associated with wind and revered by the Toltec, their predecessors in the Valley of Mexico.

Eager to expand their empire, the Aztec launched fierce wars against neighboring lands. But their primary objective was not to kill enemies or gain more territory. Instead, Aztec warriors demanded tribute and took prisoners from the people they subdued. They then sacrificed numerous captives at pyramid temples to **placate** the gods. These deities, they believed, would in turn protect them as they conducted further wars of capture, leading to more tribute and sacrifices.

Like the Inca of Peru, the Aztec imposed harsh treatment on the peoples they conquered, extracting heavy annual taxes. This ruthless policy caused outlying provinces to resent Aztec authority and made the centralized empire vulnerable to external attack. When a foreign assault prompted the empire's downfall in the early sixteenth century, the challenge came from a direction Aztec priests and generals could not predict.

> *Like the Inca of Peru, the Aztec imposed harsh treatment on the peoples they conquered, extracting heavy annual taxes.*

The Anasazi: Chaco Canyon and Mesa Verde

The great urban centers of Peru and Mesoamerica had no counterparts farther north. The peoples inhabiting North America in the millennium before Columbus never developed the levels of social stratification, urban dynamism, architectural grandeur, astronomical study, or intensive corn agriculture that characterized the Maya, Inca, or Aztec. Yet elements of all these traits appeared in North America, especially in the Southwest and the Mississippi Valley, with the emergence of increasingly settled societies and widening circles of exchange. Could north–south movements back and forth have occurred? Links of migration or trade would help to explain the dozens of ancient ball courts, similar to those in Mesoamerica, that archaeologists have excavated in Arizona. Recently, researchers have identified a north–south traffic in turquoise, highly prized in both Mexico and the Southwest.

Three identifiably different cultures were already well established in the North American Southwest by the year 500. The Mogollon occupied the dry, mountainous regions of eastern Arizona and southern New Mexico. Mogollon women were expert potters who crafted delicate bowls from the clay of the Mimbres River. Families lived in sunken pit houses that were cool in summer and warm in winter. The Hohokam, their neighbors to the west in south-central Arizona, constructed extensive canal and floodgate systems to irrigate their fields from the Gila and Salt rivers.

Farther north, where Utah and Colorado meet Arizona and New Mexico, lived the people remembered as the Anasazi, or "ancient ones." By 750 the Anasazi inhabited aboveground houses of masonry or adobe clustered around a circular ceremonial room dug into the earth. They entered this sunken religious chamber, known as a kiva, by descending a ladder through the roof. The climb back up symbolized the initial ascent of humans into the Upper World from below. European explorers later used the Spanish word for town, *pueblo*, to describe the Anasazis' multiroom and multistory dwellings.

Beginning in the 850s, Chaco Canyon in the San Juan River basin of northwest New Mexico emerged as the hub of the Anasazi world. Wide, straight roads radiating out from Chaco let builders haul hundreds of thousands of logs for use as roof beams in the nine great pueblos that still dot the canyon. The largest, Pueblo Bonito, rises five stories high in places and has 600 rooms arranged in a vast semicircle.

After 1130, a prolonged drought gripped the area, and the turquoise workshops of Chaco Canyon fell silent. Many of the inhabitants headed north, where dozens of Anasazi communities with access to better farming conditions dotted the landscape. Gradually—with populations growing, the climate worsening, and competition for resources stiffening—the Anasazi moved into sheltered cliff dwellings such as Cliff Palace at Mesa Verde in southwestern Colorado, with its 220 rooms and twenty-three kivas. Reached only by ladders and steep trails, these pueblos offered protection from enemies and shelter from the scorching summer sun. Still, another prolonged drought (1276–1299) forced the Anasazi to move once again by 1300. Survivors dispersed south into lands later occupied by the Hopi, Zuni, and Rio Grande peoples.

The Mississippians: Cahokia and Moundville

In the Mississippi Valley, the Hopewell people had prospered for half a millennium before A.D. 500 (during the era of Europe's Roman Empire). The Hopewell lived mainly in Ohio and Illinois. But their network of trade extended over much of the continent. Hopewell burial sites have yielded pipestone and flint from the Missouri River valley, copper and silver from Lake Superior, mica and quartz from Appalachia, seashells and shark teeth from Florida, and artwork made from Rocky Mountain obsidian and grizzly-bear teeth.

Hopewell trading laid the groundwork for larger mound-building societies, known as the Mississippian cultures, that emerged in the Mississippi Valley and the Southeast in roughly the same centuries as the great civilizations of Mesoamerica and the Anasazi in the Southwest. The Mississippian tradition developed gradually after 500. Then after 900, it flourished broadly for six centuries.

Shifts in technology and agriculture facilitated the rise of the Mississippians. Bows and arrows, long used in arctic regions of North America but little known elsewhere, began to see widespread use in the eastern woodlands around 700. At the same time, maize underwent a transformation from a marginal oddity to a central staple crop. Across the east, food supplies expanded as Native American communities planted corn in the rich bottomland soil along the region's many rivers. With greater productivity, commercial and religious elites took advantage of farmers and asserted stronger control over the community's increasing resources.

Separate Mississippian mound-building centers have been found as far apart as Spiro, in eastern Oklahoma, and Etowah, in northern Georgia. The largest complex was at Cahokia in the 25-mile floodplain below where the Illinois and Missouri rivers flow into the Mississippi. On Cahokia Creek, near East St. Louis, Illinois, dozens of rectangular, flat-topped temple mounds still remain after almost a thousand years. The largest mound—indeed, the largest ancient earthwork in North America—rises 100 feet in four separate levels, covering 16 acres and using nearly 22 million cubic feet of earth. Nearby, residents erected forty-eight posts in a huge circle, 410 feet in diameter. This creation, now called Woodhenge after England's Stonehenge, functioned as a calendar to mark the progression of the sun throughout each year.

IMAGE
Reconstructed View of Cahokia

Cahokia's mounds rose quickly in the decades after 1050, as the local population expanded beyond 10,000. A succession of powerful leaders reorganized the vicinity's small, isolated villages into a strong regional chiefdom that controlled towns on both sides of the Mississippi River. These towns provided the chiefdom's centralized elite with food, labor, and goods for trading. Around 1100, the population of Cahokia perhaps exceeded 15,000 people. It then waned steadily over the next two centuries as the unstable hierarchy lost its sway over nearby villages. As Cahokia declined, other regional chiefdoms rose along other rivers. The most notable appeared at Moundville in west-central Alabama, 15 miles south of modern Tuscaloosa. The site, with more than twenty flat-topped mounds, became a dominant ceremonial center in the thirteenth century. But by 1400, a century before the appearance of Europeans, Moundville's Mississippian elites had started to lose their power.

■ The most striking Mississippian earthwork to survive is the enigmatic Serpent Mound, built in the eleventh century by the Fort Ancient people in southern Ohio. The snake (holding an egg in its mouth) has links to astronomy because its curves are aligned toward key positions of the sun. The serpent may even represent Halley's Comet, which blazed in the heavens in A.D. 1066. Completely uncoiled, the earthwork would measure more than a quarter mile in length.

Linking the Continents

Estimates vary widely, but probably around one-sixth of the world's population—as many as 60 to 70 million people—resided in the Americas when Columbus arrived in 1492. Most of them lived in the tropical zone near the equator, but roughly one-tenth of the hemisphere's population (6 to 7 million) dwelt in North America, spread from coast to coast.

We cannot rule out the appearance in America of ancient ocean travelers on occasion. Around 400, Polynesian mariners sailed their double-hulled canoes from the Marquesas Islands in the South Pacific to the Hawaiian **archipelago**. Conceivably, in the millennium before 1500, one or two boats from Africa, Ireland, Polynesia, China, or Japan sailed—or were blown—to the American mainland. But any survivors of such a journey would have had little genetic or cultural impact, for no sustained back-and-forth contact between the societies occurred. Even the seafaring Norse from Scandinavia, known as Vikings, never established a lasting colony. Their brief settlement at L'Anse aux Meadows a thousand years ago is now well documented, but they remained only a few years at this coastal site in northern Newfoundland. Native American societies, therefore, knew nothing of the people, plants, animals, and microbes of the Eastern Hemisphere.

America's near isolation ended dramatically, beginning in the late fifteenth century, after innovations in deep-sea sailing opened the world's oceans as a new frontier for human exploration. Chinese sailors in the North Pacific or Portuguese mariners in the South Atlantic could well have been the first outsiders to establish ongoing contact with the peoples of the Western Hemisphere. Instead, it was Christopher Columbus, an Italian navigator in the service of Spain, who became the agent of this sweeping change. He encountered the Americas by accident and misinterpreted what he had found. But his chance encounter with a separate realm would spark new patterns of human migration, cultural transfer, and ecological exchange that would reshape the modern world.

Oceanic Travel: The Norse and the Chinese

Scandinavian settlers had colonized Ireland in the 830s and Iceland in the 870s. A century later, these seafarers—led by Erik the Red—reached Greenland in the 980s. When Erik's son Leif learned that Norse mariners blown off course had sighted land farther west, he sailed from Greenland to the North American coast. Here he explored a region near the Gulf of St. Lawrence that he named Vinland.

Around 1000, Leif Eriksson's relatives directed several return voyages to Vinland, where Norse Vikings built an outpost. The tiny colony of 160 people, including women and children, lived and grazed livestock in Vinland for several years until native peoples drove them away. The Greenlanders returned occasionally to cut timber, and they traded with inhabitants of northeastern Canada for generations. But by 1450 Norse settlements in Greenland had died out completely.

Whether sailors in Europe knew much about Norse exploits in the North Atlantic remains a mystery. What Europeans did know, vaguely, was the existence of the distant Chinese Empire. They called the realm Cathay, a term used by Italian merchant Marco Polo, who journeyed from Venice across Asia along the fabled Silk Road in the 1270s. Polo returned to Italy in 1292 to publish his *Travels*, an account of adventures in China during the reign of Kublai Khan.

Marco Polo told of many things unknown to Europeans, including rocks that burned like wood (coal) and spices that preserved meat. Asian spices such as nutmeg, cinnamon, pepper, ginger, and cloves, if they could be obtained, would offer new preservatives. When renewed Islamic power in the Middle East cut off the Silk Road to Cathay, Europeans searched for other ways to reach that far-off region.

The desire to obtain oriental spices at their source fueled European oceanic exploration, leading eventually to the transformation of the Americas. Yet it was China, not Europe, that first mastered ocean sailing on a large scale. Chinese strength in overseas exploration and trade reached its height in the early fifteenth century under Admiral Zheng He (pronounced "Jung Huh"). Between 1405 and 1433, this brilliant officer led seven large fleets to the Indian Ocean, sailing as far as east Africa. His immense treasure ships, 400 feet long and equipped with cannon, carried strange items—even giraffes—home to Asia.

Then, abruptly, China turned away from the sea, losing its opportunity to become the first global maritime power and to play a leading role in shaping oceanic trade and the destiny of North America. Within a century of Zheng He's accomplishments, the royal court grew dismissive of foreign trade and turned inward. Chinese officials destroyed the log books of earlier voyages and curtailed production of oceangoing vessels. Instead of powerful China on the Pacific, it was tiny Portugal, overlooking the Atlantic from the Iberian peninsula, that emerged as the leader in maritime innovation and exploration in the fifteenth century.

Portugal and the Beginnings of Globalization

Geography and religious zeal helped to spur Portugal's unlikely rise to world prominence. Its strategic location also exposed the tiny country to the ongoing conflict between Christianity and Islam. The religion founded by Muhammad (born at Mecca in 570) had spread rapidly across North Africa from Arabia. By the eighth century, followers of Islam (known as Muslims, Moslems, or Moors) had crossed the Straits of Gibraltar to establish a kingdom

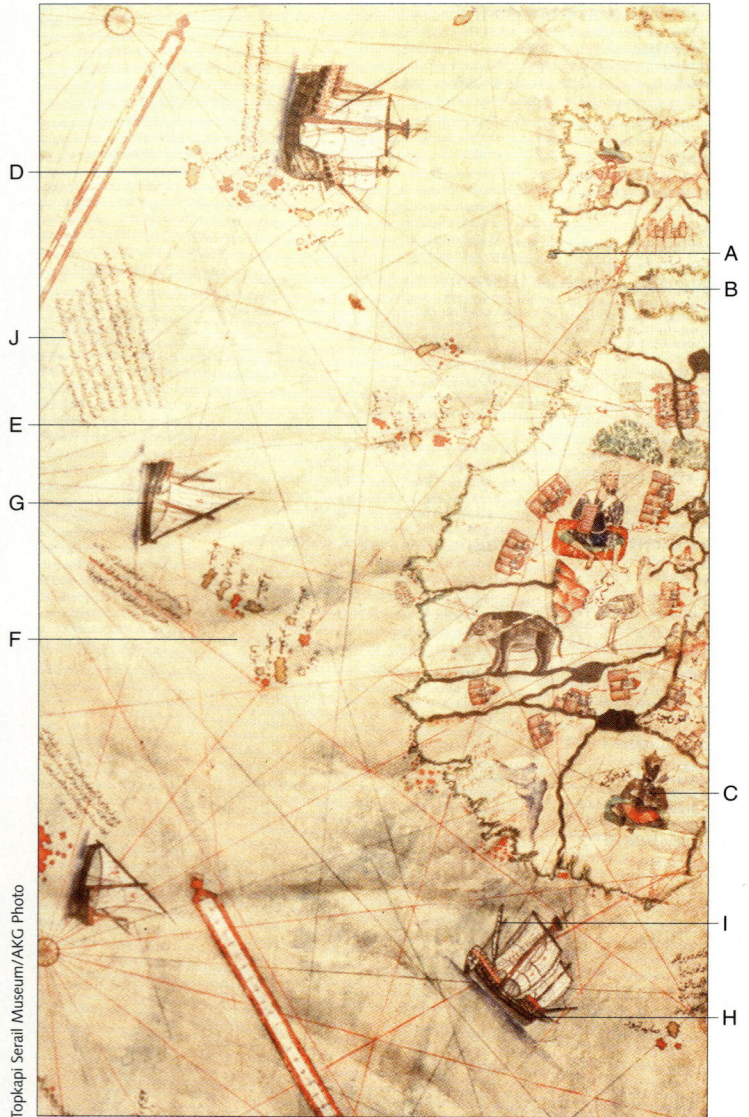

This Atlantic chart illustrates key aspects of Portuguese success in overseas exploration. Cape St. Vincent (A) where Prince Henry built his headquarters at Sagres, lies near the Strait of Gibraltar (B), the narrow entrance to the Mediterranean Sea. As Henry's mariners explored along the African coast for a sea passage to Asia, they also looked for possible allies such as Prester John, a mythical black king (C). They used the island groups of the eastern Atlantic to check their position: Azores (D), Madeiras (E), Canaries (F). Their small caravels (G) adopted the triangular lateen sail seen on traditional Arab boats in the Red Sea. Larger square-rigged ships that later sailed from Portugal to India (H) also incorporated lateen sails on a mast at the stern (I). A skilled Turkish navigator—who had never sailed on the Atlantic—made this unusual map in 1513. Piri Re'is used charts captured from a Christian ship in the Mediterranean; his inscriptions (J) are in Turkish.

in southern Spain. Centuries later, Spanish and Portuguese Christians rallied to force Islam out of the Iberian peninsula—a campaign that concluded in 1492—and to join other militant Europeans in fighting against Islamic power in the Middle East.

When Christian crusades to the holy land failed to defeat Islam and reopen overland trade routes to China, European strategists dreamed of skirting Africa by sea to reach Asia. The Portuguese were well positioned to lead this flanking movement around the areas under Muslim control. And if no such oceanic route to Asia existed, some speculated that Portuguese exploration south by sea still might provide links to a strong Christian ally. Fanciful rumors persisted regarding a wealthy black Christian ruler somewhere in Africa known as Prester John.

Intellectual and economic motives also existed for Portuguese ventures beyond the Sahara Desert, along the coast of sub-Saharan Africa. Such journeys, presenting new challenges in shipbuilding and navigation, could boost European knowledge of the unknown and open new markets. The first step involved an investment of leadership and resources, before early efforts could bear fruit and give the exploration process a momentum of it own.

Prince Henry of Portugal (1394–1460) provided these initial ingredients. In 1415 the young prince—later honored as "Henry the Navigator"—had crossed the Straits of Gibraltar to fight Muslims at Ceuta in North Africa. Committed to the campaign against Islam, Henry then waged a religiously inspired crusade-at-sea, building his headquarters at Sagres in southwest Portugal. From there, his sailors launched a far-reaching revolution in human communication and trade, perhaps the most momentous single step in a globalization process that continues to the present day.

Henry's innovative ships, known as caravels, pushed south along the African coast. Their narrow hulls were well suited for ocean sailing, and they used triangular lateen sails, an idea that Mediterranean sailors had borrowed from Arab boats on the Red Sea. The lateen sail let a vessel travel into the breeze, tacking back and forth on a zigzag course against a prevailing wind. (Vessels carryng only traditional square sails could not do this, making their voyages longer and more difficult.) Henry's experts at Sagres drew on the work of Jewish cartographers to develop state-of-the-art charts, astronomical tables, and navigational instruments. By the 1440s, his captains had mastered the winds and currents off western Africa. They began trading in gold and ivory, and, most ominously, they began buying African slaves and selling them in Europe. But when Henry died in 1460, his mariners had only sailed as far as what is now Sierra Leone.

Looking for the Indies: Da Gama and Columbus

During the 1480s, following a war with Spain, the Portuguese renewed their African designs. In 1482 they erected a trading fort called Elmina Castle on the Gold Coast (modern Ghana) to guard against Spanish competition and to support exploration toward the east. Finally, in 1487, Bartolomeu Dias rounded the southernmost tip of Africa, around the Cape of Good Hope, proving that a link existed between the Atlantic and Indian oceans. The Portuguese could now sail to India and tap into the rich spice trade. Success came a decade later with the voyage of Vasco da Gama (1497–1499). When his ship returned to Portugal from India laden with pepper and cinnamon, Europeans realized they had finally opened a southeastern sea route to the silk and spice markets of the East.

Meanwhile, the rulers of rival Spain, who were reconquering their realm from Muslim control at great expense, gambled on finding a profitable *westward* route to the Indies. In 1492, King Ferdinand and Queen Isabella finally succeeded in driving Islam from their realm by military means. The monarchs imposed Christian orthodoxy and forced Jews into exile. That same year, they agreed to sponsor an Atlantic voyage by an Italian-born navigator, Christopher Columbus. Leaving Spain with ninety men aboard three small vessels, Columbus headed for the Canary Islands and then sailed due west on September 6. After a voyage of three or four weeks, he expected to encounter the island of Cipangu (Japan), which Marco Polo had mentioned, or to reach the coast of Asia.

Why these huge misunderstandings? The mariner made several crucial mistakes. Like others, Columbus knew the world was round, not flat. He also accepted the idea of the ancient geographer Ptolemy that by using north–south lines, one could divide the globe into 360 degrees of longitude. But he questioned Ptolemy's estimate that each degree measures 50 nautical miles at the equator. (Each actually measures 60 miles.) Instead, Columbus accepted an alternative figure of 45 miles, making the circumference of his theoretical globe 25 percent smaller than the real distance around the earth. Besides *under*estimating the world's circumference, he compounded his error by *over*estimating two other crucial distances: the breadth of the Eurasian landmass and the extent of Japan's separation from China. The first distance is actually 130 degrees of longitude, and the second is 20. Columbus used authorities who suggested 225 and 30 degrees, respectively. His estimates placed Japan 105 degrees closer to Europe (at the longitude that runs through western Cuba) and well within reach.

Early on October 12, after weeks without sight of any land, the worried crew finally sighted a small island, naming it San Salvador after their Christian savior. The inhabitants proved welcoming, and Columbus recorded pleasure over the "gold which they wear hanging from their noses. But I wish to go and see if I can find the island of Cipangu." He did find a large and beautiful island (Cuba, not Cipangu), and he estimated that the Asian mainland of the Great Khan was only "a 10 days' journey" farther west. He claimed a nearby island as La Isla Española, the Spanish island, or Hispaniola (current-day Haiti and the Dominican Republic). He noted stories of hostile islanders farther south

■ Horses, absent from the Americas for nearly 10,000 years, returned aboard Spanish ships. They awed Native Americans at first and played a crucial role in European conquests. "After God," the Spanish wrote, "we owe victory to the horses."

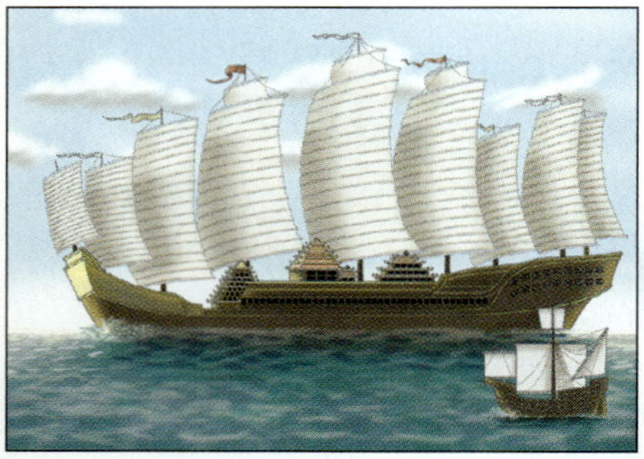

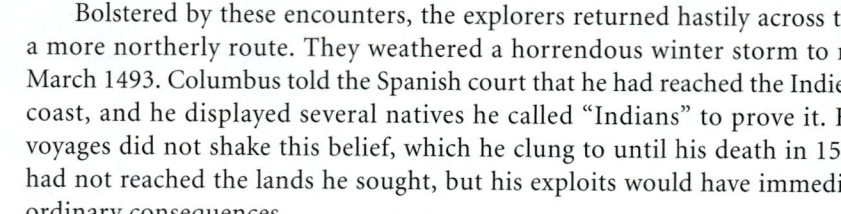

The largest Chinese vessels of Zheng He (400 ft.) were nearly five times longer than Columbus's flagship (85 ft.).

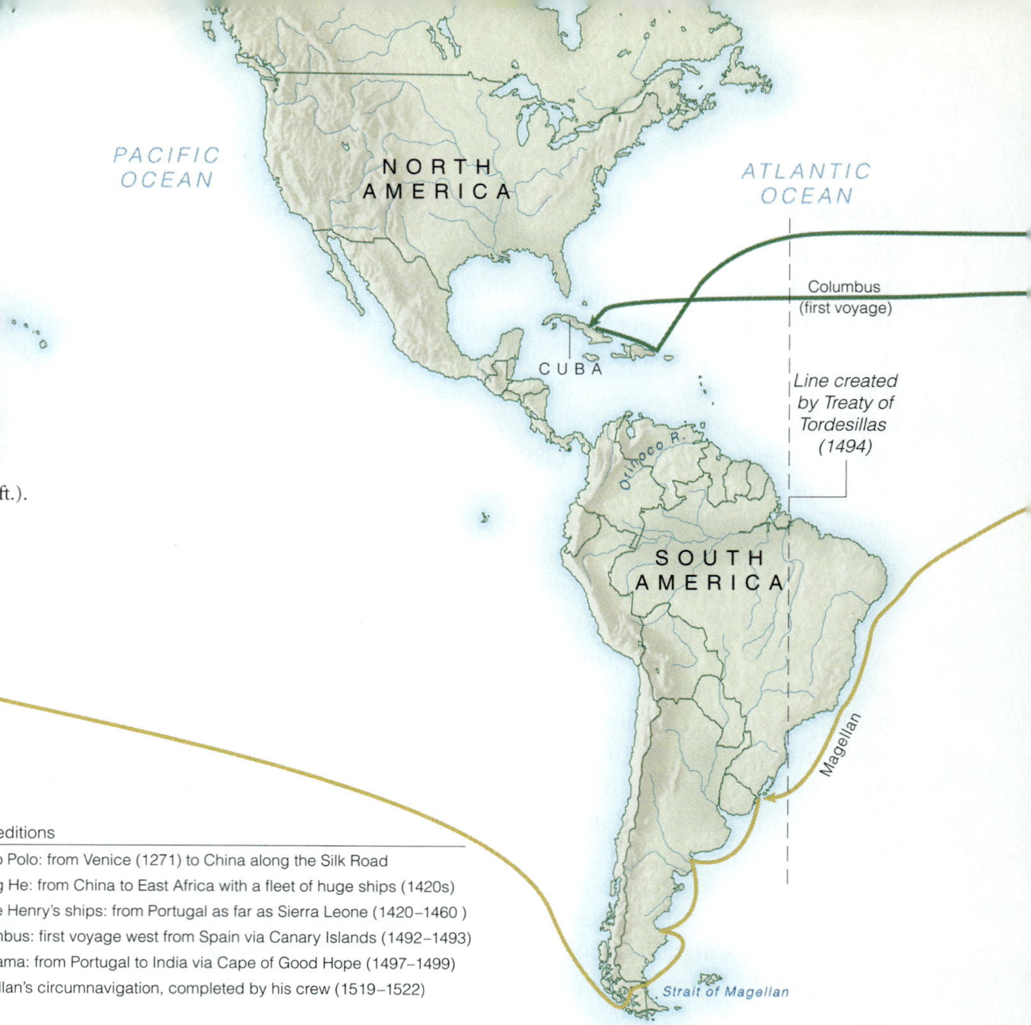

Major expeditions
- - - Marco Polo: from Venice (1271) to China along the Silk Road
——— Zheng He: from China to East Africa with a fleet of huge ships (1420s)
——— Prince Henry's ships: from Portugal as far as Sierra Leone (1420–1460)
——— Columbus: first voyage west from Spain via Canary Islands (1492–1493)
——— Da Gama: from Portugal to India via Cape of Good Hope (1497–1499)
——— Magellan's circumnavigation, completed by his crew (1519–1522)

■ MAP 1.2
OPENING NEW OCEAN PATHWAYS AROUND THE GLOBE, 1420–1520 In the 1420s, ships from Portugal and China explored opposite coasts of Africa. But China withdrew from oceanic trade, and European mariners competed to explore the world by sea. Within a century, Magellan's ship had circled the globe for Spain. The colonization in North America is a chapter in this larger saga of exploration.

From the Journal of Christopher Columbus

called Caribs, or Caniba, who were said to devour their enemies. "I repeat," he asserted, "the Caniba are no other than the people of the Grand Khan." (Upon hearing of these fierce Caribs, Europeans soon fashioned the word *cannibal* and named the region the Caribbean.)

Bolstered by these encounters, the explorers returned hastily across the Atlantic on a more northerly route. They weathered a horrendous winter storm to reach Spain in March 1493. Columbus told the Spanish court that he had reached the Indies off the Asian coast, and he displayed several natives he called "Indians" to prove it. His three later voyages did not shake this belief, which he clung to until his death in 1506. Columbus had not reached the lands he sought, but his exploits would have immediate and extraordinary consequences.

In the Wake of Columbus: Competition and Exchange

Within months of Columbus's return, the pope in Rome issued a papal bull, or decree. This pronouncement, titled *Inter Caetera*, viewed the whole world as the rightful inheritance of Christianity. It brashly divided the entire earth between two Christian powers, Spain and Portugal, by drawing a line down through the western Atlantic Ocean from the North

Pole to the South Pole. For 180 degrees west of the line, the Spanish alone could continue to seek access to Asia. East of the line, on the other half of the globe, Portugal would have a monopoly. The two Iberian powers affirmed this division of the earth in the Treaty of Tordesillas (1494).

European navigators and cartographers quickly began to comprehend the geographic reality that Columbus had so thoroughly misunderstood. When Amerigo Vespucci, another Italian in the service of Spain, crossed the South Atlantic in 1499, he described what he saw not as part of Asia but as a *Mundus Novus*, or New World. European geographers wrote his name, *America*, across their maps. Meanwhile, a third Italian navigator—John Cabot (or Caboto)—obtained a license from the English king, Henry VII, to probe the North Atlantic for access to Cathay. In 1497 Cabot sailed west from Bristol across the Atlantic to Newfoundland and perhaps Nova Scotia. Clearly, the ventures of Columbus had sparked widespread excitement and curiosity in European ports, and increasing knowledge fueled greater transatlantic contact.

After thousands of years, the long separation of the hemispheres had been broken. The destinies of the world's most divergent continents swiftly became linked. Those links fostered human migrations of an unprecedented scale. With European ships came transfers of seeds and viruses, bugs and birds, plants and animals that forever reshaped the world. Scholars call this phenomenon the **Columbian Exchange**. The term also underscores the two-way nature of the flow. West across the Atlantic went horses, cows, sheep, pigs, chickens, and honeybees and important foods such as sugar cane, coffee, bananas, peaches, lemons, and oranges. But Europeans' westbound ships also carried devastating diseases unknown in the Americas, such as smallpox, measles, malaria, and whooping cough. East in the opposite direction traveled corn, potatoes, pumpkins, chili peppers, tobacco, cacao, pineapples, sunflowers, turkeys—and perhaps syphilis. The planet and all its inhabitants would never be the same again.

Early Botanical Illustrations— New World Plants

Spain Enters the Americas

Throughout the sixteenth century, European mariners, inspired by the feats of Columbus and da Gama, risked ocean voyaging in hopes of scoring similar successes. Those who survived brought back novelties for consumers, information for geographers, and profits for ship owners. New wealth prompted further investment in exploration, and expanding knowledge awakened cultural changes for both explorers and the people they met. The dynamic European era known as the Renaissance owed much to overseas exploration. Returning mariners brought reports of surprising places and people. Their experiences challenged the inherited wisdom of traditional authorities and put a new premium on rational thought, scientific calculation, and careful observation of the natural world.

In turn, Europe's Renaissance, or rebirth, stimulated ever wider exploration as breakthroughs in technology and navigation yielded practical results. Sailing south around Africa and then east, Portuguese caravels reached China by 1514 and Japan by 1543. Sailing west, Spanish vessels learned first that the Caribbean did not offer a passage to Asia and then in 1522—through Magellan's global voyage—that the ocean beyond America was enormous. In the West Indies, and then elsewhere in the Western Hemisphere, Native Americans began to pay dearly for the exchange that ships from Spain had initiated.

The Devastation of the Indies

Spanish arrival in the West Indies in 1492 triggered widespread ecological and human disaster within decades. Well-armed and eager for quick wealth, the early colonizers brought havoc to the Taino Indians and Caribs who inhabited the islands. The strange newcomers killed and enslaved native peoples and extracted tribute from the survivors in the form of gold panned from streams. Spanish livestock trampled or consumed native gardens, prompting severe food shortages. Worse, European diseases ravaged countless villages. The West Indian population plummeted as island societies totaling more than 1 million lost nineteen of every twenty people within a generation.

This near-extinction had three consequences. First, when Dominican friars reached Cuba in 1510, these devout missionaries denounced Spanish brutality as sinful. The Indians, they argued, possessed souls that only Christian baptism could save. A Spanish soldier named Bartholomé de Las Casas, who repented and joined the Dominican order, led the outcry for reform. In his scathing exposé titled *The Devastation of the Indies*, he opposed genocide and urged conversion.

Second, in response to the steep drop in population, Spanish colonizers began importing slaves from Africa to replace the decimated Indian workforce. The same Christians who bemoaned Native American enslavement (including Las Casas) justified this initiative and overlooked the contradictions. The first importation of Africans came in 1502, following the Portuguese **precedent** in the Azores.

Third, decimation in the islands prompted the Spanish to intensify their explorations. They sought new sources of Indian labor close at hand, fresh lands to exploit, and easy passageways to the Pacific. They pushed out from the Caribbean in several directions. In 1510, they established an outpost on the Atlantic coast of Panama. From there, Vasco Núñez de Balboa pressed across the **isthmus** to glimpse the Pacific in 1513. That same year, Juan Ponce de León sailed northwest from Puerto Rico, where he had amassed a fortune as governor. Despite later tales that he sought a fountain of youth, he actually hoped the nearby land, which he named Florida, would yield new gold and slaves. But the peninsula's Indians were already familiar with Spanish raiders; they turned Ponce de León away after he claimed the region for Spain.

The Spanish Conquest of the Aztec

By 1519, the Spanish had determined that the Gulf of Mexico offered no easy passage to Asia. They needed fresh alternatives. In Spain, crown officials sought someone to sail southwest, around the South American continent that Columbus and Vespucci had encountered. For this perilous task, they recruited a Portuguese navigator named Ferdinand Magellan, who had sailed in the Indian Ocean. On his epic voyage (1519–1522), Magellan located a difficult passage through the tip of South America—now called the Strait of Magellan—and revealed the vast width of the Pacific, which covers one-third of the earth's surface. Warring factions in the Philippines killed Magellan and twenty-seven of his men, but one of his ships made it back to Spain, becoming the first vessel to circumnavigate the globe.

As news of Magellan's voyage raced through Spain in 1522, word also arrived that a Spanish soldier, or *conquistador*, named Hernán Cortés had toppled the gold-rich empire of the Aztec in central Mexico. Like other ambitious conquistadores, Cortés had followed Columbus to the Caribbean. In 1519, hoping to march overland to the Pacific as Balboa had done, Cortés sailed along Mexico's east coast and established a base camp at Vera Cruz. He quickly realized he had reached the edge of a powerful empire.

■ As the Indian population of the Caribbean plummeted in the face of new diseases and exploitation, the Spanish began importing Africans to the New World as slaves. Many were put to work mining precious metals. Here men are forced to dig for gold nuggets beside a mountain stream, then wash them in a tub and dry them over a fire, before handing them to their Spanish master to weigh in his hand-held scale.

At Tenochtitlán the Aztec emperor, Moctezuma, reacted with uncertainty to news that bearded strangers aboard "floating islands" had appeared off his coast. If the newcomers' leader was the returning god Quetzalcoatl, the court had to welcome him with the utmost care. The emperor sent basketloads of precious objects encrusted with gold to Cortés's camp. But the elaborate gifts only alerted Cortés and his men to the Aztec's wealth.

Although the Spanish numbered scarcely 600, they had several key advantages over the Aztec. Their guns and horses, unknown in America, terrified the Indians. When Cortés found coastal peoples staggering under heavy Aztec taxes, he recruited them as willing allies. An Indian woman (christened Doña Marina, or La Malinche) acted as his translator and companion. In an aggressive show of force, Cortés marched directly to the capital and seized Moctezuma as his hostage.

The Spanish still faced daunting obstacles, but sickness worked decisively to their advantage. Smallpox was a disease the Aztec had never encountered before, so they lacked any immunity. The European illness reached the mainland with the invading army, and a crushing epidemic swept the Aztec capital in 1521. The disaster let Cortés conquer Tenochtitlán (which he renamed Mexico City) and claim the entire region as New Spain.

INTERPRETING HISTORY

"These Gods That We Worship Give Us Everything We Need"

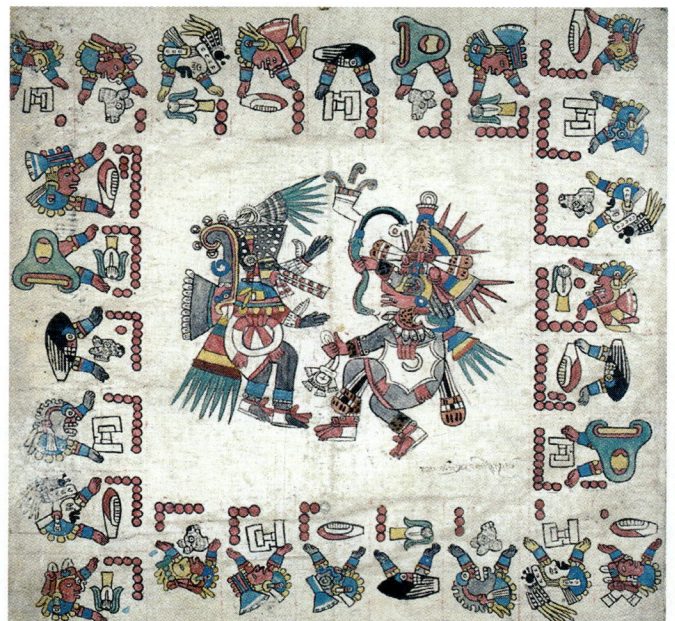

Three years after Cortés captured Tenochtitlán in central Mexico, 12 missionaries from the Franciscan Order arrived in the city to preach Christianity to the conquered Aztec. In several meetings with principal elders and priests, they explained their beliefs and laid out their plans through a translator. Similar talks would take place throughout America in later generations.

No transcript of the 1524 conversations exists, but another Franciscan, the famous preserver of Aztec culture Bernardino de Sahagún, gathered recollections of the encounter from both sides and reconstructed the dialogue. He published his version in 1564, creating parallel texts in Spanish and Nahuatl, the Aztec language. "Having understood the reasoning and speech of the twelve," Sahagún reports, the city leaders "became greatly agitated and fell into a great sadness and fear, offering no response." The next morning, they requested a complete repetition of the unsettling message. "Having heard this, one of the principal lords arose, asked the indulgence of the twelve,...and made the following long speech."

Our lords, leading personages of much esteem, you are very welcome to our lands and towns. . . . We have heard the words that you have brought us of the One who gives us life and being. And we have heard with admiration the words of the Lord of the World which he has sent here for love of us, and also you have brought us the book of celestial and divine words.

You have told us that we do not know the One who gives us life and being, who is Lord of the heavens and of the earth. You also say that those we worship are not gods. This way of speaking is entirely new to us, and very scandalous. We are frightened by this way of speaking because our forebears who engendered and governed us never said anything like this.

On the contrary, they left us this our custom of worshiping our gods. . . . They taught us how to honor them. And they taught us all the ceremonies and sacrifices that we make. They told us that. . . we were beholden to them, to be theirs and to serve countless centuries before the sun began to shine and before there was daytime. They said that these gods that we worship give us everything we need for our physical existence: maize, beans, chia seeds, etc. We appeal to them for the rain to make the things of the earth grow.

These our gods are the source of great riches and delights, all of which belong to them. . . . They live in very delightful places where there are always flowers, vegetation, and great freshness, a place...where there is never hunger, poverty, or illness. . . . There has never been a time remembered when they were not worshiped, honored, and esteemed. . . . .

It would be a fickle, foolish thing for us to destroy the most ancient laws and customs left by the first inhabitants of this land. . . . We are accustomed to them and we have them impressed on our hearts. . . . How could you leave the poor elderly among us bereft of that in which they have been raised throughout their lives? Watch out that we do not incur the wrath of our gods. Watch out that the common people do not rise up against us if we were to tell them that the gods they have always understood to be such are not gods at all.

It is best, our lords, to act on this matter very slowly, with great deliberation. We are not satisfied or convinced by what you have told us, nor do we understand or give credit to what has been said of our gods. . . . All of us together feel that it is enough to have lost, enough that the power and royal jurisdiction have been taken from us. As for our gods, we will die before giving up serving and worshiping them. This is our determination; do what you will.

Questions

1. Why would the Aztec priests fear an uprising of the common people under these circumstances? How would you respond to a similar situation?
2. As suggested near the end of this chapter, a similar religious confrontation was taking place in Europe in 1524, during the early years of the Protestant Reformation. Contrast and compare these two situations.

Source: Kenneth Mills and William B. Taylor, *Colonial Spanish America: A Documentary History* (Wilmington: Scholarly Resources, 1998), pp. 21–22.

Magellan and Cortés Prompt New Searches

Cortés's conquest of Mexico raised Spain's hopes of additional windfalls in the Americas. In 1531 Spanish raiders under Francisco Pizarro set sail from Panama for Peru, with plans to overthrow the Inca empire. Pizarro had limited resources (180 men and thirty-seven horses), but smallpox assisted him, as it had helped Cortés, and his invaders accomplished their mission. Marching overland to Cuzco in 1533, they killed the emperor, Atahualpa, and sacked the mountain capital for the gold it contained. The Spanish also pressed west across the Pacific from Mexico. One of three ships dispatched by Cortés for the Philippines actually reached its destination. Still, not until the 1560s did Spanish cargo ships, known as galleons, accomplish the arduous round trip from Acapulco to the Philippines and back across the Pacific.

In 1524, Italian navigator Giovanni da Verrazzano, sailing for the French, reached North America near modern Cape Fear, North Carolina, later cruising north to enter New York harbor and explore further along the coast. In 1526, Lucas Vásquez de Ayllón led 500 men and women from the Spanish Caribbean to the Santee River region (near present-day Georgetown, South Carolina) to settle and explore. But Ayllón fell sick and died, and the colony proved short-lived. Two years later, Pánfilo de Narváez directed an even greater disaster.

A rival of both Cortés and Ayllón, Narváez launched his expedition from Cuba in 1528. He landed near Florida's Tampa Bay, intending to bring wealth and glory to his 400 soldiers. But disease, hunger, and Indian hostilities plagued the party's journey along the Gulf Coast. Only four men—three Spanish and one North African black named Esteban—survived to make an extended trek on foot across the Southwest from Galveston Bay to Mexico City. Their leader, Álvar Núñez Cabeza de Vaca, wrote about the remarkable odyssey after he returned to Spain in 1537. Scholars now recognize Cabeza de Vaca's *Relation* (1542) as an early classic in North American literature.

Three New Views of North America

Even before Cabeza de Vaca published his narrative, Europeans initiated three more expeditions into North America. Each probed a separate region of the continent, hoping to gauge the land's dimensions, assess its peoples, and claim its resources. Together, the three enterprises made 1534 to 1543 the most extraordinary decade in the early European exploration of North America, for Native Americans and newcomers alike.

In the Northeast, Frenchman Jacques Cartier visited the Gulf of St. Lawrence in 1534 and bartered for furs with the Micmac Indians. He returned the next year and penetrated southwest up the St. Lawrence River into Canada. (The name comes from *kanata*, the Huron–Iroquois word for "village.") After a friendly reception at the large Indian town of Hochelaga near modern Montreal, the French returned downriver to camp at Stadacona, the future site of Quebec. Following a hard winter, in which he lost twenty-five men to scurvy, the explorer and his remaining crew sailed for France.

DOCUMENT

Jacques Cartier: First Contact with the Indians

Cartier came back to Quebec in 1541, seeking precious minerals and signs of a water passage farther west to the Pacific Ocean. He found neither, but a colonizing expedition followed in 1542, led by a nobleman named Roberval. It contained several hundred French settlers, including women for the first time. But again, scurvy and cold took a heavy toll at the Quebec campsite, and the weakened colony withdrew after a single winter. Despite a decade of effort, the French still had not established a beachhead in the New World. Nevertheless, they had demonstrated their resolve to challenge Spain's exclusive claim to American lands.

The Spanish, meanwhile, launched two intrusions of their own—one in the Southeast and one in the Southwest. News of Pizarro's 1533 triumph over the Incas in Peru helped renew the search for wealthy kingdoms to conquer. In 1537, Emperor Charles V of Spain granted one hardened veteran of the Peruvian campaign—Hernando de Soto—the right to explore in and beyond Florida, establishing a personal domain for himself. The conquistador spent

■ Two decades after Verrazzano's explorations, this 1547 chart shows the early claims of France in North America. It depicts the men and women of Roberval's short-lived colonizing expedition as they disembarked in 1542, watched by Native Americans. Perhaps to feature the large St. Lawrence River, the European mapmaker put North at the bottom and South at the top. Hence, the Atlantic coast seems upside-down to our eyes, with Florida appearing in the upper–right-hand corner.

most of his fortune assembling a force of more than 600 soldiers that reached Tampa Bay in 1539. The enterprise included several women and priests, along with scores of servants and African slaves, plus 200 horses. De Soto had also brought along a herd of 300 pigs that multiplied rapidly and provided food during the long march through the interior.

Over the next four years, de Soto's party traveled through parts of ten southern states. They hoped to find a city as wealthy as Cuzco in Peru or Tenochtitlán in Mexico. Instead, they encountered only scattered villages. Towns that refused to provide the intruders with porters or guides met with brutal reprisals that included the use of attack dogs. At Mabila near modern-day Selma, Alabama, de Soto's mounted army, brandishing swords and lances, killed several thousand Native Americans who had dared to attack them with bows and arrows. Still, Spanish frustrations grew due to difficult terrain, stiff Indian resistance, and failure to find riches. After exploring beyond the Mississippi River, de Soto died of a fever in 1542. His disheartened followers escaped downstream to the Gulf of Mexico the next year, leaving epidemic sickness in their wake.

At the same time, another encounter was unfolding in the Southwest. In Mexico, speculation about gold in the north had intensified after the appearance of Cabeza de Vaca. His

African companion, Esteban, guided a reconnaissance party north in 1539. Esteban was killed by the Zuni Indians, but exaggerated accounts of the region's pueblos prompted rumors about the seven golden cities known as Cibola. The next year, aspiring conquistador Francisco Vásquez de Coronado set out from northern Mexico to reach these wealthy towns before de Soto could. He left his post as a frontier governor and assembled a huge expedition with more than 300 Spanish adventurers and 1,000 Indian allies. However, his grandiose expectations were quickly dashed. The pueblos of the Zuni, he reported, "are very good houses, three and four and five stories high," but the fabled "Seven Cities are seven little villages."

The presence of Spanish forces soon imposed a heavy burden on the Pueblo Indians, as the newcomers demanded food and burned helpless towns. Desperate to get rid of Coronado, the Pueblo told him stories of a far-off, wealthy land called Quivira. They secretly recruited a Plains Indian to lead the Spaniards to some place where men and horses "would starve to death." In the spring of 1541, he guided Coronado's party northeast onto the Great Plains, with their endless herds of buffalo. But when Quivira proved to be a Wichita Indian village in what is now central Kansas, the Spanish strangled their deceitful guide and made their way back south to New Spain. At one point, as they crossed northern Texas, they even came within 300 miles of de Soto's ill-fated party in eastern Arkansas. But neither de Soto nor Coronado—nor Cartier in the north—ever discovered wealthy cities or a sea passage to the Far East.

> *Neither de Soto nor Coronado—nor Cartier in the north—ever discovered wealthy cities or a sea passage to the Far East.*

The Protestant Reformation Plays Out in America

In 1520, while Cortés vied with the Aztec for control in Mexico and Magellan maneuvered around South America, the pope excommunicated a German monk named Martin Luther. Three years earlier, Luther had mailed a list of ninety-five theses to the church door at Wittenberg, challenging papal authority. Luther's followers questioned lavish church spending and long-standing church practices such as the selling of religious pardons to raise money. They also rejected the church's elaborate hierarchy and criticized its refusal to translate the Latin Bible into modern languages. Luther's reform movement triggered the division of western Christianity into competing faiths. For their written protestations against the papacy, Luther and his fellow insurgents received the enduring name *Protestants*. Their movement became known broadly as the Reformation. Those who opposed it, siding with Rome, launched a Counter-Reformation to defend and revitalize the Roman Catholic Church.

For the first time in history, a controversy in Europe made waves that washed onto American shores. Throughout the remainder of the sixteenth century, European national and religious conflict played out in part overseas, a pattern that repeated itself in future centuries. France and Spain, competing in Europe, wrestled to claim control of Florida. England, an upstart Protestant monarchy with a rising population and an expanding navy, seized control of Ireland and launched its first attempt to plant a colony in North America.

Reformation and Counter-Reformation in Europe

Beginning in 1517, zeal for Luther's religious reforms spread across Europe, sparking armed conflict. In Switzerland, militant priests abolished the practice of confession, condemned the church calendar full of fasts and saints' days, and defied the tradition of a celibate clergy by marrying. The Swiss Reformation found its leader in a French Protestant named John Calvin who arrived in Geneva in 1541 and ruled the city as a church-centered state for more than two decades.

Calvin imposed his own strict interpretation on Lutheranism and drew dedicated followers to his church. Offended by expensive vestments and elaborate rituals, he donned a simple black "Geneva" robe. He argued that faith alone, not "good works," would lead Christians to be saved. Salvation, he preached, was determined by God, not bought by giving **tithes** to the church. Only a select few people, Calvin explained, were destined to be members of God's chosen elect. Moreover, only an informed clergy and the careful study of scripture could reveal signs of a person's status. Soon Calvinist doctrine helped shape Protestant communities across northern Europe: Huguenots in France, Puritans in England, Presbyterians in Scotland, and the Dutch Reformed Church in the Netherlands.

The Protestant Reformation that Luther had ignited coincided roughly with another important change in Europe, the emergence of the modern nation-state. Kings and queens gradually expanded court bureaucracies and asserted greater control over their subjects and economies. They strengthened their armies, gaining a near monopoly on the use of force, and they took full advantage of the new medium of printing. As religious ferment spread and local allegiances gave way to a broader sense of national identity, strong sovereigns moved to distance themselves from papal authority in Rome.

The emergence of England as a nation-state under the Tudor dynasty, founded by Henry VII in 1485, illustrates this shift in power away from Rome. In 1533, when the pope refused to grant England's next king an **annulment** of his first marriage, Henry VIII wrested control of the English church from papal hands and had Parliament approve his divorce and remarriage. The new Church of England, or Anglican Church, continued to follow much of the Catholic Church's doctrine. However, its "Protector and only Supreme Head" would now be the English monarch. During her long reign from 1558 to 1603, Henry VIII's daughter Queen Elizabeth I managed to steer the Church of England on a middle course between advocates of Catholicism and extreme Protestants.

Throughout Europe, as zealous believers on both sides of the debate staked out their positions, attempts to heal religious divisions gave way to confrontation. Challenges to the pope in Rome, whether from dissenting parishes or powerful monarchs, met with stiff resistance as Catholic leaders mobilized opposition. Their followers rallied to defend Roman Catholicism through efforts known collectively as the Counter-Reformation.

A militant new Catholic religious order called the Society of Jesus, or the Jesuits, represented one dimension of the Counter-Reformation. Led by a Spanish soldier named Ignatius Loyola and willing to give their lives for their beliefs, these dedicated missionaries and teachers helped to reenergize the Catholic faith and spread it to distant parts of the world. Another institution, the Inquisition, reflects a different side of the Counter-Reformation. In 1542, Catholic authorities established a new religious-judicial proceeding, known as the Inquisition, to help resist the spread of Protestantism. Heretics—persons accused of denying or defying church doctrine—were brought before the Inquisition's strict religious courts, and those who refused to renounce their beliefs suffered severe punishment. These heresy trials made clear to Inquisition leaders that the advent of printing was helping to spread the works of Luther and his Protestant allies. In 1557, therefore, the Vatican issued an "Index" of prohibited books.

> *In 1542, Catholic authorities established a new religious-judicial proceeding, known as the Inquisition, to help resist the spread of Protestantism.*

In Spain, King Philip II, who ruled from 1556 to 1598, led an Inquisition to root out Protestant heresy. The Spanish monarch came close to overpowering Protestant England as well. In 1588 he sent a fleet of warships—the Spanish Armada—to England in hopes of reconquering it for the Catholic Church. A timely storm and hasty mobilization by the island nation foiled the Spanish king's invasion. But Philip II's confrontation with the navy of Elizabeth I epitomized the sharp new division between Catholic and Protestant power in Europe. This deepened antagonism— religious, ideological, and economic—shaped events overseas in the second half of the sixteenth century. The struggle became especially clear in Florida, the vague region claimed by Spain that encompassed Indian lands from Chesapeake Bay to the Gulf of Mexico.

Competing Powers Lay Claim to Florida

As Spain used force to obtain the dazzling wealth of New World societies, its European rivals looked on jealously. As early as 1523, French sea raiders had captured Spanish ships returning from Mexico with Cortés's Aztec bounty of gold, silver, and pearls. Ten years later, French pirates made a similar haul. To protect the flow of riches from America, the Spanish soon initiated a well-armed annual convoy to escort their wealth from Havana to Seville. Each year, Spain's huge West Indies treasure fleet made an enticing target as it followed the Gulf Stream along the Florida coast.

> *Each year, Spain's huge West Indies treasure fleet made an enticing target as it followed the Gulf Stream along the Florida coast.*

But France had its own designs on Florida, furthered by the special concerns of French Huguenots. Unsure of their future in a religiously divided country, these Protestants took a leading role in the colonization efforts of France. In 1562 French Huguenots established a settlement at Port Royal Sound (Parris Island, South Carolina), close to the route of Spain's annual treasure fleet. The effort lasted only two years and aroused Spanish suspicions of "Lutheran" intruders.

■ In 1562, French Protestants established a short-lived colony at Port Royal Sound on the South Carolina coast. "The commander, on landing with some soldiers, found the country very beautiful, as it was well wooded with oak, cedar, and other trees. As they went through the woods, they saw Indian peacocks, or turkeys, flying past, and deer going by." Traveling upstream beyond Parris Island, they surprised an encampment of Indians, "who, on perceiving the boats, immediately took flight," leaving behind the meat "they were roasting."

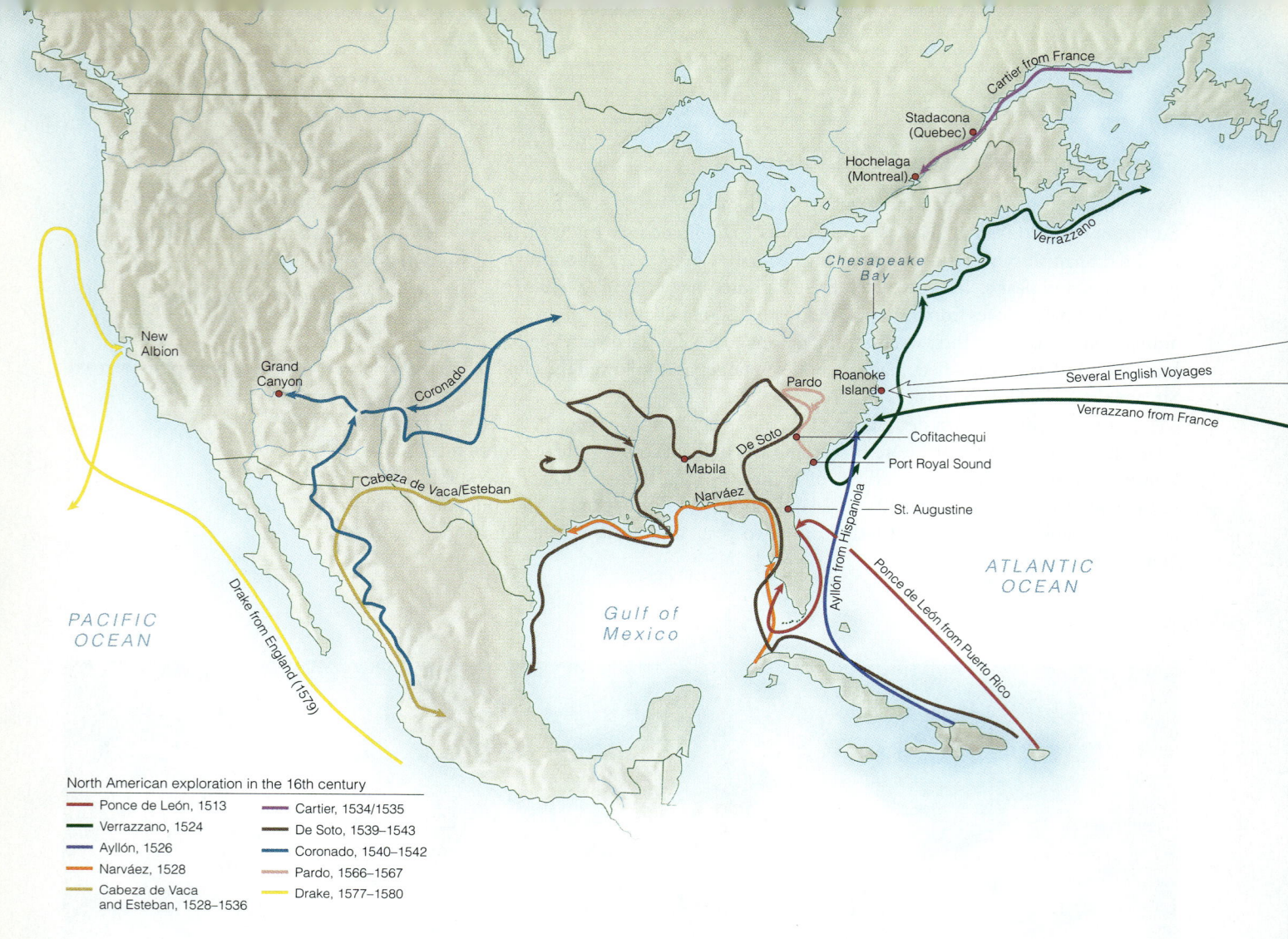

MAP 1.3
THE EXTENT OF EUROPEAN EXPLORATION OF NORTH AMERICA BY 1592
By 1592, a century after Columbus's initial voyage, European explorers and colonists had touched the edges of North America, and a few had ventured far inland. But they had not found riches or a passageway to the Pacific, and only the Spanish had managed to establish a lasting foothold along the Florida coast.

Undaunted, the French backed a larger colonizing effort to Florida in 1564. When French Protestants erected Fort Caroline on the St. John's River at present-day Jacksonville, the Spanish crown took swift action. In 1565 Philip II sent 300 soldiers and 700 colonists under Pedro Menéndez de Avilés to oust the French and secure Florida. Menéndez captured Fort Caroline and massacred hundreds of French Huguenots. The heretics, he feared, might attack the treasure fleet, forge alliances with Florida's Indians, or provoke revolt among slaves in the Spanish Caribbean. To prevent further French incursions on Florida's Atlantic coast, Menéndez established a new outpost at nearby St. Augustine. He also sent Juan Pardo far up the Savannah River to explore the interior.

With French threats defeated, the Spanish at St. Augustine attempted to plant strategic missions farther north to convert Native Americans to Christianity and secure Spain's land claims. In 1570, eight missionaries from Loyola's Society of Jesus sailed north from Florida to Chesapeake Bay. There, the Jesuits established a mission to convert local Indians and looked for "an entrance into the mountains and on to China." But the friars' rules and beliefs antagonized the Native Americans. By the time Menéndez visited the region in 1572, all the missionaries had been killed. Spain's failure to secure a foothold on Chesapeake Bay soon proved costly, as a new European rival appeared on the scene. Almost overnight, Protestant England emerged as a contending force in the Atlantic world. Now English adventurers began challenging Spanish dominance in the Caribbean and along North America's southeastern coast.

The Background of English Expansion

The voyages of John Cabot and the visits of Bristol fishing vessels to Newfoundland's Grand Banks had stimulated an early English interest in the Atlantic. But for several reasons this curiosity intensified after 1550. Henry VIII had used his power, plus the wealth he had seized from the Catholic Church, to build a sizable navy before he died in 1547. The merchant fleet grew as well, carrying English wool and cloth to Antwerp and other European ports. In addition, the English population, which had declined in the previous 150 years, grew steadily after 1500. Overall numbers more than doubled during the sixteenth century, creating pressure on limited resources, especially land. Adding to the squeeze, property owners, eager to enclose pastures for sheep grazing, pushed tenants off their land. This "enclosure movement" set even more people adrift to seek work in towns and cities. London's population soared from 50,000 in 1500 to 200,000 a century later. When Europe's saturated woolen textile market collapsed suddenly, English cloth exports fell 35 percent in 1551. Merchants searched hastily for new avenues of foreign commerce.

Starting in the 1550s, therefore, England's overseas exploration pushed in all directions. Investors in the new Muscovy Company sent ships north around Scandinavia through the Arctic Ocean, but they failed to find a northeastern route above the Asian landmass to China. Other English vessels sailed south to Morocco and the Gold Coast, challenging the Portuguese monopoly of the African trade. English mariner John Hawkins conducted three voyages to West Africa during the 1560s. Horning in on the growing transatlantic slave traffic, he purchased Africans and then sold them in Caribbean ports to Spanish buyers.

Philip II, having driven the French out of Florida, had had enough of Protestant interlopers. A Spanish fleet forced Hawkins and his young kinsman Francis Drake out of Mexican waters in 1568. But thereafter, English sea rovers, with quiet support from Queen Elizabeth I, stepped up their challenges to Spain on the high seas. Drake proved the most wide-ranging and successful. On a voyage to the Pacific (1577–1580) he plundered Spanish ports in Peru and landed near San Francisco Bay. He claimed California for England as New Albion and then sailed around the globe. In the 1580s, Drake continued, in his words, "to singe the Spaniard's beard." He sacked ports in the West Indies, encouraged slave uprisings against the Spanish, and attacked the settlement at St. Augustine. He also captured numerous treasure ships, sank two dozen enemy vessels in their home port at Cadiz, and helped to defeat Philip II's Spanish Armada in 1588.

England's anti-Catholic propagandists made Drake a national hero. Moreover, they painted Spanish cruelties toward Indians in the New World in the worst possible terms. To bolster their case, they translated the vivid writings of Las Casas into English. But the English were not blameless themselves. In the Elizabethan years, they established their own pattern of violence during their brutal conquest of Ireland. Many who played leading roles in this bloody takeover came to view a colony in America as the next logical step in England's aggressive overseas expansion.

Lost Colony: The Roanoke Experience

Sir Humphrey Gilbert, who had served in Ireland, was one Elizabethan with an eye on America. In 1576 Gilbert promoted the idea of a short northwestern passage to China, and Martin Frobisher, another veteran of the Irish campaign, undertook voyages to locate such a route. Writing an essay on "How Her Majesty May Annoy the King of Spain," Gilbert

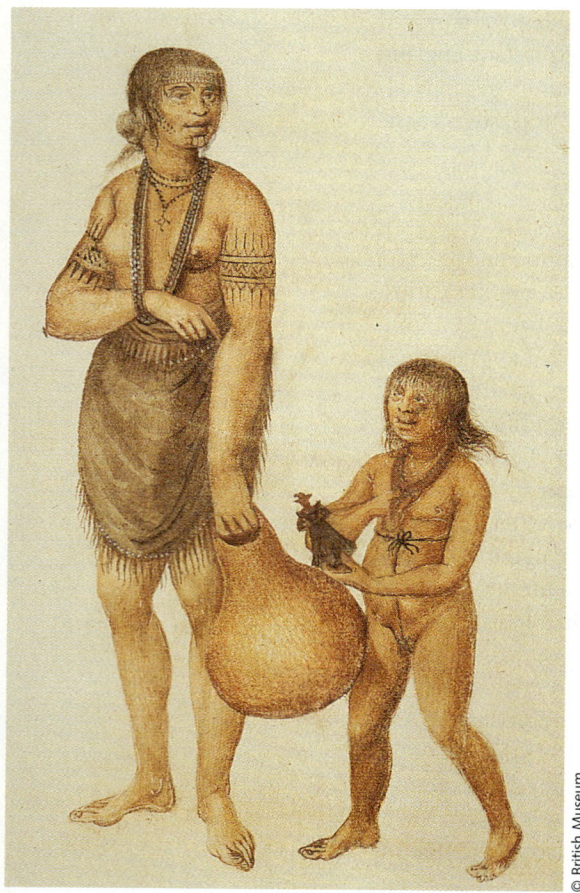

John White took part in several voyages to Roanoke Island in the 1580s. A skilled artist, the Englishman made valuable firsthand drawings of Native Americans living in what is now coastal North Carolina, including the wife and daughter of a local leader. The woman kept her "haire trussed opp in a knott," had tattoos on her arms, wore "a chaine of great pearles," and often carried "a gourde full of some kinde of pleasant liquor." The girl holds an English doll, for Indian children "are greatly Deligted with puppetts . . . brought oute of England."

DOCUMENT
Charter to Sir Walter Raleigh

proposed a colony in Newfoundland. The queen granted him a patent—a license giving him exclusive rights—for such a project. But shipwrecks and desertions doomed the venture to failure. When Gilbert died at sea on the homeward voyage, his half-brother, Walter Raleigh, obtained a similar patent to plant a colony in North America.

In 1584 Raleigh sent explorers to the Outer Banks, the string of coastal barrier islands below Chesapeake Bay that Verrazzano had glimpsed sixty years earlier. They brought back two Indian informants and positive reports about the land near Roanoke Island. The next month, Richard Hakluyt, England's foremost advocate and chronicler of overseas expansion, handed Elizabeth I an advisory paper entitled "Western Planting." The document called for the establishment of a strategic outpost on the North American coast, where the English could launch attacks against Spanish shipping, hunt for useful commodities, and convert Indians to Protestant Christianity.

Raleigh's three efforts to establish such an outpost failed in rapid succession. In 1585, he first sent Ralph Lane, a hardened veteran of the Irish campaigns, to build a fort at Roanoke Island. But storms at sea scattered his ships, and most of Lane's initial force never arrived. Those who did, including artist John White, fared badly because of scarce food, bad discipline, and hostile relations with the Indians. Francis Drake, arriving in 1586 after harassing the Spanish in the West Indies and Florida, expected to find a thriving enterprise. Instead, he carried the disheartened soldiers back to England. They had paid a price, Hakluyt commented, "for the cruelty and outrages committed by some of them against the native inhabitants of that country." A second expedition diverted to the Caribbean to prey on enemy shipping, after leaving a few men at Roanoke, who did not survive.

In May 1587 John White led a third English venture to America, with 110 people, including women and children. They planned to settle on Chesapeake Bay, but a contentious captain refused to carry them farther north after an initial stop at Roanoke Island. In August the settlers agreed to send White back to England for more supplies; they would leave a message for him if they moved. When he finally returned in 1590—delayed by England's clash with the Spanish Armada—he found the site deserted. The word *Croatoan* carved on a post suggested that survivors had joined the nearby Croatan Indians, but the Lost Colony's fate remains a source of endless speculation. The Spanish, worried by the English foray, drew up plans for a fortification at Chesapeake Bay, but warfare between Spain and England kept both countries preoccupied elsewhere until Philip II and Elizabeth I had died.

Conclusion

Over approximately 150 centuries, people of distant Asian ancestry had explored and settled the bountiful Western Hemisphere. In every region of North America, from the arctic North to the semitropical Florida Keys, they had adapted and prospered over countless generations. Then suddenly, in a single century, unprecedented intrusions by sea brought newcomers from foreign lands to the coasts of the Americas. Their numbers only increased with time. In the next century, the contest for European control of the Atlantic seaboard began in earnest.

Sites to Visit

Cahokia Mounds State Historic Site
Covering 2,200 acres just south of Highway 40 near Collinsville, in East St. Louis, Illinois, Mississippian earthworks dot this World Heritage Site. The Cahokia Mounds Museum Society conducts an archaeological field school each summer.

Chaco Culture National Historical Park
The most striking structure in this park is Pueblo Bonito, the largest building in North America until 1882. Lying in Chaco Canyon northwest of Albuquerque, New Mexico, these Anasazi ruins can be reached by driving south from Aztec (where there are several important museums) or north from Thoreau.

Makah Cultural and Research Center
This site, in Neah Bay, Washington, at the tip of Olympic Peninsula, houses thousands of artifacts from an ancestral Macah Indian village, at nearby Ozette, that was covered in a mudslide shortly before European contact and revealed by a 1970 winter storm.

Mesa Verde National Park
Located near Cortez, Colorado, this is the oldest archaeological national park in the United States. It covers 80 square miles in southwest Colorado, adjoining the Ute Mountain Indian Reservation. The park contains impressive Anasazi ruins, the most famous of which is Cliff Palace.

Moundville Archaeological Park
Located half a mile west of State Route 69, on the Black Warrior River outside Moundville, Alabama, just south of Tuscaloosa, this well-preserved Mississippian mound complex also contains an archaeological museum.

Poverty Point State Commemorative Area
A visitors' center is located near the center of the geometric earthworks from the late Archaic era on this 400-acre site on State Route 577 near Epps, Louisiana.

Pueblo Grande Museum
This downtown Phoenix, Arizona, museum, just off State Route 143, contains artifacts of the Hohokam culture. A large platform mound, a ball court, and ancient irrigation canals are preserved within the park.

Fort Raleigh National Historical Site
This site is on Route 64 at the north end of Roanoke Island, in eastern North Carolina. A reconstructed Elizabethan ship at nearby Manteo suggests the experience of England's sixteenth-century "lost colony." A drive or walk on the sandy Outer Banks (Route 12) recalls the coastline seen by Verrazzano in 1524.

Serpent Mound State Memorial
Four miles northwest of Locust Grove, Ohio, on State Route 73, this site includes a small museum and a viewing tower that allows visitors to look down on the winding effigy mound, now thought to be roughly 1,000 years old.

Digital Restorations of Ohio Valley Mounds
http://www.earthworks.uc.edu/
EarthWorks is an ongoing project at the University of Cincinnati's Center for the Electronic Reconstruction of Historical and Archaeological Sites (CERHAS). It is creating virtual reconstructions of pre-Columbian mounds and major earthen sites in the Ohio River valley, along with a CD-ROM and a videotape.

European Voyages of Exploration
www.acs.ucalgary.ca/applied_history/tutor/eurvoya/index.html
The University of Calgary has developed a course around this Web site titled "The European Voyages of Exploration: The Fifteenth and Sixteenth Centuries."

Cabeza de Vaca
www.pbs.org/weta/thewest/resources/archives/one/cabeza.htm
Read the narrative by Cabeza de Vaca of his journey across the Southwest in the 1530s.

Discoverers Web
www.win.tue.nl/cs/fm/engels/discovery/
See the "Discoverers Web" for numerous links concerning the era of European exploration.

For Further Reading

General

John Logan Allen, *North American Exploration, Vol. 1, A New World Disclosed* (1997).
Alfred W. Crosby, *Ecological Imperialism: The Biological Expansion of Europe, 900–1900* (1986; Canto edition, 1993).
Jared Diamond, *Guns, Germs, and Steel: The Fates of Human Societies* (1997).
Brian M. Fagan, *Ancient North America*, 3rd ed. (2000).
William H. Goetzmann and Glyndwr Williams, *The Atlas of North American Exploration: From the Norse Voyages to the Race to the Pole* (1992).
J. C. H. King, *First Peoples, First Contacts: Native Peoples of North America* (1999).
Charles C. Mann, *1491: New Revelations of the Americas Before Columbus* (2005).

Ancient America

Brian M. Fagan, *The Great Journey: The Peopling of Ancient America* (2004).
Francis Jennings, *The Founders of America* (1993).
Alice Beck Kehoe, *America Before the European Invasions* (2002).
Robert Silverberg, *Mound Builders of Ancient America: The Archaeology of a Myth* (1968).

A Thousand Years of Change: 500 to 1500

Sally A. Kitt Chappell, *Cahokia: Mirror of the Cosmos* (2002).
Alvin M. Josephy Jr., ed., *America in 1492: The World of the Indian Peoples Before the Arrival of Columbus* (1992).
Linda Schele and David Freidel, *A Forest of Kings: The Untold Story of the Ancient Maya* (1990).
David Hurst Thomas, *Exploring Native North America* (2000).

Linking the Continents

Alfred W. Crosby Jr., *The Columbian Exchange: Biological and Cultural Consequences of 1492* (1972).

William W. Fitzhugh and Elisabeth I. Ward, eds., *Vikings: The North Atlantic Saga* (2000).

Louise Levathes, *When China Ruled the Sea: The Treasure Fleet of the Dragon Throne* (1994).

Samuel Eliot Morison, *The European Discovery of America: The Northern Voyages, A.D. 500–1600* (1971).

J. H. Parry, *The Age of Reconnaissance: Discovery, Exploration, and Settlement, 1450–1650* (1963).

Spain Enters the Americas

Laurence Bergreen, *Over the Edge of the World: Magellan's Terrifying Circumnavigation of the Globe* (2003).

Cyclone Covey, trans. and ed., *Cabeza de Vaca's Adventures in the Unknown Interior of America* (1961).

W. J. Eccles, *France in America* (1972).

Charles Hudson, *Knights of Spain, Warriors of the Sun: Hernando de Soto and the South's Ancient Kingdoms* (1997).

Jerald T. Milanich, *Florida Indians and the Invasion from Europe* (1995).

Hugh Thomas, *Rivers of Gold: The Rise of the Spanish Empire, from Columbus to Magellan* (2003).

The Protestant Reformation Plays Out in America

Karen Ordahl Kupperman, *Roanoke: The Abandoned Colony* (1984).

Eugene Lyon, *The Enterprise of Florida: Pedro Menéndez de Avilés and the Spanish Conquest of 1565–1568* (1976).

Diarmaid MacCulloch, *The Reformation: A History* (2003).

John T. McGrath, *The French in Early Florida: In the Eye of the Hurricane* (2000).

David Beers Quinn, *England and the Discovery of America, 1481–1620* (1974).

Carl Ortwin Sauer, *Sixteenth Century America: The Land and the People as Seen by the Europeans* (1971).

For quizzes and other resources on these topics, go to www.longmanamericanhistory.com.

European Footholds in North America, 1600–1660

CHAPTER 2

IN THE SUMMER OF 1621, AN ENGLISHMAN AND AN INDIAN LEFT PLYMOUTH VILLAGE ON FOOT TO visit a Native American leader named Massasoit and secure his support for the struggling English colony. During their 40-mile journey, Stephen Hopkins and Squanto saw numerous signs of a wave of disease that had swept the New England coast four years earlier, killing thousands of Indians. Unburied skulls and bones still lay aboveground in many places. The two men who encountered these grim scenes had come together from strikingly different backgrounds.

Back in 1609, Hopkins had left England in a fleet heading for Jamestown in Virginia. When a storm wrecked his ship on the uncharted island of Bermuda, he and others rebelled against their official leader. Accused of mutiny and sentenced to hang, Hopkins pleaded his case and narrowly escaped the noose. Hopkins made it back to England and started a family, but in 1620 he decided to return to America. At the English port of Plymouth, Hopkins, his pregnant wife Elizabeth, and several children and servants became paying passengers on a ship called the *Mayflower*. The vessel had been chartered to carry a group of English Protestants to America from their exile in Holland.

During the arduous passage, tensions mounted. Hopkins was among those who muttered "mutinous speeches" and argued that "when they came ashore, they should use their own libertie, for none had power to command them." But after Elizabeth gave birth, Hopkins joined the other forty men aboard in signing the Mayflower Compact. The agreement bound all the passengers together in a "Civil Body Politic" to be governed by laws "most meet and convenient for the general good." They reached New England in early winter, and Hopkins and others laid out the village of Plymouth in the snow. There, the newcomers met Squanto, a Native American with a command of English who helped them negotiate with local Indians.

Squanto had also endured Atlantic travel. He remembered the first French and English fishing vessels, which had appeared when he was a small boy. In 1614 Squanto was among twenty-seven

■ A *Mayflower* replica is now part of the restored Plymouth Colony site.

CHAPTER OUTLINE

Spain's Ocean-Spanning Reach

France and Holland: Overseas Competition for Spain

English Beginnings on the Atlantic Coast

The Puritan Experiment

The Chesapeake Bay Colonies

Conclusion

Sites to Visit

For Further Reading

Indians taken hostage aboard an English ship. He spent time in Spain, England, and Newfoundland before returning home in 1619, only to find his entire village swept away by disease.

The *Mayflower* pilgrims, arriving a year after Squanto's return, would also suffer heavy losses. Of the 102 settlers who had begun the voyage, half of them died in Plymouth Colony by the next spring. But in New England, as elsewhere in America, death seemed to play favorites in the following years. As colonization continued, recurrent epidemics took a particularly heavy toll on Native Americans, who lacked immunity when exposed to foreign diseases for the first time. In 1622 Squanto fell sick and died of a fever, leaving no relatives behind. In contrast, Stephen and Elizabeth Hopkins lived on to see numerous children and grandchildren thrive.

By the middle of the seventeenth century, English settlements had taken root in both the Chesapeake region and New England. The success of these colonies would exert a lasting influence on the future direction of American society. But their stories unfolded as part of a far wider North American drama that included a diversity of European groups and embraced both the Atlantic and the Pacific shores. Whether confronting newcomers from Spain, France, Holland, or England, scores of Native American communities faced new challenges that altered traditional Indian ways of living and sometimes threatened their very survival.

Spain's Ocean-Spanning Reach

In 1580 Spain's Philip II laid claim to the throne of Portugal. This consolidation (which endured until 1640) unified Europe's two richest seaborne empires but also created new problems. First, combining with Portugal put huge additional burdens on the overstretched Spanish bureaucracy. Second, the global success of the combined **Iberian** empires invited challenges from envious rivals in northern Europe. The new international competition came from the French, the Dutch, and the English, aspiring naval powers with imperial ambitions that touched the Pacific as well as the Atlantic.

By 1600, for example, a Dutch ship had entered the Pacific, defying Spanish claims for control of that ocean, and had reached Japan, where the new Tokugawa dynasty (1600–1868) was consolidating its control. The pilot, an Englishman named Will Adams, visited Edo—the rising military town that would grow into modern-day Tokyo. He even built a ship for the *shogun* (ruler). Adams's experience in Japan serves as a reminder that in the decades before the *Mayflower* sailed the Atlantic, the issue of who would dominate Pacific sea lanes to America was anything but clear.

Vizcaíno in California and Japan

In April 1607, a letter from the king of Spain reached Mexico City. The king commanded his viceroy in charge of affairs in Mexico (New Spain) to create an outpost on California's Monterey Bay. Spanish galleons returning from the Philippines through the North Pacific to the west coast of Mexico desperately needed a haven along the route, after crossing the immense ocean. Monterey Bay was well supplied with water, food, and timber. The sheltering harbor would provide a perfect way station, where ships could take on supplies and make repairs before heading south.

But the viceroy in Mexico City had other ideas. He diverted the necessary funds into a search for the fabled North Pacific isles of Rica de Oro ("Rich in Gold") and Rica de Plata ("Rich in Silver"). To search for the mysterious islands, in 1611 the viceroy dispatched Sebastián Vizcaíno, a seasoned Pacific navigator who had already explored the California coast. Vizcaíno found no isles of gold and silver, but he did visit Japan. When he finally returned across the

Pacific in 1613 aboard a vessel built in Japan, he brought 180 Japanese with him to Mexico. This unique delegation was bound for Spain and Italy to open doors between East and West. However, the Tokugawas soon began to persecute the European traders and Christian missionaries who had been allowed in the Japanese islands for a generation, so the frail link between Europe and Japan through Mexico never developed further.

Tokugawa officials, it seems, feared that tolerating foreigners in Japan's ports might foster the spread of Christianity and undermine their supremacy. Moreover, developing Japanese fleets might bring guns to warlords and disrupt hard-won peace. So Japan passed up an opportunity for naval expansion, just as Ming China had done two centuries earlier after the voyages of Zheng He. Instead, the new dynasty adopted a policy of commercial and cultural isolation that lasted for more than 200 years. Otherwise, the history of North America and the world would almost certainly have taken a very different path.

> *Spain wondered whether to maintain its existing North American colony in Florida and its newest frontier province: New Mexico.*

For the Spanish, Vizcaíno's Pacific adventure consumed crucial funds, and the possibility of a Spanish settlement at Monterey quickly disappeared. Concerned that their empire had already become overextended, Spanish officials postponed plans to colonize California's coast. In addition, Spain wondered whether to maintain its existing North American colony in Florida and its newest frontier province: New Mexico.

Oñate Creates a Spanish Foothold in the Southwest

In 1598 Juan de Oñate renewed the northern efforts of Coronado's expedition several generations earlier. Setting out from New Spain, he led 500 men, women, and children north into the upper Rio Grande valley to create the province of New Mexico. Aided by Franciscan friars (organized followers of St. Francis loyal to the pope), Oñate and his colonists expected to convert the Pueblo Indians to Christianity. Expanding outward from the compact apartment-like native towns, or pueblos, the intruders hoped to open a vast new colonial realm "greater than New Spain."

But Oñate drastically underestimated the difficulties. When embittered Indians at Acoma pueblo killed eleven of his soldiers in 1599, he retaliated by bombarding the mesa-top citadel, killing 800 inhabitants and enslaving nearly 600 others. Hearing of the brutal repression of the residents of Acoma, neighboring pueblos reluctantly submitted to Spanish demands for labor and food. Colonial reinforcements arriving in 1600 were dismayed by the harsh conditions; for the colony to prosper, Oñate needed new discoveries. In 1601 he launched an expedition east into the Great Plains, but the venture proved as futile as Coronado's earlier march had been.

To make matters worse, drought gripped the Rio Grande valley, and many of the recent settlers departed, complaining that the region lacked woods, pastures, water, and suitable land. When Oñate returned from the plains, he found that two-thirds of his tiny colony had given up and returned to Mexico. Foiled on the east and weakened along the Rio Grande, Oñate next pressed west to seek a link to the Pacific. When he reached the Gulf of California in 1605, he mistook it for the great ocean and envisioned a possible link to the Pacific trade.

In fact, however, Oñate's new "Mexico" remained isolated and impoverished. The desperate colonists, strapped for food and clothing, pressed hard on the native peoples. They demanded tribute in the form of cotton blankets, buffalo hides, and baskets of scarce maize. In winter, ill-equipped Spanish soldiers stripped warm robes off the backs of shivering women and children; in summer, they scoured each pueblo for corn, torturing residents to find out where food was hidden.

Meanwhile, a few hundred Pueblo Indians—intimidated by the Spanish, desperate for a share of the food they had grown, and fearful of attacks by neighboring Apache—began to accept Christian baptism and seek Spanish protection. By 1608, when the crown threatened to withdraw support from the struggling province, the colony's Franciscan missionaries

MAP 2.1
THE SPANISH SOUTHWEST IN THE EARLY SEVENTEENTH CENTURY

appealed that their converts had grown too numerous to resettle and too dependent to abandon. Their argument may have been exaggerated, but it caught the attention of authorities. Besides, England and France were launching new colonies in Virginia and Canada. Since mapmakers still could not accurately calculate longitude (to determine east–west distances on the globe), no one was sure whether these bases created by international rivals posed a threat that was dangerously close at hand. Worried Spanish officials finally agreed with the Franciscan friars that New Mexico must carry on. They replaced Oñate with a new governor and asserted royal control over the few dozen settlers who remained in the colony.

■ Acoma, often called Sky City, sits atop a high sandstone mesa west of Albuquerque, New Mexico. The name means "place that always was," and the pueblo has been continuously inhabited for roughly 1,000 years. Acoma's Native American community survived a devastating attack by Spanish colonizers in 1599.

New Mexico Survives: New Flocks Among Old Pueblos

The Spanish decision to hold on in New Mexico reshaped life for everyone in the region. At least 60,000 Indians living in nearly sixty separate pueblos found their world transformed and their survival threatened over the next half-century. In 1610 the new governor, ruling over scarcely fifty colonists, created a capital at the village of Santa Fe. Within two decades, roughly 750 colonists inhabited the remote province, including Spanish, Mexican Indians, Africans, and mixed-race children.

The racial and ethnic diversity of New Mexico repeated the colonial pattern established in New Spain. Similarly, labor practices and religious changes also followed models established after the conquest of the Aztec in Mexico. As in New Spain, certain privileged people in the new colony received *encomiendas*; such grants entitled the holders (known as *encomenderos*) to the labor of a set number of Native American workers. With labor in short supply throughout the Spanish colonies, other settlers led occasional raids against nomadic Plains Indians, keeping some captives and shipping others south to toil as slaves in the Mexican silver mines.

Meanwhile, the number of Franciscan missionaries rose rapidly. They forbade traditional Pueblo celebrations, known as kachina dances, and destroyed sacred kachina masks. Their combination of intense zeal and harsh punishments prompted many Indians to learn Spanish and become obedient converts. However, it also drove the Indians' own religious practices

In 1621 responsibility for New Netherland—the region claimed between the Delaware and Connecticut rivers—fell to the newly chartered Dutch West India Company (DWIC). Modeled on the Dutch East India Company, the DWIC concentrated on piecing together an empire in the South Atlantic. Dutch ships seized part of sugar-rich Brazil (1632), the island of Curaçao near Venezuela (1634), and Portugal's African outpost at Elmina, on the coast of modern-day Ghana (1637). But the DWIC also laid plans for a North American colony.

To begin, the company transported a group of French-speaking Belgians to New Netherland in 1624. To secure the boundaries of the province, officials deposited farm families far up the Hudson at Fort Orange and along the Connecticut and Delaware rivers. However, Peter Minuit, the colony's director from 1626 to 1631, saw danger in this dispersal. To consolidate settlement, he purchased Manhattan Island at the mouth of the Hudson from the local Indians in 1626. By 1630 the village of New Amsterdam boasted 270 settlers at the southern tip of Manhattan.

When the company threw open the Indian trade to others besides its own agents, the careless and greedy actions of unregulated traders sparked a series of violent wars with coastal tribes. Also, the Dutch squabbled constantly with neighboring English settlers over fur-trading rights and other matters. The small colony of New Sweden, which materialized on the west side of the Delaware River in 1637, posed yet another problem. The settlers who built Fort Christina (now Wilmington, Delaware) were Swedes and Finns hoping to establish their own trade with the Indians. But in 1655, these several hundred Scandinavians were obliged to surrender to Dutch power.

"All Sorts of Nationalities": Diverse New Amsterdam

The symbol of Dutch power in the region, and the commander of the fleet that seized New Sweden, was Peter Stuyvesant. He ruled New Netherland aggressively for several decades before England seized the colony in 1664. Stuyvesant had served as governor of Dutch Curaçao, losing his right leg in a battle with the Spanish. When he arrived in New Netherland in 1647 as director general for the DWIC, he moved swiftly to assert control.

Stuyvesant limited beer and rum sales, fined settlers for promiscuity and knife fighting, and established a nine-member night watch. When a group of English Quakers, members of

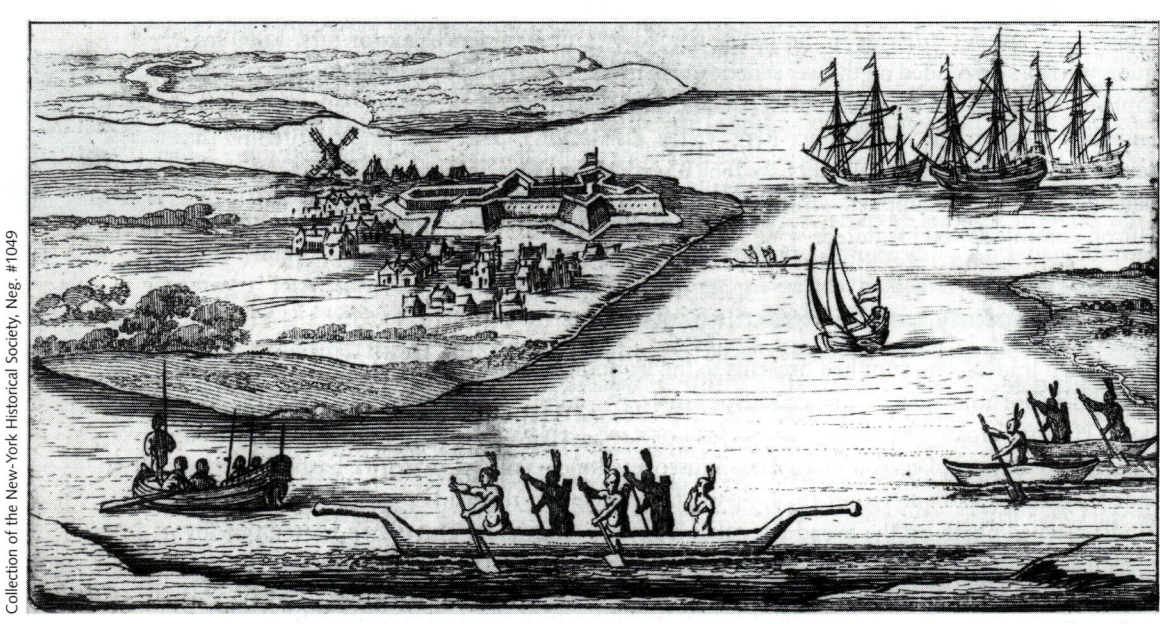

■ New Amsterdam Fort on Manhattan Island.

the newly formed Society of Friends, arrived aboard a trading vessel in 1657, he attempted to expel the radical Protestants and fine any who gave them shelter. However, Dutch residents of Flushing, on Long Island, defied his ban and signed a public letter of objection stressing religious toleration.

To address the colony's chronic labor shortage, Stuyvesant endorsed trade in African slaves and used his Caribbean connections to expand this traffic. When the Portuguese forced Holland out of Brazil in 1654 and closed that sugar colony to Dutch slave vessels, some of the ships brought their cargoes to New Amsterdam instead. Like the Dutch-speaking blacks who already lived in the colony, most of these newcomers were enslaved for life. But the DWIC, the largest importer and owner of slaves in New Netherland, granted "half-freedom" to some whom it could not employ year-round. These people, in return for an annual fee, could travel and marry freely, acquire property, and hire out their labor. By 1664 black residents made up over 10 percent of New Netherland's population and 20 percent of New Amsterdam, the colony's capital.

New Amsterdam, home to fewer than 2,000 people, also had a small Jewish contingent, the first in mainland North America. In 1654, twenty-three Sephardic Jews reached Manhattan, forced out of Brazil by the Portuguese. Stuyvesant, strident in his anti-Semitism, claimed such "blasphemers of the name of Christ" would "infect and trouble this new colony." But the DWIC, which included Jewish stockholders and was eager for newcomers of all kinds, overruled the governor's request to expel the refugees. In the end, colony officials authorized a Jewish ghetto, or segregated neighborhood, where the newcomers could pray together freely in private. At first, however, they were not allowed to construct a synagogue for public worship.

In the early 1660s, the colony continued to grow, "slowly peopled by the scrapings of all sorts of nationalities," as Stuyvesant complained. Huguenots occupied New Paltz near the Hudson; farther north, other newcomers founded Schenectady in 1661. Swedes and Finns continued to prosper along the Delaware, and numerous English had settled on Long Island. Compared with New France, New Netherland seemed far more populous, prosperous, and ethnically diverse. But whereas the French colony to the north endured for another century, the Dutch enterprise soon was absorbed by England. For, despite a slow start, the English managed to outdistance all their European rivals and establish thriving North American colonies in the first half of the seventeenth century.

> *Compared with New France, New Netherland seemed far more populous, prosperous, and ethnically diverse.*

English Beginnings on the Atlantic Coast

When Queen Elizabeth I passed away in 1603, several important elements were already in place to help England compete for colonial outposts. Thousands of rural tenants had been pushed off farms; these landless people, who flocked to urban centers in search of work, formed a restless supply of potential colonists. Also, the country had an expanding fleet of English-built ships, sailed by experienced mariners. In addition, England had a group of seasoned and ambitious leaders. A generation of soldiers (many of them younger sons of the property-holding elite known as the gentry) had fought in Europe or participated in the brutal colonization of Ireland.

Because Elizabeth I died without heirs, the king of Scotland, James Stuart, succeeded her as ruler. During the reigns of James I (1603–1625) and his son Charles I (1625–1649), religious and economic forces in England prompted an increasing number of people to consider migrating overseas. With the expansion of the country's Protestant Reformation, religious strife escalated toward civil war, which erupted in 1642. During the tumultuous 1630s, English public officials were glad to transplant Puritans and Catholics alike to foreign shores. In turn, many **ardent** believers—weary of conflict or losing hope for their cause at home—welcomed the prospect of a safe haven abroad. Economically, the development of joint stock organizations enabled merchants to raise capital and spread the high risk of colonial ventures by selling numerous shares to small investors. At the same time, the fluctuating domestic economy prompted many people to consider seeking their fortunes elsewhere.

Nor had English geographers given up on finding a sea route somewhere in the Northern Hemisphere leading to the riches of Asia. Perhaps Virginia would prove no wider than the Isthmus of Panama, or a short passage to China would reveal itself farther north. With this latter prospect in mind, England pressed Henry Hudson into service in 1610, shortly after his voyage for the Dutch. The experienced explorer ventured far to the northwest, navigating the strait and bay in northern Canada that still bear his name. But Hudson's search for a Northwest Passage failed, and he was set adrift by his mutinous crew. English attention moved elsewhere.

The Virginia Company and Jamestown

For Richard Hakluyt, England's leading publicist for overseas expansion, the proper focus seemed clear: "There is under our noses," he wrote in 1599, "the great & ample countrey of Virginia." Great and ample, indeed, especially before the rival Dutch established New Netherland. On paper, the enormous zone that England claimed as Virginia stretched north to south from the top of modern-day Vermont to Cape Fear on Carolina's Outer Banks. From east to west, it spanned North America from the Atlantic to the Pacific, however narrow or wide the continent might prove to be.

In 1606 James I chartered the Virginia Company as a two-pronged operation to exploit the sweeping Virginia claim. Under the charter, a group of London-based merchants took responsibility for colonizing the Chesapeake Bay region. Meanwhile, merchants from the English seaports of Plymouth, Exeter, and Bristol took charge of developing the northern latitudes of the American coast. In 1607 two ships from Plymouth deposited roughly a hundred colonists at the Sagadahoc (Kennebec) River in Maine. The Sagadahoc settlers erected a fort and buildings, but frostbite, scurvy, and dwindling supplies prompted a retreat home in 1608.

Mural of Jamestown Settlement

A parallel effort by the Londoners proved more enduring—but just barely. In April 1607, three ships from the Thames sailed into Chesapeake Bay carrying 105 men. They disembarked on what appeared to be a secluded island near a broad river. Within months, these subjects of James I had named the waterway the James River and established a fortified village beside it called Jamestown. In June, hoping for quick rewards, they shipped to London various stones that they thought contained precious gems and gold ore.

When the rocks proved worthless, the colonists' dreams of easy wealth evaporated. So did their fantasies about pushing west to the Pacific. During the outpost's first winter, a fire destroyed the tiny settlement, and death from hunger, exposure, and sickness cut the garrison's population in half. The governor and council appointed by the Virginia Company bickered among themselves, providing poor leadership. Fully one-third of the early arrivals claimed to be gentlemen, from England's leisure class—a proportion six times higher than in England—and most proved unaccustomed to hard manual labor. Moreover, all the colonists were employees of the company, so any profits from their labor went to repay London investors.

Despite the unsuitable make-up of the garrison, conditions improved briefly with the emergence of John Smith as a vigorous leader. Captain Smith dealt brazenly with the local Powhatan Indian confederation, numbering more than 13,000 people. He reached a tenuous accommodation with the paramount chief, Powhatan, who had been steadily expanding his power across the Tidewater region. (Later, Smith claimed to have been assisted and protected by Powhatan's young daughter, Pocahontas.) Still, the Jamestown colony limped along with meager support, living in fear of Spanish attacks.

With hopes of a swift bonanza dashed, the London merchants decided to alter their strategy. They would salvage the venture by attracting fresh capital; then they would recoup their high initial costs by recruiting new settlers who could produce staple products suited for export—perhaps grapes, sugar, cotton, or tobacco. In 1609 the company began to sell seven-year joint stock options to the English public. Subscribers could invest money or they could sign on for service in Virginia. Company officials promised such adventurers at least a hundred acres of land when their investment matured in 1616. In June 1609, 500 men and 100 women departed for the Chesapeake aboard nine ships.

"Starving Time" and the Seeds of Representative Government

When the battered fleet arrived at Jamestown, the new arrivals found insufficient supplies. Moreover, the first settlers had failed to discover a profitable staple crop. The settlers, now numbering 500, depended heavily on the Native Americans for food, and Powhatan's Confederacy proved increasingly unwilling and unable to supply it. In a grim "starving time," the ill-equipped newcomers scavenged for berries and bark. Extreme hunger drove a few to cannibalize the dead before dying themselves. By the spring of 1610, seven of every eight people had died; scarcely sixty remained alive.

John Smith, "The Starving Time"

In June these survivors abandoned their ghost town altogether. But as they set sail for England, they encountered three long-overdue ships entering Chesapeake Bay with fresh supplies and 300 new settlers. Reluctantly, they agreed to try again. More years of harsh discipline, Indian warfare, and scarce resources followed. Another force—a severe dry spell—also conspired against the hapless newcomers. Indian and English crops alike shriveled from 1607 through 1612.

Relief came from an unexpected quarter: the "bewitching vegetable" known as Orinoco tobacco. The plant, grown in parts of the West Indies and South America, had captured English taste in the previous generation. Sales of this New World product in England sent profits to the Spanish crown and prompted James I to launch a vigorous antismoking campaign in 1604. But John Rolfe, reaching Jamestown in 1610, wondered whether the "noxious weed" might provide the colonists with a viable staple crop. Rolfe, a smoker himself, suspected that sweet-flavored Orinoco tobacco could prosper in Virginia soil. Within a year, Rolfe had somehow managed to obtain seeds, and by 1612 his patch of West Indian tobacco was flourishing. Desperate settlers and impatient London investors were delighted by Rolfe's successful experiment. Soon production of the leaf soared at Jamestown, to the neglect of all other pursuits.

■ Inexperience prompted initial English difficulties at Roanoke and Jamestown, but so did poor weather. Scientists studying the region's bald cypress trees have recently shown (from certain narrow rings) that terrible droughts struck the coastal area in the late 1580s and again from 1606 through 1612. These two sequences of narrow annual rings are visible under the magnifying glass.

During Virginia's initial tobacco boom, recently starving settlers saw handsome profits within reach. Because land was plentiful, the only limitations to riches were the scarcity of workers and the related high cost of labor. Any farmer who could hire half a dozen field hands could increase his profits fivefold, quickly earning enough to obtain more land and import more servants. The company transported several shiploads of apprentices and servants to the labor-hungry colony. When a Dutch captain delivered twenty enslaved blacks in 1619, settlers eagerly purchased these first Africans to arrive in English Virginia. They also bid on the 100 women who disembarked the same year, shipped from England by the company to be sold as wives and workers. Still, men continued to outnumber women more than three to one for decades to come.

To encourage English migration further, the Virginia Company offered transportation and 50 acres to tenants, promising them ownership of the land after seven years of work. Men who paid their own way received 50 acres and an additional "**headright**" of 50 acres for each household member or laborer they transported. The Virginia Company went out of its way to assure its colonists access to such established English freedoms as the right to trial by jury and to a representative form of government. The company established civil courts controlled by English common law, and it instructed Virginia's governor to summon an annual assembly of elected **burgesses**—the earliest representative legislature in North America. First convened in 1619, the House of Burgesses wasted no time in affirming its commitment to fundamental English rights. The governor, the house said, could no longer impose taxes without the assembly's consent.

> *The Virginia Company went out of its way to assure its colonists access to established English freedoms.*

Launching the Plymouth Colony

To attract additional capital and people, the Virginia Company also began awarding patents (legal charters) to private groups of adventurers. The newcomers would live independently on a large tract, with only minimal control from the governor and his council. Two such small colonies originated among English Protestants living in exile in Holland because their separatist beliefs did not allow them to profess loyalty to the Church of England. The first group of 180, based in Amsterdam, departed for America late in 1618 on a crowded ship. Winter storms, sickness, and a shortage of fresh water destroyed the venture; scarcely fifty survivors straggled ashore in Virginia.

A second group of English Separatists, residing in the smaller Dutch city of Leiden, fared better. Most had migrated to Holland from northeast England in 1608. This group openly opposed the hierarchy, pomp, and inclusiveness of the Church of England. Instead, they wanted to return to early Christianity, where small groups of worthy (and often persecuted) believers formed their own communities of worship. After a decade in Holland, many of them had wearied of the foreign culture. Dismayed by the effect of worldly Leiden on their children, they also sensed, correctly, that warfare would soon break out in Europe. A few families pushed for a further removal to America, despite the obvious dangers of such a journey.

Possible destinations ranged from South America to Canada. But in the end, the Separatists decided to use a patent granted by the Virginia Company to a group of English capitalists. On the negative side, they had to work for these investors for seven years. They also had to take along paying passengers who did not share their beliefs. On the positive side, they received financial support from backers who paid to rent a ship. Moreover, instead of having their daily affairs controlled from London, they had the power to govern themselves.

DOCUMENT
Agreement Between the Settlers at New Plymouth (Mayflower Compact)

In September 1620, after costly delays, thirty-five members of the Leiden congregation and additional Separatists from England departed from Plymouth, along with other passengers. They were crowded aboard the *Mayflower*, a 160-ton vessel bound for Virginia. But a stormy two-month crossing brought them to Cape Cod, in modern-day Massachusetts, no longer considered part of the Virginia Company's jurisdiction. Sickly from their journey and with winter closing in, they decided to disembark at the spot they called Plymouth rather than push south to Chesapeake Bay. Earlier, they had signed a solemn compact aboard the *Mayflower* binding them together in a civil community.

William Bradford, the chronicler and longtime governor of Plymouth Colony, later recalled their plight: "They had now no friends to welcome them nor inns to entertain or refresh their weather-beaten bodies. . . . Besides, what could they see but a hideous and desolate wilderness." Bradford could scarcely exaggerate the challenge. His own wife drowned (an apparent suicide) shortly after the *Mayflower* dropped anchor. And by the time the ship departed in April, an illness had swept away half the colonists. When those remaining planted barley and peas, the English seeds failed to take hold.

Still, settlers had abundant fish and wildlife, along with ample Indian corn, and soon reinforcements arrived from England bringing needed supplies. The newcomers also brought a legal patent for the land of Plymouth Plantation. With Squanto's aid, the settlers secured peaceful relations with Massasoit's villages. When survival for another winter seemed assured, they invited Massasoit and his Indian followers to join in a three-day celebration of thanksgiving so that, according to one account, all might "rejoice together after we had gathered the fruit of our labors."

"Plymouth Colony"

The Puritan Experiment

After more than a generation of costly colonization attempts, England still had little to show for its efforts when Charles I inherited the throne in 1625. Then two forces prompted rapid change: positive publicity about America and negative developments at home. John Smith, long a key promoter of overseas settlement, drew inspiration from the early efforts at Jamestown and Plymouth. In 1624 he published a best-seller predicting future success for these regions. Ironically, the book's popularity depended in large part on the grim religious, political, and economic conditions in England that suddenly gave such literature a broad appeal.

Formation of the Massachusetts Bay Company

European Christianity had taken a number of different forms since the religious upheaval sparked by Luther a century earlier. The first Protestants had demanded a reformation of the Roman Catholic Church and had questioned papal authority over Christians. Now many non-Catholic English worshippers doubted whether the Church of England (also known as the Anglican Church) had gone far enough toward rejecting the practices of Rome. They lamented what they saw as the church's bureaucratic hierarchy, ornate rituals, and failure to enforce strict observance of the Christian Sabbath each Sunday. They scoffed at the gaudy vestments of Anglican bishops, elaborate church music, and other trappings of worship unjustified by biblical scripture. Instead, they praised the stark simplicity that John Calvin had brought to his church in Geneva.

As English Calvinists grew in number, their objections to the Church of England increased. They protested that the Anglican Church, like the Catholic Church, remained inclusive in membership rather than selective. They argued for limiting participation only to the devout, and they protested that the Church of England should be independent and self-governing rather than tied to the monarchy. This keen desire for further cleansing and purity, so common to reformers, spurred the ongoing movement known as Puritanism.

"The Puritans"

Some of the most radical members of the broad Puritan coalition (including Bradford and the Plymouth pilgrims) became known as Separatists because they were committed to an extreme position: complete separation from what they saw as the corrupt Church of England. But many more Puritans (including most of the reformers who migrated to Massachusetts Bay) resisted separation. They hoped to stay technically within the Anglican fold while taking increased control of their own congregations—a practice known as congregationalism. Unwilling to conform to practices that offended them, these nonseparating Congregationalists remained determined to save the Anglican Church through righteous example, even if it meant migrating abroad for a time to escape persecution and demonstrate the proper ways of a purified Protestant church.

An emphasis on instructive preaching by informed leaders lay at the heart of the Puritan movement. Puritans believed that the sermon should form the center of the Christian worship service. Their churches resembled lecture halls, emphasizing the pulpit more than the altar. In preaching, Puritans stressed a "plain style" that all listeners could understand. Moreover, they urged listeners to play an active role in their faith—to master reading and engage in regular study and discussion of scripture. In response to mounting public interest in these practices, Puritan ministers intensified their preaching and published their sermons. In effect, they dared authorities to silence them.

The Cambridge Agreement

Reprisals came swiftly, led by William Laud, bishop of London. Laud instructed all preachers to focus their remarks on biblical passages and avoid writing or speaking about controversial religious matters. As England's church grew more rigid and its monarchy more controlling, the nation's economy took a turn for the worse. Rents and food costs had risen more rapidly than wages, and workers paid dearly. Jobs became more scarce, and unemployed workers staged local revolts. In 1629 entrepreneurs who viewed New England as a potential opportunity teamed up with disaffected Puritans to obtain a charter for a new entity: the Massachusetts Bay Company. Through a generation of costly trial-and-error experiments, the English had amassed great expertise in colonization. And given the worsening conditions at home, especially among the Puritan faithful, proposals for overseas settlement attracted widespread attention.

"We Shall Be as a City upon a Hill"

During the next dozen years, more than 70,000 people left England for the New World. Two-thirds of them sailed to the West Indies. But a large contingent of Puritans embarked for the new Massachusetts Bay colony, adjacent to the Plymouth settlement. A loophole in the king's grant permitted them to take the actual charter with them and to hold their company meetings in America. This maneuver took them out from under the usual control of London investors and let them turn the familiar joint stock structure into the framework for a self-governing colony. By 1629 advance parties had established a post at Salem for people who "upon the account of religion would be willing to begin a foreign plantation."

In England, meanwhile, a Puritan squire named John Winthrop assumed leadership of the Massachusetts Bay Company. "God will bring some heavy Affliction upon this lande," he predicted to his wife, but the Lord "will provide a shelter & a hidinge place for us and others." In exchange, God would expect great things from these chosen people, as from the Old Testament Israelites. "We are entered into covenant with him for this work," Winthrop told his companions aboard the *Arbella* en route to America in 1630.

Winthrop laid out this higher Calvinist standard in a memorable shipboard sermon titled "A Model of Christian Charity." Far from hiding in obscurity, dedicated Puritans must set a visible example for the rest of the world, Winthrop declared. "We shall be as a city upon a hill."

The *Arbella* was one of seventeen ships that brought more than 1,000 people to New England in 1630. The English newcomers chose Winthrop as governor and established Boston as their port. By the time civil war erupted in England in 1642, nearly 20,000 people had made the journey, eager to escape the religious persecution and governmental tyranny of Charles I. Whole congregations migrated with their ministers; other people (more than 20 percent) crossed as servants. But most came as independent families, setting up stable households where

■ Port records for 1635 show that groups leaving London varied markedly, depending on their colonial destination. Young children were common aboard ships heading for New England, as were women and girls. Among passengers for New England, eight of every twenty were female. In contrast, females made up only three in twenty of those going to Virginia and one in twenty among people heading for Barbados.

INTERPRETING HISTORY

Anne Bradstreet: "The Tenth Muse, Lately Sprung Up in America"

The Puritans who migrated to America stressed literacy and education as part of their faith. They wrote down a great deal, and they left extensive records for posterity. But most of their sermons, diaries, and chronicles were drafted by men; few documents about the thoughts and experiences of New England's early migrants come from the pens of women. The poems and reflections of Anne Bradstreet provide a notable exception. "Here you may find," she reminded her children shortly before her death in 1672, "what was your living mother's mind."

The lifelong poet was born Anne Dudley in Lincolnshire, England, in 1612. She already "found much comfort in reading the Scriptures" by age seven. "But as I grew to be about 14 or 15," she recalled, "I found my heart more carnal, and . . . the follies of youth took hold of me. About 16, the Lord . . . smote me with the smallpox . . . and again restored me." That same year, she married Simon Bradstreet, the son of a minister. Two years later, despite a frail constitution, she sailed for Massachusetts Bay with her husband and her father (both future governors of the colony) aboard the *Arbella*.

Having left England at age eighteen, Anne Bradstreet was alert to all that seemed strange and different in America. When I "came into this country," she related, "I found a new world and new manners." The young couple set up housekeeping in the town of Cambridge, on the Charles River, but life was difficult at first. Anne suffered from "a lingering sickness like a consumption." Moreover, "It pleased God to keep me a long time without a child, which was a

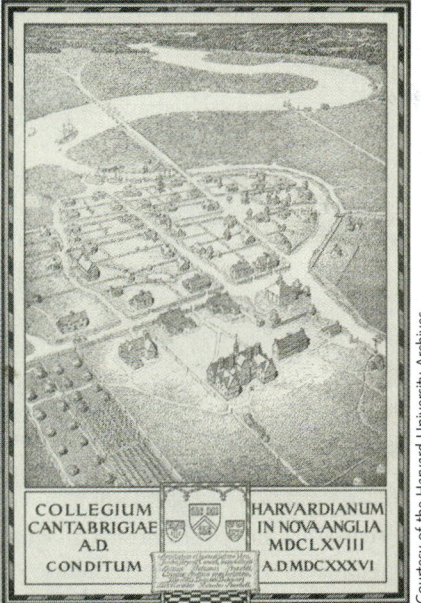

Cambridge, on the Charles River near Boston, was a small village in the 1660s. The large building in the foreground is Harvard College, founded in 1636, and the smaller brick building beside it is the Indian College, built in 1655. The village was even smaller when Anne Bradstreet resided there briefly after her arrival in Massachusetts Bay.

great grief to me and cost me many prayers and tears." Finally, she bore a son in 1633, and seven more children followed.

As the family grew and moved about, "Mistress Bradstreet" wrote poems and meditations, although detractors hinted that she should put down her quill pen and take up a sewing needle. "If what I do prove well, it won't advance," she lamented in rhyme; "They'l say it's stol'n, or else it was by chance." Nevertheless, a book of her poems was published in England in 1650, hailing her as "The Tenth Muse, Lately Sprung Up in America."

As a writer, Anne Bradstreet was more interested in spiritual improvement than literary grace. "Many speak well," she observed, "but few can do well." Throughout life, she followed a simple creed: "There is no object that we see; no action that we do; no good that we enjoy; no evil that we feel or fear, but we may make some spiritual advantage" of it.

Nothing epitomizes this belief more clearly than "some verses upon the burning of our house, July 10th, 1666." Bradstreet composed the lines on an unburned scrap of paper as she groped to make sense of the calamity. The poem helped her to mourn her loss, take stock of her blessings, and renew her faith. In part, it reads,

In silent night when rest I took,
For sorrow neer I did not look,
I waken'd was with thundring nois
And Piteous shreiks of dreadfull voice. . . .

I, starting up, the light did spye,
And to my God my heart did cry. . . .
Then coming out beheld a space
The flame consume my dwelling place.

And, when I could no longer look,
I blest his Name that gave and took,
That layd my goods now in the dust:
Yea so it was, and so 'twas just. . . .

When by the Ruines oft I past,
My sorrowing eyes aside did cast,
And here and there the places spye
Where oft I sate, and long did lye.

Here stood that Trunk, and there
   that chest;
There lay that store I counted best:
My pleasant things in ashes lye,
And them behold no more shall I. . . .

Then streight I gin my heart to chide,
And did thy wealth on earth abide?
Didst fix thy hope on mouldring dust,
The arm of flesh didst make thy trust? . . .

Thou hast a house on high erect
Fram'd by that mighty Architect. . . .
The world no longer let me Love,
My hope and Treasure lyes Above.

Questions

1. How might Anne Bradstreet's eventful life before age 20 have shaped her into a poet?
2. Imagine losing your home and belongings in a storm, flood, or fire. Would it deepen or weaken your religious beliefs? How about your need for material possessions? ■

Source: From "Verses upon the Burning of Our House," July 18th, 1666 by Anne Bradstreet.

women played important parts. They took an immediate role in crucial aspects of domestic manufacture and production, and their numerous children provided additional hands where labor was in short supply.

Initial settlers traded food, lodging, and building materials to later arrivals in exchange for textiles, tools, money, and labor. When new groups of church members wanted to establish a village, they applied for land to the General Court, a legislature made up of representatives elected from existing towns. By 1640 English settlements dotted the coast and had sprung up inland along the Connecticut River, where smallpox had decimated the Indians in 1633. There, English outposts rose at Hartford and Springfield, where English traders hoped to attract furs away from the French and Dutch.

Dissenters: Roger Williams and Anne Hutchinson

Like the biblical Hebrews before them, the Puritans—self-appointed saints—believed that God had chosen them for a special mission in the world. The Almighty, they believed, would watch carefully, punish harshly, and reward mightily. Inevitably, some devout people, raised to question authority in England, continued to dissent in New England. Not everyone accepted the idea that Puritans should dominate Indians or that women should defer to men. Roger Williams, a graduate of Cambridge University, and Anne Hutchinson, the talented daughter of an English minister, stand out as two of the earliest and most effective challengers to leadership in the Massachusetts Bay colony.

When Williams arrived in Boston, his Separatist leanings angered Bay Colony authorities, who still hoped to reform the Anglican Church rather than renounce it. Williams's other contentions proved equally distressing. The young minister argued that civil authorities, inevitably corrupt, had no right to judge religious matters. He even pushed for an unprecedented separation of church and state—to protect the church. He also contended that the colony's land patent from the king had no validity. The settlers, he said, had to purchase occupancy rights from the Native Americans. Unable to silence him, irate magistrates banished Williams from Massachusetts Bay in the winter of 1635. Moving south, he took up residence among the Narragansett Indians and built a refuge for other dissenters, which he named Providence. In 1643 he returned to London, where he persuaded leaders of England's rising Puritan revolution to grant a charter (1644) to his independent colony of Rhode Island.

A more explosive popular challenge centered on Anne Hutchinson, who had grown up in England with a strong will, a solid theological education, and a thirst for spiritual perfection. She married a Lincolnshire textile merchant and took an active part in religious discussions while also bearing fifteen children. When her Puritan minister, John Cotton, departed for New England, Hutchinson claimed that God, in a private revelation, had instructed her to follow. In 1634 the family migrated to Boston, where Hutchinson attended Cotton's church and hosted religious discussions in her home. The popularity of these weekly meetings troubled authorities, as did her argument that the "Holy Spirit illumines the heart of every true believer." Hutchinson downplayed outward conformity—modest dress or regular church attendance—as a route to salvation. Instead, she stressed direct communication with God's inner presence as the key to individual forgiveness.

Most Puritans sought a delicate balance in their lives between respected outer works and inner personal grace. Hutchinson tipped that balance dangerously toward the latter. To the colony's magistrates, especially Winthrop, such teaching pointed toward dangerous anarchy—more dangerous when it came from a woman. These officials labeled Hutchinson and her followers as Antinomians (from *anti*, "against," and *nomos*, "law"). But the vehement faction grew, attracting merchants who chafed under economic restrictions, women who questioned men's domination of the church, and young adults who resented the strict authority of their elders. By 1636 this religious and political coalition had gained enough supporters to turn Winthrop out as governor.

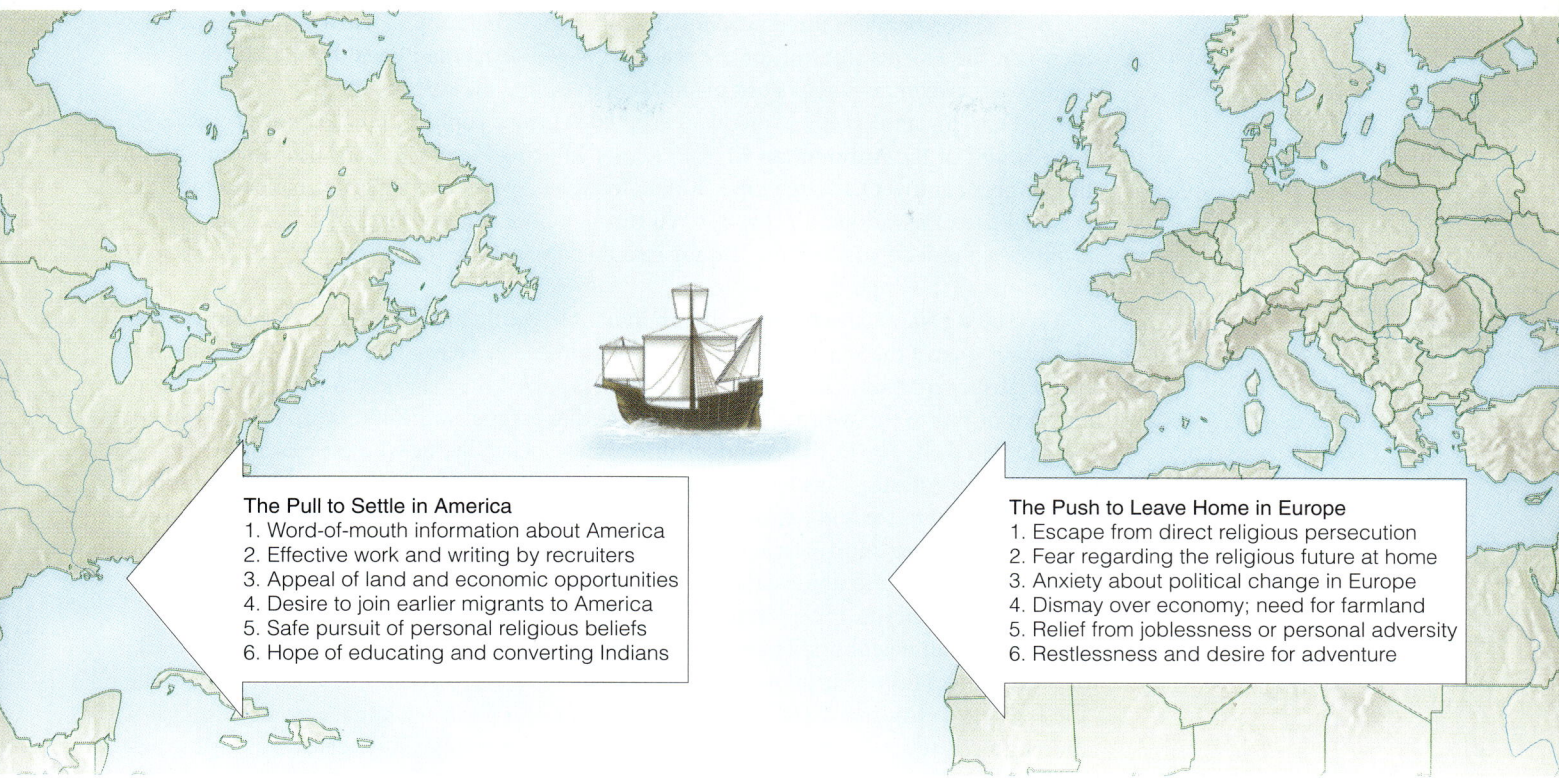

■ **FIGURE 2.1**
THE TOUGH CHOICE TO START OVER

Facing complete overthrow, members of the Puritan establishment fought back. They divided the opposition to win reelection for Winthrop, they established Harvard College to educate ministers who would not stray from the fold, they staged a flurry of trials for contempt and sedition (inciting resistance to lawful authority), and they made a special example of Hutchinson herself. After a two-day hearing in which she defended herself admirably, Winthrop sentenced his antagonist to banishment as "a woman not fit for our society." Forced into exile, Hutchinson moved first to Rhode Island and later to the vicinity of Dutch settlements near the Hudson. There she and most of her family were killed by Indians in 1643. A river and a parkway in Bronx, New York, still bear her name.

Expansion and Violence: The Pequot War

Immigration to New England slowed during the 1640s because of religious and political upheaval at home. In England, Puritans and supporters of Parliament formed an army and openly challenged royal authority during the English Civil War. After seizing power, these revolutionaries beheaded Charles I in 1649, abolished monarchy, and proclaimed England a republican Commonwealth. Settlers in Massachusetts Bay struggled to square such sweeping developments in England with Winthrop's earlier assurance that the eyes of God and humankind would be fixed on New England. Making matters worse, religious and economic controversies intensified as the next generation quickly came of age. Needing new farmland and intellectual breathing room, fresh congregations began to "hive off" from the original settlements like swarms of bees. By 1640 New Hampshire, Rhode Island, and Connecticut each had at least four new towns that would provide the beginnings for independent colonies.

But the northeastern forest was not an empty wilderness any more than the Chesapeake tidewater, the Florida interior, or the mesas of New Mexico had been. As the Hutchinsons discovered, newcomers who pushed inland were co-opting the land of longtime residents. Pressure on New England's Native Americans erupted in armed conflict in the Pequot War of 1637, at the height of the Antinomian Crisis. The neighboring Pequot Indians near the mouth of the Connecticut River had been English allies for several years, and a recent smallpox epidemic had weakened them dramatically. But Winthrop, whose son was leading a settlement effort in the area, fanned fears that the Pequot "would cause all the Indians in the country to join to root out all the English."

Recruiting Narragansett and Mohegan Indians to the English side, the colonists unleashed all-out war against the Pequot. The campaign culminated in a dawn raid on a stockaded Pequot town that sheltered noncombatants. The invaders torched the village (at Mystic, Connecticut) and shot or put to the sword almost all who tried to escape. Some 400 Indian men, women, and children died. The Puritans' Indian allies were shocked by the wholesale carnage. English warfare, they protested, "is too furious, and slaies too many men." Chastened by this intimidating display of terror and weakened by recurrent epidemics, the tribes of southern New England negotiated away much of their land over the next generation, trading furs to the expanding colonists and seeking to understand their perplexing ways.

Having gained the upper hand, the Bible-reading English made gestures to convert their Native American neighbors. The Massachusetts General Court encouraged missionary work, forbade the worship of Indian gods, and set aside land for "praying towns" to encourage "the Indians to live in an orderly way amongst us." In Roxbury, the Reverend John Eliot labored to create a 1,200-page Indian Bible. And in Cambridge, officials at Harvard, committed by their charter to the "education of the English and Indian youth of this Country," erected a well-publicized Indian College.

The Chesapeake Bay Colonies

On Chesapeake Bay, settlers' relations with the Indians remained strained at best during the first half of the seventeenth century. In 1608, in an effort to secure the support of Indian leadership, the English performed an elaborate ceremony granting a copper crown to Chief Powhatan and a scarlet cloak to replace his deerskin mantle. But two years later, suspicious that he was harboring runaway colonists, the English burned the nearest Indian villages and unthinkingly destroyed much-needed corn. One Indian woman leader, taken as a captive, watched English soldiers throwing her children in the river and shooting them in the head before she herself was stabbed to death.

For both sides, hopes of reconciliation rose briefly in 1614 with the match between Pocahontas, daughter of Powhatan, and John Rolfe, the prominent widower who had introduced tobacco. But the marriage proved brief; Pocahontas died in England three years later, after bearing one child. Leaders intended the wedding alliance as a diplomatic gesture toward peace. But it did little to curtail the settlers' bitterness over lingering dependence on Indian supplies, or Native Americans' resentment over English encroachment and arrogance.

The Demise of the Virginia Company

Powhatan's death in 1618 brought to power his more militant younger brother, Opechancanough, the leader of the Pamunkey tribe. His encounters with the English had been frequent and unfriendly. By 1618 the English tobacco crop was booming, and more newcomers were arriving annually. Over the next three years, forty-two ships brought 3,500 people to the Chesapeake colony. The influx disheartened the Indians, and Opechancanough and his followers in the Powhatan Confederacy sought ways to end the mounting intrusion. Briefly, disease seemed to work in the Indians' favor. Immigrants who made the long sea voyage with poor provisions often fell ill in the swampy and unhealthy environment of Jamestown. By 1622 the colony's inhabitants were dying almost as rapidly as newcomers arrived. Sickness had carried off 3,000 residents in the course of only three years.

Opechancanough sensed a chance to deliver the finishing blow. He planned a sudden and coordinated offensive along the lower James River. On March 22, 1622, his forces attacked the English, surprising the outlying settlements and sparing no one. Of the 1,240 colonists, nearly 350 lost their lives. Warned by an Indian, Jamestown survived the uprising, but hope for peaceful relations ended. The attack of 1622 fueled opposition to the Virginia Company among disgruntled English investors. In 1624 King James I annulled the company's charter, making Virginia a royal colony controlled by the crown. In the colony's first seventeen years, more than 8,500 people, almost all of them young, had embarked for the Chesapeake. Yet in 1624 scarcely 1,300 colonists (or three of every twenty arrivals) remained alive.

The colonists placed a bounty on Opechancanough's head, but attempts to ambush or poison him failed. The Indian leader lived on, nursing his distrust of the English. In 1644 he inaugurated a second uprising that killed some 500 colonists. But the English settlement had grown too large to eradicate. By this time old age forced the "Great General" to be carried on a litter. When the English finally captured him and brought him to Jamestown in 1646, Opechancanough was too old to walk unassisted. Still, he remained defiant until shot in the back by one of the Englishmen guarding him.

After two years of brutal warfare, the Pamunkey and their allies in the Powhatan Confederacy conceded defeat and submitted to English authority. From then on, they would pay a token annual tribute for the privilege to remain on lands that had once belonged to them. With the way cleared for expansion, land-hungry English settlers appeared in ever-increasing numbers near the shores of Chesapeake Bay. By 1660 roughly 25,000 colonists lived in Virginia and neighboring Maryland.

Maryland: The Catholic Refuge

Maryland, the smaller and the younger of the two English colonies on the Chesapeake, owed its beginnings to George Calvert. In a Protestant country, Calvert rose to become a respected Catholic member of England's government. He was named the first Baron of Baltimore, in Ireland, in 1625. Calvert, now Lord Baltimore, had a keen interest in colonization, and in 1632 he petitioned Charles I for land in the Chesapeake. The king granted him 10 million acres adjacent to Virginia, to be named Maryland in honor of the Catholic queen, Henrietta Maria. The Maryland charter gave the proprietor and his heirs unprecedented personal power, especially in the granting of lands to colonists without limitations based on religious belief.

DOCUMENT

The Charter of Maryland (1632)

Because Calvert died before the royal charter took effect, his eldest son, the second Lord Baltimore, took charge of the settlement effort. In 1634 the *Ark* and the *Dove* carried more than 200 settlers—both Protestants and Catholics—to the new colony. There, they established a capital at St. Mary's, near the mouth of the Potomac River. With the execution of the king in 1649 and the creation of an anti-Catholic commonwealth in England, the Calvert family provided a haven in Maryland for their coreligionists. However, Catholics never became a majority in the Chesapeake colony.

In 1649 Maryland's assembly passed an Act Concerning Religion, guaranteeing toleration for all settlers who professed a belief in Jesus Christ. This assertion of religious toleration, though limited, proved too broad for many to stomach. In the 1650s, supporters of the English Puritan cause seized power in Maryland, repealed the act, and briefly ended the Calverts' proprietorship. But by 1660, with the restoration of the Stuart monarchy in England, proprietary rule returned to the prosperous farming colony.

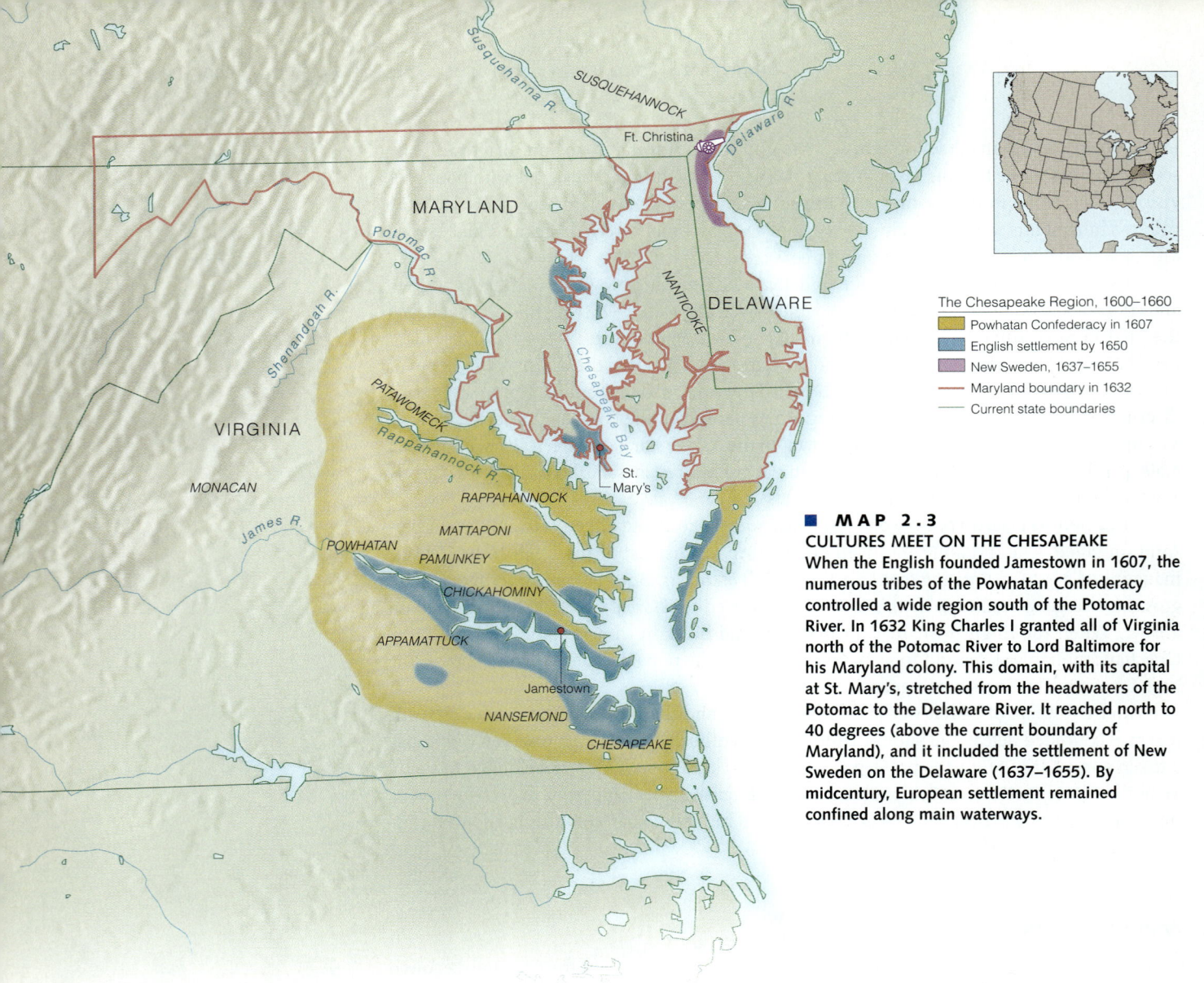

■ **MAP 2.3**
CULTURES MEET ON THE CHESAPEAKE
When the English founded Jamestown in 1607, the numerous tribes of the Powhatan Confederacy controlled a wide region south of the Potomac River. In 1632 King Charles I granted all of Virginia north of the Potomac River to Lord Baltimore for his Maryland colony. This domain, with its capital at St. Mary's, stretched from the headwaters of the Potomac to the Delaware River. It reached north to 40 degrees (above the current boundary of Maryland), and it included the settlement of New Sweden on the Delaware (1637–1655). By midcentury, European settlement remained confined along main waterways.

Tobacco Becomes a Way of Life

By 1660, Virginia and Maryland totaled roughly 35,000 settlers, scattered along the edges of the bay and its adjoining tidewater rivers. In contrast to New England, the Chesapeake still could not maintain its colonial population without steady infusions of newcomers. A sickly climate kept life expectancy low, and men continued to outnumber women by more than two to one. Early experiments with oranges, pineapples, and grapes led nowhere. Chesapeake lumber sold well at first, but it was John Rolfe's tobacco plant that emerged as the tidewater's unlikely crop of choice.

Virginia's annual tobacco exports rose from a total weight of 2,000 pounds in 1615 to 500,000 in 1626. By 1630, saturated markets and stiff taxes led to slumping tobacco prices, so Virginians diversified their efforts. The beginning of the Massachusetts Bay colony created a demand for food that Chesapeake farmers met with well-timed coastal shipments. In 1634 they reported selling to "their zealous neighbours of New England tenne thousand bushels of corne for their releefe, besides good quantities of beeves, goats and hoggs, whereof this country hath great plentie." Such diversification proved brief, however. By 1640, London was receiving almost 1.4 million pounds of tobacco annually.

Though tobacco prices remained low throughout much of the seventeenth century, newcomers to Virginia and Maryland still managed to eek out a profit. They could grow the plants amid stumps in partially cleared fields. They could learn the many necessary procedures—planting, weeding, worming, suckering, topping, cutting, stripping, and curing—as the crop progressed. In short, it took hard work, but little farming experience, to bring cured tobacco to waterfront docks. Since captains charged by volume rather than weight, planters reduced shipping costs by devising a uniform barrel size and developing ways to press more leaves into each cask.

Still, the problems were formidable. Tobacco depleted the soil rapidly, so crop yields dwindled after several years. Then farmers had to leave their plots fallow, allowing them to recover, while clearing new fields for planting. This time-consuming task forced them onto marginal land that was poorly drained and less fertile. It also moved them away from navigable rivers, raising transportation costs. Storms, droughts, and crop diseases posed constant threats, and dependence on a single product in a distant and uncertain overseas market created added dangers. By mid-century, Chesapeake planters worried about market saturation and overproduction. But by then, for better or worse, growing the noxious weed had become a way of life. Virginia and Maryland settlers found themselves enmeshed in the high-risk world of tobacco farming. Dependence on the troublesome crop would expand across the upper South for centuries to come.

Conclusion

During half a century, the French, Dutch, and English had all moved to challenge Spanish claims in North America. By 1660 all four of these maritime powers of western Europe had taken aggressive steps to establish permanent footholds on the fringes of the enormous continent. In each instance, the European colonizers benefited first from the presence of knowledgeable Native Americans and then from the sharp decline of those same people through warfare and the onslaught of new diseases.

Granted, warfare with foreign invaders and death from unknown diseases had become a part of Native American history in the preceding century. But the sixteenth century was an era of tentative European exploration. In contrast, the first half of the seventeenth century saw Europeans move beyond occasional forays to permanent colonization. Spain, France, Holland, and England each had formidable assets in Europe and on the high seas. By 1660 all had sponsored colonial settlements that had endured for several generations, and each had begun to taste the seductive fruits of empire in North America and elsewhere.

The English, slowest to become involved in overseas colonization, had caught up with their competitors by 1660. Among European countries, England had proven the most aggressive in forming expansive family-based colonies rather than military garrisons or trading outposts. By 1660 the population of England's fledgling North American colonies had already outstripped that of its rivals, and it was growing at an increasing rate. This emerging superiority in numbers was advantageous in the imperial clashes that lay ahead.

Sites to Visit

Acoma Pueblo
Located near Highway 40 west of Albuquerque, New Mexico, within the Acoma Indian Reservation, the Acoma Pueblo Visitors' Center offers guided tours of Sky City. On top of the 420-foot mesa, visitors can walk the streets of one of the oldest continuously inhabited sites in North America.

Mission San Luis Park
In northwest Tallahassee, archaeologists have excavated the Apalachee Indian town and Spanish mission that existed there in the seventeenth century. Mission San Luis Park, between Route 10 and Route 90, contains an outdoor museum with reconstructed buildings, exhibits, and guided tours.

Mashantucket Pequot Museum and Research Center
This expansive modern museum at Mashantucket in southeast Connecticut contains impressive exhibits and features a dramatic film about the Pequot War. For information, call 1-800-411-6971.

New Netherland Museum and Half Moon Visitor Center
Located in Albany, New York, the museum maintains a full-scale replica of Henry Hudson's ship the *Half Moon*, which is usually

docked at Albany and open for visitors. For information, contact the Main Office at 518-443-1609.

Plimoth Plantation
www.plimoth.org
This living history museum of seventeenth-century Plymouth is located off Route 3 south of Boston, Massachusetts. It recreates the pilgrim village as it appeared in 1627, with the *Mayflower II* and a Wampanoag Indian site nearby. Take a virtual tour at www.plimoth.org.

Historic Jamestown
www.history.org/nche/
www.ngdc.noaa.gov/paleo/drought/drght_james.html
At Historic Jamestown you can tour ruins, visit a glass-blowing exhibition, and see excavations of the original fort. Nearby, the Jamestown–Yorktown Foundation runs Jamestown Settlement, with reconstructed ships, fortifications, and Indian dwellings. These sites (busy during the 400th anniversary in 2007) are 7 miles from Williamsburg on Virginia's Colonial Parkway. They can be approached by ferry across the James River. The "Virtual Jamestown" Web site is a prize-winning educational resource on early Virginia. The severe seven-year Jamestown drought (1606–1612) is covered at the National Geographic Data Center site.

Wolstenholme Towne
This palisaded village, located near Jamestown, was destroyed in the 1622 Indian attack. The site is located at Carter's Grove Plantation, near Williamsburg. The Winthrop Rockefeller Archaeology Museum next door contains impressive exhibits on English settlement in Virginia.

Historic St. Mary's City
The site of Maryland's first capital lies off Route 5, near the mouth of the Potomac River, in southern Maryland, several hours' drive from Baltimore, Annapolis, and Washington, D.C. Since 1971 an annual summer archaeology field school has worked to excavate additional elements of the town.

For Further Reading

General
Bernard Bailyn, *The Peopling of British North America: An Introduction* (1985).
David Hackett Fischer, *Albion's Seed: Four British Folkways in America* (1989).
Henry Kamen, *Empire: How Spain Became a World Power* (2003).
Mary Beth Norton, *Founding Mothers and Fathers: Gendered Power and the Forming of American Society* (1996).
Alan Taylor, *American Colonies* (2001).

Spain's Ocean-Spanning Reach
Ramón A. Gutiérrez, *When Jesus Came, the Corn Mothers Went Away: Marriage, Sexuality, and Power in New Mexico, 1500–1846* (1991).
W. Michael Mathes, *Vizcaíno and Spanish Expansion in the Pacific Ocean* (1968).
Jerald T. Milanich, *Laboring in the Fields of the Lord: Spanish Missions and Southeastern Indians* (1999).
David J. Weber, *The Spanish Frontier in North America* (1992).

France and Holland: Overseas Competition for Spain
W. J. Eccles, *France in America* (1972).
Oliver A. Rink, *Holland on the Hudson: An Economic and Social History of Dutch New York* (1986).
Russell Shorto, *The Island at the Center of the World: The Epic Story of Dutch Manhattan and the Forgotten Colony That Shaped America* (2004).
Bruce G. Trigger, *Natives and Newcomers: Canada's "Heroic Age" Reconsidered* (1985).

English Beginnings on the Atlantic Coast
John Demos, *A Little Commonwealth: Family Life in Plymouth Colony* (1970).
Karen Ordahl Kupperman, *Indians and English: Facing Off in Early America* (2000).
Nathaniel Philbrick, *Mayflower—A Story of Courage, Community, and War* (2006).
Neal Salisbury, *Manitou and Providence: Indians, Europeans, and the Making of New England, 1500–1643* (1982).
Alden T. Vaughan, *American Genesis: Captain John Smith and the Founding of Virginia* (1975).

The Puritan Experiment
William Cronon, *Changes in the Land: Indians, Colonists, and the Ecology of New England* (1983).
Alison Games, *Migration and the Origins of the English Atlantic World* (1999).
Philip F. Gura, *A Glimpse of Sion's Glory: Puritan Radicalism in New England, 1620–1660* (1984).
Edmund S. Morgan, *The Puritan Dilemma: The Story of John Winthrop* (1958).

The Chesapeake Bay Colonies
Wesley Frank Craven, *The Southern Colonies in the Seventeenth Century, 1607–1689* (1949).
James Horn, *Adapting to a New World: English Society in the Seventeenth-Century Chesapeake* (1994).
Edmund S. Morgan, *American Slavery, American Freedom: The Ordeal of Colonial Virginia* (1975).
Helen C. Rountree, *The Powhatan Indians of Virginia* (1989).

For quizzes and other resources on these topics, go to www.longmanamericanhistory.com.

Controlling the Edges of the Continent, 1660–1715

CHAPTER

3

O N THE MONTREAL WATERFRONT IN APRIL 1704, MARGUERITE MESSIER LOADED A LARGE canoe, with help from her five children. She worked with her brother and a guide to prepare for an expedition to meet her husband at a new French outpost on the Gulf of Mexico. At twenty-eight, Messier had already been married half her life, having wed explorer-trader Pierre-Charles Le Sueur in 1690 when he was thirty-four and she was only fourteen.

Messier was deeply involved, through family ties, in the dramatic changes taking place throughout the vast North American hinterland claimed by France. Her cousin, an adventurous Canadian named Pierre Le Moyne d'Iberville, had established the French colony of Louisiana near the mouth of the Mississippi River in 1699, and three years later Iberville and his younger brother Bienville had started the village of Mobile (near present-day Mobile, Alabama) to serve as the first capital. In 1702 Messier's husband, long active in Canada's far-flung western trade, had paddled down the Mississippi, taking furs to the new outpost at Mobile. There he constructed a house for his family; then he accompanied Iberville back to France.

In 1704, confident about the future success of the Louisiana venture, Le Sueur sent word to his wife in Montreal to attempt the inland journey of nearly 2,000 miles to Mobile. He himself departed from France aboard the *Pelican* for the same destination, hoping to reunite with his family. Messier and her party set out from Montreal on April 30, 1704, making their way up the St. Lawrence and passing through Lake Ontario and Lake Erie. After more than a year, they reached Kaskaskia in southern Illinois and began to descend the Mississippi River. Messier's brother and a daughter died before the travelers finally reached their destination. When the survivors arrived at Mobile in August 1705, more bad news awaited them: the voyage of the *Pelican* had met with disaster.

Messier's husband had boarded the ship in France, joining missionaries, soldiers, and potential brides recruited to go to Mobile. But at a stopover in Cuba, he had caught yellow fever and died, along with many others, before the immigrants reached Mobile. The town—home to just 160 men and a dozen women—hardly had enough food and shelter for the sickly newcomers, and yellow fever spread quickly. The epidemic swept away forty residents in two months and decimated nearby Indian villages.

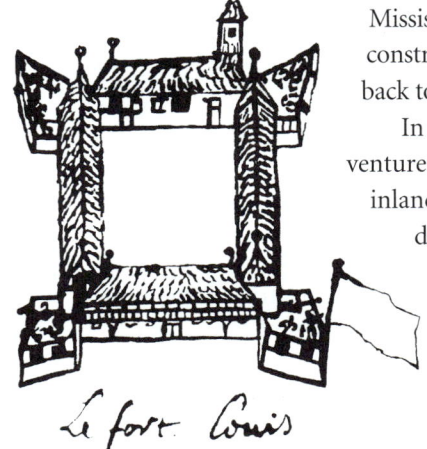

French fort at Mobile, 1705.

CHAPTER OUTLINE

France and the American Interior

The Spanish Empire on the Defensive

England's American Empire Takes Shape

Bloodshed in the English Colonies: 1670–1690

Consequences of War and Growth: 1690–1715

Conclusion

Sites to Visit

For Further Reading

55

Still, life at the outpost persisted. Townsmen welcomed the *Pelican*'s eligible young women, ages fourteen to eighteen, and priests celebrated thirteen marriages within the first three weeks. By 1705, when Marguerite Messier arrived from Montreal, new children were being born. Moving into the house her late husband had built, Messier determined to stay on and make a fresh start in the Louisiana colony.

Many of the changes that took place in North America during Marguerite Messier's lifetime occurred within a broad international context. During the second half of the seventeenth century, European maritime powers were caught up in a global race to expand and protect their overseas empires, and the chessboard was constantly changing. By the 1670s, Dutch authorities had been forced to withdraw entirely from North America, for example. As the Dutch departed, the Spanish, French, and English intensified their competition, starting towns wherever possible in order to stake out their claims.

In the East, England expanded the number and size of its coastal colonies, and English ports multiplied along the Atlantic seaboard. English newcomers also pressed inland along numerous rivers to found towns. Many of these towns (such as William Byrd's trading post that became Richmond, Virginia) appeared at the "fall line," the point where waterfalls blocked passage upstream and provided water power to run grist mills. Pushing up from the South, meanwhile, Spain struggled to retain its foothold in Florida and New Mexico and to lay claim to parts of Arizona and Texas as well. New Spanish towns appeared at Albuquerque, El Paso, and Pensacola. Of the three competing powers only France, pressing in from the St. Lawrence Valley, managed to penetrate the interior of the continent extensively. Its government created a string of forts from the Great Lakes to the Gulf of Mexico: Detroit, Peoria, and Mobile all came into being under the French flag.

One fundamental question recurred in numerous places during the decades after 1660: Who has the right to govern? Often, boundaries were vague and structures of control were tenuous; religious dissenters and political rebels who felt excluded or exploited could openly question the legitimacy of those in charge. In congregations, towns, and whole colonies, challenges to authority arose repeatedly. Disruptions and violence became familiar experiences for thousands of people inhabiting North America.

France and the American Interior

The potential wealth of the North American interior had long intrigued government ministers in France. If Canadian fur traders (known as *voyageurs*) could explore this vast domain and befriend its Indian inhabitants, France might control some of the continent's most fertile farmland and keep its extensive natural assets out of the hands of European rivals. If the French could recruit enough Native Americans as loyal allies, they might even threaten the rich mines of the Spanish empire in Mexico and challenge the growing English colonies lying to the east of the Appalachian Mountains. But for France to realize such wide ambitions, the French king, Louis XIV, would need to make North American colonization a national priority, and the extent of his commitment remained uncertain.

The Rise of the Sun King

King Louis XIV stood at the center of France's expanding imperial sphere. Indeed, so much seemed to revolve around him that he became known as the "Sun King." In 1661, at age twenty-two, he assumed personal control of a realm of 20 million people. During most of his long rule—until his death in 1715 at age seventy-seven—Louis dominated European affairs. Always a builder of monuments, he expanded the Louvre in Paris and then dazzled the French nobility and clergy with his opulent new palace at Versailles.

In religion, the Sun King challenged the Catholic pope on one hand and suppressed French Protestants (Huguenots) on the other. In politics, he centralized the monarchy's power as never before. His administration consolidated the laws of France, strengthened the armed forces, built roads, and expanded commerce. His government ministries foreshadowed modern nation-states by regulating industry and imposing tariffs and taxes.

Throughout Louis XIV's reign, his officials followed a set of policies known as **mercantilism**, a system in which a government stressed economic self-sufficiency and a favorable balance of trade. By avoiding foreign debts and drawing in valuable resources from its competitors and its own colonies, a state could pay for wars abroad and costly projects at home. The French mercantilist strategy was to exploit labor efficiently and import raw materials cheaply, while exporting expensive manufactured products, such as glassware, wine, silk, and tapestries, in exchange for gold and silver. France's colonists, like those of Spain and England, were expected to generate much-needed natural resources and to serve as eager consumers for the mother country's manufactured goods.

■ Portrait of Louis XIV, the Sun King.

In Paris, finance minister Jean-Baptiste Colbert emerged as the chief architect of this strategy of aggressive mercantilism. At home he taxed foreign imports, removed domestic trade barriers, and improved internal transportation. Moreover, he reduced worker holidays and outlawed strikes. Colbert improved France's ports and created a code to regulate maritime shipping. He expanded the naval fleet and pressed French sailors into its service. Pushing still harder, he organized overseas trading companies and provided insurance for their expensive ventures. In addition, he sanctioned France's involvement in the African slave trade. Colbert yearned to acquire new territory to increase the empire's self-sufficiency and keep overseas resources out of enemy hands. To that end, he and his successors encouraged French exploration of North America on an unprecedented scale.

The government of Louis XIV assumed direct control over New France from a private company in 1663. Colbert hoped to diversify production away from the fur trade, so he shipped artisans to the colony, along with livestock and tools. To promote domestic life and population growth, the government also transported young single women and announced cash incentives for early marriages and large families. Many of the soldiers sent to protect New France from Iroquois and English threats stayed on to establish farms.

On balance, however, Colbert's plans for a prosperous, well-populated colony failed. The small population of New France—10,000 by 1680—never grew as rapidly as French imperial strategists desired. The harsh winters and short growing seasons hindered the expansion of agriculture. Also, Louis XIV imposed restrictions to make sure that any colonist sent overseas was a pious and loyal Catholic. In 1685, when he revoked the Edict of Nantes (which had granted French Protestants their legal rights), thousands of frightened Huguenots prepared to leave the country. But the king forbade the dissenters from traveling to France's colonies. In contrast to the English, the French did not use their overseas colonies as havens for outcasts, troublemakers, and religious dissidents.

Exploring the Mississippi Valley

Encouraged by the government of Louis XIV, French Canadian explorers had probed steadily across the Great Lakes, reaching the western shores of Lake Michigan in 1634. There, Winnebego Indians (today's Ho-Chunk Nation) told of a river called the "Messisipi," and rumors of this river circulated among the French for a generation. Finally, in 1673, trader Louis Jolliet,

■ MAP 3.1
FRANCE IN THE AMERICAN INTERIOR, 1670–1720

joined by a Jesuit priest named Jacques Marquette, entered the upper Mississippi and descended the great stream to the mouth of the Arkansas River. If the Mississippi waterway flowed south into the Gulf of Mexico, instead of west to the Pacific as some explorers hoped, perhaps the river could give France a path to the wealth of New Spain and provide French settlers with access to a warm-water port.

Officials in Quebec moved to exploit these western prospects, making effective use of an experienced young adventurer: René-Robert Cavelier, Sieur de La Salle. In 1679, inspired by word of Jolliet's exploits, La Salle and his men pushed west through the Great Lakes to erect forts on the Illinois River, a tributary of the Mississippi. These outposts strengthened French trading ties with local Indians and provided a launching point for more exploration. In 1682 La Salle led a contingent of French and Indians south from the Illinois to explore the lower Mississippi. He returned to confirm that the great river indeed emptied into the Gulf of Mexico. He claimed the rich land drained by all its tributaries for Louis XIV, naming the entire river basin "Louisiana" after his king.

But La Salle, hindered by poor maps and crude navigational instruments, had mislocated the mouth of the Mississippi. Therefore, when he tried to return by sea, sailing from France with four ships and several hundred colonists, he mistakenly disembarked on the Texas coast early in 1685. Slowly, the entire colonization plan unraveled. When one ship sank near shore, the hapless settlers lost valuable supplies and any hope of relocating. Jealous lieutenants eventually killed La Salle before he could find the Mississippi River. Most of the colonists he had brought from France perished in the Texas wilderness.

King William's War in the Northeast

The French colonizers had overreached themselves. They had failed to challenge Spanish power in the Gulf of Mexico or to establish a southern port. Spread thin by the widening fur trade, French Canadians were in a weak position to repel renewed Iroquois attacks along the St. Lawrence River in the 1680s. Moreover, a strengthened Protestant regime emerged in London with the ascent of William III to the English throne in 1689. This transition started more than 100 years of conflict between Protestant England and Catholic France, an ideological and military struggle that often included North America.

■ When La Salle's colonizing expedition landed on the Texas coast in 1685, one supply ship, the *Belle*, sank in Matagorda Bay during the unloading process. Lost and discouraged, the French colony faded away within two years. In 1995 archaeologists found the *Belle* in shallow water and salvaged its remains.

The American conflict began in the Northeast with the outbreak of King William's War in 1689, when the Iroquois, well supplied with English arms, launched raids near Montreal. The French struck back, sending parties south to terrorize the English frontier, setting fire to outposts in New York and New England. At Fort Loyal (modern Portland, Maine) raiders butchered 100 English men, women, and children who had surrendered, and they took others captive. Leaving their dead unburied, the survivors fled south toward Salem and Boston in Massachusetts. Many who experienced the attack viewed it as part of a wider design to undo the Reformation and expand the authority of the Catholic Church.

After eight years of bloodshed, King William's War ended in a stalemate in 1697. Hurt by the hostilities, the Iroquois soon promised to remain neutral during any future colonial wars between France and England, a pledge they generally honored for more than half a century. The French, having strengthened their position in Canada, revived the "southern strategy" of colonization that had so obsessed Colbert and La Salle.

A turn in European events opened the door for renewed French efforts in the American heartland. King Carlos II of Spain fell ill without an immediate heir, and the royal courts of Europe competed to determine his successor. Louis XIV, eager to acquire Spain's European realm and American dominions for France, proposed that his grandson, Philip of Anjou, receive the Spanish crown. But England supported an opposing candidate, so the War of Spanish Succession (1701–1714) broke out soon after Carlos died.

Founding the Louisiana Colony

Even before new hostilities erupted in Europe in 1701, Louis XIV and his ministers took steps to secure French claims in the Gulf of Mexico, despite Spain's naval dominance in the area. By renewing La Salle's plan for a Louisiana colony, France could strengthen its hand in the impending war over succession to the Spanish throne. A colony on the Gulf of Mexico would provide a southern outlet for the French fur trade and a strategic outpost to counter Spain's new fort at Pensacola in western Florida.

England also saw advantages to establishing a base on the lower Mississippi. Such a post could challenge Spanish and French claims to the gulf region and increase English trade with the Chickasaw and other southern Indians. In 1698 a London promoter quietly made plans to transport a group of Huguenot refugees to the mouth of the Mississippi. Catching wind of this scheme, the French organized their own secret expedition to the Gulf of Mexico under an aspiring Canadian officer, Pierre Le Moyne d'Iberville.

Coming from a large and well-connected Montreal family, the Le Moynes, Iberville quickly drew several siblings into the gulf colonization plan, including his teenage brother, Bienville. Iberville and his party sailed for the Gulf of Mexico from the French port of Brest in 1699. Their ship entered the mouth of the Mississippi in time to repel the English expedition at a site on the river still known as English Turn. They also managed to build a fort at nearby Biloxi Bay before returning to France.

The two brothers were now well on their way to creating the Gulf Coast colony that La Salle and his followers had failed to establish. A second voyage let Iberville conduct further reconnaissance of the lower Mississippi. On a third trip, in 1702, he established Fort Louis, near Mobile Bay, giving French traders access to the Choctaw Indians. Young Bienville, placed in charge of Fort Louis, labored to sustain the tiny outpost at Mobile. Iberville himself left to pursue other schemes and died an early death in 1706.

Enmeshed in the War of Spanish Succession, France ignored its new Gulf colony. Epidemics took a heavy toll on Louisiana's newcomers and a far heavier toll on Indian neighbors. Settlers drawn from Canada, with prior wilderness experience, maintained close ties with local Native Americans and resented the incompetence and haughtiness of colonists sent from France. The latter complained about the poor living conditions and looked down on the uneducated Canadians. However, despite social friction and a chronic lack of supplies from France, the small community at Mobile survived, including the widow Marguerite Messier and her children.

Far to the north, additional posts reinforced French territorial claims, fostered the fur trade, and protected neighboring Indians against Iroquois raids. The village of Peoria sprang up on the Illinois River in 1691. Catholic missions appeared nearby at Cahokia (1697) and Kaskaskia (1703). Later, Fort de Chartres arose in southern Illinois in 1719. Further north, the French established two other strategic posts. In 1689 they laid out a garrison where Lake Huron joins Lake Michigan. In 1701 they created a lasting town on the strait (*le détroit* in French) connecting Lake Erie to Lake Huron. This outpost—called Detroit—was founded by a Monsieur Cadillac, who foresaw a prosperous future for the village. The Iroquois had pledged their neutrality, so the new trading post, Cadillac wrote, lay open "to the most distant tribes which surround these vast sweet water seas."

In 1712 the French crown, its resources depleted by a decade of warfare in Europe, granted control over Louisiana to a powerful Paris merchant, Antoine Crozat. Drawing Cadillac from Detroit to serve as Louisiana's governor general, Crozat hoped to develop connections

INTERPRETING HISTORY

"Marry or do not marry"

Father Jacques Gravier (1651–1708) visited French posts from Mackinac to Mobile. The Jesuit spent most of his time at Fort St. Louis (modern Peoria) among several thousand Illinois Indians, compiling a dictionary of their language and seeking to win converts. In 1691, he built a chapel outside the fort and erected a 35-foot cross. He concentrated on teaching young people, offering prizes—colored beads, needles, rosaries, small knives— to those who learned the catechism. The daughter of powerful Chief Rouensa (a girl named Aramepinchone, whom Gravier called Marie) proved especially interested. But French traders and Indian leaders remained wary of his message.

I was surprised by the indifference to instruction,…notwithstanding the politeness with which the old men received me. One of them told me in confidence that his tribesmen had resolved to prevent the people from coming to the chapel to listen to me, because I spoke against their customs. Many children and young people were sick, and I had not as free access to all of them as I would have wished…. They cry out against me as if I were the cause of the disease…. I was looked upon in most of the cabins as the bird of death; and people sought to hold me responsible for the disease and the mortality.

[In 1694 Marie's] father and mother…brought her to me in company with the Frenchman whom they wished to have for a son-in-law. [Michel Accault was a wealthy and experienced trader whom La Salle had sent to explore the Upper Mississippi in 1680. But Marie indicated] that she did not wish to marry;

An Illinois chief, holding a calumet (c. 1700). "They are tattooed behind from the shoulders to the heels, and as soon as they have reached the age of twenty-five, on the front of the stomach, the sides, and the upper arms."

Chief of an Illinois Tribe, Charles Becard de Granvelle, about 1700. New York Public Library; Astor, Lenox, and Tilden Foundations.

that she had already given her heart to God, and did not wish to share it…. I told [Accault and the parents] that God did not command her not to marry, but also that she could not be forced to do so…. The father…told me that inasmuch as I was preventing his daughter from obeying him, he would also prevent her from going to the chapel. That very night her father gathered the chiefs of the four villages, and told them that, since I prevented the French from forming alliances with them…he earnestly begged them to stop the women and children from coming to the chapel.

I thought I should not remain silent after so great an insult had been offered to God. I went to the commandant of the fort,…who answered in an insulting manner that I had drawn all this upon myself, through my stubbornness in not allowing the girl to marry the Frenchman, who was then with him. [The Jesuit demanded that the commandant support him against the chiefs. The French leader] replied coldly that he would speak to the chiefs; but, instead of assembling them at once, he waited until the afternoon of the following day, and even then I had to return to him from the purpose. [Then Gravier advised Marie:] My daughter, God does not forbid you to marry; neither do I say to you: 'Marry or do not marry.' If you consent solely through love for God, and if you believe that by marrying you will win your family to God, the thought is a good one.

Marie, age 16, married Accault and bore two sons before he died. By 1704 she had married another French trader, Michel Philippe, and moved to the new town of Kaskaskia. There Philippe turned to farming and amassed a sizable estate, including an Indian servant and five black slaves. Marie raised six more children before her death in 1725. Her will, dictated in French and then translated into the Illinois language, withheld property from one son who continued to live as an Indian. Her priest, Father Gravier, had been shot in the arm by an Indian in 1705. The arrowhead could not be removed, and he died three years later.

Questions

1. Regarding the Rouensa-Accault marriage, explore the differing motives of Marie, her parents, Michel Accault, and Father Gravier.
2. Can you recreate an argument in 1720 at Kaskaskia between Catholic Marie and the son remaining loyal to the ways of Chief Rouensa?

---

to mineral-rich Mexico and to discover precious metals in the Mississippi watershed. But probes on the upper Mississippi, the Missouri, and the Red rivers yielded no easy bonanza. Instead, explorers established three new trading posts: Natchitoches on the Red River, Fort Rosalie (at Natchez), and Fort Toulouse (near modern Montgomery, Alabama).

When Louis XIV died in 1715, the colonial population of Lower Louisiana stood at scarcely 300 people. But over two generations, the French had established a solid claim on

French America 1608–1763

> *Over two generations, the French had established a solid claim on the American interior.*

the American interior. Their position was an ongoing challenge to English and Spanish competitors. The crescent of wilderness outposts arcing north and then east from the Gulf Coast offered a useful network for additional exploration, Indian trade, and military conquest. French control of the Mississippi Valley remained a real possibility until the era of Thomas Jefferson and Napoleon Bonaparte nearly a century later.

The Spanish Empire on the Defensive

Whereas France's power expanded during Louis XIV's reign, Spain's overextended empire continued to weaken. This decline opened the door for Louis to maneuver his own grandson onto the Spanish throne in 1700 as Philip V. Meanwhile, Spanish colonizers struggled to defend vast territorial claims in North America that spread—on paper—from the Gulf of California to the Florida peninsula.

In Spain's remote colonies of New Mexico and Florida, local administration often proved corrupt, and links to imperial officials at home remained weak and cumbersome. For several generations, the Indian majority had resented the harsh treatment and strange diseases that came with colonial contact. Now, cultural disruptions and pressures from hostile Indian neighbors fanned the flames of discontent. In the late seventeenth century, a wave of Native American rebellions swept the northern frontier of New Spain.

The Pueblo Revolt in New Mexico

Pedro Hidalgo, Legal Statement (1680)

The largest and most successful revolt took place along the upper Rio Grande. There, Pueblo Indians from dozens of separate communities (or pueblos) united in a major upheaval in August 1680. They murdered twenty-one of the forty friars serving in New Mexico, ransacked their churches, and killed more than 350 settlers. After laying siege to Santa Fe, the rebels drove the remaining Spanish colonists and their Christian Indian allies south out of the province and kept them away for more than a decade. Several thousand stunned survivors took refuge at what is now El Paso and soon began questioning Indian informants to find an explanation for the fearsome uprising.

Diverse pressures had combined to ignite the Pueblo Revolt of 1680. First, a five-year drought beginning in 1666 had inflicted a famine with long-lasting effects on the peoples of New Mexico. Second, around the same time, neighboring Apache and Navajo stepped up their hostilities against the small colonial population and the numerous Pueblo Indians who had been linked with the Spanish over several generations. The attackers were embittered by the continuing Spanish slave raids that took Indian captives to work in the Mexican silver mines. In retaliation these raiding parties, riding stolen Spanish horses, killed livestock and seized scarce food. When Spanish soldiers proved unable to fend off the hit-and-run attacks, their credibility among local Pueblo Indians weakened.

Third, a smoldering controversy over religion flared during the 1670s. When an epidemic struck in 1671, Spanish missionaries could not stem the sickness with Christian prayers. In response, traditionalist Indian priests revived age-old Pueblo religious customs. Horrified, the Spanish friars and government officials punished what they saw as backsliding within a Pueblo population that seemed to have accepted key elements of the Catholic faith. At Santa Fe in 1675, they hanged three Indian leaders for idolatry and whipped and imprisoned forty-three others—including a militant leader from San Juan pueblo named Popé. Before the captives could be sold into slavery, armed Indians successfully demanded the release of Popé and the other prisoners.

Popé withdrew to Taos, the northernmost pueblo in New Mexico. From there, he negotiated secretly with like-minded factions in other pueblos, unifying resistance to Spanish dom-

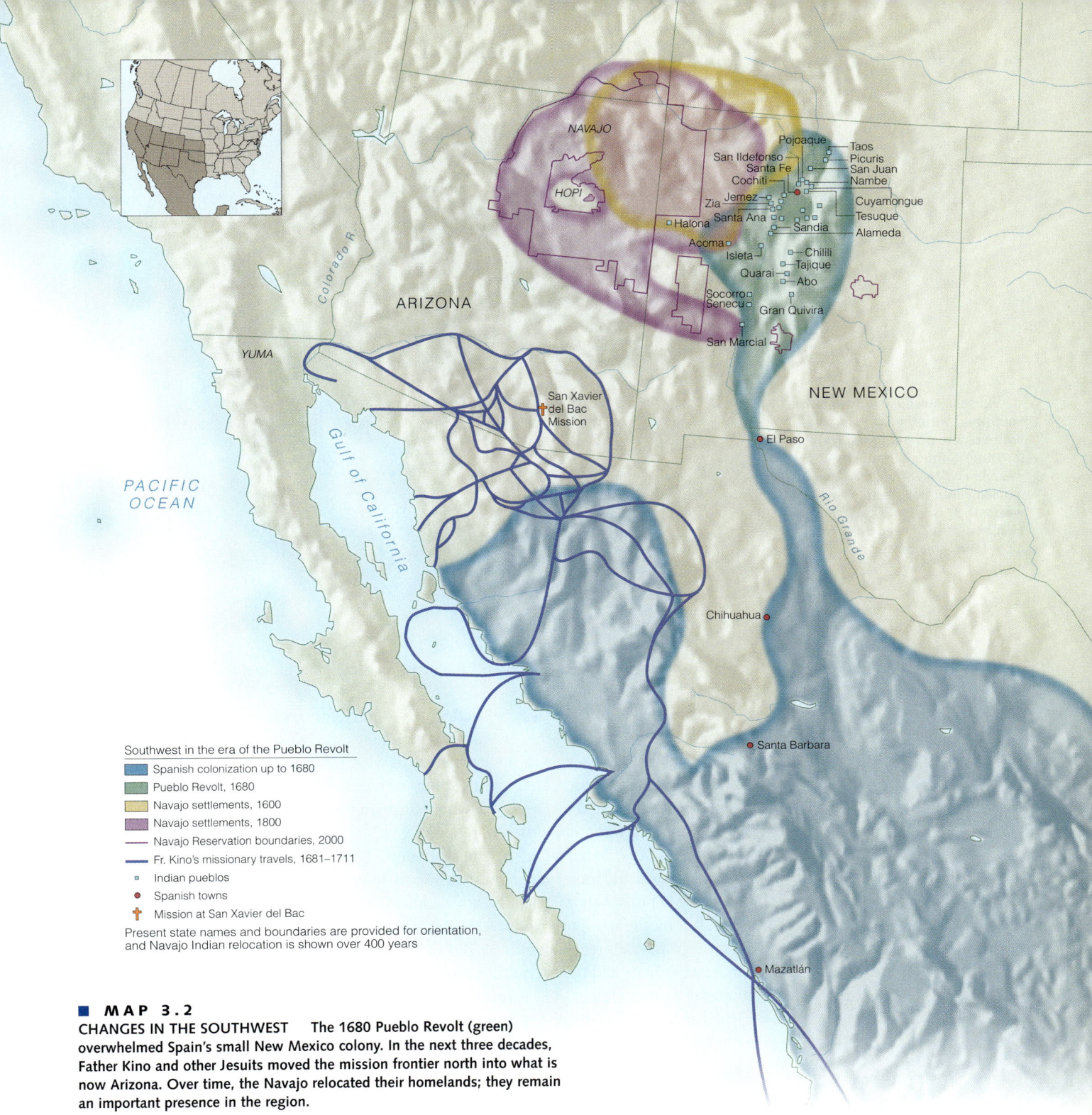

■ **MAP 3.2**
CHANGES IN THE SOUTHWEST The 1680 Pueblo Revolt (green) overwhelmed Spain's small New Mexico colony. In the next three decades, Father Kino and other Jesuits moved the mission frontier north into what is now Arizona. Over time, the Navajo relocated their homelands; they remain an important presence in the region.

ination and forging an underground movement. In part, he built support around widespread resentment of the Spanish **encomienda** system (requiring Indian communities to supply labor or pay tribute) and the Catholic Church (which forbade traditional Indian religious ceremonies). Indian women whom Spanish priests or soldiers had abused took Popé's side in this cultural clash. The movement also received covert support from numerous **mestizos** and **mulattos**, mixed-race people whose lack of "pure" Spanish blood cost them any chance for advancement. Popé sent runners to each conspiring pueblo, fixing the date for the rebellion. When the time came, his Pueblo warriors swiftly routed their adversaries. Unified in triumph,

■ Horses and sheep arrived in the Southwest with the Spanish, and both became central to the Navajo (or Diné) culture in northern Arizona and New Mexico. Navajo women continue to herd sheep and weave their wool into rugs and blankets, as they have done for more than three centuries.

the zealous victors smeared excrement on Christian altars and bathed themselves to remove the stigma of baptism.

But initial cohesion gave way to friction. The successful rebels soon quarreled over who should hold power and how best to return to ancient ways. Kivas would replace churches, and the cross would give way to the **kachina**. But what other parts of the imported culture should the Indians abandon after eight decades of intermingling with the newcomers? Various Pueblo groups could not agree on which Spanish words, tools, and customs to discard or which foreign crops and animals to retain.

In 1681 the Pueblo fended off a Spanish attempt at reconquest. But they remained divided among themselves and more vulnerable than ever to Apache raids. Within a decade, rival factions had deposed Popé, and another Spanish army, under Governor Diego de Vargas, had entered New Mexico. It took the new governor several years to subdue the province, and the Pueblo managed another full-scale rebellion in 1696. But Vargas anticipated the revolt and crushed the opposition, just as Oñate had done a century earlier. In 1706 several families established the town of Albuquerque on its present site. Learning from prior mistakes, Spanish officials did not reimpose the hated encomienda system. A new generation of Franciscan missionaries tolerated indigenous Pueblo traditions as long as the Indians also attended Catholic mass.

Navajo and Spanish on the Southwestern Frontier

The repercussions of rebellion and reconquest along the upper Rio Grande echoed through the Southwest. To the north, Pueblo refugees joined the Navajo and brought valuable experience as corn farmers. Corn, already known to the Navajo, now became an increasingly important food and sacred symbol for them. Moreover, the new arrivals had learned from the Spanish how to plant peach orchards and raise sheep. Navajo women—the weavers in their society—soon owned large flocks and created wool blankets on their traditional portable looms. The Pueblo also brought more Spanish horses, a key asset that let the Navajo spread their domain west into fine grazing country in what is now northeast Arizona. Farther north, the Ute and Comanche also acquired horses after the Pueblo Revolt. Eventually, the Comanche pressed southeast onto the Texas plains.

In Mexico City, despite limited resources, authorities sent missionaries north to spread Christianity to hostile Indians near the Gulf of California. Year by year, these friar-explorers edged toward what is now southern Arizona until they reached the cactus-studded landscape of the Sonoran Desert in the 1690s. Eusebio Kino, a tireless Jesuit missionary born in Italy and educated in Germany, spearheaded the early exploration. In 1701 this padre on horseback established a mission at San Xavier del Bac, below modern Tucson, Arizona. But Father Kino's missions languished after his death in 1711. Twenty-five years later, a silver strike at "Arizonac," near present-day Nogales on the U.S.-Mexican border, provided a new name for the region, which would eventually become the state called Arizona.

Borderland Conflict in Texas and Florida

The encounters on Spain's other North American frontiers took different forms, in part because European rivals appeared on the scene. Conflict with the French led the Spanish to found missions in Texas, a land they named after the local Tejas Indians. At first, responding to news about La Salle's ill-fated French colony, the Spanish made a brief attempt to establish a Texas mission in 1690, departing again in 1693. They renewed their effort two decades later, after Louisiana's Governor Cadillac (the founder of Detroit) sent explorers from Louisiana across eastern Texas to forge ties with Spanish communities south of the Rio Grande. Eager to open trade with the Spanish, the French visitors reached San Juan Bautista, below the modern U.S.-Mexican border, in 1714.

Spanish authorities, taken by surprise, dusted off plans for colonizing Texas. By 1717 they had established half a dozen small missions near the Sabine River, the boundary between modern Texas and Louisiana. The next year, to expand their missionary activities and secure the supply route from San Juan Bautista to these distant outposts in east Texas, the Spanish built a cluster of settlements beside the San Antonio River, at a midpoint in the trail. Within two decades, a string of missions stretched along the river. Indian converts tended herds of cattle and sheep and constructed aqueducts to irrigate new fields of wheat and corn. The earliest mission, San Antonio de Valero (1718), provided a nucleus for the town of San Antonio. Later known as the Alamo, the mission also strengthened Spanish claims to Texas against threats of French intrusion.

During the second half of the seventeenth century, the Indians of Florida, like the Pueblo in New Mexico, debated whether to reject generations of Spanish rule. The Columbian Exchange had altered their lives in dramatic ways. They ate new foods such as figs, oranges, peas, and cabbages. They used Spanish words—*azucár* (sugar), *botija* (jar), *caballo* (horse)—and metal hoes from Europe allowed them to produce more corn. But expanding contact with missionaries created major problems as well. By 1660 devastating epidemics had whittled away at Florida's Native American towns. The Indians still outnumbered the newcomers more than ten to one, but they had to expend enormous energy raising, processing, and hauling food for the Spanish. When colonists grew fearful of French and English attacks after 1670, they forced hundreds of Indians to perform even more grueling labor: constructing the stone fortress of San Marcos at St. Augustine.

Nothing proved more troubling to Florida's Indians than the spread of livestock farming. St. Augustine's elite had established profitable cattle ranches on the depopulated savannas of Timucua, near present-day Gainesville in north-central Florida. These entrepreneurs ignored requirements to keep cows away from unfenced Indian gardens, and they enforced harsh laws to protect their stock. Any Florida Indian who killed cattle faced four months of servitude; people caught raiding Spanish herds had their ears cut off.

Resentment grew in Florida's scattered mission villages. Restless Indian converts wondered whether the English, who had founded their Carolina colony in 1670, might make viable allies. The English seemed eager to trade for deerskins, and they offered the Native Americans a steadier supply of desirable goods than the Spanish could

> *During the second half of the seventeenth century, the Indians of Florida, like the Pueblo in New Mexico, debated whether to reject generations of Spanish rule.*

provide. Several Indian communities moved closer to Carolina to test this new alternative for trade. But when France and Spain joined forces against the English after 1700, Florida's Indians found themselves caught up in a struggle far larger than they had bargained for.

Ever since the days of Francis Drake, the English had schemed to oust the Spanish from St. Augustine. In 1702 English raiders from Carolina, under Governor James Moore, rampaged through the town. Yet the new stone fortress of San Marcos held firm, protecting the inhabitants. Two years later, Moore invaded Apalachee (near modern Tallahassee). His troops crushed the mission towns, killing hundreds and carrying away more than 4,000 Indian captives. Most of them were women and children, whom the English sold as slaves. By 1706 the mission villages in Apalachee and Timucua lay in ruins. "In all these extensive dominions," wrote a troubled Spanish official from St. Augustine, "the law of God and the preaching of the Holy Gospel have now ceased."

England's American Empire Takes Shape

In 1660, as Louis XIV began his long reign in France and Spanish missionaries labored in obscurity in New Mexico and Florida, England experienced a counterrevolutionary upheaval that influenced American colonial affairs dramatically. In the 1640s, amid violent civil war, rebels supporting Puritans and the Parliament had overthrown the ruling Stuart family, beheaded Charles I, and abolished hereditary monarchy altogether.

For a brief period, England became a republican commonwealth without a king. But Oliver Cromwell, the movement's dictatorial leader and self-styled Lord Protector, died in 1658. Pressures quickly mounted to undo the radical Puritan Revolution and return to monarchical government. In May 1660, a strong coalition of conservative interests welcomed the late king's son back from exile and "restored" him to the throne as King Charles II, an act known as the **Restoration**. For this reason, the last three decades of the Stuart dynasty (1660–1688) are remembered in English politics and culture as the **Restoration Era**.

The shift in London's political winds could hardly have been more sudden, and Charles II moved quickly in 1660 to underscore the end of England's Puritan experiment. He ordered the execution of those who had beheaded his father in 1649. Many who had fought to end the monarchy and strengthen Parliament sought refuge in the American colonies when their religious and political beliefs abruptly fell out of favor at home. But other elements of colonial demographics—early marriage, high birth rates, and a low level of mortality in most places—did even more to prompt expansion up and down the Atlantic coast.

Monarchy Restored and Navigation Controlled

Because most English colonists still lived within 50 miles of the Atlantic, an increase in people steadily broadened the opportunities for seaborne trade. Growing ship traffic, in turn, sparked government desires to regulate colonial navigation to bring mercantilist advantages to the restored monarchy. In 1660 Parliament passed a major new law designed to promote British shipping and trade.

The Navigation Act of 1660 laid out important conditions that shaped England's colonial commerce for generations. First, merchants could not conduct trade to or from the English colonies in foreign-owned ships. Second, key non-English products imported from foreign lands—salt, wine, oil, and naval stores (the tar, pitch, masts, and other materials used to build boats)—had to be carried in English ships or in ships with mostly English crews. Third, the law contained a list of "enumerated articles" produced overseas. The items listed—tobacco, cotton, sugar, ginger, indigo, and dyewoods—could no longer be sent directly from a colony to a foreign European port. Instead, merchants had to ship them to England first and then reexport them, a step that directly boosted England's domestic economy. Another Navigation Act, in 1663, required that goods moving from the European continent to England's overseas colonies also needed to pass through the island. Moreover, they had to arrive and depart on English ships.

Ten years later, yet another measure—the Plantation Duty Act of 1673—tried to close loopholes regarding enumerated articles. The new act required captains to pay a "plantation duty" before they sailed between colonial ports with enumerated goods. Otherwise, colonial vessels carrying such goods had to post bond before leaving harbor to ensure that they would sail directly to England. To enforce these rules, the government sent customs officers to the colonies for the first time. Backed by the Navigation Acts, England's fleets grew, and colonial trade became a major sector in England's economy.

Even the Great Plague, which swept England in 1665, could not blunt this mercantile growth. And when a catastrophic fire destroyed most of London the next year, planners redesigned the city with the broad streets and impressive buildings that suited the prosperous hub of an expanding empire. The fashionable coffee shops that sprang up as a novelty in late-seventeenth-century London became common meeting places for exchanging news and views about England's increasingly profitable activities overseas.

Dutch New Netherland Becomes New York

At the beginning of his reign, Charles II knew he had to build loyalty and strengthen an economy weakened by civil war. The king, with expensive tastes and a depleted treasury, found that he could reward loyal family members and supporters, at no cost to the crown, by granting them control over pieces of England's North American domain. With this prospect in hand, he and his ministers sought to bolster foreign trade, strengthen the royal navy, and outstrip England's commercial rivals, focusing first on the Dutch.

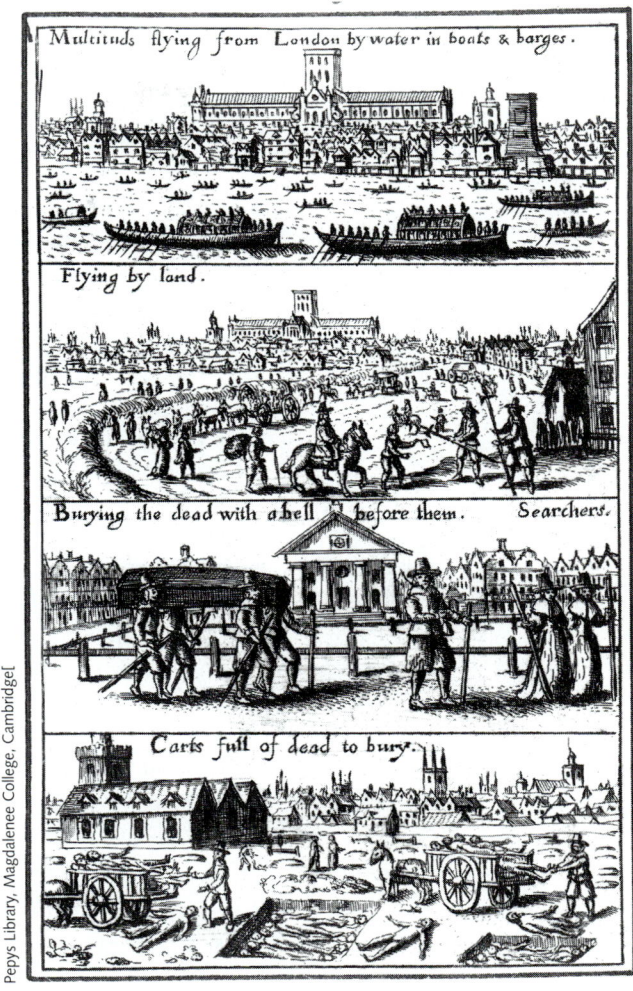

■ Images of the Great Plague in London (1665).

As London stepped up its search for new profits, English officials moved to strengthen control over existing colonies and establish (or seize) new ones wherever possible. The Navigation Acts cut sharply into the Dutch carrying trade and spurred a decade of renewed warfare between England and Holland. For the most part, these intermittent Anglo-Dutch Wars ended in stalemate. But at the final Peace of Westminster in 1674, the English emerged with several important gains in Africa and America.

In West Africa, the English captured and held several key coastal outposts: an island at the mouth of the river Gambia (renamed James Fort for the Duke of York) and Cape Coast Castle on the Gold Coast (near Elmina, the African headquarters of the Dutch West India Company). This encroachment challenged Dutch dominance of commerce with Africa for gold and ivory. It also gave England the footholds it needed to force its way into the Atlantic slave trade. Charles II had already moved to take advantage of the situation. He granted a monopoly to the Royal Adventurers into Africa (1663) and then the Royal African Company (1672) to exploit the grim but highly profitable slave traffic. Within several generations, this ruthless initiative reshaped England's American colonies at enormous human cost.

Across the Atlantic, the English had seized the Dutch colony of New Netherland and its poorly defended port of New Amsterdam. Charles II claimed that the land had belonged to

DOCUMENT

Navigation Acts

England from the time his grandfather endorsed the Virginia Company in 1606. In 1664 the king used his royal prerogative to regain control of this domain. He issued a charter putting the entire region between the Delaware and Connecticut rivers under the personal control of his brother James, Duke of York. That same year, James sent a fleet to claim his prize. When Governor Peter Stuyvesant surrendered the Dutch colony without a fight, both the province and its capital on Manhattan Island each received the name New York. Fort Orange on the Hudson became Albany because England's traditional name was *Albion*.

James now controlled an enormous domain (including the Dutch and English settlements on Long Island), and he wielded nearly absolute power over his new dukedom. He never visited New York, but as proprietor, he chose the colony's governor. That official ruled with an appointed council and enforced "the Duke's Laws" without constraint by any assembly. English newcomers to the colony resented the absence of an elected legislature, and the governor finally authorized an elected body in 1683. But when the new assemblymen approved a Charter of Liberties endorsing government by consent of the governed, the Duke of York disallowed the legislature.

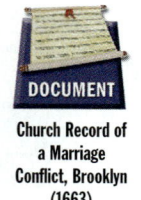
Church Record of a Marriage Conflict, Brooklyn (1663)

Married women living in the New York colony lost ground in the transition to English rule. Dutch law codes had ensured their full legal status, whereas English common law assigned wives to an inferior status (known as **coverture** or *feme covert*). They could not own property or keep control over money they earned, and they lacked any independent standing before the law.

As the English asserted political control over New York, the Dutch presence remained evident everywhere. Many English married into Dutch families and worshiped in the Dutch Reformed Church. English-speaking New Yorkers borrowed such Dutch words as *waffle*, *cookie*, *coleslaw*, and *baas* (boss). Anyone who was bilingual, such as Albany merchant Robert Livingston, had a special advantage. Livingston, an immigrant from Scotland, had learned to speak Dutch in Holland in his youth. His marriage linked him to powerful Dutch families in the Hudson Valley, and much of his early wealth came from his ability to translate commercial documents between English and Dutch.

New Restoration Colonies: New Jersey, Pennsylvania, and Carolina

Charles II had spurred England's seizure of New Netherland by issuing a charter for control of the contested region to his brother, the Duke of York. To reward supporters, the king continued issuing royal charters for American land, hoping to expand colonization at no cost to the crown. In 1670, for example, he granted a charter to the Hudson's Bay Company. The deal gave the company's proprietors a monopoly on trade, minerals, and land across northern Canada. Farther south, Charles used charters to redistribute control along major portions of the Atlantic coast. His actions prompted an unprecedented scramble for colonial property and profits. Within decades, the English launched important settlement clusters along the Delaware River valley and the Carolina coast. Each depended upon lucrative charters for a small network of friends.

> *Charles II had spurred England's seizure of New Netherland by issuing a charter for control of the contested region to his brother, the Duke of York.*

Most of these well-placed people belonged to the Councils for Trade and Plantations in London. Created in 1660, these advisory groups linked England's powerful merchants with crown officials. When Charles II issued a charter for Carolina in 1663, five of its eight initial proprietors served on those councils. In 1665 two of these same eight men became the proprietors of New Jersey. In addition, three of the eight played an active role in the Royal African Company, four became founders of the Hudson's Bay Company, and five became initial proprietors of the Bahamas. But Charles reached beyond this small group as well. In 1679 he made New Hampshire a proprietorship (an ill-fated experiment that lasted to 1708). In 1681 he paid off a debt to Quaker aristocrat William Penn by granting him a charter for Pennsylvania. (The generous arrangement included the "Lower Counties" that became Delaware in 1704.)

Penn's "holy experiment" to create a Quaker refuge benefited from earlier colonization south of New York. Dutch and Swedish settlers had inhabited the lower Delaware River valley for more than a generation. In 1665 the Duke of York carved off a portion of his vast proprietorship, granting the area between the Delaware and the Hudson to two friends: Lord John Berkeley and Sir George Carteret. They named the area New Jersey because Carteret had been born on the Isle of Jersey in the English Channel and had harbored Charles II when he took refuge there in 1649. Berkeley and Carteret promptly announced liberal "Concessions"—a representative assembly and freedom of worship—to attract rent-paying newcomers from England and the existing colonies. But their plans for profit made little headway.

In 1674 the proprietors divided these fertile lands into two separate provinces. East Jersey—where Newark was established in 1666—attracted Puritan families from New England, Dutch farmers from New York, and failed planters from Barbados. West Jersey was sold to members of the Society of Friends (including William Penn) who inaugurated a Quaker experiment along the Delaware River. Filled with egalitarian beliefs, the Quakers created a unicameral (single body) legislature, used secret ballots, and gave more power to juries than to judges. Their idealistic effort foundered within decades, and by 1702 all New Jersey came under crown control as a royal colony.

But by then, the Quakers had established a foothold in the neighboring colony of Pennsylvania. Its capital, the market town of Philadelphia, laid out by proprietor William Penn in 1682, already had more than 2,000 inhabitants. An earnest Quaker, Penn professed pacifism. He made it a point to deal fairly with the Lenni-Lenape (Delaware) Indians. After purchasing their land, he resold it on generous terms to English, Dutch, and Welsh Quakers who agreed to pay him an annual premium, called a **quitrent**. He also emphasized religious toleration. A growing stream of German Protestants and others facing persecution in Europe began to flow into Pennsylvania after 1700.

DOCUMENT

Penn, Description of Pennsylvania (1681)

Penn drew inspiration from James Harrington, the English political philosopher. Harrington's book *Oceana* (1656) argued that the best way to create an enduring republic was for one person to draft and implement its constitution. After endless tinkering, Penn devised a progressive "Frame of Government" that allowed for trial by jury, limited terms of office, and no use of capital punishment except in cases of treason and murder. But he remained ambivalent about legislative democracy. Settlers resented his scheme for a lower house that could approve acts drafted by the governor but could not initiate laws. In a new Charter of Privileges in 1701, Penn agreed to the creation of a **unicameral legislature** with full lawmaking powers. Penn's expansive proprietorship belonged to his descendants until colonial rule ended in 1776.

Anthony Ashley-Cooper, leader of the Carolina proprietors, also drew inspiration from Harrington, but for a very different undertaking. *Oceana* had stressed that distribution of land determined the nature of any commonwealth, and Ashley-Cooper (later the first earl of Shaftesbury) was eager to establish a stable aristocratic system. With his young secretary, John Locke (later an influential political philosopher), he drew up a set of "Fundamental Constitutions" in 1669. They proposed a stratified society in which hereditary nobles controlled much of the land and wealthy manor lords employed a lowly servant class of "leetmen." Their unrealistic document tried to revive the elaborate feudal hierarchy of medieval times.

The new government framework also endorsed racial slavery, declaring that "Every Freeman of Carolina shall have absolute Power and Authority over his Negro Slaves." This endorsement was not surprising, given the proprietors' involvement with England's new slave-trading monopoly in Africa and their initial recruitment of settlers in 1670 from the sugar island of Barbados. When Carolina colonists founded Charlestown (later Charleston) between the

Ashley and Cooper rivers in 1680, the proprietors had already modified aspects of their complicated scheme, setting aside feudalism to encourage greater immigration. Nevertheless, their endorsement of slavery shaped the region's society for hundreds of years.

Bloodshed in the English Colonies: 1670–1690

The appearance of English settlements along the Atlantic coast did little, in most places, to alter the traditional rhythms of life. Year after year, the daily challenges of subsistence dominated American life for Indians and colonists alike. The demanding seasonal tasks of clearing fields, planting seeds, and harvesting crops remained interwoven with the incessant chores of providing clothing, securing shelter, and sustaining community.

Over time, however, changing circumstances in America and Europe introduced new pressures up and down the Atlantic seaboard. On occasion after 1670, familiar routines gave way to episodes of bloodshed that threatened to tear whole colonies apart. Elsewhere in North America, Pueblo rebels were resisting the Spanish in New Mexico, and Iroquois warriors were challenging the French in Illinois country. The English, with their larger numbers, posed an even greater cultural and economic problem for Native American inhabitants.

> *On occasion after 1670, familiar routines gave way to episodes of bloodshed that threatened to tear whole colonies apart.*

In 1675 embittered Indians rose up across southern New England in Metacom's War (or King Philip's War). The next year, frontier tensions in Virginia sparked the upheaval known as Bacon's Rebellion. A decade later, events in England prompted further tremors. In London, mounting opposition forced the unpopular James II to surrender the English throne to William of Orange, and Parliament emerged from this "Glorious Revolution" with enhanced powers. In America, the end of rule by the Stuart dynasty was punctuated by controversy and violence in one colony after another.

Metacom's War in New England

By 1675 the Indians of southern New England, like the Pueblo in New Mexico, had endured several generations of colonization. Yet they disagreed over how much English culture they should adopt. Many used English words for trading, English pots for cooking, and English weapons for hunting. Some had converted to Christianity, living in protected "praying towns." Several young men had enrolled in Harvard's Indian College, where they learned to write English and Latin with an eye toward entering the ministry.

Massasoit, the Wampanoag **sachem** (leader) who had assisted the Pilgrims at Plymouth, made sure that his sons, Wamsutta and Metacom, learned English ways. The two men raised pigs and fired guns, and the colonists called them Alexander and Philip, after the kings of ancient Macedon. But when Wamsutta died in the 1660s, shortly after succeeding his father, Metacom (now called King Philip) suspected foul play by the English. And Metacom had other grievances. Colonial traders made the Indians drunk and then cheated them. English livestock trampled Wampanoag corn, and if Indians shot the cattle, colonial courts imposed punishments. Worst of all, colonists now outnumbered the remaining 20,000 Indians in southern New England by more than two to one.

When a white man shot and wounded a Native American in 1675, it triggered a long-expected conflict. Metacom's warriors ravaged towns along the Connecticut River valley and closer to the coast, using the victories to recruit additional Indian allies. The colonists, unprepared after forty years of peace and unchallenged dominance, were caught off guard. Distrusting even the Christian Indians, Massachusetts officials relocated whole praying towns of Indian converts to barren windswept islands in Boston Harbor.

By December, the Connecticut and Rhode Island colonies, terrified of being wiped out, united with Plymouth and Massachusetts Bay to create a force of more than 1,000 men. An Indian captive led them to a stronghold of the still-neutral Narragansett in a swamp a dozen miles west of Newport, Rhode Island. The colonists surprised and overwhelmed the fortified village, setting it ablaze during the fierce fighting. Indian survivors fled, leaving behind more than 600 dead. Many of the men, women, and children were "terribly Barbikew'd," minister Cotton Mather later recorded.

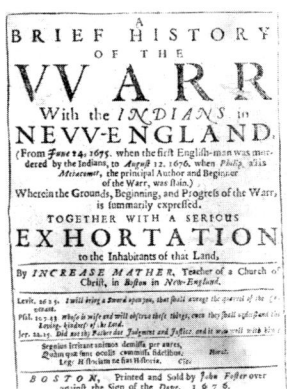

This "Great Swamp Fight," reminiscent of an earlier battle in the Pequot War, infuriated the Narragansett survivors, who joined Metacom's much-feared confederacy. But as spring arrived in 1676, the coalition weakened and the tide turned. Sickness broke out among the fighters, who lacked food and gunpowder. The powerful Mohawk of the Iroquois Confederacy opposed Metacom from the west. Numerous Christian Indians joined the colonial forces, despite their painful internment at Boston's Deer Island.

With Metacom facing defeat, defections increased. In August, a former ally betrayed the resistance leader, shot him, and delivered his head to the English. As the struggle ground to a close, the colonists captured Metacom's wife and child, selling them into slavery in the West Indies along with hundreds of other prisoners of war. New England's remaining Indians became second-class inhabitants, confined to enclaves in the areas they had once dominated, while the colonists soon rebuilt and extended their domain.

Bacon's Rebellion in Virginia

While smoke still billowed over New England, new flames broke out in Virginia. Social unrest had been growing under the stern governorship of Sir William Berkeley. England's wars with the Dutch cut into the tobacco trade, and unfree tobacco workers—more than 6,000 indentured Europeans and nearly 2,000 enslaved Africans—chafed against their harsh treatment. On the frontier, colonists resented the dependent Indians (Occaneechi, Pamunkey, and others) who traded furs in exchange for protection from enemy tribes. Settlers also feared the well-armed Susquehannock living near the Potomac River. "Consider us," Berkeley wrote to the king in 1667, "as a people press'd at our backes with Indians, in our Bowills with our Servants . . . and invaded from without by the Dutch."

By 1676 tensions in Virginia reached the breaking point. Officials had increased taxes to pay for fortifications, servant plots and mutinies abounded, and corruption ran rampant among Berkeley's close associates. The aging governor ruled from Green Spring, his huge estate near the capital, Jamestown. Fearing the hostile views of free men who did not own property, Berkeley had revoked their right to vote. He had not dared to call an election in fourteen years. He also dreaded outspoken preachers, free schools, and printing presses. "How miserable that man is," he wrote, "that Governes a People where six parts of seaven at least are Poore Endebted Discontented and Armed."

Even wealthy newcomers such as Nathaniel Bacon had trouble gaining access to Berkeley's inner circle. When Bacon arrived from England in 1674 at age twenty-seven, he received a council seat because of his connections. But rivals denied the ambitious gentleman a license to engage in the fur trade. Impatient, Bacon condemned Berkeley's ruling Green Spring faction as sponges who "have sukt up the Publique Treasure." When frontier tensions erupted into racial violence, Bacon threw himself into the conflict, challenging Berkeley's leadership and launching aggressive campaigns. His frontier followers, eager for Indian land, killed friendly Occaneechi as well as hostile Susquehannock.

■ Green Spring, the largest mansion in Virginia at the time of Bacon's Rebellion, symbolized the autocratic rule of Governor William Berkeley and his "Green Spring Faction." The estate was seized by Bacon's forces in 1676 and later restored by Berkeley's widow.

Bacon's Declaration (1676)

VIDEO
Bacon's Rebellion

Bacon's army continued to grow as backcountry leaders joined landless poor and runaway workers—both black and white—to support his anti-Indian cause. When the desperate governor called for a rare election to assert his strength, Bacon's supporters dominated the new House of Burgesses. Berkeley retreated to Virginia's eastern shore.

Throughout the summer of 1676, rumors swirled that Bacon might join malcontents in Maryland and in the Albemarle region of northeastern North Carolina to carve out an independent enclave and seek aid from the Dutch or the French. The new assembly quickly restored the vote to propertyless men and forbade excessive fees. It limited sheriffs to one year in office and passed other measures to halt corruption and expand participation in government. As an incentive for enlistment in the frontier war, the assembly granted Bacon's recruits the right to sell into slavery any Indians they captured.

For their part, slaves and indentured servants took advantage of the breakdown in public controls to leave their masters and join Bacon. Networks of "news wives" (women who used facts and rumors to fan worker discontent) spread stories of oppressive conditions. In June rebel soldiers talked openly of sharing estates among themselves, and in August they took over Green Spring Plantation, where Berkeley kept sixty horses and 400 head of cattle. A month later, Bacon's army burned Jamestown to the ground. But by October Bacon was dead, struck down by dysentery, and reinforcements for Berkeley were on the way from England. With armed vessels patrolling the rivers, Berkeley worked up enough nerve to return from the eastern shore. Soon propertied men who had joined with Bacon were changing sides again and receiving amnesty from the governor.

The revolt had been crushed, but the impact of the tumult proved huge. On the frontier, Bacon's violent campaign against the Indians had killed or enslaved hundreds and fostered bitter hatreds. In the Tidewater, the uprising had raised a frightening prospect for wealthy tobacco planters: a unified and defiant underclass of white and black workers. From then on, Virginia's gentry applied themselves to dividing the races and creating a labor force made up of African slaves. In London, the recently formed Royal African Company stood ready to further such a design.

The "Glorious Revolution" in England

No sooner had peace returned to New England and Virginia than Stuart policies brought a new round of turmoil on both sides of the Atlantic. In England, debate revived over who would succeed Charles II on the throne. The irreligious Charles, an Anglican in name only, had no legitimate children. Therefore, his brother James, a convert to Catholicism, was first in line to inherit the crown.

In 1678 rumors spread regarding a "Popish Plot" by Catholics to kill the king so that James could take power. The House of Commons, fearful of rule by a Catholic king, urged that James be excluded from the line of succession. Instead of James, House members argued, why not consider James's Protestant daughters by his first marriage: either Mary (recently wedded to her Dutch cousin, William of Orange) or Anne? Angered by such interference, Charles II dissolved Parliament in 1681 and ruled on his own for the last four years of his life.

When Charles II died in 1685, the traditional rule of succession prevailed: James II took over the English throne. In France that same year, Louis XIV revoked the Edict of Nantes, which had protected French Protestants. Fear spread among England's Protestant majority that their country's new Catholic ruler, James II, might also sanction persecution of non-Catholics. These concerns mounted when James disbanded Parliament, raised a standing army, and placed a Catholic in command of the navy. Then in 1688, James's queen gave birth to a male heir. Protestant anxieties about a pending Catholic dynasty erupted into open resistance.

United by their fear of Catholicism, rival factions among England's political elite (known for the first time as "Whigs" and "Tories") papered over their differences temporarily. They invited the Protestant William of Orange, James's Dutch son-in-law, to lead an army from Holland and take the English crown. In November 1688, he crossed the English Channel with 15,000 men, prompting James to **abdicate** the throne and escape into exile. William and Mary were proclaimed joint sovereigns in 1689, accepting a Bill of Rights that limited royal power.

Its position now enhanced, Parliament moved to grant toleration to Protestant dissenters, establish limited freedom of the press, and ensure regular parliamentary sessions. It also imposed limits on any permanent, paid military forces, known as standing armies, because they could accrue their own power and jeopardize civil authority. The English had thus preserved Protestantism and curtailed royal absolutism, all without bloodshed. Parliament hailed King William III as "our great Deliverer from Popery and Slavery." The propertied classes, who benefited most from the peaceful transition, hailed it as the "Glorious Revolution."

Jan Wyck, *William III Landing at Torbay*, 1688. National Maritime Museum Picture Library

■ Protestants in England and America opposed to King James II welcomed news that William of Orange (above) had arrived from Holland with his army in 1688 to take over the English throne.

The "Glorious Revolution" in America

The succession of James II in 1685 did not bode well for England's American colonies. The new king not only professed the Catholic faith but also cherished absolute monarchy and distrusted elected assemblies. In colonial affairs, James favored revenue-generating reforms and direct obedience to the crown. He detested the powerful leaders in Massachusetts since, as Congregationalists, they believed in a decentralized Protestant church. James also resented the fact that they disobeyed the Navigation Acts and asserted their right to self-rule, even after the crown revoked their charter in 1684. Moreover, he rejected the notion that colonists possessed the precious right claimed by the English at home: not to be taxed without giving their consent. The king envisioned an extensive reorganization of the American colonies.

When James assumed the throne, his own colony of New York automatically became a royal province. Convinced of his divine right to set policy, the king nullified the charters of certain colonies in order to bring them under his control. As the cornerstone of his reorganization plan, James linked the New England colonies (plus New York and New Jersey in 1688) into one huge *Dominion of New England*. This consolidation, under an appointed governor general, would make it easier for England to suppress dissent, enforce shipping regulations, and defend the Dominion's frontiers—at least in theory.

In practice, the effort to forge a Dominion of New England proved a disaster. The move met such stiff resistance in America that a similar design for England's southern colonies never materialized. Control of the Dominion went to a military officer, Sir Edmund Andros. The heavy-handed Andros attempted to rule from Boston through a council he appointed, made up of loyal associates, without aid or interference from any elected legislature. He asserted the crown's right to question existing land patents, and he requisitioned a Congregational church for Anglican services. Worse, he offended local leaders by strictly enforcing the Navigation Acts to collect revenue. When participants in democratic town meetings raised objections, he jailed the leaders.

> *Colonists seethed with resentment toward this revival of Stuart absolutism, which claimed total obedience to the king and his officers as a divine right for the Stuart monarchy.*

Colonists seethed with resentment toward this revival of Stuart absolutism, which claimed total obedience to the king and his officers as a divine right for the Stuart monarchy. Rumors of French invasions and Catholic plots swirled among staunch Protestants. In April 1689, welcome news that the Protestant William of Orange had invaded England inspired a revolt in Boston. Mobs showed public support for overthrowing the Stuart regime, and local leaders locked Governor Andros in jail.

The success of William and the demise of the Dominion of New England did not end royal efforts to tighten imperial control over New England. The new Massachusetts charter of 1691 consolidated neighboring Plymouth and Maine into the Massachusetts Bay colony. Moreover, it proclaimed that future governors would be appointed by the monarchy, as in other colonies. The men of Massachusetts, who had elected their own governor since the days of John Winthrop, would no longer have that right.

Emboldened by Boston's actions in 1689, New Yorkers ousted their own Dominion officials and set up a temporary government headed by Jacob Leisler. This German-born militia captain was a staunch Calvinist and hostile to the town's growing English elite. In Leisler's Rebellion, long-standing ethnic and religious rivalries merged with lower-class hostilities: Leisler's supporters resented their treatment at the hands of the rich. They freed imprisoned debtors and attacked the houses of leading merchants. After a new governor arrived to take charge in 1691, the elite fought back. They lowered artisan wages and executed Leisler as a rebel, although they could find no carpenter willing to provide a ladder for the gallows.

Similar tremors shook the Chesapeake region. In Maryland, where the Catholic proprietor ruled over a large and restive Protestant population, the governing Calvert family waited too long to proclaim its loyalty to King William. Fearing a "Popish" plot, assemblyman John Coode and a force of 250 armed Protestants marched on St. Mary's City and seized the government by force. The "happy Change in England" had replaced divine right rule with a more balanced constitutional monarchy, and Maryland settlers were determined to show their support.

Consequences of War and Growth: 1690–1715

The success of the Glorious Revolution hardly brought peace to England or its empire. On the contrary, warfare marked the reign of William and Mary and also that of Mary's sister, Queen Anne, who ruled from 1702 until her death in 1714. William immediately became involved in bloody campaigns to subdue highland clans in Scotland and overpower Catholic forces in Ireland. Moreover, English involvement against France in two protracted wars on the European continent had implications for colonists and Indians living in eastern North America. The War of the League of Augsburg in Europe became known to English colonists in America as King William's War (1689–1697), and the protracted War of Spanish Succession was experienced in America as Queen Anne's War (1702–1713).

Nowhere was the impact of these imperial wars more evident than in the rapidly growing colonies of the Northeast. Indeed, the earlier bloodshed of Metacom's (King Philip's) War, starting in 1675, had already aroused consternation and soul-searching in Bible-reading New England, and the violent decades that followed were viewed by many as a harsh test or a deserved punishment from the Almighty. They believed that the initial Puritan errand into the wilderness had been closely watched by God. Could it be, ministers now asked from the pulpit, that the Lord had some special controversy with the current generation? As communities grew more prosperous and became caught up in the pursuit of worldly success, were church members forgetting their religious roots and leading less pious lives? Invoking the Old Testament prophet Jeremiah, clerics interpreted personal and collective troubles as God's punishment for the region's spiritual decline.

But such a sweeping explanation of misfortune only raised deeper questions. New Englanders could see clearly that the consequences of rapid change were not spread equally among all towns, congregations, and families. As in most war eras, some people and localities suffered more than others. Certain individuals and groups seemed to benefit economically while others fell behind. Some anxious believers saw the hand of Satan in the day-to-day struggles of village life. Others argued that the worldly success and wartime profits of an expanding elite had undermined the community ideals of earlier generations. While flames engulfed isolated Massachusetts communities such as Deerfield and portions of the Maine frontier, fiery passions were also being aroused in older settlements, such as Salem and Boston.

DOCUMENT
Benjamin Wadsworth, from *A Well-Ordered Family* (1712)

Salem's Wartime Witch Hunt

One of the most memorable disruptions, the Salem witch hunt, occurred in Essex County, Massachusetts, a two-day ride on horseback from the embattled Maine frontier. In 1692 an outburst of witchcraft accusations engulfed the farm community of Salem Village. The strange episode remains one of the most troubling in American history.

Among European Christians, a belief in witches with a supernatural power to inflict harm stretched back for centuries. In the 1600s, witchcraft trials abounded in Europe, and in New England zealous believers had executed several dozen supposed witches in isolated cases. Three-fourths of those accused (and even more of those executed) were women. Most were beyond childbearing age, often poor or widowed, with limited power to protect themselves in the community. But the hysteria in Salem went far beyond other colonial incidents, with more than 200 people accused and twenty put to death.

Early in 1692, more than half a dozen young women in Salem Village, ranging in age from nine to twenty, began to suffer violent convulsive fits. With reduced appetites and temporary loss of hearing, sight, and memory, they also experienced choking sensations that curtailed their speech. Vivid hallucinations followed. By April the girls had accused ten people of being witches. Then some of the ten named others in their elaborate confessions, and the hysteria snowballed.

In a world where people considered satanic influence very real, frightened authorities seriously weighed the girls' stories of people appearing to them as devilish specters and apparitions. Overriding tradition, jurists allowed such "spectral evidence" in court, and convictions mounted. The court ordered public hangings on Gallows Hill that continued through September. Only when accusations reached too high in the social hierarchy and when several accusers recanted their stories did the new governor finally intervene. He emptied the jails, forbade further imprisonments, and pardoned the surviving accused until the tremor could subside.

Why this terrible outburst? Some writers wonder whether the girls' symptoms suggest food poisoning (perhaps from a fungus on rye used in baking bread) or an epidemic of mosquito-borne encephalitis (an inflammation of the brain). Others note political factions within the village. Strained relations between farm families and more prosperous urban residents nearby may have influenced the craze. Still others emphasize the zeal and gullibility of those first assigned to investigate. Some speculate that the absence of central authority, until Governor Phips arrived in the colony, allowed a troubled situation to spin out of control. Finally, commentators stress a perverse psychological dynamic that arises in any witch hunt, ancient or modern. In such cases, accused suspects often can save their own lives by supplying damaging and vivid confessions implicating others rather than by offering heartfelt denials of guilt. One or more of these factors surely came into play.

Ann Putnam, Deposition (1692)

Yet devastation on the Maine frontier also contributed to what happened in Salem Village. The little Massachusetts town had numerous links to the war zone. A recent minister, George Burroughs, much disliked in the village, had come from Maine and had returned there when the contentious parish refused to pay him. Traumatized survivors from King William's War—the current conflict against the Abenaki and French—had trickled into the community. Significantly, more than half the young women who had accused others of witchcraft had lost one or both parents in the brutal frontier wars. On February 5, just weeks before the first accusations, attackers had burned the Maine village of York 80 miles north of Salem, killing forty-eight people, and taking seventy-three captives. Word of the raid no doubt triggered shocking memories among Salem's war refugees, especially the orphans who worked as servants in local households.

Ann Putnam, Confession (1706)

Fears deepened in April when one of the accused testified that the Devil had tempted her while she had been living in Maine. Then it was reported that the specter of Reverend Burroughs "appeared" to an accuser. Charged with promoting witchcraft and encouraging the hostile Indians (whom the colonists saw as Satan's helpers), Burroughs was arrested in Maine and hanged on Gallows Hill. A servant named Mercy Short, who had been captured and orphaned by Indians, recalled disturbing dreams of the Devil. She told minister Cotton Mather that in her dreams Satan and his minions (who had "an Indian colour") had made "hideous assaults" upon her. Much of what Mather and others recorded as the work of Satan may actually have been posttraumatic stress in a frayed community during wartime.

The Uneven Costs of War

Throughout the 1690s and beyond, King William's War and then Queen Anne's War made conflict a constant element of colonial life, but the burdens fell unevenly. For many colonial families, incessant warfare brought only death and dislocation. But for others, it offered new opportunities as the colonial economies expanded. Farmers with access to port towns shifted away from subsistence agriculture and grew crops for commercial sale. In doing so, they exposed themselves to greater financial risks, given transportation costs and market fluctuations. But they hoped to reap large profits. Overseas trade and wartime smuggling offered investors even higher gains and larger risks. The crews of **privateers** (boats licensed to harass enemy shipping in wartime) made money if they captured a foreign vessel as a prize. Profits

■ For protection, the pirate Blackbeard often brought his ship into the shallow waters behind the barrier islands that form North Carolina's Atlantic coast. There, his crew bartered stolen goods at Ocracoke Island and reveled on the beach with local inhabitants.

for outright pirates were greater still. Therefore, some colonial mariners chose to become buccaneers who operated for their own gain while avoiding the arm of the law. Englishman Edward Teach, known as Blackbeard, won notoriety as a privateer-turned-pirate, haunting the Carolina coast until his death in 1718.

Everywhere, poorer families were most likely to sink under the burdens of war. **Regressive taxes**, requiring the same amount from a poor carpenter as from a rich merchant, obviously hurt impoverished people the most. So did high wartime prices for food and other basic necessities. Furthermore, many of the poor men recruited by the military became casualties of combat or disease, increasing the number of widows living in poverty. As towns expanded, the growing distance between rich and poor struck local residents. The moral ties and community obligations—known as the social covenant—that Puritan elders had emphasized two generations earlier were loosening. In their place emerged a focus on secular priorities and a new, individualistic spirit.

In Boston, troubled ministers decried the hunger and poverty that they saw deepening in their parishes alongside unprecedented displays of wealth. Between 1685 and 1715, the share of all personal wealth in the town controlled by the richest 5 percent climbed from 26 percent to 40 percent. Angry writers published irate pamphlets encouraging working people to take political action. They charged once-respected elites with studying "how to oppress, cheat, and overreach their neighbours." Predictably, when an English fleet of sixty warships carrying 5,000 men docked at Boston in 1711, powerful merchants who controlled the flow of provisions reaped huge rewards from this windfall.

Storm Clouds in the South

Peace returned to New England's frontier villages and port towns in 1711, as negotiations began for ending Queen Anne's War in America and the related War of Spanish Succession in Europe. British diplomats gained favorable terms from France and Spain when they signed a treaty at

Utrecht two years later. (The formal union of England and Scotland in 1707 under the name *Great Britain* had transformed the *English* empire into the *British* empire.) But London officials could not prevent fresh violence in North America, given the expansion of their British colonies. The Wampanoag, Narragansett, and Abenaki Indians had attempted to roll back the advancement of northeastern settlers into Connecticut, Massachusetts, and Maine. Now Native Americans in the Southeast sought to counter the encroachments of newcomers along the Carolina coast.

By the 1660s, settlers drifted into what would become the North Carolina colony. Some were English radicals fleeing the Restoration. Others, such as John Culpeper, had moved north from the Carolina settlement on the Ashley River, where they disapproved of the hierarchical plans drawn up by Shaftesbury and Locke giving Carolina proprietors firm control over the new colony. Still others were runaway servants from Virginia and refugees escaping the aftermath of Bacon's uprising. In 1677 these newcomers, led by Culpeper, seized control in the Albemarle region. The proprietors suppressed "Culpeper's Rebellion," but in 1689 they agreed to name a separate governor for the portion of Carolina "That Lies north and east of Cape Feare." Another disturbance, "Cary's Rebellion" in 1710, led to official recognition of "North Carolina, independent of Carolina," the next year. (Surveyors marked off the dividing line with Virginia in 1728.)

Native American Population Loss, 1500–1700

In 1680 Native Americans still outnumbered newcomers in eastern North Carolina by two to one, but within thirty years that ratio had been reversed. The Naval Stores Act of 1705, passed by Parliament to promote colonial production of tar and pitch for shipbuilding, drew a stream of settlers to the pine forests of eastern North Carolina. By 1710 English communities existed on Albemarle Sound, at what is now Edenton, and on Pamlico Sound, at Bath (where Blackbeard and other pirates were frequent visitors). Farther south, Protestant immigrants from Bern, Switzerland, had staked out the town of New Bern on the site of a Native American village. John Lawson, who had explored the Carolinas before helping to lay out Bath and New Bern, conceded that the Indians had been "better to us than we are to them."

Eventually, the Tuscarora Indians struck back. Frustrated by corrupt traders and land encroachment, they killed Lawson and launched a war in 1711 to drive out the intruders. But they had waited too long. Within two years, the settlers—aided by a South Carolina force of several dozen whites and nearly 500 Yamasee Indians—had crushed Tuscarora resistance. Most of the Tuscarora survivors migrated north, where they became the sixth nation within the powerful Iroquois Confederacy.

Yamasee warriors from the Savannah River region helped British colonists quell the Tuscarora uprising. But in 1715 they led their own rebellion against advancing settlers and corrupt traders linked to Charleston. They received support from Creek Indians, Spanish settlers in Florida, and French traders at the new Alabama outpost of Fort Toulouse. The still-powerful Cherokee in Appalachia opted not to join in the Yamasee War. Otherwise, the Indians might have overwhelmed the South Carolina colony.

Conclusion

European Claims in America, c. 1750

Inspired by the exploits of LaSalle and a generation of voyageurs and missionaries, the French had made inroads into the heart of the continent, glimpsing the huge Mississippi Valley. But most European intrusions remained confined to the fringes of the vast continent. The French established themselves in Louisiana, and small numbers of Spanish held onto footholds in New Mexico and Florida, while venturing into parts of Arizona and Texas.

The English newcomers, far more numerous, remained clustered along the Atlantic seaboard. When their rising numbers prompted expansion up local river valleys away from the coast, warfare with traditional inhabitants ensued. Along the length of eastern North America, from the Kennebec River to the Savannah, hundreds of settlers and Indians died violently

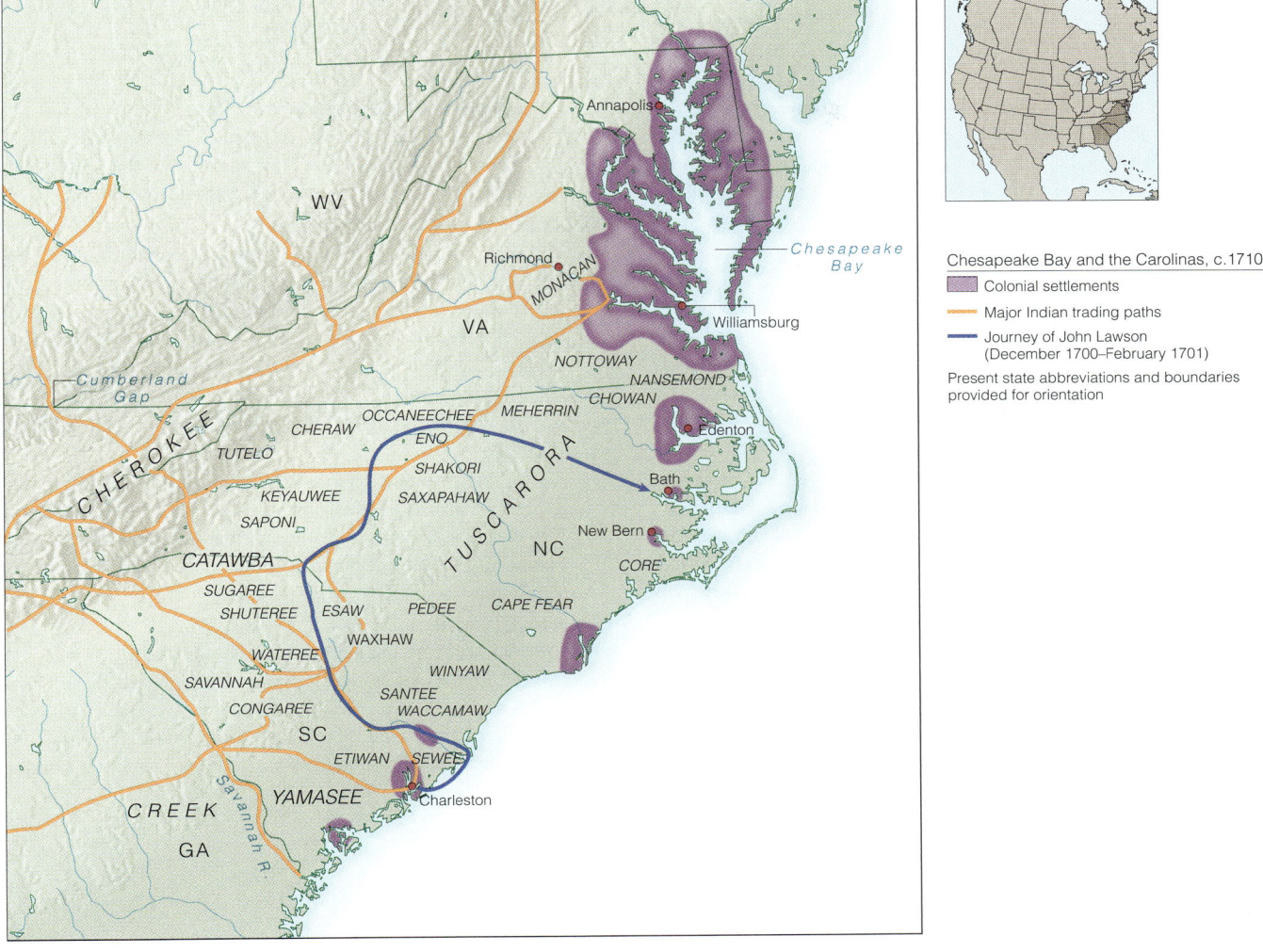

■ **MAP 3.3**
VIRGINIA AND THE CAROLINAS, c. 1710 After John Lawson made a 1,000-mile journey through the Carolina interior (1700–1701), he became an advocate for colonial growth. The expanding settlements of North Carolina and South Carolina pressed the Tuscarora and Yamasee Indians, who staged wars of resistance after 1710.

during the half-century before 1715. Often the frontier struggles became entwined with wider conflicts between the rival European empires. These wilderness skirmishes seem minute compared with the battles raging in Europe at the same time. Despite the small scale of the conflicts in North America, however, Europe's imperial wars had started to influence developments in the English colonies.

Another element of Europe's expansion overseas—the transatlantic slave trade—had also begun to alter the shape of England's North American colonies. What had seemed only a small cloud on the horizon in the early seventeenth century had grown into an ominous force, with a momentum of its own, by the early eighteenth century. The storm hit hardest along the Southeast coast, where the arrival of thousands of Africans soon shaped a distinctive and depressing world of enslavement and exploitation that endured for generations. No sooner had the English gained control along the Atlantic edge of North America than they orchestrated a "terrible transformation" that placed thousands in bondage and altered the shape of American history.

Sites to Visit

Mission San Xavier del Bac

Lying 7 miles south of Tucson, Arizona, off Interstate 19 is the mission Father Eusebio Kino founded in 1700. The current church was created in 1783. A short drive south on Highway 19, the Tumacacori National Historical Park preserves ruins of three early Spanish missions.

Jesuit Missionary Records

puffin.creighton.edu/jesuit/relations/

In the late nineteenth century, Reuben Gold Thwaites compiled and edited more than seventy volumes titled *The Jesuit Relations and Allied Documents*. Creighton University has made almost the entire English translation of these valuable documents available on this Web site. The documents are also available on CD-ROM from Quintin Publications.

Fort Toulouse

In 1717 the French built Fort Toulouse where the Coosa and Talapoosa rivers converge, just north of Montgomery, Alabama. On the third weekend each month between April and November, volunteers conduct a French Colonial Living History program in and around the reconstructed French fort, with displays of blacksmithing and musket firing.

Straits of Mackinac

The Straits of Mackinac joining lakes Huron and Michigan was once a strategic spot. Here, Interstate 75 now links Upper and Lower Michigan. North of the Mackinac Bridge, a memorial at St. Ignace honors Father Marquette. At the south end, Colonial Michilimackinac is a reconstructed village reflecting French and English frontier life.

Castillo de San Marcos

www.nps.gov/casa/home/home.htm

This stone fort guarding St. Augustine, Florida, was built in 1672–1695. The National Park Service maintains this fortress as a national monument and also provides a virtual tour online.

Old Deerfield National Historic Landmark

This site lies just east of Interstate 91 and surrounds a beautiful village in the hills of northwestern Massachusetts. Historic Deerfield, incorporated in 1952, maintains fourteen restored houses, open for a self-guided walking tour, and the Flynt Center of Early New England Life displays New England life from 1650 to 1850.

Salem Village Witchcraft

www.nhc.rtp.nc.us:8080/tserve/eighteen/ekeyinfo/salemwc.htm

A good Web introduction to "Witchcraft in Salem Village" appears as part of a project on "Religion and the National Culture" at this Web site of the National Humanities Center. Salem Village (Danvers, Massachusetts) has a memorial to victims of the 1692 witchcraft persecutions.

Eastern North Carolina

www.ah.dcr.state.nc.us/sections/hs/bath/bath.htm

North Carolina's earliest colonial ports at Edenton, Bath, and New Bern (ranging from north to south) still contain rich evidence of eighteenth-century life. This Web site for Historic Bath has links on explorer-naturalist John Lawson, Blackbeard the Pirate, and the Tuscarora War.

For Further Reading

General

Elaine G. Breslaw, *Witches of the Atlantic World: A Historical Reader and Primary Source Book* (2000).

Wesley Frank Craven, *The Colonies in Transition, 1660–1713* (1968).

Elizabeth A. H. John, *Storms Brewed in Other Men's Worlds: The Confrontation of Indians, Spanish, and French in the Southwest, 1540–1795* (1975).

Alvin M. Josephy Jr., *The Patriot Chiefs: A Chronicle of American Indian Resistance* (1969).

France and the American Interior

Marcel Giraud, *A History of French Louisiana, Vol. One: The Reign of Louis XIV, 1698–1715* (1974).

Eric Hinderaker, *Elusive Empires: Constructing Colonialism in the Ohio Valley, 1673–1800* (1997).

Robert S. Weddle, *The Wreck of the Belle, the Ruin of La Salle* (2001).

Richard White, *The Middle Ground: Indians, Empires, and Republics in the Great Lakes Region, 1650–1815* (1991).

The Spanish Empire on the Defensive

Ramón A. Gutiérrez, *When Jesus Came, the Corn Mothers Went Away: Marriage, Sexuality, and Power in New Mexico, 1500–1846* (1991).

Andrew L. Knaut, *The Pueblo Revolt of 1680: Conquest and Resistance in Seventeenth-Century New Mexico* (1995).

Jerald T. Milanich, *Florida Indians and the Invasion from Europe* (1995).

David J. Weber, ed., *What Caused the Pueblo Revolt?* (1999).

England's American Empire Takes Shape

Alan Gallay, *The Indian Slave Trade: The Rise of the English Empire in the American South, 1670–1717* (2002).

Joyce D. Goodfriend, *Before the Melting Pot: Society and Culture in Colonial New York City, 1664–1730* (1992).

Brendan McConville, *These Daring Disturbers of the Public Peace: The Struggle for Property and Power in Early New Jersey* (1999).

Gary B. Nash, *Quakers and Politics: Pennsylvania, 1681–1726* (1968).

Robert M. Weir, *Colonial South Carolina: A History* (1983).

Bloodshed in the English Colonies: 1670–1690

John Demos, *The Unredeemed Captive: A Family Story from Early America* (1994).
Jill Lepore, *The Name of War: King Philip's War and the Origins of American Identity* (1998).
David S. Lovejoy, *The Glorious Revolution in America* (1972).
Stephen S. Webb, *1676: The End of American Independence* (1984).

Consequences of War and Growth: 1690–1715

Verner W. Crane, *The Southern Frontier, 1670–1732* (1928).
Evan Haefeli and Kevin Sweeney, *Captors and Captives: The 1704 French and Indian Raid on Deerfield* (2003).
James H. Merrell, *The Indians' New World: Catawbas and Their Neighbors from European Contact Through the Era of Removal* (1989).
Gary B. Nash, *The Urban Crucible: The Northern Seaports and the Origins of the American Revolution* (1986, abridged edition).
Mary Beth Norton, *In the Devil's Snare: The Salem Witchcraft Crisis of 1692* (2002).
Marcus Rediker, *Villains of All Nations: Atlantic Pirates in the Golden Age* (2004).

For quizzes and other resources on these topics, go to www.longmanamericanhistory.com.

1672	Royal African Company (RAC) formed in London
1676	Virginia and Maryland slaves join in Bacon's Rebellion
1700	Shoshone Indians obtain horses; Sioux obtain guns
1705	Virginia Negro Act passes
1712	New York City slave revolt
1713	British receive the contract (*asiento*) to supply African slaves to Spanish colonies
1715	First whaling ventures from Nantucket
1718	French lay out New Orleans; Spanish start San Antonio
1721	Trenchard and Gordon, *Cato's Letters*
1728	Vitus Bering explores the strait between Siberia and Alaska
1734	James Oglethorpe founds Georgia as a nonslave colony Jonathan Edwards leads religious revival in Northampton, Massachusetts
1737	Delaware Indians lose land to Pennsylvania through the Walking Purchase
1739	Slave revolt in Stono, South Carolina George Whitefield's preaching tour sparks Great Awakening
1741	Bering's second voyage reaches coast of Alaska from Asia Alleged slave plot in New York City British forces capture Louisburg
1749	Spanish sign treaty with Apache at San Antonio
1751	Slavery is legalized in Georgia
1753	Moravians establish Bethabara in North Carolina
1754	War breaks out in America between French and British
1755	Braddock is defeated near Fort Duquesne
1758	Comanche attack Spanish at San Saba Mission

PART TWO

A Century of Colonial Expansion to 1775

On April 19, 1775, New England farmers battled British soldiers at Concord Bridge. The confrontation marked the start of the American Revolution. (Each spring in Massachusetts, the date is still set aside as Patriots' Day and celebrated with the running of the Boston Marathon.) But how did colonies that were weak outposts before 1700 become strong enough to challenge the power of the British Empire in the second half of the eighteenth century? The answer is not a simple one. Life changed in dramatic ways during the century before 1775, not only in New England but throughout much of North America.

The rapid spread of Spanish horses across the West allowed Native Americans, such as the Comanche and Sioux, to become mounted buffalo hunters on the Great Plains. The arrival of Russian fur traders disrupted traditional cultures on the Aleutian Islands and the coast of Alaska. At the same time, the gradual success of the new Louisiana colony gave France access to much of the Mississippi River valley. But the potential for a dominant French-speaking empire in America evaporated with the stunning defeat of French forces by the British in the Seven Years' War. As that global conflict ended in 1763, the Spanish also lost ground in North America. After claiming Florida for 200 years, they finally ceded the peninsula to the British, even as they began to extend Spanish missions up the coast of California.

Other changes were even more dramatic. In the eighteenth century, race slavery became an established aspect of colonial society in North America. Hints of coming change appeared even in the generation before 1660. During the next half century, race slavery rapidly took hold as a dominant institution in the coastal Southeast. The English had come late to the transatlantic slave trade, but they became aggressive participants in the lucrative traffic in human beings. English colonizers fashioned harsh slave-based societies in the Caribbean, then in the Chesapeake colonies of Virginia and Maryland, next in North and South Carolina, and finally, after 1750, in the recently established colony of Georgia.

"able to give a very good account of her fayth." Furthermore, she produced clear evidence that her father had sold her to Higginson for nine years. Mr. Key had demanded that Higginson not dispose of her to any other person, such as to Colonel Mottrom. Rather, he was to give her the usual "freedom portion" of corn and clothes "and lett her shift for her selfe," either in England or Virginia, when her term expired.

The local jury accepted Elizabeth Key's three-part argument and pronounced her free. But the General Court overturned the verdict on appeal, only to be overruled in turn by a committee of the General Assembly. In the end, the committee determined that "Elizabeth ought to bee free." The assemblymen also argued that her last master owed her a "freedom portion," plus back pay "for the time shee hath served longer than Shee ought to have done." Still, the matter generated debate among settlers. Several decades later, Elizabeth's case would have been decided differently. Moreover, the courts of Virginia might well have enslaved her children for life. And their offspring would have inherited slavery status as well.

A terrible transformation was under way in English colonial culture that would warp American society for centuries to come. It spread gradually, like a cancer, revealing a different pace and pattern in each mainland colony. During the 1620s and 1630s, a few black servants were working alongside white servants. But well before the end of the century, a fateful transition had occurred, and the grandchildren of those workers had been separated into two distinct categories based upon skin color and physical appearance, or race. Free blacks persisted in the English colonies, but in most communities they became anomalies, for the tide was flowing against them. From now on, people of African ancestry were to be legally enslaved for life. Elizabeth Key and her children and grandchildren experienced the painful transition firsthand.

The Descent into Race Slavery

Some major transitions in human affairs evolve gradually. This was the case for the descent of North American society into sanctioned race slavery. Nothing shaped colonial cultures more forcefully than the European colonists' commitment to the legal enslavement of hundreds of thousands of people and their descendants. It is important to examine the slippery slope that led to perpetual servitude based on race.

The Caribbean Precedent

The roots of race slavery in the Americas extend back to the era of Columbus, when warfare, sickness, and exploitation quickly decimated the native populations of the Caribbean after 1492. Hungry for human labor, the Spanish intruders began to import people from Africa to grow crops and dig for gold in the Caribbean islands. As the native population declined sharply through epidemics, the traffic in black newcomers expanded.

Spanish pressure for labor in the New World intensified further with the discovery of additional mines for precious metals in Mexico and Peru. To meet the growing demand, Spain's king even issued a contract (called the *asiento*) that allowed other European powers—such as Portugal, France, or the Netherlands—to import African slaves to the Spanish colonies. High profits drew eager participation. In the half-century between 1590 and 1640, more than 220,000 people arrived in chains from Africa at the Spanish empire's ports in Central and South America.

Meanwhile, the Portuguese purchased enslaved Africans to work their own expanding sugar plantations. They imported more than 75,000 slaves, mostly from the Congo River region of West Central Africa, to the Atlantic island of São Tomé in the sixteenth century. When

Portuguese sugar production spread to coastal Brazil, so did the exploitation of African labor. By 1625 Brazil imported the majority of slaves crossing the Atlantic each year and exported most of the sugar consumed in Europe.

Long before the 1660s, therefore, Europeans had set a precedent for exploiting African workers in New World colonies. Religious and secular authorities frowned on actively enslaving people, especially if they were fellow Christians. But they tolerated buying so-called infidels (those who followed other religions), particularly if slavery had already been imposed on them elsewhere. West African victims were non-Christians, and most had already been enslaved by others, captured by fellow Africans in war.

Confident in this rationale, the Spanish and Portuguese adapted their laws to accept the enslavement of Africans. Moreover, the condition would be passed on, with children inheriting at birth their mother's legal status. The Catholic Church backed the new labor system, though priests occasionally worked to alleviate suffering among Africans in the Americas. The pope did nothing to condemn the growing traffic, nor did the Protestant Reformation have a dampening effect. On the contrary, the rising Protestant sea powers of northern Europe proved willing to assist in the slave trade and take part in the dramatic "sugar revolution," growing sugar on a massive scale for expanding Atlantic markets.

The Dutch, for example, ruled Brazil for a generation in the first half of the seventeenth century, importing slaves to South America and exporting sugar. When the Portuguese regained control of Brazil at midcentury, they pushed out Dutch settlers. These outcasts took their knowledge about managing sugar plantations to the islands of the Caribbean. Some appeared in the new English possessions of Barbados and Jamaica, and soon they were directing African slaves in cutting, pressing, and boiling sugar cane to make molasses. The thick molasses could then be processed further to make rum and refined sugar for export. By the 1650s slavery and sugar production were engulfing England's West Indian possessions, just as these twin features had already become central to the New World colonies controlled by Spain and Portugal. A looming precedent had been set. But as late as 1660, it was not at all clear that African slavery would gain a prominent place, or even a lasting foothold, in any North American colonies.

> *As late as 1660, it was not at all clear that African slavery would gain a prominent place, or even a lasting foothold, in any North American colonies.*

Ominous Beginnings

As far back as the sixteenth century, African men had participated in Spanish explorers' forays into the Southeast, and some had remained, fathering children with Indian women. African slaves had helped to establish the small Spanish outpost at St. Augustine in 1565, but a century later no additional coastal colonies had yet appeared on the mainland anywhere south of Chesapeake Bay.

Granted, Africans were present farther north in the fledgling settlements of the French, Dutch, and English. But their numbers remained small—several thousand at most—and few of these newcomers had come directly from Africa. Most had lived for years in the Caribbean or on the mainland, absorbing colonial languages and beliefs. So they and their children, like Bess Key, were not viewed as complete outsiders by the Europeans. The legal and social standing of these early African Americans remained vague before the 1660s. Everywhere, workers were in demand, and most black newcomers found themselves laboring alongside unfree European servants, each person bound by an "**indenture**" for a period of years.

In the Massachusetts Bay colony early Puritan settlers, casting about for sources of labor and for markets, exchanged goods for slaves in the Caribbean. In 1644 seafaring New Englanders even attempted direct trade with Africa. But the following year, Massachusetts authorities ordered a New Hampshire resident to surrender a black worker he had purchased in Boston. They argued that the man had been stolen from Africa, not captured in war, and should be returned to his home. In 1652 Rhode Island passed a law limiting all involuntary service—for Europeans or Africans—to no more than ten years.

Along the Hudson River, the Dutch colonists had close ties with the sugar islands of the West Indies where race slavery was already an accepted system. In New Netherland, therefore, the laws discriminated against black workers and limited their rights. But the statutes also provided loopholes that permitted social and economic advancement to the community's Africans, most of whom spoke Dutch.

Chesapeake Bay lay even closer to the main routes of the Atlantic slave traffic. In 1619 a Dutch warship brought to Virginia more than twenty African men and women acquired as slaves in the Caribbean. Like people deported from England to the Chesapeake, they were sold as servants. Terms of service varied, and some black newcomers earned their freedom quickly and kept it. But others saw their terms extended arbitrarily. In 1640 Virginia's General Court considered punishment for "a negro named John Punch" and two other servants who had escaped to Maryland. When apprehended, the Dutchman and the Scotsman each received four additional years of service, but the African was sentenced to unending servitude "for the time of his natural life." That same year, Virginia passed a law that prevented blacks from bearing arms. A 1643 law taxing productive field hands included African American women but not white women.

These early efforts to separate Africans from Europeans by law set an ominous precedent in the use of skin color as a distinguishing marker. Still, rules governing the lives of people of color and their offspring remained ambiguous for several decades, and (as the case of Bess Key makes clear) efforts at exploitation could often be undone in court. But new forces would come into play in the mainland American colonies after 1660, consolidating the transition to hereditary African slavery.

■ This summary of an African slave-trading voyage shows wealthy planters boarding a French ship upon its arrival in the West Indies in order to buy slaves newly arrived from Angola. The crew has used an iron fence dividing the deck to protect against revolt during the voyage. The captain conducts business under an awning in the stern.

Alternative Sources of Labor

For African newcomers to English North America, their legal status became distinctly clearer and less hopeful in the decades after 1660. The transatlantic slave trade, already more than a century old, provided certain English colonies with a ready source of African workers at a time when more obvious streams of inexpensive labor—captured Native Americans and impoverished Europeans—were dwindling.

For labor-hungry colonists, Native Americans were close at hand and knew the country well. They took captives when fighting one another, so colonists could buy Indian prisoners or seize them in frontier warfare. Europeans felt they could enslave such people in good conscience, since they were non-Christians who had been taken captive in war. But Native American numbers were declining steadily, owing to epidemics. And those who did become enslaved knew the countryside well enough to escape. Besides, traffic in Indian slaves disrupted the profitable deerskin trade, undermined wilderness diplomacy, and sparked conflict on the frontier.

Efforts to maintain a steady flow of cheap labor from Europe ran into different problems. The Great Plague of 1665 devastated the English population, and the London Fire the following year created a new need for workers of all kinds to rebuild the capital. England's labor surplus, which had been a boon to the initial colonies half a century earlier, rapidly disappeared. The use of indentures persisted, whereby the poor could buy their passage by agreeing to sell their labor for a fixed term. But when these workers reached America, they served for only a few years and then had to be replaced.

Equally important, when indentured servants were mistreated, they had little difficulty in relaying their complaints home to other potential workers. The flow of ships back and forth between Europe and North America grew steadily in the century after 1660, so word of places where indentured servants were regularly abused or swindled quickly reached the other side of the Atlantic. In contrast, the African slave trade lacked any similar "feedback loop." As a result, the brutal treatment of black workers never had a chance, through accurate feedback across the Atlantic, to influence the future flow of deportations from Africa.

The Fateful Transition

In general, powerful Chesapeake tobacco planters were encouraged in 1660 by news of the Restoration of Charles II, since England's new king was likely to support their interests and reward their loyalty. These men had noticed the rising profits that sugar growers were making by using slaves in the Caribbean. In Virginia and Maryland, therefore, planters passed a series of laws that sharpened distinctions between servants working for a fixed period and slaves consigned to labor for life.

In shaping new legislation, local leaders even challenged long-standing English legal traditions, such as the right of children to inherit their father's status. In 1662 Virginia's General Assembly considered whether any child fathered "by an Englishman upon a negro woman should be slave or Free." In a crucial reversal of precedent, the legislature said that in such cases children shall be "bond or free *only according to the condition of the mother.*" From now on, the infant of any female slave would be enslaved from birth. Slavery was becoming a hereditary condition.

Could enslaved persons receive their freedom if they accepted Christianity, as sometimes happened in Spanish colonies? A 1664 Maryland law closed off that prospect. The act made clear that the legal status of non-Christian slaves did not change if they experienced religious conversion. Three years later, Virginia's government agreed that "the conferring of baptisme doth not alter the condition of the person as to his bondage." By taking religion out of the question, legislators shifted the definition of who could be enslaved from someone who was not Christian to someone who did not look European.

In scarcely a generation, black bondage had become a hereditary institution, and the conditions of life had grown markedly worse for African Americans.

In scarcely a generation, black bondage had become a hereditary institution, and the conditions of life had grown markedly worse for African Americans. Increasingly, they faced corporal punishments: whippings and mutilation. Black slaves—and often free blacks—lost their right to accuse, or even testify against, a white person in court. "And further," stated Virginia's formative slave law of 1680, "if any Negro" raises a hand, even in self-defense, "against any Christian, he shall receive thirty lashes, and if he absent himself . . . from his master's service and resist lawful apprehension, he may be killed."

The Growth of Slave Labor Camps

Over two generations, beginning in the late seventeenth century, tobacco growers in the Chesapeake and rice producers in the new colony of South Carolina embraced the system of hereditary race slavery that had developed in the Caribbean. For those forced to cut the trees, drain the swamps, and harvest the crops, the shift in production strategy represented—in modern terminology—the emergence of slave labor camps. After all, these

■ Rice plantations that emerged in coastal South Carolina around 1700 became labor camps where enslaved blacks were confined for generations, without wages or legal rights. In the 1850s, distant descendants of the region's first African workers were still being forced to plant, harvest, and process the huge rice crops that made their masters rich.

people received no wages for their labor, had no legal rights, and could be deported to some other location at any time. This deterioration in conditions occurred first, and most dramatically, in Virginia, where several thousand African Americans lived and labored by the 1670s.

Black Involvement in Bacon's Rebellion

Nothing did more to consolidate Virginia's slide toward race slavery than Bacon's Rebellion, the major uprising that shook the Chesapeake region in 1676 (see Chapter 3). The episode pitted aspiring gentry, led by Nathaniel Bacon, against beleaguered Indian groups on the frontier and an entrenched elite in Jamestown.

Free men, would-be farmers in search of land, made up part of Bacon's following, but diverse unfree workers also proved eager recruits. Such ill-treated people remained legally bound to large landholders for varying terms, and many of the Africans were undoubtedly bound for life. Together, they raised the colony's annual tobacco crop, and the backbreaking labor prompted frequent unrest. These ragged workers, however long their term of service might be, had the most to gain and the least to lose from Bacon's revolt. According to the Virginia Assembly, "many evil disposed servants . . . taking advantage of the loosenes of the tymes . . . followed the rebels in rebellion." When Bacon died in October 1676, many of his wealthier supporters reasserted their loyalty to the colonial government. But bound workers who had escaped from their masters continued the fight.

A letter reaching London that fall suggested that at the height of the rebellion Bacon had "proclam'd liberty to all Servants and Negro's." Clearly, the widespread unrest had given hope to downtrodden tobacco pickers, about a quarter of whom were black. When military reinforcements arrived in Chesapeake Bay from England in November, the commander, Captain Thomas Grantham, found hundreds of laborers still in active revolt.

Impressed by their strength, Grantham chose to use deceit when he met with 800 heavily armed rebels, both white and black, at their headquarters near the York River. Making vague promises regarding pardons and freedom, he persuaded most of the white men to surrender and return home. Only about "Eighty Negroes and Twenty English" demanded "their hoped for liberty and would not quietly laye downe their armes." But when these last holdouts boarded a sloop, Grantham disarmed the rebels and chained them below decks for return to their masters.

The Rise of a Slaveholding Tidewater Elite

With Bacon's death and the arrival of British ships, propertied Virginians had narrowly averted a successful multiracial revolution, fueled from below by workers who resented their distressed condition. But clearly some future revolt might succeed, and so the great planters of the Chesapeake region moved to tighten their hold on political and economic power. After Bacon's Rebellion, a strategy of divide and conquer seemed in order. They moved to improve conditions for poor whites in ways that would ensure deference and racial solidarity among Europeans. At the same time, they further reduced the legal status of blacks and solidified their enslavement for life.

For precedent, the aspiring planters had the model provided by slavery-based colonial societies in the West Indies, including the English sugar island of Barbados. Their uneasiness continued over importing non-Christian strangers who spoke little, if any, English. But such doubts were more than offset by the prospect of laying claim to the children of slaves and to the lives and labor of all generations to come.

Increasing life expectancy in the Chesapeake region, resulting from sturdier dwellings and more stable living conditions, meant that Africans enslaved for life would yield profitable service for an increasingly long time. And they would be more likely than ever to produce healthy offspring. Boys and girls who survived childhood could then be forced to clear more land to grow additional crops.

Among a circle of wealthy investors, the enticement of such an economic bonanza overcame any cultural anxieties or religious scruples. Seizing the moment, these aggressive entrepreneurs established themselves as the leading families of Virginia. These ambitious merchant-planters expected that the English-speaking Africans already present could assist in teaching newcomers to receive orders. They also assumed that slave laborers from diverse African societies could not communicate well enough with one another to cause dangerous disturbances. And of course, having now made skin color a determining feature of social order, they knew that black runaways could be spotted and apprehended readily in the free white community.

Closing the Vicious Circle in the Chesapeake

As the profitability of the slavery option increased, so did its appeal. By 1700 some 4,500 people were enslaved in Maryland in a total population of 35,000. And the colony's assembly was actively encouraging the importation of slaves. Growing demand meant that merchants and sea captains who had only dabbled in the transportation of slaves now devoted more time and larger ships to the enterprise. Expansion of the slave-trading infrastructure made African workers readily available and affordable.

As the supply of enslaved black newcomers grew larger, planters eager to strengthen their position manipulated the established headright system. Traditionally, under this system, the colonial government granted to any arriving head of household 50 acres for every family member or hired hand he brought into the colony. The incentive was intended to spur migration from Europe, expand the free population, and develop the land through the establishment of family farms. But the wealthy planters who saw African slavery as a profitable labor source also controlled Virginia's legal system. For their own benefit, therefore, they extended the headright system so that a land bonus also went to anyone who purchased an African arrival as a lifelong slave. Thus, before the seventeenth century closed, a Virginia investor buying twenty slaves could also lay claim to headrights worth 1,000 acres of land.

To consolidate their new regime, planters worked through the church and the legislature to separate whites from blacks socially and legally. They undermined the position of free blacks and stigmatized interracial ties. A 1691 Virginia statute decried the "abominable mixture and spurious issue" that resulted from "Negroes, mulattoes and Indians intermarrying" with English or other white people. All such couples were "banished from this dominion forever." It also prohibited masters from freeing any black or mulatto unless they paid to transport that person out of the colony within six months.

> *To consolidate their new regime, planters worked through the church and the legislature to separate whites from blacks socially and legally.*

Virginia's Negro Act of 1705 further underscored the stark new boundaries. It mandated that white servants who were mistreated had the right to sue their masters in county court. Slaves, in contrast, had no such right. Any enslaved person who tried to escape could be tortured and even dismembered in hopes of "terrifying others" from seeking freedom. When masters or overseers killed a slave while inflicting punishment, they were automatically free of any felony charge. If slaves were killed or put to death by law, the owners would be paid public funds for the loss of their "property." In scarcely forty years, a dire and long-lasting revolution had transformed the labor system of the Chesapeake with the full backing of the law.

DOCUMENT
Of the Servants and Slaves in Virginia (1705)

England Enters the Atlantic Slave Trade

The Atlantic slave trade remains the largest and longest-lasting deportation in human history. In nearly four centuries, more than 10 million people were torn from their homelands against their will and transported to the Caribbean and to Central, South, and North America. Several million more perished in transit. By 1700, more Africans than Europeans had already crossed the Atlantic to the Western Hemisphere. Their numbers grew over the following century as the traffic reached its height. The importation of Africans to North America expanded after 1700, but it remained a small proportion of the overall Atlantic slave trade.

England took little part in the trade at first. However, the development of Barbados as a lucrative sugar colony and the expansion of English overseas ambitions changed matters quickly after 1640. With the restoration of the English monarchy in 1660, Charles II immediately granted a monopoly on African trade to a small group of adventurers, and in 1672 he chartered the powerful new Royal African Company (RAC).

The RAC dispatched a steady flow of merchant ships along a **triangular trade** route. The first leg took captains to English outposts along the coast of West Africa, where they exchanged textiles, guns, and iron bars for gold, ivory, and enslaved Africans. After a transatlantic **middle passage** of one to three months, the captains sold slaves and took on sugar in the West Indies before returning to England on the final leg of the triangle. When the company's monopoly ended officially in 1698, English slave trading ballooned. By the 1730s, British ships controlled the largest share of the Atlantic slave trade. They continued to dominate the traffic for the next seventy years.

The Slave Trade on the African Coast

By the 1680s, it had been two centuries since Portuguese sailors had visited Africa's western shores and established a post at Elmina, in modern-day Ghana. Dozens of these depots, controlled by

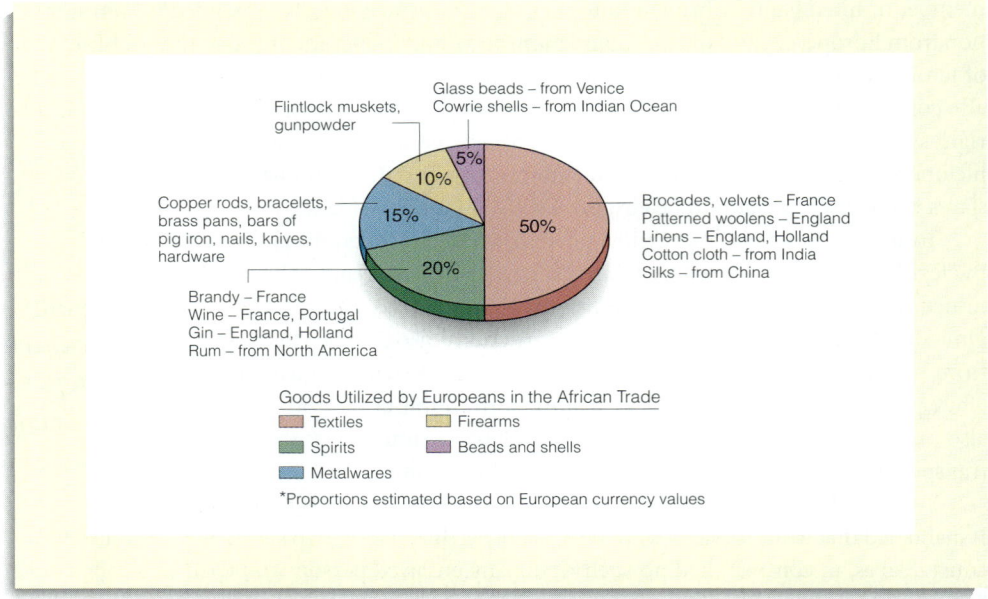

■ **FIGURE 4.1**
GOODS TRADED IN AFRICA As European ship captains expanded trade along the African coast, they tailored their cargoes to suit the demands of local markets.

rival European powers and their local allies, dotted the sub-Saharan coastline. (They became known as *factories*—an early use of the word—since a *factor*, or manager, ran each imperial trading post.) This string of European outposts began at the mouth of the Senegal River, just above Cape Verde, the continent's westernmost point; it ended below the mouth of the Congo River, in present-day Angola. In between, the coastline curved some 5,000 miles. It embraced diverse geographic environments—from open savannas to thick forests—and scores of distinctive cultures. All along this coastline, villagers caught fish and gathered salt for trade with herders and farmers living farther inland.

Generations of contact with oceangoing ships brought new pressures and opportunities to African coastal communities. Local merchants, who traded gold and ivory to sea captains for imported textiles and alcohol, formed alliances with European trading partners in response to the growing demand for human labor. They consolidated their positions near suitable harbors and navigable rivers. From there, they bartered local servants and war captives to white agents (factors). In return, they obtained linen, beads, metalwares, and muskets, items that enhanced their prestige and let them extend their inland trading networks.

Inland traders, alert to the rising demand for slaves in the port towns, annually brought thousands of captives from the backcountry to the coast. The traders traveled by land and water, binding their prisoners together in small groups to form a **coffle** (from the Arabic word for "caravan"). The overseas goods they received as payment included firearms, gunpowder, and knives, which they used to prosecute additional wars and raids to secure more captives.

By the 1660s and 1670s, the pace of deportation across the Atlantic had reached an average rate of nearly 15,000 people each year. It rose steadily to a high of more than 65,000 people per year a century later. As the traffic grew, it became increasingly organized, competitive, and routine. Shrewd African traders played one European vessel against another for the best deals. When they saw that a ship was eager to depart, they increased their prices. Hardened European agents stockpiled the wares that African traders most wanted. They also learned to curry favor with local officials and to quell unrest among captives, confined in the holding pens known as **barracoons**. Experienced captains timed their ventures to avoid the months when sickness was most rampant in the tropics. Through repeated voyages,

■ MAP 4.1
REGIONS OF THE AFRICAN SLAVE TRADE IN 1700

improved charts, and accumulated lore, they came to differentiate and exploit half a dozen major slaving regions along Africa's Atlantic coast. On occasion, they even ventured to Mozambique in southeast Africa and the nearby island of Madagascar.

The closest market where Europeans bargained for goods and slaves was Senegambia, or the northern parts of Guinea, between the Senegal River and the Gambia River. Gorée Island, off the coast of Senegal, and James Fort, located in the mouth of the Gambia, served as slave-trading centers. The long Windward Coast extending to the southeast beyond Sierra Leone became known for its pepper, grain, and ivory. Further east, from the area of Cape Three Points and Elmina to the factory at Accra, stretched the Gold Coast. There, the Portuguese had established Elmina to draw trade from the Asante gold fields in the interior. Farther east, the Slave Coast reached along the Bight of Benin to the huge delta of the Niger River. Trading depots at Whydah, Ardra, and Lagos drew captives from secondary ports in between. Beyond the Niger, where the African coast again turns south near Cameroon, lay the Bight of Biafra. English captains quickly learned the preferences for trade goods in each district, carrying textiles to the Gold Coast and metals to the Bight of Biafra.

The largest and most southerly region, known as Congo-Angola or West Central Africa, was the only one below the equator. Here, Catholic missionaries established

■ Slaves were held as prisoners in the interior before being marched to the African Coast in groups known as coffles.

footholds, and Portuguese traders exported slave labor for sugar production in Brazil and the Caribbean. Before 1700 more than half of all Atlantic slaves departed from West Central Africa. In the eighteenth century the proportion remained over one-third. Later, north of the Congo River, French and English interests came to dominate the slave traffic out of Loango and Cabinda. During the entire span of the slave trade, the Congo-Angola hinterland furnished roughly 40 percent of all Atlantic deportees: more than 4.5 million men, women, and children.

The Middle Passage Experience

Equiano, the Middle Passage (1788)

For every individual the exodus was different, a harrowing personal story. Nevertheless, the long nightmare of deportation contained similar elements for all who fell victim to the transatlantic trade. The entire journey, from normal village life to enslavement beyond the ocean, could last a year or two. It unfolded in at least five stages, beginning with capture and deportation to the African coast. The initial loss of freedom—the first experience of bound hands, harsh treatment, and forced marches—was made worse by the encounters with strange landscapes and unfamiliar languages. Hunger, fatigue, and anxiety took a steady toll as coffles of young and old were conveyed slowly toward the coast through a network of traders.

The next phase, sale and imprisonment, began when a contingent reached the sea. During this stage, which could last several months, African traders transferred "ownership" of the captives to Europeans. Many buyers subjected their new property to demeaning inspections and burned brands into their skin. Then they were put in irons alongside hundreds of other captives and guarded in a secure spot to prevent escape. From there, canoes transported the captives through the surf to a waiting vessel. (Their hands were bound, so if a canoe capsized, it meant certain drowning.) Once aboard, they might languish in the sweltering hold for weeks while the captain cruised the coast in search of additional human cargo. Crew members sometimes raised nets surrounding the deck to prevent attempts at escape or suicide.

Diagram of a Slave Ship

The ship's captain decided when to begin crossing the Atlantic, the harrowing third phase that constituted the middle passage. The Africans aboard each ship now faced an utterly alien plight, trapped in a strange wooden hull. When the crew finally raised anchor and unfurled the vessel's huge sails, the captives could only anticipate the worst. Already the crowded hold had become foul, and the large wooden buckets used as latrines had taken on a loathsome smell. The rolling of the ship on ocean swells brought seasickness and painful chafing from lying on the bare planks. Alexander Falconbridge, who sailed as a surgeon on several slave ships, recorded that "those who are emaciated frequently have their skin and even their flesh entirely rubbed off, by the motion of the ship, from the . . . shoulders, elbows and hips so as to render the bones quite bare."

Historians have documented more than 27,000 slave voyages from Africa to the Americas, and in each one an array of variables came into play to shape the Atlantic crossing. These included the exact point of departure, the planned destination, the season of the year, the length of the journey, the supplies of food and fresh water, the navigational skills of the captain and crew, the condition of the vessel, the health and resolve of the prisoners, the vagaries of piracy and ocean warfare, and the ravages of disease. A change in weather conditions or in the captain's mood could mean the difference between life and death.

England's Royal African Company maintained more than a dozen small posts along the Gold Coast. Each outpost funneled slaves to this strong seventy-four-gun fortress known as Cape Coast Castle. Cut into rock beneath the parade ground, the vaulted dungeon inside could "conveniently contain a thousand Blacks . . . against any insurrection."

While the grim details varied, the overall pattern remained the same. The constant rolling of the vessel; the sharp changes in temperature; the crowded, dark, and filthy conditions; and the relentless physical pain and mental anguish took a heavy toll. Pregnant mothers gave birth or miscarried; women were subjected to abuse and rape by the crew. Crews threw the bodies of those who died to the sharks and even used corpses as bait to catch sharks, which they fed to the remaining captives.

DOCUMENT
Falconbridge, the African Slave Trade (1788)

Saltwater Slaves Arrive in America

For the emaciated survivors of the Atlantic ordeal, two further stages remained in their descent into slavery: the selling process and the time called "seasoning." The selling process on American soil could drag on for weeks or months after the ship dropped anchor. Prospective owners examined and prodded the newcomers in dockside holding pens. Those purchased were wrenched away from their shipmates with whom they had formed strong links during their miseries at sea. Slaves often were auctioned in groups, or parcels, to ensure sale of the weak along with the strong. Then another journey brought them to the particular plantation where they were fated to work and probably to die.

IMAGE
Slave Dealers

Most newcomers did not begin their forced labor immediately. Instead, they entered a final stage, known as seasoning, which lasted several months or longer. The arrivals were distinguished as "saltwater slaves"—in contrast to "country-born slaves" who had grown up in America from birth—and seasoning gave them time to mend physically, regain their strength, and begin absorbing the rudiments of a new language. Inevitably, many suffered from what we would now describe as posttraumatic stress syndrome.

As adults and children recovered from the trauma of the middle passage, they faced a series of additional shocks. They confronted strange foods, unfamiliar tasks, and even new names. Worst of all, they encountered a master or his overseer who made every effort to break the wills of these fresh arrivals and to turn them into compliant bondservants. Repeatedly, the powerful stranger used arbitrary force to demand the slaves' obedience, destroy their hope, and crush any thoughts of resistance.

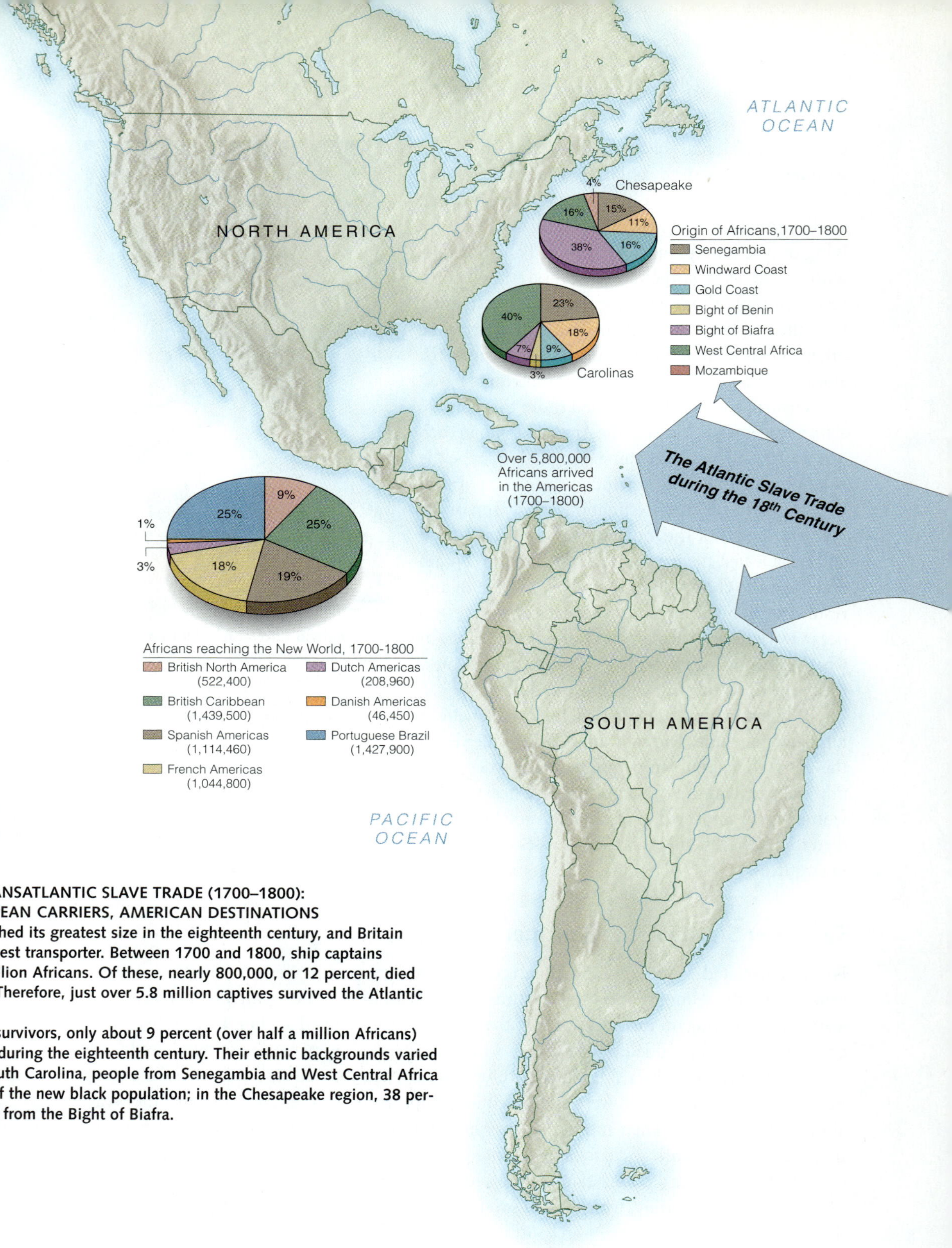

MAP 4.2
ONE CENTURY IN THE TRANSATLANTIC SLAVE TRADE (1700–1800): AFRICAN ORIGINS, EUROPEAN CARRIERS, AMERICAN DESTINATIONS

The Atlantic slave trade reached its greatest size in the eighteenth century, and Britain replaced Portugal as the largest transporter. Between 1700 and 1800, ship captains purchased more than 6.6 million Africans. Of these, nearly 800,000, or 12 percent, died during the middle passage. Therefore, just over 5.8 million captives survived the Atlantic crossing during the century.

Of these middle passage survivors, only about 9 percent (over half a million Africans) were sent to North America during the eighteenth century. Their ethnic backgrounds varied from colony to colony. In South Carolina, people from Senegambia and West Central Africa made up nearly two-thirds of the new black population; in the Chesapeake region, 38 percent of African arrivals came from the Bight of Biafra.

Survival in a Strange New Land

African Slave Trade

By 1700 race slavery was accepted throughout the mainland colonies, so Africans found themselves scattered from New England to Louisiana. But their distribution was far from even. Among roughly 247,000 slaves in the North American colonies in 1750, only 30,000 (or 12 percent) resided in the North, where they made up just 5 percent of the overall population from Pennsylvania to New Hampshire. More than one-third of these northerners (11,000) lived in the colony of New York, where they constituted 14 percent of the colonial inhabitants. All

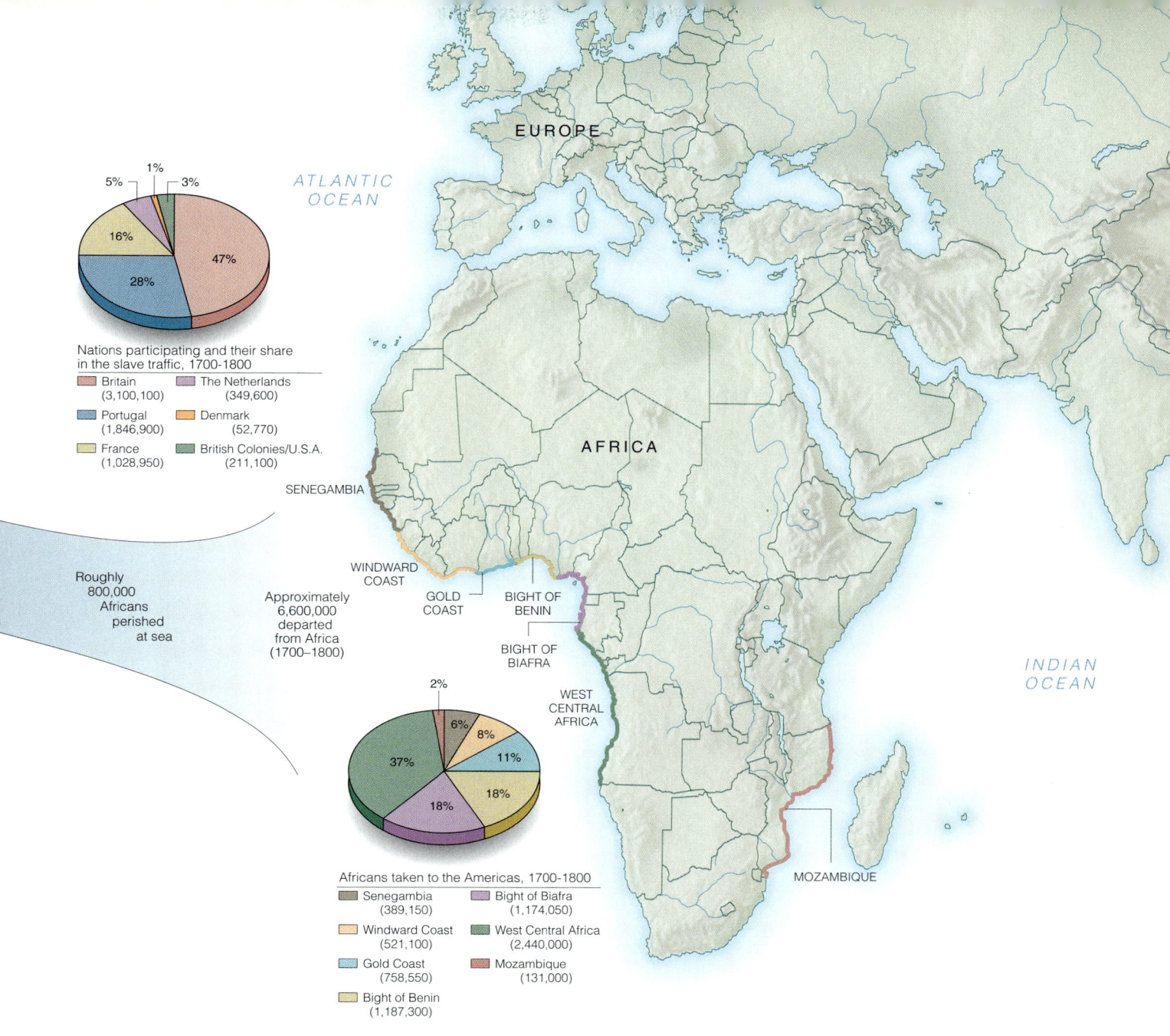

the rest of the people of African descent in North America—some 217,000 men, women, and children by the mid-eighteenth century—lived and worked in the Chesapeake region and the lower South. Fewer than 5,000 of these black southerners resided in French Louisiana.

African Rice Growers in South Carolina

Throughout the eighteenth century, by far the most North American slaves lived in Virginia or Maryland: 150,000 African Americans by 1750. But the highest *proportion* of enslaved workers lived in South Carolina, where Africans began outnumbering Europeans as early as 1708. By 1750 this black majority (40,000 people) constituted more than 60 percent of the colony's population. Almost all had arrived through the deepwater port of Charleston. Sullivan's Island, near the entrance to the harbor, with its so-called **pest house** to quarantine incoming slaves and reduce the spread of shipborne disease, has been called the Ellis Island of black America.

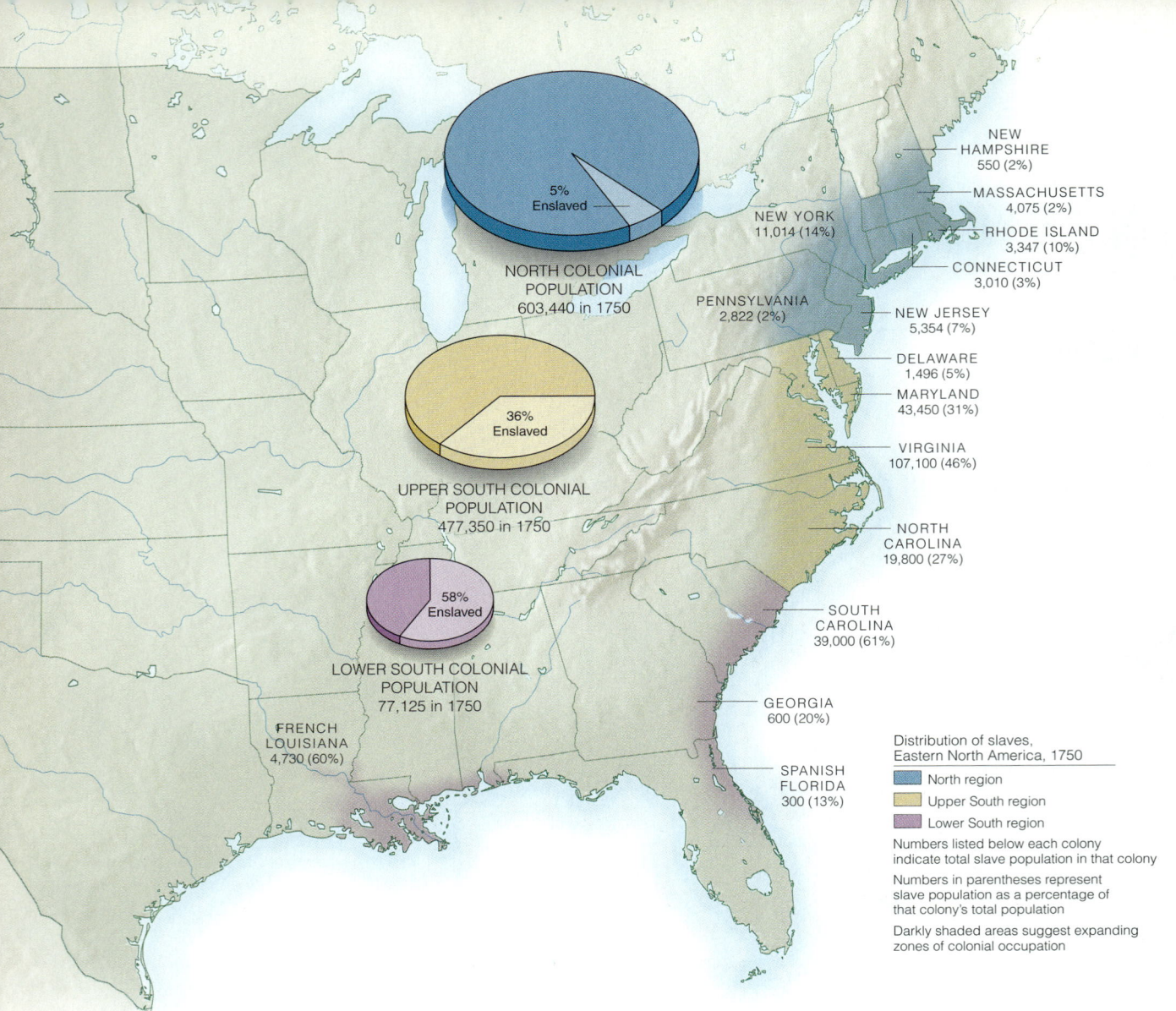

MAP 4.3
ENSLAVED PEOPLE LIVING IN NORTH AMERICA IN 1750: DISTRIBUTION BY COLONY, PERCENTAGE OF TOTAL POPULATION By 1750 nearly a quarter of a million people lived as slaves in eastern North America—more than 21 percent of the colonial population. Almost all were Africans or the descendants of Africans, along with a few thousand Native American and mixed-race slaves. In the North, slaves made up a small fraction of a large population. By far the greatest number of slaves lived in the Chesapeake area, where they made up more than a third of the total population. Enslaved people were less numerous but much more concentrated in the lower South, making up a clear majority of the overall inhabitants. White settlers had already smuggled several hundred slaves into the fledgling colony of Georgia, even though the exploitation of slave labor did not become legal there until 1751.

What explains the emergence of South Carolina's slave concentration? For one thing, the colony was closer than Virginia to Africa and to the Caribbean. Moreover, it had been founded in 1670, just as the English were embracing plantation slavery and the African trade. Indeed, some of the colony's original proprietors owned stakes in the Royal African Company. Also, some of Carolina's influential early settlers came directly from Barbados, bringing enslaved Africans and planter ambitions with them.

In the earliest days of colonization in South Carolina, newcomers lacked sufficient labor to clear coastal forests and plant crops. Instead, they let their cattle and pigs run wild. With easy foraging and warm winters, the animals reproduced rapidly. The settlers slaughtered them and shipped their meat to the Caribbean, along with firewood for boiling sugar cane and wooden barrels for transporting sugar. Ship captains also carried enslaved Native Americans to the West Indies and brought back African slaves.

The arriving Africans understood South Carolina's subtropical climate, with its alligators and palmetto trees, better than their European owners did. Many of these enslaved newcomers were already familiar with keeping cattle. Others, obliged to feed themselves, began growing rice in the fertile swamplands just as they had in West Africa. Slave owners quickly realized that this plant, unfamiliar to much of northern Europe, held the answer to their search for a profitable staple crop. Soon, people who had tended their own irrigated rice crops near the Gambia River were obliged to clear cypress swamps along the Ashley and Cooper rivers to grow rice for someone else.

Before long, merchants were shipping tons of Carolina rice to Europe, where it proved a cheap grain for feeding soldiers, orphans, and peasants. By the middle of the eighteenth century, their fortunes improved even more when indigo, another African crop, joined rice as a profitable export commodity. Outnumbered by their enslaved workers, South Carolina's landowners passed strict Negro Acts patterned on those of the Caribbean. Legislation prohibited slaves from carrying guns, meeting in groups, raising livestock, or traveling without a pass. Everywhere, mounted patrols enforced the regulations with brutal severity.

Patterns of Resistance

In South Carolina and elsewhere, enslaved African Americans pushed against the narrow boundaries of their lives. Like any other imprisoned population, they used every possible means to negotiate slivers of freedom, including spreading rumors, refusing to work, breaking tools, feigning illness, and threatening violence. In response, their owners tried to divide them in order to control them. Masters rewarded workers who were obedient and diligent or who informed on fellow slaves. They imposed harsh punishments—whipping, mutilation, sale, or death—on those suspected of taking food, sowing dissent, or plotting revolt. And they encouraged the formation of black families, not only to gain another generation of laborers at no cost but also to create the emotional ties that they knew would hold individuals in check for fear of reprisals against loved ones.

Owners confined residents in the slave labor camps with curfews and pass systems and kept them from learning to read and from communicating freely with neighbors and relatives. They also refused to allow any impartial system for expressing grievances or appealing arbitrary punishments. Faced with such steep odds, many slaves submitted to the deadening routine of the prison camp to survive. But others resorted to diverse strategies to improve their situation or undermine their masters' dominance. Running away, even for a brief period, provided relief from forced work and deprived owners of the labor they depended on. Because arson created serious damage and was difficult to detect, some slaves burned down barns at harvest time. Others succeeded in killing their masters or overseers. Such acts of pent-up rage usually proved suicidal, but they also confirmed slave owners' worst fears.

Above all, the prospect of open rebellion burned in the minds of prisoners and jailers alike. Often, therefore, it is hard to untangle episodes of white paranoia from incidents of actual revolt. Many innocent slaves were falsely accused. But countless others did discuss plans for resistance, and a few freedom fighters avoided detection or betrayal long enough to launch serious uprisings. Word of one upheaval, real or imagined, could spark others.

An early wave of slave unrest erupted in the dozen years after 1710, highlighted by violence in New York City in the spring of 1712. The leaders of the conspiracy were "Coromantee," or Akan people from Africa's Gold Coast region. Several dozen enslaved Africans and Indians, determined to obtain their freedom and kill all the whites in the town, set fire to a building. As citizens rushed to put out the blaze, the rebels attacked them with guns, clubs, pistols, staves, and axes, killing eight and wounding more. When the militia captured the insurgents, six of them committed suicide. Authorities executed eighteen, burning some at the stake, hanging others and leaving their bodies on display.

A Wave of Rebellion

A second wave of black resistance swept the mainland colonies after 1730, fueled by the largest influx of Africans to date. In Louisiana, the French had moved their capital to the new town of New Orleans on the Mississippi River (1722) and had joined their Choctaw allies in a devastating war to crush the Natchez Indians and seize their lands (1729–1731). As French landowners staked out riverfront plantations, they also imported African slaves. The several thousand black workers soon outnumbered European settlers.

Fearful of attack, Louisiana's whites broke up two presumed slave plots in 1731. One involved a scheme to rebel while Catholic colonists attended a midnight mass on Christmas. Another apparent plot was revealed by the careless boast of a black servant woman in New Orleans. It included several hundred Bambara newcomers from Senegal who aspired to massacre whites, enslave other Africans, and take control of the region. The leader was a man known as Samba Bambara, a former interpreter at Galam on the Senegal River. Bambara had lost that post and been deported to Louisiana, where he became a trusted slave, supervising workers owned by the French Company of the Indies. When torture by fire failed to force confessions from the key suspects, officials hanged the servant woman. Then Bambara and half a dozen other men were "broken on the wheel" (put to death slowly by being tied to wagon wheels and having their bones broken).

The largest slave uprising in colonial North America broke out in 1739 near the Stono River, 20 miles southwest of Charleston. Several factors fueled the Stono Rebellion. By 1739 blacks exceeded whites nearly two to one among South Carolina's 56,000 people. The proportion of recently imported slaves had reached an all-time high. In addition, working conditions had worsened steadily as rice production expanded. Moreover, for several decades the Spanish in Florida had been luring slaves from South Carolina, knowing that the promise of freedom might destabilize Carolina's profitable slave regime. More than a hundred fugitives had escaped to Florida by 1738, when Florida's governor formed them into a free black militia company at St. Augustine. Hoping to win more defections, he allowed thirty-eight African American households to settle north of the town and build a small fortress—Fort Mose.

Meanwhile, the wider commercial rivalries of the British and Spanish continued elsewhere, leading to open warfare between the two Atlantic empires in 1739. The slave uprising at Stono erupted just after word reached Charleston that war had broken out between Spain and Britain. Other factors may also have influenced the rebels' timing. An epidemic in Charleston had disrupted public activities, and a new Security Act requiring all white men to carry arms to church was to take effect before the end of September.

Early on Sunday, September 9, 1739, twenty slaves from a work crew near the Stono River broke into a local store. There they seized weapons and exe-

■ Archaeologists have recently excavated the site of Fort Mose, near St. Augustine, Florida. Dozens of slaves who escaped from South Carolina received their freedom from the Spanish and established an outpost there in the 1730s.

cuted the owners, then raised a banner and marched south, beating drums and shouting "Liberty!" The insurgents burned selected plantations, killed a score of whites, and gathered more than fifty new recruits. But armed colonists overtook them and blocked their escape to St. Augustine. Dozens of rebels died in the ensuing battle. In the next two days, militia and hired Indians killed twenty more and captured an additional forty people, whom they immediately shot or hanged.

Oglethorpe, Stono Rebellion (1739)

Yet even these reprisals could not quell black hopes. In June 1740 several hundred slaves plotted to storm Charleston and take arms from a warehouse. However, a comrade revealed the plan. According to a report, "The next day fifty of them were seized, and these were hanged, ten a day, to intimidate the other negroes." In November, a great fire of suspicious origin consumed much of Charleston.

Fire also played a role in hysteria that broke out in New York City in 1741. In March, a blaze consumed the residence of New York's governor and a local fort. Other fires soon focused suspicions on a white couple, John and Sarah Hughson, who had often entertained blacks at their alehouse. The Hughsons—thought to fence stolen goods for a black crime ring—were accused of inciting working-class unrest. In exchange for her freedom, a sixteen-year-old Irish indentured servant at the Hughsons' tavern testified that she had overheard the planning of an elaborate plot.

In a gruesome spiral of arrests and executions, New York authorities put to death thirty-four people, including four whites, and banished seventy-two blacks. On one hand, the debacle recalled the Salem witch trials, as a fearful community engaged in judicial proceedings and killings on the basis of rumors and accusations. On the other hand, the New York Slave Plot recalled Bacon's Rebellion, for evidence emerged of cooperation between impoverished blacks and whites eager to see a redistribution of property. According to his accusers, a slave named Cuffee had often observed that "a great many people had too much, and others too little." He predicted that soon his master "should have less, and that he (Cuffee) should have more." Instead, he was burned at the stake.

The Transformation Completed

The mechanisms for extorting labor from tens of thousands of people were firmly in place. But to maintain the slave labor system, local governments had to be vigilant and repressive, prompting debates within the white population. Some colonists saw slavery as too morally degrading and physically dangerous to maintain. Powerful supporters of the institution, however, found it too rewarding to give up and suggested modifications instead. Following the Stono uprising in South Carolina, for example, leaders imposed a heavy import duty on new African arrivals for several years, hoping to increase the ratio of whites to enslaved blacks in the lowcountry. At a time of growing humanitarian concerns in Enlightenment Europe, it took great effort to maintain the rationale for enslavement in America. But free people who questioned the institution met stiff resistance from those with vested interests, as the experience of the new colony of Georgia demonstrates.

Voices of Dissent

As race-based slavery expanded, white colonists treated the continuing presence of free blacks as a contradiction and a threat. As early as 1691, the Virginia assembly passed an act restricting **manumissions** (grants of individual freedom by masters) because "great inconvenience may happen to this country by setting of negroes and mulattoes free." According to the act, such people fanned hopes of freedom among enslaved blacks. Besides, when they grew old and infirm, their care at public expense could constitute "a charge upon the country." By 1723 additional Virginia statutes prevented free people of color from voting, taxed them unfairly, and prevented them from owning or carrying firearms. Lawmakers went on to prohibit all manumissions, except when the governor rewarded "meritorious service," such as informing against other enslaved workers.

While the southern slave colonies labored to intimidate, divide, and reduce their free black communities, free blacks in the North faced growing discrimination in their efforts to hold jobs, buy land, obtain credit, move freely, and take part in civic life. Northern slave populations, though small in comparison to those in the South, were growing steadily. As the North's involvement in the Atlantic slave trade expanded, its economic and legal commitment to race slavery increased. Rhode Island's slave ranks jumped from 500 in 1720 to more than 3,000 in 1750. Everywhere, new laws made manumission more difficult and African American survival more precarious. Only in the century after 1760 did northern free black communities gain the numerical and social strength to offer effective opposition to enslavement.

The Colonies to 1740

Whereas free blacks lacked the means to oppose slavery, prominent white Christians lacked the will. Even in Massachusetts, where religion remained a dominant force at the turn of the century and the number of slaves had scarcely reached 1,000 people, many leaders already owned black servants, and most ministers defended the practice. The protests that did appear were ambivalent at best. In 1700 Judge Samuel Sewell questioned African enslavement in a tract titled *The Selling of Joseph*. But he also revealed his sense of superiority and his skepticism that blacks could play a part in "the Peopling of the Land." African Americans, Sewell commented, "can seldom use their freedom well; yet their continual aspiring after their forbidden Liberty, renders them unwilling servants." Reverend Cotton Mather, a slave owner who once berated Sewell as one who "pleaded much for Negroes," was even more ambivalent. In *The Negro Christianized* (1706), the influential Puritan stressed that conversion and Christian instruction, far from earning African slaves their freedom, would make them into "better servants."

The conversion and instruction of slaves, rather than the abolition of slavery, also became a mission for pious English philanthropist Thomas Bray, a well-to-do Anglican committed to spreading the Anglican faith in America among Europeans, Indians, and Africans. In 1701 Bray established the Society for the Propagation of the Gospel in Foreign Parts (SPG). The SPG strengthened the Church of England abroad in the eighteenth century by providing dozens of ministers to serve in the colonies.

But this Anglican foothold came at a steep price. Southern planters made SPG ministers agree that any hopes they offered to slaves regarding heavenly salvation would not include hints of earthly freedom. With few exceptions, the Anglican clergy gave in, strengthening religious support of race slavery. In 1723 a heartfelt petition from a mulatto slave to the Bishop of London, in which the author protested "Cruell Bondegg" in Virginia, went unanswered. That same year, Bray set up a trust of "Associates" to carry on his work. With limited success, they focused on converting blacks in the British plantation colonies.

By the 1730s, only a few whites in Europe or America dared to press publicly for an end to slavery. Christian Priber, who arrived in the South in 1735, was one such activist. The idealistic German hoped to start a utopian community in southern Appalachia. But his radical proposal for a multiracial "Paradise" uniting Indians, Africans, and Europeans posed a huge threat to South Carolina authorities. Priber's brief career as a social agitator challenging the status quo ended in 1743, when he was arrested and brought to jail in Charleston. He died—or was killed—before his case could be heard in court.

At the same time, a New Jersey tailor and bookkeeper named John Woolman posed a less defiant but more enduring threat to race slavery. In 1743, at age twenty-three, this shy Quaker began to question his role in writing out bills of sale when his fellow Quakers purchased slaves. It struck him forcefully that "to live in ease and plenty by the toil of those whom violence and cruelty have put in our power" was clearly not "consistent with Christianity or common justice." Woolman traveled widely to Quaker meetings, north and south, pressing an issue

INTERPRETING HISTORY

"Releese Us Out of This Cruell Bondegg"

As researchers pay increasing attention to African bondage in the colonial era, new pieces of evidence continue to appear. This appeal, written in Virginia in 1723 by a mulatto Christian slave, was rediscovered in a London archive in the 1990s and transcribed by historian Thomas Ingersoll. It is addressed to Edward Gibson, the newly appointed Bishop of London, whose position gave him religious oversight over all the Anglican parishes in England's American colonies, including Virginia. Gibson, through his pamphlets, had shown an interest in the Christianization of enslaved Africans, but like many contemporary church leaders, he had less interest in the liberation of slaves. This heartfelt document, prepared with great labor and at enormous risk, was simply filed away with the bishop's vast correspondence. It never received a response or prompted any further inquiry into conditions in Virginia.

When abolition of the slave trade finally became a public issue in England in the 1780s, British artists painted scenes criticizing the traffic. But two generations earlier, pleas from New World slaves aroused no response, even from the Bishop of London, who supervised the Church of England in the American colonies.

August the forth 1723

to the Right Raverrand father in god my Lord arch Bishop of Lonnd. . . .

this coms to sattesfie your honour that there is in this Land of verJennia a Sort of people that is Calld molatters which are Baptised and brouaht up in the way of the Christian faith and followes the ways and Rulles of the Chrch of England and sum of them has white fathars and sum white mothers and there is in this Land a Law or act which keeps and makes them and there seed Slaves forever. . . .

wee your humbell and poore partishinners doo begg Sir your aid and assisttancce in this one thing . . . which is that your honour will by the help of our Sufvering [i.e., sovereign] Lord King George and the Rest of the Rullers will Releese us out of this Cruell Bondegg. . . . /and here it is to bee notd that one brother is a Slave to another and one Sister to an othe which is quite out of the way and as for mee my selfe I am my brothers Slave but my name is Secrett/

wee are commandded to keep holey the Sabbath day and wee doo hardly know when it comes for our task mastrs are has hard with us as the Egypttions was with the Chilldann of Issarall. . . . wee are kept out of the Church and matrimony is deenied us and to be plain they doo Look no more upon us then if wee ware dogs which I hope when these Strange lines comes to your Lord Ships hands will be Looket in to. . . .

And Sir wee your humble perticners do humblly beg . . . that our childarn may be broatt up in the way of the Christtian faith and our desire is that they may be Larnd the Lords prayer the creed and the ten commandments and that they may appear Every Lord's day att Church before the Curatt to bee Exammond for our desire is that godllines Shoulld abbound amongs us and wee desire that our Childarn be putt to Scool and Larnd to Reed through the Bybell

My Riting is vary bad. . . . I am but a poore Slave that writt itt and has no other time butt Sunday and hardly that att Sumtimes. . . . wee dare nott Subscribe any mans name to this for feare of our masters for if they knew that wee have Sent home to your honour wee Should goo neare to Swing upon the gallass tree.

Questions

1. In 1723, do these mulatto petitioners identify more closely with their African and non-Christian relatives who are enslaved or with their European and Anglican relations who are free? Explain.

2. Using the same kind of poor spelling and good logic, draft a paragraph or two that might further strengthen this petition and prevent the bishop of London from setting it aside. ■

Source: Thomas N. Ingersoll, "'Releese Us out of This Cruell Bondegg': An Appeal from Virginia in 1723," *William and Mary Quarterly*, Third Series, 51 (October 1994): 776–782.

that most Quakers preferred to ignore. When he drafted *Some Considerations on the Keeping of Negroes* (1754), members of the Quaker Yearly Meeting in Philadelphia published his booklet and circulated it widely. Four years later, led by Anthony Benezet, this group outlawed slaveholding among its local members. They set a precedent that many Quakers followed in the next generation, and they challenged other denominations to do the same.

Oglethorpe's Antislavery Experiment

Oglethorpe, "Establishing Georgia" (1733)

The most sustained early challenge to the slavery system in the American South came in the Georgia colony. In 1732 a group of well-connected London proprietors (known as trustees) obtained a twenty-year charter for the region between English South Carolina and Spanish Florida. Ten of the twenty-one initial trustees were members of Parliament. They included James Oglethorpe, who had recently organized and chaired a "committee on jails" to investigate the condition of debtors in English prisons. The trustees foresaw three related purposes—charitable, commercial, and military—for their experimental colony, which they named after King George II. Georgia would provide a haven for England's worthy poor, selected members of the neediest classes who could be transported across the Atlantic and settled on small farms. These grateful newcomers would then produce warm-weather commodities—olives, grapes, silk—to support the empire. Their prosperity would create a growing market for English goods. Finally, their presence would provide a military buffer to protect South Carolina from further warfare with the Yamasee and Creek Indians and from possible invasion by the Spanish in St. Augustine.

With Oglethorpe as their governor, an initial boatload of 114 settlers arrived in 1733 and began building a capital at Savannah. By 1741 the town, located on a bluff 15 miles up the Savannah River, boasted more than 140 houses. By then, more than a thousand needy English, plus 800 German, Swiss, and Austrian Protestants, had journeyed to Georgia at the trustees' expense. Another thousand immigrants had paid their own way. Like earlier colonizers, Georgia's first arrivals had trouble adjusting to a strange environment. Alligators, rattlesnakes, and hurricanes tested their resolve. Tension over governance only deepened their discouragement.

The idealistic trustees in London declined to accumulate property and profits for themselves in the colony, but they felt justified in controlling every aspect of Georgia's development. For example, they knew that gin was becoming a source of debt and disruption in Europe and that rum and brandy sold by traders was poisoning colonial relations with southeastern Indians. So in 1735 they outlawed the use of every "kind of Spirits" while still allowing consumption of wine and beer. Georgia's early experiment with prohibition of hard liquor proved difficult to implement, and officials quietly stopped enforcing the law in 1742.

Other efforts at control from above went further. The trustees refused to set up a legislature or to let settlers buy and sell land. Instead, they gave 50 acres of farm land to each family they sent over, plus a house lot in a local village, so all new towns could be well defended. But they parceled out land with little regard for variations in soil fertility. They also stipulated that owners could pass land on to sons only. To prevent the concentrations of wealth that they saw developing in other colonies, the trustees said that no one could own more than 500 acres. Prohibiting massive estates would allow for thicker settlement and therefore greater manpower to defend the colony militarily.

But the most important prohibition, by far, involved slavery. Oglethorpe began his career as a deputy governor of the Royal African Company, but he died in 1785 opposing the slave trade. His sojourn in Georgia turned him against slavery. In neighboring South Carolina, he saw firsthand how the practice degraded African lives, undermined the morals of Europeans, and laid that colony open to threats of revolt and invasion. So Oglethorpe persuaded the trustees to create a free white colony, convincing them to enact a law in 1735 that prohibited slavery and also excluded free blacks. He believed that this mandate would protect Georgia from the cor-

■ In 1729 James Oglethorpe (seated, right front) chaired a parliamentary committee exposing the harsh conditions in English jails. When William Hogarth portrayed the committee's visit to Fleet Street Prison, the artist showed Oglethorpe's concern for a dark-skinned prisoner, a hint of the philanthropist's future opposition to slavery in Georgia.

ruptions of enslavement while also making it easier to apprehend black runaways heading to Florida from South Carolina.

In 1739, the Stono Rebellion and the outbreak of war between England and Spain strengthened Oglethorpe's belief that slavery undermined the security of the English colonies by creating internal enemies who would support any foreign attackers. He saw further evidence in 1740, when he failed in a wartime attempt to capture St. Augustine from Spain. Unable to take the Florida stronghold, the governor managed to seize neighboring Fort Mose, which had been erected by anti-English slaves who had escaped from Carolina. When a Spanish force retook Fort Mose, relying heavily on Indian and African American fighters, Oglethorpe saw the intensity with which ex-slaves would fight the English, their former masters.

The next year, fearing a counterattack, Oglethorpe issued a warning to imperial officials. He predicted that if Spanish soldiers captured Georgia, a colony inhabited by "white Protestants and no Negroes," they would then send agents to infiltrate the vulnerable colonies farther north and stir black rebellion.

The End of Equality in Georgia

As Britain's war with Spain continued, few whites could deny the Georgia governor's assertion that slavery elsewhere in British America was a source of internal weakness and strategic danger. In 1742, as the governor had predicted, Spain pushed from Florida into Georgia with an eye toward destabilizing the colonies farther north. Oglethorpe's troops repulsed the invading Spanish force in the crucial Battle at Bloody Marsh on St. Simon's Island. The victory reduced the immediate threat to Britain's North American colonies, especially neighboring

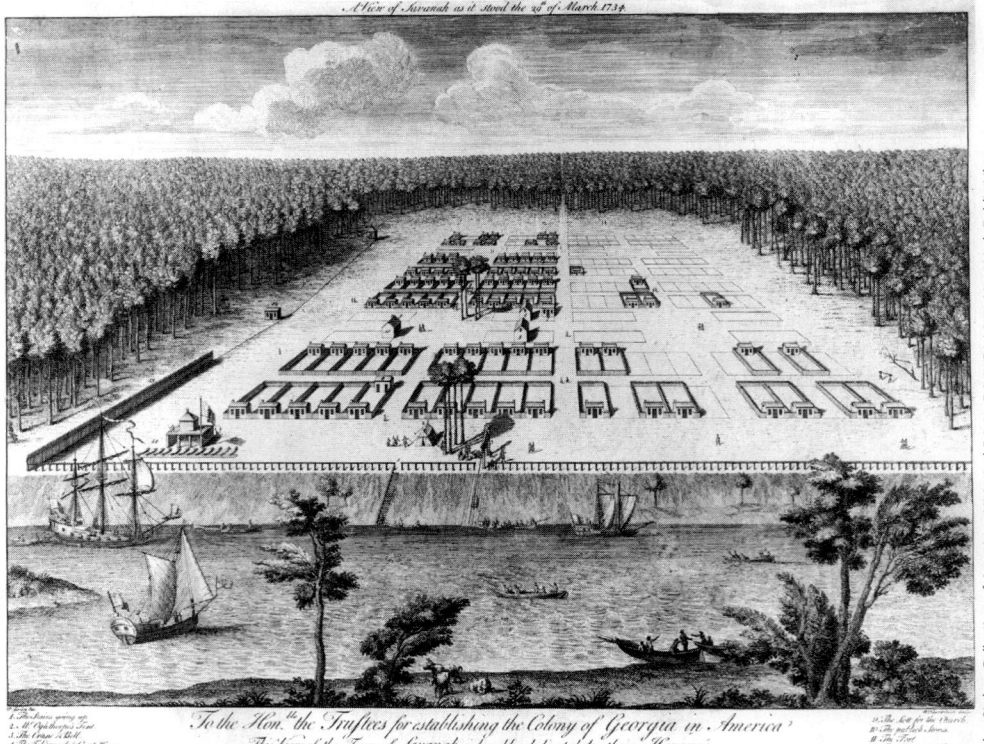

■ Savannah, the capital of Oglethorpe's Georgia, was one year old when this view was sketched in 1734. The following year, Georgia's trustees officially outlawed slavery, creating a sharp contrast with the other British colonies in North America, especially neighboring South Carolina on the opposite bank of the Savannah River.

South Carolina, where Oglethorpe and his idealistic policies had numerous powerful opponents. These opponents now joined a group of so-called Malcontents in Savannah to question Georgia's continued prohibition against slavery. When this coalition challenged the trustees' antislavery stance, it prompted the first protracted North American debate about enslavement.

In the face of numerous ills—including a sickly climate, poor soil, restrictive land policies, and lack of representative government—a well-organized Georgia faction argued that slavery was the one thing needed for the colony to prosper, since it would provide profits to slave owners regardless of Georgia's many drawbacks. Not everyone agreed. In 1739 Scottish Highlanders living at Darien on the Altamaha River had contacted Oglethorpe to lay out their practical arguments against importing Africans. Their petition expressed shock "that any Race of Mankind, and their Posterity, Should be sentenced to perpetual slavery." Immigrants from Salzburg, Germany, residing at Ebenezer on the Savannah River drafted a similar statement. But Georgia's Malcontents pushed back, demanding the right to import slaves. They drew encouragement and support from powerful merchant-planters in South Carolina, eager to expand their trade in slaves from Africa and to extend their successful rice operations into coastal Georgia.

Oglethorpe warned that the proslavery lobby, hungry to create large estates, seemed bent on "destroying the Agrarian Equality" envisioned in Georgia's initial plan. But the colony's trustees in London grew less unified, committed, and informed over time. Eventually, the persistent efforts of the proslavery pamphleteers bore fruit. In 1750 the trustees gave in on the matter of land titles. They allowed acreage to be bought and sold freely in any amount, which opened the door for the creation of large plantations. From there, it was just one more step to allowing slavery. The trustees finally gave in on the question of bondage, letting Georgians exploit slaves after January 1, 1751. The 1750 law permitting slavery made futile gestures to ensure kind treatment and Christian education for slaves, but the dam had bro-

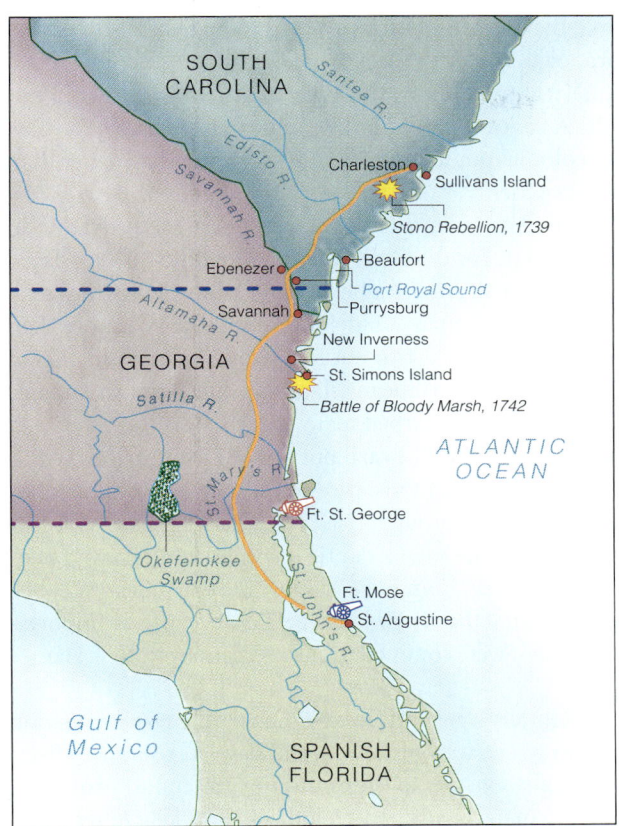

■ **MAP 4.4**
ENGLISH-SPANISH COMPETITION AND THE EXPANSION OF SLAVERY INTO GEORGIA The Spanish and the British had competing land claims along the southeast coast after 1670. Creation of the Georgia colony in 1732 intensified the rivalry. The Spanish in Florida offered freedom to any slaves who escaped from South Carolina to St. Augustine, sparking the Stono Revolt in 1739. During the war between Britain and Spain (1739–1743), Georgians defeated the Spanish at Bloody Marsh and secured the disputed "Sea Island" region for the British. Within a decade, slavery became legal in Georgia, and scores of new labor camps appeared between the Savannah and the St. Mary's River, producing rice for export.

ken. Hundreds of slave-owning South Carolinians streamed across the Savannah River to invest in land. In 1752 the trustees disbanded, their patent expiring, their vision undone. By 1754 Georgia had become a royal colony.

Slave labor camps producing rice and indigo for export soon dotted the lowcountry on both sides of the Savannah River. Georgia's assembly passed a harsh slave code in 1755, based on South Carolina's. Two years later, it legislated a system of patrols to keep the brutal new regime in place. Georgia's effort to counter race slavery in North America had failed, a case of too little too late. After holding out for nearly two decades, the colony fell victim to the same divisive institution that had already taken root elsewhere.

Slave Quarter, Hermitage Plantation, Savannah, Georgia

Conclusion

Bit by bit, the slavery system gained a firm foothold in North America during the century after 1660. In southern colonies the system shaped the entire economy and social structure, creating a society based on race slavery. Farther north, where the institution never dominated, it still persisted as a disturbing element of colonial life. Two final observations provide a wider Atlantic context. First, the influx of African slaves into English North America occurred long after the **diaspora**, or dispersion, to Mexico, Brazil, and the Caribbean was well established. The North American portion of the gigantic African traffic did not expand steadily until after the 1670s. A century later, on the eve of the American Revolution, the proportion of blacks in the colonial population (over 20 percent) was higher than it has ever been in the United States since then.

Second, even at its height, the North American trade remained marginal in relation to the wider Atlantic commerce in African labor. For example, whereas roughly 50,000 enslaved men and women reached all the docks of North America between 1721 and 1740, the small West Indian islands of English Barbados and French Guadeloupe *each* received more than 53,000 Africans during the same period. In the next two decades, while Britain's mainland colonies purchased just over 100,000 Africans, Caribbean Islands such as English Jamaica (120,000) and French Saint Domingue (159,000) absorbed many more slaves.

During this single forty-year span (1721–1760), Brazil bought 667,000 African workers—more than would reach North America during the entire slave trade. All told, scholars currently estimate that some 650,000 Africans were brought to North America over several centuries. They represented roughly 6 percent of the total Atlantic commerce in enslaved people. Still, the number of mainland slaves expanded from scarcely 7,000 in 1680 to nearly 29,000 in 1700 and to more than 70,000 in 1720. Half a century later in 1770, because of importation and natural increase, 470,000 individuals were confined to enslavement from New Hampshire to Louisiana.

A century had passed since Elizabeth Key's generation saw the terrible transformation begin. Relative openness had given way to systematic oppression, and slavery's corrosive effects were felt at every level of society. An English visitor to the South in 1759 found provincial planters "vain and imperious," subject "to many errors and prejudices, especially in regard to Indians and Negroes, whom they scarcely consider as of the human species." It took another century before pressures developed that could unseat race slavery, sanctioned by law, as a dominant institution in the land.

Sites to Visit

The Slave Trade in Global Memory
http://digital.nypl.org/lwf/flash.html

The United Nations proclaimed 2004 as the International Year to Commemorate the Struggle Against Slavery and Its Abolition. The UNESCO Slave Route Project and New York's Schomberg Center for Research in Black Culture created an exhibit and Web site entitled "Lest We Forget: The Triumph Over Slavery."

Fort Mose
http://www.oldcity.com/sites/mose/

The site of Fort Mose sits on the eastern edge of a marsh, 2 miles north of St. Augustine, Florida. Under Spanish protection, people who had escaped from slavery in South Carolina built this fortified free black community in the 1730s. Archaeologists rediscovered the site, and it is being made into an exhibition area.

Africans in America
www.pbs.org/wgbh/aia/home.html

This four-part television series prepared for PBS provides an overview of slavery from its beginnings to the end of the Civil War. Part One deals with "The Terrible Transformation," offering resources and insights on the era from 1450 to 1750.

New Hampshire's Early Black History
www.SeacoastNH.com

Billed as "the biggest website for America's smallest seacoast," this site contains an excellent section on New Hampshire's black history, which stretches back more than 350 years. Links connect to the Portsmouth Black Heritage Trail, which leads to two dozen sites in Portsmouth, describing where early black residents lived and worked.

Drayton Hall

This National Trust historic site on the Ashley River outside Charleston, South Carolina, features the oldest plantation house in America open to the public, built by Europeans and African Americans at the time of the 1739 Stono Rebellion. The staff has developed a "Gullah Connection" to explore black culture with local schools.

Cultural Landscape of the Plantation
www.gwu.edu/~folklife/bighouse/intro.html

American studies professor John Michael Vlach has created this online exhibition using images of plantation buildings from the Library of Congress and linking them with the testimonies of former slaves recorded during the 1930s.

Somerset Place

This is just one of many historic plantations across the South steadily improving the ways in which they present the slave experience. Somerset Place is a huge estate created after the American Revolution beside Lake Phelps, in Creswell, North Carolina. The site has reconstructed slave buildings, and it hosts a biannual black homecoming.

Sunken Slave Ship *Henrietta Marie*

http://melfisher.org/henriettamarie/overview.htm

The Mel Fisher Maritime Museum in Key West, Florida, explains how underwater archaeologists have recovered artifacts relating to the slave ship *Henrietta Marie*, which sank near Key West in 1700.

Images of the Atlantic Slave Trade and Slave Life

http://hitchcock.itc.virginia.edu/Slavery/

This database contains 1,000 images, arranged in 18 categories, relating to the transatlantic slave trade and slave life in the Americas.

For Further Reading

General

Ira Berlin, *Many Thousands Gone: The First Two Centuries of Slavery in North America* (1998).

———, *Generations of Captivity: A History of African-American Slaves* (2003).

David Eltis, *The Rise of African Slavery in the Americas* (2000).

Michael A. Gomez, *Reversing Sail: A History of the African Diaspora* (2005).

John Thornton, *Africa and Africans in the Making of the Atlantic World, 1400–1800* (1992).

Peter H. Wood, *Strange New Land: Africans in Colonial America* (2003).

The Descent into Race Slavery

T. H. Breen and Stephen Innes, *"Myne Owne Ground": Race and Freedom on Virginia's Eastern Shore, 1640–1676* (1980).

Kathleen M. Brown, *Good Wives, Nasty Wenches, and Anxious Patriarchs: Gender, Race, and Power in Colonial Virginia* (1996).

Winthrop D. Jordan, *White over Black: American Attitudes Toward the Negro, 1550–1812* (1968).

Edmund S. Morgan, *American Slavery, American Freedom: The Ordeal of Colonial Virginia* (1975).

Anthony S. Parent, *Foul Means: The Formation of a Slave Society in Virginia, 1660–1740* (2003).

The Growth of Slave Labor Camps

Judith A. Carney, *Black Rice: The African Origins of Rice Cultivation in the Americas* (2001).

Jay Coughtry, *The Notorious Triangle: Rhode Island and the American Slave Trade, 1700–1807* (1981).

Sylvia R. Frey and Betty Wood, *Come Shouting to Zion: African American Protestantism in the American South and British Caribbean to 1830* (1998).

Allan Kulikoff, *Tobacco and Slaves: The Development of Southern Cultures in the Chesapeake, 1680–1800* (1986).

England Enters the Atlantic Slave Trade

Madeleine Burnside, *Spirits of the Passage: The Transatlantic Slave Trade in the Seventeenth Century* (1997).

Robert Harms, *The Diligent: A Voyage Through the Worlds of the Slave Trade* (2002).

Herbert S. Klein, *The Atlantic Slave Trade (New Approaches to the Americas)* (1999).

Randy J. Sparks, *The Two Princes of Calabar: An Eighteenth-Century Atlantic Odyssey* (2004).

James Walvin, *Black Ivory: A History of British Slavery* (1994).

Survival in a Strange New Land

Michael A. Gomez, *Exchanging Our Country Marks: The Transformation of African Identities in the Colonial and Antebellum South* (1998).

Jane Landers, *Black Society in Spanish Florida* (1999).

Jill Lepore, *New York "Burning: Liberty, Slavery, and Conspiracy in Eighteenth-Century Manhattan* (2005).

Peter H. Wood, *Black Majority: Negroes in Colonial South Carolina from 1670 Through the Stono Rebellion* (1974).

The Transformation Completed

Harold E. Davis, *The Fledgling Province: Social and Cultural Life in Colonial Georgia, 1733–1776* (1976).

Gwendolyn Midlo Hall, *Africans in Colonial Louisiana: The Development of Afro-Creole Culture in the Eighteenth Century* (1992).

A. Leon Higginbotham Jr., *In the Matter of Color: Race and the American Legal Process, the Colonial Period* (1978).

Phillips P. Moulton, ed., *The Journal and Major Essays of John Woolman* (1997).

Betty Wood, *Slavery in Colonial Georgia, 1730–1775* (1984).

For quizzes and other resources on these topics, go to www.longmanamericanhistory.com.

CHAPTER 5

An American Babel, 1713–1763

CHAPTER OUTLINE

New Cultures on the Western Plains

Britain's Mainland Colonies: A New Abundance of People

The Varied Economic Landscape

Matters of Faith: The Great Awakening

The French Lose a North American Empire

Conclusion

Sites to Visit

For Further Reading

In 1749 peace seemed a welcome prospect in the Spanish settlement of San Antonio in south-central Texas. On an August morning, hundreds of people gathered in the town plaza. Captain Turibio de Urrutia, the local military commander, was there along with Father Santa Ana, who presided over the local missions. Across from them stood four Apache chiefs with many of their people. In the center of the plaza, Spanish and Indian workers began to dig a deep pit with steep sides. Those attending were about to witness one of the most important events in the town's brief history.

Three decades earlier, in the spring of 1718, a small Spanish expedition had established the town next to the San Antonio River. The newcomers built houses and excavated irrigation ditches to divert river water onto their fields. But they had occupied contested ground. In 1720 Apache bands, moving south under pressure from the Comanche, attacked several settlers. The Spanish responded with their own raids, capturing Apache women and children and selling them into Mexico as slaves.

Father Santa Ana protested such harsh tactics. The cleric hoped to make peace with the Apache and draw them into the expanding mission system, where they would learn Spanish and accept Christianity. At Santa Ana's urging, Captain Urrutia modified his approach in 1749. After the spring raids, he ordered humane treatment for the 175 prisoners brought back to San Antonio. Rather than sell them as slaves, he merely detained them and sent several captives back to Apache country with a proposal for peace.

■ Mission San Francisco de la Espada, at San Antonio, had 1,100 cattle, 80 horses, and 16 pairs of oxen when this chapel was being constructed in the 1740s. By the time the United States annexed Texas a century later (1845), the church had fallen into disrepair.

When these messengers (two women and a man) returned with word that important Apache chiefs were prepared to negotiate, the townsfolk welcomed the Apache delegation. There was feasting, important for such occasions, and the four chiefs attended a mass conducted by Father Santa Ana. After two days of discussion through translators, the Spanish released some Apache prisoners as a goodwill gesture, and both sides agreed to hold a formal peace ceremony in the plaza.

The next day all gathered to watch the workers digging the deep pit. Then the longtime adversaries buried their differences in an elaborate symbolic ritual. They lowered a live horse into the hole, along with other emblems of warfare: a lance, a hatchet, and a bundle of arrows. Next, the four chiefs linked hands and walked solemnly around the pit, accompanied by the Spanish leaders. At a signal, all the onlookers suddenly grabbed up loose earth and tossed it into the hole. The horse was completely buried—a sacrifice for peace—and the ceremony broke up with shouts and celebration.

Though striking, the encounter between the Spanish and Apache at San Antonio was not unique. During the same era, Europeans and Native Americans met to parley and trade in Detroit, Albany, Philadelphia, Charleston, St. Augustine, Mobile, New Orleans, and other colonial towns. Such formal occasions highlight a wider process of contact and interaction throughout the North American colonies in the half-century between 1713 and 1763. Everywhere, colonial expansion brought together Europeans, Africans, and Native Americans in surprising new contacts. Equally important, it forced different peoples *within* each of these three categories, despite contrasting backgrounds, to rub shoulders with one another in unfamiliar ways.

These encounters had all been set in motion by the colonization process. Spanish missionaries lived among Tejas Indians in eastern Texas; French explorers dominated, and then lost, the Mississippi Valley; escaped African slaves fought militiamen from Georgia on the outskirts of St. Augustine. Everywhere, motives differed, accents jarred, and cultures clashed. In Philadelphia, Benjamin Franklin, a newcomer from Boston, protested the way in which Germans "swarm into our settlements, and by herding together establish their language and manner to the exclusion of ours."

For many Christians, the new confusions recalled the story of Babel. The people in that biblical city, despite their high ambitions, could not undestand one another well enough to work together. Eventually, they scattered abroad across the face of the earth. Bible-reading Americans no doubt recalled that tale, especially during the great religious awakening that shook the English colonies in the 1740s, when the prospect of building something new and transcendent seemed close at hand. The German-born utopian Christian Priber even attempted to establish an egalitarian realm in Appalachia where Europeans, Africans, and Native Americans could live peaceably together. Such dreams were not to be, however. Instead, the existing colonies continued to build up regional economies of their own, under British protection, and elements of a dominant Anglo-American culture began to emerge amid the Atlantic Babel's many voices.

New Cultures on the Western Plains

It makes sense that the Apache chose to bury a horse during their elaborate ceremony at the Spanish **presidio** in 1749. By this time the horse, recently introduced to the Indians, was transforming life on the Great Plains. It also makes sense that they buried arrows and hatchets rather than guns. Traditionally, the Spanish aspired to make the Indians into loyal subjects and Christian converts. From the time of Spain's arrival in the New World, therefore, official Spanish policy had forbidden the sale of firearms to Native Americans.

In contrast, the French, Dutch, and English desired trade at almost any cost. They showed less hesitation about supplying Indians with guns in return for furs, so firearms had become familiar to many eastern Indians in the seventeenth century. In the eighteenth century, guns began to spread across the Mississippi River as well. Combined with the movement of horses from the south, this development had enormous consequences. New patterns of warfare altered Indian cultures, and more powerful hunting techniques affected the regional economies and ecologies of the Native American West.

The Spread of the Horse

Although small horses once roamed the ancient West, they migrated into Asia thousands of years ago and became extinct in America. They returned with the early Spanish explorers. Around 1600, when New Mexico's early colonists brought mares north for breeding, horse herds developed in the Rio Grande valley. After the Pueblo Revolt in 1680, horses taken from the Spanish entered Indian trading networks and rapidly moved north from one culture to another.

By 1690 the Ute had obtained horses and traded them to the Shoshone. Before the mid-eighteenth century, horses had moved west of the Rocky Mountains to the Nez Perce and north to the Blackfoot. The Apache brought horses east to the Caddoan cultures near the Red River and then north to the Pawnee, Arikara, and Hidatsa. Even tribes in the Southeast acquired Spanish horses from the West before they obtained English horses from the Atlantic coast. When a Chickasaw leader drew a regional map on deerskin in 1723, he showed a Native American leading a horse east of the Mississippi River.

For all Indians, the first horses seemed utterly strange. One elder recalled that "the people did not know what they fed on. They would offer the animals pieces of dried meat." "He put us on mind of a Stag that had lost his horns," another remembered, "and we did not know what name to give him. But as he was a slave to Man, like the dog, which carried our things, he was named the Big Dog." For generations, Native Americans had used

■ The horse offered new mobility for hunting, as in this modern painting of Navajo riders. Tribes that had once tracked buffalo on foot at the edge of the Great Plains could now pursue herds across miles of open grassland. This was true for the Cheyenne, who were living in fixed villages in what is now South Dakota in the early eighteenth century. "After they got the first horses," recalled John Stands-in-Timber, "they learned there were more of them in the South and they went there after them." Cheyenne life would never be the same again.

dogs to pull provisions and bedding on a **travois**, an A-frame device made with tent poles. A larger animal could haul bigger loads, including longer tent poles that allowed for more spacious tipis.

Whether or not a tribe used tipis as dwellings, it could readily use the horse as a new source of food and as an aid in hunting. As herds expanded and horsemanship improved, warriors rode into battle. On horses, they could conduct lightning raids over long distances. Soon, raising, trading, and stealing horses became important activities, and a family's wealth and status depended partly on the number of horses at its command.

The Rise of the Comanche

By the 1770s, mounted Comanche warriors commanded respect and fear across a vast domain. Their territory stretched south nearly 600 miles from western Kansas to central Texas, and it spanned 400 miles from eastern New Mexico to what is now eastern Oklahoma. This area, known as the Comanchería, roughly equaled all the English settlements on the Atlantic coast in size, but its origins were recent and humble. The Comanche's Shoshone-speaking ancestors had been hunter-gatherers on the high plains of Wyoming, living on small game, roots, and berries. The arrival of the horse around 1690 changed everything, allowing family bands to migrate southeast from the Rockies to hunt the buffalo herds that grazed along the western edges of the Great Plains. From there, they could trade buffalo hides for additional horses at Taos and Santa Fe.

The Comanche were not the first to make their homes in what is now eastern Colorado. For generations, groups of Apache had settled in the region near the upper reaches of the Platte and Arkansas rivers. The Apache settlements—with their irrigated gardens and herds of horses—provided easy targets for Comanche newcomers. Within two decades, the Comanche had hammered their enemies south through one river valley after another. Apache bands soon reached San Antonio, where they stole livestock from the new Spanish settlement to survive. Threatened by the Comanche moving into central Texas, the hard-pressed Apache chose to seal a pact with the Spanish at San Antonio in 1749.

Not long after they buried the horse in the plaza, the Spanish began plans for a mission and **presidio** (military post) among their Apache allies. The outpost would lie 150 miles northwest of San Antonio on the San Saba River, near present-day Menard, Texas. But the post had been established for less than a year when the Comanche attacked it in 1758. They returned the next year, capturing 700 horses. "The heathen of the north are innumerable and rich," exclaimed a Spanish officer at San Saba. "They dress well, breed horses, [and] handle firearms with the greatest skill." The Comanche onslaught continued, and the attacks finally forced the Spanish to withdraw from San Saba in 1767.

In less than two decades, the Comanche had overrun most of Texas. They continued to absorb smaller Native American groups and swell in numbers. By 1780 they had grown into a proud Indian nation of more than 20,000 people. Their domain, the Comanchería, remained a powerful entity in the Southwest for decades.

The Expansion of the Sioux

Comanche strength depended not only on mounted warfare but also on using the horse as a trade commodity to obtain guns. Because Spanish policy prohibited the sale of firearms to Native Americans, the Comanche looked east for weapons. They discovered that by selling horses to their eastern allies, such as the Wichita Indians, they could receive French muskets from Louisiana in return. But the Comanche were not alone; the Sioux also took advantage of the gun frontier as it inched steadily west.

By 1720 the French had established settlements at Peoria, Cahokia, and Kaskaskia in Illinois and at New Orleans, Natchez, and Natchitoches in Louisiana. French traders at these

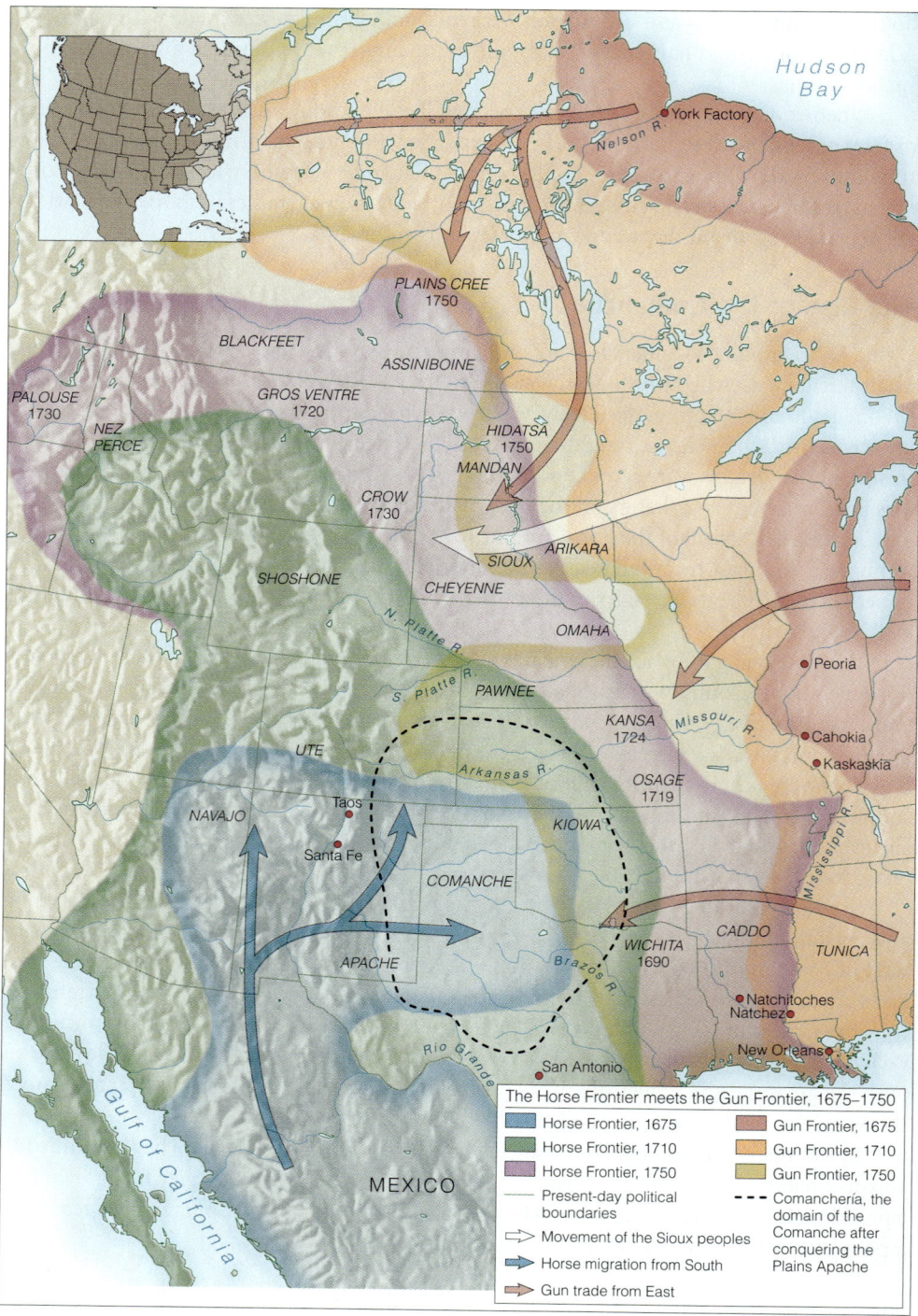

■ MAP 5.1
THE HORSE FRONTIER MEETS
THE GUN FRONTIER, 1675–1750

sites provided guns and other metal goods to Indians in exchange for salt, deerskins, beaver pelts, horses, or war captives. Native American groups that took advantage of this trade included the Tunica beside the Mississippi, the Caddo and Wichita along the Red and Arkansas rivers, and the Osage, Pawnee, and Omaha tribes near the Missouri.

Farther north, muskets carried west from French posts on the Great Lakes and south from English bases in subarctic Canada proved especially important among the Sioux peoples, who trapped game and gathered wild rice by the lakes of their northern Minnesota homeland. The

Comanche had mastered horses and then acquired guns; the Sioux, given their different location, first absorbed firearms and then adopted the horse. But the results proved equally dramatic.

When the Sioux first encountered a gun from French voyageurs in the mid-seventeenth century, they called it *mazawakan*, meaning "mysterious or sacred iron." Initially, they used the few muskets they could obtain to fight their less well-armed Indian neighbors. By 1700 French traders, moving from the east, had established direct trade with the Sioux, offering a steady supply of guns and powder in exchange for furs.

For a generation, several Sioux bands (the Teton and Yanktonai) walked between two worlds. In the summers, they followed the buffalo onto the prairies, with dogs pulling travois and women carrying heavy burdens. As cold weather approached, they retreated to the edge of the woodlands to gather firewood and seek beaver. In the spring, after trading meat and pelts to the French for guns and ammunition, they returned to the edge of the plains. They glimpsed their first horses not long after 1700. But it was several generations before the western Sioux had acquired enough mounts and developed sufficient confidence to drop their old customs and adopt a horse-centered way of life.

By midcentury, the horse frontier on the northern Great Plains had met the gun frontier. Saukamappee, a Cree Indian living with the Blackfoot, remembered vividly the surprise of the initial encounter. When he was a young man, his war party—well-armed and on foot—had gone into battle against the Shoshone. "We had more guns and iron headed arrows than [ever] before," he recalled years later. "But our enemies . . . had Misstutim [Big Dogs, that is, Horses] on which they rode, swift as the Deer."

Indian women remembered the arrival of the horse and the gun with ambivalence. These new assets improved food supplies and made travel less burdensome, but the transition brought disadvantages as well. Violent raids became more common, and young men who fought as warriors gained status in the community compared to older men and women. Also, the hard task of processing slain buffalo increased, creating new work for women even as it provided fresh resources for the whole community.

As the overlap of horse and gun proceeded after 1750, Sioux men bearing muskets continued to acquire mounts and fight for control of the buffalo grounds. Their competitors, all of whom had recently acquired horses, now had guns as well. But within several decades, the Sioux had pushed their domain west to the Missouri River. Like the Comanche farther south, they had emerged as a dominant power on the Great Plains.

Britain's Mainland Colonies: A New Abundance of People

West of the Mississippi, horses and guns brought dramatic shifts as the eighteenth century progressed. But east of the Appalachian Mountains, a different force prompted striking change: population growth. Several factors came together to push the demographic curve upward at an unprecedented rate after 1700. From our vantage point in the twenty-first century, the colonial seaports and villages appear tiny, and rural settlement seems sparse. But by the mid-eighteenth century, the coastal colonies represented the largest concentration of people that had ever occupied any portion of the continent.

On both sides of the North Atlantic, population growth characterized eighteenth-century life. But in Europe numbers rose at a gradual pace, while the population along the eastern seaboard of North America surged at an astounding rate. England in 1700 had 5.1 million people, and that figure increased a mere 14 percent to 5.8 million by 1750. In contrast, during the same half-century, the colonial population in British North America more than quadrupled, from 260,000 to nearly 1.2 million.

During these same decades, the Atlantic seaboard colonies also made a permanent and dramatic shift away from a population that was almost entirely of English origin. Never before had North America seen such extensive ethnic and racial diversity. As the numerous cultures and languages indigenous to western Europe, western Africa, and eastern North America mixed and mingled, they gave rise to an American Babel.

Population Growth on the Home Front

Natural increase—more births than deaths each year—played an important role in colonial population growth. Marriages occurred early, and the need for labor created an incentive for couples to have large families. Benjamin Franklin, who rose to become the best-known colonist of his generation, was born in Boston in 1706. He grew up in a household of seventeen children. Large families had long been commonplace, to compensate for frequent deaths among children. What made the Franklin family unusual was that all the children survived childhood and started families of their own.

Although a high birth rate typified most preindustrial cultures, it was the low death rate and long average life span that pushed up American population numbers. With no huge urban centers, colonial epidemics proved less devastating than in Europe. Food was plentiful, and housing improved steadily. Newborns who survived infancy could live a long life. (Franklin himself lived eighty-four years.) Moreover, the 1720s and 1730s proved peaceful compared to earlier decades, so soldiering did not endanger lives among men of military age. For women, death related to pregnancy and childbirth still loomed as a constant threat. (Franklin's own mother was his father's second wife; the first wife died after bearing seven children.) Yet women still outnumbered men among people living into their seventies and eighties.

Although grandparents often endured far into old age, the average age for the total population stayed remarkably young. (See Figure 5.1.) The reasons seem clear. The ratio between men and women was becoming more even over time, the marriage rates for women remained extremely high, and there was no effective means of contraception. Women could resort to sexual abstinence to avoid pregnancy, and mothers could extend the time between births by nursing their infants for a long period (since lactation reduces the chances of conception). Not surprisingly, children abounded.

"Packed Like Herrings": Arrivals from Abroad

Frequent births and improving survival rates were only part of the population story. Immigration—both forced and free—also contributed mightily to the colonies' growth. The unfree arrivals came in two different streams from two separate continents and faced very different prospects. The largest flow of unfree arrivals came from Africa, and these forced migrants faced a bleak new life with few options for improvement. By the 1730s, the expanding transatlantic slave trade brought at least 4,000 Africans to the colonies every year, and the rate increased steadily.

A separate stream of unfree laborers came to the colonies from Europe. It included prisoners forced from crowded jails and also indentured servants unable to pay their own way to America. By comparison to enslaved Africans, the long-term prospects of these European migrants were far more promising. Every year, hundreds of detainees in British jails were offered transportation to the colonies and a term of service laboring in America as an alternative to prison time or execution.

Deported felons joined the larger flow of unfree migrants from Europe: poor people, unable to pay for their own passage, who accepted transportation to America as indentured servants. All were sold to employers to serve as workers, with scant legal rights, until their indenture expired, usually after three to six years. In the 1720s, Philadelphia shippers

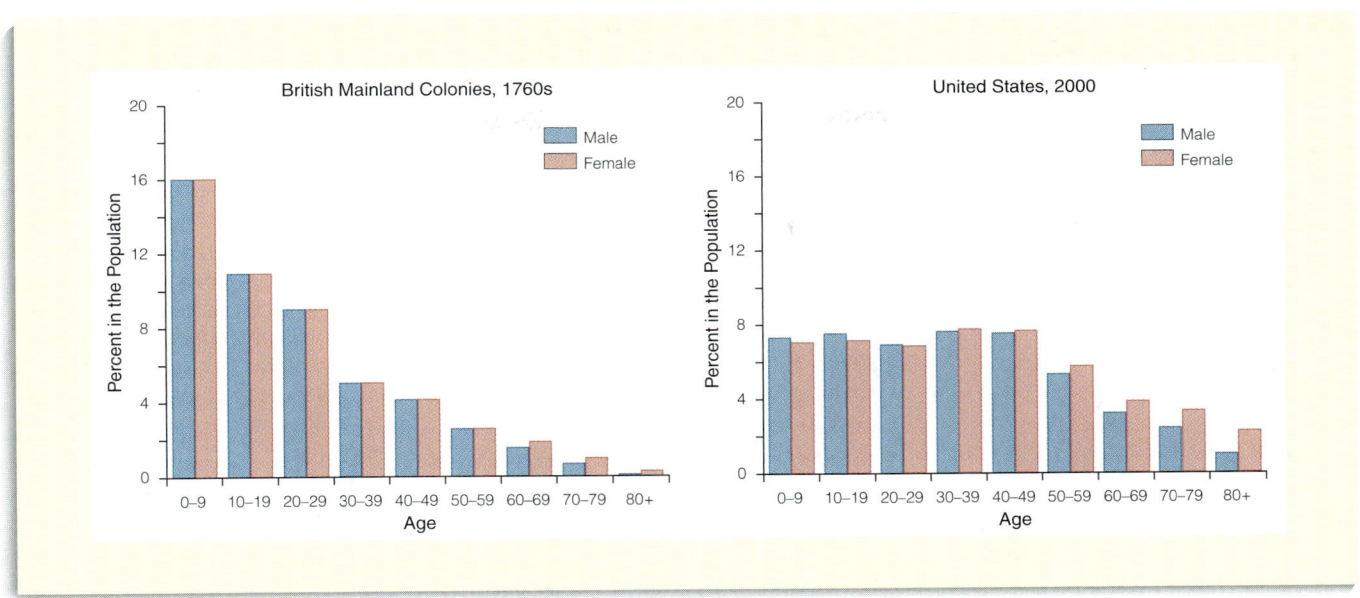

■ **FIGURE 5.1**
COMPARISON OF OVERALL POPULATION STRUCTURE BY AGE COHORT AND SEX: BRITISH MAINLAND COLONIES, 1760S, AND UNITED STATES, 2000 In the mid-eighteenth century, more than half of all people in the British mainland were under age twenty and fewer than two in ten were forty or older. In contrast, among all the living Americans at the start of the twenty-first century (281.4 million people), fewer than three in ten are under twenty, and more than four in ten are age forty or older.

devised a variation on indentures known as the redemption contract. Under this **redemption system**, agents in Europe recruited migrants by contracting to loan them money for passage and provisions. On arrival in America, the recruits could then sign a pact with an employer of their own choosing. That person agreed to pay back the shipper, "redeeming" the original loan that had been made to the immigrant. In exchange, the newcomer (called a redemptioner) promised to work for the employer for several years, receiving no more than room and board. After that, the redemptioners were on their own, and their prospects usually improved.

Besides Africans who remained unfree for life and Europeans who gained freedom after a period of service, a smaller stream of newcomers involved free families arriving from Europe who could pay their own way. Poor conditions at home pushed these risk-takers to try their luck in the New World, and glowing descriptions of abundant land at bargain rates caught their attention. American land speculators hoped to rent forest tracts to immigrant farmers who would improve the value of the land by clearing trees and building homes. Britain's imperial administrators also sought to recruit European immigrants to the American colonies. Their frontier settlements could bolster colonial defenses against foreign rivals and provide a buffer to ward off Indian attacks.

Even for those newcomers who could pay their own way, the Atlantic passage was a life-threatening ordeal. "The people are packed densely, like herrings," Lutheran minister Gottlieb Mittelberger recorded after a voyage to Pennsylvania. "During the journey the ship is full of pitiful signs of distress—smells, fumes, horrors, vomiting, various kinds of sea sickness, fever, dysentery, headaches, heat, constipation, boils, scurvy, cancer, mouth-rot, and similar afflictions." Despite such hardships, newcomers found economic opportunities awaiting them in America. They often wrote home glowing accounts of colonial life, and their letters helped boost the rising population further.

DOCUMENT
"The Passage of Indentured Servants" (1750)

INTERPRETING HISTORY

"Pastures Can Be Found Almost Everywhere": Joshua von Kocherthal Recruits Germans to Carolina

Joshua von Kocherthal grew up in southern Germany and trained to be a Lutheran minister. On a visit to London at the start of the eighteenth century, he learned of England's desire to recruit settlers to its American colonies. Because fellow Germans faced hard times at home, he led several groups to New York, where they established Neuberg (Newburgh) on the Hudson River. In 1706 Kocherthal published a German-language tract promoting migration to South Carolina. The popular booklet went through several editions in his homeland.

The winter of 1708–1709 was especially harsh east of the Rhine River. In the spring of 1709, a stream of German refugee families migrated north along the Rhine and then west to England. From there, they hoped to obtain passage across the Atlantic to South Carolina. Many carried Kocherthal's simple pamphlet, and they focused on the numerous advantages outlined in his brochure, especially the abundance of land. According to Kocherthal, the colonial government registered all land grants "to prevent errors or future arguments," and it exempted newcomers from taxes for several years. Best of all, food was plentiful, no feudal obligations or serfdom existed, and members of Protestant denominations had "freedom of religion and conscience."

South Carolina is one of the most fertile landscapes to be found…preferable in many respects to the terrain in Germany, as well as in England…. Game, fish, and birds, as well as waterfowl such as swans, geese, and ducks, occur there in such plentiful numbers that…newcomers can sustain themselves if necessary…until they have cleared a piece of land, sown seeds, and gathered in a harvest…. Among other things, there can be found in the wild so-called "Indian chickens" [turkeys], some of which weigh about 40 pounds or even more. These exist in incredible numbers….

Hunting game, fishing, and bird-catching are free to anyone, but one shouldn't cross the borders of neighbors or of the Indians [who] live in complete peace and friendship with our families. In addition, their number decreases while the number of our people (namely the Europeans) increases…. Lumber can be found there in abundance, especially the most beautiful oaks, but also many of the nicest chestnuts and nut trees which are used by many for building and are considered better than oaks. One can also find beeches, spruces, cypresses, cedars, laurels, myrtle, and many other varieties.

Hogs can be raised very easily in great numbers at little cost, because there are huge forests everywhere and the ground is covered with acorns…. Above all, the breeding of horses, cows, sheep, hogs and many other kinds of domestic livestock proceeds excellently, because pastures can be found almost everywhere, and the livestock can remain in the fields the whole year, as it gets no colder in Carolina in the middle of winter than it does in Germany in April or October…. Because of the multiplication of livestock, almost no household in Carolina (after residing there a few years) can justifiably be called poor.

Non-English Newcomers in the British Colonies

Elizabeth Sprigs, Letter to Her Father (1756)

Colonies that were thoroughly English at their origin became decidedly more varied after 1700. By far the largest change came from North America's increasing involvement in the Atlantic slave trade. By 1750, 240,000 African Americans made up nearly 20 percent of the population of the British colonies. Native Americans had been drawn into the mix in small numbers as slaves, servants, spouses, and Christian converts. But four out of five colonists were of European descent. Among them, as among the Africans and Indians, many spoke English with a different accent, or as a second language, or not at all.

The New England colonies remained the most homogenous, but even there, 30 percent of the residents had non-English roots by 1760. The new diversity was most visible in New York because of the colony's non-English origins. A 1703 census of New York City shows that the town remained 42 percent Dutch, with English (30 percent) and Africans (18 percent) making up nearly half the population. The remainder included a Jewish community (1 percent) and a growing number of French Protestants (9 percent).

The French New Yorkers had fled to America after Louis XIV ended protection for the Protestant minority of France. When the king revoked the long-standing Edict of Nantes in

In 1709, roughly 13,000 German immigrants seeking passage to America encamped for months at Blackheath, near London. The British government supplied them with tents, blankets, bread, and cheese, and churchgoers prayed for their welfare. But other Britons protested that the German strangers took "bread out of the mouths of our native handicraft men and laboring people, and increase the number of our poor which are too many and too great a burden to our nation already." Most of the refugees reached North America, serving as the vanguard for later German migration.

As far as vegetables and fruits are concerned, Indian corn predominates, thriving in such a way that one can harvest it twice a year and grow it wherever one wants to. Our local cereals such as wheat, rye, barley, and oats do well, but above all, rice thrives there as excellently as in any other part of the world, and it grows in such amounts that it can be loaded on ships and transported to other places. And as the inhabitants use rice so much and make much more profit from it than any other cereal, they are most keen on growing rice and there has been very little cultivation of other cereals.

All kinds of our fruits can be planted there, but…future arrivals would do well to bring along seedlings of any kind, or at least the seeds. . . . There can already be found different kinds of our local apples. . . . As far as cabbage, beets, beans, peas, and other garden plants are concerned, not only do our local plants grow very well, but there are also many other varieties with excellent taste that are completely unknown to us. . . . Newcomers will do well to acquire all sorts of iron tools and bring these along. . . . If someone has lived in Carolina for a time and he wants to go to another country, he may do so freely at any time.

Questions

1. Study the picture and caption regarding German refugees near London. Is that situation similar to, or different from, conditions in a modern refugee camp that you have read about or seen in the news? Be specific.
2. Do any of Kocherthal's observations about the natural world relate to the ongoing Columbian Exchange described in Chapter 1?

Source: Translations by Dorothee Lehlbach from Joshua von Kocherthal, *Ausfeuhrlicher und umstaendlicher Bericht von der beruehmten Landschaft Carolina, in dem engellaendischen American gelegen* (Frankfurt: Georg Heinrich Oehrling, 2nd ed., 1709), in the Special Collections Library of Duke University.

1685, he also prohibited Huguenot emigration, but several thousand French Protestants escaped illegally and sought refuge in America. They established small communities such as New Rochelle in New York. Everywhere, they intermarried with the English and prospered in commerce. By the 1760s, several families with humble Huguenot origins, such as the Laurenses in Charleston, had amassed enormous fortunes.

At a time when France and Great Britain were at war, another infusion of French-speaking refugees, the Acadians, fared less well. In 1755 authorities evicted French Catholics from Acadia in British Nova Scotia, fearing they might take up arms for France. Officials burned their homes and deported 6,000 of them to the various coastal colonies farther south. Mistreated for their Catholicism and feared as enemies during wartime, the Acadians struggled to get by. Resented in their new homes, many moved on to French Louisiana, where the Acadians, or Cajuns, became a lasting cultural force.

Scotland provided a much larger flow of migrants than France, stemming from two different sources. A growing stream of families, at least 30,000 people by 1770, came from Scotland itself. They were pushed by poverty, land scarcity, famines, and a failed political rebellion in 1745. In addition, a larger group known as the Scots-Irish came from Ulster

■ Like many New Yorkers of her generation, shopkeeper Mary Spratt Provoost Alexander (1693–1760) spoke both Dutch and English. Her Dutch mother had married a Scottish immigrant, and Mary was the wife of a local attorney who also came from Scotland.

in Northern Ireland. The British had encouraged these Scottish Presbyterians to settle in Ireland in the seventeenth century, displacing rebellious Irish Catholics. But the Scottish newcomers in Ulster soon faced restrictions from Parliament and the Anglican Church. By 1770 nearly 60,000 Scots-Irish had opted to leave Ireland for America.

Another stream, German-speaking immigrants, nearly equaled the combined flow of Scots and Scots-Irish settlers. They began to arrive shortly after 1700, as religious persecution, chronic land shortages, and generations of warfare pushed whole communities out of southern Germany and neighboring Switzerland. By 1770 the total had reached 85,000. These refugees generally came as whole families, and they usually took up farmland on the fringes of the colonies. Germans occupied New York's Mohawk Valley and Virginia's Shenandoah Valley, and they fanned out from Germantown across the rich farmland of Pennsylvania. Swiss founded New Bern, North Carolina, in 1710.

Almost all of the white, non-English newcomers were Protestant Christians. Many clung to their language and traditions. But most arrivals learned English, and their children intermarried with English settlers. A French visitor described a typical American "whose grandfather was an Englishman, whose wife is Dutch, whose son married a French woman, and whose present four sons have now four wives of different nations."

The Varied Economic Landscape

Colonial Products

Population growth had consequences, and the changes began at the water's edge. Ships carrying newcomers docked most often at Boston, New York, Philadelphia, or Charleston. Each of these ports grew from a village to a commercial hub, absorbing manufactured goods from Britain and shipping colonial produce abroad. All four towns developed an active coastal trade with secondary ports located on nearby rivers. In contrast, Chesapeake Bay had no single dominant port. There, Baltimore, Annapolis, Alexandria, Norfolk, and Newport News all expanded. But given the bay's many rivers, Atlantic ships often visited separate riverside plantations and villages to do business.

In Chesapeake Bay and elsewhere, inland commerce was conducted by boat wherever possible. Hartford on the Connecticut River, Albany on the Hudson, Trenton on the Delaware, and Augusta on the Savannah all become riverside trading centers. Trails and former Indian paths connected these river-based communities, easing the way for travelers in the hinterland. By the 1740s, a pathway known as the Great Wagon Road headed southwest from Philadelphia to Winchester in Virginia's Shenandoah Valley and then south through gaps in the Blue Ridge Mountains to the Piedmont region of Carolina.

Widening networks of contact, using boats and wagons, extended inland from the primary ports. And expanding fleets of ships tied each major hub to distant Atlantic ports. As a result, farmsteads and villages that had been largely self-sufficient before 1710 gradually became linked to wider markets. Local production still met most needs. But increasingly, the opportunity existed to obtain a new tool, a piece of cloth, or a printed almanac from far away. The new possibility of obtaining such goods lured farmers to grow crops for market rather than plant only for home consumption.

As local commercial systems gained coherence and strength, a string of regional economies developed along the Atlantic seaboard. Coastal vessels and a few muddy roads linked them ten-

■ In 1729 Maryland planters founded Baltimore to provide a port on Chesapeake Bay for shipping tobacco. The community had only 50 homes and 200 inhabitants when this early sketch was made in 1752, but the town grew rapidly after that.

uously to one another. But geographical and human differences caused each to take on a character of its own. Migration patterns reinforced this diversity, since arrivals from Europe often sought out areas where others already spoke their language or shared their form of worship. The influx of German farmers through Philadelphia, for example, gave unique traits to Pennsylvania. (Because the newcomers spoke German, or *Deutsch*, they became known as Pennsylvania Dutch.) Likewise, the rising importation of Africans helped shape the economy and culture of Chesapeake Bay, and the same held true for coastal South Carolina. Besides the diversity among arriving peoples, American ecological differences played a role as well. Variations in land and climate contributed to the emergence of five distinctive economic regions along the Atlantic coast: Georgia and South Carolina; North Carolina; the Chesapeake; New England; and the so-called middle colonies of New York, New Jersey, and Pennsylvannia.

Sources of Gain in the Carolinas and Georgia

Two related but distinctive regions took shape along the southeastern coast, linked respectively to the two Carolina colonies. The larger one centered on the lowcountry of coastal South Carolina. There, the warm Gulf Stream current provided a long growing season; it also assured mild winters, meaning that cattle and hogs could forage unattended for most of the year. As livestock multiplied, settlers sold meat, barrel staves, and firewood to the sugar islands of the West Indies, purchasing African slave labor in return.

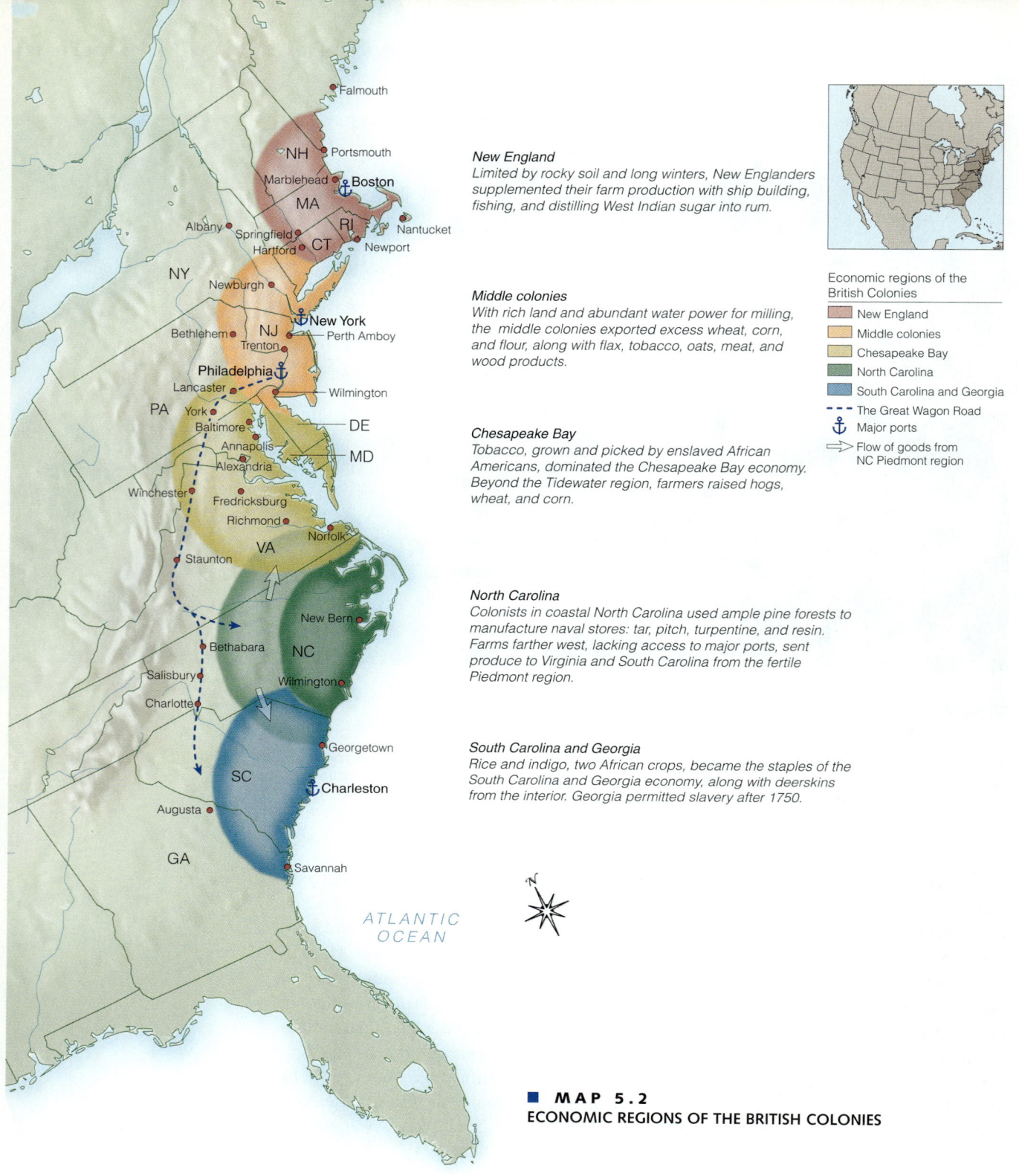

■ MAP 5.2
ECONOMIC REGIONS OF THE BRITISH COLONIES

Some of the newcomers had grown rice in Africa before their enslavement. In planting rice for their own use, they soon showed that the crop could thrive in Carolina. Once African know-how made clear the potential for rice cultivation, a system of plantation agriculture, imported from Barbados, took hold quickly after 1700. Rice production spread to Georgia after that colony legalized slavery in 1751. Another African plant, indigo, also took root as a money-making staple crop. For several generations after 1740, indigo from South Carolina provided the blue dye for England's textile industry.

On Charleston's docks, casks of deerskins piled up beside barrels of rice and indigo. The deerskin trade in South Carolina and Georgia depended on the Creek and Cherokee men who hunted the animals and the Indian women who processed hides. At the trade's height in the 1730s, Indian and white hunters killed more than a million deer per year.

In North Carolina, a second regional economy evolved. North of Cape Fear, the sandy barrier islands known as the Outer Banks prevented easy access for oceangoing vessels and hindered efforts to promote staple crop agriculture. So colonists turned to the pine forest to make a living. An extensive band of longleaf pine stretched inland for a hundred miles. With labor, this pine forest yielded naval stores: the tar and pitch used by sailors to protect their ships and rigging. Workers hauled the finished products to Wilmington on the Cape Fear River, the colony's best outlet to the sea. By the 1770s, the port was well known for exporting naval stores, and a dozen sawmills dotted the river.

Farther inland, Scots-Irish and German families moved down the Great Wagon Road after 1740 to carve out farms across the Carolina Piedmont on lands controlled largely by several absentee owners in Britain. By 1763 Ben Franklin estimated that Pennsylvania had lost 10,000 families to North Carolina. Typical of this migration were the Moravians, who established towns at Nazareth and Bethlehem, Pennsylvania, in the 1740s. In 1753 members of this German-speaking religious group bought a tract near modern-day Winston-Salem, North Carolina. They named it Wachovia, meaning "Peaceful Valley," and they quickly developed prosperous farms, a pottery shop, and a tannery around their initial settlement, called Bethabara. The newcomers bartered seeds and tools with one another and shipped extra produce overland, traveling northeast to South Carolina or northeast to coastal Virginia.

Chesapeake Bay's Tobacco Economy

North of the Carolinas, farmers in the colonies bordering Chesapeake Bay committed to tobacco production in the seventeenth century and clung to that staple crop during a long decline in its market price. After 1710, demand for tobacco revived, in part because snuff (pulverized tobacco inhaled through the nostrils) became popular among Europeans. Tobacco continued to dominate the Chesapeake economy, but local conditions in parts of Virginia and Maryland prompted crop diversification as the century progressed.

For one thing, constant tobacco planting depleted the soil. For another, most farms lay far from any navigable river, and rolling huge casks of tobacco many miles to market proved expensive. Wheat and corn thus emerged as important secondary **staples**, along with flax, hemp, and apples for making cider. The new crops provided a buffer against poor tobacco harvests and spurred related activities such as building wagons, making barrels, and constructing mills. These trades, in turn, produced widening networks of local exchange and prosperity for white **yeoman** families, with or without slaves.

Before 1700, all the mainland colonies could be described as *societies with slaves*. After that, the northern colonies continued to allow enslavement, but they never relied on it. In contrast, the southern colonies, except for certain inland farmlands settled from the north, shifted early in the eighteenth century to become something different: full-fledged *slave societies*, tied economically and culturally to slavery. By midcentury, plantation owners remained less wealthy than their counterparts in the West Indies who lived off the profits of slave-grown sugar. But on average, members of the southern elite controlled far more wealth than their counterparts in the North. The profits of the plantation system spread widely through the rest of the European American community. By the 1770s, whites in the South averaged more than twice as much wealth per person as whites in the North. An estimate for 1774 puts the average net worth among white southerners at £93, a sharp contrast to their counterparts in the middle colonies (£46) and New England (£38).

New England Takes to the Sea

North of Chesapeake Bay, two overlapping economic regions emerged: the long-established New England colonies and the somewhat newer and more prosperous middle colonies. New England faced peculiar disadvantages, beginning with the rocky soil. As imports from London increased, New Englanders found no staple crop that could be sold back directly to Britain to create a balance of trade. All the beaver had been hunted, and much of the best land had been occupied. The region's farm families had adapted well to the challenging environment and short growing seasons. Both men and women worked on handicrafts during the long, hard winters, and networks of community exchange yielded commercial prosperity in many towns. But with a rapidly growing population, successive generations had less land to divide among their children.

Increasingly, young men with little prospect of inheriting prime farmland turned to the sea for a living. In timber-rich New England, shipbuilding prospered. Colonists established shipyards at the mouth of nearly every river, drawing skilled carpenters and willing deckhands to the coast. By 1770 three out of every four ships sailing from New England to a British port were owned by colonial residents. In contrast, in the southern colonies from Maryland to Georgia, the proportion was only one in eight.

> *By 1770 three out of every four ships sailing from New England to a British port were owned by colonial residents.*

On Nantucket Island off Cape Cod, whaling became a new source of income. For generations, the islanders had cooked the blubber of beached whales to extract oil for lamps. In 1715 they outfitted several vessels to harpoon sperm whales at sea and then return with the whale blubber in casks to be rendered into oil. In the 1750s, they installed brick ovens on deck and began cooking the smelly blubber at sea in huge iron vats. This change turned the whaling vessel into a floating factory, and it allowed longer voyages in larger ships. By the 1760s, Nantucket whalers were cruising the Atlantic for four or five months at a time and returning loaded with barrels of oil.

The fishing industry prospered as well. All along the coast, villagers dispatched boats to the Grand Banks, the fishing grounds off Newfoundland. When the vessels returned, townspeople graded, dried, and salted the catch. The colonists sent the best cod fish to Europe in exchange for wine and dry goods. Yankee captains carried the lowest grade to the Caribbean sugar islands, where planters bought "refuse fish" as food for their slaves. In return, skippers brought back kegs of molasses to be distilled into rum. By 1770, 140 American distilleries, most of them in New England, produced 5 million gallons of rum annually. Much of it went to colonial taverns and Indian trading posts. But some also went to Africa, aboard ships from Britain and New England. American rum, along with various wines and spirits from Europe, made up one-fifth of the total value of goods utilized to purchase African slaves.

As the New England economy stabilized, it became a mixed blessing for women. On the farm, their domestic labors aided the household economy and helped to offset bad harvests. Mothers taught their daughters to spin yarn, weave cloth, sew clothes, plant gardens, raise chickens, tend livestock, and churn butter. The products from these chores could be used at home or sold in a nearby village to buy consumer goods. While the husband held legal authority over the home, a good wife served as a "deputy husband," managing numerous household affairs, or perhaps earning money as a midwife to help make ends meet. She took charge entirely if her husband passed away or went to sea.

But for all their labors, women seemed to lose economic and legal standing to men as New England towns became larger and more orderly. Networks of local officials, consisting entirely of men, drafted statutes and legal codes that reinforced male privileges. Women found it difficult to obtain credit or receive a business license, and the law barred married women from making contracts, limiting their chance for activities outside the home. Gradually, male apothecaries and physicians with a smattering of formal training shouldered traditional midwives away from the bedside. Overseers of the poor had the power to remove children from a widowed mother and place them in the **almshouse**, a home for persons in need of charity.

Economic Expansion in the Middle Colonies

The fifth regional economy, the one that flourished in the middle colonies between New England and Chesapeake Bay, improved upon these two neighboring worlds. The Europeans who resettled Indian lands in Delaware, Pennsylvania, New Jersey, and New York found a favorable climate, rich soil, and numerous millstreams. Unlike New Englanders, they developed a reliable staple by growing an abundance of grain. They exported excess wheat, flour, and bread as effectively as southerners shipped tobacco and rice. But unlike the planters in Virginia and Maryland, middle-colony farmers did not become locked in the vicious cycle of making large investments in enslaved workers and exporting a single agricultural staple. Instead, they developed a more balanced economy, using mostly free labor. Besides grain products, they also exported quantities of flaxseed, barrel staves, livestock, and pig iron. Large infusions of money from Britain, sent to support the war effort in America during the long conflict against France in the 1750s, gave a further lift to this prosperous economy.

Whereas the Chesapeake had no dominant seaport, the middle colonies boasted two major ports of entry. European craftsmen, unwilling to compete with unpaid slave artisans in the South, flocked to the middle-colony seaports instead. Both Philadelphia and New York grew faster than rival ports in the mid-eighteenth century, passing Boston in size in the 1750s. By 1763 Philadelphia had more than 20,000 people, New York had nearly as many, and both cities faced a set of urban problems that had already hit Boston.

As the port towns grew, so did economic and social distance between rich and poor. Large homes and expensive imports characterized life among the urban elite. In contrast, the poorest city dwellers lacked property and the means to subsist. By the 1760s, Philadelphia's almshouse and the new Pennsylvania Hospital for the Sick Poor were overflowing. In response, Philadelphia's Quaker leaders established a voluntary Committee to Alleviate the Miseries of the Poor, handing out firewood and blankets to the needy. They also built a "Bettering House," patterned on Boston's workhouse, that provided poor Philadelphians with food and shelter in exchange for work. To limit urban poverty, New York and Philadelphia authorities moved newcomers to the countryside, where Dutch and German settlers had already established an efficient farming tradition. As immigration rose, the region slowly expanded its economy far up the Hudson Valley, east into Connecticut and Long Island, and south toward Maryland.

"The Connecticut Peddler"

The farm frontier pushed west as well. The acquisitive Thomas Penn had inherited control of Pennsylvania from his more idealistic father, founder William Penn. In 1737 the young proprietor defrauded the Delaware Indians out of 1,200 square miles of potential farmland west of the Delaware River. In the infamous Walking Purchase, Penn claimed a boundary that could be walked in a day and half. Then Penn hired runners who covered more than 55 miles in 36 hours, giving him title to a huge tract. Land-hungry settlers pressed the reluctant Delaware west toward the Allegheny Mountains and occupied the rich river valleys of eastern Pennsylvania. Land agents and immigrant farmers called the fertile region "the best poor man's country."

Matters of Faith: The Great Awakening

Philadelphia epitomized the commercial dynamism of the eighteenth-century British colonies. The city was a hub in the fastest-growing economic region on the Atlantic seaboard. Ben Franklin, arriving there in 1723 at age seventeen, achieved particular success. Within seven years he owned a printing business. Within twenty-five years he was wealthy enough to retire, devoting himself to science, politics, and social improvement. He created a lending library, developed an efficient stove, promoted schools and hospitals, supported scientific and philosophical organizations, and won fame experimenting with electricity.

The outburst of scientific inquiry and religious skepticism spreading through the Atlantic world at the time became known as the Enlightenment, and its spirit of rational questioning and reason was greatly aided by the printing press. In America, Franklin and his fellow printers personified the new Age of Enlightenment. By 1760 the British mainland colonies had twenty-nine printing establishments, more presses per capita than in any country in Europe. These presses squeezed out eighteen weekly newspapers and countless public notices, fostering political and business communication throughout the colonies. But American printers also published an array of religious material, for the colonial spirit of worldly enterprise existed uneasily beside a longing for spiritual community and social perfection.

VIDEO
The Great Awakening

In the first half of the eighteenth century, colonists witnessed breakthroughs in religious toleration and controversies within the ministry. They also experienced a revivalist outpouring with roots in Europe and America, later known as the **Great Awakening**. This stirring began in the 1730s, and it gained momentum through the visits from England of a charismatic preacher named George Whitefield (pronounced Whitfield). The aftershocks of the Great Awakening persisted for a full generation.

Seeds of Religious Toleration

The same population shifts that made Britain's mainland colonies more diverse in the eighteenth century also created a new Babel of religious voices that included many non-Christians. Africans, the largest of all the new contingents, brought their own varied beliefs across the Atlantic. Some slaves from Portuguese Angola had had exposure to Catholicism in their homeland. But most Africans retained much of their traditional cultures and showed skepticism toward Christianity. Efforts to convert Native Americans also had mixed results. A minister living near the Iroquois reported that Indians would beat a drum to disrupt his services and then "go away Laughing."

Another non-Christian contingent, Jewish immigrants, remained few in number, with only several hundred families by 1770. Merchants rather than farmers, they established communities in several Atlantic ports, beginning in Dutch New Amsterdam (1654) and Newport (1658). Most were Sephardic Jews; that is, their ancestral roots were in Spain and Portugal. They came by way of the Caribbean, reaching Charleston in 1697, Philadelphia after 1706, and Savannah in 1733. A few of their children married into the Protestant culture, but more than 80 percent of Jewish young people found partners within their own small communities.

The majority of eighteenth-century newcomers to the British colonies were Christians. A few, such as the Acadians, were Catholics, but the rest had some Protestant affiliation. In the two centuries since the Reformation, numerous competing Protestant denominations had sprung up across Europe. Now this wide array made itself felt in America, as Presbyterians, Quakers, Lutherans, Baptists, Methodists, and smaller sects all increased in numbers. To attract immigrant families, most colonies did away with laws that favored a single established church. Nevertheless, New England remained firmly Congregational, and the southern gentry (plus merchant elite everywhere) concentrated within the Anglican Church.

▲ Members of the Jewish community in Newport started Touro Synagogue in 1759, a century after the arrival of their first ancestors in the Rhode Island seaport. Completed in 1763, this gem of colonial architecture is the oldest existing synagogue in the United States.

Rhode Island had emphasized the separation of church and state from the start, and Pennsylvania had likewise favored toleration, both as a matter of principle and as a practical recruitment device to attract new settlers. Since migration from Europe was a demanding ordeal, those who took the risk were often people with strong religious convictions. Such newcomers looked for assurances that they could practice their religion freely, and colonies competed to accommodate them. In many places, religious tests still limited who could hold public office, but tolerance for competing beliefs was expanding.

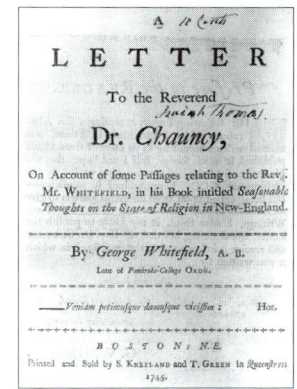

Many felt that if any institution threatened the growing religious toleration in the colonies, it was, ironically, the British king's own denomination. The monarch headed the Anglican Church, and it had influential American members, including almost every colonial governor. Therefore, repeated talk by the Church of England about installing a resident bishop in America aroused suspicions among colonists who worshipped in other denominations. This was especially true in New England, where Congregationalists had long opposed ideas of religious hierarchy. Boston, which had eighteen churches, rose up against a plan for an Anglican bishop in 1750. In a passionate sermon, Reverend Jonathan Mayhew preached that the town must keep "all imperious bishops, and other clergymen who love to lord it over God's heritage, from getting their feet into the stirrup."

The Onset of the Great Awakening: Pietism and George Whitefield

As relative toleration became a hallmark of the British colonies, no one benefited more than German-speaking Protestant groups. Numerous religious sects, such as the Moravians, Mennonites, Schwenkfelders, and Dunkers, were escaping from persecution as well as poverty at home. Their numbers multiplied after 1730, and hymns in German became a common sound on Sabbath day. In 1743, before any American printer produced an English-language Bible, a press in Pennsylvania put out a complete German edition of Luther's Bible, using type brought from Frankfurt.

Collectively, these newcomers were part of a European reform movement to renew piety and spiritual vitality among Protestant churchgoers in an age of increasing rationalism and worldliness. Pietism, as this "Second Reformation" was called, had roots in eastern Germany and stressed the need to restore emotion and intensity to worship that had become too rational and detached. The German pietists reached out after 1700 to inspire Huguenots in France and Presbyterians in Scotland. They influenced reformers in the Church of England such as John Wesley, the founder of Methodism and a teacher at Oxford University. Through Wesley, pietist ideas touched George Whitefield, a preaching prodigy in Oxford's class of 1736. Over the next decade, "the boy parson" sparked a widespread religious awakening in the American colonies.

Whitefield's mentor, Wesley, had preached briefly in Georgia. So in 1738, at age twenty-three, Whitefield spent several months in the new colony, where he laid plans for an orphanage near Savannah. Arriving back in England, Whitefield quickly achieved celebrity status, drawing large crowds with fiery sermons that criticized the Anglican Church. His popularity preceded him in 1739 when he returned to America for an extended tour, the second of seven transatlantic journeys during his career. Building upon religious stirrings already present in the colonies, Whitefield preached to huge and emotional crowds nearly 350 times in fifteen months. He made appearances from Savannah to Boston, something no public figure had ever done. "God shews me," he wrote in his journal, "that America must be my place for action."

The timing was perfect. Whitefield's brother was a wine merchant who understood the expanding networks of communication and consumption in the British Atlantic world. So Whitefield realized that in America, as newspapers multiplied and roads improved, he could advertise widely and travel extensively. He had little taste for Protestant debates over church organization and sectarian differences. Instead, he believed that an evangelical minister should simply preach the Bible fervently to a wide array of avid listeners. Everywhere he went, Whitefield served as a catalyst for religious activity.

"The Danger of an Unconverted Ministry"

The heightened commotion in American churches had local origins as well. The same tension felt in European parishes—between worldly, rational pursuits and an emotional quest for grace and salvation—also troubled colonial congregations. Occasional local revivals had taken place in America for decades. The most dramatic one occurred in Northampton, Massachusetts, in 1734–1735, spurred by a talented minister named Jonathan Edwards. As the colonies' most gifted theologian, Edwards anticipated Whitefield's argument that dry, rote "head-knowledge" made a poor substitute for "a true living faith in Jesus Christ." "Our people do not so much need to have their heads stored," Edwards observed, "as to have their hearts touched."

■ When George Whitefield visited America in 1739, his preaching spurred the Great Awakening.

In a fast-growing society, who would prepare suitable church leaders for the next generation? Candidates for the ministry could train at Harvard College (founded 1636), William and Mary (1693), Yale (1707), or one of several small academies. But these institutions could not instruct sufficient numbers. The shortage of educated ministers, combined with geographic expansion, meant that one preacher might oversee several parishes. Even if he tended only a single parish, the great distances separating parishioners made it hard for any pastor to travel widely enough to address their needs.

Edwards, "Sinners in the Hands of an Angry God"

Jonathan Edwards

Problems in the pulpit went beyond quantity to include issues of quality as well. Many college graduates had too much "head-knowledge." Their fluency in Latin and Greek often earned them more disdain than respect from down-to-earth congregations. Most foreign-born ministers, such as Anglicans sent from England and Presbyterians from Scotland, had failed to land good positions at home. Too often, they showed limited appreciation for the local church members who paid their salaries, and they resented those who criticized their ministries. One such critic was William Tennent, a Scots-Irish immigrant who arrived in Pennsylvania with his family in 1716. Dismayed by the cold, unemotional outlook of Presbyterian ministers, Tennent opened a one-room academy in a log house to train his four sons and other young men for the ministry. But local Presbyterian authorities challenged his credentials and disparaged the teachings of his "Log College." Eventually, the school moved and grew, becoming linked to the new College of New Jersey in 1746, which later evolved into Princeton University. But before this happened, Tennent's preacher sons allied themselves with Whitefield and managed to shake the colonial religious establishment to its roots.

One of Tennent's sons, Gilbert, eventually led a Presbyterian church in Philadelphia created by Whitefield's supporters. In 1740, at the time of Whitefield's triumphal tour, young Gilbert Tennent delivered a blistering sermon entitled "The Danger of an Unconverted Ministry" that became a manifesto for the revival. Cutting to the heart of the matter, he condemned the "sad security" offered by incompetent, uncaring, and greedy ministers. "They are as blind as Moles, and as dead as Stones," he charged, "without any spiritual Taste and Relish." He argued that congregations should turn away from these "Letter-learned . . . Old Pharisee-Teachers" and listen to traveling preachers instead.

The Consequences of the Great Awakening

Whitefield hailed Gilbert Tennant and his brothers as "burning and shining lights" of a new kind. All the ministers and worshipers who joined in the movement began to call themselves "New Lights." Opponents, whom they dismissed as "Old Lights," continued to defend a learned clergy, emphasized head-knowledge on the difficult road to salvation, and opposed the disruptions caused by **itinerant ministers** who moved freely from parish to parish without invitation. The New Lights, in contrast, appealed to people's emotions and stressed the prospect of a more democratic salvation open to all. They defended their itinerant wanderings, which made them more accessible to a broader public and less likely to become set in their ways. "Our Blessed Saviour was an Itinerant Preacher," they reminded their critics; "he Preach'd in no other Way."

Just as New Light preachers moved readily across traditional parish boundaries, they also transcended the lines between different Protestant sects. Their simple evangelical message reached across a wide social spectrum to diverse audiences of every denomination. Moreover, their stress on communal singing, expressive emotion, and the prospects for personal salvation drew special attention from those on the fringes of the culture, such as young people, women, and the poor. Not surprisingly, New Light ministers also made headway in spreading Christianity within various African American and Native American communities.

Members of the religious establishment, once secure as unchallenged leaders in their communities, now confronted a stark choice. Some powerful churchmen acknowledged their New Light critics and reluctantly welcomed the popular renegades into the local pulpits. Such a strategy might blunt the thrust of the revival, and it would surely raise church attendance. Other Old Lights, however, took the opposite approach; they clung to tradition and stability, challenging their new rivals openly. They condemned itinerancy and disputed the interlopers' right to preach. They mocked the faddish popularity of these overemotional zealots and even banned the New Light itinerants from local districts for the good of the parishioners.

In the end, neither tactic stemmed the upheaval, which peaked in the North in the 1740s and in the South during the 1750s and 1760s. But the long-term consequences of the Great Awakening were mixed. Zealous New Light men and women tried to transcend the competing denominations and create a broad community of Protestant believers. But the reformers could never create such unity, and they left behind no new set of doctrines or institutional structures. Nevertheless, they created an important legacy. First, they infused a new spirit of piety and optimism into American Christianity that countered older and darker Calvinist traditions. Second, they established a manner of fiery evangelical preaching that found a permanent place in American life. Finally, and most importantly, they underscored democratic tendencies in the New Testament gospels that many invoked in later years when faced with other apparent infringements of their liberties.

Zealous New Light men and women tried to transcend the competing denominations and create a broad community of Protestant believers.

The French Lose a North American Empire

In 1739, while George Whitefield launched his tour of the English colonies and the Stono slave rebellion erupted in South Carolina, the French dreamed of expanding their American empire. When Pierre and Paul Mallet set out up the Mississippi River from New Orleans that year, the two French Canadians suspected that the Missouri River, the Mississippi's mightiest tributary, stretched to New Mexico. If so, they hoped to claim a new trading route for France. Pausing in Illinois to gather seven French Canadian recruits, the Mallet brothers pushed up the Missouri, hoping it flowed from the southwest.

Jean-Pierre Lassus, *Vue et Perspective de la Nouvelle-Orléans*, 1726. C.A.O.M. Aix-en-Provence (France) DFC Louisiane 71 (pf6B)

But the river flowed from the northwest instead. Disappointed, the party left the river in Nebraska, purchased horses at an Omaha Indian village, and set off across the plains, reaching Santa Fe in July. After a nine-month stay, most of them returned east across the southern plains the next year. When the Mallets completed their enormous circuit and returned to New Orleans, they brought word from the West of Indian and Spanish eagerness to engage in greater trade. From their perspective, the future of France in America looked bright indeed. But the promise disappeared entirely within their lifetimes.

Prospects and Problems Facing French Colonists

In 1740 French colonists had grounds for cautious optimism. France already claimed a huge expanse of North America, and its wilderness empire ran strategically through the center of the continent. The potential for mineral resources and rich farmland seemed boundless. Moreover, no Europeans had shown greater skill in forging stable and respectful relations with Native Americans. French forts stretched up the Mississippi River and then east to the lower Great Lakes and the St. Lawrence Valley. These posts facilitated trade with Native Americans and secured ties between Canada and Louisiana. With Indian support, more outposts could be built farther east near the Appalachian Mountains to contain the English settlers and perhaps one day to conquer them.

At least three problems marred this scenario. First, the French population in America paled in comparison to the large number of English settlers. Canada still had fewer than 50,000 colonial inhabitants in 1740, whereas Britain's mainland colonies were rapidly approaching a million. Louisiana contained only 3,000 French people, living among nearly 4,000 enslaved Africans and 6,000 Native Americans. Second, French colonists lacked sufficient support from Paris to develop thriving communities and expand their Indian trade. The importation of goods from France was still meager and unpredictable. Finally, an ominous trickle of British hunters and settlers was beginning to cross the Appalachian chain. Carolina traders already had strong ties with the Chickasaw Indians living near the Mississippi River, and Virginia land speculators were eyeing lands in the Ohio Valley.

What seemed a promising situation for the French in 1740 was soon put to the test. Britain and France had long been on a collision course in North America. Colonial subjects of the

By 1726 New Orleans, with 100 cabins and nearly 1,000 inhabitants, was receiving shipments of trade goods from France and distributing them up the Mississippi River and its tributaries. Following a Louisiana hurricane in 1722, the levies along the waterfront were expanded, but flooding remains a threat to the low-lying city even today, as the devastation of Hurrican Katrina in 2005 made clear.

two European superpowers had already clashed in a series of wars. After several decades of peace, warfare was about to resume. King George's War (1744–1748) and the French and Indian War (1754–1763) preoccupied colonists and Native Americans alike over the next two decades. In 1763 the Treaty of Paris ended the French and Indian War, part of a far broader conflict known in Europe as the Seven Years' War. At that point, less than a quarter century after the Mallet brothers' optimistic journey through the heartlands, the British gained the upper hand. The expansive French empire in North America suddenly vanished.

British Settlers Confront the Threat from France

These colonial conflicts of the mid-eighteenth century, generally linked to wider warfare in Europe, had a significant impact on everyone living in the British mainland colonies. A few people took advantage of the disturbances to become rich. They provisioned troops, sold scarce wartime goods, sponsored profitable privateering ventures, or conducted forbidden trade with the enemy in the Caribbean. But many more people paid a heavy price because of war: a farm burned, a job lost, a limb amputated, a husband or father shot in battle or cut down by disease. From London's perspective, the Americans made ill-disciplined and reluctant soldiers. But from the colonists' viewpoint, they received too little respect and inadequate assistance from Britain.

Adding insult to injury, a hard-won victory in North America could be canceled out at the peace table in Europe. In 1745, during King George's War, Massachusetts called for an attack on Louisburg, the recently completed French fortress on Cape Breton Island that controlled access to the St. Lawrence River and nearby fishing grounds. After a long siege, New England's forces prevailed. But British diplomats rescinded the colonial victory, handing Louisburg back to France in 1748 in exchange for Madras in India.

Whatever their differences, the American colonists and the British government saw potential in the land west of the Appalachian Mountains, and both were eager to challenge French claims there. In 1747 colonial speculators formed the Ohio Company of Virginia to develop western lands. Two years later the crown granted them 200,000 acres south of the Ohio River, if they would construct a fort in the area. Moving west and north, the Virginians hoped to occupy a valuable spot (modern-day Pittsburgh, Pennsylvania) where the Monongahela and Allegheny rivers come together to form the Ohio River. But the French had designs on the same strategic location.

In 1753 the Virginia governor sent an untested young major in the colonial militia named George Washington—at age twenty-one already regarded as a promising officer—to warn the French to leave the area. The next spring Virginia workers began erecting a fort at the Fork of the Ohio, but a larger French force drove them off and constructed Fort Duquesne on the coveted site. When Major Washington returned to the area with troops, he probed for enemy forces. In a skirmish on May 28, 1754, near modern Uniontown, Pennsylvania, his men killed ten French soldiers, the first casualties in what eventually became history's first truly global war. With 450 men and meager supplies, Washington fortified his camp, calling it Fort Necessity, and dug in to prepare for a counterattack.

> "Everyone cries, a union is necessary, but when they come to the manner and form of the union, their weak noodles are perfectly distracted."

Throughout the British colonies in the early summer of 1754, fears spread about the dangers of the French offensive and the loyalties of Native American allies. Officials in London requested that all the colonies involved in relations with the Iroquois send delegates to a special congress in Albany, New York, to improve that Indian alliance. Seven colonies sent twenty-three representatives, who hoped to strengthen friendship with the Iroquois nations and also discuss a design for a union of the colonies. The delegates to the Albany Congress adopted a proposal by Benjamin Franklin for a colonial confederation. The colonies would be unified by an elected Grand Council and a president general appointed by the crown. But no colonial legislature ever ratified Franklin's far-sighted Albany Plan. "Everyone cries, a union is necessary," Franklin wrote, "but when they come to the manner and form of the union, their weak noodles are perfectly distracted."

DOCUMENT
Albany Plan of Union

The main distraction came from Pennsylvania, with word that on July 3 the French had defeated Washington's small force at Fort Necessity. But the British were not willing to give up their claims to the Ohio Valley without a fight. The crown responded by dispatching General Edward Braddock and two regiments of Irish troops to America. Early in 1755, his force arrived in Virginia, where preparations were already under way for a campaign to conquer Fort Duquesne. In June Braddock's combined British and colonial army of 2,500 began a laborious march west to face the French.

An American Fight Becomes a Global Conflict

IMAGE
The Seven Years' War

The early stages of the war in America could hardly have been more disastrous for Britain or more encouraging for France. A French and Indian force ambushed Braddock's column in the forest near Fort Duquesne, cutting it to pieces in the most thorough defeat of the century for a British army unit. Elsewhere, Indian raids battered the frontiers, spreading panic in the northern colonies. With the local militia away at war, fears of possible slave uprisings swept through the South. The French commander, the Marquis de Montcalm, struck into New York's Mohawk Valley from Lake Ontario in 1756, then pushed south down Lake Champlain and Lake George in 1757. After a seven-day siege, he took 2,000 prisoners at Fort William Henry. In an episode made famous in *The Last of the Mohicans*, France's Huron Indian allies killed more than 150 men and women after their release from the fort.

The change in British fortunes came with the new ministry of William Pitt, a vain but talented member of the House of Commons. Pitt was an expansionist committed to the growth of the British Empire at the expense of France. He brought a daring new strategy to the war effort, and he had the determination and bureaucratic skill to carry it out. Stymied in Europe by the military might of the French army, the British would now concentrate their forces instead on France's vulnerable and sparsely populated overseas colonies. Under Pitt, the British broadened the war into a global conflict, taking advantage of their superior naval power to fight on the coasts of Asia and Africa and in North America as well. By 1758 Britain had undertaken a costly military buildup in America, with nearly 50,000 troops.

To win colonial support for his plan, Pitt promised to reimburse the colonies generously for their expenses. In the South, guns, ammunition, and trade goods flowed freely to Britain's

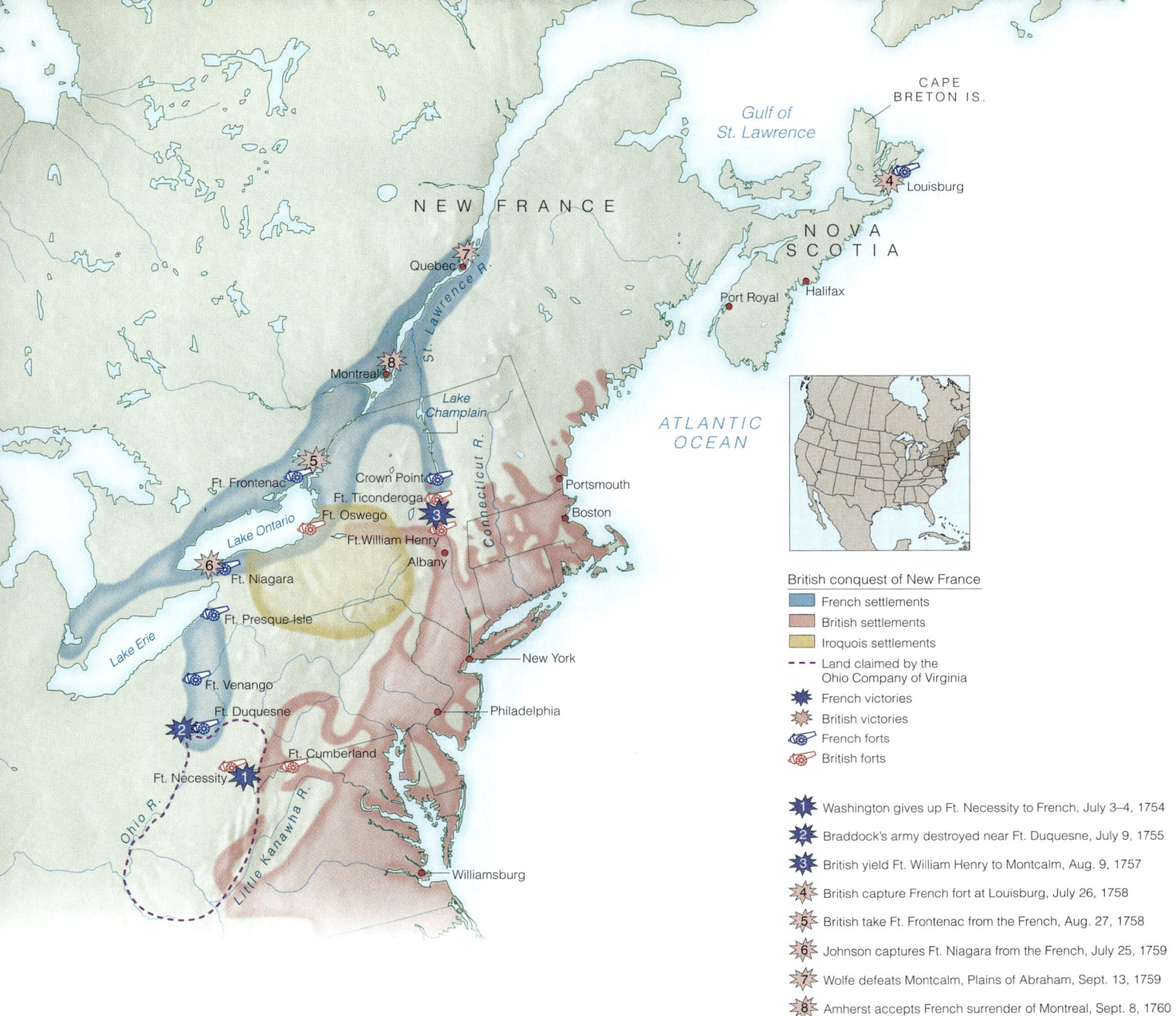

MAP 5.3
THE BRITISH CONQUEST OF NEW FRANCE, 1754–1760

Native American allies. In the North, France lost Louisburg again in July 1758. Fort Frontenac on Lake Ontario fell in August. In November, the French destroyed and abandoned Fort Duquesne. The British seized the strategic site at the Fork of the Ohio, erecting a new post (Fort Pitt), and laying out the village of Pittsburgh beside it.

In Canada, autumn brought a poor harvest, followed by the worst winter in memory. Ice in the St. Lawrence, plus a British naval blockade, cut off overseas support from France. The Marquis de Montcalm huddled in Quebec with his ill-equipped army.

In the spring of 1759, the British pressed their advantage, moving against Canada from the west and the south. Britain's superintendent of Indian affairs in the region, Sir William Johnson, sensed that many Native Americans were eager to support the winning side. Johnson successfully recruited 1,000 formerly neutral Iroquois to join 2,000 British regulars on the shores of Lake Ontario to lay siege to Fort Niagara. The fort fell in July, a British victory that effectively isolated enemy posts farther west and obliged the French to abandon them. In August, a British force under Jeffery Amherst captured Ticonderoga and Crown Point on Lake Champlain. The stage was set for an assault on Quebec.

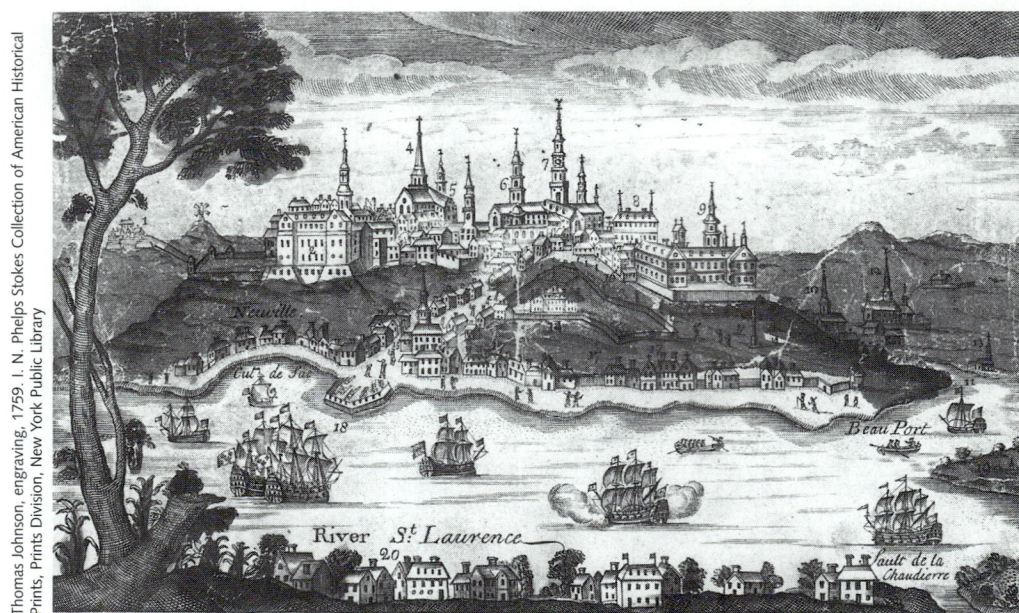

■ *Quebec, the Capital of New France,* by Thomas Johnson. A Boston printer, eager to celebrate the fall of Quebec, took an old image of the city from a French map. It shows the Catholic churches and seminaries that Louis XIV had promoted in the previous century. But in 1759 much of the town had been devastated by British cannon fire.

Quebec Taken and North America Refashioned

In London, William Pitt knew that capturing Quebec would conquer Canada. Months earlier, he had ordered James Wolfe "to make an attack upon Quebeck, by the River St. Lawrence." Wolfe's **flotilla**, with 8,500 troops, anchored near the walled city in late June. But the French held their citadel despite weeks of heavy shelling. Desperate and sick, Wolfe resorted to a ruthless campaign against the countryside that left 1,400 farms in ruins. Even this strategy failed to draw Montcalm's forces out to fight.

As a last resort, Wolfe adopted a risky plan to climb a steep bluff and attack the vulnerable west side of the city. On the night of September 12, 1759, he dispatched troops to float quietly past French sentries and scale the formidable cliffs. At daybreak, twelve British battalions emerged on a level expanse known as the Plains of Abraham. The future of the continent and its inhabitants hinged on a pitched battle between opposing European armies. Montcalm and Wolfe staked everything in the clash, and both lost their lives in the encounter. By nightfall, the British had won a decisive victory, and four days later the surviving French garrison surrendered the city of Quebec.

Montreal fell to Britain the following year, and fighting subsided in America. But Pitt continued to pour public money into the global war, and one military triumph followed another. The British conquered French posts in India, took French Senegal on the West African coast, and seized the valuable sugar islands of Martinique and Guadeloupe in the French West Indies. When Spain came to France's aid in 1762, British forces captured the Philippines and the Cuban city of Havana. But British taxpayers resented the huge costs of the war, and they worried that the effort to humiliate France and Spain could spark retaliation. Rising criticism pushed Pitt from office, and peace negotiations began.

In a matter of months, the European powers redrew the imperial map of North America. Their complex swaps constituted the largest single rearrangement of real estate in the history of the continent. First, France ceded to Spain the port of New Orleans and all of the Louisiana territory west of the Mississippi River. Then, in the 1763 Treaty of Paris, Spain turned over East Florida to Britain, receiving back Havana and the Philippines in return. France gave Britain its holdings between the Appalachians and the Mississippi River as well as the parts of Canada not already claimed by the Hudson's Bay Company. For this vast acquisition, the British returned the sugar islands of Martinique and Guadeloupe, and they allowed France to retain fishing rights off Newfoundland.

Those negotiating the peace agreed that French Canadians could choose between leaving Canada or becoming British subjects. But the Paris treaty made no mention of the thousands of Native Americans whose homelands were being reassigned. The final results were striking. Britain emerged as the world's leading colonial power, and, after two centuries, the empire of France in North America abruptly disappeared.

Conclusion

For half a century, the complex currents of colonial life had recalled the ancient tale of Babel, as told in the Book of Genesis in the Bible. A confusion of voices, interests, and cultures competed and interacted over a wide expanse in North America. In the process, a string of related economic regions emerged along the eastern seaboard. The British colonies that composed these regions varied in ethnic make-up, but they were all expanding rapidly in population. In 1763, Britain's mainland colonies contained more than 1.6 million people. The figure had quickly come to dwarf all the other population totals on the continent. Amazingly, in the thirteen years between 1750 and 1763, the British mainland colonies added more than 400,000 people. This number of new inhabitants—reflecting natural increase, European immigration, and the slave trade combined—exceeded the entire population that had been living in those same British colonies five decades earlier, in 1713.

The growth in numbers during the decades to come would be equally rapid, and the changes for the continent proved even more dramatic and long lasting. In the dozen years after 1763, the same colonies that had failed to embrace Franklin's Albany Plan of 1754 proved increasingly willing to cooperate in their opposition to new and troubling British policies. As their shared identity grew in these years leading up to the outbreak of the War of Independence in 1775, the colonists, for the first time, frequently referred to themselves—rather than to the Indians—as *Americans*.

Sites to Visit

San Saba Mission

The ruins of the mission, abandoned by the Spanish after Comanche attacks in the 1750s, lie 2 miles east of Menard, Texas, off US 190, near the San Saba River. Two miles west of Menard, on Highway 29, the fully restored San Saba Presidio contains a small museum in the rebuilt chapel. Menard is 150 miles northwest of San Antonio.

Winchester, Virginia

Founded in 1744 as a stop on the Great Wagon Road, Winchester is located 70 miles west of Washington, D.C., at Interstate 81, "where the Shenandoah Valley begins and history never ends." Young George Washington worked as a land surveyor in this frontier town, and his office is now a museum.

Old Salem

www.oldsalem.org

This reconstruction of a village founded in 1766 is in Winston-Salem, North Carolina. The site includes the Winkler Bakery, a cemetery, and the Museum of Early Southern Decorative Arts (MESDA). Take a virtual tour of the site at www.oldsalem.org. Nearby is Bethabara, a Moravian community founded in 1753, also open to the public.

George Whitefield

www.crta.org/documents/Whitefield.html

The texts of 59 sermons of the Reverend George Whitefield are available online at this Web site. The Bethesda Orphanage, founded by Whitefield in 1740, is located on 650 acres beside the Moon River outside Savannah, Georgia. It is now the Bethesda Home for Boys, America's oldest existing children's home.

Rice Museum

Located in the Old Market Building in Georgetown, South Carolina, the museum contains dioramas and exhibits describing rice cultivation. The Caw Caw Interpretive Center, west of Charleston on the Savannah Highway (Route 17S) in Ravenel, South Carolina, provides a fascinating view of eighteenth-century rice fields.

French and Indian War
    www.frenchandindianwar250.org/default.aspx

This Web site offers an introduction to the 250th anniversary of the French and Indian War. PBS has made a four-hour TV program on "The War That Made America," narrated by actor Graham Greene, an Oneida Indian whose ancestors fought in the war.

Fort William Henry and Fort Ticonderoga
    www.fort-ticonderoga.org/

Fort William Henry, at the south end of Lake George, was the location for events in 1757 depicted in the novel and film *The Last of the Mohicans*. Guided tours relating to the British–French struggle are available there and at larger Fort Ticonderoga, on Lake Champlain. Both sites are east of Interstate 87, north of Albany, New York.

Old Fort Western
    www.oldfortwestern.org/

Old Fort Western is located at 16 Cony Street on the east bank of the Kennebec River in Augusta, Maine. The fort, built in the opening year of the French and Indian War, celebrated its 250th anniversary in 2004. It is the oldest surviving wooden fort in the country and is open daily during the summer.

For Further Reading

General

John J. McCusker and Russell R. Menard, *The Economy of British America, 1607–1789* (1991).

Gary B. Nash, *The Urban Crucible: The Northern Seaports and the Origins of the American Revolution* (abridged edition, 1986).

Carla Gardina Pestana, *Liberty of Conscience and the Growth of Religious Diversity in Early America, 1636–1786* (1987).

Marcus Rediker, *Between the Devil and the Deep Blue Sea: Merchant Seamen, Pirates, and the Anglo-American Maritime World, 1700–1750* (1987).

Daniel Richter, *Facing East from Indian Country: A Native History of Early America* (2001).

New Cultures on the Western Plains

Gary Clayton Anderson, *Kinsmen of Another Kind: Dakota–White Relations in the Upper Mississippi Valley, 1650–1862* (1984).

James F. Brooks, *Captives and Cousins: Slavery, Kinship, and Community in the Southeast Borderlands* (2002).

Elizabeth A. H. John, *Storms Brewed in Other Men's Worlds: The Confrontation of Indians, Spanish, and French in the Southwest, 1540–1795* (1975).

Britain's Mainland Colonies: A New Abundance of People

Kirsten Fischer, *Suspect Relations: Sex, Race, and Resistance in Colonial North Carolina* (2002).

A. G. Roeber, *Palatines, Liberty, and Property: German Lutherans in Colonial British America* (1993).

Laurel Thatcher Ulrich, *Good Wives: Image and Reality in the Lives of Women in Northern New England, 1650–1750* (1982).

Marianne S. Wokeck, *Trade in Strangers: The Beginnings of Mass Migration to North America* (1999).

The Varied Economic Landscape

Kathryn E. Holland Braund, *Deerskins and Duffels: Creek Indian Trade with Anglo-America, 1685–1815* (1993).

Elaine Forman Crane, *Ebb Tide in New England: Women, Seaports, and Social Change, 1630–1800* (1998).

Margaret Ellen Newell, *From Dependency to Independence: Economic Revolution in Colonial New England* (1998).

Daniel Vickers, *Farmers and Fishermen: Two Centuries of Work in Essex County, Massachusetts, 1630–1850* (1994).

Michael Zuckerman, *Peaceable Kingdoms: New England Towns in the Eighteenth Century* (1970).

Matters of Faith: The Great Awakening

Patricia U. Bonomi, *Under the Cope of Heaven: Religion, Society, and Politics in Colonial America* (1986).

Philip Greven, *The Protestant Temperament: Patterns of Child-Rearing, Religious Experience, and the Self in Early America* (1977).

Timothy D. Hall, *Contested Boundaries: Itinerancy and the Reshaping of the Colonial American Religious World* (1994).

Jacob R. Marcus, *The Colonial American Jew* (1970).

The French Lose a North American Empire

Fred Anderson, *The War that Made America: A Short History of the French and Indian War,* (2005).

Fred Anderson, *A People's Army: Massachusetts Soldiers and Society in the Seven Years' War* (1984).

Colin G. Calloway, *The Scratch of a Pen: 1763 and the Transformation of North America* (2006).

John Mack Faragher, *A Great and Noble Scheme: The Tragic Story of the Expulsion of the French Acadians from Their American Homeland* (1998).

Ian K. Steele, *Betrayals: Fort William Henry and the "Massacre"* (1990).

Daniel H. Usner Jr., *Indians, Settlers, and Slaves in a Frontier Exchange Economy: The Lower Mississippi Valley Before 1783* (1992).

For quizzes and other resources on these topics, go to www.longmanamericanhistory.com.

The Limits of Imperial Control, 1763–1775

CHAPTER

6

BY THE 1760S, BOSTON HAD GROWN INTO A BUSY SEAPORT OF 16,000 PEOPLE. WITH THIS expansion, the gap between rich and poor had widened steadily, and the Seven Years' War (the French and Indian War) had only worsened the growing inequality. During the war, wealthy Boston families such as the Hancocks multiplied their fortunes, building stately homes and importing elegant fashions. In 1764 young John Hancock, heir to his uncle's vast shipping business, inherited an immense fortune of £80,000.

However, most Bostonians lived in a very different world. Half the townspeople had property and savings worth less than £40, and half of those possessed £20 or less. George Hewes, five years younger than Hancock, was born into this other Boston in 1742. At age seven, Hewes lost his father, a butcher who also sold soap and candles. But unlike Hancock, George had no rich uncle; he became an apprentice shoemaker at age fourteen.

Despite the town's growth, rich and poor still encountered one another on occasion. If anything, those contacts increased during the tumultuous decade that gave rise to the American Revolution. Politics—both imperial and local—heated up in the 1760s, opening rifts in the ruling elite. Throughout the colonies, British officials and other people who supported the crown's policies became known as Loyalists, or Tories. The wealthy among them saw social and economic dominance as their birthright and scorned their rivals for courting favor with the poor. In contrast, leaders of the emerging opposition (known as Whigs or Patriots) consisted of less conservative—often young and ambitious—members of the educated and professional

■ Some wealthy colonists, like the Hancocks of Boston, joined the Patriot opposition during the 1760s and 1770s. Gradually, out of necessity, these merchants and planters forged a loose and convenient alliance with colonial artisans and workers who came from a very different world.

CHAPTER OUTLINE

New Challenges to Spain's Expanded Empire

New Challenges to Britain's Expanded Empire

"The Unconquerable Rage of the People"

A Conspiracy of Corrupt Ministers?

Launching a Revolution

Conclusion

Sites to Visit

For Further Reading

classes. These people downplayed their rank and privilege to win popular support from those beneath them on the social scale.

In Boston, John Hancock was one such person. In 1763, after Hewes repaired an expensive shoe for Hancock, the merchant invited the young cobbler to a New Year's open house at his impressive mansion. In his old age, Hewes still recalled the occasion vividly. Intimidated by the wealth around him, he remembered being scared "almost to death" when the magnate toasted him and gave him a silver coin.

The two men met again on very different terms after a decade had passed. In December 1773 the shoemaker joined other activists, disguised as Indians, to empty chests of British tea into Boston Harbor. Recalling that night as an old man, Hewes was one of the first to refer to the event as a "tea party." And he swore that in the darkness he had rubbed elbows with Hancock himself and had joined him in smashing a crate of tea. Symbolically, the two men were now working shoulder to shoulder. They came together across class lines in a coalition that would soon challenge Europe's strongest empire, Britain, and spark the Atlantic world's first successful anticolonial revolution.

America's implausible alliance between a portion of the colonial elite and a wide spectrum of working people developed gradually and imperfectly. During the decade before 1776, class and regional interests still divided British colonists on many occasions. Urban artisans, rural farmers, enslaved African Americans, and numerous wives and widows, for example, did not necessarily share common views and concerns. Indeed, they were frequently at odds. Nevertheless, within half a generation enough of these diverse people—many as distant from one another socially as Hancock and Hewes—came together to wage a successful struggle for political independence.

What shared experiences and beliefs caused this unlikely and unstable partnership to emerge? What events shaped it and prompted it to gather momentum by July 1776, when John Hancock, as president of the Second Continental Congress, applied the first and largest signature to the American colonies' Declaration of Independence? In retrospect, we know that between 1763 and 1775, for the first time, colonists from separate regions and backgrounds began to speak of themselves as Americans—a term that had previously applied only to Indians. At times, of course, this self-conscious new identification with North America went too far, as in the creation of a *Continental* Congress; it was not, of course, a body of the entire North American continent at all.

In fact, in the Midwest in 1763, thousands of Native Americans under the leadership of Pontiac were fighting to assert their own independence from European encroachment. On the Great Plains, the Comanche and Sioux contended for new territories. Still farther west, other peoples experienced the initial shocks of colonial contact. Suddenly, inhabitants of the Hawaiian Islands and the Alaskan coast were encountering European intruders for the first time. For rival European empires, competing globally for mastery in the Atlantic, Pacific, and Indian Oceans, North America remained only one prize in a wider imperial contest.

Following the departure of the French, the push of rival powers to establish permanent control over the North American continent continued. But geographic ignorance, limited resources, weak bureaucracies, huge distances, strong-willed colonists, and resilient native inhabitants all posed limits for maintaining and expanding far-flung empires. Russia's foothold in Alaska and Spain's presence in California were new and tenuous at best. Spanish dominance at older outposts in Arizona, New Mexico, and Texas remained partial, and Spain's grip on its newly acquired Louisiana territory was even more nominal. East of the Mississippi River, long-term British control finally seemed to be assured. But even Britain, secure after its victory over France, would soon be fighting a losing battle to retain much of North America that it confidently claimed to control.

New Challenges to Spain's Expanded Empire

With Spain's acquisition of Louisiana from France in 1763, the Spanish held nominal title to the entire West, from the Mississippi to the Pacific, populated by more than one million Native Americans. But whether Spain could explore and defend this vast domain, stretching north toward Alaska, remained an open question. After all, envious rivals were already probing North America's Pacific coast. French and British exploration voyages challenged Spain's dominance in the Pacific, and Russian colonization in Alaska spurred the Spanish to establish posts along the coast of California. These rivalries, in turn, brought new pressures to bear on the West's diverse Indian peoples, even before the United States emerged as a separate entity with expansionist ambitions of its own.

Pacific Exploration, Hawaiian Contact

Defeat in the Seven Years' War removed the French from North America in 1763. Burdened with heavy war debts, France sought fresh prospects in the unexplored South Pacific. Not to be outdone, British captains pressed their own Pacific explorations. The most skilled and successful was James Cook, who ranged from the Arctic Circle to Antarctica during three momentous voyages beginning in 1768. In January 1778, during Cook's final voyage, his two vessels happened upon the Hawaiian Islands, eight major volcanic islands, plus 114 minor isles, stretching over 300 miles. More than thirteen centuries earlier (A.D. 300–500), seafaring Polynesians had migrated here in ocean-sailing canoes. They had arrived from the Marquesas Islands far to the south, and their descendants, perhaps as many as 300,000 people, lived in agricultural and fishing communities dominated by powerful chiefs.

The Hawaiians treated Cook with hospitality and respect. "No people could trade with more honisty," the captain observed. During the next twelve months, Cook cruised up the west

■ When Captain Cook anchored at Hawaii's Kealakekua Bay in 1779, he wrote in his journal that the islanders crowded aboard his two vessels and paddled around them in "a multitude of Canoes." Hundreds of others swam around the ships, along with "a number of men upon pieces of Plank." One such surfboarder is visible in the foreground.

coast of North America, two centuries after Francis Drake's visit. English mariners still hoped to find a sea passage through North America to shorten voyages from the Atlantic to Asia, but Cook encountered a solid coastline stretching all the way to Alaska. Along the way, he traded with Northwest Coast Indians for sea otter pelts.

Cook's vessels returned south in 1779, and they were again greeted with fanfare on the big island of Hawaii. But admiration turned to resentment as the English outstayed their welcome, and an angry crowd of Hawaiians killed Cook and four of his mariners. After the captain's death, his two sloops stopped at Macao in China, where the crew sold their furs at a huge profit. They then sailed back to England in 1780 with word of money to be made selling North American sea otter pelts in China. The voyagers also confirmed a disturbing rumor: Russia already had a foothold in this lucrative Pacific traffic.

The Russians Lay Claim to Alaska

In 1728 Vitus Bering, a Danish captain in the Russian naval service, completed a three-year trek across Siberia. Reaching the Kamchatka peninsula on the Pacific Ocean, he built a boat and sailed north between Asia and America through the strait that bears his name. The journey ended European speculation that Asia was linked to North America. On a second expedition in 1741, Bering visited the Alaskan mainland and claimed it for Russia. He lost his life on the return voyage after a winter shipwreck on a frozen island.

Bering's crew finally returned to Kamchatka with valuable pelts. Over the next generation, Russian merchants sent several expeditions to Alaska each year, bringing back furs that they traded with the powerful Chinese Empire. In Alaskan waters, the Russian trappers lacked the numbers and the skill to collect furs on their own. So they captured native women and children as hostages, then ransomed them back to their men in exchange for a fixed number of furs. Native Alaskans resisted these rough intruders where possible, but many eventually submitted in a desperate effort to survive.

In the quarter-century before 1780, thirty different companies sponsored expeditions to Alaskan waters. Harsh conditions and stiff competition between ships made the traffic risky for the Russians and far worse for the Aleutian Islanders. The newcomers, bringing diseases, firearms, and their brutal hostage-taking system, reduced the population of the islands. As the number of humans and animals on the Aleutian Islands declined, the Russians pushed farther east in search of new hunters and hunting grounds.

The voyages from Kamchatka were growing longer and more expensive, so a Russian organizer, Grigorii Shelikov, planned an Alaskan base to facilitate operations. Shelikov and a partner formed a new company in 1781 and founded a permanent colonial settlement on Kodiak Island east of the Aleutians in 1784, despite fierce opposition from the island's native residents. By 1799 the firm had absorbed smaller competitors to become the Russian-American Company, with a monopoly from the **czar**.

In 1790, with the Kodiak base secure, Russians forced more than 7,000 island inhabitants to embark on vast fur hunts in their versatile two-seat **kayaks**. That same year, Shelikov hired Alexander Baranov to oversee the Kodiak post and expand operations down the Alaskan coast. In 1799 Baranov established an additional outpost at Sitka in southeast Alaska. Called

■ In 1991, 250 years after Vitus Bering's voyage to Alaska, Russians from Kamchatka sailed replicas of Bering's three small vessels across the North Pacific to Alaska. Aleksandr Maslov-Bering, a descendant of the explorer, poses beside the carved bow of one boat.

New Archangel at the time, the post became the capital of Russian America in 1808. From here, Baranov eventually extended the company's reach south toward California, seeking new hunting grounds and a longer growing season.

Spain Colonizes the California Coast

The Seven Years' War had left Spain's king, Carlos III, with vast new land claims in western North America. With only limited resources, the bureaucrats administering Spanish America struggled to control the huge domain. Many of the Native Americans across the Southwest resisted several decades of military suppression and slave raids. In addition, clerics offered their own resistance to government designs. The powerful Jesuits opposed administrative reform in the colonies, and in 1767 Carlos III expelled them from the Spanish realm. Unruly colonists posed a threat of their own. French inhabitants of New Orleans led a brief rebellion against Spanish rule in 1768. Finally, officials feared challenges in the Pacific from the British and the Russians. As early as 1759, a Spanish Franciscan had published *Muscovites in California*, warning of Russian settlements.

With the threat of Russians in mind, Spanish leaders in Mexico City concentrated on establishing a token presence along the Pacific coast. In 1769 they sent a small vanguard north from lower (Baja) California, led by Gaspar de Portolá and Franciscan friar Junípero Serra, to establish an initial outpost at San Diego Bay. Portolá then pressed farther up the coast, building a presidio (or military garrison) at Monterey in 1770 to "defend us from attacks by the Russians, who," he believed, "were about to invade us."

After the removal of all Jesuits from Spanish America in 1767, numerous Franciscan missionaries, members of a competing Catholic order, expanded their work and took on new responsibilities. Following the lead of Father Serra, other Franciscans soon planted several missions between San Diego and Monterey. These included the San Gabriel mission in 1771, where colonists established the town of Los Angeles ten years later. In 1775 a Spanish captain sailed into San Francisco Bay, and the next year a land expedition laid out the presidio and mission of San Francisco. A town sprang up at nearby San José the following year. As Franciscan fathers labored to convert the coast's diverse Indians, Spanish vessels pushed far up the Pacific shoreline. Captain Ignacio de Arteaga reached the Gulf of Alaska in 1779, fourteen months after Captain Cook had been there.

Since Spanish ships had difficulty supplying the few dozen settlers in California, authorities looked for an overland supply route. In 1774 Juan Bautista de Anza set out in search of a land route to California from the presidio he commanded at Tubac, south of Tucson. Accompanied by a Franciscan named Father Garcés, he forded the Colorado River and then crossed desert and mountains to reach the coast at San Gabriel. The next year, Anza led 240 reinforcements—mostly Spanish women and children—along a similar route, pausing at San Gabriel and heading north to San Francisco Bay.

Further explorations in 1776 proved less successful. Trying to find a usable route between California and New Mexico, Father Garcés meandered through the southwestern deserts without success. Two other Franciscans, Fathers Domínguez and Escalante, left Santa Fe on horseback in July 1776. They headed northwest across Colorado and Utah in search of a more northern route to Monterey on the Pacific coast. But no such trail existed. Instead, their 1,800-mile trek revealed the huge expanse of the Great Basin.

Moreover, the path to California that Anza had established proved short-lived. The Yuma Indians, who had helped his party cross the Colorado River in 1774, soon grew to resent Spanish trespassers, and they rebelled in the summer of 1781. Father Garcés and more than 100 Spanish men, women, and children died in the bloody Yuma Revolt, and hopes for a rapid expansion of the Spanish colony in California died with them.

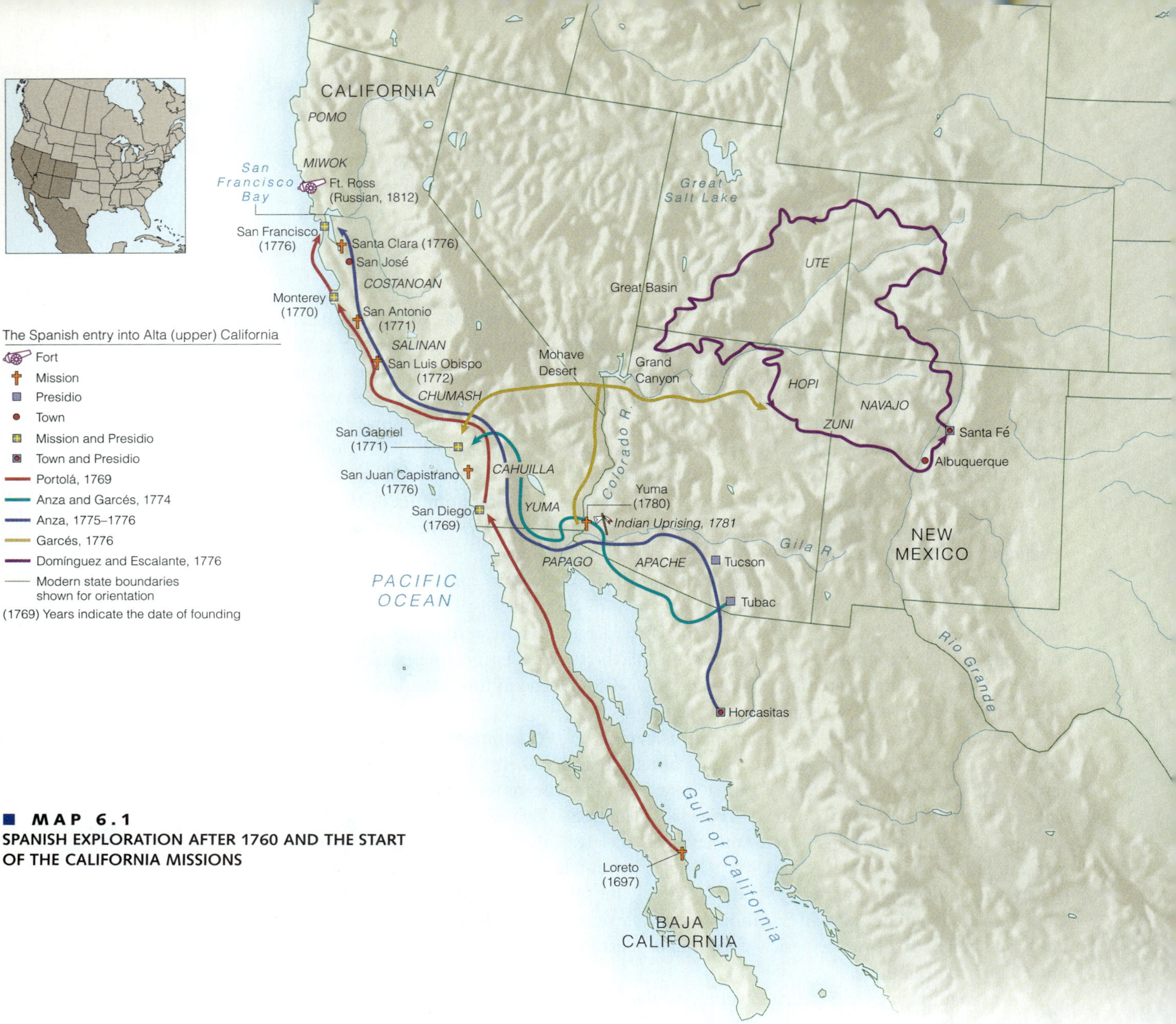

MAP 6.1

SPANISH EXPLORATION AFTER 1760 AND THE START OF THE CALIFORNIA MISSIONS

Despite these problems, Spain managed to retain control over its recently expanded North American empire. The same could not be said for the British in their own newly enlarged empire farther east. They had taken French Canada, and their military might dominated the Atlantic world. But their fortunes in North America were about to change.

New Challenges to Britain's Expanded Empire

In September 1760, French forces at Montreal submitted to British commander Jeffery Amherst. For Native Americans living east of the Mississippi, the French defeat in Canada had an immediate impact. General Amherst, who despised Indians as "contemptible," intended to alter Native American relations in the interior to reflect the new balance of power. He promptly sent James Grant to South Carolina with instructions "to chastise the Cherokees,"

who had taken up arms against the growing number of English traders and settlers in western Carolina. With 2,800 soldiers, Grant invaded Cherokee country in 1761. His men burned fifteen villages, without sparing women or children, and destroyed 1,500 acres of beans and corn.

With the Cherokee chastened in the South, Amherst turned his attention to the Indians north of the Ohio River. Here his harsh policies brought a sudden retaliation from the Native Americans that took many lives and cost Amherst his command. And if Indians in the Midwest posed fresh challenges to Britain, so did the colonists themselves.

Midwestern Lands and Pontiac's War for Indian Independence

As soon as the British unseated their French competitors in the Ohio River valley, they prohibited traffic with Indians in such goods as knives, tomahawks, muskets, powder, and lead. As French traders withdrew, the British took over their strategic posts at Detroit and at Michilimackinac. English settlers built new forts in the Ohio Valley and erected Fort Pitt over the ruins of Fort Duquesne. Indians at Niagara Falls commented in dismay at "so many Men and so much artillery passing by." Then, early in 1763, word spread among Indians that France would cede Louisiana to Spain and give up Canada and the entire Midwest to Great Britain. For Native Americans, this shocking news undercut moderate leaders willing to accommodate the English, and it strengthened the hand of pro-war factions.

Word that a treaty in far-off Paris might disrupt the entire region drew attention to Neolin, a Delaware Indian prophet urging a return to ancient ways and a sharp separation from the corrupting Europeans. Neolin's vision of renewing independence by driving out the British appealed to many Native Americans in the Midwest including Pontiac, a militant Ottawa warrior. In April, Pontiac addressed a secret council of more than 400 Ottawa, Potawatomie, and Huron, meeting within 10 miles of Fort Detroit. Invoking the Delaware Prophet's vision, he announced that the Master of Life resented the British and wanted them removed: "Send them back to the lands which I have created for them and let them stay there." By May, Pontiac had mobilized a coalition and laid siege to Detroit.

Soon Indians from eighteen nations had joined in Pontiac's widespread uprising. By mid-June 1763, both Detroit and Fort Pitt were under siege, and the British had lost every other Ohio Valley and Great Lakes outpost. As Indian raiding parties ravaged white communities in western Virginia and Pennsylvania, embittered settlers responded with racial killing. In December, white men from Paxton Creek descended on Christian families of Conestoga Indians near Lancaster, Pennsylvania, executing more than thirty peaceful converts. When easterners protested this outrage, the "Paxton Boys" marched on Philadelphia to demand increased protection on the frontier. General Amherst ordered his officers to spread smallpox if possible, and to take no prisoners. The Indians deserved extermination, he ranted, "for the good of mankind."

The violence ended in a stalemate. Without French support, Native American munitions ran short, and Detroit and Fort Pitt endured. Indian militancy waned, and Pontiac was killed by a Peoria Indian in 1765. Still, the uprising proved costly for the British and prompted a shift in policy. To avoid further expensive warfare, officials moved to restore the Indian trade, keep squatters and debt evaders out of Indian country, and prevent colonial speculation in western lands. In October 1763, Major General Thomas Gage replaced Amherst in command of British forces.

In England, the crown went further. Late in 1763, it issued a proclamation forbidding colonial settlers from moving west across the Appalachian summit. Beyond that dividing line, all the land east of the Mississippi River valley would be reserved for Indians and a few authorized British soldiers and traders. While the Proclamation Line of 1763, drawn along the crest of the Appalachians, had only limited success, it frustrated Virginia's gentry. Such prominent men as George Washington and Thomas Jefferson were investors in land companies that speculated in large western tracts, hoping to obtain property cheaply from Native Americans and sell small parcels to eager settlers at a steady profit. But the British government, fearful of sparking unified Indian opposition and additional warfare, denied the Virginians' wishes and aroused their resentment.

Grenville's Effort at Reform

In 1763 King George III appointed Robert Grenville to head a new government in London. Grenville's ministry immediately faced a series of intertwined problems. Britain's victory over the French in the Seven Years' War had proved costly, nearly doubling the national debt to a staggering £146 million. As England's postwar depression deepened, returning soldiers swelled the ranks of the unemployed. In addition, rural mobs protested a new tax on domestic cider, imposed to help whittle away at the war debt.

No one promoted opposition to the government more than John Wilkes, a flamboyant member of Parliament (MP) who published the *North Briton*, an outspoken periodical which attacked the king's peace settlement with France and the king himself. Grenville reacted by arresting the publisher, despite his status as an MP. Angered by government suppression of dissent, protesters made "Wilkes and Liberty!" a popular rallying cry.

Pressured at home, Grenville set out to impose order on Britain's growing American colonies through a series of reforms. The first step was to maintain a considerable military presence of nearly 7,000 troops in North America. The move would protect newly acquired territories while keeping young British men employed overseas rather than jobless at home. Strapped for funds, Grenville hoped to pay for the transatlantic forces with money drawn from the very colonies the troops were defending.

Raising money in this way would remind the British colonies of their subordination to the sovereign power of Parliament. Colonists had grown wealthy by sidestepping the elaborate Navigation Acts and trading illegally with foreign powers, even during wartime. Sympathetic colonial juries had looked the other way. Worse, American legislatures had used their power of the purse to withhold money from any British governor who did not favor local interests. Finally, lax customs officers assigned to colonial ports often collected their salaries while remaining in England, without even occupying their posts.

As a preliminary step, Grenville ordered absentee customs officials to their colonial stations and dispatched forty-four navy ships to assist them. Next, he moved his first reform through Parliament: the American Duties Act of 1764, also known as the Sugar Act. The new revenue law increased the duty on sugar and various other products entering the empire from non-British ports, and it cut in half the import duty of sixpence per gallon on foreign molasses. Officials hoped that New England rum distillers, who had been secretly importing cheap molasses from the French West Indies without paying customs, would be willing to pay threepence per gallon. If enforced, the act would reduce smuggling and boost revenues while saving merchants from the heavy costs of bribing port officials.

> "What has America done," protested critics, "to be stripped of so invaluable a privilege as the trial by jury?"

To ensure compliance, the Sugar Act strengthened the customs officers' authority to seize goods off arriving ships, and it established the first of several vice-admiralty courts. The court sat at Halifax, Nova Scotia, so defendants had large travel expenses, and they faced a single appointed judge instead of a favorable local jury. "What has America done," protested critics, "to be stripped of so invaluable a privilege as the trial by jury?"

Additional statutes followed quickly. The Currency Act of 1764 prohibited colonial assemblies from issuing paper money or bills of credit to be used as legal tender to pay off debts. The move only worsened the money shortage in British America, where a lopsided trade balance was already draining gold and silver from the colonies to England. Colonial merchants had to pay Grenville's new duties using scarce hard money.

The next year Parliament passed a Quartering Act that obliged colonists to assist the army by allowing soldiers to use vacant barns and other buildings as temporary quarters. The local governor was to supply the soldiers, at colonial expense, with certain basic necessities they would expect at any inn: firewood, candles, bedding, salt, vinegar, utensils, and rations of beer and cider. Colonial assemblies had willingly voted such support during colonial wars. However, these peacetime requisitions, ordered by a distant Parliament, seemed to challenge their authority and smacked of indirect taxation.

DOCUMENT

Otis, "The Rights of the British Colonies Asserted and Proved"

The Stamp Act Imposed

There was nothing indirect about Grenville's most important reform: the Stamp Act. Early in 1765, Parliament approved the new statute "for raising a further revenue" to pay for "defending, protecting, and securing" the British colonies in America. The new act was patterned on a similar law in England, and it required stamps (like those on modern packs of cigarettes) to appear on a variety of articles in America after November 1, 1765. The list included legal contracts, land deeds, liquor licenses, indentures, newspapers, almanacs, and playing cards. Colonial lawyers and printers were to purchase these stamps from designated agents; the official stamp distributor in each colony would receive a handsome fee from all stamp sales. The British treasury anticipated taking in £100,000 per year, to be spent only for government operations in America.

Stamp Act Stamps

Grenville's stamp bill generated little debate in England. Granted, colonists had no actual representation in the Parliament, but neither did the majority of subjects in England. Most of them did not have the right to vote, yet all were said to be "virtually" represented by MPs, who supposedly had the interests of the entire country at heart. If members of Parliament looked out for nonvoting subjects at home, surely they could provide the same sort of "virtual representation" for British subjects throughout the realm.

Whether or not they spoke for colonists in America, most MPs viewed Grenville's stamp measure as appropriate and well conceived. They saw no legal distinction between external duties used to regulate trade and internal taxes imposed by Parliament within the colonies themselves to raise revenue. Because the stamp tax applied to daily articles used throughout the colonies, it would be widely and evenly distributed. Even better, revenues would grow steadily and automatically as colonial economic activity continued to expand.

So as not to cause alarm in the colonies, Parliament set initial stamp prices in America lower than those charged in England, although it could always raise the rates as colonists grew accustomed to the tax. Moreover, the tax was to be gathered quietly by Americans themselves in the course of doing business rather than extracted from citizens by tax collectors. Prominent colonists were eager to accept the lucrative stamp distributorships, and no one predicted an upheaval. But the Stamp Act soon unleashed a storm of organized resistance in ports where the stamps were to be sold.

The Stamp Act Resisted

At first, colonial assemblies had mixed responses to the burdensome new tax. But in late May, the youngest member of the Virginia House of Burgesses—a rising country attorney named Patrick Henry—galvanized American resistance to the Stamp Act. As the House session was winding down, Henry introduced a series of fiery resolves challenging Parliament's right to impose taxes. The twenty-eight-year-old orator managed to gain narrow passage of five separate resolutions.

Henry's fifth and most provocative resolve asserted that Virginia's assembly had the "sole exclusive right and power to lay taxes" on the colony's inhabitants. The resolution passed by just one vote. In fact, opponents reintroduced it the next day, after Henry left town, and voted it down. But the spark had been struck. Distant newspapers were soon reprinting Henry's "Virginia Resolves," including the resolution that had been voted down plus two that had been drawn up but never introduced for a vote. These provocative draft resolutions said that Virginians were "not bound to yield obedience" to such a tax, and anyone arguing otherwise must "be deemed an enemy" to the colony.

In Massachusetts, the assembly took a different approach. It issued a call for each colony to send delegates to a Stamp Act Congress in New York in October 1765 to "implore relief" from Parliament. Local citizens, inflamed by Virginia's resolutions and squeezed by an economic depression, prepared to take more direct action. In Boston, a small group of artisans and merchants known as the Loyal Nine mobilized to force the designated stamp distributor,

1765 Stamp Act Protest

Lawyers and artisans in the Sons of Liberty encouraged demonstrations against the Stamp Act. But they ran the risk, suggested here, that poor workers, black slaves, and women in the crowds might give their own meanings to the shouts of "Liberty!"

Andrew Oliver, to resign before the stamps arrived from England. On August 16, a crowd of several thousand hanged an effigy of Oliver and tore down his Stamp Office. The protesters ransacked Oliver's elegant house, drinking his wine and smashing his furniture. The next day, Oliver resigned his appointment.

As word of the protest spread, crowds took to the streets in scores of towns. Often the mobs were encouraged by local leaders who opposed the Stamp Act. These prominent citizens had started to organize themselves in secret groups, which they called the Sons of Liberty. The crowds forced the resignation of potential stamp distributors in ports from New Hampshire to the Carolinas. When a shipment of stamps finally arrived in New York City, nearly 5,000 people risked open warfare to confiscate the hated cargo.

Throughout the second half of 1765, the Sons of Liberty promoted street violence against specific targets. But they could not always control the demonstrations, since the debtors, sailors, blacks, and women drawn to such crowds all had separate grievances of their own. For example, on August 26 in Boston, just ten days after the raid on Oliver's house, a second mob launched a broader assault. Without sanction from the Loyal Nine or the Sons of Liberty, the crowd went after the homes of several wealthy office holders, including the house of Lieutenant Governor Thomas Hutchinson. Because he also served as chief justice of the Superior Court, Hutchinson had offended townspeople by issuing numerous warrants for debtors and collecting large fees for administering bankruptcies. Hutchinson recounted how he fled when "the hellish crew fell upon my house with the Rage of devils and . . . with axes split down the doors," pillaging his entire estate.

In South Carolina several months later, the spirit of insurrection also went well beyond the careful boundaries intended by the Sons of Liberty. They were pleased when Charleston artisans hanged a stamp distributor in effigy, with a sign reading, "Liberty and no Stamp Act." And they gave tacit approval when white workers harassed the wealthy slave trader and potential stamp distributor Henry Laurens with chants of "Liberty, Liberty!" Soon, however, enslaved African Americans also took to the streets, raising their own defiant cry of "Liberty, Liberty!" Fearing an insurrection by South Carolina's black majority, the same people who had sanctioned earlier street demonstrations quickly shifted their focus, believing that ideas of freedom had spread too far. The colonial assembly temporarily banned further importation of Africans. Local leaders expanded slave patrols and placed Charleston briefly under martial law.

Elsewhere, too, the colonial elites took steps to contain the turbulence. Many moved—often reluctantly—toward more radical positions, joining the Sons of Liberty and ridiculing the British concept of virtual representation. Colonial assemblies condemned Grenville's intrusive reforms. The Stamp Act Congress passed resolutions vehemently protesting both the Sugar and Stamp acts. But even as they challenged Parliament, these same local leaders stressed their loyalty to the crown and moved to control the violence, some of which was directed at them. Such moderation appealed to cautious merchants in Atlantic seaports, who reluctantly agreed to stop ordering Britain goods. They hoped that exporters in Britain, feeling the economic pinch of a colonial boycott, might use their political strength to force a repeal of the Stamp Act and defuse the tense situation.

DOCUMENT

Franklin, Testimony Against the Stamp Act

■ MAP 6.2
BRITISH NORTH AMERICA, 1763–1766 In 1763 the British worked to govern their new provinces in Canada and Florida while suppressing an Indian uprising in the Midwest. With widely dispersed troops, they also tried to keep colonists out of the Mississippi Valley and halt opposition to the 1765 Stamp Act.

When politics in London prompted Grenville's sudden removal from office, hopes rose in America for a possible compromise resolving the Stamp Act crisis. In March 1766, these hopes were nearly fulfilled. The new ministry of Lord Rockingham, responding to merchant pressure as predicted, and also to the compelling rhetoric of William Pitt, persuaded Parliament to repeal the Stamp Act. But colonial victory had a hollow ring to it, for the repeal bill was accompanied by a blunt Declaratory Act. In it, the members of Parliament declared clearly that they reaffirmed their power "to make Laws . . . to bind the Colonists and People of America . . . in all Cases whatsoever."

"The Unconquerable Rage of the People"

As news of the Stamp Act repeal spread, the Sons of Liberty organized elaborate celebrations in British America. But word of the Declaratory Act had a sobering effect. Clearly, the problems surrounding colonial taxation and representation remained unresolved. The atmosphere of mutual suspicion and righteous indignation that had erupted during the Stamp Act crisis divided colonists further in the years ahead.

A flurry of pamphlets from colonial presses broadened awareness of the issues, sharpened arguments, and inspired new coalitions. As colonial leaders collaborated, they discovered a shared viewpoint that gave added meaning and importance to each new event. This emerging ideology had deep roots stretching back into English history.

Power Corrupts: An English Framework for Revolution

The radical ideas that had appeared during England's Civil War in the 1640s, when English subjects briefly overthrew their monarchy and proclaimed a Puritan Commonwealth, lived on long after the Restoration in 1660. English Whigs who led the Glorious Revolution in 1688 invoked some of these principles when they limited the monarchy's power and strengthened Parliament's authority. Succeeding generations hailed the rights of English subjects and congratulated themselves that Great Britain (as England and Scotland became known in 1707) had achieved a truly balanced government. They drew on the ancient Greek philosopher Aristotle to explain their accomplishment.

Magna Carta

Aristotle, his modern readers noted, had observed a cycle in politics. He believed that too much power vested in a king could eventually corrupt the monarchical form of government. Unbounded royal power led to a tyranny, misrule by a despot wielding absolute control. When nobles then asserted themselves against the tyrant (as English barons had done when they forced King John to sign the Magna Carta in 1215), the resulting aristocracy could easily turn corrupt. Abuse of power by such an oligarchy of self-serving nobles could then prompt the common people, known as the commons, to rise up. If the commons gained sway, they might build a democracy, but it too could degenerate, leaving only anarchy. Such a "mobocracy" paved the way for an opportunistic leader to once more seize the scepter of royal power and start the cycle over again.

Confident Whigs claimed that England had halted this vicious cycle by balancing the power of the nation's three estates: the king epitomized the legitimate interests of monarchy, the House of Lords represented the aristocracy, and the House of Commons represented the rest of the population. However, a few of the more radical Whig theorists continued to oppose this consensus view long after 1700. Calling themselves the Real Whigs, these skeptics charged that the existing mixed government—which claimed an ideal and lasting balance between monarchy, aristocracy, and commons—was actually less perfect and more vulnerable than most people suspected.

A truly balanced government, they argued, is hard to achieve and difficult to maintain, for power inevitably corrupts. Schemers who obtain public office can readily disrupt such a fragile system, so its protection, these critics stressed, demanded constant vigilance. They urged citizens to watch for the two surest signs of decay: the concentration of wealth in a few hands and the political and social corruption that inevitably follows. Where others saw stability in England's exuberant growth, these Real Whigs perceived sure signs of danger in the powerful new Bank of England, the expanding stock market, and the rise in public debt.

No Real Whigs proved more vigilant than John Trenchard and Thomas Gordon. The two men sensed around them the same luxury and greed that had undermined the Roman Republic. They pored over the works of ancient writers such as the Roman statesman Cato, who described and challenged corrupt behavior. In 1721 they published their own *Cato's Letters: Essays on Liberty*, cautioning against "the Natural Encroachments of Power" and warning that "public corruptions and abuses have grown upon us."

Trenchard and Gordon took special offense at Britain's corrupt patronage system. Public positions seemed designed to reward loyal support, and too many people appeared to gain a post (often in the colonies) through political ties rather than through skill or training. The authors of *Cato's Letters* saw each individual act of corruption as representing a dangerous precedent, if unopposed. They reminded their readers that tyranny is usually imposed through small, subtle steps, for "if it is suffered once, it is apt to be repeated often; a few repetitions create a habit." Before citizens realize that they are losing their liberties, the permanent "Yoke of Servitude" is in place, supported by military force. All hope of successful protest has disappeared. The encroachment of power over liberty, Trenchard and Gordon concluded, is "much easier to prevent than to cure."

Americans Practice Vigilance and Restraint

Though these writers attracted only limited attention in England, they earned a wide American following. The popularity of *Cato's Letters* and related tracts continued to spread in the colonies during the 1760s, for colonists saw disturbing parallels between the warnings of Real Whig authors and current events in America. Now, as throughout history, a government tainted by corruption might deny adequate representation, initiate unjust taxes, or replace jury trials with arbitrary courts. Officials might curtail freedoms of press or religion to consolidate their power. Moreover, weak ministers might advise the king poorly or keep citizens' pleas from reaching his ears. If the populace relaxed its guard, these ministers might even sanction a standing army in peacetime to impose arbitrary rule over their own population.

> *During the 1760s, colonists saw disturbing parallels between the warnings of Real Whig authors and current events in America.*

According to Real Whig doctrine, ordinary people must be alert but circumspect; a measured response to threats was all-important. One stubborn or mistaken act by officials did not prove a pattern of conspiracy, and it could be counterproductive to raise alarms too often. So prudent citizens should turn first to legal methods of **redress**. If the system was functioning properly, claims of real abuses would bring forth proper corrections. Even if forced to take to the streets as a last resort, crowds should be organized and purposeful, not uncontrolled. They should threaten property before people and hang effigies, not actual office holders.

For the most part, the Stamp Act demonstrations had followed this logic of restraint and had gained the desired effect. "In every Colony," wrote John Adams, "the Stamp Distributors and Inspectors have been compelled, by the unconquerable Rage of the People, to renounce their offices." But did individual demands for liberty have limits? Could slaves seek liberty from their masters? What about wives from husbands? Could tenants press for redress from rich landlords, or debtors from powerful creditors? Such questions generated widespread, heated debate in the turbulent quarter-century ahead.

Rural Unrest: Tenant Farmers and Regulators

For colonists, certain events in Europe after 1765 seemed to confirm the views that the Real Whigs had passed down. When John Wilkes was repeatedly elected to Parliament but expelled from the Commons for his radical views, his American supporters rallied on his behalf. Similarly, British colonists embraced the short-lived cause of Pasquale Paoli, who fought to free the Mediterranean island of Corsica from domination by Genoa. Many colonists christened their sons after Wilkes or Paoli, and Pennsylvanians named new towns after these overseas heroes. The two men seemed to embody the universal struggle of liberty against tyranny—a contest that often flared up closer to home as well.

In local controversies, both large and small, the "Rage of the People" frequently boiled up from below. "The People, even to the lowest Ranks, have become more attentive to their Liberties," John Adams observed, "and more determined to defend them." While stamp protesters demonstrated in New York City, aggrieved tenant farmers staged a violent revolt against powerful landholders in the Hudson River valley. They chose an Irish immigrant as their leader, established a council, organized militia companies with elected captains, and broke open jails to free debtors. They even set up their own peoaple's courts to try captured Hudson Valley gentry, before British troops finally suppressed the revolt.

Unrest also shook the Carolinas in the interior region known to colonists as the backcountry, or the Piedmont. In South Carolina, the absence of civil government beyond the coastal parishes fostered lawlessness among white settlers until the governor extended circuit courts into the interior in 1769. In North Carolina, migrants seeking fertile land moved south from Virginia and Pennsylvania in a steady stream. When they arrived in the Piedmont, they found a local elite already appointed to county posts by the governor. The newcomers disliked these grasping office holders who possessed strong family and financial ties to powerful planters and merchants farther east. They seemed to epitomize, at the local level, the sorts of corruption that had long troubled Real Whig pamphleteers.

As backcountry settlers grew in numbers, they protested against their inadequate representation in the colonial assembly. They began organizing into local groups to better "regulate" their own affairs, and they soon became known as Regulators. These small farmers, many in debt, protested loudly against regressive taxes that imposed the same burden on all colonists, regardless of their wealth. The Regulators' discontent turned into outrage when coastal planters who dominated the assembly voted public funds to build a stately mansion in New Bern for William Tryon, the colonial governor. By this act, the eastern slaveholding elite hoped to establish North Carolina's permanent capitol building on the coast, and yet Piedmont farmers would bear most of the cost of constructing the mansion.

The decision to erect "Tryon's Palace" at public expense confirmed backcountry suspicions that the governor and his associates were looking out for their own interests at the expense of the public. Both sides dug in their heels. In 1771 Governor Tryon finally called out the militia and marched into the Piedmont. After defeating several thousand angry farmers at the battle of Alamance in May 1771, Tryon hanged six Regulator leaders in Hillsborough and forced backcountry residents to swear an oath of loyalty. Many refused, migrating farther south to Georgia or west to the Appalachian Mountains. Their leader, a Quaker named Herman Husband, barely escaped with his life. In North Carolina, just as in the Hudson Valley, well-to-do members of the Sons of Liberty dismissed the organized and militant farmers as misguided rabble.

INTERPRETING HISTORY

"Squez'd and Oppressed": A 1768 Petition by 30 Regulators

In the 1760s, corruption prevailed among appointed officials in central North Carolina. Often holding numerous offices at once, these men managed elections, controlled courts, and gathered taxes. Apparently not all the tax money they collected made it to the public treasury. Nevertheless, any farmer who resisted paying might lose the plow horse or the milk cow that sustained the family. It could be "seized and sold" to cover a small tax payment or minor debt, with "no Part being ever Return'd" from the proceeds.

Banding together to better regulate their own affairs, these farmers sought relief through every possible legal means. By 1768 these organized Regulators had exhausted most avenues of peaceful protest. The western counties where they resided were badly underrepresented in the colonial assembly. As a new session prepared to convene, they fired off a final round of petitions, assuring legislators that they were law-abiding citizens willing to pay their legal share of taxes. In this message of October 4, 1768, thirty Regulators begged for the appointment of honest public officials.

In 1768 the creation of Tryon's Palace, a mansion for the North Carolina governor at New Bern, prompted backcountry protests. Irate farm families, feeling heavily taxed and poorly represented, joined the Regulator Movement. They filed petitions, withheld taxes, closed courts, and harassed corrupt officials, protesting the "unequal chances the poor and weak have in contentions with the rich and powerful."

To the Worshipful House of Representatives of North Carolina

Your Poor Petitioners [have] been Continually Squez'd and oppressed by our Publick Officers both with Regard to their fees as also in the Laying on of Taxes as well as in Collecting. . . . Being Grieved thus to have our substance torn from us [by]…such Illegal practices, we applied to our public officers to give us some satisfaction…which they Repeatedly denied us.

With Regard to the Taxes,…we labour under Extreem hardships. . . . Money is very scarce…& we exceeding Poor & lie at a great distance from Trade which renders it almost Impossible to gain sustenance by our utmost Endeavours….

To Gentlemen Rowling in affluence, a few shillings per man may seem triffling. Yet to Poor People who must have their Bed and Bedclothes, yea their Wives Petticoats, taken and sold to Defray, how Tremenious [tremendous]…must be the Consequences….Therefore, dear Gentlemen, to your selves, to your Country, and in Pity to your Poor Petitioners, do not let it stand any longer to Drink up the Blood and vitals of the Poor Distressed.

After seeking relief from existing taxes, the petitioners went on to question new burdens, such as the law imposing an additional tax "to Erect a Publick Edifice" for Governor Tryon in New Bern.

Good God, Gentlemen, what will become of us when these Demands come against us? Paper Money we have none & gold or silver we can Purchase none of. The Contingencies of Government Must be Paid, and…we are Willing to Pay, [even] if we [must] sell our Beds from under us. And [yet] in this Time of Distress, it is as much as we can support….If, therefore, the Law for that Purpose can be happily Repealed,…May the God of Heaven Inspire you with sentiments to that Purpose.

We humble Begg you would…Use your Influence with our Worthy, Virtuous Governor to discontinue…such Officers as would be found to be ye Bane of Society, and [instead to] Put in the Common Wealth [officials willing] to Encourage the Poor and…to stand [up] for them. This would Cause Joy and Gladness to Spring from every Heart. This would cause Labour and Industry to prevail over Murmuring Discontent. This would Raise your poor Petitioners…to a flourishing Opulent and Hoping People. Otherwise…disatisfaction and Melancholy must Prevail over such as Remain, and Numbers must Defect the Province and seek elsewhere an Asylum from Tyranny and Oppression….

We leave it to you…in your great Wisdom…to pass such Act or Acts, as shall be Conducive to the welbeing of a whole People over Whose welfare ye are plac'd as Guardians. . . . For the Lords Sake, Gentlemen, Exert your selves this once in our favour.

Questions

1. How, specifically, do the tone and content of this petition reflect the widespread political outlook, combining vigilance and restraint, described in Cato's Letters?

2. Pick some current issue that concerns you deeply and draft a brief, impassioned petition to your legislators. In compelling language, lay out your best arguments for action. Then see if 30 people will sign your petition.

Source: William S. Powell, James K. Huhta, and Thomas J. Farnham, eds., *The Regulators of North Carolina: A Documentary History, 1759–1776* (Raleigh: State Department of Archives and History, 1971), pp. 187–189. Some corrections have been made for readability.

A Conspiracy of Corrupt Ministers?

Numerous sharp divisions—some leading to armed conflict—continued to separate colonists of different classes and regions. But ill-timed steps by successive administrations in London attracted widening attention throughout British America, prompting uneasy new alliances. Colonists familiar with the dire warnings of Real Whig pamphleteers asked themselves a question: in the weak and short-lived ministries that succeeded Grenville's, were the leaders simply ill-informed, or were they actively corrupt? Colonists wondered whether some official conspiracy existed to chip away at American liberties. Even loyal defenders of the crown expressed frustration with new policies that appeared too harsh to calm irate colonists, yet too weak to force them into line.

Parliament's first new imposition after repeal of the Stamp Act was the Revenue Act of 1766. The act offered an additional reduction in the molasses duty, from threepence per gallon to a single penny, to further discourage smuggling and raise revenue. Colonial merchants accepted this measure as an external tax designed to regulate imperial trade. They paid the new duty, and customs revenues rose. But Real Whigs reminded them that compliance with even the most innocuous measure could set a dangerous precedent.

John Dickinson, "Letters…"

The skeptics had a point, for Parliament soon imposed new hard-line measures. Before his sudden death in 1767, Charles Townshend, the Chancellor of the Exchequer (or chief finance minister) put these distasteful statutes in motion. Townshend's new duties sparked angry responses from colonists. The most telling came from John Dickinson, a moderate Philadelphia lawyer. He drafted a series of widely circulated "Letters from a Farmer in Pennsylvania," urging colonists to respond "peaceably—prudently—firmly—jointly." He dismissed any distinction between external and internal taxation, and he also rejected the idea that Americans had virtual representation in Parliament. "We are taxed without our own consent," Dickinson proclaimed to his readers. "We are therefore—SLAVES."

The Townshend Duties

In search of funds, Parliament passed the Townshend Revenue Act of 1767, which created new duties on colonial imports of glass, paint, lead, paper, and tea. Proceeds were to be spent in the colonies for "the administration of justice, and the support of civil government," a seemingly benevolent gesture. But Dickinson and other colonists pointed out what these two phrases actually meant. "The administration of justice" cloaked expanded searches of American homes and shops in which customs officers used hated "writs of assistance" to ferret out smuggled goods. "The support of civil government" ensured that governors and appointed office holders could draw their pay directly from the new duties instead of depending on an annual salary grant from the local assembly. In short, the new act removed from colonial legislatures one of their strongest bargaining tools in dealing with the crown: the power to pay or withhold yearly salaries for key officials sent from Britain.

Similar acts and instructions followed. Asserting its sovereignty, Parliament disciplined the New York Assembly for defying the Quartering Act of 1765. The crown instructed governors in America, now less dependent for their salaries on colonial lower houses, to disapprove any measures from legislatures asserting their traditional control over how members were chosen, what their numbers should be, and when they would meet. Equally galling, the Customs Act of 1767 established a separate Board of Customs for British North America. Ominously, the commissioners would live in Boston rather than London. To strengthen the board's hand, in 1768 Britain expanded the number of vice-admiralty courts in North America from one to four, adding new courts in Boston, Philadelphia, and Charleston. Furthermore, to look after its troublesome mainland colonies, the British government created a new American Department, overseen by Lord Hillsborough. It also began to move British troops in America from remote frontier outposts to major Atlantic ports, both as a cost-cutting measure and as a show of force.

Americans found these measures threatening, especially when considered as a whole. In February 1768, the Massachusetts legislature, led by forty-six-year-old Samuel Adams, petitioned the king for redress. The legislators circulated a call to other colonial assemblies for similar protests. Condemning the Townshend Revenue Act as unconstitutional, they argued that it imposed taxation without representation. By removing control of the governors' salaries from colonial legislatures, they said, Parliament set the dangerous precedent of making royal officials "independent of the people." Lord Hillsborough demanded an immediate retraction of this provocative "Circular Letter" and ordered the dissolution of any assembly that took up the matter.

In June, events in Boston took a more radical turn. Defying Hillsborough, the Massachusetts assembly voted against rescinding its circular letter. On June 5, a dockside crowd faced down a "press-gang" from a British warship and protected local sailors from being forced (or "pressed") into naval service. Five days later, customs officials seized John Hancock's sloop, *Liberty*, and demanded that he pay import duties for a cargo of Madeira wine. This move sparked a huge demonstration as citizens dragged a small customs boat through the streets and then burned it on Boston Common. Impatient Sam Adams was heard to say, "Let us take up arms immediately and be free."

"The Liberty Song"

Emotions ran high. But most leaders sensed that any escalation of the violence would be premature and perhaps suicidal. They reined in demonstrations and instead initiated a boycott of British goods. Nonimportation plans called upon colonists to refrain from imported luxuries and opt instead for virtuous self-sufficiency. The prospect of nonviolent resistance held broad appeal. As the nonimportation movement expanded, women of all ranks, self-proclaimed Daughters of Liberty, turned to making and selling homespun garments. Local associations sprang up, pledging to forgo imported tea and London fashions. A dozen colonial assemblies voted to halt importation of selected goods. In New York, the value of imports from Britain shrank from £491,000 to just £76,000 in a single year.

> Impatient Sam Adams was heard to say, "Let us take up arms immediately and be free."

Signing an Anti-Tea Agreement

The damage to English shipping proved substantial. Britain was losing far more revenue in colonial trade than it was gaining through the expanded customs duties. Soon influential British exporters were pressing their government for relief. When Baron Frederick North, who succeeded Townshend, established a new ministry in January 1770, he received the king's consent to work toward a better arrangement with the colonies. On March 5, 1770, Lord North persuaded Parliament to repeal all the Townshend Duties except the one on tea. The move defused the colonial boycott, but it offered too little too late. Like the earlier Declaratory Act, this measure reaffirmed Parliament's disputed right to tax the colonists at will. Moreover, it came on the exact day that violence and bloodshed were escalating in Boston.

The Boston Massacre

After the *Liberty* riot in June 1768, tensions had mounted in Boston, especially with the arrival in October of two regiments of British soldiers, well armed and dressed in their traditional red coats. According to Real Whig beliefs, any appearance by a standing army in peacetime constituted danger. Artisans in a sluggish economy welcomed the increased business that the men in uniform generated, but numerous unemployed workers resented the soldiers' "moonlighting," trying to earn extra pay by applying for local jobs. With 4,000 armed men encamped in a seaport of scarcely 16,000, confrontation seemed inevitable. Affairs "cannot long remain in the state they are now in," wrote one observer late in 1769; "they are hastening to a crisis. What will be the event, God knows."

In March 1770, protesters took to the streets after a run-in between local workers and job-seeking soldiers. Rumors spread about a larger confrontation, and on March 5, around 9 p.m.,

Boston Gazette, Description of the Boston Massacre

■ In Paul Revere's image of the 1770 Boston Massacre, a moon lights up the night scene. British soldiers defend the hated customs house, which Revere labels clearly as "Butcher's Hall." The partisan engraving spread an anti-British view of the bloody event.

a crowd gathered outside the customs house. When a harassed sentry struck a boy with his rifle butt, angry witnesses pelted the guard with snowballs. As fellow soldiers pushed through the mob to assist him, firebells summoned more townspeople to the scene. The British loaded their rifles and aimed at the crowd, their bayonets fixed.

Into this tense standoff marched several dozen sailors, waving banners and brandishing clubs. Their leader was Crispus Attucks, an imposing ex-slave who stood 6 feet 2 inches. The son of a black man and an Indian woman, he had run away from his master and then taken up a life at sea. Damning the soldiers and daring them to fire, Attucks pressed his band of colonial sailors to the front, waving a long stick in the moonlight. In the mayhem, a British gun went off, prompting a volley of fire from the other soldiers. The crowd recoiled in disbelief at the sight of dead and wounded Americans lying in the street. According to a printed report, Attucks and four others had been "killed on the Spot." The anti-British cause had its first martyrs.

By grim coincidence, the bloody episode in New England occurred only hours after Lord North addressed the House of Commons to urge removal of most Townshend Duties. His effort at reconciliation immediately became lost in a wave of hostile publicity. Paul Revere, a Boston silversmith, captured the incident in an inflammatory engraving. The Sons of Liberty quickly named the event of March 5 the Boston Massacre. "On that night," John Adams remarked, "the foundation of American independence was laid."

The *Gaspee* Affair

The overzealous conduct of customs officers gave colonists further cause for distrust. In 1769, after crown agents confiscated John Hancock's vessel, the *Liberty*, and converted it into a customs vessel, citizens in Newport, Rhode Island, destroyed the sloop. In the Delaware River region, residents jailed a customs collector in 1770, and the next year local protesters stormed a customs schooner and beat up the crew. In June 1772, the *Gaspee*, another customs boat said to harass local shipping, ran aground near Pawtuxet, Rhode Island. In a midnight attack, more than a hundred raiders descended on the stranded schooner and set fire to the vessel.

The destruction of the *Gaspee* renewed sharp antagonisms. The irate Earl of Hillsborough, secretary of state for the American colonies, sent a royal commission from London to investigate and to transport suspects to England for trial. But many of the attackers, such as John Brown of Providence, came from important Rhode Island families. Even a £500 reward could not induce local inhabitants to name participants. Besides, many viewed the order to deport accused citizens to England as a denial of their fundamental right to trial by a jury of their peers.

When the colonists took action, Virginia's House of Burgesses again led the way, as it had in the Stamp Act crisis. In March 1773, Patrick Henry, Thomas Jefferson, and Richard Henry Lee pushed through a resolution establishing a standing committee to look into the *Gaspee* affair and to keep up "Correspondence and Communication with our sister colonies" regarding the protection of rights. Following Virginia's example, ten other colonial legislatures promptly established their own Committees of Correspondence. In Massachusetts, similar committees sprang up linking individual towns. Within months a new act of Parliament, designed to rescue the powerful East India Company from bankruptcy, gave these emerging communication networks their first test.

Launching a Revolution

In 1767, before Parliament imposed the Townshend Duties, Americans annually imported nearly 870,000 pounds of tea from England. But the boycott movement cut that amount to less than 110,000 pounds by 1770; colonists turned to smuggling Dutch blends and brewing homemade root teas. When nonimportation schemes lapsed in the early 1770s, purchase of English tea resumed, though a duty remained in effect. Encouraged by this apparent acceptance of parliamentary taxation, Lord North addressed the problem facing the East India Company, which owed a huge debt to the Bank of England and had 18 million pounds of unsold tea rotting in London warehouses. Many MPs held stock in the East India Company, so Parliament passed a law to assist the ailing establishment.

The Tempest over Tea

The Tea Act of 1773 let the struggling East India Company bypass the expensive requirement that merchants ship Asian tea through England on its way to colonial ports. Now they could send the product directly to the colonies or to foreign ports, without paying to unload, store, auction, and reload the heavy chests. Any warehouse tea destined for the colonies would have its English duty refunded. These steps would reduce retail prices and expand the tea market. They would also quietly confirm the right of Parliament to collect a tea tax of threepence per pound.

The company promptly chose prominent colonial merchants to receive and distribute more than 600,000 pounds of tea. These consignees would earn a hefty 6 percent commission. But wary colonists in port towns, sensing a repetition of 1765, renewed the tactics that had succeeded against the Stamp Act. Sons of Liberty vowed to prevent tea-laden ships from docking, and crowds pressured local distributors to renounce participation in the scheme. "If they succeed in the sale of that tea," proclaimed New York's Sons of Liberty, "then we may bid adieu to American liberty."

In Boston, where tea worth nearly £10,000 arrived aboard three ships in November, tension ran especially high. The credibility of Governor Thomas Hutchinson, who had taken a hard line toward imperial dissent, had suffered in June when Benjamin Franklin published private correspondence suggesting the governor's willingness to trim colonial rights. When Hutchinson's sons were named tea consignees, the appointments reinforced townspeople's suspicions. The governor could have signed papers letting the three vessels depart. But instead he decided to unload and distribute the tea, by force if necessary.

On December 16, the largest mass meeting of the decade took place at Boston's Old South Church. A crowd of 5,000, including many from other towns, waited in a cold rain to hear whether Hutchinson would relent. When word came that the governor had refused, the cry went up, "Boston Harbor a teapot tonight!" A band of 150 men, disguised as Mohawk Indians and carrying hatchets, marched to the docks and boarded the ships.

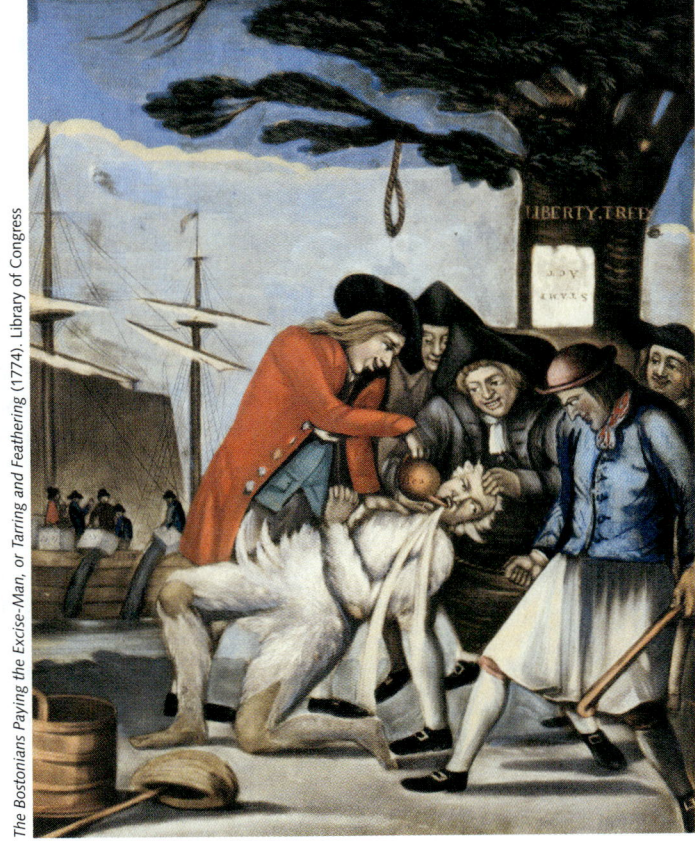

The Bostonians Paying the Excise-Man, or Tarring and Feathering (1774). Library of Congress

■ A 1774 London cartoon expressed anger that Boston's Sons of Liberty, defying British authority, could overturn the Stamp Act, tar and feather revenue agents, dump East India Company tea, and use their "Liberty Tree" to hang officials in effigy.

As several thousand supporters looked on, this disciplined crew spent three hours methodically breaking open chests of tea and dumping the contents overboard. The well-organized operation united participants representing all levels of society—from merchants such as John Hancock to artisans such as George Hewes—and news of the event spurred similar acts of defiance in other ports. Sixty years later, as one of the oldest veterans of the Revolution, Hewes still recalled with special pride his role in "the destruction of the tea."

The Intolerable Acts

"The crisis is come," wrote General Thomas Gage, commander of British forces in America, responding to the costly Tea Party in Boston Harbor; "the provinces must be either British colonies, or independent and separate states." Underestimating the strength of American resolve, Parliament agreed with King George III that only stern measures would reestablish "the obedience which a colony owes to its mother country." Between March and June 1774, it passed four so-called Coercive Acts to isolate and punish Massachusetts.

The first of the Coercive Acts, the Boston Port Act, used British naval strength to cut off the offending town's sea commerce—except for shipments of food and firewood—until the colonists paid for the ruined tea. By the Administration of Justice Act, revenue officials or soldiers charged with murder in Massachusetts (as in the Boston Massacre) could have their trials moved to another colony or to Great Britain. The Quartering Act gave officers more power to requisition living quarters and supplies for their troops throughout the colonies. Most important, the Massachusetts Government Act removed democratic elements from the long-standing Massachusetts Charter of 1691. From now on, the assembly could no longer elect the colony's Upper House, or Council. Instead, the governor would appoint council members, and he would even forbid town meetings unless he gave written permission.

Lord North's government went even further. It replaced Hutchinson with Gage, installing the general as the governor of Massachusetts and granting him special powers and three additional regiments. It also secured passage of the Quebec Act, new legislation to address nagging problems of governance in Canada after a decade of English rule. The act accommodated the Catholic faith and French legal traditions of Quebec's inhabitants. Moreover, it greatly expanded the size of the colony to draw scattered French settlers and traders under colonial government. Suddenly, Quebec took in the entire Great Lakes region and all the lands north of the Ohio River and east of the upper Mississippi River.

Expanding the province of Quebec to the Ohio River might extend British government to French wilderness outposts and help to regulate the Indian trade. But the move also challenged the western land claims of other American colonies. The Quebec Act appeared to favor French Catholics and Ohio Valley Indians—both recent enemies of the crown—over loyal English colonists. Resentment ran especially high in New England, where Protestants had long associated Catholicism with despotism. The Quebec Act, which denied the former French province a representative assembly and jury trials in civil cases, set an ominous precedent for neighboring colonies.

The Coercive Acts and the Quebec Act—lumped together by colonial propagandists as the Intolerable Acts—brought on open rebellion against crown rule. Competing pamphlets debated the proper limits of dissent. In *A Summary View of the Rights of British America*, Thomas Jefferson went beyond criticisms of Parliament to question the king's right to dispense land, control trade, and impose troops in America. Within months, Massachusetts called for a congress of all the colonies and established its own Provincial Congress at Concord, a village 17 miles west of Boston. Out of reach of British naval power, this **de facto** Massachusetts government reorganized the militia into units loyal to its own Committee of Public Safety. These farmer-soldiers became known as Minutemen for their quick response to Gage's repeated efforts to capture patriot gunpowder supplies.

■ **MAP 6.3**
BRITISH NORTH AMERICA, APRIL 1775 Rising colonial unrest brought strong countermeasures. The British government organized regional vice-admiralty courts to punish smugglers; it greatly expanded Quebec in 1774; and it reallocated troops to the Boston area. When warfare erupted there in April 1775, the news spread throughout the colonies within weeks.

From Words to Action

While Massachusetts chafed under new restrictions, shifting coalitions in each colony, ranging from conservative to radical, vied for local political control. Extralegal committees, existing outside the authorized structure of colonial government, took power in hundreds of hamlets. In Edenton, North Carolina, fifty-one women signed a pact to abstain from using imported products for the "publick good." London cartoonists mocked the action as the "Edenton Ladies' Tea Party," but women in other colonies made similar agreements to boycott British tea and textiles. During the summer, all colonies except Georgia selected representatives to the First Continental Congress.

In September 1774, fifty-six delegates convened at Carpenters Hall in Philadelphia. Most had never met before, and they disagreed sharply over how to respond to the Intolerable Acts. Joseph Galloway, a wealthy lawyer and land speculator from Pennsylvania, urged a compromise with Britain modeled on the Albany Congress of 1754. His plan called for the creation of a separate American parliament, a grand council with delegates elected by the colonial legislatures. The less conservative delegates opposed this idea for a colonial federation, under a president-general appointed by the king. Led by Patrick Henry of Virginia, they managed to table the Galloway Plan by a narrow vote.

When Paul Revere arrived from Boston on October 6, bearing a set of militant resolves passed in his own Suffolk County, further rifts appeared. Moderates from the South expressed sympathy for Massachusetts but still resisted calls for a nonexportation scheme that would withhold southern tobacco, rice, and indigo from Great Britain. By the time the Congress adjourned in late October, it had issued a Declaration of Rights and passed a range of measures that seemed to balance competing views. On one hand, the Congress endorsed the fiery Suffolk Resolves, which condemned Parliament's Coercive Acts as unconstitutional and spoke of preparation for war. On the other, it humbly petitioned the king for relief from the crisis and professed continued loyalty. But in practical terms, Galloway and the more conservative members had suffered defeat. Most importantly, the delegates signed an agreement to prohibit British imports and halt all exports to Britain except rice. They called for local committees to enforce this so-called Association, and they set a date—May 10, 1775—for a Second Congress.

DOCUMENT
"Give Me Liberty or Give Me Death"

Before delegates could meet again in Philadelphia, the controversy that had smoldered for more than a decade on both sides of the Atlantic erupted into open combat. Predictably, the explosion took place in Massachusetts, where General Gage had received secret orders to arrest the leaders of the Massachusetts Provincial Congress and regain the upper hand before the strained situation grew worse. He was to use force, even if it meant the outbreak of warfare.

■ The shots fired at dawn by British troops, dispersing local militia from Lexington's town green, were the opening volley of the American Revolution. Amos Doolittle, a Connecticut soldier who responded to the alarm, later depicted the events of April 19, 1775. The date is still honored in New England as Patriots' Day.

On April 18, Gage ordered 700 elite troops from Boston to row across the Charles River at night, march 10 miles to Lexington, and seize John Hancock and Sam Adams. Next, the soldiers were to proceed 7 miles to Concord to capture a stockpile of military supplies. Alerted by signal lanterns, express riders Paul Revere and William Dawes eluded British patrols and spurred their horses toward Lexington along separate routes to warn Hancock and Adams. Bells and alarm guns spread the word that the British were coming. By the time the British soldiers reached Lexington, shortly before sunrise, some seventy militiamen had assembled on the town green. When the villagers refused to lay down their arms, the redcoats dispersed them in a brief skirmish that left eight militiamen dead.

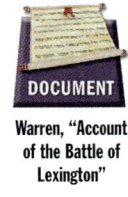

Warren, "Account of the Battle of Lexington"

The British column trudged west to Concord and searched the town for munitions. Four hundred Minutemen who had streamed in from neighboring communities advanced on the town in double file, with orders not to shoot unless the British fired first. At the small bridge over the Concord River, British regulars opened fire. "The shot heard 'round the world" killed two men. The Americans loosed a volley in return, killing three. By noon, exhausted British forces were retreating toward Boston in disarray. The redcoats made easy targets for the more than 1,000 Americans who shot at them from behind stone walls. A relief party prevented annihilation, but the British suffered severe losses: seventy-three killed and 200 wounded or missing. The Americans, with only forty-nine dead, had turned the tables on General Gage, transforming an aggressive raid into a punishing defeat.

Conclusion

For Britain, festering administrative problems in America had suddenly become a military emergency. A decade of assertive but inconsistent British policies had transformed the colonists' sense of good will toward London into angry feelings of persecution and betrayal. The years of incessant argument and misunderstanding reminded many, on both sides of the Atlantic, of watching a stable, prosperous household unravel into mutual recrimination. A once-healthy family was becoming increasingly dysfunctional and troubled. The assertive children grew steadily in strength; the aging parents chafed at their diminished respect. Predictably, authorities in London found the once-dependent colonists to be ungrateful, intemperate, and occasionally paranoid. With equal assurance, the American subjects saw Parliament, government ministers, and eventually the king himself as uninformed, selfish, and even deceitful.

Britain's overseas empire, which had expanded steadily for two centuries, now seemed on the verge of splitting apart. As the limits of imperial control in North America became more evident, colonists worked to overcome the regional and ethnic differences that had long been a fact of eighteenth-century life. Political independence no longer seemed implausible. With effort, class hostilities and urban-rural divisions could also be overcome. Redirecting old local resentments toward the British crown could increase a sense of unity among people with different personal backgrounds and resources.

Nor would British colonists be alone if they mounted a rebellion. On one hand, they could make the unlikely choice of liberating half a million slaves, empowering colonial women, and embracing the anti-British cause of Pontiac and numerous Native Americans. Such revolutionary moves would increase their strength dramatically in one direction. On the other hand, they could also take a more cautious and less democratic route. If men of substance could gain control of the forces that were being unleashed, they might curb potential idealism among slaves, women, tenant farmers, and the urban poor, giving precedence instead to policies that would win vital support from the continent of Europe in an American fight for independence. France, recently evicted from North America, and Spain, anxious about British designs in the Pacific, might both be willing allies, despite their commitment to monarchy. Such an alliance, if it ever came about, could push the limits of British imperial control to the breaking point.

Sites to Visit

Anza-Borrego Desert State Park
http://anza.uoregon.edu

This isolated and beautiful state park covers 600,000 acres 80 miles east of San Diego, California. The Web site, which focuses on the exploration of Alta, California, 1774–1776, contains maps, resources, and documents in both English and Spanish concerning Juan Bautista de Anza's two overland expeditions.

Museums in Alaska

Located near the ferry landing in Kodiak, Alaska, the Baranov Museum is housed in one of the few remaining structures from the Russian colonial era. In Fairbanks, the University of Alaska's impressive Museum of the North has added a new wing. The Anchorage Museum of History and Art contains an Alaska Gallery.

Fort Ross State Historic Park

This reconstruction of the outpost built by the Russians on the northern California coast in the early nineteenth century is located on a scenic bluff 11 miles northwest of the town of Jenner on Highway 1, about a two-hour drive from San Francisco.

Pontiac Marker

In 1977 Michigan placed a marker concerning Pontiac on a building at 3321 East Jefferson Avenue, near the Renaissance Center in downtown Detroit. It commemorates the Battle of Bloody Run, in July 1763, which marked the height of Pontiac's siege of Detroit. The city of Pontiac, named for the Ottawa leader, lies 25 miles northwest.

Boston's Freedom Trail
http://www.nps.gov/bost/freedom_trail.htm

This 2.5-mile self-guided walking tour begins at Boston Common. Stops include the Boston Massacre site, the Old South Meeting House where the Boston Tea Party began, Paul Revere's house, and the Granary Burial Ground, where Revere, John Hancock, Samuel Adams, and Crispus Attucks are all buried.

Colonial Williamsburg
http://www.history.org

This tourist site in Virginia, suitable for all ages, features shops, homes, and public buildings as they existed in the 1770s. In the Capitol Building on Duke of Gloucester Street, Patrick Henry stirred the House of Burgesses to oppose the Stamp Act in 1765. Costumed guides offer interpretations and candlelight tours.

Tryon's Palace

Governor William Tryon erected this building in New Bern, North Carolina, in 1768 over the protests of Regulators. The Georgian mansion, with a handsome garden overlooking the Trent River, served as the colony's first capitol. Now restored, Tryon Palace Historic Sites and Gardens is 112 miles east of Raleigh, the current capital.

Alamance Battleground

At this site, located on Route 62 near Burlington, North Carolina, Governor Tryon's forces defeated the Regulators in 1771. In historic Hillsborough, 30 miles east, a plaque on a hillside at the end of King Street on the east side of the town marks the site where Regulator leaders were hanged.

For Further Reading

General

Jack P. Greene, ed., *Colonies to Nation: A Documentary History of the American Revolution* (1975).

Merrill Jensen, *The Founding of a Nation: A History of the American Revolution, 1763–1776* (1968).

Pauline Maier, *From Resistance to Revolution: Colonial Radicals and the Development of American Opposition to Britain, 1765–1776* (1972).

Robert Middlekauff, *The Glorious Cause: The American Revolution, 1763–1789* (1982).

Alfred F. Young, ed., *The American Revolution: Explorations in the History of American Radicalism* (1976).

New Challenges to Spain's Expanded Empire

John Francis Bannon, *The Spanish Borderlands Frontier, 1513–1821* (1970).

Lydia T. Black, *Russians in Alaska, 1732–1867* (2004).

Richard Hough, *Captain James Cook* (1994).

John L. Kessell, *Spain in the Southwest: A Narrative History of Colonial New Mexico, Arizona, Texas, and California* (2002).

Mark Santiago, *Massacre at the Yuma Crossing: Spanish Relations with the Quechans, 1779–1782* (1998).

Barbara Sweetland Smith and Redmond J. Barnett, eds., *Russian America: The Forgotten Frontier* (1990).

New Challenges to Britain's Expanded Empire

John K. Alexander, *Samuel Adams: America's Revolutionary Politician* (2002).

John L. Bullion, *A Great and Necessary Measure: George Grenville and the Genesis of the Stamp Act, 1763–1765* (1982).

Colin G. Calloway, *The Scratch of a Pen: 1763 and the Transformation of North America* (2006).

Arthur H. Cash, *John Wilkes: The Scandalous Father of Civil Liberty* (2006).

Gregory E. Dowd, *A Spirited Resistance: The North American Indian Struggle for Unity, 1745–1815* (1992).

Edmund S. Morgan and Helen M. Morgan, *The Stamp Act Crisis: Prologue to Revolution*, 3rd ed. (1995).

"The Unconquerable Rage of the People"

Bernard Bailyn, *The Ideological Origins of the American Revolution* (1967).

Edward Countryman, *A People in Revolution: The American Revolution and Political Society in New York, 1760–1790* (1981).

Ronald Hoffman, *A Spirit of Dissention: Economics, Politics, and the Revolution in Maryland* (1973).

Marjoleine Kars, *Breaking Loose Together: The Regulator Rebellion in Pre-Revolutionary North Carolina* (2002).

A Conspiracy of Corrupt Ministers?

Bernard Bailyn, *The Ordeal of Thomas Hutchinson* (1974).

Woody Holton, *Forced Founders: Indians, Debtors, Slaves, and the Making of the American Revolution in Virginia* (1999).

Peter D. G. Thomas, *The Townshend Duties Crisis: The Second Phase of the American Revolution, 1767–1773* (1987).

John W. Tyler, *Smugglers and Patriots: Boston Merchants and the Advent of the American Revolution* (1986).

Launching a Revolution

David Hackett Fischer, *Paul Revere's Ride* (1994).

Benjamin Woods Labaree, *The Boston Tea Party* (1964).

Peter D. G. Thomas, *Tea Party to Independence: The Third Phase of the American Revolution, 1773–1776* (1991).

Alfred F. Young, *The Shoemaker and the Tea Party: Memory and the American Revolution* (1999).

For quizzes and other resources on these topics, go to www.longmanamericanhistory.com.

1776	Thomas Paine, *Common Sense*
	Declaration of Independence
	New Jersey gives women holding property the right to vote
	Washington crosses the Delaware
1777	Burgoyne surrenders at Saratoga
1778	United States forges an alliance with France
1779	Sullivan's campaign against the Iroquois
1780	Charleston falls to the British
1781	Articles of Confederation ratified
	Cornwallis surrenders at Yorktown
1783	Treaty of Paris
	Newburgh Conspiracy is thwarted
1785	Land Ordinance of 1785
1786	Shays's Rebellion
1787	Constitutional Convention meets in Philadelphia
	Northwest Ordinance creates Northwest Territory
	Constitution of the United States is signed
1789	George Washington is elected the first president of the United States
	U.S. Constitution goes into effect after ratification by nine states
	Judiciary Act of 1789
1790	First U.S. Census enumerates population of 4 million
	Congress restricts citizenship to "free white persons"
	Northern states take steps to abolish slavery
	Miami Chief Little Turtle scores victory over U.S. troops

PART THREE

The Unfinished Revolution, 1775–1803

IN 1775 GREAT BRITAIN STILL POSSESSED ALL OF NORTH AMERICA EAST of the Mississippi River, from Hudson Bay to the Gulf of Mexico. If the British could suppress the troublesome rebellion along the Atlantic seaboard, their prospects for expansion in America looked promising. Farther west, Spain had recently acquired the vast Louisiana Territory from France. The Spanish retained their dominance in the Southwest, and they were finally beginning to expand their claim to California by building a series of new missions and presidios.

By 1803, however, the broad picture had changed markedly. In the Pacific Ocean, Europeans had encountered the Hawaiian Islands for the first time, Russian fur traders had consolidated their hold in Alaska, and Spanish vessels along the Pacific coast faced increasing competition from the ships of rival nations. The British still held Canada and Florida, but the thirteen rebellious colonies had become an independent republic and had started to acquire new territories. The most spectacular acquisition was the Louisiana Territory, which the United States purchased in 1803, after Spain returned the region to the control of France.

Few could have foreseen such an unlikely series of events in such a brief span of time. Thomas Jefferson drafted the Declaration of Independence in 1776 at age thirty-three. His generation had reluctantly become the effective leaders of a revolutionary movement by the mid-1770s. They contended ably with those who pushed for greater democratization, those who desired the stability of military rule, and even those who longed for the protection of the British monarchy.

These unlikely revolutionary leaders were by no means united in all their views and actions. They argued fervently over constitutional issues, domestic policies, and foreign alignments. Most managed to reap personal rewards from the new society's collective success. And they saw to it that these rewards reached far beyond their own households. Urban artisans, frontier farmers, and immigrant newcomers benefited from the removal of monarchy.

Such positive developments inspired optimism for many, both at home and abroad. Yet although the revolutionary era fulfilled the expectations of numerous citizens, it failed to meet the hopes and aspirations of other

Americans. Many American merchants and planters, indebted to British interests before 1776, gained by the separation from Great Britain as creditors and investors in the new society. Many frontier farmers and army veterans, on the other hand, faced burdensome debts after the Revolutionary War.

Women worried that the numerous written constitutions of the period were unresponsive to their interests. In 1776 New Jersey gave the vote to "all free inhabitants" who were also property holders. This included some single women, and in 1790 the state's election law referred specifically to "he or she" among voters. But this novel provision was undone a generation later, in 1807, when New Jersey men objected to the idea of any women having the right to vote. From New Hampshire to Georgia, committed "Daughters of Liberty" had made possible colonial boycotts through their industry and had managed families, farms, and businesses during the dislocations of war. Female access to education and the courts improved somewhat in the last quarter of the eighteenth century, but for most American women the advances were more symbolic than real.

For African Americans the disappointments were greater still. British offers of freedom prompted thousands of southern slaves to take up the Loyalist cause at great personal risk. Other free blacks and slaves, primarily in the North, shouldered arms for the Patriots, drawn by the rhetoric of liberty and the prospect of advancement. Even though they had chosen the winning side, they reaped few benefits. Although the number of free blacks expanded after the Revolutionary War, the African slave trade to the United States resumed and gained official protection. Slavery itself gained renewed significance with the transition to cotton production in the South and a federal constitution that sanctioned the power of slaveholders. Even in the North, where gradual emancipation became the norm by the end of the century, free blacks found their welcome into white churches and schools to be so half-hearted that many began organizing their own separate institutions.

Eastern Indians, like African Americans, had good reason to distrust the Revolution and its leaders. The majority, including most Iroquois and Cherokee warriors, sided with the British and paid a steep price in defeat. Throughout the Mississippi Valley, Native Americans who still remembered the benefits of French trade and British military support faced relentless pressure as American speculators, soldiers, and settlers dissected their homelands. After 1803, government officials promised that the newly acquired lands beyond the Mississippi would become an Indian Territory, providing a refuge for displaced eastern tribes. If so, what was to become of the Native American nations that already inhabited the western plains?

Like most political upheavals, the American Revolution left many questions unanswered and much business unfinished. Even the new federal government itself, in operation for little more than a decade by 1803, remained a work in progress. The specific roles and relative power of the government's three separate branches spurred endless debate, as did the proper place of the military and the most suitable direction for foreign policy. The Constitution ratified in 1789 seemed promising, but it remained an uncertain and largely untested framework.

1791	Bill of Rights is ratified Saint Domingue slave revolt Alexander Hamilton, "Report on the Subject of Manufactures" Samuel Slater constructs first spinning machine on U.S. soil Bank of the United States is chartered
1792	Washington is reelected president Mary Wollstonecraft, *Vindication of the Rights of Woman*
1793	Washington issues Neutrality Proclamation Eli Whitney invents the cotton gin
1794	U.S. troops defeat forces of Ohio Confederacy Whiskey Rebellion
1795	Jay's Treaty Treaty of San Lorenzo
1796	Washington's farewell address John Adams is elected president
1797	XYZ Affair
1798	Quasi War with France (to 1800) Alien and Sedition Acts Kentucky and Virginia Resolutions (1798–1799)
1799	Seneca Leader Handsome Lake proclaims *gai'wiio*, or "Good Message"
1800	Thomas Jefferson is elected president Gabriel plot is exposed in Richmond, Virginia
1801	Judiciary Act of 1801 War against Barbary pirates Spain secretly cedes Louisiana Territory to France
1803	Louisiana Purchase *Marbury v. Madison*

CHAPTER 7

Revolutionaries at War, 1775–1783

CHAPTER OUTLINE

"Things Are Now Come to That Crisis"

Declaring Independence

The Struggle to Win French Support

Legitimate States, a Respectable Military

The Long Road to Yorktown

Conclusion

Sites to Visit

For Further Reading

In 1775 African-born Thomas Peters was a thirty-seven-year-old slave in Wilmington, North Carolina. As a young man, he had been taken from what is now Nigeria and shipped to Louisiana aboard a French slave ship. Forced to cut sugar cane, Peters rebelled so often that his owner sold him to a merchant on North Carolina's Cape Fear River. There he received his English name, operated a grist mill, and started a family. Still enslaved, Peters was working as a millwright and living with his wife, Sally, age twenty-two, and their four-year-old daughter, Clairy, by the eve of the Revolutionary War.

During the fifteen years between Peters's abduction from Africa in 1760 and the outbreak of hostilities between America and Britain in 1775, nearly 225,000 people had streamed into the British mainland colonies. More than half came from the British Isles (125,000), and another 15,000 arrived from elsewhere in Europe. But the remaining 85,000 newcomers—or four in every ten—had all been purchased in Africa and enslaved in the coastal South. Thomas Peters, entering from Louisiana, was among the recent arrivals in British America.

In the summer of 1775, Peters must have heard talk about possible slave revolts in Virginia and the Carolinas. Before the end of the year, he certainly knew that Virginia's governor, Lord Dunmore, had offered freedom to slaves who would take up arms for the British. The following March, ships of the Royal Navy arrived at Cape Fear River. The fleet offered to provide safe haven for any slaves escaping from Patriot masters. Joining other black

■ Escaped slave Thomas Peters took part in the British fleet's unsuccessful attempt to seize control of Charleston Harbor in June 1776. A South Carolina soldier painted this view of British ships afire the morning after the attack.

164

families, Tom and Sally Peters risked arrest to gain their personal liberty by bolting to the British vessels.

Peters was with the British fleet when General Henry Clinton's forces tried to take Charleston, South Carolina, in June 1776. Throughout the war, Peters served in a unit called the Black Pioneers. Wounded twice, he rose to the rank of sergeant and earned the promise of a farm in British Canada. In 1783, as defeated Loyalists left New York City at the end of the war, he joined other Black Pioneers aboard the *Joseph James*, bound for Nova Scotia. With him were Sally, Clairy, and eighteen-month-old John. Departing in November, the ship was blown off course by foul weather. The ex-slaves spent the winter at Bermuda before finally joining 3,500 other black Loyalists in Nova Scotia in May 1784.

After he and others had been stripped of promised farmland in Nova Scotia, Peters ventured to London in 1790 to protest their treatment. In England, he met with British abolitionists who were planning a colony of former slaves in West Africa. Returning to Canada with this news, he led 1,200 African Americans to Sierra Leone, where he died at Freetown in 1792. In thirty-two years, Peters had seen New Orleans, Wilmington, Charleston, Philadelphia, New York, Bermuda, Halifax, and London. (See Map 7.1.) He had escaped after sixteen years of enslavement and gone to war, fighting for his freedom and for the safety of family and friends.

Though Thomas Peters's saga is unusual, it helps to illustrate that the War of American Independence was not a two-sided struggle, with English colonists unified to oppose the English monarchy. Instead, like most revolutions, it was a conflict fought by shifting coalitions. In a time of strife, there were countless possibilities for forging political "marriages of convenience" between different regions, groups, and interests.

Within each small community, and within the Atlantic theater as a whole, alliances often proved the old adage that "My enemy's enemy is my friend." Thomas Peters escaped servitude to join the British in part because the man holding him in slavery was a leading member of the local Sons of Liberty. Likewise, powerful merchants like John Hancock and Henry Laurens threw in their lot with the people because they had grown disillusioned with Parliament's political and commercial controls. On the international scale, the monarchies of France and Spain swallowed their dislike for American rhetoric to join in a war that allowed them an opportunity to attack their long-standing rival, Britain. On the other hand, many Cherokee and Iroquois Indians, disillusioned by contact with land-hungry settlers, cast their lot with the British forces from overseas.

These numerous alliances remained problematic and incomplete. Not all Iroquois warriors or African slaves sided with the British, and by no means all New England merchants or Virginia planters embraced the Patriot cause. In a landscape marked by uncertainty, large numbers of people at all levels of society opted for cautious neutrality as long as they could, while others shifted their allegiance as the winds changed. The final outcome of the conflict, therefore, remained a source of doubt. Looking back, Americans often view the results of the Revolutionary War as inevitable, perhaps even foreordained. In fact, the end result—and thus independence itself—hung in the balance for years.

Patriots and Slaves Toppling Statue of George III

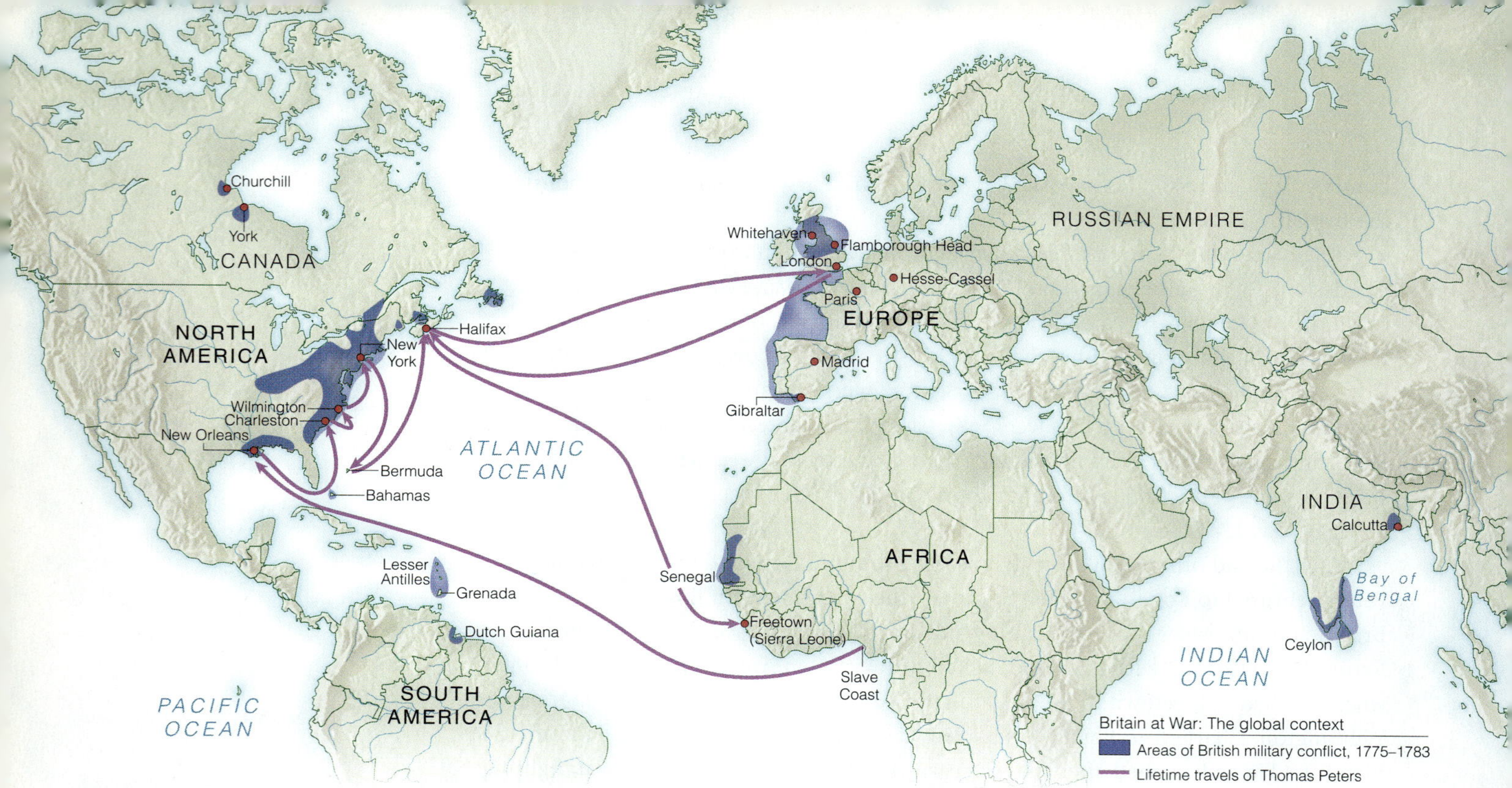

■ **MAP 7.1**

BRITAIN AT WAR: THE GLOBAL CONTEXT, 1778–1783 For Britain, the war that began in 1775 expanded into a worldwide conflict against rival European powers within three years. By 1783 the British lost American colonies while expanding their hold in India. The lifetime journey of African-born Thomas Peters, shown here, is clearly exceptional, but extensive movements figured in many lives during these years of warfare. General Cornwallis, for example, went on to serve the British in India after his defeat at Yorktown in 1781.

"Things Are Now Come to That Crisis"

New England's Minutemen had rallied swiftly at Lexington. In the ensuing months, Congress took the initial steps to form a Continental Army. It also launched efforts to force the British out of Boston and to pull Canada into the rebellion. If these predominantly Protestant rebels hoped to draw the French Catholics of Quebec into their revolt, would free whites also be eager to include the blacks of Boston, Williamsburg, and Charleston in the struggle for liberty? Or would it be the British who recruited more African Americans such as Thomas Peters and furnished them with arms? The answers to such questions became clear in the fifteen months between the skirmish at Lexington and the decision of Congress to declare political independence from Britain in July 1776.

The Second Continental Congress Takes Control

Enthusiasm ran high in Philadelphia in May 1775 as the Second Continental Congress assembled, and the delegates moved quickly to put the colonies on a wartime footing. They instructed New York to build fortifications, and they paid for a dozen companies of riflemen to be sent north to aid the Minutemen surrounding Boston. They created an Army Department under the command of a New York aristocrat, General Philip Schuyler, and approved an issue of $2 million in currency to fund the military buildup.

In late May, word arrived from Lake Champlain in New York of a victory for soldiers under Benedict Arnold of Connecticut and for the Green Mountain Boys, Vermont-area farmers led by Ethan Allen. They had captured Fort Ticonderoga, along with its cannons, and the new Army Department badly needed all such heavy arms. This initiative not only secured the Hudson Valley against a British attack from the north; it also allowed Schuyler to propose a strike against Montreal and Quebec via Lake Champlain. Congress approved the assault, to be led by General Richard Montgomery. It also approved a daring scheme submitted by Arnold. He planned to lead separate forces up the Kennebec River. They would assist Montgomery in seizing Quebec and winning Canada before the region could become a staging ground for British armies.

But no single action by Congress had greater implications than the one taken on June 15, 1775. That day, members voted unanimously to appoint George Washington, a forty-three-year-old delegate from Virginia, "to command all the continental forces." Colonel Washington already headed a committee drawing up regulations to run the new army, and he had notable military experience. But his strongest asset may have been his southern roots. Northern delegates sensed the need to foster colonial unity by placing a non–New Englander in charge of the army outside Boston. In military and political terms, the selection of Washington proved auspicious. The tall, imposing planter from Mount Vernon emerged as a durable and respected leader in both war and peace. But putting a slaveholder in command also closed certain radical options. It signaled the beginning of an important alliance between the well-to-do regional leaders of the North and South, contributing to the particular shape of the Federal Constitution a dozen years later.

■ In June 1775, Congress selected a wealthy Virginia planter to command its army. The choice of George Washington reassured southern slave owners and disappointed blacks and whites in the North who saw slavery as a contradiction in the struggle for freedom.

"Liberty to Slaves"

The selection of Washington sent a strong message to half a million African Americans, spurring many of them to risk siding with the British. For their part, the British sensed an opportunity to undermine rebellious planters. In June 1775, the British commander in America, Thomas Gage, wrote to London: "Things are now come to that crisis, that we must avail ourselves of every resource, even to raise the Negros, in our cause."

In the South, rumors of liberation swept through the large African American community during 1775. Slaveholding rebel authorities countered with harsh measures to quell black unrest. In South Carolina that spring, attention focused on a prominent free black man named Thomas Jeremiah, a skilled pilot in the busy port of Charleston. In April, Jeremiah supposedly told an enslaved dockworker of a great war coming and urged slaves to seize the opportunity. Weeks later, nervous Patriot planters made the well-known free black into a scapegoat, accusing him of involvement in a plot to smuggle guns ashore from British ships to support a slave uprising. In August 1775, despite a lack of hard evidence against him, Jeremiah was publicly hanged and then burned.

That September, a Georgia delegate to Congress made a startling comment. If British troops were to land on the southern coast with a supply of food and guns, he said, and offer freedom to slaves who would join them, 20,000 blacks from Georgia and South Carolina would materialize in no time. In November, the beleaguered royal governor of Virginia, Lord Dunmore, attempted just such a scheme. Dunmore issued a proclamation granting freedom to the slaves of rebel masters who agreed to take up arms on behalf of the king. Hundreds responded to Dunmore's proclamation. They formed the Ethiopian Regiment and wore sashes proclaiming "Liberty to Slaves."

The Siege of Boston

In the North, British forces had been confined in Boston ever since the Battle of Lexington. They would remain isolated on the town's main peninsula for nearly a year, supported by the Royal Navy. In early July 1775, Washington arrived at nearby Cambridge to take up his command and oversee the siege of Boston. He quickly set out to improve order among his men, tightening discipline, calming regional jealousies, and removing incompetent officers. In addition, he wrote scores of letters to civilian political leaders and the president of Congress to muster support for his feeble army.

Washington made clear that nearly everything was in short supply, from tents and uniforms to muskets and cannons. He dispatched twenty-five-year-old Henry Knox, a former bookseller and future general, to retrieve the cannons captured at Ticonderoga. The Patriots' siege could not succeed without heavy fieldpieces to bombard the city from the heights at Dorchester and Charlestown that lay across the water from Boston.

Even before Washington's arrival, the British and the Americans had vied for control of these strategic heights. Indeed, General Gage drew up plans to secure Charlestown peninsula by seizing its highest point, Bunker Hill. But the Patriots learned of the scheme. On the night of June 16, 1775, they moved to fortify the area. The next afternoon, 1,500 Patriots confronted the full force of the British army in the Battle of Bunker Hill.

Gage might easily have sealed off Charlestown peninsula with his naval power. Instead, he used 2,500 British infantry to launch three frontal attacks from the shoreline. The first two uphill charges fell back, but a third assault finally dislodged the Americans. Although the battle of Bunker Hill was technically a British victory, success came at a terrible price. The encounter left forty-two percent of British troops (1,054 men) wounded or dead—the worst casualty figures of the war. Gage lost his command, replaced by General William Howe, and the Royal Army no longer appeared invincible.

With Washington and his army encamped outside Boston, Henry Knox worked to retrieve the British **ordnance** captured at Ticonderoga. Using oxen, sledges, and local volunteers, he hauled forty-three heavy cannons east, across trails covered with snow and ice, from the Hudson Valley to the coast. His men delivered the guns in late winter, and in March 1776 the Americans, in a surprise move, placed them on Dorchester Heights, where they could bombard the enemy huddled in Boston. Threatened, and unable to counterattack, Britain's General Howe evacuated his army, retreating by ship to Halifax, Nova Scotia. There, he made plans to attack the rebels again at New York, where Loyalist support was stronger.

Declaring Independence

As Washington laid siege to Boston, other Americans converged on British forces in Canada. General Montgomery's troops seized Montreal in November 1775. They then descended the St. Lawrence River to join Benedict Arnold's men, who had struggled north toward Quebec under brutal winter conditions. Their combined force attacked the walled city during a fierce snowstorm on the night of December 30. But their assault failed, and Montgomery perished in the fighting. When British reinforcements reached Quebec in May, the Americans retreated toward Lake Champlain. They left behind most of their baggage and hundreds of sick companions, dying from smallpox. Hundreds more died during the withdrawal or spread the deadly pox as they returned to New England towns. Everywhere, strained loyalty to the British was turning to explosive anger.

DOCUMENT
"Common Sense" by Thomas Paine

"Time to Part"

In January 1776, a brilliant pamphlet, *Common Sense*, captured the shifting mood and helped propel Americans toward independence. The author, a former corsetmaker named Thomas

Paine, had endured personal and economic failures in England before sailing to Philadelphia in 1774 at age thirty-seven. To this passionate man, with his gift for powerful prose, America represented a fresh start, and Paine poured his energy into bold newspaper essays.

Common Sense sold an amazing 120,000 copies in three months. Paine promised to lay out "simple facts, plain arguments, and common sense" on the precarious American situation. He lambasted "the so much boasted constitution of England," attacking hereditary monarchy and the divine right of kings. "One honest man," Paine proclaimed, is worth more "than all the crowned ruffians that ever lived." He urged the creation of an independent constitutional republic that could become "an asylum for all mankind." "Reconciliation is now a fallacious dream," he argued: "'TIS TIME TO PART."

Paine's **avid** readers agreed. In the spring of 1776, one colony after another instructed its representatives to the Second Continental Congress to vote for independence. But many among the well-to-do held strong social and economic ties to London. They feared the loss of British imperial protection and the startling upsurge of democratic political activity among the lower orders. At first, Congress vacillated. Finally, with no sign of accommodation from England, most members agreed with Robert Livingston of New York that "they should yield to the torrent if they hoped to direct its course." In early June, young Livingston, age thirty, joined the committee assigned to prepare a formal statement declaring independence from Great Britain. The Committee of Five also included Benjamin Franklin, John Adams, Roger Sherman, and the second youngest member of the Continental Congress, Thomas Jefferson.

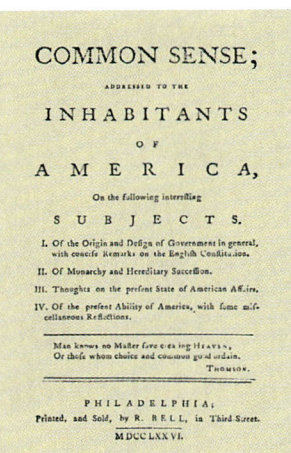

The thirty-three-year-old Jefferson willingly took responsibility for crafting the document. He framed a stirring preamble, drawing on British philosopher John Locke's contract theory of government. Locke (1632–1702) believed that the sovereign power ultimately resided not in government but in the people themselves, who chose to submit voluntarily to civil law to protect property and preserve basic rights.

According to Locke, rulers possessed conditional, not absolute, authority over the people. Citizens therefore held the right to end their support and overthrow any government that did not fulfill its side of the contract. For any people facing "a long train of abuses," Jefferson wrote, "it is their right, it is their duty, to throw off such government and to provide new guards for their future security." He went on to catalogue the "repeated injuries and usurpations" committed by King George III. On July 2, when Congress voted on a statement affirming that "these United Colonies are, and of right, ought to be, Free and Independent States," twelve colonies approved, with the New York delegation abstaining. Having made the fundamental decision, the delegates then considered how to "declare the causes" behind their momentous choice to separate from Great Britain.

John Adams to Abigail Adams (July 3, 1776)

Over the next two days, Congress members edited the draft declaration submitted by the Committee of Five. They kept Jefferson's idealistic assertion that "all men are created equal." But they removed any reference to slavery, except for the charge that the king had "excited domestic insurrections amongst us," a veiled reference to the Thomas Jeremiah debacle in Charleston and to Lord Dunmore's proclamation. With other changes in place, they finally voted to approve the revised Declaration of Independence on July 4, 1776.

Declaration of Independence

John Hancock, the president of the Congress, signed the document with a flourish, and printers hastily turned it into a published broadside. The other signatures (contrary to folklore) came two weeks later, after New York had finally offered its approval. Then fifty-six delegates gathered to sign their names to "The unanimous declaration of the thirteen United States of America." They did so at great risk, for signing the document exposed them to charges of treason, punishable by death.

Signing of the Declaration of Independence

The British Attack New York

While the Second Continental Congress debated independence, the British maneuvered to suppress the rebellion. Strangling the revolt with a naval blockade appeared impossible, given

INTERPRETING HISTORY

"Revoking Those Sacred Trusts Which Are Violated": One of Many Proclamations of Independence (South Carolina, May 1776)

Throughout the late spring of 1776, provincial assemblies, town meetings, and grand juries in the thirteen colonies began issuing their own pronouncements regarding a break with Great Britain. The authors drew on historical precedent, legal tradition, and emotional sentiment. They mixed lofty theory and Real Whig ideology with local concerns. They also incorporated rhetoric and ideas from current pamphlets, speeches, and newspaper essays.

At least ninety of these proclamations survive. Most are more impressive for their strong feelings than for their literary merit. But taken together, they suggest the sentiments, arguments, and words that were in the air when Jefferson drafted the Declaration of Independence. This document was drawn up and signed by fifteen members of the Cheraw District grand jury who came together for their regular court session in Long Bluff, South Carolina, on Monday, May 20, 1776.

Young Martha Ryan used her cipher-book to do more than practice writing. She also drew American ships and flags and embellished the popular rallying cry, "Liberty or Death."

The Presentments of the Grand Jury of and for the Said District

I. When a people, born and bred in a land of freedom and virtue…are convinced of the wicked schemes of

---

the length of the American coastline. But two other strategies emerged—one southern and one northern—that shaped British planning throughout the conflict.

The southern design rested on the assumption that loyalty to the crown remained strongest in the South. If the British could land forces below Chesapeake Bay, support from white loyalists and enslaved blacks might enable them to gain the upper hand and push north to reimpose colonial rule elsewhere. In June 1776, troops under General Henry Clinton arrived off the South Carolina coast with such a mission in mind. On June 28, British ships bombarded Sullivan's Island, at the mouth of Charleston harbor. But the Americans' log fortress withstood the cannon fire, and the attackers withdrew. The British did not renew their southern design for several years, concentrating instead on a separate northern strategy.

According to Britain's northern plan, troops would divide the rebellious colonies in two at the Hudson River valley, seizing New York City and advancing upriver while other forces pushed south from Canada. Then, having sealed off New England, they could finally crush the radicals in Massachusetts who had spearheaded the revolt while restoring the loyalties of inhabitants farther south. Lord George Germain, the aggressive new British cabinet min-

their treacherous rulers to fetter them with the chains of servitude, and rob them of every noble and desirable privilege which distinguishes them as freemen,—justice, humanity, and the immutable laws of *God,* justify and support them in revoking those sacred trusts which are so impiously violated, and placing them in such hands as are most likely to execute them in the manner and for the important ends for which they were first given.

II. The good people of this Colony, with the rest of her sister Colonies, confiding in the justice and merited protection of the King and Parliament of *Great Britain,* ever…esteemed such a bond of union and harmony as the greatest happiness. But when that protection was wantonly withdrawn, and every mark of cruelty and oppression substituted;…self-preservation, and a regard to our own welfare and security, became a consideration both important and necessary. The Parliament and Ministry of *Great Britain,* by their wanton and undeserved persecutions, have reduced this Colony to a state of separation from her…as the only lasting means of future happiness and safety…. Cast off, persecuted, defamed, given up as a prey to every violence and injury, a righteous and much injured people have at length appealed to *God!* and, trusting to his divine justice and their own virtuous perseverance, taken the only and last means of securing their own honour, safety, and happiness.

III. We now feel every joyful and comfortable hope that a people could desire in the present Constitution and form of Government established in this Colony; a Constitution founded on the strictest principles of justice and humanity, where the rights and happiness of the whole, the poor and the rich, are equally secured; and to secure and defend which, it is the particular interest of every individual who regards his own safety and advantage.

IV. When we consider the publick officers of our present form of Government now appointed, as well as the method and duration of their appointment, we cannot but declare our entire satisfaction and comfort; as well in the characters of such men, who are justly esteemed for every virtue, as their well-known abilities to execute the important trusts which they now hold.

V. Under these convictions,…we…recommend it to every man…to secure and defend with his life and fortune a form of Government so just, so equitable, and promising;…that the latest posterity may enjoy the virtuous fruits of that work, which the integrity and fortitude of the present age had, at the expense of their blood and treasure, at length happily effected.

VI. We cannot but declare how great the pleasure, the harmony, and political union which now exists in this District affords; and having no grievances to complain of, only beg leave to recommend that a new Jury list be made for this District, the present being insufficient.

And lastly, we beg leave…that these our presentments be printed in the publick papers.—PHILIP PLEDGER, Foreman [and 14 other signatures]

Questions

1. While Thomas Jefferson was preparing the Declaration of Independence (see the text of the document in the Appendix, pp. A-3–A-4), many local presentments were in circulation. How does the South Carolina example compare in form, content, emotion, and clarity to Jefferson's document?

2. If many ideas and arguments present in the Declaration of Independence were indeed commonplace in the colonies early in 1776, how does this information enhance or alter your understanding of Thomas Jefferson's accomplishment?

Source: Pauline Maier, *American Scripture: Making the Declaration of Independence* (New York: Knopf, 1997), pp. 229–231.

---

ister in charge of American affairs, favored this plan. An overwhelming strike, he asserted, could "finish the rebellion in one campaign."

Early in 1776, Germain set out to generate a land and sea offensive of unprecedented scale. He prodded the sluggish admiralty for ships, and he rented troops from abroad. Russia declined a request for 20,000 soldiers, but the German states produced 18,000 mercenaries. Eventually, 30,000 German troops traveled to America, so many of them from the state of Hesse-Cassel that onlookers called all of them Hessians. Canada, having already repulsed an American invasion, could provide a loyal staging ground in the north. "I have always thought Hudson's River the most proper part of the whole continent for opening vigorous operations," observed "Gentleman Johnny" Burgoyne, the dapper and worldly British general who arrived at Quebec with reinforcements in May 1776.

But plans for a strike south from Canada had to wait. Britain made its first thrust toward the mouth of the Hudson River by sea. In June, a convoy under General William Howe sailed from Halifax to Staten Island, New York, with 9,000 soldiers. By August, the general had received 20,000 reinforcements from across the Atlantic. His brother, Admiral Richard Howe, hovered nearby with 13,000 sailors aboard seventy naval vessels. On

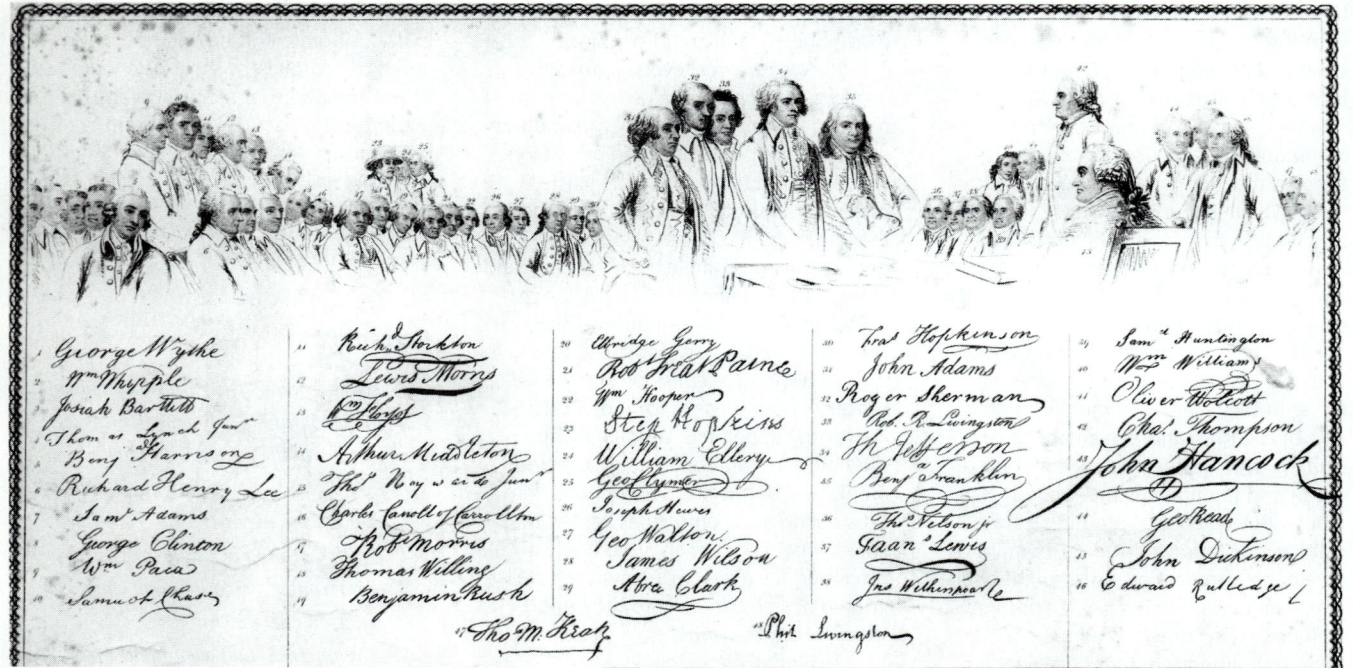

John Trumbull spent years gathering portraits for his famous painting *The Declaration of Independence*. This engraving identifies individuals in the painting with their signatures. The artist placed the Drafting Committee in the center (31–35). He omitted signers for whom he had no likeness, and he included several nonsigners, such as John Dickinson.

orders from Congress, General Washington moved south to defend New York City, a difficult task made harder by ardent Loyalist sentiment. Short on men and equipment, the general weakened his position further by dividing his troops between Manhattan and Brooklyn Heights on nearby Long Island.

A month after Congress members signed the Declaration of Independence, Washington nearly lost his entire force—and the cause itself. General Howe moved his troops by water from Staten Island to the Brooklyn area and then outflanked and scattered the poorly trained Americans in the Battle of Long Island on August 27. Remarkably, the British leader called off a direct attack that almost certainly would have overrun the American batteries on Brooklyn Heights. When his equally cautious brother failed to seal off the East River with ships, rebel troops escaped disaster by slipping back to New York City in small boats under cover of night and fog.

"Victory or Death": A Desperate Gamble Pays Off

New York Burning (1776)

Washington's narrow escape from Long Island in August 1776 was the first of numerous retreats. His army left New York City on September 15. The rebels withdrew from upper Manhattan and Westchester in October and from Fort Washington and Fort Lee on the Hudson—with heavy losses—in November. The Americans "fled like scared rabbits," one Englishman wrote. With winter at hand, the Continental forces retreated southwest toward Philadelphia.

As the ragged American army withdrew from New York late in 1776, General William Howe repeatedly failed to press his advantage. The British commander and his brother had received a commission from Lord North, who headed the government in London, permit-

■ This picture showing the noise and movement of the American victory at the Battle of Princeton was created by deaf painter William Mercer, whose father, Brigadier General Hugh Mercer, died in the battle.

ting them to negotiate a peace settlement with the Americans whenever possible. They hoped that a strong show of force, without a vicious offensive that might alienate civilians, could bring the enemy to terms. Howe's troops offered pardons to rebels and encouraged desertions from Washington's army. In early December, the dwindling American force hurried through Princeton and slipped across the Delaware River into Pennsylvania. Confident of victory, the British failed to pursue them, instead making camp at Trenton. Washington realized that unless circumstances changed quickly, "the game will be pretty well up."

Distressed by civilian talk of surrender, Tom Paine again took up his pen. In the *Pennsylvania Journal* for December 19, he launched a new series of essays ("The American Crisis") that began with the ringing words "These are the times that try men's souls." Paine mocked "the summer soldier and the sunshine patriot" who shrank from extreme trials. "Let it be told to the future world, that in the depth of winter, when nothing but hope and virtue could survive," vigilant citizens, "alarmed at one common danger, came forth to meet and to repulse it."

Action soon followed words. On Christmas Day 1776, Washington issued a new code phrase for sentinels: "Victory or Death." He ordered Paine's words read aloud to the troops. Then, after dark, his men recrossed the windswept Delaware River in a driving snowstorm and advanced on Trenton. Holiday festivities and foul weather had left the enemy unprepared, and intelligence of the impending attack seems to have been ignored. The Americans inflicted a startling defeat, killing several dozen and capturing more than 900 Hessian soldiers. As Washington advanced again on December 30, Howe sent fresh troops forward under Charles Cornwallis to confront the rebels, pinning them down near Trenton. But when the British paused before attacking, the Americans left their campfires burning and slipped out of reach. They then circled behind Cornwallis to defeat his reinforcements at Princeton on January 3. It was not the last time that Washington bested Cornwallis.

The Struggle to Win French Support

Revolutionary War: Northern Theater, 1775–1780

The success at Trenton and Princeton restored a glimmer of hope for the tattered Continental Army and its supporters. As American forces took up winter quarters at Morristown, Howe withdrew his army from much of New Jersey to await the spring campaigns. As a result, anxious civilians in the region who had sworn their loyalty to the crown felt deserted. Public sentiment again swung toward the rebels.

More importantly, news of the victories spurred support overseas for the American cause. French officials, eager to see their European rival bogged down in a colonial war, dispatched secret shipments of munitions to aid the revolutionaries.

One young aristocrat, the idealistic Marquis de Lafayette, was already on his way from France to volunteer his services to General Washington. But drawing forth an official French commitment to the American cause would take a larger show of success. That triumph finally came at the end of the next campaign season, with the Americans' stunning victory at Saratoga, deep in the Hudson Valley, 185 miles above New York City.

Breakdown in British Planning

Among the Americans, two years of grim conflict had dampened the initial zeal that had prompted citizens to enlist. Washington believed that the armed resistance could scarcely continue unless many more men made longer commitments to fight. He also insisted that his soldiers needed tighter discipline and better pay. In response, Congress expanded his disciplinary powers and offered a bonus to those who enlisted for a three-year term.

In a slumping economy, numerous recruits answered the call, including immigrants and unemployed artisans. All lacked training, supplies, and experience. Many rural recruits also lacked immunity to smallpox, since they had never been exposed to the disease. When smallpox broke out among the soldiers at Morristown, Washington ordered a mass inoculation. Because the process brings on a mild case of the disease, he anxiously counted the days until his rebuilding army could be ready to fight. "If Howe does not take advantage of our week state" Washington Commented on April 1777, "he is very unfit for his trust."

> *By seeking a decisive blow and a negotiated settlement in 1776, the British had achieved neither objective.*

Despite American vulnerability, the British were slow to move. Lord North's ministry had fallen victim to its own contradictions. By seeking a decisive blow *and* a negotiated settlement in 1776, the British had achieved neither objective. They had also underestimated the persistence of Washington's army. During the 1777 campaigns, they learned further lessons about the difficulty of their task and the need for coordinated plans.

General Burgoyne, returning to London for the winter, won government support for a major new offensive. He planned to lead a large force south from Canada, using the Hudson Valley to drive a wedge through the rebellious colonies. In support, a combined British and Indian force would strike east from Lake Ontario, capturing Fort Stanwix and descending eastward among the Mohawk River to meet Burgoyne at Albany. William Howe would push north from New York City to complete the design.

But General Howe had formed a different plan. Assuming Burgoyne would not need his help in the Hudson Valley, he intended to move south against Philadelphia. The two generals

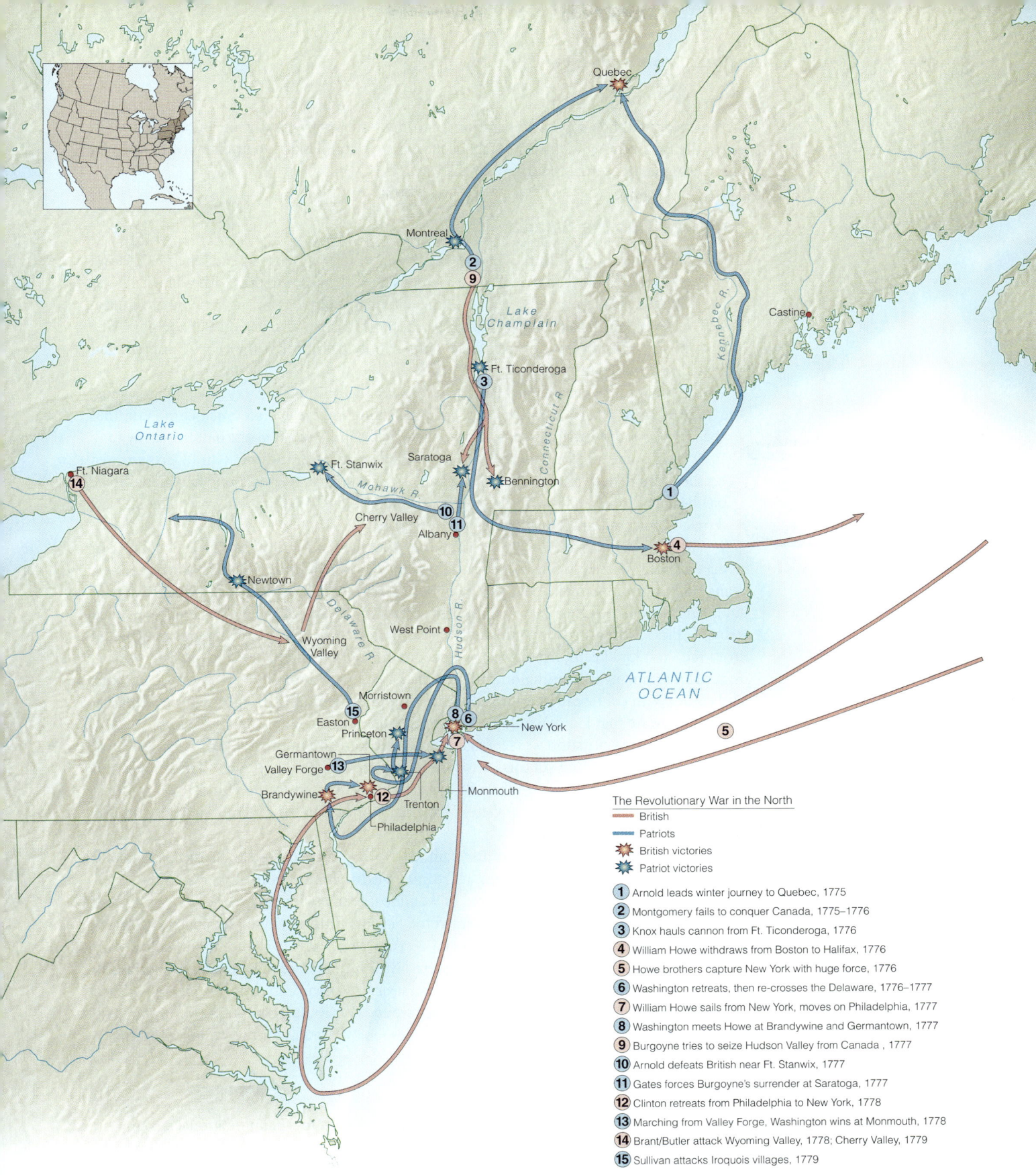

■ MAP 7.2
THE REVOLUTIONARY WAR IN THE NORTH

never integrated their separate operations, and the results were disastrous. In one six-month span, the British bungled their best chance for victory and handed their enemies an opening that permanently shifted the course of the war.

Saratoga Tips the Balance

The isolated operations of Burgoyne and Howe got off to slow starts in late June 1777. Howe took two months to move his troops by sea from New York harbor to the headwaters of Chesapeake Bay. This delay gave the Americans time to march south, but an engagement at Brandywine Creek on September 11, 1777, failed to check the British advance on Philadelphia. The British finally entered the city in late September only to find that the rebel Congress had retreated to York, Pennsylvania.

At Germantown, just north of Philadelphia, Washington launched a surprise attack against the large Hessian garrison on October 4, but morning fog created so much confusion that the inexperienced Patriot troops allowed victory to slip away. Yet as the battered army took up winter quarters at nearby Valley Forge, the defeats at Brandywine and Germantown seemed worth the price. The Americans had gained combat experience and had made Howe pay heavily for his hollow capture of Philadelphia. "Now," Washington wrote, "let all New England turn out and crush Burgoyne."

Moving south from Canada in late June, "Gentleman Johnny" saw little likelihood of being crushed. The British officers believed their huge army to be invincible. The worried Americans fell back from Crown Point and Ticonderoga on Lake Champlain. But as British supply lines lengthened, the crown's army grew less certain of victory. Burgoyne's soldiers expended valuable time cutting a roadway through the wilderness. Also, the reinforcements anticipated from the West had been turned back by Benedict Arnold's men at Fort Stanwix. Even worse, American militia near Bennington badly mauled a British unit of 600 sent to forage for corn and cattle. With cold weather approaching and supplies dwindling, Burgoyne pushed toward Albany, unaware that Howe would not be sending help up the Hudson to meet him.

As Burgoyne's situation worsened, the American position improved. An arrogant British proclamation demanding submission from local residents only stiffened their resolve and drew out more rebel recruits. While Burgoyne's army crossed to the Hudson River's west bank at Saratoga, General Horatio Gates's American forces dug in on Bemis Heights, 10 miles downstream.

On September 19, 1777, Patriot units under two aggressive officers, Benedict Arnold and Daniel Morgan, confronted the enemy at Freeman's Farm, not far from Saratoga. In the grueling battle, British forces suffered 556 dead or wounded, nearly twice the American losses. Gates's refusal to commit reinforcements prevented the Patriots from achieving total victory. Nevertheless, the American ranks swelled with new recruits who sensed a chance to inflict losses on Burgoyne's forces. On October 7, the beleaguered British tried once more to smash southward, only to suffer defeat in a second battle at Freeman's Farm. Morgan and Arnold once again played key roles, though Arnold suffered a crippling leg wound. When Burgoyne's entire army of 5,800 surrendered at nearby Saratoga ten days later, Gates took full credit for the stunning triumph.

Forging an Alliance with France

Ever since declaring independence, Congress had maneuvered to win international recognition and aid for the new nation. It sent Benjamin Franklin to Paris as part of a commission seeking European support. Uncertain about the rebellion's chances for success, especially after the fall of Philadelphia, the French government moved cautiously, confining itself to covert assistance in money and arms.

Word of the American victory at Saratoga suddenly gave Franklin greater leverage. When he hinted to the French that he might bargain directly with London for peace, France's foreign minister, Comte de Vergennes, moved immediately to recognize American independence. France agreed to renounce forever any claim to English land in North America, and Franklin promised that the Americans would help defend French holdings in the Caribbean. Both parties pledged to defend the liberty of the new republic, and each agreed not to conclude a separate peace with Great Britain or to cease fighting until U.S. independence had been ensured by formal treaty. In May 1778 the Continental Congress approved this alliance. The next month, France entered the war, adding its enormous wealth and power to the American cause. A year later, Spain—unwilling to ally itself directly with the upstart republic but eager to protect its vast American assets from Great Britain—entered the war on the side of France.

For the British, what had been a colonial brushfire swiftly flared into a global conflict reminiscent of the Seven Years' War. These new hostilities with France meant possible invasions at home and inevitable attacks on outposts of Britain's empire. French ships seized Senegal in West Africa, took Grenada in the West Indies, and burned trading posts on Hudson Bay in Canada. London's annual war expenditures climbed from £4 million in 1775 to £20 million in 1782.

As war costs mounted in Britain, domestic opposition to the conflict in America intensified. Some members of Parliament pushed for a swift settlement. In 1778 a peace commission led by Lord Carlisle offered concessions to the Continental Congress, hoping to tear the French alliance apart. But the Carlisle Commission failed to win a reconciliation. Other Britons went further in opposing the war. Their diverse reasons included fear of French power, desire for American trade, disgust over war profiteering, ties to friends in America, and idealistic belief in the revolution's principles. Many drank toasts to General Washington and openly supported the American cause.

Faced with growing economic and political pressure, the king and his ministers briefly considered withdrawing all troops from the rebellious colonies and focusing on the French threat. But instead, when General Howe resigned as commander in chief in America, they instructed his successor, Sir Henry Clinton, to retreat from Philadelphia to New York and devote his main resources to attacking the French in the Caribbean. Over the next four years, discontent within Britain continued to escalate, and no strategy proved sufficient to pacify the Americans or to crush their rebellion.

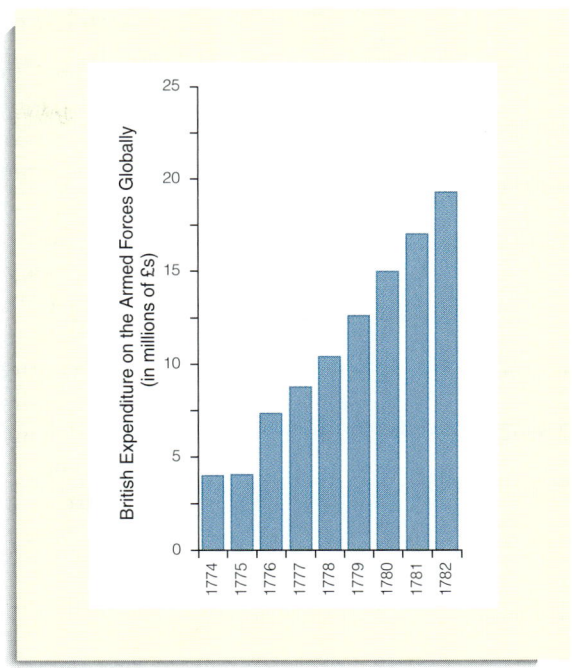

■ **FIGURE 7.1**
BRITISH GOVERNMENT EXPENSES ON ARMED FORCES THROUGHOUT THE WORLD (IN MILLIONS OF POUNDS), 1774–1782 Britain's war budget soared after France entered the conflict in 1778, but major resources flowed toward India and the Caribbean, limiting the share available for North America.

Legitimate States, a Respectable Military

Even with the new French alliance, the rebellious American states faced serious challenges on both the civilian and military fronts. They had thrown out their colonial governors and embarked on a dangerous war, but two fundamental questions still confronted them: How would the once-dependent colonies govern themselves? And how could they shape a military force with enough unity and resources to offer protection but not so powerful and unchecked as to seize control from their new civil governments?

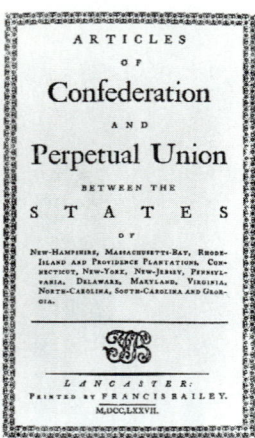

The Articles of Confederation

The Continental Congress that the rebelling states created had taken prompt initiative. Without clear authority, it had declared independence, raised an army, issued currency, borrowed money from abroad, and negotiated an alliance with France. Then it moved to bring greater stability and legitimacy to its work. In 1777, one month after the victory at Saratoga, it approved Articles of Confederation and presented this formal plan for a lasting and unifying government to the states for ratification. In every region, citizens were already debating how much authority each new state government would have in relation to the larger federation. Who would have the power to levy taxes, for example, and who would control the distribution of land?

The Articles declared "The United States of America" to be a "firm league of friendship" between the thirteen former colonies. The final document proposed a weaker confederation than the one outlined in an earlier draft by John Dickinson. In the finished charter, each state would retain all independent rights and powers not "expressly delegated" to the Confederation Congress. Indeed, ties between the sovereign states seemed so loose that France considered sending thirteen separate ambassadors to America.

According to the Articles, Congress could not collect taxes or regulate trade; it could only requisition funds from the states. Proportions would vary depending on each state's free population. Moreover, the Confederation had no separate executive branch; executive functions fell to various committees of the Confederation Congress. In addition, to the dismay of land speculators, the Congress would not control the western domains that several large states had claimed. Maryland, a small state without western claims, protested this arrangement and refused to ratify. To win the required approval from all thirteen states, drafters changed the plan and granted the Confederation control of western lands. After four years, the Articles finally won ratification in 1781.

Articles of Confederation

Given the importance of the states, the task of designing new state governments seemed a higher priority to many than inventing a confederation structure. Some leaders in the Continental Congress returned home to help implement this state-level process. In May 1776, for example, two of Jefferson's friends in the Virginia delegation in Philadelphia departed for Williamsburg. They left their younger colleague behind, but they carried his written draft for a possible state constitution. Those already at work in Virginia accepted Jefferson's proposed preamble, and on June 29, 1776, Virginia led the way, adopting the first republican state constitution.

Virginia had already pioneered in another respect. Two weeks earlier, Virginia representatives approved a Declaration of Rights drawn up by George Mason. He affirmed the revolutionary concepts that all power derives from the people and that magistrates are their servants. He went on to endorse trial by jury, praise religious freedom, and condemn hereditary privilege. Over the next eight years, many states adopted a similar bill of rights to enumerate the fundamental limits of government power.

Creating State Constitutions

Though diverse, the thirteen states shared practical needs. Each had removed a functioning colonial government and needed to reestablish the rule of law under a new system. Britain possessed no written constitution, but the colonists had been ruled under published charters, and they believed in the value of such clear and open arrangements. Thus they readily envisioned an explicit controlling document, or constitution, for each new state. Besides, the novel idea that government flowed from the people—as an agreement based on the consent of the governed—called for some all-encompassing, written legal contract.

A new written constitution, whether for a state or a union of states, represented something more fundamental and enduring than a regular law. It needed to be above day-to-day legal statutes and political whims. Somehow, the people, through chosen representatives, had to prepare a special document that citizens would affirm, or ratify, only one time. After the new government structure was in place, the constitution itself would be difficult, though not impossible, to change.

In 1779 Massachusetts legislators, under pressure from the public, fixed upon a method for providing the elevated status and popular endorsement for such a new document. Local voters in town meetings chose representatives for a specific constitution-drafting convention. These delegates, building on a model suggested by John Adams, crafted a suitable document, and their proposed constitution was then submitted to all the state's free men (regardless of race or property) for ratification. This widened constituency was intended to give special weight to the endorsement process.

John Adams, Thoughts on Government

Approval of the Massachusetts document was hotly debated. Many objected to the limits on popular power that were part of Adams's novel design. A reluctant revolutionary, Adams had composed a tract titled *Thoughts on Government* to counter the democratic enthusiasm of Tom Paine's *Common Sense*. Adams argued that "interests" (like-minded groups), rather than people, should receive equal representation. In addition, he proposed sharing legislative responsibilities between a house, a senate, and a chief executive. Property requirements for these offices were steep, so wealthy interests would have power far beyond their numbers. The Massachusetts state constitution, ratified by a narrow margin, implemented these ideas. They signaled a turn away from the strongest popular radicalism of 1776 and foreshadowed the more conservative balance of interests that James Madison championed in the federal Constitution drafted in 1787.

This extended experiment in constitution writing was unprecedented. Never before in history, John Adams observed, had several million people had numerous opportunities "to form and establish the wisest and happiest government that human wisdom could contrive." Initial state efforts yielded varied results as citizens debated novel approaches to self-government. By 1780 the desire of prominent and well-established elites to rein in democratic power was evident. Yet in comparison to the overseas monarchy they had rejected, even the most conservative new state constitutions seemed risky and bold.

At least three common threads ran through all the documents. First, fearing executive might, drafters curtailed the power of state governors to dismiss assemblies, raise armies, declare war, fill offices, or grant privileges. Colonial governors had been appointed from above, by proprietors or the crown, and they could serve terms of any length. In contrast, state governors would now be elected annually, usually by the assembly. Moreover, their service was subject to impeachment and controlled by term limits. In Pennsylvania, the most radical of the new constitutions did away with a single governor altogether, placing executive power in the hands of a twelve-member council elected by the people.

Second, drafters expanded the strength of legislatures and increased their responsiveness to the popular will. They made elections more frequent, and they enlarged the size of assemblies to allow greater local involvement. They also reduced property requirements for holding office and changed limits on the right to vote to allow wider participation.

Third, the constitution-makers feared the possible corruptions that came when people held more than one office at the same time. Having experienced these glaring conflicts of interest firsthand, they stressed the separation of executive, legislative, and judicial posts. Preventing members of the executive branch from also holding a legislative seat removed any prospect for a cabinet-style government along the lines of the British model.

Tensions in the Military Ranks

A new republican order, whatever its nature, could not defend itself without a suitable fighting force. Just as defunct colonial administrations gave way to new state governments after much debate, colonial militia companies transformed into state militia amid serious arguments. In the state militias and in Washington's national army, which was controlled and paid by the Continental Congress, tensions emerged from the start. Animated discussions erupted as to what

George Washington at Valley Forge

constituted equitable pay, appropriate discipline, suitable tactics, and a proper distribution of limited supplies. Others argued over whether wealth, popularity, vision, military experience, political savvy, European training, or influential ties should play a role in determining who received, or retained, the cherished right to command.

One heated topic involved the election of officers. Wealthy gentry assumed that they would command the state militias, while citizen soldiers demanded the right to choose their own leaders. Another source of tension concerned the right of a prosperous individual to buy exemption from military service or to send a paid substitute. In 1776, as Washington's army had retreated into Pennsylvania, militia in Philadelphia had chastised "Gentlemen who formerly Paraded in our Company and now in the time of greatest danger have turn'd their backs." They asked whether state authorities meant "to force the poorer kind into the field and suffer the Rich & the Great to remain at home?"

Three years later, some of these same Philadelphia militia, bitter that the burdens of the war always fell disproportionately on the poor, took part in what became known as the Fort Wilson Riot. Staging a demonstration in October 1779 spurred by soaring food prices, they intentionally marched past the stately home of James Wilson, where wealthy Patriots had gathered. "The time is now arrived," the demonstrators' handbill proclaimed, "to prove whether the suffering friends of this country, are to be enslaved, ruined and starved, by a few overbearing Merchants, . . . Monopolizers and Speculators." Shots were exchanged, and six died in the melee at "Fort Wilson." (Wilson himself went on to become a leader of the 1787 Constitutional Convention.)

Subtle class divisions also beset the Continental Army, where jealousies over rank plagued the status-conscious officer corps. Congressional power to grant military commissions, often on regional and political grounds, only intensified disputes. Also, Americans representing Congress abroad were empowered to promise high military posts to attract European officers. Some of these recruits served the American cause well, such as Johann de Kalb and Friedrich von Steuben (both born in Germany) and Thaddeus Kosciusko and Casimir Pulaski from Poland. In France, at age nineteen, the Marquis de Lafayette secured a commission to be a major general in America, and he assisted Washington impressively throughout the war.

In contrast, other foreign officers displayed arrogance and spread dissension. Irish-born Thomas Conway, for example, courted congressional opponents of Washington and encouraged the desires of General Horatio Gates to assume top command. Whether or not a concerted "Conway Cabal" ever existed, Washington managed to defuse tensions from Valley Forge during the hard winter of 1777–1778. His numerous letters helped to consolidate his position with Congress and to patch frayed relations with Gates.

Another rival for command of the army, English-born Charles Lee, met disfavor several months later, when Washington ordered him to attack the rear guard of Clinton's army as it withdrew from Philadelphia to New York. Lee mismanaged the encounter at Monmouth, New Jersey, on June 28, 1778, and only Washington's swift action stopped a premature retreat. The Battle of Monmouth ended in a draw, but American troops claimed victory and took pride in their swift recovery and hard fighting.

Shaping a Diverse Army

George Washington at Valley Forge

The army's improved effectiveness came in large part from the efforts of Friedrich von Steuben, a European officer recruited by Benjamin Franklin after charges of homosexuality disrupted his German military career. He had arrived at Valley Forge in February 1778, offering to serve without pay. There he found soldiers with poor food, scant clothing, and limited training. Many Americans still wanted to see a more democratic citizen army, with elected officers and limited hierarchy. But Washington hoped to mold long-term soldiers into a more "Europeanized" force, and Steuben suited his needs. The German worked energetically to drill soldiers who, in turn, trained others.

■ More than a century after the grim winter at Valley Forge, artist Edwin Abbey composed this mural of Steuben drilling Washington's soldiers in February 1778.

New discipline helped boost morale. Still, terms of service and wage levels remained sources of contention. So did the disparities in treatment and pay between officers and enlisted men. There were other grievances: inept congressional committees overseeing the war effort, incompetent officers filling political appointments, and a frustrating shortage of new recruits. Arguments also persisted over whether women or African Americans could serve in the army.

Women organized in diverse ways to assist the war effort, making uniforms and running farms and businesses for absent husbands. A few American women, such as Deborah Sampson of Massachusetts, disguised themselves as men and fought. Far more accompanied the troops to cook and wash in the camps. Earning scant pay, they carried water to the weary and wounded on the battlefield. Serving in these capacities, they formed a presence in both armies. As many as 20,000 women may have accompanied the American army during the war. Mary Hays, wife of a Pennsylvania soldier, endured the winter at Valley Forge and later hauled pitchers of water on the battlefield at Monmouth. When her husband was wounded, she is said to have set down her jug and joined her gun crew, earning folk legend status as the cannon-firing "Molly Pitcher."

After petitioning to fight, free blacks were allowed to join the revolutionary army. Rhode Island even formed an African American regiment. But repeated proposals to arm southern slaves met with defeat. South Carolina and Virginia went so far as to move in the opposite direction, offering to give away slaves captured from Loyalist planters as a bonus to white recruits. Thus it is no surprise that thousands of enslaved people, especially in the South, risked their lives to escape to British lines.

Letter from a Revolutionary War Soldier

The War at Sea

Even as the Americans' army grew into a respectable force, their lack of naval strength proved a constant disadvantage. As early as October 13, 1775, the Continental Congress had agreed to arm two vessels to prey on British supply ships. The vote marked the birth of the American navy. Despite objections, Congress promptly appointed a committee to acquire sailing craft, and most of the thirteen states built up their own small navies, adding to the confusion. The lack of central coordination proved deadly. When Massachusetts sent its ships along the Maine coast to challenge a Loyalist buildup at Castine in 1779, British vessels cornered the fleet at Penobscot Bay and crushed the enterprise.

Despite its strength, the British navy faced increasing challenges as more European powers joined the fray: France in 1778, Spain in 1779, and Holland in 1780. The English feared possible invasion, and French corsairs harassed Britain's coastline, joined by American captains. One such captain, a Scottish immigrant named John Paul Jones, arrived in European waters from America in early 1778. In April, Jones raided the port of Whitehaven in his native Scotland, and the propaganda triumph of an American success in British waters proved huge. The brazen young captain won an even greater victory the next year when his crew managed to board Britain's sleek new H.M.S. *Serapis* and capture the frigate before their own vessel sank.

In all, the Continental Navy equipped more than fifty vessels and captured nearly 200 British craft as prizes. But these numbers pale in comparison to the activities of American privateers. More than a thousand private shipowners obtained licenses from Congress to seize enemy ships and divide the proceeds among themselves and their crew. With international commerce curtailed, shipowners and sailors were eager to try their luck. Their small, quick boats swarmed the Atlantic like troublesome gnats, frustrating England's mighty navy. By war's end the British had surrendered 2,000 ships, 12,000 men, and goods valued at £18 million. And privateering drew merchant investors into the Patriot war effort, helping to bind the coastal elite more firmly to the American cause.

The Long Road to Yorktown

By July 1778, Clinton's British forces had returned to New York City, and their situation had not improved. Frustrated in New England and the middle tier of states, Clinton revived the southern strategy discussed at the beginning of the war. Less thickly settled than the North, the South appeared more vulnerable. It supposedly contained a wide array of Loyalists who would offer support. Also, the South's lengthy growing season meant more fodder for wagon horses and cavalry mounts. The long southern coastline had little protection, and Washington's distant army would have trouble defending the region. Moreover, nearly 500,000 slaves posed a threat to Patriot planters and represented potential support for British invaders. Finally, the same whites who dreaded slave rebellion also feared war with Native Americans, so the possible use of Indian allies also entered Britain's strategic calculation.

Indian Warfare and Frontier Outposts

Most Native Americans in eastern North America remained loyal to the British. Exceptions existed, such as the Oneida, Tuscarora, and Catawba, but many Indians had long-standing grievances about white encroachments. In Appalachia, colonial land investors and colonists had defied the king's Proclamation Line for more than a decade. When dissident Cherokee, led by a young war chief named Dragging Canoe, attacked intruders on the Watauga River in July 1776, whites struck back. In all, 6,000 troops from four southern states pushed into the mountains, laying waste to Cherokee villages.

Daniel Boone had already led migrants through Cumberland Gap in western Virginia to establish a fort on the Kentucky River at Boonesborough in 1775. By 1777 these pioneer families faced Indian adversaries who were fighting for their homelands. The Native Americans were also being urged on by Henry Hamilton, the British commandant at far-off Detroit. In one six-month span, Hamilton, who became known as the Hair Buyer, received seventy-seven prisoners and 129 scalps from this frontier warfare. Along the upper Ohio, violence escalated in 1777, when Americans killed Shawnee leader Cornstalk and his son during a truce. The next

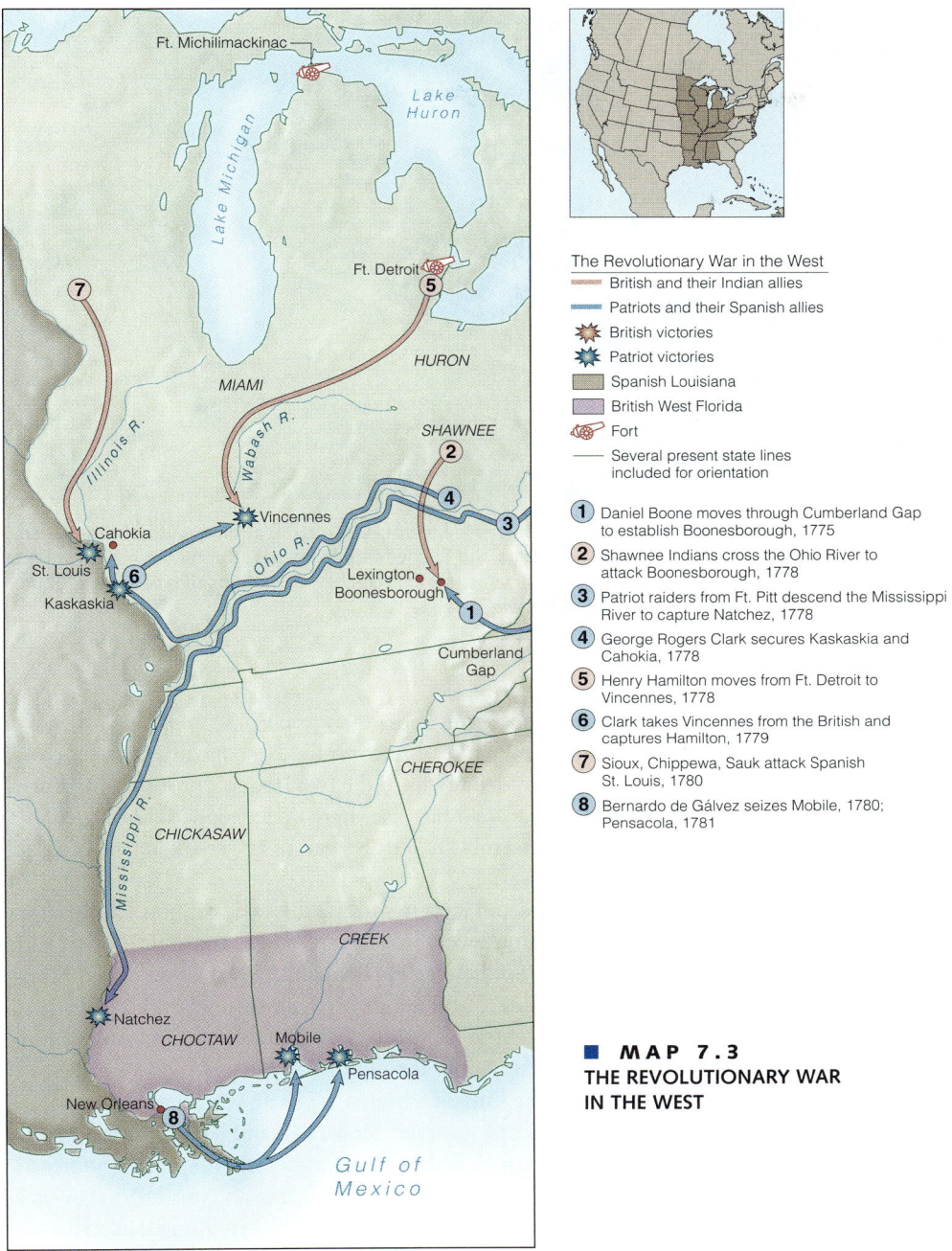

MAP 7.3
THE REVOLUTIONARY WAR IN THE WEST

year, they murdered the neutral Delaware leader, White Eyes. Four years later, at the village of Gnadenhutten (south of modern-day Canton, Ohio), militia from Pennsylvania massacred 100 peaceful Delaware men, women, and children who had been converted to Christianity by missionaries of the Moravian Church.

By then, conflict involving Native Americans had also flared farther north. Joseph Brant, a mixed-race Mohawk leader educated in New England and loyal to the British, pushed south from Fort Niagara on Lake Ontario, attacking poorly guarded frontier settlements. First in the Wyoming Valley of northeastern Pennsylvania and later in New York's Cherry Valley, the raiders killed hundreds of non-Indian settlers. In the summer of 1779, American General John Sullivan led a campaign to annihilate Indian towns in reprisal.

■ The British used Fort Niagara (on the southwest edge of Lake Ontario, at the mouth of the Niagara River) to launch attacks on American settlements and to shelter Indian allies. During the harsh winter of 1779–1780, 5,000 Iroquois refugees, made homeless by the scorched-earth campaign of General John Sullivan, camped near the fort in 5 feet of snow.

Sullivan's revenge-minded troops, numbering more than 4,000, destroyed forty villages of the four tribes in the Iroquois Confederacy most linked to the British cause: the Mohawk, Onondaga, Cayuga, and Seneca. They avoided towns of the two Iroquois groups sympathetic to the Americans—the Oneida and Tuscarora—but elsewhere they chopped down orchards, torched crops, and sent Indian refugees streaming to Fort Niagara. Hunger and retaliatory raids haunted the region until the end of the war.

While the British were passing arms and supplies to the divided Iroquois Confederacy through Fort Niagara, they were also using several western posts to arm other Indian allies and seek an advantage in the interior. Soldiers at Fort Michilimackinac recruited Sioux, Chippewa, and Sauk warriors for an unsuccessful attack on Spanish-held St. Louis in 1780. At Fort Detroit, Hamilton continued to equip war parties of Ottawa, Fox, and Miami Indians to attack American newcomers migrating into the Ohio Valley.

In 1778, with support from his home state of Virginia, a young Patriot surveyor named George Rogers Clark organized a foray west to counter these raids and lend support to Spanish and French allies in the upper Mississippi Valley. He secured settlements on the Mississippi River, and in February 1779 he led a grueling winter march to the fort at Vincennes in southern Indiana. In surprising that outpost on the Wabash River, the Americans managed to capture Henry Hamilton, but they failed to seize Detroit.

The Unpredictable War in the South

The rebel war effort beyond the Appalachian Mountains expanded south in 1778, when Patriot raiders captured Natchez on the lower Mississippi and seized property in British West Florida. But it was the energetic governor of Spanish Louisiana, Bernardo de Gálvez, whose actions proved decisive. Living in New Orleans, Gálvez maintained a careful neutrality between the Americans and their British rivals through 1778. But when Spain allied with France and declared war on Britain the next year, the governor acted quickly to keep the British from gaining ground on the Gulf Coast.

Moving from west to east, Governor Gálvez drove the British from the Mississippi River in 1779, seized their fort at Mobile in 1780, and conquered Pensacola, the capital of British West Florida, in 1781. The fall of Mobile and Pensacola cut British supply lines to the southeast-

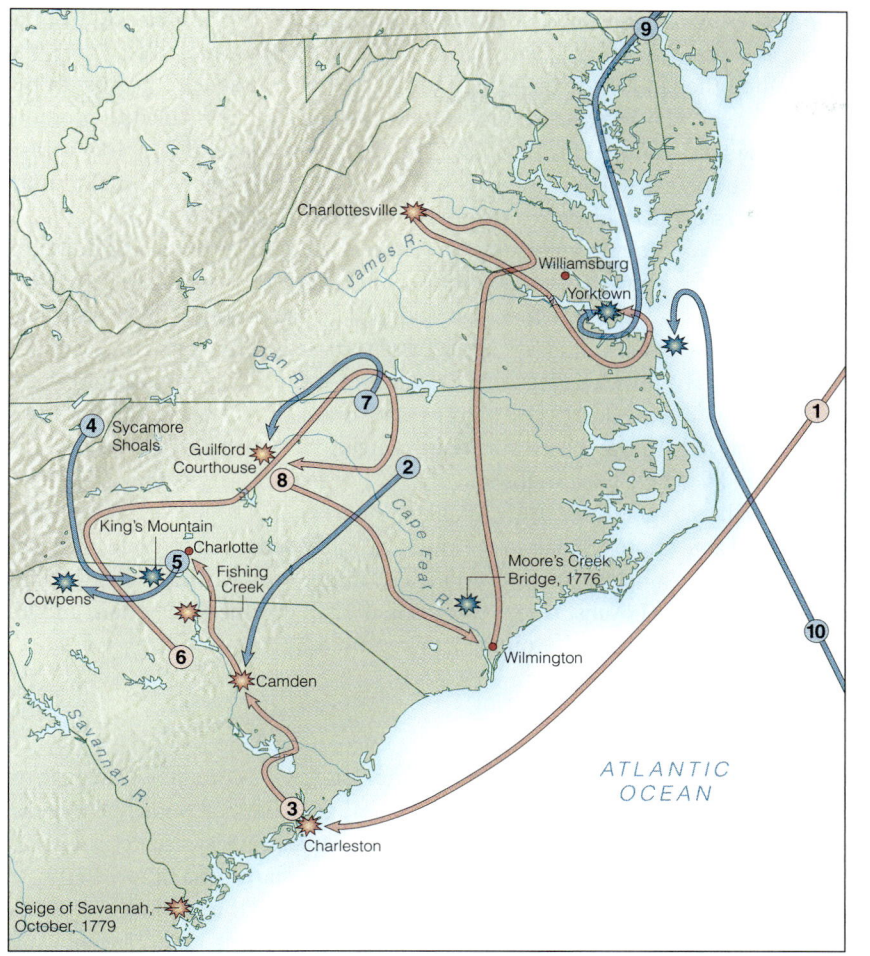

MAP 7.4
THE REVOLUTIONARY WAR IN THE SOUTH

ern interior, hurting Creek and Cherokee warriors. Without additional guns, knives, and powder, the Indians could offer little assistance in Britain's ambitious plan to win back the South. It was support the British could ill afford to lose.

Still, the crown's forces regained control of most of Georgia from the rebels in 1778. The next year, they blocked American and French efforts to retake Savannah. Early in 1780, British generals Clinton and Cornwallis ferried troops by sea from New York to South Carolina, and by May they had isolated Charleston and forced the surrender of 5,500 American troops—the largest loss of American men and weapons during the entire war. A confident Clinton returned to New York, leaving Cornwallis in command in South Carolina as fierce fighting erupted across the state. Banastre Tarleton's British cavalry, along with Loyalist supporters, went head to head against the guerrilla bands led by Thomas Sumter, Andrew Pickens, and Francis Marion.

In June 1780, Congress appointed Horatio Gates to take command of southern operations, and he hurried to the Carolinas with fresh troops. On August 16, Gates's army confronted Cornwallis at Camden, South Carolina, 120 miles north of Charleston. The Americans, short on rest, food, and leadership, suffered another huge defeat. Two days after the Camden disaster, as Gates fled north, Tarleton's cavalry landed another blow. They surprised Sumter's band of 800 partisans at Fishing Creek near the Catawba River and took 300 prisoners. Suffering almost no losses themselves, the cavalry inflicted 150 casualties and freed several hundred Loyalists and British regulars.

That September, as Washington absorbed word of the defeats at Camden and Fishing Creek, he received another rude shock. Benedict Arnold—in command of West Point, the key outpost controlling the Hudson River—had plotted to defect and yield the post to the British. An admired leader, Arnold was also self-centered. When Congress failed to promote him, he became alienated from the Patriot cause. The capture of General Arnold's British contact, Major John André, alerted Washington to the scheme. He hanged the major as an enemy spy, but Arnold escaped and received command of British troops.

Five years of war left Washington and Congress facing severe problems: soaring inflation, scarce resources, sinking citizen morale, and mounting disobedience among enlisted men. Early in 1780, soldiers from Massachusetts, New York, and Connecticut had mutinied in separate incidents. Members of the Pennsylvania and New Jersey Lines soon staged similar strikes over disputed terms of enlistment. The British had reason for optimism as Cornwallis pressed into North Carolina in the fall of 1780. But the next twelve months saw a dramatic reversal in their fortunes.

That reversal began in October with a surprising Patriot victory at King's Mountain in the southern backcountry, where Cornwallis had sent Major Patrick Ferguson with a troop of South Carolina Loyalists to guard the army's flank and **harry** rebel supporters. More than 800 frontiersmen rallied at Sycamore Shoals in the Watauga Valley and raced south to challenge the British. On October 6, just below North Carolina's southern border, these sharpshooters surrounded and decimated the Loyalist troops. Ferguson died in the one-sided affair, and his force lost more than 1,000 men—killed, wounded, or captured.

The Final Campaign

A shrewd change in American leadership followed the victory at King's Mountain. Congress, on Washington's advice, replaced Gates in the southern command with General Nathanael Greene, an experienced Rhode Islander who had served as the army's quartermaster general. Greene arrived in Charlotte, North Carolina, in December 1780, taking charge of a tattered army of 1,600. Shocked by the violence of partisan warfare and conscious of the need to win public support, he urged restraint on such experienced guerrilla fighters as Sumter and Marion while weaving them into his overall plans to conduct an elusive "fugitive war." Greene decided to divide his small army and send half his men into South Carolina under the seasoned Daniel Morgan to harass the British flank. "It makes the most of my inferior force," he explained, "for it compels my adversary to divide his, and holds him in doubt as to his own line of conduct."

Cornwallis took the bait and dispatched Tarleton, who caught up with Morgan at Hannah's Cowpens, west of King's Mountain, on January 17, 1781. The outnumbered rebel militia lacked experience and discipline, but Morgan turned this weakness to an advantage at the Battle of Cowpens. He stationed the militia units in front of his Continental forces with orders to fire two rounds and fall back. Sensing an enemy retreat, the British force of 1,100 advanced too far too fast. Morgan's men promptly overwhelmed them. Tarleton managed to escape, but he left behind 100 dead, 800 prisoners, and most of his horses and ammunition. Morgan's victorious Patriot force suffered only 148 casualties. He rightly called the Battle of Cowpens "a devil of a whipping."

Though frustrated, Cornwallis clung to the belief that "a successful battle may give us America." He discarded all excess baggage and pursued the rebel army 200 miles across North Carolina. Greene, continuing his elusive "fugitive war," directed a speedy retreat over swollen rivers to the Virginia border. Then he doubled back to confront the weary British in the Battle of Guilford Courthouse on March 15. Although the American forces eventually withdrew from the field, Cornwallis sustained such heavy losses that he was forced to alter his plans.

The British retreated to the coast at Wilmington, North Carolina, and then marched north in early summer 1781 to Yorktown, Virginia. There, Cornwallis hoped to obtain reinforcements by sea, rally Loyalists in the Chesapeake region, and divide the rebelling colonies. The design's success hinged on naval superiority and timely support from General Clinton in New York. But Cornwallis could be assured of neither.

■ The joint American-French victory at the siege of Yorktown, Virginia, in October 1781 ended British hopes for preventing American independence. As Cornwallis's troops marched out to lay down their arms, a band played "The World Turned Upside Down." "Finally," Lafayette wrote proudly, "everything came together at once, and we had a sensational turn of events. . . . The play is over."

In August the French fleet in the Caribbean set out for Chesapeake Bay. Admiral François De Grasse planned to spend eight weeks in North American waters. The move gave Washington (still in the north) brief access to impressive naval power, and he seized his chance. He sent word south to Lafayette in Virginia to keep Cornwallis contained at Yorktown. Then, to hold Clinton's forces in New York, he ordered his men to make a show as if preparing for a lengthy siege. But instead of besieging New York City, American soldiers and their French allies slipped away, secretly marching south to lay a trap for the British army.

Admiral De Grasse reached Chesapeake Bay with two dozen ships at the end of August. On September 5, he repulsed a British fleet off the mouth of the bay, dashing Cornwallis's hopes for relief by sea and allowing Washington to tighten the noose. When 9,000 Americans and 7,800 French converged on Yorktown in late September, they outnumbered their 8,000 opponents by more than two to one, and the siege proved brief. Plagued by sickness and shortages of food and munitions, the British surrendered on October 19, 1781. For Washington and his army, Yorktown was a stunning victory. Intermittent warfare continued for another year. But the Americans finally had powerful leverage to bargain for peace and force Britain to recognize their independence.

Winning the Peace

After Yorktown, the final phase of the war played out in European courts. There, the diplomatic maneuvering proved complicated and risky, with Benjamin Franklin, John Adams, and John Jay as the key American players. Often at odds, the three men nevertheless managed to achieve a final triumph that proved as unlikely and momentous as Washington's victory in Virginia. They did it, wrote the immodest Adams, "in spite of the malice of enemies, the finesse of Allies, and the mistakes of Congress."

For the British, the road to the peace table had been long and unpleasant. Early feelers about a negotiated settlement—from the Howes in 1776 and the Carlisle Commission in 1778—had not mentioned independence. But conditions changed drastically after Yorktown. Domestic unrest in Britain had already boiled into riots, and the expanded war was going poorly in India and the West Indies. "O God, it is all over!" Lord North muttered when he received the news of Cornwallis's defeat in Virginia.

The American Revolution

The final American victory in the War of Independence came at the peace table, when negotiators John Jay, John Adams, and Benjamin Franklin won favorable terms in the 1783 Treaty of Paris. Benjamin West's unfinished painting also includes the absent Henry Laurens (rear) and Franklin's grandson (right), the delegation's secretary.

Within months, Sir Guy Carleton replaced Clinton in command of the remaining British forces in America, the hawkish Lord Germain stepped down from the Cabinet, and North resigned after twelve years as prime minister. Even the king spoke of abdicating. But instead, he approved a new ministry more suited to the rising antiwar sentiment in Parliament. The Earl of Shelburne became prime minister in July 1782. Even before he assumed office, he had authorized peace discussions with his old acquaintance, Benjamin Franklin.

Franklin was in a difficult position. The crucial alliance he had negotiated with France stated that the Americans would not sign a separate peace with Britain. Moreover, Congress, grateful for vital French military and financial support, had instructed the American negotiators to defer to the wishes of Vergennes. The Americans did not realize that the French foreign minister had already entertained thoughts of a truce that would leave London in control of all the territory it currently held in America, including New York City and parts of the lower South. Vergennes opposed the Americans' republican principles, and he refused to treat the American diplomats as equal partners.

Still, the American peace commissioners fared surprisingly well in the treacherous waters of European diplomacy, starting with Franklin's first informal talks with the British. He laid out four "necessary" points, leading with the recognition of American independence. To this he added the removal of British troops, the right to fish in Newfoundland waters, and the revision of the Canadian border, which the Quebec Act of 1774 had pushed south to the Ohio River. Franklin then noted some "desirable" items for later bargaining. The British, he suggested, should consider paying an indemnity for war damages, an act that would officially acknowledge their own blame for the war. Perhaps they should cede Canada to the United States as well.

For its part, Britain sought compensation for roughly 70,000 American Loyalists who had been driven from their homes, plus the right to collect old debts that colonists had owed to British merchants before 1776. Hoping to disrupt the American-French alliance and to reestablish trade with their former colonies, the British negotiated preliminary peace terms with the Americans in November 1782. In return for independence, troop withdrawal, and fishing rights, the Americans agreed vaguely that their Congress would "recommend" that individual states approve compensation for confiscated Loyalist property.

On the Canadian boundary question, the Americans scored another success, but one that came at the expense of Indian nations. By giving up their bid for all of Canada, the negotiators persuaded Britain to relinquish the Ohio Valley and accept a northern boundary for the United States defined by the Great Lakes and the St. Lawrence River. In the west, the United States would reach to the Mississippi River, and Americans would gain free navigation on that waterway, despite Spanish opposition. In the South, the thirty-first parallel, above East and West Florida, would provide the American boundary.

The diplomats endorsed the final peace terms at Versailles, France, in September 1783. Amid all the other treaty terms, the British yielded East and West Florida to Spain. In the process, however, they made no mention of the Indians who had served as allies in the American conflict. Abandoned, the Native Americans had to confront their new situation alone. To end up "betrayed to our Enemies & divided between the Spaniards and the Amer-

Territorial Campaigns in Eastern America after Treaty of Paris

icans is Cruel & Ungenerous," protested the Creek leader, Alexander McGillivray. His people had been "most Shamefully deserted."

Conclusion

The War for Independence that began at Lexington had lasted eight years. Like any lengthy armed struggle, it took a heavy toll on combatants and noncombatants alike. Personal survival was far from certain, as encounters with sickness and the enemy carried off enlisted men. American forces lost an estimated 25,000 soldiers, a huge number in proportion to the small overall population.

For those who avoided death, lesser dangers abounded. Uprooting from home became commonplace, losses of property were extensive, and indebtedness proved widespread. Despite constant uncertainties at the individual level, a makeshift revolutionary army, learning as it marched, had forced the British to concede American independence.

As in all wars, some of the most decisive action occurred far from the battlefield. In London, weakness in the chain of command, a lumbering bureaucracy, and divided public sentiment undermined the British war effort. Elsewhere in Europe, skillful American diplomats built the international alliances needed to secure victory and won peace terms that promised survival to the new confederation of states. A flurry of constitution writing unprecedented in history had launched more than a dozen newly independent states, and the Articles of Confederation, approved after long delay, had knit them together into a formal league with a common Congress. The new and difficult art of republican self-government remained a work in progress, with some of the most difficult and contentious choices still to come. The fragile unity built on fighting a common enemy would be strained to the limit as new debates erupted over the meaning and direction of the unfinished revolution.

Sites to Visit

Saratoga National Historical Park

The National Park Service maintains a visitor center and has arranged a self-guided battlefield tour that includes the locations for the British and American camps during the crucial engagement of October 1777 at this park, which is located 10 miles south of Saratoga Springs, New York, on Route 50.

Brandywine Battlefield State Park

This park is located on Highway 202 west of Philadelphia, Pennsylvania, not far from the borders of Delaware and Maryland. (At nearby Chadds Ford, the Wyeth Museum celebrates one of America's great artistic families.)

The Continental Congress
http://lcweb2.loc.gov/ammem/amlaw/lawhome.html

This Web site in the American Memory series of the Library of Congress contains materials, starting from 1774, that concern the First and Second Continental Congress.

Virginia Runaways Project
http://people.uvawise.edu/history/runaways/

This digital database of runaway slave and servant advertisements contains transcripts and images of all runaway ads placed in Virginia newspapers from 1736 to 1777. It contains a new search interface and updated support material.

Cowpens National Battlefield
http://www.nps.gov/cowp/index.htm

The actual site of the battle where Daniel Morgan's troops defeated Banastre Tarleton's British forces (January 17, 1781) is located 10 miles west of Gafney, South Carolina, off Highway I-85. The battle was dramatized in Hollywood's film *The Patriot* (2000).

Spy Letters of the American Revolution
http://www.si.umich.edu/spies/index-timeline.html

This Web site, maintained by the Clements Library at the University of Michigan, contains facsimiles and transcriptions of diverse spy letters contained in the Sir Henry Clinton collection and provides some context for each letter.

Old Fort Niagara
http://www.oldfortniagara.org/

This New York State Historic Site overlooks Lake Ontario at the mouth of the Niagara River. Built by the French in 1727, the fort is located just off the Robert Moses Parkway, not far from Niagara Falls, at Youngstown, New York.

Birth of the Navy of the United States
http://www.history.navy.mil/

Visit the Naval Historical Center Web site (Early History Branch) to learn about the history of the U.S. Navy in the Revolutionary era.

For Further Reading

General
Colin G. Calloway, *The American Revolution in Indian Country: Crisis and Diversity in Native American Communities* (1995).
Gregory Fremont-Barnes and Richard Alan Ryerson, *The Encyclopedia of the American Revolutionary War: A Political, Social, and Military History*, 5 vols. (2006).
Don Higginbotham, *The War of American Independence* (1971).
Piers Mackesy, *The War for America, 1775–1783* (1965).
Robert Middlekauff, *The Glorious Cause* (1982).
Gordon S. Wood, *The Creation of the American Republic, 1776–1787* (1969).
Alfred F. Young, ed., *Beyond the American Revolution: Explorations in the History of American Radicalism* (1993).

"Things Are Now Come to That Crisis"
Ira D. Gruber, *The Howe Brothers and the American Revolution* (1972).
Mary Beth Norton, *Liberty's Daughters: The Revolutionary Experience of American Women, 1750–1800* (1980).
Ray Raphael, *A People's History of the American Revolution: How Common People Shaped the Fight for Independence* (2001).
Richard A. Ryerson, *The Revolution Is Now Begun: The Radical Committees of Philadelphia, 1765–1776* (1978).
Simon Schama, *Rough Crossings: Britain, the Slaves, and the American Revolution* (2006).

Declaring Independence
David Hackett Fischer, *Washington's Crossing* (2004).
Eric Foner, *Tom Paine and Revolutionary America* (1976).
Pauline Maier, *American Scripture: Making the Declaration of Independence* (1997).
Barnet Schecter, *The Battle for New York: The City at the Heart of the American Revolution* (2002).
Gordon S. Wood, *The Americanization of Benjamin Franklin* (2004).

The Struggle to Win French Support
Wayne Bodle, *The Valley Forge Winter: Civilians and Soldiers at War* (2002).
Stephen Conway, *The British Isles and the War of American Independence* (2000).
Jonathan R. Dull, *A Diplomatic History of the American Revolution* (1985).
Sylvia R. Frey, *The British Soldier in America: A Social History of Military Life in the Revolutionary Period* (1981).
Max M. Mintz, *The Generals of Saratoga: John Burgoyne and Horatio Gates* (1990).

Legitimate States, a Respectable Military
Willi Paul Adams, *The First American Constitutions: Republican Ideology and the Making of the State Constitutions in the Revolutionary Era* (1980).
Jeff Broadwater, *George Mason: Forgotten Founder* (2006).
Elisha P. Douglass, *Rebels and Democrats: The Struggle for Equal Political Rights and Majority Rule During the American Revolution* (1955).
Charles Patrick Neimeyer, *America Goes to War: A Social History of the Continental Army* (1996).
Evan Thomas, *John Paul Jones: Sailor, Hero, Father of the American Navy* (2003).
Alfred F. Young, *Masquerade: The Life and Times of Deborah Sampson, Continental Soldier* (2004)

The Long Road to Yorktown
Robert M. Calhoon, *The Loyalists in Revolutionary America, 1760–1781* (1973).
Max M. Mintz, *Seeds of Empire: The American Revolutionary Conquest of the Iroquois* (1999).
Richard B. Morris, *The Peacemakers: The Great Powers and American Independence* (1965).
Steven Rosswurm, *Arms, Country, and Class: The Philadelphia Militia and the Lower Sort During the American Revolution* (1987).
J. Barton Starr, *Tories, Dons, and Rebels: The American Revolution in British West Florida* (1976).
Carl Van Doren, *Mutiny in January: The Story of a Crisis in the Continental Army* (1943).

For quizzes and other resources on these topics, go to www.longmanamericanhistory.com.

New Beginnings: The 1780s

CHAPTER

8

DURING THE REVOLUTIONARY WAR YEARS, BETWEEN 1775 AND 1782, A HUGE SMALLPOX epidemic ricocheted relentlessly across broad sections of North America. At times the epidemic entwined itself with the war, traveling on supply ships and moving with marching troops. In the Northeast, it struck during the siege of Boston and the attack on Quebec. In the South, it cut down hundreds of Virginia slaves who had escaped at the start of the war to join Governor Dunmore's "Ethiopian Regiment." The disease found additional victims during the British siege of Charleston in 1780.

Like the war itself, smallpox erupted first in Massachusetts. But the devastating contagion spread far more widely than the military destruction, proving truly continental in scope. It gained a foothold in New Orleans, Mexico City, and the trading posts that dotted the Canadian interior. In 1781 the disease ravaged Indian villages on the Northwest Coast, devastated missions on the Baja Peninsula, and erupted at California's San Gabriel Mission, where Spanish-speaking newcomers were building a village named Our Lady of the Angels (the start of modern-day Los Angeles). On the Atlantic coast, smallpox menaced Virginia as French and American troops surrounded the British at Yorktown. As the War of Independence ended, the transcontinental epidemic also drew to a close.

The contagion left a patchwork of destruction from the Atlantic to the Pacific. Smallpox losses were greatest among Native Americans, and few groups or regions remained untouched. British sea captain George Vancouver, probing Puget Sound in 1792, observed numerous skulls, ribs, and other human remains "scattered about the beach."

■ Smallpox "spread like lightning through all the missions," causing "havoc which only those who have seen it can believe. The towns and missions were . . . deserted, and bodies were seen in the road." Time and again, "the poor little children, abandoned beside the dead, died without help" (Father Luis Sales, Baja California, 1781). This modern photo shows that smallpox persisted until its global eradication in the 1970s.

CHAPTER OUTLINE

Beating Swords into Plowshares

Competing for Control of the Mississippi Valley

Debtor and Creditor, Taxpayer and Bondholder

Drafting a New Constitution

Ratification and the Bill of Rights

Conclusion

Sites to Visit

For Further Reading

■ **MAP 8.1**
THE SPREAD OF SMALLPOX ACROSS NORTH AMERICA, 1775–1782 A great smallpox epidemic swept North America during the Revolutionary era. In 1781 it moved up the Baja Peninsula with settlers heading for San Gabriel, the Spanish mission that became Los Angeles, California.

When Vancouver's pilot, Peter Puget, pressed farther into the sound that is named for him, he found deserted villages that only a dozen years earlier had bustled with people. In its eight-year course, the fearsome virus took more than 130,000 North American lives, many times the total of 25,000 Americans lost in service during the Revolution.

As the dual scourges of epidemic and war subsided, fresh problems confronted North America's inhabitants. Great Britain's mainland colonies had won their independence, but questions remained as to which European powers would exert the most influence on the huge continent. British power ruled Canada; Spanish authority claimed much of the West; and French officials still dreamed of regaining control over the Mississippi Valley. In the North Pacific, Russians intruded on the Alaskan coast, and soon the prospect of trade with China lured sea captains from the United States to seek furs along the Northwest Coast.

In the woodlands between the Appalachian Mountains and the Mississippi River, Indians whom Pontiac had sought to unify once again endured sudden transfers of their ancestral land between distant powers. But now the rapid incursion of American settlers added new urgency to their situation. Farther east, inhabitants of the Atlantic seaboard faced an array of thorny problems after warfare and smallpox loosened their grip. Half a million people remained legally enslaved, and they were potential allies for any European power seeking to disrupt the fragile new **federation**.

In addition, members of the Confederation's Continental Congress in Philadelphia had a restless army to pay, a weak government to reform, and enormous war debts to confront. Acceptance of the Articles of Confederation in 1781 had not come easily, and all assumed that the basic structure of governance would demand further revision and adjustment. However, few could foresee that within eight years it would be set aside for a more centralized federal design.

Beating Swords into Plowshares

At first, in the wake of military victory over Britain, the short-term survival of the new United States of America seemed assured, thanks to years of intense fighting and skillful diplomacy. The former colonies had banded together under the Articles of Confederation, finally ratified in 1781, which placed specific governmental powers in the hands of an elected national legislature, or Continental Congress. But deeper questions persisted regarding the new republican experiment. With peace at hand, how would citizens transform their "swords into plowshares," as urged by the Biblical prophet, Isaiah? Should power rest primarily with the victorious army, the wealthy merchants, or the artisans and farmers central to the revolutionary movement? Should authority be consolidated in the hands of a well-educated, new national elite, or should it be widely dispersed, with local communities and states empowered to manage their own affairs? Equally important, what cultural patterns would take hold within the fledgling society in these postwar years?

Women Petition for War Compensation

Will the Army Seize Control?

After their triumph at Yorktown, Washington's men had moved north to press British forces to evacuate New York City. More than 10,000 American troops and 500 officers encamped at Newburgh, on the Hudson River. Exhausted soldiers were eager to receive long-overdue pay and return home. Clearly, they could negotiate best for promised wages while they were still together and armed. Officers were especially reluctant to disband without certain assurances of money. In 1780 they had extracted from the Congress a promise of half pay for life. In December 1782, with no sign of compensation in sight, disgruntled officers sent a delegation to Philadelphia to press their claims.

Within Congress, the men around financier Robert Morris, including James Wilson and Alexander Hamilton, wanted to bolster and centralize the Confederation's finances. To that end, they sought a new duty of 5 percent on imported goods to raise money from the states. Revenue from this "continental impost" could make the Confederation solvent and allow it to

INTERPRETING HISTORY

Demobilization: "Turned Adrift Like Old Worn-Out Horses"

Joseph Plumb Martin was born in western Massachusetts in 1760. He enlisted in the Continental Army before his sixteenth birthday and was encamped at West Point, New York, when peace finally arrived. Later, in a compelling narrative of his wartime experiences, he recalled the **demobilization** process from the perspective of a common soldier.

[On April 19, 1783,] we had general orders read which satisfied the most skeptical, that the war was over and the prize won [after] eight tedious years. But the soldiers said but little about it; their chief thoughts were closely fixed upon their situation. . . . Starved, ragged and meager, not a cent to help themselves with, and no means or method in view to remedy or alleviate their condition. This was appalling in the extreme. . . .

At length, the eleventh day of June 1783, arrived. "The old man," our captain, came into the room, with his hands full of papers. . . . He then handed us our discharges, or rather furloughs, . . . permission to return home, but to return to the army again if required. This was policy in government; to discharge us absolutely in our present pitiful, forlorn condition, it was feared, might cause some difficulties. . . .

Some of the soldiers went off for home the same day that their fetters were knocked off; others stayed and got their final settlement certificates, which they sold to procure decent clothing and money. . . . I was among those. . . . I now bid a final farewell to the service. I had obtained my settlement certificates and sold some of them and purchased some decent clothing, and then set off from West Point. . . .

When those who engaged to serve during the war enlisted, they were promised a hundred acres of land, each. . . . When the country had drained the last drop of service it could screw out of the poor soldiers, they were turned adrift like old worn-out horses, and nothing said about land to pasture them upon. . . . Congress did, indeed, appropriate lands, . . . but no care was taken that the soldiers should get them. [Instead,] a pack of speculators. . .were driving about the country like so many evil spirits, endeavoring to pluck the last feather from the soldiers. The soldiers were ignorant of the ways and means to obtain their bounty lands. . . . It was, soldiers, look to yourselves; we want no more of you.

We were, also, promised six dollars and two thirds a month. . . . And what was six dollars and sixty-seven cents of this "Continental currency," as it was called, worth? It was scarcely enough to procure a man a dinner. . . . I received one month's pay in specie while on the march to Virginia, in the year 1781, and except that, I never received any pay worth the name while I belonged to the army. . . . It is provoking to think of it. The country was rigorous in exacting my compliance to *my* engagements. . .but equally careless in performing her contracts with me, and why so? One reason was that she had all the power in her own hands and I had none. Such things ought not to be.

After the war, Martin settled on the Maine frontier, and a speculator bought his right to 100 acres of bounty land in Ohio. In 1818, as a disabled laborer with a large family, he successfully petitioned Congress for a small pension to support the household. He died poor in 1850.

Questions

1. Why did the government worry about discharging soldiers such as Martin in 1783, and why did many of them sell their final settlement certificates?
2. Do elements in Martin's complaints relate to the situation of modern American combat veterans?

Source: James Kirby Martin, ed., *Ordinary Courage: The Revolutionary War Adventures of Joseph Plumb Martin,* 2nd ed. (New York: Brandywine Press, 1999), pp. 159–164.

William Ranney painted *Revolutionary War Veterans Returning Home* in 1848, when the United States was at war with Mexico. The image offered a positive reminder of earlier American military success. But some soldiers leaving the Continental Army in 1783 had clearly fared better than others.

assume responsibility for paying off war debts. In turn, this commitment would tie the interests of wealthy citizens to the Confederation government's success. Morris even threatened to resign his post if the "nationalists" did not get their way. Rumblings from the officer corps would help these politicians push through the impost measure, crucial to their long-term goals. So they quietly encouraged the military dissidents in Newburgh.

In March 1783, anonymous petitions circulated among officers encamped at Newburgh. These inflammatory "addresses" contained a veiled threat of military takeover in order to impose stability after a turbulent revolution. They suggested that officers should sit tight, neither fighting nor laying down their arms, until Congress guaranteed their payment. Without Washington's approval, the officers at Newburgh arranged a meeting to discuss their plight.

If the plotters hoped to draw Washington into the scheme, they were sorely disappointed. He did attend the officers' meeting on March 15, but he used his commanding presence to discredit the ill-advised plan. His eyes weakened by endless wartime correspondence, he drew a pair of spectacles from his pocket, a surprising gesture that underscored his years of dedication and sacrifice. He then read a letter from Congress containing assurances of support, and he urged his officers not to take any actions that would undermine the honor they had earned. Within Congress, the frightening prospect of a coup dissolved resistance to certain demands from the officers. Chastised by Washington, the officers disavowed the "infamous propositions" and accepted a congressional offer of full pay for the next five years. In April 1783, word spread that preliminary articles of peace had been signed in Paris. By June most soldiers were headed home.

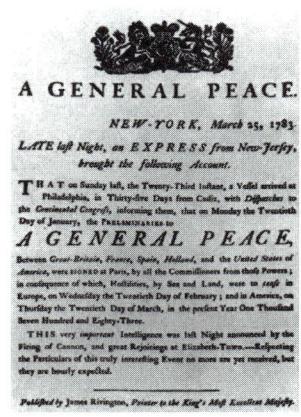

George Washington, The Newburgh Address

The Society of the Cincinnati

Washington's strong stance against the suspected Newburgh conspiracy reminded his admirers of the familiar story of Cincinnatus, a general in Rome's early Republic. The Roman Senate called Cincinnatus from his farm to command an army against invaders. After defeating the enemy, he put down his sword and took up his plow again rather than seize power as a military ruler. His selfless act earned Cincinnatus the lasting respect of the Roman people. Similarly, at a crucial moment for the American republic, Washington urged fellow officers to respect the fragile principle of civilian control over the military. Your action, Thomas Jefferson told Washington, "has probably prevented this revolution from being closed as most others have been by a subversion of that liberty it was intended to establish."

Still, Jefferson and others had grounds to fear that some military officers might meddle in politics while hiding behind the noble name of Cincinnatus. In May 1783, General Henry Knox announced formation of the Society of the Cincinnati. The new organization invoked the name of the famous Roman, in a plural form, to put its members in the best light. But it was open only to officers in the Continental Army, their descendents, and invited honorary members, so some onlookers sensed that the "Cincinnati Club" had a sinister purpose. After all, members contributed to a charitable fund that resembled a political **war chest**, and they maintained contact with each other through newsletters concerning "the general union of the states." Critics feared a separate, self-perpetuating aristocracy of the very kind Americans had fought to erase.

Washington was automatically a member of the society, but Jefferson and other friends urged the general not to accept a leadership position. Struck by this "formidable" opposition, Washington suggested changes in the society, including doing away with the hereditary and honorary memberships. However, he never played a central role in the organization, and Washington's well-publicized alterations were never implemented. The Cincinnati exerted influence as a pressure group before receding from politics in future generations.

Renaming the Landscape

The controversy over the Society of the Cincinnati represented part of a larger debate about the direction of postwar life. Many Americans—despite continuing disagreements—set out to build a national culture and a shared identity. Like the Puritans before them, they aspired to provide new models for the Atlantic world.

They began with names. Everywhere, people christened new towns, counties, streets, and schools and renamed old ones. They replaced numerous British names, such as those of hated prewar governors, so Virginia's Dunmore County received the Indian name *Shanando* (later spelled *Shenandoah*). Because most people found references to royalty distasteful, King Street in Boston quickly became State Street. Still, royal figures who had aided the revolution received their due. Newcomers on the Ohio River named their town Louisville, honoring America's wartime alliance with King Louis XVI of France.

Political leaders popularized Christopher Columbus as well. For generations, the English had downplayed the explorer's importance as they contested Spanish claims in the Western Hemisphere. Now, American writers coined the ringing term *Columbia* for their land to stress its separation from Britain. In South Carolina, citizens named their new capital Columbia in 1786. Five years later, the proposed national capital was christened the District of Columbia. In New York City, when King's College reopened in 1784 under local governance, it was called Columbia College (later Columbia University).

Of all the new names, those honoring individual war heroes became the most popular. Citizens hailed foreign supporters of the revolution—such as Lafayette, Pulaski, and Steuben—by using their names on streets and towns. They saluted American officers the same way. Washington's name was used most often, but those of Montgomery, Wayne, Greene, Lincoln, Mercer, Marion, and others popped up as well. North Carolina named one of its trans-Appalachian forts on the Cumberland River Nashborough, after General Francis Nash, who had died at the battle of Germantown. Citizens changed the fort's name to Nashville in 1784. Two years later, inhabitants of a site on the Tennessee River named their new town Knoxville in honor of General Knox, who had become the Confederation's secretary of war the previous year.

An Independent Culture

New names were just part of the story. Many felt that the American language needed to be made more independent and accessible. Noah Webster, a schoolteacher who had fought against Burgoyne, believed that "as an independent nation, our honor requires us to have a system of our own, in language as well as government." In his *American Spelling Book* (1783), Webster championed a simple, uniform written language that rejected English conventions. Words such as *colour* and *labour* lost their silent *u*, *theatre* became *theater*, and *plough* was shortened to *plow*. The New Englander followed this success with an influential grammar book and a popular reader. Webster went on to produce *An American Dictionary of the English Language* (1828) that incorporated 5,000 new words, many of them reflecting Indian origins (*tomahawk*) and American nature (*rattlesnake*).

> Noah Webster believed that "as an independent nation, our honor requires us to have a system of our own, in language as well as government."

Webster also joined other reformers in lobbying state legislatures for copyright laws to protect the literary works that poured from the pens of ambitious writers. Philip Freneau, a classmate of James Madison at Princeton, drafted a poem titled "The British Prison Ship" (1781), about his war experiences. Authors living near Hartford, known as the Connecticut Wits, wrote similarly nationalistic poetry. Timothy Dwight, future president of Yale College, created "The Conquest of Canaan" (1785), and Joel Barlow composed an epic titled "The Vision of Columbus" (1787), heralding a bright future.

Increasingly, the land itself captured the imagination of Americans. In 1784 a Connecticut silversmith engraved the first map of the new United States, and a recent Yale graduate, Jedidiah Morse, published *Geography Made Easy*, which went through twenty-five editions. (Five years later, Morse created *The American Geography* and earned his reputation as the "Father of American Geography.") In Philadelphia, Quaker naturalist William Bartram drafted a pioneering nature book about his travels throughout the Southeast, and the versatile painter and patriot Charles Willson Peale launched a museum to promote interest in art and the natural world. At Monticello, Thomas Jefferson corresponded with Peale and pursued his own fascination with the American landscape. He promoted exploration, tested new crops, and excavated ancient Indian mounds. In *Notes on the State of Virginia* (1785), Jefferson detailed his region's geography, society, and natural history.

In 1782 Hector St. John de Crèvecoeur, a Frenchman who made his home in America, published *Letters from an American Farmer*, posing the question "What is an American?" According to Crèvecoeur, free people flourished in America because of "a new mode of living, a new social system" that nurtured community growth. Societies for bettering jails, assisting debtors, and building libraries had existed before independence, but after the war Crèvecoeur watched a new generation creating voluntary associations at an unprecedented rate. Reformers launched more than thirty new benevolent organizations between 1783 and 1789, offering aid to the poor, the sick, and the disabled.

In 1785 prominent New Yorkers John Jay and Alexander Hamilton joined like-minded citizens to form a Society for the Promotion of the Manumission of Slaves. In Connecticut, citizens banded together in an early temperance organization to stop the abuse of liquor. Similar efforts to reform and improve the new nation sprang up everywhere. Amid such optimism, no sooner had the former British colonists disentangled themselves from the British Empire than they began to speak of shaping an expansive empire of their own.

■ Exploring near the Altamaha River in Georgia, John Bartram and his botanist son William found "several curious shrubs, one bearing beautiful good fruit." They named it the Franklin tree after their scientist friend in Philadelphia, Benjamin Franklin. William drew a watercolor of the rare plant and saved seeds to protect the species.

Competing for Control of the Mississippi Valley

"It has ever been my hobby-horse," John Adams wrote in 1786, "to see rising in America an empire of liberty, and a prospect of two or three hundred millions of freemen, without one noble or one king among them. You say it is impossible. . . . I would still say, let us try the experiment." Westward expansion became a persistent American theme. But during the postwar decade, interest and activity centered mostly on the land just beyond the Appalachian Mountains, territory reserved for Indians by the British until Britain ceded the lands to the United States at the end of the Revolution.

In the South in the 1780s, pioneer families searching for land pushed west through Cumberland Gap and spread out across parts of the lower Mississippi River valley, a region that eventually became known as the Old Southwest. These homesteaders promptly faced resistance from Native American inhabitants and their Spanish supporters. At the same time, north of the Ohio River, other American migrants were flocking to newly claimed woodlands later remembered as the Old Northwest. They, too, met stiff opposition from Native Americans and their British allies in neighboring Canada. By the time the Constitutional Convention met in Philadelphia in the summer of 1787, the Continental Congress of the existing Confederation government was busy revising an elaborate plan to draw this territory into the Union.

■ **MAP 8.2**
SOUTHERN LAND DEBATES AFTER 1783 Following the Revolution, competing forces collided in the trans-Appalachian South. The United States claimed land reaching the Mississippi River down to 31 degrees latitude, and the Spanish claimed territory north to the Tennessee River. Although major Indian tribes continued to possess much of the region, coastal states also claimed sweeping jurisdiction. In Georgia, for instance, settlement remained confined near the Savannah River, but the state sold speculators large tracts as far west as the Yazoo River.

Disputed Territory: The Old Southwest

For a generation, Spain had been rebuilding its position north of the Gulf of Mexico and east of Texas in the Old Southwest. The Spanish had acquired Louisiana from France in 1763 and had conquered West Florida. In a 1783 treaty, Britain gave back East Florida to the Spanish and agreed that Spain would retain West Florida as well. The Spanish occupied St. Augustine, Pensacola, New Orleans, and Natchez, as well as St. Louis farther north.

Because Spain controlled both banks of the lower Mississippi, the Spanish determined who could use the huge river for trade. Since 1763 they had let British subjects navigate freely on the Mississippi, so trans-Appalachian fur traders had become accustomed to using this thoroughfare. Louisiana merchants paid for goods in Spanish silver, and settlers upriver needed the hard currency. During the Revolutionary War, Americans had retained access to the river, and the Spanish in New Orleans depended on produce from the north. Still, Spanish authorities feared American expansion into the Mississippi Valley. They debated whether to resist migrants pushing from the east, or to co-opt newcomers and profit from their trade.

In 1783 Spain was shocked when Britain, through its separate treaty with the United States, granted the Americans a generous southern boundary: the thirty-first parallel. The treaty terms also included the right of Americans to navigate the Mississippi. The Spanish believed that they should be the only ones to decide whose boats had access to the Mississippi. Moreover, Spain had good reason to claim that its West Florida province stretched north *above* 31 degrees at least to the mouth of the Yazoo River and perhaps as far as the Tennessee River.

For its part, the new Confederation had the force of numbers working to its advantage. The threat of Indian attacks had dammed up westward expansion since 1775. After the war, Americans migrated by the thousands to three existing centers of Anglo settlement in the Old Southwest. By 1785, 10,000 recent migrants clustered along several rivers above Knoxville. Nearly three times that many newcomers had already staked claims to the rich land between Lexington and Louisville. In addition, another 4,000 were clearing farms along the Cumberland River around Nashville, and aggressive Americans talked about pushing even farther. They imagined establishing a foothold on the Mississippi at Chickasaw Bluffs (modern Memphis) or perhaps seizing Natchez or New Orleans.

American Claims and Indian Resistance

Powerful land speculators pressed southern legislatures to support expansion. Georgia, unlike many other states, had not relinquished its western lands to the Confederation. The state's 35-million-acre Yazoo claim stretched west from the Chattahoochee River (Georgia's present boundary with Alabama) to the Mississippi River and from the lower border of modern-day Tennessee to the thirty-first parallel. "I look forward to a time, not very far distant," wrote Judge George Walton, when Georgia "will be settled and connected . . . from the shores of the Atlantic to the banks of the Mississippi." By 1789 Walton had been elected governor of the state, and the land business boomed. During his tenure, Walton signed warrants for huge tracts up to 50,000 acres, sometimes selling unusable or even nonexistent acreage.

Unlike Georgians, pioneers from Virginia and the Carolinas faced a rugged mountain barrier. But they still trekked west through Cumberland Gap. In the decade after the war, backwoodsman Daniel Boone worked as a surveyor for these migrants in the trans-Appalachian region of Virginia that became Kentucky in 1792. During that same decade, North Carolina issued more land patents than it had created during the entire colonial era, most of them deeds for homesteads west of the mountains. Some of North Carolina's western landholders tried to create their own separate jurisdiction: the mountain state of Franklin. Without recognition from the Confederation government, their venture soon failed. Instead, all of North Carolina's western territory—from the Appalachians to the Mississippi—became the state of Tennessee in 1796.

> *Native American southerners, living in all these lands, suddenly found themselves caught between the competing claims of Spain and the United States.*

Native American southerners, living in all these lands, suddenly found themselves caught between the competing claims of Spain and the United States. The Cherokee, Creek, Choctaw, and Chickasaw—numbering roughly 40,000 people—all debated over which leaders and strategies to follow. Some responded to their new situation by selecting leaders with European-American ties. Among the Creek, for example, Alexander McGillivray rose to prominence. The son of a wealthy Scottish trader and a Creek woman, he had been raised on his father's Georgia plantation before becoming the Creek leader in 1782. He was well equipped to bargain with Spanish and American officials.

The renegade Cherokee warrior Dragging Canoe, who had split with tribal elders before the Revolution broke out, offered a different approach. Hundreds of militant Indians, discouraged by the compromises of their leaders, had joined his band of guerrilla fighters known as the Chicamauga living along the Tennessee River. From this well-protected location—near where Alabama, Georgia, and Tennessee now meet—the Chicamauga recruited allies and led forays to stop American encroachment. But Dragging Canoe died in 1792 before he could build a strong alliance with Indians north of the Ohio River.

"We Are Now Masters": The Old Northwest

Native Americans in the North also struggled to maintain their way of life and resist the newcomers. But white Americans lost no time in claiming Indian domains ceded by Britain in the 1783 Treaty of Paris. "We are now Masters of this Island," General Philip Schuyler boasted to the Iroquois, "and can dispose of the Lands as we think proper." Britain refused to vacate western forts on the pretext that Americans still owed prewar debts to London merchants. Even so, the British could provide little material support to the region's Indians.

American delegations moved quickly to draft treaties with the Iroquois and the Ohio Valley tribes. Delegates bluntly asserted the right of the new United States government to Indian lands, treating the Native Americans as dependents rather than equals. The negotiators even took hostages to force the Indians to accept their terms. Ordinary Americans sealed these claims with a surge of migration into western Pennsylvania and beyond. "The Americans . . . put us out of our lands," Indian leaders complained to the Spanish in 1784, "extending themselves like a plague of locusts in the territories of the Ohio River which we inhabit."

Western Land Claims Ceded by the States

Americans initially remained divided among themselves over who would control the region. Connecticut retained a "western reserve" of 4 million acres south of Lake Erie that it used to satisfy claims from the state's war veterans. Similarly, Virginia held onto land rights for an even larger "military district" to repay soldiers and war victims. But one by one, the states of Massachusetts, New York, Connecticut, and Virginia ceded large territorial claims to the Confederation government.

These western acquisitions transformed the Confederation into something more than a league of states. With lands of its own to organize, the Confederation government took on attributes of a sovereign ruling body. As the number of cessions increased, Congress put Thomas Jefferson in charge of a committee to draft "a plan for the temporary Government of the Western territory." Before he departed for Europe to replace Benjamin Franklin as the American minister to France, Jefferson drew up a design for western land distribution.

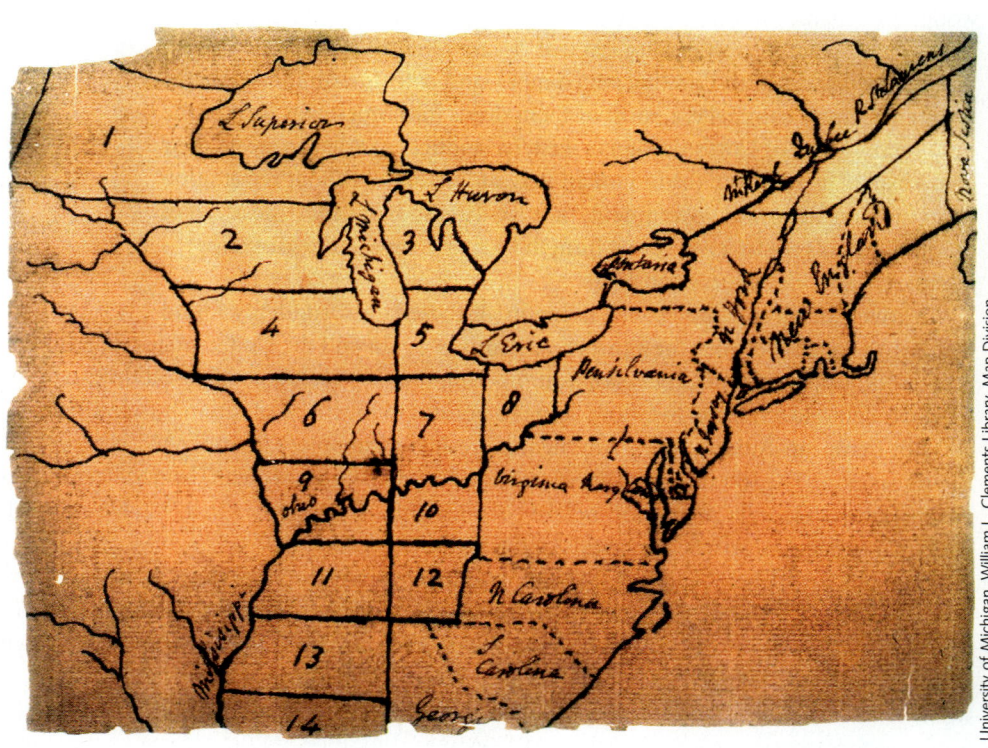

■ A sketch by Congressman Thomas Jefferson shows his proposal to divide the new interior territories into fourteen states (with Number 7 to be named Saratoga after the crucial Revolutionary War victory). By suggesting numerous compact states, Jefferson hoped to maximize the congressional voting power of western farmers. Others, eager to limit western power in Congress, pushed successfully for fewer, larger states.

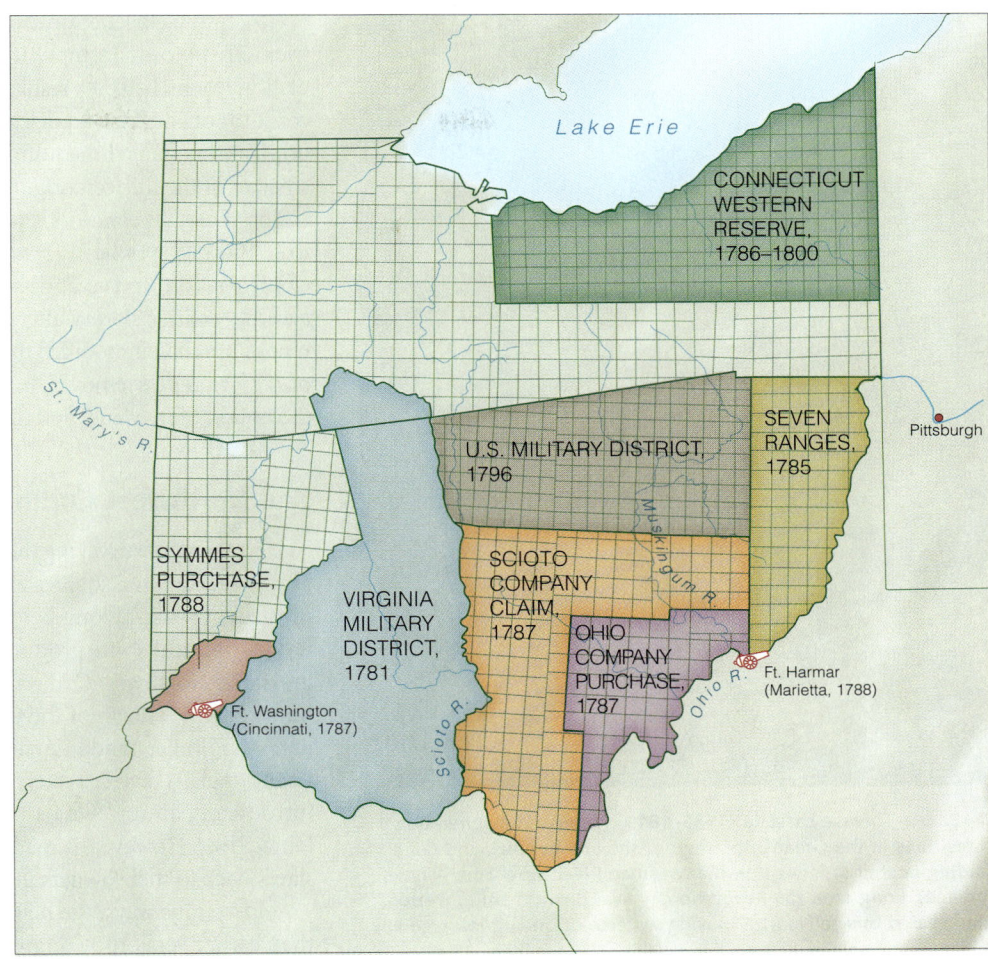

■ MAP 8.3
SETTLERS' OHIO, AFTER 1785   In 1785 the American government began to impose a novel grid system on the territory northwest of the Ohio River. Later, surveyors laid our similar straight geometric boundaries for states and counties accorss the natural landscape of the American West.

After Jefferson sailed for France, his report became the basis for the Land Ordinance of 1785. Jefferson knew that in the South, where surveyors often staked out piecemeal claims on a first-come, first-served basis, the best property had gone to wealthy investors. Moreover, boundary **litigation** over odd-shaped lots had proved endless. To avoid these complications, the 1785 ordinance called for surveyors to lay out a grid of adjoining townships, beginning at the point where the Ohio River flowed out of Pennsylvania. A township would contain thirty-six numbered sections, each 1 mile square (640 acres). The ordinance reserved the income from one valuable section near the heart of every township to support public education.

But orderly surveying and public education were just parts of Jefferson's plan. Hoping to populate the region with self-sufficient yeomen farmers, he proposed that the government give away land in small parcels. He envisioned self-government for these new inhabitants, not colonial status. For Jefferson, the more weight these independent farmers obtained in the American government the better, so he urged the rapid entry of numerous new territories into the Union on an equal footing with the thirteen original states. He suggested creating up to fourteen small, rectangular districts in the west. At least nine would be north of the Ohio River, and each could become a separate state with voting rights in Congress.

■ Marie-Thérèse Lasselle (1735–1819) witnessed a generation of transitions in the Great Lakes region. She and her husband ran a trading post at Kekionga on the Maumee River (now Fort Wayne, Indiana). Long after the Revolutionary War drove them to Detroit, she created this self-portrait, using watercolor on embroidered silk.

According to Jefferson's report, the first settlers arriving in a district were to form a temporary government. When the local population reached 20,000, residents could call a convention, frame a constitution, and send a delegate to Congress. When the district's population equaled the number of free inhabitants living in the smallest of the thirteen original states, that district could enter the Union if certain conditions were met. Each new state must agree to support a republican form of government, remain part of the Confederation, and accept a share of the federal debt. It must also agree to exclude slavery after 1800. Congress accepted Jefferson's report, but then it modified the plan greatly. In its Land Ordinance of 1785, Congress removed his call for numerous districts, dismissed the notion of free land, and dropped the idea of ending slavery.

The Northwest Ordinance of 1787

The huge task of surveying the wilderness north of the Ohio River into neat geometric squares would take years to complete. Almost immediately—and long before the initial ordinance could take hold—political shifts produced an entirely new law from Congress: the Northwest Ordinance of 1787. This law determining how territories north of the Ohio River would be governed contained a number of additional changes to Jefferson's original plan. For example, it reversed direction on the slave question once again, introducing an immediate prohibition of slavery north of the Ohio River. However, it made arrangements to deport fugitive slaves back to their owners in slaveholding states.

In various ways, the new ordinance proved less democratic than earlier versions. Congress cut the possible number of new states from the Old Northwest, specifying there could be only three

Northwest Ordinance (1787)

to five new states. This move limited the potential political weight of the vast territory. In addition, the ordinance increased property requirements for citizens who wanted to vote or hold office. It also slowed the process by which new states could gain admission to the Union. Eventually, Congress granted statehood to five new entities, but the process took more than half a century.

Most members of Congress feared democratic governance in the Old Northwest and the prospect of giving a strong voice to people with different regional interests. To retain control over the domain, they provided for the appointment of territorial officials—a governor, a secretary, and three judges—instead of allowing elected governments. Even when territorial legislatures formed, the governor would have veto power over their actions. James Monroe, head of the committee that moved the bill through Congress, wrote candidly to Jefferson, "It is in effect to be a colonial gover[nme]nt similar to wh[at] prevailed in these States previous to the revolution."

These changes benefited eastern speculators—some of whom were members of Congress—who hoped to control these lands for profit. In 1786 former army officers in New England, joined by five surveyors, organized the Ohio Company to buy up western land. They dispatched Massachusetts minister Manasseh Cutler to lobby Congress to sell a huge tract at bargain rates. Cutler joined forces with congressional insiders associated with another venture, the Scioto Company. Together, they engineered a deal providing 1.5 million acres to the Ohio Company and another 5 million acres for Scioto investors.

Whatever suspicious bargains surrounded congressional passage of the Northwest Ordinance of 1787, the new law still granted basic rights to western residents. These guarantees—following state bills of rights—included religious freedom, trial by jury, and access to common-law judicial proceedings. Most important, the western territories were assured of full entry into the Union as equal states rather than receiving dependent status as permanent colonies. This system established an orderly method for bringing new regions into the Union, starting when Vermont became the fourteenth state in 1791.

Debtor and Creditor, Taxpayer and Bondholder

The end of the Revolutionary War brought widespread economic depression. The money spent by foreign armies for goods and services dried up, and the split with Britain disrupted established patterns of commerce. When peace returned, merchants and artisans scrambled to find new markets and to locate new routes of profitable trade. At the same time, those who had preserved their holdings or made money during the war paid to buy goods from abroad that had been scarce during the fighting. These foreign purchases drained hard currency away from the states and increased the Confederation's debt.

Citizens everywhere felt the **brunt** of the postwar slump as prices dropped and the money supply shrank. As credit tightened, merchants called in their loans and unpaid bills. Families in debt, especially poor artisans and subsistence farmers, suddenly faced the threat of **foreclosure** and loss of their property. They fought back in local elections, in state legislatures, and even in the streets. Violence broke out in state after state, from New Hampshire to Georgia, as hard-pressed people, many of them veterans, decried fiscal policies that favored wealthy bondholders. Onerous taxes were being used to pay annual interest on bonds held by members of the moneyed classes. When armed conflict erupted in Massachusetts, the rebellion helped prompt a drastic effort to restructure and strengthen the national government through a special, closed-door convention in Philadelphia.

New Sources of Wealth

In 1783, the British government managed to fire one parting shot at the former colonies. To nurture Britain's maritime trade and punish New England shippers, it restricted Americans from trading with the British West Indies. The move barred American ships from a key portion of Britain's imperial commerce, forcing merchants to seek out new avenues of trade. In 1784 an American vessel entered the Baltic Sea and established trade relations with Russia. Meanwhile, the seaports of Nantucket and New Bedford stepped up their search for whales to provide oil for American lamps. Captains had no trouble finding sailors in need of work, and ships sailed wherever they sensed possible profits.

Early in 1783, a Savannah merchant named Joseph Clay commented that a "vast number" of slaves had fled the South in wartime. As rice plantations renewed production, African workers were "exceeding scarce and in demand." Sensing a profit, foreign slave traders shipped 15,000 Africans to Georgia and South Carolina by 1785. New England captains soon joined in, sailing ships to Africa in hopes of renewing a trade that had been interrupted during the war. Antislavery sentiment had increased with the idealism of the Revolution, and several states, including Virginia, had outlawed slave imports. Still, American ships transported Africans to the Spanish West Indies, South Carolina, and Georgia. "The Negro business is a great object with us," Clay reported in 1784. "It is to the Trade of this Country, as the Soul to the body."

Financier Robert Morris took a global perspective, realizing that profits could be made by opening new trade routes to the Orient. The project would take an enormous investment—ten times the amount needed to send a ship to Europe—but the potential rewards were irresistible. Morris's first vessel, the *Empress of China*, left New York harbor for Canton by way of the Indian Ocean early in 1784. It carried almost 30 tons of ginseng root—procured from western Virginia—highly prized by the Chinese. The ship also carried 2,600 furs, and $20,000 in hard currency, a huge drain on New York's economy.

■ This painting on glass shows Northwest Coast Indians menacing the American ship *Columbia* from their large war canoes. Captain Robert Gray was conducting trade for sea otter pelts to transport across the Pacific Ocean to China, where the soft fur was highly valued.

In six months, the American ship reached Canton, China's outlet for foreign commerce. "The Chinese had never heard of us," one sailor noted, "but we introduced ourselves as a new Nation" and gave them "a description of our Country." Chinese merchants welcomed trade with "the new people" and called their strange country "the flowery flag kingdom" because the stars on the American flag resembled blossoms. In May 1785 the *Empress of China* returned to New York loaded with tea, chinaware, and silk. Morris and his partners raked in a hefty 20 percent return on their investment.

Other traders took notice. In 1787 the Browns, wealthy merchants in Providence, diverted a slave ship from the African trade to the China tea trade. That same year, six Boston investors sent several vessels around Cape Horn to trade for furs on the American Northwest Coast, pioneering new Pacific routes for American ships. Among the Nootka Indians, Captain Robert Gray exchanged cloth and iron goods for sea otter pelts. Then he sailed the *Columbia* across the Pacific, pausing at Hawaii for supplies. Reaching Canton in 1789, Gray traded profitably and proceeded home through the Indian Ocean, making the *Columbia* the first American ship to circumnavigate the globe.

Because Gray's voyage affirmed the rewards of trade along the Northwest Coast, a diplomatic controversy flared the following year at Nootka Sound, on the west side of Vancouver Island. Although Spain protested British and American trading activities in the area, Gray was back on the Northwest Coast by 1792. He entered a powerful stream—where Washington and Oregon now meet—and named it the Columbia River, after his ship. When he planted the American flag at the mouth of this major waterway, his action foreshadowed later territorial claims by the United States in the Oregon region.

While American merchants probed for new markets abroad, they also moved to strengthen their economic and political position at home. Some wealthy investors bought up a variety of loan certificates, paper notes, and wartime securities issued by state governments and the Continental Congress, paying only a small fraction of the original value. Certificates issued to soldiers at the end of the war became part of this speculative market when the original recipients sold their notes to prosperous speculators for needed cash. In Maryland, for example, the claims on $900,000 owed by the state became concentrated in the hands of only 318 people by 1790. Moreover, sixteen of these people controlled more than half of the total value, and these wealthy investors took an increasing interest in political events. They realized that whoever controlled the reins of power at the state and national levels would determine how the various notes of credit might be redeemed. Speculators who had purchased large quantities of these notes for a fraction of their face worth stood to reap enormous profits from any government that would pay interest on, and then buy back, all these paper arrangements at their original high value.

"Tumults in New England"

The few people who had acquired most of the paper securities wanted their holdings redeemed for hard money. But the majority of citizens, faced with rising debts amid an economic downturn, resented the heavy taxes needed to pay interest on the debt to these wealthy speculators. Favoring much easier credit, they urged their states to issue new paper money. But local elites wanted to limit paper money in ways that favored their new position as powerful creditors and holders of wartime certificates. Their opponents argued that issuing paper money could take the pressure off cash-strapped farmers and help retire enormous war debts. In seven states, these advocates of economic relief carried the day. State government presses put additional notes in circulation.

Local battles over debt, credit, and currency issues hit hardest in the Northeast. In Massachusetts, a legislature sympathetic to creditors consolidated the state's huge war debts in a way that placed extreme tax burdens on ordinary citizens. Also, Britain's move to ban American ships from the British West Indies cut off the lucrative trade that New Englanders had created. For generations, these American captains had sold fish, grain, and lumber to the islands in exchange for hard currency. Sudden exclusion from Britain's Caribbean colonies dried up the flow of much-needed cash into New England and undermined that region's economy.

Sudden exclusion from Britain's Caribbean colonies dried up the flow of much-needed cash into New England and undermined that region's economy.

These changes had an immediate impact. In New Hampshire courts, debt cases rose sixfold from 1782 to 1785. Even if the debts themselves were not large, the heavy costs of traveling to court and paying high legal fees pushed thousands of rural families into bankruptcy. Judges routinely ordered the seizure and sale of property. Embittered farmers watched as their horses, cows, wagons, and household goods disappeared in auction at low prices. Hard times often spark drastic responses, and New England's pot soon boiled over. Early in 1787, Washington's secretary in Virginia noted that the "tumults, insurrections, and *Rebellion* in New England have of late much engrossed the minds of the people here."

Newspaper accounts told of disturbing events in Rhode Island. There, rural politicians seeking relief for indebted farmers swept into power during the elections of April 1786. Their triumph freed the assembly from its longtime domination by rich Providence merchants. The newcomers, elected on their paper-money platform, wasted no time in implementing their ballot-box revolution. The Rhode Island region had a withered economy, and the state government carried a burdensome war debt. To address these matters, assemblymen approved a huge outlay of paper money: £100,000. The assembly planned to distribute the new money among the towns and lend it to citizens on equitable terms. The revenue received back in taxes as the economy rebounded would then be used to pay off the state's debts and retire the paper currency. To ensure the plan's success, legislators declared the money as legal tender that all creditors had to accept as payment.

Not surprisingly, creditors and speculators resented Rhode Island's currency law. Moreover, they fumed at the new legislature's unwillingness to assume a share of the national debt and pay interest to wealthy bondholders, as other states had done. Without control over the legislature, these speculators feared they would be left holding all the continental securities they had acquired. They took swift action. Though heavily outnumbered, members of the moneyed class in Providence used their economic strength to fight back. Many merchants closed their stores rather than accept payments in the new medium of exchange. Some even left the state to avoid being forced to accept debt payments in paper money. When the controversial new statute expired, creditors everywhere sighed with relief. Their elite newspapers condemned the "Rogues' Island" currency law as a dire example of the dangers of democracy.

The Massachusetts Regulation

In Massachusetts and New Hampshire, unlike Rhode Island, powerful merchants retained control over the state assemblies, and they resisted public pressure to generate more paper money. Instead, these creditors pushed to enforce debt collection by the courts. As in other states, wealthy speculators had bought up, at bargain rates, most of the public securities and certificates issued during the war. They anticipated huge profits if a government they controlled could redeem these notes, in gold and silver, at their full face value.

In New Hampshire, by 1785, securities valued at nearly £100,000 belonged to just 4.5 percent of the state's adult male population: 1,120 men among approximately 25,000. A mere 3 percent of this group—thirty-four men—controlled more than a third of this vast speculative investment. Most of these men had close ties to the prevailing government, situated in Exeter, near the coast. When farmers organized conventions to voice their economic grievances, merchants infiltrated and disrupted their meetings. In September 1786, 200 citizens, many of them armed war veterans, marched on Exeter to demand money reforms before conditions "drive us to a state of desperation." Officials organized cavalry units to confront the furious citizens, arresting their leaders from the crowd "as a butcher would seize sheep in a flock." As soon as the state's president, General John Sullivan, had suppressed the dissenters, he issued a proclamation forbidding further conventions. He then wrote to Massachusetts governor James Bowdoin, offering to help crush similar unrest in the neighboring state.

DOCUMENT
Military Reports on Shays' Rebellion

Early in 1786, the Commonwealth of Massachusetts had imposed a heavy direct tax on its citizenry. Western farmers lacked sufficient cash and already faced a wave of foreclosures for debt. They protested the tax law at town meetings and county conventions. When their complaints fell on deaf ears, they took action, "regulating" events as the North Carolina Regulators had done two decades earlier. The Massachusetts Regulation became known as Shays's Rebellion when a former army officer named Daniel Shays emerged as one of its popular leaders. At first, these New England Regulators focused on closing the courts. In August 1786, 1,500 farmers marched against the Court of Common Pleas in Hampshire County and shut it down. The next month, another band closed the court in Worcester.

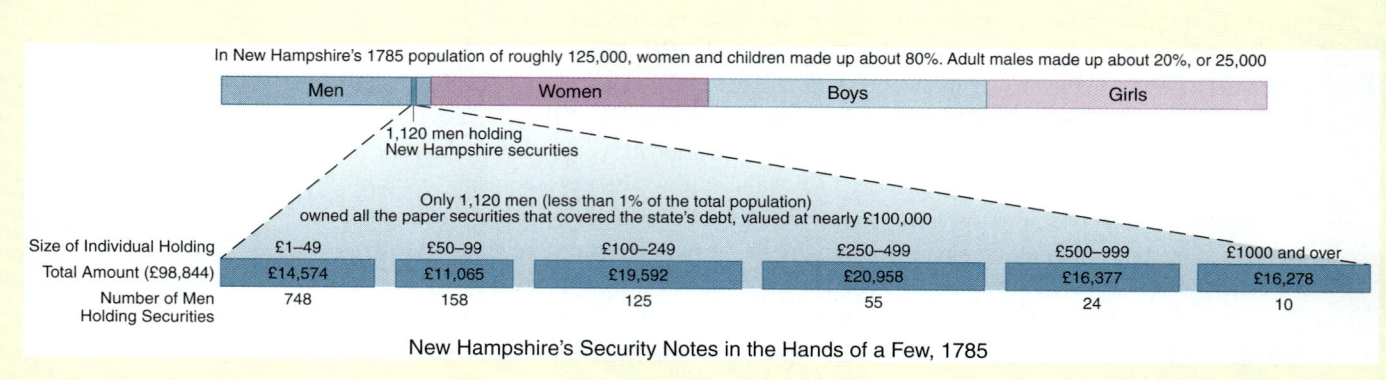

■ **FIGURE 8.1**
CONCENTRATION OF SECURITY NOTES IN THE HANDS OF A FEW: THE EXAMPLE OF NEW HAMPSHIRE IN 1785

The confrontation escalated as winter set in. By January more than 1,000 Shaysites, knowing that their allies in New Hampshire had been defeated, moved to seize the federal arsenal in Springfield. But Governor Bowdoin had mobilized an army, financed largely by wealthy merchants in Boston. This private militia overpowered the westerners and forced all who did not flee to sign an oath of allegiance. Disarmed but not silenced, the dissidents succeeded in extracting some relief from the legislature. They also managed to defeat Bowdoin in the next election and replace him with a more popular governor, John Hancock.

The unrest in New England played into the hands of those advocating a stronger national government. (Rumors even circulated that nationalists had provoked the violence to rally support for their cause.) In May 1787, Henry Knox expressed fear to General John Sullivan that "we are verging fast to anarchy." He urged Sullivan to send delegates from New Hampshire to a crucial meeting that was about to begin in Philadelphia.

> *The unrest in New England played into the hands of those advocating a stronger national government. (Rumors even circulated that nationalists had provoked the violence to rally support for their cause.)*

Drafting a New Constitution

Even before Yorktown, Alexander Hamilton, Washington's youthful Caribbean-born aide-de-camp, had proposed a convention to restructure the national government. Now he worked with another young nationalist, James Madison, and their energetic supporters to bring it about. Congress had made earnest efforts toward reform, but any changes to the Confederation's governing articles required approval from all thirteen states. Thus, vital amendments—which would let Congress regulate commerce, raise revenue, and establish a judiciary, for example—proved nearly impossible. For some powerful leaders, especially merchants and creditors, a major political revision seemed in order.

Alexander Hamilton – Portrait

"Many Gentlemen both within & without Congress," wrote Madison, desire a "Convention for amending the Confederation." Still, it would take impressive leadership—Madison provided much of it—to seize the initiative and then generate enough momentum to change the rules of national government. Extensive compromise, both between elite factions and toward resistant popular forces, would be necessary at every stage. After all, it would take an enormous push to engineer such a convention, to guide it to restructure the government along nationalist lines, and finally to persuade voting Americans to ratify the proposed changes and accept their legitimacy. To begin such a task, would-be reformers needed to convince the Confederation Congress to allow their revision plans to move forward. For that, they needed to recruit the enormous prestige of George Washington.

Statue of George Washington

Philadelphia: A Gathering of Like-Minded Men

The path began at Mount Vernon in 1785 when Washington hosted commissioners appointed by Maryland and Virginia to resolve state boundary disputes regarding the Potomac River. During the gathering, these men (including James Madison) scheduled a broader meeting on Chesapeake trade for the next year at Annapolis, Maryland. They invited all the states to send representatives. Only twelve delegates from five states showed up at Annapolis in September 1786, but news of the unrest in New England prompted talk of a more extended meeting.

Mount Vernon

Alexander Hamilton, as a representative from New York, persuaded the other delegates to call for a convention in Philadelphia the following May to discuss commerce and other matters. Madison won endorsement for the proposal from the Virginia legislature and then from Congress. Reform-minded congressmen, such as James Monroe, saw an opportunity to amend and improve the existing Confederation structure. But when the states sent delegates to Philadelphia the following spring, many of the appointees thought that amendments might not go far enough. They were open to the more sweeping changes that Madison and other nationalists had in mind. So the gathering called to consider commercial matters and propose improvements to the Articles of Confederation soon became a private meeting to design and propose an entirely new structure for governing the United States.

Madison reached Philadelphia in early May 1787. He immediately began drafting plans for drastic change and lobbying delegates, some of whom came early to attend a secret gathering of the Society of the Cincinnati. On May 25, when representatives from seven states had arrived, they launched the convention and unanimously chose Washington as the presiding officer. Participants agreed that they would operate behind closed doors and each state delegation would have one vote. There would be no public discussion or official record of their proceedings. Soon, delegates from twelve states had joined the gathering. Only Rhode Island opted not to send representatives.

The fifty-five delegates had much in common. All were white, male, and well educated, and many already knew one another. These members of the national elite included thirty-four lawyers, thirty public creditors, and twenty-seven members of the Society of the Cincinnati. More than a quarter of the participants owned slaves, and nearly a dozen had done personal business with financier Robert Morris of the Pennsylvania delegation. Not surprisingly, all seemed to agree that the contagion of liberty had spread too far. Indeed, Elbridge Gerry of Massachusetts called the current situation "an excess of democracy."

Specifically, these men feared recent legislation that state assemblies had adopted to assist hard-pressed citizens: laws that delayed tax collection, postponed debt payments, and issued paper money. Most delegates hoped to replace the existing Confederation structure with a national government capable of controlling finances and creating creditor-friendly fiscal policy. To be effective, they believed, a strengthened central government must have greater control over the states. Only Robert Yates and John Lansing of New York and Luther Martin of Maryland staunchly resisted expanding central power.

Many delegates, especially those from heavily populated states, thought the national legislature should be based on proportional representation according to population rather than each state receiving equal weight regardless of its numbers. Also, most wanted to see the single-house (unicameral) Congress of the Confederation replaced by an upper and lower house that would reflect the views and values of different social classes. John Adams had helped create such a two-house (bicameral) system in the Massachusetts constitution, thereby limiting pure democracy and giving more political power to propertied interests.

Besides calling for checks within the legislative branch itself, Adams had also laid out strong arguments for separating, and checking, the powers of each competing branch of government. For a sound and lasting government, Adams had argued, there should be **separation of powers**; the legislative branch should be balanced by separate executive and judicial branches that are equally independent. Most delegates agreed with this novel system of **checks and balances**, intended to add stability and remove corruption.

Compromise and Consensus

DOCUMENT

The Debates in the Federal Convention of 1787 reported by James Madison

The Philadelphia gathering, which lasted through the entire summer, would later be known as the Constitutional Convention of 1787. Even as a consensus emerged within the small meeting, countless personal, practical, and philosophical differences persisted. Hamilton delivered a six-hour speech in which he staked out an extremely conservative position. He underscored "the imprudence of democracy" and stressed a natural separation between "the few and the many"—the "wealthy well born" and the "turbulent and changing" people. Hamilton's conservative oration called for the chief executive and the senators to be chosen indirectly, by elected representatives rather than by the people themselves, and he recommended that these high officials should serve for life. Such ideas undoubtedly appealed to many of his listeners, but all of the delegates knew that a majority of citizens would never accept such proposals. Pierce Butler of South Carolina invoked Solon in ancient Greece, "who gave the Athenians not the best government he could devise but the best they would receive."

This attentiveness of convention members to what the public would accept is illustrated by their approach to voting rights. Property ownership was no longer a universal voting requirement, and state constitutions varied on whether religion, race, or gender could determine eligibility. James Wilson of Pennsylvania, second only to Madison in working to build a practical nationalist majority in the convention, pointed out that "it would be very hard and disagreeable" for any person, once franchised, to give up the right to vote. Accordingly, the delegates proposed that in each state all those allowed to vote for the "most numerous branch of the state legislature" would also be permitted to cast ballots for members of the House of Representatives. But they shied away from accepting direct election for the Senate or the president, and they deferred suffrage matters to the states.

Time and again during the sixteen-week convention, these like-minded men showed their willingness to bargain and compromise. Lofty principles and rigid schemes often gave way to balancing and improvisation. The unlikely creation of the electoral college for selecting a president is one example. Delegates who differed over the length for the chief executive's term of office and right to run for reelection also disagreed on the best method of presidential selection. Some of them suggested that ordinary voters should elect the president; others proposed that the state governors, or the national legislature, or even electors chosen by the lower house should choose the chief executive.

Finally, the aptly named Committee on Postponed Matters cobbled together an acceptable system: a gathering (or "college") of chosen electors from each state would cast votes for the presidency. This **electoral college** plan had little precedent, but it managed to balance competing interests. Under the scheme, state legislatures would set the manner for selecting electors. The least populous states would get a minimum of three electoral votes, and states with more people would choose more electors in proportion to their numbers, giving them added weight in the decision. The people could also participate in the voting process, though only if their state legislatures called for it. If no candidate won a majority in the electoral college, the House of Representatives had the right to determine the president, with each state having one vote. The system was far from elegant or democratic, but it placated varied interests, and it won prompt approval.

Questions of Representation

As deliberations stretched across the long, hot summer of 1787, two central issues threatened to unravel the convention: political representation and slavery. Questions of representation pervaded almost every discussion, pitting the states with the largest populations, such as Virginia, Pennsylvania, and Massachusetts, against the less populated states. Madison's well-organized Virginians offered a comprehensive blueprint outlining a new national government that would have three separate branches. This design, called the "Virginia Plan," recommended a bicameral national legislature with proportional representation in each body. The House of Representatives would be chosen by popular election, the Senate by the lower house.

> *As deliberations stretched across the long, hot summer of 1787, two central issues threatened to unravel the convention: political representation and slavery.*

Madison's system clearly favored populous states. Not surprisingly, a coalition of small-state delegates led by William Paterson of New Jersey submitted an alternative "New Jersey Plan." This less sweeping revision built on the current Articles of Confederation. It called for a continuation of the existing unicameral legislature, in which each state received an equal vote. A committee chaired by Benjamin Franklin managed to break the impasse. The idea of an upper house, or Senate, would be retained, and each state, whatever its size, would hold two senate seats. Seats in the House of Representatives would be determined proportionally, according to the relative population of each state. Moreover, this lower house would have the power to initiate all bills dealing with finance and money matters.

To implement proportional representation in a fast-growing society, the delegates devised a radical innovation: a national census every ten years. This regular headcount in turn raised a thorny question. Should slaves—people enumerated in the census yet denied the rights of citizens—be counted in determining a state's proportional representation in the national government? Slaveholding states wanted their human property to count because that would give those states more representation. The convention resolved this dilemma in mid-July with a "three-fifths" formula that made every five enslaved people equivalent to three free people in apportionment matters.

In an ironic twist, the same week the Constitutional Convention delegates approved the notorious three-fifths clause, the existing government of the United States leaned in the opposite direction. Meeting in New York, members of the Confederation's Congress passed the Northwest Ordinance, which outlawed slavery in the new territory above the Ohio River. Because there was much contact between the two meetings, some scholars speculate that powerful Southerners agreed to give away the prospect of slavery north of the Ohio River in exchange for more support of slavery within the new plan taking shape in Philadelphia.

Slavery: The Deepest Dilemma

During the debate over the three-fifths clause, Madison commented that the greatest division in the United States "did not lie between the large & small States: it lay between the Northern & Southern," owing to "the effects of their having or not having slaves." This highly charged issue continued to simmer beneath the surface for most of the summer.

In late August, with most other matters resolved, delegates could no longer postpone questions surrounding slavery. Yet again, a committee deliberated, and a bargain was struck. But this time, hundreds of thousands of human lives were at stake. Planter delegates from Georgia and South Carolina refused to support any document that regulated the slave trade or curtailed slavery itself. They asserted that such a charter could never win acceptance at home.

In part they were bluffing. Constraints against slavery had wide popular appeal in the expanding backcountry of the Deep South, where independent farmers outnumbered planters, ministers questioned slavery, and pioneers wanted national support in confronting powerful Indians.

■ In a crucial decision, members of the Constitutional Convention chose to protect the slave trade and preserve slavery. One African American who had already taken matters in her own hands was Mumbet, a slave in Massachusetts and widow of a Revolutionary War soldier. In 1781 she sued for her freedom on the grounds that "all were born free and equal." Her court victory proved a landmark in New England. Proudly, she took the name Elizabeth Freeman.

Yet few delegates challenged the proslavery posture, possibly because strong antislavery opinions could have prolonged or even deadlocked the convention. Weary participants were eager to complete their work and fearful of unraveling their hard-won consensus. Rather than force the matter, even those who disapproved of slavery rushed to compromise, heaping a huge burden on future generations. Southern delegates dropped their protests against giving Congress the power to regulate international shipping. In exchange, the framers approved a clause protecting the importation of slaves for at least twenty years. They also added a provision governing fugitive slaves that required the return of "any person held to service or labor." Through a calculated bargain, delegates had endorsed slavery and drawn the South into the Union on terms that suited that region's leaders. The word *slave* never appeared in the finished document.

In early September, the convention members put the finishing touches on their proposal and wondered whether Americans would accept it. Winning state-by-state approval would involve an uphill battle, especially given the absence of a bill of rights. George Mason, who had drawn up Virginia's Declaration of Rights eleven years earlier, reminded members that such a set of guarantees "would give great quiet to the people." But in the convention's closing days, many delegates resisted the notion, and all were eager to adjourn. They overwhelmingly voted down Mason's suggestion.

Without a bill of rights, Mason and Gerry refused to endorse the final document, along with Edmund Randolph of Virginia. Other delegates who dissented had already departed. Of the seventy-four delegates chosen at the convention's outset, fifty-five actually attended the proceedings, and only thirty-nine agreed to sign the finished plan. It was approved "by the unanimous consent of the States present" on September 17, 1787.

Ratification and the Bill of Rights

Committed nationalists now faced their most difficult task: winning public acceptance for an alternative structure that defied existing law. After all, the proposed constitution ignored the fact that the Articles of Confederation—the document governing the United States at the time—could be amended only with the approval of all thirteen states. Instead, the text drafted in Philadelphia stated that ratification (acceptance through voting) by conventions in any nine states would make the new document take effect in those places. Moreover, the proposed ratification process left no room for partial approval or suggested revisions. Each state, if it wanted to enter the debate at all, had to accept or reject the proposed frame of government as offered.

The Campaign for Ratification

The Confederation Congress had acquiesced in allowing the 1787 convention to occur in the first place. Most congressional representatives had expected the meeting to produce proposals for amending the current government, not discarding it. But now that the Philadelphia **conclave** had ended, the Congress sitting in New York City balked at endorsing the revolutionary document. To avoid a lengthy and troublesome debate, proponents of the new constitution urged Congress simply to receive the frame of government as a possible proposal and then transmit it to the states without an endorsement. Congress did so on September 28, 1787, and the document's advocates portrayed the unanimous vote as an expression of approval.

Supporters had no time to lose because Pennsylvania's assembly was set to adjourn on the next day. An early victory in that large and central state would be crucial in building momentum, so they rushed the congressional letter of transmittal from New York to Philadelphia. There, the assembly faction dominated by Robert Morris won a hasty vote to schedule a state ratifying convention. Over the next three months, towns and counties elected delegates, a convention met, and Pennsylvania voted to approve the new plan. Delaware had approved it unanimously on December 7, and New Jersey and Georgia followed suit. By the end of January, Connecticut had also ratified. Other states had called elections and scheduled conventions. Only Rhode Island, which had not sent delegates to the drafting convention, refused to convene a meeting to debate ratification.

By seizing the initiative early, the proponents of the new framework shaped the terms of debate. The drafters, anything but a cross-section of society, worked to portray themselves as such. They noted that their document began with the ringing phrase "We the people of the United States," a last-minute addition by Gouverneur Morris of New York. And Madison told the public that the text sprang from "*your* convention."

Most important, in a reversal of logic and contemporary usage, the nationalists who supported the new constitution took for themselves the respected name of **Federalists**. They gave their opponents the negative-sounding term **Anti-Federalists**. The Federalists then used their ties to influential leaders to wage a media war for public support. They dashed off letters and published essays praising the proposed constitution.

The strongest advocacy came from Alexander Hamilton and James Madison. The two men composed eighty essays for the New York press under the pen name *Publius*. John Jay added five more, and in the spring of 1788 the collection appeared as a book titled *The Federalist*.

DOCUMENT

Madison Defends the Constitution

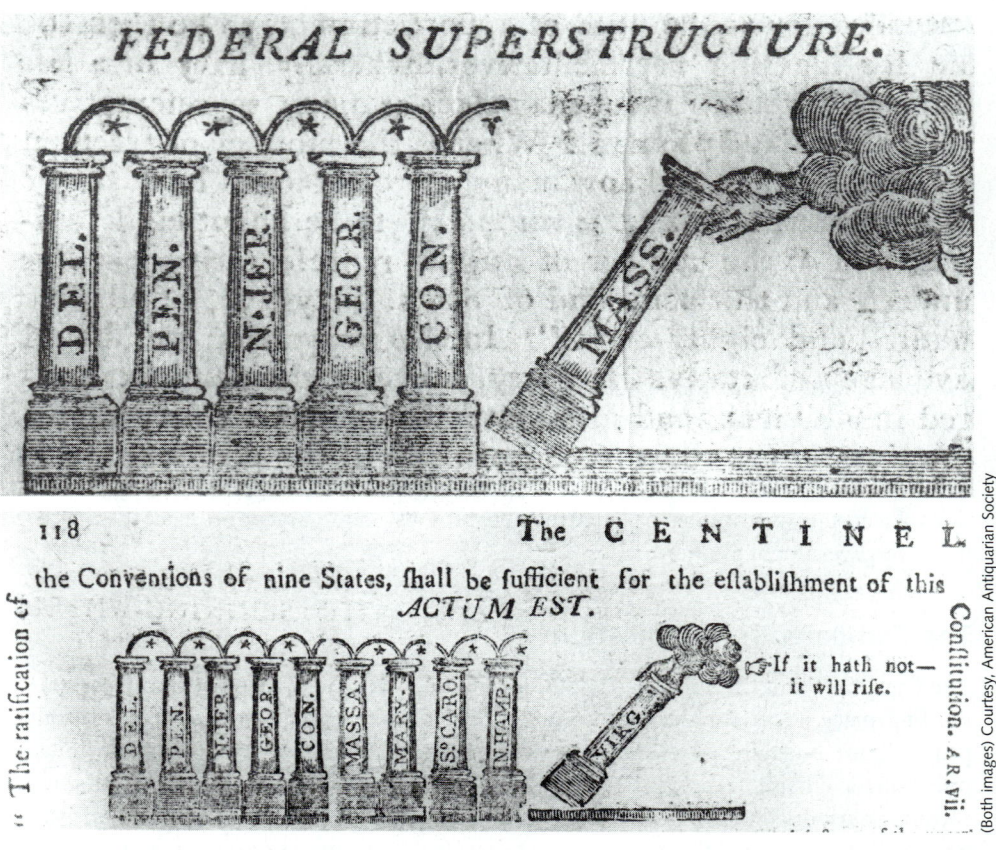

■ In 1788 newspapers tracked ratification of the new "federal superstructure" state by state. Massachusetts ratified the proposed U.S. Constitution in March—apparently aided by the Hand of God! New Hampshire provided the "ninth and sufficient pillar" in June, followed by Virginia four days later.

In the most famous piece, "Number 10," Madison challenged the widely accepted idea that a republic must be small and compact to survive. Turning the proposition around, he argued that minority opinions would fare better in a large nation, where diverse competing interests would prevent a unified majority from exerting control.

Dividing and Conquering the Anti-Federalists

Opponents of the new plan found themselves on the defensive from the start. Many of them had supported some government change, and most conceded the presence of economic difficulties. But Federalist predictions of impending chaos seemed exaggerated. "I deny that we are in immediate danger of anarchy," one Anti-Federalist writer protested.

Henry, Against the Ratification of the Constitution

Richard Henry Lee, president of the Confederation Congress, condemned the Federalists as a noisy "coalition of monarchy men, military men, aristocrats and drones." Other prominent figures joined him in opposition: George Clinton in New York; Luther Martin in Maryland; and Patrick Henry, George Mason, and Benjamin Harrison in Virginia. Such notables became the spokespeople for a far wider array of skeptics.

Many opponents of the proposed constitution protested the plan's perceived threat to local political power. Despite Madison's reassurances in *Federalist* Number 10, they believed that local and state governments represented voters more fairly and responded to their needs more quickly than a distant national authority could. For some critics this belief expressed a radical democratic principle; for others it represented their provincial bias. In short, Anti-Federalists were too diverse to speak with a single voice. Their ranks included subsistence farmers living far from urban markets and war veterans who saw their influence in republican government diminished by the proposed system. Many indebted people also opposed ratification, fearing that a strong national government would favor the interests of bondholders and foreign creditors ahead of the economic well-being of ordinary citizens.

If Anti-Federalists were numerous in the remote countryside, Federalists predominated in coastal commercial centers. Using a variety of tactics, they pressed their advantages in the fight to control state ratifying conventions. They lured prominent Anti-Federalist delegates with hints of high office, and they ridiculed vocal opponents as Shaysite extremists. In state after state, they forged coalitions linking commercial farmers living near towns and rivers with aspiring artisans and city-based entrepreneurs. Through intensive politicking, they garnered approval in Massachusetts in February 1788, but only by a thin margin (187 votes to 168 in the ratifying convention). This commitment from "the Bay State" helped to sway Maryland in April, South Carolina in May, and New Hampshire in June. The Federalists could now claim the nine states needed to implement their plan, and in July they staged parades to hail the new Constitution of the United States.

■ Celebrations in July 1788 hailed the new Constitution of the United States. "Columbus" on horseback led New York City's parade, followed by artisan groups. The silk banner of the pewterers proclaimed that under the Federal Plan, "All Arts Shall Flourish in Columbia's Land, And All Her Sons Join as One Social Band."

The approved Constitution promptly became the law of the land. But in Massachusetts, the Federalists had triumphed only by promising to add an explicit bill of rights that gave written protection for valued civil liberties. They had to make similar assurances to secure slim majorities in Virginia (89 to 79) and New York (30 to 27). North Carolinians had voted down the proposed frame of government at their first ratifying convention because it lacked a bill of rights. A second North Carolina convention, called in 1789, withheld approval until a bill of rights had actually been introduced into the first Federal Congress as proposed amendments to the Constitution. In 1790, Rhode Island narrowly voted approval for the new framework (34 to 32) rather than risk being left in economic and political isolation.

Adding a Bill of Rights

In a society consisting of almost 3 million people, the franchise remained a limited privilege, open primarily to white men with property. All told, only about 160,000 voters throughout the country took part in choosing representatives to the state ratifying conventions. And only about 100,000 of these people—less than 7 percent of the entire adult population—cast votes for delegates who supported the Constitution. Federalists knew, therefore, that they would have to fulfill their pledge to incorporate a bill of rights. Madison, goaded by Jefferson, promised Virginians that he would push for the inclusion of specific rights as amendments to the Constitution. He had several motives. First, he hoped to ensure his own election to the nation's new House of Representatives. Second, he wanted to head off talk of another convention "for a reconsideration of the whole structure of government."

In compiling a list of protections, or bill of rights, Madison drew from scores of proposals for explicit amendments put forward by the state ratifying conventions. He selected those, mostly dealing with individual rights, that could pass a Federalist-dominated Congress and would not dilute any of the proposed new government's powers. He set aside suggestions for limiting the government's right to impose taxes, raise a standing army, or control the time and place of elections. True to his word, he pushed twelve less controversial statements through the Congress as constitutional amendments, despite congressional apathy and opposition. Within two years, three-fourths of the states ratified ten of these short but weighty pronouncements. Hence, the first ten amendments—the Bill of Rights—quickly became a permanent part of the U.S. Constitution.

Many of the protections provided by the **Bill of Rights** harked back to lessons learned in earlier struggles with Parliament. The ten amendments guarded the right of the people to bear arms, limited government power to quarter troops in homes, and banned unreasonable searches or seizures. They also ensured the right to trial by jury, outlawed excessive bail and fines, and prohibited "cruel and unusual punishments." The First Amendment secured freedom of speech and of the press, protected people's right to assemble and petition, and prohibited Congress from meddling in the exercise of religion. By securing these freedoms, Madison engineered a final set of compromises that ensured the acceptance and **longevity** of the Constitution he had done so much to frame.

Conclusion

The War for Independence exhausted the new nation. Managing the difficult task of demobilization and reconstruction consumed American energy and resources in the 1780s. So did the new western domain, where Americans had to balance prospects for national expansion against the military threats posed by European empires and Native American groups that claimed the region. Also, economic differences set aside during the war quickly reemerged; questions of wealth and property loomed large.

Therefore, when confederation leaders imposed unprecedented taxes to pay off the war bonds gathered up by wealthy speculators, irate farmers and veterans protested that Congress was gouging "the Many" to enrich "the Few." These numerous dissenters pressured state governments to provide debt relief and issue paper money. But wealthy creditors reacted forcefully: these like-minded men maneuvered to create a new and stronger central government that could support their interests and override state-level economic measures favoring the common people. Sidestepping the existing government, they drafted a new constitution at a closed convention in Philadelphia in 1787, and they campaigned successfully for its ratification by 1789.

The reins of power, which nearly slipped from the hands of established American leaders during the tumultuous 1770s, had been securely restored by the end of the 1780s, in the face of bitter and varied opposition. But the fierce debate over ratification of the constitution raised fresh uncertainties about the long-term survival of the union. Much hinged on selection of the first president. Inevitably, George Washington emerged as the overwhelming favorite to become the first chief executive of the new republic.

Sites to Visit

Washington's Newburgh Headquarters

For sixteen months in 1782–1783, the farmhouse of Jonathan Hasbrouck served as Washington's headquarters in Newburgh, New York, 12 miles north of West Point. The state of New York purchased the stone building on Lafayette Street in 1850 and opened it as the first publicly operated historic site in the United States.

Fraunces Tavern

http://www.francestavernmuseum.org/index.html

Here, at 54 Pearl Street near the tip of Manhattan, Washington bid farewell to his officers in 1783. From 1785 to 1787, while New York served as the capital city, the building held the departments of foreign affairs, the treasury, and war. Now it houses a museum with exhibits relating to the eighteenth century.

Mount Vernon
www.mountvernon.org/

During the nineteenth century, concerned women rallied to preserve Mount Vernon, George Washington's estate on the Potomac River. It is still maintained by the Mount Vernon Ladies' Association. If you cannot visit the plantation itself, 8 miles south of Alexandria, Virginia, you can visit the Web site.

Independence National Historical Park in Philadelphia
http://www.nps.gov/inde/

Covering 45 acres and containing twenty buildings, this site includes Independence Hall, where the Constitutional Convention met in the summer of 1787. The Visitor Center is at Third and Walnut Streets. On the Market-Frankfurt Subway, use the 5th Street and Market station.

Natchez Trace Parkway
http://www.nps.gov/natr/

Running 444 miles from Natchez, Mississippi, to the outskirts of Nashville, Tennessee, this one-time Chickasaw Indian trail became a pathway for boatmen returning north after floating their goods down the Mississippi. It is now a scenic road maintained by the National Park Service.

Congress and the Constitution
http://lcweb2.loc.gov/ammem/amlaw/lawhome.html

This Library of Congress Web site has the complete text of Max Farrand's *Records of the Federal Convention*, published in 1911, plus Paul H. Smith's *Letters of Delegates to Congress*, and many excellent post-1789 documents.

James Madison: His Legacy
http://www.jmu.edu/madison/madison.htm

The James Madison Center at James Madison University in Virginia maintains this Web site, which provides ready access to materials on Madison's life and interests, along with links to numerous documents and Web sites.

Historic Bartram's Garden
http://www.ushistory.org/tour/index.html

This Web site is part of LibertyNet's Virtual Tour of Historic Philadelphia. The garden itself, located at 54th Street and Lindbergh Boulevard, is run by the John Bartram Association, named for William Bartram's botanist father. Visit www.bartramtrail.org/ to learn more about backpacking Bartram's Trail through the South.

For Further Reading

General

Merrill Jensen, *The New Nation: A History of the United States During the Confederation, 1781–1789* (1948).
Richard B. Morris, *The Forging of the Union, 1781–1789* (1987).
Kenneth Silverman, *A Cultural History of the American Revolution* (1976).
Larry E. Tise, *The American Counterrevolution: A Retreat from Liberty, 1783–1800* (1998).
Gordon S. Wood, *The Creation of the American Republic, 1776–1787* (1969).

Beating Swords into Plowshares

Elizabeth A. Fenn, *Pox Americana: The Great Smallpox Epidemic of 1775–82* (2001).
Richard H. Kohn, *Eagle and Sword: The Federalists and the Creation of the Military Establishment in America, 1783–1802* (1975).
Henry F. May, *The Enlightenment in America* (1976).

Competing for Control of the Mississippi Valley

Gregory Evans Dowd, *A Spirited Resistance: The North American Indian Struggle for Unity, 1745–1815* (1992).
R. Douglas Hurt, *The Ohio Frontier: Crucible of the Old Northwest, 1720–1830* (1996).
Peter S. Onuf, *Statehood and Union: A History of the Northwest Ordinance* (1987).
Arthur Preston Whitaker, *The Spanish American Frontier, 1783–1795* (1927, reprinted 1969).

Debtor and Creditor, Taxpayer and Bondholder

E. James Ferguson, *The Power of the Purse: A History of American Public Finance, 1776–1790* (1961).
Jackson Turner Main, *The Anti-Federalists: Critics of the Constitution, 1781–1788* (1961).

Edmund S. Morgan, *Inventing the People: The Rise of Popular Sovereignty in England and America* (1988).
Leonard L. Richards, *Shays' Rebellion: The American Revolution's Final Battle* (2002).

Drafting a New Constitution

Charles A. Beard, *An Economic Interpretation of the Constitution of the United States* (1913).
Carol Berkin, *A Brilliant Solution: Inventing the American Constitution* (2002).
Christopher Collier and James Lincoln Collier, *Decision in Philadelphia: The Constitutional Convention of 1787* (1986).
Leonard W. Levy and Dennis J. Mahoney, eds., *The Framing and Ratification of the Constitution* (1987).
John P. Kaminski, ed., *A Necessary Evil? Slavery and the Debate over the Constitution* (1995).
Jack N. Rakove, *Original Meanings: Politics and Ideas in the Making of the Constitution* (1996).

Ratification and the Bill of Rights

Akhil Reed Amar, *The Bill of Rights: Creation and Reconstruction* (1998).
Saul Cornell, *The Other Founders: Anti-Federalism and the Dissenting Tradition in America, 1788–1828* (1999).
Michael Kammen, *A Machine That Would Go by Itself: The Constitution in American Culture* (1986).
Richard E. Labunski, *James Madison and the Struggle for the Bill of Rights* (2006).
Garry Wills, *Explaining America: The Federalist* (1981).
David Siemers, *The Antifederalists: Men of Great Faith and Tolerance* (2003).

For quizzes and other resources on these topics, go to www.longmanamericanhistory.com.

CHAPTER 9

Revolutionary Legacies, 1789–1803

CHAPTER OUTLINE

Competing Political Visions in the New Nation

People of Color: New Freedoms, New Struggles

Continuity and Change in the West

Shifting Social Identities in the Post-Revolutionary Era

The Election of 1800: Revolution or Reversal?

Conclusion

Sites to Visit

For Further Reading

AMERICA'S REVOLUTIONARY WAR WAS OVER, BUT COMPETING IDEAS OF LIBERTY AND EQUALITY swirled throughout the Atlantic world, reinforced by the rhetoric of the French Revolution of 1789. In August 1800, Gabriel Prosser, an enslaved blacksmith in Richmond, Virginia, plotted to seize the state capitol and overthrow the slave regime. His plan gave voice to the egalitarian principles articulated in Philadelphia in 1776 and then in the Caribbean island of Saint-Domingue in 1791, when slaves had staged a bloody revolution against their French masters. (In 1804 they renamed the country Haiti.) Gabriel's rebels used the words of the nation's founders to justify their actions, rallying around the cry "Death or Liberty." One even compared himself to George Washington in his struggle to "obtain the liberty of [his] countrymen." Gabriel's plans failed when informants betrayed him and a hurricane-force storm washed out any hope for the uprising's success. Yet Gabriel's rebellion, even though foiled, is indicative of the ongoing struggles among almost all Americans regarding the legacy of the Revolution.

Among Native Americans, the American Revolution destroyed one Indian confederation and led to the creation of another. The Iroquois Confederacy in present-day New York State had suffered greatly during the war. Then, in the late 1780s, some survivors migrated westward, away from their ruined fields and still smoldering villages. Regrouping in Detroit, they forged a new political alliance, this time with other Indians living along the Ohio River and in the Great Lakes region. Mohawk leader Joseph Brant urged the Algonquin, Shawnee, Delaware, and others to join in common purpose to resist U.S. territorial aggression. Members of the Ohio Confederacy, he claimed, should "eat out of one bowl with one spoon." Gaining military strength from political unity (just as the American colonists had done), they could now resist the tide of newcomers sweeping into the trans-Appalachian West—the area that is today Kentucky, Ohio, Indiana, and Michigan. Their resistance proved effective, drawing the army of the infant nation into an expensive and bloody war.

■ Artist Gilbert Stuart painted this portrait in 1786 of Mohawk leader Joseph Bryant (born Thayendanegea).

Slaves and Native Americans were not the only ones wrestling with the unfinished revolution. As the century ended, a number of groups challenged dominant notions about race, gender, wealth, and standing in the community. In New England and the Upper South, a rapidly growing class—free people of color—struggled to assert their rights. Throughout the new states, some women maintained a high degree of political engagement; New Jersey even granted well-to-do women the right to vote, if only for a brief period. Artisans also sought to wield new political clout, taking part in the new and surprising formation of national parties. Free blacks, women voters, and artisan-politicians all revealed the social tensions mounting in the new republic as well as the promise it offered to these same groups.

The first census of the United States, conducted in 1790, tallied 4 million people. Of this number, 750,000 (more than 18 percent) were black. People of various ethnicities clustered together in pockets throughout the states. German-born people accounted for one-third of all Pennsylvanians, and almost one-fifth of New York residents were Dutch. Numbers of Northerners and Southerners were about equal. However, ethnic and regional differences proved less significant in shaping the emerging two-party system than the persistent split between urban-based merchants and rural interests such as southern planters. The Revolution also unleashed enormous creative energy, as some people, unfettered by restrictions imposed by the crown, pursued new economic opportunities. In contrast, many artisans and small farmers continued to stagger under a burden of debt and new federal taxes. For them, the Revolution was a betrayal of their vision for America.

Competing Political Visions in the New Nation

In the first two decades of the new nation, domestic politics remained entwined in relations with the great European powers. For all their bold talk of freedom and liberty, the heirs of the Revolution continued to formulate public policies based upon the models offered by Great Britain and France. Specifically, some Americans found much to admire in British traditions of social order and stability, traditions shaped by a strong central authority in the form of a monarchy. Other Americans derived inspiration from the French Revolution, which began in 1789. They believed that, for all its bloody excesses, the revolution represented an ideal of true democracy, an ideal at odds with entrenched privilege in the form of monarchies and aristocracies. The British model appealed to Federalists, supporters of a strong central government. In contrast, the French model appealed to Anti-Federalists, soon to be called Democratic-Republicans, supporters of the rights of the states and of the active participation of ordinary citizens in politics. These divergent views shaped both foreign and domestic policy in the 1790s.

Within this contentious atmosphere, George Washington assumed the presidency in 1789, backed by the unanimous endorsement of the electoral college. Neither the ratification of the Constitution nor Washington's election silenced the continuing debate over civil liberties and the nature of the national government. Responding to the concerns of the Anti-Federalists, Congress quickly passed ten amendments to the Constitution, collectively called the Bill of Rights. Ratified by the necessary number of states in 1791, the amendments were intended to protect white men from the power of government, whether local, state, or national. The Judiciary Act of 1789 established a national, federal court system that included a five-member Supreme Court and the office of attorney general, charged with enforcing the nation's laws.

Like other public figures of the time, Washington believed that ideological differences between political leaders should never become institutionalized in the form of separate parties. These leaders believed politicians should debate issues freely among themselves, without being bound by partisan loyalty to one view or political candidate over another. However, by the late 1790s, the intense rivalry between Alexander Hamilton, Washington's secretary of the treasury, and Thomas Jefferson, his secretary of state, had produced a **two-party system** that proved remarkably durable. Representing two competing political visions, Hamilton and his supporters (known as Federalists) and Jefferson and his supporters (called Democratic-Republicans) disagreed on foreign diplomacy and domestic economic policies. Hamilton advocated a strong central government that would promote commerce and manufacturing. In contrast, Jefferson favored states' rights bolstered by small, independent farmers who would serve as the nation's moral and political center.

The Hamiltonian System

In 1792 Washington ran for and won a second term. Four years later, Washington declined to run for a third term. His successor was his vice president, John Adams, an unabashed Federalist who rankled Jefferson and other more egalitarian-minded citizens. Between 1789 and 1800, the clash between the Federalists and the Democratic-Republicans reverberated on the high seas, in Indian country, and in the halls of Congress.

Federalism and Democratic-Republicanism in Action

An outspoken Federalist, Hamilton took bold steps to advance the commercial interests of the new nation. In 1789, as Washington's secretary of the treasury, he persuaded Congress to enact the first U.S. **tariff** on imported goods. He argued this move would encourage home manufactures and raise money for the treasury.

Alexander Hamilton, "Bank"

Hamilton also sought to strengthen the federal government through **monetary policy**. At his prodding, in 1790 Congress agreed to fund the national debt—that is, to assume responsibility for repaying the government's creditors including paying interest on the debt (a total of $54 million). Congress also assumed responsibility for debts that the individual states had incurred during the Revolution. To pay for all this, federal officials stepped up debt collection and imposed new taxes on individuals. In 1791 Congress also issued a twenty-year charter to the first Bank of the United States. Hamilton believed this institution, modeled after the Bank of England, would help stimulate the economy by circulating surplus funds held by the government.

An advocate of agricultural interests and the power of individual states, Jefferson disagreed with Hamilton on all these issues. Jefferson bitterly opposed the Bank of the United States, arguing that only the states could issue charters for financial institutions. He favored a lower tariff, urging that high-priced imports hurt farmers and other small consumers. The leader of the Democratic-Republicans believed that the government should not interfere in the lives of its citizens by imposing new taxes on individual households or on imported goods. According to Jefferson, governments, like individuals, should exercise restraint in their spending and should avoid accumulating debt. Hamilton and Jefferson's opposing views of government shaped the American political party system for generations to come.

The different views epitomized by Hamilton and Jefferson found expression in American reactions to Europe's political turmoil surrounding the French Revolution. Since France had recently been a crucial wartime ally, most Americans at first supported the dramatic events unfolding there in 1789. By imposing constitutional constraints on their king, Louis XVI, the French seemed engaged in a heroic struggle much like that of the Patriots of 1776, who had challenged the enormous power of the British monarch. But when French radicals launched what became known as the Reign of Terror, American public opinion grew more critical.

In January 1793, leaders in Paris beheaded the French king and went on to execute aristocrats and presumed opponents of the revolution. In response, Federalist politicians argued that the bloody excesses in France should push American citizens toward a moderate and stable central government for the United States, more like that of Great Britain. Months later, when

France and England went to war over territorial claims in Europe and the West Indies, American public opinion was divided. Fearing dangerous entanglements, President Washington issued a Proclamation of Neutrality at the outbreak of the war, but few Americans could resist taking sides.

Tensions between France and the United States took a turn for the worse when France's first envoy to the United States, Citizen Edmund Genêt, ignored the Neutrality Proclamation and tried to enlist American support for French designs on Spanish Florida and British Canada. Nor did Britain endear itself to its former American subjects during these years. Pursuing French military forces in 1793, the British navy seized 300 American merchant ships plying the West Indian seas, forcing American sailors into service. In a practice known as **impressment**, British sea captains boarded American ships and captured sailors at gunpoint. Meanwhile, along the United States' northwest border, British officials were supplying the Indians of the Ohio Confederacy with guns, alcohol, and encouragement in their fight against the Americans. Feeling squeezed by foreign powers in such ways, many Americans hoped that economic growth could assist the fledgling United States in resisting pressures from European rivals.

Planting the Seeds of Industry

During the late eighteenth century, most manufacturing still took place in individual households. Master artisans employed journeymen (skilled workers) and apprentices as well as their own wives and children. Throughout New England and the Mid-Atlantic, family businesses made everything from soap and candles to cloth and shoes.

In the 1790s, however, signs of a novel manufacturing economy emerged, especially in the region stretching from New England to New York, New Jersey, and Pennsylvania. This area had all the ingredients for an American Industrial Revolution: water power from rushing rivers, a faltering agricultural economy that western producers would soon eclipse, capital from successful merchants, and a dense population offering both workers and consumers.

Key individuals helped spark the early changes, including Samuel Slater, a twenty-one-year-old English inventor who arrived in the United States in 1791. With financial support from Moses Brown, a wealthy merchant of Providence, Rhode Island, Slater constructed the first American machine for spinning cotton thread and launched his Steam Cotton Manufacturing Company in nearby Pawtucket. The nine boys and girls (ages seven to twelve) hired by Slater to operate the machinery were among America's first factory workers.

In 1793 another innovator, Massachusetts-born Eli Whitney, invented the cotton gin. This machine gave a tremendous boost to both the southern plantation economy and the fledgling northern industrial system. By quickly removing the seeds and other impurities from raw cotton, Whitney's cotton gin fostered the emergence of a new cotton economy. Southern planters expanded their holdings in land and slaves, rushing to meet the rising demand for cotton from mill owners in both England and New England.

By the mid-1790s, Hamilton and his supporters were praising the nation's economic growth and regional specialization. Traditional

■ Elijah Boardman of New Milford, Connecticut, poses at his desk in 1789. The portrait highlights Boardman's success as a merchant. His business prospered because wealthy Americans wanted to dress fashionably, as he did, with his ruffled sleeves, silk stockings, and fancy shoe buckles. By the late eighteenth century, New England merchants were at the center of a thriving worldwide exchange of goods between Europe, the United States, and China. Their profits helped to finance the country's industrial revolution.

This logo advertises the Hampshire machine. A precursor of the canal lock, the machine consisted of a pulley that carried a canal barge in a cart up an inclined plane. Invented in 1795, it was used on the Connecticut River in western Massachusetts. However, it proved too cumbersome in the long run. Most canals used locks, sections closed off with gates so that the water level could be raised or lowered.

products of the Atlantic seaboard—tar and turpentine in North Carolina, tobacco in the Chesapeake region, wheat in the Mid-Atlantic states—flourished once again, as early canal and turnpike construction encouraged new markets. In New England, shipbuilding prospered, free from earlier British restrictions, and the fishing and whaling fleets expanded. The forests of Maine and New Hampshire produced wood for hulls, masts, planks, and barrels. In the Deep South, enslaved workers raised cotton, first in South Carolina and Georgia, later in the fertile lands of Alabama and Mississippi. Between 1792 and 1800, annual cotton production jumped from 3 million to 35 million pounds. The figure would soar to 93 million pounds by 1815.

The Whiskey Rebellion: A Tax Revolt in the Countryside

Despite Hamilton's optimism about the economy, Washington's administration faced violent resistance on occasion, particularly with regard to Hamilton's "hard money" policy. By favoring **hard currency** (coinage) and limiting paper money, the government constricted financial credit. With less money to lend, creditors charged high interest rates for loans. Courts forced debtors such as small farmers to repay loans, even when money was extremely scarce. Those who could not pay their taxes or repay their loans faced foreclosure on their property.

Eager to strengthen the federal government and reduce the national debt, Hamilton devised a federal excise tax on whiskey. The plan was aimed at distillers rather than consumers, and it imposed a higher rate on small producers. Therefore, the tax fell especially hard on backcountry farmers, who distilled their bulky grain harvest into whiskey for efficient shipment to eastern markets. In 1794, opposition boiled over into a defiant "Whiskey Rebellion" in Pennsylvania, where cash-strapped farm families felt they were being saddled with an unfair burden.

Washington Whiskey Rebellion Address

These farmers, using the tactics of the Stamp Tax rioters a generation earlier, attacked officials and tarred and feathered a man charged with collecting the whiskey tax. They closed courts, blocked roads, and organized mass protests.

Hamilton, believing that a show of force would strengthen the federal government, urged the president to make western Pennsylvania a test case for enforcing the tax. In September, the government federalized 13,000 men from state militias to subdue the rebellion. To underscore the supremacy of the national government over the states, Washington personally led the troops into western Pennsylvania. However, when the soldiers arrived, they found that organized resistance had collapsed.

Washington claimed that the Whiskey Rebellion had been incited by ignorant men who perverted the facts with their "suspicions, jealousies, and accusations of the whole government." Yet he failed to gauge the extent of country dwellers' economic distress. By defying federal authority so openly, the farmers expressed the general grievances of westerners who felt underrepresented in state legislatures and the halls of Congress. They also revealed the deep current of resentment against Federalist policies that was running through rural America.

Securing Peace Abroad, Suppressing Dissent at Home

The Jay Treaty (1794)

In 1795 the president sent Chief Justice John Jay to England to negotiate a key treaty. The negotiations were intended to address four problems: British forts in the Northwest Territory, American debts owed to British creditors, British seizure of American ships and sailors in the West Indies, and the right of individual Americans to trade freely with European belligerents in wartime. Jay obtained a treaty but failed to extract meaningful compromises from England.

England grudgingly agreed to evacuate its northern forts and to stop seizing American ships. Jay, however, acquiesced to English demands that individual Americans pay the debts they had owed to English creditors since before the Revolution. The Americans believed that

Frederick Kemmelmeyer, *General George Washington Reviewing the Western Army at Fort Cumberland the 18th of October*, c. 1794. Winterthur Museum (58.2780)

■ This 1794 painting seemingly evokes the American Revolution, when General Washington reviewed American troops. However, in this scene, President Washington is surveying some of the 13,000 state militiamen he commanded in an effort to suppress the Whiskey Rebellion in western Pennsylvania. Farmers objected to the new government tax on whiskey. With cries of "Liberty and No Excise," the protesters harassed federal tax collectors, reminiscent of anti–Stamp Act demonstrations three decades before. The Whiskey Rebellion melted away quickly. Critics objected to Washington's willingness to use such a huge force against the protesters.

their victory in the war exempted them from long-standing financial obligations to their English creditors. The Democratic-Republicans took alarm at Jay's concessions. In their view, the new agreement humiliated all Americans and threatened southern planters in particular.

Western agricultural interests did better with the Pinckney Treaty of 1795 (the Treaty of San Lorenzo). Under this agreement, Spain allowed the United States to navigate the Mississippi River freely and to land goods at New Orleans free of taxes for three years.

With their eye on the next presidential election, the Democratic-Republicans began a vigorous campaign in favor of their own candidate, Virginia's Thomas Jefferson. They contrasted Jefferson, the friend of the small farmer, with the Federalists' choice, Vice President John Adams of Massachusetts, an advocate of strong central government run by the educated and wellborn. Jefferson's party expressed particular dismay over Washington's haste to crush the rebellious Pennsylvania farmers in 1794 and over Jay's Treaty. Backed by the New England states, Adams won the election, though narrowly. Because Jefferson received the second largest number of electoral votes—68 to Adams's 71—the Virginian became the new vice president according to the terms of the Constitution then in effect (Article II, section I).

DOCUMENT

The Treaty of San Lorenzo

In his farewell address, printed in newspapers but not delivered in person, Washington warned against the "insidious wiles of foreign influence" and against entangling alliances with foreign powers that could compromise America's independence and economic well-being. Nevertheless, upon assuming the presidency in 1797, Adams found that European powers still had a hold on American domestic and foreign relations. France began to seize American merchant vessels (300 of them by mid-1797) in retaliation for what it saw as favoritism toward England in Jay's Treaty. In October of that year, President Adams sent John Marshall and Elbridge Gerry to join the U.S. ambassador to France, Charles Pinckney, to negotiate a new treaty with France. However, French intermediaries (referred to only as X, Y, and Z in the Americans' dispatches) demanded that the three U.S. commissioners arrange for a loan of $12 million to France and pay a $250,000 bribe. Only then would the envoys be allowed to speak to the foreign minister, Charles Talleyrand. The sentiments of the American public, outraged at the idea of paying a bribe and willing to defend their new nation against all aggressors, were captured in the cry "Millions for defense, but not one cent for tribute." Adams called the commissioners home, ending the "XYZ Affair."

TABLE 9-1
The Election of 1796

Candidate	Political Party	Electoral Vote
John Adams	Federalist	71
Thomas Jefferson	Democratic-Republican	68
Thomas Pinckney	Federalist	59
Aaron Burr	Democratic-Republican	30

Federalists throughout the country called for war against France, and the Adams administration sought to shore up the country's military forces by creating the Navy Department and the Marine Corps. Hoping to rid U.S. coastal waters of French ships that were preying on American vessels, in May 1798 Congress authorized American captains to seize such armed "pirates" sent from the Republic of France. Over the next two years, the undeclared so-called Quasi War pitted the American navy against its French counterpart until the two nations signed a treaty, called the Convention of 1800, in Paris.

Conflicts also continued to simmer on the domestic front. The Federalist-dominated Congress passed the Alien and Sedition Acts in 1798 to suppress the rising chorus of criticism from rural people, Democratic-Republican leaders, and newspaper editors. Such dissent, they charged, amounted to **sedition**—an act of insurrection against the government. These new laws made it more difficult for immigrants to become resident aliens, gave the president the power to deport or imprison aliens, and branded as traitors any people (U.S. citizens included) who "unlawfully combine or conspire together, with intent to oppose any measure or measures of the government of the United States."

The Alien and Sedition Acts

Even though the Alien and Sedition Acts were unconstitutional—they violated the First Amendment's guarantee of freedom of speech—the Federalist-dominated Supreme Court upheld them. Consequently, Democratic-Republicans were by definition guilty of treason, for they advocated policies and supported candidates opposed by the Federalists, the party in power.

Ten newspaper editors were convicted, and many others charged and jailed, under the Sedition Act. Some Democratic-Republican lawmakers also spent time in jail because their speech offended their partisan rivals. Congressman Matthew Lyon of Vermont (founder of a newspaper called Scourge of Aristocracy) went to prison for suggesting that President Adams showed "unbounded thirst for ridiculous pomp, foolish adulation, and selfish avarice."

In 1798 and 1799, the state legislatures of Kentucky and Virginia issued a series of resolutions condemning the Alien and Sedition Acts. Outraged at what they saw as the Federalists' blatant power grab, the two legislatures proposed that individual states had the right to declare such measures "void and of no force." Thomas Jefferson (for Kentucky) and James Madison (for Virginia) wrote the actual resolutions. In declaring that states could essentially ignore congressional authority, the two Founding Fathers unwittingly laid the theoretical framework for Southerners to attempt to nullify federal laws in the future.

The Virginia and Kentucky Resolutions

People of Color: New Freedoms, New Struggles

In the late eighteenth century, despite the rhetoric of equality, North American elites demonstrated a preoccupation with race as a means of categorizing people. Spanish officials in colonial New Mexico conducted a 1790 census that divided the population into groups based on ethnicity, with specific terms to designate varieties of mixed-race parentage. In the United States, a 1790 Naturalization law limited naturalized U.S. citizenship to "free white persons," mocking the oft-heard claim that all people were equal under the law.

The crosscurrents of the revolutionary legacy showed themselves most obviously in the status of African Americans. Most remained enslaved, and their numbers were increasing

■ After the Revolution and well into the early nineteenth century, African Americans, both enslaved and free, served as sailors in disproportionate numbers. This picture suggests the dangers faced by all men who labored on whaling ships. By the 1790s, American whalers were searching for sperm whales as far away as the South Pacific. These whales were the source of several prized substances, including sperm oil (a fuel), spermaceti (used to make candles), and ambergris (an ingredient in expensive perfumes). During the heyday of the sperm whale industry, American fleets were killing 10,000 whales annually.

annually, due to the continuation of the Atlantic slave trade. But even free African Americans faced an uphill struggle in their efforts to achieve political rights and economic well-being. Free people of color created educational and religious institutions that affirmed their sense of community and shared heritage. But persistent white prejudice, sanctioned by law, limited their employment options and condemned many to poverty. For them, the Revolution remained an unfulfilled promise, not to be forgotten. According to Jeremiah Asher, an African American born in New Jersey in 1785, "my first ideas of the right of the colored man to life, liberty, and the pursuit of happiness" came from "the lessons taught me by the old black soldiers of the Revolution."

Blacks in the North

Between 1790 and 1804, all the northern states abolished slavery. Some, such as New York and New Jersey, did so gradually, stipulating that the children of slaves must serve a period of time (as long as twenty-eight years in certain states) before they could gain their freedom. In 1800 over 36,500 blacks in the North were still enslaved, and some 47,000 were free. Pennsylvania did not liberate its last slave until 1847. Yet throughout the North, blacks—whether enslaved or free—were only a small percentage of the total population, ranging from less than 1 percent in Vermont to almost 8 percent in New Jersey. Most black men worked as farm hands or manual laborers, most black women as domestic servants or laundresses. Nevertheless, some whites saw black men as rivals for their jobs and as a threat to the well-being of the white population.

At both the state and national levels, most free blacks lacked basic citizenship rights. In 1792, two years after Congress limited naturalized U.S. citizenship to "free white persons," it restricted the militia to white men. State legislatures in New England and the Mid-Atlantic region imposed various other restrictions on free people of color. These measures limited blacks' right to vote, serve on juries, and move from place to place. Rectifying an "oversight" in their state constitutions, New Jersey and Connecticut later took special pains to disfranchise African American men. Massachusetts offered free blacks the most rights, including the right to vote (for men) and the right of blacks and whites to intermarry.

As slaves, African Americans had served in a variety of skilled capacities in the North. Yet as free people, they faced mounting pressures in trying to live independently. Certain jobs, such as those with the federal postal service, remained closed to them by law. And municipal authorities refused to grant them licenses to ply their trades, such as wagon driving. Lacking the means to buy tools and equipment and the ability to attract white customers, many black artisans had to take menial jobs. Increasingly, free black men worked as laborers, sailors, and domestic servants, and black women worked mostly as domestic servants and laundresses.

Still, free blacks in the North set about creating their own households and institutions. They moved out of the garrets and back rooms in houses owned by whites and set up housekeeping on their own. In Boston in 1790, one in three African Americans lived outside white households; thirty years later, eight in ten did so. In response to efforts of white Methodists to segregate church seating, Philadelphia black leaders formed the Free African Society in 1787. The first independent black church in the North, St. Thomas Protestant Episcopal Church, was founded in Philadelphia in the early 1790s. Black people also continued to celebrate their own festivals, typically featuring parades in which black people came together to strut their finery, play drums and other African musical instruments, and proclaim their identity as a free people. The festivals gave men and women alike an opportunity to escape the confines of the workplace, even if only for a short time, and eat, drink, and dance with other people of color.

An anonymous artist captured this scene, probably in the slave quarters of a South Carolina plantation, in 1800. It is unknown what kind of entertainment or celebration the musicians and dancers are engaged in. The two men on the right are playing musical instruments of west African origin: a banjo and a *quaqua*, or skin-covered gourd used as a drum. On large lowcountry plantations especially, Africans and their descendants preserved traditional musical forms and social rituals.

Manumissions in the South

In 1782 the Virginia state legislature lifted a fifty-nine-year-old ban on manumission, a process by which owners released selected people from bondage. Over the next ten years, approximately 10,000 Virginia slaves gained their freedom through manumission. Some planters believed that the Revolution was the will of God, and they came to believe that slavery violated their religious principles. Some, taking to heart the rhetoric of the Revolution, objected to the glaring contradiction between the ideal of liberty and the reality of bondage. In 1802 a Maryland woman freed her slaves because, she said, the institution went against "the inalienable Rights of Mankind."

In the Upper South, especially, private manumissions dramatically increased the free black population. There, the emergence of a more diversified economy, including craft shops and grist mills, had lowered slave prices and encouraged abolitionist sentiment among some lawmakers, clergy, and slave owners.

Virginia planters George Washington and Robert Carter were unusual in terms of the numbers of slaves they manumitted (several hundred) and their efforts to ease the transition to freedom for people who possessed neither land nor financial resources. Providing for manumission in his will, Washington arranged apprenticeships for younger freed blacks and pensions for aged ones. In 1792 Carter granted his older slaves small plots of land. In general, however, newly emancipated men and women had difficulty finding employment as free workers. Nor was their freedom guaranteed: the 1782 Virginia manumission law provided that black debtors could be returned to slavery.

Some slaves, inspired by the growing community of free people of color in their midst and by the example of the black revolutionaries in Saint-Domingue in 1791, freed themselves. They ran away, heading for the anonymity of a nearby town or a haven such as Philadelphia or New York. Despite the growth in the free black population, the number of slaves actually increased in the Upper South, from over 520,000 in 1790 to almost 650,000 in 1810. In the South, slavery proved to be an extraordinarily durable institution.

■ MAP 9.1

THE NORTHWEST TERRITORY After the Revolution, the Northwest Territory became a battleground. Indians—both long-term residents and newcomers—as well as European American squatters and speculators vied for control of the land. The Northwest Ordinance of 1787 provided for territorial governments before an area could apply for statehood. The present-day states of Ohio, Indiana, Michigan, Illinois, and Wisconsin were carved out of the Northwest Territory. All had gained statehood by 1848, but only after almost sixty years of bloodshed between Indians and U.S. troops in the region.

Continuity and Change in the West

Western communities tended to duplicate their eastern counterparts. The opening of federal lands proved a boon for speculators, who extended credit to homesteaders and profited from the sale of small land parcels. Charged high prices for their purchases and forced to buy expensive supplies transported across the Appalachians, some newcomers rapidly sank into debt. Nor did black Americans fare well, whether slave or free. Before 1800, many white families seeking a fresh start in the trans-Appalachian South took slaves with them into the new states of Kentucky and Tennessee. Even in the Northwest Territory (above the Ohio River), where slavery was prohibited by law, African American arrivals faced the same prejudices that shaped social relations in the East. Rather than extend the bounds of liberty, western settlement solidified ideas about white supremacy.

From the Canadian border to Georgia, the trans-Appalachian West had become a cultural battlefield. European Americans warred against Indians, but Indian leaders also disagreed bitterly with one another about how to respond. Should they defend their hunting grounds to the death or seek refuge elsewhere? For most, the answer was neither total resistance nor complete **capitulation** to an alien culture. Yet one generalization holds true for all inhabitants: the abundance of land and natural resources, combined with the clash of cultures and the prevalence of armed men of different backgrounds, made life particularly dangerous in the borderlands.

Indian Wars in the Great Lakes Region

Native Americans residing in the Northwest Territory in the 1790s included peoples who had long occupied the Great Lakes region and the Upper Midwest, such as the Miami, Potawatomi, Menominee, Kickapoo, Illinois, Fox, Winnebago, Sauk, and Shawnee. Also present were refugees from the East: Ottawa, Ojibway, Wyandot, Algonquin, Delaware, and Iroquois displaced by the Revolutionary War. As they resettled in villages, they managed to retain some elements of their cultural identity, but in the seven years immediately after the Revolution, thousands died in Indian-white clashes in the region.

What caused this violence? By encouraging European Americans to stake their claim to the area, the Northwest Ordinance inflamed passions on both sides: whites' determination to occupy and own the land and Indians' equal determination to resist this incursion. In 1790, under orders from President Washington, Brigadier General Josiah Harmar led a force of about 1,500 men into the Maumee River Valley in the northwest corner of modern-day Ohio. Orchestrating two ambushes in September, Miami chief Little Turtle and his men killed 183 of Harmar's troops, driving the general back in disgrace. The next year, Washington chose another officer, General Arthur St. Clair, to resume the fight. But when St. Clair's men met Little Turtle's warriors in November 1791 near the upper Wabash River, the Americans suffered an even greater defeat, losing over 600 men.

Washington tried once more to find a commander equal to Little Turtle. This time he chose General Anthony Wayne, a Revolutionary War hero dubbed "Mad Anthony" for his bold recklessness. Wayne mobilized a force of 3,000 men and constructed a string of new forts as well. At the battle of Fallen Timbers in August 1794, near present-day Toledo, hundreds of Indians perished before Wayne's forces. The withdrawal of British support helped to doom the Ohio Confederacy. On August 3, 1795, 1,100 Indian leaders met at Fort Greenville (in western Ohio) and ceded to the United States a vast tract of Indian land: all of present-day Ohio and most of Indiana. Little Turtle helped negotiate the agreement.

Indian Acculturation in the West

White newcomers swiftly made clear their belief that men should farm and herd sheep and cattle, while women should milk cows, raise chickens, tend the garden, spin thread, and weave cloth. However, Indian groups differed in their responses to the various attempts to persuade—or force—them to "acculturate" by adopting novel customs. At first, all learned from each other, as newly arrived settlers and indigenous peoples traded foodways, folk remedies, and styles of dress, adopting foreign habits while still retaining some old ways. Little Turtle himself chose among European American cultural traits; he drank tea and coffee, kept cows, and shunned leather breeches in favor of white men's clothing. The fact that his wife made butter suggested that she was skilled in the ways of European American homemakers.

Adopting some habits of European Americans—for example, liquor consumption—amounted to self-destruction. Alcohol was a prized trade item. Moreover, European Americans and Indians often used it to lubricate political negotiations and cultural rituals. Yet conflicts over liquor, and tensions vented under the influence of liquor, became increasingly common—and deadly. Some Indian leaders, such as Joseph Brant and Little Turtle, came to view the drinking of alcohol as a full-blown crisis among their people. Both believed that Indians must reject the white man's bottle if they were to survive.

But liquor was only one piece of a larger cultural puzzle, as the experience of the Cherokee, Chickasaw, Choctaw, Creek, and Seminole Indians in the southeastern United States revealed. The migration of whites into their hunting grounds rapidly depleted their game supply and devastated their crop fields. Unable to hunt efficiently for food, many in these groups took up new forms of agriculture after the Revolution, and they became known to whites as the Five Civilized Tribes. Women, who had traditionally tended crops using hoes, gave way in the fields to men, often using plows provided by the federal government. Protestant missionaries encouraged Indian women to learn to spin thread and weave cloth. For more than a generation, the willingness of these southern tribes to accommodate themselves to European American law and divisions of labor allowed them to stay in their homeland and retain key elements of their cultural identity.

In southwest and far west borderland areas, Spanish officials met with mixed success in their attempts to convert Indians to Christianity and encourage them to engage in **sedentary farming**. For example, between 1772 and 1804, Spanish priests established five missions among the Chumash, hunter-gatherers living in permanent villages along the California coast. When large numbers of the Indians moved to these settlements, they forfeited their traditional kin and trade networks, and their distinctive culture began to fade. Birth rates plummeted due to disruptions in family life (more women than men lived in the missions), and mortality rates increased dramatically as contact with the Spanish introduced new diseases.

In contrast, along the Texas Gulf Coast, the Spanish made little headway in their efforts to bring the Karankawa Indians into the missions. Members of this nomadic tribe arrived at the mission gates only when their own food reserves were low; in essence, the Karankawa simply included the missions in their seasonal migrations between the Gulf Coast and the coastal prairie.

Land Speculation and Slavery

The West was not necessarily a place of boundless economic opportunity for all people who settled there. Eager investors and creditors thwarted many homesteaders' quest for cheap land. Schemes such as the Ohio Company of Associates foreshadowed the significance of **land speculation** in shaping patterns of settlement and property ownership further west in later generations. With backing from wealthy investors, the Ohio Company quickly bought up tracts of land and then sold parcels to family farmers at inflated rates. A similar venture was initiated in Georgia in 1795, when speculators bribed state legislators for the right to resell huge tracts to the west of the state, land that the state did not even own. The state legislature passed the so-called Yazoo Act (named for a Georgia river) because of these bribes. The act resulted in the defrauding of thousands of buyers, whose land titles were worthless.

By protecting slavery and opening new territory to European American settlement, the new nation condemned southern blacks to a kind of legal bondage that stood in stark contrast to revolutionary principles. Many settlers relied on slave labor. By the late eighteenth century, Kentucky slaves numbered 40,000—more than 18 percent of the state's total population. On wilderness homesteads, where farmers owned just one or two slaves, African Americans faced a kind of isolation unknown on large plantations in the East.

Patterns of land use directly affected the spread of slavery into the West. Despite eastern planters' use of European soil conservation techniques (crop rotation, use of manure as fertilizer), many of them had to contend with depleted soil in the Upper South. Generations of tobacco growers had worn out the land, depriving it of nutrients. As a result, many growers were forced to abandon tobacco. Some of them moved west into Indian lands in the Mississippi Territory to cultivate cotton. The scarcity of labor motivated slave owners to push work-

■ In 1791, an artist made this sketch of the wife of a Spanish soldier stationed at the presidio, or military garrison, in Monterey, California. Many elite Spaniards in the Americas went to great lengths to dress like their European counterparts. This woman is wearing the elegant dress, elaborate jewelry, and dainty shoes that befit her status. One eighteenth-century resident of New Mexico wrote that, despite the hot climate, European Americans "will go up to their ears in debt simply to satisfy their pride in putting on a grand appearance." However, most *nuevomexicanos* adopted some elements of Indian-style clothing, such as practical leather moccasins and garments made of buckskin and coarse woolens.

Courtesy, Museo de America, Madrid. Photo by Iris Engstrand

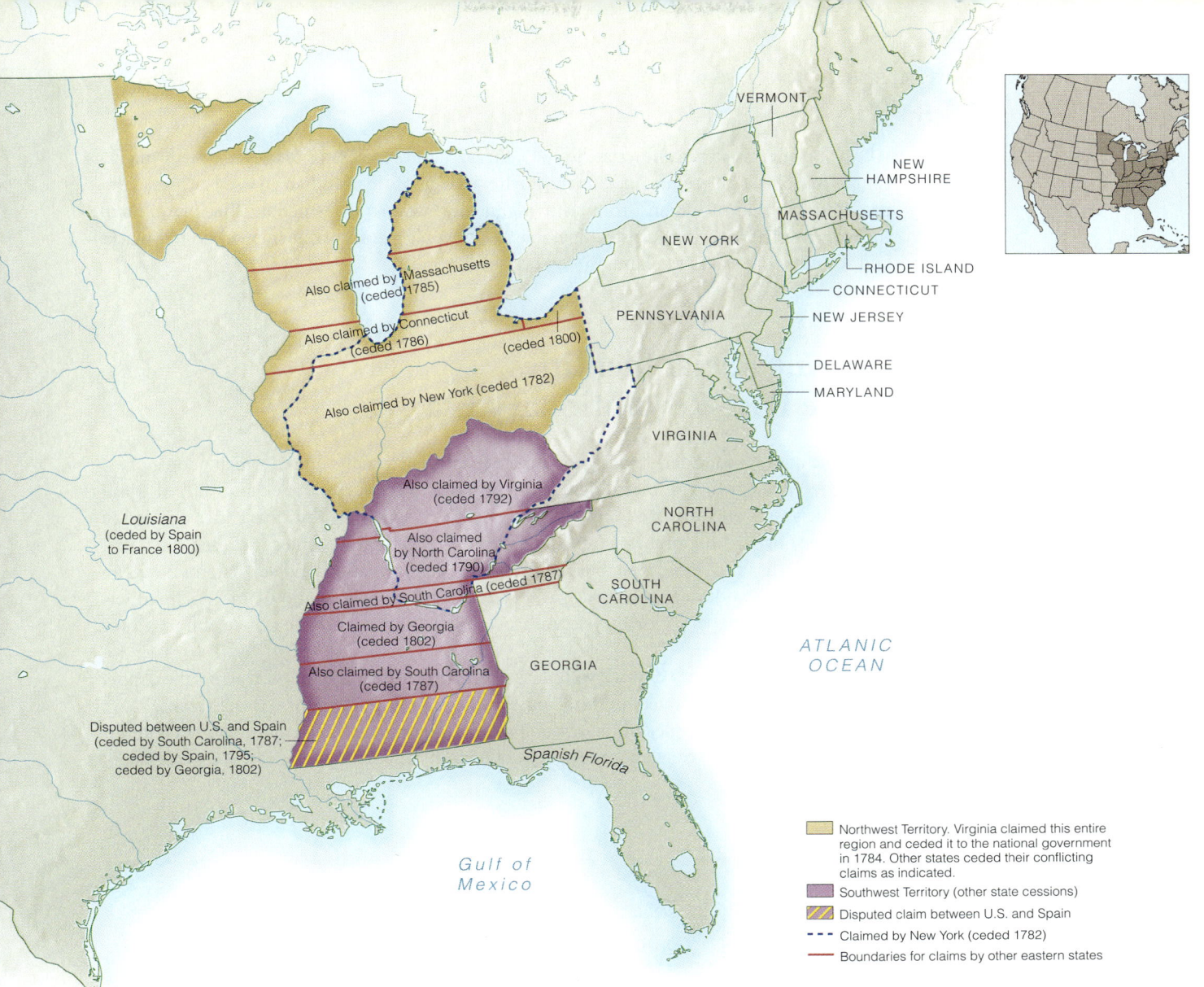

■ **MAP 9.2**
WESTERN LAND CLAIMS OF THE STATES Several of the original thirteen colonies, including Massachusetts, Connecticut, New York, Virginia, South Carolina, North Carolina, and Georgia, claimed land west of the Appalachian mountains. By 1802 these states had ceded their western lands to the federal government. The Land Ordinance of 1785 provided that this expanse be auctioned off in parcels no less than 640 acres each, with a minimum price of one dollar per acre—too expensive for many family homesteaders, thus opening the way for investors to purchase and profit. Hoping to raise money through land sales, the federal government did not object to speculation.

ers to the limits of their endurance. Slaves cleared potential farmland, rooted out tree stumps, and prepared the ground for cultivation. Once cotton could be planted, these same slaves worked in gangs under the sharp eye of a white overseer or black driver. Men, women, and children labored as human machines, planting, hoeing, and harvesting as much cotton as quickly as possible.

Many free people of color also found a less than hospitable welcome in the West. In 1802 delegates to the first Ohio territorial convention moved to restrict blacks' economic and political opportunities, even though fewer than 400 were living in Ohio at the time. Although slavery was outlawed in Ohio and other territories, blacks still lacked the right to vote. Soon after Ohio became a state in 1803, the legislature took steps to prevent the in-migration of free blacks altogether. In 1803 the territorial legislature of Indiana passed a "black law" prohibiting blacks or Indians from testifying in court against white people. Black families in the Northwest Territory were also vulnerable to kidnapping: some white men seized free blacks and sold them as slaves to plantation owners in the South.

Shifting Social Identities in the Post-Revolutionary Era

The nation's founders had argued for an egalitarian society, one in which people prospered according to their talents and ambition. Of course, their definition of egalitarianism encompassed only white men. Still, it was a revolutionary idea and led to challenges of social hierarchies after the Revolution. These hierarchies included the patriarchal (male-headed) family, established Protestant denominations, power systems based on social standing, and ideas about race and gender. Ordinary men and women penned letters to local newspapers, glorifying common laborers and questioning the claim to power of elite citizens.

In the early nineteenth century, voluntary reform organizations multiplied across the nation. As their numbers proliferated, both the possibilities and limitations of reform became clear. Some groups—for example, white working men—sought to advance their own self-interest without showing much concern for the plight of African American laborers. In other cases, peo-

■ Men and women participate in a Shaker worship service in New Lebanon, New York. The formal name of the church was the United Society of Believers in Christ's Second Appearance. The group's more familiar name derived from their peculiar worship style, which involved trembling and shaking. Members of the group reconfigured traditional family relations. They forbade marriage and sexual intercourse, depending on new converts to expand their ranks. Like several other Protestant denominations, encouraged congregants to call each other brothers and sisters.

ple banded together to target the behavior of a specific group: drunkards, slave owners, the irreligious, or prostitutes. These moral reform groups welcomed diversity among members, as long as new converts supported the cause.

Artisan-Politicians and the Plight of Post-Revolutionary Workers

In the decades after the Revolution, residents of port cities along the eastern seaboard grew accustomed to public parades marking special occasions: a visit from George Washington, the ratification of the Constitution, the Fourth of July. Most of these parades consisted of groups of artisans marching together, carrying the banners of their respective occupations. As one example, the bricklayers' flag declared, "Both Buildings and Rulers Are the Works of Our Hands."

Proud of their role in the Sons of Liberty and other revolutionary organizations, bricklayers—along with tanners, carpenters, glassblowers, weavers, and other groups of artisans—proclaimed themselves the proud citizens of the new nation. American worker organizations built on a distinct revolutionary heritage that stressed the equality of all (white) freeborn men. Master artisans in several cities—including Boston, Albany, Providence, Portsmouth, Charleston, Savannah, and New York—created organizations called the General Society of Mechanics and Tradesmen that brought together skilled workers from a variety of fields. The proliferation of newspapers let these artisans participate in a new, more open public forum. Such participation in turn helped them to gain greater influence within local politics. In some towns, as many as 85 percent of adult men owned property of some kind and thus were eligible to vote. Indeed, artisans' organizations soon became quasi-political groups, extending their reach in ways that pre-Revolutionary trades-based associations had not.

But not all workers were so secure. The diggers who constructed the early canals of the 1790s included men from all walks of life: part-time farmers, indentured servants, slaves, and white transients. Moving around in search of work, they led an unsettled existence that contrasted greatly with the more predictable life of urban artisans. Canal diggers represented a transition workforce of sorts, bridging the worlds of traditional, outdoor work with the more disciplined, regimented pace of the factory.

The plight of menial laborers (in the countryside and the cities) suggests the ironies that accompanied the decline of indentured servitude and the rise of the "free laborer." To be sure, master artisans attained a degree of economic independence. But for men and women who lacked skills, money, and wealthy patrons, freedom often meant financial insecurity and, in some cases, reliance on public or private charity. Those who did find work usually had the kinds of jobs that came with the booming economy of the late eighteenth century: moving goods from one place to another, building new structures, and providing personal services for the merchants who profited from all this commercial activity.

"Republican Mothers" and Other Well-Off Women

Some well-educated women in the United States read English writer Mary Wollstonecraft's *Vindication of the Rights of Woman* published in England and America in 1792. In that manifesto, Wollstonecraft argued that young men and women should receive the same kind of education. She objected to a special female curriculum that exclusively emphasized skills such as needlepoint and musical accomplishments; this "false system of education," she charged, left women "in a state of perpetual childhood."

In 1801 an anonymous "American Lady" published an essay titled "A Second Vindication of the Rights of Woman." In it, she claimed that "a good kitchen woman [that is, a household drudge], very seldom makes a desirable wife, to a man of any refinement." The anonymous "American Lady" and others who shared her opinion celebrated a new kind of woman—the

INTERPRETING HISTORY

A Sailmaker Discusses "Means for the Preservation of Public Liberty" on the Fourth of July, 1797

Urban skilled artisans (also called mechanics) played a significant role in the American fight for independence. In the years after the conflict, many artisans remained active in politics. They believed that the success of the new nation depended on the ability of its citizens to remain informed about and engaged in the political process.

In a speech delivered on July 4, 1797, a New York sailmaker, George James Warner, warned that citizens must strive to preserve the hard-won gains of the Revolution.

We must guard as a most valuable privilege, the freedom and rights of election. WHEREVER the wealthy by the influence of riches, are enabled to direct the choice of public officers, *there* the downfall of liberty cannot be very remote. It is our own fault if an influence so dangerous, has become in any measure prevalent among us. It would not be the case if the people did not consent to become the dupes of design. It is because tradesmen, mechanics, and the industrious classes of society consider themselves of TOO LITTLE CONSEQUENCE to the body politic that *any thing* belonging to the system of oppression at all obtains. We ought to spurn from us with disdain, the individual who would not solicit our vote, from motives of personal consideration. He ought not to be listened to, who would *demand* it as the price of friendship, or who would *expect* it from regard to his superior riches. It too often happens that men only capable of attracting public notice by an ostentatious display of their wealth, are deemed best qualified to protect the rights of the people, and consequently receive their suffrages; while our choice ought only to be directed to men of TALENTS and VIRTUE whatever their situation in life might be. The *possession* of riches is not necessarily accompanied by superior understanding or goodness of heart. On the contrary, the experience of ages confirms this opinion, that a state of mediocrity is more favorable to them both.

If, instead of improving on it original plan, our government, at any future period, should be irresistibly impelled in an unalterable course toward despotism, the dividing line between the *rich* and the *poor* will be distinctly marked, and the *latter* will be found in a state of vassallage [slavery] and dependence on the former.

Be it your care then, my fellow-citizens, to guard with unceasing vigilance against the growth of this evil; assume the native dignity of your character and maintain with a modest but determined spirit, the liberty of opinion. Suffer no one to DICTATE imperiously what line of conduct you are to pursue; but at the same time let no one be sacrificed at the alter of public vengeance, for a candid and liberal expression of his sentiments....

We must endeavor to acquaint ourselves with the political situation and relative interests of our country. Without this information, we shall either be unable to form an accurate opinion on our own, or often become the dupes of the designing. The PUBLIC PRINTS naturally present themselves as the vehicles of this necessary knowledge. Those conducted in a spirit of liberality, yet altogether consonant to the principles on which our revolution was achieved, should employ the public attention and meet its decided support. It will be found, that a JUST and EQUAL GOVERNMENT will ever derive additional stability, as the PEOPLE obtain a more general knowledge of its principles and operations. The result is, that every sincere friend to our NATIONAL CONSTITUTION ought sedulously to promote the dissemination of this knowledge, as a barrier to

"**Republican mother**"—who provided cultured companionship for her husband and reared her children to be virtuous, responsible members of society. This image of womanhood led to a new notion: that well-off women should dedicate themselves to tending the home fires rather than aspiring to a more public role in business or politics.

Prior to the Revolution, women tended to bear many children, since additional hands were needed to labor in the fields. But as the sons of farmers became store managers and bookkeepers, they had less need for the unpaid labor of their own children. The decline in white women's fertility rates after the Revolution suggests that the economy had shifted. And some women could now buy products their grandmothers had made at home. In particular, a small but influential group of well-to-do women in the cities were shedding their roles as producers of candles, soap, and textiles. Instead, they became consumers of these staples and of luxury goods, and they managed household servants. As "Republican mothers," these women participated in the public life of the new nation as the guardians of the home and the socializers of children.

The New York City Mechanics' Society was founded in 1785 and incorporated in 1792. The society included many different kinds of artisans. In addition to representing the interests of skilled artisans, it served as a mutual aid association, lending money to members and distributing charity to the poor. This certificate of membership combines the traditional symbol of arts and crafts, the arm and hammer, with images of American patriotism (the eagle in the center foreground) and prosperity (waterways and fields on the left, urban townhouses on the left). Children are prominently featured here. In 1820 the General Society opened a school for the children of its members, and began offering classes to women in 1821.

the risings of sedition, as well as to the encroachments of arbitrary power.

In his speech, Warner also called for "the practice of all the moral virtues" and the education of children "as to the RIGHTS which they possess, and the DUTIES which they owe society." Warner himself became active in New York's Democratic-Republican party.

Questions

1. According to Warner, in what ways do wealthy politicians threaten to undermine a robust form of democracy?
2. How are the principles of an educated citizenry and a free press related to the preservation of American liberty?
3. How would an African American sailor react to Warner's speech? How would a New York woman employed as a domestic servant react to Warner's speech?

Source: George James Warner, *Means for the Preservation of Public Liberty* (New York, 1797); reprinted in Howard B. Rock, *The New York City Artisan, 1789–1825* (Albany: State University of New York Press, 1989), pp. 6–11.

But the idea of the "Republican mother" also suggested a more radical notion. If such a woman wanted to earn the respect accorded all intelligent human beings, she must strive for an education equal to that of men. In the 1790s, a number of academies for "young ladies" opened in New England. These schools offered courses in such "womanly pursuits" as needlework, etiquette, and music. But many also offered a classical curriculum consisting of mathematics, foreign languages, and geography. This system of study encouraged young women to think for themselves. In this respect, female academies challenged the view that women were intellectually inferior to and necessarily dependent on men.

A Loss of Political Influence: The Fate of Nonelite Women

Many Native American women, feeling the pressure of non-Indian cultures, found their traditional roles had been weakened by the end of the eighteenth century. For example, among

■ James Peale completed this painting of his family in 1795. Peale came from a distinguished family of artists. The picture represents the ideal of post-Revolutionary citizenship and family life. Husband and wife are both featured prominently, although their roles differ. The husband represents the household in the public, political sphere. The wife, a devoted mother, is responsible for preparing the children to be virtuous citizens of the new republic. Growing up in a well-to-do home, these playful children are exempt from the hard labor associated with childhood in the colonial period and, in the 1790s, still characteristic of childhood among enslaved, rural, and poor families.

the Cherokee, the introduction of a European American division of labor lessened women's customary political influence as leaders and diplomats. Most European Americans believed that only men should serve in positions of authority, and so Cherokee women felt pressed to refrain from taking part in political negotiations and to subordinate themselves to men.

In the West, Indian women registered the brunt of ongoing conflicts between their own people and European American settlers. In New Mexico, female Indian captives from Plains tribes (such as the Apache, Comanche, and Kiowa) became *indios servientes* in Hispanic households. In the East, Native American women dispossessed of their land pieced together a meager existence. For example, in Natick, Massachusetts, women turned to weaving and peddling baskets and brooms while their men scrounged for wage labor.

For some Americans, the postwar years brought unprecedented opportunities to buy, sell, and trade. However, commercial development, combined with race and gender discrimination, offered only modest possibilities for many impoverished women and women of color. Like other free blacks, Chloe Spear of Boston "worked early and late" at a number of jobs, such as laundering and ironing clothes. Eventually, she managed to purchase her own home. In Rhode Island, Elleanor Eldrige started her work career at age ten in 1795. Thereafter, she worked as a domestic servant, spinner, weaver, dairymaid, and nurse. She finally went into business, first as a soapboiler and then as a wallpaperer and house painter. However, like many free blacks, Eldrige remained vulnerable to the machinations of white men who tried to defraud her of her hard-won earnings.

Some white women also felt the effects of fluctuations in the market economy. In Philadelphia in the mid-1790s, two former servants—Polly Nugent (married to a blacksmith who had just lost his job) and Grace Biddle (newly widowed)—had to plead for assistance from their former mistress, Elizabeth Drinker. The city's "Bettering House" for indigent people housed men and women, blacks and whites. Many women had neither the resources nor the opportunities to improve their lot after the Revolution.

> *Commercial development, combined with race and gender discrimination, offered only modest possibilities for many impoverished women and women of color.*

The Election of 1800: Revolution or Reversal?

The campaign of 1800 pitted Thomas Jefferson and his vice-presidential running mate, Aaron Burr, against the incumbent, John Adams, and his vice-presidential nominee, Charles Pinckney. Certain elements of the campaign were predictable. The Democratic-Republicans blasted Alexander Hamilton's economic policies and the Adams administration's military buildup. Jefferson's party also condemned the Alien and Sedition Acts, used to silence Adams's political opponents. For their part, the Federalists portrayed Jefferson as a godless supporter of the French Revolution. They also charged that he had fathered children by one of his slaves, Sally Hemings. (Two centuries later, DNA evidence suggested that this assertion might be true.)

Jefferson prevailed in the 1800 election, but his victory did not come easily. The electoral college allowed delegates to vote separately for president and vice president, and as a result Jefferson tied with Burr. Each man received 73 votes. Then the decision went to the House of Representatives, which was dominated by Federalists. After a series of tied votes, Jefferson finally gained a majority. His selection in February 1801 marked the orderly transfer of power from the Federalists to the Democratic-Republicans, a peaceful revolution in American politics.

As chief executive, Jefferson did little to change the direction of the country. Aware of his razor-thin victory, he retained many Federalist appointees. And his eagerness to expand the boundaries of the United States—which culminated in the Louisiana Purchase of 1803—solidified the Hamiltonian principles that favored commerce and trade over agrarian values.

TABLE 9-2

The Election of 1800

Candidate	Political Party	Electoral Vote
Thomas Jefferson	Democratic-Republican	73
Aaron Burr	Democratic-Republican	73
John Adams	Federalist	65
Charles C. Pinckney	Federalist	64

The Enigmatic Thomas Jefferson

Who was Thomas Jefferson? In 1800 Jefferson, the presidential candidate, wrote, "I have sworn upon the altar of God eternal hostility against every form of tyranny over the mind of man." Yet Jefferson's own views on ordinary people were less heroic. Specifically, his deep skepticism about African American equality and the viability of Indian cultures helped to justify violent assaults on both groups in the early nineteenth century.

Many Americans know Jefferson as the author of the Declaration of Independence. But he also sought to justify slavery as a central institution in the new republic, and he regarded blacks as lacking in imagination and intelligence. Jefferson wrote much about the noble calling of the yeoman farmer. Yet he assigned the task of tilling the soil on his own estate (Monticello, near Charlottesville, Virginia) to his enslaved workers.

The president's views on Indians also did nothing to reverse the course of aggression in the West. He believed that land ownership created the stable institutions necessary for civilized behavior. Yet the system of private property, and the violent methods that whites used to enforce it, spelled the destruction of traditional Indian ways of life.

"Jefferson and Liberty"

It is tempting to excuse Jefferson's racist beliefs by saying he merely reflected his time. But in fact, a significant number of Jefferson's contemporaries were voicing their misgivings about slavery. While Jefferson acknowledged their arguments, he did not share their beliefs. A citizen of a trans-Atlantic "republic of ideas," he corresponded with political thinkers—from John Adams to the Marquis de Lafayette—who understood the inherent tension between freedom for whites and slavery for blacks. Obviously, Jefferson knew that some of the northern states had written constitutions that incorporated the sentiments of the Declaration of Independence in ways that justified the abolition of slavery. Moreover, a notable number of Jefferson's wealthy Virginia compatriots (including George Washington) had chosen to free their slaves, either by their own hand or through provisions of their wills, to practice in their own households what they preached to British tyrants.

The United States provided the political theory and rhetoric to inspire abolitionists around the globe, but within the new nation, the debate over the institution of slavery continued to rage.

Jefferson lived in an age when revolutionary enthusiasm was sweeping the western world. Challenges to slavery had rocked Europe; France outlawed the practice in 1794, although Napoleon later reinstated it. Abolition had also transformed the Western Hemisphere with the successful rebellion of the Saint-Domingue slaves in 1791. The United States provided the political theory and rhetoric to inspire abolitionists around the globe, but within the new nation, the debate over the institution of slavery continued to rage. The southern states, in particular, took decisive steps to solidify the institution within their own boundaries.

Protecting and Expanding the National Interest: Jefferson's Administration to 1803

As president, Jefferson reconsidered his original vision of the United States: a compact country in which citizens freely pursued modest agrarian interests without interference from the national government or distractions from overseas conflicts. Indeed, during his years in office, the federal government moved toward increasing its power.

Just before Jefferson assumed the presidency, the Federalist-dominated Congress had strengthened the national court system by passing the Judiciary Act of 1801. The act created sixteen circuit (regional) courts, with a judge for each, and bolstered support staff for the judicial branch in general. President Adams appointed these judges (so-called midnight judges because they were appointed right before Jefferson took office). Before stepping down, Adams had also appointed Secretary of State John Marshall as chief justice of the Supreme Court.

Adams's last-minute acts had long-term consequences. Marshall remained on the bench for thirty-four years. He presided over the court when it rendered its landmark *Marbury v. Madison* decision in 1803, which established the judiciary's right to declare acts of both the executive and legislative branches unconstitutional. Chief Justice Marshall wrote: "It is emphatically the province and duty of the judicial department to say what the law is."

In the realm of international affairs, Jefferson asserted his own authority. Challenges from foreign powers prompted the Democratic-Republican president to take bold steps to protect U.S. economic and political interests abroad and along the country's borders. In 1801 Jefferson's administration launched a war against Barbary pirates in North Africa when Tripoli (modern-day Libya) demanded ransom money for kidnapped American sailors. (Together, the North African kingdoms of Tunis, Tripoli, Algeria, and Morocco were known as the Barbary States.) The war against Tripoli, which spanned four years, revealed the extent of U.S. trade interests even at this early point in the nation's history. The United States signed a peace treaty with Tripoli in 1805 and paid $60,000 for the release of the American captives.

At the beginning of the nineteenth century, the European powers continued their operations in the territory west of the United States. In 1801 Napoleon persuaded the King of Spain to secretly cede the trans-Mississippi region called Louisiana to France. Retaining control of New Orleans, Spain denied Americans the right to use that city as a depository for goods awaiting shipment. In 1803 Jefferson sent his fellow Virginian, and prominent Anti-Federalist, James Monroe to Paris. Together with American ambassador Robert Livingston, Monroe set out to secure American trading rights to New Orleans. To the Americans' surprise, Napoleon agreed to sell the whole area to the United States. At the time, Louisiana included most of the territory between the Mississippi River and the Rocky Mountains—a total of 828,000 square miles. The United States agreed to pay $15 million for the Louisiana Purchase.

Louisiana Purchase

The Louisiana Purchase reversed the roles of Jefferson and his Federalist rivals. The president advocated territorial expansion, but his opponents remained suspicious of the move. Devoted to a strict interpretation of the Constitution, Jefferson traditionally favored limiting federal authority. Yet he sought to justify the purchase by pointing out that it would finally rid the area of European influence. He proposed shifting Indians from the Mississippi Territory (part of present-day Alabama and Mississippi) to the West so that American newcomers could have the eastern part of the country to themselves. For their part, the Federalists feared that Louisiana would benefit mainly agrarian interests and eventually dilute New England's long-standing political influence and power. They suspected Jefferson of attempting to expand the influence of his own political party.

Conclusion

In his first inaugural address, Jefferson suggested that both parties, despite their differences, shared similar views about the role of government and the importance of economic opportunity for ordinary people. Seeking unity after a partisan campaign, he reminded political leaders, "We are all Republicans, we are all Federalists." Indeed, most public officials at the time held a common suspicion of groups that professed religious beliefs that lay outside the mainstream of Protestantism or liberal Deism (a general belief in God without ties to a particular religious denomination). Most considered slavery less a moral issue than a political matter that individual states must address. And most agreed that women, as well as black and Indian men, should have no formal voice in governing the nation.

Despite such widely shared assumptions, officeholders often defined political interests in "either-or" terms: either the French system of political equality or the British monarchy; either the individual states or the federal government; either the farm or the factory. Such thinking suited the emerging two-party system, and was reinforced by that system's growth. But it also promoted narrow views regarding the promise of the United States, already a society of great economic and ethnic diversity. After all, a candidate's political victory depended on his winning more votes than his opponent, and the electoral system provided no avenues for different groups to share power. This system made it extremely difficult for people who had no place in it to find their own political voice and claim the Revolutionary legacy as their own.

At the same time, the new nation gave white men opportunities practically unknown in the rest of the world. Regardless of their background, many white men could aspire to own property, to enjoy impressive legal rights, and to participate in the political process. The federal government supported economic growth by facilitating territorial expansion, technological innovation, and the protection of private property. As much for the prosperity it promoted as for the noble ideas it nourished, the Revolution continued to inspire liberation movements within the United States and throughout the world.

Sites to Visit

Thomas Jefferson
www.pbs.org/jefferson/
This site is the companion to the Public Broadcasting System series on Jefferson. The site includes material on how people understand Jefferson today.

Archiving Early America
earlyamerica.com
Old newspapers provide a window into the issues of the past. This site includes the Keigwin and Matthews collection of early newspapers.

Alexander Hamilton
http://www.alexanderhamiltonexhibition.org
This site, developed by the New York Historical Society, provides an introduction to Hamilton's life and influence in the United States.

XYZ Affair
gi.grolier.com/presidents/aae/side/xyzaffr.html
This site examines the XYZ affair.

Whiskey Rebellion
www.whiskeyrebellion.org
This site devoted to the 1794 Whiskey Rebellion includes a narrative of events and a timeline.

Native Languages of the Americas
www.geocities.com/bigorrin/miam.htm
This site provides information on the language of the Miami and Illinois Indians, a dialect of the same Algonquin language spoken in Indiana and later in Oklahoma.

The Quasi War, 1798–1800
www.yale.edu/lawweb/avalon/quasi.htm
This site for the Avalon Project at the Yale Law School explores the Quasi War between the United States and France.

Marshall Cases
odur.let.rug.nl~usa/D/1801-1825/marshallcases/marxx.htm
John Marshall, and the cases he heard, shaped the form and function of the judicial system in the United States.

National Museum of the American Indian
www.si.edu/nmai
The Smithsonian Institution maintains this site, which provides information about the new museum in Washington D.C., that is dedicated to the history and culture of Native Americans.

For Further Reading

General Works

Joyce Appleby, *Inheriting the Revolution: The First Generation of Americans* (2000).
Joseph J. Ellis, *Founding Brothers: The Revolutionary Generation* (2000).
Richard H. Kohn, *Eagle and Sword: The Beginnings of the Military Establishment in America* (1975).
Richard White, *The Middle Ground: Indians, Empires, and Republics in the Great Lakes Region, 1650–1815* (1991).
Bernard A. Weisberger, *America Afire: Jefferson, Adams, and the Revolutionary Election of 1800* (2000).

Competing Political Visions in the New Nation

Joyce Appleby, *Capitalism and the New Social Order: The Republican Vision of the 1790s* (1984).
Albert Bowman, *The Struggle for Neutrality: Franco-American Diplomacy During the Federalist Era* (1974).
William Hogeland, *The Whiskey Rebellion* (2006).
James Roger Sharp, *American Politics in the Early Republic: The New Nation in Crisis* (1995).

People of Color: New Freedoms, New Struggles

Ira Berlin, *Slaves Without Masters: The Free Negro in the Antebellum South* (1981).
Douglas R. Egerton, *Gabriel's Rebellion: The Virginia Slave Conspiracies of 1800 and 1802* (1993).
James O. Horton and Lois Horton, *In Hope of Liberty: Culture, Community, and Protest Among Northern Free Blacks, 1700–1860* (1997).
Leon Litwack, *North of Slavery: The Negro in the Free States, 1790–1860* (1961).
Matthew Mason, *Slavery and Politics in the Early Republic* (2006).

Continuity and Change in the West

Henry W. Bowden, *American Indians and Christian Missions: Studies in Cultural Change* (1981).
Gregory Evans Dowd, *A Spirited Resistance: The North American Indian Struggle for Unity, 1745–1815* (1992).
Robert V. Hine and John Mack Faragher, *The American West: A New Interpretive History* (2000).
Reginald Horsman, *Expansion and American Indian Policy, 1783–1812* (1967).

Shifting Social Identities in the Post-Revolutionary Era

Paul Gilje, *Liberty on the Waterfront: American Maritime Culture in the Age of Revolution* (2003).

Nathan O. Hatch, *The Democratization of American Christianity* (1989).

Linda Kerber, *Women of the Republic: Intellect and Ideology in Revolutionary America* (1980).

William G. McLaughlin, *Cherokee Renascence in the New Republic* (1986).

Billy G. Smith, *The "Lower Sort": Philadelphia's Laboring People, 1750–1800* (1990).

The Election of 1800: Revolution or Reversal?

Doron Ben-Atar and Barbara B. Oberg, eds., *Federalists Reconsidered* (1998).

Gordon S. Brown, *Toussaint's Clause: The Founding Fathers and the Haitian Revolution* (2005).

Joseph J. Ellis, *American Sphinx: The Character of Thomas Jefferson* (1996).

John Ferling, *Adams vs. Jefferson: The Tumultuous Election of 1800* (2004).

Peter S. Onuf, *Jefferson's Empire: The Language of American Nationhood* (2000).

Garry Wills, *"Negro President": Jefferson and the Slave Power* (2003).

For quizzes and other resources on these topics, go to www.longmanamericanhistory.com.

1803	South Carolina reopens slave trade Louisiana Purchase *Marbury v. Madison*
1804	Lewis and Clark expedition (1804–1806)
1805	British Navy defeats French and Spanish fleets at Battle of Trafalgar
1806	Congress authorizes funds for construction of National Road
1807	Jefferson places embargo on all U.S. exports to Europe U.S.S. *Chesapeake* attacked by British vessel Robert Fulton pilots first steamboat up the Hudson River
1808	Congressional ban on slave trade takes effect Non-Intercourse Act prevents exports to France and England Tecumseh and Tenskwatawa found Prophet Town in Indiana
1810	Macon's Bill No. 2
1811	Battle of Tippecanoe Revolt of 400 slaves in Louisiana
1812	War of 1812 begins
1813	Red Sticks battle U.S. troops at Battle of Horseshoe Bend
1814	British forces attack Washington, D.C.
1815	Treaty of Ghent ends War of 1812 Battle of New Orleans
1816	Tariff of 1816
1817	Rush-Bagot Agreement
1818	Andrew Jackson battles Seminoles in Florida African Methodist Episcopal Church founded in Charleston, S.C.
1819	Spain cedes Florida to United States Tallmadge Amendment Panic of 1819
1820	Missouri Compromise Washington Irving, *Legend of Sleepy Hollow*
1821	Mexico gains independence from Spain Sequoyah completes Cherokee syllabary
1822	Charleston officials convict and hang blacks in Vesey "plot"
1823	Monroe Doctrine Catharine Beecher establishes Hartford Female Seminary Lowell textile mills open
1824	Erie Canal opens

PART FOUR

Expanding the Boundaries of Freedom and Slavery, 1803–1848

IN THE FIRST HALF OF THE NINETEENTH CENTURY, FEW IF ANY NATIONS could rival the United States' remarkable record of growth. At its founding, the country consisted of 4 million people living in thirteen states that hugged the eastern seaboard of North America. By the mid-nineteenth century, the nation's population had grown to 22.5 million people as a result of reproduction, foreign immigration, and the conquest of indigenous and Spanish-speaking peoples. Because of a mix of diplomatic pressure and military aggression, dramatic geographic expansion accompanied the burgeoning population growth. By 1850 the country sprawled the breadth of the continent to the Pacific Ocean.

Territorial expansion, economic growth, and increasing ethnic diversity profoundly shaped American politics in the first half of the nineteenth century. Innovations in transportation (the steamboat), communication (the telegraph), and the production of crops and textiles (reapers and mechanical looms) allowed Americans to move materials, people, and information more quickly and to produce food and goods more efficiently. Meanwhile, the immigration of large numbers of western Europeans, the rapid expansion of the free black population, and the conquest of Spanish-speaking peoples in the Southwest in 1848 challenged the United States' view of itself as an exclusively Anglo-Protestant nation.

Some citizens declared that the United States had a God-given duty and God-given right to expand its borders in opposition to the British and Russians in the Northwest and in opposition to Spain and later Mexico in the South and Southwest. Thus, territorial expansion brought the United States into conflict with other countries and groups that claimed the land. America's victory in the War of 1812 secured the nation's Great Lakes border and at the same time proved that American soldiers and sailors were the equal of England's seasoned fighting forces.

In 1823, fearful that European powers would take advantage of independence movements in Latin America, the United States issued the Monroe Doctrine, stating that the era of colonization of the Americas was over.

Nevertheless, Indian tribes continued to resist the incursion of European Americans who believed that land was a commodity to be wrested from native peoples and then bought and sold. In the southern part of the country, the Five Civilized Tribes and other Native American groups occupied territory coveted by both gold seekers and cotton growers. Many American voters demanded that their political leaders work to expand the nation's boundaries through a variety of means: treaty, negotiation, or military force.

Andrew Jackson, who assumed the presidency in 1828, seemed a fitting symbol and a representative politician of the age. Determined to expand the power of the executive branch of government, Jackson claimed to represent the interests of ordinary people in his political battles against the Second Bank of the United States and the Supreme Court and in his forceful removal of Indian tribes from the Southeast to Indian Territory (present-day Oklahoma). Like other politicians of the time, Jackson conceived of citizenship as a system of rights and privileges for white men only.

Still, European Americans trumpeted the arrival of a new era of egalitarianism. Western settlers laid claim to political power, and suffrage restrictions based on property ownership crumbled in the wake of egalitarian legislation and rhetoric. Americans were restless, moving out west and back east again, around the countryside, and in and out of cities. Believing that people could and should work together to reform society, many created reform associations, embraced new religious beliefs, and joined political parties. New forms of association yielded new kinds of communities in an era characterized by great geographic mobility.

At the same time, two distinct power systems coalesced to ensure that certain groups would monopolize the political and economic life of the country. In the South, cotton planters launched an aggressive defense of the institution of slavery. In the North, an emerging class system extended the differences between the political influence and material well-being of factory owners and machine operatives.

For the country, therefore, growth brought great promise and great peril. Abolitionists, associations of working people, nativists (people hostile to immigrants), women's rights advocates, and a variety of other groups proclaimed their agendas for social change. Most significantly, by 1848 it was becoming more difficult for national legislators to resolve the question of whether to allow slavery in the territories. As passions rose, few could imagine a political compromise that would satisfy abolitionists and proslavery advocates alike. As midcentury approached, more and more Americans seemed prepared to express their convictions—or their prejudices and resentment—through violent means.

1826	American Society for the Promotion of Temperance founded
1827	Workingmen's Party founded in Philadelphia
1828	*Cherokee Phoenix* begins publication
1829	Gold discovered on Cherokee lands in Georgia
1831	Nat Turner leads slave rebellion in Virginia William Lloyd Garrison publishes *The Liberator*
1832	Nullification crisis *Worcester v. Georgia* Jackson vetoes Second Bank of the United States Black Hawk War
1833	Great Britain abolishes slavery National Road completed
1834	Cyrus McCormick patents reaper First strike at Lowell mills Whig Party organized
1835	Alexis de Tocqueville, *Democracy in America* Texas revolts against Mexico
1836	Congress passes gag rule on antislavery petitions Republic of Texas founded
1837	Panic of 1837 John Deere invents steel plow
1838	Pennsylvania revokes black male suffrage Cherokee removal begins; Trail of Tears
1840	Liberty Party founded
1841	John Tyler assumes presidency after death of William Henry Harrison Supreme Court rules in favor of *Amistad* Africans
1844	Mormon leader Joseph Smith killed by mob in Nauvoo, Illinois
1845	Irish potato famine Frederick Douglass, *Narrative of the Life of Frederick Douglass* Texas becomes twenty-eighth state
1846	Great Britain cedes southern part of Oregon Country to United States Mexican-American War begins
1847	United States wins battles of Buena Vista, Vera Cruz, Mexico City Capture of San Patricio soldiers, Battle of Churubusco
1848	Treaty of Guadalupe Hidalgo ends Mexican-American War Women's Rights convention in Seneca Falls, New York Popular revolutions sweep Europe

CHAPTER 10

Defending and Expanding the New Nation, 1803–1818

Louisiana Purchase and Exploration of the Trans-Mississippi West

CHAPTER OUTLINE

The British Menace

The War of 1812

The "Era of Good Feelings"?

The Rise of the Cotton Plantation Economy

Conclusion

Sites to Visit

For Further Reading

I N EARLY NOVEMBER 1804, A GROUP OF SOLDIERS WORKED FEVERISHLY TO CONSTRUCT A ROUGH military garrison on the north bank of the Missouri River, near several Mandan Indian villages just west of modern Washburn, North Dakota. The soldiers knew they had to work quickly. Within a month, winter would descend on the northern Great Plains, and the temperature would plummet. In fact, not long after Fort Mandan was completed, the temperature registered at 45 degrees Fahrenheit below zero.

The garrison provided shelter for an expedition party led by Meriwether Lewis and William Clark. Both captains in the U.S. Army, Lewis and Clark had been commissioned by President Thomas Jefferson to explore the upper reaches of the newly acquired Louisiana Territory, which had doubled the size of the country. With the ultimate goal of reaching the Pacific Coast in what today is Oregon, their party spent the winter at Fort Mandan and joined the buffalo hunts and nightly dances sponsored by their hosts, the Mandan Indians. Between November 1804 and March 1805, Lewis and Clark also found time to record their observations on all manner of things natural and cultural. In their journals and their letters to President Jefferson, they described the language of the Hidatsa Indians and the beadwork of the Arikara, the medicinal properties of native plants, and the contours of the Missouri River. In a shipment prepared for the president, they included deer horns, pumice stones, and the pelt of a white weasel. Among an assortment of live animals, only a magpie and a prairie dog survived the journey to Washington, D.C.

Lewis and Clark's trek took twenty-eight months to complete and covered 8,000 miles. Their expedition's purpose was partly scientific, but Jefferson had also commissioned them to chart a northwestern waterway

■ Captain Meriwether Lewis posed in Indian dress for this watercolor completed in 1807 by French artist C. B. J. Févret de Saint-Mémin.

■ MAP 10.1
LEWIS AND CLARK This map, showing the route of the Lewis and Clark expedition, suggests the importance of interior waterways in facilitating travel and exploration in the West. Spain feared, rightly, that the Americans would use western rivers to establish trade links with the Indians and thereby challenge Spain's northern border with the United States.

passage to the Pacific coast. The president hoped to divert the profitable fur trade of the far Northwest away from British Canada and into the hands of Americans by locating a river connecting this larger Northwest directly to eastern U.S. markets. Jefferson also instructed Lewis and Clark to initiate negotiations with various Indian groups, to pave the way for miners and ranchers to move into the area.

Lewis and Clark's party consisted of a diverse group of people, including British and Irish enlisted men, and Lewis's African American slave, York. At Fort Mandan, the group picked up Toussaint Charbonneau, a French Canadian, and his fifteen-year-old wife, Sacajawea, a Shoshone Indian. The explorers came to rely on Sacajawea's skills as an interpreter. And because women never traveled with Indian war parties, Sacajawea's presence reassured suspicious Native Americans that the goal of the expedition was peaceful.

During the first two decades of the nineteenth century, the United States faced a number of challenges from within and outside its borders, challenges that had long-lasting political and economic effects. Indians in general were a persistent threat to the new nation. Indeed, in the Great Lakes region, various tribes maintained political

The Louisiana Purchase

and military alliances with the British in Canada. Nevertheless, in this period the United States successfully met its most severe test to date: a war with Great Britain that raged from 1812 to 1815. The effects of this so-called Second American Revolution were far-reaching. The conflict eliminated the British from the Old Northwest once and for all. The war also spurred industrialization and stimulated commerce. In the South, the cotton plantation system began to shape the political and economic life of the entire region, in the process stimulating the expansion of human bondage.

The British Menace

In the election of 1804, Democratic-Republican Thomas Jefferson and his vice-presidential running mate, George Clinton, easily defeated their Federalist opponents, Charles C. Pinckney and Rufus King. Developments overseas preoccupied Jefferson during his second term in office. England and France continued to challenge each other as the reigning powers of Europe. In 1805 the British navy, under the command of Lord Nelson, defeated the French and Spanish fleets in the Battle of Trafalgar off the coast of Spain. That same year, France reveled in its own triumph on land when Napoleon conquered the Austrian and Russian armies at the Battle of Austerlitz. Supreme on the seas, England in 1806 passed the Orders in Council, which specified that any country that wanted to ship goods to France must first send them to a British port and pay taxes on them. Many Americans believed that England's policies amounted to acts of military and economic aggression against the United States.

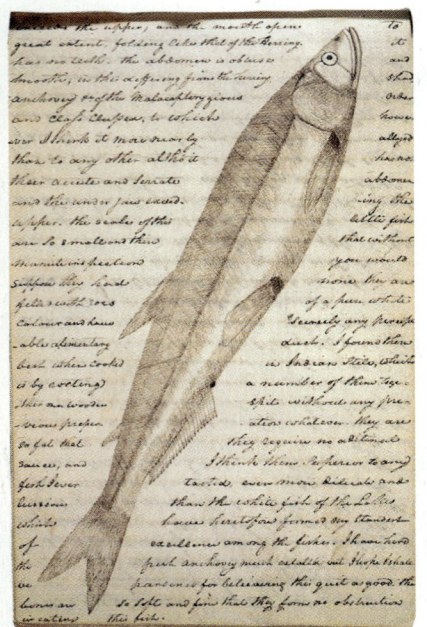

■ Lewis and Clark were not only explorers; they were also pioneering naturalists committed to gathering, recording, and studying plants and animal life in the West. William Clark drew this sketch of a eulachon, also called a candlefish, as part of his journal entry for February 25, 1806. Pacific Indians dried the oily fish and used it as a torch.

William Clark, *Eulachon (T. Pacificus)*, 1806, Voorhis Journal #2. William Clark Papers, Missouri Historical Society Archives

The Embargo of 1807

Not content to control trade across the Atlantic as decreed by the 1806 Orders in Council, the British also seized sailors from American ships, claiming that these men were British seamen who had been lured away from their own vessels by American captains promising them higher wages. In some cases these claims were probably true. However, U.S. political leaders charged that an estimated 6,000 U.S. citizens had been seized by the British navy between 1808 and 1811, including an unknown number of African Americans, many of whom were working as mariners. With limited economic opportunities on shore, black sailors accepted the danger and long absences from home. However, neither black nor white sailors had bargained for enforced service in His Majesty's Royal Navy. Seizure, or impressment, reminded Americans of their pre–Revolutionary War days, when British "press gangs" prowled the docks of American port cities and seized colonial merchant sailors. In 1807 the tensions over impressment erupted into violence. Just 10 miles off the shore of Virginia, the American ship *Chesapeake* came under attack from a British vessel. British naval officers claimed that the Americans were harboring four British deserters. In the ensuing exchange of cannon fire, three Americans were killed and eighteen wounded. Jefferson demanded that England leave American sailors and ships alone, but he was rebuffed.

TABLE 10-1

The Election of 1804

Candidate	Political Party	Electoral Vote
Thomas Jefferson	Democratic-Republican	162
Charles C. Pinckney	Federalist	14

In 1807 President Jefferson decided to place an **embargo** on all exports to the European powers in an effort to force those nations to respect the rights of Americans on the high seas. The Embargo Act passed by Congress halted the shipment of goods from the United States to Europe. Because Europe—including England—relied heavily on American grain and timber, Jefferson hoped that the move would force England to respect American independence. The president saw this measure as preferable to either war or capitulation to England. But the move aroused intense opposition in Federalist-dominated New England, where the regional economy depended heavily on foreign trade. As the effects of the embargo took hold, the New England grain growers saw the markets for their products dry up, and the timber industry suffered when local shipbuilding ground to a standstill. Southern tobacco and cotton planters faced similar hardship because of the embargo. By 1808 some of them had joined with Northerners to circumvent the embargo by moving their goods through Canada and then to Europe.

Yet Jefferson held his course, prodding Congress to enforce the unpopular act. His efforts provoked a backlash as New England politicians threatened to take their states out of the union. Despite all the uproar, the embargo did benefit Americans by promoting industrialization at home. At the same time, the embargo seemed only to intensify, not lessen, tensions between England and the United States.

On the Brink of War

Both the Federalists and the Democratic-Republicans suffered a blow to their leadership in 1804. That year, the Federalist party lost one of its original leaders with the death of Alexander Hamilton at the hand of his rival, Aaron Burr. Both successful New York attorneys, the two men had risen together through the political ranks in the 1780s and 1790s. Burr served as Jefferson's running mate in the election of 1800; four years later he ran for governor of New York. Incensed by a report that Hamilton had claimed he was "a dangerous man, and one who ought not to be trusted with the reins of government," as well as "still more despicable rumors," Burr challenged his antagonist to a pistol duel at Weehawken, New Jersey, in July 1804. Hamilton, mortally wounded in the affair, died the next day, and Burr's political career fell into ruin.

Jefferson, declining to run for a third presidential term in 1808, left the stage as well. Soon after the inauguration of the new president, James Madison, Congress repealed Jefferson's embargo and replaced it with the Non-Intercourse Act, which eased the complete ban on exports to Europe. This measure permitted American exporters to ship their goods to all European countries except for France and England, still at war with one another. New Englanders opposed even this limited embargo.

The original partisan division within Congress—the Federalists, with their emphasis on a strong national government, against the localist Democratic-Republicans—gradually eased. By 1810 a different split had emerged—between young, hotheaded representatives from the West and their more conservative seniors from the eastern seaboard. The western group, or "**war hawks**," called on the nation to revive its former glory. Americans must uphold U.S. honor, they declared, by opposing European, especially British, claims to military dominance. The war hawks also yearned to vanquish the Indians who impeded settlement of the area west of the Mississippi.

TABLE 10-2

The Election of 1808

Candidate	Political Party	Electoral Vote
James Madison	Democratic-Republican	122
Charles C. Pinckney	Federalist	47
George Clinton	Democratic-Republican	6

Looking eastward, the war hawks saw an England determined to defile the honor of their young nation. Looking westward, these same men saw an equally threatening menace: the rise of an ominous Indian resistance movement that blended military strength with native spirituality. The movement was led by Shawnee brothers Tecumseh and Tenskwatawa (also known as the Prophet), who founded Prophet's Town in Indiana in 1808. They envisioned a sovereign Indian state and the preservation of Native American culture. Tenskwatawa spoke of a time and place where Indians would reject alcohol and scorn "the food of whites" as well as the "wealth and ornaments" of commercial trade. Tecumseh set out to deliver the message to as many Indian groups as possible, traveling the broad swath of territory from Florida to Canada.

In 1809, the territorial governor of Indiana, William Henry Harrison, plied a group of Indian leaders with liquor, then got them to agree to sell 3 million acres to the U.S. government for just $7,600. Upon hearing of the deal, Tecumseh decried a new form of American aggression: "treaties" between U.S. officials and Indians who lacked the authority to sell their people's homeland. "All red men," Tecumseh proclaimed, must "unite in claiming a common and equal right in the land, as it was at first, and should be yet; for it never was divided, but belongs to all, for the use of each."

In November 1811, Harrison led 1,000 U.S. soldiers in an advance on Prophet's Town. But before they could reach the settlement, several hundred Shawnees under the command of Tenskwatawa attacked their camp on the Tippecanoe River. The Indians suffered a sound defeat before the superior U.S. weapons, and Harrison burned Prophet's Town to the ground.

■ This lithograph of the Prophet (Tenskwatawa) was based on an 1824 painting of the Shawnee mystic and holy man. Early in life, he suffered an accident with bows and arrows, losing his right eye. He and his older brother Tecumseh called on all Indians to resist the encroachment of their lands by whites and to renounce the way of life followed by whites, including the use of liquor. After the Indians' defeat at the Battle of Tippecanoe in 1811, the Prophet retreated to Canada. He returned to the United States in 1826. By that time he no longer wielded influence as a leader of the Shawnee.

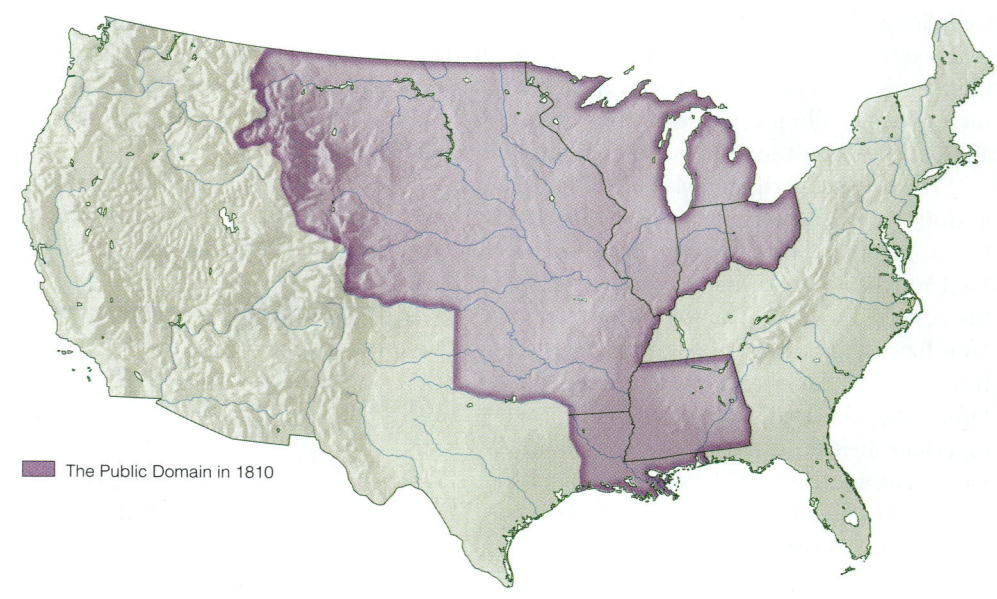

■ MAP 10.2
THE PUBLIC DOMAIN IN 1810
This map indicates the expanse of western lands owned by the U.S. government in 1810, after the Louisiana Purchase. American war veterans received land warrants in return for military service in the Revolutionary War and the War of 1812. A warrant entitled the bearer to settle a specific number of acres of unoccupied lands. Warrants could be transferred, sold, and traded like stocks and bonds. After the War of 1812, the government issued 29,186 land warrants for a total of 4.8 million acres.

The Public Domain in 1810

The War of 1812

The defeat of the Shawnees at Tippecanoe encouraged western war hawks' resolve to break the back of Indian resistance altogether. But to achieve this goal, the United States would have to invade Canada and eliminate the British arms suppliers who had been trading with the Indians. Claiming the mantle of patriotism, western and southern members of the House of Representatives agitated for a war that would eliminate both the British threat on the high seas and the Canada-based Indian-British alliance. These Americans wanted a war that would win for them a true independence once and for all. "On to Canada! On to Canada!" became the rallying cry of the war hawks.

TABLE 10-3
The Election of 1812

Candidate	Political Party	Electoral Vote
James Madison	Democratic-Republican	128
De Witt Clinton	Federalist	89

The War of 1812

In a secret message sent to Congress on June 1, 1812, President Madison listed Americans' many grievances against England: the British navy's seizure of American citizens, the blockades of American goods, and continued conflict "on one of our extensive frontiers," the result of "savages" who had the backing of British traders and military officials. Madison left it up to Congress whether Americans would continue to endure these indignities or would act "in defense of their natural rights." Seventeen days later, the House voted 79 to 49 and the Senate voted 19 to 13 to declare war on England and, by extension, the western Indians.

While uniting Americans behind a banner of national expansion, the War of 1812 also exposed dangerous divisions between regions of the country and between political viewpoints. Many New Englanders saw the conflict as a plot by Virginia Democratic-Republicans primarily to aid France in opposition to England and to add agrarian (that is, slave) states to the Union. In an ironic twist, the New England Federalists—usually staunch defenders of the national government—argued that states should control their own commerce and militias.

Pushing North

Although the Americans were better armed and organized than the western Indians, they were at a disadvantage when they took on the soldiers and sailors of the British Empire. The United States had not invested in the military and thus was ill-prepared for all-out war. The American navy consisted merely of a fleet of tiny gunboats constructed during the cost-conscious Jefferson administration. The charter for the Bank of the United States had expired in 1811, depriving the country of a vital source of financial credit. Suffering from a drop in tax revenues as a result of the embargo on foreign trade, the nation lacked the funds to train and equip the regular army and the state militias. Nevertheless, in the fall of 1812, the Americans launched an ambitious three-pronged attack against Canada, striking from Niagara, Detroit, and Lake Champlain. All three attempts failed miserably.

In the West in late 1812, Tecumseh (who had accepted a commission as a brigadier general in the British army) and British General Isaac Brock captured Detroit. Yet the Americans scored some notable successes in 1813. That September, Commodore Oliver

■ In 1815 approximately 6,000 American prisoners of war were confined to Britain's dank Dartmoor Prison in Devonshire, England. Many of them were African Americans, who represented one-fifth of all sailors who fought in the war. Among that group was Richard Crafus. An imposing man, Crafus earned the title "King Dick" by serving as the leader of the central barracks at Dartmoor, where blacks were held. He strolled through the cell block, carrying a large club and settling disputes between the prisoners.

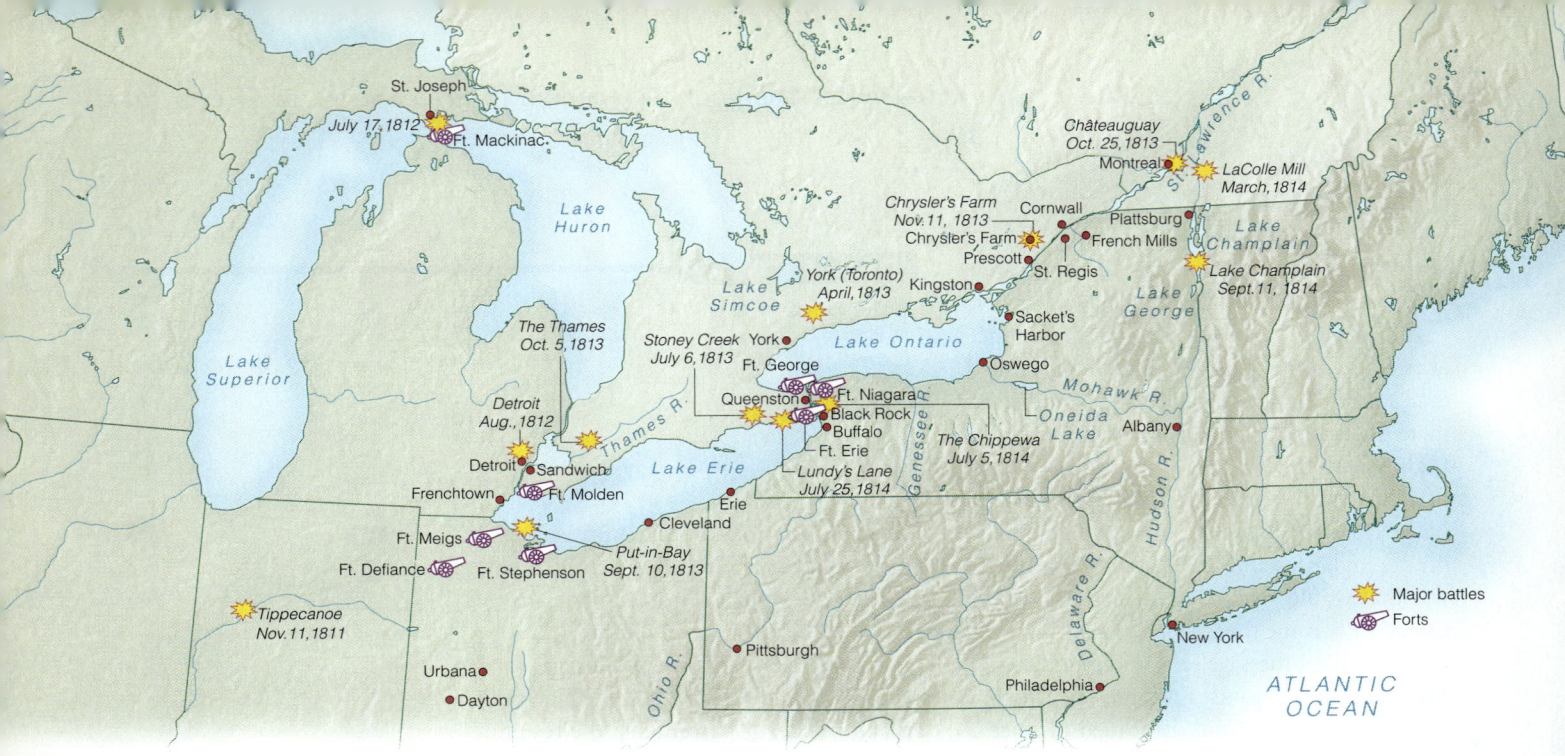

MAP 10.3
THE NORTHERN FRONT, WAR OF 1812 Much of the fighting of the War of 1812 centered in the Great Lakes region. It was there, the war hawks charged, that the British were inciting Indians to attack American settlements. Conducted in 1812 and 1813, the campaign against Canada was supposed to eliminate the British threat and, some Americans hoped, win Canadian territory for the United States.

H. Perry defeated a British fleet at Put-in-Bay on Lake Erie. Exhilarated, he declared, "We have met the enemy and they are ours." Perry's hard-won victory forced the British back into Canada, over Tecumseh's objections. General William Henry Harrison followed in hot pursuit. British Colonel Henry Proctor marched his troops to eastern Ontario, leaving Tecumseh to try holding the Americans at bay. At the Battle of the Thames that October, Harrison defeated the Indians. Many perished, Tecumseh among them.

Later that autumn, an American campaign against Montreal failed. The Americans trudged back into New York state, the British close behind them. Flush with their victory in Montreal, the British captured Fort Niagara and set Buffalo and other nearby towns aflame.

By mid-1814, the English and their allies had also crushed Napoleon in Europe. This success freed up 15,000 British troops, who promptly sailed for North America. Still, in July 1814 the Americans, under the leadership of Major General Jacob Brown and Brigadier General Winfield Scott, managed to defeat the British at the Battle of Chippewa, across the Niagara River from Buffalo. But by the end of that year, the Americans had withdrawn to their own territory and relinquished their goal of invading and conquering Canada. The arrival of fresh British troops forced the Americans to defend their own soil.

Fighting on Many Fronts

For the Americans, the most humiliating episode of the war came with the British attack on the nation's capital. On August 24, 1814, the British army, backed by the Royal Navy, sailed into Chesapeake Bay. At the Battle of Bladensburg, Maryland, they scattered the American troops they encountered. The Redcoats then advanced to Washington, where they torched the Capitol building and the White House, causing extensive damage to both structures.

Residents of the capital city had received word that the British were advancing. On Sunday, August 21, public officials frantically packed up their books and papers. Private citizens gathered up their furniture and other belongings and left town. By Tuesday, the city stood nearly empty. As a ragtag American force succumbed to the British, a Baltimore newspaper reported, President Madison "retired from the mortifying scene, and left the city on horseback."

Yet the Americans rallied, pursued the British, and bested them in the Battle of Baltimore. This victory inspired an observer, Francis Scott Key, to write "The Star Spangled Banner" as he watched "the bombs bursting in air" over Baltimore's Fort McHenry. The Americans scored another crucial victory in September, when U.S. naval commander Thomas McDonough crushed the British fleet on Lake Champlain near Plattsburgh, New York.

In the Southeast, Tecumseh's message of Indian unity had resonated with particular force among Native Americans once the war broke out. Some Cherokee and Choctaw cast their lot with the United States. However, a minority of Creek were emboldened by Tenskwatawa's call to war against the whites. By 1813 a group of warriors called Red Sticks (for their scarlet-painted weapons) stood ready to do battle with U.S. forces. Yet they faced opposition from some of their own people, the White Sticks, who counseled peace. The Red Sticks finally decided to attack Fort Mims, north of Mobile.

In response, Andrew Jackson, leader of the Tennessee militia, received a commission as major general. His mission was to retaliate against the Indians. Jackson had speculated in Indian lands in Mississippi Territory, and he called Native Americans "blood thirsty barbarians." Even in a country where anti-Indian sentiment ran high, his views were extreme. He often boasted about collecting the scalps of all his Indian victims, and he relished his new assignment.

DOCUMENT

Dolley Madison to Her Sister as the British Approach (1814)

■ This engraving, published in 1814, depicts the bombardment of Fort McHenry by British warships in September of that year. When he witnessed the battle, Francis Scott Key, a Washington lawyer, was aboard a prisoner exchange boat in Baltimore Harbor. He was seeking release of a friend captured by the British. After penning the poem "The Star Spangled Banner," Key set the words to music, using the tune of a popular English drinking song. Congress declared the song the national anthem in 1931.

Jackson's 3,500 troops laid waste to Creek territory. Regiments of Cherokee, Choctaw, and Chickasaw Indians, as well as White Sticks, helped them. During a monumental battle in March 1814, more than three-quarters of the 1,000 defending Red Sticks and a number of Indian women and children died at Horseshoe Bend (in modern-day Alabama). In the Treaty of Horseshoe Bend that followed, the Americans forced the Creek Nation to give up 23 million acres. The remnants of the Red Sticks fled to the swamps of Florida, where they joined additional Creeks, other Florida Indians, and numerous fugitive slaves in an emerging group known as the Seminoles.

Jackson next marched to New Orleans to confront the British. Knowing he would be facing some of Europe's finest soldiers, he assembled 7,000 men, U.S. soldiers and militiamen from the states of Louisiana, Kentucky, and Tennessee. Two Kentucky regiments consisted of free Negro volunteers, about 400 men in total. The Battle of New Orleans, fought on January 8, 1815, began with a ferocious assault by British soldiers. But within just half an hour, 2,000 of them lay dead or wounded. The Americans lost only seventy. Jackson's back country sharpshooters had vanquished the army of Europe's greatest military power.

Later, many Americans associated Andrew Jackson with the war's decisive battle and most glorious victory. But in fact, American and British negotiators had actually signed a peace agreement ending the war two weeks before the British defeat in New Orleans. The Battle of New Orleans might have been a glorious victory for the Americans, but it was hardly the decisive battle of the war.

An Uncertain Victory

In the fall of 1814, Madison had decided to end the war. He dispatched John Quincy Adams, son of former president John Adams, to the Belgian city of Ghent to start negotiations. Representative Henry Clay and three other American envoys accompanied Adams. At first, English representatives at the meeting made two demands. The Americans, they said, must agree to the creation of an Indian territory in the upper Great Lakes region. They must also cede much of the state of Maine to England. The Americans refused, and the negotiations dragged on.

In the meantime, the New England states had grown increasingly impatient with what they called "Mr. Madison's war." As with the embargo, they saw the effort as a mistake and a threat to their regional commercial interests. In December 1814, Massachusetts, Connecticut, Rhode Island, New Hampshire, and Vermont sent delegates to a gathering in Hartford, Connecticut, to consider a course of action. The delegates demanded that the federal government give their states financial aid to compensate for the revenue they had lost as a result of disrupted trade. Some delegates even hinted that their states wanted to secede from the union. Although most delegates shied away from immediate action, the majority of them apparently wanted to leave open the possibility of actual **secession**.

After Congress ratified the Treaty of Ghent in February 1815, the Americans and the British never again met each other across a battlefield as enemies.

Back in Ghent, the British had reversed their initial position by late December. They had lost recent battles in upper New York and in Baltimore and, as always, were still worried about new threats from France. They dropped their demands for territory and for an Indian buffer state in the upper Midwest. They also agreed to an armistice that, in essence, represented a draw: both combatants would retain the same territory they had possessed when the war began. The British made no concessions to the Americans' demands that they stop impressing American sailors and supplying the western Indians with arms or that they revoke the Orders in Council. Still, most U.S. citizens considered the war a great victory for the United States. After Congress ratified the Treaty of Ghent in February 1815, the Americans and the British never again met each other across a battlefield as enemies.

The Treaty of Ghent (1814)

The "Era of Good Feelings"?

In the 1816 presidential election, Democratic-Republican candidate James Monroe benefited from several developments that had mortally wounded the Federalist party: the War of 1812 victory, presided over by a Democratic-Republican chief executive; the New England Federalists' flirtation with secession (and treason) during the war years; and the strong nationalist tendencies of both the Jefferson and Madison administrations, which had stolen the Federalists' thunder.

Addressing Congress in December 1817, President Monroe expressed optimism about the state of the nation. The country's boundaries were secure, and the Indians had little choice but to retreat farther and farther west. The president predicted that, shortly, "Indian hostilities, if they do not altogether cease, will henceforth lose their terror." Equally inspiring, the Americans had once again defied the British Empire and won. Two treaties with Britain—the Rush-Bagot of 1817 and the pending Convention of 1818—set the U.S.-Canadian border at the forty-ninth parallel and provided that the two countries would jointly occupy Oregon Territory for ten years.

TABLE 10-4
The Election of 1816

Candidate	Political Party	Electoral Vote
James Monroe	Democratic-Republican	183
Rufus King	Federalist	34

Monroe called on Congress to acknowledge "the vast extent of territory within the United States [and] the great amount and value of its productions" and to facilitate the construction of roads and canals. It was this "happy situation of the United States," in Monroe's words, that ushered in what some historians called "The Era of Good Feelings." Although voters continued to disagree over some issues of the day—such as the national bank, sectionalism, and **internal improvements**—they did not necessarily express those disagreements in the form of bitter partisan wrangling. Still, the term "good feelings" may fully apply only to a narrow group of **enfranchised citizens**, men who shared common beliefs about territorial expansion and economic development.

DOCUMENT

Western Country Ohio (1816)

Praise and Respect for Veterans After the War

American veterans of the War of 1812 won the praise of a grateful nation. Even the British expressed a grudging respect for Americans' fighting abilities. One British naval officer admitted, "I don't like Americans; I never did, and never shall." He had "no wish to eat with them, drink with them, or consort with them in any way." But, he added, he would rather not fight with "an enemy so brave, determined, and alert, as they have always proved." To reward veterans for their service, Congress offered them 160-acre plots of land in the territory between the Illinois and Mississippi rivers. These grants did much to encourage families to emigrate west and establish homesteads.

Some military heroes of the war parlayed their success into impressive political careers. Andrew Jackson won election to the presidency in 1828 and 1832, as did William Henry Harrison in 1840. Countless others earned recognition within their own community, and European American veterans were not the only ones to gain status and influence as a result of the conflict. For example, a Cherokee leader named the Ridge earned the gratitude of American officials for his contributions to the war effort. He had accepted the government's attempts to press the Cherokee to adopt European American ways, settling in a log cabin rather than in a traditional Cherokee dwelling when he married a Cherokee woman named Susanna Wickett in the early 1790s. During the war against the Red Sticks, the Ridge served under Andrew Jackson and earned the title of major. For the rest of his life, the Cherokee leader was known as Major Ridge. His wife devoted herself to tending an orchard, keeping a garden, and sewing clothes,

INTERPRETING HISTORY

Cherokee Women Petition Against Further Land Sales to Whites in 1817

In traditional Cherokee society, men took responsibility for foreign affairs while women focused on domestic matters, leading to a roughly equal division of labor. However, European American diplomats, military officials, and traders dealt primarily with Indian men. As a result, beginning in the eighteenth century, Cherokee women's traditional influence was eroding within their own communities. In this new world, Indian warriors wielded significant power.

Nevertheless, Cherokee women insisted on presenting their views during the crisis of 1817–1819, when men of the group were deciding whether to cede land to U.S. authorities and move west. The following petition was supported by Nancy Ward, a Cherokee War Woman. This honorific title was bestowed on women who accompanied and attended to the needs of war parties. Ward had supported the colonists' cause during the American Revolution.

Amovey [Tennessee] in Council 2nd May 1817

The Cherokee Ladys now being present at the meeting of the Chiefs and warriors in council have thought it their duties as mothers to address their beloved Chiefs and warriors now assembled.

Our beloved children and head men of the Cherokee nation we address you warriors in council we have raised all of you on the land which we now have,

In 1987, Wilma Mankiller became the first woman to be elected Principal Chief of the Cherokee Nation of Oklahoma.

which God gave to us to inhabit and raise provisions we know that our country has once been extensive but by repeated sales has become circumscribed to a small tract, and [we] never have thought it our duty to interfere in the disposition of it till now, if a father or mother was to sell all their lands which they had to depend on which their children had to raise their living on which would indeed be bad and to be removed to another country we do not wish to go to an unknown country [to] which we have understood some of our children wish to go over the Mississippi but this act of our children would be like destroying your mothers. Your mothers your sisters ask and beg of you not to part with any more of our lands, we say ours. [Y]ou are our descendants and take pity on our request, but keep it for our growing children for it was the good will of our creator to place us here and you know our father the great president [James Monroe], will not allow his white children to take our country away for if it was not they would not ask you to put your hands to paper for it would be impossible to remove us all for as soon as one child is raised, we have others in our arms for such is our situation and will consider our circumstance.

Therefore children don't part with any more of our lands but continue on it and enlarge your farms and cultivate and raise corn and cotton and we your mothers and sisters will make clothing for you which our father the president has recommended to us all we don't charge anybody for selling any lands, but we have heard such intentions of our children but your talks become true at last and it was our desire to forewarn you all not to part with our lands.

Nancy Ward to her children[:] warriors to take pity and listen to the talks of your sisters, although I am very old yet cannot but pity the situation in which you will hear of their minds. I have great many grand children which I wish they do well on our land.

In addition to Nancy Ward, 12 Cherokee women signed the petition. Their names suggest the varying degrees of assimilation to white ways on the part of Cherokees in general. Petitioners included Cun, o, ah and Widow Woman Holder, as well as Jenny McIntosh and Mrs. Nancy Fields.

It is unclear what effect, if any, this petition had on Cherokee male leaders. The Cherokee nation did halt land cessions to whites between 1819 and 1835.

Questions

1. How and why did motherhood confer authority on Cherokee women?
2. What is the significance and meaning of the land in Cherokee culture?
3. Does this petition provide evidence for the view that early nineteenth-century Cherokee men and women were adopting elements of European American culture? If so, what elements, and in what ways?

Source: Cherokee Women to Cherokee Council, May 2, 1817, series 1, Andrew Jackson Presidential Papers, Library of Congress Manuscripts Division, Washington, D.C. Reprinted in Nancy F. Cott, Jeanne Boydston, Ann Braude, Lori Ginzberg, and Molly Ladd-Taylor, eds., *Root of Bitterness: Documents of the Social History of American Women* (Boston: Northeastern University Press, 1996), pp. 177–178.

---

tasks traditionally performed by European American but not Native American women. Eventually, the family prospered, bought African American slaves, and became Christians as well.

The Ridge's battlefield experiences earned him the respect of other Cherokee who embraced the "civilization" program that missionaries and government officials promoted. At the same time, the Ridge vehemently resisted U.S. officials' attempts to persuade the Chero-

■ Southeastern Indians varied widely in their willingness to adopt European American ways. Some argued that the best way to preserve their community and remain on the land of their forebears was to accommodate themselves to white practices of trade, textile production, and farming. This 1805 painting shows Benjamin Hawkins, a government Indian agent, at a Creek settlement near Macon, Georgia. Hawkins expresses evident satisfaction with the Indians' neat cabins, well-tended fields, flocks of sheep, and bountiful harvest of vegetables.

kee to give up their lands to whites and move west. He believed that his people should adopt some elements of white culture but should also hold fast to their native lands in opposition to white settlers and politicians.

A Thriving Economy

The end of the War of 1812 saw an upsurge in internal migration. New Englanders, especially, pushed west in search of new opportunities. Between 1800 and 1820, the population of Ohio grew from 45,000 to 581,000. New means of transportation—and new means to fund them—facilitated the movement of goods and people. In 1807 an entrepreneur named Robert Fulton piloted the *Clermont*, his new kind of boat powered by steam, up the Hudson River from New York City. Steamboats traveled upriver, against the current, ten times faster than keelboats, which had to be pushed, pulled, or hauled by men or mules. Within a few years, therefore, such vessels were plying the Mississippi River and its major tributaries.

Improvements in land transportation stimulated economic growth. The profits that the Philadelphia and Lancaster Turnpike raked in by charging travelers tolls inspired other local private corporations to invest in roads. By 1810 several thousand such corporations were building roads up and down the East Coast. Funding came from a variety of sources, both public and private. Philadelphia textile mill owners financed transportation links with the city's **hinterland** (rural areas to the west) to carry their goods to the largest number of customers. Individual cities also invested in routes westward. The state of Virginia authorized a board of public works to expend funds for roads and other internal improvements. Western politi-

Improvements in land transportation stimulated economic growth.

cians flexed their political muscle in 1806 by securing congressional authorization for the building of the Cumberland (later National) Road, which snaked through the Allegheny Mountains and ended at the Ohio River.

The acceleration of commerce in the West, combined with the disruption in trade from Europe that had come with the Embargo of 1807 and the War of 1812, stimulated manufacturing throughout the United States. Philadelphia's growth proved particularly dazzling. During the war, the city's craft producers did not have to worry about foreign competition. Local merchant-financiers, who otherwise might have been pouring their money into trade ventures, began to invest in manufacturing. As early as 1808, the city's new factories had compensated for the glass, chemicals, shot, soap, lead, and earthenware that no longer flooded in from England. Philadelphia soon took the lead in production of all kinds, whether carried out in factories, artisans' shops, or private homes. Metalworking, ale brewing, and leather production counted among the array of thriving industries that made Philadelphia the nation's top industrial city in 1815. Still, in 1820 about two-thirds of all Philadelphia workers labored in small shopd employing fewer than six people.

Transformations in the Workplace

Even the earliest stages of the Industrial Revolution transformed the way people lived and worked. Some crafts—for example, the production of leather, barrels, soap, candles, and newspapers—expanded from small shops with skilled artisans into larger establishments with unskilled wage earners. In these cases, production was reorganized; now wage earners under the supervision of a boss replaced apprentices and journeymen who had formerly worked alongside a master artisan. These workers performed a single task many times a day instead of using their specialized skills to see a production process through to completion.

New England rapidly became the center of mechanized textile production in the United States. By the late eighteenth century, Boston shippers were making handsome profits by supplying Alta California (the area north of San Diego, encompassing present-day California, Nevada, and parts of Arizona and Utah) with cloth, shoes, and tools, selling western otter pelts in China, and returning home laden with Chinese porcelains and silks. These profits helped to finance New England's mechanized textile industry. By 1813 seventy-six cotton mills housing over 51,000 spindles were operating within the vicinity of Providence, Rhode Island.

Faced with a shortage of adult men (many were moving west), New England mill owners sought other local sources of labor. The Rhode Island system of production had relied on child spinners working in small mills. This system gave way to the Lowell model, based in Waltham and Lowell, Massachusetts, which brought young women from the surrounding countryside to work in gigantic mills. Many of the women were eager to earn cash wages and to escape the routine of farm life. Still, New England mill owners realized that they had to reassure Yankee parents that their daughters would find the factories safe, attractive places to work. Mill owners offered the young women housing in dormitory-like boardinghouses staffed by older women, called matrons, who looked after them.

The Market Revolution

In the North, wage earning gradually replaced family labor and indentured servitude as the dominant labor system. Factory workers quickly and efficiently proccessed raw materials—leather into shoes, cotton into clothing. With the advent of steamboats and toll roads, traditional barriers separating farms from towns and the West from the East began to crumble. Together, all of these rapid economic transformations in the early nineteenth century fueled what some scholars have called the **Market Revolution**. Driven by improvements in transportation, increasing commercialization, and the rise of factories, powerful economic changes affected ordinary Americans and their everyday routines at home and on the job.

The gradual changes of the Market Revolution were driven by investment. Wealthy New England merchants led the way, but a wide variety of private individuals and public institutions proved willing to invest their money and energy in new economic opportunities. Profits from foreign trade helped to build the textile factories that dotted the northeastern landscape. States and even towns used the money of taxpayers and private investors to build turnpikes and later to finance canals and railroads. **Entrepreneurs** pioneered the **putting out** system, a form of production (of hats and other forms of clothing, for example) that enlisted the efforts of single women in the cities, as well as farm families during the winter season. These workers received raw materials from a **merchant-capitalist** and engaged in piecework in return for wages. Combined public-private investment in new forms of business organization and technology spurred American economic growth.

These changes spilled over into American social and religious life, encouraging some people to adopt an optimistic worldview about the possibilities inherent in American life—possibilities that included moving from one place to another, making money by selling new products, altering the natural landscape to make way for canals or factories, and aspiring to buy goods rather than produce goods at home. Foreign visitors often commented on the "restlessness" of Americans, their "acquisitiveness," and their impatience with tradition.

Not all Americans adopted this new way of looking at the world, but almost all groups felt its effects. Slave owners pushed black men, women, and children to work even harder in the fields of the South so that more cotton and rice could be exported to northern and European markets. Western Indians suffered the effects of European American conquest, as whites chopped down forests and cleared the land for farms, violently displacing native populations in the process. In New England textile mills, women and children operated the machines that produced cloth. These operatives served as the vanguard of the Industrial Revolution in America.

By the second decade of the nineteenth century, America had clearly defined itself as a nation that embraced many different kinds of change in transportation and technology. Yet traditional forms of inequality and hierarchy endured, serving as distinguishing features of the Market Revolution.

The Rise of the Cotton Plantation Economy

The growth and spread of the cotton economy redefined the institution of slavery, the southern political system, and, ultimately, all of American history. With the invention of the cotton gin and the acquisition of the Louisiana Territory, cotton production boomed, and the enslaved population expanded. About 700,000 slaves resided in the United States in 1790; just two decades later, that figure had jumped to 1.1 million. Beginning in 1808, the United States outlawed the importation of new slaves. However, the astounding profitability of cotton heightened the demand for labor. Planters began to rely on the domestic slave trade—the forced migration of slaves from the upper South to the lower South.

The institution of slavery was marked by increasingly sharp regional variations, reflecting the impact of cotton cultivation on local economies. At the same time, the contours of an African American culture emerged. This culture had certain characteristics regardless of place, such as strong ties that bound nuclear and extended family members, rich oral and musical traditions heavily influenced by West African customs, and individual and collective resistance to slavery. White people as a group understood little of this culture; they viewed black people primarily as workers who would never become citizens. As U.S. military strength and nationalistic pride grew, southern planters imposed a harsher, more regimented system of slavery on the black population. The tension between the rhetoric of freedom and equality and the reality of slavery continued to shape southern—and American—life for the next four decades.

Regional Economies of the South

Throughout the South, shifts in production methods transformed the demographic and economic make-up of specific regions. For example, by the early nineteenth century, the Chesapeake tobacco economy had declined as a result of worn-out lands and falling prices. In its place arose a more diversified economy based on crafts, the cultivation of corn and wheat, and the milling of flour. Owners put enslaved men to work making barrels and horseshoes while forcing their wives, sisters, and daughters to labor as spinners, weavers, dairymaids, personal servants, and livestock tenders.

Plantation and Southern Commerce

The lower South states of Georgia and South Carolina also saw their economies change during this period. The indigo export business never recovered from the Revolution, since colonial cultivators of the plant had relied heavily on British **subsidies** to shore up their profits. European customers now had to turn to Louisiana and Central America for indigo. In contrast, the lowcountry (coastal) South Carolina rice economy recovered and flourished after the war. In a particularly rich rice district, All Saints Parish, one out of two slaves lived on a plantation with more than a hundred slaves in 1790; thirty years later, four out of five lived on such large establishments. In these areas, the plantation owners themselves often lived elsewhere, and black people constituted almost the entire population.

Adding to the wealth of South Carolina and Georgia was the rapid development of cotton cultivation, especially in the interior, away from the coast. There, prosperous cotton planters began to rival their lowcountry rice-growing counterparts in social status and political influence, and these slaveholders pushed steadily for further western expansion. Cotton planters rushed into the newly-purchased Louisiana Territory after 1803. They accelerated an economic process that had begun in the late eighteenth century: the replacement of a frontier exchange economy with plantation agriculture. (Sugar dominated the New Orleans region; cotton, the rest of the lower Mississippi Valley.) By 1800 slaves in lower Louisiana were producing 4.5 million pounds of sugar annually and more than 18,000 bales of cotton.

The reaches of the lower Mississippi took on an increasingly multicultural flavor. A strong Spanish influence persisted as a vestige of colonial days. French-speaking planter-refugees and their slaves from revolutionary Saint-Domingue came to New Orleans while the city was still in French hands (1800 to 1803). Between 1787 and 1803, nearly 3,000 slaves arrived from Africa, Spanish West Florida, and the Chesapeake to be sold in New Orleans, followed by even larger numbers of slaves from the North after 1803. Slave owners who settled in Natchez, on the banks of the Mississippi River, grew cotton—and grew rich.

Black Family Life and Labor

The number of enslaved persons in the United States grew from 700,000 in 1790 to more than 1.5 million in 1820 and continued to increase rapidly over the next four decades. Since importation of Africans ended officially in 1808, these numbers suggest a tremendous rate of natural increase. Some planters continued to buy slaves brought into the country illegally after 1808. But most of the increase stemmed from births. The preferences of both slave owners and slaves account for this development. Southern planters encouraged black women to bear many children. At the same time, enslaved African Americans valued the family as a social unit; family ties provided support and solace for a people deprived of fundamental human rights. Even under harsh conditions, black people fell in love, married (albeit informally, without the sanction of law), had children, and reared families. Despite the lack of protection from local, state, and national authorities, the slave family proved a remarkably resilient institution.

> *Enslaved African Americans valued the family as a social unit; family ties provided support and solace for a people deprived of fundamental human rights.*

The stability of individual slave families depended on several factors, including the size and age of the plantation and the fortunes and life cycle of the slave owner's family. Very large

■ **British artist John Antrobus titled his 1860 painting *Plantation Burial*. Held at night, after the workday, slave funerals provided an opportunity for the community—including slaves from nearby plantations—to come together in mourning. Planters remained suspicious of such gatherings, which were marked by African musical forms and religious rituals. Whites feared that slaves would conspire under the cover of darkness.**

or long-established plantations had more two-parent slave families than did the small or newer holdings, which tended to have more unrelated people. Slave families were broken up when whites died and their "property" was bequeathed to heirs. Slaves might also be sold or presented to other family members as gifts. Many slave families suffered disruption in response to the growing demand for slaves in the fresh cotton lands of Alabama and Mississippi. The forced migration from upper South to lower South necessarily severed kin ties, but slaves often reconstituted those ties in the form of symbolic kin relationships. Families adopted new, single members of the slave community, and the children called these newcomers "Aunt" or "Uncle."

Since plantations functioned as slave labor camps, owners generally showed little or no inclination to take family relationships into account when they parceled out work assignments to men, women, and children. Rather, those assignments, and the conditions under which slaves performed them, reflected the size and crops of a particular plantation. An estimated 75 percent of (prewar) **antebellum** slaves worked primarily as field hands. On large plantations the division of labor could be quite specialized. Men served as skilled carpenters, blacksmiths, and barrelmakers, and women worked as cooks, laundresses, nursemaids, and personal maids.

Rice slaves continued to work under the task system. Each day, after they completed a specific assigned task, they spent their time as they chose, within limits. Even in the cotton-growing regions, where blacks labored under the regimented gang system, slaves tried to work for themselves in the little free time they had on Saturday afternoons and Sunday. In Louisiana, one white observer noted that the slave man returning to his living quarters after a long, hot day in the fields "does not lose his time. He goes to work at a bit of the land which he has planted with provisions for his own use, while his companion, if he has one, busies herself in preparing some for him, herself, and their children." Family members who grew or accumulated a modest surplus—of corn, eggs, vegetables—in some cases could sell their wares in a nearby market or to slaves on another plantation.

Some slaves appropriated goods from their master's storeroom and barn and sold or traded them to other slaves or to poor whites. These transactions often took place under the cover of darkness. Planters complained of slaves who stole their cattle, hogs, chickens, sacks full of cotton, farm equipment, and stores of ham and flour. Thus slaves' various forms of labor fell into at least three categories: work performed at the behest of and directly under the supervision of whites, labor performed by and for family members within the slaves' living quarters, and the sale (or sometimes clandestine exchange) of goods with masters, other slaves, and poor whites.

Resistance to Slavery

In 1817 the New Orleans City Council decreed that slaves could sing and dance at a stipulated place—Congo Square—every Sunday afternoon. Thereafter, a variety of groups came together to make music. These groups included recent émigrés from Saint-Domingue and slaves newly imported from Africa; slaves from neighboring plantations, in town for the day; and free people of color (**Creoles**), who often blended Spanish and French classical music traditions. In towns and on plantations throughout the South, black people drew from West African musical styles, using drums as well as banjolike instruments, gourd rattles, and mandolins. Over the generations several uniquely American musical styles flowed from Congo Square and other southern gathering places: the blues, gospel, ragtime, jazz, swing, and rock 'n' roll.

In their artistic expression, dress, hairstyles, and language, slaves sought to preserve their cultural uniqueness and create an existence that slaveholders could not touch. In the South Carolina lowcountry, slaves spoke Gullah. Originally a pidgin—a blend of words and grammatical structures from West African languages and English—Gullah later developed into a more formal Creole language. Slaves throughout the United States also mixed West African religious beliefs with Christianity. In slave quarters, spiritual leaders not only preached a Christianity of equality but also told fortunes and warned away "haunts" (spirits of the dead).

Black resistance to slavery took many forms. Slaves might work carelessly in an effort to resist a master's or mistress's demands. During the course of their workday, some slaves broke hoes and other farm implements. A cook might burn the biscuits, thus spoiling a special dinner party for her mistress. Striking out more directly, the African-influenced "conjurer"—often a woman who had a knowledge of plants and herbs—could wreak havoc on a white family by concocting poisons or encouraging disruptive behavior among slaves.

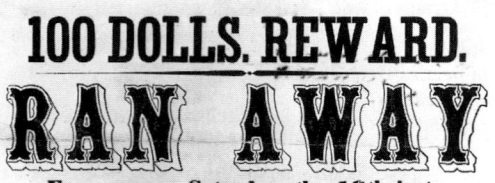

■ From colonial times through the abolition of slavery in 1865, runaways were a persistent problem for slaveholders. This advertisement was published in the Centerville, Maryland, *Times and Eastern-Shore Public Advertiser*. Typically, the owner describes the runaways in terms of their height, skin color, and ther distinguishing characteristics.

Slaves also stole goods from their masters and at times stole themselves by running away. (This practice was more common among young, unmarried men than among those who had family obligations.) Despite the extraordinary peril involved, some slaves revolted. In St. Charles and St. John the Baptist parishes in Louisiana, an 1811 revolt of 400 slaves cost two whites their lives and left several plantations in flames. The original participants, led by a free man of color, Charles Deslondes, acquired new members as they marched toward New Orleans. U.S. troops cut their advance short, killing sixty-six of them. In the Southeast in 1817 and 1818, 400 to 600 runaway slaves converged on the swamps of central Florida, uniting with Indian refugees from the Red Stick War. Together, they raided Georgia plantations until Andrew Jackson and his soldiers halted them in April 1818.

To justify their own behavior, masters and mistresses created a number of myths about the black people they exploited. Whites had a vested interest in believing that their slaves felt gratitude toward them. Skilled in the so-called deference ritual, some slaves hid their true feelings and acted submissively in the presence of white people. Owners and overseers alike interpreted this behavior as a sign of black contentment.

Although some planters boasted of their fatherly solicitude for their slaves, most slave owners harbored deep fears about the men and women they held in bondage. These fears explain the barbaric punishments that some owners inflicted on men, women, and children. Even in "respectable" southern families, slave owners branded, mutilated, and beat enslaved workers for resisting discipline or to deliver a warning to other potentially defiant slaves. In the slave South, American cries of freedom, equality, opportunity, and the blessings of citizenship rang hollow.

Conclusion

In the first two decades of the nineteenth century, striking historical developments stirred the spirit of American nationalism. The Louisiana Purchase magnified the natural wealth of the young nation, and the federal government encouraged citizens to exploit that wealth through trade and settlement. The Embargo of 1807 and the War of 1812 freed the country from the British menace in the Northwest Territory and on the high seas. The war also bolstered the American economy by stimulating technological innovation and the growth of manufacturing. Territorial expansion combined with economic development created new jobs for a burgeoning population.

Southern cotton planters and northern factory owners derived their newfound prosperity from very different sources: staple crop agriculture on one hand and the emerging industrial system on the other. At the same time, these two groups had much in common. As they expanded their operations, whether sprawling plantations or gigantic mill complexes, they displaced smaller landowners and raised land prices. Members of both elite groups proved restless entrepreneurs, eager to move around to find the freshest lands and the cheapest labor. Their personal wealth and their political power set them apart from the people under them—the slaves and wage earners—who produced that wealth. And both the southern "lords of the lash" and the northern "lords of the loom" depended on large numbers of slaves to grow cotton. Producing and processing cotton yielded tangible benefits for a few and created a new, harsher world of work for many.

Sites to Visit

Lewis and Clark Expedition
www.cp.duluth.mn.us/~tmcs/lewsclrk1.htm
This site offers assorted materials treating the expedition that explored the Louisiana Territory.

Barbary Treaties
www.yale.edu/lawweb/avalon/diplomacy/barbary
This site includes the texts of treaties between the United States and the Barbary states, 1789–1816.

Documents from the War of 1812
www.yale.edu/lawweb/avalon/19th.htm
This site includes important documents from the War of 1812.

Whole Cloth: Discovering Science and Technology Through American Textile History
www.si.edu/lemelson/centerpieces/whole_cloth/
The Jerome and Dorothy Lemelson Center for the Study of Invention and Innovation and Society for the History of Technology assembled this site. It includes excellent activities and sources related to early American manufacturing and industry.

Indian Affairs: Laws and Treaties
http://digital.library.okstate.edu/kappler/
This digitized text at Oklahoma State University includes preremoval treaties with the Five Civilized Tribes and other groups.

For Further Reading

General

Stephen E. Ambrose, *Undaunted Courage: Meriwether Lewis, Thomas Jefferson, and the Opening of the American West* (1996).

Joanne P. Melish, *Disowning Slavery: Gradual Emancipation and "Race" in New England, 1780–1860* (1998).

Carroll Pursell, *The Machine in America: A Social History of Technology* (1995).

David J. Weber, *The Spanish Frontier in North America* (1992).

The British Menace

Robert J. Allison, *The Crescent Obscured: the United States and the Muslim World, 1776–1815* (1995).

W. Jeffrey Bolster, *Black Jacks: African-American Seamen in the Age of Sail* (1997).

Thomas J. Fleming, *Duel: Alexander Hamilton, Aaron Burr and the Future of America* (1999).

Burton Spivak, *Jefferson's English Crisis: Commerce, Embargo, and the Republican Revolution* (1974).

John Sugden, *Tecumseh: A Life* (1998).

The War of 1812

Donald R. Hickey, *The War of 1812: A Forgotten Conflict* (1989).

Robert V. Remini, *The Battle of New Orleans* (1999).

Robert Allen Rutland, *The Presidency of James Madison* (1990).

David C. Skaggs and Larry L. Nelson, eds., *The Sixty Years' War for the Great Lakes, 1754–1814* (2001).

The "Era of Good Feelings"?

Frank Lawrence Owsley, Jr. and Gene A. Smith, *Filibusters and Expansionists: Jeffersonian Manifest Destiny, 1800–1821* (1997).

Theda Perdue, *Cherokee Women: Gender and Culture Change, 1700–1835* (1998).

Kirkpatrick Sale, *The Fire of His Genius: Robert Fulton and the American Dream* (2001).

Ronald Schultz, *The Republic of Labor: Philadelphia Artisans and the Politics of Class, 1720–1830* (1993).

The Rise of the Cotton Plantation Economy

Eugene D. Genovese, *Roll, Jordan, Roll: The World the Slaves Made* (1976).

Charles W. Joyner, *Down by the Riverside: A South Carolina Slave Community* (1984).

Michael Mullin, *Africa in America: Slave Acculturation and Resistance in the American South and British Caribbean* (1992).

Jeffrey Robert Young, *Domesticating Slavery: The Master Class in Georgia and South Carolina, 1670–1837* (1999).

For quizzes and other resources on these topics, go to www.longmanamericanhistory.com.

Expanding Westward: Society and Politics in the "Age of the Common Man," 1819–1832

CHAPTER

11

CAMPAIGNING FOR POLITICAL OFFICE IN TENNESSEE IN THE 1820S WAS NOT AN ACTIVITY FOR THE faint of heart. Candidates competed against each other in squirrel hunts, the loser footing the bill for the barbecue that followed. A round of speechmaking often was capped by several rounds of whiskey enjoyed by candidates and supporters alike. Into this boisterous arena stepped a man unrivaled as a campaigner. David Crockett ran successfully for several offices, including local justice of the peace in 1818, state legislator in 1821 and 1823, and U.S. congressman in 1827, 1829, and 1833. The plainspoken Crockett knew how to play to a crowd and rattle a rival. He bragged about his skill as a bear hunter and ridiculed the fancy dress of his opponents. He condemned closed-door political caucuses (small groups of party insiders who hand-picked candidates) and praised grassroots democracy. Crockett claimed he could out-shoot, out-drink, and out-debate anyone who opposed him. If his opponent lied about him, why, then, he would lie about himself: "Yes fellow citizens, I can run faster, walk longer, leap higher, speak better, and tell more and bigger lies than my competitor, and all his friends, any day of his life." Crockett's blend of political theater and folksy backwoods banter earned him the allegiance of voters like him—men who, though having little formal education, understood the challenges of carving a homestead out of the dense thickets of western Tennessee.

Davy Crockett, Advice to Politicians (1833)

During the 1820s, European American settlers in the trans-Appalachian West transformed the style and substance of American politics. In 1790, 100,000 Americans (not including Indians) lived west of the Appalachians; half a century later that number had increased to 7 million, or about four out of ten Americans. Beginning with Kentucky in 1792, western states began to relax or abolish property requirements for adult male voters. Even the English that Americans spoke changed. New words introduced into the political vocabulary reflected the roughhewn, woodsman quality of western electioneering: candidates hit the campaign trail, giving "stump" speeches along the way. They supported their party's platform with its "planks" (positions on the issues). As legislators, they voted for "pork-barrel" projects that would benefit their constituents at home. Emphasizing his modest origins,

■ John Gadsby Chapman painted this portrait of Davy Crockett.

CHAPTER OUTLINE

The Politics Behind Western Expansion

Federal Authority and Its Opponents

Real People in the "Age of the Common Man"

Ties That Bound a Growing Population

Conclusion

Sites to Visit

For Further Reading

David Crockett became widely known as Davy Crockett. (It is hard to imagine anyone calling the Sage of Monticello Tommy Jefferson.)

Western settlers attacked what they considered centralized, eastern-based institutions of wealth and privilege. They scorned a six-person Supreme Court that could overturn the laws of Congress and the individual states. They charged that the privately owned Second Bank of the United States enriched its own board of directors at the expense of indebted farmers. Western voters rejoiced with the 1828 election of Andrew Jackson to the presidency; here, they claimed, was a man who would battle eastern financiers and at the same time support white settlers' claims to Indian lands in the West. Jackson held out the promise that ordinary people would have a political voice and access to expanding economic opportunities.

During his two terms in office (1828–1836), Andrew Jackson of Tennessee so dominated the American political landscape that historians have called him the symbol of an age and the representative man of his time. Born in humble circumstances, orphaned at age fourteen, Jackson achieved public acclaim as a lawyer, military officer, and finally president. He promoted a strong central government, and the authority of the chief executive in particular, and he had fought against foreign military forces (the British in the War of 1812) and Native Americans. He clashed with southern states' rights advocates.

Democracy had its limits during this period. While voter participation in presidential elections soared, from 25 percent of eligible voters in 1824 to 50 percent in 1828, even most free people could not vote, including Native Americans, women, and free people of color. Further complicating this age was the rise of distinct social classes. Acquiring great economic and political significance, the class system seemed to mock the idea of equality. The outlines of this system appeared in the 1820s in the Northeast, where business and factory managers received salaries, not hourly wages, and their wives were full-time homemakers and mothers. New forms of popular literature, such as the *Ladies Magazine*, published in Boston, glorified the middle-class family, especially the pious wife and mother who held moral sway over it.

The "age of the common man" was thus rife with irony. Jackson himself embodied many apparent contradictions. An Indian-fighter, he adopted a young Indian boy as his ward. A foe of privilege, he was a slave owner. A self-professed champion of farmers and artisans, he expressed contempt for their representatives in Congress. He also took steps to expand the power of the executive branch. The 1820s revealed these larger contradictions as national leaders pursued a more democratic form of politics on one hand and supported a system based on class and racial differences on the other. The resulting tensions shaped American society and politics in the third decade of the nineteenth century.

The Politics Behind Western Expansion

DOCUMENT
Expanding America and Internal Improvements

As the United States gained new territory through negotiation and conquest and people moved west, the nation felt the impact. President Monroe warned Europeans not to intervene any longer in the Western hemisphere. Americans settling west of the Appalachian mountains found a spokesman in Andrew Jackson. Once in the West, settlers faced the same kinds of conflicts that increasingly preoccupied Easterners, especially those between masters and slaves and debtors and creditors. Congressional debates over whether Missouri should be admitted to the Union as a slave or free state sent shock waves throughout the country. Of the political conflict over the fate of slavery in the territories, the elderly Thomas Jefferson wrote, "This momentous question, like a firebell in the night, awakened and filled me with terror. I considered it at once as the death knell of the Union."

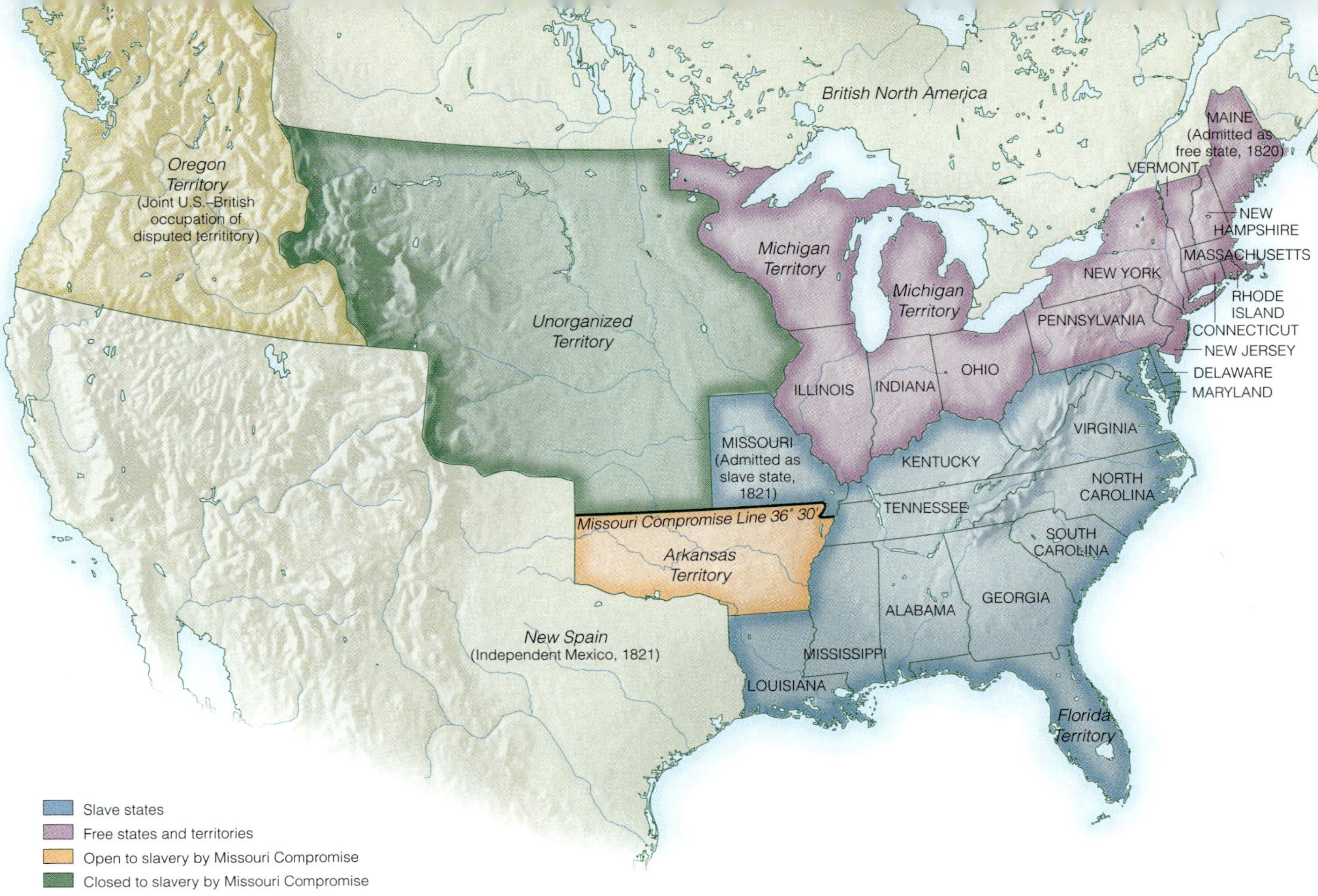

MAP 11.1

THE MISSOURI COMPROMISE Missouri applied for statehood in 1819, threatening the balance between eleven free and eleven slave states. According to a compromise hammered out in Congress, Missouri was admitted as a slave state, and Maine, formerly part of Massachusetts, was admitted as a free state. Slavery was banned above the 36°30′ parallel.

The Missouri Compromise

In 1819 the United States consisted of twenty-two states. Slavery was legal in half of them. Late that year, the territory of Missouri applied for statehood. This move set off panic in both the North and South because a twenty-third state was bound to upset the delicate balance of senators between slave and free states. The debate over the future of Missouri occupied Congress from December 1819 to March 1820.

In the Senate, Rufus King of New York claimed that Congress had the ultimate authority to set laws governing slavery. However, his colleague William Pinckney of Maryland retorted that new states possessed the same rights as the original thirteen; that is, they could choose whether to allow slavery. Maine's application for admission to the Union suggested a way out of the impasse. Speaker of the House of Representatives Henry Clay of Kentucky successfully proposed a plan. Missouri would join the Union as a slave state at the same time that Maine, originally part of Massachusetts, would become the twenty-fourth state and be designated a free one. In the future, slavery would be prohibited from all Louisiana Purchase lands north of latitude 36°30′, an area that included all territory north of present-day Missouri and Oklahoma.

The day Congress sealed the compromise, Secretary of State John Quincy Adams of Massachusetts walked home from the Capitol with Senator John C. Calhoun of South Carolina. The two men engaged in a muted but intense debate over slavery. Calhoun claimed that the institution "was the best guarantee to equality among the whites." Slavery, he asserted, demonstrated that all white men were equal to one another and superior to all blacks. Unnerved by Calhoun's

Missouri Compromise of 1820–1821

MAP 11.2

PRINCIPAL CANALS BUILT BY 1860 Many canals were expensive ventures and, in some cases, engineering nightmares. The Erie Canal had a competitive advantage because it snaked through the Mohawk Valley, the only major level pass through the mountain chain that stretched from Canada to Georgia. In contrast, the Pennsylvania Main Line Canal, which ran from Harrisburg to Pittsburgh, used a combination of inclined planes and steam engines in ten separate locations to haul boats up and down the Allegheny Mountains.

comments, Adams concluded that the debate over Missouri had "betrayed the secret of [Southerners'] souls." By reserving backbreaking toil for blacks, wealthy planters fancied themselves aristocratic lords of the manor. Adams confided in his diary that night, "They look down upon the simplicity of a Yankee's manners, because he has no habits of overbearing like theirs and cannot treat negroes like dogs." Adams feared that North-South conflicts might someday imperil the nation itself.

Ways West

Missouri was just one of the territories west of the Mississippi whose population had increased during this period. Through land grants and government financing of new methods of transportation, Congress encouraged European American migrants to push their way west and south. The Land Act of 1820 enabled westerners to buy a minimum 80 acres at a price of $1.25 an acre in cash—even in those days, a bargain homestead. Built with the help of government legal and financial aid, new roads and canals, steamboats, and, after the early 1830s, railroads facilitated migration. Between 1820 and 1860, the number of steamboats plying the

The rich bottomlands of the Mississippi Delta proved ideal for growing cotton. After the forced removal of the Five Civilized Tribes from the Old Southwest, slave owners established expansive plantations in the delta. This scene, painted in 1842 by artist William Henry Brown, shows a group of slaves bringing in "the whole weeks picking" of cotton on the Vick plantation near Vicksburg, Mississippi.

William Henry Brown, *Hauling the Whole Weeks Picking*, 1842. Historic New Orleans Collection (1975.93.1 & 1975.93.2)

Mississippi River jumped from 60 to more than 1,000. Canals linked western producers to eastern consumers of grains and cattle and connected western consumers to eastern producers of manufactured goods. Shipping costs and times between Buffalo and New York shrank. Cities such as Rochester and Syracuse, New York, and Cincinnati, Ohio, flourished because of their location along key waterways.

The most important of these man-made water highways was the Erie Canal. Completed in 1825, this engineering marvel used 83 **canal locks** to link the Great Lakes directly to the East Coast by way of the Hudson River. Public acclaim was thunderous. Upstate New York's economy thrived. And New York City, at the mouth of the Hudson, emerged as the most important port and financial center in the country.

"The Erie Canal"

Americans took a variety of routes west. In the 1820s, desperate planters moved out of the exhausted lands of the upper South (the states of Virginia and Maryland), the Carolinas, and Georgia, westward into Alabama, Arkansas, Louisiana, and Mississippi. This migration across the Appalachian Mountains furthered the nationalist idea of the "expansion of liberty and freedom," a view held by many white men regardless of political affiliation. Yet it also spread slavery. The sight of slave coffles—groups of men, women, and children bound together in chains, hobbling down a city street or a country road—became increasingly common in this western region. In 1821 Virginia, North Carolina, South Carolina, and Georgia had produced two-thirds of the nation's cotton crop; the rest came from recently settled areas. Just a dozen years later the proportions shifted: Tennessee, Louisiana, Alabama, Mississippi, and Florida together produced two-thirds of all cotton, and the remaining one-third came from older areas.

The westward expansion of cotton farming continued the European process of clearing the land had started in the early colonial period. This, combined with hunting game with firearms, had altered the backwoods **ecology** east of the Mississippi. When farmers dammed rivers, drained ponds and swamps, and chopped down trees, they unavoidably destroyed the places where wildlife lived and the food supply they ate. European demands for beaver hats led to the near-extinction of beaver east of the Mississippi River.

■ MAP 11.3
MEXICO'S FAR NORTHERN FRONTIER IN 1822 This map shows Mexico's far northern frontier in 1822. When Moses Austin died suddenly in 1821, the task of supervising the settlement of in-migrants from the United States fell to his son Stephen. The Mexican government authorized the younger Austin to act as empresario of the settlement. He was responsible for the legal and economic regulations governing the settlements clustered at the lower reaches of the Colorado and Brazos rivers.

European Americans also migrated across the border into Mexican territory. In 1821 Spain approved the application of a U.S. citizen, Moses Austin, to settle 300 American families on 200,000 fertile acres along the Colorado and Brazos river bottoms in southeastern Texas. Austin died soon after, but his son Stephen carried on his legacy. Within two years, the younger Austin had received permission (now from the government of newly independent Mexico) to bring in another 100 families. These settlers, together with **squatters**, numbered about 1,500 people. Although the Mexican constitution prohibited slavery, some of the newcomers brought their slaves with them, and some free people of color came on their own. All these migrants from the United States called themselves **Texians** to distinguish themselves from the *Tejanos*, or Spanish-speaking residents of the region. These newly arrived Texians agreed to adopt the Roman Catholic faith and become citizens of Mexico. During the rest of the decade, 900 additional families sponsored by Austin arrived in Texas. They were followed by 3,000 more squatters. Mexican officials feared that they would lose authority over the mass of American newcomers within their borders.

The Panic of 1819 and the Plight of Western Debtors

In 1819 a financial panic swept across the nation, followed by an economic depression that hit western states and territories particularly hard. The Second Bank of the United States played a major role in triggering this economic downturn, which came to be called the Panic of 1819. Granted a twenty-year charter by Congress in 1816, the Second Bank resembled its predecessor, seeking to regulate the national economy through loans to state and local banks. In 1819 the bank clamped down on small, local **wildcat banks**, which had extended credit to many people who could not repay their loans. Many homesteaders were not self-sufficient farmers but producers of staple crops or proprietors of small enterprises. They relied on credit from banks and local private lenders. As a result, the bank's crackdown on wildcat banks had a devastating impact on western households. Debtors unable to meet their obligations had their mortgages foreclosed, their homes seized, and their crops and equipment confiscated. Ruined by the Panic of 1819, many western farmers developed an abiding hatred of the Bank of the United States and a deep resentment of eastern financiers.

Davy Crockett's own family history suggests the plight of families dependent on bank credit to create homesteads out of western territory. The son of a propertyless squatter, Crockett had an intense fear of debt. Although he campaigned as a hunter and a farmer, he had built several enterprises on land he leased or owned on Shoal Creek in south-central Tennessee: a water-powered grist mill, a gunpowder factory (worked by slaves), an iron ore mine, and a liquor distillery. For each venture, he had to borrow money from local creditors. Spending much of his time away from home, Crockett relied on his wife, Elizabeth, and his children to manage these businesses. (He had three children by his first wife, Polly, who died in 1815, and eventually would have a total of nine by Elizabeth.)

The depression of 1819 cut off Crockett's sources of credit, and in 1822 a flash flood swept away his grist mill and powder factory. Without milled grain, the distillery could no longer operate. Creditors immediately set upon the family, demanding payment of their debts. The Crocketts were fortunate enough to own land they could sell, using the proceeds to repay their debts and then moving farther west in Tennessee.

Others were not so lucky. Small farmers who lost their land through foreclosure in the Panic of 1819 could not produce crops for the eastern market, contributing to the rise in the price of food. Deprived of credit, small shopkeepers also felt the effects of the depression. With rising unemployment, consumers could not afford to buy cloth, and as the demand for cotton fell, southern plantation owners, too, felt the contraction. Within a few years Andrew Jackson would capitalize on the fears and resentments of working men, farmers, planters, and tradesmen, as he championed the "common man" in opposition to what debtors called the "eastern monied interests." In doing so he would transform the two-party system.

The Monroe Doctrine

Despite the troubled economy, James Monroe won reelection easily in 1820. On the international front, his second term opened on a tense note. Foreign nations had started claiming land or promoting their own interests near U.S. borders. The United States remained especially wary of the Spanish presence on its southern and western borders. In 1818 President Monroe had authorized General Andrew Jackson to broaden his assault on the Seminole Indians—a group composed of Native Americans and runaway slaves—in Florida. For the past two years, U.S. troops had pursued fugitive slaves into Spanish-held Florida. Now Jackson and his men seized the Spanish fort at Pensacola and claimed all of western Florida for the United States. The United States demanded that Spain either suppress the Seminole population or sell all of east Florida to the United States. With the Transcontinental Treaty of 1819, Spain gave up its right to both Florida and Oregon (although Britain and Russia still claimed land in Oregon). In 1822 General Jackson became the first governor of Florida Territory.

In 1821 the czar of Russia forbade non-Russians from entering the territory north of the fifty-first parallel and the open sea 100 miles off the coast of what is now Canada and Alaska.

TABLE 11-1

The Election of 1820

Candidate	Political Party	Electoral Vote
James Monroe	Democratic-Republican	231
John Quincy Adams	Democratic-Republican	1

The Russians had established trading posts up and down that coast, some almost as far south as San Francisco Bay. Meanwhile, rumors circulated that European monarchs were planning new invasions of Latin America.

Fearful of an alliance between Russia, Prussia, Austria, Spain, and France, President Monroe and Secretary of State John Quincy Adams formulated a policy that became a landmark in American diplomatic history. Adams rejected a British proposal that Great Britain and the United States join forces to oppose a further Spanish encroachment in Latin America. He convinced Monroe that the United States must stand alone against the European powers—Spain in the south and Russia in the northwest—if it hoped to protect its own interests in the Western Hemisphere. In his annual message to Congress in December 1823, the president declared that the era of Europe's colonization of the Americas had ceased. Henceforth, he said, foreign nations would not be allowed to intervene in the Western Hemisphere.

The United States conceived the so-called Monroe Doctrine as a self-defense measure aimed specifically at Russia, Spain, and Britain. With the Russo-American Treaty of 1824, Russia agreed to pull back its claims to the area north of 54°40′, the southern tip of the present-day Alaska panhandle. However, the United States did not have the naval power to back up the Monroe Doctrine with force.

The doctrine was at first more a statement of principle than a blueprint for action, intended to discourage European powers from political or military meddling in the Western Hemisphere. The doctrine would have greater international significance in the late nineteenth century, when the United States developed the military might to enforce it.

The Monroe Doctrine (1823)

Andrew Jackson's Rise to Power

The election of 1824 provided a striking contrast to the bland affair four years earlier in which Monroe had been elected. In 1824 the field of presidential nominees was crowded, suggesting a party system in disarray. Although all the candidates called themselves "Democratic-Republicans," the label meant little more than the fact that most politicians sought to distance themselves from the outmoded "Federalist" label, which hearkened back to the post-Revolutionary period rather than pointing forward to the nation's new challenges. Nominees included Secretary of State John Quincy Adams, Representative Henry Clay of Kentucky, and Andrew Jackson, now a senator from Tennessee. Jackson received the highest number of electoral votes (99), but no candidate achieved a majority. As a result, the election went to the House of Representatives.

Clay withdrew from the race. He had promised Jackson his support but then endorsed Adams, whom the House subsequently elected. When Adams named Clay secretary of state, Jackson's supporters cried foul. The election, they charged, amounted to nothing more than a corrupt deal between two political insiders.

Haunted by these charges, Adams served his four-year term under a cloud of public distrust. A member of a respected New England family and the son of former president John Adams, the new chief executive had served with distinction in Monroe's cabinet. Still, Adams proved ill suited to the rough-and-tumble world of what came to be called the New Democracy. Adams advocated a greater federal role in internal improvements and public education, a variation on Henry Clay's "American System," a set of policies which promoted a national bank, public funding of canals and turnpikes, and a high tariff to protect domestic manufactures.

Adams's party, which called itself the National Republicans, faced a formidable chal-

TABLE 11-2

The Election of 1824

Candidate	Political Party	Popular Vote (%)	Electoral Vote
John Quincy Adams	Democratic-Republican	30.5	84
Andrew Jackson	Democratic-Republican	43.1	99
William H. Crawford	Democratic-Republican	13.1	41
Henry Clay	Democratic-Republican	13.2	37

■ Some commentators disapproved of what they considered the excessively lively inauguration gala for President Jackson in 1829. One described the affair this way: "On their arrival at the White House, the motley crowd clamored for refreshments and soon drained the barrels of punch, which had been prepared, in drinking to the health of the new Chief Magistrate. A great deal of glassware was broken, and the East Room was filled with a noisy mob."

lenge in the election of 1828. Having seethed for four long years, Andrew Jackson's supporters (the Democratic-Republicans) now urged "the people" to reclaim the White House. The campaign was a nasty one. Jackson's opponents attacked his personal morality and that of his wife and his mother. Jackson's supporters countered with the charge that Adams himself was corrupt and that he and his cronies must be swept from office.

Jackson won a stunning victory, with his supporters hailing the well-to-do slaveholder as the president of the "common" (meaning white) man. In office, Jackson tightened his party's grip on power by introducing a national political spoils system. Through this process, successful candidates rewarded their supporters with jobs and tossed their rivals out of appointed offices. The spoils system let the Democratic-Republicans—now called the Democrats—build a nationwide political machine. Not surprisingly, it also provided fertile ground for corruption.

DOCUMENT

Andrew Jackson, First Annual Message to Congress (1829)

TABLE 11-3
The Election of 1828

Candidate	Political Party	Popular Vote (%)	Electoral Vote
Andrew Jackson	Democratic	56.0	178
John Quincy Adams	National Republican	44.0	83

Federal Authority and Its Opponents

When Americans defeated the British in the War of 1812, they ensured the physical security of the new nation. However, the war's end left a crucial question unanswered: what role would federal authority play in a republic of states? During Andrew Jackson's tenure, Congress, the chief executive, and the Supreme Court all jockeyed for influence over one another and over the states. Jackson claimed a broad popular mandate to increase the power of the presidency, and used it to end the charter of the Second Bank of the United States.

At the same time, militant southern sectionalists regarded the growth of federal executive and judicial power with alarm. If the president could impose a high tariff on the states and if the Supreme Court could deny the states the authority to govern Indians within their own borders, might not high-handed federal officials someday also threaten the South's system of slavery?

Judicial Federalism and the Limits of Law

In a series of notable cases, the Supreme Court, under the leadership of Chief Justice John Marshall, sought to limit states' power to control people and resources within their own boundaries. In *McCulloch v. Maryland* (1819), the Court supported Congress's decision to grant the Second Bank of the United States a twenty-year charter. The state of Maryland had imposed a high tax on notes issued by the bank. Declaring that "the power to tax involves the power to destroy," the Supreme Court ruled the state's action unconstitutional. The court justices held that, although the original Constitution did not mention a national bank, Congress retained the authority to create such an institution. This fact implied that Congress also had the power to preserve it. This decision relied on what came to be called a "loose construction" of the Constitution to justify "implied powers" of the government, powers not explicitly stated in the Constitution.

In 1832 a case involving the rights of the Cherokee nation brought the Court head to head with President Jackson's own brand of federal muscle-flexing. With the expansion of cotton cultivation into upland Georgia in the early nineteenth century, white residents of that state increasingly resented the presence of their Cherokee neighbors. At the same time, some Cherokee worked and worshipped in ways similar to European Americans: they cultivated farmland, converted to Christianity, and established a formal legal code. On July 4, 1827, Cherokee leaders met in convention to devise a republican constitution. In the grand tradition of the Patriots of 1776, the group proclaimed the Cherokee a sovereign nation, responsible for its own affairs and free of the dictates of individual states.

By the late 1820s, however, certain white people, including the president, were calling for the removal of the Cherokee from the Southeast. The 1829 discovery of gold in the Georgia hills brought 10,000 white miners to Cherokee territory in a gold rush that the Indians called the "Great Intrusion." President Jackson saw the very existence of the Cherokee nation as an affront to his authority and a hindrance to Georgia's economic well-being. He resented the fact that the Cherokee considered themselves a sovereign nation, independent of the U.S. president. Jackson, in fact, favored removing all Indians from the Southeast to make way for whites. He declared that Georgia should be rid of "a few thousand savages" so that "towns and prosperous farms" could develop there. In 1830, with the president's backing, Congress passed the Indian Removal Act. The act provided for "an exchange of lands with the Indians residing in any of the states or territories, and for their removal west of the river Mississippi."

Outraged by this naked land grab, the Cherokee nation refused to sign the removal treaties specified by Congress as part of the Indian Removal Act. In a petition to Congress in 1830, members of the group declared, "We wish to remain on the land of our fathers. We have a perfect and original right to claim this, without interruption or molestation." In an effort to protect their land titles, the Cherokee first tried to take their case to Georgia courts, but Georgia refused to allow them to press their claim. The Georgia legislature maintained that it had authority over all the Indians living within the state's borders, and that the Cherokee nation lacked jurisdiction over its own people. The Cherokee nation appealed to the Supreme Court.

DOCUMENT
Memorial of the Cherokee Nation (1830)

The Cherokee hoped that the Supreme Court would support their position that they were an independent entity, not bound by the laws of Georgia. In a set of cases—*Cherokee Nation v. Georgia* (1831) and *Worcester v. Georgia* (1832)—the Court agreed that Georgia's authority did not extend to the Cherokee nation. The Court proclaimed that Indian self-

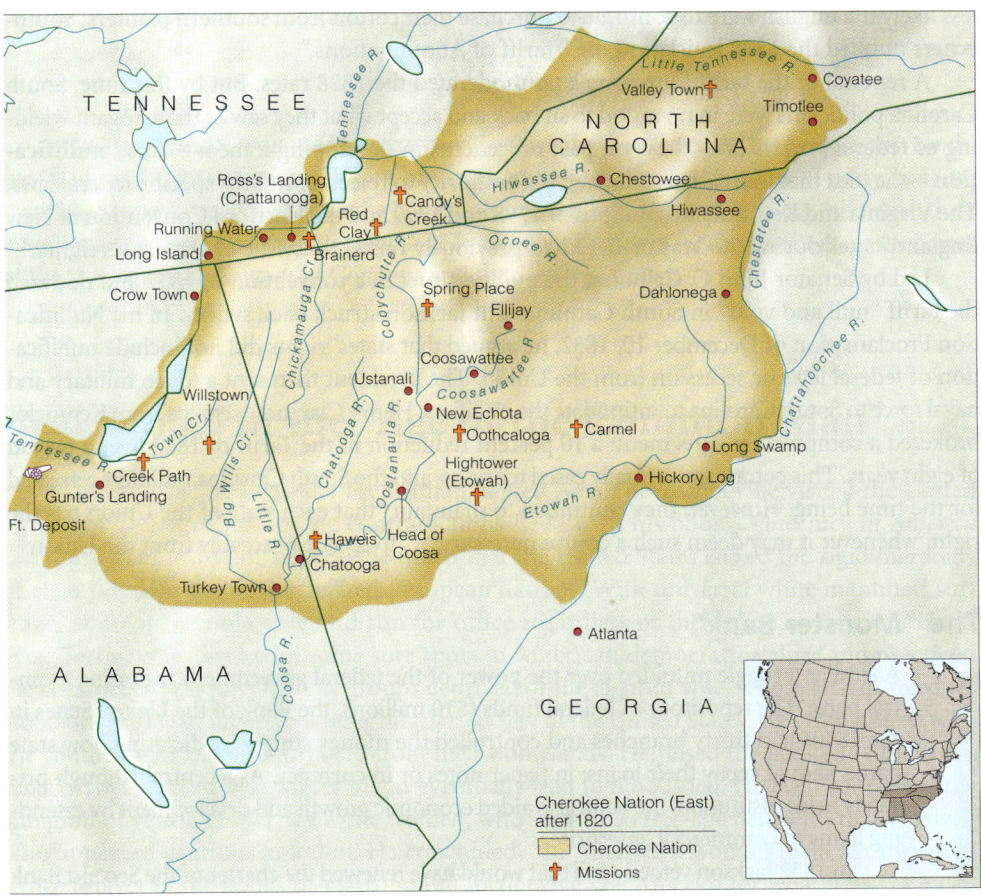

■ MAP 11.4
THE CHEROKEE NATION AFTER 1820   This map shows the Cherokee nation on the eve of removal to Indian Territory (present-day Oklahoma). The discovery of gold in the region sparked a constitutional battle over control of Cherokee land. In 1832 the Supreme Court ruled that the federal government had ultimate authority over Indian nations. The state of Georgia ignored the ruling and sought to enforce its own laws in Cherokee territory.

governing bodies were "domestic dependent nations" under the authority of the U.S. government, not the individual states. Under this ruling, Georgia lacked the authority to force Indians from their land. More generally, the states must defer to the federal government in issues related to the welfare and governance of the Indians. The governor of Georgia rejected these Supreme Court rulings, as did Jackson. Of the *Worcester* decision, Jackson declared, "John Marshall has made his decision. Now let him enforce it." In 1832 the president instead sent troops to Georgia to begin forcing the Indians out of their homeland.

The "Tariff of Abominations"

Besides engineering the removal of the Cherokee, Jacksonian Democrats continued the post–War of 1812 policy of high tariffs. In 1828 they pushed through Congress legislation that raised fees on imported manufactured products and raw materials such as wool. Facing a disastrous decline in cotton prices after the Panic of 1819, Southerners protested: to survive, they had to both sell their cotton on the open world market and buy high-priced supplies from New England or Europe. In their view, the higher the tariff on English goods, the

Artist Charles Bird King painted this portrait of Sequoyah while the Indian leader was in Washington, D.C., in 1828. Government officials honored him for developing a written form of the Cherokee language. He is wearing a medal presented to him by the Cherokee nation in 1825. He later settled permanently in Sallisaw, in what is today Sequoyah County, Oklahoma.

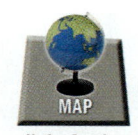

Native American Land Cessions to 1829

According to the committee, when European settlers depleted reserves of wildlife, Indians as a group would cease to exist.

Members of the Cherokee nation bitterly denounced these assertions. "The Cherokees do not live upon the chase [for game]," they pointed out. Neither did the Creek, Choctaw, Chickasaw, and Seminole—the other members of the Five Civilized Tribes, so called for their varying degrees of conformity to white people's ways.

In parts of California, Spanish missionaries conquered Indian groups, converted them to Christianity, and then forced them to work in the missions. In missions up and down the California coast, Indians worked as weavers, tanners, shoemakers, bricklayers, carpenters, blacksmiths, and other artisans. Some herded cattle and raised horses. Indian women cooked for the mission, cleaned, and spun wool. They wove cloth and sewed garments.

Nevertheless, even Indians living in or near missions resisted the cultural change imposed by the intruders. Catholic missionaries complained that Indian women such as those of the Chumash refused to learn Spanish. The refusal among some Indians to completely assimilate signaled persistent, deep-seated conflicts between native groups and incoming settlers. In 1824 a revolt among hundreds of newly converted Indians at the mission *La Purisima Concepción* north of Santa Barbara revealed a rising militancy among native peoples.

After the War of 1812, the U.S. government had rewarded some military veterans with land grants in the Old Northwest. Federal agents tried to clear the way for these new settlers by ousting Indians from the area. Overwhelmed by the number of whites, some Indian groups such as the Peoria and Kaskaskia gave up their lands to the interlopers. Others took a stand against the white intrusion. In 1826 and 1827, the Winnebago attacked white families and boat pilots living near Prairie du Chien, Wisconsin. Two years later, the Sauk chief Black Hawk (known to Indians as Ma-ka-tai-me-she-kia-kiak) assembled a coalition of Fox, Winnebago, Kickapoo, and Potawatomi. Emboldened by the prospect of aid from British Canada, they clashed with federal troops and raided farmers' homesteads and miners' camps.

In August 1832 a force of 1,300 U.S. soldiers and volunteers struck back, killing 300 Indian men, women, and children encamped on the Bad Axe River in western Wisconsin. The massacre, the decisive point of what came to be called the Black Hawk War, marked the end of armed Indian resistance north of the Ohio River and east of the Mississippi.

Slaves and Free People of Color

Southern whites perceived free blacks, like Indians, as an unwelcome and dangerous presence, especially given the possibility that they would conspire with slaves to spark a rebellion. For these reasons some states began to outlaw private manumissions (the practice of individual owners freeing their slaves) and to force free blacks to leave the state altogether. In the 1820s the small proportion of free blacks within the southern population declined further.

One free black who inspired such fears was Denmark Vesey. Born on the Danish-controlled Caribbean island of St. Thomas in 1767, Vesey was a literate carpenter as well as a religious leader. In 1799 he won $1,500 in a Charleston, South Carolina, lottery and used some of the money to buy his freedom. In the summer of 1822, a Charleston court claimed to have unearthed evidence of a "diabolical plot" hatched by Vesey together with plantation slaves from the surrounding area.

Yet the historical record strongly suggests that no plot ever existed. Black "witnesses" who feared for their own lives provided inconsistent and contradictory testimony to a panel of judges. Authorities never located any material evidence of a planned uprising, such as stockpiles of weapons. Under fire from other Charleston elites for rushing to judgment, the judges redoubled their efforts to embellish vague rumors of black discontent into a tale of a well-orchestrated uprising and to implicate growing numbers of black people. As a result of the testimony of several slaves, thirty-five black men were hanged and another eighteen exiled outside the United States. Of those executed, Vesey and twenty-three other men said nothing to support even the vaguest charges of the court.

DOCUMENT
An Account of the Late Intended Insurrection Among a Portion of Blacks of this City

In the North, some blacks were granted the right to vote after emancipation in the late eighteenth century; however, many of those voting rights were lost in the early nineteenth century. New Jersey (in 1807), Connecticut (1818), New York (1821), and Pennsylvania (1838) all revoked the legislation that had let black men cast ballots. Free northern blacks continued to suffer under a number of legal restrictions. Most were not citizens and therefore perceived themselves as oppressed like the slaves in the South.

A new group of black leaders in the urban North began to link their fate to that of their enslaved brothers and sisters in the South. In Boston, North Carolina–born David Walker published his fiery *Walker's Appeal to the Coloured Citizens of the World* in 1829. Walker called for all blacks to integrate fully into American society, shunning racial segregation whether initiated by whites or by blacks themselves. Reminding his listeners of the horrors of the slave trade, he declared that black people were ready to die for freedom: "I give it as a fact, let twelve black men get well armed for battle, and they will kill and put to flight fifty whites."

Northern black leaders disagreed among themselves on the issues of integration and black separatism—for example, whether blacks should create their own schools or press for inclusion in the public educational system. A few leaders favored leaving the country altogether, believing that black people would never find peace and freedom in the United States. Founded by whites in New Jersey in 1817, the American Colonization Society (ACS) paid for a small number of black Americans to settle Monrovia, later named Liberia, on the west coast of Africa. The ACS drew support from a variety of groups, including whites in the upper South who wanted to free their slaves but believed that black and white people could not live in the same country, and some slaves and free people of color convinced that colonization would give them a fresh start. A small number of American-born blacks settled in Liberia. However, most black activists rejected colonization. They had been born on American soil, and their forebears had been buried there. Maria Stewart of Boston declared, "Before I go [to Africa] the bayonet shall pierce me through."

> *Northern black leaders disagreed among themselves on the issues of integration and black separatism.*

Northern whites sought to control black people and their movements. Outspoken black men and women such as Walker and Stewart alarmed northern whites who feared that if blacks could claim decent jobs, white people would lose their own jobs. African Americans who worked outdoors as wagon drivers, peddlers, and street sweepers were taunted and in some cases attacked by whites who demanded deference from blacks in public. In October 1824, a mob of white men invaded a black neighborhood in Providence, Rhode Island. They terrorized its residents, destroyed buildings, and left the place "almost entirely in ruins." The catalyst for the riot had come the previous day, when a group of blacks had refused to yield the inside of the sidewalk—a cleaner place to walk—to white passersby.

In the South, whites in 1831 took steps to reinforce the institution of slavery, using both violent and legal means. That year Nat Turner, an enslaved preacher and mystic, led a slave revolt in Southampton, Virginia. In the 1820s, the young Turner had looked skyward and had seen visions of "white spirits and black spirits engaged in battle . . . and blood flowed in streams." Turner believed that he had received divine instructions to lead other slaves to freedom, to "arise and prepare myself, and slay my enemies with their own weapons." In August he and a group of followers that eventually numbered eighty moved through the countryside, killing whites wherever they could find them. Ultimately, nearly sixty whites died at the

INTERPRETING HISTORY

José Agustin de Escudero Describes New Mexico as a Land of Opportunity, 1827

In the early nineteenth century, many people believed that the West afforded abundant economic opportunities for those willing to work hard. However, in most areas of the trans-Appalachian West, farming was a risky venture. Farmers needed cash or credit to hire hands—or to buy slaves—to clear dense underbrush and make other improvements on the land. Floods and droughts could wipe out a year's hard work and ruin even the most industrious family.

Nevertheless, certain frontier livelihoods did not take large investments in labor or equipment. In 1827 José Agustin de Escudero, a lawyer from the Mexican state of Chihuahua, visited the northern reaches of his country and reported on the partido system of sheep raising in the colony of New Mexico. He reported that the quality and expanse of the land meant that young men of modest means could prosper after a few years without securing large loans.

Merino sheep

It can be asserted that there were no paupers in New Mexico at that time, nor could there be any. At the same time, there were no large-scale stockmen who could pay wages or make any expenditure whatever in order to preserve and increase their wealth in this branch of agriculture. A poor man, upon reaching the age when one generally starts a family, would go to a rich stockman and offer to help him take care of one or more herds of sheep. These flocks were composed of *a thousand* ewes and *ten* breeding rams, which were never separated from the herd as is the practice of stock raisers in other countries. Consequently, in each flock, not a single day would go by without the birth of two or three lambs, which the shepherd would

---

hands of Turner's rebels. Turner himself managed to evade capture for more than two months. After he was captured, he was tried, convicted, and executed.

After the Turner revolt, a wave of white hysteria swept the South. In Virginia near where the killings had occurred, whites assaulted blacks with unbridled fury. The Virginia legislature seized the occasion to defeat various antislavery proposals. Thereafter, all the slave states moved to strengthen the institution of slavery. For all practical purposes, public debate over slavery ceased.

DOCUMENT
The Confession of Nat Turner (1831)

The Legal and Economic Dependence of Women

Regardless of where they lived, enslaved women and Indian women had almost no rights under either U.S. or Spanish law. However, legal systems in the United States and the Spanish borderlands differed in their treatment of women. In the United States, most of the constraints that white married women had experienced in the colonial period still applied in the 1820s. A husband controlled the property that his wife brought to the marriage, and he had legal authority over their children. Indeed, the wife was considered her husband's possession. She had no right to make a contract, keep money she earned, vote, run for office, or serve on a jury. In contrast, in the Spanish Southwest, married women could own land and conduct business on their own. At the same time, however, husbands, fathers, and local priests continued to exert much influence over the lives of these women.

European American women's economic subordination served as a rationale for their political inferiority. The "common man" concept rested on the assumption that men had the

put with the ewe and force the female to suckle without the difficulties which he would have had with a larger number of offspring. The shepherd would give the owner ten or twenty per cent of these sheep and an equal amount of wool, as a sort of interest, thus preserving the capital intact.

From the moment he received the flock, the shepherd entered into a contract in regard to the future increase, even with his own overseer. As a matter of fact, he usually contracted it at the current market price, two reales per head [an advance from the stockman], the future increase to be delivered in small numbers over a period of time. With this sum, which the shepherd had in advance, he could construct a house, and take in other persons to help him care for and shear the sheep, which was done with a knife instead of shears. The milk and sometimes the meat from the said sheep provided him sustenance; the wool was spun by his own family into blankets, stockings, etc., which could also be marketed, providing an income. Thus the wealth of the shepherd would increase until the day he became, like his overseer, the owner of a herd. He, in turn, would let out his herds to others after the manner in which he obtained his first sheep and made his fortune. Consequently, even in the homes of the poorest New Mexicans, there is never a dearth of sufficient means to satisfy the necessities of life and even to afford the comfort and luxuries of the wealthiest class in the country.

José de Escudero was a visitor to, not a resident of, New Mexico. It is possible that he oversimplified the partido shepherds' self-sufficiency in this region. Soon after winning its independence from Spain, Mexico opened New Mexico to U.S. traders. By the mid-1820s, traders were leading mule trains along the Santa Fe Trail, which ran from Franklin, Missouri, to Santa Fe, New Mexico. In his account here, Escudero indirectly highlights the roles of wives and mothers (as spinners and weavers of cloth) in preserving the economic independence of the shepherds' households.

Nevertheless, Escudero's observations suggest that a combination of factors, including the nature of the landscape (in this case suitable for sheep grazing) and the amount of initial capital necessary to the enterprise (in this case a minimal amount of cash), were crucial elements in providing young men and their families with economic opportunities on the frontier.

Questions

1. In what way does Agustin de Escudero link economic opportunity to the life cycle of rural New Mexican families?
2. What are some of the problems that a young sheep owner might encounter as he tried to build up his flock and provide for his family?
3. How might the appearance of the railroad in a few years change this sheep-herding economy?

Source: H. Bailey Carroll and J. Villasana Haggard, trans. and ed., *Three New Mexico Chronicles* (Albuquerque, 1942), pp. 41–42.

---

largest stake in society because only they owned property. That stake made them responsible citizens.

Yet women contributed to the economy in myriad ways. Although few women earned cash wages in the 1820s, almost all adult women worked. In the colonial period, society had highly valued women's labor in the fields, the garden, and the kitchen. However, in the early nineteenth century, work was becoming increasingly identified as labor that earned cash wages. This attitude proved particularly common in the Northeast, where increasing numbers of workers labored under the supervision of a boss. As this belief took root, men began valuing women's contributions to the household economy less and less. If women did not earn money, many men asked, did they really work at all?

In these years, well-off women in the northeastern and mid-Atlantic states began to think of themselves as consumers and not producers of goods. They relied more and more on store-bought cloth and household supplies. Some could also afford to hire servants to perform housework for them. Privileged women gradually stopped thinking of their responsibilities as making goods or processing and preparing food. Rather, their main tasks were to manage servants and create a comfortable home for their husbands and children.

In contrast, women in other parts of the country continued to engage in the same forms of household industry that had characterized the colonial period. In Spanish settlements, women played a central role in household production. They made all of their family's clothes by carding, spinning, and weaving the wool from sheep. They tanned cowhides and ground blue corn to make tortillas, or *atole*. They produced their own candles and soap, and they

> *In the early nineteenth century, work was becoming increasingly identified as labor that earned cash wages.*

plastered the walls of the home. In the Spanish mission of San Gabriel, California, the widow Eulalia Pérez cooked, sewed, ministered to the ill, and instructed children in reading and writing. At Mission San Diego, Apolonaria Lorenzana worked as a healer and cared for the church sacristy and priestly vestments.

Indian women also engaged in a variety of essential tasks. Sioux and Mandan women, though of a social rank inferior to men, performed a great deal of manual labor in their own villages. They dressed buffalo skins that the men later sold to traders. They collected water and wood, cooked, dried meat and fruit, and cultivated maize (corn), pumpkins, and squash with hoes made from the shoulderblades of elk. These women worked collectively within a network of households rather than individually within nuclear families.

Some women worked for cash wages during this era. New England women and children, for example, were the vanguard of factory wage-earners in the early manufacturing system. In Massachusetts in 1820, women and children constituted almost a third of all manufacturing workers. In the largest textile factories, they made up fully 80 percent of the workforce.

The business of textile manufacturing took the tasks of spinning thread and weaving cloth out of the home and relocated those tasks in factories. The famous "Lowell mill girls" are an apt example. Young, unmarried white women from New Hampshire, Vermont, and Massachusetts, these workers moved to the new company town of Lowell, Massachusetts, to take jobs as textile machine operatives. In New England, thousands of young men had migrated west, tipping the sex ratio in favor of women and creating a reserve of female laborers. But to attract young women to factory work, mill owners had to reassure them (and their parents) that they would be safe and well cared for away from home. To that end, they established boarding houses where employees could live together under the supervision of a matron—an older woman who served as their mother-away-from-home. Many young women valued the friendships they made with their coworkers and the money they made in the mills. Some of these women sent their wages back home so that their fathers could pay off the mortgage or their brothers could attend school.

Most ordinary women received little in the way of formal education. Yet elite young women had expanded educational opportunities, beginning in the early nineteenth century. Emma Willard founded a female academy in Troy, New York, in 1821, and Catharine Beecher established the Hartford (Connecticut) Female Seminary two years later. For the most part, such schools catered to the daughters of wealthy families, young women who would never have to work in a factory to survive. Hailed as a means to prepare young women to serve as wives and mothers, the schools taught geography, foreign languages, mathematics, science, and philosophy, as well as the "female" pursuits of embroidery and music.

Out of this curriculum designed especially for women emerged women's rights activists, women who keenly felt both the potential of their own intelligence and the degrading nature of their social situation. Elizabeth Cady, an 1832 graduate of the Troy Female Seminary, later went on to marry Henry B. Stanton and bear seven children. But by the 1840s, she strode onto the national stage as a tireless advocate of women's political and economic rights.

Ties That Bound a Growing Population

As the nation expanded westward, population growth and migration patterns disrupted old bonds of community. When people left their place of birth, they often severed ties with their family and original community. New forms of social cohesion arose to replace these traditional ties. New religions sought to make sense of the changing political and economic landscape. High literacy rates among the population created a new community of readers—a dispersed audience for periodicals as well as for a new, uniquely American literature. Finally, opinionmakers used the printed word to spread new ideas and values across regional boundaries. These ideas, such as glorification of male ambition, helped knit together far-flung segments of the population, men and women who began to speak of an "American character."

New Visions of Religious Faith

New forms of religious faith arose in response to turbulent times, offering one path to social cohesion. During the Indian Wars in the Old Northwest, a Winnebago prophet named White Cloud helped Black Hawk create a **coalition** of Winnebago, Potawatomi, Kickapoo, Sauk, and Fox Indians. A mystic and medicine man, White Cloud preached against white people and exhorted his followers to defend their way of life, an Indian way that knew no tribal boundaries. White Cloud, the religious leader, and Black Hawk, the military leader, surrendered together to federal troops on August 27, 1832, their alliance signifying the spiritual component in the Indians' militant resistance to whites.

Religious Revivalism and Reform

New religious enthusiasms took hold in other parts of the country as well. In the late 1820s and early 1830s, the Second Great Awakening swept western New York. The fervor of religious revivals so heated the region that people began to call it "the Burned-Over District." Hordes of people of various Protestant denominations attended week-long prayer meetings, sat together on the "anxious bench" for sinners, and listened, transfixed, as new converts told of their path to righteousness.

What explains this wave of religious enthusiasm? A major factor was a clergyman named Charles Grandison Finney, who managed to tap into the wellspring of hope and anxiety of the time. A former lawyer, Finney preached that people were moral free agents, fully capable of deciding between right and wrong and doing good in the world. Finney's message had great appeal during this period of rapid social, economic, and technological change. In New England and New York, for example, canals were bringing new kinds of goods to rural areas and longtime residents were departing for the Midwest. Traditional social relationships seemed threatened.

Throughout the country, religious institutions also grappled with questions about slavery. As the fear of possible black uprisings spread, white clergy in the South began to turn away from their former willingness to convert anyone. Instead, they began seeking respectability in the eyes of the well-to-do, slave-owning class. Incorporating masculine imagery into their sermons, they strove to reinforce the power of husband over wife, parent over child, and master over slave, relations that defined the typical plantation household.

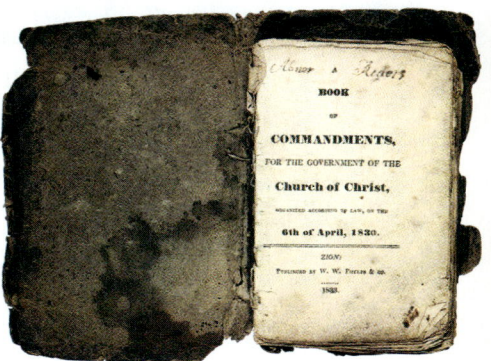

Elsewhere, some church leaders sought to purge Christianity of what they saw as its too-worldly nature and to revive the early, simple church that Jesus and his disciples had established. On April 6, 1830, a young farmer named Joseph Smith founded the Church of Jesus Christ of Latter-Day Saints (also called the Mormons) in Fayette, New York. Smith said that, in a vision, an angel named Moroni presented him with the text of a holy book originally written by a Native American historian more than 1,400 years earlier. The text was called the *Book of Mormon*. Together with the Old and New Testaments, it formed the basis of a new faith. Over the next few years, the Mormon Church grew rapidly, claiming 8,000 members by the mid-1830s. However, the young church also aroused intense hostility among mainstream Protestant denominations that regarded the new group's theology and textual inspiration with suspicion.

Literate and Literary America

Around the same time, a young widow named Sarah Hale broke new ground for women. In 1821 she became the first woman to edit an American periodical when she accepted

■ The Rev. John Atwood and family reading the Bible, 1845.

"Old Ironsides" by Oliver Wendell Holmes Jr.

responsibility for editing the Boston-based *Ladies Magazine*, later renamed *Godey's Lady's Book*. Once a hatmaker but now a published poet and novelist, Hale portrayed women as especially devout and thus powerful: men might claim as their domain "the government and the glory of the world," she wrote in 1832, "but nevertheless, what man shall become depends upon the secret, silent influence of women." That influence, Hale and other men and women like her believed, derived from women's roles as nurturers and caretakers. Thousands of similar magazines—most short-lived—appeared between 1825 and 1850.

Just as sentimental fiction and poetry attracted a large readership among women, a number of male writers staked their claim to emerging American literature. Washington Irving, James Fenimore Cooper, and William Cullen Bryant all explored regional histories and landscapes in their works. In *Rip Van Winkle* (1819) and the *Legend of Sleepy Hollow* (1820), Irving wrote about the legends of upstate New York. Cooper explored the western New York middle ground contested by the British, Americans, French, and Indians in the late eighteenth century in such works as *The Spy* (1821) and *The Last of the Mohicans* (1826). Bryant, inspired by the sight of the Illinois plains in 1832, penned "The Prairies," a praise-song to the vast plains as beautiful and "quick with life."

Along with this new American literary tradition, small towns across the nation began publishing newspapers to educate, inform, and entertain readers. News stories about national elections and legislation, about foreign monarchs and conflicts, reached log cabins in the West as well as elegant townhouses in Boston and Philadelphia. Wrote Washington Irving in 1820, "Over no nation does the press hold a more absolute control than over the people of America, for the universal education of the poorest classes makes every individual a reader."

Newspapers, books, and magazines promoted a set of values that writers claimed described an enduring American character. The ideal American supposedly was ambitious—ready to seize opportunity wherever it could be found—and at the same time devoted to home and family. In fact, these values strongly resembled those adopted by the British middle classes at the same time. Indeed, the United States spawned its own brand of middle-class sensibility called Victorianism, after the English queen who reigned from 1837 to 1901.

> *The ideal American supposedly was ambitious—ready to seize opportunity wherever it could be found—and at the same time devoted to home and family.*

Five core values defined early American Victorianism. First, the Victorians believed in the significance of the individual. People should be judged on the basis of their character, not on the circumstances of their birth. This belief, however, generally applied only to white men. Second, individuals should have the freedom to advance as far as their talents and ambition took them; no person should claim advantages over others by virtue of a noble title or aristocratic lineage. Third, work was intrinsically noble, whether performed by a canal digger wielding a pick-axe or a merchant using a quill pen. All people, regardless of their trade, deserved to reap the fruits of their labor. Fourth, everyone should exercise self-control and restraint in activities such as drinking and engaging in sexual relations. Finally, men and women occupied separate but complementary spheres. American society could be orderly and stable only if men could find a haven from the heartless world of work in their own homes. There, wives tended the hearth and infused the household with their love, self-sacrifice, and religious devotion.

Conclusion

Western settlement infused American politics with raw energy in the 1820s. Andrew Jackson was the first in a long line of presidents who boasted of their humble origins and furthered their careers by denouncing what they called the privileges enjoyed by wealthy Easterners. The challenges faced by western settlers in establishing homesteads and paying their debts emerged as national, not purely local, issues. Through the sheer force of his personality, Andrew Jackson exemplified these dramatic changes in the political landscape. Almost single-handedly, he extended the limits of executive power and remade the American party system in the process.

However, the contradictions in Jacksonian politics became glaring in the coming years. As the nation expanded its borders and diversified its economy, distinctions between social classes sharpened. The country also staked its claim to foreign territory, using violence to advance democratic values. Meanwhile, the North and South eyed each other with increasing distrust. And the contrast between those who moved from place to place voluntarily and those who were forced to move became even more dramatic.

Sites to Visit

The Second Bank of the United States, 1816–1936
odur.let.rug.nl/~usa/E/usbank/bank04.htm
The political conflict surrounding the Second Bank of the United States contributed to the rise of the Whig party.

The Erie Canal
www.canals.state.ny.us/culture/history
This official New York State site presents the Erie Canal as the stimulus for enormous economic and social change.

The Cherokee Nation
www.cherokee.org/culture/history.asp
This is the official Web site of the Cherokee nation based in Talequah, Oklahoma.

Commerce of the Prairies
www.kancoll.org/books/gregg/index.html#contents
This University of Kansas site includes information on life and commerce on the frontier between the United States and Mexico; including the Santa Fe Trail.

Pioneering the Upper Midwest: Books from Michigan, Minnesota, and Wisconsin, ca. 1820–1910
memory.loc.gov/ammem/umhtml/umhome.html
This Library of Congress site looks at first-person accounts, biographies, promotional literature, ethnographic and antiquarian texts, colonial archival documents, and other works from the seventeenth to the early twentieth century. It covers many topics and issues related to Americans and the settlement of the upper Midwest.

The Settlement of African Americans in Liberia
www.loc.gov/exhibits/african/afam002.html
This site contains images and text relating to the colonization movement sponsored by the American Colonization Society.

African American Women Writers from the Nineteenth Century
http://digital.nypl.org/schomburg/writers_aa19/toc.html
The New York Public Library Schomburg Center for Research in Black Culture site contains texts of literature by African American women of the nineteenth century.

For Further Reading

General
Stuart R. Blumin, *The Emergence of the Middle Class: Social Experience in the American City, 1760–1900* (1989).
Daniel Feller, *The Jacksonian Promise: America, 1815–1840* (1995).
Melvyn Stokes and Stephen Conway, eds., *The Market Revolution in America: Social, Political, and Religious Expressions, 1800–1880* (1996).
David J. Weber, *The Spanish Frontier in North America* (1992).

The Politics Behind Western Expansion
James W. Covington, *The Seminoles of Florida* (1993).
Mark Derr, *The Frontiersman: The Real Life and Many Legends of Davy Crockett* (1993).
Timothy Matovina, *Tejano Religion and Ethnicity: San Antonio, 1821–1860* (1995).
Ronald E. Shaw, *Canals for a Nation: The Canal Era in the United States, 1790–1860* (1990).

Federal Authority and Its Opponents
William W. Freehling, *Prelude to Civil War: The Nullification Controversy in South Carolina, 1816–1836* (1966).
Michael F. Holt, *Political Parties and American Political Development from the Age of Jackson to the Age of Lincoln* (1992).
Lawrence Frederick Kohl, *The Politics of Individualism: Parties and the American Character in the Jacksonian Era* (1989).
Robert V. Remini, *Andrew Jackson and His Indian Wars* (2001).

Real People in the "Age of the Common Man"
Thomas Dublin, *Transforming Women's Work: New England Lives in the Industrial Revolution* (1994).
Albert L. Hurtado, *Intimate Frontiers: Sex, Culture and Gender in California* (1999).
Walter Licht, *Industrial America: The Nineteenth Century* (1995).
Julie Winch, *Philadelphia's Black Elite: Activism, Accommodation, and the Struggle for Autonomy, 1787–1848* (1988).

Ties That Bound a Growing Population
Jeanne Boydston, *Home and Work: Housework, Wages, and the Ideology of Labor in the Early Republic* (1990).
Richard L. Bushman, *Joseph Smith and the Beginnings of Mormonism* (1984).
Nathan O. Hatch, *The Democratization of American Christianity* (1989).
Christine L. Heyrman, *Southern Cross: The Beginnings of the Bible Belt* (1997).

For quizzes and other resources on these topics, go to www.longmanamericanhistory.com.

Peoples in Motion, 1832–1848

CHAPTER

12

I N THE SPRING OF 1847, JANNICKE SAEHLE LEFT HER HOME IN BERGEN, A CITY ON THE WESTERN coast of Norway, and boarded a ship bound for New York City. From New York, the young woman traveled by steamship up the Hudson River to Albany. There she boarded a train to Milwaukee, Wisconsin. Although arduous, the journey had its pleasures. Piloted by a charming captain, the steamship resembled, in Saehle's words, "a complete house four stories high, and very elegantly furnished, with beautiful rugs everywhere." On the train, the passengers enjoyed each other's company as well as "the noteworthy sights that we rushed past." By the summer, Saehle was living with and working as a domestic servant for a Norwegian family, the Torjersens, in Koshkonong in southeastern Wisconsin. Founded in 1840, Koshkonong was a rapidly growing settlement of Norwegian immigrants farming the fertile prairie.

Jannicke Saehle was eager to make a new life for herself in the United States. For just a few months of service in the Torjersen household, she received the harvest of 3 acres of wheat for three years. In the fall, she found a job washing and ironing at a tavern in Madison. For the first five weeks, she earned a dollar a week. Then she received a raise of twenty-five cents a week, with the promise of another raise, and relief from washing, at the end of the winter. Although she could not speak English, she was pleased to "enjoy the best treatment" from the tavern owners and patrons.

■ Norwegian immigrants to the United States, 1880s.

In September 1847, Jannicke Saehle wrote of her good fortune in America in a letter to her family back in Norway. She described "the superabundance of food" in the Torjersen home. On his 40-acre farm, Torjersen kept swine and produced "tremendous amounts" of wheat, potatoes, beans, cabbage, cucumbers, onions, and many other kinds of vegetables. At the Madison tavern, she had "food and drink in abundance" and dined on the same fare served to the guests: for breakfast, "chicken, mutton [lamb], beef or pork, warm or cold wheat bread, butter, white cheese, eggs, or small pancakes, the best coffee, tea, cream and sugar." For supper she feasted on "warm biscuits, and several kinds of cold wheat bread, cold meats, bacon, cakes, preserved apples, plums, and berries, which are eaten with cream, and tea and coffee." Saehle felt heartbroken to see excess food thrown to the chickens and pigs, for, she wrote, "I

CHAPTER OUTLINE

Mass Migrations

A Multitude of Voices in the National Political Arena

Reform Impulses

The United States Extends Its Reach

Conclusion

Sites to Visit

For Further Reading

think of my dear ones in Bergen, who like so many others must at this time lack the necessaries of life."

Jannicke Saehle was just one of the more than 13,000 immigrants from Norway, Sweden, and Denmark who arrived in the United States during the 1840s. This migration continued to increase over the course of the nineteenth century. In the 1880s, more than 655,000 Scandinavians, fleeing poverty and military conflict, came to America. Many traveled to Wisconsin and Minnesota, where they farmed small homesteads and found the cold winter climate similar to that of their homeland.

In the 1830s and 1840s, patterns of settlement and employment among immigrant groups varied widely in the United States. For example, most Irish immigrants lacked the resources to move much farther west than the eastern seaboard ports where they landed. In contrast, many Germans arrived with enough money to buy farmland in the Midwest or take up a trade in eastern cities. Many immigrants relied for jobs and housing on compatriots who had already arrived. Communities of immigrants built their own religious institutions and **mutual aid societies**.

In the 1830s and 1840s, the United States was home to many peoples in motion. Groups of Indians in the Southeast and Midwest and slaves in the upper South were forced at gunpoint to move from one region of the country to another. From western Europe came poor and persecuted groups drawn to the United States by the demand for labor and the promise of religious and political freedom. Some Americans eagerly pulled up stakes and moved to nearby cities or towns in search of better jobs. Migrants with enough resources made the long journey across the Sonoran Desert in the Southwest to California or to the Oregon Territory in the Northwest.

Population movements and economic change generated new forms of community and group identity. In their native lands, many newcomers to the United States had lived and labored as peasants under the control of aristocratic landlords. Now in America these immigrants worked as wage earners or as small farmers. Urban workers founded the National Trades Union, an organization that tried to help laboring people wield political influence. Some women and men challenged basic institutions such as the **nuclear family**, slavery, and white supremacy. Some reformers established new communities based on alternative notions of marriage and child-rearing.

In politics, the so-called Second Party system had emerged by 1836, as Jacksonian Democrats squared off against the Whigs on familiar issues including tariffs and new systems of transportation. Some Americans turned to violence to advance or defend their causes. Urban mobs vented their wrath against African Americans, abolitionists, and Irish immigrants and other Roman Catholics. The government itself sponsored violence, which peaked in the late 1830s with the forced removal of southeastern Indians to the West, and again in the late 1840s, when the United States wrested a vast expanse of land from Mexico. Indeed, within the larger society, physical force seemed to be an acceptable means of resolving disputes; politicians of all persuasions followed Andrew Jackson's lead and staked their claim to national leadership on the basis of their records as soldiers, military officers, and Indian-killers.

Mass Migrations

When foreign visitors called Americans a "restless" people, they were referring to patterns of both immigration and migration within the country. Between 1830 and 1850, 2.3 million immigrants entered the United States, up from a total of

152,000 during the two previous decades. Most newcomers came from Ireland, Germany, England, Scotland, and Scandinavia. In the United States itself, individuals and families moved around the country with almost dizzying frequency in search of better jobs. They migrated from rural to urban areas, from one city to another, out west and then back to the East. In the late 1840s, almost half of all urban residents moved within a twelve-month period. For the country as a whole, an estimated one family in five moved every year, and on average every family moved once every five years. Many westward migrants had enough money to move overland and buy a homestead once they arrived in Wisconsin or Oregon. However, much of the population turnover in urban areas stemmed from landless people's relentless quest for higher wages and cheaper places to rent.

Some people moved because other people forced them to—under the crack of a whip and in manacles. Slave traders in the upper South transported thousands of slaves to the lower South for sale "on the block." U.S. soldiers forced Indians to walk from their homelands in the southeast to Indian Territory (now the state of Oklahoma). In the less settled West, however, older identities of race and ethnicity sometimes gave way to new identities forged from mixing cultures.

Newcomers from Western Europe

During this period, hardships in Western Europe led to increased immigration to the United States, especially from Ireland and the German states. For the long-suffering people of Ireland, life had become more precarious than ever by the early nineteenth century. Over the generations, small farm plots had been subdivided among heirs to the point that most holdings consisted of fewer than 15 acres each. At the same time, the population of Ireland had grown exponentially—to more than 4 million people in 1800. England treated Ireland like a colony that existed purely for the economic gain of the mother country (or, in the eyes of the Irish, an occupying power). A series of English laws and policies mandated that farmers export most of the island's grain and cattle, leaving the impoverished people to subsist mainly on a diet of potatoes. Then, beginning in 1845, a blight devastated the potato crop. In the next five years, 1 million people died and another million fled to the United States. The great Irish migration had begun.

> *During this period, hardships in Western Europe led to increased immigration to the United States, especially from Ireland and the German states.*

Large numbers of poor Irish had settled in the United States even before the potato famine of the mid-1840s. In the 1820s, about 50,000 such immigrants arrived; the following decade saw a spike in numbers to more than 200,000. Then as the 1840s and 1850s unfolded, 1.7 million Irish men, women, and children emigrated to the United States. This exodus continued over the next century as more than 4.5 million Irish arrived.

By the 1870s, the Irish constituted fully 20 percent of the population of New York City, 14 percent of Philadelphia, and 22 percent of Boston (the "hub of Gaelic America"). The newcomers quickly formed mutual aid associations and other community organizations. In cities across America, the Sisters of Mercy, a Roman Catholic order founded in Dublin, established homes to provide lodging for single women and day nurseries for the children of working mothers.

Most Irish immigrants lacked the resources to move much farther west than the eastern seaport cities where they landed, and they soon realized that their struggle against poverty, discrimination, and religious persecution would not end in the United States. The arrival of large numbers of Irish immigrants in the 1830s threatened the jobs of native-born Protestants, who reacted with resentment and violence. Employers posted signs outside their doors reading "No Irish Need Apply." Despised for their Roman Catholicism and their supposed clannishness, the Irish competed with African Americans for the low-paying jobs at the bottom of the economic ladder. In 1834 a mob destroyed the Ursuline convent in Charlestown, near Boston, after terrifying the women and children residents and ransacking the building.

Nevertheless, by the 1850s, the Irish had gained a measure of influence. They filled many high positions in the U.S. Catholic Church and became active in the Democratic party. They

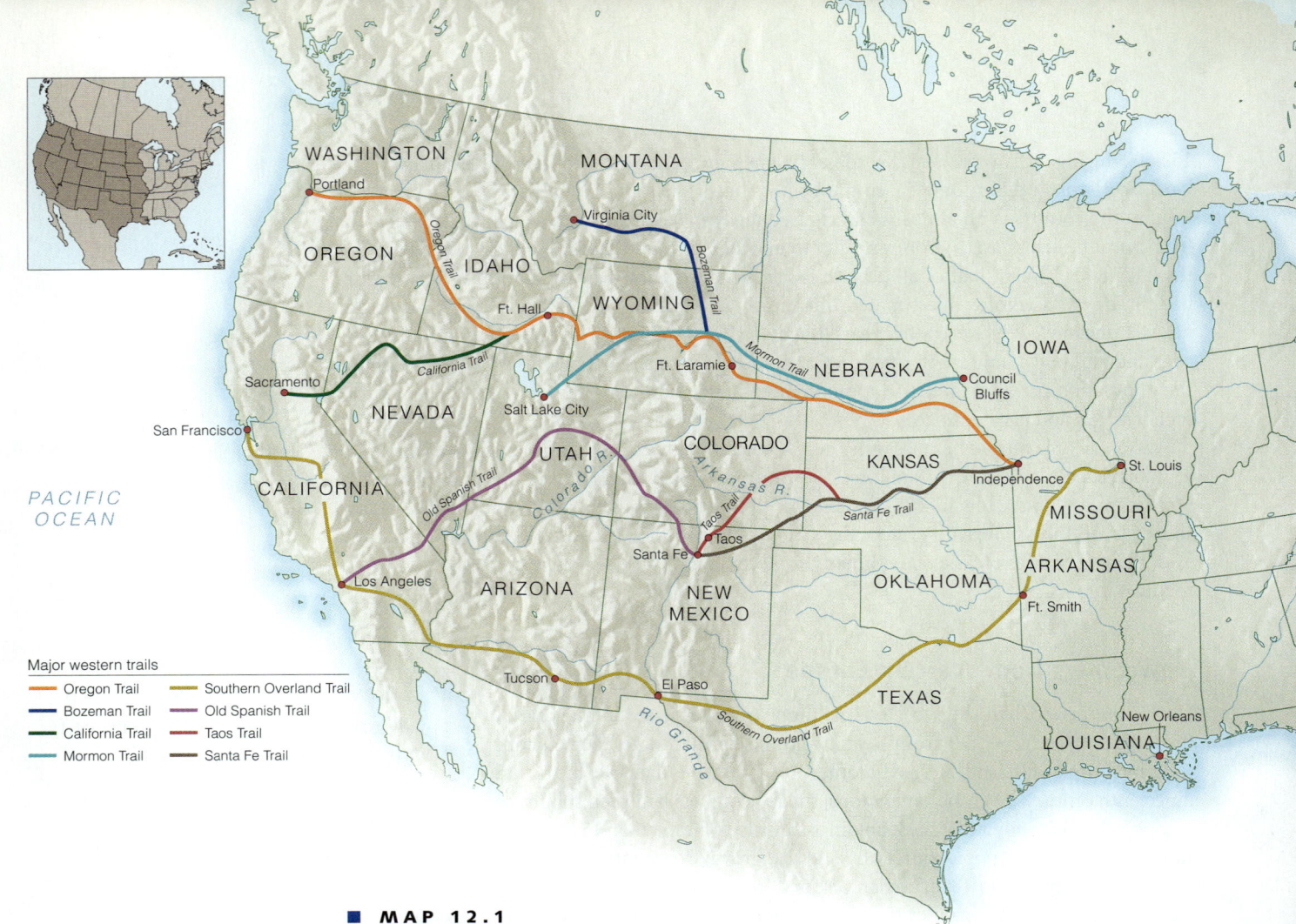

■ **MAP 12.1**
WESTERN TRAILS This map shows the major trails followed by western emigrants in the nineteenth century. Settlers endured long and dangerous journeys. For example, beginning at Independence, Missouri, and stretching to Portland, Oregon, the Overland Trail was 2,000 miles long. Covering the entire trail could take four to six months. Wagon trains had to traverse rocky terrain, scale mountains, and ford rivers. Along the way, outposts such as Fort Laramie and Fort Hall gave travelers a chance to refresh their supplies, rest their livestock, and repair their wagons. Though resentful of such incursions, Indians rarely attacked large wagon trains.

claimed that their white skin entitled them to distance themselves from blacks and lay claim to full American citizenship.

The hardship endured by the Irish in the early nineteenth century mirrored the political and economic distress of many other people living in Europe at the time. The revolutions of 1848 in France, the German states, the Austrian Empire, and parts of Italy struck out against monarchy and called for constitutional government. Rising unemployment and dramatic population increases made food scarce in both rural and urban areas, stimulating immigration across the Atlantic.

Between 1831 and 1850, more than half a million Germans arrived in the United States. Those numbers exploded in the next few decades. An uprising against the authoritarian Prussian state had failed in 1848, and German intellectuals, farmers, and workers alike fled across the ocean. Wilhelm Stille came to Ohio in the mid-1830s. In letters home, he praised the vitality of the local German immigrant community, the bountiful soil, and the "feel for freedom" that infused even the most recent newcomers.

The Slave Trade

Forced migration of enslaved workers increased during this period as the slave trade became big business. Many wealthy traders made regular trips between the upper and lower South. Traders transported men, women, and children by boat down the eastern seaboard or down the Mississippi River or chained and forced them to walk as much as 20 miles a day for seven or eight weeks at a time in the chill autumn air. Eventually, slaves stood on the block in the markets of New Orleans, Natchez, Charleston, and Savannah, where white men inspected them for health, strength, and compliance.

Between 1800 and 1860, the average price of slaves quadrupled, revealing a growing demand for bound labor. As many as one out of every ten slave children in the upper South was sold to the lower South (many to cotton planters) between 1820 and 1860. Slave households in Virginia bore the brunt of these forced separations. There, an estimated three-quarters of the people sold never saw their spouse, parents, or children again.

> *Between 1800 and 1860, the average price of slaves quadrupled, revealing a growing demand for bound labor.*

It was sometimes worse if they did. Moses Grandy, standing on a sidewalk one day, saw his wife in chains, in a coffle passing by. He recalled the scene in his 1844 autobiography:

> Mr. Rogerson was with them on his horse, armed with pistols. I said to him. "For God's sake, have you bought my wife?" He said he had; when I asked him what she had done, he said she had done nothing, but that her master wanted money. He drew out a pistol and said that if I went near the wagon where she was, he would shoot me. I asked for leave to shake hands with her which he refused, but said I might stand at a distance and talk with her. My heart was so full that I could say very little. . . . I have never seen or heard from her from that day to this. I loved her as I love my life.

Voluntary migrations of African Americans formed the counterpoint of the slave trade as runaways and free people of color made their way out of the old slave states. An estimated 50,000 enslaved workers tried to escape each year, but few made it to the North and freedom. Some southern free people of color headed to northern cities. By 1850 more than half of all Boston blacks had been born outside Massachusetts. Of those migrants, about one-third had been born in the South, most in Virginia, Maryland, and the District of Columbia. Slave runaways who lived in fear of their safety and their lives eluded census takers, but by mid-century as many as 600 fugitives lived in Boston.

Slavery in the South

Regardless of their place of origin, many migrants took up residence with other blacks, who helped ease the newcomers' transition to city life. These boarding arrangements strengthened ties between the enslaved and the free communities. For example, when authorities arrested the runaway George Latimer in Boston in 1842, free blacks in that city took immediate action. They posted signs condemning the police as "human kidnappers." Some tried to wrench him physically from his captors. Still others sponsored protest meetings in the local African Baptist Church and made common cause with white lawyers sympathetic to abolition. Finally a group of blacks and whites raised enough money to buy Latimer from his owner and free him.

Meanwhile, throughout the urban North, whites began eyeing blacks' jobs. Irish immigrants in particular desperately sought work. Skilled black workers found it increasingly difficult to ply their trades as cooks, hotel and boat stewards, porters, brickmakers, and barbers. In 1838, 656 black artisans in Philadelphia reported that they had to abandon their work because white customers would no longer patronize them. White factory owners in Philadelphia preferred white laborers. In that same city, a bustling site of machine shops and textile factories, almost no blacks did industrial labor of any kind.

Trails of Tears

Like enslaved blacks, many Indians were forced to migrate. In 1835 President Andrew Jackson made a puzzling declaration. The removal of eastern Indian groups to Indian Territory,

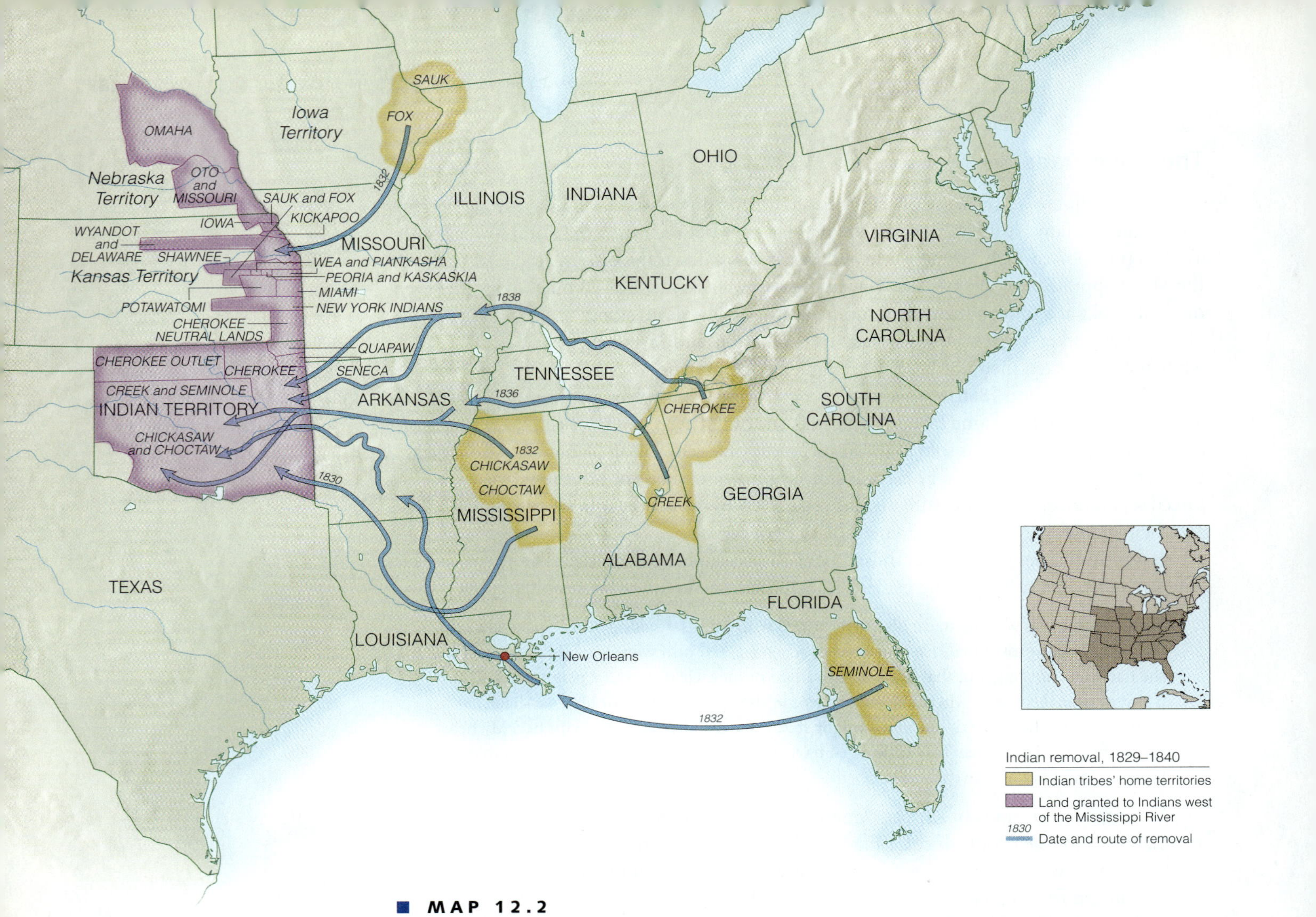

■ **MAP 12.2**

INDIAN REMOVAL This map shows the routes of forced migration of the Five Civilized Tribes in the 1830s. By the 1870s, several groups of Plains Indians, including the Cheyenne, Arapaho, Comanche, and Kiowa, had joined them in Indian Territory (present-day Oklahoma).

Native American Removal

he said, would ensure their "physical comfort," "political advancement," and "moral improvement." Rarely have a chief executive's words contrasted so starkly with reality.

Throughout the 1830s, the U.S. government pursued the policy of removing Indians from the Southeast by treaty or by force. The 1832 Treaty of Payne's Landing, negotiated by the Seminole Indians and James Gadsden, a representative of Secretary of War Lewis Cass, aimed to force the Seminole out of Florida and into Indian Territory (present-day Oklahoma). The federal government promised to give individual Indians cash, plus blankets for the men and dresses for the women, in exchange for their lands. Government authorities also hoped to recapture the large number of runaway slaves who had sought refuge in Seminole villages, deep in the swamps of central Florida.

Three years later, in 1835, many of the Indians had departed for the West. But a small number withdrew deeper into the Everglades and held their ground. They were led by a young man named Osceola, who with his followers waged a **guerrilla war** (based on ambush tactics rather than traditional conventions of European American warfare) against better-armed U.S. troops. Osceola's resistance, called the Second Seminole War, dragged on for seven years. Eventually, the government forced 3,000 Seminole to move west, but not until it had spent $20 million, and 1,500 U.S. soldiers had lost their lives.

The Choctaw of the southern Alabama–Mississippi region, the Chickasaw directly to the north of them, the Creek in central Georgia and Alabama, and the Cherokee of north Georgia suffered the same fate in the 1830s. The Creek remained bitterly divided among themselves on the issue of removal, as did the Cherokee. Major Ridge, his son John Ridge, and Elias Boudinot, leaders of the so-called Treaty Party of the Cherokee nation, urged their people to give up their homeland and rebuild their nation in the West. John Ross and others like him opposed the Ridges and Boudinot. The Cherokee must remain in Georgia at all costs, Ross insisted. He claimed that he spoke for a majority of Cherokee. To silence him, the U.S. government threw him in prison. Then it concluded negotiations with the Treaty Party, which agreed to sell Cherokee land to the federal government for $5 million. Elias Boudinot said, "We can die, but the great Cherokee Nation will be saved." Within a few years, the Ridges and Boudinot died at the hands of anti–Treaty Party Cherokee assassins.

In 1838 General Winfield Scott, with 7,000 troops under his command, began rounding up the citizens of the Cherokee nation. U.S. troops held men, women, and children in concentration camps before forcing them to march west. During the period from 1838 to 1839, nearly 16,000 Indians began a journey that they called the Trail on Which We Cried. Four thousand of them died of malnutrition and disease in the course of the 116-day forced march. U.S. troops confiscated or destroyed the material basis of Cherokee culture: sawmills, cotton gins, barns, homes, spinning wheels, meetinghouses, flocks, herds, and the printing press used to publish the *Cherokee Phoenix*.

Rebecca Neugin later recalled how the army troops "drove us out of our house to join other prisoners in a stockade." The soldiers let Rebecca's mother take a few cooking utensils with her; the family lost everything else. Still, Neugin's family remained intact. Many others did not. A soldier who participated in the operation saw children "separated from their parents and driven into the stockade with the sky for a blanket and the earth for a pillow."

U.S. officials claimed that troops had carried out the removal with "great judgment and humanity." However, an internal government report completed in 1841 revealed that the United States had reneged on even its most basic treaty promises. "Bribery, perjury, and forgery, short weights, issues of spoiled meat and grain, and every conceivable subterfuge was employed by designing white men." Many government agents seized goods such as blankets and food intended for Indians and sold these goods for profit. Military authorities suppressed the report, and the public never saw it.

Migrants in the West

For many native-born migrants seeking a new life west of the Mississippi, the road proved neither smooth nor easy. For example, as the Mormon community moved west from New York, they met with religious persecution. The founder of the church, Joseph Smith, aroused the anger of his neighbors in Nauvoo, Illinois. They took alarm at the Nauvoo Legion, a military company formed to defend the Mormon community. They also heard rumors (for the most part true) that Smith and other Mormon leaders engaged in plural marriage or polygamy, allowing men to marry more than one wife.

In 1844 the Nauvoo Legion destroyed the printing press owned by a group of rebellious church members who objected to what they considered Smith's authoritarian tactics. Civil authorities charged Smith and his brother Hyrum with the destruction of private property and arrested and jailed the two men in the nearby town of Carthage. In June 1844, an angry mob of non-Mormons broke into the jail and lynched the brothers.

By 1847 Brigham Young, who had inherited the mantle of leadership from Smith, determined that the Mormons could not remain in Illinois. Migrants, some of them pushing handcarts loaded with personal belongings, set out for the West. By 1852, 10,000 Mormons had settled in Salt Lake City in what is present-day Utah. With their large numbers and

■ This picture of the Whitman mission at Waiilatpu, Oregon, in 1845 shows the missionaries' house on the left, a mill in the background, a blacksmith shop in the right center, and a gathering place for worshippers on the far right. By this time the Whitmans had turned their attention from converting Indians to preaching to European American emigrants recently arrived from the East.

church-inspired discipline, the community prospered. They created an effective irrigation system and turned the desert into a thriving agricultural community.

The Mormons had not settled an uninhabited wilderness. Around Salt Lake, Canadian trappers, Paiute Indians, and Spanish speakers from New Mexico crossed paths, some to hunt, others to gather roots and berries, herd sheep, or trade captives. A Christmas dinner celebrated near Great Salt Lake around this time revealed the multicultural mix of western life. The guests included Osborne Russell (a European American trader), a Frenchman married to a Flathead woman, and various other intermarried Cree, Snake, and Nez Perceé Indians. The group feasted on the meat of elk and deer, a flour pudding, cakes, and strong coffee. After the meal, the women cleared the table. The men smoked pipes and then went outside and conducted target practice with their guns.

European Americans also migrated to the Northwest during this period. Protestant missionaries initially settled Oregon beginning in 1834. But in contrast to the Mormons, these northwestern colonists found themselves in the midst of hostile Native Americans. One young doctor and his wife from western New York, Marcus and Narcissa Whitman, established a mission near present-day Walla Walla, Washington. More than a thousand more emigrants from the East followed the Whitmans to Oregon during the "Great Migration" of 1843.

The U.S. government aided this westward movement when it commissioned its Topographical Corps of Engineers to survey the Oregon Trail. That task fell to an expedition headed by John Charles Frémont in 1843–1844. The expedition's final report had immense practical value for the emigrants, for it mapped the way west and provided crucial information about pasture, sources of water, and climate.

The Oregon settlements founded by missionaries were fragile affairs. Discouraged and overwhelmed by homesickness, Narcissa Whitman eagerly awaited copies of the latest *Mothers'*

Magazine sent to her by female relatives in the East. After 1843 the influx of newcomers brought her some consolation but also brought outbreaks of measles, to which the Native Americans had no immunity. An ensuing epidemic among the Cayuse claimed many lives. In 1847, blaming the missionaries for the deaths of their people, several Indians attacked the Whitman mission, killing twelve whites, including Narcissa and Marcus Whitman.

New Places, New Identities

The Midwest, the West, and the borderlands between U.S. and Spanish territories were meeting places for many different cultures. Leaving established communities behind, some migrants challenged rigid definitions of who was black, Indian, Hispanic, or European American. Moving from one place to another enabled—or forced—people to adopt new individual and group identities.

People who fell into one racial category in the East sometimes acquired new identities in the West. Some people classified as "black" in the South became "white" outside the region. In 1831 George and Eliza Gilliam decided to leave their home in Virginia and make a new life for themselves in western Pennsylvania. Eliza died in 1838, and George remarried nine years later. He prospered over the course of his lifetime. He worked as a doctor and druggist and invested in and sold real estate. George and his second wife, Frances, eventually moved to Illinois, and the couple finally settled in Missouri. Several of the Gilliam children attended college in Ohio. In 1870 the census listed the value of his estate at $95,000 (the equivalent of $2 million dollars today).

Leaving established communities behind, some migrants challenged rigid definitions of who was black, Indian, Hispanic, or European American.

George Gilliam was the son of a white father and a black mother. Although he and his first wife Eliza were very light-skinned, the commonwealth of Virginia classified them both legally as black. Beginning their married life near Petersburg, they were well aware of Virginia's tightening restrictions on free people of color and their uncertain future in Virginia, where local officials knew who they were and who their parents were. In contrast, the public records in their new home states of Pennsylvania, Illinois, and Missouri listed family members as white. Outside the slave South, the Gilliams managed to reinvent themselves and embrace opportunities sought by many other Americans in this era of migration.

Throughout the West, migrants forged new identities as a matter of course. For example, many people straddled more than one culture in the western borderlands. In 1828 Mexican military officer Jose Maria Sanchez described the *Tejano* settlers (Spanish-speaking natives of Mexico) he met in the province of Tejas (Texas): "Accustomed to the continued trade with the North Americans, they have adopted their customs and habits, and one may say truly that they are not Mexican except by birth, for they even speak Spanish with a marked incorrectness." In other provinces of northern Mexico, European American Protestant traders and travelers mingled with Catholic native Spanish speakers.

In parts of the West, traditional social identities yielded to new ones, based less on a single language or ethnicity than on a blend of cultures and new ways of making a living from the land. The 1830s and 1840s marked the height of the Rocky Mountain fur trade. The trade could generate huge profits for the eastern merchants who controlled it. Individual trappers fared more modestly, ranging freely across national boundaries and cultures, going wherever the bison, bear, and beaver took them. These men demonstrated a legendary ability to navigate among Spanish, French, European American, and Native American communities. Westerners coined new terms to describe the people representative of new kinds of cultural identity within trading communities. Some white men became "white Indians," and the children they had with Indian women were called "métis" (mixed bloods). William Sherley "Old Bill" Williams, a convert to the religion of the Osage Indians of the southeastern Plains, was not unusual in the ways he crossed cultural boundaries. He married an Osage woman, and when she died, he wed a New Mexican widow. His third wife was a Ute woman. Williams's life story suggests the ways that Indian and Hispanic women could serve as cultural mediators between native peoples and European American traders.

A Multitude of Voices in the National Political Arena

The increasing diversity of the American population, combined with specialized regional economies, also heightened tensions within and between different groups and sections of the country. The Second Party system, which replaced the Federalist–Anti-Federalist rivalry of the early nineteenth century, was characterized by intense competition between the Jacksonian Democrats and anti-Jackson Whigs. But this new system could not accommodate the old or new conflicts based on race, religion, ethnicity, regional loyalties, and political beliefs. Social and cultural disputes between nativists and immigrants, and between abolitionists and defenders of slavery, spilled out of the courthouse and the legislative hall and into the streets. Public demonstrations ran the gamut from noisy parades to bloody clashes. During these displays, resentments between ethnic and religious groups, arguments over political issues, and opposition to reformers often blended together.

Whigs, Workers, and the Panic of 1837

Clay, "Defense of the American System"

One polarizing force, Andrew Jackson—ill with tuberculosis—did not run for a third term in 1836. The Democrats nominated Jackson's vice president and friend Martin Van Buren of New York for president. The Jackson-haters, led by Senator Henry Clay and other congressmen, formed a political party called the Whigs. They drew their support from several groups: advocates of Clay's American System (policies that supported a national bank, public funding of canals and turnpikes, and protective tariffs), states' rights Southerners opposed to Jackson's heavy-handed use of national power, and merchants and factory owners in favor of the Second Bank of the United States. **Evangelical Protestants** from the middle classes also joined the anti-Jackson forces; they objected to his rhetoric stressing class differences because they believed that individual religious conviction, not a group's material status, should shape politics and society. Still somewhat disorganized, these allied groups fielded three candidates: Hugh White of Tennessee, Senator Daniel Webster of Massachusetts, and General William Henry Harrison of Indiana. Benefiting from the Whigs' disarray, Van Buren narrowly won the popular vote but swept the electoral college.

During this period, political candidates of all persuasions in northeastern cities began to court the allegiance of workers aligned with a new trade union movement. People worried about making a living tended to favor the Democratic party, which spoke against class privilege and the wealthy. In the late 1820s and early 1830s, a variety of trade organizations had formed to advance the interests of skilled workers (the "producing classes," they called themselves). These unions pressed for a ten-hour workday, the abolition of debtors' prisons and paper money (so that workers would receive their wages in hard currency rather than bank notes), and higher wages.

The founding of the National Trades Union (NTU) in 1834 made workers more politically visible. The union represented workers as diverse as jewelers, butchers, bookbinders, and factory work-

TABLE 12-1
The Election of 1836

Candidate	Political Party	Popular Vote (%)	Electoral Vote
Martin Van Buren	Democratic	50.9	170
William Henry Harrison	Whig		73
Hugh L. White	Whig	49.1	26
Daniel Webster	Whig		14
W.P. Magnum	Independent	—	11

ers. In Philadelphia in the early 1830s, for example, the local NTU organization, called the General Trades Union, consisted of fifty trade societies and supported a number of successful strikes. Both Whigs and Democrats professed allegiance to the union, but neither party went out of its way to represent the interests of workers over other groups, such as farmers and bookkeepers.

A major depression, the Panic of 1837, created even larger troubles for the trade union movement. Brought on by **overspeculation**—in canals, turnpikes, railroads, and slaves—the panic deepened when large grain crops failed in the West. British creditors worsened matters when they recalled loans they had made to American customers. The depression lasted until the early 1840s and devastated the NTU and its constituent organizations. Up to one-third of all Americans lost their jobs when businesses failed. Those fortunate enough to keep their jobs were in no position to press for higher wages. Not until the Civil War era did members of the laboring classes recapture political momentum at the national level.

Suppression of Antislavery Sentiment

Enslaved black workers were also at the center of contention in these years. In 1831 a Boston journalist named William Lloyd Garrison launched *The Liberator*, a newspaper dedicated to "immediate emancipation" of all slaves. Two years later, a group of sixty blacks and whites formed the American Anti-Slavery Society. That same year, Great Britain had abolished slavery in the British West Indies. This move encouraged like-minded Americans eager to cooperate with their British counterparts to abolish slavery everywhere. In the United States, the abolitionist movement enlisted the energies of a dedicated group of people who believed not only that slavery was immoral but also that the federal government must take immediate steps to destroy this "peculiar institution."

Garrison, First issue of *The Liberator*

Both northern communities of free people of color and white women and men provided moral and financial support to the society. All the supporters showed a great deal of courage within a larger American society indifferent to the issue of slavery. Well-to-do black leaders, including Henry Highland Garnet, Charles Lenox Remond, and his sister Sarah Parker Remond, spoke out on behalf of southern blacks in chains. Fugitive slaves, including Frederick Douglass, Solomon Northup, and William and Ellen Craft, electrified northern abolitionist audiences with their firsthand accounts of the brutality of slavery and of their own daring escapes from bondage.

A few white women also became active in the abolitionist cause. Sarah and Angelina Grimké, for example, left the household of their slave-owning father in Charleston, South Carolina, and moved to Philadelphia. The Grimké sisters spoke before groups composed of men and women, blacks and whites in the North, an act offensive to many other whites. They were struck by what they considered the similar legal constraints of slaves and white women. White men considered both groups to be unworthy of citizenship rights, childlike in their demeanor, well-suited for domestic service, and inherently unintelligent.

Abolitionist activities provoked outrage not only from southern slave owners but also from anti-abolitionists and their allies in Congress—in other words, most northern whites. In Washington, D.C., the House of Representatives imposed a gag rule on antislavery petitions, forbidding them to be read aloud or entered into the public record. Supporters of slavery also resorted to violence. In 1834 a mob of whites attacked a school for young women of color operated by a white teacher, Prudence Crandall, near New Haven, Connecticut. A local paper charged that the school was fostering "levelling [egalitarian] principles, and intermarriage between whites and blacks." The next year in Boston a different mob attacked the *Liberator* founder, William Lloyd Garrison, tying a rope around him and parading him through the streets of that city while onlookers jeered. In 1837 in Alton, Illinois, a group of whites murdered outspoken abolitionist Rev. Elijah

■ Born a slave in Maryland in 1818, Frederick Douglass became a leading abolitionist speaker, editor, and activist. Not content to condemn southern slaveholders exclusively, he also criticized northern employers for not hiring blacks. Trained as a ship caulker, Douglass faced job discrimination in the shipyards of New Bedford, Massachusetts, where he and his wife, Anna, settled soon after he escaped slavery and they moved north (in 1838).

■ The artist titled this print *New Method of Assorting the Mail, as Practised by Southern Slave-Holders*. In July 1835, a proslavery mob broke into the U.S. post office in Charleston, South Carolina, and burned abolitionist literature. The sign on the side of the building offers a "Reward for Tappan." The brothers Arthur and Lewis Tappan were wealthy New York City merchants who funded abolitionist activities. Southern slaveholders hoped to stem the North-South flow of abolitionist literature, which took the form of sermons, pamphlets, periodicals, and resolutions.

P. Lovejoy. Hounded out of Missouri because of his antislavery pronouncements, Lovejoy had moved directly across the river to Alton, in free-state Illinois, where he published the *Alton Observer* and organized the Illinois Anti-Slavery Society. Antiblack riots broke out in New York City, Philadelphia, and Cincinnati in 1834, and again in Philadelphia in 1842.

Still, these dramatic episodes had little noticeable impact on the two major political parties. In 1840 the Democrats renominated Van Buren, although many people blamed him for the depression. Eager to find a candidate as popular as Andrew Jackson, the Whigs selected William Henry Harrison; his supporters called him "Old Tippecanoe" in recognition of his defeat of Indians at the battle of the same name in 1811. As Harrison's running mate the Whigs chose John Tyler, who had been both governor of and a senator from Virginia. To counter their reputation as well-heeled aristocrats, which in fact they were, the Whigs promoted Harrison as a simple, humble man living in a log cabin and drinking hard cider. They rallied around the slogan "Tippecanoe and Tyler Too."

By this time, the Whigs had gained strong support among wealthy southern planters, who worried that Van Buren would not protect their interests in slavery. Harrison won the election, but he contracted pneumonia at his inauguration and died within one month of taking office. Ridiculed as "His Accidency," Tyler assumed the presidency and soon lost his core constituency, Whigs who favored a strong central government, by vetoing bills for both a national bank and higher tariffs. The new president represented members of the Whig party who were ardent supporters of states' rights. As a result, he proved a poor standard-bearer for the numerous nationalist-minded Whigs. Tyler learned a hard lesson: that members of his own party were a loose coalition of groups with varying views on a range of issues rather than a unified party bound to a single idea or principle.

Abolitionists could claim few victories, either real or symbolic, during these years. However, they did take heart from the *Amistad* case. In 1839 Spanish slave traders attempted to transport fifty-three illegally purchased Africans to Havana, Cuba, on a ship named *Amistad*. En route to Havana, the Africans, under the leadership of a young man named Cinqué, rebelled, killed the captain, and took over the ship. Soon after, U.S. authorities captured the ship off the coast of Long Island. President Van Buren wanted to send the blacks to Cuba. However, a federal district court judge in Hartford, Connecticut, ruled that because the African slave trade had been illegal since 1808, the Africans had been wrongfully enslaved. The U.S. government appealed the case to the Supreme Court.

To raise funds for the *Amistad* case, Philadelphia black leader Robert Purvis paid to have Cinqué's portrait painted; then antislavery activists sold copies for $1 each. In 1841 former president John Quincy Adams argued the Africans' case before the high court. The court ruled in their favor. Of the original fifty-three men, women, and children, thirty-five had survived the ordeal, and they returned to Africa. Slavery advocates and abolitionists alike pondered the question: Could the law be used to dismantle slavery?

TABLE 12-2
The Election of 1840

Candidate	Political Party	Popular Vote (%)	Electoral Vote
William Henry Harrison	Whig	53.1	234
Martin Van Buren	Democratic	46.9	60
James G. Birney	Liberty	<1	—

Nativists as a Political Force

Immigration, like slavery, aroused strong feelings. Among the active players on the political scene in the early nineteenth century were the **nativists**, who opposed immigration and immigrants. The immigrants who came to the United States were a varied group in terms of their jobs, religion, and culture. Some farmed homesteads in Michigan, and others worked in northeastern factories. But to nativists, these distinctions made little difference: all immigrants were foreigners and thus unwelcome. Some nativists were also **temperance** advocates calling for the prohibition of alcohol; they objected to the Irish drinking in taverns and the Germans drinking in their *Biergarten*. Protestants worried that large numbers of Catholic immigrants

■ Abolitionists hailed the eventual freeing of the *Amistad* captives as one of their few successes in the fight against slavery before the Civil War. This picture shows the Spanish slave ship, commandeered by the captives under the leadership of Cinqué, anchored off Culloden Point, Long Island, in 1839. Initially charged with the murder of the ship's captain, the Africans were held in New Haven, Connecticut, until a U.S. Supreme Court ruling led to their release and return to Africa in 1842.

would be loyal to the pope in Rome, the head of the Catholic Church, and thus undermine American democracy. Members of the working classes, black and white, feared the loss of their jobs to desperate newcomers who would accept low, "starvation" wages. But nativists objected just as much when immigrants kept to themselves—in their Catholic schools or in their German *Turnverein* (gymnastics clubs). They also complained when immigrants participated in U.S. politics as individual voters and members of influential voting blocs.

Samuel F. B. Morse, the artist and inventor, was among the most vocal nativists. In the early 1840s, he ceased painting portraits and turned his creative energies to developing a form of long-distance electric communication. Congress financed construction of the first telegraph line, which ran from Washington to Baltimore. In May 1844, Morse sent a message in code, "What hath God wrought!" and the modern telegraph was born. The precursor of all later communication innovations, the telegraph revolutionized the spread of information and tied the country together.

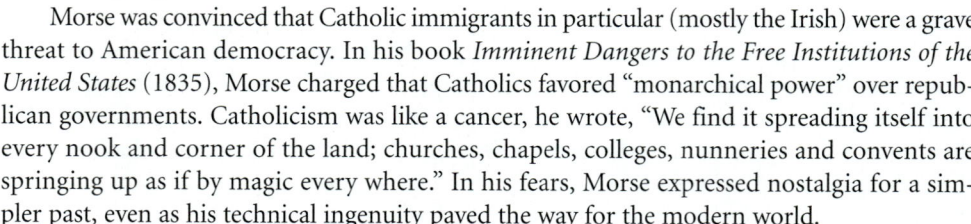
Morse, Foreign Immigration

Morse was convinced that Catholic immigrants in particular (mostly the Irish) were a grave threat to American democracy. In his book *Imminent Dangers to the Free Institutions of the United States* (1835), Morse charged that Catholics favored "monarchical power" over republican governments. Catholicism was like a cancer, he wrote, "We find it spreading itself into every nook and corner of the land; churches, chapels, colleges, nunneries and convents are springing up as if by magic every where." In his fears, Morse expressed nostalgia for a simpler past, even as his technical ingenuity paved the way for the modern world.

In 1844 an openly nativist political organization, the American Republican party, elected six of its candidates to Congress and dozens of others to local political offices. In 1849 nativists founded the Order of the Star-Spangled Banner. Also called the Know-Nothing party, the group got its name by cautioning its members to profess ignorance when asked about its existence.

■ Taken on May 9, 1844, this daguerreotype is one of the first American photographs to record an urban civil disturbance. A crowd gathers outside Philadelphia's Girard Bank, at the corner of Third and Dock streets. At the time, soldiers called in to quell the riot were occupying the bank. Called the Bible Riots, the clash between Protestant and Catholic workers revealed tensions arising from nativism, temperance activism, and the use of the Protestant version of the Bible in the public schools.

Anti-Catholic prejudices in particular helped to justify territorial expansion. Many U.S. Protestants believed the government was justified in seizing the land of Spanish-speaking Catholics in the West. They claimed religious and cultural superiority over Hispanics. As Protestant explorers, traders, and travelers reported on their experiences in the Southwest, their condemnation of Mexican Roman Catholics set the stage for the U.S. conquest of northern Mexico in the late 1840s.

Reform Impulses

In August 1841, writer Lydia Maria Child recorded a striking scene in New York City: a march sponsored by the Washington Society, a temperance group, was snaking its way through the streets. The procession stretched for 2 miles and consisted of representatives from "all classes and trades." The marchers carried banners depicting streams and rivers (the pure water favored over liquor) and poignant scenes of the grateful wives and children of reformed drunkards. Stirred by the martial sounds of trumpets and drums, Child wrote that the music was "the voice of resistance to evil." She added, "Glory to resistance! for through its agency men become angels."

Inspired by faith in the perfectibility of human beings and heartened by the rapid pace of technological progress, many Americans set about trying to "make angels out of men," in Child's words. In the process, various reform associations targeted personal habits such as dress and diet, conventional beliefs about sexuality and the status of women, and institutions such as schools, churches, and slavery. Their efforts often brought women out of the home and into public life. Yet not all Americans shared the reformers' zeal, and even those who did rarely agreed about the appropriate means to transform society.

Public Education

In the eyes of some Americans, a growing nation needed new forms of tax-supported schooling. As families moved from one area of the country to another, public education advocates pointed out, children should be able to pick up in one school where they had left off in another. Members of a growing middle class wanted to provide their children with schooling beyond basic literacy instruction (reading and writing skills) and had the resources to do so.

Horace Mann, a Massachusetts state legislator and lawyer, was one of the most prominent educational reformers. In 1837 Mann became secretary of the first state board of education. He stressed the notion of a **common school system** available to all boys and girls regardless of class or ethnicity. In an increasingly diverse nation, schooling promoted the acquisition of basic knowledge and skills. But it also provided instruction in what Mann and others called American values: hard work, punctuality, and sobriety.

How exactly would educators teach reading and writing skills and moral values? The dictionary of Connecticut's Noah Webster (published in 1828) and the McGuffey's *Reader* series, first published in 1836, provided a way. In his books, William H. McGuffey, a college professor and Presbyterian minister, combined lessons in reading with lessons in moral behavior: "Beautiful feet are they that go / Swiftly to lighten another's woe." Over the next twenty years, the McGuffey series sold more than 7 million copies.

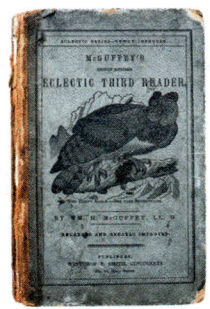

By the 1840s, public school systems attended by white children had cropped up across the North and the Midwest. Local school boards eagerly tapped into the energies of women as teachers. School officials claimed that women were naturally nurturing and could serve as "mothers away from home" for small children. Furthermore, schools could pay women only a fraction of what men earned. Between the 1830s and 1840s, the number of female schoolteachers in Massachusetts jumped more than 150 percent. In 1846 writer and educator Catharine Beecher created a Board of National Popular Education, which sent unmarried female New England teachers to the Midwest.

> Despite the lofty goals of Mann and other reformers, public schooling did not offer a "common" experience for all American children.

Despite the lofty goals of Mann and other reformers, public schooling did not offer a "common" experience for all American children. Almost exclusively, northern white children benefited from public school systems. Slightly more than one-third of all white children attended school in 1830; twenty years later, the ratio had increased to more than one-half. In northern cities, these proportions were considerably higher; there reformers were able to provide elementary-school instruction for relatively large numbers of white children, both immigrant and native-born.

By contrast, few black children had the opportunity to attend public schools. In the South, slave children were forbidden by law to learn to read and write. Recalled one former slave many years later, "dey [owners] didn't teach 'em nothin' but wuk [work]." By the 1830s, schools for even the children of free people of color had to meet in secret. In the North, many black households needed the labor of children to survive, resulting in black school-attendance rates well below those of whites. Throughout the Northeast and Midwest, black children remained at the mercy of local officials, who decided whether they could attend the schools their parents' tax dollars helped to support.

All over the country, education remained an intensely grassroots affair, belying the reformers' call for uniform systems. Local communities raised money for the teacher's salary, built the schoolhouse, and provided wood to heat the building. Southern states did not develop uniform public education systems until the late nineteenth century. Lacking local, popular support for tax-supported schooling, poor white children remained illiterate, while wealthy parents hired tutors for their own children or sent them to private academies.

Other forms of education also multiplied. The number of colleges more than doubled (46 to 119) between 1830 and 1850. Founded in 1837, Mount Holyoke, a college for women in Massachusetts, and Oberlin in Ohio, which accepted black men as well as women of both races, were unusual for their liberal admission policies. Lyceums—informal lectures offered by speak-

■ Artist Albertus Browere titled this 1844 painting *Mrs. McCormick's General Store*. These barefoot boys are getting into trouble. Reformers advocated universal, compulsory schooling as one way to rid street corners of young mischief makers. Had these youngsters lived in the country, they probably would have been working in the fields.

ers who traveled from place to place—attracted hordes of adults regardless of their formal education. By the mid-1830s, approximately 3,000 local lecture associations, mostly in New England and the Midwest, were sponsoring such series. In addition, local agricultural fairs offered informal practical instruction to rural people.

Formal training for professionals such as physicians and lawyers also changed during this period. By the 1830s, almost all states required that doctors be licensed. The only way to attain such a license was to attend medical school, and these schools still excluded women. In regions of the country where medical schools appeared, the self-taught midwife gradually yielded to the formally educated male physician. In contrast, in rural communities of black and white Southerners, Native Americans, and Hispanics, women continued to practice time-honored ways of midwifery and healing.

Alternative Visions of Social Life

As in education, the crosscurrents of reform showed up clearly in debates about sexuality, the family, and the proper role of women. For example, reformer Sylvester Graham argued that even husbands and wives must monitor their sexual activity. Sexual excess between husband and wife, he claimed, caused ills ranging from headaches, chills, and impaired vision, to loss of memory, epilepsy, insanity, and "disorders of the liver and kidneys." Graham also promoted a diet of special crackers made of wheat flour (now called Graham crackers) and fruit (in place of alcohol and meat) in addition to a regimen of plain living reinforced with cold showers.

The crosscurrents of reform showed up most clearly in debates about sexuality, the family, and the proper role of women.

Other reformers disagreed with Graham's notion that people must repress their sexuality to lead a good and healthy life. Defying conventional standards of morality, sponsors of a number of experimental communities discouraged marriage-based monogamy (a legal commitment between a man and a woman to engage in sexual relations only with each other) and made child-rearing the responsibility of the entire community rather than just the child's parents. These communities were **communitarian**—seeking to break down exclusive relations between husband and wife, parent and child, employer and employee—in an effort to advance the well-being of the whole group, not just individuals within it. These communities were also **utopian**, seeking to forge new kinds of social relationships that would, in the eyes of the reformers, serve as a model for the larger society.

Many of these communities explicitly challenged mainstream views related to property ownership and the system of wage labor as well as rules governing relations between the sexes. The Scottish industrialist and socialist Robert Owen founded New Harmony in Indiana in 1825, basing his experiment on principles of "cooperative labor." In 1826 Owen released his "Declaration of Mental Independence," which condemned private property, organized religion, and marriage. By this time, 900 persons had joined the New Harmony order.

Several other prominent communitarian experiments that challenged conventional marital relations were vehemently criticized, and participants were sometimes physically attacked by their neighbors. Salt Lake City Mormons, who practiced plural marriage, continued to meet intense hostility from outsiders. Another group, the Oneida Community, founded in upstate New York near Utica in 1848 by John Humphrey Noyes, went even further than the Mormons in advocating an alternative to monogamy. At its peak, Oneida consisted of 300 members who endorsed the founder's notion of "complex marriage," meaning communal sexual unions and community-regulated parent-child relations. Charges of adultery eventually forced Noyes to flee the country and seek refuge in Canada.

Utopian Communities before the Civil War

Network of Reformers

Many moral reforms overlapped with and reinforced each other. For example, women's rights advocates often supported temperance. Husbands who drank, they pointed out, were more likely to abuse their wives and children. Sarah and Angelina Grimké gained prominence as both abolitionists and advocates for women's rights. They also followed Sylvester Graham's program, and for a short time they sported "bloomers" (loose fitting pants, popularized by dress reformer Amelia Bloomer) in place of cumbersome dresses.

Dorothea Dix spearheaded a major reform effort that gained the support of a variety of politicians and activists. As a young woman, Dix had worked as a teacher and writer. In 1836 she visited England, where she met several prominent British reformers. Five years later she volunteered to teach a Sunday school class for women at an East Cambridge jail not far from Boston. Her first day there, in March 1841, changed her life—and the face of American antebellum reform—forever.

Dix found among the inmates not only women accused of prostitution and vagrancy, but also women who were clearly mentally ill. All of them were miserable, shivering in the cold. Dix was horrified that insane persons were imprisoned with criminals. She set out on a campaign to investigate the conditions under which the mentally ill were confined. Over the next 18 months, she investigated every prison, almshouse, and asylum in Massachusetts. She kept careful notes, which later formed the basis of her petitions, or "memorials," demanding better treatment for all insane persons. At one place she found people "confined…in *cages, closets, cellars, stalls, pens! Chained, naked, beaten with rods,* and *lashed* into obedience." Dix presented her findings to the Massachusetts state legislature. Heartened by the public outcry she had inspired, she widened her investigation to include the states of Rhode Island and New York. In the late 1840s, she traveled to another dozen states in the South, Mid-Atlantic, and Midwest.

DOCUMENT
Trial of Susan B. Anthony

The organized women's rights movement drew its greatest inspiration from the abolitionist cause. Elizabeth Cady Stanton, for example, and other American women attended the 1840 World Anti-Slavery Convention in London. Male leaders of the British and Foreign Anti-Slavery Society relegated the women delegates to a balcony and excluded them from the formal deliberations. Eight years later, Cady Stanton worked with Lucretia Mott, a Quaker minister, Susan B. Anthony, a women's rights activist, and other similarly inclined men and women to organize a women's rights convention at Seneca Falls, New York.

Women's rights advocates made some progress independent of the abolitionist movement. For instance, in 1839 Mississippi passed the nation's first Married Women's Property Law. The ruling was intended to protect the fortunes of the married daughters of wealthy planters. In 1848 both New York and Pennsylvania passed legislation giving married women control over any real property (land) or personal property they brought to marriage.

Massachusetts resident Margaret Fuller explored many reform impulses of the day during her brief life (1810–1850). Educated in the classics by her father at home in Cambridge, in the 1830s she embraced a new intellectual sensibility called Transcendentalism. Fuller cultivated friendships with two other famous Transcendentalists living in the Boston area: Ralph Waldo Emerson and Henry David Thoreau. Transcendentalists believed in the primacy of the spirit and the essential harmony between people and the natural world. They took their inspiration from European Romantics, who celebrated the beauty of nature in art, music, and literature. In 1845 Fuller published *Woman in the Nineteenth Century*, one of the first feminist essays written by an American. "I would have Woman lay aside all thought, such as she habitually cherishes, of being led and taught by men," wrote Fuller. She then embraced the role of investigative journalist, writing about the plight of slaves, Indians, and imprisoned women for the New York *Tribune*.

The United States Extends Its Reach

Efforts to reform society at home went hand-in-hand with a determination to expand the nation's borders, especially in the Southwest. In the mid-1840s, the editor of the *New York Morning News* declared that the United States had a "manifest destiny" to "overspread the continent" and claim the "desert wastes." Those inhabiting the "desert wastes"— Mexican settlers and a variety of Indian groups—apparently would have little say in the matter.

The term *manifest destiny* soon became a catchall phrase, justifying American efforts not only to conquer new territory but also to seek out new markets for its goods across the oceans.

Global Trade

International political developments and technological innovations led to expanded opportunities for trading. In 1846 Britain repealed its exclusionary Corn Laws, which had protected its own agricultural markets from foreign competition. As a result, farmers in the U.S. Midwest had fresh incentive to produce wheat for export. The invention of the swift clipper ship, which ushered in "the golden age of American shipping," also helped in the expansion of global trade. Narrow-bodied vessels topped with large sails on towering masts, the new ships "clipped off" the miles. American merchants used them to import tea from China and wool from Australia. Investors from the eastern United States financed trading companies that sold antelope skins, beaver pelts, and cured beef to markets in Cuba and Europe.

Among all American exports to foreign countries, cotton was king, accounting for half of the total goods shipped after 1840. Southern planters and northern merchants alike made huge profits from the cotton trade. In 1840 English textile manufacturers depended on the fiber, and the American South produced about three-quarters of their supply. No wonder then that southern slave owners were eager to extend their land holdings into Texas. They were joined in that hope by residents of the western states, men such as former Tennessee politician Davy Crockett, hoping to press into the fresh lands of the far West and Southwest.

The Lone Star Republic

In the early 1830s, the Mexican government became alarmed by the growing number of American emigrants to Texas. Worried that the settlers would refuse to pledge allegiance to Mexico, that country closed the Texas border to further in-migration. By 1835 only one out of every eight residents of Texas was a *Tejano* (that is, a native Spanish speaker); the rest, numbering 30,000, hailed from the United States. The U.S.-born Texians, together with some prominent *Tejanos*, had become increasingly well armed and militant. They organized volunteer patrols to attack Indian settlements. These forces became the precursor of the Texas Rangers, a statewide organization of law enforcement officers.

> *In the early 1830s, the Mexican government became alarmed by the growing number of American emigrants to Texas.*

In 1836 the Texians decided to press for independence from Mexico. Only by becoming a separate nation, they believed, could they trade freely with the United States, establish their own schools, and collect and spend their own taxes. The pro-independence Texians included Davy Crockett, who had moved there in late 1835. A few months later, Crockett and other armed Texians retreated to a Spanish mission in San Antonio called the Alamo. In March 1836, a military force led by Antonio López de Santa Anna, president of the Republic of Mexico and a general in the army, battled them for thirteen days. All 187 Texians died at the hands of Santa Anna and his men; the Mexican leader lost 600 of his own troops. Historians disagree on whether all of the Alamo defenders died fighting or if some were executed by Mexican soldiers.

In April a force of Texians and their *Tejano* allies, including military leader Juan Seguin, surprised Santa Anna and his men at the San Jacinto River and killed another 600 of them. The victors captured Santa Anna and declared themselves a new nation. Sam Houston, former U.S. congressman from Tennessee and commander in chief of the Texian army, became president of the Republic of Texas (also called the Lone Star Republic) in 1837. Some *Tejanos* who objected to Mexican high-handedness joined in supporting the new republic, including Jose Antonio Navarro, Francisco Ruiz, and Lorenzo de Zavala, who became its vice president.

In the northern territories of Mexico, many Spanish speakers had long felt abandoned by the Mexican government, which had made no provisions for their self-government and, as in the case of Texas, inhibited trade relations with the United States. Although other Mexican provinces protested the way they were treated by the government, Texas was the only Mexican state to launch a successful rebellion against Mexico.

Texas's independence raised the fears of U.S. abolitionists and imperiled blacks living in the new republic. In contrast to Mexico, which had abolished slavery in 1829, Texas approved a constitution that not only legalized slavery but also prohibited free blacks from living in the country. Greenbury Logan, a black man who owned a farm near Austin, petitioned to stay. He wrote, "Every privilege dear to a free man is taken away." But **vigilantes** forced him to leave. They also forced out many *Tejanos*. Among them was Juan Seguin, who had helped defeat Santa Anna at the Battle of San Jacinto and was now the mayor of San Antonio. Not until 1981 did another *Tejano*, Henry Cisneros, hold the office of mayor of the city of San Antonio.

The Election of 1844

As an independent republic, Texas became a hotly contested political issue in the United States. During the election of 1844, politicians began to debate whether the United States should annex Texas. Van Buren was outspoken in his opposition to the idea. As a result, the frankly expansionist Democrats spurned the former president as a candidate and nominated James K. Polk of Tennessee. They called for the "reannexation" of Texas and the "reoccupation" of Oregon. Their rallying cry became "Fifty-Four Forty or Fight," a reference to their desire to own the area (expressed in terms of its longitude and latitude coordinates) claimed by the British in present-day Canada south of Alaska and west of the Continental Divide. Kentucky congressman Henry Clay received the Whig nomination after he announced he was against the **annexation** of Texas. But under pressure from Southerners, he later changed his mind, to the disgust of party leaders.

TABLE 12-3

The Election of 1844

Candidate	Political Party	Popular Vote (%)	Electoral Vote
James K. Polk	Democratic	49.6	170
Henry Clay	Whig	48.1	105
James G. Birney	Liberty	2.3	—

Neither the Democrats nor the Whigs had shown an interest in addressing the issue of slavery directly in the last presidential election. Yet in 1844, the controversy over the annexation of Texas made it impossible for the two parties to ignore the growing controversy over bound labor. Under the banner of the young Liberty party, some abolitionists charged that territorial expansion would mean the continued growth and prosperity of the slave system; they pointed to the public pronouncements of southern planters, who were outspoken in their desire to expand their slaveholdings into the fertile lands of Texas.

DOCUMENT
James K. Polk's First Inaugural Address

For their part, Democrats and Whigs believed, correctly, that most voters would ignore slavery when they cast their ballots. Thus members of both parties tried to silence both sides of the slavery debate. They turned a deaf ear to the proslavery advocates on one hand and squelched northern abolitionist opinion by ignoring petitions to Congress on the other. In the end, Polk won the election. The expansionists had elected one of their most ardent champions to the highest office in the land.

Still, Polk was not interested in going to war with Great Britain over the vast territory of Oregon. In 1846 the two countries reached a compromise. Britain would accept the 49th parallel as the border between Canada and the United States and retain the disputed islands off the coast of Vancouver. The United States settled for one-half of its original claim to Oregon. Thereafter, it was free to turn its full attention to extending its southern and western borders.

War with Mexico

VIDEO
Moving West and the Mexican-American War

Texian leaders wanted to become part of the United States. In 1845, as one of his last acts as president, Tyler invited Texas to become the twenty-eighth state. He also understood that annexing Texas was a way to goad Mexico into open hostilities; Mexico had warned the United States that such a move would mean war. A joint resolution of both houses of Congress confirmed Texas statehood in December 1845.

MAP 12.3

THE U.S.-MEXICAN WAR During the U.S.-Mexican War, American troops marched deep into the interior of Mexico. General Winfield Scott raised the American flag over Mexico City on September 14, 1847. The treaty that concluded the war was named after the village of Guadalupe Hidalgo, a few miles north of the Mexican capital. The U.S. army withdrew the last of its troops from foreign soil in July 1848.

The boundaries between Mexico and the new state of Texas remained in dispute. Mexico recognized the Nueces River as the boundary for Texas. In contrast, Texians and U.S. politicians envisioned the boundary a hundred miles to the south at the Rio Grande. Complicating matters further, the new president, James K. Polk, had sent an envoy, John Slidell, to purchase California and a disputed section of Texas from Mexico. Mexico refused the deal. Nevertheless, around this time, Polk wrote in his diary that if he could not acquire all of New Mexico and California through diplomatic negotiation, he was determined to obtain them by force. The stage was set for war.

Armed conflict broke out in January 1846. U.S. troops, under the command of General Zachary Taylor (a veteran of wars against Tecumseh, the Seminole, and Black Hawk), clashed

INTERPRETING HISTORY

Senator John C. Calhoun Warns Against Incorporating Mexico into the United States

In January 1848, Senator John C. Calhoun delivered a speech, addressing his remarks to President Polk and to his fellow lawmakers. He urged them to resist calls to incorporate all of a conquered Mexico into the United States. Calhoun favored the spread of slavery into new territories. However, here he expresses the fear that residents of Mexico were incapable of becoming suitable U.S. citizens for "racial" reasons.

It is without example or precedent, either to hold Mexico as a province, or to incorporate her into our Union. No example of such a line of policy can be found. We have conquered many of the neighboring tribes of Indians, but we never thought of holding them in subjection—never of incorporating them into our Union. They have either been left as an independent people amongst us, or been driven into the forests.

I know further, sir, that we have never dreamt of incorporating into our Union any but the Caucasian race—the free white race. To incorporate Mexico, would be the first instance of the kind of incorporating an Indian race; for more than half of the Mexicans are Indians, and the other half is composed chiefly of mixed tribes. I protest such a union as that! . . .

Sir, it is a remarkable fact, that in the whole history of man, as far as my knowledge extends, there is no instance whatever of any civilized colored races being found equal to the establishment of free popular government, although by far the largest portion of the human family is composed of these races. . . . Are we to associate with ourselves as equals, companions, and fellow-citizens, the Indians and mixed race of Mexico? Sir, I should consider such a thing as fatal to our institutions.

Calhoun then moves on to another theme. He disputes the notion that Mexico can begin as a territory and then work its way up to statehood, following the standards Congress set for other western territories.

You can establish a Territorial Government for every State in Mexico, and there are some twenty of them. You can appoint governors, judges, and magistrates. You can give the people a subordinate government, allowing them to legislate for themselves, whilst you defray the cost. So far as the law goes, the thing is done. There is no analogy between this and our Territorial Governments. Our Territories are only an offset of our own people, or foreigners from the same regions from which we came. They are small in number. They are incapable of forming a government. It would be inconvenient for them to sustain a government, if it were formed; and they are very much obliged to the United States for undertaking the trouble, knowing that, on the attainment of their majority—when they come to manhood—at twenty-one—they will be introduced to an equality with all other members of the Union. It is entirely different with Mexico. You have no need of armies to keep your Territories in subjection. But when you incorporate Mexico, you must have powerful armies to keep them in subjection.

---

with a Mexican force near the mouth of the Rio Grande near Matamoros. Taylor had deliberately moved his troops across the Nueces River into disputed territory; his intention was to provoke an armed response from Mexico. A skirmish ensued, eleven Americans were killed, and Taylor pulled back. Polk used this military action as justification for a declaration of war against Mexico. The president declared, "American blood has been shed on American soil."

Not all Americans supported the war. Transcendentalists such as Henry David Thoreau objected to what they saw as a naked land grab. Refusing to pay taxes for what he considered a war to expand slavery, Thoreau went to jail. Nativists also objected to the war, fearing that the United States would have to assimilate thousands of Indians and Spanish-speaking Roman Catholics. Some members of Congress, including a newly elected U.S. Representative from Illinois named Abraham Lincoln, also condemned Polk's "act of aggression."

Predictably, opponents of slavery were among Polk's most outspoken critics. Soon after the outbreak of war, Representative David Wilmot of Pennsylvania attached an amendment to a bill appropriating money for the war. Called the Wilmot Proviso, the measure declared that "neither slavery nor involuntary servitude shall ever exist" in territories the United States acquired from Mexico. Though a member of the Democratic party, Wilmot spoke primarily as a white Northerner; he wanted to preserve the West for "the sons of toil of my own race and color." Wilmot's views show how racial prejudice and antislavery sentiment coexisted in the minds of many white Northerners. The House approved the proviso, but the Senate did not. Southern Democrats claimed that Congress had no right to deprive slaveholders of their private property anywhere in the nation.

> **The Wilmot Proviso declared that "neither slavery nor involuntary servitude shall ever exist" in territories the United States acquired from Mexico.**

Corwin, "Against the Mexican War"

Portrait of John C. Calhoun by Charles Bird King, c. 1818–1825.

You may call it annexation, but it is a forced annexation, which is a contradiction in terms, according to my conception. You will be involved, in one word, in all the evils which I attribute to holding Mexico as a province. In fact, it will be but a Provincial Government, under the name of a Territorial Government. How long will that last? How long will it be before Mexico will be capable of incorporation into our Union? Why, if we judge from the examples before us, it will be a very long time. Ireland has been held in subjection by England for seven or eight hundred years, and yet still remains hostile, although her people are of kindred race with the conquerors. A few French Canadians on this continent yet maintain the attitude of hostile people; and never will the time come, in my opinion, Mr. President, that these Mexicans will be reconciled to your authority. . . . Of all nations of the earth they are the most pertinacious—have the highest sense of nationality—hold out the longest, and often even with the least prospect of effecting their object. On this subject also I have conversed with officers of the army, and they all entertain the same opinion, that these people are now hostile, and will continue so. . . .

We make a great mistake, sir, when we suppose that all people are capable of self-government. We are anxious to force free government on all; and I see that it has been urged in a very respectable quarter, that it is the mission of this country to spread civil and religious liberty over all the world, and especially this continent. It is a great mistake. None but people advanced to a very high state of moral and intellectual improvement are capable, in a civilized state, of maintaining free government; and amongst those who are so purified, very few, indeed, have had the good fortune of forming a constitution capable of endurance.

Calhoun also warns that "these twenty-odd Mexican States" would eventually have power in Congress. He asks his listeners whether they would want their own states "governed by" these peoples.

Questions

1. Why does Calhoun assume that, if the United States incorporates Mexico into its territory, the federal government "must have powerful armies to keep them [Mexicans] in subjection"?
2. How might Calhoun's more extreme expansionist colleagues—those in favor of seizing all of Mexico—have countered his arguments against such action?

Source: Clyde A. Milner, ed., *Major Problems in the History of the American West: Documents and Essays* (1989), pp. 219–221.

Meanwhile, Polk launched a three-pronged campaign against Mexico. He sent Taylor into northern Mexico and ordered General Stephen Watts Kearny into New Mexico and then into California. Following the third directive of the campaign, General in Chief of the U.S. Army Winfield Scott coordinated an **amphibious landing** of 10,000 soldiers at Vera Cruz, on the Gulf of Mexico coast. Mexican forces tried to defend their homeland using guerrilla tactics. But U.S. soldiers overcame them in part by terrorizing civilians. Scott acknowledged that the men under his command had "committed atrocities to make Heaven weep and every American of Christian morals blush for his country. . . . Murder, robbery and rape of mothers and daughters in the presence of tied-up males of the families."

In September 1847, Mexico City surrendered, and the war ended. Mexico had been in no shape to resist superior U.S. firepower. The United States paid for Scott's victory with 13,000 lives and $100 million. The Mexicans lost 20,000 lives. In the Treaty of Guadalupe Hidalgo (approved by the Senate in 1848) Mexico agreed to give up its claims to Texas. The United States gained all of Texas and half of the territory of Mexico: the area west of Texas, comprising present-day New Mexico, Arizona, Utah, Nevada, and California. Male residents of areas formerly held by Mexico were given one year to decide whether to stay in the United States and become citizens or return to Mexico. They were also entitled to retain their titles to the land, a provision that proved difficult to enforce in the face of European American land hunger.

The U.S. government paid Mexico $18,250,000. Of that amount, $15 million was designated as payment for land lost; the rest was **restitution** to U.S. citizens who might bring claims against Mexico for damaged or destroyed property during the war. Americans had conflicting views of

Mexican-American War, 1846–1848

■ This painting shows the U.S. Navy going up the Tuxpan River in Mexico during the U.S.-Mexican War. Located on the Gulf Coast halfway between Vera Cruz and Tampico, Tuxpan was the last significant Mexican port to be seized by U.S. forces by the spring of 1847. Commodore M. C. Perry assembled a formidable force of marines and infantry to take over the town on April 19, 1847.

the treaty. Abolitionists saw it as a blood-drenched gift from American taxpayers to slaveholders. Others argued that Polk had squandered a rare opportunity to seize all of Mexico.

Conclusion

In the 1830s and 1840s, mass population movements affected almost every aspect of American life. Immigrants from western Europe helped to swell the nation's labor force in midwestern farming communities and eastern cities. The arrival of the Roman Catholic Irish provoked a backlash among native-born Protestants and spawned a nativist political movement. Reformers in the United States and Europe went back and forth across the Atlantic, exchanging ideas related to women's rights, abolition, and utopian communities. As European Americans pushed the boundaries of the country west and south, they clashed with Indians and with foreign powers that claimed those lands as their own. Thus migration and immigration had profound consequences for American politics, ideas, society, and economics.

Most striking was the restlessness among land-hungry slave owners and antislavery forces alike. The war with Mexico in general and the clash over the Wilmot Proviso in particular opened a new chapter in the debate over slavery. In considering the proviso, congressmen gave up their party loyalties as Democrats or Whigs and began to think of themselves as Southerners and Northerners. When Wilmot proclaimed that he wanted to preserve the West for his "own color," he revealed that even antislavery Northerners did not necessarily embrace black people as equals. When Southerners indicated that even the vast expanse of Texas would not satisfy their desire for land, they revealed that the conflict over slavery was far from over. In fact, that conflict was about to enter a new and ominous stage.

Sites to Visit

The American Whig Party, 1834–1856
odur.let.rug.nl/~usa/E/uswhig/whigsxx.htm
This site explores the rise and fall of the anti-Jackson Whig party.

Alexis de Tocqueville Tour: Exploring Democracy in America
www.tocqueville.org/
Text and images are part of this companion site to C-SPAN's programming on Tocqueville.

America's First Look into the Camera: Daguerreotype Portraits and Views, 1839–1864
memory.loc.gov/ammem/daghtml/daghome.html
The Library of Congress's daguerreotype collection consists of more than 650 photographs from the 1839–1864 period. The collection includes portraits, architectural views, and some street scenes.

Influence of Prominent Abolitionists
www.loc.gov/exhibits/african/afam006.html
This Library of Congress exhibit includes pictures and text related to abolitionists.

Western Trails Project
http://skyways.lib.ks.us/KSL/trails/
This site provides primary sources and images related to the Oregon Trail and other trails and European Americans' early movement westward.

Mountain Men and the Fur Trade
www.xmission.com/~drudy/amm.html
This site includes private correspondence from early settlers in the area west of the Mississippi River.

Exploring *Amistad*
amistad.mysticseaport.org/main/welcome.html
The Mystic Seaport Museum in Mystic, Connecticut, maintains this site, which includes collections of historical documents related to the slave revolt aboard the *Amistad* and the trial that followed.

Native Americans
www.americanwest.com/pages/nathome.htm
A collection of links to homepages of Native American nations.

American Presidency: A Glorious Burden
americanhistory.si.edu/presidency/index.html
The Smithsonian Institution maintains this site on American presidents.

"Been Here So Long": Selections from the WPA American Slave Narratives
newdeal.feri.org/asn/index.htm
A site devoted to the interviews of former slaves conducted in the late 1930s.

The U.S.-Mexican War, 1846–1848
www.pbs.org/Kera/usmexicanwar/
This bilingual site explores the causes, course, and outcome of the Mexican-American War.

For Further Reading

General

Michael Holt, *The Rise and Fall of the American Whig Party: Jacksonian Politics and the Onset of the Civil War* (1999).
Mary P. Ryan, *The Cradle of the Middle Class: The Family in Oneida County, New York, 1790–1865* (1983).
Charles G. Sellers, *The Market Revolution: Jacksonian America, 1815–1846* (1991).
David J. Weber, *The Spanish Frontier in North America* (1992).

Mass Migrations

John Ehle, *Trail of Tears: The Rise and Fall of the Cherokee Nation* (1988).
John Mack Faragher, *Women and Men on the Overland Trail* (1979).
Walter Johnson, *Soul by Soul: The Inside of the Antebellum Slave Market* (1999).
Philip J. Schwarz, *Migrants Against Slavery: Virginians and the Nation* (2001).

A Multitude of Voices in the National Political Arena

Donald B. Cole, *Martin Van Buren and the American Political System* (1984).
Paul A. Gilje, *The Road to Mobocracy: Popular Disorder in New York City, 1763–1834* (1987).
Daniel Walker Howe, *The Political Culture of the American Whigs* (1979).
David R. Roediger, *The Wages of Whiteness: Race and the Making of the American Working Class* (rev. ed., 1999).

Reform Impulses

Charles Capper, *Margaret Fuller: An American Romantic Life* (1992).
Carl Kaestle, *Pillars of the Republic: Common Schools and American Society, 1780–1860* (1983).
Henry Mayer, *All on Fire: William Lloyd Garrison and the Abolition of Slavery* (1998).
Shirley J. Yee, *Black Women Abolitionists: A Study in Activism, 1828–1860* (1992).

The United States Extends Its Reach

Arnoldo De León, *The Tejano Community, 1836–1900* (1982).
Richard Griswold Del Castillo, *The Treaty of Guadalupe Hidalgo: A Legacy of Conflict* (1990).
David Alan Johnson, *Founding the Far West: California, Oregon, and Nevada, 1840–1890* (1992).
Paul D. Lack, *The Texas Revolutionary Experience: A Political and Social History, 1835–1836* (1992).

For quizzes and other resources on these topics, go to www.longmanamericanhistory.com.

1848	Gold is discovered in California
Women's Rights Convention, Seneca Falls, New York
Free Soil party is founded
1849	"Forty-Niners" migrate to California
1850	Clayton-Bulwer Treaty
Compromise of 1850; Fugitive Slave Law
1851	Fort Laramie Treaty
Indiana Constitution bars in-migration of African Americans
1852	American (Nativist) party is founded
Abolitionists free fugitive slave Shadrach
Harriet Beecher Stowe, *Uncle Tom's Cabin*
1853	Gadsden Purchase
Matthew Perry's fleet enters Tokyo Harbor
1854	Kansas-Nebraska Act
Republican party is founded
Cyrus McCormick patents mechanical reaper
Henry David Thoreau, *Walden*
1855	William Walker captures Granada, Nicaragua
Pottowatamie Creek massacre
Walt Whitman, *Leaves of Grass*
1856	Lecompton (Kansas) Constitution
1857	*Dred Scott* Supreme Court Case
George Fitzhugh, *Cannibals All*
1858	Lincoln-Douglas debates
1859	Harpers Ferry raid
Harriet Wilson, *Our Nig*
Cortina's War in Texas
1860	South Carolina secedes from Union
1861	Confederate States of America is formed
Civil War begins
U.S. Sanitary Commission is founded
1862	Minnesota (Santee) Sioux uprising
Congress passes Homestead, Morrill, and Pacific Railroad acts
Battle of Antietam
1863	Emancipation Proclamation
Richmond bread riots
Battle of Gettysburg
Northern antidraft riots
Lincoln delivers Gettysburg Address

PART FIVE

Disunion and Reunion

THE CIVIL WAR WAS THE COUNTRY'S GREATEST POLITICAL AND MORAL crisis. By 1860 the two-party system could no longer contain the dispute between proslavery and antislavery forces. That dispute centered on the fate of slavery in new western territories. Tensions accompanied large-scale migration to the west, and the 1849 Gold Rush pushed California—and the issue of slavery there—to the forefront of the nation's attention. Several dramatic developments—the secession of southern states from the Union, the formation of the Confederate States of America, and a Confederate attack on a federal fort in Charleston Harbor—precipitated all-out war. In the spring of 1861, few people could have anticipated that the conflict would drag on for four long years and claim more than 600,000 lives.

The Second Party system, based on divisions between Whigs and Democrats, unraveled in the 1850s. Both parties represented coalitions of groups that expressed cultural, not sectional, sensibilities. Yet a series of events led to a **realignment** of parties into northern and southern camps. Many Northerners chafed under the Fugitive Slave Act of 1850, which required that all citizens assist law enforcement agents in retrieving runaway slaves for their owners. The founding of the Republican party in 1854 gave a political voice to Northerners hoping to preserve the western territories for family farmers who would not have to compete for land and labor with large slaveholders. In 1857 the Supreme Court ruled that black people had no rights that any court was bound to respect. Violent conflicts between proslavery and antislavery forces in Kansas and a failed raid by abolitionists on Harpers Ferry, Virginia, in 1859 revealed that legislators' resolutions and maneuverings were insufficient to stave off bloodshed.

In pursuing a militant nationalism, Confederates hoped to compensate for their relative weakness in terms of population and industrial capacity compared with the North. They believed that they could use a large, docile black labor force to grow food and serve as a support system for the army. They anticipated that European nations, dependent on southern cotton, would extend them diplomatic recognition and that white civilians would rally to the defense of their homeland no matter what the price in money or blood. Confederates also believed that western Indians would gladly assist them in their cause against a hated U.S. army and that brilliant southern generals could indefinitely outstrategize a huge, lumbering invading army. On all these counts they miscalculated, but their miscalculations were revealed gradually.

During the war, white Southerners had to contend with two major unanticipated consequences of the conflict. First, war mobilization efforts across the South required the centralization of government and economic policymaking. Principled states' rights supporters opposed these efforts. Second, slaves and free blacks alike proved traitorous to the Confederate cause. In myriad ways—running away from their owners and spying for the enemy, slowing their work pace in the fields, and fighting for the Union army—black people served as combatants in the war. They fought for their families and their freedom and for a country that would grant them full citizenship rights. In the North, only in late 1862 did President Abraham Lincoln announce that the United States aimed to destroy slavery, but violent antidraft, antiblack riots in several cities showed that the northern population was deeply divided over emancipation.

Soon after the end of the war and Lincoln's death, in April 1865, congressional Republicans began to challenge President Andrew Johnson's plan for reconstructing the South; they considered it too lenient toward the former Confederate states. In 1867 these political leaders had enough votes to enact their own plan, calling for the enfranchisement of black men in the South, the reorganization of southern state governments under leadership loyal to the Union, and the enactment of a labor contract system between southern landowners and black laborers.

Members of the Republican party backed a strong Union, a federal system in which the central government would ensure that individual men could pursue their own self-interest in the marketplace of goods and ideas. Yet the Civil War era exposed the limits of the Republican vision. The Plains Indians sought not citizenship but freedom from federal interference. Women and working people challenged various components of the Republican ideal, with its emphasis on unbridled individualism and federal subsidies of business. African Americans aspired to own property, vote, and send their children to school, just as other nineteenth-century Americans did. They wanted to farm their own land and care for their own families free from white intrusion. Yet congressional Republicans did not enact large-scale land redistribution programs; most thought that once the rebels were subdued and slavery abolished, their duty was done.

Civil strife persisted into the postwar period. Union generals turned from quelling the southern rebellion to putting down armed resistance among the Plains Indians. Former rebels formed vigilante groups to attack black voters and their allies in the South. By the early 1870s, most Northerners had lost interest in the welfare of the former slaves and acquiesced as former Confederates reclaimed state governments. The last occupying forces withdrew from the South in 1877. In welding the country together as a single economic and political unit, the Republicans had triumphed. However, white Southerners retained control over their local social and political affairs. The revolution to secure African American civil rights was stalled for nearly 100 years.

1864	Fort Pillow massacre of African American (Union) soldiers Sand Creek (Colorado) massacre Sherman's march to the sea
1865	Freedmen's Bureau is formed Confederacy is defeated Lincoln is assassinated; Andrew Johnson becomes president Thirteenth Amendment is ratified
1866	Civil Rights Act of 1866 National Labor Union is founded Equal Rights Association is founded Ku Klux Klan is organized Congress approves Fourteenth Amendment
1867	National Grange is founded United States purchases Alaska from Russia Reconstruction Act of 1867
1868	Johnson is impeached and acquitted U.S.-China Burlingame Treaty Colored Labor Union is founded Fourteenth Amendment is ratified
1869	Congress approves Fifteenth Amendment Transcontinental Railroad is completed National Woman Suffrage Association and American Woman Suffrage Association are formed Knights of Labor is founded
1870	Fifteenth Amendment is ratified
1871	Ku Klux Klan Act
1872	Apex Mining Act of 1872 Congress creates Yellowstone National Park Susan B. Anthony attempts to vote Crédit Moblier scandal
1873	Timber Culture Act Onset of depression
1874	Freedman's Savings Bank fails
1875	Civil Rights Act Resumption Act Whiskey Ring is exposed
1876	Battle of Little Big Horn Contested presidential election between Rutherford B. Hayes and Samuel J. Tilden
1877	Compromise of 1877 California Workingmen's party is formed Great Railroad Strike

CHAPTER 13

The Crisis over Slavery, 1848–1860

O N JANUARY 24, 1848, HENRY WILLIAM BIGLER TOOK A BREAK FROM BUILDING A SAWMILL FOR JOHN Sutter in California's Sacramento Valley and penned in his pocket diary, "This day some kind of mettle was found . . . that looks like goald."

GOLD! News of the discovery at Sutter's mill spread like wildfire. Immigrants from all over the world and migrants from all over the United States began to pour into the foothills of the Sierra Nevada Mountains in 1849. Dubbed "the Forty-Niners," they journeyed westward across the mountains, from the **tenements** of New York City and the great plantations of Mississippi; north from Mexico; and over the oceans, from western Europe, China, and South America. Equipping themselves with simple mining tools, the Forty-Niners began to dig for buried treasure, determined to stake a claim and make a fortune.

During the Gold Rush years of 1848 to 1859, various cultural groups were thrown in close proximity to each other. People from Belgium, France, Germany, Scotland, Chile, and Long Island learned to appreciate flour and corn tortillas (*tortillas de harina* and *tortillas de maiz*) and beef cooked in chile, staples of the Mexican diet. The disproportionate number of men permitted small numbers of women to challenge European American gender conventions. A gold miner might take a break from washing his clothes, straighten his aching back, and watch a Mexican woman and her daughter, well mounted on their horses, rounding up a herd of near-wild cattle. An-Choi, a Chinese immigrant woman, earned a tidy sum by opening a brothel that catered to gold miners. Biddy Mason, an enslaved woman, successfully sued for her freedom and became the first African American homesteader in Los Angeles.

■ Chinese and European American miners pan for gold in the Auburn Ravine in California in 1852.

California became part of the United States as a result of the U.S.-Mexican War. In the 1848 Treaty of Guadalupe Hidalgo, Mexico agreed to hand over territory stretching from Texas northwest to California. As a result, the United States obtained a vast expanse of land—almost 530,000 square miles—called the Mexican Cession. In addition to the land, the nation added to its population large numbers of men, women, and children already living in the area—13,000 Spanish speakers and 100,000 Indians (all former Mexican

CHAPTER OUTLINE

Regional Economies and Conflicts

Individualism vs. Group Identity

The Paradox of Southern Political Power

The Deepening Conflict over Slavery

Conclusion

Sites to Visit

For Further Reading

citizens) in California alone. After 1848 many new settlers streamed into California, and the migrants pressed for statehood. The Gold Rush exacerbated tensions over slavery, pushing the nation down the road toward the Civil War.

California became a state in 1850, but only after a bitter Congressional debate over the extension of slavery. The resulting Compromise of 1850 included several provisions bearing on the issue of slavery: California would be admitted as a free state; slave-trading would be outlawed in the District of Columbia; carved out of the Mexican Cession, the Utah and New Mexico territories could decide for themselves whether or not to legalize slavery. Finally, a new, harsh, fugitive slave law provided for the capture and return of slaves who found their way to free states in the North or West, including California. Though called a compromise, in fact these provisions inflamed the passions on both sides of the slavery debate—abolitionists in the North and slave owners in the South.

Despite California's status as a free state, the principle of free labor was often violated. In 1850 the state enacted a law that provided for the indenture or apprenticeship of Indian children to white men for indeterminate periods of time. The law also allowed for the hiring out, to the highest bidder, of adult Indians deemed guilty of **vagrancy**.

California's Fugitive Slave Law of 1852 decreed that, regardless of his or her current status, a black person who entered the state as a slave and thereafter attempted to remain on free soil was a fugitive slave. That year, three African American gold miners, Robert Perkins, Carter Perkins, and Sandy Perkins, all former slaves who had been freed by their owner, were arrested under the law and ordered re-enslaved in their native Mississippi.

Other California labor systems revealed that the principle of free labor was not carried out in practice. Chinese immigrants to California entered the country organized in companies, or district associations, indebted to merchants for their transportation and bound to work for an employer until the debt was repaid. Fearing competition from cheap labor, alarmed European Americans labeled these Asian workers "coolies" (i.e., enslaved laborers). By 1852 the Chinese in California (almost all of them men) had been pushed out of mining as a result of the discriminatory Foreign Miners Tax, a measure leveled with special force against both Chinese and Mexican miners. Although the Treaty of Guadalupe Hidalgo guaranteed U.S. citizenship rights to Mexicans, those rights were not enforced under the law. Many Mexicans found themselves vulnerable to violence and land **dispossession** perpetrated by the growing European American majority.

Continued European American migration into the Midwest, the Great Plains, and the Southwest intensified conflicts over land with Native Americans and Latinos. Rapid population growth, the coming together of many different cultures, and dramatic economic changes all fueled the conflict over slavery. All over the nation, Americans gradually united around a radical proposition: whether human beings could be held as private property was an issue on which there could be no compromise.

Regional Economies and Conflicts

It is tempting to view the decade of the 1850s with an eye toward the impending firestorm of 1861. However, in the early 1850s, few Americans could have anticipated the Civil War. At midcentury, the United States was going through a period of rapid transition. New developments such as railroads, the factory system, and more efficient farm equipment led to significant changes in regional economies and began to give shape to an emerging national economy. Migration into the Midwest accelerated. Slavery shaped life in the South, though most

United States Territorial Expansion in the 1850s

white southerners were not plantation owners. Annexation of land in the Southwest and West and the conquest of Indians on the Plains produced wrenching social upheavals for Native Americans in those regions. Meanwhile, Americans continued to wrestle with the role of slavery in this rapidly changing society, while a free labor ideology grew stronger in the North.

Native American Economies Transformed

On the Plains, Indians confronted wrenching transformations in their way of life. Forced to relocate from the Southeast to Indian Territory (present-day Oklahoma), the Five Southern ("Civilized") Tribes, the Cherokee, Choctaw, Creek, Chickasaw, and Seminole, grappled with the task of rebuilding their political institutions. By the 1850s, the Cherokee had established a new capital at Talequah, along with public schools. They published a Cherokee newspaper (the *Advocate*) and created a flourishing print culture in their own language.

To the north and west of Indian Territory, Plains Indian tribes such as the Sioux, Kiowa, and Arapaho exploited the horse, which had been introduced by Europeans in the Southwest in the seventeenth century. By raiding, trading, and breeding, these groups increased their stock of horses, which they used to hunt bison and transport their lodges and food from site to site. With abundant food and the means to trade with whites, these groups prospered for a brief period in the mid-nineteenth century. Their beadwork and animal-skin painting exemplified the artistic vitality of their cultures.

In the 1850s, U.S. officials negotiated treaties with various Plains Indian groups to enable European Americans to move west without fear of attack. Most settlers were bent on heading straight for California or the Northwest, traversing the Plains, which they called the Great American Desert in the mistaken belief that the absence of trees there demonstrated the infertility of the soil. The Fort Laramie Treaty of 1851 and the Treaty of Fort Atkinson three years later provided that the government could build roads and establish forts along western trails and that, in return, Indians would be compensated with supplies and food for their loss of hunting rights in the region. A young Cheyenne woman, Iron Teeth, recalled "the government presents" to her people in these terms: "We were given beef, but we did not care for this kind of meat. Great piles of bacon were stacked upon the prairies and distributed to us, but we used it only to make fires or to grease robes for tanning." She and her family sought out other items from government trading posts: "brass kettles, coffee-pots, curve-bladed butcher knives, boxes of black and white thread."

Land Conflicts in the Southwest

To the Southwest, the United States had gained control over a vast expanse of land, provoking legal and political conflicts over the rights and labor of the people who lived there, both natives and newcomers. Under the terms of the Treaty of Guadalupe Hidalgo, Mexico **ceded** not only California but also the province of New Mexico, territory that included the present-day states of New Mexico, Arizona, Utah, Nevada, and western Colorado. In 1853 the United States bought an additional tract of land from Mexico, 55,000 acres located in the area south of the Gila River (in present-day New Mexico and Arizona). Overseen by the U.S. secretary of war, a Mississippi planter named Jefferson Davis, the agreement was called the Gadsden Purchase (after James Gadsden, a railroad promoter and one of the American negotiators).

In Texas newly arrived European Americans battled native *Tejanos* (people of Mexican origin or descent) for political and economic supremacy. White migrants from the southern United States brought their slaves with them to the region, claiming that the institution of slavery was crucial for commercial development. German immigrants came to central and east Texas, founding towns with German names such as Fredericksburg, Weimar, and Schulenburg. During the 1850s, **commercial farming** continued to replace **subsistence homesteading** as the

▲ MAP 13.1 TERRITORIAL EXPANSION IN THE NINETEENTH CENTURY
As a result of the Mexican War (1846–1848), the United States won the territory west of Texas by conquest. In 1853, James Gadsden, U.S. ambassador to Mexico, received congressional approval to pay Mexico $15 million for 55,000 square miles in present-day southern Arizona and New Mexico. That year marked the end of U.S. continental expansion.

cattle industry spread and the railroads penetrated the region. Although European Americans monopolized the courts and regional political institutions, *Tejanos* retained cultural influence throughout Texas, dominating the cuisine and styles of music and architecture.

Some Spanish-speaking residents in the Southwest reacted forcefully when U.S. courts disregarded the land titles held by *Californios* and *Tejanos*. In the early 1850s, California authorities battled Mexican social bandits such as Joaquin Murrieta, who, with his men, raided European American settlements. Murrieta and others argued that they were justified in stealing from privileged European Americans who, they claimed, disregarded the lives and property of Mexicans. In 1859 in the Rio Grande Valley of Texas, tensions between the *Tejano* majority and groups of European American law enforcement officers known as the Texas Rangers erupted into full-scale warfare. Juan Cortina, who had fought on the side of Mexico during the Mexican War, orchestrated attacks on European Americans and their property in the vicinity of Brownsville. U.S. retaliation led to Cortina's War, pitting the Mexican leader against a young U.S. colonel, Robert E. Lee. Cortina became a hero to *Tejanos*. "You have been robbed of your property, incarcerated, chased, murdered, and hunted like wild beasts," he declared, "to me is entrusted the work of breaking the chains of your slavery."

Ethnic and Economic Diversity in the Midwest

Migrants to the Midwest in these years encountered less resistance. The Yankee Strip (named for the northeasterners who migrated there) ran through northern Ohio, Indiana, and Illinois and encompassed the entire states of Michigan, Wisconsin, and Minnesota. Here migrants from New England settled and established public schools and Congregational churches. Immigrants from western Europe also made a home in this region—the Germans, Belgians, and Swiss in Wisconsin, the Scandinavians in Minnesota. At times cultural conflict wracked even the smallest rural settlements. In some Wisconsin villages, equally matched numbers of Yankees and Germans contended for control over the local public schools, with the group in power posting notices for school board elections in its own language, hoping that its rivals would not show up at the polls.

The lower Midwest, including the southern portions of Ohio, Indiana, and Illinois, retained strong cultural ties to the southern states, from which many settlers had migrated. Though residing in free states, they maintained broad support for the institution of slavery. In some cases, they outnumbered their Yankee counterparts and managed to shape the legal system in a way that reflected a distinct antiblack bias. For example, Indiana's state constitution, approved in 1851, prohibited black migrants from making contracts with whites, testifying in trials that involved whites, voting, and entering the state.

Most rural midwestern households followed the seasonal rhythms characteristic of traditional systems of agriculture. However, by the mid-nineteenth century, family farming had become dependent on expensive machinery and hostage to the national and international grain markets. John Deere's steel plow (invented in 1837) and Cyrus McCormick's horse-drawn mechanical reaper (patented in 1854) boosted levels of grain production. Improved agricultural efficiency meant that the Midwest, both upper and lower, was fast becoming the breadbasket of the nation.

Regional Economies of the South

Like the Midwest, the South at midcentury had its own diversity. The South Atlantic states encompassed a number of regional economies. Bolstered by the high price of cotton on the world market, slave plantations prospered in the Black Belt, a wide swath of fertile soil stretching west from Georgia. In many areas of the South, planters concentrated their money and energy on cotton, diverting slaves from nonagricultural labor to toil in the fields. During the 1850s, enslaved Virginia sawmill laborers, South Carolina skilled artisans, and Georgia textile mill operatives all found themselves reduced to the status of cotton hands. In some cases, white laborers took their places in mills and workshops. In other parts of the South, slaves combined field work with nonagricultural work.

Increasingly, northern critics described the South as a land of economic extremes, with wealthy planters enjoying their white-columned mansions while degraded blacks slaved obediently in the fields. The reality was more complicated. Even among whites, there were huge variations in material conditions and daily experiences. A large amount of wealth in land and slaves was concentrated among a small percentage of the white population, and many non-slaveholding whites were **tenant farmers**, leasing their land, mules, and implements from wealthy planters. In some areas, as many as one of five farms was operated by tenant farmers.

At the same time, about half the total southern white population consisted of **yeoman** farmers, families that owned an average of 50 acres and produced most of what they consumed themselves, with the occasional help of a hired hand (a leased slave or a wage-earning white person). In upcountry Georgia and South Carolina, yeoman farmers maintained local economies that were little affected by the cotton culture of the great planters in the Black Belt. These families grew what they needed: corn for themselves and their livestock and small amounts of cotton that the women spun, wove, and then sewed into clothing. Men and women alike labored in neighborhood networks of exchange, trading farm produce such as milk and eggs for services such as shoemaking and blacksmithing.

The institution of slavery discouraged immigrants from moving to the rural South in large numbers. German artisans realized that slave labor would undercut their own wages, and Scandinavian farmers understood that they could not compete with large planters in terms of landowning or slave owning. However, the ethnic diversity of southern port cities offered a striking contrast to the countryside, where native-born Protestants predominated. In 1860, 54 percent of all skilled workers and 69 percent of unskilled workers in Mobile, Alabama, were immigrants.

Throughout the slave states, black people continued to challenge the underpinnings of white supremacy. On the back roads of the plantation counties, late at night, poor workers of both races colluded to deprive the planter elite of their ill-gotten gain. Slaves swapped hams pilfered from smokehouses and bags of cotton lifted from storehouses for cash and goods offered by landless whites.

Southern blacks were a diverse group. In the cities, planters allowed highly skilled slaves to hire themselves out and keep part of the money they earned for themselves. In their pride of craft and in their relative freedom to come and go as they pleased, these people inhabited a world that was neither completely slave nor completely free. Located primarily in the upper South and in the largest towns, communities composed of free people of color supported churches and clandestine schools, mocking the white notion that all black people possessed a childlike temperament and were incapable of caring for themselves.

A Free Labor Ideology in the North

In reaction to the southern slave system, the rural areas of the Northeast and Mid-Atlantic spawned a potent **free labor ideology**, which held that workers should reap what they sow, unfettered by legal systems of slavery and indentured servitude. Free labor advocates glorified the family farmer, the sturdy landowner of modest means, the husband and father who labored according to the dictates of the season and owed his soul—and his vote and the land he tilled—to no master. Nevertheless, the reality that sustained this ideal was eroding in the North during the 1850s.

More and more Northerners were earning wages by working for bosses, rather than tilling their own land. Faced with competition from Midwestern farmers and burdened by unfavorable growing conditions imposed by rocky soil and a long winter, New Englanders were migrating to nearby towns and mill villages and to the West. By 1860 the region's textile and shoemaking industries were largely mechanized. From New Hampshire to Rhode Island, growing numbers of water-powered factories perched along the **fall line**, where rivers spilled swiftly out of the foothills and into the coastal plain. The all-white factory workforce included men and women, adults and children, Irish Catholics and native-born Protestants, failed farmers and young men and women eager to leave the uncertain, hardscrabble life of the countryside for the promise of the mill towns and the seaport cities.

Although Northerners in general contrasted themselves to the "backward slave South," their region of the country retained elements of unfree labor systems. New Jersey did not officially emancipate the last of its slaves until 1846, and throughout the North, vestiges of slavery lingered through the mid-nineteenth century. As a group of disproportionately poor people, blacks in New England, the Mid-Atlantic, and the Midwest were vulnerable to labor exploitation, including indentured servitude and a system of "apprenticeship" whereby black children were taken from their parents and forced to work for whites.

Many nonslave workers did not receive pay for their labors. As is the case today, wives and mothers throughout the country performed almost all of their work in the home without monetary compensation, although the measure of a white man was rendered

■ Maine textile workers, with their shuttles, pose for a formal portrait around 1860. Although women factory workers developed a collective identity distinct from that of middle-class wives, most young, native-born women eventually married and withdrew from the paid labor force. Many male factory workers were skeptical that women could or should play an effective role in labor organizations such as unions. Nevertheless, women workers in a number of industries, including textiles and shoes, formed labor organizations in the antebellum period.

more and more in cash terms. On farms and in textile mills such as those of Pawtucket, Rhode Island, children played a key role in the livelihood of individual households but received little or nothing in cash wages. Some members of the white working classes began to condemn "**wage slavery**," a system that deprived them of what they considered a fair reward for their labors and left them at the mercy of merchant capitalists and factory bosses. These workers charged that they were paid so little by employers that their plight was similar to that of black slaves in the South.

Different regions developed specialized economies. In turn, these regions relied on each other for the production of staple crops and manufactured goods. The result was a national economy. Southern slaves produced the cotton processed in New England textile mills. Midwestern farmers grew the grain that fed eastern consumers. California Forty-Niners discovered the gold that expanded the national currency supply. Yet these patterns of economic interdependence were insufficient to resolve the persistent political question: Which groups of people are entitled to American citizenship, with all the rights and privileges that the term implies?

Individualism vs. Group Identity

In every region of the country, discriminatory ideas and practices increasingly exerted force. People were defined ever more strongly on the basis of their nationality, language, religion, and skin color. They were more and more limited in their legal status and the

■ Just as American writers explored questions of national identity, American artists portrayed everyday scenes related to the vitality of American enterprise and democracy. This painting, *Raftsmen Playing Cards* (1847), was one from George Caleb Bingham's series of pictures of Missouri rivermen. A contemporary observer speculated that the youth on the right is "a mean and cunning scamp, probably the black sheep of a good family, and a sort of vagabond idler." Large rivers such as the Missouri and Mississippi remained powerful symbols of freedom in the American imagination.

jobs they could obtain. Degrading images of legally vulnerable groups—blacks, Chinese, Hispanos—became a part of popular culture, in the songs people sang and the pictures they saw in books and magazines. Through these means, native-born Americans of British stock sought to distance themselves from people of color and from immigrants.

Paradoxically, some writers began to highlight the idea of American individualism during this time. Such authors extolled what they considered the universal qualities embedded in American nationhood. They believed that the United States consisted not of distinctive and competing groups, but of a collection of individuals, all bent on pursuing their own self-interest, variously defined. They believed that the "representative" American was ambitious and acquisitive, eager to make more money and buy new things.

Yet not everyone could afford to embrace this optimistic form of individualism. Many who were marginalized found emotional support, and in some cases even political power, in a strong group identity. For example, on the Plains, the Sioux Indians resisted the idea that U.S. officials could carve up territory and sell land to individual farmers at the expense of a people that pursued the buffalo across artificial political boundaries. During negotiations at Fort Laramie in 1851, Black Hawk, a leader of the Oglala Sioux, condemned the whites with his understatement, "You have split my land and I don't like it." In contrast to the Plains Indians, who wanted no role in American politics, African Americans and white women strove for full citizenship rights. These groups looked forward to the day when each person was accorded the same rights and was free to pursue his or her own talents and ambitions.

Putting into Practice Ideas of Social Inferiority

By promoting ideas related to the supposed inferiority of African Americans, Hispanos, and immigrants, European American men could justify barring these groups from the rights of citizenship and landownership as well as from nonmenial kinds of employment. In California, U.S. officials justified the exclusion of blacks, Indians, Chinese, and the poorest Mexicans from citizenship rights by claiming that members of these groups were nonwhite or, in the words of one state judge writing in 1854, "not of white blood." (Of course, the concept of "white blood" has no scientific basis because the different blood types—A, B, AB, and O—are found among all peoples.)

> *The precarious social status of various groups was revealed in patterns of their work.*

The precarious social status of various groups was revealed in patterns of their work. In California, white men pursued opportunities on farms and in factories while increasing numbers of Chinese men labored as laundrymen and domestic servants. Indians toiled as field hands under white supervision. In rural Texas, Anglos established plantations and ranches while more and more Mexicans worked as *vaqueros* (cowboys), shepherds, sidewalk vendors, and **freighters**. In Massachusetts mill towns, white men and women served as the forefront of an industrial labor force while many African Americans of both sexes and all ages were confined to work in kitchens and outdoors as sweepers, cart drivers, and hawkers of goods.

Despite the divergent regional economies that shaped them, emerging ideologies of racial inferiority were strikingly similar. European Americans stereotyped all Chinese, Mexicans, and African Americans as promiscuous, crafty, "degraded," and intellectually inferior to whites. Such prejudices, in places as diverse as Boston, San Antonio, and San Francisco, prevented many people of color from reaching the limits of their own talents in mid-nineteenth-century America.

"A Teeming Nation"—America in Literature

Ideas about ethnic and racial difference coexisted with notions of American individualism, which stressed forms of universal equality. The variety of voices that gave expression to the national ideals of personal striving and ambition suggested the growth, energy, and vitality of the United States in the 1850s. In the Northeast, writers such as Ralph Waldo

DOCUMENT

"Moby Dick" by Herman Melville

INTERPRETING HISTORY

Professor Howe on the Subordination of Women

Antebellum southern elites prized what they called "natural" hierarchical social relations: the authority of fathers and husbands over daughters and wives, parents over children, rich over poor, and whites over blacks. According to slaveholders, clergy, and scholars, these relationships provided social stability and ensured that the weak and dependent would receive care from the rich and powerful. In July 1850, George Howe, professor of biblical literature at the Theological Seminary at Columbia, South Carolina, addressed the graduating class of a private women's academy. Howe suggested that the roles of women (elite white women) were enduring and never-changing.

The Endowments, Position and Education of Woman. An Address Delivered Before the Hemans and Sigourney Societies of the Female High School at Limestone Springs

The duties of life to all human beings are arduous, its objects are noble—each stage of its progress is preparatory to some other stage, and the whole a preparation to an interminable existence, upon which, in one sense, we are hereafter to enter, and in another, have already entered. Others may slightly regard the employments, trials and joys of the school girl. I am disposed to put on them a higher value. Our wives, sisters, and our mothers were in the same position yesterday. You will occupy a like [position] with them tomorrow. Whatever of virtue, of patient endurance, of poignant suffering, of useful labor, of noble impulse, of generous endeavor, of influence exerted on society for its good, has been exhibited in their example, in a few short years we shall see exhibited also in yours.

To woman, . . . there must be ascribed . . . acuteness in her powers of perception, . . . instincts . . . and emotions. When these are powerfully excited there is a wonderful vigor and determination of will, and a ready discovery of expedients to accomplish her wishes. She has readier sympathies, her fountain of tears is nearer the surface, but her emotions may not be so constant and permanent as those of man. She has greater readiness and tact, purer and more noble and unselfish desires and impulses, and a higher degree of veneration for the virtuous and exalted, and when she has found the way of truth, a heart more constant and more susceptible to all those influences which come from above. To the gentleness and quiet of her nature, to its affection and sympathy, that religion which pronounces its benediction on the peace-makers and the merciful, which recommends to them the ornament of a meek and quiet spirit, which, in the sight of the Lord, is of a great price, addresses itself with more force and greater attraction than it addresses man. Born to lean upon others, rather than to stand independently by herself, and to confide in an arm stronger than hers, her mind turns more readily to the higher power which brought her into being. . . .

Providence, then, and her own endowments mark out the proper province of woman. In some cases she may strive for the mastery, but to rule with the hand of power was never designed for her. When she thus unsexes herself she is

DOCUMENT
"Walden" by Henry David Thoreau

Emerson, Henry David Thoreau, Herman Melville, and Walt Whitman promoted a robust sensibility attuned to the challenges posed by the rigors of both the external world of natural beauty and the inner world of the spirit.

Some forms of literature offered an explicit critique of American materialism. According to Emerson, people were too concerned about possessions; as he put it, things were "in the saddle," riding everyone. During the 1850s, Thoreau's work became more explicitly focused on nature, as in his book *Walden* (1854). An appreciation of the wonders of nature—wonders that could be felt and tasted, as well as seen—amounted to a powerful force of democratization; anyone and everyone could participate. In turn, Thoreau actively supported the abolition of slavery; his love of nature formed the foundation of his belief in the universal dignity of all people in general and the cause of freedom for black people in particular.

In contrast, other writers celebrated busy-ness, whether in the field or workshop. In the introduction to his book of poetry titled *Leaves of Grass* (1855), Walt Whitman captured the restlessness of a people on the move: "Here is not merely a nation but a teeming nation of nations. Here is action . . . magnificently moving in vast masses." To Whitman, the expansiveness of the American landscape mirrored the American soul, "the largeness and generosity of the spirit of the citizen." His sensuous "Song of Myself" constituted an anthem for all Americans poised, gloriously diverse in their individuality, to exploit the infinite possibilities of both body and spirit.

despised and detested by man and woman alike. England's Queen Victoria at the present moment, if not more feared, is far more beloved in the quiet of her domestic life, than Elizabeth was, the most feared of her female Sovereigns.

Howe ends his address by drawing an implicit comparison between the South and the North. Like many Southerners, he associated the North with labor radicalism, abolitionism, and challenges to the "natural" position of women.

When women go about haranguing promiscuous assemblies of men, lecturing in public, either on infidelity or religion, on slavery, on war or peace—when they meet together in conventions and pass resolutions on grave questions of State—when they set themselves up to manufacture a public opinion for their own advantage and exaltation—when they meet together in organized bodies and pass resolutions about the "rights of woman," and claim for her a voice and a vote in the appointment of civil rulers, and in the government, whether of Church or State, she is stepping forth from her rightful sphere and becomes disgusting and unlovely, just in proportion as she assumes to be a man.

Louisa McCord was a member of an elite slaveholding family in South Carolina. She was an ardent supporter of slavery. Though an accomplished essayist herself, she believed that white women should remain subordinate to their fathers and husbands. In 1856 she wrote, "The positions of women and children are in truth as essentially states of bondage as any other, the differences being in degree, not kind." She added that the "true definition of slavery" thus "applies equally to the position of women in the most civilized and enlightened countries."

Questions

1. Does Professor Howe believe that women are naturally inferior to men? Why or why not?
2. Why would Howe argue against citizenship rights for women, including the right to vote and serve on juries?
3. What were the tensions implicit in white women's status, considering that they were neither full citizens like their husbands nor slaves like the workers who toiled on their behalf? ■

Source: George Howe, *The Endowments, Position and Education of Woman. An Address Delivered Before the Hemans and Sigourney Societies of the Female High School at Limestone Springs*, July 23, 1850 (Columbia, SC: I. C. Morgan, 1850), pp. 5, 9, 10–11.

Challenges to Individualism

Many men and women remained skeptical of—and, in some cases, totally estranged from—the wondrous possibilities inherent in Whitman's phrase "Me, Me going in for my chances." In northern cities, individualism spawned the kind of creative genius necessary for technological innovation and dynamic economic change, but it had little meaning for Native Americans in the West, most of whom were desperately seeking a collective response to new threats in the form of cattle ranchers and the U.S. cavalry. On the Great Plains, groups such as the Mandan and Pawnee performed ceremonies and rituals that celebrated kinship and village life above the individual.

African Americans in the North forged a strong sense of group identity. Though they rejected notions of white people's "racial" superiority, blacks had little choice but to think of themselves as a group separate and distinct from whites. In northern cities, blacks took in boarders and joined mutual-aid societies in order to affirm the collective interests of the larger black community. In contrast, well-to-do whites were increasingly emphasizing the sanctity of the nuclear family, composed solely of parents and children. Charismatic black Boston preacher Maria Stewart denounced the twin evils of racial and gender prejudice for condemning all black women to a life of menial labor: "How long shall the fair daughters of Africa be compelled to bury their minds and talents beneath a load of iron pots and kettles?"

■ Isabella Baumfree was born into slavery in New York State in 1797. Thirty years later she escaped from bondage and became a preacher. In 1843 she changed her name to Sojourner Truth. A powerful orator, she spoke on behalf of abolition and urged white women's-rights activists to embrace the cause of enslaved women. Truth sold small cards, called *cartes de visite*, to support herself. On this card, a portrait taken in 1864, she notes that she must sell her image ("the Shadow") to make a living.

Some groups of women embraced a collective identity of womanhood, although the definition of that identity took several forms. In the North, writers such as Catharine Beecher articulated a vision of female self-sacrifice fueled by family obligations and emotional relationships. Beecher declared that self-sacrifice formed the "grand law of the system" by which women should live their lives. Informed by religious devotion and sustained by labors of love in the home, this female world offered an alternative to the masculine individualism necessary to profit-seeking, whether on the family farm or in the bank or textile mill. Middle-class women believed they could take pride in rearing virtuous citizens and caring for overworked husbands. Sarah Willis Parton (Fanny Fern) cautioned her readers in a series of sketches published in 1853 (*Fern Leaves from Fanny's Portfolio*) that marriage is "the hardest way on earth of getting a living. You never know when your work is done."

Other groups of women cherished different kinds of aspirations. Organizers of the country's first conference devoted to the status of women, the Seneca Falls Convention held in upstate New York in 1848, derived inspiration from the abolitionist movement and protested the efforts of white men to exclude women from formal participation in it. In their demands for women's rights, Elizabeth Cady Stanton and Lucretia Mott linked the plight of the slave with the plight of free women, arguing that white men exploited and denigrated members of both groups. Stanton, Mott, and others received crucial support from African American leaders such as Sojourner Truth and Frederick Douglass. Delegates to Seneca Falls approved a document called the "Declaration of Sentiments," modeled after the Declaration of Independence: "We hold these truths to be self-evident: that all men and women are created equal." This group of women claimed for themselves a revolutionary heritage and all the rights and privileges of citizenship: to own property in their own names, to vote, to attend schools of higher learning, and to participate "in the various trades, professions, and commerce."

Many women, including enslaved workers throughout the South and hard-pressed needleworkers toiling in cramped New York City tenements, could not devote themselves full time to the care of hearth and home, nor could they aspire to a career of public agitation. In her autobiographical novel *Our Nig; or, Sketches from the Life of a Free Black, in a Two-Story White House, North* (1859), Harriet Wilson wrote bitterly of the fate of women such as her mother, a woman "early deprived of parental guardianship, far removed from relatives . . . left to guide her tiny boat over life's surges alone and inexperienced." Like the book's main character, Alfrado, Wilson herself had suffered at the hands of tyrannical white women employers, but at the end of the story Alfrado achieves a measure of dignity and independence for herself by setting up a small business. She thus offered an explicit challenge to both the arrogance of propertied white men and the homebound sentimentality of wealthy white women.

The Paradox of Southern Political Power

At the center of debates about hierarchies and equality, the institution of slavery needed to expand to survive. Decades of intensive cultivation were exhausting the cotton fields in the South. The planter elite was counting on the admission of new territories as slave states to preserve their threatened power in Congress. To slave owners, northern-sponsored efforts to block their expansion amounted to a death sentence for all that the white South held dear. In defense of the slave system, the white South had to mount a strong offense or die.

Slavery in the South

In the early 1850s, proslavery forces maintained firm control over all branches of the federal government. This derived in large part from the "three-fifths clause" of the Constitution, which gave disproportionate representation to the slave states, where each slave was counted as three-fifths of a person. Nevertheless, southern planters felt increasingly defensive as the country expanded westward. They warned against "the abolition excitement," which would necessarily upset the delicate balance between slave and free states. Gradually, this tension between southern strength and southern fears led to the fraying and then unraveling of the Jacksonian American party system, which had relied on a truce maintained between Whigs and Democrats on the issue of slavery. A new party, the Republicans, fused the democratic idealism and economic self-interest of native-born Northerners in such a powerful way that white Southerners believed that the institution of slavery was in danger of succumbing to the Yankee onslaught. And so a clash of ideas gradually slipped out of the confines of the polling place and into the realm of armed conflict.

The Party System in Disarray

In 1848, eight years after the appearance of the antislavery Liberty party, cracks in the second two-party system of Whigs versus Democrats opened wider with the founding of the Free-Soil party. Free-Soilers challenged the prevailing notion that the Whigs and Democrats could continue to smooth over the question of slavery in the territories with a variety of patchwork policies and piecemeal compromises. The Free-Soil platform promoted a forthright no-slavery-in-the-territories policy and favored the Wilmot Proviso (introduced in Congress in 1846), which would have banned slavery from all land acquired as a result of the Mexican War.

TABLE 13-1
The Election of 1848

Candidate	Political Party	Popular Vote (%)	Electoral Vote
Zachary Taylor	Whig	47.4	163
Lewis Cass	Democratic	42.5	127
Martin Van Buren	Free-Soil	10.1	—

In the presidential election of 1848, the Free-Soil party nominated former President Martin Van Buren, Democrat of New York. At the same time, Free-Soilers extended their appeal to the Whig party by supporting federal aid for internal improvements, free western homesteads for settlers, and protective tariffs for northern manufacturers.

Nevertheless, the two major parties persisted in avoidance politics. The Democrats nominated General Lewis Cass, the "father of **popular sovereignty**," a doctrine allowing citizens of new states to decide for themselves whether to permit slavery within their borders. The Whigs put forth General Zachary Taylor, although the Louisiana slaveholder and Mexican War veteran had never held elected office. Taylor managed to parlay his military record into a close win in the fall of 1848. But Taylor died after a year and a half as president and was replaced by his vice president, Millard Fillmore.

In 1849 white Southerners confronted a disturbing reality. Although slave owners controlled the presidency and the Supreme Court and outnumbered the North in the House of Representatives, California's application for statehood in 1849 raised the specter of an unbalanced federal system consisting of sixteen free states and fifteen slave states. The abolitionist threat appeared in other guises as well: the territories of Utah and New Mexico apparently preparing to ban slavery once they became states, abolitionists clamoring for the immediate emancipation of all slaves, and black men and women, including former slave Harriet Tubman, working with abolitionists in the upper South and the North to facilitate the escape of slaves through a network of safe stops called the Underground Railroad. The "railroad" consisted of northerners, white and black, who sheltered fugitives from southern slavery in their flight to the North or, in some instances, to Canada.

The Compromise of 1850

Against this backdrop of sectional controversy, Congress debated the terms under which California would enter the Union in 1850. A young Democratic senator from Illinois, Stephen Douglas, helped cobble together the Compromise of 1850, under which California would enter the Union as a free state that year. New Mexico and Utah would eventually submit the slavery question to voters and thus put the idea of popular sovereignty to a practical test. The federal government would abolish the slave trade in Washington, D.C. (a move that did not affect the status of slaves already living there), and shore up the Fugitive Slave law of 1793 with a new, harsher measure.

The Fugitive Slave Law of 1850 essentially did away with the notion of the North as free territory, for it required local and federal law enforcement agents to retrieve runaways no matter where they sought refuge in the United States. Blacks were denied a trial or the right to testify on their own behalf. Fugitive slave commissioners earned $10 for each runaway they returned to a claimant. By compelling ordinary citizens to aid in the capture of alleged fugitives, the law brought the issue of slavery to the doorstep of northern whites.

Despite these dramatic events, the presidential campaign of 1852 was a lackluster affair. The Democrats nominated an unknown lawyer, Franklin Pierce. Although he hailed from New Hampshire, Pierce supported slavery. The Whigs turned their back on the undistinguished President Fillmore and chose as their nominee General Winfield Scott, who had gained fame during the Mexican War. Yet the Whigs split into regional factions during the election, Northerners resenting Scott's support of the Fugitive Slave Law and Southerners doubting his devotion to slavery. This split foreshadowed the end of national political parties and the emergence of regional parties, an ominous development indeed.

TABLE 13-2
The Election of 1852

Candidate	Political Party	Popular Vote (%)	Electoral Vote
Franklin Pierce	Democratic	50.9	254
Winfield Scott	Whig	44.1	42
John P. Hale	Free-Soil	5.0	—

Expansionism and Political Upheaval

The interests of southern planters affected not only domestic politics, but debates and policies related to foreign affairs as well. Even as Congress was heatedly discussing the Compromise of 1850, Southerners were contemplating ways to extend their reach across and even beyond the continental United States. They wanted to find new, fresh, fertile lands for cotton cultivation, and they hoped to incorporate those lands into the United States. Such expansion would also help to bolster the political power of slave owners in Congress by someday adding new slave states to the Union.

In 1850 the United States and Great Britain signed the Clayton-Bulwer Treaty, agreeing that neither country would seek to control the rights to any future canal spanning the Panama-

Nicaragua isthmus. In 1848 President Polk had made a gesture to buy Cuba from Spain, an offer that was rebuffed but one that did not discourage two privately financed expeditions of proslavery Americans from making forays into Cuba in an effort to seize the island by force on behalf of the United States. In 1854 the American ambassadors to Great Britain, France, and Spain met in Ostend, Belgium, and issued a statement declaring that, if Spain would not sell Cuba, the United States would be justified in taking control of the island. According to the Americans, the Monroe Doctrine gave license to the United States to rid the Western Hemisphere of European colonial powers. Noting that two of the three ambassadors hailed from slave states, abolitionists charged that the Ostend Manifesto was just one more ploy to extend the power of slaveholders throughout the Northern Hemisphere.

In 1855 a young proslavery American adventurer, Tennessee-born William Walker, gathered a band of fifty-eight mercenaries and managed to capture Granada, Nicaragua. Declaring himself president of Nicaragua, Walker encouraged the institution of slavery and won U.S. recognition for his regime in 1856. Walker was driven out of the country a year later, but his arrogance and bold move helped set the stage for the Nicaraguan anti-American movement that would resurface in the twentieth century.

The Gadsden Purchase of 1853 marked the end of westward land acquisition on the continent, but in a commercial sense, expansion continued past the edge of the continental United States. Americans saw the Pacific Ocean as a trade route and East Asia as a trading partner. Commodore Matthew Perry commanded a fleet of U.S. Navy ships that steamed into Tokyo Harbor in 1853. The treaty Perry helped arrange with Japan in 1854 protected American whaling ships, sailors, and merchants in that part of the world and opened the door to an increase in trade later in the century.

By the mid-1850s, the uniting of the continent into what would eventually become the forty-eight contiguous states was a source of sectional tension as well as national pride. Fewer and fewer Northerners supported what they considered proslavery charades, so-called legislative compromises. And the territory of Nebraska, poised on the brink of statehood, forced national lawmakers to confront again the political problem of the expansion of slavery. Once more Senator Douglas from Illinois stepped in to fill the breach. Douglas believed that mutual accommodation between North and South demanded a constant process of negotiation and flexibility on both sides. Thus he argued that the gigantic territory be split into two new states, Kansas and Nebraska, whose respective voters would decide the issue of slavery for themselves. His proposal necessitated that part of the Missouri Compromise of 1820, the part that forbade slavery above the 36°30′ line, would have to be repealed.

> By the mid-1850s, the uniting of the continent into what would eventually become the forty-eight contiguous states was a source of sectional tension as well as national pride.

The Kansas-Nebraska Act became law in 1854, enraging northern Free-Soilers by dismantling the 1820 agreement. They became convinced that what they called the Slave Power Conspiracy would stop at nothing until slavery overran the entire nation. The measure also had a profound effect on the Plains Indians, for it deprived them of fully one-half the land they had been granted by treaty. Specifically, the act wrought havoc on the lives of Ponca, Pawnee, Arapaho, and Cheyenne on the southern and central plains. European American settlers poured into the region, provoking Indian attacks. In September 1855, 600 American troops staged a retaliatory raid against an Indian village, Blue Water, in Nebraska, killing eighty-five Sioux and leading to an escalation in violence between Indians and settlers in the area.

The Compromise of 1850 and the Kansas-Nebraska Act

In their impatience with the two major parties, Free-Soilers were not alone in the early 1850s. The nativist American party, or Know-Nothings, condemned the growing political influence of immigrants, especially Roman Catholics. With its ranks filled with former Whigs, the party tapped into a deep wellspring of resentment against immigrants on the part of urban, native-born workers as well as Protestant farmers anxious about retaining their influence in public affairs.

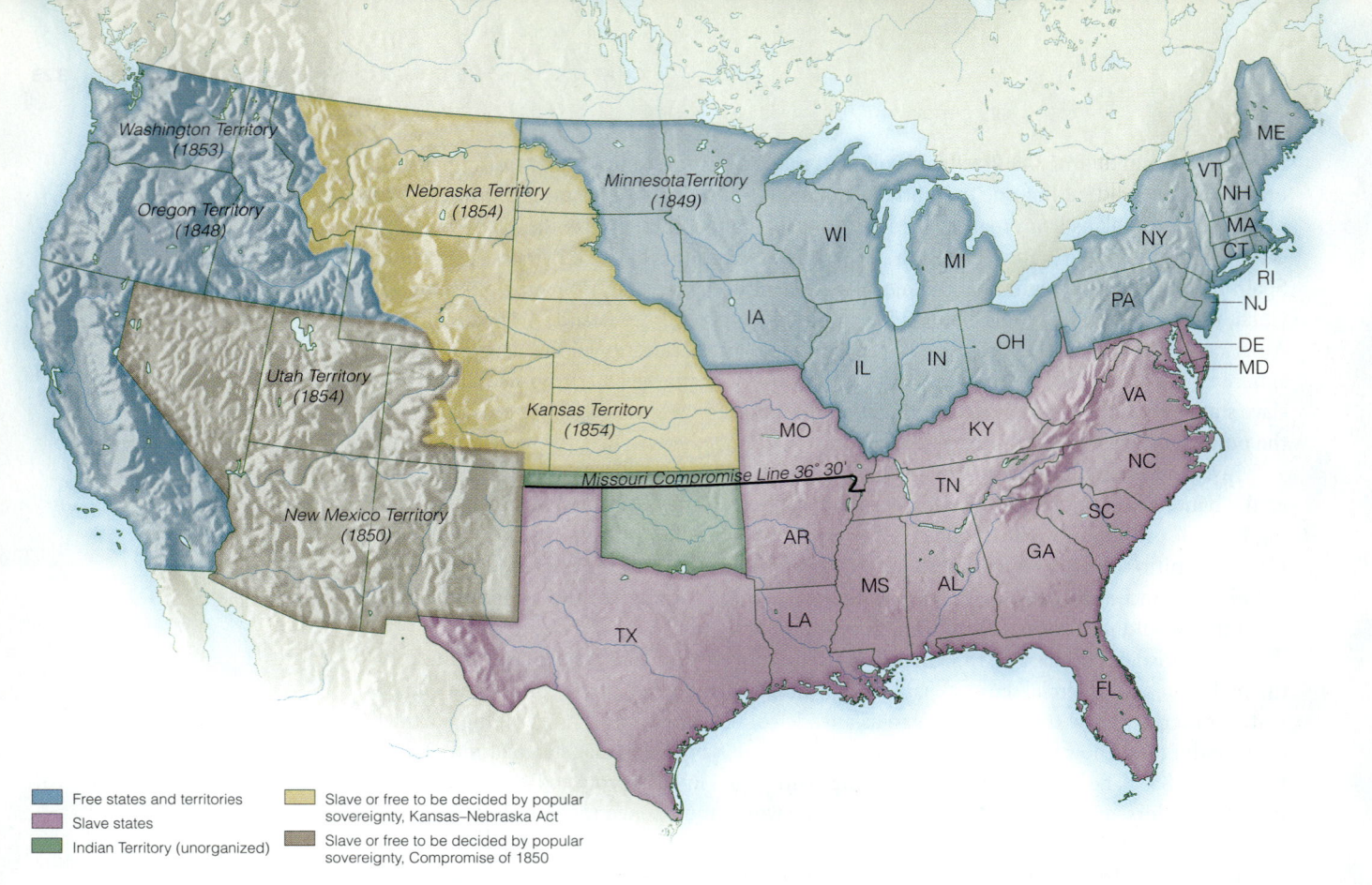

■ MAP 13.2
THE KANSAS-NEBRASKA ACT, 1854 Stephen A. Douglas, senator from Illinois, proposed the Kansas-Nebraska Act of 1854. Douglas hoped to ensure that any transcontinental railroad route would run through Illinois and benefit his constituents. To secure southern support for the measure, proponents of the bill repealed part of the Missouri Compromise of 1820. As a result of the act, settlers displaced many Plains Indians from their lands. In the mid-1850s, the territory of Kansas became engulfed in an internal civil war that pitted supporters of slavery against abolitionists.

The Republican Alliance

The rapid rise of the Know-Nothings further indicated that voters had grown disillusioned with the two-party system. Confirmation of that fact appeared on March 20, 1854, in the small town of Ripon, Wisconsin, when a group of disaffected Whigs created a new party called the Republicans. One core idea informed the party: that slavery must not be allowed to spread into the western territories. From this base, the Republicans built an organization so powerful that it would capture the presidency within six years.

The genius of the Republican party resided in its ability to create and maintain an alliance between groups with vastly different goals. Now forced by the Fugitive Slave Act of 1850 to serve slaveholders (by returning runaway slaves to them) and fearful of the potential of slaveholding Southerners to capture their party, some northern Democrats cast their lot with the Republicans. From the ranks of antislavery men—the long-suffering adherents of the Liberty and Free-Soil parties—came another wing of the Republicans. These party members openly proclaimed their belief in the power of the federal government to halt the relentless march of slavery and ensure that, throughout the land, free soil would be tilled by free labor, free men and women.

Yet antislavery Republicans were by no means unified on major issues apart from the extension of slavery. Many Northerners were willing to tolerate slavery as long as it could be confined to the southern states; they cared little or nothing for the rights of black people, slave or free. In fact, in the Midwest, Republicans saw no contradiction in calling for the end of slavery in one breath and for the end of black migration to the area in the next. They feared that as job competitors, blacks would force whites to work for less money than they were accustomed to, or would push whites out of jobs altogether.

From the ranks of the newly formed Illinois state Republican party emerged a formidable leader. Born in 1809 in Kentucky, Abraham Lincoln came from a modest background and followed a checkered path into Illinois Whig politics: from youthful plowhand and log-splitter, to local postmaster and county surveyor, and finally self-taught lawyer and member of the state legislature (1834–1842). Although his 6-foot 4-inch frame and humble background drew ridicule from wealthy people—a Philadelphia lawyer described him as "a tall rawly boned, ungainly back woodsman, with coarse, ill-fitting clothing"—Lincoln made good use of his oratorical gifts and political ambition in promoting the principles of free soil.

The presidential election of 1856 revealed the full dimension of the national political crisis. The Democrats nominated James Buchanan, a "dough-face" (i.e., proslavery Northerner) from Pennsylvania, with John Breckinridge of Tennessee as his running mate. In their platform, they took pains to extol the virtue of sectional compromise on the slavery issue, by this time a very unpopular position. Meanwhile, the enfeebled Whigs could do little but stand by helplessly and declare as their "fundamental article of political faith, an absolute necessity for avoiding geographical parties," another plank decidedly out of favor with a growing number of voters. The Know-Nothings cast their lot with former President Millard Fillmore, offering voters little more than an anti-immigrant platform.

TABLE 13-3

The Election of 1856

Candidate	Political Party	Popular Vote (%)	Electoral Vote
James Buchanan	Democratic	45.3	174
John C. Frémont	Republican	33.1	114
Millard Fillmore	American	21.6	8

Drawing on former members of the Free-Soil and Whig parties, the Republicans nominated John C. Frémont of California for president. Their platform stated in no uncertain terms the party's opposition to the extension of slavery, as well as Republican support for a transcontinental railroad and other federally sponsored internal improvements such as roads and harbors. The document also included the bold, noble rhetoric—in favor of "the blessings of liberty" and against "tyrannical and unconstitutional laws"—that would be the hallmark of the Republican party in the decade to come. Buchanan won the election, but Frémont's carrying eleven of the sixteen northern states boded well for the Republican party and ill for the slaveholders' union. In Illinois, Frémont had benefited from the tireless campaigning of Abraham Lincoln, who electrified ever-growing crowds of people with the declaration that "the Union must be preserved in the purity of its principles as well as in the integrity of its territorial parts."

The Deepening Conflict over Slavery

Only a small subset of Americans—adult white men—participated directly in the formation of new political parties that set the terms for congressional debates over territorial expansion and slavery. Nevertheless, during the 1850s, increasing numbers of ordinary people were drawn into the escalating conflict over the South's "peculiar institution" as some Northerners mounted concerted challenges, violent as well as peaceful, to the Fugitive Slave Law. The western territory of Kansas became a bloody battleground as abolitionists and proslavery forces fought for control of the new state government. Sites of struggle over the slavery issue also included the streets of Boston, the Supreme Court of the United States, political rallies in Illinois, and a federal arsenal in Harpers Ferry, Virginia. No longer would the opposing sides confine their disagreements to congressional debates over the admission of new states. Nor would words be the only weapons. The country was rushing headlong into nationwide armed conflict.

VIDEO
Slavery

The Rising Tide of Violence

Reminiscences of the Underground Railroad (1880)

The Fugitive Slave Law of 1850 caused fear and alarm among many Northerners. In response to the measure, some African Americans, hiding in northern cities, fled to Canada, often with the aid of conductors on the Underground Railroad. Abolitionists, white and black, made dramatic rescue attempts on behalf of men and women sought by their self-proclaimed southern owners. In Boston in 1851, a waiter named Shadrach Minkins was seized at work and charged with running away from a Virginia slaveholder. During a court hearing to determine the merits of the case, a group of blacks stormed in, disarmed the startled authorities, and, in the words of a sympathetic observer, "with a dexterity worthy of the Roman gladiators, snatched the trembling prey of the slavehunters, and conveyed him in triumph to the streets of Boston." Shadrach Minkins found safety in Montreal, Canada, and a Boston jury refused to convict his lawyers, who had been accused of masterminding his escape. The spectacular public rescue of Minkins, and other such attempts, both successful and unsuccessful, throughout the North, brought the issue of slavery into the realm of public performance in northern towns and cities.

Gradually, the war of words over slavery cascaded out of small-circulation abolitionist periodicals and into the consciousness of a nation. In particular, author Harriet Beecher Stowe managed to wed politics and sentiment in a most compelling way. Her novel *Uncle Tom's Cabin* (1852) sold more than 300,000 copies within ten months and a million copies over the next seven years. The book, originally serialized in a magazine, *The National Era*, introduced large numbers of Northerners to the sufferings of an enslaved couple, Eliza and George. Slavery's greatest crime, in Stowe's eyes, was the forced severance of family ties between husbands and wives, parents and children.

Southern slaveholders were outraged at Stowe's attempt to portray their way of life as an unmitigated evil. A South Carolina slave-holding woman, Louisa McCord, wrote "We proclaim it [slavery], on the contrary, a Godlike dispensation, a providential caring for the weak, and a refuge for the portionless." Another Southerner, George Fitzhugh, took this argument to its logical conclusion. In his book *Cannibals All! Or, Slaves Without Masters* (1857), Fitzhugh claimed that civil society demanded the enslavement of the masses, whether white or black: "Some were born with saddles on their backs, and others booted and spurred to ride them—and the riding does them good." Fitzhugh also argued that slaves, whom he claimed were cared for by benevolent planters, were better off than northern factory workers, whom he asserted were exploited and neglected by indifferent employers.

Meanwhile, the territory of Kansas was becoming engulfed in a regional civil war. Proslavery settlers, aided and abetted by their compatriots (called Border Ruffians) from Missouri, installed their own territorial government at Shawnee Mission in 1855. Opposing these proslavery settlers were the Free-Soilers, some of whom had organized into abolitionist groups, such as the New England Emigrant Aid Company, and armed themselves with rifles.

This dangerous situation soon gave way to terrorism and insurrection on both sides. In 1855, in retaliation for a proslavery raid on the "Free-Soil" town of Lawrence, Kansas, an Ohio abolitionist named John Brown, together with his four sons and two other men, hacked to death five proslavery men at Pottowatamie Creek. The massacre only strengthened the resolve of proslavery advocates, who in the next year drew up a constitution for Kansas, which effectively nullified the principle of popular sovereignty over the issue of slavery. Called the Lecompton Constitution, the document decreed that voters might approve or reject slavery, but even if they chose to

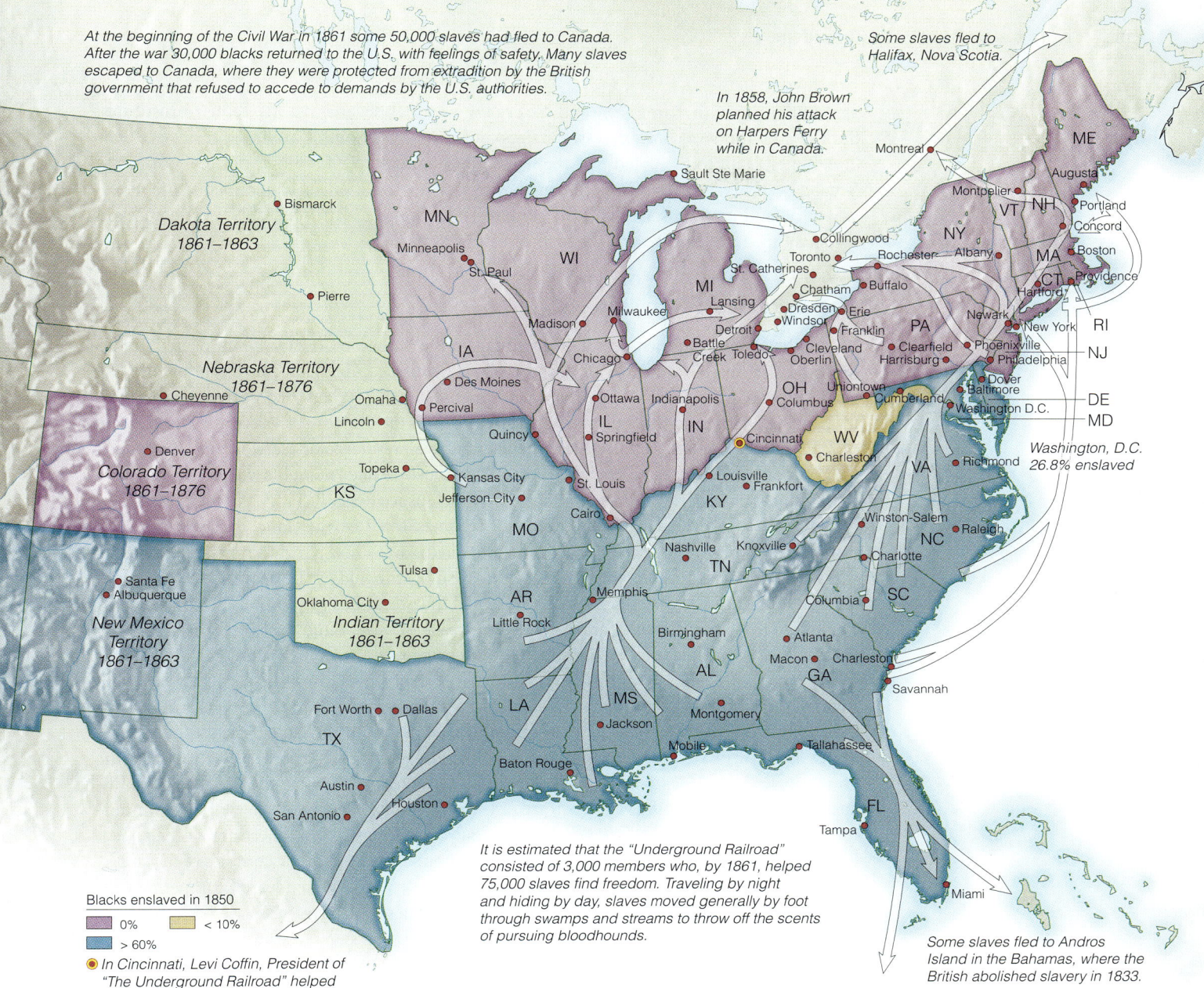

MAP 13.3
THE UNDERGROUND RAILROAD
The Underground Railroad consisted of a network of people who helped fugitives in their escape from slavery en route to the North or Canada. An escaped slave named Harriet Tubman made an estimated nineteen separate trips to the South to help an estimated 300 slaves escape to freedom. Like Tubman, most "conductors" on the Underground Railroad were blacks, many of them free men and women living in the North.

reject it, any slaves already in the state would remain slaves under the force of law. By throwing his support behind the Lecompton Constitution, President Buchanan alienated northern members of his own party, and the Democrats descended into North-South factionalism.

The spilling of blood over slavery was not confined to the Kansas frontier. In 1856 Senator Charles Sumner of Massachusetts, an outspoken abolitionist, delivered a speech on the floor of the United States Senate condemning "The Crime Against Kansas" (the Lecompton Constitution) and the men who perpetrated it, men he characterized as "hirelings picked from the drunken spew and vomit of an uneasy civilization," men who (like his own colleague Senator Butler of South Carolina) loved slavery the way that degenerates loved their prostitutes. Shortly after this speech, Congressman Preston S. Brooks of South Carolina, a relative of Senator Butler, leapt to the defense of the white South and attacked Sumner on the floor of the Senate, beating him into unconsciousness with a cane. Abolitionists contemplated the necessity of defending themselves and their interests, from the courtrooms of New England and the small towns of the West to the halls of Congress itself.

The *Dred Scott* Decision

The Supreme Court, *Dred Scott v. Sanford*

Across the street from the Capitol, proceedings in the Supreme Court were more civil but no less explosive. In 1857 a former slave named Dred Scott sued in federal court, claiming that he was a citizen of Missouri and a free man. Scott maintained that he had become free once his master had taken him onto free soil (the state of Illinois and the territory of Wisconsin). In the case of *Dred Scott v. Sanford* (1857), the court ruled that even residence on free soil did not render a slave a free person, for, regardless of their status, black people had "no rights which the white man was bound to respect." With this single decision, Chief Justice Roger B. Taney and the Court threw off the hard-won balance between slave and free states. In effect, the Court declared unconstitutional the Compromise of 1820, which had banned slavery in the region north of Missouri's southern boundary, because, the justices held, slave owners could not be deprived of their property without due process. This decision threatened the precarious freedom of the South's quarter million free people of color and extended the reach of slavery into the northern states.

Most white people residing outside the South never read the Court's ruling, but if they had, they probably would have agreed with the justices' claim that, since the earliest days of the Republic, blacks "had been regarded as beings of an inferior order, and altogether unfit to associate with the white race, either in social or political relations." At the same time, northern opinion makers warned that the decision made Northerners complicit in the slave system. Of the "slave power," the *Cincinnati Daily Commercial* thundered, "It has marched over and annihilated the boundaries of the states. We are now one great homogeneous slaveholding community." Even nonabolitionists had good reason to fear the long-term implications of the ruling, for it suggested that the institution of slavery was about to spill out of the confines of the southern states and into the rest of the country. Free white men and women feared competing with slaves in the workplace, whether in the West or East. These concerns increased with the onset of a depression in 1857 in the northeastern and midwestern states, as the mining of California gold produced inflation in the East.

The Lincoln-Douglas Debates

The Lincoln-Douglas Debates of 1858

Against this backdrop of economic turmoil and political conflict, the congressional elections of 1858 assumed great significance. In particular, the Senate contest in Illinois pitted incumbent Stephen A. Douglas against challenger Abraham Lincoln. In a series of seven public debates, the two men debated the political conflict over slavery as it had been shaped during the tumultuous decade after the Mexican War. Though no friend of the abolitionists, Douglas was quickly falling from favor within the Democratic party; the Supreme Court had nullified his proposal for popular sovereignty in the territories, and he had parted ways from his southern brethren when he denounced Kansas's Lecompton Constitution.

Lincoln ridiculed the doctrine of popular sovereignty, which he maintained was as thin as the "soup that was made by boiling the shadow of a pigeon that had starved to death." He had no desire to root out slavery in the South, but, "I have said, and I repeat, my wish is that the further spread of [slavery] may be arrested, and that it may be placed where the public mind shall rest in the belief that it is in the course of ultimate extinction." According to a reporter present, this last remark provoked great applause. And this was no minor confrontation between two candidates; it is estimated that in six of the seven debates, the two men spoke before crowds exceeding 10,000 people each. Lincoln lost the election (in which blacks were not allowed to vote as a matter of Illinois law), but, more significantly, he won the loyalty of Republicans all over the North and put the white South on notice that the days of compromise were almost over. Meanwhile, with the admission as free states of Minnesota in 1858 and Oregon in 1859, Congress began to reflect a distinct antislavery bias.

Harpers Ferry and the Presidential Election of 1860

On a Sunday night in October 1859, John Brown and nineteen other men (including at least five African Americans) launched a daring attack on the federal arsenal in Harpers Ferry, Virginia. They had received guns and moral support from some of the North's leading abolitionists, and their plan was to raid the arsenal and distribute firearms to slaves in the surrounding area, thereby inciting a general rebellion that, they hoped, would engulf the rest of

■ The election of 1858 pitted Stephen A. Douglas, Democratic senator from Illinois, against his Republican challenger, a lawyer named Abraham Lincoln. The debates between the two candidates revealed the increasing divisiveness of the slavery question. Douglas maintained that compromise on the issue was still possible; he argued that the European American men residing in territories should decide the question for themselves. Although Lincoln lost this election, he articulated a view that was rapidly gaining support throughout the North: the idea that slavery must not be allowed to spread outside the South.

■ Augustus Washington, son of a former slave, took this picture of John Brown in 1846, thirteen years before the raid on Harpers Ferry, Virginia. A pioneer daguerreotypist, Washington operated a successful studio in Hartford, Connecticut. After the passage of the Fugitive Slave Law in 1850, Washington emigrated with his family to Liberia, an African settlement for American freeborn blacks and former slaves, founded as a republic in 1847.

the South. The Virginia militia and a U.S. Marines force, commanded by Lieutenant Colonel Robert E. Lee, captured Brown and his surviving followers, but not before the insurrectionist had killed seven people and injured ten others. Brown was convicted of treason against the United States for his raid on the federal arsenal, murder, and inciting an insurrection. On December 2, 1859, before being led to the gallows, Brown handed a scrap of paper to one of his guards: "I John Brown am now quite *certain* that the crimes of this *guilty land: will* never be purged *away:* but with Blood." Brown failed as the instigator of a slave rebellion, but he succeeded as a prophet.

The raid on Harpers Ferry cast a shadow over the party conventions held in the summer of 1860. By then it was apparent that the national party system had all but disintegrated. Southerners in effect seceded from the Democratic party by walking out of their Charleston convention rather than supporting Stephen Douglas as candidate for president. Within a few weeks, representatives of both the northern and the southern wings of the party reconvened in separate conventions in Baltimore. Northerners gave the nod to Douglas and Southerners chose as their standard-bearer John C. Breckinridge, a proponent of extending slavery into the territories and annexing Cuba. Representing the discredited strategy of compromise was the candidate of the Constitutional Union party, John Bell of Tennessee.

In Chicago, the Republicans lined up behind Abraham Lincoln and agreed on a platform that had something for everybody, including measures to boost economic growth (as promoted by Henry Clay's American System earlier in the century): a proposed protective tariff, a transcontinental railroad, internal improvements, and free homesteads for western farmers. The Republicans renounced the Know-Nothings. Lincoln himself took the lead in admonishing Republicans who sought to curtail the voting rights of European immigrants, such as the Germans and Scandinavians.

Yet Republicans held out little hope for other groups demanding the rights and protection that flowed from American citizenship. Spanish-speaking residents of California, Chinese immigrants, free people of color throughout the North, Indian tribes from North Carolina to the northwestern states, the wives and daughters of men all over the country—these groups were not included in the Republicans' grand design for a country based on the principles of free labor.

Abraham Lincoln was elected president in 1860, although he received support from only 40 percent of the men who cast ballots. Lincoln won the electoral college, and he also received a plurality of the popular vote. However, ten southern states had refused to list him on the ballot; in that region of the country, he received almost no votes. Stephen Douglas won almost 30 percent of the popular vote; together, Douglas and Breckinridge outpolled Lincoln (2.2 million votes to 1.85 million). Nevertheless, the new president had swept New England, New York, Pennsylvania, and the upper Midwest. The regional interests of North and South took precedence over national political parties. By the end of 1860, South Carolina had seceded from the Union, and the nation headed toward war.

TABLE 13-4

The Election of 1860

Candidate	Political Party	Popular Vote (%)	Electoral Vote
Abraham Lincoln	Republican	39.8	180
Stephen A. Douglas	Democratic	29.5	12
John C. Breckinridge	Democratic	18.1	72
John Bell	Constitutional Union	12.6	39

Conclusion

During the 1850s, Americans on both sides of the slavery issue voiced their opinions, and their frustrations, in ever more dramatic ways. People all over the country came to feel that the debate over slavery had relevance to their lives. In the slave states, black workers remained yoked to a system that denied their humanity and mocked the integrity of their families. In the nonslave states, free people of color understood that northern racial prejudice was but a variation of the slaveholders' theme of domination. New England farm families looking to move west were convinced that western homesteads would not improve their economic security if these homesteads were surrounded by plantations cultivated by large numbers of enslaved workers. Republicans promoted a future full of hope, a future that would fulfill the long-thwarted promise of the young country as a "republic of equal rights, where the title of manhood is the title to citizenship."

In contrast, southern whites of various classes agreed on a rallying cry that stressed independence from Yankee interlopers and freedom from federal interference. Yet this unifying rhetoric carried different meanings for different groups of Southerners. The owners of large plantations were desperate to preserve their enslaved labor forces, and also hungry for fresh lands and renewed political power; these men scrambled to maintain their own privileges in the face of growing northern influence in Congress. Non-slaveholding farmers sought to produce all household necessities themselves and remain independent of the worldwide cotton market economy so crucial to the wealth of slave masters and mistresses. Yet almost all southern whites, rich and poor, stood allied, determined to take up arms to protect their households and their distinctive "southern way of life."

The Fitful Fifties

Slave Population Patterns, 1790 and 1860

Sites to Visit

Secession Era Editorial Project
history.furman.edu/~benson/docs/
  Furman University is digitizing editorials about the secession crisis and already includes scores of them on this site.

John Brown Trial
www.law.umkc.edu/faculty/projects/ftrials/Brown.html
  For information about the John Brown trial, this site provides a set of excellent links.

Lincoln-Douglas Debates of 1858
www.nps.gov/liho/debates.htm
  This National Park Service site includes the texts of these crucial public debates.

Compromise of 1850 and Fugitive Slave Act
www.pbs.org/wgbh/aia/part4/title.html
  From the PBS series on Africans in America, an analysis of the Compromise of 1850 and the effect of the Fugitive Slave Act on black Americans.

Words and Deeds in American History
memoryloc.gov/ammem/mcchtml/corhome.html
  A Library of Congress site containing links to sites on Frederick Douglass; the Compromise of 1850; speeches by John C. Calhoun, Daniel Webster, and Henry Clay; and other topics from the Civil War era.

Harriet Beecher Stowe and *Uncle Tom's Cabin*
xroads.virginia.edu/~HYPER/STOWE/stowe.html
  This site provides both text and descriptions of Stowe's important books and information about the author's life.

For Further Reading

General Works
Eric Foner, *Free Labor, Free Soil, Free Men: The Ideology of the Republican Party Before the Civil War* (1970).
William W. Freehling, *The Road to Disunion* (1990).
James Oliver Horton and Lois E. Horton, *In Hope of Liberty: Culture, Community and Protest Among Northern Free Blacks, 1700–1860* (1997).
Peter Kolchin, *A Sphinx on the Ameican Land: The Nineteenth-Century South in Comparative Perspective* (2003).
Nancy Isenberg, *Sex and Citizenship in Antebellum America* (1998).

Regional Economies and Conflicts
Joan Cashin, *A Family Venture: Men and Women on the Southern Frontier* (1991).
Susan Lee Johnson, *Roaring Camp: The Social World of the California Gold Rush* (2000).
John D. Majewski, *A House Dividing: Economic Development in Pennsylvania and Virginia Before the Civil War* (2000).
David Montejano, *Anglos and Mexicans in the Making of Texas, 1836–1986* (1987).

Individualism vs. Group Identity
Tomás Almaguer, *Racial Faultlines: The Historical Origins of White Supremacy in California* (1994).
Bonnie S. Anderson, *Joyous Greetings: The First International Women's Movement, 1830–1860* (2000).
Yong Chen, *Chinese San Francisco, 1850–1943: A Trans-Pacific Community* (2000).
Frances Levine, *Our Prayers Are in This Place: Pecos Pueblo Identity over the Centuries* (1999).

The Paradox of Southern Political Power
Avery O. Craven, *The Growth of Southern Nationalism, 1848–1861* (1953).
Robert E. May, *The Southern Dream of a Caribbean Empire, 1854–1861* (1973).
Leonard Richards, *The Slave Power: The Free North and Southern Domination, 1780–1860* (2000).

The Deepening Conflict over Slavery
David Herbert Donald, *Lincoln* (1995).
William E. Gienapp, *The Origins of the Republican Party, 1852–1856* (1987).
Michael F. Holt, *The Rise and Fall of the American Whig Party: Jacksonian Politics and the Onset of the Civil War* (1999).
Kate Clifford Larson, *Bound for the Promise Land: Harriet Tubman, Portrait of an American Hero* (2004).
Albert J. Von Frank, *The Trials of Anthony Burns: Freedom and Slavery in Emerson's Boston* (1998).

For quizzes and other resources on these topics, go to www.longmanamericanhistory.com.

"To Fight to Gain a Country": The Civil War

CHAPTER

14

CHAPTER OUTLINE

Mobilization for War, 1861–1862

The Course of War, 1862–1864

The Other War: African American Struggles for Liberation

Battle Fronts and Home Fronts in 1863

The Prolonged Defeat of the Confederacy, 1864–1865

Conclusion

Sites to Visit

For Further Reading

PENSACOLA, FLORIDA, WAS THE SITE OF A DRAMATIC COURT-MARTIAL TRIAL IN APRIL 1862, WHEN five men were found guilty of treasonous acts against the Confederate States of America. "Possessed of information well calculated to aid the enemy," and thus capable of "giving intelligence" to the enemy, the defendants had endangered the security of Confederate troops stationed in the area, according to the chief prosecutor. Later, the presiding officer claimed that coastal communities were engulfed in a "general stampede" as planters tried to move slaves and livestock out of the way of the encroaching Union army. At stake in this trial was the very fate of the would-be new nation.

All of the defendants—George, Robert, Stephen, Peter, and William—were runaway slaves. The specific charges lodged against them read, "That the said slaves are intelligent beings possessing the faculties of Conveying information which would prove useful to the enemy and detrimental to the Confederate States." The charges suggest that the Confederates were forced to repudiate elements of their own proslavery beliefs, which held that black people were childlike and servile, incapable of acting on their own, and grateful for the guidance and protection of southern whites.

■ Sgt. F. L. Baldwin, a Union soldier, poses with an American flag as a backdrop.

Prosecuting officers believed that "strong measures" were needed to prevent the nefarious activities of "spys whether white or black." These officials therefore were unprepared for the firestorm of criticism that followed the announcement of the verdict. The owner of the slaves, General Jackson Morton, expressed outrage that two of his men were marked for summary execution. In a formal complaint to Confederate authorities, Morton denounced the hearing as "vulgar and improper." By the time the controversy faded, an impressive array of Confederate military officers (from sentinels to a lieutenant, a captain, a colonel, a major general, and a general) had had to justify their actions in convening the trial. In the words of one official, "The sacrosanctity of slave property in this war has operated most injuriously to the Confederacy."

Though at a distinct disadvantage compared to the North in terms of troops and materiel, the white South managed to fight on for four long, bloody years. Early on, politicians hailed slaves as a tremendous asset, an immense, easily managed labor force that would grow food and dig trenches.

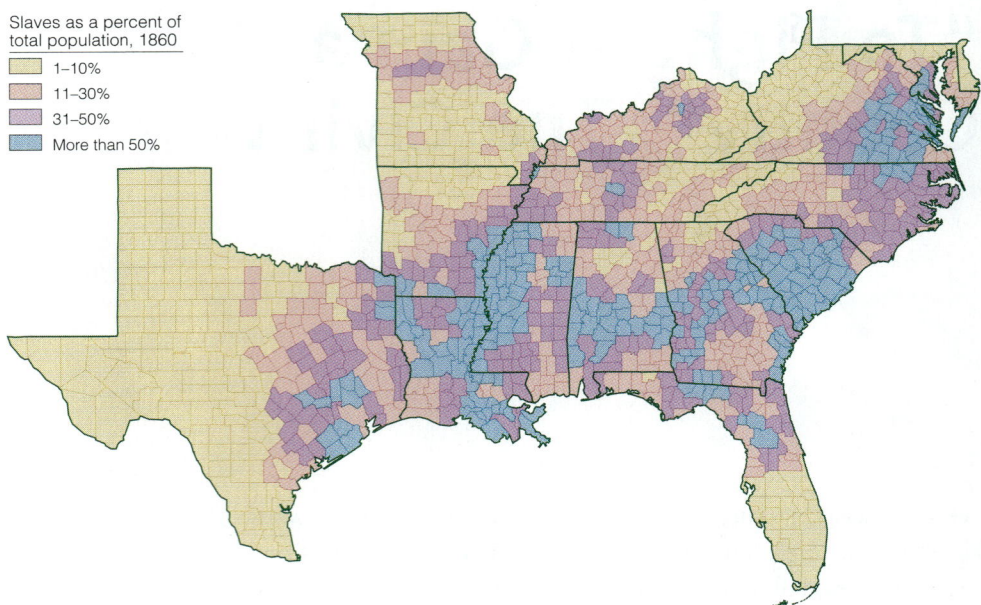

MAP 14.1
SLAVERY IN THE UNITED STATES, 1860 In the South, the areas of the greatest concentration of slaves were also the areas of greatest support for the Confederacy. During the war, the Appalachian mountain region and the upper Piedmont—the area between the mountains and the broad coastal plain—were home to people loyal to the Union and to people who became increasingly disaffected with Confederate policies as the war dragged on.

Instead, African American men and women became freedom fighters, a source of subversion in the heart of the Confederacy. In October 1862, in response to the crisis of wartime slave management, the Confederate Congress passed a measure that exempted from military service one white man for every twenty slaves on a plantation. Many slave owners used this law to shield themselves or their sons from combat duty. In turn, the Twenty-Negro Law inflamed resentment among non-slaveholding small farmers, who charged that this rich man's war was actually a poor man's fight.

As defenders of slavery, the Confederates cast themselves as rebels in an age when the principle of individual rights was gaining ground. The citizens of France, Germany, and Italy were agitating on behalf of modern, democratic nation-states, and systems of serfdom and slavery throughout Europe and the Western Hemisphere were under siege. By early 1865, desperate southern leaders were themselves considering offering slaves their liberty in return for military service.

The Republican conduct of the war revealed the party's nationalistic guiding principles. Yet several groups besides white Southerners objected to a strong federal government, one that would weld the country together geographically as well as economically. The Lincoln administration met bitter resistance from Indian tribes as diverse as the Santee Sioux of Minnesota, the Cheyenne of Colorado, and the Navajo and Apache of the Southwest. In northeastern cities, Irish immigrants battled federal draft agents and attacked black women, men, and children, their supposed competitors in the workplace. The Civil War, then, was less a "brothers' war" between the white farmers of the North and South exclusively and more a conflict that pitted diverse groups against each other over the issues of slavery, territorial expansion, federal power, and local control. Yet by the end of the war in April 1865, the Republican vision of a Union forged in blood had prevailed, at the cost of more than 600,000 lives.

Mobilization for War, 1861–1862

On December 20, 1860, less than eight weeks after Abraham Lincoln was elected president of the United States, South Carolina seceded from the Union, determined, in the words of its own Declaration of Independence, to "resume her separate and equal place among nations." By February 1, 1861, Mississippi, Florida, Alabama, Georgia, Louisiana, and Texas (all states dependent on slave-based staple-crop agriculture) had also withdrawn from the United States of America. Three days later, representatives of the seven states met in Montgomery, Alabama, and formed the Confederate States of America. They also adopted a new constitution for their new nation. Though modeled after that of the United States, this document invoked the power of "sovereign and independent states" instead of "we, the people." Delegates to the Montgomery convention elected as their president Jefferson Davis, a wealthy Mississippi planter with an impressive record of public service. Davis was a graduate of West Point, a veteran of the Mexican War, and a former United States congressman, senator, and secretary of war.

Confederate Constitution (1861)

The Secession Impulse

In some respects, the Civil War seems difficult to explain, for the two sides shared a great deal. Most of the people in the North and South were English-speaking Protestants with deep roots in the culture of the British Isles. Together they celebrated a revolutionary heritage, paying homage to George Washington and the other Founding Fathers.

The Union Severed

Why, then, was the white South, especially the slave South, so fearful of Abraham Lincoln? Although Lincoln enjoyed a broad electoral college victory, he won only 40% of the popular vote. Lincoln had made it clear that, as president, he would possess neither the authority nor the desire to disturb slavery as it existed in the South. However, he summed up his philosophy before the secession crisis this way: "As I would not be a *slave*, so I would not be a *master*. This expresses my idea of democracy. Whatever differs from this . . . is not democracy."

Not surprisingly, then, southern elites felt threatened by Lincoln in particular and the Republicans in general, pointing to the new president's oft-repeated promise to halt the march of slavery into the western territories. Although he was in no position to achieve this goal by executive order, Lincoln did have the power to expand the Republican base in the South by dispensing **patronage** jobs to a small group of homegrown abolitionists. He could also make appointments to the Supreme Court as openings became available. The Republican party was not a majority party; it was a sectional party of the North and the upper Midwest. But this sectional party had managed to seize control of the executive branch of government, tipping the **antebellum** balance of power between slave and free states decisively in favor of the North. Slave owners feared that John Brown's 1859 raid on the federal arsenal at Harpers Ferry, Virginia, was just the first in a series of planned attacks on the slave South.

Two last-ditch efforts at compromise failed to avert a constitutional crisis. In December 1860, as South Carolina was seceding and other states were preparing to join it, neither northern Republicans nor lower South Democrats showed any interest in a series of proposed constitutional amendments that would have severely curtailed the federal government's ability to restrict the interstate slave trade or the spread of slavery. Called the Crittenden Compromise (after its sponsor, Senator John J. Crittenden, a Whig from Kentucky), this package of proposed amendments was defeated in the Senate on January 16, 1861. A peace conference, organized by the Virginia legislature and assembled in February, revised the Crittenden Compromise, but key players were missing: the seven Confederate states and five northern states. Congress rejected the conference's recommendations at the end of February. By this time, many Americans, radicals and moderates, Northerners and Southerners, were in no mood to compromise on the issue of slavery, especially its extension into the West.

■ **MAP 14.2**
THE SECESSION OF SOUTHERN STATES, 1860–1861 The southern states seceded from the Union in stages, beginning with South Carolina in December 1860. Founded on February 4, 1861, the Confederate States of America initially consisted of only that state and six Deep South states. The four upper South states of Virginia, Arkansas, Tennessee, and North Carolina did not leave the Union until mid-April, when Lincoln called for 75,000 troops to put down the civil rebellion. The slave states of Delaware, Maryland, Kentucky, and Missouri remained in the Union, but each of those states was bitterly divided between Unionists and Confederate sympathizers.

"Lee at Fredericksburg" (1886) by J. Horace Lacy

> *In his inaugural address of March 4, Lincoln appealed to the South to refrain from any drastic action.*

In his inaugural address of March 4, Lincoln appealed to the South to refrain from any drastic action, invoking the historic bonds of nationhood, the "mystic chords of memory, stretching from every battle-field, and patriot grave, to every living heart and hearthstone." For the most part, Lincoln's plea for unity fell on deaf ears. However, among the Southerners who initially resisted the secessionists' call to arms was the West Point graduate and Mexican War veteran Robert E. Lee of Virginia. Later, after Virginia seceded, Lee cast his lot with the Confederacy: "I cannot raise my hand against my birthplace, my home, my children," he declared. By his home, Lee meant the Commonwealth of Virginia, not the collection of disaffected states.

Indeed, in early April, the Confederacy was a rhetorical powerhouse, full of blustering firebrands. But it was also a poor excuse for an independent nation, with only one-third of the U.S. population and almost no industrial capacity. Over the next few weeks, as the seven Confederate states attempted to coax the upper South to join their revolution, Lincoln emerged as an unwitting ally in their effort.

Located in Charleston Harbor, Fort Sumter was one of two Union forts in southern territory, and in the spring of 1861 it was badly in need of supplies. On April 12, Lincoln took the high moral ground by sending provisions but not troops to the fort. The Confederates found the move provocative nonetheless and began firing on the fort. After a thirty-three-hour Confederate bombardment, the heavily damaged fort surrendered without a fight. In response, many white Southerners, such as Mary Boykin Chesnut, the wife of a high Confederate official, cheered and embraced the "pomp and circumstance of glorious war."

Three days after the capture of Fort Sumter, Lincoln (anticipating a conflict no longer than ninety days) called for 75,000 northern volunteers to quell a civil uprising "too powerful to be suppressed by the ordinary course of judicial proceedings." By the end of the month, he had ordered a blockade of southern seaports. Condemning these moves as acts of "northern aggression," the upper South, including Virginia (deprived of its western part, which now formed a new state called West Virginia), Tennessee, Arkansas, and North Carolina all seceded from the Union by May 20. Grateful for the newfound loyalty of Virginia and eager to appropriate the Tredegar Iron Works in Richmond, the Confederacy moved its capital from the down-at-the-heels Montgomery to the elegant Richmond on May 11.

Certain segments of the southern population early demonstrated that they would withhold their support from the Confederacy. Yeoman farmers in the upcountry, Louisiana sugar planters dependent on world markets for their product, and people in the hill country of east Tennessee all voted for Unionist delegates to their respective state conventions that chose secession. Enslaved black workers, of course, could hardly be counted on to defend those who kept them in bondage. The Border States of Missouri, Kentucky, Maryland, and Delaware remained within the Union, although among their residents were many outspoken people who openly sympathized with the South.

Preparing to Fight

Poised to battle each other, the South and the North faced similar challenges. Both sides had to inspire—or force—large numbers of men to fight. Both had to produce massive amounts of cannon, ammunition, and food. And both had to devise military strategies that would, they hoped, ensure victory. In early 1861, white Southerners were boasting of the stockpiles of cotton that, if needed, would serve as leverage for military support, diplomatic recognition, and financial assistance from the great European powers. Plantations brimming with hogs and corn, it was hoped, would sustain both masters and slaves, in contrast to the North, where cotton mills would lie idle and workers would soon descend to poverty and starvation.

From the beginning of the war, Confederates aimed for a strategy calculated to draw on their strengths. They would fight a purely defensive war with small units of troops deployed around the South's 6,000-mile border. Seasoned officers such as Robert E. Lee and Thomas J. Jackson would lead the charge to crush Union armies that ventured into Confederate territory. Finally, the South could command 3 million black people (a third of its total population of 9 million), all of whom, it was assumed, would do the bidding of planters and military men. Whereas the North would have to conquer the South to preserve the Union, the Confederacy would only have to survive to win its independence.

At first, the North was inclined to think little past the numbers: in 1860, it possessed 90 percent of the manufacturing capacity and three-quarters of the 30,000 railroad miles in the United States. Its population, 22 million, dwarfed that of the South. The North retained control of the (admittedly less than formidable) U.S. Navy and all other resources of the federal government, including a bureaucratic infrastructure to facilitate troop deployment and communication. Its diversified economy yielded grain as well as textiles; it could not only mobilize a large army but count on feeding it as well.

Early on, the North had a plan, but one that could hardly be dignified by the term *strategy*. It would defend its own territory from southern attack and target Confederate leaders, under the assumption that latent Union sentiment in the South would arise to smash the rebellion before it went too far. Union gunboats positioned along the East Coast and up and down the Mississippi River would seal off the Confederacy from foreign supply lines. The North would also launch a political offensive calculated to undermine Confederate sympathizers by bolstering Unionist sentiment everywhere. Lincoln, for example, continued to appeal to slaveholders loyal to the Union, whether those slaveholders lived in the Border States or deep in the heart of the Confederacy.

INTERPRETING HISTORY

A Virginia Slaveholder Objects to the Impressment of Slaves

During the Civil War, some southern slave owners bitterly resisted Confederate slave impressment policies. On December 4, 1861, John B. Spiece, an Albemarle County, Virginia, slaveholder and lawyer, wrote to the Confederate attorney general and protested government policy.

Dr Sir, Although a stranger to you, yet in consequence of the excitement and distress in this section of the country, in reference to a certain matter; I am constrained to address you, not merely on my own account; but on behalf of a large number of most respectable citizens....

A practice has prevailed for some considerable time in *this* section of the country of impressing into service of the confederate army, the horses wagons and *slaves* belonging to the people.

The "Press masters" will go to their houses, and drag off their property to Just Such an extent as they choose; until it has not only created great excitement and distress; but bids fair to produce wide spread ruin. And I am told that these "Press masters" are paid by the Government the enormous price of *two dollars and fifty cents for each team which they impress*;—hence their anxiety and untiring exertions to increase the number;—thus making thirty or forty dollars pr day—

While I do not controvert the right of the Government to impress into its service *wagons and teams*; yet I do controvert the right to impress *Slaves*—It does seem to me that no one can be impress'd into military service of any kind, unless he is subject to military duty: because this whole business is relating to the Army, and is purely a military matter.—

The people in this section of the country are much attached to their slaves, and treat them in a humane manner—consequently they are exceedingly pained at having them dragged off at this inclement season of the year, and exposed to the severe weather in the mountains of north western Virginia.... Some have already died, and others have returned home afflicted with Typhoid fever, which has spread through the family to a most fatal and alarming extent.—

I am a practicing lawyer myself, but these "Press masters" will hear nothing from any one residing amongst the people.—

Therefore Sir, in consequence of the distress produced by the causes before mentioned, I am constrained to write to you; requesting you if you please, to give your opinion upon the questions involved.

To wit—If a man's wagon and team should be impress'd into Service, can his slave be impress'd to drive the said team—

Secondly—If a man has neither wagon or team can his slave be impress'd to drive some other team (*some* of the "Press masters" yield this *last* point, whilst others do not, and contend that they can impress just as many slaves as they choose from any plantation, taking all the negro men if they think proper.)—

Some few of the people have not been able to sow their grain this fall:— and there is deep dissatisfaction amongst the people—therefore I deem it proper and expedient that the authorities should know it—

Spiece goes on to cite the laws of the Commonwealth of Virginia, as amended in 1860, "by which it seems there is no power to impress Slaves." In the absence of Confederate congressional legislation to that effect, he argues, government authorities lack the legal right to take slaves from their owners. Spiece concludes his letter by suggesting that in taking slaves far from their homes, Confederate authorities were endangering the security of the would-be-new nation.

There is also a serious evil in impressing slaves for the service in North western

---

Northerners also invoked a Revolutionary heritage to justify their cause. However, they downplayed the issue of unjust taxation and instead stressed the glories of the Union—in Lincoln's words, "the last, best hope of mankind" in an age of kings and emperors.

Barriers to Southern Mobilization

On July 21, 1861, at Manassas Junction (Bull Run), about 30 miles southwest of Washington, D.C., Union and Confederate forces encountered each other on the field of battle for the first time. This was the fight that earned Thomas "Stonewall" Jackson his nickname and burnished his reputation, for Union troops skirmished briefly with the enemy and then turned and fled back to the capital, disgraced. In the coming weeks, Northerners gave up the idea that

These slaves are unloading ships at City Point, Virginia. Field hands impressed to work in Confederate factories, on wharves, and in mines experienced a new way of life off the plantation and out of the sight of their owners.

Virginia:—whilst there they get to talking with *Union men* in disguise, and by that means learn the original cause of the difficulty between North & South: then return home and inform other negroes:—not long since one of my neighbors negro men went to his master, and desired to let him go again to the north western army—adding "I wish you to let me go further than I went before["]—I have the honor to be most respectfully your Obt Servt.

It is unknown whether Confederate officials responded to Spiece's letter.

Questions

1. *How does John Spiece demonstrate his talents as a lawyer in this letter?*

2. *In what ways does Spiece's reaction to slave impressment suggest changes in, or challenges to, southern planters' ideology of paternalism?* ■

Source: Ira Berlin, Barbara J. Fields, Thavolia Glymph, Joseph P. Reidy, and Leslie S. Rowland, eds., *Freedom: A Documentary History of Emancipation, 1861–1867*, Series 1, Vol. 1, *The Destruction of Slavery* (1985), pp. 782–783.

---

the effort to suppress the rebels would be an easy one, and Lincoln began to reorganize the country's officer corps and fortify its armies.

To win this initial victory, the Confederates had relied on the massing of several huge forces: those of Generals Joseph Johnston and P. G. T. Beauregard, as well as Stonewall Jackson. Consequently, southern military strategists decided they must continue to defend southern territory while going on the offensive against the Yankees (the "offensive-defensive" strategy was used for the duration of the conflict). In other matters, however, the South learned life-and-death lessons more slowly. Only gradually did the central paradox of the Confederate nation become abundantly clear: that a country founded on an agrarian ideal of "states' rights" needed to industrialize its economy and centralize its government operations to defeat the Union.

■ Farmer's cabin, Block House, New Braunfels, Texas.

The first weeks of the war revealed that the South would pursue its antebellum aims of conquering western territory for slavery. An early victory of Texas forces over Union troops in New Mexico led to the formation of what slaveholders in that region called the Confederate Territory of Arizona. Over the next year, the Confederates launched successful assaults on the cities of Albuquerque and Santa Fe, in present-day New Mexico. However, southern troops amounted to little more than a band of plunderers; in Rio Abajo, for example, farmers and ranchers switched their allegiance to the Union after the rebels raided their homesteads.

Deprived of money raised from customs duties (the U.S. Navy blockade brought a halt to established patterns of overseas trade), the Confederacy relied on floating bonds ($400 million worth), raising taxes, and a 10 percent tax on farm produce. The Confederate Treasury printed money at a furious rate ($1 billion over the course of the conflict), but its value declined precipitously; near the end of the war one Confederate dollar was worth only 1.6 cents.

Raising a volunteer army and impressing slave labor (forcing slaves to labor for the military) met with stiff resistance from various quarters of southern society. For yeoman farm families, long defensive of the independence of their own households, Confederate mobilization efforts came as a rude shock. Antebellum Southerners believed that white fathers should protect and retain control over their dependents at all times. Planters expressed a well-founded fear that slaves impressed for a wide range of tasks, whether saltmaking or chopping trees or tending brick kilns, were difficult to control now that plantation discipline had been loosened. When the Confederate call for volunteers failed to produce the number of soldiers (and menial laborers) needed to fight the Union, the Richmond government in March 1862 implemented a military conscription law (all men between ages eighteen and thirty-five—later it became forty-five—were called up for three years of service). The law exempted certain kinds of workers, such as railroad employees, schoolteachers, miners, and druggists, and allowed the buying of **substitutes** by draftees who could afford the $300 price for them. This last type of exemption allowed wealthy men to pay someone to fight in their place.

These provisions provoked anger not only among ordinary citizens but also among principled states' rights advocates such as governors Joseph Brown of Georgia and Zebulon Vance of North Carolina. Brown exempted large numbers of men from the draft, claiming that the Confederacy posed a greater threat to states' rights than did the Union. On January 1, 1862, 209,852 southern men were present for duty. Yet the northern force was more than twice as large, with 527,204.

Indians and Immigrants in the Service of the Confederacy

Just as the Confederates failed in their attempt to use fully the labor of enslaved workers, so they failed to reap much gain from the vaunted military prowess of Indians, especially those in Indian Territory (present-day Oklahoma). In 1861 southern military officials appealed to the Cherokee and the other Five Tribes for support, promising them arms and protection from Union forces in return. Only gradually and reluctantly did Cherokee leader John Ross commit his men to the Confederacy: "We are in the situation of a man standing alone upon a low naked spot of ground, with the water rising all around him." More devoted to the Confederate cause was Cherokee leader Stand Watie, who, backed by many Cherokee slaveholders, proceeded to mobilize what he called the "United Nations of Indians" as a fighting force on behalf of the Confederacy. Among those responding to the call to arms were Chocktaw and Chickasaw men, who formed Company E of the 21st Mississippi Regiment, "the Indian Brigade."

■ Stand Watie

Although Indian Territory was considered of great strategic value to the Confederacy, southern military officials at times expressed frustration with the traditional battle tactics of Indian warriors. They were unused to military encounters that pitted long, straight rows of men on foot against each other. At the Battle of Elkhorn Tavern (Pea Ridge) in March 1862, Indian troops abandoned the battlefield in the face of cannon fire, leading their commander, Albert Pike, to demand that in the future they be "allowed to fight in their own fashion" rather than "face artillery and steady infantry on open ground." By the summer of 1862, the Confederacy lost its advantage in Indian Territory; the Cherokee and Creek were divided in their loyalties, with some joining Union forces. By this time, the Comanche and Kiowa, resentful of the Confederacy's broken promises (guns and money diverted from them), had joined Union troops and were threatening to invade Texas.

Like Native Americans, immigrants and ethnic minorities in the South were divided in their loyalties. A Jewish lawyer and slaveholder, Judah Benjamin, served as a cabinet member and trusted adviser to Jefferson Davis. Prominent southern military officers included some from Ireland, Prussia, and France. German and Irish workmen from southern cities helped fill the ranks of the Confederate army, as did an estimated 2,500 Hispanos. But ethnic loyalties could also disrupt services deemed necessary to Confederate manufacturing and transportation. The Confederate railroad director in Selma, Alabama, contended with a labor force of immigrants (most probably from Germany and Ireland), men who "do not feel identified in any great degree with the South" and who demanded high wages. They were constantly threatening to run away to Union lines, where they believed they could make more money and enjoy the luxuries denied them in war-torn Alabama.

The Course of War, 1862–1864

When the time came to marshal resources in the service of the national state, Northerners were at a distinct advantage over the states' rights men who dominated the Confederacy. Not only did the Union have more resources, but the Republicans' support for the centralization and consolidation of power also facilitated the war-mobilization process. In Congress, the Republicans took advantage of their new majority status and expanded federal programs in the realm of the economy, education, and land use. However, like Davis, Lincoln encountered vehement opposition to his wartime policies. Meanwhile, on the battlefield, Union losses were mounting. The United States confronted an uncertain fate.

The Republicans' War

Worried about disloyalty in the vicinity of the nation's capital, on April 27, 1861, Lincoln gave General Winfield Scott the power to suspend the writ of habeas corpus (a legal doctrine designed to protect the rights of people arrested) in Baltimore. By the end of the year, this policy, which allowed the incarceration of people not yet charged with a crime, was being applied in almost all of the loyal United States. Chief among those targeted were people suspected of interfering with war mobilization of men and supplies. Democrats stepped up their opposition to the president, denouncing him as a tyrant and a dictator. Meanwhile, from the other side of the political spectrum, abolitionists expressed their frustration with the administration's conciliatory policy toward the South in general and toward Unionist slaveholders in particular. Lincoln insisted that his objective was "to save the Union, and . . . neither to save or destroy slavery."

Wartime manufacturing and commerce proved to be a boon to enterpreneurs. In Cleveland a young commission-house operator named John D. Rockefeller was earning enough money to hire a substitute to serve in the army for him. In the middle of the war, he shifted his business from trading grain, fish, water, lime, plaster, and salt to refining the crude oil (used in kerosene lamps) recently discovered in western Pennsylvania. War profiteers seized their opportunities in both the North and the South. In 1862 the *Southern Cultivator*, a magazine published in Augusta, Georgia, ran an article titled "Enemies at Home," denouncing the "vile crew of speculators" who were selling everything from corn to cloth at exorbitant prices.

The Republicans' willingness to centralize wartime operations led in 1861 to the formation of the U.S. Sanitary Commission, which recruited physicians, trained nurses, raised money, solicited donations, and conducted inspections of Union camps on the front. During the war,

■ Ulysses S. Grant

■ William Sherman

Robert E. Lee

Stonewall Jackson

as many as 20,000 white and black women served as nurses, cooks, and laundresses in Union military hospitals. Black women worked primarily in the latter two categories. A long-time advocate of reform on behalf of the mentally ill during the antebellum period, Dorothea Dix, served as superintendent of nurses.

The Republicans believed that the federal government should actively promote economic growth and educational opportunity, and they enacted measures previously thwarted by Democratic presidents and Congresses. In July 1862, the Homestead Act granted 160 acres of western land to each settler who lived on and made improvements to the land for five years. Congress also passed the Morrill Act, which created a system of land grant colleges. (Many of these colleges eventually became major public universities, including Colorado State University, Kansas State University, and Utah State University.) Also approved in 1862, the Pacific Railroad Act appropriated to the Union Pacific and the Central Pacific railroads a 400-foot right-of-way along the Platte River route of the Oregon Trail and lent them $16,000 to $48,000 (depending on the terrain) per mile.

During the first year and a half of war, Union military strategy reflected a prewar Republican indifference to the rights and welfare of both northern and southern blacks. In September 1861, Lincoln revoked a directive released by General John Frémont that would have authorized the seizure of property and the emancipation of slaves owned by Confederates in the state of Missouri. The president feared that such a policy would alienate slaveholders who were considering switching their allegiance to the Union. Later that fall, the capture of Port Royal, South Carolina, allowed Union soldiers to treat blacks as "**contraband** of war," denying slaveholders their human property but failing to recognize blacks as free people with rights.

> Union military strategy reflected a prewar Republican indifference to the rights and welfare of both northern and southern blacks.

As Union forces pushed deeper into Confederate territory, U.S. officers devised their own methods for dealing with the institution of slavery. By early 1862, the North had set its sights on the Mississippi River valley, hoping to bisect the Confederacy and cut off supplies and men bound from Texas, Arkansas, and Louisiana to the eastern seaboard. In February, General Ulysses S. Grant captured Fort Henry and Fort Donelson on the Tennessee and Cumberland rivers, the Union's first major victory of the war; in April,

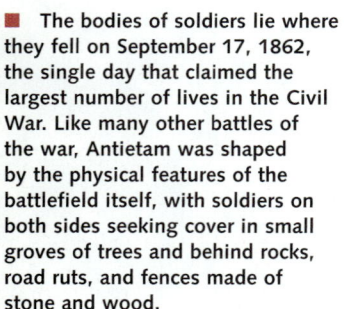
The bodies of soldiers lie where they fell on September 17, 1862, the single day that claimed the largest number of lives in the Civil War. Like many other battles of the war, Antietam was shaped by the physical features of the battlefield itself, with soldiers on both sides seeking cover in small groves of trees and behind rocks, road ruts, and fences made of stone and wood.

New Orleans fell to Admiral David Farragut. In New Orleans, General Benjamin Butler attempted to retain the loyalty of Unionist slaveholders by returning runaway slaves to them. This policy was not always greeted with enthusiasm within Union ranks. A Massachusetts soldier, restless under the command of an officer sympathetic to "slave catching brutes," vowed, "I never will be instrumental in returning a slave to his master in any way shape or manner."

The Ravages of War: The Summer of 1862

The Civil War
Part I: 1861–1862

In the summer of 1862, the South suffered a hemorrhaging of its slave population as the movement of Union troops up and down the eastern seaboard opened the floodgates to runaways. Yet over the course of the summer the Confederacy persevered on the battlefield, aided by the failure of Union armies to press their advantage. In June, General George McClellan was turned back on the outskirts of Richmond, which convinced Lincoln not only of the incompetence of his chief general but also of the value of a less forgiving approach toward the South. But General John Pope, brought in from the western campaign to command the 50,000-man Army of the Potomac, did little better.

In other parts of the country, the Yankee war against the Confederates spilled over into savage campaigns against Indian tribes. An uprising among the Santee Sioux, in Minnesota killed 500 whites before the state militia quashed the rebellion at Wood Lake in the fall of 1862. General James H. Carleton routed the Texas Confederates who had been occupying New Mexico and Arizona, and then provided what he called a "wholesome lesson" to the Mescalero Apache and Navajo who had been menacing Spanish American *placitas* (communities) in the area. Carleton's Union soldiers forced the Mescaleros to accept reservation status at Bosque Redondo in the Pecos River valley. Meanwhile, Colonel Kit Carson conducted a campaign of terrorism against the Navajo, burning *hogans* and seizing crops and livestock, claiming that "wild Indians could be tamed." Many of the survivors undertook the "Long Walk" to Bosque Redondo, a forced march reminiscent of the Cherokee Trail of Tears a generation before.

On the banks of Antietam Creek in northern Virginia, on September 17, the bloodiest single day of the war claimed 20,000 lives and resulted in a Union victory, although a costly one.

To journalists and soldiers alike, battles could offer stirring sights of long rows of uniformed men arrayed against each other, their arms at the ready, regimental flags unfurled in the wind. Yet for the women of Shepardstown, Maryland, left to clean up after the Antietam slaughter, there was no talk of the glory of war, only a frantic, round-the-clock effort to feed the Confederates and bind their wounds. Surveying the battlefield wreckage, one observer, Maria Blunt, lamented the carnage: the dead but also men "without arms, with one leg, with bandaged sides and backs; men in ambulances, wagons, carts, wheelbarrows, men carried on stretchers or supported on the shoulder of some self-denying comrade." All over the South, white women established temporary hospitals in barns, private homes, and churches and mourned each human sacrifice to the cause: "A mother—a wife—a sister had loved him."

The extraordinarily high casualty rate in the war stemmed from several factors. Confederates and Federals alike fought with new kinds of weapons (rifles and sharpshooters accurate at up to 1,000 yards) while troops massed in old-style (that is, close) formation. Soft minie balls punctured and lodged in limbs, leading to high rates of amputation that in turn fostered deadly infections. One Alabama soldier observed in 1862, "I believe the Doctors kills more than they cour [cure]." In fact, twice as many Civil War soldiers died of infection and disease—diarrhea, dysentery, typhoid, pneumonia, and malaria—as were killed in combat.

■ Kate Cumming of Mobile, Alabama, earned the gratitude of the Confederacy for her work as a hospital matron during the war. Before and during the Civil War, many people believed that respectable women should not work in hospitals. Physicians claimed that women were likely to faint at the sight of blood and that they were not strong enough to turn patients over in their beds. Yet, as the war progressed, more and more northern and southern women defied these stereotypes and served in hospitals as nurses, administrators, and comforters of the ill and dying. Noted Cumming soon after she first entered a hospital, "The foul air from this mass of human beings at first made me giddy and sick, but I soon got over it." Still, in southern hospitals, soldiers and enslaved workers handled much of the direct patient care.

The Emancipation Proclamation

Appalled by the loss of life but heartened by the immediate outcome of Antietam, Lincoln took a bold step. In September he announced that on January 1, 1863, he would proclaim all slaves in Confederate territory free. Lincoln used the Emancipation Proclamation to bolster northern morale by infusing the conflict with moral purpose and at the same time to further the Union's interests on the battleground by encouraging Southern blacks to join the U.S. army. The measure left slavery intact in the loyal Border States and in all territory conquered by the Union. Consequently, nearly 1 million black people were excluded from its provisions. Skeptical of the ability of blacks and whites to live together, Lincoln remained committed to the colonization of freed blacks outside the United States (in Central America or the West Indies).

In the congressional elections of 1862, the Democrats had picked up strength in New York, Pennsylvania, and Ohio and carried Illinois. The lower Midwest in general harbored large numbers of Democrats who opposed the war (especially now that it was an "abolition war") and called for peace with the South; these so-called Copperheads disrupted Union enlistments and encouraged military desertions. The Emancipation Proclamation electrified abolitionists, but the war effort and the growing casualties were taking their toll among the laboring classes. Especially aggrieved were the working people who paid higher taxes (relative to those paid by the wealthy) to keep the war machine running, and the dockworkers and others who lost their livelihoods when trade with foreign countries ceased. Their resentment boiled over in the summer of 1863.

DOCUMENT

Barton, Memoirs about Medical Life at the Battlefield (1865)

Persistent Obstacles to the Confederacy's Grand Strategy

From the beginning of the war, the North's effort to blockade 3,500 miles of southern coastline met with fierce resistance on the high seas. The South made up in resourcefulness what it lacked in a navy, relying for supplies on swift steamers manned by privateers (British arms smuggled onto remote southern beaches could bring up to 700 percent in profits). Seemingly invincible Confederate ships such as the ironclad *Merrimack* and the well-fortified British-built warships *Alabama* and *Florida* prowled the southeastern seaboard, sinking Union vessels and protecting the blockade runners. Nevertheless, by December 1861, Union forces had established beachheads in Confederate territory up and down the East Coast.

In November 1861, Union naval forces intercepted a British packet ship, the *Trent*, and seized two Confederate diplomats, James Mason and John Slidell, who were en route to London and Paris, where they planned to plead the South's case in a bid to gain diplomatic recognition. To avoid a rift with England, Lincoln and Secretary of State William H. Seward released the two men. In the process, Mason and Slidell lost whatever influence they might have had with European governments, and Lincoln enjoyed the praise of the British public for his moderation in handling the *Trent* affair.

More generally, Confederate hopes for diplomatic recognition foundered on the shoals of European politics and economics, in England and in the Western Hemisphere. English textile mills drew on their own immense prewar stockpiles of raw cotton and sought out new sources of fiber in Egypt and elsewhere. Also, English workers flexed their political muscle in a successful effort to forestall recognition of the slaveholders' nation. Early in the war the Confederates, who counted 2,500 Hispanics among their ranks, recognized the strategic importance of Mexico, both as a trade route for supplies and as a means of access to ports. In approaching Mexican President Benito Juarez for aid in late 1861, however, Confederate envoy John T. Pickett discovered that, although Mexicans still smarted from their defeat on their own land thirteen years before, the Juarez administration remained an ally of the United States.

By the summer of 1862, Britain and France were inclined to mediate peace in favor of Confederate independence, for the two powers assumed that the South's impressive victories in Virginia and Tennessee signaled a quick end to the war. Nevertheless, the Confederacy's autumn setbacks of Antietam and Perryville (in Kentucky), combined with ennobling rhetoric of the soon-to-be-announced Emancipation Proclamation, proved that the Union was still very much alive. The diplomatic recognition the white South so desperately craved remained elusive.

The Other War: African American Struggles for Liberation

From the onset of military hostilities, African Americans, regardless of whether they lived in the North or the South, perceived the Civil War as a fight for freedom. Although they allied themselves with Union forces, they also recognized the limitations of Union policy in ending slavery. Therefore, blacks throughout the northern and southern states were forced to take action to free themselves as individuals, families, and communities. Twenty-year-old Charlie Reason recalled his daring escape from a Maryland slave master and his decision to join the famous 54th Massachusetts Infantry composed of black soldiers: "I came to fight *not* for my country, I never had any, but to gain one." Soon after the 54th's assault on Fort Wagner (outside Charleston Harbor) in July 1863, Reason died of an infection contracted when one of his legs had to be amputated. In countless ways, black people throughout the South fought to gain a country on their own terms.

Enemies Within the Confederacy

Like the Revolutionaries of 1776, slaveholding whites were shocked when they could not always count on the loyalty of "petted" domestics. Soon after the war began, South Carolina's Mary Boykin Chesnut had expressed unease about the enigmatic behavior of one of her trusted house slaves, Laurence, asking herself of all her slaves, "Are they stolidly stupid or wiser than we

■ All over the South, black people watched and waited for opportunities to claim their own freedom. The movement of Union troops into an area often prompted slaves to flee from the plantation. Individuals and extended families sought safety behind Union lines or in nearby towns or cities, or began the quest for long-lost loved ones.

are, silent and strong, biding their time?" A few months later, Chesnut's cousin was murdered while sleeping, bludgeoned by a candlestick; the cousin's slaves William and Rhody were charged with the crime. Of her own mulatto servant, one of Chesnut's women friends remarked, "For the life of me, I cannot make up my mind. Does she mean to take care of me—or to murder me?" Now rising to the surface, such fears put whites on alert, guarding against enemies in their midst.

Yet no single white man or woman could halt the tide of freedom. Given the chance to steal away at night or walk away boldly in broad daylight, black men, women, and children left their masters and mistresses, seeking safety and paid labor behind Union lines. Throughout the South, black people waited and watched for an opportunity to flee from plantations, their actions depending on the movement of northern troops and the disarray of the plantations they lived on. In July 1862, the Union's Second Confiscation Act provided that the slaves of rebel masters "shall be deemed captives of war and shall be forever free," prompting Union generals to begin employing runaway male slaves as manual laborers. Consequently, military authorities often turned away women, children, older adults, and the disabled, leaving them vulnerable to spiteful masters and mistresses. For black men pressed into Union military and menial labor service, and for their families still languishing on plantations, "freedom" came at a high price indeed.

The Ongoing Fight Against Prejudice in the North and South

In the North, the Emancipation Proclamation spurred the enlistment of black men in the Union army and navy. Eventually, about 33,000 northern blacks enlisted, following the lead of their brothers-in-arms from the South. For black northern soldiers, military service opened up a wider world. Some learned to read and write in camp, and almost all felt the satisfaction of contributing to a war that they defined in stark terms of freedom versus slavery. They wore their uniforms proudly.

Union wartime policies revealed, however, that African Americans would continue to fight prejudice on many fronts. Some northern whites approved recruiting blacks, reasoning that for each black man killed in battle, one white man would be spared. Until late in the war, black soldiers were systematically denied opportunities to advance through the ranks and were paid less than whites. Although they showed loyalty to the cause in disproportionate numbers compared with white men, most blacks found themselves barred from taking up arms at all, relegated to **fatigue work** deemed dangerous and degrading to whites. They intended to labor for the Union, but, in the words of a black soldier from New York, "Instead of the musket it is the spade and the Whelbarrow and the Axe cuting in one of the horable swamps in Louisiana stinking and misery." For each white Union soldier killed or mortally wounded, two died of disease; the ratio for blacks was one to ten.

Many northern military strategists and ordinary enlisted men showed indifference at best, contempt at worst, for the desire of black fugitives to locate lost loved ones and begin to labor on their own behalf. In the course of the war, Union experiments with free black labor—on the South Carolina Sea Islands under the direction of northern missionaries, and in Louisiana, under the direction of generals Nathaniel Banks and Benjamin Butler—emphasized converting the former slaves into staple crop wage workers under the supervision of Yankees. Some of these whites, in their eagerness to establish "order" in former Confederate territory, saw blacks only as exploitable labor—if not cannon fodder, then hands to dig ditches and grow cotton.

Former slave Susie King Taylor recalled the heady, dangerous days of 1862, when she fled from Savannah and found refuge behind Union lines off the coast of Georgia. Despite little pay and poor treatment in the First South Carolina Volunteers (later known as the 33rd United States Colored Cavalry), Taylor gained a great deal of satisfaction from conducting a school for black children on St. Simon's Island and performing a whole host of tasks for the fighting men, from cleaning rifles to washing clothes and tending the ill. She understood that her own contributions to the war effort showed "what sacrifices we can make for our liberty and rights."

Battle Fronts and Home Fronts in 1863

In 1863 the North abandoned the strategy of conciliation in favor of an effort to destroy the large southern armies and deprive the Confederacy of its slave labor force. By this time, the war was causing a tremendous hardship among ordinary white folk in the South. Meanwhile, Lincoln found himself caught between African American freedom fighters who resented the poor treatment they received from many white commanders, and white Northerners who took their opposition to the war in general and the military draft in particular into the streets. Deprivation at home and the mounting casualty rates on the battlefields were reshaping the fabric of American society, North and South.

Disaffection in the Confederacy

The Civil War assaulted Southerners' senses and their land. Before the war, slave owners and their allies often contrasted the supposed tranquility of their rural society with the rude, boisterous noisiness of the North. According to this view, the South was a peaceful place of contented slaves toiling in the fields, whereas the North was the site of workers striking, women clamoring for the vote, and eccentric reformers delivering streetcorner harangues.

The war exploded on the southern landscape with ferocious force, and the rumble of huge armies on the march shook southern society to its foundations. For the first time many Southerners smelled the acrid odor of gunpowder and the stench of rotting bodies. They heard the booms of near and distant cannon and the mournful sounds of church bells tolling for the dead. They saw giant encampments of soldiers cover what used to be cotton fields. Seemingly overnight, both armies constructed gorge-spanning train trestles and huge riverside docks and warehouses, all in preparation for conflict. As soldiers withdrew from the battlefield, they left behind a scarred and blood-spattered land, cornfields mowed down, fires smoldering in their wake.

These sights and sounds were especially distressing to Southerners who objected to the war as a matter of principle or because of its disastrous effects on their households. Scattered throughout the South were communities resistant to the policies of what many ordinary whites considered the Richmond elite—the leaders of the Confederacy. In western North Carolina, a group calling themselves Heroes of America declared their loyalty to the Union. In northern Alabama, the "Free State of Jones [County]" raised troops for the Yankee army. Throughout the rural South, army deserters were welcomed home by their impoverished wives and children; it is estimated that during much of the war, as many as one-third of all Confederate soldiers were absent without leave at any particular time.

During much of the war, as many as one-third of all Confederate soldiers were absent without leave at any particular time.

Groups of poor women resisted the dictates of the Davis administration, wealthy men and women who flaunted an extravagant wartime lifestyle of lavish dinners and parties. Women from Virginia to Alabama protested a Confederate 10 percent "tax-in-kind" on produce grown by farmers and the food shortages that reached crisis proportions. In April 1863, several hundred Richmond women, many of them wives of Tredegar Iron Works employees, armed themselves with knives, hatchets, and pistols and ransacked stores in search of food: "Bread! Bread! Our children are starving while the rich roll in wealth."

Whereas some white women resisted the Confederacy, others leaped to the fore to provide essential goods and services to the beleaguered new nation. Virginia's Belle Boyd kept track of Union troop movements and served as a spy for Confederate armies. Poor women took jobs as textile factory workers, and their better-educated sisters found employment as clerks for the Confederate bureaucracy. Slaveholding women busied themselves running plantations, rolling bandages, and knitting socks for soldiers. Still, many women thought their labors were in vain. Of the Confederacy's stalled progress, Georgia's Gertrude Thomas noted, "Valuable lives lost and nothing accomplished."

The Tide Turns Against the South

In the fall of 1862, Lincoln replaced General McClellan with General Ambrose E. Burnside and then General Joseph ("Fighting Joe") Hooker. In early May 1863, Lee and Jackson encountered Hooker at Chancellorsville, Virginia. The battle left Hooker reeling, but it also claimed the life of Jackson, mistakenly shot by his own men on May 2 in the early evening twilight. The South had lost one of its most ardent champions.

Lee decided to press his advantage by invading Pennsylvania and, it was hoped, encouraging northern Peace Democrats and impressing the foreign powers. The ensuing clash at Gettysburg was a turning point in the war. Drawn by reports of a cache of much-needed shoes, Confederate armies converged on the town, in the south-central part of the state and across the border from Maryland. Union forces pursued. In a three-day battle that began on July 1, the 92,000 men under the command of General George G. Meade were arrayed against the 76,000 troops of Robert E. Lee.

Gettysburg later came to represent the bloody consequences of a war fought by men with modern weapons under commanders with a premodern military sensibility. On the last day of the battle, the men under Confederate Major General George Pickett moved slowly into formation, passing hastily dug graves and the fragments of bodies blown to bits the day before. At 3 p.m., a mile-wide formation of 15,000 men gave the rebel yell and charged three-quarters of a mile across an open field to do battle with Union troops well fortified behind stone walls. Within half an hour, Pickett had lost two-thirds of his soldiers and all thirteen of his colonels. The battle's three-day toll was equally staggering: 23,000 Union and 28,000 Confederate soldiers wounded or killed. Fully one-third of Lee's army was dead or wounded.

What made men of both sides fight on under these conditions? Some remained devoted to a cause. Others cared less about the Confederacy or the Union and more about proving their manhood and upholding their family's honor. Still others sought to memorialize comrades slain in battle or to conform to standards of discipline drilled into them. Some prayed merely to survive.

The Union victory at Gettysburg on July 3 brought rejoicing in the North. The next day, General Ulysses S. Grant captured Vicksburg on the Mississippi River, a move that earned him the rank of lieutenant general (conferred by Congress). Within a year, he assumed the position of supreme commander of the Union armies.

Civil Unrest in the North

Brewster, Three Letters from the Front (1862)

Not all segments of northern society joined in the celebration. Even principled supporters of the Union war effort were growing weary of high taxes and inflated consumer prices, not to mention the sacrifices of thousands of husbands, sons, and brothers. In May, federal soldiers had arrested the defiant and outspoken Copperhead Clement Vallandigham at his home in Dayton, Ohio. Subsequently convicted of treason (he had declared the conflict "a war for the freedom of blacks and the enslavement of whites"), Vallandigham was banished to the South.

Following a military draft imposed on July 1, 1863, the northern white working classes erupted. Enraged at the wealthy who could buy substitutes, resentful of the Lincoln administration's high-handed tactics, and determined not to fight on behalf of their African American competitors in the workplace, laborers in New York City, Hartford, Troy, Newark, and Boston (many of them Irish) went on a rampage. The New York City riot of July 11–15 was especially savage as white men directed their wrath against black men, women, and children. Members of the mob burned the Colored Orphan Asylum to the ground and then mutilated their victims, before the federal government deployed 20,000 troops to New York to quell the violence and discourage other men from resisting the draft elsewhere. On August 19, the draft resumed.

The Desperate South

Meanwhile, the South had to contend not only with dissent and disaffection at home but also with the stunning battle and territorial losses it suffered at Gettysburg and Vicksburg. On August 21, Jefferson Davis proclaimed a day of "fasting, humiliation and prayer." Even as Davis was invoking the name of the Almighty, 450 rebels under the command of William Clarke Quantrill were destroying the town of Lawrence, Kansas (long a hotbed of abolitionist sentiment), and killing 150 of its inhabitants. With the exception of Quantrill and John Singleton Mosby (whose squads of men roamed northern Virginia attacking Union posts and troops in 1863), Confederate military leaders shunned guerrilla warfare, preferring to meet the enemy on a field of honor.

Before the year was out, Davis faced other setbacks as well. Grant's successes at Missionary Ridge and Lookout Mountain, in Tennessee, caused both France and England to draw back from offering overt support to the Confederacy in the form of sales of navy warships or diplomatic recognition. The Confederate president had long counted on securing the support of the great European powers; now those hopes were dashed.

Dedicating the national cemetery at Gettysburg on November 19, 1863, Lincoln delivered a short address that affirmed the nation's "new birth of freedom" and its commitment that "the government of the people, by the people, for the people, shall not perish from the earth." Lincoln's speech is one of the rhetorical masterpieces of American politics. In it he elevated the Civil War from a military conflict exclusively to a great moral struggle against slavery. Meanwhile, Grant, the hero of Vicksburg was poised at the border of northern Georgia, ready to push south to the sea and cut in half what was left of the Confederacy.

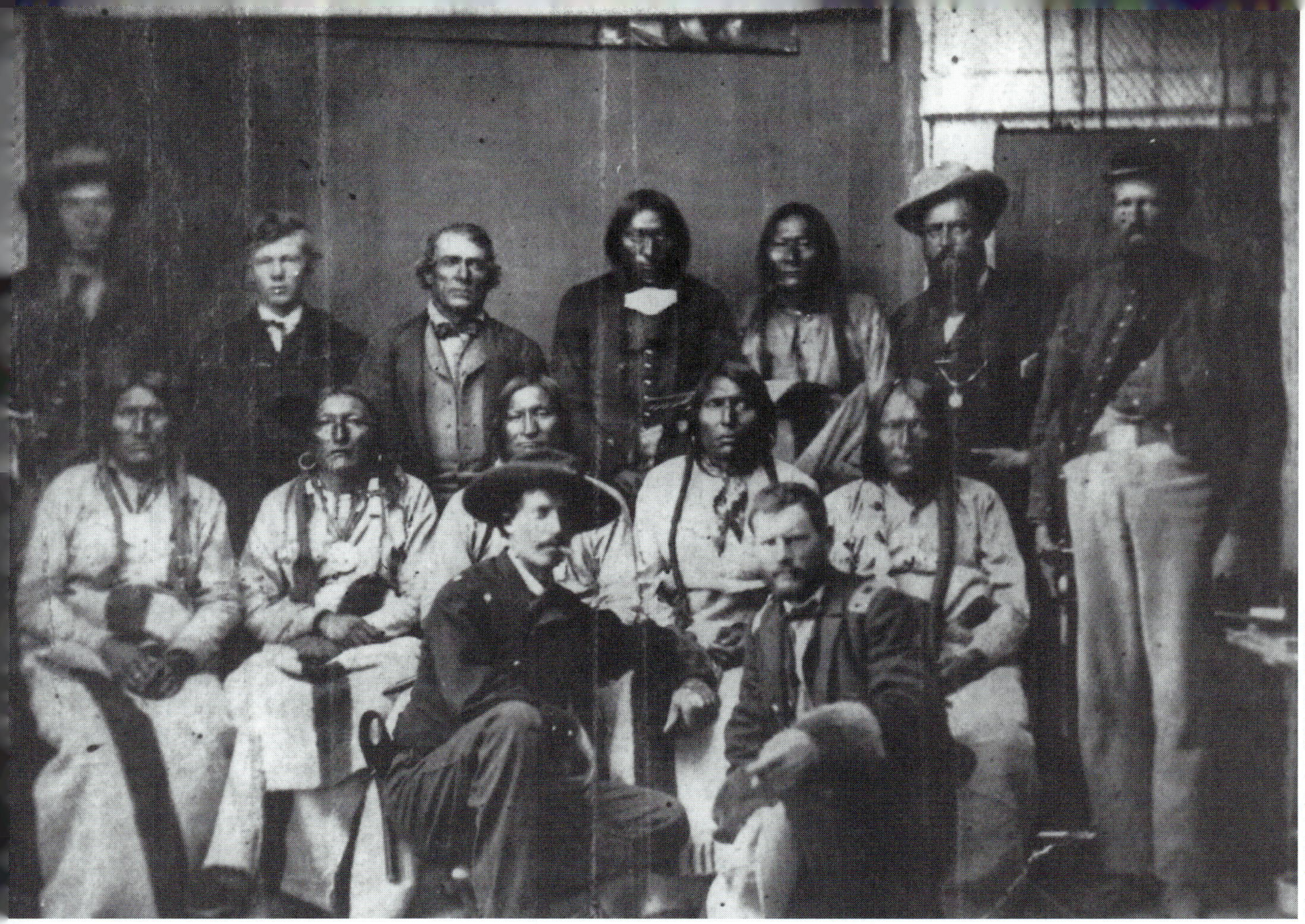

■ In September 1864, the Indian chiefs Black Kettle and White Antelope, with other Cheyenne and Arapaho leaders, met with Colonel John M. Chivington at Camp Weld, Colorado. The purpose of the meeting was to secure a truce between the Indians and European Americans in the area. Two months later, Chivington attacked an encampment of these Indians on the banks of Sand Creek, about 100 miles southeast of Denver.

The Prolonged Defeat of the Confederacy, 1864–1865

By 1864 northern generals, with Lincoln's blessing, had decided to fight a "hard war" against their tenacious enemy. Union troops were authorized to live off the land (denying southern civilians the necessities of life in the process), to seize livestock and other supplies indiscriminately, and to burn everything that the Confederates might find useful. The purposes of this strategy were twofold: to irreparably harm what was left of Confederate morale, and to facilitate the movement of northern troops through hostile territory. If northern troops could sever the area west of Georgia from the Confederacy and take Richmond and destroy its surrounding armies, the Union would be safe at last.

"When This Cruel War Is Over"

White Men's "Hard War" Toward African Americans and Indians

The policy of "hard war" should not be confused with total war, characterized by state-approved terrorism against civilians. However, Confederate policies toward black soldiers and Union policies toward Indian insurgents in the West did show elements of total war against particular segments of the population. In April 1864, Confederate General Nathan Bedford Forrest destroyed

Fort Pillow, a Union garrison on the Mississippi River. After surrendering, black soldiers were systematically murdered. Wounded survivors were bayoneted or burned to death. Among southern generals, conventions of war (providing for the detention and exchange of prisoners of war) did not apply to African American soldiers.

Nor were Indians accorded the minimal respect shown to most white combatants. In the early fall of 1864, a group of Cheyenne and Arapaho were camped along Sand Creek in the southeastern corner of Colorado. Black Kettle, a chief of the Cheyenne, had received promises from Union Colonel John M. Chivington and others stationed at Camp Weld in Denver that the two sides would remain at peace with each other. Therefore, on the morning of November 29, 1864, when Black Kettle saw Chivington leading a Colorado volunteer militia toward his settlement, he waved a white flag and stood his ground.

Chivington did not come in peace. That day he and his men massacred 125 to 160 Indians, mostly women, children, and old people, returning later to mutilate the bodies. In response, the Sioux, Arapaho, and Cheyenne launched their own campaigns against white migrants traveling the South and North Platte trails. Chivington declared that it was "right and honorable" to kill Indians, even children, using any means.

"Father Abraham"

The election of 1864 proceeded without major incident, although Lincoln faced some opposition within his own party. Together with his new running mate, a former slave owner from Tennessee named Andrew Johnson, Lincoln benefited from a string of preelection military victories won for him by Admiral David G. Farragut at Mobile, Alabama, and by General Philip Sheridan in Virginia's Shenandoah Valley. As a result, he defeated the Democratic nominee, his own former general, George McClellan, who managed to garner 45 percent of the popular vote. One of the keys to Lincoln's success was the "peace platform" that the Democrats had drafted at their convention the summer before. Support among Union soldiers for "Little Mac" dropped precipitously as a result, and Lincoln won three-quarters of the army's vote.

Despite his limited military experience, Lincoln possessed a strategic sense superior to that of many of his generals. He played down his own military experience, making light of his minor part in the Black Hawk War of 1832. In that conflict, he reminisced, he had engaged in "charges upon wild onions... [and] bloody struggles with the Musquetoes." However, he cared deeply about ordinary soldiers and talked with them whenever he had the opportunity. In return, Union troops gave "Father Abraham" their loyalty on the battlefield and, especially during the election of 1864, at the ballot box.

TABLE 14-1
The Election of 1864

Candidate	Political Party	Popular Vote (%)	Electoral Vote
Abraham Lincoln	Republican	55.0	212*
George B. McClellan	Democratic	45.0	21

*Eleven secessionist states did not participate.

The Last Days of the Confederacy

Union General William Tecumseh Sherman's forces overtook Atlanta in September 1864 and swept southeast toward the coast, living off the land and denying Confederate soldiers and civilians alike food and supplies along the way. En route to Savannah, Sherman's men liberated Andersonville Prison, a 26-square-acre Confederate camp that held 33,000 prisoners in the summer of 1864. Unable to feed their own armies and so unwilling to commit large supplies of food to the prison, the Confederate commander, Henry Wirz, stood by while 13,000 died of starvation, disease, and exposure. Wirz was the only Confederate officer to be tried, convicted, and executed for war crimes by the U.S. government.

■ **MAP 14.3**
SHERMAN'S MARCH TO THE SEA, 1864–1865   General William T. Sherman's famous march to the sea marked the final phase of the Union effort to divide and conquer the Confederacy. Sherman's men burned Atlanta to the ground in September 1864. In late December, they made their triumphant entry into the city of Savannah. Sherman followed a policy of "hard war" in these final months of the war; he ordered his troops to seize from civilians any food and livestock they could use and to destroy everything else, whether rail lines, houses, or barns. White Southerners expressed outrage over these tactics. Still, Sherman never systematically attacked civilians, a characteristic of the Union's "total war" against Native American peoples in the West.

After presenting Lincoln with the "Christmas gift" of Savannah in December, Sherman took his 60,000 troops north, slogging through swamps and rain-soaked terrain to confront the original secessionists. Later, he recalled with satisfaction, "My aim then was to whip the rebels, to humble their pride, to follow them to their inmost recesses, and make them fear and dread us." By mid-February, South Carolina's state capital, Columbia, was in flames. African American troops were among the triumphant occupiers of the charred city.

By early April 1865, Grant had overpowered Lee's army in Petersburg, Virginia. Withdrawing, Lee sent a telegram to Davis, who was attending church in Richmond, warning him that the fall of the Confederate capital was imminent. Davis and almost all other whites fled the city. Arriving in Richmond on April 3, only hours after the city had been abandoned, was the commander in chief of the Union army, Abraham Lincoln. Lincoln calmly walked the streets of the smoldering city (set afire by departing Confederates), flanked by a group of ten sailors.

The Civil War
Part II:
1863–1865

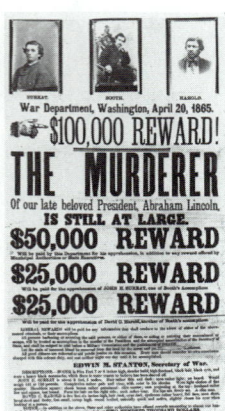

Throngs of black people greeted the president, exclaiming, "Glory to God! Glory! Glory! Glory!" When a black man kneeled to thank Lincoln, the president said, "Don't kneel to me. That is not right. You must kneel to God only, and thank Him for the liberty you will enjoy hereafter."

On April 9, Lee and his demoralized and depleted army of 35,000 men found themselves outnumbered by Grant and Meade, and Lee surrendered his sword at Appomattox Courthouse in northern Virginia. Union officials ensured rebel soldiers protection from future prosecution for treason, and allowed the cavalry to keep their horses for use in spring planting. When the ragtag members of the so-called Stonewall Brigade—men who had entered the war with Stonewall Jackson four years before—came forward to lay down their arm, the Union army gave them a salute of honor, acknowledging their bravery.

Watching a comedy with his wife, Mary, at Ford's Theater in Washington on the night of April 14, Lincoln was one of the last casualties of the war. Shot by John Wilkes Booth, a Confederate loyalist fearful that the president was bent on advancing "nigger citizenship," Lincoln lingered through the night but died the next morning. Booth was caught and shot within a matter of days. Of the departed president, Secretary of State Seward said, "Now he belongs to the ages."

Conclusion

Rather than asking why the South lost the Civil War, we might wonder why it took the North four years to win it. Despite all the political dissent and social conflict in the white South, despite the crumbling of the institution of slavery and the lack of support from the European powers, the Confederacy was able to mobilize huge armies under the command of brilliant tacticians such as Lee and Jackson. The war was fought on the battlefield by regiments of soldiers, not on the sea by navies or in the countryside by guerrillas. Therefore, as long as Confederate generals could deploy troops and outwit their foes during brief but monumental clashes, the Confederacy could survive to fight another day.

In terms of soldiers' lives lost—620,000—the Civil War was by far the costliest in the nation's history. (The death toll among American military personnel in the Revolution was 26,000; in World War I, 116,000; in World War II, 400,000; in Vietnam, 58,000.) At the end of the war, the Union was preserved and slavery was destroyed. Yet, in their quest for true freedom, African Americans soon learned that military hostilities were but one phase of a wider war, a war to define the nature of American citizenship and its promise of liberty and equality. Thus April 1865 marked not so much a final judgment as a transition to new battlefields.

Sites to Visit

Valley of the Shadow: Living the Civil War in Pennsylvania and Virginia
http://valley.vcdh.virginia.edu/

This project tells the histories of two communities on either side of the Mason-Dixon line during the Civil War. It includes narrative and an electronic archive of sources.

The Civil War in Charleston, South Carolina
www.awod.com/gallery/probono/cwchas/cwlayout.html

This site covers the history of the Civil War in and around Charleston.

Abraham Lincoln Association
www.alincolnassoc.com/

This site includes digital versions of Lincoln's papers.

United States Civil War Center
www.cwc.lsu.edu/

Maintained by Louisiana State University, this site aims to promote the study of the Civil War by making available "all appropriate private and public data" related to the conflict.

Civil War Women

scriptorium.lib.duke.edu/collections/civil-war-women.html

This Duke University library site includes original documents, links, and biographical information about several women and their lives during the Civil War.

Library of Congress Civil War Documents and Photographs

memory.loc.gov/ammem/

This Library of Congress site includes a wealth of texts and images related to the history of the Civil War.

Civil War Timeline

www.historyplace.com/civilwar/index.html

This site offers a comprehensive Civil War timeline that includes photographs.

National Civil War Association

www.ncwa.org/

This site documents the activities of one of the many Civil War reenactment organizations in the United States.

For Further Reading

General

David Herbert Donald, *Lincoln* (1995).

Steven Hahn, *A Nation Under Our Feet: Black Political Struggles in the Rural South from Slavery to the Great Migration* (2003).

Edward Hagerman, *The American Civil War and the Origins of Modern Warfare* (1988).

James M. McPherson, *Battle Cry of Freedom: The Civil War Era* (1988).

Reid Mitchell, *Civil War Soldiers: Their Expectations and Experiences* (1988).

Mobilization for War, 1861–1862

Gabor Borit, ed., *Lincoln's Generals* (1994).

Drew Gilpin Faust, *The Creation of Southern Nationalism: Ideology and Identity in the Civil War South* (1988).

Joseph L. Harsh, *Confederate Tide Rising: Robert E. Lee and the Making of Southern Strategy, 1861–62* (1998).

Wilfrid Knight, *Red Fox: Stand Watie and the Confederate Indian Nations During the Civil War Years in Indian Territory* (1988).

The Course of War, 1862–1864

Stephen Ash, *When the Invaders Came: Conflict and Chaos in the Occupied South, 1861–1865* (1996).

Howard Jones, *The Union in Peril: The Crisis over British Intervention in the Civil War* (1992).

Elizabeth Leonard, *All the Daring of the Soldier: Women of the Civil War Armies* (1999).

Heather Cox Richardson, *The Greatest Nation on Earth: Republican Economic Policies During the Civil War* (1997).

The Other War: African American Struggles for Liberation

Ira Berlin et al., *Freedom: A Documentary History of Emancipation*: Series 1, Vol. I: *The Destruction of Slavery*; Series 2: *The Black Military Experience* (1982).

Jacqueline Jones, *Labor of Love, Labor of Sorrow: Black Women, Work, and the Family Since Slavery* (1985).

William S. McFeely, *Frederick Douglass* (1991).

Willie Lee Rose, *Rehearsal for Reconstruction: The Port Royal Experiment* (1964).

Battle Fronts and Home Fronts in 1863

Stephen V. Ash, *Middle Tennessee Society Transformed, 1860–1870: War and Peace in the Upper South* (1988).

Iver Bernstein, *The New York City Draft Riots: Their Significance for American Society and Politics in the Age of the Civil War* (1990).

Drew Gilpin Faust, *Mothers of Invention: Women of the Slaveholding South in the American Civil War* (1996).

J. Matthew Gallman, *The North Fights the War: The Home Front* (1994).

The Prolonged Defeat of the Confederacy, 1864–1865

Michael B. Ballard, *A Long Shadow: Jefferson Davis and the Final Days of the Confederacy* (1997).

Mark Grimsley, *The Hard Hand of War: Union Military Policy Toward Southern Civilians, 1861–1865* (1995).

James M. McPherson, *For Cause and Comrades: Why Men Fought in the Civil War* (1997).

J. Tracy Power, *Lee's Miserables: Life in the Army of Northern Virginia from the Wilderness to Appomattox* (1998).

For quizzes and other resources on these topics, go to www.longmanamericanhistory.com.

CHAPTER 15

Consolidating a Triumphant Union, 1865–1877

IN SAVANNAH, GEORGIA, IN MID-DECEMBER 1864, AFRICAN AMERICAN MEN, WOMEN, AND children rejoiced when the troops of Union General William Tecumseh Sherman liberated the city: the day of jubilee had come at last! The city's black community immediately formed its own school system under the sponsorship of a new group, the Savannah Education Association (SEA). The association owed its creation to the desire of freedpeople of all ages to learn to read and write. A committee of nine black clergy began by hiring fifteen black teachers and acquiring buildings (including the Old Bryan Slave Mart) for use as schools. By January 1, 1865, Savannah blacks had raised $800 to pay teachers' salaries, enabling several hundred black children to attend classes free of charge.

Following hard on the heels of the Union army, a group of northern white missionaries arrived in Savannah to seek black converts for two Protestant denominations, the Presbyterians and the Congregationalists. On the first day of school, in January 1865, these northern newcomers watched a grand procession of children wend its way through the streets of Savannah. The missionaries expressed amazement that the SEA was an entirely black-run organization. These whites had believed the former slaves incapable of creating such an impressive educational system.

In March 1865, the federal government, under the auspices of the newly formed Bureau of Refugees, Freedmen, and Abandoned Lands (Freedmen's Bureau), agreed to work with missionaries in opening schools for black children throughout the former Confederate states. In Georgia, missionaries and government officials soon became alarmed that black leaders were willing to accept financial aid from them but not willing to relinquish control of SEA schools to the whites in return. The Northerners were also distressed by the militancy of certain local black leaders. One of these leaders was Aaron Bradley, who, armed with a pistol and bowie knife, was urging other black men to vote as a bloc in all elections.

In an effort to wrest control of the SEA from Savannah blacks, northern missionaries and agents of the Freedmen's Bureau decided to withhold funds from the association. By March 1866,

■ In Savannah, African American Sunday school pupils pose for photographer William Wilson in 1890. After the Civil War, many southern black communities created, or enlarged and solidified, their own institutions, including schools and churches.

CHAPTER OUTLINE

The Struggle over the South

Claiming Territory for the Union

The Republican Vision and Its Limits

Conclusion

Sites to Visit

For Further Reading

these efforts had paid off: the city's black community, swollen by a refugee population, was no longer able to support its own schools. Northern whites took over SEA operations, and the association ceased to exist.

Postwar political interest in the South unleashed a major conflict between supporters of African American rights and supporters of southern white privilege. Republican congressmen hoped to *reconstruct* the South by enabling African Americans to own land and to become full citizens. Southern freedpeople sought to free themselves from white employers, landlords, and clergy and to establish control over their own workplaces, families, and churches. In contrast, President Andrew Johnson appeared bent on *restoring* the antebellum power relations that made southern black people field laborers dependent on white landowners. For their part, many southern whites were determined to prevent black people from becoming truly free. Most former rebels remained embittered about the outcome of the war and vengeful toward the freedpeople.

After the war, western economic development presented new challenges for men who had fought for the Union. In order to open the West to European American miners and homesteaders, the U.S. army clashed repeatedly with Native Americans. On the Plains and in the Northwest, Indians resisted white efforts to force them to abandon their nomadic way of life and take up sedentary farming. William Tecumseh Sherman, Philip H. Sheridan, and George Custer were among the U.S. military officers who had commanded troops in the Civil War and now attempted to subdue the Plains Indians and further white settlement. Sherman declared, "We must act with vindictive earnestness against the Sioux, even to their extermination, men, women and children." The former head of the Freedmen's Bureau, General Oliver O. Howard, oversaw the expulsion of Chief Joseph and his people, the Nez Perce, from their homeland in southeast Washington's Walla Walla Valley in 1877.

The Civil War hardened the positions of the two major political parties. The Republicans remained in favor of a strong national government, one that promoted economic growth. The Democrats tended to support states' efforts to manage their own affairs, which included regulating relations between employers and employees, whites and blacks. The railroad industry represented a robust, Republican-sponsored partnership between private enterprise and the federal government. Between 1862 and 1872, the government gave the industry subsidies that included millions of dollars in cash and more than 100 million acres of land. During the postwar period, federal government officials attempted to complete the political process that the military defeat of the South had only begun: the consolidation of the Union, North and South, East and West. This process encompassed the nation as a whole.

The Struggle over the South

The Civil War had a devastating impact on the South in physical, social, and economic terms. The region had lost an estimated $2 billion in investments in slaves; modest homesteads and grand plantations alike lay in ruins; and gardens, orchards, and cotton fields were barren. More than 3 million former slaves eagerly embraced freedom, but the vast majority lacked the land, cash, and credit necessary to build family homesteads for themselves. Hoping to achieve social and economic self-determination, African American men and women traveled great distances, usually on foot, in efforts to locate loved ones and reunite families that had been separated during slavery. At the same time, landowning whites considered black people primarily as a source of agricultural labor; these whites resisted the idea that the freedpeople should be granted citizenship rights.

In the North, Republican lawmakers disagreed among themselves how best to punish the defeated but defiant rebels. President Abraham Lincoln had indicated early that after the war the government should bring the South back into the Union quickly and painlessly. His successor wanted to see members of the southern planter elite humiliated, but resisted the notion that freedpeople should become independent of white landowners. In Congress, moderate and radical Republicans argued about how far the government should go in ensuring the former slaves' freedom.

Wartime Preludes to Postwar Policies

Wartime experiments with African American free labor in Union-occupied areas foreshadowed bitter postwar debates. As early as November 1861, Union forces had occupied the Sea Islands off Port Royal Sound in South Carolina. In response, wealthy cotton planters fled to the mainland. Over the next few months, three groups of northern civilians landed on the Sea Islands with the intention of guiding blacks in the transition from slave to free labor. Teachers arrived intent on creating schools, and missionaries hoped to start churches. A third group, representing Boston investors, had also settled on the Sea Islands to assess economic opportunities; by early 1862, they decided to institute a system of wage labor that would reestablish a staple crop economy and funnel cotton directly into northern textile mills. The freed slaves, however, preferred to grow crops for their families to eat rather than cotton to sell, relying on a system of barter and trade among networks of extended families. Their goal was to break free of white landlords, suppliers, and cotton merchants.

Meanwhile, in southern Louisiana, the Union capture of New Orleans in the spring of 1862 enabled northern military officials to implement their own free (that is, nonslave) labor system. General Nathaniel Banks proclaimed that U.S. troops should forcibly relocate blacks to plantations "where they belong"; there they would continue to work for their former owners in the sugar and cotton fields, but now for wages supposedly negotiated annually. The Union army would compel blacks to work if they resisted doing so. In defiance of these orders, however, some blacks went on strike for higher wages, and others refused to work at all. Moreover, not all Union military men relished the prospect of forcing blacks to work on the plantations where they had been enslaved. Thus, federal policies returning blacks to plantations remained contested even within the ranks of the army itself.

> *Not all Union military men relished the prospect of forcing blacks to work on the plantations where they had been enslaved.*

The Lincoln administration had no hard-and-fast **Reconstruction** policy to guide congressional lawmakers looking toward the postwar period. In December 1863, the president outlined his Ten Percent Plan. This plan would allow former Confederate states to form new state governments once 10 percent of the men who had voted in the 1860 presidential election had pledged allegiance to the Union and renounced slavery. Congress instead passed the Wade-Davis Bill, which would have required a majority of southern voters in any state to take a loyalty oath affirming their allegiance to the United States. By refusing to sign the bill before Congress adjourned, Lincoln vetoed the measure (through a **pocket veto**). However, the president approved the creation of the Freedmen's Bureau in March 1865. The bureau was responsible for coordinating relief efforts on behalf of blacks and poor whites loyal to the Union, for sponsoring schools, and for implementing a labor contract system on southern plantations. At the time of his assassination, Lincoln seemed to be leaning toward giving the right to vote to southern black men.

Presidential Reconstruction, 1865–1867

When Andrew Johnson, the seventeenth president of the United States, assumed office in April 1865 after Lincoln's death, he brought his own agenda for the defeated South. Throughout his political career, Johnson had seen himself as a champion of poor white farmers in oppo-

■ Freedmen's Bureau agents distributed rations to former slaves and southern whites who had remained loyal to the Union. Agents also sponsored schools, legalized marriages formed under slavery, arbitrated domestic disputes, and oversaw labor contracts between workers and landowners. This photo shows the bureau office in Petersburg, Virginia.

sition to the wealthy planter class. A man of modest background, he had been elected U.S. senator from Tennessee in 1857. He alone among southern senators remained in Congress and loyal to the Union after 1861. Lincoln first appointed Johnson military governor of Tennessee when that state was captured by the Union in 1862 and then tapped him as his running mate for the election of 1864.

Soon after he assumed the presidency, Johnson disappointed congressional Republicans who hoped that he would serve as a champion of the freedpeople. He welcomed back into the Union those states reorganized under Lincoln's Ten Percent Plan. He advocated denying the vote to wealthy Confederates, though he would allow individuals to come to the White House to beg the president for special pardons. Johnson also outlined a fairly lenient plan for readmitting the other rebel states into the Union. Poor whites would have the right to vote, but they must convene special state conventions that would renounce secession and accept the Thirteenth Amendment abolishing slavery. Further, they must repudiate all Confederate debts. The president opposed granting the vote to the former slaves; he believed that they should continue to toil as field workers for white landowners. In fact, many former rebels gradually came to see Johnson as their postwar political ally.

Johnson failed to anticipate the speed and vigor with which former Confederate leaders would move to reassert their political authority. In addition, he did not gauge accurately the resentment of congressional Republicans, who thought his policies toward the defeated South were too forgiving. The southern states that took advantage of Johnson's reunification policies passed so-called **Black Codes**. These state laws were an ill-disguised attempt to institute a system of near-slavery. They aimed to penalize "vagrant" blacks, defined as those who did not work in the fields for whites, and to deny blacks the right to vote, serve on juries, or in some cases even own land. The Black Code of Mississippi restricted the rights of a freedperson to "keep or carry fire-arms," ammunition, and knives and to "quit the service of his or her employer before the expiration of his or her term of service without good cause." The vagueness of this last provision threatened any blacks who happened not to be working under the supervision of whites at any given moment. People arrested under the Black Codes faced imprisonment or forced labor.

The Mississippi Black Code

At the end of the war, congressional Republicans were divided into two camps. Radicals wanted to use strong federal measures to advance black people's civil rights and economic independence. In contrast, moderates were more concerned with the free market and private property rights; they took a hands-off approach regarding former slaves. But members of both groups reacted with outrage to the Black Codes. Moreover, when the legislators returned to the Capitol in December 1865, they were in for a shock: among their new colleagues were four former Confederate generals, five colonels, and other high-ranking members of the Confederate elite, including former Vice President Alexander Stephens, now under indictment for treason. All of these rebels were duly elected senators and representatives from southern states. In a special session called for December 4, a joint committee of fifteen lawmakers (six senators and nine members of the House) voted to bar these men from Congress.

By January 1865, both houses of Congress had approved the Thirteenth Amendment to the Constitution, abolishing slavery. The necessary three-fourths of the states ratified the measure by the end of the year. However, President Johnson was becoming more openly defiant of his congressional foes who favored aggressive federal protection of black civil rights. He vetoed two crucial pieces of legislation: an extension and expansion of the Freedmen's Bureau and the Civil Rights Bill of 1866. This latter measure was an unprecedented piece of legislation. It called on the federal government—for the first time in history—to protect individual rights against the willful indifference of the states (as manifested, for example, in the Black Codes). Congress managed to override both vetoes by the summer of 1866.

In June of that year, Congress passed the Fourteenth Amendment. This amendment guaranteed the former slaves citizenship rights, punished states that denied citizens the right to vote, declared the former rebels ineligible for federal and state office, and voided Confederate debts. This amendment was the first to use gender-specific language, guarding against denying the vote "to any of the male inhabitants" of any state.

Even before the war ended, Northerners had moved south, and the flow increased in 1865. Black and white teachers volunteered to teach the former slaves to read and write. Some white Northerners journeyed south to invest in land and become planters in the staple crop economy. White southern critics called all these migrants **carpetbaggers**. This derisive term suggested that the Northerners hastily packed their belongings in rough bags made of carpet scraps and then rushed south to take advantage of the region's devastation and confusion. To many freedpeople, whether they worked for a carpetbagger or a Southerner, laboring in the cotton fields was but a continuation of slavery.

Some former southern (white) Whigs, who had been reluctant secessionists, now found common ground with northern Republicans who supported government subsidies for railroads, banking institutions, and public improvements. This group consisted of some members of the humbled planter class as well as men of more modest means. Southern Democrats, who sneered at any alliances with the North, scornfully labeled these whites **scalawags** (the term referred to a scrawny, useless type of horse on the Scottish island of Scalloway).

INTERPRETING HISTORY

A Southern Labor Contract

After the Civil War, many southern agricultural workers signed labor contracts. These contracts sought to control not only the output of laborers but also their lives outside the workplace.

On January 1, 1868, the planter John D. Williams assembled his workers for the coming year and presented them with a contract to sign. Williams owned a plantation in the lower Piedmont county of Laurens, South Carolina. He agreed to furnish "the said negroes" (that is, the three black men and two black women whose names were listed on the document) with mules and horses to be used for cultivating the land. The workers could receive their food, clothing, and medical care on credit. They were allowed to keep one-third of all the corn, sweet potatoes, wheat, cotton, oats, and molasses they produced. Presumably, they would pay their debts to Williams using proceeds from their share of the crop.

According to the contract, Williams's workers promised to

bind them Selves to be steady & attentive to there work at all times and to work at keeping in repair all the fences on Said plantation and assist in cuting & taking care of—all the grain crops on Said plantation and work by the direction of me [Williams] or my Agent....

And should any of them depart from the farm or from any services at any time with out our approval they shall forfeit one dollar per day, for the first time and for the second time without good cause they shall forfeit all of their interest in the crop their to me the enjured person—they shall not be allowed to keep firearms or deadly wapons or ardent Spirits and they shall obey all lawful orders from me or my Agent and shall be honest—truthful—sober—civel—diligent in their business & for all wilful Disobedience of any lawful

After the Civil War, many rural southern blacks, such as those shown here, continued to toil in cotton fields owned by whites.

orders from me or my Agent drunkenness moral or legal misconduct want of respects or civility to me or my Agent or to my Family or any elce, I am permitted to discharge them forfeiting any claims upon me for any part of the crop....

Moses Nathan	1 full hand
Jake Chappal	" "
Milly Williams	½ " "
Easter Williams	" "
Mack Williams	" "

At the end of the contract is this addition:

We the white labores now employed by John D. Williams on his white plains plantation have lisened and heard read the foregoing Contract on this sheet of paper assign equal for the black laborers employed by him on said place and we are perfectly Satisfied with it and heare by bind our selves to abide & be Governed & Controwed by it

Wm Wyatte	1 full hand
John Wyatte	1 full hand
Packingham Wyatte	½ " "
Franklin Wyatte	½ " "
R M Hughes	1 full hand
B G Pollard	1 full hand
George Washington Pollard	1 full hand

To sign the contract, all of the blacks and two of the whites "made their marks"; that is, they signed with an "X" because they were illiterate.

Questions

1. In what ways did sharecropping differ from wage labor?
2. Do you see evidence that family or kin members worked together on Williams's plantation?
3. What is the significance of the contract addendum signed by white laborers?

Source: Rosser H. Taylor, "Postbellum Southern Rental Contracts" [from Furman University library, Greenville, South Carolina], *Agricultural History* 17 (1943): 122–123.

■ Residents of Edisto Island, off the coast of South Carolina, pose with a U.S. government mule cart immediately after the Civil War. U.S. troops captured the island in November 1861. The following March, the government began to distribute to blacks the lands abandoned by their former masters. In October 1865, President Andrew Johnson halted the program. A group of angry and disappointed blacks appealed to the president, claiming, "This is our home, we have made these lands what they are." After meeting with the group, General Oliver O. Howard noted, "I am convinced that something must be done to give these people and others the prospect of homesteads."

Soon after the war's end, southern white vigilantes launched a campaign of violence and intimidation against freedpeople who dared to resist the demands of white planters and other employers. Calling itself the Ku Klux Klan, a group of Tennessee war veterans soon became a white supremacist terrorist organization and spread to other states. In May 1866, violence initiated by white terrorists against blacks in Memphis, Tennessee, left forty-six freedpeople and two whites dead, and in July, a riot in New Orleans claimed the lives of thirty-four blacks and three of their white allies. These bloody encounters demonstrated the lengths to which ex-Confederates would go to reassert their authority and defy the federal government.

Back in Washington, Johnson vetoed the Fourteenth Amendment, traveling around the country and urging the states not to ratify it. He argued that policies related to black suffrage should be decided by the states. The time had come for reconciliation between the North and South, maintained the president. (The amendment would not be adopted until 1868.)

Congressional Republicans fought back. In the election of November 1866, they won a two-thirds majority in both houses of Congress. These numbers allowed them to claim a mandate from their constituents and to override any future vetoes by the president. Moderates and radicals together prepared to bypass Johnson to shape their own Reconstruction policies.

The Postbellum South's Labor Problem

While policymakers maneuvered in Washington, black people throughout the South aspired to labor for themselves and gain independence from white overseers and landowners. Yet white landowners persisted in regarding blacks as field hands who must be coerced into working. With the creation of the Freedmen's Bureau in 1865, Congress intended to form an agency that would mediate between these two groups. Bureau agents encouraged workers and employers to sign annual labor contracts designed to eliminate the last vestiges of the slave system. All over the South, freed men, women, and children would contract with an employer on January 1 of each year. They would agree to work for either a monthly wage, an annual share of the crop, or some combination of the two.

> *While policymakers maneuvered in Washington, black people throughout the South aspired to labor for themselves and gain independence from white overseers and landowners.*

Most freedpeople understood they must find a way to provide for themselves first and foremost. They thought of freedom in terms of welfare for their family rather than just for themselves as individuals. Men and women embraced the opportunity to live and work together as a unit. For many couples, their first act as free people was to legalize their marriage vows. Black women shunned the advice of Freedmen's Bureau agents and planters that they continue to pick cotton. These women withdrew from field labor whenever they could afford to do so. Enslaved women had been deprived of the opportunity to attend to family life. Now freedwomen sought to devote themselves to caring for their families.

Blacks along the Georgia and South Carolina coast were determined to cultivate the land on which their forebears had lived and died. They urged General Sherman to confiscate the land owned by rebels in the area. In response, in early 1865, Sherman issued Field Order Number 15, mandating that the Sea Islands and the coastal region south of Charleston be divided into parcels of 40 acres for individual freed families. He also decreed that the army might lend mules to these families to help them begin planting. Given the provisions of this order, many freed families came to expect that the federal government would grant them "40 acres and a mule."

As a result of Sherman's order, 20,000 former slaves proceeded to cultivate the property once owned by Confederates. Within a few months of the war's end, however, the War Department bowed to pressure from the white landowners and revoked the order. The War Department also provided military protection for whites to return and occupy their former lands. In response, a group of black men calling themselves Commissioners from Edisto Island (one of the Sea Islands) met in committee to protest to the Freedmen's Bureau what they considered a betrayal. Writing from the area in January 1866, one Freedmen's Bureau official noted that the new policy must be upheld but regretted that it had brought the freedpeople in "collision" with "U.S. forces."

Southern Skepticism of the Freedmen's Bureau (1866)

During its brief life (1865 to 1868), the Freedmen's Bureau compiled a mixed record. The individual agents represented a broad range of backgrounds, temperaments, and political ideas. Some were former abolitionists who considered northern-style free labor to be "the noblest principle on earth." These men tried to ensure safe and fair working arrangements for black men, women, and children. In contrast, some agents had little patience with the freedpeople's drive for self-sufficiency. Some bureau offices became havens for blacks seeking redress against abusive or fraudulent labor practices, but other offices had little impact on the postwar political and economic landscape. For agents without means of transportation (a reliable horse), plantations scattered throughout the vast rural South remained outside their control. Because white landowners crafted the wording and specific provisions of labor contracts, the bureau agents who enforced such agreements often served the interests of employers rather than laborers.

A Sharecrop Contract

The outlines of **sharecropping**, a system that defined southern cotton production until well into the twentieth century, were visible just a few years after the Civil War. Poor families, black and white, contracted annually with landlords, who advanced them supplies, such as crop seed, mules, plows, food, and clothing. Fathers directed the labor of their children in the fields. At the end of the year, many families remained indebted to their employer and, thus, entitled to nothing and obliged to work another year in the hope of repaying the debt. If a sharecropper's demeanor or work habits displeased the landlord, the family faced eviction.

Single women with small children were especially vulnerable to the whims of landlords in the postbellum period. Near Greensboro, North Carolina, for example, planter Presley George Sr. settled accounts with his field worker Polly at the end of 1865. For her year's expenses, Polly was charged a total $69 for corn, cloth, thread, and board for a child who did not work. By George's calculations, Polly had earned exactly $69 for the labor she and her three children (two sons and a daughter) performed in the course of the year, leaving her no cash of her own. Under these harsh conditions, freedpeople looked to each other for support and strength.

Building Free Communities

Soon after the war's end, southern blacks set about organizing themselves as an effective political force and as free communities devoted to the social and educational welfare of their own people. Differences among blacks based on income, jobs, culture, and skin color at times inhibited institution-building. Some black communities found themselves divided by class, with blacks who had been free before the war (including many literate and skilled light-skinned men) assuming leadership over illiterate field hands. In New Orleans, a combination of factors contributed to class divisions among people of African heritage. During the antebellum period, light-skinned free people of color, many of whom spoke French, were much more likely to possess property and a formal education than were enslaved people, who were dark-skinned English speakers. After the Civil War, the more privileged group pressed for public accommodations laws, which would open the city's theaters, opera, and expensive restaurants to all blacks for the first time. However, black churches and social organizations remained segregated according to class.

"Free At Last"

For the most part, postbellum black communities united around the principle that freedom from slavery should also mean full citizenship rights: the ability to vote, own land, and educate their children. These rights must be enforced by federal firepower: "a military occupation will be absolutely necessary," declared the blacks of Norfolk, "to protect the white Union men of the South, as well as ourselves." Freedpeople in some states allied themselves with white yeomen who had long resented the political power of the great planters and now saw an opportunity to use state governments as agents of democratization and economic reform.

Networks of freedpeople formed self-help organizations. Like the sponsors of the Savannah Education Association, blacks throughout the South formed committees to raise funds and

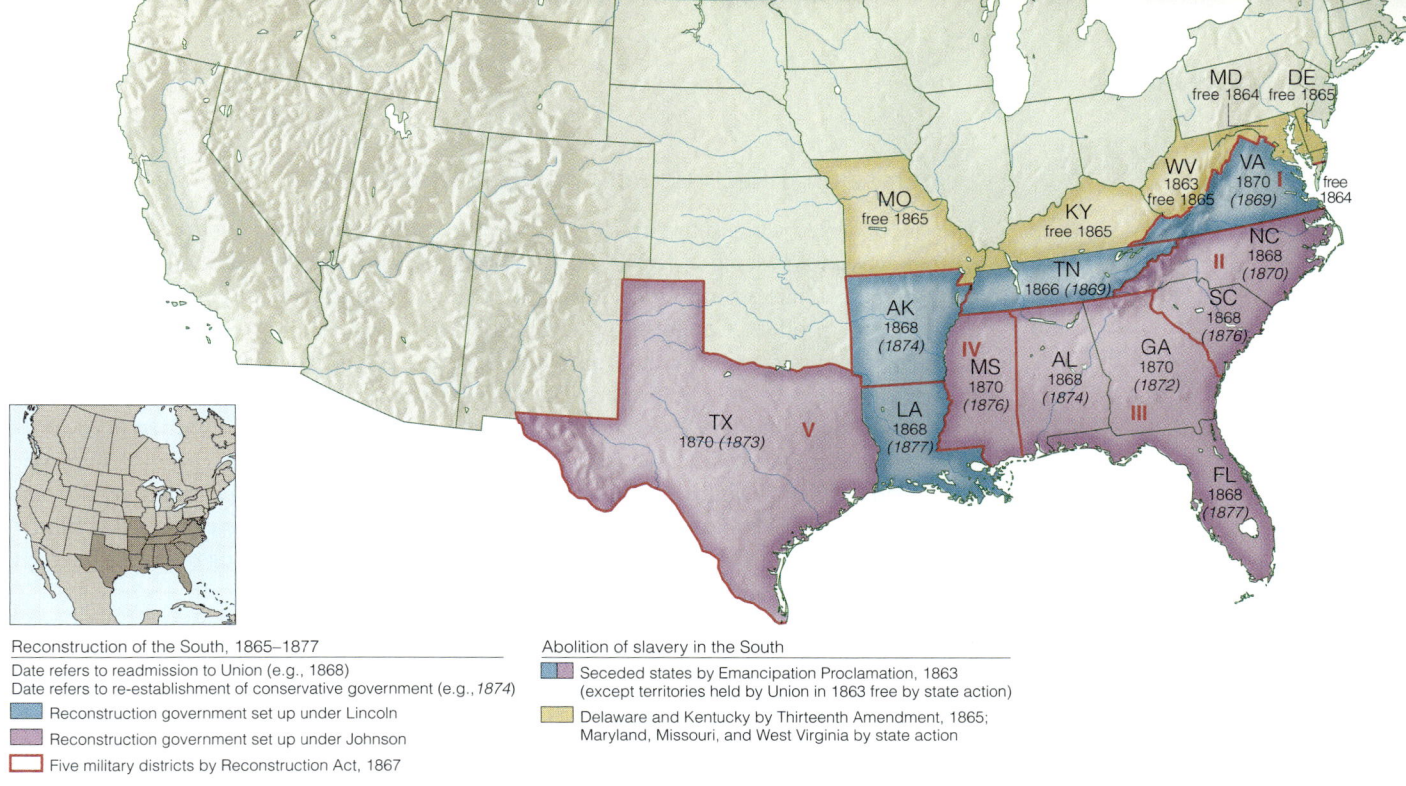

MAP 15.1
RADICAL RECONSTRUCTION Four of the former Confederate states, Louisiana, Arkansas, Tennessee, and Virginia, were reorganized under President Lincoln's Ten Percent Plan in 1864. Neither this plan nor the proposals of Lincoln's successor, Andrew Johnson, provided for the enfranchisement of the former slaves. In 1867 Congress established five military districts in the South and demanded that newly reconstituted state governments implement universal manhood suffrage. By 1870 all of the former Confederate states had rejoined the Union, and by 1877 all of those states had installed conservative (i.e., Democratic) governments.

hire teachers for neighborhood schools. Small Georgia towns, such as Cuthbert, Albany, Cave Spring, and Thomasville, with populations no greater than a few hundred, raised up to $70 per month and contributed as much as $350 each for the construction of school buildings. Funds came from the proceeds of fairs, bazaars, and bake sales; subscriptions raised by local school boards; and tuition fees. In the cash-starved postbellum South, these amounts represented a great personal and group sacrifice for the cause of education.

All over the South, black families charted their own course. They elected to take in orphans and elderly kin, pool resources with neighbors, and arrange for mothers to stay home with their children. These choices challenged the power of former slaveholders and the influence of Freedmen's Bureau agents and northern missionaries and teachers. At the same time, in seeking to attend to their families and to provide for themselves, southern blacks resembled members of other mid-nineteenth-century laboring classes who valued family ties over the demands of employers and landlords.

Tangible signs of the new emerging black communities infuriated most southern whites. A schoolhouse run by blacks proved threatening in a society where most white children had little opportunity to receive an education. Black communities were also quick to form their own churches, rather than continue to occupy an inferior place in white churches. Other sights proved equally unsettling: on a main street in Charleston, an armed black soldier marching proudly or a black woman wearing a fashionable hat and veil, the kind favored by white women of the planter class. These developments help to account for the speed with which whites organized themselves in the Klan and various other vigilante groups, aiming to preserve "the supremacy of the white race in this Republic."

Congressional Reconstruction: The Radicals' Plan

The rise of armed white supremacist groups in the South helped spur congressional Republicans to action. On March 2, 1867, Congress seized the initiative. A coalition led by two radicals, Senator Charles Sumner of Massachusetts and Congressman Thaddeus Stevens of Pennsylvania, prodded Congress to pass the Reconstruction Act of 1867. The purpose of this measure was to purge the South of disloyalty once and for all. The act stripped thousands of former Confederates of voting rights. The former Confederate states would not be readmitted to the Union until they had ratified the Fourteenth Amendment and written new constitutions that guaranteed black men the right to vote. The South (with the exception of Tennessee, which had ratified the Fourteenth Amendment in 1866) was divided into five military districts. Federal troops were stationed throughout the region. These troops were charged with protecting Union personnel and supporters in the South and with restoring order in the midst of regional political and economic upheaval.

Congress passed two additional acts specifically intended to secure congressional power over the president. The intent of the Tenure of Office Act was to prevent the president from dismissing Secretary of War Edwin Stanton, a supporter of the radicals. The other measure, the Command of the Army Act, required the president to seek approval for all military orders from General Ulysses S. Grant, the army's senior officer. Grant also was a supporter of the Republicans. Both of these acts probably violated the separation of powers doctrine as put forth in the Constitution. Together, they would soon precipitate a national crisis.

During the Reconstruction period, approximately 2,000 black men of the emerging southern Republican party served as local elected officials, sheriffs, justices of the peace, tax collectors, and city councilors. Many of these leaders were of mixed ancestry, and many had been free before the war. They came in disproportionate numbers from the ranks of literate men, such as clergy, teachers, and skilled artisans. In Alabama, Florida, Louisiana,

■ This drawing by famous political cartoonist Thomas Nast depicts the first black members of Congress. Left to right, front row: Senator Hiram Revels of Mississippi (the first African American to serve in the U.S. Senate), Representatives Benjamin S. Turner of Alabama, Josiah T. Walls of Florida, Joseph H. Rainey of South Carolina, Robert B. Elliott of South Carolina. Back row: Representatives Robert G. DeLarge of South Carolina, Jefferson Long of Georgia.

Mississippi, and South Carolina, black men constituted a majority of the voting public. Throughout the South, 600 black men won election to state legislatures. However, nowhere did blacks control a state government, although they did predominate in South Carolina's lower House. Sixteen black Southerners were elected to the U.S. Congress during Reconstruction. Most of those elected to Congress in the years immediately after the war were freeborn. However, among the nine men elected for the first time after 1872, six were former slaves. All of these politicians exemplified the desire among southern blacks to become active, engaged citizens.

Newly reconstructed southern state legislatures provided for public school systems, fairer taxation methods, bargaining rights of plantation laborers, racially integrated public transportation and accommodations, and public works projects, especially railroads. Nevertheless, the legislative coalitions forged between Northerners and Southerners, blacks and whites, were uneasy and, in many cases, less than productive. Southern Democrats (and later, historians sympathetic to them) claimed that Reconstruction governments were uniquely corrupt, with some carpetbaggers, scalawags, and freedpeople vying for **kickbacks** from railroad and construction magnates. In fact, whenever state legislatures sought to promote business interests, they opened the door to the bribery of public officials. In this respect, northern as well as southern politicians were vulnerable to charges of corruption. In the long run, southern Democrats cared less about charges of legislative corruption and more about the growing political power of local black Republican party organizations.

In Washington in early 1868, President Johnson forced a final showdown with Congress. He replaced several high military officials with more conservative men. He also fired Secretary of War Stanton, in apparent violation of the Tenure of Office Act. Shortly thereafter, in February, a newly composed House Reconstruction Committee impeached Johnson for ignoring the act, and the Senate began his trial on March 30. The president and Congress were locked in an extraordinary battle for political power.

The final vote was thirty-five senators against Johnson, one vote short of the necessary two-thirds of all senators' votes needed for conviction. Nineteen senators voted to acquit Johnson of the charges. Nevertheless, to win acquittal, he had had to promise moderates that he would not stand in the way of congressional plans for Reconstruction. Johnson essentially withdrew from policymaking in the spring of 1868. That November, Republicans urged Northerners to "vote as you shot" (that is, to cast ballots against the former Confederates) and elected Ulysses S. Grant to the presidency.

Political reunion was an uneven process, but one that gradually eroded the newly won rights of former slaves in many southern states.

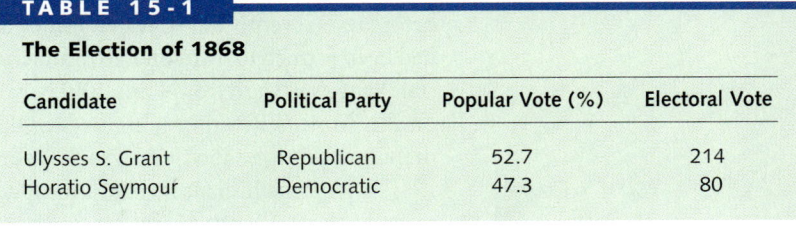

TABLE 15-1

The Election of 1868

Candidate	Political Party	Popular Vote (%)	Electoral Vote
Ulysses S. Grant	Republican	52.7	214
Horatio Seymour	Democratic	47.3	80

By the end of 1868, Arkansas, North Carolina, South Carolina, Louisiana, Tennessee, Alabama, and Florida had met congressional conditions for readmission to the Union, and two years later, Mississippi, Virginia, Georgia, and Texas followed. The Fifteenth Amendment, passed by Congress in 1869 and ratified by the necessary number of states a year later, granted all black men the right to vote. However, in some states, such as Louisiana, reunification gave Democrats license to engage in wholesale election fraud and violence toward freed men and women. In 1870–1871, a congressional inquiry into the Klan exposed pervasive and grisly assaults on Republican schoolteachers, preachers, and prospective voters, black and white. The Klan also targeted men and women who refused to work like slaves in the fields. In April 1871, Congress passed the Ku Klux Klan Act, which punished conspiracies intended to deny rights to citizens. But Klan violence and intimidation had already taken their toll on Republican voting strength.

VIDEO
Legacies of Reconstruction

Claiming Territory for the Union

While blacks and whites, northerners and southerners struggled for power in the south, poet Walt Whitman celebrated the "manly and courageous instincts" that propelled a brave, adventurous people west. Whitman hailed the march across the prairies and over the mountains as a cavalcade of progress. He and other Americans believed that the postbellum migration fulfilled a mission of national regeneration begun by the Civil War. Kansas's population grew by 240 percent in the 1860s, Nebraska's by 355 percent.

To unite the entire country together as a single economic and political unit was the Republican ideal. The railroads in particular served as vehicles of national integration. When the Central Pacific and Union Pacific Railroads met at Promontory Point, Utah, in 1869, the hammering of the spike that joined the two roads produced a telegraphic signal received simultaneously on both coasts, setting off a national celebration.

Meanwhile, regular units of United States cavalry, including two regiments of blacks, were launching attacks on Indians on the Plains, in the Northwest, and in the Southwest. Between 1865 and 1890, U.S. military forces conducted a dozen separate campaigns against western Indian peoples and met Indian warriors in battle or attacked Indian settlements in more than 1,000 engagements. In contrast to African Americans, who adamantly demanded their rights as American citizens, defiant western Indians battled a government to which they owed no allegiance.

Federal Military Campaigns Against Western Indians

In 1871 the U.S. government renounced the practice of seeking treaties with various Indian groups. This change in policy opened the way for a more aggressive effort to subdue native populations. It also hastened the expansion of the reservation system, an effort begun in the antebellum period to confine specific Indian groups to specific territories.

In the Southwest, clashes between Indians and U.S. soldiers persisted after the Civil War. In 1867 at Medicine Lodge Creek in southern Kansas, the United States signed a treaty with an alliance of Comanche, Kiowa, Cheyenne, Arapaho, and Plains Apache. This treaty could not long withstand the provocation posed by the railroad, as Indians continued to attack the surveyors, supply caravans, and military escorts that preceded the railroad work crews. The year before, the Seventh U.S. Cavalry, under the command of Lieutenant Colonel George Custer, had been formed to ward off native attacks on the Union Pacific, snaking its way across the central Plains westward from Kansas. In November 1868, Custer destroyed a Cheyenne settlement on the Washita River, in present-day Oklahoma. Custer's men murdered women and children, burned tipis, and destroyed 800 horses.

Geronimo and Natiche Surrender (1886)

The Apache Indians managed to elude General George Crook until 1875. Crook employed some of these Apache to track down the war chief Geronimo of the Chiricahua. Like many other Indian leaders, Geronimo offered both religious and military guidance to his people. He believed that a spirit would protect him from the white man's bullets and from the arrows of Indians in league with government troops. Yet Geronimo was tricked into a momentary surrender in 1877, and was held in irons for several months before gaining his release and challenging authorities for another nine years.

In 1874 Custer took the Seventh Cavalry into the Black Hills of the Dakotas. Supposedly, the 1868 Treaty of Fort Laramie had rendered this land off-limits to whites. Custer's mission was to offer protection for the surveyors of the Northern Pacific Railroad and to force Indians onto reservations as stipulated in the 1868 treaty. However, the officer lost no time trumpeting the fact that Indian lands were filled with gold. This report prompted a rush to the Black Hills, lands sacred to the Sioux. Within two years, 15,000 gold miners had illegally descended on Indian lands to seek their fortunes. The federal government proposed to buy the land, but leaders of the Sioux, including Red Cloud, Spotted Tail, and Sitting Bull, spurned the offer.

During the morning of June 25, 1876, Custer and his force of 264 soldiers attacked a Sun Dance gathering of 2,500 Sioux and Cheyenne on the banks of the Little Big Horn River in Montana. Custer foolishly launched his attack without adequate backup, and he and his men were easily overwhelmed and killed by Indian warriors, led by the Oglala Sioux Crazy Horse and others. Reacting to this defeat, U.S. military officials reduced the Lakota and Cheyenne to wardship status, ending their autonomy.

Indians throughout the West maintained their distinctive ways of life during these turbulent times. Horse holdings, so crucial for hunting, trading, and fighting, varied from group to group, with the Crow wealthy in relation to their Central Plains neighbors the Oglala and the Arikara. Plains peoples engaged in a lively trading system. They exchanged horses and their trappings (bridles and blankets) for eastern goods such as kettles, guns, and ammunition. Despite their differences in economy, these groups held similar religious beliefs about an all-powerful life force that governed the natural world. People, plants, and animals were all part of the same order.

The Postwar Western Labor Problem

In 1865 the owners of the Central Pacific Railroad seemed poised for one of the great engineering feats of the nineteenth century. In the race eastward from California, they would construct trestles spanning vast chasms and roadbeds traversing mountains and deserts. Government officials in Washington were eager to subsidize the railroad. What the owners lacked was a dependable labor force. The Irish workers who began the line in California struck for higher wages in compensation for brutal, dangerous work. These immigrants dropped their shovels and hammers at the first word of a gold strike nearby—or far away. As a result, in 1866 the Central Pacific had decided to tap into a vast labor source by importing thousands of Chinese men from their native Guangdong province.

■ With this 1870 photograph, the Kansas Pacific Railroad advertised the opportunity for western travelers to shoot buffalo from the comfort and safety of their railroad car. The company's official taxidermist shows off his handiwork. Railroad expansion facilitated the exploitation of natural resources while promoting tourism.

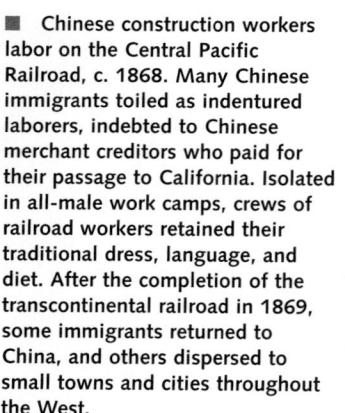
Chinese construction workers labor on the Central Pacific Railroad, c. 1868. Many Chinese immigrants toiled as indentured laborers, indebted to Chinese merchant creditors who paid for their passage to California. Isolated in all-male work camps, crews of railroad workers retained their traditional dress, language, and diet. After the completion of the transcontinental railroad in 1869, some immigrants returned to China, and others dispersed to small towns and cities throughout the West.

The Chinese toiled to extend the railroad tracks eastward from Sacramento, California, up to 10 miles a day in the desert, only a few feet a day in the rugged Sierra Nevada Mountains. In nerve-wracking feats of skill, they lowered themselves in woven baskets to implant nitroglycerine explosives in canyon walls. Chinese laborers toiled through snowstorms and blistering heat to blast tunnels and cut passes through granite mountains. With the final linking of the railroad in Utah in 1869, many Chinese returned to California.

Signed in 1868, the Burlingame Treaty, named for Anson Burlingame, an American envoy to China, had supposedly guaranteed government protection for Chinese immigrants as visitors, traders, or permanent residents. Most immigrants were men. (Six out of ten California Chinese women were listed in the 1870 census as prostitutes, most the victims of their compatriots.) Yet the treaty did not inhibit U.S. employers, landlords, and government officials from discriminating against the Chinese.

By 1870, 40,000 Chinese lived in California and represented fully one-quarter of the state's wage earners. They found work in the cigar, woolen-goods, and boot and shoe factories of San Francisco; in the gold mining towns, now as laundry operators rather than as miners as they had before the Civil War; and in the fields as agricultural laborers. White workers began to cry unfair competition against this Asian group that was becoming increasingly integrated into the region's economy.

As a group, Chinese men differed from California Indians, who remained trapped in the traditional agricultural economy of unskilled labor. Whites appropriated Indian land and forced many men, women, and children to work as wage earners for large landowners. Deprived of their familiar hunting and gathering lands, and wracked by disease and starvation, California Indians had suffered a drastic decline in their numbers by 1870, from 100,000 to 30,000 in twenty years.

Land Use in an Expanding Nation

As with the labor force, the end of the Civil War prompted new conflicts and deepened long-standing ones over the use of the land in a rich, sprawling country. In the South, staple crop planters began to share political power with an emerging elite, men who owned railroads and textile mills. Despairing of ever achieving antebellum levels of labor efficiency, some landowners turned to mining the earth and the forests for saleable commodities. These products, obtained through extraction, included phosphate (used in producing fertilizer), timber, coal, and turpentine.

As European Americans settled in the West and Southwest, they displaced natives who had been living there for generations. For example, the U.S. court system determined who could legally claim property. Western courts also decided whether natural resources such as water, land, timber, and fish and game constituted property that could be owned by private interests. In the Southwest, European American settlers, including army soldiers who had come to fight Indians and then stayed, continued to place Hispanic land titles at risk. Citing prewar precedents, American courts favored the claims of recent squatters over those of long-standing residents. In 1869, with the death of her husband (who had served as a general in the Union army), Maria Amparo Ruiz de Burton saw the large ranch they had worked together near San Diego slip out of her control. The first Spanish-speaking woman to be published in English in the United States, de Burton was a member of the Hispanic elite. Nevertheless, she had little political power. California judges backed the squatters who occupied the ranch.

In the 1870s, the so-called Santa Fe Ring wrested more than 80 percent of the original Spanish grants of land from Hispanic landholders in New Mexico. An alliance of European American lawyers, businesspeople, and politicians, the Santa Fe Ring defrauded families and kin groups of their land titles and speculated in property to make a profit. Whereas many ordinary Hispanic settlers saw land—with its crops, pasture, fuel, building materials, and game—as a source of livelihood, groups such as the Santa Fe Ring saw land primarily as a commodity to be bought and sold.

Seemingly overnight, boom towns sprang up wherever minerals or timber beckoned: southern Arizona and the Rocky Mountains west of Denver, Virginia City in western Nevada, the Idaho-Montana region, and the Black Hills of South Dakota. In all these places, increasing numbers of workers operated sophisticated kinds of machinery, such as rock crushers. When the vein was exhausted or the forests depleted, the towns went bust.

Railroads facilitated not only the mining of minerals but also the growth of the cattle-ranching industry. Rail connections between the Midwest and East made it profitable for Texas ranchers to pay cowboys to drive their herds of long-horned steers to Abilene, Ellsworth, Wichita, or Dodge City, Kansas, for shipment to stockyards in Chicago or St. Louis. Cattle drives were huge; an estimated 10 million animals were herded north from Texas alone between 1865 and 1890. They offered employment to all kinds of men with sufficient skills and endurance. Among the cowhands were African American horsebreakers and gunmen and Mexicans skilled in the use of the *reata* (lasso). Blacks made up about 25 percent and Hispanics about 15 percent of all cowboy outfits.

In knitting regional economies together, federal land policies were crucial to the Republican vision of a developing nation. The Mineral Act of 1866 granted title to millions of acres of mineral-rich land to mining companies, a gift from the federal government to private interests. The Timber Culture Act of 1873 allotted 160 acres to individuals in selected western states if they agreed to plant one-fourth of the acreage with trees. Four years later, the Desert Land Act provided cheap land if buyers irrigated at least part of their parcels.

The Apex Mining Act of 1872 legalized traditional mining practices in the West by validating titles approved by local courts. According to the law, a person who could locate the apex of a vein (its point closest to the surface) could lay claim to the entire vein beneath the surface.

TABLE 15-2
Estimates of Railroad Crossties Used and Acres of Forest Cleared, 1870–1910

Year	Miles of Track	Ties Renewed Annually (millions)	Ties Used on New Construction (millions)	Total Ties Annually (millions)	Acres of Forest Cleared (thousands)
1870	60,000	21	18	39	195
1880	107,000	37	21	58	290
1890	200,000	70	19	89	445
1900	259,000			91	455
1910	357,000			124	620

Source: Michael Williams, *Americans and Their Forests* (1989), 352.

The measure contributed to the wholesale destruction of certain parts of the western landscape as mining companies blasted their way through mountains and left piles of rocks in their wake. It also spurred thousands of lawsuits as claimants argued over what constituted an apex or a vein.

It was during this period that a young Scottish-born naturalist named John Muir began to explore the magnificent canyons and mountains of California. He contrasted nature's majesty with the artificial landscape created by and for humans. In the wilderness, there is nothing "truly dead or dull, or any trace of what in manufactories is called rubbish or waste," he wrote; "everything is perfectly clean and pure and full of divine lessons."

Muir was gratified by the creation of the National Park system during the postwar period. Painters and geologists were among the first Easterners to appreciate the spectacular vistas of the western landscape. In 1864 Congress set aside a small area within California's Yosemite Valley for public recreation and enjoyment. Soon after the war, railroad promoters forged an alliance with government officials in an effort to block commercial development of particularly beautiful pockets of land. Northern Pacific railroad financier Jay Cooke lobbied hard for the government to create a 2-million-acre park in what is today the northwest corner of Wyoming. As a result, in March 1872, Congress established Yellowstone National Park. Tourism would continue to serve as a key component of the western economy.

Muir and others portrayed the Yosemite and Yellowstone valleys as wildernesses, empty of human activity. In fact, both areas had long provided hunting and foraging grounds for native peoples. Yellowstone had been occupied by the people now called the Shoshone since the fifteenth century. This group, together with the Bannock, Crow, and Blackfoot, tried to retain access to Yellowstone's meadows, rivers, and forests after it became a national park. However, U.S. policymakers and military officials persisted in their efforts to mark off territory for specific commercial purposes, while Indians were confined to reservations.

Buying Territory for the Union

Before the war, Republicans had opposed any federal expansionist schemes that they feared might benefit slaveholders. However, after 1865 and the outlawing of slavery, some Republican lawmakers and administration officials advocated the acquisition of additional territory. Secretary of State William Seward led the way in 1867 by purchasing Alaska from Russia. For $7.2 million (about 2 cents an acre), the United States gained 591,004 square miles of land. Within the territory were diverse indigenous groups—Eskimo, Aleut, Tlingit, Tsimshian, Athabaskan, and Haida—and a small number of native Russians. Though derided at the time as "Seward's icebox," Alaska yielded enough fish, timber, minerals, oil, and water power in the years to come to prove that the original purchase price was a tremendous bargain.

The impulse that prompted administration support for the Alaska purchase also spawned other plans for territorial acquisitions. In 1870 some Republicans joined with Democrats in calling for the annexation of the Dominican Republic. These congressmen argued that the tiny Caribbean country would make a fine naval base, provide investment opportunities for American businesspeople, and offer a refuge for southern freedpeople.

However, influential Senator Charles Sumner warned against a takeover without considering the will of the Dominican people, who were currently involved in their own civil war. Some congressmen, in a prelude to foreign policy debates of the 1890s, suggested that the dark-skinned Dominican people were incapable of appreciating the blessings of American citizenship. In 1871 an annexation treaty failed to win Senate approval.

The Republican Vision and Its Limits

After the Civil War, victorious Republicans envisioned a nation united in the pursuit of prosperity. All citizens would be free to follow their individual economic self-interest and to enjoy the fruits of honest toil. In contrast, some increasingly vocal and well-organized groups saw the expansion of legal rights, and giving black men the right to vote in particular, as only initial, tentative steps on the path to an all-inclusive citizenship. Women, industrial workers, farmers, and African Americans made up overlapping constituencies pressing for equal political rights and economic opportunity. Together they challenged the mainstream Republican view that defeat of the rebels and destruction of slavery were sufficient to guarantee all people prosperity.

Government-business partnerships also produced unanticipated consequences for Republicans committed to what they believed was the collective good. Some politicians and business leaders saw these partnerships as opportunities for private gain. Consequently, private greed and public corruption accompanied postwar economic growth. Thus, Republican leaders faced challenges from two very different sources: people agitating for civil rights and people hoping to reap personal gain from political activities.

Postbellum Origins of the Woman Suffrage Movement

After the Civil War, the nation's middle class, which had its origins in the antebellum period, continued to grow. Dedicated to self-improvement and filled with a sense of moral authority, many middle-class Americans (especially Protestants) felt a deep cultural connection to their counterparts in England. Indeed, the United States produced its own "Victorians," so called for the self-conscious middle class that emerged in the England of Queen Victoria during her reign from 1837 to 1901.

At the heart of the Victorian sensibility was the ideal of domesticity: a harmonious family living in a well-appointed home, guided by a pious mother and supported by a father successful in business. Famous Protestant clergyman Henry Ward Beecher and his wife were outspoken proponents of this domestic ideal. According to Eunice Beecher, women had no "higher, nobler, more divine mission than in the conscientious endeavor to create a *true home.*"

Yet the traumatic events of the Civil War only intensified the desire among a growing group of American women to participate fully in the nation's political life. They wanted to extend their moral influence outside the narrow and exclusive sphere of the home. Many women believed that they deserved the vote and that the time was right to demand it.

In 1866 veteran reformers Elizabeth Cady Stanton, Susan B. Anthony, and Lucy Stone founded the Equal Rights Association to link the rights of white women and African Americans. Nevertheless, in 1867, Kansas voters defeated a referendum proposing **suffrage** for both blacks and white women. This disappointment convinced some former abolitionists that the two causes should be separated—that women should wait patiently until the rights of African American men were firmly secured. Frederick Douglass declined an invitation to a women's suffrage convention in Washington, D.C., in 1868. He explained, "I am now devoting myself to a cause [if] not more sacred, certainly more urgent, because it is one of life and death to the long enslaved people of this country, and that is: negro suffrage." But African American activist and former slave Sojourner Truth warned, "There is a great stir about colored men getting their rights, but not a word about the colored women; and if colored men get their rights, and not colored women get theirs, there will be a bad time about it."

In 1869 two factions of women parted ways and formed separate organizations devoted to women's rights. The more radical wing, including Cady Stanton and Anthony, bitterly denounced the Fifteenth Amendment because it gave the vote to black men only. They helped to found the National Woman Suffrage Association (NWSA), which argued for a renewed commitment to the original Declaration of Sentiments passed in Seneca Falls, New York, two decades earlier. They favored married women's property rights, liberalization of divorce laws, opening colleges and trade schools to women, and a new federal amendment to allow women to vote. Lucy Stone and her husband, Henry Blackwell, founded the rival American Woman Suffrage Association (AWSA). This group downplayed the larger struggle for women's rights and focused on the suffrage question exclusively. Its members supported the Fifteenth Amendment and retained ties to the Republican party. The AWSA focused on state-by-state campaigns for women's suffrage.

In 1871 the NWSA welcomed the daring, flamboyant Victoria Woodhull as a vocal supporter, only to renounce her a few years later. Woodhull's political agenda ranged from free love and dietary reform to legalized prostitution, working men's rights, and women's suffrage. (In the nineteenth century, free love advocates denounced what they called a sexual double standard, one that glorified female chastity while tolerating male promiscuity.)

In 1872 one of Woodhull's critics successfully challenged her. Woodhull spent a month in jail as a result of the zealous prosecution by vice reformer Anthony Comstock, a clergyman who objected to her public discussions and writings on sexuality. Comstock assumed the role of an outspoken crusader against vice. A federal law passed in 1873, and named after him, equated information related to birth control with pornography, banning this and other "obscene material" from the mails.

Susan B. Anthony used the 1872 presidential election as a test case for women's suffrage. She attempted to vote and was arrested, tried, and convicted as a result. By this time, most women suffragists, and most members of the NWSA for that matter, had become convinced that they should focus on the vote exclusively; they therefore accepted the AWSA's policy on this issue. In the coming years, they would avoid other causes with which they might have allied themselves, including black civil rights and labor reform.

> *The economic developments that allowed factory managers and owners of large wheat farms to make a comfortable living for themselves did not necessarily benefit agricultural and manufacturing workers.*

Workers' Organizations

Many Americans benefited from economic changes of the postwar era. Railroading, mining, and heavy industry helped fuel the national economy and in the process boosted the growth of the urban managerial class. In the Midwest, many landowning farmers prospered when they responded to an expanding demand for grain and other staple crops. In Wisconsin, wheat farmers cleared forests, drained swamps, diverted rivers, and profited from the booming world market in grain. Yet the economic developments that allowed factory managers and owners of large wheat farms to make a comfortable living for themselves did not necessarily benefit agricultural and manufacturing workers.

■ A Norwegian immigrant extended family in the town of Norway Grove, Wisconsin, poses in front of their imposing home and up-to-date carriage in this photograph taken in the mid-1870s. Linking their fortunes to the world wheat market, these newcomers to the United States prospered. Wrote one woman to her brother back home in Norway, "We all have cattle, driving oxen, and wagons. We also have children in abundance."

Indeed, during this period growing numbers of working people, in the countryside and in the cities, became caught up in a cycle of indebtedness. In the upcountry South (above the fall line, or Piedmont), formerly self-sufficient family farmers sought loans from banks to repair their war-damaged homesteads. To qualify for these loans, the farmer had to plant cotton as a staple crop, to the neglect of corn and other foodstuffs. Many sharecroppers, black and white, received payment in the form of credit only; for these families, the end-of-the-year reckoning yielded little more than rapidly accumulating debts. Midwestern farmers increasingly relied on expensive threshing and harvesting machinery and on bank loans to purchase the machinery.

Several organizations founded within five years of the war's end offered laborers an alternative vision to the Republicans' brand of individualism and nationalism. In 1867 Oliver H. Kelly, a former Minnesota farmer now working in a Washington office, organized the National Grange of the Patrons of Husbandry, popularly known as the Grange. This movement sought to address a new, complex marketplace increasingly dominated by railroads, banks, and grain elevator operators. The Grange encouraged farmers to form **cooperatives** that would market their crops and to challenge discriminatory railroad rates that favored big business.

Founded in Baltimore in 1866, the National Labor Union (NLU) consisted of a collection of craft unions and claimed as many as 600,000 members at its peak in the early 1870s. The group welcomed farmers as well as factory workers and promoted legislation for an eight-hour workday and the arbitration of industrial disputes.

In 1873 a nationwide depression threw thousands out of work and worsened the plight of debtors. Businesspeople in agriculture, mining, the railroad industry, and manufacturing had overexpanded their operations. The free-wheeling loan practices of major banks had contributed to this situation. The inability of these businesspeople to repay their loans led to the failure of major banks. With the contraction of credit, thousands of small businesses went bankrupt. The NLU did not survive the crisis.

However, by this time, a new organization had appeared to champion the cause of the laboring classes in opposition to lords of finance. Founded in 1869 by Uriah Stephens and other Philadelphia tailors, the Knights of Labor eventually aimed to unite industrial and rural workers, the self-employed and the wage earner, blacks and whites, and men and women. The Knights were committed to private property and to the independence of the farmer, the entrepreneur, and the industrial worker. The group banned from its ranks "nonproducers," such as liquor sellers, bankers, professional gamblers, stockbrokers, and lawyers.

This period of depression also laid the foundation for the Greenback Labor party, organized in 1878. Within three years after the end of the Civil War, the Treasury had withdrawn from circulation $100 million in wartime paper currency ("greenbacks"). With less money in circulation, debtors found it more difficult to repay their loans. The government also ceased coining silver dollars in 1873, despite the discovery of rich silver lodes in the West. To add insult to injury, the Resumption Act (1875) called for the government to continue to withdraw paper greenbacks. Thus, hard money became dearer, and debtors became more desperate. In 1878 the new Greenback Labor party managed to win 1 million votes and elect fourteen candidates to Congress. The party laid the foundation for the Populist party that emerged in the 1890s.

Several factors made coalition building among these American workers difficult. One was the nation's increasingly multicultural workforce. Unions, such as the typographers, were notorious for excluding women and African Americans, a fact publicized by both Frederick Douglass and Susan B. Anthony, to no avail. In 1869 shoe factory workers (members of the Knights of St. Crispin) went on strike in North Adams, Massachusetts. They were soon shocked to see seventy-five Chinese strikebreakers arrive by train from California. Their employer praised the new arrivals for their "rare industry." The shoemakers' strike collapsed quickly after the appearance of what the workers called this "Mongolian battery." Employers would continue to manipulate and divide the laboring classes through the use of ethnic, religious, and racial prejudices.

Political Corruption and the Decline of Republican Idealism

Out of the new partnership between politics and business emerged an extensive system of bribes and kickbacks. Greedy politicians of both parties challenged the Republicans' high-minded idealism.

In the early 1870s, the *New York Times* exposed the schemes of William M. "Boss" Tweed. Tweed headed Tammany Hall, a New York City political organization that courted labor unions and contributed liberally to Catholic schools and charities. Tammany Hall politicians routinely used bribery and extortion to fix elections and bilk taxpayers of millions of dollars. One plasterer employed on a city project received $138,000 in "payment" for two days' work. After the *Times* **exposé**, Tweed was prosecuted and convicted. His downfall attested to the growing influence of newspaper reporters.

Another piece of investigative journalism rocked the political world in 1872. In 1867 major stockholders of the Union Pacific Railroad had formed a new corporation, called the Crédit Mobilier, to build railroads. Heads of powerful congressional committees received shares of stock in the new company. These gifts of stock were bribes to secure the legislators' support for public land grants favorable to the new corporation. The *New York Sun* exposed a number of the chief beneficiaries in the fall of 1872, findings confirmed by congressional investigation. Among the disgraced politicians was Grant's vice president, Schuyler Colfax.

The 1872 presidential election pitted incumbent Grant against the Democratic challenger, *New York Tribune* editor Horace Greeley. Many Republicans, disillusioned with congressional corruption and eager to press forward with civil service reform, endorsed the Democratic candidate. Greeley and his Republican allies decried the patronage (or "spoils") system by which politicians rewarded their supporters with government jobs. Nevertheless, Grant won the election.

By 1872, after four bloody years of war and seven squandered years of postwar opportunity, the federal government seemed prepared to hand the South back to unrepentant rebels. The North showed what one House Republican called "a general apathy among the people concerning the war and the negro." The Civil Rights Act of 1875 guaranteed blacks equal access to public accommodations and transportation. Yet this act represented the final, half-hearted gesture of radical Republicanism. The Supreme Court declared the measure unconstitutional in 1883 on the grounds that the government could protect only political and not social rights. White Southerners reasserted their control over the region's political economy.

The presidential election of 1876 intensified public cynicism about deal making in high places. A dispute over election returns led to what came to be known as the Compromise of 1877. In the popular vote, Democrat Samuel J. Tilden outpolled Republican Rutherford B. Hayes, a former Ohio governor. However, when the electoral votes were counted, the Democrat had only 184, one short of the necessary number. Nineteen of the twenty votes in dispute came from Louisiana, South Carolina, and Florida, and these three states submitted two new sets of returns, one from each of the two main parties. A specially appointed congressional electoral commission, the Committee of Fifteen, was charged with resolving the dispute. It divided along

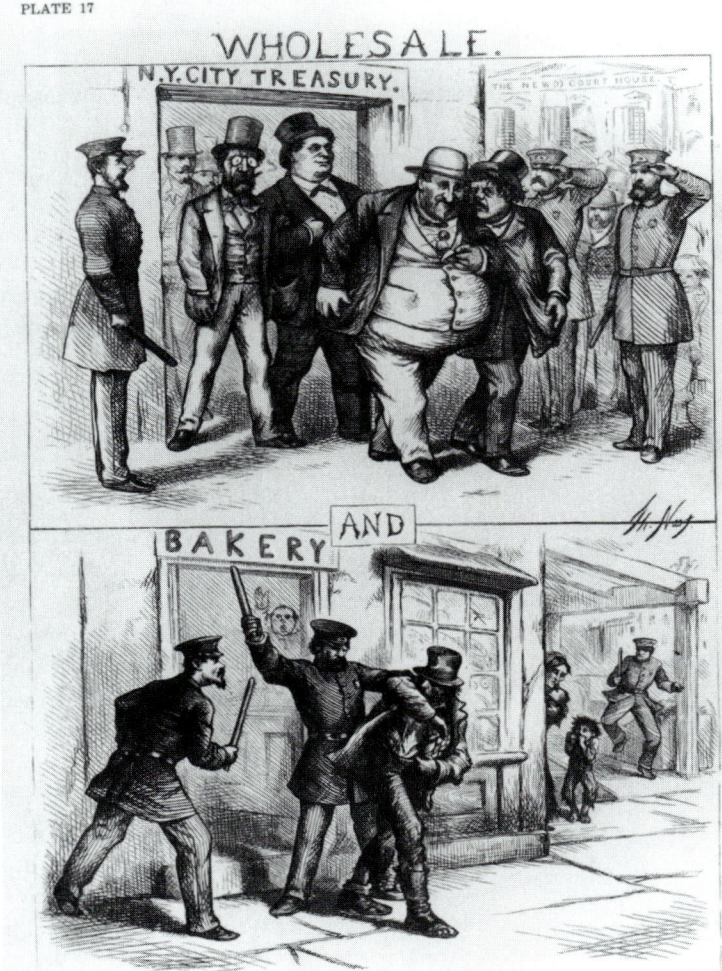

■ In 1871 Thomas Nast drew a series of cartoons exposing the corruption of New York City Democratic boss William M. Tweed and his political organization, Tammany Hall. In this drawing, published in *Harper's Weekly* in 1871, Nast depicts Tweed and his cronies engaging in a "wholesale" looting of the New York City treasury with the assistance of compliant police officers. Those same officers stand ready to crack down on the impoverished father who robs a bakery to feed his family. By portraying Tweed as an enemy of the poor, Nast ignored the fact that the political boss gained a large following among immigrant voters.

TABLE 15-3

The Election of 1872

Candidate	Political Party	Popular Vote (%)	Electoral Vote
Ulysses S. Grant	Republican	55.6	286
Horace Greeley	Democratic, Liberal Republican	43.9	66

TABLE 15-4
The Election of 1876

Candidate	Political Party	Popular Vote (%)	Electoral Vote
Rutherford B. Hayes	Republican	48.0	185
Samuel J. Tilden	Democratic	51.0	184

Samuel Tilden's Speech to the Manhattan Club Conceding the Election of 1876

partisan lines. The eight Republicans outvoted the seven Democrats to accept the Republican set of returns from Florida.

To break the logjam, the Democrats agreed that Hayes could assume office in return for the withdrawal of all remaining federal troops from the South. The Republicans tacitly agreed that their work there was finished and that blacks in the region should fend for themselves. Hayes declined to enforce the Civil Rights Act of 1875. White Southerners were free to uphold the principle of states' rights that had been traditionally invoked to deny blacks their rights in the region.

Conclusion

During the dozen or so years after the Civil War, both northern Republicans and southern Democrats registered a series of spectacular wins and crushing losses. Though humiliated by the Union victory, southern white supremacists eventually won for themselves the freedom to control their own local and state governments. As landlords, sheriffs, and merchants, these men defied the postwar federal amendments to the Constitution and deprived African Americans of basic citizenship rights. By the end of Reconstruction, northern Republicans had conceded local power to their former enemies. Even an aggressive nationalism, it turned out, could accept traditional southern hierarchies: white over nonwhite, rich over poor.

On the other hand, at the end of Reconstruction, Republicans remained in firm control of national economic policy. The white South had secured its right to conduct its own political affairs, but the Republican vision of economic growth and development had become the law of the land. This vision was a guiding principle of historic national and, increasingly, international significance. Economic innovation in particular proved to be a force of great unifying power, stronger than all the federal military forces deployed during and after the Civil War.

Sites to Visit

Impeachment of Andrew Johnson
www.impeach-andrewjohnson.com

This HarpWeek site about the impeachment includes images and text from the Reconstruction period.

Diary and Letters of Rutherford B. Hayes
www.ohiohistory.org/onlinedoc/hayes/index.cfm

The Rutherford B. Hayes Presidential Center in Fremont, Ohio, maintains this searchable database of his writings.

Freedmen and Southern Society Project (University of Maryland, College Park)
www.history.umd.edu/Freedmen/index.html

This site contains a chronology and sample documents from several collections of primary sources about emancipation and freedom in the 1860s.

History of the Suffrage Movement
www.rochester.edu/SBA/

This site includes a chronology, important texts relating to women's suffrage, and bibliographical information about Susan B. Anthony and Elizabeth Cady Stanton.

Indian Memorial at Little Big Horn Battlefield National Monument
www.nps.gov/libi/indmem.htm

The Smithsonian Institution maintains this site, providing information about the museum.

National Museum of the American Indian
www..nmai.si.edu

The Smithsonian Institution maintains this site, providing information about the museum.

Northern Great Plains, 1880–1920: Photographs from the Fred Hulstrand and F. A. Pazandak Photograph Collections
www.memory.loc.gov/ammem/award97/ndfahtml/ngphome.html

This American Memory site from the Library of Congress contains two collections from the Institute for Regional Studies at North Dakota State University with 900 photographs of rural and small-town life at the turn of the century. Included are images of sod homes and the people who built them, farms and the machinery that made them prosper, and one-room schools and the children who were educated in them.

For Further Reading

General Works

Eric Foner, *Reconstruction: America's Unfinished Revolution, 1863–1877* (1988).

David Montgomery, *Beyond Equality: Labor and the Radical Republicans, 1862–1872* (1967).

Amy Dru Stanley, *From Bondage to Contract: Wage Labor, Marriage, and the Market in the Age of Slave Emancipation* (1998).

Ronald Takaki, *A Different Mirror: A History of Multicultural America* (1993).

Richard White, *"It's Your Misfortune and None of My Own": A History of the American West* (1991).

The Struggle over the South

Peter Bardaglio, *Reconstructing the Household: Families, Sex and the Law in the Nineteenth-Century South* (1995).

Ira Berlin and Leslie S. Rowland, eds., *Families and Freedom: A Documentary History of African-American Kinship in the Civil War Era* (1997).

Dwight B. Billings, *Planters and the Making of a "New South": Class, Politics, and Development in North Carolina, 1865–1900* (1979).

Frederick Cooper, Thomas C. Holt, and Rebecca J. Scott, eds., *Beyond Slavery: Explorations of Race, Labor, and Citizenship in Post-Emancipation Societies* (2000).

Michael Golay, *A Ruined Land: The End of the Civil War* (1999).

Thomas C. Holt, *Black over White: Negro Political Leadership in South Carolina During Reconstruction* (1977).

Jacqueline Jones, *Soldiers of Light and Love: Northern Teachers and Georgia Blacks, 1865–1873* (1980).

Claiming Territory for the Union

Stephen E. Ambrose, *Nothing Like It in the World: The Men Who Built the Transcontinental Railroad, 1863–1869* (2000).

Orin G. Libby, ed., *The Arikara Narrative of the Campaign Against the Hostile Dakotas, June, 1876* (1998).

Ruth B. Moynihan, Susan Armitage, and Christiane Fischer Dichamp, eds., *So Much to Be Done: Women Settlers on the Mining and Ranching Frontier* (1990).

Larry Sklenar, *To Hell with Honor: Custer and the Little Bighorn* (2000).

Robert Wooster, *The Military and United States Indian Policy, 1865–1903* (1988).

Judy Yung, *Unbound Feet: A Social History of Chinese Women in San Francisco* (1995).

The Republican Vision and Its Limits

Leon Fink, *Workingmen's Democracy: The Knights of Labor and American Politics* (1983).

Barbara Goldsmith, *Other Powers: The Age of Suffrage, Spiritualism, and the Scandalous Victoria Woodhull* (1998).

Heather Cox Richardson, *The Death of Reconstruction: Race, Labor and Politics in the Post-Civil War North* (2001).

Lyde Cullen Sizer, *The Political Work of Northern Women Writers and the Civil War* (2000).

Irwin Unger, *The Greenback Era: A Social and Political History of American Finance, 1865–1879* (1964).

For quizzes and other resources on these topics, go to www.longmanamericanhistory.com.

1877	All federal troops withdrawn from the South, ending Reconstruction
	"Great Uprising" of railroad employees and other workers
1878	Thomas Edison patents the phonograph
	San Francisco Workingmen's party stages anti-Chinese protests
1879	First telephone line connects two American cities (Boston and Lowell, Massachusetts)
1880	New York City streets lit by electricity
1881	Charles Guiteau assassinates President Garfield
1882	Standard Oil Trust is created
	Chinese Exclusion Act
1883	Pendleton Act (civil service reform)
1884	Mark Twain, *The Adventures of Huckleberry Finn*
1885	Geronimo leads Apache to Sierra Madres in Mexico
1886	Accused Haymarket bombers tried and convicted
	Geronimo and his followers are sent to Fort Marion, Florida; the children are sent to the government Indian school in Carlisle, Pennsylvania
1887	Interstate Commerce Act creates Interstate Commerce Commission
	Dawes Severalty Act
	United States claims right to Pearl Harbor, leases it as a coaling and repair station

1888	Edward Bellamy, *Looking Backward*
1889	First All-American football team, consisting of players from Yale, Harvard, and Princeton
	National Farmers' Alliance is founded
1890	Sherman Anti-Trust Act
	Wyoming admitted to the Union, first state to enfranchise women
	National American Woman Suffrage Association is formed
	Wounded Knee Massacre

PART SIX

The Emergence of Modern America, 1877–1900

THE UNITED STATES BECAME A MODERN NATION DURING THE LAST quarter of the nineteenth century. Vast reserves of coal, timber, and water helped fuel a growing industrial economy. Railroad lines criss-crossed the nation and knit together regional economies. Large numbers of immigrants, many from eastern Europe, arrived in the United States, drawn by America's rising standard of living, high demand for labor, and religious and political freedom.

To raise the money needed to purchase expensive equipment and machinery, coal and oil producers and railroad owners formed modern corporations, businesses that were owned by stockholders rather than individuals. The largest businesses sought to dominate the marketplace by eliminating their competitors. Managers could cut production and operating costs by slashing the wages of workers or by installing labor-saving machinery. Either way, workers paid the price.

The generation that came of age after the Civil War witnessed a series of violent confrontations between workers and employers. Standards of industrial work discipline required workers to labor for long hours at dangerous, disagreeable jobs. Some workers formed new kinds of labor unions to combat the power of big business. Some organizations, such as the Knights of Labor, were national in scope and inclusive in their membership; others represented the interests of specific groups of workers. Employers, local and state law enforcement officials, and judges used a variety of means to suppress strikes and other forms of collective action among workers. Nevertheless, local communities often supported the strikers, who were their friends and neighbors.

During the late nineteenth century, the national economy began to shift to the production of consumer goods. New products gave Americans new ways to spend their money. Manufacturers of everything from toothpaste to bathtubs advertised their goods to a mass market. In cities, department stores offered a dazzling array of goods.

Even as the country was becoming more ethnically diverse, advertisers promoted a single standard of physical beauty and material well-being. At the same time, some scholars and politicians seized on a revolutionary new theory of natural history to argue for the superiority of white, middle-class Americans. Social Darwinism served as the intellectual justification for unfettered economic growth and for the subjugation of darker-skinned peoples, at home and abroad.

Many Americans rejected the trends toward economic standardization and cultural homogeneity. Native Americans in the West continued to resist the railroad and its profound threat to their way of life. By 1890 the U.S. military had forcibly subdued most of these Indians, relegating many to reservations. Together with industrial workers throughout the nation, Hispanic villagers in the Southwest and African American sharecroppers in the South disputed the notion that progress could be defined exclusively in terms of economic growth and development.

Middle-class reformers sought to mediate between what they perceived to be two dangerous groups: arrogant industrialists and discontented workers. These reformers feared that rapid urban and industrial growth would cause rifts in the social fabric. Middle-class women pioneered in the founding of social settlements and other urban institutions to ease the transition of immigrants into modern American society.

The lines between national standards and local cultural interests often blurred. For example, for a short time Sioux chief Sitting Bull (Tatanka Iyotake) appeared with William ("Buffalo Bill") Cody's "Wild West" show, which played to enthusiastic audiences in the United States and Europe. Yet this Indian leader also led the Plains Indians as they attempted to resist U.S. military authorities. Some groups of Americans who sought to preserve their own cultural traditions nonetheless aspired to a middle-class way of life and its material comforts. Elite Hispanic families in the Southwest remained devoted to their Roman Catholic faith and at the same time followed up-to-date clothing fashions marketed by East Coast department stores.

The promise and the conflicts inherent in the emerging modern social order met head on in the 1890s. A new political party called the Populists mounted a brief but potent challenge to entrenched economic and political power. The Populists failed in their attempt to capture the presidency in 1896, but they offered a vision of a new kind of political party, one that would bring black and white farmers and industrial workers together in opposition to landlords, employers, and bankers.

In 1898, in an effort to protect its interests in the Western Hemisphere and to extend those interests into the Pacific, the United States went to war with Spain. This imperialist venture suggested the links among several impulses, including missionary outreach, commercial expansion, and white supremacist racial ideologies. By 1900 the United States was fast becoming a world leader in terms of manufacturing, technological innovation, and the rapid growth of its prosperous middle class.

1891	Populist party formed Eleven Italian immigrants are lynched in New Orleans
1892	Ellis Island opens as screening site for immigrants Miners strike in Coeur d'Alene, Idaho Steelworkers strike at Carnegie's Homestead plant near Pittsburgh
1893	Columbian Exposition opens in Chicago Pro-American interests stage a successful coup against Queen Liliuokalani of Hawaii Worst nationwide depression to date
1894	Coxey's Army marches on Washington, D.C. Pullman workers strike
1896	Supreme Court decides *Plessy v. Ferguson*, upholds segregation W. E. B. Du Bois is first black person to receive a Ph.D. from Harvard
1898	United States annexes Hawaii *Maine* blows up in Havana Harbor  United States defeats Spain in Spanish-American-Cuban-Filipino War Spain cedes Guam and Puerto Rico to United States, turns over Philippines in return for $20 million
1899	Gen. Emilio Aguinaldo leads Filipino revolt against 70,000 U.S. occupying forces
1900	U.S. troops sent to China to crush Boxer Rebellion 

CHAPTER 16

Standardizing the Nation: Innovations in Technology, Business, and Culture, 1877–1890

ANDREW CARNEGIE EVENTUALLY BECAME THE RICHEST MAN IN THE WORLD, but he began life in modest circumstances. In 1835 Will and Margaret Carnegie were living in the village of Dunfermline, Scotland, where Will was a skilled weaver. The couple had two sons—Andrew, born in 1835, and Tom, born eight years later. When steam-powered textile looms threw Will Carnegie and other handweavers out of work, the family emigrated to the United States and settled in Pittsburgh, Pennsylvania. Eager to work hard, Andrew took a series of jobs to help support the family: bobbin boy in a textile mill, tender of a steam boiler in a factory, clerk and then messenger in a telegraph office. By the time he was 18 years old, he was personal assistant to Thomas Scott, superintendent of the Western Division of the Pennsylvania Railroad. Three years later, after the death of his father, Andrew assumed the role of family breadwinner; he also took over the job of Thomas Scott, who became president of the railroad.

Working for the railroad, Andrew Carnegie learned a great deal about running a gigantic business efficiently and profitably. He also invested in oil and railroads. In 1872 he visited England and gained firsthand information about the production of steel, a lighter, stronger material than iron. Three years later he opened his own steel plant in Pittsburgh, then proceeded to buy rival steel mills.

CHAPTER OUTLINE

The New Shape of Business

The Birth of a National Urban Culture

Thrills, Chills, and Bathtubs: The Emergence of Consumer Culture

Defending the New Industrial Order

Conclusion

Sites to Visit

For Further Reading

In his business life, Andrew Carnegie was a man of strong principles. In 1868 he had promised himself that he would not hoard the money he made; instead he would promote the "education and improvement of the poorer classes." Earning $25 million a year by the early 1890s, he nonetheless believed that "The amassing of wealth is one of the worst species of idolatry." During the course of his career, Carnegie gave away 90 percent of his fortune, founding the Carnegie Endowment for International Peace, as well as many public libraries around the country.

It was significant that Carnegie spent his formative years in business learning about railroads. These lessons paved the way for his own success in the steel industry. By 1877 the emergence of a national rail system signaled the rise of big business. The railroad industry produced Amer-

■ When Andrew Carnegie retired in 1901, he sold the Carnegie Steel Company to American banker and financier J. P. Morgan for $480 million. Carnegie's personal fortune was about $500 million.

The "Great Labor Uprising" of July 1877 was the first national strike in U.S. history. As railroad lines proliferated, owners slashed wages in a bid to remain competitive. Railroad workers in some cities destroyed trains, tracks, and other equipment. Spreading eventually to fourteen states, the conflict claimed the lives of more than 100 people and resulted in the loss of millions of dollars worth of private property.

ica's first business bureaucracies, employing gigantic workforces to maintain, schedule, operate, and staff trains that traversed 93,000 miles of track. By 1890 the Pennsylvania Railroad had become the nation's largest employer, with 110,000 workers on its payroll. About one out of seven people worked in the rail industry. The personnel in charge of coordinating these vast operations were among the country's first professional, salaried managers.

The railroad industry was both a great centralizer and a great standardizer. Trains ran on schedules that were set by a central office, and those schedules relied on definitions of actual time that were standard throughout the nation. Moreover, trains broke down regional boundaries by transporting goods to all areas of the country. For the first time, trains carried brand-name goods and commodities to a national market. A California wheat farmer could purchase replacement parts for his McCormick reaper manufactured in Chicago. An Iowa farm family ordered a new cookstove through a mail-order catalogue. Levi-Strauss, a small clothier in San Francisco, shipped its famous denim pants to cowboys in Texas. Pillsbury Flour of Minnesota distributed its products to bakeries throughout the Midwest. Armour Meatpacking of Chicago sent its sausages to the East Coast. With the introduction of the new refrigerated railroad car, trains also began carrying larger loads of fruits and vegetables over longer distances. The new traffic in produce stimulated commercial agriculture in the South and on the West Coast.

Few Americans amassed the fabulous fortunes of rich industrialists like Carnegie, yet most people aspired to a better life, even in modest terms. Proprietors, managers, and office workers filled the ranks of the comfortable middle class, men and women freed of the danger and drudgery of manual labor. Between 1880 and 1900, clerical workers tripled in number, and business managers increased from 68,000 to more than 318,000. Enjoying steady work and cash salaries, middle-class employees began to move their families out of the city. Urban areas were becoming increasingly befouled by smokestacks and congested with new factories and workshops.

Providers of goods and services celebrated a "standard" American viewed as white, native born, middle class, heterosexual, and Protestant. This image assumed special significance in the marketing of consumer products and in the appeal of new forms of leisure activities. With technical innovations came novel ways for people to spend their money. Athletic contests, traveling road shows, and amusement parks provided exciting sensory experiences for young and old alike. At the same time, the mass marketing of goods gave rise to a consumer culture that valued newness, fashion, and luxury.

Mass advertising techniques heightened distinctions that European Americans drew between themselves and people they considered inferior, exotic, or foreign. Yet the energy and vitality associated with American popular culture served as a magnet for people all over the world. Beginning in the 1880s, eastern European immigrants streamed to the United States. They were also eager to partake of the country's plentiful jobs, material prosperity, and democratic openness. Well into the twentieth century, the nation still showed the ethnic and cultural diversity that was shaped by patterns of immigration during the late nineteenth century.

The New Shape of Business

In 1882 prospectors discovered gold in the creeks of Idaho's Coeur d'Alene region (in Indian territory, about 90 miles east of Spokane, Washington). Multiethnic boomtowns mushroomed in the region. The Northern Pacific Railway promoted settlement, and the primitive techniques that had been used in surface mining soon yielded to far more efficient hydraulic methods of extraction (a process in which powerful water hoses wash the soil away to expose gold deposits).

The mining industry in the region soon emerged as a big business. In 1885 an unemployed carpenter named Noah S. Kellogg set in motion a dramatic chain of events. Kellogg discovered a lode containing not only gold but also zinc and lead. In short order, he sold his mines to a Portland businessman, who paid a whopping $650,000 for them. A group of eastern and California investors, and finally several large corporations, soon controlled major interests in the mines. By the mid-twentieth century, mining companies had dug more than a billion dollars' worth of metal out of Noah Kellogg's original stake.

> *Population growth spurred the growth of industries that exploited nature.*

Population growth spurred the growth of industries that exploited nature. Immigrants streamed to American shores, particularly from eastern and southern Europe. Between 1880 and 1890, the U.S. population grew from 50 million people to almost 63 million, and six new states entered the Union: North Dakota, South Dakota, Montana, and Washington (all in 1889) and Idaho and Wyoming (both in 1890). Increased demand in turn hastened large-scale commercial mining, logging, and fishing.

Crucial to the process of innovation were engineers, who mastered the technical aspects of construction and design. Many American engineers were trained in Germany, but others attended such schools as the Massachusetts Institute of Technology (MIT) or Cornell University, in New York State, both of which introduced electrical engineering into their curricula in 1882. American engineers, such as those who worked in Mexico under the auspices of mining companies and the railroads, served as the vanguard of American capitalism throughout the world.

Advocates of standardized industrial processes and mass marketing hoped to break down regional barriers and create an integrated national economy. Whether they specialized in railroads or shoes, wheat or steel, business owners and managers who possessed the necessary resources and resourcefulness pursued similar goals: to mine, grow, manufacture, or process large quantities of goods and then market them as widely, cheaply, and quickly as possible. Business put a premium on technological innovation, on the efficient use of workers, and on the reduction of uncertainties that accompanied a competitive marketplace. These guiding principles, formulated during the late 1870s and 1880s, laid the foundations of economic progress in late nineteenth-century America.

New Systems and Machines—and Their Price

The free enterprise system thrived on innovation. Indeed, during the 1880s, new machines, new technical processes, new engineering feats, and new forms of factory organization fueled the growth and efficiency of U.S. businesses. Many devices that became staples of American life appeared during this period. Alexander Graham Bell invented the telephone in 1876. Thomas A. Edison developed the phonograph in 1877 and the electric light in 1879. Cash registers, stock tickers, and typewriters soon became indispensable tools for American businesses. Beginning in the 1880s, railroad cars installed steam heat and electric lights, boosting the comfort of passengers.

DOCUMENT

Edison, "The Success of the Electric Light"

During this period, more and more businesses perfected the so-called American system of manufacturing, which dated back half a century and relied on the mass production of interchangeable parts. Factory workers made large numbers of a particular part, each part exactly the same size and shape. This system enabled manufacturers to assemble products more cheaply and efficiently, to repair products easily with new parts, and to redesign products quickly. The engineers who designed the modern bicycle (which has wheels of equal size) used the American system to make their product affordable to almost anyone who wanted one. The bicycle craze of the late nineteenth century resulted from the novelty and cheapness of this new form of transportation and recreation, one enjoyed by males and females of all ages. Production techniques used to make bicycles were later adapted to the manufacture of automobiles.

New technical processes also facilitated the manufacture and marketing of foods and other consumer goods. Distributors developed pressure-sealed cans, which enabled them to market agricultural products in far-flung parts of the country. Innovative techniques for sheet metal stamping and electric resistance welding transformed a variety of industries. By 1880, 90 percent of American steel was made by the Bessemer process, which injected air into molten iron to yield steel.

The agriculture business benefited from engineering innovations as well, which often reached across national boundaries. As just one example, the first modern irrigation systems in the Southwest were constructed by Native Americans and *mestizos* (people of both indigenous and Spanish ancestry). And in the 1870s, Japan began importing American farm implements and inviting U.S. engineers to construct dams and canals for new steam- and water-powered gristmills and sawmills. Technology was a universal language, one that many peoples around the globe sought to master.

Long active in territorial exploration and land surveying, the federal government continued to assume a leading role in applied science. In 1879 the U.S. Geological Survey (USGS) was formed, charged with compiling and centralizing data describing the natural landscape, an effort that had originated in 1804 with the Lewis and Clark expedition. In the 1880s, the federal government also began to systematize and disseminate information useful to farmers through the U.S.

MAP 16.1
AGRICULTURAL REGIONS OF THE MIDWEST AND NORTHEAST By 1890 several Midwestern cities served as shipping centers, getting wheat and corn to the growing metropolitan areas of the Northeast and Mid-Atlantic. Farmers complained that the railroads gave discounts to large shippers, such as Standard Oil, and discriminated against small producers.

Resources and Conflict in the West

Department of Agriculture. In 1881, for example, the department's Entomology Bureau began to combine current research on insects with practical techniques for pest control.

Like factory machines, new agricultural machinery benefited consumers, but the need for hired hands evaporated. Early in the nineteenth century, producing an acre of wheat took fifty-six hours of labor; in 1880 that number dropped to twenty hours. One agricultural worker in Ohio observed, "Of one thing we are convinced, that while improved machinery is gathering our large crops, making our boots and shoes, doing the work of our carpenters, stone sawyers, and builders, thousands of able, willing men are going from place to place seeking employment, and finding none. The question naturally arises, is improved machinery a blessing or a curse?"

Alterations in the Natural Environment

Innovation altered the natural landscape and hastened the depletion of certain natural resources. By the mid-1870s, Texas had new steam-powered lumber mills equipped with saw rigs that could produce up to 30,000 board feet a day. This capacity made Texas lumbering a big business, especially when it was combined with infusions of capital and the expansion of railroad lines into the piney woods region, along the eastern edge of the state. Texas lumber mills were poised to benefit from the exhaustion of the great forests of the eastern and Great Lakes states.

In the Chesapeake Bay, dredge boats were becoming more efficient in harvesting oysters, and shellfish reserves began to decline. In the mid-1880s, oyster harvesters took a record 15 million bushels from the bay; the shellfish simply could not replenish themselves. New means of commercial fishing also reduced supplies of salmon in the Northwest.

■ Following the wholesale slaughter of buffalo on the Great Plains, settlers earned money by gathering the skeletons. "The bones are shipped East by the carloads," reported the Dodge City *Times*, "where they are ground and used for fertilizing and manufactured into numerous useful articles." This mound of buffalo bones at the Michigan Carlson Works in Detroit, c. 1880, suggests the extent of the devastation.

In 1884 in California, a federal court issued a permanent injunction against hydraulic mining, because it contributed to soil erosion and water pollution. Hydraulic mining had washed an estimated 12 billion tons of earth into San Francisco Bay, raising the floor of the bay several feet. At the same time, mercury flowing into nearby streams from gold mines in the San Jose hills was poisoning fish in the bay, creating pollution that would be felt well into the twentieth century. Similar cases of industrial pollution despoiled other parts of the country. In the absence of any laws to restrain them, Chicago meatpackers befouled the Chicago River with the byproducts of sausage, glue, and fertilizer.

By stimulating manufacturing and **extractive enterprises** alike, the railroads powered these great environmental transformations, for better or worse. Since buffalo herds impeded rail travel, railroads promoted the shooting of buffalo from trains, a "sport" that almost eradicated the species. By the mid-1880s, the great herds had disappeared, victims of ecological change (the incursion of horses into grazing areas), disease (brucellosis spread by domestic livestock), and commercial enterprise. Sioux leader Black Elk decried the slaughter and the "heaps of bones" left to rot in the sun.

Innovations in Financing and Organizing Business

As agents of economic development and cultural change, the railroads knew no peer. As private enterprises, however, they faced the same challenges that all big businesses ultimately must address. The proliferation of independent lines and the high fixed costs associated with the industry made profits slim and competition intense. As a result, railroad companies began to come together in informal pools to share equipment and set prices industrywide. In the 1880s,

these pools gave way to consolidation, a process by which several companies merged into one large company.

In these years, U.S. businesses grew larger and more quickly than their western European counterparts. This difference stemmed in large part from America's astonishing population growth and its rich natural resources. Equally significant, the United States possessed a social and legal culture favorable to big business. The absence of an entrenched, conservative elite, along with the spread of state and national laws that protected private property, stimulated the entrepreneurial spirit. The U.S. government refrained from owning industries, although it heavily subsidized the railroad industry. It taxed business lightly and did not tax individual incomes at all until 1913. Finally, American bankers such as J. P. Morgan aggressively promoted growth through their lending practices and bond sales.

Several large enterprises began to conquer not just local but also national markets. Examples include Bell Telephone (founded in Boston), the Kroger grocery business (Cincinnati), Marshall Field department store (Chicago), and Boston Fruit Company. In the South, Midwest, and West, investors rushed to finance gigantic mining operations and agribusinesses, such as the 1.5 million acres devoted to rice cultivation in southeastern Louisiana and bonanza wheat farms (as large as 38,000 acres) in the Red River valley of North Dakota.

Owners of these enterprises devised new forms of business organization that helped their companies grow and survive in a dynamic economy. By combining, or integrating, their operations, manufacturers cut costs and monopolized an entire industry in the process. Unable to withstand the ruthless competition that favored larger enterprises, smaller companies folded. The two icons of American big business in the 1880s—Andrew Carnegie in steel and John D. Rockefeller in petroleum—proved master innovators in both the managerial and technical aspects of business.

In 1875 Carnegie opened the Edgar Thomson Steelworks in Pittsburgh. Within a year, he was producing steel at half the prevailing market price. Carnegie excelled at vertical integration, in which a single firm controls all aspects of production and distribution. Carnegie employed laborers in the Lake Superior region to mine the raw material, and he owned the ships and railroads that brought the ore to the mills in Pittsburgh.

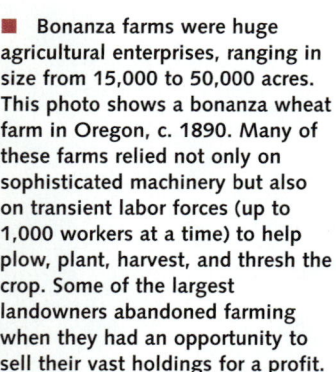

■ Bonanza farms were huge agricultural enterprises, ranging in size from 15,000 to 50,000 acres. This photo shows a bonanza wheat farm in Oregon, c. 1890. Many of these farms relied not only on sophisticated machinery but also on transient labor forces (up to 1,000 workers at a time) to help plow, plant, harvest, and thresh the crop. Some of the largest landowners abandoned farming when they had an opportunity to sell their vast holdings for a profit.

Another form of business consolidation was horizontal integration, in which a number of companies producing the same product merge to reduce competition and control prices. In 1882 John D. Rockefeller, a former bookkeeper, horizontally integrated the petroleum industry by forming Standard Oil Trust. Stockholders in small companies turned over their shares to Standard Oil, which then coordinated operations and eliminated competition from other smaller firms. Standard Oil also practiced vertical integration. Soon Rockefeller had positioned himself to buy out his rivals—or ruin them. **Trusts** placed a premium on efficient production, but they also worked to the disadvantage of consumers, who were hostage to high prices within industries that lacked competition.

New Labor Supplies for a New Economy

To operate efficiently, expanding industries needed expanding supplies of workers to grow crops, extract raw materials, and produce manufactured goods. Many of these workers came from abroad. The year 1880 marked the leading edge of a new wave of immigration to the United States. Over the next ten years, 5.2 million newcomers entered the country, almost twice the previous decade's level of 2.8 million.

In the mid-nineteenth century, most immigrants hailed from western Europe and the British Isles—from Germany, Scandinavia, England, and Ireland. Between 1880 and 1890, Germans, Scandinavians, and the English kept coming, but they were joined by numerous Italians, Russians, and Poles. In fact, these last three groups predominated among newcomers for the next thirty-five years, their arrival rates peaking between 1890 and 1910. At the same time, immigrants from Asia, especially from China, were making their way to the Kingdom of Hawaii, which was annexed by the United States in 1898. Between 1852 and 1887, 26,000 Chinese arrived on the islands. Almost 40 percent of all immigrants to the United States during this period were known as "birds of passage," men who were recruited by American employers and who, after earning some money, migrated back to their native land.

> *The year 1880 marked the leading edge of a new wave of immigration to the United States. Over the next ten years, 5.2 million newcomers entered the country, almost twice the previous decade's level of 2.8 million.*

Many of the new European immigrants sought to escape oppressive economic and political conditions in Europe, even as they hoped to make a new life for themselves and their families in the United States. Russian Jews fled discrimination and violent **antisemitism** in the form of pogroms, organized massacres conducted by their Christian neighbors and Russian authorities. Southern Italians, mostly landless farmers, suffered from a combination of declining agricultural prices and high birth rates. Impoverished Poles chafed under cultural restrictions imposed by Germany and Russia. Hungarians, Greeks, Portuguese, and Armenians, among other groups, also participated in this great migration; members of these groups too were seeking political freedom and economic opportunity.

Immigrants replenished America's sense of itself as a haven for the downtrodden, a place where opportunity beckoned to hard-working and ambitious people. "The New Colossus," written by American poet Emma Lazarus in 1883, pays tribute to the "huddled masses yearning to breathe free"—people from all over the world who sought refuge in the United States. The words of her poem are inscribed on the Statue of Liberty at the entrance to New York harbor.

The story of Rosa Cassettari, a young woman who emigrated from northern Italy to the United States in 1884, suggests the challenges that faced many newcomers during this period. Rosa's husband, Santino, had preceded her to America. He had settled in an iron mining camp in Missouri. Leaving her son with relatives, Rosa received the assurances of friends and relatives: "You will get smart in America. And in America you will not be so poor."

Life in the iron camp proved harsh—nothing like what Rosa had expected. Her husband, who was much older than she, neglected her; he preferred the company of prostitutes in the

■ MAP 16.2
POPULATION OF FOREIGN BORN, BY REGION, 1880   After the Civil War, large numbers of immigrants settled in northeastern cities. In addition, the upper Midwest and parts of the western mining frontier drew many newcomers from western Europe. The area along the country's southwestern border was home to immigrants from Mexico. Cuban cigar makers established thriving communities in southern Florida.

town. The iron was almost depleted, and some workers and their wives had moved on to a new mine in Michigan. Rosa's days centered on caring for her new baby and cooking for thirteen of the miners.

Despite these realities, within a couple of years, Rosa grew used to America and considered herself an American. She returned briefly to her hometown in Italy but expressed impatience with the rigid social etiquette that separated the rich from the poor. She also yearned for the hearty meals that had become her staple in the iron camp. Back in Missouri, she mustered enough courage to leave Santino, traveling to Chicago and making a new life for herself in the Italian *colonia* (community) there. She eventually married another Italian man (the two had fallen in love in Missouri) and found work as a cleaning woman at Chicago Commons, a social settlement house.

Specific groups of immigrants often gravitated toward particular kinds of jobs. For example, many Poles found work in the vast steel plants of Pittsburgh, and Russian Jews went into the garment industry and street-peddling trade in New York City. California fruit orchards and vegetable farms employed numerous Japanese immigrants. Cuban immigrants rolled cigars in Florida. In Hawaii, the Chinese and Japanese labored in the sugar fields; after they had accumulated a little money, they became rice farmers and shopkeepers. In Boston and New York City, second-generation Irish took advantage of their prominent place in the Democratic party to become public school teachers, firefighters, and police officers.

The experience of Kinji Ushijima (later known as George Shima) graphically illustrates the power of immigrant niches. Shima arrived in California in 1887 and, like many other Japanese immigrants, found work as a potato picker in the San Joaquin Valley. Soon, Shima moved up to become a labor contractor, securing Japanese laborers for the valley's white farmers. With the money he made, he bought 15 acres of land and began his own potato farm. Eventually he built a large potato business by expanding his holdings, reclaiming swampland, and investing in a fleet of boats to ship his crops up the coast to San Francisco. Taking advantage of a Japanese niche, Shima prospered through a combination of good luck and hard work.

Efficient Machines, Efficient People

The Industrial Revolution

By the late nineteenth century, the typical industrial employee labored within an immense, multistory brick structure and operated a machine powered by water or steam. Smoky, smelly kerosene lamps gave way to early forms of electric lighting, first arc and then incandescent light bulbs. Long-standing industries, such as textiles and shoes, were now fully mechanized. The new products flooding the economy—locomotives and bicycles, cash registers and typewriters—streamed from factories designed to ensure maximum efficiency from both machines *and* the people who tended them.

In the 1880s, a few factory managers hired efficiency experts. The experts' goal was to cut labor costs in the same way that industry barons had shaved the costs of extracting raw materials or distributing final products. With huge quantities of goods flowing from factories, even modest savings in wages could mean significant profits in the long run. Frederick Winslow Taylor, chief engineer for the Midvale Steel Plant outside Philadelphia, pioneered in the techniques of efficient "scientific management."

By the late nineteenth century, the typical industrial employee labored within an immense, multistory brick structure and operated a machine powered by water or steam.

Southern textile mill owners in the Piedmont region of South Carolina and Georgia devised their own strategies for shaping a compliant workforce. They employed only white men, women, and children as machine operators, but threatened to hire blacks if the whites protested low wages and poor working conditions. Poor whites lived in company housing, their children attended company schools, and they received cash wages. In contrast, blacks remained in the countryside, impoverished and without the right to vote. In the cities of the North as well as the textile villages of the South, factory workers remained exclusively white until well into the twentieth century.

The Birth of a National Urban Culture

In the 1880s, visitors to the territory of Utah marveled at the capital, Salt Lake City, where Mormon pioneers had made the desert bloom. Situated at the foot of the magnificent snow-covered Wasatch Range, this oasis in the Great Salt Basin boasted a built landscape almost as impressive as the natural beauty that surrounded it. In the heart of Salt Lake City lay Temple Square. This broad plaza contained the Mormon Tabernacle, a huge domed structure. Next to it stood the Mormon Temple, a soaring six-spired granite cathedral still under construction. The city had the advantage of rail service (Promontory Point, where the transcontinental railroad was joined, was not far away). Mines in nearby Bingham Canyon yielded rich lodes of silver and large local smelters refined copper ores. Irrigation systems made the city self-sufficient in the production of foodstuffs. A settlement inspired by religious faith, Salt Lake City was at the same time thoroughly modern.

Not just Salt Lake City, but other cities around the country began to assume monumental proportions. In New York, the 1880s marked the completion of Central Park and the Brooklyn Bridge and the arrival of the Statue of Liberty from France. Chicago, rebuilding after a disastrous fire in 1871, became a sprawling rail hub dotted with yards for western cattle, northern timber, and the

■ Admirers hailed New York City's Brooklyn Bridge as the eighth wonder of the world when it was completed in 1883. With a central span of 1,595 feet, it became the largest suspension bridge in the world. Built over fourteen years, the bridge linked Brooklyn to Manhattan across the East River, using steel suspension cables that are nearly 16 inches thick. Its total cost was about $18 million.

trains that hauled them. In 1885 Chicago also became the location for a major architectural breakthrough by engineer William LeBaron Jenney. He designed the ten-story Home Insurance Building, the world's first metal frame skyscraper. The steel skeleton weighed only one third as much as the thick stone walls needed to support a similar masonry building, and the design left room for numerous windows. Urban architecture would never be the same again.

Cities in general represented American notions of progress and prosperity; they were places where innovation, consumer culture, and new forms of entertainment grew and flourished. From 1875 to 1900, American cities developed increasingly sophisticated systems of communications and transportation. Streetlights, transportation networks, and sewer lines provided basic services to swelling populations of immigrants and rural in-migrants. Cities also represented a new cultural diversity in American life. And they required larger local governments to manage the services necessary for daily life.

Economic Sources of Urban Growth

Northeastern and mid-Atlantic cities emerged as centers of concentrated manufacturing activity. Yet, with the aid of eastern capital, western cities also flourished. New York's Wall Street and Boston's State Street, home to the nation's largest investment bankers, financed the Main Streets of the Midwest and West. Some urban areas prospered through milling, mining, or other enterprises, such as lumber and flour milling in Minneapolis and ore smelting in Denver. Others focused on manufacturing to serve a growing western population. Chicago was rivaled only by New York in terms of its industrial economy and the vast territory that it supplied with raw materials, processed food, and manufactured goods. Salt Lake City produced goods for the so-called Mormon Corridor of settlements that stretched west from the city to southern California. By the 1880s, San Francisco had a commercial reach that encompassed much of the West as well as Hawaii and Alaska.

No trend supported urban growth more than the arrival of newcomers from abroad. To stoke its furnaces, mill its lumber, and slaughter its cattle, Chicago relied on immigrants from Ireland, Slovakia, Germany, Poland, and Bohemia. The three cities with the highest percentage of foreign-born residents in 1880 were San Francisco (45 percent), Chicago (42 percent), and New York (40 percent). Yet all large cities also attracted migrants from America's own countryside, as native-born men and women fled the hardships of life on the farm. Moreover, the use of increasingly efficient agricultural machines meant that rural workers had fewer job opportunities. Most of the immigrants from rural areas to the cities were young women; they included Yankee girls from the hardscrabble homesteads of New England, daughters of Swedish immigrants in Minnesota, and native-born farm tenants in Indiana.

Rural folk sought the steady work and wages afforded by jobs in the city, but they were also drawn to the excitement that had become the hallmark of the urban scene. In the early nineteenth century, Thomas Jefferson had located the heart of America in its sturdy yeoman farmers. By the late nineteenth century, that heart had shifted to the city.

Building the Cities

The American city was emerging as a technological marvel. Through a combination of money and engineering skill, cities managed to provide an adequate water supply for private and commercial purposes, move large numbers of people and goods efficiently, get rid of waste materials, and illuminate thoroughfares at night. Professionals, such as landscape contractors, construction architects, and civil engineers, designed the parks, bridges, public libraries, and museums that made cities so attractive to many.

Cities grew upward and outward as a result of developments in mass production and technology. Elevators extended living and office spaces upward. The invention of the electric streetcar in 1888 permitted cities to spread out. Soon, residential suburbs cropped up many miles from urban commercial cores. Wealthy and middle-class urban residents followed the streetcar lines out of the city, hoping to find a green refuge from the grime and noise of downtown while maintaining a manageable commute to work.

As cities expanded, the challenges associated with providing services also grew more complex and expensive. A polluted water supply, for example, meant epidemics of diphtheria and cholera, so city taxpayers demanded waterworks that delivered drinkable water through intricate systems of dams, pumps, reservoirs, and pipes. Chicago had long pumped its sewage into Lake Michigan, the source of its drinking water. In the 1880s, the city financed the building of a canal and the reversal of the flow of the Chicago River. These changes sent the city's sewage away from Lake Michigan and westward into the Mississippi River instead. Begun in 1889, the 28-mile Chicago Sanitary and Ship Canal was completed seven years later. One awed observer marveled at the "powerful machinery for digging and hoisting, steam shovels, excavators, inclines, conveyors, derricks, cantilevers, cableways, channelers, steam drills, pumps, etc." The cost: $54 million.

Local Government Gets Bigger

These new systems of services, combined with the mushrooming immigrant neighborhoods, changed both the quality and the quantity of urban problems. Zoning issues—who could build what, where, and when—became flashpoints for conflict as the interests of homeowners, developers, and municipal engineers collided. Urban political leaders struggled to improve the city's public works while meeting the needs of multiple ethnic groups. Governing a city was an expensive, full-time enterprise and one that had the potential to be very lucrative to businesspeople and politicians alike.

Although New York's "Boss" Tweed had been convicted on charges of corruption in the early 1870s, the infamous Tammany Hall gang carried on his legacy. The Democratic officials associated with this social and political organization perfected a system of kickbacks linked to municipal construction projects. Under this system, contractors paid politicians for city construction contracts. For example, a New York City courthouse that was supposed to cost a quarter of a million dollars ended up costing taxpayers fifty-two times that amount, or twice as much as the United States paid Russia for Alaska! In the 1880s, secretive networks of corruption linking law enforcement personnel, city officials, and construction contractors flourished in many cities. These webs, or "machines," characterized urban life for decades to come.

> *In the 1880s, secretive networks of corruption linking law enforcement personnel, city officials, and construction contractors flourished in many cities.*

Urban machines existed to secure jobs for their loyal supporters and line the pockets of those at the highest levels of power. Deal-making blurred the lines between private enterprise and public service as everyone from mayors to local ward organizers benefited from the modernization of the American city. In the process, urban bosses ensured that the streets were paved, tenement buildings erected, sewer lines laid, and trolley tracks extended. But taxpayers footed the bill, which included outrageous amounts of money used for bribes and kickbacks.

Money-grubbing politicians, judges, and police extorted "hush money" from brothels, gambling parlors, and unlicensed taverns. Urban bosses also had a vested interest in sponsoring new money-making venues for professional sports and supporting other forms of commercialized leisure activity. Baseball parks, boxing rings, and race tracks yielded huge sums in the form of kickbacks from contractors. Once built, stadiums and boxing rings generated profits indefinitely as fans filled the stands.

Thrills, Chills, and Bathtubs: The Emergence of Consumer Culture

On a hot summer day in 1890, a young mother named Emily Scanlon, with her three-year-old daughter in tow, paid the 5-cent admission fee to a popular ride called the Toboggan Slide at the Brandywine Springs Amusement Park near Wilmington, Delaware. The two of them ascended a stairwell to the top of the three-story-high structure and then stepped into a car that ran on a wooden trough. When the attendant released the brakes, the car descended, pulled by gravity. It moved slowly at first, then picked up speed around a curve. Suddenly, Emily Scanlon stood up in the car (perhaps to retrieve her hat, which had blown off), and she and her daughter were thrown from the car. Mrs. Scanlon died instantly of a broken neck, but the youngster survived. Significantly, the tragedy did not provoke a shutdown of the ride or the installation of safety measures. Instead, park managers simply posted a sign that read, "Passengers must keep their seats." Patrons continued to enjoy the thrills of the toboggan.

Brandywine Springs boasted an ornate gateway that proclaimed "Let All Who Enter Here Leave Care Behind." In cities around the country, amusement parks brought men and women, girls and boys together to enjoy merry-go-rounds, prizefights, and circus sideshows. By 1880 railroads and steamships were transporting crowds out of Manhattan to Coney Island, where working-class people mingled with the self-proclaimed "respectable" middle classes.

Americans of all kinds began to sample a new realm of sensual experience—one of physical daring, material luxury, and visual fantasy—either as participants or as observers. Central to this emerging consumer culture was mass advertising, a form of appeal that sought to instill in consumers the desire for things that were new and visually attractive. Colorful spectacles of all kinds—whether in the form of a department store window or a well-publicized athletic event—became an integral part of American life.

Shows as Spectacles

Public officials, college administrators, and ambitious entrepreneurs alike discovered that Americans craved new and stimulating forms of entertainment and were willing to pay for them. The traveling circus provides a case in point. By the 1870s, such shows were erecting their tents in small towns and big cities alike. The largest shows employed hundreds of people as performers, cooks, carpenters, and wagon drivers. Circus owners provided their customers with exciting sights and sounds—death-defying lion-tamers, gravity-defying gymnasts and tightrope walkers, exhibits of wild animals such as elephants and tigers, rollicking brass bands, and the hilarious antics of clowns.

In the quarter-century after Reconstruction, three major sports began to attract large national audiences. Organized baseball had existed since 1846, when the Knickerbocker Base Ball Club of New York met the New York Nine in Hoboken, New Jersey. (The score was 23 to 1, in favor of the Nine.) The National Baseball League, consisting of eight professional teams, was founded in 1876, the American League in 1900. In the 1880s, several new regulations—those governing the overhand pitch, foul balls, and swingless strikes—helped to standardize the game.

Also in the 1880s, Walter Camp, a former Yale University football player, introduced rules—for instance, the system of downs and the center snap to the quarterback—that made that sport quicker and more competitive. Camp was also behind the selection of the first "All America" team (1889) to stimulate fan interest. By this time towns, high schools, and colleges were fielding football teams.

Likewise, boxing emerged as a national, regulated sport. John L. Sullivan, an American, won renown as the world's bare-knuckled champion in 1882, even as more and more fighters had started wearing gloves. Sullivan then joined a traveling theatrical group and demonstrated gloved boxing to enthusiastic crowds all over the country. In 1889, Sullivan defeated an opponent in a seventy-five-round match, the last heavyweight, bare-knuckled championship.

Performances based on skills of all kinds gained national audiences, as the career of William "Buffalo Bill" Cody reveals. Born in Iowa in 1846, Cody parlayed his early years as a Pony Express postal rider, cavalry scout, Indian fighter, and buffalo hunter into a form of mass entertainment. In his "Buffalo Bill Combination" show, cowboy and Indian actors performed skits depicting dramatic events in western history (from a European American point of view, at least).

In 1882 Cody produced "Buffalo Bill's Wild West," a traveling road show that featured sharpshooter Annie Oakley, cowboy musicians, and Sioux warriors performing authentic Native American dances. Sioux leader Sitting Bull (Tatanka Iyotake), long an admirer of Annie Oakley (he called her "Little Sure Shot"), joined the show in 1885. Like other Indians who worked for Cody, Sitting Bull took advantage of the opportunity to escape the confines of the reservation (in his case, Standing Rock in North Dakota). As a member of the "Wild West" troupe, he also enjoyed decent food and accommodations. At a time when whites were denigrating Indian culture, Sitting Bull affirmed that culture by demonstrating his shooting and riding skills. However, white audiences jeered him—they saw him as less an entertainer and more an enemy warrior—and he left after just a year. By the 1890s, Cody was playing to audiences in Europe as well as the United States, dramatizing a West that was fast disappearing.

■ "Buffalo Bill" Cody and Sitting Bull pose for a promotional photo for the 1885 season of the "Wild West." Cody refrained from calling the production a "show," maintaining that it demonstrated frontier skills and recreated historical encounters (such as Custer's Last Stand and stagecoach robberies). The "Wild West" toured Canada and Europe and inspired many imitators.

Mass Merchandising as Spectacle

During the late nineteenth century, the act of shopping in cities for goods, especially luxury goods, became an adventure in itself. A new piece of the cityscape, the department store, welcomed customers into a world of luxury and abundance, a place of color, light, and glamour. These "palaces of consumption" showcased a variety of technological innovations. In Marshall Field's "Grand Emporium" (Chicago), Wanamaker's (Philadelphia), and Lord & Taylor (New York), shoppers glided from story to story on escalators and in elevators. Warmed by central heating, they browsed display cases, racks, and tables laden with enticing goods and illuminated by arc lighting. Their money streamed into cash registers or to a central clerk through cash conveyors.

Thus, department stores not only offered a dazzling array of goods but also made shopping an exciting experience. This appealed particularly to middle-class women, who had the leisure time and the cash to indulge in day-long shopping excursions. In 1880 a New Yorker could arrive at Macy's by taking the Sixth Avenue elevated train and spend the morning exploring any number of specialized departments: ribbons, women's and children's muslin underwear, toys, candy, books, men's furnishings, china and glassware, and so on. Fatigued at noon, she might visit the lunchroom to partake of a modest meal and then devote the rest of her day to examining the colored dress silks, a new department established the year before.

■ Refugio Amador and her five daughters, Emilia, Maria, Clotilde, Julieta, and Corina, were members of an elite Hispanic family in Las Cruces, New Mexico. Her husband, Martin Amador, was a prominent politician, merchant, hotel owner, and freighter. A subcontractor for the U.S. government, he supplied military troops in the area. The family shopped by mail-order catalogue from Bloomingdale's Department Store in New York City.

The department store was an exclusively urban phenomenon, but mass merchandising reached far beyond cities. The material riches of American society became accessible to rural people through the mail-order catalogue. This marketing device was pioneered in 1872 by the Chicago company Montgomery Ward, the official supply house for the Farmers' Grange. On homesteads throughout the Midwest, family members gathered to pore over the thousands of items displayed in "The Great Wish Book." The company's motto? "Satisfaction guaranteed or your money back." Farm wives delighted in the latest Parisian fashions, their husbands pondered the intricacies of McCormick threshing machinery, and the children studied the newest line of toys and fishing rods. Late in the decade, a competitor appeared on the scene in the form of the Sears, Roebuck Catalogue.

The mass production needed to satisfy eager customers depended on mass advertising, an enterprise still in its infancy in the 1880s. Yet some of the principles that would shape the future of this business were in place even at this early date. For instance, soon after the Civil War, the makers of Sozodont dentifrice (toothpaste) plastered the name of their product all over weekly religious magazines and more mainstream publications, such as *Harper's* and *Scribner's*. They labeled the natural landscape as well. Indeed, the word *Sozodont* on Maiden's Rock in Red Wing, Minnesota, was so large that steamboat passengers on the Mississippi River three miles away could plainly read it.

"Rural Free Delivery Mail"

Defending the New Industrial Order

By the late 1870s, as consumer culture expanded, intense conflict over fundamental issues all but evaporated from national politics. Although ethnic and cultural loyalties continued to inflame local and state elections, Republicans and Democrats at the national level disagreed about little except the tariff. Adhering to tradition, Republicans favored a higher tariff that would benefit domestic businesses by making imported goods more expensive. In contrast, Democrats argued that a higher tariff, and resulting higher prices for goods produced in the United States, would harm consumers. Members of the Republican party called themselves the Grand Army of the Republic; they "waved the **bloody shirt**"—that is, reminded voters that many of their Democratic opponents, especially those in the South, had supported secession a generation before. Still, the two major parties openly shared a similar goal: to win as many jobs as possible for their respective supporters. Politics served as a vehicle for patronage and favors rather than as a conduit for ideas and alternative visions of the nation's future.

Many politicians also shared a belief in the idea of *laissez-faire* (a French phrase meaning to leave alone, referring to the absence of government interference in the economy). Laissez-faire was actually a flexible concept, invoked to justify government indifference in some areas but government intervention in others. Indeed, politicians tended to favor laissez-faire in social matters more than in the economy. Thus, support for manufacturers and railroads in the form of tariff protection and land grants, for example, was justified. At the same time, however, Congress, the president, and the Supreme Court were reluctant to enact bold measures to redress the growing gap between rich and poor. In fact, certain clergy, businesspeople, and university professors sought to explain and defend the inequality between the captains of industry and the masses of ill-paid laborers. Their theory of **Social Darwinism** viewed the system of industrial capitalism as desirable because it was "natural."

In his first novel, *The Gilded Age* (1873), writer Mark Twain (Samuel Clemens) satirized the trend toward corruption in public affairs and the wild financial speculation that produced both poverty and great wealth. The growth of large businesses that received economic and political support from government officials served to enrich employers, investors, and politicians at the expense of workers and farmers. The term *Gilded Age* became synonymous with the excess and extravagance on the part of politicians and businessmen alike during the last quarter of the nineteenth century.

The Contradictory Politics of Laissez-Faire

In 1880 the undistinguished President Rutherford B. Hayes chose not to run for office again. That summer the Republicans nominated James A. Garfield of Ohio, a former mule driver who had become a Civil War general. To counter the "bloody-shirt" effect, Democrats put forth their own former Union general: Winfield S. Hancock, who had been wounded at Gettysburg. Garfield won the popular vote by a narrow margin but overwhelmed Hancock in the electoral college.

Garfield's arrival in the White House set off a race for patronage jobs among loyal Republicans. Indeed, overwhelmed by office-seekers, the new president remarked, "My God! What is there in this place that a man should ever want to get into it?" Then on July 2, 1881, Charles J. Guiteau, who had unsuccessfully sought the position of U.S. consul in Paris, shot Garfield in a Washington, D.C., train station. Garfield languished for a few months, finally dying on September 19.

Vice President Chester A. Arthur, a former New York politician, assumed the reins of government. Arthur's administration supported certain forms of government intervention in society, or "social engineering." Arthur and others believed that laissez-faire policies had their limits; strong measures were needed to counter what they and other conservatives considered immoral personal behavior. In 1882 Congress passed the Edmunds Act. Targeting Mormons, the act outlawed polygamy (the practice of having more than one wife at a time), took the right to vote away from the law's offenders, and sent a five-member commission to Utah to oversee local elections.

TABLE 16-1
The Election of 1880

Candidate	Political Party	Popular Vote (%)	Electoral Vote
James A. Garfield	Republican	48.5	214
Winfield S. Hancock	Democratic	48.1	155
James B. Weaver	Greenback-Labor	3.4	—

That same year, Congress responded to pressure from West Coast European American politicians, the San Francisco Workingmen's Party in particular, and approved the Chinese Exclusion Act. The act became the first piece of legislation to bar a particular group from entering the United States. Most Chinese immigrants took jobs that native-born whites shunned. Moreover, unemployment among California white manufacturing workers in the 1870s was caused not by Chinese competitors, but by the flood of cheap eastern-made goods carried into the state by the transcontinental railroad. As eastern goods entered California, manufacturers in the West laid off workers and closed factories. The Chinese thus became scapegoats for groups hit hard by larger economic changes.

In 1883 the Supreme Court hurt the cause of blacks' civil rights by declaring the Civil Rights Act of 1875 unconstitutional. The five cases involved in the Court's decision focused on exclusions of blacks from hotels, railroad cars, and theaters. The Court held that state governments could not discriminate on the basis of race but that private individuals could do so. This decision put an official stamp of approval on racist practices of employers, hotels, restaurants, and other providers of jobs and services.

Arthur surprised his critics by embracing the cause of civil service reform. This movement sought to inject professional standards into public service and rid the country of the worst excesses of the corrupt "spoils system," where political victors put loyal supporters into public jobs regardless of their qualifications. In response to Garfield's assassination by Guiteau, the disappointed patronage-seeker, Congress passed the Pendleton Act (1883). This measure established a merit system for federal job applicants and created the Civil Service Commission, which administered competitive examinations to candidates in certain classifications.

In 1884 Arthur fell ill (he would die shortly), and the Republicans nominated James G. Blaine of Maine as their candidate for the presidency. Blaine, who had benefited from corrupt deals in the past, offended the sensibilities of a group of reform-minded Republicans, who called themselves Mugwumps. (The term reportedly had its roots in an Indian word that meant "holier than thou.") As a result, Blaine was bested in the national election by the former mayor of Buffalo, Grover Cleveland, who became the first Democratic president in twenty-eight years.

TABLE 16-2
The Election of 1884

Candidate	Political Party	Popular Vote (%)	Electoral Vote
Grover Cleveland	Democratic	48.5	219
James G. Blaine	Republican	48.2	182

Resources and Conflict in the West

Throughout the 1880s, Congress and the chief executive applied the laissez-faire principle selectively—for example, to the status of Indians. Like other critics of federal Indian policy, writer Helen Hunt Jackson in her 1881 book *A Century of Dishonor* called for applying the "protection of the law to the Indian's rights of property." Moved to act, Congress passed the Dawes General Allotment (Severalty) Act in 1887. The new act was intended to improve the economic condition of Indians by eliminating common ownership of tribal lands in favor of a system of private property. The law distributed plots of land to individual Indians who renounced traditional customs. The law also encouraged these landowners to become sedentary farmers and to adopt "other habits of civilized life." In the end, however, the act amounted to little more than a land-grab on the part of whites; between 1887 and 1900, Indian-held lands decreased from 138 million acres to 78 million acres.

The Dawes Act

By the 1880s, local citizens, through the Grange and their elected public officials, were calling for the states to restrict the monopolistic practices of the railroads. Nevertheless, in *Wabash v. Illinois* (1886), the Supreme Court invalidated a state law regulating railroads, ruling that only Congress, and not the states, could control interstate transportation. The next year Congress passed the Interstate Commerce Act of 1887. This legislation mandated that the railroads charge all shippers the same rates and refrain from giving rebates to their largest customers. The act also established the Interstate Commerce Commission to oversee and stabilize the railroad industry. Congress thus acknowledged that the public interest demanded some form of business regulation, although enforcement of the act was less than vigorous.

Interstate Commerce Act

Cleveland invoked laissez-faire principles in 1887 when he vetoed legislation that would have provided seeds for hard-pressed farmers in Texas. As the president put it, "Though the people support the government, the government should not support the people." Cleveland also favored lower tariff rates, but most Americans favored government protection of domestic manufacturing in the form of higher tariffs. The Republicans exploited Cleveland's unpopular views on this issue in the 1888 campaign, nominating Benjamin Harrison, grandson of President William Henry ("Tippecanoe") Harrison. The younger Harrison defeated his rival in the electoral college but not in the popular vote.

TABLE 16-3

The Election of 1888

Candidate	Political Party	Popular Vote (%)	Electoral Vote
Benjamin Harrison	Republican	42.9	233
Grover Cleveland	Democratic	48.6	168
Clinton B. Fisk	Prohibition	2.2	—
Anson J. Streeter	Union Labor	1.3	—

The principle of government laissez-faire was of little use in addressing a central paradox of the late nineteenth century: the free enterprise system was being undermined by the very forms of business organization it had spawned and nourished. **Trusts** and combinations were inherently hostile to competition. In 1890 Congress passed a piece of landmark legislation, the Sherman Anti-Trust Act, designed to outlaw trusts and large business combinations of all kinds.

Social Darwinism and the "Natural" State of Society

In the late nineteenth century, human-made devices and engineering feats helped create a new social order, one marked by a few very wealthy industrialists, a growing middle class, and an increasingly diverse workforce of ill-paid field and factory hands. Brazenly borrowing from the theories of Charles Darwin, a British naturalist who had pioneered the study of evolution, some prominent clergy, businesspeople, journalists, and university professors sought to defend this new order as God-ordained or "natural." These observers drew parallels between Darwin's theory of "survival of the fittest" and the workings of modern society. (In his book *The Origin of Species*, Darwin had discussed the study of animals, not people or societies.) In the United States, Social Darwinists warned that "unnatural" forms of intervention—specifically, labor unions or social welfare legislation—were misguided, dangerous, and ultimately doomed to failure. In essence, Social Darwinists distorted a compelling scientific theory, misusing it to justify exploitation of the poor and laboring classes.

Herbert Spencer, Social Darwinism (1857)

The ideology of Social Darwinism evolved in response to class conflict and other forms of social turbulence in the 1870s and 1880s. Famed Brooklyn minister Henry Ward Beecher cited what he called "the great laws of political economy" to preach the virtues of poverty ("it was fit that man should eat the bread of affliction") and the evils of labor unions. Beecher and like-minded thinkers agreed that the government had the right and the obligation to come to the rescue of private companies threatened by angry workers or consumers. These observers also made a distinction between public subsidies to railroads and tariff protection for domestic manufacturers on one hand and public intervention on behalf of workers on the other.

Yale sociologist William Graham Sumner declared that society was like a living organism. For the species to remain healthy, individuals must prosper or decline according to their inherent characteristics. "Society, therefore, does not need any care or supervision," Sumner wrote in his 1883 treatise *What the Social Classes Owe to Each Other*. These views

INTERPRETING HISTORY

Andrew Carnegie and the "Gospel of Wealth"

In an article titled "Wealth," published in the *North American Review* in 1889, steel manufacturer Andrew Carnegie defended the amassing of large fortunes on the part of a few. He hailed this trend as a sign of progress.

The conditions of human life have not only been changed, but revolutionized, within the past few hundred years. In the former days there was little difference between the dwelling, dress, food, and environment of the chief and those of his retainers. The Indians are to-day where civilized man then was. When visiting the Sioux, I was led to the wigwam of the chief. It was just like the others in external appearance, and even within the difference was trifling between it and those of the poorest of his braves. The contrast between the palace of the millionaire and the cottage of the laborer with us to-day measures the change which has come with civilization.

This change, however, is not to be deplored, but welcomed as highly beneficial. It is well, nay, essential for the progress of the race, that the houses of some should be homes for all that is highest and best in literature and the arts, and for all the refinements of civilization, rather than that none should be so. Much better this great irregularity than universal squalor. . . . Whether the change be for good or ill, it is upon us, beyond our power to alter, and therefore to be accepted and made the best of. It is a waste of time to criticise the inevitable.

This *Judge* cartoon depicts Andrew Carnegie dispersing his fortune. Many of his donations were used for the establishment of public libraries, a worthy cause according to Carnegie's "gospel of wealth."

Carnegie believed that wealthy people had the responsibility to give away their money before they died, although he had distinct ideas about to whom—or to what—such money should be given. He elaborated on what came to be called the "gospel of wealth":

There remains, then, only one mode of using great fortunes; but in this we have the true antidote for the temporary unequal distribution of wealth, the reconciliation of the rich and the poor—a reign of harmony—another ideal, differing indeed, from that of the Communist in requiring only the further evolution of existing conditions, not the total overthrow of our civilization. . . . Under its sway we shall have an ideal state, in which the surplus wealth of the few will become, in the best sense, the property of the many, because it is administered for the common good, and this wealth, passing through the hands of the few, can be made a much more potent force for the elevation of our race than if it had been distributed in small sums to the people themselves. Even the poorest can be made to see this, and to agree that the great sums gathered by some of their fellow-citizens and spent for public purposes, from which the masses reap the principal benefit, are more valuable to them than if scattered through the course of many years in trifling amounts.

In 1901 Carnegie sold his steel company to banker J. P. Morgan for $480 million. By the time of his death, Carnegie had given away an estimated $350 million to a variety of causes and institutions.

Questions

1. How does Carnegie link extremes of wealth and poverty with progress?
2. Why did Carnegie focus his philanthropic energies on building public libraries?
3. Why would Carnegie have rejected as impractical and unreasonable the argument that he should have paid his workers higher wages rather than distributing his profits to charity?

Source: Andrew Carnegie, "Wealth," *North American Review* (1889).

---

rationalized not only the hierarchies of the workplace but also the triumph of "Anglo Saxons" on the North American continent and beyond. Editors of the *New York Times* interpreted Darwin's ideas as suggesting that "the red man will be driven out, and the white man will take possession. This is not justice, but it is destiny." In his book *Our Country* (1885), the Reverend Josiah Strong also drew on the ideas of Social Darwinism to claim that just as the fittest plants and animals endure in the natural kingdom, so "civilized" whites would eventually displace "barbarous," dark-skinned peoples, whether on the High Plains of South Dakota or on the savannas of Africa.

Conclusion

Some historians suggest that the great captains of industry were the chief representatives of widely held values in late-nineteenth-century America. Men such as Carnegie and Rockefeller had the vision and personal ambition necessary to build large corporate enterprises. They became fabulously wealthy by providing the United States with the ingredients necessary to an economic revolution: steel, oil, and other materials. Their ideology of unbridled individualism encouraged many people to aspire to entrepreneurial independence: the tailor's hope that he would someday own his own store, the waiter's dream of opening his own restaurant. The explosion of economic activity during this period—a second American industrial revolution—widened the middle class and lent credence to the notion of widespread upward mobility, modest though it was in most cases.

Nevertheless, a case can be made that engineers were the true representatives of the age. As designers of railroad routes, gravity-defying skyscrapers, and new systems of shop-floor management, they oversaw the technical aspects of economic growth and development. Engineers melded science with mass production to yield a form of capitalism that thrived on consumers' deepest desires and anxieties, despite resistance from some who rejected standardization in favor of local tradition or new forms of collective action.

Sites to Visit

Alexander Graham Bell Family Papers
www.memory.loc.gov/ammem/bellhtml/bellhome.html

This Library of Congress site contains papers from 1862 to 1939 as well as a chronology, images, selected documents, and interpretive essays about Bell.

John D. Rockefeller and Standard Oil
www.micheloud.com/FXM/SO/

This study with accompanying images by François Micheloud tells of the rise of Rockefeller and his mammoth company.

Transcontinental Railroad
www.sfmuseum.org/hist1/rail.html

This virtual Museum of the City of San Francisco site has excellent information on the railroad.

Touring Turn-of-the-Century America: Photographs from the Detroit Publishing Company, 1880–1920
www.memory.loc.gov/ammem/detroit/dethome.html

This Library of Congress collection has thousands of photographs from turn-of-the-century America.

African American Perspectives: Pamphlets from the Daniel A. P. Murray Collection, 1818–1907
www.memory.loc.gov/ammem/aap/aaphome.html

This collection includes writings of famous African Americans, including Frederick Douglass, Booker T. Washington, Ida B. Wells-Barnett, Benjamin W. Arnett, Alexander Crummel, and Emanuel Love.

Evolution of the Conservation Movement, 1850–1920
www.memory.loc.gov/ammem/amrvhtml/conshome.html

This American Memory site brings together scores of primary sources and photographs about the historical formations and cultural foundations of the movement to conserve and protect America's natural heritage.

Inside an American Factory: The Westinghouse Works, 1904
www.memory.loc.gov/ammem/papr/west/westhome.html

Part of the American Memory project at the Library of Congress, this site provides a glimpse inside a turn-of-the-century factory.

For Further Reading

General Works

Alfred D. Chandler, *The Visible Hand: The Managerial Revolution in American Business* (1977).
Jon Gjerde, *The Minds of the West: Ethnocultural Evolution in the Rural Middle West, 1830–1917* (1997).
Andrew C. Isenberg, *The Destruction of the Bison: An Environmental History, 1750–1920* (2000).
T. Jackson Lears, *Fables of Abundance: A Cultural History of Advertising in America* (1994).
Walter Licht, *Industrializing America: The Nineteenth Century* (1995).

The New Shape of Business

James R. Barrett, *Work and Community in the Jungle: Chicago's Packinghouse Workers, 1894–1922* (1987).
Ron Chernow, *Titan: The Life of John D. Rockefeller, Sr.* (1998).
Wendy Gamber, *The Female Economy: The Millinery and Dressmaking Trades, 1860–1930* (1997).
Thomas Parke Hughes, *American Genesis: A Century of Invention and Technological Enthusiasm, 1870–1970* (1989).
David E. Nye, *Electrifying America: Social Meanings of a New Technology, 1880–1940* (1990).

Donald J. Pisani, *Water, Land, and Law in the West: The Limits of Public Policy, 1850–1920* (1996).

C. J. Schmitz, *The Growth of Big Business in the United States and Western Europe, 1850–1939* (1993).

The Birth of a National Urban Culture

Edwin G. Burrows and Mike Wallace, *Gotham: A History of New York City to 1898* (1999).

Howard P. Chudacoff and Judith E. Smith, *The Evolution of American Urban Society*, 5th ed. (2000).

William Cronon, *Nature's Metropolis: Chicago and the Great West* (1991).

Robert V. Hine and John Mack Faragher, *The American West: A New Interpretive History* (2000).

Eric Monkkonen, *America Becomes Urban: The Development of U.S. Cities and Towns, 1780–1980* (1988).

David Nasaw, *Going Out: The Rise and Fall of Public Amusements* (1993).

Thrills, Chills, and Bathtubs

Bessie Louise Pierce, *As Others See Chicago: Impressions of Visitors 1673–1933* (2004).

Allen Guttmann, *A Whole New Ball Game: An Interpretation of American Sports* (1988).

John F. Kasson, *Amusing the Millions: Coney Island at the Turn of the Century* (1978).

Joy S. Kasson, *Buffalo Bill's Wild West: Celebrity, Memory and Popular History* (2000).

William Leach, *Land of Desire: Merchants, Power, and the Rise of a New American Culture* (1993).

Defending the New Industrial Order

Thomas L. Haskell, *The Emergence of Professional Social Science: The American Social Science Association and the Nineteenth-Century Crisis of Authority* (1977).

Richard Hofstadter, *Social Darwinism in American Thought, 1860–1914*, rev. ed. (1955).

Valerie S. Mathes, *Helen Hunt Jackson and Her Indian Reform Legacy* (1990).

Louis Menand, *The Metaphysical Club: A Story of Ideas in America* (2001).

For quizzes and other resources on these topics, go to www.longmanamericanhistory.com.

Challenges to Government and Corporate Power, 1877–1890

CHAPTER 17

In the spring of 1889, men in San Miguel County, northern New Mexico territory, armed themselves and donned masks. Mounting their horses, they rode out to attack their enemies. As members of a secret organization called *las Gorras Blancas* (the Whitecaps), they banded together in the dead of the night and destroyed the fences of local cattle ranchers, chopping the wooden posts to pieces and scattering the barbed wire. In some of their raids, the rebels shot and wounded ranchers. Over the next year and a half, *las Gorras Blancas* broadened their targets. They burned bridges, haystacks, and piles of lumber; cut telegraph wires; and took axes to electric light poles and to railroad ties belonging to the Atchison, Topeka, and Santa Fe Railroad. The membership of the group overlapped with that of the Knights of Labor, a national labor union that boasted twenty local assemblies in San Miguel County, east of Santa Fe. On the night of March 11, 1890, *las Gorras Blancas* nailed pieces of paper to the buildings of East Las Vegas, the largest town in the county. These pages, copies of the insurgents' "platform," declared, "Our purpose is to protect the rights and interests of the people in general; especially those of the helpless classes."

Who were these determined nightriders? They consisted of Hispanos—Spanish-speaking natives of the area. Their movement began when Juan Jose Herrera, together with his two brothers, Pablo and Nicanor, organized their neighbors in an effort to block European American ranchers from fencing their land. Labeled *las masas de los hombres pobres* (the masses, the poor people) by a local newspaper, *las Gorras Blancas* were desperately struggling to preserve a traditional way of life that was rapidly disappearing. Fenced lands prevented the area's Hispanic settlers from grazing their stock herds in the customary, open-range manner.

Many Hispanos lived in adobe (baked-clay) dwellings in small river-valley villages surrounded by breathtaking mesas, ponderosa pine forests, and high dry plains. In addition to raising chickens and grazing sheep, families grew chiles, pinto beans, squash, and wheat. Together, villagers relied on the common lands that had come down to them from their ancestors—land originally bestowed through grants from Spain and then Mexico. After the Civil War, European American interlopers—

■ By 1889 Santa Fe had seen several centuries of cultural conflict.

CHAPTER OUTLINE

Resistance to Legal and Military Authority

Revolt in the Workplace

Crosscurrents of Reform

Conclusion

Sites to Visit

For Further Reading

sheep and cattle ranchers, lawyers, speculators, commercial lumberers, and the railroads—began to encroach on these common lands. Through local courts, the newcomers installed a system of private property that granted exclusive ownership to single individuals. It was these groups, with their fences and their laws governing land title registration, that *las Gorras Blancas* targeted.

Las Gorras Blancas had only mixed success. They managed to discourage new European Americans from settling in the area, and they prevented the railroads from buying more rail ties in northern New Mexico. Yet the nightriders could not stem the tide of land loss throughout the Southwest. The Court of Private Land Claims, established in 1891 by the U.S. government, resolved land disputes between Hispanic and European American claimants. Of the more than 35 million acres of land in dispute in the early 1890s, Hispanic claimants received title to little more than 2 million acres—barely one-twentieth of the land they had held in common.

Las Gorras Blancas represented a unique response to local conditions. But it was also part of a growing, nationwide movement against the standards imposed by industrialization and capitalism. Around the country, a wide variety of individuals and organizations emerged in the late 1870s and the 1880s to challenge employers, landlords, and military and government officials. Members of these latter groups responded with a challenge of their own: business, they proclaimed, must be allowed to develop fully and freely without "unnatural" intervention in the form of regulatory legislation or grassroots rebellions such as that of *las Gorras Blancas*.

> *Around the country, a wide variety of individuals and organizations emerged in the late 1870s and the 1880s to challenge employers, landlords, and military and government officials.*

It is difficult to generalize about those who contested the emerging order. Even their own names could be misleading. In the early 1890s, another group called "white caps," this one in Mississippi, consisted of whites who terrorized black landowners and mill workers. And although the Knights of Labor was a national union, it shaped its program in accordance with local issues. In San Miguel County, for instance, the issue was land—who controlled it and under what conditions. In Washington, D.C., the Knights' concern was the welfare of workers in the building trades. The Richmond, Virginia, Knights pioneered interracial organizing, living up to the group's motto, "An injury to one is an injury to all." In contrast, the San Francisco Knights spearheaded the move to bar Chinese laborers from the United States and to limit job opportunities for those who remained. Indeed, groups that challenged the authority of government and large business interests often disagreed among themselves about goals and strategies for change.

Resistance to Legal and Military Authority

America's march toward national economic centralization and integration was not steady. On the battlefield and in the courts, European Americans pressed their advantage, but these efforts met with stiff resistance from a variety of aggrieved groups. Members of these groups rightly believed they had much to lose from so-called progress. European Americans repeatedly used the notion of "racial" difference as a justification for depriving darker-skinned peoples of their claims to land, jobs, and even life itself. For example, California lawmakers approved legislation that discriminated against the Chinese as workers and as parents of school-aged children. In an effort to seek redress, some Chinese took their claims to court.

In a similar vein, prejudice against African Americans assumed the form of discriminatory legislation and random violence. Blacks chafed under restrictions intended to bar them from good jobs and from associating with white people on an equal basis. Varieties of black resistance to white authority included migration out of the South to the West, creation of community institutions, and violent retaliation.

For their part, during the late 1880s, the Plains Indians responded to encroaching railroads, settlers, and military regiments by embracing a movement of spiritual regeneration. On the Plains, whites, and especially U.S. military officers, perceived this movement as more dangerous than an armed uprising, and they reacted accordingly.

Chinese Lawsuits in California

Throughout California, job-hungry whites agitated for the violent expulsion of Chinese from jobs. (Most of these immigrants received two-thirds the wages of their white counterparts for the same work.) Opposition to the Chinese hardened in the 1880s. In San Francisco, the Knights of Labor and the Workingmen's Party of California helped to engineer the passage of the Chinese Exclusion Act, approved by Congress in 1882. This measure denied any additional Chinese laborers entry into the country while allowing some Chinese merchants and students to immigrate. In railroad towns and mining camps, vigilantes looted and burned Chinese communities, in some cases murdering or expelling their inhabitants. In 1885 in Rock Springs, Wyoming, white workers massacred twenty-eight Chinese and drove hundreds out of town in the wake of an announcement by Union Pacific officials that the railroad would begin hiring the lower-paid immigrants. Cheered on by others, a mob burned the Chinese section of town to the ground.

Whites held that the Chinese, with their distinctive customs, would never fit into American life. Nevertheless, early on the Chinese demonstrated an understanding and appreciation of American political and legal processes. Beginning in Gold Rush days, Chinese immigrants had taken their grievances to court. In 1862 in San Francisco, Ling Sing protested

DOCUMENT

Farwell, The Chinese at Home and Abroad

■ In the West, Chinese mining companies used water-management techniques based on traditional Chinese machinery such as the waterwheel. This photo shows a Chinese river-mining operation in Siskiyou, California, c. 1890. Chinese workers also constructed flumes, dams, canals, tunnels, and pumps to drain areas efficiently.

the $2.50 personal tax levied on Chinese exclusively. The California Supreme Court agreed (in *Ling Sing v. Washburn*) that the group could not be singled out for special taxes. In the 1870s, Chinese merchants used the provisions of the Civil Rights Act to challenge state and local laws that forbade them from holding certain jobs, living in white neighborhoods, and testifying in court.

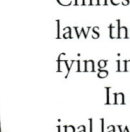
Yick Wo v. Hopkins

In San Francisco in 1885, laundry operator Yick Wo was convicted under an 1880 municipal law prohibiting the construction of wooden laundries without a license. A native of China, Yick Wo had arrived in the United States in 1861. By the time of his arrest, he had operated a legal laundry for twenty-two years. When he applied for a license, the board of supervisors turned him down, just as the board had denied licenses to all Chinese laundry operators who applied. In 1885 his lawyers petitioned the California Supreme Court, which upheld Yick Wo's arrest. The lawyers continued their appeal to the U.S. Supreme Court, maintaining that the board of supervisors intended to bar Chinese from independent laundry work altogether. In *Yick Wo v. Hopkins* (1886), the Supreme Court reversed the state court's decision. The higher court held that the San Francisco laundry-licensing board had engaged in the discriminatory *application* of a law that on the surface was nondiscriminatory.

Still, many cases challenging discriminatory laws never made it to the nation's highest court. And state and local courts in general often refused to acknowledge that Chinese immigrants had any civil rights at all. (Chinese immigrants were not granted citizenship until World War II, although their children born in this country qualified as citizens.) In 1885 the California Supreme Court heard the case *Tape v. Hurley*, brought by Joseph and Mary Tape on behalf of their daughter Mamie. Joseph Tape was a Chinese immigrant with some standing in the San Francisco Chinese community. Mary Tape had been raised in a Shanghai orphanage and had come to the United States with missionaries when she was eleven years old. She grew up to speak English fluently and dressed as a European American. Their daughter Mamie was quite westernized as well.

Even so, Mamie Tape was barred from the city's public school system. The school board claimed that Mamie's presence in the classroom would be "very mentally and morally detrimental" to her classmates. The Tapes sued the city and won, but the school board retaliated by creating a separate school for children of Asian descent within Chinatown. Mary Tape wrote an angry letter to the board: "Dear Sirs, Will you please to tell me! Is it a disgrace to be Born a Chinese? Didn't God make us all!!! What right! have you to bar my children out of the school?" In the end, the Tapes decided to enroll their two children in the segregated school. Yet their legal protest kept alive the ideal of equality under the law.

Blacks in the "New South"

In 1886 Henry Grady, the young editor of the Atlanta *Constitution*, traveled north to deliver a speech to the New England Society of New York. Grady hailed what he called the "New South." The former Confederate states, he claimed, were now forward looking, prepared to embrace industrialization and promote the reconciliation of blacks and whites. According to the journalist, it was time for the South to march forward and join with a larger, modernizing America.

Grady's speech about the "New South" provided a label that stuck. Yet he doubtless spoke too soon and in terms too grandiose. True, he could point with pride to some dramatic industrial developments in the South. Soon after James Bonsack invented a cigarette-rolling machine in 1880, James Buchanan Duke's Durham, North Carolina, company was selling 400,000 machine-made cigarettes each day. The southern textile labor force more than doubled between 1880 and 1890. And by the mid-1880s, with the backing of the Tennessee Coal, Iron, and Railway Company, the city of Birmingham, Alabama, specialized in pig iron production.

Factory and professional work in towns and cities offered new opportunities in the South as industry developed. However, these jobs were dominated by white men. Low-paid heavy

Some Chinese made a prosperous life for themselves in the United States. This photo shows Ah Sue, her husband, Ah Quin, and their twelve children. Ah Sue found refuge in the San Francisco Chinese Mission Home in 1879. Two years later she and Ah Quin celebrated their Christian wedding in the Mission Home. Ah Quin rose from the position of cook to become a successful railroad contractor and merchant in San Diego.

labor, primarily in rural areas, continued to be the primary source of work for black men. The hardest and lowest-paid jobs, such as digging ore out of a hill in northern Alabama or constructing a railroad through the swamps of Florida, often went to convicts whom private employers had leased from the state. Most of these "convict lease" workers were black men who had been arrested on minor charges and then bound out when they could not pay their fines or court costs. In Mississippi a black man could be picked up for "some trifling misdemeanor," in the words of one observer, fined $500, and compelled to work off the fine (at a rate of 5 cents a day) for a local planter. With an almost unlimited supply of such workers, employers had little incentive to ease the brutal living and working conditions endured by these convicts.

Some blacks fled the countryside and settled in southern cities, where good jobs were still limited but personal freedom was greater. Gradually, a new black elite arose. These physicians, lawyers, insurance agents, and undertakers reached out to an exclusively black clientele. They also nourished a sense of community. Black men and women continued to sustain their own institutions, such as schools, lodges, benevolent societies, burial organizations, and churches.

In the late 1880s, white Democrats feared the assertiveness of the new black elite. According to whites, this generation of men and women born as free persons and not as slaves must be "put in their place," quite literally. As a result, new state and local laws mandated separate water fountains for blacks and whites, restricted blacks to separate railroad cars and other forms of public transportation, and excluded them altogether from city parks and other public spaces. Long-standing customs barring black people from white-owned theaters, restaurants, and hotels now carried the weight of law. There were two separate school systems, one white and well funded, one black and starved of cash. Legal discrimination against blacks came to be called the **Jim Crow** system.

By the 1890s, a rising tide of lynching engulfed the South, but white officials did little or nothing to halt it. Black men, women, and children were all vulnerable to the fury of the white lynch mob—on the most flimsy pretext. Blacks throughout the segregated South rightly feared that they would be targeted if they spoke out against lynching. Yet northern blacks did not hesitate to highlight the hypocrisy of the federal government, which turned a blind eye toward this practice. Frances Ellen Watkins Harper, an educator and writer living in Philadelphia, issued the following challenge to an audience of white club women: "A government which has the power to tax a man in peace, draft him in war, should have the power to defend his life in the hour of peril." Harper condemned "the government which can protect and defend its citizens from wrong and outrage and does not."

"Jim Crow" in the West

Racial segregation was not limited to the South. The U.S. military enforced its own set of Jim Crow regulations. In 1869 Congress created the 24th and 25th Infantries (Colored), composed of African American soldiers. White officers were appointed to lead these segregated units. Consequently, black men who aspired to positions of military leadership found their way blocked. Some white officers, such as George Custer, refused to command black troops.

Military officials assigned black soldiers to the West, where they became known as buffalo soldiers. (The origins of the term are unclear. It may refer to the buffalo robes worn by many of the soldiers or to Plains Indians' respect for the black men's skills on horseback.) Many of these men were proud to wear a U.S. soldier's uniform, an emblem of their newly won citizenship rights. They helped to construct new roads and forts, protect wagon trains of settlers, and patrol the border between the United States and Mexico. They were an integral part of campaigns to subdue the Cheyenne, Comanche, Sioux, Ute, Kiowa, and Apache. They were among the soldiers deployed to quash strikes among workers (silver miners in Idaho, for example) and to fight forest fires in the Northwest.

■ Among the "buffalo soldiers" who served with the U.S. military were these Seminole scouts. The Seminole traced their history to the eighteenth century, when Creek Indians and runaway slaves of African descent established communities together in Florida. After the Seminole Wars (1818–1858), many Seminole were relocated to Indian Territory (present-day Oklahoma). Some fled to Mexico before the Civil War. In 1870 they were recruited by U.S. Army officers to serve as scouts. Their unit was disbanded eleven years later. Discriminatory policies of the military caused some to return to Mexico.

Often the buffalo soldiers encountered hostility from local townspeople, who resented their patronage of local establishments. In 1881 black Tenth Cavalry troops stationed at Fort Concho near San Angelo, Texas, reacted angrily when a local white man killed a black soldier in a saloon. Another soldier had died at the hands of a local white within the previous two weeks. In the absence of justice for the murderers, the soldiers blanketed San Angelo with handbills. Signed "U.S. soldiers," the message read, "If we do not receive justice and fair play . . . someone will suffer, if not the guilty, the innocent. It has gone far enough." When some of the soldiers attacked one of the men they believed guilty, the Texas Rangers entered the town to restore order. The army transferred the black companies out of the area and disciplined the leaders of the protest.

Once they were mustered out of the army, some black soldiers decided to settle permanently in the West. There they joined thousands of black migrants who were fleeing the Jim Crow South. In the late 1870s, 20,000 blacks from Tennessee, Mississippi, and Louisiana, called "Exodusters," migrated into western Kansas. The migrants cited the South's convict lease system, poor schools, and pervasive violence and intimidation as reasons for their flight. Some of these migrants established all-black towns in Kansas, Colorado, Nebraska, and New Mexico. Though generally small and poor, such towns provided places for blacks to live life on their own terms.

The Ghost Dance on the High Plains

Their lands and way of life threatened by whites, western Indians sought desperately to revitalize their culture and protect themselves. In 1889 an Indian named Wovoka offered the Plains Indians a mystical vision of the future, a vision that promised a return to the beloved past. A leader of the Paiute in Nevada, Wovoka preached what came to be called the Ghost Dance, part religion and part resistance movement. In 1889 a solar eclipse occurred while Wovoka was wracked by fever, and he claimed that the conjunction of the two events enabled him to glimpse the afterworld. The Indians could usher in a new day of peace, Wovoka proclaimed, and this new day would be a time free of disease and armed conflict. The buffalo would return, he promised, and the Indian men and women who had died would come back to replenish depleted villages.

VIDEO
Sioux Ghost Dance

Many of the Indians who performed the Ghost Dance fell into a trance-like state, bringing inspiration to impoverished and disheartened reservation communities. However, as the ritual spread across the Plains, U.S. military officials grew anxious. In November 1890, E. B. Reynolds, a Special U.S. Indian Agent, described to his superiors in Washington the strange, seemingly dangerous behavior that had gripped the Indians on Pine Ridge Reservation in South Dakota: "The religious excitement aggravated by almost starvation is bearing fruits in this state of insubordination; Indians say they had better die fighting than to die a slow death of starvation, and as the new religion promises their return to earth, at the coming of the millennium, they have no fear of death."

VIDEO
Westward Expansion and the Native Americans

As tensions between whites and Indians mounted, Sitting Bull emerged as a spiritual and political leader. After leading his followers into Canada, Sitting Bull returned to the United States in 1881 and later performed briefly with Buffalo Bill Cody in the Wild West show (see page 395). He surrendered at Fort Buford, Dakota Territory, where he was held prisoner for two years. Sitting Bull offered a pointed critique of the sedentary, materialistic way of life promoted by whites:

> The life of white men is slavery. They are prisoners in towns or farms. The life my people want is a life of freedom. I have seen nothing that a white man has, houses or railways or clothing or food, that is as good as the right to move in open country, and live in our own fashion.

Sitting Bull rejected white notions of "progress" in favor of his people's traditions.

In mid-December 1890, military officials ordered Indian police to arrest Sitting Bull at his cabin on the Standing Rock Reservation in South Dakota. Alarmed by what they perceived as rising Indian militancy, white settlers in Nebraska and South Dakota pressured the

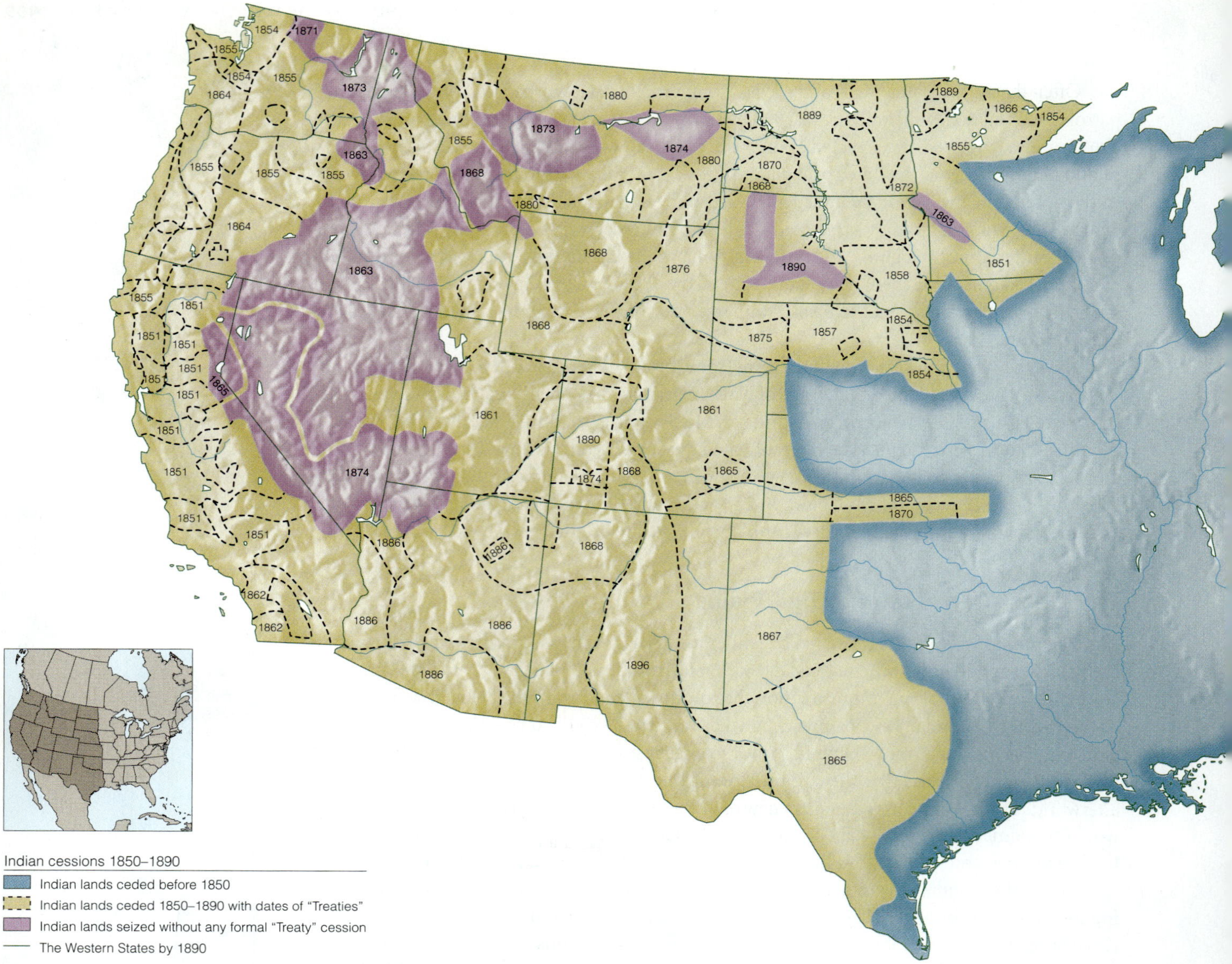

Indian cessions 1850–1890
- Indian lands ceded before 1850
- Indian lands ceded 1850–1890 with dates of "Treaties"
- Indian lands seized without any formal "Treaty" cession
- The Western States by 1890

■ **MAP 17.1**
INDIAN LANDS LOST, 1850–1890 Between 1850 and 1890, many "treaties" signed by Indian groups and the U.S. government provided that Indians turn over land in exchange for cash payments. Yet U.S. military forces seized a large portion of western Indian lands by force, without signing any treaty agreements at all. By 1890 many Indians lived on reservations, apart from European American society.

Accounts of the Wounded Knee Massacre

government to rid the area of the "savages . . . armed to the teeth," men who were "traitors, anarchists, and assassins." While arresting Sitting Bull, his Indian captors killed him.

A week later, on December 28 and 29, soldiers of the Seventh Cavalry under Colonel James Forsyth attacked Indians at Wounded Knee Creek, South Dakota. Estimates of the number of Indians killed range from 150 to 250. More than sixty women and children were among those slain as they fled the oncoming troops. The massacre at Wounded Knee proved the last major violent encounter between Plains Indians and U.S. cavalry forces. By this time, many Indians throughout the Midwest lived on reservations and engaged in farming. Government agents, eager to create independent farmers, instructed Indian men in the use of the plow. But plowing became a collective effort, as bands would work together until their task was done. Thus some Indian groups attempted to maintain customs of collective endeavor in opposition to the European Americans' glorification of ambition and individualism.

Revolt in the Workplace

Workers launched different kinds of challenges against the system of industrial capitalism, which, many charged, enriched a few industrialists and bankers at the expense of the vast majority of laboring people. Workers joined together in unions, and in many cases they fought the violence of private company security forces with violence of their own. Some men and women destroyed the machinery that threatened to replace them in the workplace. By the early 1890s, critics of the new industrial and agribusiness order—a system driven by technological innovation—had come together in the form of a new political group, the People's party, or Populists. This organization aimed to bring together urban and rural, male and female, agricultural and industrial workers to protest the hardships suffered by laborers of all kinds and to demand that the federal government take strong action in rectifying social ills.

Nevertheless, in workplace conflicts, the lines were not always strictly drawn between employees and employers. For example, the late-nineteenth-century laboring classes never achieved the level of unity called for by the Populists. White workers often expressed intense hostility toward their African American and Chinese counterparts. Within small towns, shopkeepers and landlords at times showed solidarity with striking workers; in these cases, community ties were stronger than class differences. Also, despite their critique of big business, workers often embraced the emerging consumer culture. In fact, many of them fought for shorter work days and higher wages so that they could enjoy their share of the material blessings of American life—in department stores, movie theaters, and amusement parks. In the end, Populism was primarily a rural movement composed of small farmers, sharecroppers, and wage hands.

Trouble on the Farm

In the late summer of 1878, the combined effects of the recent national economic depression and the loss of jobs to labor-saving technology catalyzed a rash of machine breaking throughout rural Ohio. In the Midwest, displaced farmhands burned the reapers, mowers, and threshers of their former employers. Some wealthy farmers responded by abandoning their machinery and rehiring their farmhands. Technology, one noted, "ought to be dispensed with in times like these." By contrast, critics charged the machine-breakers with "short-sighted madness." The protests revealed that even family farming had become a business. Now farmers needed to secure bank loans, invest in new machinery, and worry about the price of crops in the world market.

In the mid-1880s, the plight of Plains farmers worsened when a series of natural disasters highlighted their vulnerability to the elements. Drought and declining wheat prices drove half the population of western Kansas and Nebraska back east to Iowa and Illinois between 1888 and 1892. Meanwhile, the bitterly cold winter of 1886–1887 decimated cattle herds throughout the region.

Things took a radical turn in the 1880s, when a national movement of farmers emerged and tapped into a wellspring of anger and discontent in farming regions throughout the nation. The Southern Alliance in Louisiana, Texas, and Arkansas pressed for an expanded currency, taxation reform, and government ownership of transportation and communication lines. Its members tended to ally with the Democratic party. The Northern Alliance from the Plains states also focused on the expansion of the currency supply—specifically, the coinage of silver—but advocated the formation of a third political party to advance its interests. Both of these large regional groups found adherents in the mountain West. There, miners and farmers joined together to protest the monopolistic powers of the railroads, privately owned water companies, and silver mining interests. These monopolies drove up consumer prices and depressed workers' wages.

A Nebraska farm family poses proudly with their new windmill, c. 1890. Such devices powered water pumps that reached deep into the earth. Though expensive, windmills were necessities for drought-stricken farmers on the Plains, especially during the harsh years of the mid-1880s to the mid-1890s.

Most Alliance men and women farmed modest parcels of land. As small producers, they felt powerless to influence the businesspeople and politicians who affected their livelihoods and their life possibilities. Members of the Alliance also presented themselves as the last line of defense for the noble yeoman in the face of the corrupting influences of modern corporate capitalism. In rural Alabama, where the Farmers' Alliance had links with local schools and churches, the group's newspapers railed against the "filthy city," a "wicked place" of vice, crime, and dissipation. Farm folk thus distanced themselves from the "New South Creed," which promoted materialism and industrialization.

Suffering from a recession in the late 1880s, farmers in the Dakotas, Nebraska, Kansas, and Texas began to mobilize into a new political party. Organizing work among Alliance members at the local level laid the foundation for the creation of the People's, or Populist, party. By representing the financial interests of all farmers and highlighting the vulnerabilities of debtors, the organization foreshadowed the wider national appeal of the Populist party in the 1890s.

Militancy in the Factories and Mines

The new economy wrought profound hardship on members of the urban laboring classes as well as on small farmers. Many industrial workers faced layoffs and wage cuts during the depressions of the 1870s and 1880s. The great railroad strikes of 1877 (see Chapter 16) foreshadowed an era of bitter industrial conflict. Because no laws regulated private industry, employers could impose ten- to fifteen-hour workdays, six days a week. Industrial accidents were all too common, and some industries lacked safety precautions. Steelworkers labored in excessive heat, and miners and textile mill employees alike contracted respiratory diseases. With windows closed and machines speeded up, new forms of technology created new risks for workers.

The Chicago meatpackers, who wielded gigantic cleavers in subfreezing lockers, and the California wheat harvesters, who operated complex mechanical binders and threshers, were among those confronting danger on the job.

Women wage-earners also faced dangerous working conditions. In 1884 the Massachusetts Bureau of Statistics of Labor issued a report outlining the occupational hazards for working women in the city of Boston. In button-making establishments, female workers often got their fingers caught under punch and die machines. Employers provided a surgeon to dress an employee's wounds the first three times she was injured; thereafter, she had to pay for her own medical care. Women operated heavy power machinery in the garment industry and exposed themselves to dangerous chemicals and processing materials in paper-box making, fish packing, and confectionery manufacturing.

Some women workers, especially those who monopolized certain kinds of jobs, organized and struck for higher wages. Three thousand Atlanta washerwomen launched such an effort in 1881 but failed to get their demands met. Most women found it difficult to win the respect not only of employers but also of male unionists. Leonora Barry, an organizer for the Knights of Labor, sought to change that. Barry visited mills and factories around the country. At each stop, she highlighted women's unique difficulties and condemned the "selfishness of their brothers in toil" who resented women's intrusion into the workplace. Barry was reacting to men such as Edward O'Donnell, a prominent labor official who claimed that wage-earning women threatened the role of men as family breadwinners.

For both men and women workers, the influx of 5.25 million new immigrants in the 1880s stiffened job competition at worksites throughout the country. To make matters worse, vast outlays of capital needed to mechanize and organize manufacturing plants placed pressure on employers to economize. Many of them did so by cutting wages. Like the family farmer who could no longer claim the status of the independent yeoman, industrial workers depended on employers and consumers for their physical well-being and very survival.

■ Mining was one of the most hazardous occupations in the United States. Below-surface miners worked with explosives and sophisticated kinds of machinery. As a result, the chances of explosions, cave-ins, rockslides, and fires increased. These conditions help to account for the labor militancy of miners throughout the country. This photo shows a mining operation at Marysville, near Helena, Montana, c. 1885.

Organizing American Labor in the Late 19th Century

Not until 1935 would American workers have the right to organize and bargain collectively with their employers. Until then, laborers who saw strength in numbers and expressed an interest in a union could be summarily fired, **blacklisted** (their names circulated to other employers), and harassed by private security forces. The Pinkerton National Detective Agency, founded in 1850 by a Scottish immigrant named Allan Pinkerton, initially found eager clients among the railroads. The Pinkertons, as they were called, served as industrial spies and policemen during some of the most bitter and violent strikes of the late nineteenth century.

The Knights of Labor under the leadership of Terence V. Powderly made impressive gains in the 1880s. In appealing to many different kinds of workers around the country, the Knights blended a critique of the late-nineteenth-century wage system with a belief in the dignity of labor and a call for collective action. According to the Knights, business monopolies and corrupt politicians everywhere shared a common interest in exploiting the labor of ordinary men and women. The Knights advocated a return to the time when workers controlled their own labor and received a just price for the products they made. "We declare an inevitable and irresistible conflict between the wage system of labor and republican system of government," the Knights proclaimed.

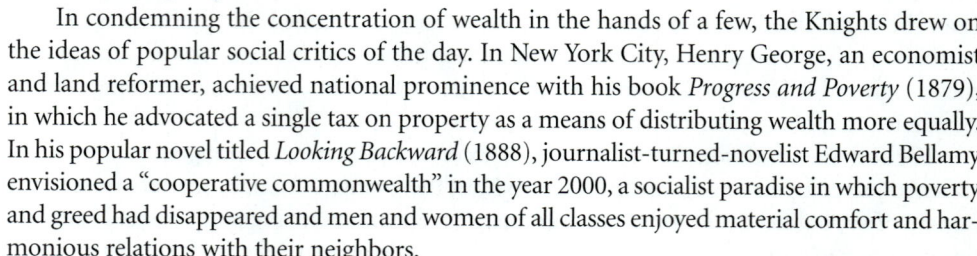
Bellamy, from *Looking Backward*

In condemning the concentration of wealth in the hands of a few, the Knights drew on the ideas of popular social critics of the day. In New York City, Henry George, an economist and land reformer, achieved national prominence with his book *Progress and Poverty* (1879), in which he advocated a single tax on property as a means of distributing wealth more equally. In his popular novel titled *Looking Backward* (1888), journalist-turned-novelist Edward Bellamy envisioned a "cooperative commonwealth" in the year 2000, a socialist paradise in which poverty and greed had disappeared and men and women of all classes enjoyed material comfort and harmonious relations with their neighbors.

Between 1885 and 1886, the Knights undertook the difficult task of organizing black workers. Many blacks remained suspicious of white-led unions, and for good reason. Historically, the white labor movement had conceived itself as a way to exclude black men and women from stable, well-paying jobs. Throughout the South, segregation was the norm within biracial unionism. Whites, whether New Orleans dockworkers, Birmingham District coal miners, or lumber workers in East Texas and Louisiana, insisted on separate locals from blacks. Yet African Americans did not necessarily acquiesce to this arrangement.

In 1886 workers around the country began to mobilize on behalf of the eight-hour day. "Eight hours to constitute a day's work" was their slogan. The issue had broad appeal, but the growing diversity of the labor force made unity difficult. In 1880, between 78 and 87 percent of all workers in San Francisco, St. Louis, Cleveland, New York, Detroit, Milwaukee, and Chicago were either immigrants or the children of immigrants. In many places, the laboring classes remained vulnerable to divisive social and cultural animosities. The diversity of ethnic groups, coupled with the fact that many newcomers from Europe adopted racist ideas to become "Americans," drove wedges between workers.

The Haymarket Bombing

The year 1886 marked the end of an era dominated by the Knights of Labor as the organization experienced the difficulties of overcoming its members' diverse crafts, racial loyalties, and political allegiances. Industrialists dug in their heels and, with the aid of hired detectives, took union leaders to court on charges of sabotage, assault, conspiracy, and murder.

On May 1, 1886, 350,000 workers in 11,562 business establishments went out on a one-day strike as part of the eight-hour workday movement. In Chicago, home to militant labor anarchists (men and women who opposed government authority of any kind), 40,000 workers participated in the strike. Among the Chicago leaders was Albert Parsons. A descendant of New England Puritans and a printer by trade, Parsons had lived in Waco, Texas, where he

INTERPRETING HISTORY

"Albert Parsons's Plea for Anarchy"

On August 10, 1886, the *New York Herald* published an essay by convicted Haymarket defendant Albert R. Parsons. In it, Parsons defends his views on anarchism. His theories on the inevitable clash between workers and capitalists echo the arguments of Karl Marx, the German political theorist. Marx predicted that the capitalist system would inevitably self-destruct and that the working classes would rise to rule the world.

So much is written and said nowadays about socialism or anarchism, that a few words on the subject from one who holds to these doctrines may be of interest to the readers of your great newspaper.

Anarchy is the perfection of personal liberty or self-government. It is the free play of nature's law.... It is the negation of force or the domination of man by man. In the place of the law maker it puts the law discoverer and for the driver, or dictator, or ruler, it gives free play to the natural leader. It leaves man free to be happy or miserable, to be rich or poor, to be mean or good. The natural law is self-operating, self-enacting, and cannot be repealed, amended or evaded without incurring a self-imposed penalty....

The capitalist system originated in the forcible seizure of natural opportuni-

Albert Parsons

ties and rights by a few, and converting these things into special privileges, which have since become vested rights formally entrenched behind the bulwarks of statute law and government....

And what of the laborer who for twelve or more hours weaves, spins, bores, turns, builds, shovels, breaks stones, carries loads, and so on? Does his twelve hours weaving, spinning, boring, turning, building, shoveling, etc. represent the active expression or energy of his life? On the contrary, life begins for him exactly where this activity, this labor of his ceases—viz: at his meals, in his tenement house, in his bed. His twelve hours work represents for him as a weaver, builder, spinner, etc., only so much earnings as will furnish him his meals, clothes, and rent.... The wage slaves are "free" to compete with each other for the opportunity to serve capital and capitalists to compete with each other in monopolizing the laborer's products.

Parsons argues that it is only a matter of time before the capitalist system "will collapse, will fall of its own weight, and fall because of its own weakness." He asserts that the fall of capitalism will usher in a new era of socialism, a system in which all property is held in common and workers can govern themselves. He concludes:

To quarrel with socialism is silly and vain. To do so is to quarrel with history; to denounce the logic of events; to smother the aspirations of liberty. Mental freedom, political freedom, industrial freedom—do not these follow in the line of progress? Are they not the association of the inevitable?

Ten days after this essay was published, Albert Parsons and the other Haymarket defendants were found guilty and sentenced to be hanged. Four of them, including Parsons, were executed on November 11, 1887. The true identity of the bomb-thrower remains a mystery to this day.

Questions

1. What is the significance of Parsons's claim that the triumph of socialism is "inevitable" and "natural"?
2. Why did many Americans identify anarchists with violence?

---

met his future wife, Lucia Gonzalez, an Afro-Latina (probably born a slave). In 1873 the Parsonses moved to Chicago to avoid Texas laws against "race mixing," which prohibited interracial marriage. There Albert joined the International Typographical Union, and Lucia took up dressmaking. They were counted among the most famous and feared radicals in the city.

On May 4, things took a bloody turn. Strikers called a rally in Chicago's Haymarket Square to protest the murder of two McCormick Reaper strikers the day before. During the rally, a bomb went off, killing a police officer and wounding seven others, who later died. Although the identity of the culprit was never discovered, eight **anarchists**, including Albert Parsons, were arrested, tried, and sentenced to death for conspiring to provoke violence.

The Haymarket hangings demoralized the labor movement nationwide. Now associated in the minds of the middle class with wild-eyed bomb throwers, the Knights saw their ranks plummet from 700,000 in 1886 to 100,000 by 1890. With the demise of the Knights of Labor,

DOCUMENT

Engel, Address by a Haymarket Anarchist

the American Federation of Labor (AFL) emerged to become the most powerful national labor movement. Samuel Gompers, an English immigrant cigarmaker, had founded the new group in 1886 partly in response to the Knights' attempts to usurp the Cigar Makers' International Union with a socialist-dominated local. The AFL garnered the allegiance of skilled trade workers (most of them white men) and promoted basic goals such as better wages and working conditions.

Yet the radical labor tradition persisted. Meeting in Paris in 1889, a congress of world socialist parties voted to set aside May 1, 1890, as a day of worldwide celebrations in support of labor and demonstrations in favor of the eight-hour workday. (May 1 became an international labor day, celebrated annually.) In the United States, the United Mine Workers (founded in 1890) and the American Railway Union (1893) followed the radical labor-organizing principles of the Knights of Labor long after the AFL attained its ascendancy.

Crosscurrents of Reform

In the 1880s, a young Danish-born journalist named Jacob Riis prowled New York's East Side slum district in search of stories for the New York *Tribune* and the Associated Press bureau. In this part of the city, more than 37,000 tenement buildings housed more than 1 million people in inhuman living conditions. In 1890 Riis published a collection of his own photographs, along with explanatory notes, under the title *How the Other Half Lives*. His book galvanized the public in support of slum clearance and housing codes. *How the Other Half Lives* is a powerful indictment of greedy landlords, indifferent city officials, and unscrupulous sweatshop owners.

■ Jacob Riis titled this photograph *Street Arabs in Sleeping Quarters [Areaway, Mulberry St.]*. Riis's photos, collected in his book *How the Other Half Lives*, exposed the poverty and wretched living conditions endured by many immigrants in New York's Lower East Side. In certain cases, Riis carefully positioned his subjects before photographing them. It is doubtful that these little boys were sleeping while the photographer noisily set up his equipment a few feet away.

During the last decades of the nineteenth century, reformers adopted a range of causes. Some, like Riis, focused on the plight of the urban poor. Others challenged the Indian reservation system, which, they charged, left Indians poor and dependent on the federal government. Settlement house workers aimed to improve the lives of immigrant families. Middle-class women sought to protect and empower women by aiding abused or vulnerable wives and mothers, promoting temperance in alcohol use, and supporting women's suffrage. Many reformers participated in a transatlantic community of ideas, learning about reform strategies and institutions from their European counterparts.

One factor leading to reform was middle-class Americans' fear that the poor would lash out in angry frustration in order to call attention to social injustice. The reformers reasoned that even modest improvements in the lives of the poor would stave off violent conflict between the classes. Dramatic labor disputes, from the railroad workers' "great uprising" of 1877 to the Haymarket bombing of 1886, frightened many well-to-do people, especially in the nation's largest cities. Although reformers professed to favor the full integration of various ethnic groups into American life, at times they could hardly help but look down on the people they aimed to help. Yet many reformers were also motivated by a genuine sense of concern for less privileged groups.

Transatlantic Networks of Reform

American reformers derived ideas and inspiration from their European counterparts. This transatlantic exchange of ideas was greatly facilitated by improvements in sea transportation. During the 1870s and 1880s, ocean travel became cheaper and safer as well as more efficient and comfortable. Writer Henry James (1843–1916) traveled extensively in Europe before making his home in London in the mid-1870s.

Contacts between European and American scholars, students, artists, clergy, writers, and reformers enriched the intellectual life of the United States and bolstered the reform impulse. American women's rights supporters conferred with their counterparts in London. American college students attended classes at German universities. Out of these contacts emerged the Social Gospel, a moral reform movement that stressed the responsibility of Christians to address the ills of modern urban life.

Contacts between European and American scholars enriched the intellectual life of the United States and bolstered the reform impulse.

An idealistic graduate of Rockford (Illinois) Female Seminary, Jane Addams journeyed to Europe for the first time in 1883. The sight of large numbers of poor people in London's East End made a lasting impression on her. In 1888 she went again to England and visited Toynbee Hall, a social settlement founded to alleviate the problems of the laboring classes. Back in Chicago, she and her friend and former classmate Ellen Gates Starr decided to open a settlement house of their own in 1889. Called Hull House, it was located in the Nineteenth Ward, home to 5,000 Greek, Russian, Italian, and German immigrants.

Social settlement houses—so-called because their goal was to help immigrants with the transition of settling in the United States—provided a variety of services for immigrants, including English language classes, neighborhood health clinics, after-school programs for children, and instruction in personal hygiene and infant care. In 1891 six settlements were in operation. By 1900 the number stood at 200.

The Goal of Indian Assimilation

In the mid-nineteenth century, many European Americans, including government officials, believed that the reservation system was a much-needed reform to protect western Indians. Whites reasoned that reservation Indians would remain separate from the rest of American society, to the benefit of everyone. Indians could preserve their own culture, and they would remain safe from the attacks of both homesteaders and U.S. Army troops. By segregating this

■ Susan LaFlesche was the first Indian woman to become a physician in the United States. Together with her sisters Marguerite and Lucy, Susan attended Hampton Institute in Virginia, a vocational school for African Americans and Indians. This photo, c. 1885, shows Hampton students performing in a pageant at the school. Susan, center, and the woman on the right represented "Indians of the Past." The other students represented "Indians of the Present." Hampton's mission was to prepare its students for farming and the skilled trades.

group, European Americans were free to settle on rich farmlands, mine for gold and silver, and take advantage of timber resources in the West.

By the 1870s, the harsh reality of the reservation system had prompted a group composed of both Native Americans and European Americans to call for reform. The reformers pointed out that many western Indians had previously roamed the Plains in search of buffalo and other sources of food, clothing, and shelter. Confining whole tribes to reservations meant that they lost not only their traditional means of feeding and housing themselves but their entire way of life. Reservation lands were often unsuitable for farming, leaving the residents to depend on supplies of food, blankets, and clothing provided by the federal government. Kept apart from the rest of American society, denied the rights of citizenship such as education and the vote, many Indians fell victim to self-destructive behavior, including alcoholism and suicide.

AUDIO
Omaha Funeral Song

Convinced that the reservation system was a failure, in 1879 reformers began to call for the assimilation of Native Americans into American life. This cause was promoted by some Indians as well as Protestant missionaries. In 1879 Ponca chief Standing Bear toured the East Coast, speaking before large, receptive audiences in Chicago, Boston, New York, Philadelphia, and Washington.

Standing Bear's appeal helped to galvanize eastern reformers. The campaign for Indian assimilation bore a marked resemblance to the antislavery crusade before the Civil War. Both movements focused on the wrongs perpetrated by the U.S. government (slavery and the Indian reservation system). Both argued that the group in question deserved full citizenship rights. And both promoted the ideal of group self-sufficiency: blacks and Indians tilling the soil, embracing mainstream Christianity, and learning trades.

Beginning in 1883, advocates of Indian assimilation sponsored annual conferences at Lake Mohonk, New York, to plot strategy for the coming year. These conferences brought together scholars, clergy, reformers, and politicians, all of whom considered their cause as part of the tradition of Protestant missionary outreach work. The reformers believed that the values of white middle-class Protestants provided the best guide for Indians seeking to rid themselves of the hated reservation system. Advocates of assimilation also received support from people who simply wanted the Plains Indians removed from their land to make way for European American settlers.

Out of these conflicting impulses—one on behalf of the Indians' welfare, the other in support of the destruction of Indians' claims to large tracts of land—came two major initiatives that would shape federal Indian policy in the years to come. The first was the Indian boarding school movement, begun in 1879 with the founding of a school near Carlisle, Pennsylvania. The purpose of the movement was to convert Indian children to Christianity, and to force them to abandon their native culture and learn literacy skills. The second was the Dawes Severalty Act of 1887, allowing reservation land to be divided into separate farms for individual Native American families. Moreover, ambitious land speculators and corrupt government officials sought to enrich themselves from the provisions of the act which allowed the sell-off of Indian lands to white buyers.

Women Reformers: "Beginning to Burst the Bonds"

Like the Indian assimilation movement, women's reform work in general during this period had a strong missionary strain. In San Francisco, the Occidental Branch of the Women's Foreign Missionary Society enlisted the aid of well-to-do women in sponsoring a rescue home for Chinese prostitutes. Without the protection of traditional kin ties, these immigrants remained vulnerable to sexual and physical abuse. The rescue home enabled the young women to escape the men who exploited them and, in some cases, to reenter society, now as married women, factory wage-earners, or small merchants.

In Salt Lake City, a group of women challenged the Mormon practice of plural marriage. In 1886 their Industrial Christian Home Association received a subsidy from Congress to provide shelter for "women who renounce polygamy and their children of a tender age." That same year some Denver women founded the Colorado Cottage Home, a rescue home for pregnant girls and women.

The Women's Christian Temperance Union (WCTU) is an apt example of the missionary impulse behind late-nineteenth-century reform. Though best known for its antialcohol crusade, the WCTU also sponsored homes for unwed mothers and day and night nurseries for the children of working women. It also stressed the need for women's "purity," claiming that women and children were the chief victims of men's alcohol consumption. But the group went further to denounce women's victimization at the hands of men in general.

By the 1870s, the issue of women's suffrage had captured the attention of men and women throughout the country. The issue had special resonance in the West for several reasons. When European American women overcame the hardships associated with the challenge of settling the trans-Mississippi West, they considered themselves worthy of having an equal voice in the polling booth. Reflecting on her hard life as a settler in Circle Valley, Utah, Mrs. L. L. Dalton wrote in 1876 that she was "proud and thankful" to see women "beginning to burst the bonds of iron handed custom" and asserting their "co-heirship" with fathers, brothers, and husbands. Abigail Scott Duniway, who sympathized with the plight of overworked and often lonely farm wives, published a women's rights journal, *New Northwest*, in Portland, Oregon, from 1871 to 1887.

■ Frances Willard (1839–1898) grew up on a farm in Wisconsin Territory. She served as the first dean of women at Northwestern University in Illinois. In the mid-1870s, she decided to devote her life to the cause of temperance. From 1879 until her death, she was president of the Woman's Christian Temperance Union. Willard developed what she called a "Do-Everything policy." Under her leadership, the WCTU addressed a range of issues, including women's suffrage and workers' rights.

Western politics pitted cattle ranchers against farmers, and religious and cultural groups against each other. These conflicts prompted the men of various groups to seek allies wherever they could find them—within their own households if necessary. The territorial legislature of Wyoming granted women the right to vote in 1869. Utah Territory followed suit in 1870, and Washington Territory in 1883. Then came the states of Wyoming (1890), Colorado (1893), and Utah and Idaho (1896).

Conclusion

In the 1870s and 1880s, the Americans who challenged the power of government and big business represented a wide spectrum of ideologies, tactics, and goals. Some resisted violently. Others formed new institutions such as settlement houses, reform associations, or political parties. Some people hoping to effect social change used the language of evangelical Protestantism, echoing the reform activities of persons who called for the abolition of slavery before the Civil War. Others collected data and interviewed specific groups of workers, women, or immigrants in an effort, first, to expose the conditions under which these groups lived and labored and, second, to propose specific legislation to remedy those conditions. Plains Indians embraced religious mysticism in a failed attempt to halt the incursion of European Americans into their ancient hunting grounds. Thus, powerful groups encountered much resistance from people opposed to their narrow idea of progress—the idea that bigger factories, more efficient farm machinery, and a nationwide network of railroad lines would bring prosperity to all Americans.

As Americans began to think more broadly about their place in the world, some men and women hoped to apply the principles of moral and civic reform to other countries west of the United States. The 1880s laid the foundations for a trans-Pacific empire of missionary work and trade. In the process, a new ideology of expansionism emerged, one that blended elements of economic gain, national security, and Christian missionary outreach to peoples in far-off lands.

Sites to Visit

Anarchy Archives at Pitzer University
dwardmac.pitzer.edu/Anarchist_Archives/archivehome.html

This archive includes classic anarchist texts, especially information about and graphics of the Haymarket Riot.

Labor-Management Conflict in American History
http://www.publichistory.org/reviews/view_review.asp?DBID=93

This Ohio State University site includes primary accounts of some of the major events in the history of the labor-management conflict in the late nineteenth and early twentieth centuries.

Samuel Gompers Papers at the University of Maryland
http://www.history.umd.edu/Gompers/index.html

This site includes information about the papers project. It also has a photo gallery, selected documents, and a brief history of the first president of the American Federation of Labor.

African American Perspectives: Pamphlets from the Daniel A. P. Murray Collection, 1818–1907
http://memory.loc.gov/ammem/aap/aaphome/html

This collection includes writings of famous African Americans, including Frederick Douglass, Booker T. Washington, Ida B. Wells-Barnett, Benjamin W. Arnett, Alexander Crummel, and Emanuel Love.

The Haymarket Affair Digital Collection
http://www.chicagohistory.org/hadc/index.html

The Chicago Historical Society maintains this site about a pivotal moment in American labor history.

African American Women Writers of the Nineteenth Century
digital.nypl.org/schomburg/writers_aa19/

The New York Public Library's Schomburg Center for Research in Black Culture maintains this site, which contains a large number of digital texts by African American women of the nineteenth century.

For Further Reading

General Works

Edward L. Ayers, *The Promise of the New South: Life After Reconstruction* (1992).

Sarah Deutsch, *No Separate Refuge: Culture, Class, and Gender on an Anglo-Hispanic Frontier, 1880–1940* (1987).

Lawrence Goodwyn, *Democratic Promise: The Populist Moment in America* (1976).

Patricia N. Limerick, *The Legacy of Conquest: The Unbroken Past of the American West* (1987).

David Montgomery, *The Fall of the House of Labor: The Workplace, the State, and American Labor Activism, 1865–1925* (1987).

Elizabeth Sanders, *Roots of Reform: Farmers, Workers, and the American State, 1877–1917* (1999).

Resistance to Legal and Military Authority

Tomás Almaguer, *Racial Fault Lines: The Historical Origins of White Supremacy in California* (1994).

Dee Brown, *Bury My Heart at Wounded Knee: An Indian History of the American West* (1970).

Steven Hahn, *A Nation Under Our Feet: Black Political Struggles in the Rural South from Slavery to the Great Migration* (2003).

Leon Litwack, *Trouble in Mind: Black Southerners in the Age of Jim Crow* (1998).

Robert J. Rosenbaum, *Mexicano Resistance in the Southwest: The Sacred Right of Self-Preservation* (1981).

Alexander Saxton, *The Indispensable Enemy: Labor and the Anti-Chinese Movement in California* (1971).

Robert M. Utley, *The Lance and the Shield: The Life and Times of Sitting Bull* (1993).

Revolt in the Workplace

Leon Fink, *Workingmen's Democracy: The Knights of Labor and American Politics* (1983).

Philip S. Foner, *The Great Labor Uprising of 1877* (1977).

Jacquelyn Dowd Hall, James Leloudis, Robert Korstad, Mary Murphy, LuAnn Jones, and Christopher B. Daly, *Like a Family: The Making of a Southern Cotton Mill World* (1987).

Stuart B. Kaufman, *Samuel Gompers and the Origins of the American Federation of Labor, 1848–1896* (1973).

Theodore R. Mitchell, *Political Education in the Southern Farmers' Alliance, 1887–1900* (1987).

Bruce Nelson, *Beyond the Martyrs: A Social History of Chicago's Anarchists, 1870–1900* (1988).

Richard Steven Street, *Beasts of the Field: A Narrative History of California Farmworkers, 1769–1913* (2004).

Crosscurrents of Reform

Jean Bethke Elshtain, *Jane Addams and the Dream of American Democracy* (2001).

Paula Giddings, *When and Where I Enter: The Impact of Black Women on Race and Sex and America* (1984).

Frederick E. Hoxie, *A Final Promise: The Campaign to Assimilate the Indians, 1880–1920* (1984).

Peggy Pascoe, *Relations of Rescue: The Search for Female Moral Authority in the American West, 1874–1939* (1990).

Jacob Riis, *How the Other Half Lives: Studies Among the Tenements of New York* (1971).

Daniel T. Rodgers, *Atlantic Crossings: Social Politics in a Progressive Age* (1998).

For quizzes and other resources on these topics, go to www.longmanamericanhistory.com.

CHAPTER 18

Political and Cultural Conflict in a Decade of Depression and War: The 1890s

CHAPTER OUTLINE

Frontiers at Home, Lost and Found

The Search for Alliances

American Imperialism

Conclusion

Sites to Visit

For Further Reading

IN THE EARLY 1890s, LUTHER STANDING BEAR, A YOUNG MAN OF LAKOTA SIOUX ORIGIN, FOUND himself suspended between two worlds. Born in 1868 in South Dakota, he had learned to hunt buffalo in the traditional manner of the western Sioux. In 1879 he bowed to the wishes of his father, Standing Bear, who insisted that he learn the ways of "Long Knives," or whites. And so the youth was among the first pupils to attend the new federal Indian boarding school in Carlisle, Pennsylvania.

Called Ota Kte, or Plenty Kill, at home, now he was required to pick a new first name from among those listed on a classroom blackboard. He chose Luther. His teachers took away his blanket and moccasins and gave him a coat, pants, and vest to wear. They forbade him to speak his native language, and they cut his long hair. Like most other youths at Carlisle, Standing Bear learned to read and write English and to practice a craft (in his case, tin-smithing). His teachers encouraged him to embrace Christianity.

In 1884, as part of his government-sponsored training, Luther Standing Bear traveled to Philadelphia to work at the Wanamaker department store. After spending a year stocking shelves and performing other tasks at the famous store, Standing Bear returned to South Dakota. There he taught Sioux schoolchildren and married the daughter of an Indian mother and a white father.

After the massacre at Wounded Knee, South Dakota, in December 1890, the young man moved with his family to the nearby Pine Ridge Reservation, where he began work as a shopkeeper and postal clerk. In the late 1890s, Luther Standing Bear served

■ This group of Chiricahua Apache students arrived at the Carlisle Indian boarding school in 1890. Government-sponsored Indian education included dressing them in European American clothing and cutting their hair.

as an interpreter for Buffalo Bill's "Wild West" show during its tour in London. By 1912 he had become an American citizen and settled in southern California, where he began his acting career in the new motion picture industry. He appeared in some of the first movie westerns and became an Indian activist, speaking out against the "government prison" known as the reservation.

In the 1890s, Luther Standing Bear's journey took place amid economic depression, civil strife, and war. Throughout the decade, workers and owners showed that the United States was not immune to the bloody class conflict that had long plagued Europe. Some scholars lamented the closing of the western frontier, prompting fears that America's unique dynamic of growth and social improvement had come to an end. Native-born whites began to seize upon new categories of racial difference to draw distinctions between various groups in the United States and around the world. Faced with declining consumer demand at home, politicians and businesspeople joined forces to expand American markets and American influence abroad. America's imperialistic ventures would reveal a blend of economic interests and missionary outreach, particularly in Cuba and the Philippines.

> *Native-born whites began to seize upon new categories of racial difference.*

Whereas some Americans tried to define rigid racial and nationalistic boundaries, others sought avenues of connections. A new political party, the Populist, or People's, party, aimed to bring together men and women of all backgrounds and regions. By advocating **grassroots democracy** as well as government action to regulate the economy, the party paved the way for the Progressive reforms of the early twentieth century.

Frontiers at Home, Lost and Found

In 1893 historian Frederick Jackson Turner proposed a new way of thinking about American history. According to Turner, the process of settling the West had shaped all of American history. He argued that during the colonial period, the rigors of taming the land had transformed English colonists into more resourceful, more democratic people—in other words, into Americans. With each successive wave of western settlement, American society renewed itself. In his view, the West served as a safety valve, a place of opportunity that beckoned people out of crowded eastern cities. However, Turner noted, an 1890 Census Report had concluded that the frontier—the unsettled area of the western part of the country—had recently disappeared. "And now," Turner concluded, "four centuries from the discovery of America, at the end of a hundred years of life under the Constitution, the frontier has gone, and with its going has closed the first period in American history."

Turner's thesis promoted the idea of American "exceptionalism": the idea that its individualism and democratic values made the United States unique among the nations of the world. Yet, in his celebration of the sturdy frontiersman, Turner ignored the bloody legacy of western settlement and its devastating effects on native and Spanish-speaking peoples.

Nevertheless, at the end of the nineteenth century, Turner and others were asking questions. Did America need to conquer new lands and "tame" certain peoples to preserve its distinctive character? Now that the frontier had disappeared, what was to prevent the United States from becoming more like Europe? These urgent concerns led to efforts to assimilate and Americanize certain groups of people and to tighten systems of legal discrimination against others. In addition, some Americans turned their attention to "interior" frontiers of psychology, art, and spirituality.

■ Frederick Jackson Turner's 1893 announcement that the western frontier had disappeared was premature. Here, homesteaders in Washington State cut down trees to carve a farm out of the forest, c. 1900. Felling gigantic hardwoods in the Northwest was a formidable challenge to family farmers.

Claiming and Managing the Land

As less and less land was available for cultivation, grazing, and mining, the politics of rural development entered a new phase. In the early 1890s, the last great parcel of Indian land was opened to European American farmers. Congress established the Territory of Oklahoma in 1890. Three years later, the Cherokee Outlet in the north-central part of the territory, combined with Tonkawa and Pawnee reservations, was thrown open to settlers and oil developers. On September 16, 1893, 100,000 people claimed 6.5 million newly opened acres in a single day. The "sooners," people who rushed to claim the land, gave the state of Oklahoma its nickname. The "Sooner State" was admitted to the Union in 1907.

Congress took other steps to manage western lands during the 1890s. The Court of Private Land Claims (1891) oversaw land disputes in New Mexico, Colorado, and Arizona. This court favored recent European American claimants over the Hispanic settlers who had received title to the lands from either Spain or Mexico generations earlier.

Land courts were only one example of an expanded federal role in the settlement of the West and management of the land. During the 1890s, the federal government continued to provide information and services for farmers through the U.S. Department of Agriculture. Policymakers argued over the proper balance between conserving natural resources for use by farmers, loggers, and oilmen and preserving the beauty of unspoiled panoramas for the enjoyment of all. In 1890 Congress established a national park in California's spectacular Yosemite Valley, where the Yosemite Indians had lived for hundreds of years. The 1891 Forest Reserve Act set aside forest reserves in the **public domain** (that is, vast tracts of land still owned by the federal government). Logging companies were allowed to exploit these areas for their timber.

With his appointment as chief of the Division of Forestry in 1898, Gifford Pinchot sought to bring the issue of natural resource conservation to national attention. He believed that a managed forest could provide lumber and then renew itself. By contrast, John Muir and others argued that uninhabited regions should be preserved in their natural state, unmarred by dams, mines, or logging operations. In 1892 Muir founded the Sierra Club, a group devoted

■ **MAP 18.1**
INDIAN RESERVATIONS, 1900 The Dawes Severalty Act, passed by Congress in 1887, intended to abandon the reservation system and integrate Indians into mainstream American society. Nevertheless, many reservations remained intact. As a group, Indians lived apart from European Americans. By the early twentieth century, the Indian as a "vanishing American" had become a stock character in novels and films. Yet Indian activists continued to press the cause of their people: to preserve native cultures and, at the same time, protest persistent poverty.

to preserving wilderness. In 1899 both Muir and the Northern Pacific Railroad lobbied successfully for two new national parks, Mount Rainier in Washington and Glacier in Montana, highlighting the ongoing significance of railroad tourism. "Rusticating," or hiking and enjoying the beauty of nature, became a popular pastime for many Americans in the 1890s.

The Tyranny of Racial Categories

The supposed closing of the western frontier, and with it the disappearance of the "safety valve" for restless Easterners, highlighted urban America's increasing class and cultural diversity. In an effort to categorize social groups, many national opinion-makers—scholars, journalists, and politicians—claimed that people should be distinguished from one another by their inborn, "natural" characteristics, ranging from skin color to facial bone structure and intelligence. Supposedly, these differences defined specific racial categories, such as Caucasoid, Mongoloid, and Negroid. In fact, so-called racial differences between groups were cultural differences. Late-nineteenth-century scientific racists ranked "superior" and "inferior" races on an elaborate hierarchy encompassing all groups, native and foreign born. Identification of racial categories pervaded the nation's popular, political, and legal cultures.

Several factors account for this renewed obsession with race in the 1890s. European and American efforts to colonize and explore the far reaches of the globe brought whites face to face with darker-skinned peoples, whom scholars in the new discipline of **anthropology** studied and classified. The "New Immigration" from eastern Europe raised concerns about conferring citizenship on non-Anglos, such as Russian Jews, Poles, and Italians. Persistent violence along the U.S.-Mexican border, combined with the resistance of Indians and African Americans to the authority of white people, alarmed local and federal officials. Theories of "racial difference" were used to justify attempts to subordinate these groups, by violence if necessary.

In the South, the doctrine of white supremacy had disastrous consequences for African Americans. Beginning with Mississippi in 1890, over the next twenty years, white Democrats in all the southern states met in state constitutional conventions and imposed restrictions on the voting rights of African American men, including literacy requirements and poll taxes (fees that people had to pay to vote).

In 1896 the Supreme Court put its stamp of approval on segregated schools, trains, and streetcars in its *Plessy v. Ferguson* opinion. By a seven-to-one majority, the Supreme Court ruled that such Jim Crow laws did "not necessarily imply the inferiority of either race." Justice John Marshall Harlan dissented from the majority view, pointing out the obvious: "The white race deems itself to be the dominant race," a view that conflicted with the "colorblind" U.S. Constitution.

■ A middle-class Powhatan Indian family in Virginia poses for the camera, c. 1900. Since the seventeenth century, the Powhatan had intermarried with the Nanticoke of Delaware as well as African Americans of the mid-Atlantic region. Communities such as these defied the efforts of scientists and others to rigidly categorize people according to race.

Between 1882 and 1901, more than 100 people, most of them black men, were lynched every year in the United States; the year 1892 set a record of 230 deaths. In the South, lynch mobs targeted black men and women who refused to subordinate themselves to whites. Many black men victimized by lynch mobs were falsely accused of raping white women. Black Memphis newspaper editor Ida B. Wells charged that accusations of rape were merely a pretext for the murder of black men. The southern white man, wrote Wells, "had never gotten over his resentment that the Negro was no longer his plaything, his servant, and his source of income." Death threats forced the editor to move north.

Yet even in the South, racial definitions were never as clear-cut or self-evident as racists, scientific or otherwise, claimed. For example, Italians and Jews occupied a **middle ground** between black and white, as class issues intermingled with racial categories. In 1891 in New Orleans, the lynching of a group of eleven Italian prisoners accused of conspiring to murder the city's chief of police met with no public outcry. Instead, a local newspaper condemned the "lawless passions" and "the cutthroat practices" that it claimed were characteristic of all Italian immigrants. However, the Italian government protested loudly against the incident. Armed conflict between the two nations was averted only when the United States agreed to compensate the victims' families.

At the same time, Jewish shopkeepers and merchants in the South gained a conditional entry into the ranks of "whites." In Natchez, Mississippi, the small but prosperous Jewish community owned forty-five businesses, about a third of all in the town. However, living in an overwhelmingly Protestant region of the country, many southern Jews found themselves barred from local social organizations.

New Roles for Schools

Between 1890 and 1899, nearly 3.7 million immigrants entered the United States, fewer than 1.4 million of them English speakers from the United Kingdom and Ireland; nearly 2.3 million were non-English speakers from Germany, Italy, Austria-Hungary, and Russia. During this period, public displays of patriotism became increasingly characteristic of American life. The recitation of the Pledge of Allegiance was introduced into public classrooms and courtrooms in the 1890s.

Victorians (in England and the United States) saw formal education as a great equalizer of social groups. Moreover, many younger immigrants and the children of immigrants eagerly embraced American schooling as a means of upward mobility. However, schools did not always fulfill their promise as agents of equal opportunity for all. Increasingly, schools separated and grouped children according to their culture, religion, and class as well as race.

At the Carlisle Indian school, boys learned to make harnesses, tin pots and pans, wagons, and carriages, among other products, many of which were sold to local residents to raise money for the school. Girls took in laundry and ironed, also part of the school's money-making effort. The goal of such activities was to enable the pupils to become self-supporting upon graduation.

The school as a vehicle for vocational instruction also found support among northern philanthropists concerned about education for southern black children and young people. A generation after the Civil War, the persistent poverty of many rural southern blacks convinced northern reformers that this group of Americans should be educated for a distinct form of second-class citizenship. Philanthropists, such as Julius Rosenwald of Chicago, upheld the notion of segregated public education. They created new institutions, or modified existing ones, to stress the trades and "domestic arts" at the expense of such subjects as philosophy, mathematics, and foreign languages.

This emphasis on vocational training evoked varied reactions from African American leaders. Born a slave in 1858, Booker T. Washington had labored in a West Virginia coal mine before attending Hampton Normal (teacher-training) and Agricultural Institute in Virginia. In 1881 he assumed the leadership of Tuskegee Institute, an Alabama school for blacks founded on the Hampton model. Speaking at the Cotton States Exposition, a fair held in Atlanta in 1895, Washington urged southern blacks to "Cast down your buckets where you are"—in other words, to remain in the South and to concentrate on acquiring manual skills that would bring a measure of self-sufficiency to black families and communities. In the same address, Washington proposed that blacks refrain from agitating for civil rights, such as the vote. In return, whites should refrain from attacking innocent men, women, and children. Ignoring this last part of the speech, whites hailed Washington's "Atlanta Compromise" proposal as one that endorsed racial segregation and second-class citizenship for blacks.

DOCUMENT
Booker T. Washington, Atlanta Exposition Address

Challenging Washington's message, northern scholar-activist W. E. B. Du Bois ridiculed the notion that blacks should be content to become maids, carpenters, and sharecroppers. Similarly, in 1896 John Hope, a young professor at Roger Williams University in Nashville, Tennessee, and future president of Morehouse College and later Atlanta University, renounced Washington's apparent **accommodationist** stance: "If we are not striving for equality, in heaven's name for what are we living?" he demanded. "Rise, Brothers! Come let us possess this land. Never say, 'Leave well enough alone.'"

In many urban areas, Roman Catholic nuns founded and staffed **parochial** (parish) **schools** that appealed to certain immigrant communities. By 1900 Catholics constituted the largest single denomination in the country, with 9 million members from diverse backgrounds.

New forms of schooling reinforced class and cultural distinctions. No longer dependent on the income their children might earn in the workplace, late-nineteenth-century urban middle-class families could allow their sons and daughters to prolong their schooling. High school came to be considered a logical extension of public schooling. Between 1890 and 1900, the number of students graduating from high school doubled, from 43,731 to 94,883.

The spread of private institutions of higher education reflected the wealth of a new industrial owner class and new forms of socialization for young people of privilege. In 1891 Central Pacific Railroad builder Leland Stanford founded Stanford University in California in honor of his recently deceased son. The previous year, Standard Oil's John D. Rockefeller established the University of Chicago.

College life was becoming associated with a particular stage of personal development, a stage marked not only by academic endeavors, but also by uniquely American group activities, such as playing with or cheering for the school football team. The game of basketball was invented in 1891, and soon after, many colleges formed teams that played the new sport. In 1893 an editorial in the *Nation* magazine decried "the inordinate attention given to athletics in college" and suggested that "debt, drink, and debauchery" were the natural consequence. The writer singled out athletic scholarships and the recruitment of college baseball players by professional scouts as especially unfortunate developments.

Connections Between Consciousness and Behavior

In the 1890s, some scholars and writers proposed that, although America's geographic frontier was closed, the "interior" frontier (of the human will and imagination) still attracted the curious. In Vienna, professor-physician Sigmund Freud pioneered the study of the human unconscious, the mysterious realm of thought and feeling that lies hidden beneath the mundane activities of everyday life. Freud's *The Interpretation of Dreams* (1900) suggested that dreams reveal the dreamer's unconscious desires and that these desires shape routine behavior. In the United States, the new discipline of psychology owed much to the work of Harvard University professor William James. In his *Principles of Psychology* (1890), James described the human brain as an organism constantly adjusting itself to its environment; people's surroundings profoundly influence their behavior, he argued.

Novelist Stephen Crane combined an unflinching look at reality—a blood-soaked Civil War battlefield or the slums of New York City—with a sensitive probing of human psychology. In *The Red Badge of Courage* (1894), Crane explores the fears and self-delusions of a Union soldier, basing his account on firsthand descriptions of the fighting a generation before. By stripping the story of all ideology—northern soldiers are hardly distinguishable from southern soldiers, and political issues are never mentioned—Crane suggests that the real war was that of the combatants battling their own private demons.

The new discipline of psychology owed much to the work of Harvard University professor William James.

Kate Chopin's novel *The Awakening* (1899) prompted outrage among critics. They objected to the sympathetic portrayal of the wealthy married heroine, Edna Pontellier, who anguishes over her inability to reconcile her artistic, free-spirited temperament with her roles of wife and mother. At the end of the story, set in New Orleans, she chooses to commit suicide rather than submit to a life of convention. The novel focuses on Edna's reaction to the expectations other people have of her and on her gradual awakening to the idea that she must live life—or die—on her own terms.

Religious leaders also explored the uncharted territory of the mind. In the late nineteenth century, the Church of Christ, Scientist, founded by Mary Baker Eddy in 1879, prospered and grew. Eddy held that physical illness was a sign of sin and that such illness could be healed by Christian faith and prayer. In 1892 she reorganized her Christian Science faith around a mother church in Boston. Through branch churches, the American-born sect spread to more than sixty countries throughout the world.

The Search for Alliances

In the 1890s, groups of Americans seemed to be estranged from each other as they rarely had been before. A few were enjoying the fruits of astonishing wealth, building for themselves magnificent, multimillion-dollar "summer cottages" reminiscent of glittering European palaces. In 1899 University of Chicago sociologist Thorstein Veblen coined the term **conspicuous consumption** to describe the expensive tastes of the ostentatious rich. Meanwhile, working men and women toiled long hours under dangerous conditions—when they had jobs. In 1895 the average worker was unemployed for three months of the year. Categories of race pitted various groups, native born and immigrant, against one another. Self-styled sophisticated city folk derided the **hayseeds** on the farm.

Still, the prosperous middle class hoped that certain unifying forces would connect different classes and ethnic groups. Businessmen, lawyers, and other professionals placed their faith in public schools, such cultural institutions as public museums and libraries, and the desire for a more comfortable life to instill "American" values in newcomers and the poor. The 1890s also witnessed some remarkable alliances between groups of people who had never before found common ground. The Populist party had a profound impact on the nation's political landscape in the 1890s. And women, through their local and national organizations, helped to blend domestic concerns with politics, offering a new model of civic involvement.

Class Conflict

Congress passed the Pension Act of 1890 to provide pensions for all disabled men who had served in the Union army during the Civil War. To pay for the pensions, Congress imposed a high tariff (named the McKinley Tariff after Representative William McKinley of Ohio) on a wide variety of imported goods. The northeastern states, dependent on domestic manufacturing, traditionally supported a high tariff. Western states supported the McKinley Tariff in return for the Sherman Silver Purchase Act of 1890, under which the federal government promised to buy a total of 4.5 million ounces of silver each month and to issue banknotes for that amount redeemable in gold or silver. As a result, Westerners benefited from the infusion of federal cash used to purchase silver mined in the West.

VIDEO
Political and Cultural Conflicts—1890s

However, the pairing of a high tariff with the purchase of silver produced explosive political and economic results. The tax on imported manufactured goods hurt consumers, and when wages did not keep pace with prices, workers revolted. In 1892 steel magnate Andrew Carnegie and his company chairman Henry Clay Frick initiated a drastic wage cut at the Carnegie Steel Company's Homestead plant, near Pittsburgh. Workers struck in June. They armed themselves with rifles and dynamite and engaged in a pitched battle with some 300 detectives from the Pinkerton agency, men hired by Frick to break the strike. (Homestead town officials had refused Frick's request to subdue the strikers.) Ten people died, and sixty were wounded. In response to the violence, the governor of Pennsylvania mobilized the state's

■ MAP 18.2
MANUFACTURING IN THE UNITED STATES, 1900   During the late nineteenth century, most manufacturing took place in the northeastern United States. Exceptions included flour milling in Minneapolis, the growing textile industry in the southern Piedmont, and the emergence of steel production in Birmingham, Alabama, thanks to rich local deposits of coal and iron ore.

National Guard. The troops escorted strikebreakers to work. The company cut its workforce by 25 percent and reduced the wages of the strikebreakers. The steelworkers' union lay in ruins. Gloated Frick, "Our victory is now complete and most gratifying."

In the West, gold, copper, and silver miners faced daunting barriers to labor organization from within and outside their ranks. Protestants harbored suspicions of Roman Catholics. Ancient hatreds prevented the Irish from cooperating with the English. European Americans disdained Mexicans and the Chinese. However, the workers in Idaho's Coeur d'Alene mines managed to overcome these animosities and strike for union recognition. In March 1892, mine owners in the region formed a "protective association" and slashed wages. When workers walked off the job, the owners imported strikebreakers from other areas of the West. The strikers retaliated by blowing up a mine with dynamite. Fifteen hundred state and federal troops arrived on the scene, and the resulting clash left seven miners dead. The troops confined 300 striking miners in bullpens, where they remained for several weeks before their trials. In this case, too, the strikers met with defeat. However, out of this conflict came a new organization, founded in Butte, Montana, in 1893: the Western Federation of Miners.

Widespread discontent over the tariff and simmering resentment on the part of debtors clamoring for unlimited coinage of silver helped unseat President Harrison in the election of 1892. The victorious Democratic candidate, Grover Cleveland, took office once more in 1893 (the only defeated president to be reelected). A new and noteworthy player in the election of 1892 was the People's (Populist) party, whose first national convention took place in Omaha, Nebraska, that summer. The party had emerged from the Farmers' Alliances that had so effectively organized black and white midwestern and southern farmers in the 1880s. In the 1890s, the plight of western farmers reflected the state of American agriculture in general. The price of wheat had been a dollar a bushel in 1870, but it was only 35 cents twenty years later. Dakota farmers lost 15 cents on every bushel of wheat they sent to market.

The Populist party platform endorsed at the Omaha convention supported "free and unlimited coinage of silver and gold at the present legal ratio of sixteen to one"; a graduated income tax; government ownership of railroad, telegraph, and telephone companies; and an end to land speculation. The delegates condemned government subsidies to private corporations and called for the direct election of U.S. senators. The Populists' 1892 platform also included resolutions sympathizing "with the efforts of organized workmen to shorten the hours of labor" to an eight-hour workday (many workers were forced to toil twelve to fourteen hours daily) and expressing solidarity with the Knights of Labor in their struggles against "tyrannical" employers.

TABLE 18-1
The Election of 1892

Candidate	Political Party	Popular Vote (%)	Electoral Vote
Grover Cleveland	Democratic	46.1	277
Benjamin Harrison	Republican	43.0	145
James B. Weaver	Populist	8.5	22
John Bidwell	Prohibition	2.2	—

The Populists gained strength when a national economic depression hit in 1893. This dramatic downturn stemmed from several causes. As debtors clamored for "free silver," foreign investors in the United States became nervous, and European bankers began to call in their loans. A bubble of overbuilding and land speculation burst.

The effects of the depression were widespread. Within six months, 8,000 businesses failed. As many as 20 percent of all workers lost their jobs. In 1894 Jacob S. Coxey, an Ohio quarry owner, dubbed himself a "general" and mobilized 5,000 men to march to Washington, D.C. There, "Coxey's Army" protested the failure of the federal government to provide relief, now that the country was in the midst of the worst depression ever.

Also in 1894, Eugene V. Debs, head of the American Railway Union (ARU), inspired the union's 150,000 members to protest conditions at the Pullman Palace Car Company. Employees in the company town of Pullman, near Chicago, felt squeezed when Pullman cut their wages by one-third but left intact the rents on their company-owned houses. The resulting strike crippled railroads from Chicago to California. President Cleveland declared that he could not stand by while the strikers interfered with the delivery of the U.S. mail. The president sent troops to quell the uprising, crushing the strike. For the first time, a federal court issued an **injunction** to force workers to go back to their jobs. Debs and other ARU leaders defied the order and went to jail.

To workers all over the country, the response to the Pullman strike signaled a troublesome alliance between government and big business, two powerful forces that the poor and the unemployed could not hope to counter. Judicial decisions confirmed the belief of many farmers and workers that all branches of the federal government were conspiring to favor the rich at the expense of the poor. In 1895 the Supreme Court rendered two opinions that favored big business and the wealthiest Americans. In *United States v. E. C. Knight*, the court ruled that the Sherman Anti-Trust Act of 1890 applied only to interstate commerce and not to manufacturers. The court had decided in favor of the subject of the suit, the sugar trust that controlled 98 percent of the industry. In *Pollock v. Farmers' Loan and Trust Company*, the court struck down a modest federal income tax (2 percent on incomes over $4,000 per year). These decisions helped set the stage for the showdown between the Populists and the two major parties in 1896.

Demise of the Populists

In 1896 the Republicans nominated Congressman William McKinley of Ohio, whose name had graced the widely unpopular tariff bill of 1890. The Democrats turned their back on Cleveland, regarded as a pariah by members of his own party for his ties to big business and his high-handed tactics against the Pullman strikers. Without an obvious presidential candidate at their convention in Chicago in July, the Democrats seemed at loose ends. Then, out of the audience, a young man rose to address the 15,000 delegates. William Jennings Bryan, a thirty-six-year-old Populist from Nebraska, electrified the assembly with his passionate denunciation of arrogant industrialists and indifferent politicians. The country must abandon the gold standard once and for all, he thundered: "You shall not press down upon the brow of labor this crown of thorns, you shall not crucify mankind upon a cross of gold." One awestruck listener, an alternate member of the Nebraska delegation, later said of Bryan's "Cross of Gold" speech, "There are no words in our language to picture the effect it produced upon the vast multitude which heard it." The next day, the Democrats chose Bryan as their candidate for president, too.

TABLE 18-2
The Election of 1896

Candidate	Political Party	Popular Vote (%)	Electoral Vote
William McKinley	Republican	51.1	271
William J. Bryan	Democratic	45.5	176

By nominating this eloquent upstart, the Democrats took on the Populist cause of free silver. Conservative Democrats bolted the party or sat out the election. Meeting in their own convention later in the summer, the Populists chose Bryan as their candidate for president.

In the general election, McKinley received much support from his friend and political supporter Marcus (Mark) Hanna. A wealthy iron magnate and chair of the Republican National Committee, Hanna coordinated an effort to raise large sums of money for the Republicans ($16 million in total, compared with the Democrats' $1 million). Hanna charged that Bryan as president would mean disaster for businessmen, bankers, and other creditors, who would now be at the mercy of working people, small farmers, and other debtors. McKinley triumphed in November and, as a national force, the People's party rapidly disintegrated after the election of 1896.

As a political movement encompassing disparate elements, the Populists left a mixed legacy. In some areas of the country, the party yielded some remarkable, if short-lived, interracial coalitions. In North Carolina, Republican-Populist **fusion** captured the state legislature in 1894 and the governorship in 1896. Throughout the South, however, the black population was growing—from 4.5 million on the eve of the Civil War to a total of 10 million people in 1890. Frightened by this development, white southern Democrats campaigned to disfranchise black men, beginning in the 1890s. Landless blacks and whites would find no common political ground again until the 1930s.

Barriers to a U.S. Workers' Political Movement

In the 1890s, workers in Europe were forging new political parties to represent their interests and, in some cases, to press a bold socialist agenda, in the forum of national politics. Although late-nineteenth-century America showed dramatic evidence of bitter class conflict, it produced no viable workers' party or socialist movement. Why? The answer is not simple. Together, farmers and members of the industrial laboring classes aspired to self-sufficiency, a life free of debt that released their wives and children from unremitting toil and provided some measure of material comfort. Nevertheless, both groups found it difficult to unify themselves.

The large influx of immigrants meant that competition for even low-paying jobs remained fierce among wage-earning men and women. Employers manipulated racial, ethnic, and religious prejudices among workers to keep them estranged. White Protestant workers seized on ethnic and religious distinctions to win for themselves advantages in the workplace. Their unions excluded certain racial and ethnic groups altogether. Even somewhat egalitarian unions fell prey to racial prejudice. In addition, skilled workers, taking pride in their craft and its traditions, distanced themselves from those who tended machines.

Many American workers, regardless of ethnicity, religion, or industry, continued to believe that they could eventually own their own businesses. They resisted casting their lot permanently with unions or other working-class organizations. High rates of **geographic mobility** also prevented workers from committing themselves to a particular union in a particular place. And the power of antistrike forces proved daunting. Private security agencies, such as the Pinkertons, as well as state-deployed National Guard troops, backed up the authority of employers, judges, mayors, and governors.

Challenges to Traditional Gender Roles

In the 1890s, the women's suffrage, club, missionary, and social settlement movements emerged as significant political forces. In 1890 the two major national women's suffrage associations, the National Woman Suffrage Association and the American Woman Suffrage Association, merged to form the National-American Woman Suffrage Association (NAWSA). Elizabeth Cady Stanton served as the new group's first president for two years. But the suffrage movement exhibited contradictory impulses. On one hand, it brought together supporters from around the country and yielded striking examples of international cooperation. On the other hand, white native-born Protestant American suffragists distanced themselves from the poor, immigrants, African Americans, and the laboring classes within their own country.

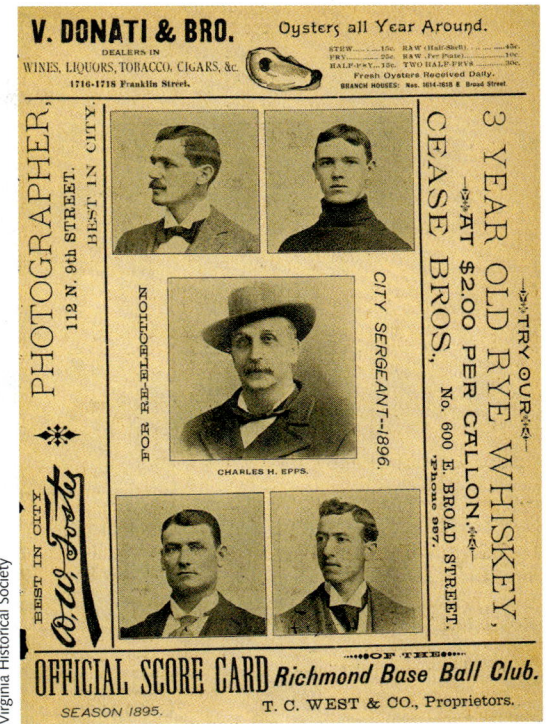

■ In 1896 Charles H. Epps, the city sergeant of Richmond, Virginia, ran for reelection. He distributed these cards to prospective voters. The cards suggest the masculine nature of politics at this time. This one doubled as a scorecard for the city's professional baseball team and carried advertisements for a local whiskey manufacturer and liquor and tobacco store.

Identifying themselves primarily as wives and mothers, some women entered the political realm through local women's clubs. They believed that personal intellectual development and group political activity would benefit both their own families and society in general. In the 1880s, the typical club focused on self-improvement through reading history and literature. By the 1890s, many clubs had embraced political activism. They lobbied local politicians for improvements in education and social welfare and raised money for hospitals and playgrounds. The General Federation of Women's Clubs (GFWC), founded in 1892, united 100,000 women in 500 affiliate clubs throughout the nation.

Women's Suffrage before the 19th Century

Yet the GFWC specifically excluded African American clubs. Black women formed their own national federation, the National Association of Colored Women (NACW), in 1896. Through club work, they spoke out against lynch mobs and segregationists and worked to improve their local communities. In some areas of the country, black and white women did make common cause—to further the goals of temperance, for example—although white women embraced these alliances uneasily.

In the West, Protestant-sponsored "mission homes" ministered to women in need. The San Francisco Presbyterian Chinese Mission Home offered a safe haven for Chinese women fleeing abuse and exploitation. Eastern women supported not only the San Francisco mission but also shelters for unwed mothers and abused girls in other cities, in the name of virtuous womanhood.

■ The diversity of the American workforce and the American economy inhibited the development of a national workers' political party. By the 1890s, some industries were fully mechanized. Others relied on traditional forms of manual labor. In California, Asian workers faced persistent discrimination from labor unions. These immigrants are picking oranges near Santa Ana, c. 1895.

Social settlements were unique institutions, founded and staffed by well-educated women, many of whom had attended elite women's colleges. The daily operations of the settlement house reflected the priorities of its founders, who often brought activists, public health officials, journalists, and laboring men and women together around the dinner table to discuss problems of the poor. Settlement house workers hoped to instill in poor women the values of domesticity and pride in American citizenship. By 1900 more than 200 social settlement houses were helping to acculturate immigrants by offering classes in a variety of subjects, including English, health, and personal hygiene.

Although often associated with immigrants in the largest cities, settlement houses reached diverse populations. In the late 1890s, a coalition of the Kentucky Federation of Women's Clubs and other organizations sponsored several teachers who organized a summer settlement called Camp Cedar Grove in the eastern part of the state. This venture provided the foundation for the Hindman Settlement School. The school, still in existence, initially aimed to **acculturate** mountain people to middle-class ways in dress, eating habits, and manners and to preserve traditional mountain music and crafts.

Sensitive to the racial prejudices of their clients and their neighbors, most early settlements failed to reach out to African Americans. This policy stimulated the development of black-led settlements, such as the Phyllis Wheatley Settlement in Minneapolis and the Neighborhood Union in Atlanta. Founded by Lugenia Burns Hope in 1908, the Neighborhood Union aimed "to bring about a better understanding between the races."

Some women challenged traditional gender relations that relegated women to dependence on men. Emma Goldman, a Russian immigrant and self-proclaimed anarchist, paired the sexual liberation of women with the rights of workers to live a decent life. A radical by any measure, Goldman was, nevertheless, not alone in rejecting the idea that marriage should always be permanent. Between 1890 and 1900, the divorce rate increased from one out of every seventeen new marriages to one out of twelve. More and more couples, middle class and working class, native born and immigrant, were seeking means to dissolve marriages that had failed.

Charlotte Perkins Gilman was among the most prolific and well-known critics of the conventional division of labor in the home. She proclaimed that women, no longer content to remain dependent on men, must take their rightful place within the economy, working as equals with their brothers and husbands. Gilman proposed that housework be divided into its specialized tasks to be performed by professionals. This system would free women from the unpaid, mind-numbing task of combined "cook-nurse-laundress-chambermaid-housekeeper-waitress-governor." In her critique of gender conventions, Gilman anticipated the feminist movement of the 1960s.

Men also pondered the effects of industrializing society on their own roles. As assistant secretary of the U.S. Navy in the late 1890s, Theodore Roosevelt worried that, in this age of machines, young men lacked the opportunities for "the strenuous life" their grandfathers had enjoyed. He argued that unapologetic masculine bravado provided the key to American

> *The daily operations of the settlement house reflected the priorities of its founders.*

strength and **rejuvenation** on both a national and personal level. In his multivolume history *The Winning of the West* (1889–1896), Roosevelt extolled America's relentless march to the Pacific: "The rude, fierce settler who drives the savage from the land lays all civilized mankind under a debt to him." Imperialism at home and abroad, he declared, was a "race-important work," one that should claim the energies of men as politicians and soldiers.

American Imperialism

In the 1890s, the United States began to extend its political reach and economic dominance to other parts of the world. Americans looked beyond their borders and saw exotic peoples who represented a variety of opportunities—as consumers of American goods, producers of goods Americans wanted to buy, and objects of American benevolence. This view represented an extension of the reform impulse at home.

The country's mighty industrial manufacturing sector demanded new markets and a wider consumer base. The depression of 1893, in particular, raised fears that manufacturers would have to contend with surpluses of goods that Americans could not afford to buy. American businesspeople and State Department officials established a partnership that combined private economic self-interest with national military considerations. Some molders of public opinion used the new languages of race and masculine virility to justify an "Anglo-Saxon" mission of conquest of "childlike" peoples. Meanwhile, European countries were carving up Africa and making economic inroads into China. Many Americans believed their own country should join the "race" for riches and "march" to glory as part of the international competition to exploit the natural resources and trade potential of weaker countries.

> *American businesspeople and State Department officials established a partnership that combined private economic self-interest with national military considerations.*

Cultural Encounters with the Exotic

In early October 1897, 30,000 spectators paid their 25-cent fee to enter New York's Excursion Wharf and observe the strange cargo of the recently arrived steamship *Hope*. Arctic explorer Robert Peary had returned from Greenland, bringing with him six Greenland Eskimo and a 37.5-ton meteorite dislodged from the Cape York region. The American public hailed the intrepid explorer Peary as a hero. The American Museum of Natural History put the Eskimo on display, and New Yorkers regarded their odd clothing, language, and eating habits with intense curiosity.

During the late nineteenth century, Americans were fascinated by artifacts and images dealing with far-away places, especially Africa, the Middle East, and Asia. This impulse, revealed in high art as well as popular culture, stereotyped darker-skinned, non-Christian peoples as primitive, sensual, and inscrutable. Chicago's Columbian Exposition of 1893 featured exhibits depicting harems, spice merchants, and turbaned warriors and performances of "hootchy kootchy dancers," scantily clothed young women writhing to the music of exotic instruments.

Throughout the late nineteenth century, photographers took pictures of Middle Eastern nomads and African villagers. American artists traveled abroad to render romantic scenes of deserts, ancient ruins, and mysterious peoples in oils and in watercolors. These cultural tendencies could be used to sell products and entertainment. The glassmaker-jeweler Tiffany and Co. evoked Islamic art in its tea services and silver patterns. Tobacco companies marketed mass-produced cigarettes with "Oriental" brand names: "Fatima," "Omar," and "Camel."

The Greenland Eskimo Minik is shown here soon after his arrival in New York City in 1897 at age 7. Minik was devastated by the death of his widowed father, Qisuk; the two were among six Eskimo brought to New York by Arctic explorer Robert E. Peary. Later in his life, Minik spoke of his father to a newspaper reporter, saying, "He was dearer to me than anything else in the world, especially when we were brought to New York, strangers in a strange land."

Thus, a fascination with the exotic encompassed a wide range of impulses in American life and letters, bringing together explorers, scientists, artists, and advertising agents.

Initial Imperialist Ventures

The opening of Asia to American trade, combined with the military challenges posed by the major European imperial powers, stimulated the growth of the U.S. Navy in the 1880s. In his book *The Influence of Sea-Power in History, 1660–1763* (1890), Captain Alfred Thayer Mahan contended that if the United States aspired to be a world power, it must control the seas.

Seeking way stations for its ships, the United States negotiated control over both Pearl Harbor in Hawaii and the harbor at Pago Pago in Samoa in 1887. Three years later, Secretary of State James G. Blaine hosted the first Pan-American Conference in Washington, D.C., a gathering of representatives from nineteen independent Latin American republics.

In 1895 the United States signaled to Great Britain that it was prepared to go to war to bar Europeans from colonizing or intervening in the Americas, a policy outlined in the Monroe Doctrine more than seventy years before. Britain had persisted in its long-standing claims to the jungle boundary between its colony of British Guiana and the country of Venezuela on the north coast of South America. President Cleveland made clear his intention to enforce the Monroe Doctrine. Britain, sensitive to other threats posed by European imperial powers to the far-flung British empire, backed down. Thereafter, Britain began to concentrate on strengthening its diplomatic ties with the United States.

Meanwhile, in the Pacific, the Hawaiian Islands seemed to pose both a threat and an opportunity for American interests. Located 2,000 miles from the California coast, Hawaii had a population of 150,000 in 1890. In 1875 sugar planters and merchants, many of whom were related to missionaries, had negotiated a treaty with the United States that let them ship the crop to the United States duty free. Production of Hawaiian sugar increased from less than 10,000 tons in 1870 to 300,000 tons thirty years later.

By this time, Chinese, Koreans, Filipinos, Puerto Ricans, Japanese, and Portuguese had made their way to the Hawaiian Islands. These groups formed the bulk of the plantation labor force, for disease had decimated the native population. In the fields and in their barracks, immigrant contract workers followed a disciplined regimen under the supervision of mounted, whip-wielding overseers called *lunas*. Indeed, these laborers' workday bore a marked resemblance to that of sharecroppers on the largest cotton plantations of the U.S. South.

The McKinley Tariff of 1890 raised duties on imports of the islands' sugar. This served to overturn the 1875 pro-planter treaty, causing planters (mostly Americans) to panic about their livelihood. They received no support from the islands' native leader, Queen Liliuokalani, who believed foreigners should be barred from running the country. In 1893 the planters, backed by American marines, launched a successful revolt that deposed the queen. They then called for the United States to annex the islands as a territory. When President Cleveland discovered that native Hawaiians opposed annexation, he refused to agree to the move. His refusal incurred the wrath of American imperialists, who claimed that the "Hawaiian pear" had been "ripe for the plucking." Those seeking to expand American influence also looked just south of Florida.

The Spanish-American-Cuban-Filipino War of 1898

Activities of the United States in the Caribbean, 1898–1930s

In the Caribbean, Cuban nationalists staged an uprising against the island's Spanish colonial authorities in 1895. Native *insurrectos* under the leadership of José Martí burned crops of sugar cane and attacked passenger trains. American companies with large investments in the Cuban sugar industry (a total of about $50 million) were outraged at the destruction of their property; they had no sympathy for the *insurrectos*. Yet the arrival of Spanish military officials, who herded the rebels into barbed-wire concentration camps, inflamed public opinion in the United States. By 1897, both businesspeople and humanitarians urged President McKinley to intervene in Cuba.

Two major American newspaper publishers, William R. Hearst and Joseph Pulitzer, highlighted Spanish atrocities against Cubans. On February 9, 1898, Hearst published a letter written by the Spanish minister in Washington, D.C., Dupuy de Lôme, in which de Lôme denounced President McKinley as a spineless politician. Six days later, the American battleship *Maine*, which had been sent to Havana harbor to evacuate Americans should the need arise, exploded and sank. Two hundred sixty officers and men were killed. Subsequent investigations concluded that the heat from one of the coal bins had ignited an adjacent powder magazine. But the Hearst papers implied that the Spanish were responsible for the blast. Attempting to expand their readership, the Hearst and Pulitzer newspapers engaged in **yellow journalism**: sensational news reporting that blurred the line between fact and fiction, spontaneous reality and staged theater. War sold papers.

McKinley responded to American businesspeople who feared for their interests in Cuba and to other Americans who decried Spain's brutality toward the *insurrectos*. On April 11, 1898, McKinley called on Congress to declare war against Spain. To war supporters, much was at stake: the large American sugar investment, trade with the island, and American power and influence in the Western Hemisphere. Congress responded to McKinley's message by adopting

■ The battleship *Maine* exploded and sank in Havana harbor on February 15, 1898.

■ **MAP 18.3**
THE SPANISH-AMERICAN-CUBAN-FILIPINO WAR OF 1898 In Cuba, the United States combined a blockade of the island with an army invasion to defeat Spanish forces. In the Philippines, the U.S. triumph over the Spanish opened a wider war between American occupying forces and native Filipinos.

the Teller Amendment, which declared that the United States would guarantee Cuba its independence once the Spanish were driven from the island. America went to war on April 29.

McKinley hoped to hobble the Spanish navy by making a **preemptive attack** on the fleet in the Spanish colony of the Philippines. Commodore George Dewey, stationed with the American Asiatic Squadron in Hong Kong, was dispatched with his ships to Manila Bay, where on May 1, 1898, his force of four battleships sank all ten rickety Spanish vessels, killing 400, with only a few minor American casualties. Dewey waited in the harbor until American reinforcements arrived in August. Then, with the help of Filipino nationalists led by Emilio Aguinaldo, U.S. forces overran Manila on August 13.

Meanwhile, congressional Republicans had found the necessary votes to annex Hawaii. They claimed that the United States needed the Pacific islands to secure a refueling way station for Dewey's troops. McKinley signed the congressional resolution on July 7, 1898. Hawaiian residents were granted citizenship rights, and the islands became an official U.S. territory in 1900.

Earlier, in the summer of 1898, 17,000 American troops prepared for their incursion into Cuba. Among them were the Rough Riders, volunteers organized by Lieutenant Colonel Theodore Roosevelt, who had resigned his post as assistant secretary of the navy to serve as an officer. The troops landed near Santiago, Cuba, in late June. On July 1, Roosevelt and his men engaged an unprepared Spanish force of about 2,000 men at El Caney and San Juan Hill. The Rough Riders charged up nearby Kettle Hill (they were on foot, not on horses) and into American legend. They received crucial backup support from two African American regiments

Roosevelt's Rough Riders

that day. By late July, American warships had destroyed the Spanish fleet in Santiago Bay. According to Secretary of State John Hay, it had been "a splendid little war," just 113 days long. Battles claimed 385 American lives.

On August 12, 1898, Spain signed an **armistice** and later in the year ceded its claim to remnants of its empire, including Cuba and Puerto Rico in the Caribbean and the island of Guam in the Pacific. The United States forced Cuba to incorporate into its constitution (written in 1901) the so-called Platt Amendment, which guaranteed continuing U.S. influence over the country, including the stationing of American troops at a naval station on Guantanamo Bay. Meeting with Spanish negotiators in Paris, the United States agreed to pay $20 million for the Philippines.

World Colonial Empires, 1900

But Filipino rebels were not about to bow to a new colonial power. Over the next two years, the United States committed 100,000 troops to subdue the rebels, using tactics that foreshadowed the U.S. war in Vietnam seventy years later. Hunting down guerrillas hiding in the jungle, American soldiers torched villages and crops. They forced water down the throats of suspected rebel leaders—a form of torture known as the "water cure"—in an effort to extract information. Four thousand Americans and 20,000 Filipinos died in combat. As many as 600,000 Filipino civilians succumbed to disease and starvation.

Ownership of the Philippine Islands gave the United States a foothold in Asia. In 1894–1895, Japan had waged a successful war against China, and European traders rushed in to China to monopolize local markets and establish their own **spheres of influence**. Secre-

INTERPRETING HISTORY

Proceedings of the Congressional Committee on the Philippines

In January 1900, Congress established the Committee on the Philippines. Senator Henry Cabot Lodge of Massachusetts was appointed chair. The committee's task was to review the American conduct of the war. The testimony of two U.S. officers, which follows, foreshadows the difficulties faced by the United States in fighting a guerrilla war in Vietnam six decades later.

Brigadier General Robert P. Hughes testified in response to questions posed by committee members:

Q: In burning towns, what would you do? Would the entire town be destroyed by fire or would only offending portions of the town be burned?
GEN. HUGHES: I do not know that we ever had a case of burning what you would call a town in this country; but probably a *barrio* or a *sitio*; probably a half dozen houses, native shacks, where the *insurrectos* [rebels] would go in and be concealed, and if they caught a detachment passing they would kill some of them.
Q: What did I understand you to say would be the consequence of that?
GEN. HUGHES: They usually burned the village.
Q: All of the houses in the village?
GEN. HUGHES: Yes, every one of them.
Q: What would become of the inhabitants?
GEN. HUGHES: That was their lookout....The destruction was as a punishment.
Q: The punishment in that case would fall, not upon the men, who would go elsewhere, but mainly upon the women and little children.
GEN. HUGHES: The women and children are part of the family, and where you wish to inflict a punishment you can punish the man probably worse in that way than in any other.
Q: But is that within the ordinary rules of civilized warfare? Of course you could exterminate the family, which would be still worse punishment.

Gen. Hughes: These people are not civilized.

Sergeant Charles S. Riley also testified in response to the committee's questions:

Q: During your service there [in the Philippine Islands] did you witness what is generally known as the water cure?
A: I did.
Q: When and where?
A: On November 27, 1900, in the town of Igbaras, Iloilo Province, Panay Island.

Riley described to the committee a Filipino man, 40–45 years of age, stripped to the waist, with his hands tied behind him.

Q: Do you remember who had charge of him?
A: Captain Glenn stood there beside him and one or two men were tying him.... He was then taken and placed under the tank, and the faucet was opened and a stream of water was forced down or allowed to run down his throat; his throat was held so he could not prevent swallowing the water, so that he had to allow the water to run into his stomach.... When he was filled with water it was forced out of him by pressing a foot on his stomach or else with their hands....

---

tary of State John Hay issued a communication called the Open Door note in the summer of 1899; in it, he urged the imperial powers to respect the trading interests of all nations. In 1900 the Boxer Uprising in China prompted cooperation among the western powers. The Boxers, radical Chinese nationalists, killed 200 foreign missionaries and other whites in an effort to purge China of outsiders. Together, the Germans, Japanese, British, French, and Americans sent 18,000 troops to quell the revolt. The United States and European nations continued to compete for the China market well into the twentieth century.

Critics of Imperialism

Theodore Roosevelt seemed to personify the late-nineteenth-century idea of American manifest destiny: the notion that the core of the nation's history was a militant mission to expand its territorial reach. However, not all Americans agreed with Roosevelt. New York financier Mark Hanna called him a "madman" and "that damned cowboy." Writer Mark Twain believed him "clearly insane" and "insanest upon war and its supreme glories." Twain and other prominent people founded the Anti-Imperialist League in 1898 in an attempt to stem the rising tide of militarism.

It is difficult to generalize about the politics of anti-imperialists during this period. Some critics of imperialism advocated a hands-off policy toward other nations in the belief that all peo-

This photograph of a United States soldier during the War of 1898 is titled *The Church Saint sat on by a Washington "Johnnie" [soldier]*. During the war, photographers produced vivid images that conveyed the dramatic effects of the U.S. invasion on the society and culture of the Philippines. Led by Emilio Aguinaldo, insurrectionists fought for Philippine independence, beginning in January 1899. Two years later, American forces captured Aguinaldo and established a colonial government in the country.

Q: What had been his crime?
A: Information had been obtained from a native source as to his being an insurgent officer. After the treatment he admitted that he held the rank of captain in the insurgent army—an active captain....

Q: His offense was treachery to the American cause?
A: Yes, sir.

Questions

1. In what ways did the Filipino insurrection challenge the conventions of what congressional committee members called "civilized warfare"?
2. How did General Hughes justify the destruction of whole villages as part of the U.S. effort to suppress the insurrectionists?
3. What are the arguments for and against the practice of torture as a means of extracting information from enemy combatants? ■

Source: Proceedings of the Congressional Committee on the Philippines, in Harvey Graff, ed., *American Imperialism and the Philippine Insurrection* (Boston, 1969), pp. 64–79.

---

ples were entitled to self-determination. In contrast, other anti-imperialists such as Social Darwinists used arguments about racial hierarchies to justify their opposition to expansion.

In the summer of 1900, the Democrats and Republicans prepared for the upcoming presidential election. Receiving the Democratic nomination once again, William Jennings Bryan was eager to press the outdated cause of free silver. He also condemned the American presence in the Philippines, although this issue, too, was rapidly losing the attention of the electorate. At the Republican convention, Roosevelt's supporters managed to win for him the slot as McKinley's running mate. That fall, the former Rough Rider waged an exuberant campaign. Accompanied by a retinue of gun-toting cowboys, he wrapped the Republicans in the American flag. When McKinley swept to reelection in the fall, few Americans could have anticipated how central Roosevelt's vision would become to the country over the next two decades.

Conclusion

As Americans greeted the twentieth century, they might have marveled at the dramatic changes that had occurred in their country over the last 100 years. In 1800 the United States was home to 5.3 million people who lived in sixteen states. One hundred years later, the country included forty-five states and boasted a population of 76 million people. Many workplaces, fields as well as factories, were dominated by machines and the people who tended them. The economy was shifting toward the mass production of consumer goods.

In 1900 the United States exerted control over the land and peoples of Alaska, the Hawaiian and Samoan Islands, the Philippines, Guam, Puerto Rico, and (through the Platt Amendment) Cuba as well. These holdings, notable for their strategic significance, illustrated the growing willingness of the United States to extend its influence and economic reach—by armed force if necessary—to the far corners of the earth. The new drive for worldwide economic and political power was fast eclipsing America's revolutionary heritage, with its values of democracy and self-determination.

Sites to Visit

Spanish-American War
www.loc.gov/rr/hispanic/1898

This site provides resources and documents about the Spanish-American War, the period before the war, and the people who participated in the fighting or commented on it.

The Age of Imperialism
www.smplanet.com/imperialism/toc.html

Focusing on the late nineteenth and early twentieth centuries, this site includes much information about American imperialism.

Hispanic Voices/Voces Hispanas
bancroft.berkeley.edu/collections/latinamericana.html

This interactive site on Latinos in California is maintained by the Bancroft Library in Berkeley. The autobiographical narratives include late-nineteenth-century oral histories with Latinos.

Late Nineteenth-Century Authors
xroads.virginia.edu/~hyper/hypertex.html

This University of Virginia site includes material on prominent nineteenth-century writers, including William Dean Howells, Mark Twain, and Joel Chandler Harris.

Mary Baker Eddy
www.tfccs.com/index.jhtml;jsessionid

Sponsored by the Christian Science Church, this site looks at the founding of Christian Science.

National Arts and Crafts Archives
www.arts-crafts.com/index.html

This site serves as a guide to materials related to the Arts and Crafts movement, which lasted from about 1890 to 1929.

Era of William McKinley
http://history.osu.edu/projects/McKinley/default.cfm

This Ohio State University site contains a bibliography and numerous images from various periods of McKinley's career. It also includes an excellent collection of McKinley-era cartoons.

"Votes for Women" Suffrage Pictures
http://lcweb2.loc.gov/ammem/vfwhtml/vfwhome.html

This site, part of the Library of Congress American Memory Series, includes images of parades and picket lines, as well as anti-suffragist activity.

Hawaii's Last Queen
http://www.pbs.org/wgbh/amex/hawaii/index.html

This site complements the PBS program on the overthrow of Hawaii's hereditary monarchy in 1893.

For Further Reading

General

Glenda Elizabeth Gilmore, *Gender and Jim Crow: Women and the Politics of White Supremacy in North Carolina, 1896–1920* (1996).

Matthew Frye Jacobson, *Barbarian Virtues: The United States Encounters Foreign Peoples at Home and Abroad, 1876–1917* (2000).

Emily S. Rosenberg, *Spreading the American Dream: American Economic and Cultural Expansion, 1890–1945* (1982).

Robert W. Rydell, *All the World's a Fair: Visions of Empire at American International Expositions, 1876–1916* (1984).

Frontiers at Home, Lost and Found

David Wallace Adams, *Education for Extinction: American Indians and the Boarding School Experience, 1875–1928* (1995).

Matthew Frye Jacobson, *Whiteness of a Different Color: European Immigrants and the Alchemy of Race* (1998).

Neil R. McMillen, *Dark Journey: Black Mississippians in the Age of Jim Crow* (1989).

Mark David Spence, *Dispossessing the Wilderness: Indian Removal and the Making of the National Parks* (1999).

David B. Tyack, *Managers of Virtue: Public School Leadership in America, 1820–1980* (1982).

Michael J. Pfeifer, *Rough Justice: Lynching and American Society, 1874–1947* (2004).

Jonathan Sarna, *American Judaism: A New History* (2004).

The Search for Alliances

Paul Buhle, *From the Knights of Labor to the New World Order: Essays on Labor and Culture* (1997).

Sarah Deutsch, *Women and the City: Gender, Space, and Power in Boston, 1870–1940* (2000).

Patricia R. Hill, *The World Their Household: The American Woman's Foreign Mission Movement and Cultural Transformation, 1870–1920* (1985).

Seymour Martin Lipset and Gary Marks, *It Didn't Happen Here: Why Socialism Failed in the United States* (2000).

Vicki L. Ruiz and Ellen Carol DuBois, eds., *Unequal Sisters: A Multicultural Reader in U.S. Women's History* (2000).

American Imperialism

Robert L. Beisner, *Twelve Against Empire: The Anti-Imperialists, 1898–1900* (1968).

H. W. Brands, *Bound to Empire: The United States and the Philippines* (1992).

Kenn Harper, *Give Me My Father's Body: The Life of Minik, the New York Eskimo* (2000).

Walter LaFeber, *The American Search for Opportunity, 1865–1913* (1993).

William Appleman Williams, *The Tragedy of American Diplomacy* (1972).

For quizzes and other resources on these topics, go to www.longmanamericanhistory.com.

1901	McKinley is assassinated; Vice President Theodore Roosevelt becomes president
1902	Newlands Act spurs dam building and irrigation in the Southwest
1903	First motorized flight by Orville and Wilbur Wright Henry Ford founds Ford Motor Company
1904	Roosevelt Corollary to Monroe Doctrine
1905	Industrial Workers of the World (IWW) founded Japan defeats Russia
1906	San Francisco earthquake Upton Sinclair, *The Jungle* Pure Food and Drug Act
1907	"Gentlemen's Agreement" with Japan Oklahoma (former Indian Territory) becomes state Indiana becomes first state to pass compulsory sterilization law
1908	*Muller v. Oregon* limits maximum hours for working women
1909	New York City garment workers' "Uprising of the 20,000" Peary-Henson expedition reaches North Pole with four Greenland Inuit

National Association for the Advancement of Colored People (NAACP) founded

1910	Mexican Revolution begins
1911	Triangle Shirtwaist Company fire, New York City Society of American Indians founded
1912	Theodore Roosevelt helps form Progressive party Woodrow Wilson elected president
1913	Federal Reserve Act Sixteenth Amendment (federal personal income tax) ratified
1914	U.S. troops block German arms shipment to Mexico War breaks out in Europe

PART SEVEN

Reform at Home, Revolution Abroad, 1900–1929

MANY AMERICANS GREETED THE FIRST YEARS OF THE TWENTIETH century with optimism. Developments at home and abroad seemed to promise a new era of prosperity and progress. The mass manufacturing of automobiles proved a boon to the economy and transformed patterns of travel, leisure, and consumption. The beginning of commercial air flights heralded a revolution in communication and transportation. Moving pictures and new musical forms such as jazz delighted millions.

Focused on the new challenges of urbanization and industrialization, Progressive reformers sought to use science to solve a wide range of problems related to public health and welfare. Some advocated overhauling the system of public education; others pressed for legislation banning the sale and distribution of alcohol. Some lobbied for worker health and safety legislation, and still others sought to exercise social control through eugenics and state-mandated sterilization.

A variety of groups challenged white men's exclusive claim to civil rights. African Americans took the national stage to argue for equality under the law and for freedom from state-sanctioned violence in the form of lynching and servitude for debt. Beginning with the Great Migration of World War I, southern blacks abandoned the cotton fields to seek jobs in northern cities.

The changing roles of women bolstered the women's suffrage movement. Growing numbers of women were becoming labor organizers, reformers, and college professors. Rising divorce rates and the emergence of birth control as a political as well as a medical issue signaled challenges to the traditional patriarchal family. At the same time, conflicts among reformers emerged. For example, white middle-class suffragists hoped to maintain their "respectability" in an effort to win the support of reluctant male leaders; in the process, these women distanced themselves from members of the working class and even the African American women active in the suffrage movement. Suffragists' efforts paid off in 1920, with the ratification of the Nineteenth Amendment to the Constitution.

With its lively consumer culture and rising standard of living, the United States continued to attract newcomers from abroad. Immigrants from Mexico and eastern Europe sought refuge from poverty, oppression, and civil strife at home. In 1914, 1.2 million immigrants came to America, the largest number in a single year before or since that date. Between 1900 and 1930, more than 1 million Mexicans migrated north, most settling in existing Mexican American communities in the Southwest or creating new communities there or in the Midwest.

World War I shattered the belief among many Progressives that conflicts could be solved in a rational, peaceful way. The end of the war had permanently entangled U.S. interests in European affairs. Moreover, revolutions in Mexico (1910) and Russia (1917) affected the United States directly, the former by spurring immigration across the country's southwest border, the latter by challenging the nation's system of industrial capitalism. Nevertheless, many Americans remained convinced that the country could and should isolate itself from world affairs.

Natural forces also remained beyond the control of reformers and government officials. The San Francisco earthquake of 1906, the great Mississippi flood of 1927, and the Florida hurricane of 1928 exacted devastating tolls in terms of human life and property damage. The local communities that were directly affected struggled for years to recover from these disasters.

But for many Americans, the 1920s were a period of peace and prosperity. New household appliances and conveniences lightened the burdens of housework. Radios and movies proved to be popular forms of entertainment. Traditional social mores gave way to expressions of sexual freedom. Progressive impulses waned as business values rose to take their place.

The decade after the end of World War I revealed both the persistence of old conflicts and the emergence of new conflicts within American society. Conservatives branded labor union organizers and socialists as unpatriotic and subversive. Asian immigrants on the West Coast and blacks in the rural South and urban North faced continued legal discrimination in the workplace and in the courts. Protestant fundamentalists challenged the move toward secularism and rationalism, claiming that religious faith, not science, set the standard for morality in modern life. Responding to those who feared that foreign immigration represented a threat to American society, Congress imposed immigration restrictions in 1924. Put into effect in 1920, the Eighteenth Amendment to the Constitution prohibited the sale and distribution of alcoholic beverages. The three Republican presidents who served during the 1920s—Harding, Coolidge, and Hoover—retreated from the activist stance favored by their predecessors, including Theodore Roosevelt and Woodrow Wilson.

The stock market crash of 1929 revealed fundamental weaknesses in the American economy. A tide of bank failures engulfed individual American families even as it threatened businesses abroad. As the depression deepened, Americans looked to the federal government to address the crisis.

1915	U.S. Marines occupy Haiti Germans sink *Lusitania* Film *Birth of a Nation* released
1916	Jeannette Rankin elected first female member of Congress U.S. Marines occupy Dominican Republic
1917	U.S. enters World War I U.S. Marines occupy Cuba Russian Revolution Residents of Puerto Rico granted U.S. citizenship
1918	Spanish influenza epidemic kills 20 million worldwide Sedition Act Wilson's "Fourteen Points" speech to Congress
1919	Versailles Treaty ends World War I U.S. Senate rejects League of Nations Eighteenth Amendment (prohibition) ratified
1920	Nineteenth Amendment (women's suffrage) ratified
1921	Tulsa whites attack black community Sheppard-Towner Act
1922	Five-Power Naval Treaty
1923	Equal Rights Amendment proposed
1924	Johnson-Reid Act Portable radio introduced
1925	Scopes trial, Dayton, Tennessee F. Scott Fitzgerald, *The Great Gatsby*
1926	Gertrude Ederle is first woman to swim across English Channel
1927	Charles Lindbergh flies nonstop from New York to Paris Al Jolson stars in *The Jazz Singer*, first talking movie Sacco and Vanzetti executed *Buck v. Bell* upholds compulsory sterilization laws
1928	Tamiami Trail across Florida Everglades completed
1929	Stock market crash

CHAPTER 19

The Promise and Perils of Progressive Reform, 1900–1912

CHAPTER OUTLINE

Immigration: The Changing Face of the Nation

Work, Science, and Leisure

Reformers and Radicals

Expanding National Power

Conclusion

Sites to Visit

For Further Reading

"I AM A WORKING GIRL," DECLARED CLARA LEMLICH IN HER NATIVE YIDDISH, "ONE OF THOSE striking against intolerable conditions." Still in her teens, the petite young woman took the podium on the night of November 22, 1909, in front of thousands of striking workers in New York, and roused them with her passionate, direct call for action: "I am tired of listening to speakers who talk in generalities. What we are here for is to decide whether or not to strike. I offer a resolution that a general strike be declared—now." The next morning, 15,000 garment workers went on strike, demanding that the work week be reduced to fifty-two hours, with overtime pay and union recognition. Soon, the strikers swelled in number to more than 20,000. Observers at the time were astonished to see lively, fashionably dressed young women filling the picket lines. Ninety percent of the striking workers were women; they were overwhelmingly young Jewish immigrants, with Italian women constituting about 6 percent.

The strike was a demand for union recognition, reasonable wages and hours, and safe and decent working conditions, including an end to sexual harassment on the job. But at the same time, the strikers insisted that they should be treated as "ladies" and have access to the consumer goods and leisure culture taking shape in American cities. Ultimately, the strike ended with a failed compromise when the striking workers overwhelmingly rejected an offer of better wages and working conditions that did not include recognition of their union. Calling the strikers "socialists," their more moderate allies broke from the union and left the young female workers vulnerable to the power of the company owners. The coalition of support fell apart, and most of the strikers eventually went back to work.

■ Victims of the Triangle Shirtwaist Company fire.

Less than two years later, a fire broke out in the top floors of the Triangle Shirtwaist Company, one of the centers of the 1909 strike. Eight hundred workers, most of them young Jewish and Italian women, were trapped in the inferno because company officials had locked interior doors to prevent the women from taking unauthorized breaks or leaving work early. The flames tore through the building in less than half an hour, leaving 146 young women dead. Those who did not succumb to flames and smoke jumped to their deaths. One reporter wrote, "I looked upon the dead bodies and I remembered these girls were the shirtwaist makers. I remembered their great strike of last year in which the same girls had demanded more sanitary conditions and more safety precautions in the shops. Their dead bodies were the answer." In the investigation that followed, the owner of the factory was never charged with a crime or held responsible for the tragedy. He claimed that his building was in full compliance with safety laws, but compliance with the laws did not ensure safety for the workers. No laws required sprinklers, adequate fire escapes, or fire drills. Just a few months before the fire, the building had been inspected and declared "fireproof."

The "uprising of twenty thousand," as the 1909 strike came to be called, and the tragic factory fire that ignited in its aftermath, are two among many dramatic episodes in the early twentieth century that expose the fractures and tensions within the nation at the time. Immigrants and racial minorities demanded the full promise of American life; workers struggled against the exploitation, poor pay, and dangerous conditions that characterized industrial jobs; young women insisted on respect at work and access to the playful environment of urban fashion and popular culture; female voices called for full citizenship and the vote and claimed their right to be heard by male bosses and union leaders; and activists across the political spectrum tried to control and manage the changes taking place around them in accord with their widely differing values.

■ An earthquake devastated San Francisco on April 18, 1906. Here a Chinese immigrant watches as the city goes up in flames. Chinatown was destroyed, along with much of the downtown.

During the first years of the twentieth century, the nation began to emerge as something profoundly different than it had been in the past. Even the landscape changed as cities continued to grow not only outward but also upward, with the construction of towering skyscrapers, and downward, with the creation of subway systems. But human enterprise continued to be vulnerable to the forces of nature. On April 18, 1906, an earthquake virtually leveled San Francisco. The earthquake symbolized American life at the dawn of the twentieth century, as did one word: upheaval. The dramatic changes taking place in the nation at the dawn of the new century, from industry and technology down to the most intimate levels of life, sparked equally dramatic efforts to control, tame, and regulate them. Because of the flurry of reform activity during this period, historians call it the Progressive Era. Politicians from all parties participated in the wide range of reform efforts known as Progressivism, fueled by a faith in progress and a belief in the possibility for social improvement.

Immigration: The Changing Face of the Nation

Between 1900 and 1910, nearly 9 million immigrants entered the United States, the largest number for any single decade in the nation's history until the 1990s. They came particularly from southern and eastern Europe, as well as Mexico and Asia. The United States was one of several potential destinations for these courageous and hopeful sojourners. It was particularly appealing because of its often exaggerated, but nonetheless

Ellis Island Immigrants, 1903

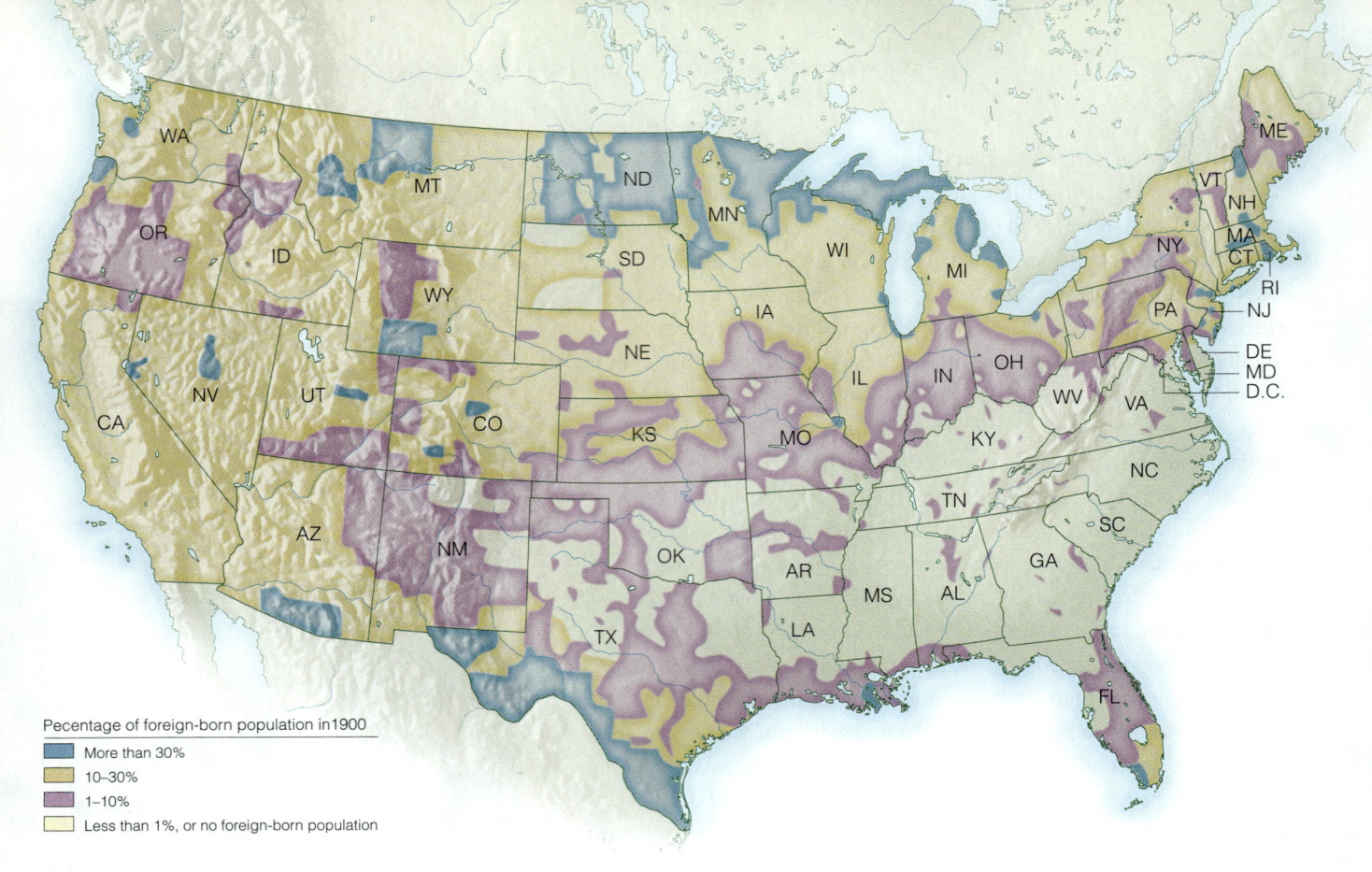

■ **MAP 19.1**

FOREIGN-BORN POPULATION, 1900 Although the most famous points of entry for immigrants during the turn-of-the-century decades were New York's Ellis Island for people from Europe, and Angel Island in San Francisco Bay for people from Asia, most immigrants actually settled in the upper Midwest and the southwestern region bordering Mexico.

real, opportunities for jobs and economic advancement, its official commitment to freedom of religion and political thought, and its reputation as a nation that welcomed newcomers from abroad.

On arrival, many found that the "promised land" was not the paradise they expected. They faced crowded living conditions in urban tenements, jobs in sweatshops and factories with long hours, low wages, and miserable working conditions, and a hostile reception. Many Americans—including some whose own parents or grandparents had come to the United States as immigrants—looked down on the newcomers as "racially inferior" and morally suspect, feared competition for jobs, and worried that the masses of poor foreigners in their midst would become a burden on taxpayers and public institutions. The Statue of Liberty may have held up the torch of welcome, but many citizens, from union halls to legislative chambers, wanted the newcomers to leave.

Many did leave. One-third of immigrants to the United States returned to their home countries. Some came for only a few years and returned to their native lands, including nearly 90 percent of migrants from the Balkans. Other groups, especially those who faced severe hardships in the lands of their birth, were more likely to make the United States their permanent home, settling with their families and building communities. Only 11 percent of the Irish and 5 percent of the Jews returned between 1908 and 1923.

The Heartland: Land of Newcomers

At the dawn of the twentieth century, it was not the coastal cities, with their visible immigrant ghettos, but the settlements in the upper Midwest, along with the lower Southwest, where the greatest concentration of foreign-born residents lived. In the growing towns and cities of the Midwest, newcomers from central Europe and Italy joined the earlier settlers from Germany and Scandinavia to form farming and mining communities on the rich soil and abundant iron deposits of the region.

In the 1890s, the upper Midwest was sparsely settled. As a result of the Dawes Act of 1887, which divided tribal lands into individual parcels, much of the land originally held by Indians had been divided and sold. Most of the Indians who were native to that region were removed to reservations. The iron-rich areas near Lake Superior, previously the hunting, fishing, and gathering areas of the Native Americans, were now inhabited by lumberjacks who cut the forests. Mining companies discovered the iron deposits and began recruiting workers, first from northern Europe and then, after 1900, from southern and eastern Europe. By 1910 the iron range was home to thirty-five European immigrant groups. Gradually, these cohesive working-class communities, like others elsewhere, developed their own brand of ethnic Americanism, complete with elaborate Fourth of July celebrations and other festivities that expressed both their distinctive ethnic identities and their allegiance to their adopted country.

■ An immigrant family manages the daily routines of life in a tenement flat in 1910. Crowded conditions, poor ventilation, and inadequate plumbing made it impossible for impoverished residents such as these to maintain a clean and healthy environment.

The Southwest: Mexican Borderlands

In 1904 a train carrying Irish orphans from a Roman Catholic **foundling home** in New York chugged westward to deliver its small passengers to waiting Catholic families in Clifton and Morenci in the Arizona territory. Church officials at the New York orphanage had screened the families carefully to be certain that the couples hoping to adopt these children were devout churchgoing Catholics, industrious workers, and respectable members of the community. The local parish priest approved these couples, and on the appointed day, they waited eagerly as the orphans, dressed in their best clothes with their pink cheeks scrubbed clean, departed from the train. But when the Anglo-Protestant residents of the town discovered that Mexican Catholic foster parents claimed these fair-skinned children, they were outraged.

That night, the Anglo women gathered to mobilize their husbands into a vigilante posse. In the middle of the night, during a driving rainstorm, the men went to the homes of the Mexican couples and kidnapped the children at gunpoint. The next day, the children were distributed to the vigilantes' wives and other Anglo foster parents. Although the Catholic foundling home that had placed the children with the Mexican couples fought a lengthy legal battle to regain custody of the children, the Anglos managed to keep the orphans. The Arizona Supreme Court validated the kidnapping in the name of the "best interests of the children," and the U.S. Supreme Court let the ruling stand.

The struggle over the orphans reflected tensions and divisions in the region along lines of class as well as race. Longtime residents of this borderland region of Arizona included many

Mexicans, mainly farmers, ranchers, and miners. In the early twentieth century, Mexico's deteriorating economy and prolonged revolution after 1911 prompted large numbers of Mexicans to migrate to California and the Southwest, looking for work. The year before the arrival of the orphans, Mexican mine workers had struck for better wages and working conditions against the Anglo owners of the Arizona Copper Company. The owners put down the strike, and the conflict left bitter feelings on both sides. The vigilante kidnapping of the orphans was, in part, retaliation against the Mexican workers who had organized the strike the previous year.

Asian Immigration and the Impact of Exclusion

Asians continued to face the most severe restrictions on immigration. The Chinese Exclusion Act of 1882, which prohibited most Chinese from immigrating to the United States, was renewed and extended in 1902. As a result, the mostly bachelor Chinese community in the United States declined by nearly half between 1890 and 1920. Many died or returned to China, reducing the numbers from more than 107,000 to about 61,000. The sex ratio remained severely unbalanced, with about fourteen men for every woman.

During the exclusion era, certain categories of Chinese immigrants were allowed entry. Wives of Chinese men already in the United States could enter, as could teachers, students, and merchants. More than 20,000 Chinese arrived during the first decade of the new century. One such emigrant was Sieh King King, an eighteen-year-old student. In 1902, at a meeting of the Protect the Emperor Society, a reform party that advocated restoring the deposed emperor and establishing a constitutional monarchy in China, she addressed a packed hall in San Francisco's Chinatown. The *San Francisco Chronicle* reported that she "boldly condemned the slave girl system, raged at the horrors of foot-binding [a traditional Chinese practice in which girls' feet were tightly bound to keep them small] and, with all the vehemence of aroused youth, declared that men and women were equal and should enjoy the privileges of equals." Like Clara Lemlich, her eastern European Jewish peer in New York, Sieh King King expressed

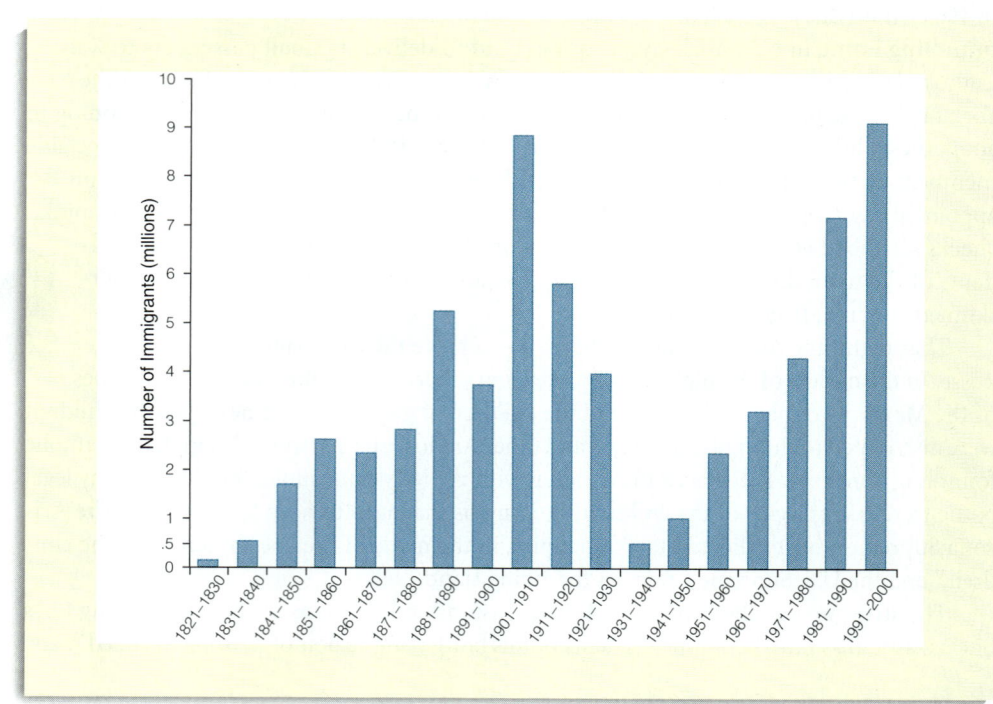

■ **FIGURE 19.1**
NUMBER OF IMMIGRANTS ENTERING THE UNITED STATES, 1821–2000 The number of immigrants entering the United States spiked in the first decade of the twentieth century and then dropped drastically as a result of the immigration restriction laws passed by Congress in the 1920s. Immigration increased again as laws changed after World War II, allowing new immigrant groups to enter.

■ MAP 19.2

AREAS EXCLUDED FROM IMMIGRATION TO THE UNITED STATES, 1882–1952 In 1882 the United States barred Chinese immigrants from entering the country; Japanese and Koreans were barred in 1924. In 1917 the exclusion was extended to people from India, Indonesia, and the Arabian Peninsula. Those laws remained in effect until 1943 and 1952, respectively.

ideas that were emerging among urban radicals in the United States but also reflected political movements in their home countries.

Individual Chinese could also immigrate if they had family members in the United States. As a result, American-born Chinese frequently traveled back and forth, claiming on their return that they left a child in China and requesting permission for their offspring to emigrate. In this way they created spaceholders for imaginary kin, allowing other Chinese to enter the country. The American authorities knew of this system of "paper sons" and "paper fathers" and tried to stop the practice with elaborate and lengthy investigations that could last a year or more while hopeful Chinese immigrants waited as virtual prisoners in wretched conditions on Angel Island, the immigrant gateway in San Francisco Bay.

In the 1880s, there were only about 3,000 Japanese immigrants in mainland United States. Japanese immigrants could still enter the country, and nearly 300,000 did so between 1890 and 1920, when opportunities for higher-paying jobs in Hawaii and California offered an alternative to the economic crisis they faced in Japan. Marriages in Japan generally were arranged by families, and some men returned to Japan to meet and marry their brides. But cost and distance often prevented those meetings. Some women came to the United States as "picture brides" after an exchange of photographs. Although some women were disappointed with their often much older husbands, most accepted their fate as they would have accepted an arranged marriage in Japan. Others were delighted with the opportunity for adventure and life in the new land. As one picture bride explained, many of the people from her village had already gone

■ This young woman was a "picture bride" whose photograph secured her betrothal to her distant future husband. In this way, many men who emigrated from Asia arranged to marry women they had never met. The young fiancée then left her home to join a strange man in a strange land, hoping for the best.

to the United States, and she wanted to go, too: "I didn't care what the man looked like."

Although the Japanese comprised less than 1 percent of California's population, they faced intense nativist hostility. The Japanese in California protested against the discrimination they faced, and in one case they successfully turned a local case of school segregation into an international incident. In response to the segregation of Japanese children in San Francisco, the Japanese government expressed its extreme displeasure. Hoping to avoid a confrontation with Japan—a significant military power that had just won a war with Russia—President Theodore Roosevelt interceded and convinced the San Francisco school board to rescind its segregation order. This incident led to the "Gentlemen's Agreement" of 1907, in which the Japanese government agreed to limit the number of immigrants to the United States. The numbers of immigrants from Japan dwindled, and Japanese immigrants instead began to settle in Brazil.

Newcomers from Southern and Eastern Europe

Eastern European Jews were among the most numerous of the "new" immigrants in the early twentieth century. In 1880 there were about 250,000 Jews in America; by 1920, there were 4 million, the vast majority from eastern Europe. During those forty years, a number of factors motivated Jews to leave their small towns, or *shtetls*. Economic turmoil and restrictions on Jewish land ownership, trade, and business left many Jews impoverished. Antisemitic policies in Russia and eastern Europe confined many Jews to live in restricted areas. Even more devastating was the increase in antisemitic violence in the form of riots, or *pogroms*, in which Jewish towns were attacked and many Jews were beaten and killed. Many young Jewish boys emigrated to avoid being conscripted into the czar's army.

One such immigrant was young Morris Bass. At age twelve, he left his family and ventured alone across the Atlantic. He did not wander long in the crowded Jewish ghetto of New York before a butcher offered him a job and a place to sleep on a straw mat behind the shop. Like many others, Morris prospered modestly. After a few years, he was able to strike out on his own as a pushcart peddler. Eventually, he sent home enough money to bring his parents and siblings to America. Some Jewish immigrants struggled to retain the faith and practices of Jewish orthodoxy that had defined their lives in the *shtetl*. But Morris was among those who wanted to assimilate into American life. He retained Jewish cultural practices but abandoned many religious rituals, such as refraining from work on Saturdays (the Jewish Sabbath) and wearing distinctive clothes.

Foreign-Born Population, 1890

Italian immigration also reached its peak between 1900 and 1914. While 90 percent of the Jews who migrated from Russia came to the United States, Italians ventured to many countries around the world. Turmoil in their home country, resulting from the political and economic consequences of unification of the Italian peninsula, prompted 27 million Italians—a third of Italy's population—to emigrate between 1870 and 1920. The majority of Italians who came to the United States arrived with their families and settled permanently, establishing strong communities and mutual aid societies. Most Italians were committed Roman Catholics, and they preserved their rituals, festivals, and faith in the new country.

■ At Ellis Island this immigrant family received identification tags, indicating that they had been examined and declared healthy. Those who were ill, or youngsters without relatives to meet them, were sent to quarantine houses. Some were refused entry and sent back to their home countries.

Work, Science, and Leisure

As the nineteenth century gave way to the twentieth, working women and men—both immigrants and native-born—could increasingly expect to be employed in industry rather than farms, in large organizations rather than small shops, and in enterprises that relied more on efficiency than craftsmanship. Towering skyscrapers began to dot the urban landscape, symbolic of the triumph of commerce and corporate power. Science and technology reigned, changing the nature of work as well as the fruits of production. Professional organizations of educators, social workers, physicians, and scientists emerged, while experts with academic credentials became leaders of many public institutions. It seemed as though science could solve virtually any problem. Advances in medical science contributed to improved public health. But in some cases, experts relied on scientific principles to address social problems rather than confronting the underlying structural causes, such as widespread poverty.

This more urban society developed new forms of leisure and entertainment. The film industry emerged in Hollywood, a suburb of Los Angeles. Amusement parks and nightclubs provided new venues for greater intimacy between unmarried men and women. And American art and literature began to emphasize the vitality and diversity of life in the nation's cities.

The Uses and Abuses of Science

Breakthroughs in science and medicine led to improvements in public health. Reformers exposed the dangers of potions and remedies sold by street vendors, as standards for medications improved. But crowding and lack of sanitation still fostered the spread of disease, especially among the poor. Lack of access to clean water was one of the major causes of disease, along with crowding, lack of medical care, and other chronic problems of poverty. Improved

INTERPRETING HISTORY

Defining Whiteness

Naturalization laws pertaining to immigrants in the early twentieth century were based on racial categories. Asian immigrants, classified racially as "Mongolians," were not allowed to apply for U.S. citizenship. Naturalization was available only "to aliens being free white persons and to aliens of African nativity and to persons of African descent." Because racial theories were imprecise and fluid, and racial identities were not linked to nationality, immigrants occasionally challenged their racial classification to claim that they were "white." John Svan, who was Finnish, petitioned in federal court to contest the labeling of Finns as Mongolians, claiming that he was white and, therefore, allowed to apply for U.S. citizenship. The petition demonstrates the acceptance of racial definitions based on phenotype—particularly skin color—as well as the imprecise nature of those definitions. In the case of "John Svan vs. the United States Government," the court granted Svan's petition, legally changing his racial identity from Mongolian to white and reclassifying Finns as white people. Here is the court's 1908 memorandum, which allowed Svan to become a citizen:

John Svan was born in Finland and calls himself a Finn. . . . According to ethnologists, the Finns in very remote times were of Mongol origin; but the various groupings of the human race into families is arbitrary and, as respects any particular people, is not permanent but is subject to change and modification through the influences of climate, employment, intermarriage and other causes. There are indications that central and western Europe was at one time overrun by the Finns; some of their stock remained, but their racial characteristics were entirely lost in their remote descendants, who now are in no danger of being classed as Mongols. The Osmanlis, said to be of Mongol extraction, are now among the purest and best types of the Caucasian race. Changes are constantly going on and those occurring in the lapse of a few hundred years with any people may be very great.

The chief physical characteristics of the Mongolians are as follows: They are short of stature, with little hair on their body or face; they have yellow-brown skins, black eyes, black hair, short, flat noses, and oblique eyes. In actual experience we sometimes, though rarely, see natives of Finland whose eyes are slightly oblique. We sometimes see them with sparse beards and sometimes with flat noses; but Finns with a yellow or brown or yellow-brown skin or with black eyes or black hair would be an unusual sight. They are almost universally of light skin, blue or gray eyes, and light hair. No people of foreign births applying

---

public sanitation alleviated the problem considerably in the early years of the twentieth century, reducing the incidence of typhoid fever by 70 percent. Among those who contributed to better conditions were community nurses. In 1900 the New York Charity Organization Society hired Jessie Sleet Scales, the first African American public health nurse, to address problems related to tuberculosis. Scales and other public health professionals implemented sanitation standards and provided care for poor communities, helping to control the spread of disease. Public sanitation remained a problem, however, especially in crowded cities.

Reflecting an impulse to blame social problems on allegedly flawed individuals or groups was the eugenics movement, which advocated scientific breeding to improve the nation's racial stock. Drawing on theories of white racial superiority and unscientific notions of genetic inheritance, eugenicists believed that character traits were inherited, including tendencies toward criminality, sexual immorality, and lack of discipline leading to poverty. Eugenicists claimed that social problems resulted from the high birthrate of immigrants and others they considered to be racially inferior to educated middle-class Anglo-Saxon Americans with their low birthrate.

President Theodore Roosevelt was an outspoken advocate of eugenics reform. One of his major concerns was that Americans were shirking their duty to create a robust citizenry for the future. Alarmed by the dramatic decline in the birthrate of native-born Americans and the tendency of some college-educated women to remain single and childless, he feared that the immigrants, with their much higher birthrate, would overrun the nation. Roosevelt called upon Anglo-Saxon women to prevent what he called **race suicide**, much as male citizens had an obligation to defend the country if called to military duty.

These Finnish men living in Minnesota were among those whose racial classification was changed from "Mongolian" to "White" as the result of one Finnish immigrant's petition. Along with the Jews, Italians, Irish, and other immigrant groups now considered "white," Finns were classified as nonwhite until the laws and customs changed. Racial categories were fluid and imprecise, but whiteness conferred status and privileges.

in this section of the country for the full rights of citizenship are lighter-skinned than those born in Finland. In stature they are quite up to the average. Confessedly, Finland has often been overrun with Teutons and by other branches of the human family, who, with their descendants, have remained within her borders and are now called Finns. They are in the main indistinguishable in their physical characteristics from those of purer Finnish blood. Intermarriages have been frequent over a very long period of time. If the Finns were originally Mongols, modifying influences have continued until they are now among the whitest people in Europe. It would, therefore, require a most exhaustive tracing of family history to determine whether any particular individual born in Finland had or had not a remote Mongol ancestry. This, of course, cannot be done and was not intended. The question is not whether a person had or had not such ancestry, but whether he is now a "white person" within the meaning of that term as usually understood. This is the practical construction which has uniformly been placed upon the law. . . . Under such law Finns have always been admitted to citizenship, and there is no occasion now to change the construction.

The applicant is without doubt a white person within the true intent and meaning of such law.

The objections, therefore, in my opinion should be overruled and it will be so ordered.

Questions

1. According to the court, what might cause changes in the "groupings of the human race into families" over time? How does the court's opinion reflect prevailing attitudes toward race during the Progressive Era?
2. How did the court explain the transformation of Finns from the classification as "Mongols" to becoming "among the whitest people in Europe"?

Some eugenics crusaders proposed compulsory sterilization of those they deemed unfit for parenthood. Indiana enacted a eugenic sterilization law in 1907, and other states soon followed. These laws gave legal sanction to the surgical sterilization of thousands of men and even greater numbers of women whom government and medical officials deemed "feebleminded." The criteria for determining "feeblemindedness" were vague at best; often sexual impropriety or out-of-wedlock pregnancy landed young women—generally poor and often foreign-born—in institutions for the feebleminded, where the operations took place. The Supreme Court upheld compulsory sterilization laws in the 1920s. Increasingly, women of color were targeted, and the practice continued well into the 1980s.

Scientific Management and Mass Production

In 1911 Frederick Winslow Taylor wrote *The Principles of Scientific Management*, a guide to increased efficiency in the nation's industries. Taylor began his career as a laborer in the Midvale Steel Works near Philadelphia in 1878 and rose through the ranks to become the plant's chief engineer. There he developed a system to improve mass production in factories in order to make more goods more quickly. Taylor's principles included analysis of each job to determine the precise motions and tools needed to maximize each worker's productivity, detailed instructions for workers and guidelines for their supervisors, and wage scales with incentives to motivate workers to achieve high production goals. Over the next decades, industrial managers all over the country drew on Taylor's studies. Business leaders rushed to embrace Taylor's principles, and Taylor himself became a pioneering management consultant.

Taylor, Scientific Management

Henry Ford was among the most successful industrialists to employ Taylor's techniques. Born in 1863 on a farm near Dearborn, Michigan, the mechanically inclined Ford became an apprentice in a Detroit machine shop in 1879. Although he did not invent the automobile—the first motor cars were manufactured in Germany—he developed design and production methods that brought the cost of an automobile within the reach of the average worker. Experimenting with the new internal combustion engine in the 1890s, he built his first automobile in 1896. In 1903 Ford established the Ford Motor Company and began a profitable business. He introduced the popular and relatively inexpensive, mass-produced Model T automobile in 1908, which sold for $850. In 1913 Ford introduced the **assembly line**, a production system in which each worker performed one task repeatedly as each automobile in the process of construction moved along a conveyor. The assembly-line manufacturing increased production while cutting costs. In 1914 Ford increased his workers' wages to $5 per day at a time when industrial laborers averaged only $11 per week. By 1916 the price of the Model T dropped to $360. In this sense Ford was a pioneer not only in production but also in consumption.

New Amusements

As Americans increasingly moved from rural to urban areas, and from farms to factories, new institutions of leisure emerged in the growing cities. Consumer culture was the flip side of business culture in the early twentieth century. One of the great ironies of American history in the twentieth century is that its popular culture—which more than anything else identifies the United States to the rest of the world—was largely a creation of immigrants and people of color. During the very years when these groups faced intense discrimination, they developed the cultural products that came to define America itself.

The motion picture industry is a case in point. In 1888 Thomas Edison invented the kinetoscope, the early motion picture camera. The pragmatic Edison thought that his new device might be used in education and industry. But he did not see much commercial potential for the gadget. Not until the early twentieth century did the moving picture begin to reach a wide audience. Moviemakers left the East Coast and moved to the West, taking advantage of the even climate, cheap land, and nonunion labor. Within a few years, the moviemakers, mostly Jewish immigrants from Europe, established the film industry. Hollywood emerged as a major center of American popular culture, sending its products across the nation and abroad.

The first audiences for the motion pictures were in the working-class neighborhoods of the growing cities. In New York alone, by 1910, there were 1,000 small storefront theaters and fun houses known as penny arcades where there had been none twenty years earlier. The number of saloons also increased from 7,000 to 9,000, while the Coney Island amusement park drew thousands to its shimmering lights and thrilling rides. During these same years, the sounds of African American music began to attract audiences among immigrants as well as native-born whites, as youths from all ethnic groups flocked to dance halls. Glamorous nightclubs, known as cabarets, also began to appear, offering dining, dancing, music, and entertainment to the wealthy.

Coney Island, 1904

"Sex O'Clock in America"

The sexual mores and behavior of Americans seemed to be changing so dramatically that one observer announced that "sex o'clock" had struck. Indeed, the codes of the past were challenged at every turn. Among the middle class, unchaperoned dating began to replace the previous system of a man "coming to call" at the home of a woman he hoped to court.

Immigrants often brought traditional courtship patterns to the new world and extended them into the next generation. One Italian man described his thwarted efforts to woo his fiancée in private. When he visited her home, "She sat on one side of the table, and I at the other.

They afraid I touch." Finally, less than a month before their wedding, he got permission to take her to the theater. But the family was unwilling to let them go alone. "We came to the aisles of the theater. My mother-in-law go first, my fiancée next, my little sister, my father in law. I was the last one. I had two in between. . . . I was next to the old man." He tried to steal a kiss a few days before the wedding, but his fiancée rebuffed him: "No, not yet."

In spite of efforts by their elders, native-born as well as immigrant youth challenged the sexual codes of the past. Increasing sexual intimacy between unmarried men and women reflected heightened expectations for sexual satisfaction—for women as well as men. These years also witnessed a rise in the proportion of brides who were pregnant at marriage, from a low of 10 percent in the mid-nineteenth century to 23 percent by 1910.

Marriage increasingly held the promise not only of love, intimacy, and mutual obligation, as it had in the nineteenth century, but of sexual fulfillment and shared leisure pursuits. However, some women did not marry but instead formed lifelong attachments to other women. Rarely identified as lesbian but often described as **Boston marriages**, these unions signified long-term emotional bonds between women who lived together. The widely admired reformer Jane Addams shared her life with Mary Rozet Smith for more than thirty years. Meanwhile, lesbians, as well as gay men, gained greater visibility in the cities. They frequented bars and clubs in such places as Greenwich Village and Harlem, hoping to avoid the attention of police, who were likely to arrest them for indecent conduct.

> *Marriage increasingly held the promise not only of love, intimacy, and mutual obligation, but of sexual fulfillment and shared leisure pursuits.*

Artists Respond to the New Era

Artists of all kinds contributed to enriching, expressing, interpreting, and transforming the urban industrial landscape. Among the most controversial was a group of painters who focused their attention on portrayals of life in the cities—including urban amusements and diverse

■ *The Café Francis*, by George Luks, c. 1909. Luks was one of the "Ashcan School" artists who celebrated urban street life and popular culture. Their raw and sensual depictions of city entertainments stirred controversy among art critics at the time.

working-class subjects. This art exuded the vitality of urban life and conveyed a gritty reality without moral condemnation. Contemptuous critics referred to them as the "Ashcan School," a label they embraced.

Theodore Dreiser's 1900 novel *Sister Carrie* narrates the story of an independent young woman who comes to Chicago and uses her sexuality to advance her ambition. Contrary to the morality tales popular at the time, Carrie does not suffer for her sins. Rather, she prospers, while her male lovers are destroyed by their infatuation with her. Because of the novel's scandalous content, Dreiser's publisher did not promote the book, although it was revived and republished in later years.

Photography also began to exhibit a new realism. Documentary photographer Lewis Hine photographed immigrants, industrial work, and urban street life. Avant-garde artists Alfred Stieglitz and Edward Steichen drew inspiration from artistic innovations in Europe, such as Cubism. Popular music flourished in the first decade of the century, especially jazz. From its roots in African musical traditions, slave songs, spirituals, and ragtime, jazz brought together the various strains of African American music and developed new forms, centered in New Orleans.

Reformers and Radicals

The broad movement for social reform known as **Progressivism** included two distinct impulses. On the one hand, many Anglo-Saxon Protestants tried to impose order on a rapidly changing nation. They hoped to stem the tide of immigration, bolster rapidly eroding sexual codes, and quell the movements for social change. On the other hand, women's rights activists, workers, and African Americans struggled to achieve the rights and privileges available to white men of property and standing. The tensions between these two very different approaches to reform shaped the politics of the era.

Muckraking, Moral Reform, and Vice Crusades

In the early twentieth century, a group of investigative journalists, the **muckrakers**, began to expose the ills of industrial life. Their best-known works illuminated corruption in business and politics. Ida Tarbell wrote a powerful exposé of the ruthless business practices of John D. Rockefeller, who transformed the Standard Oil Company into a monopoly. Lincoln Steffens unearthed scandals in city and state politics. Upton Sinclair's novel *The Jungle*, published in 1906, tells the story of Jurgis Rudkus, a Lithuanian immigrant, and his family and friends and provides a grim exposé of the squalid working conditions in the meatpacking plant where Rudkus worked. It led to the passage of the Pure Food and Drug Act (1906) and a Meat Inspection Act, which prohibited adulterated or fraudulently labeled food and drugs from interstate commerce.

Steffens, from *The Shame of the Cities*

Child labor was another concern of reformers. Children worked in fields and factories across the country, picking cotton in Texas, mining coal in West Virginia, working in the textile mills of North Carolina, and sewing buttons in urban sweatshops. Children of immigrants and rural migrants often assisted parents on farms or in shops, their labor an accepted part of the household economy. But the sorts of jobs available to children in the urban industrial world often were dangerous and unhealthy, characterized by long hours, low pay, and miserable working conditions. Reformers attempted to improve the conditions under which children worked and to establish age limits so that children could attend school and spend time in healthful recreation rather than in grim sweatshops and factories. Ultimately, child labor activists succeeded in passing legislation at the state level that restricted child labor, although these efforts were more successful in northern states than in the South.

Mother Jones, "The March of the Mill Children"

Protective legislation for women was also controversial. Reformers campaigned for laws that would establish minimum wages, maximum hours, regulations against night work, and restrictions on heavy lifting. When they were unable to secure such safety measures for all workers, they argued that women needed special protections because of their physical frailty and their role as future mothers. Women's rights activists disagreed over these measures. Some argued that they were necessary to protect women from exploitation and dangerous working conditions. Others claimed that women should be treated the same as men, arguing that protective legislation implied that women needed special care and were not suited for particular kinds of work. The Supreme Court affirmed the ten-hour working day for women—and the principle of protective legislation—in its landmark 1908 decision *Muller v. Oregon*.

One noted reformer was Helen Keller, whose work on behalf of the blind called attention to the needs of the disabled. Keller lost her sight and hearing from an illness at the age of nineteen months and learned to communicate through Braille and sign language, which she mastered through touch, with the help of her extraordinary teacher, Anne Sullivan. Keller went on to study at schools for the deaf and graduated with honors from Radcliffe College in 1904. A passionate socialist and advocate of women's rights along with other radical causes, Keller wrote several books and lectured widely all over the world, with the assistance of interpreters.

Most Progressive reformers were prosperous American-born Anglo-Saxon Protestants. Along with their efforts to improve living and working conditions and alleviate the suffering of the poor, they also hoped to eradicate vice from their society. Vice crusaders in most of the nation's large cities tried to eliminate prostitution and to patrol dance halls, movie theaters, and saloons. Vice crusading culminated in the passage of the Mann Act in 1910, which made it illegal to transport women across state lines for "immoral purposes."

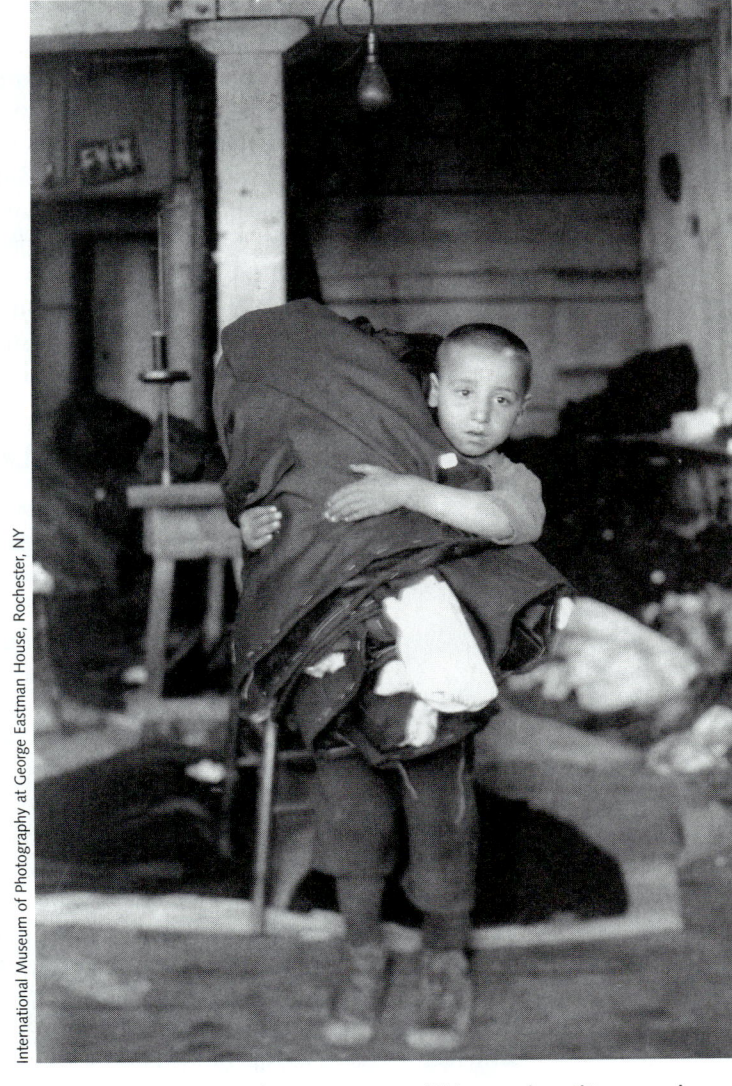

■ In the early twentieth century, many children such as this young boy worked long hours doing hard labor. Photographer Lewis Hine, who took this picture, worked for the National Child Labor Committee. His photographs documented the exploitation of child workers and helped to generate support for child labor laws.

Women's Suffrage

The movement for women's rights, including the effort to gain the vote, was already more than half a century old by 1900. But the movement gained momentum at the dawn of the twentieth century. A new generation of women's rights leaders came together in the suffrage movement. The militancy of the suffrage movement in England inspired American activists to develop new tactics and international alliances. These activists achieved legislative success when several western states granted women the right to vote: Washington in 1910, California in 1911, and three more states in 1912. Eventually the movement united around the goal of enacting a federal amendment.

The suffrage movement, for all its radicalism, was largely a movement of white middle-class women. White suffrage leaders feared that any alliance with women of color would alienate Southern voters whom they needed for ratification of the Nineteenth Amendment. They also hoped to win over to their cause racist and nativist critics in the North who feared that granting the vote to women would enfranchise "undesirable" voters, specifically immigrant and minority women. The suffrage movement also gained the support of conservatives who believed that women would vote for conservative causes such as prohibition and immigration restriction.

Many minority women, such as Hispana activist Adelina Otero Warren, supported the suffrage movement even though white leaders kept their distance and refused to embrace the antiracist campaigns of their nonwhite sisters. The African American antilynching activist Ida B. Wells (also known by her married name as Ida B. Wells-Barnett) supported women's suffrage but was unable to convince the white women's rights leaders to denounce lynching. Ultimately, the passage of the Nineteenth Amendment resulted from a combination of factors, including radical activism, strong support of a wide range of reformers, and an alliance with conservative, racist, and anti-immigrant forces.

Radical Politics and the Labor Movement

Progressive reformers believed that American capitalist democracy was a fundamentally sound system that simply needed to be fixed to achieve its full promise. Radicals of the era, by contrast, believed that the system itself was flawed and needed to be fundamentally transformed. Emma Goldman, a Russian Jewish immigrant, was one of many radical activists who gained both fame and notoriety for her outspoken support of radical causes. Like Sieh King King and Clara Lemlich, Goldman was among the growing numbers of women who were leaders in the labor struggles of the day, although women were excluded from most unions.

Socialism was never as strong in the United States as it was in Europe, but it did gain strength at the turn of the century. Socialists promoted labor unions and the rights of women and formed their own political party. Socialist leader Eugene V. Debs, who had gained national fame for his role in the 1894 railroad strike, became the spokesperson and leader of the Socialist party. Between 1900 and 1920, he was the party's candidate for president, gaining nearly a million votes, or 6 percent of the electorate, in the 1912 election. Although the socialists never gathered a large enough following to win national elections, they elected hundreds of candidates to local office.

Logo for the Industrial Workers of the World

The Industrial Workers of the World (IWW), also known as the **Wobblies**, offered another possibility for labor radicalism. It was organized in 1905 by socialists and labor militants. The IWW included women, blacks, immigrants, and unskilled and migratory laborers, workers generally shunned by the American Federation of Labor (AFL). The Wobblies organized workers in the mines of the Rocky Mountain states, in the lumber camps of the Pacific Northwest and the South, and in the eastern textile and steel mills. IWW membership reached about 3 million people, although no more than 150,000 were members at any one time.

Resistance to Racism

The Progressive Era was anything but progressive for nonwhite Americans. Although there were notable exceptions, such as Jane Addams, many white Protestant reformers were either indifferent to racial minorities or actively hostile to them. Moreover, most blacks lived in the rural South, not in northern cities where Progressives were most active. Lynching continued into the twentieth century, with nearly 100 lynchings per year between 1900 and 1910. African Americans were the primary targets of lynch mobs, although other minorities were also vulnerable. Between 1850 and 1930, 597 Mexicans died at the hands of vigilante mobs, half of them in Texas. Black leaders spoke out against lynching and other forms of racial injustice. Ida B. Wells-Barnett, who had launched an international crusade against lynching in the 1890s, worked to establish local and national networks of black women's clubs. Although she was unable to persuade white suffrage leaders to support the cause of racial justice, she worked closely with Jane Addams to prevent the establishment of segregated schools in Chicago.

A number of other black leaders came to prominence in the first decade of the twentieth century. In 1905 scholar and civil rights leader W. E. B. Du Bois joined with other black leaders to form the Niagara Movement, which called for an end to segregation and discrimination in unions, the courts, and public accommodations, as well as for equal economic and educational opportunity. In 1909 prominent African Americans joined with white progressive allies to establish the National Association for the Advancement of Colored People (NAACP). The new organization adopted the platform of the Niagara Movement, and Du Bois became the editor of its journal, *The Crisis*.

Expanding National Power

Along with flourishing radical and reform movements at the grassroots, the Progressive Era gave rise to a reformist impulse at the national level. The person who most fully embodied the national Progressive movement was Theodore Roosevelt, president from 1901 to 1908. Roosevelt used his power to regulate big business, intervene in labor disputes, control the uses of the natural environment, and extend the reach of the nation across the world. His hand-picked successor in the White House, William Howard Taft, followed mostly similar policies.

Theodore Roosevelt: The "Rough Rider" as President

Roosevelt rose to prominence in the Republican party in the 1880s and held a number of important political posts, including assistant secretary of the U.S. Navy (1897–1898) and governor of New York (1899–1900). In 1900 Roosevelt became vice president. But in September 1901, President McKinley was assassinated, and at age forty-two, Roosevelt became the youngest person ever to occupy the Oval Office. Roosevelt was a strong proponent of American military and commercial presence in the world. He expanded the power of the federal government both at home and abroad and used the "bully pulpit" of the presidency to exert moral leadership.

Using the Sherman Anti-Trust Act of 1890, which gave the federal government the power to break up monopolies, Roosevelt in 1902 ordered the Justice Department to prosecute the Northern Securities Company, a $400-million monopoly that controlled all railroad lines and traffic in the Northwest. Within a year, the company was dissolved. Although this bold act earned Roosevelt the title of "trust-buster," it was not his intention to weaken big business. In fact, he believed that a strong country needed large, powerful industries, and he hoped to regulate them to keep big business strong.

TABLE 19-1

The Election of 1900

Candidate	Political Party	Popular Vote (%)	Electoral Vote
William McKinley	Republican	51.7	292
William Jennings Bryan	Democratic-Populist	45.5	155

The same year that Roosevelt took on the Northern Securities Company, he also used the powers of the federal government to intervene in a labor dispute. Striking coal miners in eastern Pennsylvania wanted recognition of their union, a 10 to 20 percent increase in wages, and an eight-hour day. But the mine owners refused to negotiate. Roosevelt summoned the mine owners and John Mitchell, president of the United Mine Workers union, to the White House for a meeting. He threatened to send in troops if the mine owners did not agree to the union's request for arbitration. The mine owners backed down, and the arbitrators negotiated a compromise that awarded the miners a 10 percent wage increase and a nine-hour day.

Roosevelt's efforts to strengthen the state and foster American nationalism extended to his attitudes toward immigrants. He believed that discrimination against loyal newcomers harmed democracy: "It is a base outrage to oppose a man because of his religion or birthplace." He was proud of appointing a cabinet in which "Catholic and Protestant and Jew sat side by side." But

Lumberjacks topple a giant spruce tree in a forest in Washington state around 1900. President Theodore Roosevelt believed that the federal government should manage timberlands and other natural resources to prevent depletion while allowing their use. Roosevelt preserved some Pacific Northwest forests in national parks and refuges but allowed others to be cultivated for timber.

to Roosevelt, becoming an American meant renouncing any loyalties to one's original homeland or culture. He did not believe in cultural pluralism, the idea that the United States could include citizens who retained their ethnic heritage. Rather, Roosevelt promoted the idea of a melting pot that would blend all diverse cultures into a unique American "race." Although Roosevelt was a firm believer in Anglo-Saxon superiority, he was also the first president to invite an African American leader, Booker T. Washington, to the White House.

Protecting and Preserving the Natural World

Industrial smoke had long been a problem in both European and American cities, and Progressive Era reformers established organizations in major cities to fight air pollution. At the same time, mining and other industries were depleting natural resources while destroying the natural beauty of the land. More than any previous president, Roosevelt used the federal government to manage the natural world. Although his actions did not please everyone on all sides of the debate, Roosevelt's environmental efforts were among his most enduring legacies.

Roosevelt advocated both preservation and conservation. His preservation policies doubled the number of national parks, created sixteen national monuments, and established fifty-one wildlife refuges. At the same time, he shared the view of **conservationists** that timberlands, areas for livestock grazing, water, and minerals needed federal government management. Roosevelt transferred 125 million acres of public land into the forest reserves to prevent the depletion of timber, and he set aside land for dam sites, oil and coal reserves, and grazing. John Muir and the Sierra Club campaigned to protect the beautiful Hetch Hetchy Valley in Yosemite National Park, but Congress passed the Raker Act in 1913, allowing the city of San Francisco to build a dam and a reservoir, flooding the valley. Residents of the Owens Valley in eastern California also protested the building of an aqueduct to divert water to the Los Angeles area. Dams, reservoirs, and aqueducts brought water and electricity to arid regions, allowing such cities as Las Vegas and Los Angeles to flourish in environments that would otherwise be unable to support large populations.

Expanding National Power Abroad

The decades surrounding the turn of the twentieth century marked the high point of European and American imperial expansion, bringing 75 percent of the world's land under the control of Europeans or their descendants. Roosevelt hoped to stengthen the federal government at home, develop the nation's military and commercial might, and extend American power abroad. To further these ends, he sent troops to China as part of the international expedition to crush the nationalist Boxer Uprising in 1900. He also proposed the construction of a canal across the Isthmus of Panama, which Congress approved in 1902. But Panama was still a province of Colombia, and Roosevelt was unhappy with the Colombia government's negotiating position regard-

TABLE 19-2
The Election of 1904

Candidate	Political Party	Popular Vote (%)	Electoral Vote
Theodore Roosevelt	Republican	57.9	336
Alton B. Parker	Democratic	37.6	155
Eugene V. Debs	Socialist	3.0	—

ing an American canal project. So he encouraged and aided Panamanian nationalists who seceded from Colombia in 1903. In return, the U.S. president got his canal deal with a newly independent Panama.

In 1904 Roosevelt further increased the authority of the United States to intervene in the affairs of nations in the Western Hemisphere through what came to be known as the Roosevelt Corollary to the Monroe Doctrine of 1823. Fearing political uprisings that might threaten American commercial interests, Roosevelt asserted that "chronic wrongdoing" might require the intervention by "some civilized nation" in the affairs of another. "In the Western Hemisphere," he concluded, this "may force the United States . . . to the exercise of an international police power." The Roosevelt Corollary justified later interventions in the Dominican Republic, Cuba, Nicaragua, Mexico, and Haiti. While the Monroe Doctrine had told Europeans to stay out of the hemisphere, the Roosevelt Corollary declared that the United States would intervene where it wanted to.

The bloody U.S. war against Filipino nationalists that began in 1899 lasted four years before the Americans crushed the revolt and established firm colonial rule in the Philippines. William Howard Taft became the colony's first governor-general in 1901. Taft developed a program of public works that included an infrastructure of roads, bridges, and schools. He also transferred government functions to those Filipinos who cooperated with American colonial powers. Although the United States promised to grant Philippine independence, that promise was deferred until 1946.

William Howard Taft: The One-Term Progressive

Roosevelt declined to run for reelection in 1908. The Republicans selected Roosevelt's hand-picked successor, William Howard Taft. Prior to his service in the Philippines, Taft had been a federal circuit judge. In 1904 Roosevelt appointed him secretary of war. Taft was a loyal ally who worked closely with Roosevelt on foreign and domestic policies. Roosevelt assumed that Taft, after his victory in the general election, would fulfill Roosevelt's reform agenda.

Taft's respect for the separation of powers spelled out in the U.S. Constitution made him dubious about some of Roosevelt's extensions of the powers of the presidency. Nevertheless, Taft initiated far more antitrust suits than Roosevelt had during his presidency. Despite similar political inclinations, Roosevelt's support for his protégé cooled. Although Roosevelt counted major business leaders among his own advisors, he was displeased when Taft appointed corporate lawyers rather than activist reformers to his cabinet. Taft departed from Roosevelt's foreign policy as well. In contrast to Roosevelt, who emphasized military might, Taft claimed that "Dollar Diplomacy"—"substituting ballots for bullets"—was the best way for the United States to exert influence in the world. Taft took Roosevelt's military rule of the Philippines a step further by establishing U.S. business interests there.

TABLE 19-3
The Election of 1908

Candidate	Political Party	Popular Vote (%)	Electoral Vote
William H. Taft	Republican	51.6	321
William Jennings Bryan	Democrat-Populist	43.1	162
Eugene V. Debs	Socialist	2.8	—

DOCUMENT

Dollar Diplomacy—William Howard Taft (1912)

When Taft signed the higher Payne-Aldrich Tariff in 1909, he disappointed progressive Republicans and aligned himself with the conservative old guard of the party, those who had been most critical of Roosevelt. The breach between Taft and the Progressives widened when Taft's secretary of the interior, Richard A. Ballinger, opened up for commercial development 1 million acres of land that Roosevelt had placed under federal protection. In a further affront to conservationists, Gifford Pinchot, still head of the National Forest Service, discovered that Ballinger had sold Alaskan coal deposits to corporate moguls J. P. Morgan and David Guggenheim. When Taft defended Ballinger, Pinchot leaked the news to the press and called for a congressional investigation. Taft subsequently fired Pinchot, but Roosevelt publicly supported Pinchot and signaled his break from Taft.

Roosevelt returned from big-game hunting in Africa to enter the political spotlight once again. He toured the country in 1910, describing his plan for a "New Nationalism," a far-reaching expansion of the federal government to stabilize the economy and institute social reforms. The election of reformers of both parties to Congress in 1910 encouraged Roosevelt to challenge Taft for leadership of the Republican party. When the old guard managed to renominate Taft at the Republican National Convention, Roosevelt and his supporters withdrew from the Republican party and formed the Progressive party. Roosevelt boasted, "I am as strong as a bull moose," inspiring his followers to call themselves the **Bull Moosers**. Their reformist platform called for extensive controls on corporations, minimum wage laws, child labor laws, a graduated income tax, and women's suffrage.

TABLE 19-4
The Election of 1912

Candidate	Political Party	Popular Vote (%)	Electoral Vote
Woodrow Wilson	Democratic	41.9	435
Theodore Roosevelt	Progressive	27.4	88
William H. Taft	Republican	23.2	8
Eugene V. Debs	Socialist	6.0	—

Roosevelt argued for a "New Nationalism," in which a strong federal government would regulate the trusts and, if necessary, curb their power. Democratic candidate Woodrow Wilson, reluctant to vest so much power in the government, called his own approach the "New Freedom," believing that the government should dismantle the trusts and then revert to limited powers. The Republican vote split between Taft and Roosevelt, and the victory went to Wilson, former president of Princeton University and governor of New Jersey. Wilson took office amid an overwhelming popular mandate for reform.

Conclusion

When Woodrow Wilson entered the White House in 1913, the nation looked and behaved differently than it had at the turn of the century. Millions of immigrants from Europe, Asia, and Mexico had arrived in the United States and settled in towns and cities across the nation. Growing urban areas with new amusements and increasingly diverse populations emerged as centers of a national mass culture. New developments in science and technology brought the automobile and the motion picture to American consumers. At the same time, industrial production contributed to environmental damage, pollution, and dangerous working conditions.

Progressive reformers and labor activists mounted efforts to curb the ill effects of urban industrial society. Faith in science and expertise gave rise to pervasive optimism that social problems could be solved. Muckrakers exposed corruption, women's rights activists pushed for the vote, and African American leaders organized for civil rights and against lynching. In the West and Southwest, Mexicans and Asians challenged discriminatory laws and labor practices. At the same time, moralists and vice crusaders sought to tame what they considered dangerous challenges to the social order.

These years also witnessed a major expansion of national power. Presidents Roosevelt and Taft strengthened the role of the federal government through new efforts to regulate big business and by extending America's military and economic presence abroad. By 1912 most Americans supported a strong reform agenda. But within a few years, the nation became embroiled in a major world war that would challenge the inherent optimism of Progressivism, signaling the end of an era.

Sites to Visit

Touring Turn-of-the-Century America: Photographs from the Detroit Publishing Company, 1880–1920.
memory.loc.gov/ammem/detroit/dethome.html

This Library of Congress site includes thousands of photographs from turn-of-the-century America.

Coal Mining in the Gilded Age and Progressive Era
http://ehistory.osu.edu/osu/mmh/gildedage/default.cfm

This Ohio State University site examines the development of the coal industry, including experiences of miners and sometimes violent labor-management conflict.

W. E. B. Du Bois Resources
http://webdubois.org

Included here are writings by and about the great African American intellectual and civil rights leader W. E. B. Du Bois.

Triangle Shirtwaist Factory Fire, March 25, 1911
www.ilr.cornell.edu/trianglefire/

Oral histories, cartoons, images, and essays about the fire are included here.

Inside an American Factory: Films of the Westinghouse Works, 1904
lcweb2.loc.gov/ammem/papr/west/westhome.html

This site provides a glimpse inside a turn-of-the-twentieth-century factory.

Theodore Roosevelt
www.ipl.org/ref/POTUS/troosevelt.html

This Internet Public Library site contains biographical information about Theodore Roosevelt and his election to the presidency and links to Internet biographies and resources about him.

William Howard Taft
www.ipl.org/ref/POTUS/whtaft.html

This Internet Public Library site contains biographical information about William Howard Taft and his election to the presidency and links to Internet biographies and resources about him.

Emma Goldman Papers
sunsite3.berkeley.edu/Goldman/

This site includes information about the famous immigrant radical and selections of writings by and about her.

For Further Reading

General Works

Gail Bederman, *Manliness and Civilization: A Cultural History of Gender and Race in the United States, 1800–1917* (1995).

Steven J. Diner, *A Very Different Age: Americans of the Progressive Era* (1998).

Sara Evans, *Born for Liberty: A History of Women in America* (1989).

Gary Gerstle, *American Crucible: Race and Nation in the Twentieth Century* (2001).

Immigration: The Changing Face of the Nation

Matthew Frye Jacobson, *Barbarian Virtues: The United States Encounters Foreign Peoples at Home and Abroad* (2000).

Erika Lee, *At America's Gates: Chinese Immigration During the Exclusion Era, 1882–1943* (2003).

Riv-Ellen Prell, *Fighting to Become Americans: Jews, Gender, and the Anxiety of Assimilation* (1999).

Vicki L. Ruiz, *From Out of the Shadows: Mexican Women in Twentieth-Century America* (1998).

Ronald Takaki, *Strangers from a Different Shore: A History of Asian Americans* (1989).

Work, Science, and Leisure

John D'Emilio and Estelle Freedman, *Intimate Matters: A History of Sexuality in America* (1988).

Elaine Tyler May, *Great Expectations: Marriage and Divorce in Post-Victorian America* (1980).

Lary May, *Screening Out the Past: The Birth of Mass Culture and the Motion Picture Industry* (1980).

Stephen Meyer III, *The Five Dollar Day: Labor Management and Social Control in the Ford Motor Company, 1908–1921* (1981).

David Van Drehle, *Triangle: The Fire That Changed America* (2003).

Reformers and Radicals

Jane Addams, *Twenty Years at Hull House* (1910).

W. E. B. Du Bois, *The Souls of Black Folk* (1903).

Nan Enstad, *Ladies of Labor, Girls of Adventure: Working Women, Popular Culture, and Labor Politics at the Turn of the Twentieth Century* (1999).

Dorothy Herrmann, *Helen Keller: A Life* (1999).

Expanding National Power

Kathleen Dalton, *Theodore Roosevelt: A Strenuous Life* (2002).

Richard Drinnon, *Facing West: The Metaphysics of Indian-Hating and Empire-Building* (1980).

Richard Hofstadter, *The Age of Reform* (1960).

Walter LaFeber, *The American Search for Opportunity, 1865–1913* (1993).

Edmund Morris, *Theodore Rex* (2002).

Robert Weibe, *The Search for Order* (1967).

For quizzes and other resources on these topics, go to www.longmanamericanhistory.com.

CHAPTER 20

War and Revolution, 1912–1920

ON THE MORNING OF APRIL 6, 1909, SIX PEOPLE ARRIVED AT THE TOP OF THE WORLD. THEY HAD fulfilled at last the dream of two generations of Arctic explorers to reach the North Pole. Exhausted from a month of walking across the treacherous ice of the Arctic Sea, they rested for thirty hours at their polar camp. Then they turned south—the only direction available—and raced for their lives against the brutal cold that threatened to kill them.

Who were these men? Four were Greenland Inuit ("Eskimo"), for whom the Arctic region was home, even if they rarely ventured out on the frozen sea that covered the last 400 miles to the Pole. Two were American. The leader of the party, Bowdoin College graduate and renowned Arctic adventurer Robert Peary, had already built a reputation as a leading figure in the explorations of the Earth's last remote places. The other American to reach the North Pole that day received no such fame. Yet by the accounts of his fellow travelers, Matthew Henson was the one person Peary said he could not get along without. Henson was also African American.

■ American Robert Peary led the first expedition to reach the North Pole.

Twelve years after Henson and Peary stood together to plant the American flag in the Inuit world of the far North, the relations between white and black Americans appeared in a sharply different light in Oklahoma. The former Indian Territory had become a state in 1907 and had more than 50,000 Cherokee and other Native American residents, more than any other state. The discovery at the turn of the century of vast oil reserves along the Arkansas River made Tulsa a boom town, with all the social tensions that accompany rapid growth. The vibrant African American section of the segregated city along Greenwood Avenue offered a strong example of black economic independence.

That entire community was destroyed on the night of May 31, 1921, in the largest American race riot of the twentieth century. In previous years, similar riots had erupted in St.

■ American Matthew Henson accompanied Peary on the epic 1909 expedition.

CHAPTER OUTLINE

A World in Upheaval

The Great War and American Neutrality

The United States Goes to War

The Struggle to Win the Peace

Conclusion

Sites to Visit

For Further Reading

Louis, Chicago, and elsewhere, when white resentment over black mobility and declining deference exploded around a petty pretext. That night in Tulsa, white terrorists executed as many as 300 African Americans and burned the entire Greenwood district to the ground.

The decade that stretched from the discovery of the North Pole to the Tulsa race riot was marked by unusual turbulence in American life. From 1910 to 1914, optimism about solving the nation's social problems rose as reformers attempted to ameliorate some of the worst aspects of modern industrial life. International developments then turned American attentions abroad. Traumatic social revolutions swept through Mexico, China, and Russia, and the conflagration of the Great War—World War I—consumed all of Europe and eventually drew in the United States. What President Woodrow Wilson called the war "to make the world safe for democracy" encouraged people of color, both in the vast European-ruled colonies of Asia and Africa and in the segregated United States, to claim a place of greater equality. But at home the war also created pressures for conformity and intolerance for dissent. The United States emerged from the war with great prestige and power, although the Versailles Treaty ending World War I failed to create a lasting structure for world peace.

A World in Upheaval

American politics in the 1910s and the U.S. involvement in World War I must be understood within the context of change and uncertainty in the international system. While world affairs were still dominated by the wealthy nations of western Europe and North America, the first wave of the great revolutions of the twentieth century was beginning to wash away much of the old order. Tensions also sharpened within the United States over traditional hierarchies of color, gender, and class. The struggle between reform and reaction pervaded public life in the United States and much of the rest of the world.

The Apex of European Conquest

On the eve of World War I, all but a quarter of the world's population lived under the rule of Europeans or their descendants. Explorations of the most remote parts of the globe filled in the last blank spaces on world maps, including the North (1909) and South (1911) poles. The granting of statehood to Arizona and New Mexico in 1912 filled out the forty-eight mainland states.

Technological innovations in transportation and communication tied the world more closely together. Just as the Suez Canal (1870) and the trans-Siberian railroad (1904) linked Europe more directly to Asia, the Panama Canal (1914) cut in half the travel time by water between the East and West coasts of the United States. Cables laid on the floor of the Atlantic Ocean in 1914 inaugurated telephone service between Europe and the United States.

The competition that arose from the expansion of European power sowed the seeds of World War I. Germany, France, Britain, Italy, and Russia raced each other for new colonies and greater influence across Africa and Asia. The central rivalry emerged between a newly unified Germany (1871) and traditionally dominant Britain. Anticipating trouble, each of the major European powers sought allies to bolster its position. Britain, France, and Russia formed the Triple **Entente** against the Triple Alliance of Germany, Austria-Hungary, and Italy (when war came in 1914 Italy switched sides, and the Ottoman Empire—modern Turkey—joined Germany and Austria-Hungary as the Central Powers).

The United States emerged as a global power in this same period around the turn of the century. Fifteen years after the United States seized an overseas empire in 1898, U.S. economic growth was stunning. U.S. consumption of energy from modern fuels (coal and oil) in 1913 equaled that of Britain, Germany, France, Russia, and Austria-Hungary combined. The United States also brought a different history to the world stage. It had been born in 1776 in the first successful revolution by colonies against a European empire. Americans had long understood themselves as a people who opposed empires and supported self-government. The events of 1898 contradicted this legacy, and Americans remained ambivalent about their country's imperial venture. The U.S. Congress in 1916 promised eventual independence to the Philippines and granted U.S. citizenship to residents of Puerto Rico in 1917.

> *The United States had been born in the first successful revolution by colonies against a European empire.*

Confronting Revolutions Abroad

As nationalist movements in China, Russia, and Mexico overturned weak central governments controlled by foreign investors, American economic and security interests seemed to be at stake on three continents. In Asia, the Chinese deeply resented exclusive foreign enclaves that dominated their nation's coastal region and exempted foreigners from the constraints of Chinese laws. In 1911 nationalist revolutionaries inspired by Sun Yat-sen, a Hawaiian-educated democratic reformer, overthrew the Manchu dynasty that had proven unable to resist western incursions.

The American desire for an open door into China's trade—a door that no other powerful nation could close at will—conflicted with the rising imperial power of the region: Japan. The Tokyo government, which had annexed Korea in 1910, responded to the outbreak of World War I by seizing the valuable German-held Shantung Peninsula in northeastern China. In its Twenty-One Demands to China, issued in January 1915, Japan made clear its plans to dominate the development of the Chinese economy. The American relationship with both China and Japan was undercut at home by continued discrimination and violence against immigrants from Asia.

Revolutionary struggles with implications for America also threatened the monarchs who ruled eastern Europe. For Russians, defeat at the hands of Japan in 1905 helped precipitate a thwarted revolution that year, followed by two years of political turmoil. The **czar** survived to rule another decade, and thousands of political activists—unionists, anarchists, and socialists—joined a growing wave of immigration from Russia to the United States. The wave crested in 1914 at 1.2 million people, most of them from east or south of the Alps. That same year, the assassination of the heir to the Austro-Hungarian throne by a Serbian nationalist in Sarajevo provided the spark that ignited the Great War.

The most important region of the world for the United States before World War I was Latin America, especially Central America and the Caribbean islands. This area guarded the nation's strategic southern flank, and American citizens and corporations invested more money in Latin America than in any other region of the world. American anxieties about stability to the south centered on Mexico. "Land for the landless and Mexico for the Mexicans" became the slogan of revolutionaries there between 1910 and 1920. U.S. stakes in the Mexican revolution were high. American investors owned 43 percent of all Mexico's wealth (other foreigners owned another 25 percent), and more than half of the country's trade flowed north to the United States. Moreover, by 1921 Mexico was the world's second largest exporter of oil. Almost a million Mexicans crossed their northern border during the revolutionary decade, tripling the number of Americans with recent roots south of the Rio Grande.

■ MAP 20.1
U.S. INTERESTS AND INTERVENTIONS IN THE CARIBBEAN REGION, 1898–1939   By its size, wealth, and military power, the United States dominated the Caribbean region to its south. American capitalists invested heavily in Mexico, Central America, and the Caribbean islands, and U.S. troops often intervened to protect those investments. Puerto Rico (by acquisition from Spain) and the Panama Canal Zone (by lease from Panama) became particularly important territories ruled by the United States.

Many came through El Paso, the "Ellis Island" for immigrants from the south. Fleeing poverty and violence, they found both discrimination and employment. Whereas most immigrants sought unskilled positions, members of Mexico's professional classes came north for political asylum as well, including teachers, architects, and lawyers. New arrivals of all classes joined Mexican Americans who had lived in the region since it was part of Mexico. They had not crossed the border; in 1848 the border had crossed them.

Wilson sought unsuccessfully to reestablish in Mexico a political order respectful of the rights of foreign property owners. Wilson twice sent U.S. troops into Mexico, at Veracruz in April 1914 to block a German arms shipment and then in pursuit of Francisco ("Pancho") Villa and his army after their 1916 assault on Columbus, New Mexico. The American forces under General John J. Pershing withdrew in early 1917 as the president

> Mexican Americans had lived in the region since it was part of Mexico. They had not crossed the border; in 1848 the border had crossed them.

prepared to enter the much larger war in Europe. Land redistribution and national control of Mexico's abundant mineral wealth, particularly oil, were written into the new constitution passed a few days later, and the revolutionary upheaval ended by 1920.

Conflicts over Hierarchies at Home

Just as social upheaval threatened monarchies and international investors abroad, less privileged Americans contested traditional lines of hierarchy and control in the United States. The Wilson administration's "New Freedom" slogan did not apply to African Americans, who faced continuing discrimination in employment and housing. The president filled his cabinet with white Southerners who segregated the few federal agencies that had employed blacks. When Wilson took office, African Americans continued to be murdered publicly by vigilante mobs across the South at a rate of more than one person per week. But the president ignored requests from the recently formed NAACP for an antilynching law, and the United States remained one of the few societies in which human beings were burned at the stake.

Women of all colors lived under particular burdens of discrimination. Their uniquely intimate relationships—as daughters, wives, mothers—to those who did not treat them as equals complicated their efforts at reform. So did their dilemma about women's roles in society: some sought full legal equality with men, while others wanted special protections for women on the grounds that they were fundamentally different.

American women's long struggle to vote came to a head in this decade. By 1912 a growing number of European nations and nine American states, all in the West, granted the franchise to citizens of both sexes. The moderate National American Women Suffrage Association under the leadership of Carrie Chapman Catt worked within the political system, building an alliance

■ In February 1917, as the United States broke relations with Germany and began to prepare to enter World War I, supporters of women's suffrage continued to picket on the sidewalk outside the White House. College women joined the effort to ensure that winning liberty at home would go hand in hand with fighting for democracy abroad.

with President Wilson after he endorsed women's suffrage in 1916 and supporting the U.S. entry into World War I the next year. Alice Paul and other militants formed the National Women's party and opposed the war effort as inherently undemocratic because half the adult population could not vote. In 1918 suffragist organizers helped elect a more sympathetic Congress that passed the Nineteenth Amendment, ending sex discrimination in voting two years later.

Most adult Americans—workers—continued to find themselves in frequent conflict with the owners who employed them. Industrial capitalism's efficiency produced great material wealth, but 60 percent of it belonged to 2 percent of the population, whereas two-thirds of Americans owned only 2 percent of the wealth. The anticapitalist aspirations of the Socialist party and the Industrial Workers of the World frightened both industrialists and the more conservative labor leaders of the American Federation of Labor, especially when the western-based IWW led two major strikes in the East, one a success in Lawrence, Massachusetts, in 1912 and the other a failure in Paterson, New Jersey, in 1913. The campaign against a wage cut at the vast Lawrence textile factory was especially impressive in uniting 20,000 workers of forty different national backgrounds.

■ The coal miners' tent colony outside Ludlow stood on the high plains of south-central Colorado, at the base of the mountains of the Front Range. Winter snows and cold temperatures made for a difficult life, as did the grueling and dangerous work of mining coal that was common across the state. Strikers along with their wives and children died in the Ludlow massacre on April 20, 1914.

Some business owners sought to undercut union campaigns by providing better working conditions and even company-run "unions." These carrots of concession were accompanied by the stick of force. Bolstered by sympathetic federal courts and state governors, companies usually refused to negotiate with workers who went on strike. This pattern reached a shocking climax on Easter night in 1914 outside Ludlow, Colorado, in a mining camp owned by John D. Rockefeller Jr.'s Colorado Fuel and Iron Company. State militia and company guards broke a strike there with torches and machine guns, burning the miners' tent colony and killing two women and eleven children.

Such brutality by owners against workers and their families appalled most Americans. The Wilson administration slowly began supporting the right of laborers to organize for collective bargaining with their employers. Wilson's strong backing from Samuel Gompers and the AFL in the 1912 election initiated the modern Democratic-labor alliance.

The Great War and American Neutrality

Most Americans had roots of some kind in Europe and had long defined themselves in relation to life on "the continent." But they also considered themselves part of the New World that was separate from the Old World of kings, castles, and rigid social classes. When Europe stepped off the precipice in August 1914 into a war larger than any previously fought or imagined, few Americans wanted any part of it. Make "no entangling alliances," George Washington had urged his fellow citizens. Europeans must stay out of our hemisphere, the Monroe Doctrine had declared. Americans focused instead on domestic political reforms and on an economy revived by European demands for war-related goods, which created new jobs that lured many black Southerners north. But international ties proved too important to the well-being of Americans for the country to remain indefinitely on the sidelines of World War I.

"The One Great Nation at Peace"

Following traditional U.S. policy, Wilson urged Americans to remain neutral "in fact as well as in name" to promote an eventual "peace without victory." Neutrality was profitable. Wilson stoutly defended the rights of neutrals to trade with belligerents, the same principle that had led the United States into the War of 1812 against England. After the recession of 1913–1914, war-related demands from abroad for American farm and factory products jump-started the economy. In the course of World War I, American bankers extended $10 billion in loans to the Entente (primarily Britain and France), and the United States changed from a debtor nation to the world's largest creditor.

The nature of the fighting in Europe bolstered the American determination to avoid being drawn into the conflict. Industrialized warfare brought fiendish new ways to kill human beings, including machine guns and poison gas. Gone were the days of bold maneuvers and dashing cavalry charges; now was the time of trench warfare, with its unrelenting misery, terror, and helplessness. Eight and a half million young men lost their lives and another 21 million were wounded, devastating an entire generation of European society. Eight million civilians also died as a result of the fighting, and an international outbreak of influenza in 1918 killed another 20 million around the world.

In the United States, neutrality also made political sense. Immigrants from every part of Europe lived and voted in the United States, so Americans had blood ties to all the belligerents. Commercial and political elites tended to identify with Britain and France, as did many other Americans. But among two of the largest groups of Americans, those with roots in Germany and Ireland, many took a different view. Few Irish Americans equated England with the cause of democracy after centuries of British rule in Ireland. Native-born white Americans were already concerned with preserving unity in their increasingly varied and urban society. Allowing in the hatreds from Europe's battlefields would only exacerbate the ethnic and class tensions that worried social reformers and many politicians, including President Wilson.

Reform Priorities at Home

Americans traditionally considered powerful government a primary threat to individual liberty, but the rise of mammoth corporations at the start of the twentieth century altered that calculation. Competition was disappearing, particularly in critical sectors of the economy such as oil production and railroads. Laissez-faire policies, by which federal agencies encouraged economic expansion, were no longer adequate; only government could balance the new might of the largest companies. This meant modest regulation of some aspects of the marketplace. Wilson's first term also encouraged such democratic reforms as the ratification of the Seventeenth Amendment for the direct popular election of U.S. senators (1913), previously chosen by state legislatures.

Three areas topped the Wilson administration's reform agenda: taxes, the money system, and monopolies. The Underwood-Simmons Tariff of 1913 cut duties—taxes—on imported goods by almost one-half, helping American consumers and promoting freer trade. The Sixteenth Amendment (1913) allowed a federal income tax, which the 1916 Revenue Act put into effect. This was a progressive tax, one that took a larger percentage of the income of the rich than it took from the poor. The legislation also levied higher taxes on corporate profits and created the first federal estate tax on inheritances.

Congress moved to regulate money in another new way as well. The absence of a centrally managed money system had long contributed to the exaggerated boom-and-bust cycles in the American economy. The Federal Reserve Act of 1913 created a system of twelve Federal Reserve Banks to control the amount of currency in circulation, increasing it in deflationary times and decreasing it when inflation threatened. The system aimed to abolish depressions and prevent bank closures. It did not fully succeed, as the years after 1929 showed, but the

■ The body of a soldier lies caught in barbed wire in the "no-man's-land" between opposing trenches on the western front. Technological advances in weaponry helped make the fighting in World War I vastly more destructive than previous wars. The sheer scale of the slaughter stunned combatants and observers, both in Europe and America, and helped turn many in the postwar generation to deep skepticism regarding the use of military force.

Federal Reserve System stabilized the American banking industry and helped position the dollar to become the central global currency.

No issue so dominated American politics between 1913 and 1915 as the tension between huge new corporations and the nation's antimonopoly tradition. The size and market share of companies such as U.S. Steel, American Tobacco, and Du Pont (chemicals) inhibited competition. Congress created the Federal Trade Commission (1914) to investigate business practices that unfairly prevented competition. The Clayton Antitrust Act of 1914 supplemented the 1890 Sherman Antitrust Act by outlawing specific unfair business practices such as local price cutting and granting rebates to undermine competitors.

TABLE 20-1

The Election of 1916

Candidate	Political Party	Popular Vote (%)	Electoral Vote
Woodrow Wilson	Democratic	49.4	277
Charles E. Hughes	Republican	46.2	254
A. L. Benson	Socialist	3.2	—

Another kind of legislation focused on preserving natural landscapes. An increasingly urban, industrial society looked to its most beautiful rural places for solace. Local and state governments set aside parklands throughout the Progressive Era. Wilson followed in Roosevelt's conservationist footsteps by creating the National Park Service in 1916 to provide unified management of such new national treasures as Glacier National Park in Montana (1910), Rocky

Mountain National Park in Colorado (1915), Lassen Volcanic National Park in California (1916), and Acadia National Park in Maine (1919).

The Great Migration

Most African Americans lived in the South, where segregation and discrimination trapped the majority in poverty. Many therefore seized the unprecedented opportunity offered by the outbreak of the Great War. War-related orders created huge needs for workers in northern factories, and the war also closed the spigot of European immigration, drying up the standard source of new labor. Along with other cities, Chicago and Detroit became centers of the **Great Migration** of more than half a million African Americans out of Dixie during the war years.

African American Population, 1910 and 1950

Black Southerners still found plenty of discrimination in the urban North. But the large black communities of Philadelphia, Cleveland, and New York offered far greater independence than the rural South they left behind. African Americans could vote, earn higher wages, send their children to better schools, and even sit where they wanted on streetcars. One woman newly arrived in Chicago was stunned the first time she boarded a trolley and saw black people sitting next to whites. "I just held my breath, for I thought any minute they would start something. Then I saw nobody notices it, and I just thought this is a real place for Negroes."

When war in Europe shut off most Atlantic immigration after 1914, it opened the door to newcomers who did not have to cross the submarine-infested ocean. Blacks who boarded trains for the North were joined by a similar number of white Southerners leaving rural poverty to look for jobs. A small stream of French Canadians found work in New England factories. A much larger stream of Mexicans and Mexican Americans flowed to jobs across the American Southwest and Midwest. World War I and the Mexican Revolution increased their num-

■ A migrant family from the South arriving in Chicago, c. 1916. Southerners of all colors, like Europeans, were drawn by the lure of better jobs to the industrial cities of the American Northeast and Midwest. With immigration from Europe slowed to a trickle by the onset of World War I, industry's demand for southern immigrants increased sharply.

bers sharply, with the growing cities of Los Angeles, San Antonio, and El Paso remaining particular magnets for new immigrants. The number of Mexican Americans in Los Angeles soared from 6,000 in 1910 to nearly 100,000 in 1930.

Limits to American Neutrality

A steady undertow of interests and inclinations pulled against American neutrality after 1914. Most Americans who paid attention to events abroad favored the Entente over the Central Powers. The diversity of Americans' ethnic roots across Europe, Africa, Asia, and Latin America could not mask fundamental cultural and linguistic connections to England, the one-time "mother country." President Wilson deeply admired British political values and institutions, and most influential newspaper editors supported the British cause. Even Americans critical of the British Empire did not want to see the European continent under the autocratic rule of the German Kaiser.

Concrete economic interests also tied the United States to the Entente. During three years of neutrality, American bankers lent 85 times as much to the Entente nations as to the Central Powers ($2.3 billion versus $27 million), and agricultural and industrial workers earned decent wages in filling Entente war orders.

Certain powerful Americans, concentrated on the East Coast, tried from the start to prepare the country for entering the war. They emphasized that the U.S. military was much smaller than the forces of European states because of Americans' traditional aversion to large standing armies. Republicans such as Theodore Roosevelt and former Secretary of State Elihu Root led the war preparedness movement.

Progressives themselves split over the war. More radical reformers opposed joining it as a matter of principle. "Let the capitalists do their own fighting and furnish their own corpses," Socialist Eugene Debs wrote in 1914, "and there will never be another war on the face of the earth." They feared, presciently, that going to war would take the wind out of the sails of domestic reform.

DOCUMENT
Debs, Critique of World War I

Most Progressives followed President Wilson's leadership, opposing U.S. involvement in Europe at first but gradually shifting to support it. The president squeaked by conservative Republican nominee Charles Evans Hughes in the 1916 election, winning a second term in the White House. "He kept us out of war," his supporters declared, but Wilson himself was less optimistic. He knew where German submarine warfare might lead: "Any little German lieutenant can put us into the war at any time by some calculated outrage."

The United States Goes to War

Like Lyndon Johnson in 1964 regarding Vietnam, Wilson won reelection as a liberal reformer and a man of peace, only to go to war within six months. On April 2, 1917, Wilson asked Congress for a declaration of war against Germany "to make the world safe for democracy." Congress agreed by a large majority, and four days later the United States entered the Great War. Mobilization went slowly. The government limited anti-war criticism, and it took almost a year before American soldiers in large numbers saw combat in the trenches of northern France. But American foodstuffs and munitions arrived more quickly, as did American naval ships protecting cargo vessels bound for England. The U.S. entry into the war ultimately provided the narrow margin of victory against the Central Powers.

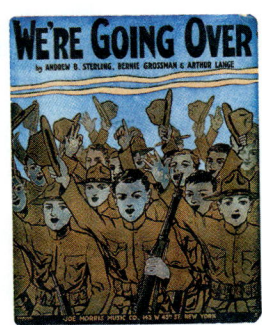

The Logic of Belligerency

Wilson's insistence on the traditional rights of neutral nations to trade with belligerents clashed with German and British efforts to prevent trade destined for their enemy. The German use

DOCUMENT
Wilson's War Message to Congress

of the new submarines, or U-boats (from the German *Unterseeboote*), against superior British surface forces pulled Americans into the war. Submarines were extremely vulnerable when not submerged. Before firing on a merchant or passenger ship that might be armed or carrying contraband (war materials), they refused to surface and warn civilian passengers—as required under international law—to evacuate on lifeboats. With Britain arming merchant ships and stowing munitions in the holds of passenger ships, U-boats were the key element in the German campaign to weaken the enemy. The British navy, in turn, seized American goods bound for Germany. But Britain's blockade of the German coastline and neutral ports nearby did not endanger civilians in the same way. "One deals with life; the other with property," Secretary of State Robert Lansing explained.

The deaths of civilians without warning on the high seas shocked and angered the American public, especially the sinking of the magnificent British ocean liner *Lusitania* in May 1915, which killed 128 U.S. citizens and a thousand others. Hoping not to draw the United States into the war, the German government twice put its unrestricted submarine warfare on hold. But by January 1917 the British blockade had reduced German food rations per person to less than half the prewar level. Facing imminent starvation, Berlin decided to take one last chance with unrestricted submarine warfare. The German government calculated that it could force a British and French surrender before enough American assistance arrived.

Preparing for war with the Americans, German Ambassador Arthur Zimmermann secretly offered German aid to the revolutionary Mexican government "to reconquer the lost territory in Texas, New Mexico, and Arizona" if it joined the Central Powers. Mexico declined, but the Zimmermann telegram leaked to the press on March 1 and outraged Americans. One last hindrance to joining the Entente disappeared with the revolution that same month in Russia, which replaced the monarchy with a democratic government.

Still guarding American autonomy and wary of close identification with the French, British, and Russian empires, however, Wilson took the nation into war as an "Associated" power rather than a full-blown member of the Entente. The president believed that the United States, unique among the belligerents, sought only to defend principles rather than to acquire territory. "We have no quarrel with the German people" but only with the "Prussian autocracy" whose U-boats were engaged in "a warfare against mankind," Wilson declared in calling Americans to a great crusade in Europe.

Mobilizing the Home Front

America and the Great War

Going to war entailed a complete reorientation of the American economy. For the army and navy to succeed abroad, mass production of war materials had to be centrally planned, and only the federal government could fulfill this role. The Wilson administration created several new agencies to manage the war effort at home. The Selective Service Act established local boards to draft young men into the military. The U.S. Railroad Administration took control of the nation's primary transportation system to solve railroad tie-ups caused by heavy demands for war materials. The War Industries Board supervised all war-related production, allowing large manufacturers to coordinate their schedules without fear of antitrust action. The War Labor Board resolved disputes between workers and employers. The Committee on Public Information had the task of inspiring and maintaining public support for Wilson's war policies.

The close cooperation between industry and government, combined with strong demand for American goods from the Entente governments, caused corporate earnings to soar. "We are all making more money out of this war than the average human being ought to," one steel company official admitted privately. And some of the war gains were spread, for a collaborative effort entailed keeping workers productive and content. Taking a position unprecedented in the U.S. government, the War Labor Board promoted an eight-hour workday and the right of workers to form unions.

European demand for war-related goods brought the U.S. economy out of the deep recession of 1913–1914 and created hundreds of thousands of new jobs. U.S. entry into the war in April 1917 took several million men into the armed forces, opening better-paying opportunities in manufacturing to many women. Four workers at the Westinghouse Electric Company pause from their labors in 1918.

Ensuring Unity

The deaths of U.S. soldiers and sailors made support for the war an emotional issue, and a pattern of repressing dissent took hold that outlasted the war. Several states banned teaching the German language. Sauerkraut became "liberty cabbage," frankfurters became hot dogs, and many German Americans anglicized their names. Temperance reformers cited German beer drinking in their successful campaign for a constitutional prohibition of alcohol production. Congress approved the controversial Eighteenth Amendment in December 1917 as a way to save grain for the war effort, and the states ratified it in 1919. Anti-German sentiment led to sometimes deadly violence against Americans of German descent by the summer of 1918. Congress passed sharply restrictive immigration legislation in 1917 as anti-German feelings fed broader prewar fears of new immigrants.

Most African Americans agreed with W. E. B. Du Bois's call to "close our ranks shoulder to shoulder" with white fellow citizens in support of the war effort, despite escalating antiblack violence. The arrival of half a million black Southerners in northern cities increased competition for jobs and housing, causing resentment among many whites. Employers contributed to tensions by recruiting African Americans as strikebreakers and pitting them against white workers. Whites rioted in East St. Louis on July 1, 1917, causing at least forty-seven fatalities, most of them black. Black soldiers from the North at times rebelled against the Jim Crow restrictions they found on southern military bases.

DOCUMENT

Buffington, "Friendly Words to the Foreign Born"

INTERPRETING HISTORY

African American Women in the Great War

Just as black American men served in the American Expeditionary Forces in France in 1917–1918, black American women served in auxiliary organizations such as the Red Cross and the Young Men's and Women's Christian Associations (YMCA and YWCA), which worked to boost the soldiers' morale. They staffed canteens set up to provide social and educational support for American troops as an alternative to entertainments such as prostitution and gambling. Addie W. Hunton and Kathryn M. Johnson felt a particular calling to encourage African American soldiers, who suffered from discrimination and segregation even as they fought for democracy. As devout Christians, the two women believed they must model a life of service and compassion, even in the face of persecution. An account of their time in Europe published soon after they returned to the United States suggests some of the complications of a segregated society sending people abroad.

Two Colored Women with the American Expeditionary Forces

The relationship between the colored soldiers, the colored welfare workers, and the French people was most cordial and friendly and grew in sympathy and understanding, as their associations brought about a closer acquaintance. It was rather an unusual as well as a most welcome experience to be able to go into places of public accommodation without having any hesitations or misgivings; to be at liberty to take a seat in a common carrier, without fear of inviting some humiliating experience; to go into a home and receive a greeting that carried with it a hospitality and kindliness of spirit that could not be questioned.

These things were at once noticeable upon the arrival of a stranger within the gates of this sister democracy, and the first ten days in France, though filled with duties and harassed with visits from German bombing planes, were nevertheless a delight, in that they furnished to some of us the first full breath of freedom that had ever come into our limited experience.

The first post of duty assigned to us was Brest. Upon arriving there we received our first experience with American prejudices, which had not only been carried across the seas, but had become a part of such an intricate propaganda, that the relationship between the colored soldier and the French people is more or less a story colored by a continued and subtle effort to inject this same prejudice into the heart of the hitherto unprejudiced Frenchman.

[An order posted by a white officer of a black battalion read:] "Enlisted men of this organization will not talk to or be in company with any white women, regardless of whether the women solicit their company or not."

[Another order read:] "There are two Y.M.C.A.'s, one near the camp, for white troops, and one in town, for the colored troops. All men will be instructed to patronize their own Y."

The account also describes segregation imposed during the return voyage to the United States:

Quite a bit of unpleasantness was experienced on the boats coming home.... On [one] boat there were nineteen colored welfare workers; all the women were placed on a floor below the white women, and the entire colored party was placed in an obscure, poorly ventilated section of the dining-room, entirely separated from the other workers by a long table of Dutch civilians. The writer immediately protested; the reply was made that the southern white workers on board the ship would be insulted if the colored workers ate in the same section of the dining-room with them, and, at any rate, the colored people did not expect any such treatment as had been given them by the French.

Questions

1. How did serving in France affect the ways African American men and women viewed their own country?
2. What might the impact of blacks' service in France have been on American society when they returned home after the war?

American women supported the war effort in many ways, including working in munitions factories, buying war bonds, single-parenting while husbands were away in the military, and volunteering as nurses for the armed forces in France. Here, African American women entertain black soldiers with music in a service club in Newark, New Jersey, 1918.

Source: Addie W. Hunton and Kathryn M. Johnson, *Two Colored Women with American Expeditionary Forces* (New York: Brooklyn Eagle Press, 1920), pp. 28–30, 182–183, 186.

■ **MAP 20.2**
WORLD WAR I IN EUROPE AND THE WESTERN FRONT, 1918 By the time U.S. troops arrived in force on the western front in northern France, the new Bolshevik (Communist) government of Russia had made peace with the Germans and withdrawn from the war. Germany now faced enemies only on one front—the western front—and moved all its troops there. In this dire situation for the French and British, American soldiers helped fill the gap in 1918.

The War in Europe

When the United States entered the war in Europe in 1917, crisis gripped the Entente. In the east, much of the war effort collapsed in the confusion of Russia's revolution against the czar. In the west, forty-nine divisions of the French army mutinied, refusing orders to make further suicidal advances. In the south, at Caporetto, Austro-Hungarian forces inflicted a disastrous defeat on the Italian army. It was not clear whether the Americans had joined soon enough to stave off defeat.

World War I

No battle-ready American army waited at ports for immediate shipment to the trenches of northern France. U.S. commanders instead had to conscript and train nearly 5 million young men for an American Expeditionary Force (AEF) under General Pershing, and 16,000 young women volunteered for service overseas as nurses and Red Cross workers. Although the veteran French and British lines had to stand largely on their own against the final German spring offensive, American soldiers later engaged in fierce combat at Belleau Wood, Château-Thierry, and St. Mihiel, ultimately losing 114,000 men. As the only army growing stronger in 1918, the AEF contributed crucially to the fall offensive that convinced Germany to surrender on November 11.

Events in Russia provoked the greatest long-term concerns. In October 1917, Vladimir Lenin and his fellow **Bolsheviks** seized control of the government, building a dictatorship of the Communist party in the name of the working class. The Bolsheviks opposed the Great War as a struggle among rival capitalists. In the czar's archives, they found and published the secret prewar treaties of the Entente for dividing up their prospective conquests after the war, both in Europe and in the colonies overseas. While Wilson spoke of a war for democracy, the Bolsheviks asked Russians, "Are you willing to fight for this, that the English capitalists should rob Mesopotamia and Palestine?"

The answer, as Wilson feared, was no. In January 1918, the president gave the famous "Fourteen Points" speech to the U.S. Congress, outlining his aims of a postwar world built not on expansion and revenge but on national self-determination, open diplomacy, and freedom of commerce and travel, to be guaranteed by a new League of Nations. He hoped to dissuade the Bolsheviks from making a separate peace with Germany that would allow Germany to move all its troops to the western front. But Lenin, facing civil war at home, conceded huge swaths of the old czarist empire in eastern Europe to the Germans to gain peace with the Brest-Litovsk Treaty of March 3, 1918.

The competing visions of Wilson and Lenin for world order contained the roots of the Cold War that would dominate American life after 1945. They agreed that the old diplomacy of imperialist states competing for pieces of property around the globe would no longer work and that only the creation of democratic states would prevent further wars. But they understood democracy very differently. For Wilson, it meant self-governing nations with capitalist economies and republican political practices (at least in Europe and North America, and eventually elsewhere). For Lenin, it meant workers in every land overthrowing the owners of capital and setting up Soviet governments. Whereas Wilson viewed the world as a collection of nations, Lenin saw it as a battleground between two classes.

■ **"Comrade Lenin Sweeps the Globe Clean."** This Bolshevik (Communist) drawing shows Vladimir I. Lenin (1870–1924), the leader of the Russian revolution and founder of the world's first Communist government, ridding the world of capitalists and monarchs. But Lenin also sought western trade and investment, especially from the United States, as a stimulus to reconstructing the devastated postwar economy of the new Union of Soviet Socialist Republics (USSR).

The Struggle to Win the Peace

World War I killed more than 16 million people and wrought immeasurable physical, social, and psychological damage. Was it worth it? Citizens of the belligerent nations emerged from 1918 convinced that only a future free of war could legitimate such suffering. Some put their hopes in the radical solution unfolding in Russia. Some in the Entente states believed that severe measures against Germany would ensure peace. Most looked to Woodrow Wilson in the winter and spring of 1919, with his vision of a more peaceful, democratic postwar order. The president sailed for Europe in January to lead the

MAP 20.3
EUROPE AFTER WORLD WAR I The outcome of World War I led to significant changes in the boundaries of Europe, particularly its eastern parts. Four great empires in the region—Russia, Germany, Austria-Hungary, and the Ottomans—collapsed. Negotiations at Versailles created a band of new nations, providing both self-determination and a bulwark against Russian communism.

conference that would shape the peace. Vast crowds greeted him enthusiastically as he toured England, Italy, and France.

Peacemaking and the Versailles Treaty

War and revolution destroyed the four great empires of Russia, Germany, Austria-Hungary, and the Ottomans (based in modern Turkey). Meeting in Paris from January to

June 1919, the "Big Three" of Wilson, French President Georges Clemenceau, and British Prime Minister David Lloyd George took on two major tasks to shape the postwar order. First, the three leaders redrew the map of eastern and central Europe to create nation-states out of the vanished empires. Second, they had to decide what to do about a defeated Germany. The possible spread of revolution gave the negotiations a particular urgency. Anticolonial revolts broke out in India and China, and pro-Soviet workers' councils seized power briefly in Hungary and southern Germany. "We are running a race with Bolshevism," Wilson warned, "and the world is on fire."

To put out the fire, the Big Three created a string of new nations running from Finland in the north to Yugoslavia in the south. Eastern Europeans were to be self-governing within the new political boundaries. How far would "self-determination" go? Secretary of State Lansing worried that the president's language of democracy was "loaded with dynamite." The world's nonwhite majority wondered whether it applied to them. The Big Three created the mandate system to provide for eventual self-determination for colonies after a period of tutelage under an established power, and they rejected Japan's proposal to include racial equality as a principle of the new League of Nations.

The German question predominated at the Paris conference. To create a long-term peaceful order in Europe, Wilson wanted lenient terms for Germany. But the French and British had lost much more in the war than the Americans, and they believed Germany must pay for that. To satisfy France and England, Germany had to admit guilt for causing the war and pay $33 billion in reparations, while losing much of its eastern territory to the new states of Poland and Czechoslovakia. For Wilson the League of Nations was the key: this new and unprecedented global organization would keep the peace by ensuring collective security for all nations.

DOCUMENT
Henry Cabot Lodge's Objections to Treaty of Versailles

Most Republicans objected on principle to one key aspect of the Versailles Treaty (named for the estate of King Louis XIV, where it was signed): Article 10 of the League of Nations charter, guaranteeing ahead of time a collective response to defend any member's territory from attack. Treaty opponents were determined to preserve complete American autonomy, including freedom of action in Latin America. Henry Cabot Lodge Jr. of Massachusetts, the powerful Republican chair of the Senate Foreign Relations Committee, organized the two Senate votes rejecting American membership in the league. Hoping to stave off defeat for his idealistic plan, Wilson undertook an ill-advised national speaking tour to promote the league. His strenuous effort failed to win American participation in the league, and it ultimately broke his fragile health. Wilson suffered a stroke on October 2, 1919, that left him incapacitated for the rest of his presidency.

Waging Counterrevolution Abroad

Soon after Russia withdrew from the war, Britain, France, and the United States intervened in the civil war there between the Bolsheviks (the "Reds") and the various counterrevolutionary forces (the "Whites"). The initial military rationale in the summer of 1918 was to reopen the eastern front against Germany. The United States landed 7,000 troops in Vladivostock, on Russia's far Pacific coast. In conjunction with the British, 5,000 U.S. soldiers went ashore at Archangel in northern Russia. They quickly became involved in fighting the Red Army. The Wilson administration meanwhile funneled money and military intelligence to leaders of the White forces.

The Bolsheviks rejected certain values cherished by most Americans: the sanctity of private property and contracts, political liberty, and religious freedom. They liberalized divorce laws and legalized abortion, challenging conservative American attitudes about the relationships between women and men. And they established the Comintern in 1919 to promote similar revolutions around the world. Intervention in the Russian civil war failed to overthrow Lenin's government, and American troops pulled out in 1920.

The Red and Black Scares at Home

Meanwhile, in the United States, the scale of industrial unrest provoked fears of a Soviet-style revolution. Four million American workers, one out of every five, went out on strike in 1919—the highest proportion of the workforce ever. They sought improved wages and working conditions as well as recognition of the right to collective bargaining. In Seattle a walkout by shipyard workers mushroomed into a general strike that shut down most of the city for a week. In Pittsburgh the AFL led a bitter strike against U.S. Steel in pursuit of union recognition. The United Mine Workers led walkouts by hundreds of thousands of coal miners, which evolved into open warfare between miners and coal companies in West Virginia over the next two years. In Boston three-quarters of the police force went on strike to protest wages lower than those of common laborers. Between April and June, anarchists mailed or delivered bombs to thirty-six prominent public figures, including Attorney General A. Mitchell Palmer. All were defused except two.

■ The Seattle General Strike Committee took on the responsibility of keeping essential services running in the city. Here its members issue groceries to union families, January 1919. The cooperation necessary among organized workers to keep a strike going offered a different model of community interaction than did the individualism often touted by wealthier Americans.

Whereas many Americans sympathized with struggles for unionization, others viewed them as dangerous to private property and social order. They associated strikes with radical immigrants and anarchists and considered them "un-American." The **Red Scare** of 1919 associated reform and social justice of any kind with subversion. Attorney General Palmer directed the deportation to Russia of 249 foreign-born radicals aboard the *Buford* in December 1919, including anarchist and feminist Emma Goldman. "Palmer raids" led to the arrest of thousands more within a month.

Violence against workers extended to African Americans after World War I. An upsurge in lynching included at least ten black veterans still in uniform and was not limited to the South. White mobs burned entire black communities to the ground, including Tulsa's Greenwood neighborhood in 1921 and the all-black town of Rosewood, Florida, in 1923. The Red Scare merged with the "Black Scare" in Phillips County, Arkansas, where black sharecroppers, many of them veterans, formed a union in 1919 to pursue equitable crop settlements from landlords. Fearing insurrection, local white leaders used 2,500 federal troops and white vigilantes to massacre more than 200 sharecroppers. But any inclination toward deference in the face of brutality was gone, and African Americans fought back fiercely against white marauders in deadly riots in Washington and Chicago in the summer of 1919.

Where was the president during this turmoil? Incapacitated by his stroke, he lay resting in his bed in Washington, the administration managed largely by his wife, Edith, and his secretary, Joseph Tumulty. In any case, Wilson's segregationist policies suggested that he would have been unlikely to provide effective leadership in bridging the nation's racial divides.

Conclusion

How much success could a varied generation of Progressive reformers claim? Women had won the vote with the Nineteenth Amendment. Daily life for Americans of darker hue continued to entail picking one's way through a maze of discrimination. Most union campaigns stalled by 1920, beaten back by the physical force and cleverness of corporate employers and their government sympathizers. When the Red Scare dissipated, Americans did not return to the reform spirit of Progressivism. Voter turnout in 1920 dipped below 50 percent for the first time in a century. Those who did vote that year gave the Republican party a sweeping victory and put Ohio Senator Warren G. Harding in the White House. His speeches may have been, as one rival said, "an army of pompous phrases moving over the landscape in search of an idea," but most of the nation sought calm after the upheavals of the previous decade.

American contributions to democracy abroad were similarly ambivalent. Whereas eastern Europeans named streets in their newly independent nations for President Wilson, few Latin Americans believed that U.S. invasions of Caribbean and Central American countries promoted self-government. Russians admired much about American society and the U.S. economy while resenting American troops in their land. Above all hung the problem of Germany, still the most potentially powerful single nation in Europe. The Versailles Treaty imposed harsh terms and embittered a generation of German people. "If I were a German, I think I should not sign it," Wilson admitted privately. The Weimar Republic that replaced the abdicated German Kaiser lasted through the 1920s. But the storms of the Great Depression after 1929 swamped Germany's republican experiment and gave rise to Adolph Hitler.

Sites to Visit

The Great War, 1914–1918
www.pitt.edu/~pugachev/greatwar/ww1.html
This site offers an array of narratives, photos, documents, statistics, maps, and bibliography, plus links to other useful World War I sites.

Women and Social Movements in the United States, 1600–2000
womhist.binghamton.edu
Maintained by two Binghamton University historians, this site has a rich trove of documents on the history of American women as well as excellent links to others.

Avalon Project at Yale Law School: Documents in Law, History and Diplomacy
www.yale.edu/lawweb/avalon/avalon.htm
Researchers can find here the texts of a large number of the most important primary documents illuminating U.S. relations with other countries, including materials on American responses to the Bolshevik revolution in Russia.

Temperance and Prohibition
prohibition.osu.edu/
Cartoons, newspaper articles, and other primary documents available here illuminate the struggle over whether to prohibit the sale of alcoholic beverages.

Emma Goldman Papers
sunsite3.berkeley.edu/Goldman/
This site has photos and excerpts from the writings and speeches of one of America's most influential radicals and feminists.

Religion Online
www.religion-online.org/
This site has essays by prominent scholars on diverse aspects of Christian theology and American church history.

Up South: African American Migration in the Era of the Great War
www.ashp.cuny.edu/video/south.html
Maintained by the American Social History Project at the Graduate Center of the City University of New York, this site offers details of the mass migration of rural black Southerners to the urban north during World War I.

Influenza Pandemic of 1918
www.stanford.edu/group/virus/uda/
A variety of information, documents, and photos of the deadly global outbreak of the "Spanish flu" can be found here.

For Further Reading

General

Kendrick A. Clements, *Woodrow Wilson: World Statesman* (1987).
John M. Cooper, *Pivotal Decades: The United States, 1900–1920* (1990).
Alan Dawley, *Changing the World: American Progressives in War and Peace* (2003).
Nell Irvin Painter, *Standing at Armageddon: The United States, 1877–1919* (1987).

A World in Upheaval

John Mason Hart, *Empire and Revolution: The Americans in Mexico since the Civil War* (2002).
Arthur Link, ed., *Woodrow Wilson and a Revolutionary World* (1982).
Joseph A. McCartin, *Labor's Great War: The Struggle for Industrial Democracy and the Origins of Modern American Labor Relations, 1912–1921* (1997).

George J. Sánchez, *Becoming Mexican American: Ethnicity, Culture, and Identity in Chicano Los Angeles, 1900–1945* (1993).

The Great War and American Neutrality

John W. Coogan, *The End of Neutrality: The United States, Britain, and Maritime Rights, 1899–1915* (1981).

Steven J. Diner, *A Very Different Age: Americans of the Progressive Era* (1998).

James Grossman, *Land of Hope: Chicago, Black Southerners, and the Great Migration* (1989).

Vicki I. Ruiz, *From Out of the Shadows: Mexican Women in Twentieth-Century America* (1998).

The United States Goes to War

Edward M. Coffman, *The War to End All Wars: The American Military Experience in World War I* (1987).

Martin Gilbert, *The First World War: A Complete History* (1994).

David M. Kennedy, *Over Here: The First World War and American Society* (1980).

Kathleen Kennedy, *Disloyal Mothers and Scurrilous Citizens: Women and Subversion During World War I* (1999).

The Struggle to Win the Peace

Alfred W. Crosby, *America's Forgotten Pandemic: The Influenza of 1918*, 2nd ed. (2003).

David S. Foglesong, *America's Secret War Against Bolshevism: U.S. Intervention in the Russian Civil War, 1917–1920* (1995).

Thomas J. Knock, *To End All Wars: Woodrow Wilson and the Quest for a New World Order* (1992).

Gordon N. Levin Jr., *Woodrow Wilson and World Politics: America's Response to War and Revolution* (1968).

William M. Tuttle Jr., *Race Riot: Chicago in the Red Summer of 1919* (1970).

For quizzes and other resources on these topics, go to www.longmanamericanhistory.com.

CHAPTER 21

The Promise of Consumer Culture: The 1920s

CHAPTER OUTLINE

The Business of Politics

The Decline of Reform

Hollywood and Harlem: National Cultures in Black and White

Science on Trial

Consumer Dreams and Nightmares

Conclusion

Sites to Visit

For Further Reading

IN THE SUPERIOR COURT OF LOS ANGELES IN 1920, LORIMER LINGANFIELD, A RESPECTABLE BARBER, filed for divorce. Although his wife, Marsha, held him in "high regard and esteem as her husband," there were "evidences of indiscretion" in her conduct. She wore a new bathing suit, "designed especially for the purpose of exhibiting to the public the shape and form of her body." To his further humiliation, she was "beset with a desire to sing and dance at cafes and restaurants for the entertainment of the public." When Lorimer complained about her "appetite for beer and whisky" and extravagant tastes for luxury, she replied that he was "not the only pebble on the beach, she had a millionaire 'guy' who would buy her all the clothes, automobiles, diamonds and booze that she wanted." The ultimate insult was her refusal to have any sexual intercourse, claiming that she did not want any "dirty little brats around her." The judge was sympathetic, and Lorimer Linganfield won his suit.

The Linganfields' difficulties represent a larger struggle as Americans shifted from the **producer economy** of the nineteenth century, complete with clearly defined gender roles and sexual mores, to the **consumer economy** of the twentieth century and to new amusements, changing sexual behavior, and flamboyant "new women." Marsha Linganfield was a "**flapper**," one of the young women of the 1910s and 1920s who broke from time-honored conventions. With short, "bobbed" hair, knee-length dresses, and boyish styles unencumbered by layers of petticoats, flappers flirted, petted, and danced "wild" dances like the Charleston, an African American dance brought north from South Carolina **juke joints**. Flappers blurred the line between "good girls" and "bad girls" that had previously defined proper female behavior.

■ Gertrude Ederle swims the English Channel.

New forms of popular entertainment that developed in the 1920s, especially Hollywood movies and jazz music, became defining features of the nation itself. The popular arts offered Jews and blacks a space for innovation. At a time when white, Anglo-Saxon, Protestant (WASP) men had control of nearly all government and business institutions, Jewish moviemakers and African American musicians were creating the culture that would soon represent the nation.

The great heroes of the 1920s were celebrities admired for their individual achievements in sports and adventure. In 1927, the same year that Babe Ruth hit a record sixty home runs, Charles Lindbergh flew his small monoplane, *The Spirit of St. Louis*, nonstop from New York to Paris in thirty-three and one-half hours, a feat that electrified the world and made him an instant hero. Professional sports came of age in the 1920s. In 1926, nineteen-year-old Olympic gold medalist Gertrude Ederle became the first woman to swim the English Channel. She broke the world's record with her time of fourteen hours and thirty-one minutes, two hours shorter than those of the six men who had preceded her. On her return to the United States, 2 million cheering fans lined the streets of New York City to welcome her home. The nation idolized this new generation of heroes, who dominated headlines and drew cheering crowds wherever they went.

> *The great heroes of the 1920s were celebrities admired for their individual achievements in sports and adventure.*

The glamorous life, however, was out of reach for many. Often characterized as the "roaring twenties" of giddy prosperity and reckless good times, these were also years of widespread poverty, especially in rural areas and urban ghettos. But at the end of the decade, almost half of all households did own a car or a radio; almost a third owned a washing machine or a vacuum cleaner real wages rose steadily.

Conservative politics at the national level prevailed throughout the decade. An antiradical immigrant Red Scare followed World War I, and Prohibition made alcohol consumption illegal until 1933. High-profile court cases revealed public ambivalence about the use of new scientific knowledge. Business values of material acquisition spread as the expansion of consumer credit weakened the traditions of saving and frugality. For those with money to invest, Wall Street beckoned. The stock market rose to perilous heights, only to collapse at the end of the decade.

The Business of Politics

In 1924 President Calvin Coolidge declared, "The business of America is business." Despite its many critics, with the support of national political leaders, business reigned. After an initial recession following World War I, the Republican U.S. economy grew steadily. The Gross National Product (GNP) increased 5.5 percent per year, from $149 billion in 1922 to $227 billion in 1929. Official unemployment remained below 5 percent throughout the decade, and real wages rose 15 percent. These trends fueled the popularity of the conservative, business-friendly presidents of the 1920s. Economic interests also drove foreign policy during the decade. After World War I, with much of Europe in shambles, the United States made loans to foreign countries, becoming the world's leading creditor nation. International markets opened up for American-made products, leading to a tremendous expansion in foreign trade.

Warren G. Harding: The Politics of Scandal

Warren G. Harding, a former newspaper editor and Republican U.S. senator from Ohio, won the 1920 presidential election by the biggest landslide since 1820. He established the conservative agenda that would last throughout the decade. Harding supported immigration restriction and opposed labor unions. In the wake of World War I, Harding distanced himself from Woodrow Wilson's peace settlement but promoted international treaties. In 1921 and 1922, Secretary of State Charles Evans Hughes achieved the first major disarmament accord, the Five-Power Treaty, signed by Japan, Britain, France, Italy, and the United States at the Washington Conference. The

Warren G. Harding

five nations agreed to scrap more than 2 million tons of warships in the first such pact of its kind. Hughes extended the power of the United States abroad through economic ties, encouraging banks to provide loans to war-ravaged Europe.

But Harding's presidency was marred by scandal. He had built his political base by handing out favors and deals to his friends, and he continued to do so as president. His buddies used their offices and influence for personal gain, while Harding caroused with them, drinking, despite Prohibition, and engaging in notorious extramarital affairs. At first, the press ignored these abuses, but by 1923, the many scandals finally broke. Harding's cronies were exposed for selling government appointments and providing judicial pardons and police protection for bootleggers.

TABLE 21-1

The Election of 1920

Candidate	Political Party	Popular Vote (%)	Electoral Vote
Warren G. Harding	Republican	60.4	404
James M. Cox	Democratic	34.2	127
Eugene V. Debs	Socialist	3.4	—

The most serious scandal of Harding's presidency involved the large government oil reserves at Teapot Dome, Wyoming, and Elk Hills, California. At the urging of Secretary of the Interior Albert Fall, Harding transferred control over the reserves from the U.S. Navy to the Department of the Interior. After accepting a bribe of nearly $400,000 from two oil tycoons, Harry F. Sinclair and Edward L. Doheny, Fall secretly issued leases to them without opening up the competition to other oil companies. Fall went to jail for a year as a result. In another scandal, Charles R. Forbes, head of the Veteran's Bureau, went to prison for swindling the government out of $200 million worth of hospital supplies. When he learned of the scandals that occurred in his close circle, Harding grew deeply worried. The stress probably contributed to the illness that killed him in 1923.

Calvin Coolidge: The Hands-Off President

Harding's vice president, Calvin Coolidge, took over the presidency. Sober and serious, this aloof New Englander was not vulnerable to scandal as his predecessor had been. Coolidge believed that the government should meddle as little as possible in the affairs of the nation. He took long naps every day and exerted little presidential leadership. Known mostly for his hostility to labor unions and his laissez-faire attitude toward business, he was a popular president during the complacent mid-1920s.

DOCUMENT
Inaugural Address, Calvin Coolidge (March 1925)

Not everyone was pleased with Coolidge's probusiness politics, and opposition mobilized for the 1924 election. Progressive Republicans formed a new Progressive party and nominated Robert M. La Follette of Wisconsin for president. The Progressive platform promoted conservation measures, higher taxes on the wealthy, doing away with the electoral college in favor of direct election of the president, and the abolition of child labor. The Democrats deadlocked between Catholic candidate Alfred E. Smith, an urban politician from New York, and Protestant William G. McAdoo, who had a base of support in the South and West. On the 103rd ballot, the delegates finally chose a compromise candidate, John W. Davis, a corporation lawyer. The Republicans nominated Coolidge, who claimed responsibility for the nation's prosperity and won easily, receiving more votes than the other two candidates combined.

TABLE 21-2

The Election of 1924

Candidate	Political Party	Popular Vote (%)	Electoral Vote
Calvin Coolidge	Republican	54.0	382
John W. Davis	Democratic	28.8	136
Robert M. LaFollette	Progressive	16.6	13

Coolidge took pride in measures that prevented the government from interfering in the economy, such as his vetoes of the 1926 and 1928 McNary-Haugen bills, which would have provided government subsidies to farmers if farm prices dropped. The passage of the Revenue

Act of 1926, a form of **trickle-down economics** intended to boost the economy, reduced the high income and estate taxes that Progressive reformers had put into place during World War I.

Herbert Hoover: The Self-Made President

The 1928 election was a major turning point for the presence of ethnic minorities in politics, for the Democrats broke tradition by selecting an Irish Roman Catholic, Alfred E. Smith, governor of New York, as their candidate. It was the first time a major party had nominated a Catholic for president. Coolidge decided not to run for reelection in 1928, and the Republican party selected Secretary of Commerce Herbert Hoover as its nominee. Prohibition—the Eighteenth Amendment banning the manufacture and sale of alcohol—figured prominently in the 1928 presidential campaign. Although the Democratic platform gave lukewarm support to the continuation of Prohibition, Smith made no secret of his support for the repeal of the Eighteenth Amendment. By contrast, Republican Herbert Hoover praised Prohibition as "a great social and economic experiment." The other major issue of the campaign was religion. Anti-Catholic sentiment was strong throughout the country, especially in the South, where Democrats either sat out the election or voted Republican. Smith's opponents attacked his Catholicism, charging that he was more loyal to the Vatican than to the United States.

TABLE 21-3

The Election of 1928

Candidate	Political Party	Popular Vote (%)	Electoral Vote
Herbert Hoover	Republican	58.2	444
Alfred E. Smith	Democratic	40.9	87
Norman Thomas	Socialist	0.7	—

Herbert Hoover epitomized the values of the self-made man. He was orphaned as a child and raised by relatives of modest means. After graduating from newly established Stanford University, Hoover went into mining and rose through the ranks to become a wealthy corporate leader. By age forty, he was already a millionaire. Hoover began his career in government during World War I, when he earned widespread admiration for handling the distribution of food relief to European war refugees. He then served ably as secretary of commerce in the Harding and Coolidge administrations. Shortly after the election, President Hoover predicted, "We in America today are nearer to the final triumph over poverty than ever before in the history of any land." But less than a year into his presidency, his optimism, along with the nation's economy, came crashing down.

The Decline of Reform

Reformers who had championed the causes of the marginalized and disadvantaged lost influence in the business-dominated 1920s. After achieving the vote, the women's rights movement splintered as younger women sought new freedoms not through politics but through a social and sexual revolution. Widespread hostility toward immigrants and various ethnic groups was at the root of the outlawing of liquor, new laws restricting immigration, and the rise of the Ku Klux Klan. But progressive political impulses did not entirely disappear, especially among African Americans, who continued to mobilize and organize for civil rights.

Women's Rights After the Struggle for Suffrage

One indication of the waning of progressive reform was the fragmentation of women's rights activism in the 1920s. The more radical wing of the suffrage movement, the National Woman's Party (NWP), in 1923 launched a campaign for the Equal Rights Amendment (ERA), which declared simply: "Equality of rights under the law shall not be denied or abridged by the United States or by any state on account of sex."

The debate over the ERA in the 1920s reflected the fundamental divide that would permeate women's rights activism throughout the rest of the twentieth century. On one side were those who believed that women were fundamentally the same as men and deserved equal rights; on the other side were those who argued that women were different and deserved special privileges and protections. Many women's rights activists opposed the ERA because it would undercut efforts to gain special legislative protections for women based on their presumed physical weakness and their potential for childbearing, such as maximum hours, regulations against night work, and limitations on the weights they could lift. These women disapproved of the goals and tactics of the NWP and formed their own nonpartisan organization, the League of Women Voters, which promoted social and political reform.

Marital breakdown still carried a heavy negative stigma, especially for women. Nevertheless, the divorce rate doubled between 1900 and 1920 and continued to rise throughout the 1920s, in part the result of women's increasing independence. As job opportunities for women increased, more women felt able to abandon unhappy marriages.

Prohibition: The Experiment That Failed

The Eighteenth Amendment, prohibiting the manufacture and sale of alcohol, went into effect in January 1920. Several diverse interests came together to promote the ban on liquor. Temperance crusaders in the Anti-Saloon League and the Women's Christian Temperance Union had argued since the late nineteenth century that women and children suffered when men spent their paychecks at the saloon and returned home drunk and violent. World War I prompted others to support a ban on the manufacture of liquor to save grain for the war effort. Anti-immigrant "drys" had political motives for promoting prohibition. They hoped to undercut the power bases of immigrant and ethnic

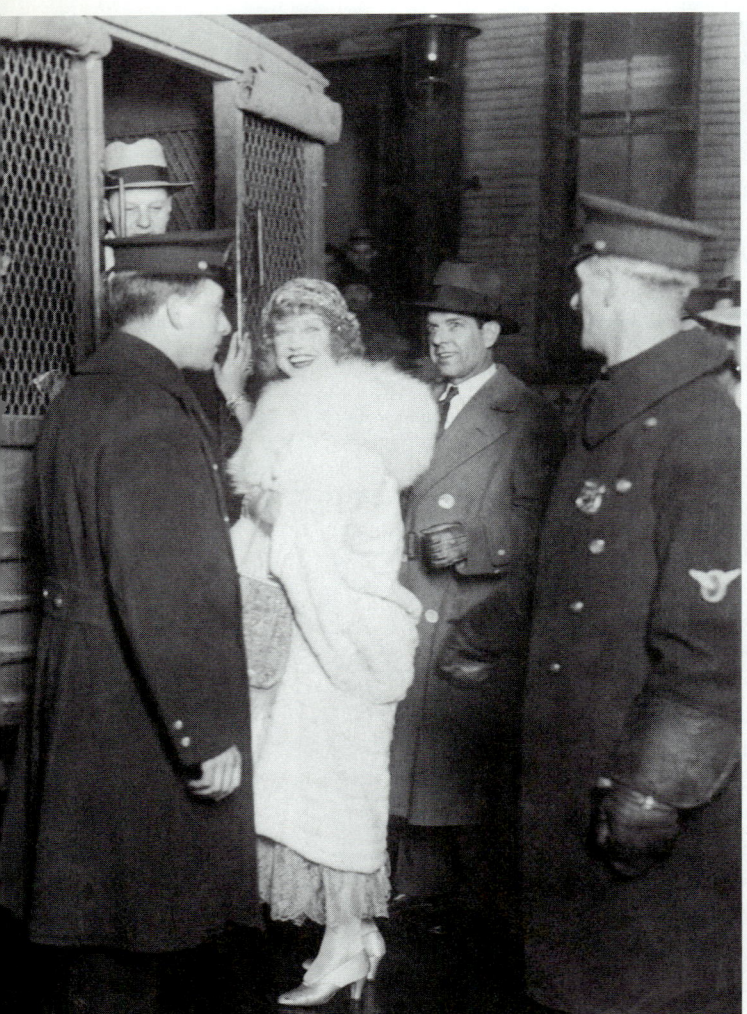

■ Speakeasy hostess Mary Louise Guinan appears unrepentant as she is arrested for selling alcohol during the Prohibition era. Law enforcement was futile because speakeasies that were raided and closed simply reopened in new locations.

DOCUMENT
Eighteenth Amendment—Prohibition of Intoxicating Liquor (January 16, 1919)

politicians who used local saloons to forge their constituencies and **political machines**. The "wets" included alienated intellectuals, Jazz Age rebels, and many city dwellers whose social lives revolved around neighborhood pubs, especially in Irish and German communities.

Enforcement was impossible. Federal agents had responsibility for enforcing the law, but their numbers were inadequate. In order to be effective, federal agents had to work closely with local law enforcement officials. In some urban areas, local officials refused to cooperate with federal agents. Americans who wanted to drink liquor found many ways to acquire it. Illegal "speakeasies" abounded where customers could buy drinks delivered by rumrunners who smuggled in liquor from Canada, Mexico, and the West Indies. Many people concocted their own "bathtub gin" or "moonshine whiskey," homemade brews using readily available ingredients and household equipment.

Prohibition was intended to cure society's ills. Instead, it provided vast opportunities for crime and profit. Organized crime received a major boost when violence erupted in the scramble to profit from illegal liquor. Chicago witnessed 550 gangland killings in the 1920s, with few arrests or convictions. By 1929 Chicago mob king Al Capone controlled a massive network of speakeasies that raked in $60 million annually.

Prohibition failed to live up to its promise. Although alcohol consumption declined by two-thirds within a year of the passage of the amendment, by 1929 the consumption of alcohol had climbed back up to 70 percent of its pre-Prohibition level.

"Prohibition is a Failure"

Reactionary Impulses

The Red Scare after World War I (see Chapter 20) inaugurated a decade of hostility to political radicals and foreigners. Shoemaker Nicola Sacco and fish peddler Bartolomeo Vanzetti were both: Italian **aliens** and self-proclaimed anarchists. In May 1920, the paymaster and guard of a South Braintree, Massachusetts, shoe company was robbed and murdered, and Sacco and Vanzetti were arrested and charged with the crime. Sacco testified that he was in Boston at the time, applying for a passport, and his alibi was corroborated. Both men proclaimed their innocence and insisted that they were on trial for their political beliefs rather than the crime itself. Their Italian accents and advocacy of anarchism in the courtroom did not help their case with many Americans suspicious of foreign radicals, including the judge presiding at their trial. Despite a weak case against them, Sacco and Vanzetti were convicted of first-degree murder and sentenced to death.

Lawyers for the two anarchists appealed the case several times to no avail. The convictions sparked outrage among Italian Americans, political radicals, labor activists, and liberal intellectuals who believed the two men were falsely convicted. The case soon generated mass demonstrations, appeals for clemency, and petitions from around the world. In response, the governor of Massachusetts appointed a commission to review the case, but the commission concluded that there were no grounds for a new trial. Finally, on August 23, 1927, Sacco and Vanzetti were executed by electric chair at Charlestown State Prison.

The case of Sacco and Vanzetti underscored the anti-immigrant sentiment that prevailed in the 1920s. In 1924 Congress passed the Johnson-Reid Act, imposing a limit of 165,000

■ Nicola Sacco and Bartolomeo Vanzetti, Italian aliens and self-proclaimed anarchists, were accused of murder in May 1920. The men and their supporters claimed they were on trial not for the crime but for their political beliefs and their immigrant status. After all appeals failed, the two were executed in 1927.

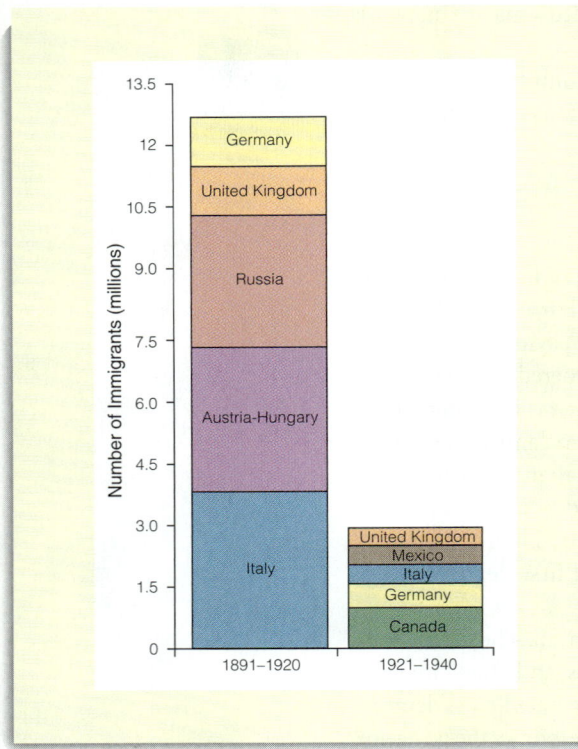

■ **FIGURE 21.1**
NUMBER OF IMMIGRANTS AND COUNTRIES OF ORIGIN, 1891–1920 AND 1921–1940 Before the immigration restriction laws passed in the 1920s, many immigrants came from Russia and southern and eastern Europe. After immigration restriction, most came from western Europe and Canada.

immigrants from countries outside the Western Hemisphere and using a quota system for each country based on the year 1890, a time when British, German, and Scandinavian immigrants dominated the foreign-born population. The Johnson-Reid Act limited entry every year to 2 percent of the total number of immigrants from each country who were present in 1890. This measure effectively barred Jews, Slavs, Greeks, Italians, and Poles because their numbers were so small in 1890. In addition, the 1924 law reaffirmed the exclusion of Chinese immigrants and added Japanese and other Asians to the list, effectively closing the door to all migrants from Asia.

Agricultural interests in California and Texas lobbied hard to keep the door open to Mexicans because of the low-wage labor they provided. In the aftermath of the Mexican Revolution, many Mexicans hoped to find stability and jobs in the United States. Between 1910 and 1930, more than 1 million Mexicans, nearly one-tenth of Mexico's population, migrated to the United States, where they found work on farms, on railroads, and in mines.

One of the most reactionary developments of the 1920s was the revival of the Ku Klux Klan (KKK), which became the most powerful white supremacy group in the nation, remaining active throughout the twentieth century. Klan membership included laborers, businesspeople, physicians, judges, social workers, and women who felt that their homogenous small-town Protestant culture was threatened by the evils of modern life, brought on by the presence and influence of morally suspect outsiders. The Klan wielded considerable power in the 1920s in certain states, particularly Texas, Oklahoma, Oregon, and Indiana.

Marcus Garvey and the Persistence of Civil Rights Activism

In the midst of a decade of reactionary policies toward outsiders and political activists, African Americans continued their struggle for civil rights. Jamaican-born black nationalist Marcus Garvey moved to New York City's Harlem in 1916 and opened a branch of his Universal Negro Improvement Association (UNIA). Garvey urged black people to establish their own nation-state in Africa: "Africa was peopled with a race of cultured black men, who were masters in art, science, and literature. . . . Africa shall be for the black peoples of the world." By the 1920s, the UNIA had nearly 1 million followers and called for political justice and labor rights for black Americans.

In keeping with his belief in black-owned businesses, Garvey established the Black Star Line and encouraged his followers to invest in the shipping company. Nearly 40,000 African Americans invested three-quarters of a million dollars to purchase shares of Black Star stock. But the business ran into problems. Managers purchased ships that needed extensive and costly repairs, and the company ran up huge debts. Garvey claimed that he had paid for a ship that was never delivered. In 1922 Garvey was arrested and charged with mail fraud for advertising and selling stock for a ship that did not exist. Although the government lacked any concrete evidence to prove the case against him, Garvey was convicted and sentenced to five years in prison. Garvey kept up his political activities from prison, then was released after two years and deported to Jamaica as an undesirable alien. Nevertheless, the momentum he sparked continued.

Hollywood and Harlem: National Cultures in Black and White

In 1920, for the first time, the majority of Americans lived in towns and cities with populations greater than 2,500. Although this shift often is considered a watershed in the transformation from rural to urban America, it is worth noting that because the census defined any town with more than 2,500 inhabitants as urban, the majority of Americans still lived in small and ethnically homogeneous towns. Many small-town Americans still viewed big-city life with suspicion. They feared the decline of traditional Protestant American values of hard work, thrift, and discipline. Yet they were drawn to the new urban life.

Hollywood on the West Coast and Harlem on the East Coast became centers of cultural innovation that spanned the nation. Eventually, the artistic productions of both centers attracted audiences of all racial, class, and regional backgrounds. Increasingly, as Americans moved from place to place, they encountered similar entertainments, music, arts, and consumer products. Movies, automobiles, radios, and advertising all fostered this emerging national culture.

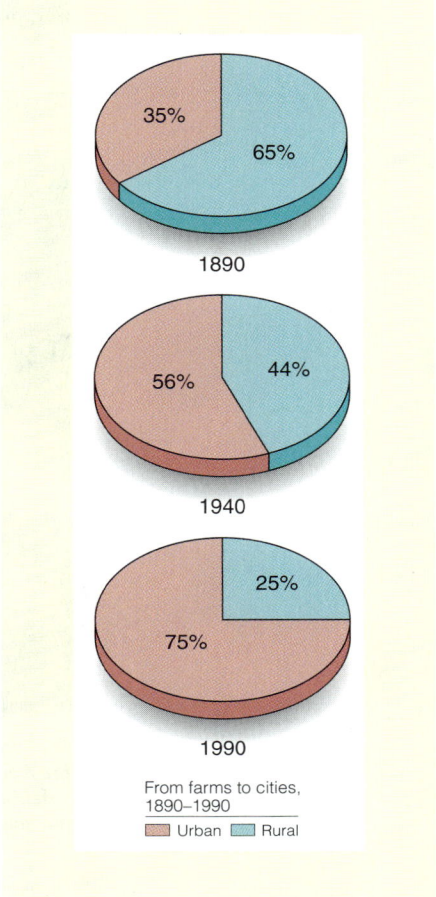

■ **FIGURE 21.2**
URBAN AND RURAL POPULATION, 1890–1990 In the nineteenth century, the American population was primarily rural. During the twentieth century, the population became predominantly urban.

Hollywood Comes of Age

As movie theaters spread into towns and cities across the country, the messages of Hollywood began to reach a mass audience and forge a nationwide popular culture. Movie stars and their films provided models for how to adopt new styles of manhood and womanhood. Douglas Fairbanks showed middle-class men how to break free from the humdrum of white-collar work into the world of leisure. His attire of sports clothes changed the way men dressed in their off-work hours. Female stars, such as Clara Bow, epitomized the flapper and taught female viewers how to be "naughty but nice."

Ironically, as the nation closed its doors to immigrants, foreigners on screen captivated the imagination of a native-born population drawn to the allure of the outsider. Movie stars like Greta Garbo from Sweden, Dolores del Rio, Lupe Velez, and Ramon Navarro from Mexico, and Rudolph Valentino from Italy drew audiences with their foreignness. And yet, because movies were silent until the late 1920s, their accented voices were not heard. Sound arrived in the late twenties, bringing the voices and dialects of ethnic performers into the movies. For native-born Americans watching films in small towns and cities, sound movies brought the diverse voices of the cities into their communities. For immigrants, sound movies carried their own familiar accents and allowed for a greater sense of identification with the stars on the screen.

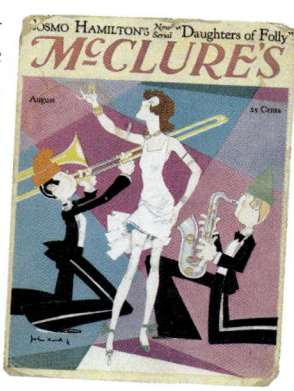

The Harlem Renaissance

While Hollywood in the 1920s developed on the West Coast, a flourishing center of African American culture emerged on the East Coast. The black arts movement known as the Harlem Renaissance drew on European as well as African and African American artistic traditions and gathered white as well as black intellectuals and artists. The young black poet Arna Bontemps was among the many artists drawn to Harlem. In 1924 he described Harlem as "a foretaste of paradise. A blue haze descended

■ Rudolph Valentino dances the tango in this famous scene from the 1920 film *The Four Horsemen of the Apocalypse*. Films in the 1920s featured exotic locales with foreign stars such as the Italian-born Valentino. In keeping with the public's taste for grandeur, lavish movie palaces emerged in cities across the country.

Roaring 20's

at night and with it strings of fairy lights on the broad avenues. From the window of a small room in an apartment on Fifth and 129th Street, I looked over the rooftops of Negrodom and tried to believe my eyes. What a city! What a world!"

Harlem Renaissance writers laid claim to their identity as Americans while articulating the culture, aesthetics, and experiences of African Americans. The poet Langston Hughes challenged white America to accept African Americans in his 1925 poem "I, too, sing America:"

> I, too, sing America
> I am the darker brother
> They send me to eat in the kitchen
> When company comes,
> But I laugh
> And eat well
> And grow strong
> Tomorrow,
> I'll be at the table
> When company comes
> Nobody'll dare
> Say to me,
> "Eat in the kitchen,"

Then.
Besides,
They'll see how beautiful I am
And be ashamed—
I, too, am America.

The music of black America was such an important marker of the era that it provided the decade with its most lasting moniker, the Jazz Age. Emanating not from Harlem but from New Orleans, Chicago, and St. Louis, jazz was, nevertheless, central to the black arts movement and the emerging national culture. With the help of the recording industry and radio, jazz and the blues began to reach a wide audience, primarily among blacks but increasingly among whites as well. Blues lyrics expressed themes of working-class protest and resistance to racism. Women who sang the blues, including Bessie Smith, Ma Rainey, and Ethel Waters, asserted their sexuality, their passion for men or for women, their resistance to male domination, their sorrows, and their strength.

Radios and Autos: Transforming Leisure

Radio played a major role in linking people across regions through shared information, advertising, and entertainment. Annual radio production increased from 190,000 in 1923 to almost 5 million in 1929. Radios brought jazz and other forms of popular music to the airwaves, transforming the way music was enjoyed in American homes. Americans became more inclined to listen to music on their Victrolas and radios than to make music themselves. By the mid-1920s, sales of records surpassed those of sheet music; production and sales of pianos also dropped precipitously.

The number of radio stations soared from thirty in 1922 to 556 the following year, and national broadcasts began to supersede local ones. Airwaves became so cluttered that by the mid-1920s, the federal government, through the leadership of Secretary of Commerce Herbert Hoover, created the Federal Radio Commission to regulate and organize access. Meanwhile, American Telephone and Telegraph (AT&T) and the National Broadcasting Company (NBC) combined to form the first national network system, which gave programs and advertisers access to audiences across the country.

■ Poet Langston Hughes as a student at Lincoln University, Pennsylvania, in 1927. One of the major literary figures of the Harlem Renaissance, Hughes expressed the hopes, dreams, and sorrows of black Americans.

As radios entered millions of American homes, automobiles began to extend the mobility of Americans. The automobile offered the possibility of commuting to work without relying on public transportation, encouraging the expansion of suburban communities. The number of passenger cars in the nation more than tripled during the twenties. The Federal Highways Act of 1916 had produced a network of roads all over the country, providing construction jobs and a slew of new roadside businesses, from restaurants to garages. Automobiles also stimulated the tourist industry; Florida, California, and Arizona became vacation destinations in this period.

Automobile production also revolutionized the consumer industry. The pragmatic Henry Ford built inexpensive, functional automobiles that he expected his workers to be

"Oh, I *beg* your pardon! I thought you were extinct."

■ This cartoon from *The New Yorker* reflects the intrusive aspects of tourism that developed in the Southwest, as well as the widespread erroneous assumption that Native American communities had died out by the twentieth century.

able to purchase and keep. But Ford faced serious competition from General Motors' Alfred P. Sloan Jr., who developed the concept of **planned obsolescence** and put a new emphasis on auto styling to encourage customers to trade in their old cars for newer and more expensive models.

The automobile was part of a consumer society increasingly focused on leisure, pleasure, and intimacy. Courtship patterns changed, and sexual activity increased as young couples abandoned the front porch for the back seat. Women gained new freedom and autonomy when they, too, took the wheel. Moralists worried that the automobile would provide youth with too much independence and privacy. One juvenile court judge announced that "the automobile has become a house of prostitution on wheels."

Science on Trial

Although advances in technology and medicine improved the quality of life for many Americans in the early twentieth century, scientific efforts to alter the natural world did not always lead to expected social benefits. One case in point was the engineering project to build levees along the Mississippi River to prevent flooding. Scientific ideas were also tested in the nation's courtrooms. Two major cases, the Scopes trial and the Supreme Court's decision in *Buck v. Bell*, subjected scientific ideas to judicial and cultural scrutiny. Although decisions in both cases resolved the immediate legal issues, the questions they raised continued to generate controversy and debate throughout the rest of the century.

Wembridge, "Petting and the Campus"

The Great Flood of 1927

For half a century the engineers of the Mississippi River Commission had adhered to a policy of building levees, assuming that strong barricades against the river's banks would prevent flooding. Presumably, the levees would allow the rich soil of the floodplains along the river to be settled and farmed rather than leaving the basins empty to provide places for the river to expand and contract with seasonal rains. But the levee policy proved to be a disastrous example of human efforts to master the natural contours of the land. In March 1927, the rains came, and the river rose. Public authorities and river experts assured those who watched and worried that the levees would hold. They were wrong. Torrential rains caused the river to rage across the levees and the land beyond, submerging 26,000 square miles of prime farmland in 170 counties across seven states. More than 900,000 people were forced from their homes. The flood caused more than $100 million in crop losses and $23 million in livestock deaths. Journalists at the time called it "America's greatest peacetime disaster."

With the help of the Department of Commerce and the National Guard, the Red Cross set up 154 relief camps for flood victims. The camps were racially segregated. Refugees in the white camps were free to come and go and had more comfortable and generous accommodations

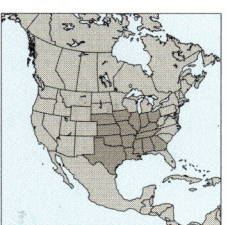

■ MAP 21.1
THE MISSISSIPPI RIVER FLOOD OF 1927   The Mississippi River flood in 1927 sent water across a huge area of the South, extending as far west as Texas, covering most of Louisiana, Arkansas, and Mississippi, and reaching north into Kansas, Illinois, and Indiana.

and rations than those in the black camps. Armed guards patrolled the camps for black refugees and restricted people attempting to enter or leave. Black laborers had to register and give the names of their employers to receive any shelter or assistance. Federal authorities, including Secretary of Commerce Herbert Hoover, refused to intervene in local camp management. As a result, southern whites were able to force black sharecroppers back to work on their plantations. Despite the prisonlike conditions, many African American refugees managed to escape and made their way north.

The Triumph of Eugenics: *Buck v. Bell*

Many Americans, including large numbers of policymakers, believed in white racial superiority. Supposedly scientific theories of race bolstered claims that distinct, biologically based characteristics divided humans into superior and inferior races. These theories had no scientific merit and were later thoroughly discredited. But in the 1920s, these dubious theories of racial superiority supported measures such as immigration restriction and eugenic sterilization laws. Eugenics was a pseudo-science based on notions of racial superiority. Eugenicists claimed that the Anglo-Saxon Protestant "race" was superior to all others, including Jews, Southern Europeans, and Catholics, as well as nonwhites. Racial superiority, according to eugenic reformers, might be compromised not only by mixing with inferior groups but also by the propagation of individuals whose mental or moral condition rendered them inferior, and whose offspring would diminish the quality of the Anglo-Saxon "stock."

Several states had enacted eugenic laws that allowed the state to sterilize "inferior" individuals without their knowledge or consent. These laws authorized government and medical officials to determine whether or not an individual was inferior, or "feebleminded," and to order that the person be sterilized. Opponents of eugenic sterilization, mostly Catholic activists, challenged these laws in several states. In an effort to put an end to such challenges, eugenic advocates decided to test the constitutionality of the Virginia compulsory sterilization law. Their plan was to bring the case all the way to the U.S. Supreme Court, which they expected to uphold the law.

The proponents of the law selected the case of Carrie Buck, in part because she was white. Eugenic advocates did not want race to be at the center of the case, especially because eugenic sterilization laws did not target particular races; they simply targeted the "feebleminded." Feeblemindedness was a loosely defined criterion often used to label poor, immigrant, or minority women who were sexually active. At the age of seventeen, Carrie Buck, the daughter of an unmarried woman, was raped and became pregnant; as a result, she was sent to a state institution for the feebleminded. Buck was labeled as feebleminded because she had borne a child out of wedlock and was therefore deemed morally unfit for parenthood.

Carrie Buck was sterilized in 1927. The following year, Buck's sister Doris was taken to the Virginia Colony for Epileptics and the Feebleminded and sterilized at age sixteen. She was told that she had had an appendectomy. Later, Doris Buck married and tried to get pregnant. None of the physicians she consulted told her why she could not conceive. She finally learned the truth in 1979. "I broke down and cried. My husband and I wanted children desperately. We were crazy about them. I never knew what they'd done to me."

No evidence established that Carrie Buck, her mother, or her daughter was below normal intelligence. Buck's daughter died as a child, but her teachers described the girl as bright. In writing the majority opinion for the Supreme Court that upheld the law, Justice Oliver Wendell Holmes wrote, "Three generations of imbeciles are enough." Within the next few years, thirty states had compulsory sterilization laws, and the number of operations rose dramatically. In the 1930s, the Nazis in Germany modeled their sterilization policies on the California law. Finally, in the 1980s, a rare alliance of traditional Catholics and feminist activists succeeded in repealing compulsory sterilization laws.

Science, Religion, and the Scopes Trial

Populist leader and longtime reformer William Jennings Bryan was among those troubled by eugenics. In his last public crusade, Bryan opposed another scientific theory in a courtroom in Dayton, Tennessee, in July 1925. Tennessee had recently enacted the Butler Act, which made it illegal to teach the theory of evolution in the schools. The American Civil Liberties Union (ACLU) announced that it would defend any teacher charged with violating the Butler Act. A twenty-four-year-old science teacher from the local high school, John Thomas Scopes, agreed to test the law. Using a state-approved textbook, Scopes taught a lesson on evolutionary theory on April 24 to his Rhea County High School science class. He was arrested on May 7 and quickly indicted by a grand jury. Bryan agreed to represent the prosecution; famed Chicago criminal lawyer Clarence Darrow headed the ACLU's team of defense lawyers.

Bryan did not oppose science, but he objected to its misapplication. Darrow did not oppose religion. But he argued that religious fundamentalists—"creationists" who believed in the literal interpretation of the Bible—should not determine the way science was taught in the schools. Reporters at the time, and since, cast the trial as a struggle between religion and science, with rural and small-town Americans on the side of creationism and secular urbanites supporting evolution. But the divide was not so clear-cut. Almost all advo-

> *Almost all advocates on both sides of the Scopes trial were Christians who disagreed over how to interpret the Bible.*

The Rise and Fall of Man

■ This satiric political cartoon, published during the Scopes trial, depicts the theory of evolution as the development of humans from their origins as apes to the "survival of the fittest," portrayed as William Jennings Bryan. Bryan argued the case against evolution in the famous courtroom drama.

cates on both sides of the Scopes trial were Christians who disagreed over how to interpret the Bible. They were also believers in science; those opposed to the teaching of evolution considered it to be an unscientific theory.

The Scopes trial also contained elements of popular entertainment. Dubbed "the Monkey trial" because Darwin's theory of evolution demonstrated that humans evolved from an earlier primate form from which monkeys and chimpanzees also descended, the trial was one of the first national media events. The judge invited reporters from around the country, including broadcast journalists. The Scopes trial was the first jury trial broadcast on live radio. More than 900 spectators packed the courtroom, and hundreds more gathered in the streets, where a carnival atmosphere prevailed, complete with souvenir stands, food vendors, itinerant preachers, and hucksters, including numerous chimpanzees accompanied by their trainers.

The jury reached a guilty verdict in just nine minutes. Bryan technically won the case, but most reporters deemed the spectacle a victory for Darrow and the teaching of evolution. That assessment was premature. The Tennessee Supreme Court overturned the verdict on a technicality, robbing Darrow of his chance to take the case to the U.S. Supreme Court. Before the trial, most science textbooks included discussion of evolution; after the trial, material on evolution began to disappear. Laws against the teaching of evolution remained on the books until the U.S. Supreme Court overturned an Arkansas law in 1968.

The Scopes trial did not resolve the debate between creationists and evolutionists, and the controversy continued throughout the century. As late as 2000, the Board of Education in Kansas ruled that creationism and evolution were both unproven theories and that both could be taught in the schools.

Consumer Dreams and Nightmares

Unlike faith and politics, the material prosperity of many in the Jazz Age seemed a unifying force. During the 1920s, spending on recreation nearly doubled. Faith in continuing prosperity promoted the extension of consumer credit to unprecedented heights. Previously, the only major item routinely purchased on credit was a house. But in the twenties, installment buying became the rage for a wide range of consumer goods, from autos and radios to household appliances. Consumer debt rose from $2.6 billion in 1919 to $7.1 billion in 1929. As one official in a midwestern loan company remarked, "People don't think anything nowadays of borrowing sums they'd never have thought of borrowing in the old days. They will assume an obligation for $2,000 today as calmly as they would have borrowed $300 or $400 in 1890." This habit of buying on credit boosted the standard of living for many but also left families in a precarious situation and vulnerable to the vagaries of the broader economy. The stock market crash and subsequent depression made that vulnerability vividly clear.

Marketing the Good Life

DOCUMENT
Advertisements from 1925 and 1927

Advertising fueled much of the new spending. As one contemporary reporter noted, "Advertising is to business what fertilizer is to a farm." According to advertisers, consumer goods promised health, beauty, success, and the means to eliminate personal and embarrassing flaws, such as bad breath or dandruff. Cigarette companies used advertising to promote smoking as a symbol of independence for women and as a means to achieve beauty. Clever advertising campaigns promised women that if they would "reach for a Lucky Strike" instead of a sweet, they would remain slim, healthy, and sexually appealing.

Advertising also fostered a vision of big business as a benevolent force, promoting individual happiness. In his 1925 best-seller *The Man That Nobody Knows*, advertising executive Bruce Barton portrayed Jesus as a businessman who gathered a group of twelve followers who believed in his enterprise and, through effective public relations and advertising, sold his product to the world. The consumer culture had its temples: movie palaces, department stores, and the 1920s innovation, the shopping center. Kansas City's elegant Country Club Plaza was the first shopping center in the nation.

A much less successful venture was the Florida land boom, based on fantasies of a consumer paradise. When World War I closed off routes to the European playgrounds of American elites, shrewd developers in the sunshine state sparked a frenzy of investment in Florida real estate. To create "earthly paradises" and resorts, developers rushed to construct roads and find new land on which to build.

Human folly and nature's fury contributed to the Florida land boom and bust. The boom peaked in 1925 and quickly collapsed. In 1926 a hurricane hit Miami, killing 130 people and causing millions of dollars of property damage. Another hurricane in 1928 killed more than 1,000 people and destroyed several towns. The destruction wrought by the hurricanes, and the exposure of exaggerated promotional advertisements and inflated prices, quickly put an end to land speculation in Florida.

■ In the 1920s, advertisers used sexualized images to sell all sorts of products. This advertisement for automobile tires provides very little information about the product but evokes images of fun and romance to capture consumers' attention.

Writers and Critics

Some social critics claimed that consumerism fostered not only economic disasters such as the Florida land boom but also a stifling conformity. Sinclair Lewis was one of several novelists of the twenties whose books expressed biting criticism of the frantic pursuit of material gain and status. George Babbitt, the protagonist of Lewis's novel *Babbitt* (1922), struggles to become accepted and successful in his small town by conforming to the empty materialism and standardized opinions accepted and prized by his neighbors.

F. Scott Fitzgerald wrote not about small-town conformity, as Lewis did, but about the modern urban life that was its antithesis. Fitzgerald glamorized, criticized, and in many ways embodied the giddy nightlife and status seeking of the Jazz Age. Born in St. Paul, Minnesota, into a family of modest means, he grew up admiring and emulating the wealthy. He married glamorous flapper Zelda Sayre, daughter of a prominent Alabama judge, and together they embraced the dizzy, indulgent, free-spirited life of the decade. But Fitzgerald's novels, including *This Side of Paradise* (1920), *The Beautiful and the Damned* (1922), and *The Great Gatsby* (1925), criticized the era's obsessions with success, glamour, consumerism, advertising, and status. The Fitzgeralds, along with other writers who were critical of American superficiality and conformity, moved to Paris. Eventually, the life Fitzgerald both lived and criticized caught up with him. By the end of the decade, he—like the nation—was broken by his excesses. In 1931 he came home to Baltimore an alcoholic; Zelda was diagnosed with schizophrenia and spent the rest of her life in mental institutions.

Poverty amid Plenty

Most Americans in the 1920s were neither investing in Florida real estate nor frequenting expatriate American writer Gertrude Stein's Paris salon. Even so, they were not immune to the desires and dreams that the consumer society sparked. The middle class and the more prosperous members of the working class enjoyed many of the comforts, amusements, and appliances that the booming economy made available. The poor, by contrast, struggled just to make ends meet. Throughout the twenties, the nation's poorest people continued to be the most mobile, moving in search of jobs, security, and a place they could settle and call home. Henry Crews, son of a white Georgia sharecropper, longed for "that single house where you were born, where you lived out your childhood . . . your anchor in the world." But he never had such a

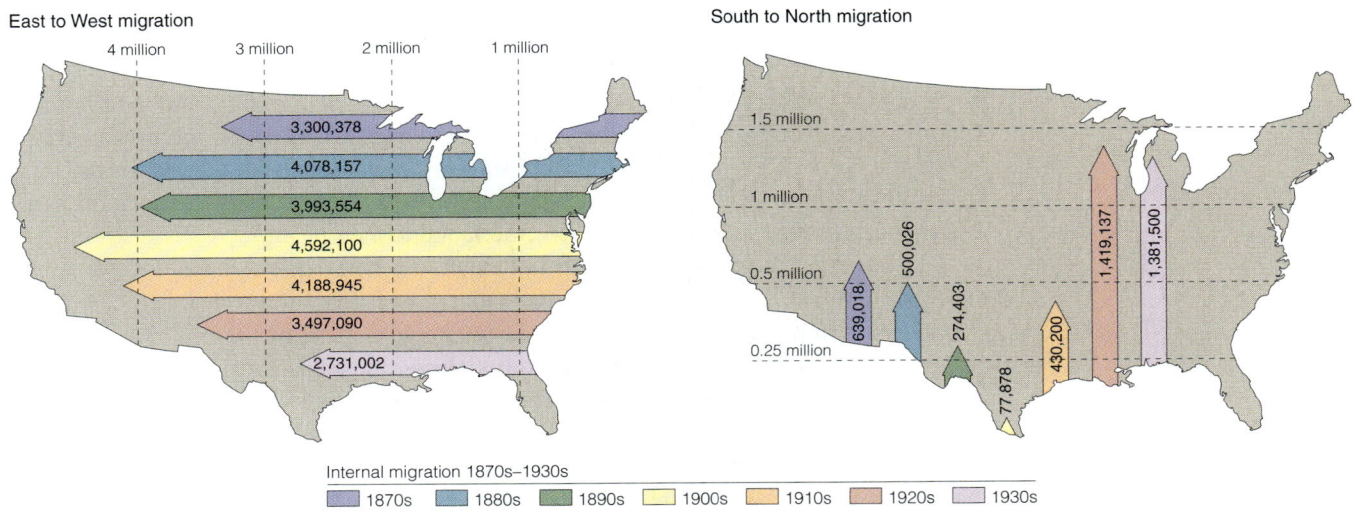

■ **MAP 21.2**
AMERICANS ON THE MOVE, 1870s–1930s Between the 1870s and the 1930s, millions of Americans moved around the country, mostly from East to West, but also from South to North.

home. Like that of many other hardworking sharecroppers and factory workers, his family moved frequently in search of a better life, a dream that often proved elusive.

Sharecropping required hard work and careful planning to carve out a meager life, but many did so with pride. Ed Brown, a young black sharecropper, had no formal education but considered himself "pretty schemy." He worked on six different plantations, moving about in search of better circumstances or to escape from debt or threats of violence. Although he and his wife, Willie Mae, were never able to buy a place of their own, they did improve their circumstances over time. When they finally got out of debt and secured a bit of cash, they used it to adorn their meager cabin. In 1929 they bought an old Model T Ford. But finding it too costly to maintain, they swapped it for a cow and a butter churn and dasher, which provided more practical benefits. Meanwhile, Ed took odd jobs to earn extra money, while Willie Mae took care of the children, picked cotton, took in laundry, and, as Ed noted with appreciation, kept "things . . . lookin very pretty."

Industrial workers struggled throughout the decade, especially in a political climate hostile to unions. With the crushing of labor radicalism in the Red Scare after World War I, union organizing and strikes declined. But workers continued to protest low wages and poor working conditions. In March 1929, young women textile workers in Elizabethton, a small town nestled in the Blue Ridge Mountains of eastern Tennessee, closed down the American Glanzstoff plant in protest against low wages, petty rules, and arrogant employers. Soon, the protest spread to textile mills across the region. At Glanzstoff, the strikers returned to work when the company promised better pay and agreed not to discriminate against union members. But the employers broke their promises, so the women struck again. The governor sent in the National Guard, armed with machine guns. More than 1,000 people were arrested in confrontations with the troops.

The Stock Market Crash

The symbolic end of the 1920s arrived on "Black Tuesday," October 29, 1929, when the inflated and overextended stock market came crashing down. In one day, stocks fell in value $14 billion. By the end of the year, stock prices were down 50 percent; by 1932, they had dropped another 30 percent. In three years, $74 billion of the nation's wealth had vanished. The effect on the economy was catastrophic. Industrial production fell by half. More than 100,000 businesses went bankrupt. Banks failed at an alarming rate: more than 2,000 closed in 1931 alone. Unemployment rose to staggering levels, reaching 25 percent by 1932 and rarely dropping below 17 percent throughout the 1930s.

In keeping with the social policies that had prevailed throughout the 1920s, relief efforts were slim. No federal relief or welfare, no unemployment insurance, no Social Security, no job programs existed to help those who had lost their jobs, their savings, and their homes. Although many wealthy people lost their fortunes, which had been built on speculative investments, the poor suffered the most. People who lost their homes and farms moved into makeshift shelters in shantytowns, which they nicknamed "**Hoovervilles**" to mock the ineffectual efforts of President Herbert Hoover to respond to their plight.

The causes of the stock market crash and the decade-long depression that followed were complex and varied. Stock prices had risen dramatically, especially at the end of the 1920s. Speculators had been purchasing stocks on 10 percent margins, meaning they put down only 10 percent of the cost and borrowed the rest from brokers and banks. The popularity of installment buying in the consumer goods market had devastating effects when applied in this manner to the stock market. Investors expected to get rich quickly by selling their stocks at a higher price and paying back the loans from their huge profits. This system worked for a few years, encouraging investors with limited funds to make risky investments in the hope of gaining large fortunes. When the price of stocks spiraled out of control, far beyond their actual value, creditors demanded repayment of their loans, and investors were unable to pay their debts.

INTERPRETING HISTORY

Mario Puzo, *The Fortunate Pilgrim*

Italians, like most other European immigrants, established households where almost everyone worked to support the family. Fathers earned wages, mothers often took in boarders or did piecework at home to earn extra money, and sons and daughters found jobs in sweatshops and factories. Most immigrants married within their own ethnic groups. Often, immigrant families were torn by fierce generational conflicts, as old-world parents tried to maintain traditional ways while their American children struggled to break free. This generational struggle beset nearly every immigrant group.

Mario Puzo, the Italian American novelist best known for The Godfather, was among the many children of immigrants to express the cultures and experiences of newcomers through the arts. His autobiographical novel The Fortunate Pilgrim is a portrait of life in the Italian community of New York City in the early years of the century. The book depicts the struggles and triumphs of an Italian immigrant family. The men work long hours for meager wages while the women struggle to maintain the family. Mothers gather on tenement stoops to bemoan the behavior of their Americanized children, yet they dream the American dream of a better life. At the end of the book, the mother's dream comes true, and the family moves to a suburban home in Long Island. Yet it is a bittersweet ending, for she and her family realize the loss of the vibrant community that, for all its hardship and poverty, had sustained them in the city.

Each tenement was a village square; each had its group of women, all in black, sitting on stools and boxes and doing more

Mario Puzo, author of *The Fortunate Pilgrim* and *The Godfather*.

than gossip. They recalled ancient history, argued morals and social law, always taking their precedents from the mountain village in southern Italy they had escaped, fled from many years ago. And with what relish their favorite imaginings! Now: What if their stern fathers were transported by some miracle to face the problems *they* faced every day? Or their mothers of the quick and heavy hands? What shrieks if *they* as daughters had dared as these American children dared? If *they* had presumed.

The women talked of their children as they would of strangers. It was a favorite topic, the corruption of the innocent by the new land. Now: Felicia, who lived around the corner of 31st Street. What type of daughter was she who did not cut short her honeymoon on news of her godmother's illness, the summons issued by her own mother? A real whore. No no, they did not mince words. Felicia's mother herself told the story. And a son, poor man, who could not wait another year to marry when his father so commanded? Ahhh, the disrespect. *Figlio disgraziato.* Never could this pass in Italy. The father would kill his arrogant son; yes, kill him. And the daughter? In Italy—Felicia's mother swore in a voice still trembling with passion, though this had all happened three years ago, the godmother recovered, the grandchildren the light of her life—ah, in Italy the mother would pull the whore out of her bridal chamber, drag her to the hospital bed by the hair of her head. Ah, Italia, Italia; how the world changed and for the worse. What madness was it that made them leave such a land? Where fathers commanded and mothers were treated with respect by their children.

Each in turn told a story of insolence and defiance, themselves heroic, long-suffering, the children spitting Lucifers saved by an application of Italian discipline—the razor strap or the *Tackeril*. And at the end of each story each woman recited her requiem. *Mannaggi a America!*—Damn America. But in the hot summer night their voices were filled with hope, with a vigor never sounded in their homeland. Here now was money in the bank, children who could read and write, grandchildren who would be professors if all went well. They spoke with guilty loyalty of customs they had themselves trampled into dust.

Questions

1. What seem to be the particular contrasts between cultural values in a southern Italian village and in New York City that these mothers worry most about?
2. Can you think of other, more recent immigrant groups in the United States who might be wrestling with similar dilemmas arising from inevitable cultural tensions in the immigrant experience? ■

Source: Mario Puzo, *The Fortunate Pilgrim* (New York: Random House, 1997), pp. 10–11.

The collapse of the stock market alone would not necessarily have caused such a severe and prolonged depression. Poor decision making by financial and political leaders exacerbated underlying weaknesses in the economy. The Federal Reserve curtailed the amount of money in circulation and raised interest rates, making it more difficult for people to get loans and pay off their debts. These policies had profound worldwide implications and contributed to an international crisis. Banks in Germany and Austria, for example, depended on loans from the United States, and many went bankrupt, causing a ripple effect across Europe. The Hawley-Smoot Tariff of 1930 also contributed to the downward spiral. The new high tariff was intended to protect American commodities from competition from cheaper foreign goods. Foreign governments retaliated by raising their own tariffs to keep out American goods. These monetary and trade policies backfired, and the economic crisis spread throughout the western industrial world.

"Prosperity of the 1920s and the Great Depression"

Within the United States, the unequal distribution of wealth exacerbated the effects of the economic downturn. The nation may have looked prosperous, but most of the wealth was concentrated in the hands of a small number of people. If average Americans had been able to buy more cars, household appliances, and other products, those industries might have survived, and the economy might have recovered more quickly. Political leaders, and the business-oriented public policies they had promoted throughout the decade, left the country ill prepared to address the crisis and meet the needs of families deprived of their means of livelihood.

Conclusion

The stock market collapse, and the prolonged depression that followed, revealed the flaws in the economic system that spurred the apparent prosperity of the 1920s. Beneath the visible affluence was the hidden poverty that prevailed throughout the decade. National leaders promoted business interests and paid little attention to social welfare, the environment, or the need to regulate the economy. By the end of the 1920s, it was clear that Prohibition was a dismal failure and that the federal government was ill equipped to enforce it.

Although political reform withered, cultural vitality flowered. Hollywood emerged as a major industry, and the Jazz Age reflected the widespread appeal of African American music. A black arts movement flourished, centered in Harlem, and writers—disenchanted with the status quo—gathered in Greenwich Village or moved to France. Across the country, a youth culture challenged the gender and sexual mores of the past. Consumer culture expanded as increasing numbers of families purchased cars, radios, and new fashions. Few who were involved in the private preoccupations of the decade could have foreseen the disaster ahead, when the stock market crashed and the Depression set in.

Sites to Visit

Harlem: Mecca of the New Negro
etext.lib.virginia.edu/harlem/
   This site is the online text of the March 1925 *Survey Graphic Harlem Number*, which includes writings of many Harlem Renaissance writers.

Calvin Coolidge
www.ipl.org/div/POTUS/ccoolidge.html
   This site contains basic information about Coolidge's election and presidency and online biography.

Warren G. Harding
www.ipl.org/div/POTUS/wgharding.html
   This site contains basic information about Harding's election and presidency and online biography.

Herbert Hoover
www.ipl.org/div/POTUS/hchoover.html
   This site contains basic information about Hoover's election and presidency and online biography.

Harlem, 1900–1940: An African American Community
www.si.umich.edu/CHICO/Harlem/

This site of the New York Public Library's Schomburg Center for Research in Black Culture includes information and articles about the history of Harlem as a center of African American cultural life.

Scopes Trial
xroads.virginia.edu/~UG97/inherit/1925home.html

This site from the University of Virginia's American Studies program includes images, documents, and articles relating to the Scopes Trial.

Temperance and Prohibition
prohibition.osu.edu/

This site from Ohio State University covers the history of temperance and prohibition in the United States.

Jazz Age: Flapper Culture and Style
www.geocities.com/flapper_culture/

This site includes images, descriptions, and information on famous "flappers" of the 1920s.

For Further Reading

General
Ann Douglas, *Terrible Honesty: Mongrel Manhattan in the 1920s* (1995).
Lynn Dumenil, *The Modern Temper: American Culture and Society in the 1920s* (1995).
David J. Goldberg, *Discontented America: The United States in the 1920s* (1999).
Robert S. Lynd and Helen Merrell Lynd. *Middletown* (1929).

The Business of Politics
Kendrick A. Clements, *Hoover, Conservation, and Consumerism: Engineering the Good Life* (2000).
John Kenneth Galbraith, *The Great Crash, 1929* (1955).
William E. Leuchtenberg, *The Perils of Prosperity, 1914–1932* (1958, 1993).
David Farber, *Sloan Rules: Afred P. Sloan and the Triumph of General Motors* (2002).

The Decline of Reform
Nancy Cott, *The Grounding of Modern Feminism* (1987).
Matthew Frye Jacobson, *Whiteness of a Different Color: European Immigrants and the Alchemy of Race* (1998).
Desmond S. King, *Making Americans: Immigration, Race, and the Origins of the Diverse Democracy* (2000).
Nancy MacLean, *Behind the Mask of Chivalry: The Making of the Second Ku Klux Klan* (1994).

Hollywood and Harlem
Beth Bailey, *From Front Porch to Back Seat: Courtship in Twentieth-Century America* (1988).
Ray Batchelor, *Henry Ford, Mass Production, Modernism and Design* (1994).
Nathan Irvin Huggins, *The Harlem Renaissance* (1971).
Virginia Scharff, *Taking the Wheel: Women and the Coming of the Motor Age* (1991).

Science on Trial
John M. Barry, *Rising Tide: The Great Mississippi Flood of 1927 and How It Changed America* (1997).
Daniel Kevles, *In the Name of Eugenics: Genetics and the Uses of Human Heredity* (1985).
Garry Wills, *Under God: Religion and American Politics* (1990).

Consumer Dreams and Nightmares
William Frazer and John J. Guthrie Jr., *The Florida Land Boom: Speculation, Money, and the Banks* (1995).
Jacqueline Jones, *The Dispossessed: America's Underclass from the Civil War to the Present* (1992).
Jackson Lears, *Fables of Abundance: A Cultural History of Advertising in America* (1994).

For quizzes and other resources on these topics, go to www.longmanamericanhistory.com.

1930	Beginning of construction of Hoover Dam Hawley-Smoot Tariff 1,352 U.S. banks fail
1931	Nine young African Americans (the "Scottsboro Boys") arrested on charges of rape
1932	Black unemployment rates reach 50 percent "Bonus Army" marches on Washington, D.C.
1933	Initial New Deal ("Hundred Days") legislation: AAA, FERA, CCC, TVA, NIRA Adolf Hitler becomes chancellor of Germany Twenty-First Amendment ratified
1934	Indian Reorganization Act Securities and Exchange Commission (SEC) created Federal Housing Authority created
1935	National Labor Relations (Wagner) Act Social Security Act Committee of Industrial Organizations (CIO) organized
1936	Civil war in Spain Hoover Dam on Colorado River completed, creating Lake Mead
1937	Japan invades China 170,000 workers participate in sit-down strikes FDR's court-packing plan fails
1938	Boxer Joe Louis defeats Max Schmeling Fair Labor Standards Act Congress creates Special Committee on Un-American Activities
1939	First meeting of El Congreso de Pueblos de Habla Española Germany invades Poland World War II begins
1940	Smith Act Germany invades Denmark, Norway, Holland, Belgium, Luxembourg, and France
1941	A. Philip Randolph's March on Washington Movement FDR's "Four Freedoms" speech Japan bombs Pearl Harbor
1942	Executive Order 9066 (internment of Japanese and Japanese Americans) Congress of Racial Equality (CORE) founded Japan conquers the Philippines

PART EIGHT

From Depression and War to World Power, 1929–1953

THE GREAT DEPRESSION AND WORLD WAR II TESTED AMERICANS' faith in their federal government to a degree unmatched in the nation's history. Economic collapse in the 1930s and the threat of Nazi and Japanese aggression from 1941 to 1945 presented challenges beyond the reach of ordinary citizens, local communities, and businesses acting alone. The federal government began to take more responsibility for economic and social well-being at home and for the spread of American values around the world.

The Great Depression resulted in a fundamental reordering of American politics. President Franklin Delano Roosevelt (FDR), who took office in 1933, believed that the federal government must assume an active role in banking, agriculture, and social welfare. He sponsored a large number of federal initiatives, known collectively as the New Deal. The New Deal aimed to put people back to work, restore faith in American businesses, boost purchasing power among consumers, and cushion the effects of economic downturns on industrial workers.

The effects of the New Deal were uneven. Many workers, including domestic servants, agricultural laborers, and part-time and seasonal employees, did not qualify for Social Security and other benefits. In the South, government policies that discouraged landowners from planting crops led to the displacement of many black and white sharecropping families. On the other hand, employees of many large companies won higher wages and improved job security as a result of militant labor protests. African American civil rights activists, local communist organizations such as urban Unemployed Councils, and southern sharecroppers' and tenants' unions gave voice to the groups hit hardest by the Depression.

The New Deal did not end the Depression. On the morning of December 7, 1941, the Japanese conducted a surprise air attack on the U.S. Pacific naval fleet stationed in Pearl Harbor, Hawaii. Americans reacted with shock and outrage to what the president called this "day of infamy." The U.S. entry into World War II put large numbers of Americans back to work, many of them in the expanding defense industries.

The conflict brought Americans together in shared hardship, sacrifice, and national purpose. At the same time, the war placed strains on the social fabric. All over the country, family members separated from one another to search for work. In the Midwest, blacks and whites competed for scarce wartime resources, such as housing. On the West Coast, more than 100,000 Japanese immigrants and U.S. citizens of Japanese descent were forced into internment camps.

Elected to an unprecedented fourth term in 1944, Roosevelt proved to be a commanding leader during wartime as well as economic depression. In the last stages of the war, the president met several times with his British and Soviet counterparts, Winston Churchill and Josef Stalin, to plan for the postwar reconstruction of Europe and Asia. Roosevelt's death in April 1945 catapulted Vice President Harry S. Truman into the presidency. Germany surrendered to the Allies the next month. In August 1945, the new president authorized the dropping of atomic bombs on the Japanese cities of Hiroshima and Nagasaki, effectively ending the war in the Pacific. Together, the two bombs killed 120,000 Japanese civilians and wounded at least 130,000 more. The Atomic Age ushered in a new chapter in the history of human warfare.

Together with its allies, the United States emerged victorious from the war, but unlike its allies, America escaped physical destruction. Yet in many respects the postwar world was radically different from the world of the 1930s. The Soviet Union, an ally in the war against Germany and Japan, emerged as America's greatest enemy. The development of weapons of mass destruction introduced a new and profound threat to the natural environment, as well as to humans. To secure its supremacy in world affairs, the United States helped to form the North Atlantic Treaty Organization (NATO). For the first time, Americans were part of a multinational peacetime alliance, one that required them to defend a member of the alliance even if they themselves were not attacked.

World War II also profoundly altered life in the United States. The perceived communist threat led some Americans to suspect domestic groups of internal subversion: African Americans agitating for their civil rights, labor leaders attempting to organize southern factories, and leftists who expressed support for communism in general and the Soviet Union in particular. Supported by government contracts, the defense industry became an integral part of the nation's economy.

Recovering quickly from the disruptions of war, returning soldiers and their wives hoped to settle down to a normal family life. These couples produced the baby boom, a generation that shaped American culture and society in significant ways. In the new and growing suburbs, many (predominantly white) Americans achieved their dream of home ownership, and businesses found plenty of room to expand in new industrial parks. Yet, not all Americans shared in this newfound prosperity and security, and not all were willing to forgo their rights to free speech and free assembly in the struggle against communism.

1943 Smith-Connally Act
Zoot-suit riots in Los Angeles. Attacks on blacks in Detroit

1944 Normandy invasion on D-Day (June 6)
Servicemen's Readjustment Act (GI Bill)

1945 Harry S. Truman becomes president upon death of Roosevelt
First test of atomic bomb, Alamogordo, New Mexico
Atomic bombs dropped on Hiroshima and Nagasaki
V-E Day (May 7); V-J Day (Sept. 2)
United Nations created

1946 *Morgan v. West Virginia* outlaws segregation in interstate transportation
Winston Churchill gives "Iron Curtain" speech, Fulton, Missouri

1947 Jackie Robinson joins Brooklyn Dodgers
Taft-Hartley Act
Truman Doctrine of containing communism announced

1948 New Mexico and Arizona grant Indians right to vote
Modern state of Israel founded
Armed Services desegregated
Organization of American States (OAS) founded

1949 Billy Graham launches his first evangelical crusade in Los Angeles
Establishment of People's Republic of China
USSR acquires nuclear weapons

1950 North Korean troops invade South Korea
Internal Security Act of 1950
Senator Joseph McCarthy accuses State Department of harboring communists

1951 Ethel and Julius Rosenberg convicted of treason

1952 McCarran-Walter Act
Puerto Rico becomes self-governing commonwealth

1953 Korean War ends
Soviet leader Josef Stalin dies

CHAPTER 22

Hardship and Hope in the 1930s: The Great Depression

CHAPTER OUTLINE

The Great Depression

Presidential Responses to the Depression

The New Deal

A New Political Culture

Conclusion

Sites to Visit

For Further Reading

WILL ROGERS WAS A CHEROKEE, A COMEDIAN, A PLAINSPOKEN CRITIC OF THE NATION'S RICH and powerful, a movie star, a journalist, and an adviser to President Franklin Delano Roosevelt (FDR). Rogers articulated a new vision of American national identity that took shape in the 1930s. In contrast to an earlier notion of the United States as an Anglo-Saxon country into which newcomers might assimilate, this new Americanism included ethnic minorities, particularly those of European immigrant background. The Great Depression tarnished the status of the nation's business elite and opened up the political process to party realignments and new leaders. The popular culture expressed and reflected this new Americanism; Will Rogers was its most prominent voice.

In the 1930s, the Great Depression gave rise to a cultural and political upheaval that helped propel Rogers to stardom and political influence. President Franklin Roosevelt coveted his support, and Rogers obliged by promoting the New Deal, the president's program for economic recovery. However, Rogers also pushed the president to the left by advocating such measures as taxing the rich and redistributing wealth. In 1932 Oklahoma nominated Rogers for president as the state's favorite son; three years later, California Democratic leaders urged him to run for the Senate. But in 1935, before any of these possibilities could come to fruition, Rogers died in a plane crash.

The response to Rogers's death illustrates his stature as a national leader and spokesperson for a new multicultural Americanism. Congress adjourned in his memory, President Roosevelt sent a well-publicized letter to Rogers's family, the governor of California proclaimed a day of mourning, flags flew at

■ Presidential candidate Franklin Delano Roosevelt (left) delighted in the support of comic Will Rogers (right) in 1932.

half staff, bells rang in Rogers's honor in more than 100 cities, and nearly 100,000 people filed by his coffin at Forest Lawn Cemetery. Radio stations across the country broadcast his memorial service from the Hollywood Bowl, presided over by a Protestant minister and a Catholic priest, while a

Yiddish performer sang a Hebrew mourning chant. Across town, Mexican American citizen groups placed a wreath on Olvera Street that read "Nosotros Lamentamos la Muerte de Will Rogers" ("We Mourn the Death of Will Rogers"). In the predominantly black Los Angeles community of Watts, an African American fraternal group called the Friends of Ethiopia joined black performers from Rogers's films in a parade to honor the Cherokee movie star who had spoken out publicly against Italy's 1935 invasion of Ethiopia. Back in his hometown of Claremore, Oklahoma, Cherokee Indians performed a death dance in memory of their fallen kinsman.

This massive national grieving reveals not only Rogers's popularity, but also the culture of 1930s America. The economic crisis unleashed changes in society that opened the door for a politically radical Cherokee Indian to become one of the most popular figures of the Great Depression. Millions of Americans experienced poverty—many for the first time. The shared experience of loss and suffering permeated the country.

Roosevelt drew a new political coalition into the Democratic party that elected him to the presidency four times. The Great Depression gave him the opportunity to forge a strong national government and to promote a more representative democracy. His inclusiveness efforts brought citizens of recent immigrant background into the political mainstream but stopped short of the color line. Nevertheless, African American voters abandoned the Republican party to vote for FDR.

> *The economic crisis opened the door for a politically radical Cherokee Indian to become one of the most popular figures of the Great Depression.*

The New Deal, a package of remedies put together by Franklin Roosevelt to address the problems of the Depression, provided relief to many Americans in need but did not eradicate poverty or end the Depression. Yet, as American families from every region of the country drew around their radios to hear the president's **fireside chats**, as they made heroes of Will Rogers and other outsider celebrities, and as they held onto their faith in the nation's promise in spite of its worst economic crisis, they helped forge a more inclusive nation.

The Great Depression

The Great Depression defined the 1930s in the United States. Part of a global economic crisis, it shaped American culture, the political life of the nation, the public policies that resulted, and the cultural expressions that reflected the spirit of the people during a time of national crisis. Its effects permeated the lives of Americans from the mansions of the wealthy to the shanties of the poor and from the boardrooms to the bedrooms. The Depression drove thousands of farmers from the drought-striken southern Great Plains to California. But the story is not simply one of despair and hardship. It is also one of strong communities, resourcefulness, and hope.

> *The story of the Depression is not simply one of despair and hardship. It is also one of strong communities, resourcefulness, and hope.*

Causes of the Crisis

The Great Depression of the 1930s was the worst economic depression in the nation's history. But it was neither the first nor the last. **Capitalism**, the economic system that forms the basis of the American economy, has cycles of ups and downs. Under capitalism, the free market operates with minimal interference from the government. In the United States, prior to the 1930s, the government stepped in to regulate the

■ Margaret Bourke-White in this 1937 photograph, "At the time of the Louisville Flood," depicts the painful irony of poverty in the midst of affluence. Here, hungry Americans line up at a breadline in front of a billboard proclaiming American prosperity.

economy primarily to protect economic competition. Progressive Era reforms prevented corporations from establishing monopolies, so that competition could flourish. In the free market economy, consumers would determine which companies would succeed, based on the quality of their products and services. Because the government did not determine the levels of industrial or agricultural productivity, and did not set the prices, the economy was subject to changing circumstances that led to times of prosperity and times of recession or, in the case of severe economic downturns, depression.

Before the 1930s, the United States provided no **welfare-state** benefits, such as medical care, relief from poverty, income for the unemployed, or old-age insurance. Without any policies that would serve as a safety net for workers who lost their jobs, many wage earners and their families fell into poverty during times of economic downturn. In the Great Depression of the 1930s, the economic crisis was so severe that one-quarter of the nation's workers, nearly 14 million people, lost their jobs, leaving them and their families—40 million people in all—without any income or security. Many of these people had never known poverty before. Among the newly poor were thousands of middle-class Americans who now faced the loss of their homes and savings. For working-class and poor Americans, the impact of the Depression was devastating because they had little economic security to begin with.

The Depression was a global economic catastrophe. Of the major world powers, only the Soviet Union—as a communist society, with state-directed labor, agriculture, and industry—was immune to the collapse of the capitalist system after 1929. In fact, its economy grew throughout the 1930s. The relative health of the Soviet economy led many people in troubled capitalist systems to look to communism as an alternative. Socialism also gained many converts across Europe.

The Great Depression

For many Americans, the Depression really began in the 1920s. Food production and distribution stumbled along weakly throughout the 1920s, leaving widespread rural poverty in its wake. During the 1920s, 1,200 big corporations absorbed more than 6,000 independent businesses. By 1929, 200 corporations controlled nearly half of all industry, which limited competition and made it difficult for new, smaller businesses to flourish.

Although the economy looked healthy on the surface, prosperity rested on an unsound foundation. Many people obtained consumer goods on credit, so when people lost their jobs, they could not pay their debts. Throughout the 1920s, the gap between the rich and poor increased. Nearly 80 percent of the nation's families had no savings at all. Americans with high annual incomes of $10,000 or more—2.3 percent of the people—held two-thirds of all savings. The concentration of wealth among the richest Americans during the 1920s contributed to the persistence of the crisis in the 1930s.

International factors also played a role in the economic collapse. American overseas loans soared in the 1920s, reaching $900 million by 1924 and $1.25 billion by 1928. Germany was a large borrower, for example. Following its defeat in World War I, Germany had been required to make large reparation payments to France and other countries. The United States provided loans to Germany to help the country make its payments. When the stock market crashed, foreign economies like that of Germany also weakened and could not repay their debts. To make matters worse, the United States had established high tariffs to keep foreign goods out of the country so that Americans would buy only American-made goods. This, in turn, encouraged other countries to establish their own tariff barriers. American exports fell sharply.

Surviving Hard Times

In human terms, the Depression of the 1930s dealt a devastating blow to large numbers of Americans: crushing poverty, hunger, humiliation, and loss of dignity and self-worth. Many felt a profound shame that they could no longer earn a living and support their families. The few jobs available often went to the young, strong, well-fed, and well-groomed. Thousands of citizens poured out their hearts in letters to the president, hoping that the government could provide some assistance. In 1934 an Oklahoma woman lamented, "The unemployed have been so long without food-clothes-shoes-medical care-dental care etc—we look prety bad—so when we ask for a job we dont' get it. And we look and feel a little worse each day—when we ask for food they call us bums—it isent our fault . . . no we are not bums."

Families provided the first line of defense against disaster, especially in the early days of the crisis. Many families adapted to hard times by abandoning time-honored gender roles. As men lost jobs, women went to work. Working women did not take jobs from men; rather, they held jobs defined as "traditional women's work" as secretaries, nurses, and waitresses. These jobs offered lower wages than most jobs held by men. A white woman working for wages earned, on average, 61 percent of a white man's wages; a black woman earned a mere 23 percent. Still, they provided at least a modicum of much-needed income.

Many parents struggled to provide for their families under difficult conditions, sometimes risking their health and safety to do so. Erminia Pablita Ruiz Mercer remembered when her father was injured while working in the beet fields in 1933. "He didn't want to live if he couldn't support his family," so he risked experimental back surgery and died on the operating table. Young Erminia then dropped out of school to work as "a doughnut girl" to support her mother and sisters.

Enduring Discrimination

For many poor families, hard times were nothing new. As one African American noted, "The Negro was born in depression. It only became official when it hit the white man." Throughout the 1930s, black Americans suffered the impact of economic hard times disproportionately. By 1932 black unemployment reached 50 percent. With local white authorities in charge of relief, impoverished southern blacks had few places to turn for assistance. African Americans also faced increasing violence; the number of lynchings increased from eight in 1932 to twenty in 1935.

Many poor people joined the growing ranks of **hobos**, riding the rails from town to town, looking for work. But poverty did not erase racial hierarchies or sexual codes, especially for nine young African Americans who came to be known as the "Scottsboro Boys." On March 25, 1931, the youths, ranging in age from thirteen to twenty-one, were taken from a train in Paint Rock, Alabama, after a fight with a group of white men. Two white women, also on the train, accused the nine of rape. Narrowly avoiding a lynching, the youths were taken to jail in Scottsboro, where they began a long ordeal. Within two weeks, an all-white jury convicted them of rape, and they were sentenced to death. But in November 1932, the U.S. Supreme Court ordered a new trial on the grounds that the defendants did not get a fair trial.

The first defendant to be retried was quickly convicted again and sentenced to death. At this point, the case became a major rallying point for civil rights activists, liberals, and radicals throughout the 1930s. Support for the young men came from all over the world, including the British Parliament and the Communist party. In 1935 the U.S. Supreme Court reversed the second set of convictions on the grounds that excluding blacks from the jury denied the defendants due process. Yet, in the next two years, five of the defendants were again tried and found guilty. Although none of the Scottsboro Boys was executed, they all spent long years in prison.

Mexican American families could barely survive on the low wages paid to Mexican laborers. According to a 1933 study, working children's earnings constituted more than one-third of their families' total income. The work was often grueling. Julia Luna Mount recalled her first day at a Los Angeles cannery: "I didn't have money for gloves so I peeled chilies all day long by hand. After work, my hands were red, swollen, and I was on fire! On the streetcar going home, I could hardly hold on my hands hurt so much." Young Julia was lucky—her father saw her suffering and did not make her return to the cannery. But Carmen Bernal Escobar's father could not afford to be soft-hearted about work: "My father was a busboy and to keep the family going . . . in order to bring in a little more money . . . my mother, my grandmother, my mother's brother, my sister and I all worked together" at the cannery.

Those with cannery work, hard as it was, were among the fortunate. Many more Mexicans were deported. Between 1931 and 1934, more than 500,000 Mexicans and Mexican Americans—approximately one-third of the Mexican population in the United States—were sent to Mexico. Most were children born in the United States. Throughout the century, the United States opened or closed its doors to Mexican immigrants depending on the need for their labor. They were deported during the Depression when unemployment was high, then recruited again during the labor shortage of World War II.

Interview about Life in a Government Camp

The Dust Bowl

Severe drought exacerbated the difficulties of farmers across Oklahoma, Texas, Kansas, Colorado, and New Mexico, an area that came to be known as the **Dust Bowl**. Farmers had used the land mainly for grazing until high grain prices during World War I enticed them to plow

■ **MAP 22.1**
DUST AND DROUGHT, 1931–1939 Drought cut a giant swath across the middle of America during the years of the Great Depression. The hardest hit region was the Dust Bowl area of Oklahoma, Texas, New Mexico, Colorado, and Kansas. Many people fled the afflicted areas, abandoning farms, piling their belongings on their cars, and driving along Route 66 to California.

under millions of acres of natural grasslands to plant wheat. Plowing removed root systems from the soil, and years of little rainfall caused the land to dry up. By the middle of the decade, high winds picked up the loose topsoil, creating dust storms across the open plains. The ecological disaster drove 60 percent of the population out of the region.

Migrant farm families fleeing the Dust Bowl came to symbolize the suffering wrought by the Depression. The photographs of Dorothea Lange, the songs of Woody Guthrie, and the writings of John Steinbeck all immortalized their plight. Steinbeck's Pulitzer prize–winning novel *The Grapes of Wrath* (1939) and its film version have remained classics of American popular art. Writing in *The Nation* in 1936, Steinbeck described the Dust Bowl migrants streaming into California:

> Poverty-stricken after the destruction of their farms, their last reserves used up in making the trip, they have arrived so beaten and destitute that they have been willing at first to work under any conditions and for any wages offered. . . . They are not drawn from a peon class, but have either owned small farms or been farm hands in the early American sense, in which the "hand" is a member of the employing family. They have one fixed idea, and that is to acquire land and settle on it. . . . They are not easily intimidated. They are courageous, intelligent, and resourceful. Having gone through the horrors of the drought and with immense effort having escaped from it, they cannot be herded, attacked, starved, or frightened.

Thousands of **Okies** piled belongings on their cars and made their way to California in hopes of starting over. There they joined Mexican migrant farm workers, African American laborers, and others down on their luck, hoping for work.

■ An Oklahoma farmer and his sons try to find shelter from the storm of dust that blew across the plains in 1935. Severe drought after years of excessive plowing created dry loose topsoil that was picked up by high winds. More than half of the residents of the Dust Bowl moved out of the area as a result of the devastation.

Arthur Rothstein, 1936. Library of Congress

Presidential Responses to the Depression

Until the collapse of the economy, President Herbert Hoover's political achievements had earned wide admiration. He seemed the perfect embodiment of the spirit of the prosperous 1920s. But his ideas about politics and economics were ill suited to the crisis of the 1930s. Dissatisfaction with Hoover's response to the Depression gave Franklin Delano Roosevelt a landslide victory in the 1932 presidential election. Promising to take action to ease the nation's suffering, the optimistic Roosevelt seemed to embody hope for an end to the crisis.

Herbert Hoover: Tackling the Crisis

Had prosperity continued, Hoover might have left a legacy of presidential leadership to match his earlier achievements as a Progressive administrator of food relief in Europe. Declaring that "excessive fortunes are a menace to true liberty," he favored steeply graduated inheritance and income taxes on the wealthy, with no tax burden on the poor. He believed that society had a responsibility to care for those in need and that the prosperous should bear much of the burden. After the stock market crash, Hoover increased spending for public works—programs in which the government created jobs for people who needed employment—to the unprecedented sum of $700 million. He established the Reconstruction Finance Corporation to make government credit available to banks and other financial institutions. Seeking to restore confidence in the economy, he strove for a balanced budget by raising taxes and cutting spending—a strategy that underestimated the depth of the Depression and made the situation worse.

As the Depression set in and brought widespread misery, Hoover fully expected that charitable organizations would step in and provide aid to the poor. He believed that government relief to the needy had demoralizing effects on people. Even when it was clear that the crisis was beyond the help of charitable groups, Hoover remained strongly opposed to direct relief for the poor. Private giving did increase to record levels; unfortunately, it was not sufficient.

Hoover's popularity reached its lowest ebb in 1932. A group of World War I veterans in Portland, Oregon, organized a march on Washington, D.C., called the Bonus March. The veterans were due to receive a bonus of $1,000 each in 1945. The group had asked to have their bonuses early, in 1932, to help ease their suffering during the Depression. Hoover refused. More than 20,000 veterans traveled to Washington to petition Congress. The House passed a bill to pay the bonus immediately, but the Senate refused to follow suit. The determined veterans set up a tent city and settled in with their families. On the last day of the congressional session, when Hoover again refused to meet with the protesters, the veterans began to leave. But some did not depart quickly enough, and a police officer began shooting at the unarmed demonstrators, killing one person.

Army Chief of Staff Douglas MacArthur stepped in and escalated the violence. His troops used tear gas and bayonets to prod the veterans and their families to vacate the area, then set fire to the tent city. The attack injured more than 100 people and killed one baby. The image of federal troops assaulting a group of peaceful veterans stunned the public. Although MacArthur had ordered the brutality, the public directed its outrage against Hoover. As most people saw it, Hoover had heartlessly spurned the veterans' legitimate request. By the time of the 1932 election, Hoover had lost most of his public support.

IMAGE

Bonus Expeditionary Force March on Washington

Franklin Delano Roosevelt: The Pragmatist

In contrast to Hoover, Franklin Delano Roosevelt was born into a family of wealth and privilege whose ancestors included European aristocrats and passengers on the *Mayflower*. Pampered as a child, at age fourteen he went to Groton, then the nation's most exclusive boarding school; from there he attended Harvard College and Columbia Law School. In 1905, during his first year at Columbia, he married a distant cousin, Eleanor Roosevelt, the niece of President Theodore Roosevelt. Like Franklin, Eleanor came from a sheltered, upper-class background. But her early life, unlike his, was filled with sadness. Both her parents died when she was a young child, and at age ten she went to live with her grandmother, who left her in the care of a harsh governess. The young

■ Franklin Delano Roosevelt during a radio broadcast, October 14, 1938. Roosevelt mastered the medium of radio and used it effectively to communicate directly to the people. In what came to be known as "fireside chats," Roosevelt addressed his millions of listeners as "my friends."

INTERPRETING HISTORY

Songs of the Great Depression

Popular songs expressed the spirit, sorrows, and longings of Depression Era Americans. According to folk-music historian Alan Lomax, the 12-year-old daughter of a striking Harlan County, Kentucky, mineworker wrote "Which Side Are You On?" in 1937. The song became a popular anthem for labor militancy.

Woody Guthrie (1912–1967) wrote more than a thousand songs about the struggles of common people and the dispossessed. As a teenager, Guthrie left home to hitchhike, ride the rails, live in hobo camps, and follow migrant workers around the country. His song "Union Maid" expresses the hopes and spirit of union workers, and "So Long, It's Been Good to Know Yuh" captures the sorrows of Dust Bowl migrants.

Woody Guthrie, singer and songwriter, immortalized the spirit of ordinary Americans during the struggles of the Great Depression. His songs became anthems of the era and remain classics of American folk music.

Which Side Are You On? By Florence Reece (sung to the tune of an old English song, "Jack Munro")

Come all of you good workers
Good news to you I'll tell
Of how the good old union
Has come in here to dwell.

Chorus
Which side are you on,
Tell me, which side are you on?

My daddy was a miner,
He's now in the air an' sun,
Stick with him, brother miners,
Until this battle's won.

They say in Harlan County
There are no neutrals there
You'll either be a union man,
Or a thug for J. H. Blair.

O gentlemen, can you
  stand it,
O tell me if you can,

---

woman began to flourish when she went abroad to study. The rigorous education developed her strengths and confidence, which would serve her well during her marriage to FDR.

Franklin Roosevelt was elected to the New York State Senate in 1911, and in 1913 he became Assistant Secretary of the Navy. He ran unsuccessfully as the Democratic vice presidential nominee in 1920. His political plans derailed suddenly in 1921 when he was stricken with polio. The painful and incapacitating illness threw the normally ebullient young man into despair. He had always assumed that he would control his own destiny. Now he could no longer use his legs. The formerly athletic Roosevelt depended on braces, crutches, and a wheelchair to move around. But his upbringing had given him extraordinary reserves of self-confidence and optimism, and these qualities helped to sustain him in the face of his paralysis.

FDR's bout with polio did nothing to dampen his political ambitions. He became governor of New York in 1928, following in the footsteps of Theodore Roosevelt. But, unlike

TABLE 22-1
The Election of 1932

Candidate	Political Party	Popular Vote (%)	Electoral Vote
Franklin D. Roosevelt	Democratic	57.4	472
Herbert Hoover	Republican	39.7	59
Norman Thomas	Socialist	2.2	—

Will you be a lousy scab,
Or will you be a man?

Don't scab for the bosses,
Don't listen to their lies,
Us poor folks haven't got a chance,
Unless we organize.

Source: "Which Side Are You On?" by Florence Reece © 1947 by Stormking Music, Inc. All rights reserved. Used by permission.

Union Maid By Woody Guthrie (first verse and chorus)

There once was a union maid
Who never was afraid
Of goons and ginks and company finks
And the deputy sheriffs who made the raids;
She went to the union hall
When a meeting it was called
And when the company boys came 'round
She always stood her ground.

Chorus

Oh, you can't scare me.
I'm sticking to the union, (3 times)
Oh, you can't scare me.
I'm sticking to the union, (2 times)
Till the day I die.

Source: "Union Maid." Words and music by Woody Guthrie. TRO-© Copyright 1961 (Renewed) 1963 (Renewed) Ludlow Music, Inc., New York, NY. Used by permission.

"So Long, It's Been Good to Know Yuh (Dusty Old Dust)" By Woody Guthrie (selected verses and chorus)

I've sung this song, but I'll sing it again,
Of the place that I lived on the wild, windy plains,
In the month called April, the county called Gray
And here's what all of the people there say:

Chorus

So long, it's been good to know ye; (3 times)
This dusty old dust is a-getting my home,
And I've got to be driftin' along.

A dust storm hit, and it hit like thunder;
It dustedus over, and it covered us under;
Blocked out the traffic and blocked out the sun.
Straight for home all the people did run.

The sweethearts sat in the dark and they sparked,
They hugged and kissed in that dusty old dark,
They sighed and cried, hugged and kissed

Instead of marriage, they talked like this:
Honey, so long, it's been good to know ye…

Now, the telephone rang, and it jumped off the wall;
That was the preacher a-making his call.
He said, "Kind friend, this may be the end;
You've got your last chance of salvation of sin."

The churches was jammed, and the churches was packed,
And that dusty old dust storm blowed so black;
The preacher could not read a word of his text,
And he folded his specs and he took up collection, said:
So long, it's been good to know ye. . . .

Source: "So Long It's Been Good To Know Yuh (Dusty Old Dust)." Words and music by Woody Guthrie. TRO-© Copyright 1940 (Renewed) 1950 (Renewed) 1963 (Renewed) Folkways Music Publishers, Inc., New York, NY. Used by permission.

Questions

1. What makes the songs emblematic of the era in which they were written?
2. How are issues of class addressed in these folk tunes?

---

his Republican cousin, Franklin was a Democrat. In the 1932 presidential campaign, FDR made few specific proposals, but promised the American people a "New Deal."

"Nothing to Fear but Fear Itself"

In his inaugural address, Roosevelt endeavored to ease the nation's anxieties with reassuring words: "Let me assert my firm belief that the only thing we have to fear is fear itself—nameless, unreasoning, unjustified terror which paralyzes needed efforts to convert retreat into advance." Roosevelt launched his advance immediately. Panic had prompted many Americans to pull out their bank savings, causing many banks to fail. To stop the run on banks, FDR called Congress into a special session and announced a "bank holiday," temporarily closing all the nation's banks. He could have nationalized the banking system, a move toward socialism that would likely have received widespread support. But Roosevelt favored government regulation, not government ownership. He proposed the Emergency Banking Bill, providing government support for private banks. Congress passed the bill instantly, to the applause of the bankers who helped draft it.

In the first of his "fireside chats" to millions of radio listeners, whom he addressed as "my friends," Roosevelt assured citizens that the banks that reopened were sound. He

DOCUMENT

Franklin D. Roosevelt, First Inaugural Address (1933)

Franklin Roosevelt, fireside chat (September 6, 1936)

used the medium of radio skillfully to explain his policies and to communicate comforting and reassuring messages that reached people in the intimate setting of their homes. The next day, bank deposits exceeded withdrawals as a result of the confidence he inspired.

The New Deal

The New Deal drew on Progressive Era reform impulses to extend the reach of the federal government to solve social problems. It provided assistance to many Americans suffering the effects of the Depression and established the welfare state that would last half a century. Based on pragmatism, experimentation, and shrewd political calculation, FDR's plan began with a flurry of activity in the first 100 days of his administration and developed into a more progressive agenda by 1935, often called the **second New Deal**. New Deal programs countered the cyclical nature of capitalism and offered a safety net for industrial workers. They legitimized labor unions and established a system of regulation and cooperation between industry and labor. They won Roosevelt a resounding reelection in 1936. Many New Deal programs failed, but those that succeeded created the foundation of the modern American state. The broad-based reform effort, however, did not end the Depression nor eradicate poverty.

The First Hundred Days

Roosevelt acted quickly and pragmatically. As one of his first acts, he encouraged Congress to repeal Prohibition. In 1933 the states quickly ratified the Twenty-First Amendment, repealing the Eighteenth. Repeal of Prohibition helped the economy by providing additional tax revenues from liquor sales, since they were once again legal, and a market for farmers' corn and wheat, which were used in the production of liquor. Congress created the Securities and Exchange Commission (SEC) to oversee the stock market and the Federal Deposit Insurance Corporation (FDIC) to reform the banking system and provide insurance for deposits.

One of FDR's most pressing challenges was to prop up prices for producers while keeping them low enough for consumers. Poverty in the midst of plenty was one of the Depression's cruelest ironies. Because farmers could no longer afford to transport their goods to market, food rotted while millions of people went hungry. Through the Agricultural Adjustment Act, the government sought to prop up farm prices by limiting supply. That is, it paid farmers to destroy livestock and take acreage out of production.

■ Dorothea Lange took photographs for the Farm Security Administration (FSA), documenting the lives of Depression-era migrants. This 1939 photo, "Mother and Children on the Road, Tulelake, Siskiyou County, California," is one of Lange's many portraits of impoverished families.

Most Americans in need desperately wanted to work. They considered government relief a sign of failure and a source of deep shame and humiliation. Many citizens searched for ways to preserve their pride. One woman wrote to Eleanor Roosevelt asking to borrow money in order to avoid charity:

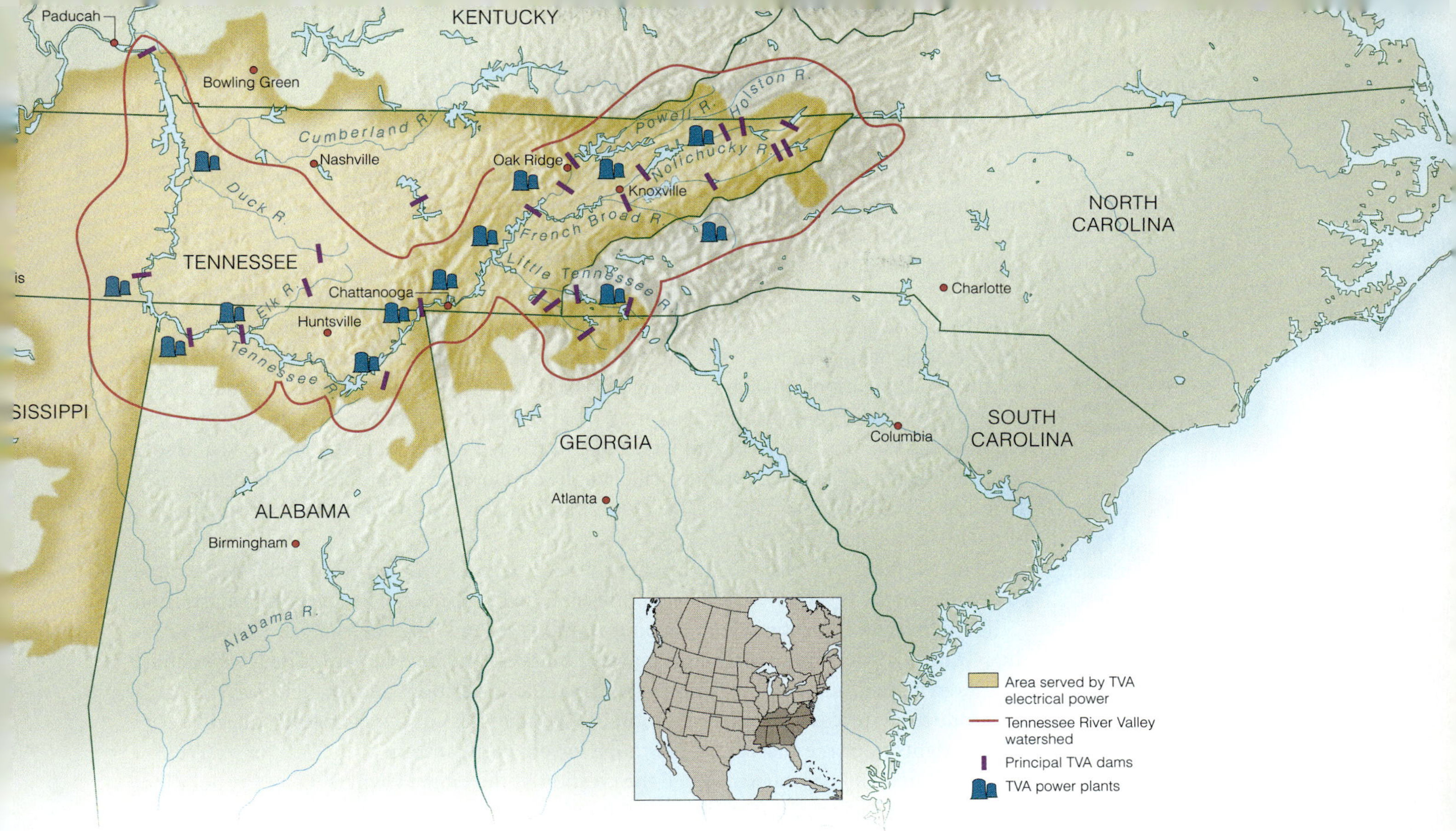

■ **MAP 22.2**
AREAS SERVED BY THE TENNESSEE VALLEY AUTHORITY The Tennessee Valley Authority (TVA) brought electricity to a large area in western Appalachia, one of the poorest regions in the country. The government-owned project strengthened the economy and improved living conditions in the area.

Please Mrs. Roosevelt, I do not want charity, only a chance from someone who will trust me. . . . I am sending you two of my dearest possessions to keep as security, a ring my husband gave me before we were married, and a ring my mother used to wear. . . . If you will consider buying the baby clothes, please keep them (rings) until I send you the money you spent. It is very hard to face bearing a baby we cannot afford to have, and the fact that it is due to arrive soon, and still there is no money for the hospital or clothing, does not make it any easier. I have decided to stay home, keeping my 7 year old daughter from school to help with the smaller children when my husband has work. . . . The 7 year old one is a good willing little worker and somehow we must manage—but without charity.

In March 1933, Congress passed the Federal Emergency Relief Administration (FERA), which provided $500 million in grants to the states for aid to the needy. Roosevelt placed Harry Hopkins in charge. Hopkins, an energetic and brash young reformer, disbursed $2 million during his first two hours on the job. He then persuaded Roosevelt to launch a temporary job program, the Civil Works Administration (CWA). The CWA provided government-sponsored jobs for more than 4 million workers. But the program came under fire from conservatives, and FDR ended it a few months later.

The New Deal included two major programs that addressed conservation and environmental issues. In 1933 Roosevelt combined his interest in conservation with his goal of providing work for unemployed young men. The Civilian Conservation Corps (CCC) operated under the control of the Army. CCC workers lived in camps, wore uniforms, and conformed to military discipline. They planted millions of trees, dug canals and ditches, built

VIDEO
New Deal

more than 30,000 wilderness shelters, stocked rivers and lakes with nearly 1 billion fish, and preserved historic sites. Their work revived depleted forests and provided flood control. By 1935 the CCC had employed more than 500,000 young men and kept them, in FDR's words, "off the city street corners."

The Tennessee Valley Authority

Another measure that linked natural resources to the recovery effort was the Tennessee Valley Authority (TVA), an experiment in government-owned utilities that brought power to rural areas along the Tennessee River in seven states in western Appalachia—among the poorest areas in the nation. This far-reaching government-owned project offered a radical alternative to American capitalism, based on private enterprise. Under the TVA, the government built five dams, improved twenty others, and constructed power plants; it produced and sold electricity to the valley's farmers and facilitated the development of industry in the region. The TVA also provided flood control. The TVA became one of the largest and cheapest suppliers of power in the nation.

Tennessee Valley Authority Act

The National Industrial Recovery Act (NIRA), passed by Congress in 1933, became the centerpiece of the first New Deal. The NIRA established the National Recovery Administration (NRA) to oversee regulation of the economy. In his second "fireside chat," Roosevelt called the NRA "a partnership in planning" between business and government. The NRA enabled businesses in each sector of the economy to form trade associations and set their own standards for production, prices, and wages. Section 7(a) of the NIRA also guaranteed collective bargaining rights to workers, sparking new hope for union organizers.

FDR's first 100 days also included the creation of the Home Owners' Loan Corporation, providing refinancing of home mortgages at low rates. Because the plan helped stem the tide of foreclosures and also guaranteed the repayment of loans, it pleased homeowners, banks, and real-estate interests. It helped gain for FDR the support of a large segment of the middle class.

One of the boldest New Dealers was John Collier, whom Roosevelt appointed as Commissioner of Indian Affairs. Collier opposed the policy of land allotment that the Dawes Act of 1887 had enacted. Under allotment, Native American land holdings had dwindled from 130 million acres to 49 million acres—much of it desert. Collier rejected the assumption that Indians' survival depended on their assimilation into white culture. He altered the government

■ On October 28, 1935, John Collier, Commissioner of Indian Affairs, stands with a group of Flathead Indian chiefs as Secretary of the Interior Harold L. Ickes signs the first constitution providing for Indian self-rule. Franklin Roosevelt appointed Collier to bring the New Deal to Native Americans.

boarding schools' curriculum to include bicultural and bilingual education and eliminated military dress and discipline.

Collier's ideas came to fruition in the 1934 Indian Reorganization Act, which recognized the autonomy of Indian tribes, did away with the allotment program, and appropriated funds to help Indians add to their land holdings. It also provided for job and professional training programs as well as a system of agricultural and industrial credit. In keeping with Collier's goal of Indian self-government, each tribe decided whether to accept the terms of the Indian Reorganization Act. In the end, 181 tribes voted to accept the law, while seventy-seven opted out of it.

Monumental Projects Transforming the Landscape

The New Deal years gave rise to monumental construction projects that altered the landscape and affected the natural environment. In addition to the dams built as part of the TVA, gigantic new dams provided electricity and irrigation in the arid West. Construction on Hoover Dam on the Colorado River 30 miles from Las Vegas began in 1931. The huge Grand Coulee Dam across the Columbia River in Washington State provided electricity to much of the Northwest and irrigation for over half a million acres of land in the Columbia basin.

The Golden Gate Bridge, another Depression-era project, spanned the entrance to San Francisco Bay. When the bridge opened in 1937, 32,000 vehicles and 19,000 pedestrians passed over the picturesque engineering marvel on the first day. Monumental architecture also soared skyward in other cities. In 1930, construction began on the Empire State Building in New York City, the tallest building in the world up to that time.

Protest and Pressure from the Left and the Right

Despite these accomplishments, challenges to Roosevelt's New Deal took many forms. In spite of FDR's efforts to help businesses survive and remain profitable during the Depression, many business leaders continued to oppose the New Deal, charging that FDR was a dictator and that his program amounted to socialism. At the same time, FDR faced criticism from the left. Many people believed that Roosevelt's policies did not go far enough to ease the suffering caused by the economic crisis. Some thought that New Deal policies aimed at bolstering capitalism were ill-advised, and that capitalism itself was the problem. Disenchantment with capitalism drew many Americans to the cause of socialism and swelled the ranks of the small Communist party.

Many people believed that Roosevelt's policies did not go far enough to ease the suffering caused by the economic crisis.

By 1934 and 1935, much of the pressure on Roosevelt came from workers, whose hopes that the NIRA would guarantee collective bargaining rights were dashed by the intransigence of employers. In 1934 nearly 1.5 million workers participated in 1,800 strikes. Although most African Americans supported FDR and the Democratic party during the Depression, between 3,000 and 4,000 members of the black community of Birmingham, Alabama, joined the Communist party and related organizations during the 1930s. One successful effort at biracial organizing occurred in the Arkansas delta in 1934. The Southern Tenant Farmers' Union (STFU) brought together black and white tenants and sharecroppers to fight for better working conditions.

In addition to the communists, socialists, labor unions, and grassroots organizations that sprang up all over the country, a number of individuals proposed alternatives to Roosevelt's program and gained large followings. The most influential of these were Dr. Francis Townsend, Father Charles E. Coughlin, and Senator Huey P. Long. In 1934 Townsend, a retired physician and health commissioner from Long Beach, California, introduced an idea for a pension plan that sparked a nationwide grassroots movement. Townsend proposed a 2 percent national sales tax that would fund a pension of $200 a month for Americans over age sixty. The **Townsend Plan** became hugely popular, especially among elderly Americans. In 1936 a national survey indicated that half of all Americans favored the plan. Though the plan was never implemented, the groundswell of support that it generated probably hastened the development and passage of the old-age insurance system contained in the 1935 Social Security Act.

Coughlin also inspired a huge following. A Catholic priest from Canada, he served as pastor of a small church outside Detroit, Michigan. He began to broadcast his sermons on the radio, using his magnetic personality to address political as well as religious issues. Soon he became a media phenomenon, broadcasting through twenty-six radio stations to an audience estimated at 40 million. The "Radio Priest" called for a redistribution of wealth and attacked Wall Street, international bankers, and the evils of capitalism. But his message turned from social justice populism to right-wing bigotry. His virulent anti-Semitism and admiration for the fascist regimes of Adolf Hitler in Germany and Benito Mussolini in Italy drove away many of his followers. By 1940 Coughlin had ceased broadcasting and abandoned all political activities, under orders of the Catholic Church.

Huey P. Long was among the most powerful, and colorful, politicians of the era. He rose from modest origins to become a lawyer and a public service commissioner. In 1928 Long won the governorship of Louisiana. His progressive leadership inspired tremendous loyalty, especially among poor workers and farmers. He did more for the underprivileged people of Louisiana than any other governor. He expanded the state's infrastructure; developed social services; built roads, hospitals, and schools; and changed the tax code to place a greater burden on corporations and the wealthy. He proved unique among southern politicians in that his public statements were free of racial slurs. But he also trampled the democratic process. His ambition had no bounds, and he used any means to accumulate power.

> *Huey P. Long was among the most powerful, and colorful, politicians of the era.*

In 1932 Long resigned the governorship and won election to the U.S. Senate. Soon, he gained a huge national following. Initially he supported FDR, but by 1933 he had broken with the president and forged his own political movement based on his Share-Our-Wealth Plan. Giving voice to the resentments many Americans felt toward "wealthy plutocrats," Long advocated a radical redistribution of the nation's wealth. He called for new taxes on the wealthy and proposed to use the funds to guarantee a minimum annual income of $2,500 for all those in need. As he put it, "How many men ever went to a barbecue and would let one man take off the table what was intended for nine-tenths of the people to eat? The only way you'll ever be able to feed the balance of the people is to make that man come back and bring back some of the grub he ain't got no business with." By 1935 he was planning to challenge FDR in the next presidential election. But he never had the chance. In September 1935, the son-in-law of one of his vanquished political opponents assassinated him.

Eleanor Roosevelt also pushed FDR to the left, particularly on the issue of civil rights. Although FDR was reluctant to support an antilynching bill in Congress for fear of alienating southern white voters, the First Lady campaigned vigorously against lynching. When the Daughters of the American Revolution (DAR) denied the African American opera star Marian Anderson the right to perform at Constitution Hall in Washington, D.C., Eleanor promptly resigned from the DAR in protest and arranged for Anderson to perform at the Lincoln Memorial on Easter Sunday 1939, where a huge audience stood in the cold to hear her sing.

The Second New Deal

FDR was careful not to alienate southern Democrats by cultivating African American voters. However, he did reach out to industrial workers. In the spring of 1935, Congress passed the National Labor Relations Act, also known as the Wagner Act, which strengthened and guaranteed collective bargaining and gave a huge boost to labor unions.

Also in 1935, Congress passed the Social Security Act, perhaps the most important and far-reaching of all New Deal programs. The act established a system of old-age pensions,

TABLE 22-2

Key New Deal Legislation, 1933–1938

Year	Act or Agency	Key Provisions
1933	Emergency Banking Act	Reopened banks under government supervision
	Civilian Conservation Corps (CCC)	Employed young men in reforestation, flood control, road construction, and soil erosion control projects
	Federal Emergency Relief Act (FERA)	Provided federal funds for state and local relief efforts
	Agricultural Adjustment Act (AAA)	Granted farmers direct payments for reducing crop production; funds for payment provided by a processing tax, later declared unconstitutional
	Farm Mortgage Act	Provided funds to refinance farm mortgages
	Tennessee Valley Authority (TVA)	Constructed dams and power projects and developed the economy of a seven-state area in the Tennessee River Valley
	Home Owners' Loan Corporation	Provided funds for refinancing home mortgages of nonfarm homeowners
	National Industrial Recovery Act (NIRA)	Established a series of fair competition codes; created National Recovery Administration (NRA) to write, coordinate, and implement these codes; NIRA's Section 7(a) guaranteed labor's right to organize (act later declared unconstitutional)
	Public Works Administration (PWA)	Sought to increase employment and business activity by funding road construction, building construction, and other projects
	Federal Deposit Insurance Corporation (FDIC)	Insured individual bank deposits
	Civil Works Administration (CWA)	Provided federal jobs for the unemployed
1934	Securities and Exchange Act	Created Securities and Exchange Commission (SEC) to regulate trading practices in stocks and bonds according to federal laws
	Indian Reorganization Act	Restored ownership of tribal lands to Native Americans; provided funds for job training and a system of agricultural and industrial credit
	Federal Housing Administration (FHA)	Insured loans provided by banks for the building and repair of houses
1935	Works Progress Administration (WPA)	Employed more than 8 million people to repair roads, build bridges, and work on other projects
	National Youth Administration (NYA)	WPA program that provided job training for unemployed youths and part-time jobs for students in need
	Federal One	WPA program that provided financial assistance for writers, artists, musicians, and actors
	National Labor Relations Act (Wagner Act)	Recognized the right of employees to join labor unions and to bargain collectively, reinstating the provisions of NIRA's Section 7(a); created the National Labor Relations Board (NLRB) to enforce laws against unfair labor practices
	Social Security Act	Created a system of social insurance that included unemployment compensation and old-age survivors' insurance; paid for by a joint tax on employers and employees
1938	Fair Labor Standards Act	Established a minimum wage of 25 cents an hour and a standard work week of 44 hours for businesses engaged in interstate commerce

unemployment insurance, and welfare benefits for dependent children and the disabled. The framework of the Social Security Administration shaped the welfare system for the remainder of the century. But the welfare state established by the Social Security Act left out many of the most needy. It also established a two-track system of welfare. One track provided workers with unemployment insurance and support in their old age (the Social Security program). But Social Security did not cover domestics, seasonal or part-time workers, agricultural laborers, or housewives. The other track made matching funds available to states to provide relief for the needy, mostly dependent women and children with no means of support. Unlike Social Security, which was provided to all retired workers regardless of their circumstances, relief programs, which came to be known as "welfare," were administered according to need.

The architects of this welfare system included top New Deal advisers, many of them women who had been active reformers, such as Eleanor Roosevelt. These advocates hoped to protect women and children from the destitution that almost certainly resulted if a male breadwinner lost his job, deserted his family, or died. The system presumed that a man ordinarily earned a **family wage** that let him support his wife and children and that women were necessarily economically dependent on men. Thus, a deeply entrenched gender system prevailed through the 1930s. As a result, some—though not all—male breadwinners received benefits like Social Security. Impoverished women and children, on the other hand, received public charity. These payments were usually meager, not enough to lift a woman and her children out of poverty.

Because there were no nationally established guidelines on how to distribute welfare funds, states could determine who received assistance. As a result, the Social Security Act did little to assist African Americans, especially in the South, where black women were deliberately excluded by local authorities who preferred to maintain a pool of cheap African American labor rather than to provide relief for black families.

WPA Project at Tonawanda Reservation

In 1935 Congress allocated the huge sum of nearly $5 billion for the Emergency Relief Appropriation. Roosevelt used a significant portion of the money to expand his public works program. By executive order, he established the Works Progress Administration (WPA), which provided millions of jobs for the unemployed. The project mandated that WPA jobs would make a contribution to public life and would not compete with private business. The jobs included building streets, highways, bridges, and public buildings; restoring forests; clearing slums; and extending electricity to rural areas. The WPA National Youth Administration gave work to nearly 1 million students.

The most effective WPA program was Federal One, which provided financial support for writers, musicians, artists, and actors. The Federal Theater Project, under the direction of Hallie Flanagan, former head of Vassar College's Experimental Theater, shaped the project into an arena for experimental community-based theater. The Federal Theater Project included sixteen black theater units. Federal One supported thousands of artists and brought the arts to a wide public audience through government-funded murals on public buildings, community-theater productions, local orchestras, and the like.

The New Deal did not reach everyone. Programs were geared toward full-time industrial workers, most of whom were white men. Domestic workers, Mexican migrant laborers, black and white sharecroppers, Chinese and Japanese truck farmers—all were among those ineligible for Social Security, minimum wages and maximum hours, unemployment insurance, and other New Deal benefits. But the New Deal established the national welfare state and provided assistance and security to millions of working people along with disabled, dependent, and elderly Americans. Such sweeping programs also solidified Roosevelt's popularity among the poor, workers, and much of the middle class.

FDR's Second Term

In the 1936 campaign, FDR claimed that the election was a battle between "the millions who never had a chance" and "organized money." He boasted that the "forces of selfishness and of lust for power" had united against him: "They are unanimous in their *hate* for *me—and I welcome their hatred.*" His strategy paid off. Roosevelt won the election by a landslide of more than 60 percent of the popular vote. Six million more voters cast ballots than had done so in

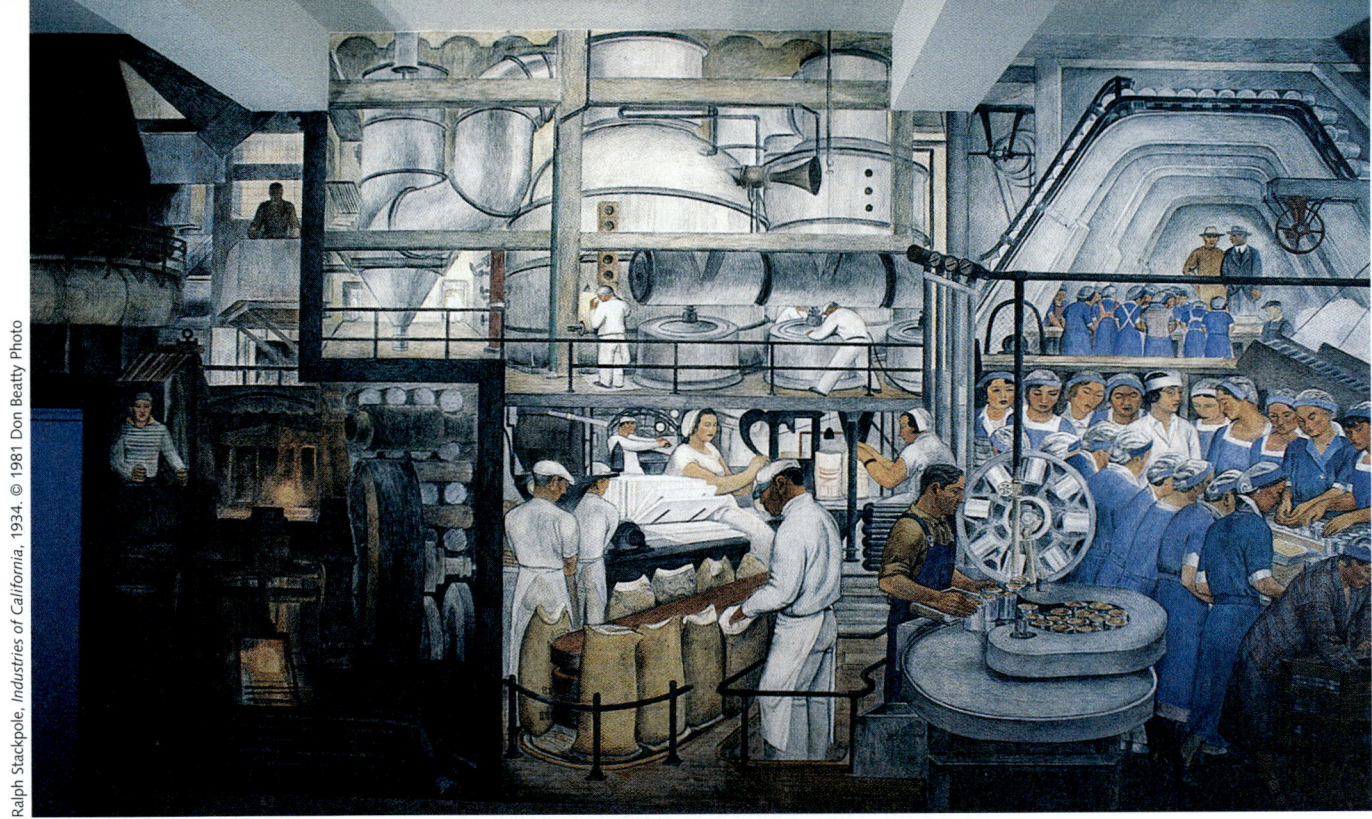

■ In this mural on San Francisco's Coit Tower, "Industries of California," Works Projects Administration (WPA) artist Ralph Stackpole depicts the city's diverse workforce. Across the country, government-funded artists created works of public art that portrayed life in local communities.

1932, and 5 million of those new votes went to Roosevelt. His strongest support came from the lower ends of the socioeconomic scale. The election also swept Democrats into Congress, giving them a decisive majority in both the House and the Senate.

With such a powerful mandate, Roosevelt was well positioned to promote a new legislative program. As his first major effort, he took on the Supreme Court. Dominated by conservative justices, the Court had invalidated some major legislation of Roosevelt's first term, including the AAA and the NIRA. Roosevelt feared that the justices would unravel the New Deal by striking down its progressive elements. To shift the balance of power on the Court, he proposed a measure that would let the president appoint one new justice for every one on the Court who had at least ten years of service and who did not retire within six months after turning seventy.

Emboldened by his landslide victory, FDR believed that he could persuade Congress and the nation to go along with any plan he put forward, but he was mistaken. Many viewed his "court packing" plan as a threat to the fundamental separation of powers and feared that it would set a dangerous precedent. Powerful Republicans in Congress forged an alliance with conservative Democrats, mostly from the South, to defeat the plan. This informal alliance dominated Congress for the following two decades. The Court blunder cost Roosevelt considerable political capital and empowered his opponents. In the end, his plan proved unnecessary anyway. The Court did not undercut the New Deal. Within the next few years, retirements allowed Roosevelt to appoint several new justices who tipped the balance in his favor.

TABLE 22-3
The Election of 1936

Candidate	Political Party	Popular Vote (%)	Electoral Vote
Franklin D. Roosevelt	Democratic	60.8	523
Alfred M. Landon	Republican	36.5	8
William Levine	Union	1.9	—

A New Political Culture

FDR continued to face strong opposition from conservatives on the right and from radicals, communists, and socialists on the left. But his political fortunes benefited from the emergence of a new and more inclusive national culture. This new Americanism emanated from the working class and found expression in the labor movement, the popular culture, and the political coalition that came together in the Democratic party. These nationalizing forces cut across lines of class and region and occasionally challenged hierarchies of gender and race.

The Labor Movement

The labor insurgency that erupted during the early years of the New Deal demonstrated the need for a new national labor movement. The American Federation of Labor (AFL), restricted to skilled workers, left out most of the nation's less skilled industrial laborers. John L. Lewis of the United Mine Workers (UMW) and Sidney Hillman of the Amalgamated Clothing Workers of America were among several union leaders from a number of industries—including mining, steel, rubber, and automobile—who left the AFL to form a new and more broad-based labor organization, the Congress of Industrial Organizations (CIO). Hillman and others argued that higher wages were good for the economy because workers would then be able to purchase consumer products, benefiting industry as well as workers. Lewis and Hillman played key roles in the CIO's growth into a national force, but the impetus came from the workers themselves.

The CIO's first major action came in 1936 in Akron, Ohio, where workers in the rubber industry organized a **sit-down strike**, a new strategy whereby laborers stopped work and simply sat down, shutting down production and occupying plants so that strikebreakers could not enter and take their jobs. Sit-down strikes became a prominent labor tactic during 1936 when forty-eight strikes broke out across the nation. The numbers shot up the following year to about 500 strikes that lasted more than one day.

The most powerful demonstration of workers' discontent came in the automobile industry, where speed-ups of the assembly line drove workers to rebellion. In 1936 a spontaneous strike erupted against General Motors in Atlanta; it soon spread to Kansas City, Missouri; Cleveland, Ohio; and the main plants at Flint, Michigan. Two weeks into the strike, workers clashed with police. Frank Murphy, Michigan's pro-labor governor, refused to use National Guard troops against the strikers, and Roosevelt declined to send in federal troops. John L. Lewis negotiated on behalf of the workers, who demanded recognition of their union.

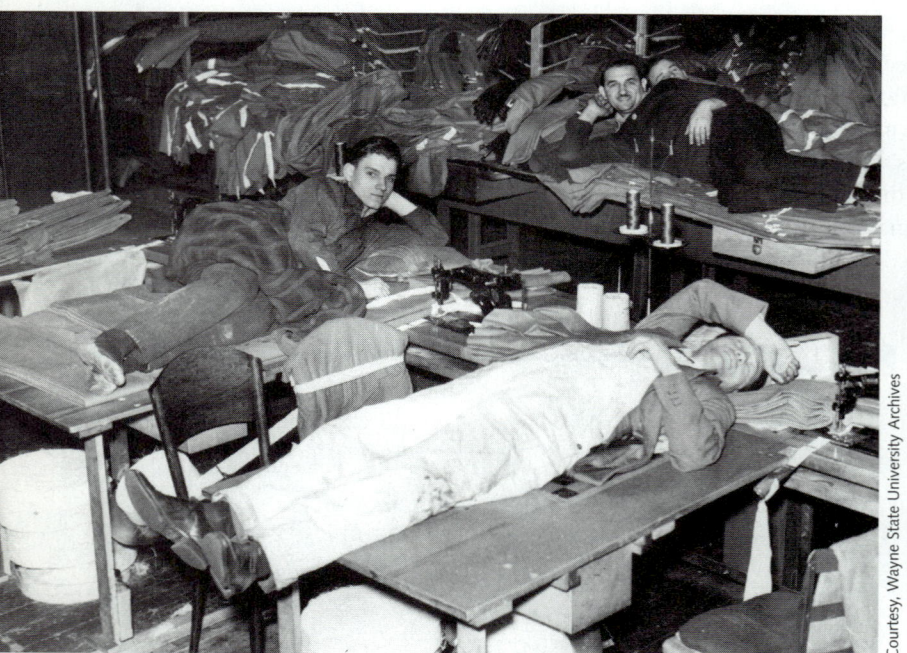

■ These sit-down strikers at the Dodge Main plant in Hamtramck, Michigan, slept on their sewing tables while occupying the factory, shutting down production. The sit-down strike became an effective form of labor protest during the 1930s.

Women as well as men participated actively in the Flint strike. Twenty-three-year-old Genora Johnson Dollinger, wife of a striker and mother of two young sons, organized 500 women into the Women's Emergency Brigade, made up primarily of strikers' wives, sisters, and girlfriends. Wearing red berets and armbands, they ran soup kitchens and first-aid stations. They also entered the fray when necessary, as when they broke plant windows so that the company could not use tear gas effectively against the strikers inside.

Dollinger arranged a children's picket line as well, in which her two-year-old carried a sign that read, "My daddy strikes for us little tykes."

The sit-down strike at Flint lasted forty-four days and forced General Motors to recognize the United Auto Workers (UAW), which was a CIO union. The strike scored a clear victory for the workers and boosted the CIO's stature as a national union of industrial workers. Membership in the UAW quadrupled in the next year. Bowing to the formidable power of the national union in the wake of the UAW success, U.S. Steel conceded to the CIO even without a strike, ending its policy of hiring nonunion workers and signing an agreement with the Steel Workers' Organizing Committee. The CIO brought together workers from all over the country. Most of its member unions were open to racial and ethnic minorities and women.

The New Deal Coalition

FDR's support of labor unions brought workers solidly into the Democratic fold. They joined a coalition that included voters who had never before belonged to the same party, particularly northern blacks and southern whites. Although African Americans in the South were disenfranchised, blacks in the North had voted Republican for sixty years, loyal to the party of Lincoln. In a dramatic shift, black voters in northern cities overwhelmingly backed FDR in 1936 and remained in the Democratic party for the rest of the century.

Other racial and ethnic minorities also joined the New Deal coalition. In 1939 Latinos organized their first national civil rights assembly, El Congreso de Pueblos de Habla Española (the Spanish-Speaking People's Congress), which opened with a congratulatory telegram from Eleanor Roosevelt. Immigrants from Europe and their children also became loyal Democratic voters.

In spite of this diverse coalition, many Americans remained bitterly opposed to FDR. On the left, socialists and communists criticized the New Deal for patching up capitalism rather than transforming the economic system. On the right, conservative business leaders despised Roosevelt for the constraints he placed on business and the intrusion of the government into the economy. Critics from the political right considered the New Deal akin to communism. In 1938 Congress created the House Un-American Activities Committee (HUAC), chaired by Martin Dies of Texas. Formed ostensibly to investigate American fascists and Nazis in the United States, the committee instead pursued liberal and leftist groups throughout World War II and the Cold War.

A New Americanism

The New Deal coalition reflected not only Roosevelt's popularity but also a new and more inclusive American identity. An expanding mass culture fostered this sensibility, spread largely through the national media. It is no accident that Franklin Roosevelt found his way into the homes and hearts of Americans through his "fireside chats" over the radio; his mastery of that technology made him the first media-savvy president. During the 1930s, 70 percent of all households owned a radio—more than owned a telephone. The motion-picture industry also expanded into small towns across the country. Talking films brought vernacular speech and a variety of accents to diverse audiences who gathered in neighborhood theaters.

Movie plots portrayed the triumph of common people over the rich and powerful and celebrated love across class and ethnic lines. Although racial stereotypes persisted in motion pictures throughout the decade, notable exceptions, such as Will Rogers's films, featured strong minority characters. Popular movies also challenged traditional gender and class hierarchies. Female stars, such as Katharine Hepburn, Rosalind Russell, Bette Davis, and Mae West, portrayed feisty, independent women.

New sports celebrities also embodied the nation's diversity. Baseball star Joe DiMaggio, son of an Italian immigrant fisherman, became a national hero. African American boxer Joe Louis, the "Brown Bomber" who was born into a sharecropper family in Alabama, became

Amelia Earhart was the first woman to fly solo across the Atlantic. The legendary aviator gave preliminary flying lessons to her friend Eleanor Roosevelt. FDR convinced his wife not to take up flying, but the First Lady always regretted her decision.

heavyweight champion of the world at age twenty-three. In 1938, when Louis fought German boxer Max Schmeling at Yankee Stadium, the fight attracted 70,000 fans and grossed more than $1 million. When the black fighter knocked out Schmeling in the first round, he seemed to strike a blow for America against Hitler's Nazi Germany.

A number of women also became heroes in the 1930s for their daring exploits, personal courage, and physical prowess. Athletes like tennis champion Helen Wills and Olympic track star and brilliant golfer "Babe" (Mildred) Didrikson (later Zaharias) greatly expanded the popularity of women's sports. Renowned aviator Amelia Earhart, the first woman to fly solo across the Atlantic, devoted her life to advancing both feminism and commercial aviation. When her plane disappeared during an attempted round-the-world flight in 1937, many of her admirers were so convinced of her invincibility that they refused to believe she had died. Even today, people still speculate about her fate.

Conclusion

The New Deal set in place a welfare state that established the principle of government responsibility for the well-being of vulnerable citizens. Before the New Deal, people suffered the fluctuations of the market economy with no recourse beyond the assistance of kin, communities, and charities. Older Americans who could no longer work had no government-guaranteed pensions and often faced poverty in old age. Bank failures could wipe away life savings. Unemployment could mean starvation for a worker's family. The New Deal provided Social Security for the elderly, unemployment compensation for workers who had lost their jobs, minimum standards for hours and wages, and economic aid to women and children who had no means of support. It established national economic regulations and regulatory agencies as well as the right of workers to unionize and engage in collective bargaining. These government protections offered many Americans an unprecedented level of economic security.

Most New Deal policies protected factory workers in large companies. The safety net did not extend to many of the neediest Americans, including Mexican American migrant workers, African American and white sharecroppers, seasonal agricultural laborers, and domestic workers. FDR was reluctant to press for antilynching legislation for fear of alienating southern congressmen who still retained enormous power. Although FDR's conservative opponents accused him of socialist leanings, the New Deal actually rescued and shored up capitalism.

The New Deal was the Roosevelt administration's response to a global economic crisis. With the exception of the communist Soviet Union, which had already abandoned capitalism, all industrialized nations responded to the Depression by increasing the role of the state in the economy. Italy, Germany, and Japan moved to fascism and the nearly total state direction of the economy, while Britain and France established welfare states that would become more fully developed after World War II. The U.S. system of social welfare was not as extensive and inclusive as those that emerged in some western European democracies. But it was part of a larger trend toward government intervention in the economy and greater protections for citizens.

Sites to Visit

African American Odyssey: The Depression, New Deal, and World War II
memory.loc.gov/ammem/aaohtml/exhibit/aopart8.html

This Library of Congress site covers the history of African Americans during the years of the Depression and World War II.

Southern Mosaic: The John and Ruby Lomax 1939 Southern States Recording Trip
memory.loc.gov/ammem/lohtml/lohome.html

This site from the American Folklife Center, Library of Congress, provides audio, text, and photos of the Lomax collection of American folk songs collected and recorded across the South.

Voices from the Dust Bowl: The Charles L. Todd and Robert Sonkin Migrant Worker Collection, 1940–1941
memory.loc.gov/ammem/afctshtml/tshome.html

This Library of Congress site includes Farm Security Administration studies of migrant work camps in California in 1940 and 1941, with audio, images, manuscripts, and publications.

New Deal Network
newdeal.feri.org

This site includes images, documents, texts, artifacts, and other materials from the New Deal era.

Crash of 1929
www.btinternet.com/~dreklind/thecrash.htm

This site includes a discussion of the causes of the 1929 stock market crash, along with audio clips of songs related to the crash.

Franklin D. Roosevelt Presidential Library and Museum
www.fdrlibrary.marist.edu/

This site includes documents, images, audio, and other primary source material from the Franklin D. Roosevelt Library.

New Deal for the Arts
www.archives.gov/exhibits/new_deal_for_the_arts/index.html

This site of the National Archives includes artwork, documents, photographs, and information from the New Deal programs that funded artists in the 1930s.

For Further Reading

General

Steve Fraser and Gary Gerstle, eds., *The Rise and Fall of the New Deal Order, 1930–1980* (1989).
Robert S. McElvaine, *The Great Depression: America, 1929–1941* (1984, 1993).
James R. McGovern, *And a Time for Hope: Americans in the Great Depression* (2000).
Studs Terkel, *Hard Times: An Oral History of the Great Depression* (1986).

The Great Depression

Glen Elder Jr., *Children of the Great Depression: Social Change in Life Experience* (1974).
Robert S. McElvaine, ed., *Down and Out in the Great Depression: Letters from the Forgotten Man* (1983).
Vicki L. Ruiz, *From Out of the Shadows: Mexican Women in Twentieth-Century America* (1998).
Judith Smith, *Family Connections: A History of Italian and Jewish Immigrant Lives in Providence, Rhode Island, 1900–1940* (1985).

Presidential Responses to the Depression

Edward D. Berkowitz, *America's Welfare State: From Roosevelt to Reagan* (1991).
Blanche Wiesen Cook, *Eleanor Roosevelt* (1999).
Frank Friedel, *Franklin D. Roosevelt: A Rendezvous with Destiny* (1990).
Lawrence W. Levine and Cornelia R. Levine, *The People and the President: America's Conversation with FDR* (2002).

The New Deal

Anthony Badger, *The New Deal* (1988).
Alan Brinkley, *Voices of Protest: Huey Long, Father Coughlin and the Great Depression* (1982).
Steven Fraser, *Labor Will Rule: Sidney Hillman and the Rise of American Labor* (1991).
Linda Gordon, *Pitied but Not Entitled: Single Mothers and the History of Welfare* (1994).

A New Political Culture

Lizabeth Cohen, *Making a New Deal: Industrial Workers in Chicago, 1919–1939* (1992).
Michael Denning, *Cultural Front: The Laboring of American Culture in the Twentieth Century* (1998).
Lary May, *The Big Tomorrow: Hollywood and the Politics of the American Way* (2000).

For quizzes and other resources on these topics, go to www.longmanamericanhistory.com.

CHAPTER 23

Global Conflict: World War II, 1937–1945

O N DECEMBER 7, 1941, KEITH LITTLE WAS OUT HUNTING RABBITS WITH FRIENDS AT THEIR boarding school on the Navajo reservation of Ganado, Arizona. When they heard the news that the Japanese had attacked the U.S. naval base in Hawaii at Pearl Harbor, the teenage boys pledged to fight for their country. The next morning, Little and his friends showed up with their hunting rifles at the office of the reservation superintendent, ready to enlist. The previous year, the Tribal Council had voted unanimously to defend the United States against invasion. "There exists no purer concentration of Americanism than among the First Americans," the council declared.

Little and about 400 other Navajo became part of a special unit that developed an intricate code, based on the Navajo language, to transmit top-secret information without risk of detection. The Navajo language was particularly well suited to code because very few people besides Navajo knew it. In a process code named "Magic," the all-Navajo 382nd Platoon of the U.S. Marine Corps encoded and decoded sensitive military information almost instantly and flawlessly. In two days on the Pacific island of Iwo Jima, six "Code Talkers" transmitted more than 800 messages, working around the clock, without a single error. Signal Officer Major Howard Conner recalled, "Without the Navajos the Marines would never have taken Iwo Jima."

The experiences of the Navajo "Code Talkers" echo many larger themes of America's involvement in World War II. Along with other ethnic and racial minorities, the Navajo willingly fought—and many died—

■ Navajo "Code Talkers" operate a portable radio in the Pacific combat zone in 1943.

CHAPTER OUTLINE

Mobilizing for War

Pearl Harbor: The United States Enters the War

The Home Front

Race and War

Total War

Conclusion

Sites to Visit

For Further Reading

for a country that had treated them as second-class citizens. African Americans also joined the war effort, though in segregated units, to fight for the **Double V**—victory against fascism abroad and racial discrimination at home. Young Japanese Americans left internment camps where their families had been forcibly detained to join a war against the land from which their parents came.

World War II was a global war, affecting countries and peoples all over the world. The huge scale of destruction was unlike that of any previous war. At least 55 million people died, including 25 million in the Soviet Union, 10 million in China, and 6 million in Poland. In the Holocaust, Nazi

Germany's campaign of genocide, 6 million European Jews perished along with thousands of Romani (Gypsies), Poles, mentally and physically disabled people, homosexuals, and others deemed "racially inferior." The war also had a tremendous impact on countries under colonial rule. Germany's bombardment of England and occupation of France, Holland, and Belgium weakened these countries' hold over their vast colonies. Japan's defeat of the American, British, Dutch, and French forces in Southeast Asia from 1940 to 1942 shocked the Western powers and ended white rule in the region, setting in motion a wave of decolonization in Asia and Africa after the war.

The United States was the only major combatant that did not suffer massive destruction on its home territory. It had two powerful advantages: an ocean barrier on its east and west coasts, plus tremendous natural resources that could provide the materials needed for modern warfare, such as steel and oil. In order to minimize American casualties, President Franklin Delano Roosevelt (FDR) pursued a strategy to make the United States the "arsenal of democracy," providing armaments and supplies to the other Allied powers so that their armies would do most of the fighting. Although the Soviet Union carried the largest burden of fighting the war and suffered the highest losses, millions of Americans also fought, and many died in the conflict. Military service had a leveling effect on social relations, as soldiers came together from all classes and ethnic groups. The vast majority of the troops—more than 85 percent—were white men from a wide variety of backgrounds. Soldiers of color generally fought in segregated units, but their battlefield successes and sacrifices gave them a sense of belonging to the nation and fueled postwar movements for equality and civil rights.

> *The United States was the only major combatant that did not suffer massive destruction on its home territory.*

No bombs dropped on the American mainland, yet the war reached into every aspect of national and personal life. Although wartime brought prosperity, the rationing of essential goods and the scarcity of consumer products brought nearly all Americans into the war effort. As soldiers and war industry workers moved around the country, local and regional sensibilities gave way to a stronger national identity. The U.S. military and defense establishment expanded to the formidable scale it would maintain during and after the war, making the United States the most powerful nation in the world.

Mobilizing for War

During the 1930s, the rise of **fascism** and militarism in Italy, Germany, and Japan created a terrible dilemma for Americans. Disillusioned by World War I and preoccupied with the hardships of the Great Depression, they disagreed strongly with each other about how to respond to overt aggression in Africa, Europe, and Asia. The ensuing "Great Debate" became a turning point in the nation's relationship with the outside world. Mobilizing for the enormous crusade of World War II gave rise to a unity of purpose that lasted throughout the war and into the postwar era.

The Rise of Fascism

In the 1930s, Depression-era Americans grappled with their problems at home and avoided entanglements abroad. But they found it difficult to ignore events in Europe and Asia. In Italy, Spain, and Germany, where a weak economy and high unemployment created political unrest, fascist leaders rose to power with strong popular support. These new leaders promised economic recovery through strengthening military and national expansion. They also encouraged intense nationalist sentiments, urging people to identify strongly with the state. Fascist governments were antidemocratic, antiparliamentary, and frequently antisemitic. These governments generally ruled by police surveillance, coercion, and terror.

Germany emerged as the most powerful fascist state in Europe. After Germany's defeat in World War I and the severe economic depression that Germany experienced in the 1920s, Adolf Hitler's National Socialist (Nazi) party won broad support in the weakened country. On January 30, 1933, Hitler became chancellor of Germany. Extolling fanatical nationalism and the racial superiority of "Aryan" Germans, Hitler blamed Jews for Germany's problems. He began a campaign of terror against Jews, homosexuals, suspected communists, and anyone else he saw as promoting "un-German" ideas. Hitler vowed to unite all German-speaking peoples into a new empire, the "Third Reich."

The fascist governments forged alliances to increase their power and launched campaigns of aggression and expansion. In 1935 Italy invaded Ethiopia, the sole independent African nation. The following year, Nazi troops occupied the Rhineland, in the western region of Germany, in violation of the Versailles agreement. Hitler and Mussolini signed the **Axis Pact**, and Japan forged an alliance with Germany. Soon after that, civil war erupted in Spain. Hitler and Mussolini extended aid to the fascist General Francisco Franco, who was trying to overthrow Spain's republican government.

Although Spanish republicans appealed to antifascist governments for help in the fight against Franco, only the Soviet Union came to their assistance. The United States maintained an official policy of neutrality. American Catholics and State Department conservatives believed that the anticommunist Franco would promote social stability. Many on the left, including large numbers of writers and intellectuals, championed the beleaguered Spanish government and denounced the fascists. Some joined Soviet-organized international forces to fight against Franco.

Aggression in Europe and Asia

In the spring and summer of 1938, Hitler annexed Austria to the Third Reich and then demanded that the Sudetenland be turned over to Germany. In the breakup of the Austro-Hungarian Empire after World War I, this German-speaking area had become part of the newly formed Czechoslovakia. Soviet leader Josef Stalin offered to join France and Britain to keep Hitler out of the Sudetenland and halt his aggression. But the leaders of France and Britain rebuffed Stalin's suggestion. In September they met with Hitler in Munich and agreed to let him have the Sudetenland in return for his promise that he would seek no more territory. Stalin feared that the anticommunist leaders of France and Britain were trying to turn Hitler's aggression toward the Soviet Union. To prevent that possibility, Stalin signed a nonaggression pact with Hitler. Eventually, Hitler broke all his promises. Throughout the war and after, the Munich meeting became the symbol of "appeasement," a warning that compromise with the enemy leads only to disaster.

Hitler and Mussolini in Munich, 1940

In 1939, with the help of the Soviet Union and in violation of the Munich agreement, Germany invaded Poland, which fell quickly. At that point Britain and France declared war on Germany. That same year, Madrid finally fell to Franco's forces.

By 1940 Hitler was sweeping through Europe, invading Denmark, Norway, Holland, Belgium, Luxembourg, and then France. In just six weeks, the Nazis had seized most of western Europe. Hitler then turned his forces on Great Britain. In the summer and fall of 1940, German raids on British air bases nearly destroyed the British Royal Air Force (RAF). Hitler ordered the bombing of London and other English cities, attacking civilians day and night in what came to be called the Battle of Britain.

In the Far East, events had taken an equally alarming turn. Nationalistic militarists gained control of the Japanese government in Tokyo and began a course of expansion. In 1931–1932,

Japanese troops occupied the large Chinese province of Manchuria. Five years later, the Japanese launched a full-scale war against China. The United States extended aid to China and discontinued trade with Japan. In 1940 Japan joined Germany and Italy in the Axis alliance and invaded the French colony of Indochina.

The Great Debate: Americans Contemplate War

In the mid-1930s, the overwhelming majority of Americans opposed intervention in foreign conflicts. Congress passed the Neutrality Acts of 1935, 1936, and 1937, outlawing arms sales or loans to nations at war and forbidding Americans from traveling on the ships of belligerent powers. In 1937 a Gallup poll indicated that 70 percent of Americans believed that the United States should have stayed out of World War I.

When Japan invaded China in 1937, FDR refused to comply with the provisions of the latest Neutrality Act, on the technicality that neither combatant had officially declared war. By creatively interpreting the law, he was able to offer loans to the embattled Chinese. Roosevelt felt strongly that the United States should actively help to resist the Axis powers.

The largest organization to oppose Roosevelt's effort was the America First Committee. With 450 chapters, the group claimed several hundred thousand members, including famed aviator Charles Lindbergh. Centered largely in the Midwest, the America Firsters included some active Nazi supporters. But conservative businesspeople also took part. Some members believed that war would impede American prosperity. Others, long opposed to Roosevelt and the New Deal, feared that war would give additional power to the already strong federal government. In 1940, the popular FDR nonetheless became the first president elected to a third term.

Despite intense nonintervention sentiments, public opinion began to shift. Many Americans were shocked when Hitler swiftly conquered much of Europe. News reports of the German occupation of France and the intense bombardment of England in the Battle of Britain bolstered FDR's efforts to take action. In his "Four Freedoms" speech to Congress in January 1941, FDR cited the four freedoms he considered necessary for the postwar world: freedom of speech and expression, freedom of worship, freedom from want, and freedom from fear. At that time, the United States was not yet officially at war. But the president pledged his support for England against the Nazis. A few months later, Congress approved the Lend-Lease agreement to lend rather than sell munitions to the Allied countries.

When Hitler broke his promise to Stalin and attacked the Soviet Union in June 1941, FDR extended Lend-Lease to the Soviets. During the summer, FDR and British Prime Minister Winston Churchill met on a ship off the coast of Newfoundland

TABLE 23-1

The Election of 1940

Candidate	Political Party	Popular Vote (%)	Electoral Vote
Franklin D. Roosevelt	Democratic	54.8	449
Wendell L. Willkie	Republican	44.8	82

■ Norman Rockwell's depiction of the "Four Freedoms," which adorned the cover of the *Saturday Evening Post*, inspired the purchase of war bonds and came to symbolize the democratic values for which the nation was fighting. These four scenes by the popular artist evoked an American ideal of close families and harmonious communities.

to develop a joint declaration known as the Atlantic Charter. The two leaders announced that the United States and Britain sought no new territories, they recognized the right of all peoples to choose their own form of government, and they called for international **free trade** and navigation. Realizing the possible cost of losing colonies, Churchill retreated from the global implications of the charter, while Roosevelt walked a fine line between contradicting Churchill and supporting the idea of empire. However, the charter emboldened anticolonial activists around the world.

Pearl Harbor: The United States Enters the War

The Japanese attack on Pearl Harbor shocked the nation and catapulted the United States immediately into World War II. President Roosevelt somberly told millions of Americans gathered around their radios that the day of the attack would "live in infamy." Most former doubters now joined the war effort. The entire nation shifted into high gear to defeat brutal, aggressive regimes intent on conquering much of the world. For some, wartime mobilization offered new opportunities; for others, it brought sacrifice.

December 7, 1941

For nearly a decade, tensions had been mounting between the United States and Japan as American leaders tried to contain Japan's expansion in Asia. Roosevelt assumed that a strong U.S. military presence in the Pacific would persuade Japan's premier, General Hideki Tojo, to avoid a confrontation with the United States. When Japan continued its aggression in Asia, FDR froze Japanese assets in the United States, putting trade with Japan under presidential control. This move, he hoped, would bring Japan to the bargaining table. Instead, on November 25, the Japanese dispatched aircraft carriers toward Hawaii and sent troops to the border of Malaya in the South Pacific.

Although U.S. intelligence sources had broken the codes with which the Japanese encrypted messages about their war plans, they did not realize that the Japanese intended to strike Hawaii. At 7:55 a.m. on December 7, Japanese planes swooped over Pearl Harbor and bombed the naval base. The assault caught the American forces completely off guard and destroyed most of the U.S. Pacific fleet. Only a few aircraft carriers that were out at sea survived. Two hours after the attack on Pearl Harbor, the Japanese also struck the main U.S. base at Clark Field in the Philippines, destroying half of the U.S. Air Force in the Far East.

At roughly the same time that Keith Little heard the news about Pearl Harbor at his Navajo reservation boarding school, another sixteen-year-old, John Garcia, watched flames rising at Pearl Harbor from his house four miles away. The young Hawaiian reached the scene in time to witness the second round of bombings. "I spent the rest of the day swimming inside the harbor, along with some other Hawaiians. I brought out I don't know how many bodies, and how many were alive and how many dead. . . . We worked around the clock for three days."

When the smoke cleared, 2,323 American service personnel were dead. Congress immediately declared war against Japan. Three days later, Germany and Italy declared war against the United States.

Japanese American Relocation

The assault on Pearl Harbor sparked widespread rumors along the U.S. West Coast that Japanese and Japanese Americans living there planned to sabotage the war effort. Although no charges of criminal activity or treason were ever brought against any Japanese Americans, powerful white farming interests eager to eradicate Japanese American competition pushed for an evacuation.

Not everyone supported the internment idea. U.S. Attorney General Francis Biddle protested that there was "no reason" for a mass relocation. J. Edgar Hoover, director of the FBI, also opposed the plan, arguing that it reflected "hysteria and lack of judgment." Nevertheless, the Roosevelt administration gave in to the pressure, with the support of California Attorney General Earl Warren. In February 1942, Roosevelt signed Executive Order 9066, which suspended the civil rights of American citizens of Japanese descent. The order authorized the removal of 110,000 Japanese and Japanese Americans from the West Coast. Of those, 70,000 were *Nisei*, native-born American citizens. Families received at most a week's notice to evacuate their homes and move to prisonlike camps surrounded by barbed wire and guarded by armed soldiers. There were ten such camps in seven states, most of them located in arid, desolate spots in the West. At the camps, internees lived in makeshift wooden barracks, where entire families crowded into one room.

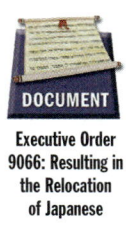

DOCUMENT

Executive Order 9066: Resulting in the Relocation of Japanese

While the internment experience alienated some Japanese Americans, fully 33,000 joined the armed services—including 1,200 who enlisted from the internment camps—and proved their patriotism on the battlefield. In the Pacific, their knowledge of the Japanese language proved critical in translating intercepted Japanese military documents. General Charles Willoughby, chief of intelligence in the Pacific, estimated that Japanese American military contributions shortened the war by two years. The Japanese also served ably in Europe, suffering huge casualties. The Japanese Americans of the 442nd Regiment lost one-fourth of their soldiers in battles in North Africa and Italy. They suffered another 800 casualties rescuing the Texan "Lost Battalion," 211 men surrounded by German troops in the Vosges Mountains of France. As one Texan recalled, "We were never so glad to see anyone as those fighting Japanese Americans."

■ On December 7, 1941, the Japanese launched a surprise attack on the U.S. naval base at Pearl Harbor, Hawaii. The attack brought the United States immediately into World War II and was the only time that the war came to American soil.

■ **MAP 23.1**
INTERNMENT OF JAPANESE AMERICANS DURING WORLD WAR II After the Japanese attack on Pearl Harbor, President Franklin Delano Roosevelt signed an order authorizing the removal of people of Japanese descent from the West Coast. These Japanese Americans were relocated to internment camps built in arid and isolated areas in the West, as well as in two locations in Arkansas.

Nevertheless, the U.S. government would take its time acknowledging that the internment had been a grave injustice. The Supreme Court upheld the constitutionality of the policy, and Roosevelt would not rescind the evacuation order until after his reelection in 1944. The camps finally closed in 1945. All told, Japanese Americans lost property valued at $500 million. In 1988 Congress enacted legislation awarding restitution payments of $20,000 each to 60,000 surviving internees—a small gesture for Americans whose only "crime" was their Japanese ancestry.

Foreign Nationals in the United States

Although Japanese Americans were the only U.S. citizens interned solely on the basis of their ancestry, German and Italian nationals living in the United States were also subject to new regulations, and in some cases relocation and incarceration. The Smith Act of 1940 required all foreign-born residents to be registered and fingerprinted, and broadened the grounds for deportation.

Six hundred thousand Italians and 314,000 Germans living in the United States were subject to these requirements. Several hundred were deemed potentially dangerous and interned for the duration of the war. Approximately 10,000 Italian nationals were forced to relocate from their homes on the West Coast. A few hundred German and Italian immigrants who were naturalized U.S. citizens were also relocated from designated coastal areas.

Wartime Migrations

Even before the United States officially entered World War II, the conflict had begun to change the face of the nation. The sleepy town of Richmond, California, perched near the north end of San Francisco Bay, underwent a profound transformation when the nation stepped up war production. The town's mostly white population of 23,000 ballooned to 120,000 after industrialist Henry Kaiser constructed four shipyards there. The yards employed over 150,000 workers, more than one-fourth of them African American. Most were young, married migrants from the South, and there were slightly more women than men. They came to Richmond attracted by the better pay and benefits, along with the opportunity for greater freedom than they had known in the Jim Crow South.

■ The family pictured here was among thousands of loyal citizens of Japanese ancestry removed from their homes on the West Coast and relocated to internment camps. Here, the Hirano family, George, Hisa, and Yasbei (left to right), pose at the Colorado River Relocation Center in Poston, Arizona. Hisa holds a photo of her son, an American soldier, who is off fighting the war.

Many cities, however, were ill equipped to handle the influx of migrants. An estimated 60,000 African Americans moved into Chicago, for example, causing an enormous housing crisis. Many newcomers lacked even a modicum of privacy as they crowded into basements and rooms rented from total strangers. Huge numbers of whites also came north, many leaving hardscrabble farms and hoping to prosper in booming war industries.

Wartime also saw new migration from abroad and a reversal of earlier immigration policies. Because of the alliance with China in the war against Japan, in 1943 Congress repealed the Chinese Exclusion Act, and migrants from China became eligible for citizenship for the first time. An executive agreement between the United States and Mexico created the **bracero** program, under which 300,000 Mexican laborers, mostly agricultural workers, came to rural areas like California's San Joaquin Valley. By the mid-1960s, nearly 5 million Mexicans had migrated north under the program.

The Home Front

Wartime mobilization brought Americans from all regions and backgrounds together in shared service and sacrifice. Automobile manufacturers stopped making cars and instead turned out tanks, jeeps, and other military vehicles. Citizens made do with government-rationed basic staples, from food to gasoline. As able-bodied men left their jobs to fight the war, new work opportunities opened up for women as well as for disabled Americans. Cities and centers of war production brought together young women and men who found new opportunities for sexual experimentation, while gay men and lesbians discovered newly visible communities in both military and civilian life. The war raised expectations of women and minorities that they would achieve full inclusion in the American promise.

Many Americans hoped that the liberal spirit of the New Deal would endure during the war; others were eager for an end to what they perceived as Depression-era class conflict and hostility to business interests. To some extent, both sides got their wish. Full employment, the increasing strength of unions, and high taxes on the wealthy pleased New Deal liberals. Profit guarantees, freedom from antitrust actions, no-strike pledges, and low-cost imported labor gratified probusiness conservatives. And Roosevelt was elected to an unprecedented fourth term in 1944.

TABLE 23-2
The Election of 1944

Candidate	Political Party	Popular Vote (%)	Electoral Vote
Franklin D. Roosevelt	Democratic	53.5	432
Thomas E. Dewey	Republican	46.0	99

Building Morale

The United States, like all other major powers involved in the conflict, mounted a propaganda drive to promote support for the war effort. Roosevelt created the Office of War Information (OWI) in 1942 to coordinate morale-boosting and censorship initiatives. Working in partnership with the motion picture industry and other media outlets, the OWI sponsored movies, radio programs, publications, and posters. These productions portrayed the war as a crusade to preserve the "American way of life" and encouraged American women and men to work in war industries, enlist in the armed forces, and purchase war bonds. Eric Johnston, head of the Motion Picture Producers' Association and FDR's business adviser, insisted that Hollywood remove class conflict from its films: "We'll have no more *Grapes of Wrath*, we'll have no more *Tobacco Roads*, we'll have no more films that deal with the seamy side of American life. We'll have no more films that treat the banker as a villain."

Within the United States, government censors made sure that no photographs showing badly wounded soldiers or mutilated bodies reached the public. The censors also removed any images that might elicit sympathy for the enemy, such as pictures of injured or frightened enemy soldiers suffering at the hands of American soldiers. Photographs that appeared in the American media generally sanitized the horror of war, depicting noble American soldiers and a shadowy, faceless enemy. Rarely, if ever, did those on the home front see the true extent of the war's destructiveness and brutality. When men returned home severely traumatized by what they had seen, even their trauma was censored. As just one example, for more than three decades, the army suppressed John Huston's *Let There Be Light*, a film documentary of World War II veterans in a psychiatric hospital suffering from post-traumatic stress disorder.

Home Front Workers, "Rosie the Riveter," and "Victory Girls"

Wartime opened up new possibilities for jobs, income, and labor organizing, for women as well as for men, and for new groups of workers. Disabled workers entered jobs previously considered beyond their abilities, fulfilling their tasks with skill and competence. Norma Krajczar, a visually impaired teenager from North Carolina, served as a volunteer aircraft warden where her sensitive hearing gave her an advantage over sighted wardens in listening for approaching enemy planes. Deaf people streamed into Akron, Ohio, to work in the tire factories that became defense plants, making more money than they ever made before.

Along with new employment opportunities, workers' earnings rose nearly 70 percent. Income doubled for farmers and then doubled again. Labor union membership grew 50 per-

■ Eight American presidents elected consecutively following World War II were veterans of that war. Pictured in wartime service, from top left, are: Dwight D. Eisenhower, John F. Kennedy, Lyndon Johnson, Richard Nixon, Gerald Ford, Jimmy Carter, Ronald Reagan, and George H. W. Bush.

cent, reaching an all-time high by the end of the war. Women and minorities joined unions in unprecedented numbers. Energetic labor organizers like Luisa Moreno and Dorothy Ray Healy organized Mexican and Russian Jewish workers at the California Sanitary Canning Company into a powerful CIO cannery union that achieved wage increases and union recognition.

World War II ushered in dramatic changes for American women. Wartime scarcities led to increased domestic labor as homemakers made do with rationed goods, mended clothing, collected and saved scraps and metals, and planted "victory gardens" to help feed their families. Employment opportunities for women also increased. As a result of the combined incentives of patriotism and good wages, many women took "men's jobs" while the men went off to fight.

Rosie the Riveter became the heroic symbol of the woman war worker. Pictures of attractive "Rosies" building planes or constructing ships graced magazine covers and posters. Future Hollywood star Marilyn Monroe first gained attention when her photograph appeared in *Yank*, a magazine for soldiers. The magazine pictured her not as the sex goddess she later became, but as a typical Rosie the Riveter clad in overalls, working at her job in a defense plant.

For the first time, married women joined the paid labor force in droves and public opinion supported them. During the Depression, 80 percent of Americans had objected to the idea of wives working outside the home; by 1942 only 13 percent still objected. However, mothers of young children found very little help. In 1943 the federal government finally responded to the needs of working mothers by funding some day-care centers. But meager to begin with and conceived as an emergency measure, government funding for child care would end after the war.

New opportunities for women also opened up in the armed services. All sectors of the armed forces had dwindled in the years between the two wars and needed to gain size and strength. Along with the 10 million men aged twenty-one to thirty-five drafted into the armed services and the 6 million who enlisted, 140,000 women volunteered for the Women's Army Corps (WACs; originally the Women's Army Auxiliary Corps, WAAC) and 100,000 for the Navy WAVES (Women Accepted for Voluntary Emergency Service).

Most female enlistees and war workers enjoyed their work and wanted to continue after the war. The extra pay, independence, camaraderie, and satisfaction that their jobs provided had opened their eyes to new possibilities. Edith Speert, like many others, was never again content as a full-time housewife and mother. Edith's husband, Victor, was sent overseas in 1944. During the eighteen months of their separation, they penned 1,300 letters to each other, sometimes two or three times a day. The letters revealed the love and affection they felt for one another, but Edith did not hesitate to tell Victor how she had changed. In a letter from Cleveland, dated November 9, 1945, she wrote:

> Sweetie, I want to make sure I make myself clear about how I've changed. I want you to know *now* that you are not married to a girl that's interested solely in a home—I shall definitely have to work all my life—I get emotional satisfaction out of working; and I don't doubt that many a night you will cook the supper while I'm at a meeting. Also, dearest—I shall never wash and iron—there are laundries for that! Do you think you'll be able to bear living with me? . . .
> I love you, Edith

Wartime upheaval sent the sexual order topsy-turvy. For many young women, moving to a new city or taking a wartime job opened up new possibilities for independence, excitement, and sexual adventure. Some young women, known as "victory girls," believed that it was an act of patriotism to have a fling with a man in uniform before he went overseas. The independence of these women raised fears of female sexuality as a dangerous, ungoverned force. The worry extended beyond the traditional concern about prostitutes and "loose women" to include "good girls" whose sexual standards might relax during wartime. Public health campaigns warned enlisted men that "victory girls" would have their fun with a soldier and then leave him with a venereal disease, incapable of fighting for his country.

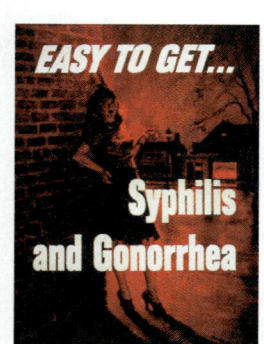

Wartime also intensified concerns about homosexuality. Urban centers and the military provided new opportunities for gay men and lesbians to form relationships and build communities. Although the military officially banned homosexuals from the forces, many served by keeping their orientation secret. If discovered, gay men faced severe punishment, including confinement in cages called "queer stockades" or in psychiatric wards. Lesbians faced similar sanctions, although the women's corps, in an effort to assure the civilian world of their recruits' femininity, often looked the other way.

Race and War

The Holocaust, Nazi Germany's campaign to exterminate European Jews, demonstrated the horrors of racial hatred taken to its ultimate extreme. The U.S. government did little to help Jewish refugees or to stem the slaughter of Jews in Europe. Official indifference and widespread antisemitism prevailed throughout the war. Nevertheless, Nazi policies against the Jews discredited racial and ethnic prejudice, forcing Americans to confront the reality of racism in their own country. Anthropologist Ruth Benedict, in her 1943 book *The Races of Mankind*, urged the United States to "clean its own house" and "stand unashamed before Nazis and condemn, without confusion, their doctrines of a Master Race." As black leader W. E. B. Du

Bois noted, World War II was a "War for Racial Equality" and a struggle for "democracy not only for white folks but for yellow, brown, and black."

The Holocaust

Hitler's war aims included conquering all of Europe and destroying European Jewry. Throughout the war, Nazi anti-Jewish policies escalated from persecution and officially sanctioned violence to imprisonment in concentration camps, slave labor, and ultimately Hitler's "Final Solution," genocide. Nazis developed increasingly efficient means of killing Jews. In the infamous Nazi death camps, guards herded prisoners into "shower rooms" that were actually gas chambers.

Nazi Murder Mills

American officials knew of the Nazi persecution of the Jews but did little about it. Throughout the 1930s, American Jewish groups pressured the Roosevelt administration to ease immigration laws to allow Jewish refugees to enter the country. But the United States raised the legal quota of Jewish immigrants only slightly.

When the Nazis began their policy of extermination in 1941, they tried to keep it a secret. U.S. State Department officials heard reports of the Holocaust but decided to keep the information quiet. Despite official silence, Rabbi Stephen S. Wise, a prominent American Jewish leader, heard the news and held a press conference in November 1942. But the American press, preoccupied with military events and reluctant to publish stories of atrocities without official verification, gave the Holocaust little coverage. Meanwhile, despite reports of Nazi genocide, the U.S. government turned away boatloads of Jewish refugees, sending them back to Germany to their deaths.

Nazi persecution of the Jews raised American sensitivity to the issue of racism but did little to diminish antisemitism within the United States. In fact, American hostility toward Jews reached new heights during World War II and exceeded the level of prejudice against any other group. In 1944, when asked to identify the greatest "menace" to the nation, 24 percent of Americans polled listed Jews—more than those who listed Germans, Japanese, radicals, Negroes, and foreigners. In Europe, American military strategists knew of the existence and location of Nazi death camps, but they chose not to try to bomb them or the railroad lines leading to the camps.

The U.S. government turned away boatloads of Jewish refugees, sending them back to Germany to their deaths.

Racial Tensions at Home

Throughout the war years, racial tensions within the United States persisted. Black workers, who were excluded from the best-paying jobs in the defense industry, mobilized against discrimination on the job. Their most powerful advocate was African American civil rights leader A. Philip Randolph, who had organized the overwhelmingly black Brotherhood of Sleeping Car Porters and won the union a contract with the railroads in 1937. At the beginning of American involvement in the war in 1941, Randolph pressured FDR to ban discrimination in defense industries. He threatened to organize a massive march on Washington if Roosevelt did not respond. Roosevelt issued Executive Order 8802, which created the Fair Employment Practices Commission (FEPC) to ensure that blacks and women received the same pay as white men for doing the same job. The FEPC narrowed pay gaps somewhat, but it did not solve the problem. The American Federation of Labor, which included the highest-paid workers, still refused to accept blacks as members and fought with the FEPC over the equal-pay policy.

Randolph, "Why Should We March"

Sometimes the presence of racial minorities in previously all-white work settings led to hostilities. In 1943 in Detroit, white workers at the Packard auto plant walked off the job when three black employees were promoted. With increasing numbers of white and black Southerners arriving to work in the city's war industries, overcrowding strained the boundaries of traditionally segregated neighborhoods. Clashes at a new housing complex escalated into several days of rioting, resulting in thirty-four deaths and 1,800 arrests.

INTERPRETING HISTORY

Zelda Webb Anderson, "You Just Met One Who Does Not Know How to Cook"

Zelda Webb Anderson became one of the first black women to enter military service during World War II. She served as an officer in the Women's Army Auxiliary Corps (WAACS), renamed the Women's Army Corps (WAC) in 1943. After the war she earned a doctorate in education at the University of California, Berkeley. Her 42-year career in education included a stint teaching at the University of East Africa in Dar-es-Salaam, Tanzania. She related her wartime experiences to the University of Nevada Oral History Program in 1995.

I reported for duty in January 1942. . . . This was so exciting to me. We had black officers, and our basic training was the same as for men. They would simply tell us, "You wanted to be in a man's army, so now you got to do what the men do." We learned military courtesy, history, how to shoot an M-1, go on bivouac, bathe in a teacup of water, eat hardtack rations. . . .

Every evening troops of male soldiers would march by our barracks en route to the mess hall. I told the commanding officer that we would like to have some shades at the windows. "Oh, no. You wanted to be in the man's army. Fine—you have to do what the men do." I told all the girls, "Listen, they won't give us any shades. So I want you to get right in front of the windows buck naked." The next day we had shades at all the windows. . . .

They pulled me out of basic training the third week and sent me to officer training in Des Moines. All of the instruc-

Zelda Webb Anderson

tors were white, but white and black officers were being trained in the same facility, in the same classes, and we slept in the same barracks. After OCS I was assigned to a laundry unit.

A black enlisted WAAC could either be in the laundry unit or she could be in the hospital unit. In the laundry unit, if she had a college degree, she could work at the front counter. . . . If she had less than that, then she did the laundry—very demeaning. And in the hospital unit they let her wash walls, empty basins, wash windows—all that menial work. . . .

I was assigned to duty at Fort Breckenridge, Kentucky. The post commander's name was Colonel Throckmorton. In a pronounced southern accent he told me, "You're going over to that colored WAC company, and you're going to be the mess officer."

I said, "Sir, I have not had any mess training."

"All you nigras know how to cook."

I said, "You just met one who does not know how to cook; but if you send me to Fort Eustis, Virginia, for training I will come back and be the best mess officer you have on this post."

"I ain't sending you to no school, and you're going over there to be a mess officer." When I about-faced, I kept on going. I didn't even salute him. . . .

[Much later, after developing a more cordial relationship with Colonel Throckmorton,] I told him that segregation has not allowed white people to know black people: "We know you very intimately, but you don't know how we think, how we react, and so you just try to push your stuff on us, not giving a damn about how we feel about this. And then when we rebel, or you meet somebody like me, who decides that you can't do this to me, then you think I'm cantankerous; you think I'm an agitator. I'm just trying to give you an education. . . ."

I lived out the rest of my days very happy in the Army. If I had succumbed to the treatment that they had given other blacks before, and not spoken up for myself, my morale would have been down. . . . In this life, you've got to speak up for yourself. You can't go around shuffling your feet with your head hung down acting apologetic. If you see something you want, you must go after it. One day somebody will recognize it, and it's a victory for you, especially when it's somebody who has denigrated you because of your race. . . .

Our country has not solved all of its problems. You have to live democracy before you can preach democracy. I've got four granddaughters, and I don't want them put in a position where they don't have equal opportunities, equal chances, and then they have to fight the same old battles that I fought again.

Questions

1. Why do you think Anderson, as a woman and an African American, would choose to enlist in the U.S. Army during World War II?
2. According to Anderson, in what ways did the segregation of the armed forces distort white officers' views of blacks?

In Los Angeles, the death of a Mexican American youth, José Diaz, at a gravel pit called Sleepy Lagoon sparked sensational news coverage and whipped up anti-Mexican fervor. Although police never determined the cause of Diaz's injuries, they filed first-degree murder charges against twenty-two Mexican American boys from the neighborhood. The jury found the young men guilty, but an appeals court overturned the convictions. Nevertheless, hostility continued to mount against Mexican American youths, particularly **pachucos** who sported **zoot suits**, distinctive attire with flared pants, long coats, and wide-brimmed hats. Pachucos wore the zoot suit as an expression of ethnic pride and rebelliousness, as well as incipient political consciousness.

For eight days in June 1943, scores of soldiers hunted zoot-suiters in Los Angeles bars, theaters, dance halls, and even in their homes, pulling off their clothes and beating them. Soon the attacks expanded to all Mexican Americans, and then to African Americans as well, some of whom also wore the zoot-suit style. The Los Angeles police sided with the rioters. They stood by during the beatings and then arrested the naked and bleeding youths and charged them with disturbing the peace. The rioting raged until the War Department made the entire city of Los Angeles off limits to military personnel.

Fighting for the "Double V"

In spite of discrimination at home, members of minority groups responded enthusiastically to the war effort. The numbers of blacks in the U.S. army soared from 5,000 in 1940 to 700,000 by 1944, with an additional 187,000 in the U.S. Navy, Coast Guard, and Marine Corps. Four thousand black women joined the WACs. Almost all soldiers fought in segregated units, despite protests by the NAACP that "a Jim Crow army cannot fight for a free world." African Americans fought for the "Double V"—victory over fascism abroad and racial discrimination at home.

Like Keith Little and his boarding-school buddies who became Navajo "Code Talkers" (described at the beginning of this chapter), American Indians all over the country declared their willingness to fight for the cause. Fully 25,000 Native Americans, including 800 women, served in the military during the war. By 1945 nearly one-third of all able-bodied Native American men between eighteen and fifty had served. Five percent of them were killed or wounded in action. Native Americans enlisted at a higher rate than the general population, prompting the *Saturday Evening Post* to editorialize, "We would not need the Selective Service if all volunteered like the Indians."

In addition to those who enlisted, half of all able-bodied Native American men not in the service and one-fifth of women left reservations for war-industry jobs. At the beginning of the war, men on reservations earned a median annual income of $500, less than one-fourth the national average. One-third of all Native American men living off reservations were unemployed. Worse, the average life expectancy for Native Americans in 1940 was just thirty-five years, compared with sixty-four years for the population at large. Like others who found new opportunities during the conflict, Native Americans hoped that the economic progress they had made would be permanent. But the boom would end for them when the war ended. Fewer than 10 percent of Native Americans who relocated to cities found long-term employment after the war.

Total War

World War II consisted of two wars, one centered in Europe and the other in the Pacific. Combatants in both conflicts engaged in **total war**—the targeting of civilian as well as military targets. Of all the combatants, only the United States escaped physical destruction on its own national soil (with the exception of Pearl Harbor). Coming out of the war physically unscathed, economically sound, and politically strong, the United States became the most prosperous and powerful nation in the world.

World War II in Europe

The War in Europe

The attack on Pearl Harbor brought the United States immediately into the war in both Europe and the Pacific. The leaders of the Allied powers, including the United States, Britain, and the Soviet Union, had to develop a strategy to defeat the Axis powers. But the **Allies** did not always agree on how to conduct the war, and relations between the United States and the Soviet Union remained strained. Unable to fully overcome the hostility and suspicion that had marked their earlier encounters, leaders of both countries fought the war with postwar power considerations in mind.

Like the United States at Pearl Harbor, the Soviet Union suffered a shocking blow when Germany launched a surprise invasion in June 1941 in violation of the nonaggression pact Hitler had signed with Stalin in 1938. With the full might of the Nazi forces now concentrated on the front lines against the Russians in eastern Europe, Soviet premier Joseph Stalin wanted the United States to open a second front in western Europe to divert the Nazis toward the west and relieve pressure on the Soviet

■ **MAP 23.2**
WORLD WAR II IN EUROPE Along the eastern front of the war in Europe, Soviet troops did the bulk of the Allied fighting in Europe and sustained the highest casualties. The Battle of Stalingrad, in which Soviet troops finally drove back the Nazis after months of brutal fighting, was a major turning point in the war.

Union. In May 1942, Roosevelt assured Stalin that the United States would support an Allied invasion across the English Channel into France. But the British prime minister, Winston Churchill, persuaded FDR to delay that dangerous maneuver and instead to launch an invasion of French north Africa, which was controlled by the Nazi occupation forces in Vichy, France.

While the Allies turned their attention to north Africa, the Soviets managed single-handedly to force the German army into retreat at Stalingrad, where fierce fighting lasted from August 1942 to January 1943. The Battle of Stalingrad was a major turning point in the war. Axis soldiers in north Africa also surrendered in May 1943. The following summer, the Allied forces overran the island of Sicily and moved into southern Italy. Italians overthrew Mussolini and opened communication with General Dwight D. Eisenhower, commander of the Allied forces in Europe. By 1944 the Allied forces reached Rome.

A photograph taken on D-Day, June 6, 1944, as U.S. troops waded to shore from their landing craft and faced German artillery fire on Omaha Beach. This is a rare surviving photograph from the initial Normandy invasion because so many of the photographers, along with thousands of soldiers, died at the scene.

The long-awaited Allied invasion across the English Channel finally began on June 6, 1944, code named D-Day. At dawn, in the largest amphibious landing in history, more than 4,000 Allied ships descended on the French beaches at Normandy. As the troops splashed onto shore, they met a barrage of German fire. Many thousands died on the beach that day. Over the next ten days, more than 1 million soldiers landed at Normandy, along with 50,000 vehicles and more than 100,000 tons of supplies, opening the way for an advance into Nazi-occupied France.

In the months after D-Day, the western Allies liberated Paris and went on to defeat the Germans in Belgium at the Battle of the Bulge, sending the Nazis into full retreat. The Allied armies then crossed the Rhine River and headed for Berlin. Eisenhower stopped his troops at the Elbe River to let Soviet troops take Berlin. Eisenhower hoped that giving the Soviets the final triumph would ease postwar relations with the Soviet Union—but he also wanted to save American lives. Huge numbers of Soviet troops died in the siege of Berlin, but the war in Europe was nearly over. With the Soviets approaching his bunker in April 1945, Hitler committed suicide. Germany surrendered on May 7, 1945—V-E (Victory in Europe) Day. FDR himself had died suddenly of a cerebral hemorrhage on April 12, 1945.

The War in the Pacific

As the conflict in Europe came to an end, the war in the Pacific continued to rage. Following the attack on Pearl Harbor, Japan continued its conquests in the Pacific. In April 1942, General Douglas MacArthur, driven from the Philippines to Australia, left 12,000 American and 64,000 Filipino soldiers to surrender on the Bataan peninsula and the island of Corregidor. On the infamous "Bataan Death March" to the prison at Camp O'Donnell, the Japanese beat, tortured, and shot the sick and starving troops. As many as 10,000 men died on the march.

Now in control of Indochina, Thailand, the Philippines, and the chain of islands from Sumatra to Guadalcanal, Japan's military leaders planned to destroy what remained of the U.S. fleet. But MacArthur marshaled his forces and achieved a major victory in the Battle of the Coral Sea in May 1942. U.S. intelligence sources discovered that the Japanese were planning a massive assault on Midway Island, a naval base key to Hawaii's defense. Under the command of Admiral Chester Nimitz, the United States launched a surprise air strike on June 4,

World War II in the Pacific

■ **MAP 23.3**
WORLD WAR II IN THE PACIFIC During World War II, the Japanese occupied vast territories in Asia and the Pacific. The Battle of Midway in 1942 was the first major victory for the United States in the Pacific and helped turn the tide of the war in favor of the Allies.

1942, sinking four Japanese carriers, destroying 322 planes, and virtually eliminating Japanese offensive capabilities. Two months later, Nimitz's forces landed at Guadalcanal in the Solomon Islands, subduing the Japanese in five months of brutal fighting. Having seized the offensive, U.S. troops continued toward Japan. MacArthur's forces took New Guinea, and, by February 1944, Nimitz secured the Marshall Islands and the Marianas. Next came Saipan, Iwo Jima, and Okinawa in the spring of 1945.

The war in the Pacific was particularly vicious. Racism on both sides fueled acts of extreme brutality. Japan's leaders believed that their racial superiority gave them a divine mission to conquer Asia. The Japanese tortured prisoners of war and civilians in their conquered lands. They tested biological weapons and conducted medical experiments on live subjects. Japanese troops forced Chinese and Korean women into sexual slavery, euphemistically calling them "**comfort women**."

Racial hostility also promoted American battlefield savagery. U.S. troops in the Pacific often killed the enemy instead of taking prisoners and desecrated the enemy dead with disrespect equal to that meted out by the Japanese on the bodies of their foes. War correspondent Ernie Pyle explained that "in Europe we felt that our enemies, horrible and deadly as they were, were still people. But . . . the Japanese were looked upon as something subhuman and repulsive, the way some people feel about cockroaches or mice."

The End of the War

Allied leaders met several times to plan for the postwar era. Roosevelt hoped to ensure American dominance and to limit Soviet power. At a conference in Teheran, Iran, in 1943, Roosevelt insisted that the eastern European states of Poland, Latvia, Lithuania, and Estonia should be independent after the war. As the war wound down, Churchill, Stalin, and Roosevelt met again at Yalta, in Ukraine, in February 1945. They agreed to demand Germany's unconditional surrender and to divide the conquered nation into four zones to be occupied by Britain, the Soviet Union, the United States, and France. It became obvious at Yalta that separate spheres of influence would prevail after the war. Poland was a source of contention. Although Stalin nominally agreed to allow free elections in eastern Europe, he intended to make sure that the countries bordering the Soviet Union would be under his control. He also pledged to enter the war against Japan and received assurances that the Soviet Union would regain the lands lost to Japan in the 1904–1905 Russo-Japanese War.

DOCUMENT
Manhattan Project Notebook

In July 1945, the newly sworn-in American president, Harry Truman, joined Stalin and Churchill (replaced by Clement Attlee after Churchill's election loss) at Potsdam, near Berlin. The three leaders issued a statement demanding "unconditional surrender" from Japan while privately agreeing to let Japan retain its emperor. The rest of the conference focused on postwar Europe.

As the war ended in Europe, Allied troops liberated the Nazi concentration camps. At that moment, the world finally learned the extent of Hitler's "Final Solution." Among the soldiers who first entered the camps were a number of Japanese Americans. Ichiro Imamura described the sight at Dachau: "When the gates swung open, we got our first good look at the prisoners. . . . They were like skeletons—all skin and bones. . . . They were sick, starving and dying." Some of the survivors saw the Japanese American soldiers and feared that they were Japanese allies of the Germans. A *Nisei* soldier reassured them, "I am an American soldier, and you are free."

The atomic bomb offered Truman a new means to end the war. In 1942 Roosevelt had authorized the Manhattan Project, the research program to develop nuclear weapons, at a top-secret laboratory in Los Alamos, New Mexico. The building of the bomb was the work of 125,000 people and cost nearly $2 billion.

When Truman learned of the successful test on July 16, 1945, while at the Potsdam conference, he hoped to avoid an invasion of Japan that would have cost the lives of many American soldiers, and he wanted to send a message to the Soviet Union that the United States would be the dominant power in the postwar world. But some of the scientists who had developed the bomb urged a "demonstration" in a remote, unpopulated area that would impress the Japanese but would not cause loss of life. General George C. Marshall and other military leaders argued in favor of dropping the bomb on military or industrial targets, with ample warning ahead

■ On V-J Day, August 14, 1945, New Yorkers of Italian descent celebrate Japan's surrender. Although the United States fought against the country of their ancestors, these Americans showed their spirited support for the Allied cause.

of time to enable civilians to leave target areas. But others agreed with Truman that dropping the bomb on a major city, without warning, would be the only way to persuade the Japanese to surrender unconditionally.

When the first bomb exploded over Hiroshima on August 6, 1945, and the second on Nagasaki two days later, the horrifying destructiveness of nuclear weapons became apparent. Even though the American public saw few images of the carnage on the ground, the huge mushroom cloud and the descriptions of cities leveled and people instantly incinerated shocked the nation and the world. In addition to the immediate devastation wreaked by the bomb, deadly radioactive fallout remained in the atmosphere, causing illness and death for months and even years after the attack. On August 14, 1945—V-J (Victory in Japan) Day—the Japanese agreed to surrender, and the official ceremony of surrender took place on September 2.

Conclusion

World War II left massive devastation in its wake all across the globe. Although 400,000 Americans died in the conflict, American casualties were far below those suffered by other countries. The wartime economy provided full employment and brought the nation out of the Great Depression.

The war changed life for Americans in profound ways. Although wartime forged a sense of unity as the nation came together to fight against fascism, it also highlighted fissures within American society. Members of minority groups fought in segregated units. Racial tensions and conflicts erupted at home, even as the country fought against a racist foe. Women joined the paid labor force and the armed services in unprecedented numbers, while at the same time being bombarded by official and cultural messages reminding them that their ultimate service to the nation was as wives and mothers.

While life at home changed dramatically, so did the place of the United States in the world. The war's conclusion did not usher in the era of peace Americans expected. European empires staggered on the brink of collapse. Only the United States and the Soviet Union remained as major military powers, shifting the international balance of power from a multipolar to a bipolar system. For the next half-century, the fallout from World War II, as well as the power struggle between the United States and the Soviet Union, would shape political relationships across the globe.

Sites to Visit

Powers of Persuasion—Poster Art of World War II
www.archives.gov/exhibits/powers_of_persuasion/powers_of_persuasion_home.html
This Library of Congress site includes posters created during World War II to encourage support for the war and to build morale.

A-Bomb WWW Museum
www.csi.ad.jp/ABOMB/
This site includes information about the impact of the atomic bombs dropped on Japan during World War II as well as materials and images about the development of nuclear weapons.

A People at War
www.archives.gov/exhibits/a_people_at_war/a_people_at_war.html
This National Archives site includes materials and images about the contributions millions of Americans made to the war effort.

U.S. Holocaust Memorial Museum
www.ushmm.org/
This official Web site of the U.S. Holocaust Memorial Museum in Washington, D.C., covers the history and documents of the Holocaust.

Tuskegee Airmen
www.wpafb.af.mil/museum/history/prewwii/ta.htm
This site of the Air Force Museum at Wright-Patterson Air Force Base includes information and photographs of the African American pilots of World War II.

Abraham Lincoln Brigade Archives
www.alba-valb.org/aboutalb.htm
This site has information and articles about the Spanish Civil War and the unit of American volunteers who fought in it.

Zoot Suit Riots
www.pbs.org/wgbh/amex/zoot/
This Web site from the Public Broadcasting Service (PBS) documentary series *The American Experience* covers the World War II Zoot Suit riots in Los Angeles.

William P. Gottlieb Photographs of the Golden Age of Jazz
memory.loc.gov/ammem/wghtml/wghome.html
This Library of Congress site includes images, audio, and articles from *Down Beat* magazine in the 1940s.

For Further Reading

General
Paul Fussell, *Wartime: Understanding and Behavior in the Second World War* (1989).
John Keegan, *The Second World War* (1990).
Studs Terkel, *"The Good War": An Oral History of World War II* (1984).

Mobilizing for War
Justus D. Doenecke, *Storm on the Horizon: The Challenge to American Intervention, 1939–1941* (2000).
Thomas J. Fleming, *The New Dealers' War: Franklin D. Roosevelt and the War Within World War II* (2001).
Cecelia Lynch, *Beyond Appeasement: Interpreting Interwar Peace Movements in World Politics* (1999).

Pearl Harbor: The United States Enters the War
Allan Berube, *Coming Out Under Fire: The History of Gay Men and Women in World War Two* (1990).
Akira Iriye, *Pearl Harbor and the Coming of the Pacific War: A Brief History with Documents and Essays* (1999).
Michael S. Sherry, *The Rise of American Air Power: The Creation of Armageddon* (1987).

The Home Front
John Morton Blum, *V Was for Victory: Politics and American Culture During World War II* (1976).
Lewis A. Erenberg and Susan E. Hirsch, *The War in American Culture* (1996).
Elaine Tyler May, *Pushing the Limits: American Women, 1940–1961* (1994).

Race and War
Beth Bailey and David Farber, *The First Strange Place: The Alchemy of Race and Sex in World War II Hawaii* (1992).
Aaron Berman, *Nazism, the Jews and American Zionism, 1933–1948* (1990).
John W. Dower, *War Without Mercy: Race and Power in the Pacific War* (1987).
Barbara Dianne Savage, *Broadcasting Freedom: Radio, War, and the Politics of Race, 1938–1948* (1999).

Total War
Ronald Powaski, *March to Armageddon: The United States and the Nuclear Arms Race, 1939 to the Present* (1987).
George H. Roeder Jr., *The Censored War: American Visual Experience During World War Two* (1993).
Michael S. Sherry, *In the Shadow of War: The United States Since the 1930s* (1995).
Gerhard L. Weinberg, *A World at Arms: A Global History of World War II*, 2nd ed. (2005).

For quizzes and other resources on these topics, go to www.longmanamericanhistory.com.

The retreat of European colonialism and American competition with the Soviet Union nonetheless encouraged many white Americans to acknowledge the contradiction between leading the "free world" and limiting the freedoms of Americans of color. A series of Supreme Court decisions validated the long-term strategy of the National Association for the Advancement of Colored People (NAACP) for contesting segregation in the courts. Court rulings outlawed segregation in voting primaries (*Smith v. Allwright*, 1944), interstate transportation (*Morgan v. Virginia*, 1946), contracts for house sales (*Shelley v. Kraemer*, 1948), and graduate schools (*Sweatt v. Painter* and *McLaurin v. Oklahoma*, 1950).

Popular culture moved in the same direction of breaking down racial barriers. *Billboard* magazine in 1949 changed the category of "race music" to "rhythm and blues" as white record producers and radio disc jockeys such as Alan Freed began to bring the early rock 'n' roll of African American musicians to mainstream white audiences. By 1955 young white musicians such as Bill Haley and Elvis Presley joined black stars such as Chuck Berry and Little Richard in creating a wildly popular sound that transcended racial categories. Professional baseball erased its color line when Jackie Robinson, a former four-sport star at the University of California–Los Angeles and lieutenant in the U.S. Army, joined the Brooklyn Dodgers in 1947.

Native Americans and Mexican Americans faced similar discrimination in the Southwest and elsewhere. With war veterans in the fore, they also organized to contest unfair education and election practices. "If we are good enough to fight, why aren't we good enough to vote?" asked returning Navajo soldiers in New Mexico and Arizona, where the state constitutions prohibited Indian residents from voting, until successfully challenged in 1948. The League of United Latin American Citizens (LULAC) followed a strategy similar to that of the NAACP regarding educational discrimination, leading to a federal Court's decision in *Mendez v. Westminster* (1946) outlawing segregated schools for Mexican Americans in California. In parallel fashion, indigenous Alaskans organized in the Alaska Native Brotherhood successfully lobbied the territorial legislature in Juneau to pass an antidiscrimination law in 1945.

Class Conflict

In many ways, 1946 seemed like 1919. A world war had just ended, in which corporations had made handsome profits. American workers had enjoyed nearly full employment and improving wages and had joined unions in large numbers. In 1946 one-third of the workforce held a union card, the largest portion ever. But the end of war-related orders led to job cuts and the loss of overtime wages, and by the spring of 1946, 1.8 million workers were out on strike.

Mirroring World War I, the conclusion of hostilities in 1945 revealed rising tensions between the United States and the Soviet Union. The spread of leftist revolutions abroad amplified fears of communist influence in American unions, especially because a few of the most effective Congress of Industrial Organizations (CIO) organizers were Communist party members or at least sympathetic to an emphasis on class conflict between owners and workers. As in 1919, a Red Scare began to develop, egged on by a business community that used the supposed threat of the tiny U.S. Communist party to weaken the much larger and less radical union movement. In contrast to the end of World War I, however, federal law guaranteed the right of workers to bargain collectively, and the strikes of 1946 resulted in some negotiated wage increases.

The tide turned against unions as anticommunism intensified. The Republican party claimed a sweeping victory in the 1946 congressional elections, taking control of both the House and the Senate in a stark rejection of Truman's leadership. Republicans and conservative Democrats then passed the Taft-Hartley Act in 1947 over the president's veto, weakening unions by prohibiting secondary boycotts (against the products of a company whose workers were on strike) and requiring union officials to swear anticommunist oaths. Two years later, the increasingly conservative CIO expelled eleven unions that still had leftist and communist leadership. At the same time, the expanding U.S. economy after 1947 pulled many skilled workers up into the middle class and gave them a larger stake in the status quo.

The Quest for Security

On February 21, 1947, a British official in Washington informed the U.S. government that Britain could no longer provide financial assistance to the anticommunist governments of Greece and Turkey. This marked a watershed in modern world history. Long the greatest imperial power and the dominant outside force in the Middle East, Britain was beginning a protracted, slow retreat. Left in its wake were vacuums of power, particularly in the Middle East, South Asia, and Africa. President Truman and his advisers believed that either Soviet or American influence would flow into these regions. The Truman administration formulated a policy to contain communism in the eastern Mediterranean that it quickly expanded to encompass the entire noncommunist world. Powerful new nuclear weapons increased anxieties about the nation's security.

Redefining National Security

U.S. policymakers had ended World War II with one primary goal. They were determined to revive the global capitalist economy that had nearly dissolved in the Great Depression of the 1930s and had then been battered by the war. American prosperity and freedom, they believed, depended on a world system of free trade because Americans simply could not consume all the products of their efficient farms and factories. If they could not sell the surplus abroad, the United States would slide back into an economic depression.

"National security" was expanding to mean something very different from simply defending the nation's territory against invasion. For the disproportionately powerful United States, national security after 1945 came to be identified with the creation and preservation of a free-trading capitalist world order. American national security was seen to be at stake almost everywhere around the globe.

The primary threat to that security came from the Soviet Union. The danger lay in Soviet encouragement, by example and assistance, of revolutions that rejected market economies and individualist ethics. Demoralized by the war's destruction and by grim postwar economic conditions, western Europeans and others seemed to be considering the paths of socialism and communism. "Hopeless and hungry people," Secretary of State Dean Acheson warned, "often resort to desperate measures."

> *"Hopeless and hungry people," Acheson warned, "often resort to desperate measures."*

Conflict with the Soviet Union

The antifascist alliance of the Soviet Union and the United States dissolved rapidly as their conflicting interests reemerged after the war. Long skeptical of the capitalist world it wanted to replace, the Soviet government viewed expansive U.S. interests as evidence of "striving for world supremacy." Yet Moscow was just as clearly expanding its own sphere of national security, with Soviet troops remaining in areas they had occupied during the war: Manchuria, northern Korea, Iran, and especially eastern and central Europe. Each side spoke of the other's goal as "world domination."

Contrasting experiences in World War II amplified historical and ideological differences. Whereas the war brought the United States out of the global capitalist depression (which the

Soviets had avoided), it brought the USSR into a depression caused by the invading Germans' destruction of the western portion of the country. With a decimated population, a battered economy, and minimal air and naval forces, the postwar Soviet Union remained a regional power based on its army. The United States was the only truly global power, with a vast naval armada and air force projecting military might onto every continent, undergirded by the most productive economy in world history.

The two nations' visions of the postwar world order reflected these relative positions. Americans sought an open world for the free flow of goods and most ideas and proved willing to tolerate and even embrace dictatorial governments as long as they were anticommunist and open to foreign trade and investment. Meanwhile, the Soviets called for a more traditional division into separate spheres of influence for the great powers.

Conflicts over specific areas liberated from the Nazis hastened the onset of the Cold War in the first eighteen months after the end of World War II. Whereas the Soviets wanted reparations and a deindustrialized Germany that could never threaten it again, the United States considered a rebuilt industrial German state crucial for a healthy, integrated western European economy. Britain and France had gone to war in defense of an independent Poland, but for Stalin control of Poland was not negotiable because it had been "the corridor for attack on Russia." Moscow and Washington also clashed over Iran, where the Soviets briefly encouraged a leftist uprising in the northern part of the oil-rich country to counteract British and American influence in the capital city of Teheran. U.S. policymakers worried about Soviet requests to Turkey for greater control of the straits leading out of the Black Sea into the Mediterranean.

The Policy of Containment

Churchill's "Iron Curtain" Speech

Diplomat George Kennan best articulated the policy of **containment** in an influential telegram sent from his post at the U.S. embassy in Moscow in February 1946. Kennan explained Soviet hostility as a function of traditional Russian insecurity overlaid with newer Marxist justifications. He called for "the adroit and vigilant application of counterforce" against all Soviet efforts at expanding their influence. One month later, on March 5, 1946, former British prime minister Winston Churchill warned that a Russian "iron curtain" had descended across Europe, imprisoning all those to the east of it. "The reins of world leadership are fast slipping from Britain's competent but now very weak hands," the State Department argued. "These reins will be picked up either by the United States or by Russia."

> "The reins of world leadership are fast slipping from Britain's . . . hands. These reins will be picked up either by the United States or by Russia."

Picking up those reins meant a fundamental reorientation for the United States. No longer just the dominant force in the Western Hemisphere, it would have to maintain its wartime projection of military forces around the globe—permanently. In an address to Congress on March 12, 1947, asking for $400 million in aid for Greece and Turkey, Truman simplified the world system into two "ways of life," those of "free peoples" and those of "terror and oppression" under communist rule. All nations must choose between them, he declared, and the United States must support "free peoples who are resisting attempted subjugation by armed minorities or outside pressures."

The **Truman Doctrine**, as it became known, exaggerated a real problem in order to win public support for a new international role for the United States. It funded the governments of Turkey and Greece, but it framed the new policy broadly, opening the path to supporting anticommunist regimes and opposing revolutions around the world for decades to come. The most important immediate step was the reconstruction of a vibrant, reintegrated western European economy. The United States provided $13 billion

MAP 24.1

EUROPE DIVIDED BY THE COLD WAR For centuries Europe had controlled much of the rest of the world. After 1945, Russians occupied the eastern half of the continent and Americans wielded dominant influence in the western half. This division of Europe into communist and noncommunist blocs lasted until the end of the Cold War in 1989.

between 1948 and 1952 to fund the European Recovery Program, commonly known as the Marshall Plan for its chief architect, Secretary of State George Marshall (1947–1949).

Ensuring western European security against the Red Army also entailed the first U.S. military alliance in peacetime. The victors of World War II divided a defeated Germany into separate zones of occupation. The British, French, and American decision in March 1948 to create

DOCUMENT

The Marshall Plan

a unified state out of the western sectors of Germany led a few months later to a year-long Soviet blockade of western access to Berlin and fears of a general war. The creation of the North Atlantic Treaty Organization (NATO) in 1949 made the American military commitment to Europe permanent. The point of NATO for western Europe, its British first secretary general said, was to "keep the Americans in, the Russians out, and the Germans down."

Video: The Onset of Cold War

The onset of the Cold War determined the fate of the defeated powers of World War II. The Truman administration was committed to "push ahead with the reconstruction of those two great workshops of Europe and Asia—Germany and Japan." This agenda replaced initial concerns about rooting out Nazism and punishing war criminals, as at the Nuremberg trials of surviving Nazi leaders in 1945–1946. The American occupation of Japan under General Douglas MacArthur initially (1945–1947) emphasized democratization of Japanese society, including building labor unions, weakening corporate monopolies, ensuring women's political rights, and punishing war criminals. But rising U.S. tensions with the Soviets and the imminent victory of the Communist forces in China's civil war prompted American officials to shift course by 1948. Henceforth, they focused on rebuilding as quickly as possible Japan's industrial economy as the hub of capitalist Asia.

Colonialism and the Cold War

The world's nonwhite majority still lived under European colonial control, and for them the struggle for national independence and racial equality was the great issue of the late 1940s and 1950s. In this North-South conflict, as opposed to the East-West conflict of the Cold War, the United States held an awkward position. Its primary NATO partners included the greatest colonial powers: Britain, France, Belgium, the Netherlands, and Portugal. Racial segregation in the United States further undercut American leadership of the "free world."

> *For the world's nonwhite majority, the struggle for national independence and racial equality was the great issue of the late 1940s and 1950s.*

With European rule in Asia and Africa on the way out, the Truman administration sought a gradual transfer of colonial rule into the hands of local pro-West elites. The U.S. grant of official independence to the Philippines in 1946 was offered as a model, as was the British departure from India a year later. However, the importance of Europe for America meant supporting even those imperialists who did not leave peacefully, such as the French who dug in against communist-led revolutionaries in Vietnam (part of French Indochina).

Document: Press Release Announcing U.S. Recognition of Israel

The British withdrawal from Palestine in 1948 created a peculiar dilemma for the United States. Jewish settlers—primarily from Europe and often survivors of the Holocaust—proclaimed the new state of Israel against the wishes of the Arab majority. Secretary of State Marshall and others urged Truman not to recognize Israel in order to avoid imperiling U.S. relations with the Arab oil-producing states. The president sympathized with the Jewish desire for a homeland, however, and understood the importance of American Jews as constituents of the Democratic party in the 1940s. His decision to recognize Israel, which most Middle Easterners viewed as a new colonial state, set the United States on a course of enduring friendship with that nation and enduring conflict with Israel's Arab neighbors and the Palestinians.

The Impact of Nuclear Weapons

Scientists in the 1940s dramatically increased Americans' sense of personal safety by introducing the use of antibiotics. "Miracle drugs" such as penicillin cured common bacterial infections that had previously been debilitating or fatal. What science gave with one hand

■ Soldiers watch as "Dog," a 21-kiloton nuclear device, is dropped from a bomber at the Nevada Test Site at Yucca Flat, northwest of Las Vegas, in November 1951. U.S. atomic specialists tested nuclear weapons first in the Marshall Islands of the western Pacific Ocean, especially the Bikini atoll, beginning in 1946, and then in Nevada beginning in January 1951. Residents downwind from the test sites suffered various adverse health effects from radiation exposure, including high cancer rates.

it threatened to take away with the other, however. The use of atomic weapons on Japan foreshadowed a future of utter insecurity in which instantaneous destruction of entire nations could occur without warning.

Even without being fired again in war after 1945, nuclear weapons altered the American environment. Weapon tests released vast quantities of radiation into the atmosphere. Local cancer rates spiked upward for Bikini Islanders in the Pacific, where the first tests occurred, and then for farmers and ranchers in Utah and Nevada, when tests began 65 miles northwest of Las Vegas in 1953. Navajo Indians mining uranium in the Southwest paid dearly for their intensive exposure to the poisonous material, as did thousands of workers involved in nuclear weapon production. Weapon assembly plants in Hanford, Washington, and Rocky Flats, Colorado, leaked radioactivity into the groundwater. In combination with the nuclear power industry, atomic weapon development resulted in an enormous supply of radioactive waste—deadly for 10,000 more years—that the U.S. government still does not know how to dispose of safely.

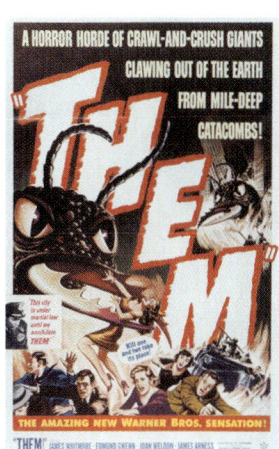

The government offered reassurances about the safety of the atom, and the Atomic Energy Commission covered up evidence of radioactivity's ill effects. But many Americans were deeply anxious about this destructive new power that loomed over their lives, especially as the Soviet-American arms race intensified. Science fiction movies painted

Duck and Cover

frightening pictures of a future devastated by nuclear war and haunted by exposure to radiation. Concerns about a nuclear world escalated with the successful 1952 test of an American hydrogen bomb, a thousand times more powerful than the device that destroyed Hiroshima.

A Cold War Society

Expanding economic opportunities and narrowing political freedoms characterized American society in the first decade of the Cold War. A withering fire of anticommunist repression pushed dissident views to the margins of the nation's political life. Americans largely accepted this new conformity for two reasons: their desire to support their government during international crises, especially the Korean War (1950–1953), and a consumer cornucopia that surrounded them with attractive material goods. Americans moved to the suburbs, and to the South and West.

> *Expanding economic opportunities and narrowing political freedoms characterized American society in the first decade of the Cold War.*

By 1947 the United States was launching into an era of extraordinary economic expansion that continued for twenty-five years. Since Ben Franklin's time, Americans had been known for thrift in their pursuit of wealth, but after 1945 the long-cherished principle of delaying gratification declined steeply. "Buy now, pay later," General Motors urged as it offered an installment plan to customers. Diner's Club introduced the first credit card in 1950. In a formulation breathtaking for its distance from Puritan and immigrant traditions of saving for the future, writer William Whyte observed that "thrift is now un-American."

Family Lives

Levittown

Many white Americans embraced the opportunity to move to the suburbs after World War II. Seeking larger homes and yards and quieter neighborhoods, they flocked to new developments such as Levittown outside New York City on Long Island. Suburbs were not for everyone, however. Even as federal courts struck down segregation laws in some spheres of American life, agencies such as the Veterans Administration and the Federal Housing Administration were encouraging residential separation by race. Private banks did the same. Other government policies, including highway construction and tax benefits for homeowners, promoted the growth of suburbs at the cost of cities. A third epoch in American residential history began by 1970 when more Americans resided in suburbs than cities, parallel to the 1920 shift from a rural majority to an urban one.

Suburban life encouraged a sharpening of gender roles among the growing middle class. Men commuted to work while women were expected to find fulfillment in marriage and motherhood, including a nearly full-time job of unpaid housework. "We married what we wanted to be," one female college graduate recalled. "If we wanted to be a lawyer or a doctor we married one." Despite this partial retreat from wartime employment, however, fully one-third of American women continued to work for pay outside the home. The economic circumstances of most black women offered them little choice, and most wound up doing double housework: their own and that of families employing them as domestics.

From 1946 to 1964, women giving birth at a younger age to more children created the demographic bulge known as the baby boom. Large families reinforced the domestic focus of most women, putting the work of child-rearing at the center of their lives. Fatherhood became increasingly a badge of masculinity. Family physician Benjamin Spock published *Baby and Child Care* (1946), a runaway best seller that helped shift the emphasis in American parenting from strictness to greater nurturance.

Married mothers were celebrated, but unmarried ones were rebuked. Despite the greater freedom of the war years, the sexual double standard remained in place, with women's virtue linked directly to virginity in a way that men's was not. Birth control devices such as the diaphragm were legal only for married women and only in certain states. Women seeking to terminate unwanted pregnancies had to consider illegal abortions, the only kind available before 1970; millions did so, including one-fifth of all married women and a majority of single women who became pregnant. Two studies of American sexual behavior by Dr. Alfred Kinsey of Indiana University in 1948 and 1953 shocked the public with their revelation of widespread premarital and extramarital sexual intercourse as well as homosexual liaisons.

The Growth of the South and the West

Before World War II, American cultural, industrial, and financial power had always been centered in the urban North, but federal expenditures during the war began to change this. The U.S. Army built most of its training bases in the South, where land close to the coasts was thinly populated and inexpensive. Military bases and defense industries sprang up along the West Coast to project power into the Pacific against Japan. U.S. troops built the Alcan (Alaska–Canada) Highway, and millions of GIs passed through Hawaii en route to the Pacific battlefront. Fighting against the Japanese to defend Pearl Harbor and the Aleutian Islands brought the once-distant territories of Hawaii and Alaska more into Americans' consciousness, setting them on the path to statehood in 1959.

■ A new cloverleaf intersection on a freeway arches across the northern New Jersey suburbs in 1949. Multilane, limited-access highways became common after World War II. A new word, "smog" (neither smoke nor fog), appeared to describe the urban pollution caused by trucks and commuter vehicles.

Population Shifts, 1940—1950

The **Sunbelt** of the South, the Southwest, and California grew rapidly after the war, whereas older Rustbelt cities of the Northeast and Midwest such as Buffalo and Detroit began to lose manufacturing jobs and population. Like the 440,000 people who moved to Los Angeles during the war, postwar migrants to California and Arizona appreciated the weather and the economic opportunities. Military spending underwrote half the jobs in California during the first decade of the Cold War. Migrants from south of the border, meanwhile, found work primarily in California's booming agricultural sector.

Two industries particularly stimulated the growth of the Sunbelt: cars and air conditioning. Automobiles helped shape the economies of western states, where new cities were built out of sprawling suburbs. New car sales shot up from 70,000 in 1945 to 7.9 million in 1955. Inexpensive gasoline, refined from the abundant crude oil of Texas and Oklahoma, powered this fleet. Automobile exhaust pipes replaced industrial smokestacks as the primary source of air pollution. Air conditioning also became widely available after World War II and contributed to the breakdown of the South's regional distinctiveness. From Miami and Atlanta to Houston and Washington, D.C., the new Sunbelt depended on the indoor comfort brought by controlling summertime heat and humidity.

Harry Truman and the Limits of Liberal Reform

On the political front, the onset of the Cold War narrowed the range of American political discourse. In seeking to consolidate the New Deal legacy, President Truman found himself boxed in by conservative Republican opponents. Allied governments in western Europe had embraced the idea that access to health care was a right of every citizen in a modern democratic state. But when Truman proposed a system of national health care, conservatives quashed the legislation in Congress.

Perhaps the most blatant omission of the New Deal had been protection against racial discrimination. As the Cold War intensified, the fact that millions of Americans still lacked basic guarantees for their civil rights was an embarrassing contradiction to rhetoric about ensuring rights and liberties throughout the "free world." Truman campaigned for reelection in 1948 on a platform of support for civil rights that was unprecedented in the White House. That summer he ordered the desegregation of the armed forces and the federal civil service.

African American voters in Chicago, Cleveland, and other northern cities played a key role in swing states; their solid support lifted Truman to a narrow and surprising victory over the heavily favored Republican candidate, New York governor Thomas Dewey. Truman's reelection was all the more impressive because of the fracturing of the Democratic party. Alienated by the civil rights plank, white Southerners walked out of the Democratic convention and ran South Carolina governor Strom Thurmond as an independent candidate. The "Dixiecrats" won four states in the Deep South, foreshadowing the abandonment by white Southerners of the party of their parents in the 1960s. Truman won as a man of the moderately liberal center, fierce against communism, usually supportive of the rights of organized labor, and opposed to discrimination.

The Cold War at Home

In a pattern that became known as **McCarthyism**, mostly Republican conservatives attributed communist successes abroad—especially in China and Korea—to liberal Democrats in the Truman administration, accusing them of sympathizing with and even spying for the Soviet Union. The hunt for domestic subversives to explain international setbacks was grounded in the reality of a handful of actual Soviet spies, most notably Julius Rosenberg (who was executed for treason in 1953 along with his apparently innocent wife, Ethel) and nuclear scientist Klaus Fuchs. But this second Red Scare expressed primarily the frustration of being unable to translate vast U.S. power into greater control of world events. And it served, above all, to cast suspicion on the patriotism of liberals at home.

Despite his general support for civil liberties, Truman helped set the tone for pursuing suspected traitors. In an unsuccessful effort to fortify his right flank against Republican attacks, he established a federal employee loyalty program in March 1947 as the domestic equivalent of the Truman Doctrine. Attorney General Tom Clark drew up a list of supposedly subversive organizations that the FBI and state committees on "un-American activities" then hounded. In a case with sobering implications for free speech, federal courts in 1949 convicted the leaders of the U.S. Communist party of promoting the overthrow of the U.S. government. Words alone, the courts ruled, could be treasonable—the same logic as the wartime Sedition Act of 1918 (see Chapter 20).

Republicans reaped the benefits of the Red Scare. Most Americans who had sympathized in any way with the Soviet Union in the Depression years were by the late 1940s merely liberal Democrats, but the House Un-American Activities Committee (HUAC) zeroed in on their earlier records. Investigating Hollywood, the television industry, and universities as well as the executive branch of the U.S. government, HUAC destroyed the careers of prominent figures as well as average Americans.

The era found its name in the previously obscure junior senator from Wisconsin, Republican Joseph McCarthy. With a single speech in Wheeling, West Virginia, on February 9, 1950, this ambitious politician soared to prominence. "I have here in my hand a list of 205" Communist party members working in the State Department, he declared. Over the next four years, the numbers and names changed as McCarthy stayed one step ahead of the evidence while intimidating witnesses before his Senate Permanent Subcommittee on Investigations. He talked about communists, but his show was about Democrats. As the war in Korea raged, he mercilessly red-baited (attacked as "soft" on communism) the Truman administration. But after the Republican electoral victory in 1952, his excesses lost their partisan utility. With the end of the war in Korea and his ill-advised attacks on the U.S. Army as supposedly infiltrated by communists (the Army-McCarthy hearings), he was at last censured by his Senate colleagues in 1954 and died an early, alcohol-related death in 1957.

TABLE 24-1
The Election of 1948

Candidate	Political Party	Popular Vote (%)	Electoral Vote
Harry S. Truman	Democratic	49.5	304
Thomas E. Dewey	Republican	45.1	189
J. Strom Thurmond	State-Rights Democratic	2.4	38
Henry A. Wallace	Progressive	2.4	—

DOCUMENT
McCarthy, Wheeling, West Virginia Speech

> *McCarthy talked about communists, but his show was about Democrats. As the war in Korea raged, he mercilessly red-baited the Truman administration.*

Who Is a Loyal American?

The Cold War politics of inclusion and exclusion established a new profile for loyal Americans. Private familial and material concerns were expected to replace public interest in social reform. Anticommunists launched a withering assault on homosexuals as "perverts" and threats to the nation's security. Church membership climbed in tandem with condemnations of "godless communism," and Congress added the words "under God" to the Pledge of Allegiance. Discrimination against Roman Catholics and Jews, though still evident, declined as Catholics such as McCarthy proved intensely anticommunist and as pictures and stories emerged to reveal the horrors of the Nazi Holocaust against the Jews. More inclusive references to the "Judeo-Christian tradition" became common.

■ From 1951 to 1953, Mexican American miners went on strike against the Empire Zinc Mining Company in Silver City, New Mexico. Women took on major roles in this labor action, which inspired a famous movie, *Salt of the Earth*. Defiant in the face of police and company shotguns and billy clubs, Elvira Molano (center) served as cochair of the union negotiating committee and became known as "the most arrested woman" during the strike.

American leadership of the global anticommunist cause strengthened the struggle for racial equality at home, within certain limits. The **NAACP** and most African Americans took an anticommunist position in accord with Truman, in return for his support of civil rights. They downplayed their concern for colonial independence in Africa and Asia to support NATO. The American GI Forum (Latino veterans) and the Japanese American Citizen League also worked within the confines of Cold War politics to end discrimination.

For impoverished Native Americans, the government seemed to give with one hand and take away with the other. In 1946 Truman established the Indian Claims Commission to consider payment for lands taken and treaties broken. But Dillon S. Myer, director of the Bureau of Indian Affairs, closed reservation schools, withdrew support for traditional cultural activities, and launched an urban relocation program, all intended to move Native Americans into the mainstream and get the government "out of the Indian business."

Immigrants, too, received mixed messages. The McCarran-Walter Act (1952) ended the long-standing ban on allowing people of Asian descent not born in the United States to become U.S. citizens. But it preserved the discriminatory 1924 system of "national origins" for allocating numbers of immigrants from different countries. The bill also strengthened the attorney general's authority to deport aliens who were suspected of subversive intentions. The powerful 1953 film *Salt of the Earth*—with its pro-union, pro-socialist, pro-feminist, and pro-Latino sympathies—was condemned as subversive and rarely screened until the 1970s.

The United States and Asia

Japan did not conquer independent nations in its sweep southward at the start of World War II. Instead it defeated the forces of imperial powers: the French in Indochina, the Dutch in Indonesia, the British in Singapore and Malaya, and the Americans in the Philippines. In a single swoop, Japanese soldiers demonstrated the absurdity of white supremacy and cleared the way for the end of colonialism in Asia. Then Japan's retreat in 1945 left vacuums of power throughout the region. Into them flowed two contenders: the returning but gravely weakened European imperialists, and Asian nationalists such as Ho Chi Minh in Vietnam. Americans were not passive observers of this struggle, as they sought to establish a new free-trading order in the region. As communist forces won a civil war in China, the U.S. government bulked up its military and intelligence capacities and went to war in Korea.

The Chinese Civil War

Americans had long felt a special connection to China. Half of the thousands of Christian missionaries sent out by American churches in the early twentieth century had been posted there. Entrepreneurs eyed the Chinese market, home to one-fifth of the world's potential consumers. During World War II, Chinese resistance to Japan's invasion occupied millions of Tokyo's soldiers who would otherwise have been shooting at American GIs. The close U.S. alliance with the government of Jiang Jieshi seemed to confirm American hopes that Asia's largest nation would follow a pro-American path.

But the partisans of the Chinese Communist Party (CCP) under Mao Zedong's leadership fought more effectively against the Japanese than Jiang's soldiers did. Japan's withdrawal from China in 1945 initiated four years of warfare between the Communists and Jiang's anticommunist Nationalists. The Truman administration provided $3 billion in aid to Jiang. Americans watched in frustration as the CCP defeated the Nationalists, who retreated to the island of Taiwan. On October 1, 1949, Mao announced the establishment of the People's Republic of China (PRC).

This was the first communist government created without the presence of Soviet troops. Profound suspicions on both sides prevented any Sino-American accommodation, and the U.S. government refused to recognize the People's Republic. Faced with U.S. hostility and sharing a common ideology with the Soviet Union, Mao papered over historic Chinese-Russian tensions and signed a mutual defense pact with Moscow in February 1950. The so-called loss of China increased the importance for American policymakers of building capitalist societies in the rest of Asia, particularly Japan and—fatefully—South Korea and Vietnam. China's revolution also became a major issue in American politics. "Who lost China?" Republicans demanded rhetorically and effectively, presuming that it had once been America's to lose.

The Creation of the National Security State

A week before Mao's announcement that China had become a communist country, President Truman shared some equally grim news with the American public: the Soviet Union had

■ Were all communists conspiring together against the United States and its interests? New Chinese leader Mao Zedong (left) helps Soviet ruler Josef Stalin celebrate his birthday on December 21, 1949. Two months later, the two men signed a mutual defense treaty. But, as their expressions suggest, they shared little personal warmth. Conflicting Chinese and Russian national interests soon strained—and eventually broke—their alliance.

detonated its first nuclear device. The United States had lost the atomic monopoly that for four years assured Americans of their unique position of military strength. Truman asked his advisers for a full reevaluation of the nation's foreign policy.

The result was the top-secret National Security Council document 68 (**NSC-68**), which articulated the logic of what became the **national security state**: a government focused on the imperatives of military power, global involvement, and radically increased defense spending. NSC-68 argued that the United States had entered an era of permanent crisis because of the expansion of communism and the hostile intentions of the Soviet Union. America's worldwide interests meant that it must oppose revolutions or radical change anywhere on the globe. NSC-68 went beyond the containment policy of the Truman Doctrine to call instead for fostering "a fundamental change in the nature of the Soviet system." This armed struggle necessitated secrecy and centralization of power in the hands of the federal government.

The National Security Act of 1947 and its 1949 amendments created the institutions of the new national security state. The Central Intelligence Agency (CIA) organized spying and covert operations, the Department of Defense unified the separate branches of the military, and the National Security Council (NSC) coordinated foreign policy information for the president. NSC-68's call for secrecy encouraged government deception of the public in the interest of "national security," with a consequent decline in democratic input into the nation's foreign relations.

At War in Korea

Two months after NSC-68 arrived on the president's desk, troops from communist North Korea poured across the thirty-eighth parallel into South Korea on June 25, 1950. The alarmist recommendations of NSC-68 now seemed fully justified to U.S. policymakers. But the origins of the conflict on the Korean peninsula were complicated.

INTERPRETING HISTORY

NSC-68

Concerned about the trend of international events in the wake of the Communist revolution in China and the Soviet Union's acquisition of nuclear weapons, President Truman ordered his National Security Council on January 31, 1950, to conduct "a reexamination of our objectives in peace and war and of the effect of these objectives on our strategic plans." The resulting study, known as NSC-68, called for a military buildup to counter Soviet expansionism. Some specialists on the USSR, such as George Kennan, questioned NSC-68's accuracy regarding Soviet intentions and successes. But the subsequent North Korean invasion of South Korea seemed to confirm the idea of "international communism" on the march.

From NSC-68: U.S. Objectives and Programs for National Security (April 14, 1950)

The Soviet Union, unlike previous aspirants to hegemony, is animated by a new fanatic faith, antithetical to our own, and seeks to impose its absolute authority over the rest of the world. . . .

Any substantial further extension of the area under the domination of the Kremlin would raise the possibility that no coalition adequate to confront the Kremlin with greater strength could be assembled. It is in this context that this Republic and its citizens in the ascendancy of their strength stand in their deepest peril.

The issues that face us are momentous, involving the fulfillment or destruction not only of this Republic but of civilization itself. . . . The assault on free institutions is world-wide now, and in the context of the present polarization of power a defeat of free institutions anywhere is a defeat everywhere. . . .

Our policy and actions must be such as to foster a fundamental change in the nature of the Soviet system. . . . In a

Workers at the Douglas Aircraft Company's Santa Monica factory assemble Nike guided missiles for the U.S. Army in 1955. Large military contracts proliferated during the Cold War and stimulated the growth of Sunbelt states like California.

shrinking world, which now faces the threat of atomic warfare, it is not an adequate objective merely to seek to check the Kremlin design, for the absence of order among nations is becoming less and less tolerable. . . .

The integrity of our system will not be jeopardized by any measures, covert or overt, violent or non-violent, which serve the purposes of frustrating the Kremlin design, nor does the necessity for conducting ourselves so as to affirm our values in actions as well as words forbid such measures. . . .

The total economic strength of the U.S.S.R. compares with that of the U.S. as roughly one to four. . . . The military budget of the United States represents 6 to 7 percent of its gross national product (as against 13.8 percent for the Soviet Union). . . . This difference in emphasis between the two economies means that the readiness of the free world to support a war effort is tending to decline relative to that of the Soviet Union.

It is true that the United States armed forces are now stronger than ever before in other times of apparent peace; it is also true that there exists a sharp disparity between our actual military strength and our commitments. . . . It is clear that our military strength is becoming dangerously inadequate. . . .

In summary, we must . . . [engage in] a rapid and sustained build-up of the political, economic, and military strength of the free world.

Questions

1. What is the precise problem that the United States faces, according to NSC-68?
2. How does NSC-68's analysis of the Soviet threat in 1950 compare with American understandings today of the threat from Islamic terrorist organizations such as Al Qaeda? ■

■ Near Haktong-ni, Korea, on August 28, 1950, an Army corpsman fills out casualty tags while one American soldier comforts another who has just seen a friend killed in action. Men who fought together on the front lines in Korea, as in other wars, experienced physical and psychological traumas unparalleled in civilian life. They often developed strong friendships with each other but sometimes had difficulty making the transition back to peacetime routines at home.

Korea had been colonized by Japan since 1910. After Japan's defeat in 1945, Soviet and U.S. forces each occupied half of the peninsula. In the north, the Soviets installed a dictatorial Communist regime under Kim Il Sung, who had fought with the Chinese Communists in their common struggle against Japan. In the south, the Americans established an authoritarian capitalist regime led by Syngman Rhee, who had lived in the United States most of the previous four decades. The thirty-eighth parallel was an arbitrary dividing line for a nation that had been unified for 1,300 years, and both governments sought to reunite Korea under their control. Border skirmishes intensified after the Soviets and Americans withdrew in 1948, and leftist rebellions continued across much of the south. Some 100,000 Koreans lost their lives in the fighting between 1945 and 1950.

U.S. forces arrived in late June 1950, just in time to prevent the South Korean army from being driven off the peninsula, and then slowly pushed the North Koreans back toward the thirty-eighth parallel in hard fighting. Truman received UN approval for this "police action," along with a small number of troops from several other nations.

Americans assumed the North Korean invasion had been orchestrated by Moscow as part of a plan of worldwide communist aggression. The Truman administration considered defense of South Korea crucial to demonstrate the credibility of U.S. power. The U.S. government took preemptive actions against possible aggression elsewhere. It sent the Seventh Fleet to defend Taiwan, which it had previously assumed China would eventually conquer and reabsorb; it increased assistance to anticommunist forces in the Philippines and Vietnam; and it rearmed West Germany as part of NATO. The U.S. annual military budget increased from $13 billion in 1950 before the war to $50 billion in 1953, setting a pattern for vast military expenditures ever since.

General Douglas MacArthur's brilliantly executed landing of fresh U.S. and UN troops at the port of Inchon behind North Korean lines on September 15, 1950, created a turning point in the war. South Korea was retaken; containment had succeeded. Should American commanders now shift to rolling back communism by proceeding north of the thirty-eighth parallel? The opportunity was irresistible, despite Truman's determination to keep this a limited war. MacArthur ignored signals that the Chinese would not allow U.S. soldiers to come all the way to their border at the Yalu River—the equivalent for Americans of having the Soviet Army arrive at the Rio Grande. On November 27, 200,000 Chinese soldiers struck hard, driving American soldiers south of the thirty-eighth parallel again in the longest retreat in U.S. military history.

MacArthur wanted to take this "entirely new war" directly to the Chinese, using conventional or nuclear bombing campaigns against the People's Republic of China. His growing insubordination forced Truman to fire the popular general in April 1951 because the president had no desire to start a larger war that would draw in the USSR. The bloody fighting in Korea stalemated that spring close to the original dividing line, where the front remained as the two sides negotiated for two years before signing a ceasefire in July 1953. American deaths totaled 37,000, and China lost nearly a million soldiers. Three million Koreans on both

TABLE 24-2
The Election of 1952

Candidate	Political Party	Popular Vote (%)	Electoral Vote
Dwight D. Eisenhower	Republican	55.1	442
Adlai E. Stevenson	Democratic	44.4	89

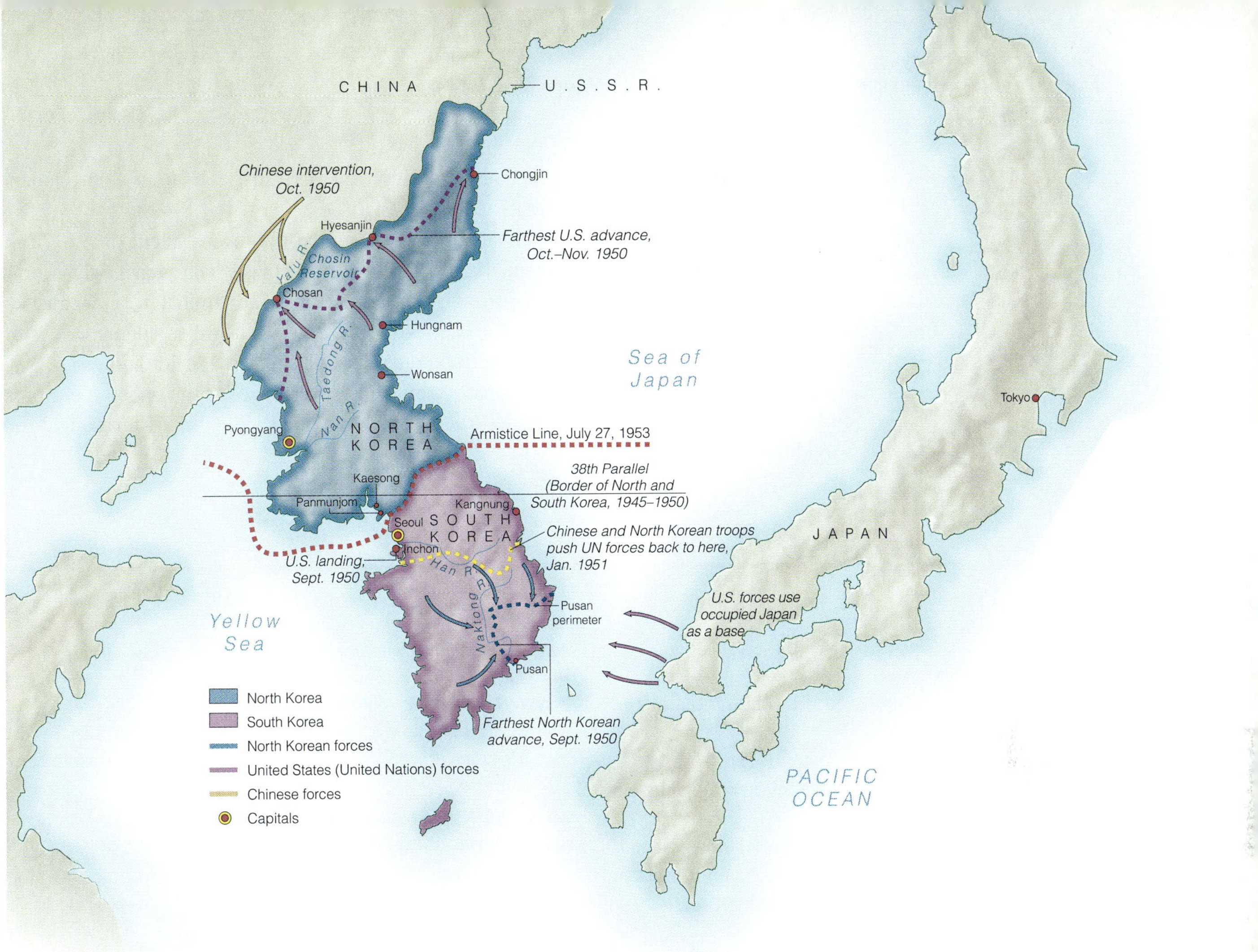

■ **MAP 24.2**

THE KOREAN WAR, 1950–1953 The strategic location of the Korean peninsula enhanced the importance of what had originally been a civil conflict among Koreans. Korea's close proximity to China, the Soviet Union, and U.S.-occupied Japan made the outcome of that conflict very important to all of the great powers. The Americans and Chinese wound up doing the bulk of the fighting against each other in the full-scale war that unfolded in 1950.

The Korean War, 1950–1953

sides died—10 percent of the population of the peninsula—and another 5 million were made refugees. Containment succeeded at enormous cost, and the Korean peninsula is still divided and heavily armed today.

The Korean War shaped subsequent American politics and society in critical ways. The stalemate frustrated Americans, who agreed with MacArthur that there was "no substitute for victory." But the ominous threat of nuclear weapons meant that wars had to be limited. The fighting in Korea enabled McCarthy and the Red Scare to dominate political life in the United States. Republican presidential nominee General Dwight Eisenhower was perhaps the most popular American alive because of his leadership of the Allied victory in Europe in World War II, and he swept into the White House in 1952 over Democrat Adlai Stevenson, the governor of Illinois.

Conclusion

The war in Korea ensured a generation of hostility between the United States and China. It tied the People's Republic more closely to the USSR, strengthening the common belief that international communism was a unified movement. The United States committed itself to defending Taiwan from recapture by the Beijing government. The Korean War also jump-started the moribund Japanese economy as American dollars poured into Japan, where the U.S. war effort was based.

Frustrations with the course of war in Korea affirmed the inward focus of American society in the 1950s. Despite the organizing efforts of political activists such as civil rights workers, most citizens seemed to look increasingly to their personal and familial lives for satisfaction and meaning. From the powerful U.S. economy flowed an unprecedented river of consumer goods, including the new artificial materials—plastic, vinyl, nylon, polyester, Styrofoam—that have pervaded and polluted American life ever since. As the ceasefire in Korea ended the fighting, and U.S. soldiers returned from across the Pacific, Americans sought the good life at home.

Sites to Visit

National Security Archive at George Washington University
www.gwu.edu/~nsarchiv/
This superb site includes the most recent declassified documents on the making of U.S. foreign policy.

Cold War International History Project
http://wilsoncenter.org/index.cfm?fuseaction=topics.home&topic_id=1409
The Woodrow Wilson International Center for Scholars maintains this excellent site, which offers newly released documents and up-to-date interpretive essays on the American-Soviet struggle.

The Ad*Access Project of Duke University Library
scriptorium.lib.duke.edu/adaccess/
This site presents images from over 7,000 advertisements in U.S. and Canadian newspapers and magazine between 1911 and 1955, offering insights into popular culture and consumer life.

Truman Presidential Museum and Library
www.trumanlibrary.org/index.php
The Harry Truman Presidential Library maintains this site, which contains an especially useful collection of documents regarding foreign policy decisions in the early Cold War.

Avalon Project at the Yale Law School: Documents in Law, History, and Diplomacy
www.yale.edu/lawweb/avalon/avalon.htm
Researchers can find here the texts of a large number of the most important primary documents illuminating U.S. relations with other countries.

Korea + 50: No Longer Forgotten
www.trumanlibrary.org/korea/
The Truman Library's site on the Korean War has documents, photos, and interpretative essays by prominent historians.

Bancroft Library Collections
bancroft.berkeley.edu/collections/
The Bancroft Library of the University of California at Berkeley has extensive collections, exhibits, and links revealing the history of California, the nation's most populous state.

For Further Reading

General

William H. Chafe, *The Unfinished Journey: America Since World War II*, 5th ed. (2006).
Alonzo Hamby, *Man of the People: A Life of Harry S. Truman* (1995).
Godfrey Hodgson, *America in Our Time* (1976).
Walter LaFeber, *America, Russia, and the Cold War, 1945–2002*, 9th ed. (2002).
James T. Patterson, *Grand Expectations: The United States, 1945–1974* (1996).

The Uncertainties of Victory

Thomas Borstelmann, *The Cold War and the Color Line: American Race Relations in the Global Arena* (2001).
Robert R. Korstad, *Civil Rights Unionism: Tobacco Workers and the Struggle for Democracy in the Mid-Twentieth-Century South* (2003).
Melvyn P. Leffler, *The Specter of Communism: The United States and the Origins of the Cold War, 1917–1953* (1994).

Suzanne Mettler, *Soldiers to Citizens: The G.I. Bill and the Making of the Greatest Generation* (2005).
Thomas Sugrue, *The Origins of the Urban Crisis: Race and Inequality in Postwar Detroit* (1996).

The Quest for Security

Carolyn Woods Eisenberg, *Drawing the Line: The American Decision to Divide Germany, 1944–1949* (1996).
Walter Isaacson and Evan Thomas, *The Wise Men: Six Friends and the World They Made: Acheson, Bohlen, Harriman, Kennan, Lovett, McCloy* (1986).
Melvyn P. Leffler, *A Preponderance of Power: National Security, the Truman Administration, and the Cold War* (1992).
Thomas G. Paterson, *On Every Front: The Making and Unmaking of the Cold War* (1992).

A Cold War Society

Paul S. Boyer, *By the Bomb's Early Light: American Thought and Culture at the Dawn of the Atomic Age* (1985).

Kenneth T. Jackson, *Crabgrass Frontier: The Suburbanization of the United States* (1985).

Elaine Tyler May, *Homeward Bound: American Families in the Cold War Era* (1988).

Ellen Schrecker, *Many Are the Crimes: McCarthyism in America* (1998).

Stephen J. Whitfield, *The Culture of the Cold War* (1991).

The United States and Asia

Warren I. Cohen, *America's Response to China: A History of Sino-American Relations*, 4th ed. (2000).

Jon Halliday and Bruce Cumings, *Korea: The Unknown War* (1988).

Michael J. Hogan, *A Cross of Iron: Harry S. Truman and the Origins of the National Security State, 1945–1954* (1998).

Christine Klein, *Cold War Orientalism: Asia in the Middlebrow Imgaination, 1945–1961* (2003).

Walter LaFeber, *The Clash: A History of U.S.-Japan Relations* (1997).

For quizzes and other resources on these topics, go to www.longmanamericanhistory.com.

PART NINE

The Cold War at High Tide, 1953–1979

1953	CIA engineers coup in Iran, restores shah to power
1954	*Brown v. Board of Education* Founding of Southeast Asia Treaty Organization (SEATO) French leave Vietnam, which is divided into South Vietnam and North Vietnam
1955	Polio vaccine approved for use Disneyland opens in Anaheim, California Montgomery, Alabama, bus boycott begins
1956	Interstate Highway Act
1957	Central High School, Little Rock, Arkansas, integrated USSR launches *Sputnik* satellite Eisenhower Doctrine
1958	National Defense Education Act
1959	Nixon-Khrushchev Kitchen Debate Cuban Revolution
1960	Oral contraceptive pill comes on the market Beginning of lunch counter sit-ins (Greensboro, North Carolina) American U-2 spy plane shot down over USSR
1961	First American launched into space Bay of Pigs invasion of Cuba Berlin Wall constructed Freedom Rides begin
1962	Rachel Carson, *Silent Spring* Cuban missile crisis Students for a Democratic Society (SDS) founded
1963	Lyndon B. Johnson becomes president after assassination of John F. Kennedy Equal Pay Act of 1963 Betty Friedan, *The Feminine Mystique*
1964	Gulf of Tonkin Resolution Civil Rights Act of 1964 (employment) Wilderness Act
1965	Civil Rights Act of 1965 (voting rights) *Griswold v. Connecticut* legalizes birth control for married couples Watts (Los Angeles) riot
1966	Clean Water Act National Organization for Women (NOW) founded
1967	Thurgood Marshall appointed first African American to Supreme Court Detroit and Newark riots

DURING THE THIRD QUARTER OF THE TWENTIETH CENTURY, THE Cold War cast a long shadow over the United States and the rest of the world. Tensions mounted at home and abroad as the United States and the Soviet Union vied for power among the world's nations. In poor Third World countries, insurgents attempted to throw off the yoke of colonialism and play the two superpowers against each other. The United States used a variety of strategies to counter Soviet influence in Latin America, Africa, the Middle East, and Southeast Asia, including military force in Korea and Vietnam, white-knuckle diplomacy in Cuba, extensive aid to nonaligned countries, and covert operations worldwide.

Soviet advances in science and technology spurred the U.S. government to sponsor bold new domestic initiatives in the areas of public education and space exploration. The Cold War even helped to shape a post–World War II domestic ideal: a nuclear family living in a house in the suburbs, with a breadwinner father and a full-time homemaker mother. Many Americans believed that their prosperous, consumer-oriented economy, with its emphasis on individualism and personal choice, was a key weapon in the fight against communism.

In a feverish arms race, both the United States and the USSR rushed to stockpile weapons of mass destruction. Constant innovations in the technology of nuclear weaponry (such as intercontinental ballistic missiles) made the bombers used in World War II obsolete. The hydrogen bomb, tested successfully for the first time in 1953, dwarfed the power of the atomic bomb that had leveled Hiroshima. Nevertheless, citizens who criticized the arms buildup risked being branded unpatriotic. More than ever before, domestic policy was intertwined with foreign policy.

The rise of multinational corporations meant that large, impersonal institutions, whether government or private, were shaping American life. Middle-level managers—men in "grey flannel suits"—represented the corporate ethos of loyalty to the company above all else. At the same time, many Americans sought to work within their local communities for social and political change. In the South, African American men and women launched a dramatic assault on the system of legal segregation known as "Jim Crow." Working at the grassroots level, these activists boycotted buses, marched, engaged in sit-ins at lunch counters, and went to jail. Their efforts provoked the courts and Congress to act, culminating in the Civil Rights Acts of 1964 and 1965. For the first time in American history, the federal government assumed responsibility for eliminating discrimination in the workplace and guaranteeing all its citizens the right to vote.

Other groups also organized and entered the political arena. Indians, disabled Americans, California farm workers, and gay men and lesbians all formed organizations to counter discrimination and advance their civil rights. The women's movement affected all aspects of American society, enabling women to play a fuller role in the political and economic life of the country. A new environmental movement secured legislation protecting wilderness areas and endangered species and ensuring that Americans had clean air to breathe and clean water to drink.

Lyndon B. Johnson assumed the presidency after the assassination of John F. Kennedy in 1963. Johnson hoped to revitalize the New Deal legacy by expanding social welfare programs. His program, called the Great Society, sought to address seemingly intractable problems such as poverty, lack of health care for the elderly, and the deterioration of inner-city neighborhoods. But Johnson also expanded the U.S. military presence in Vietnam, an effort that cost an increasing number of American lives. Even constant bombing proved futile to stem the civil war that pitted Americans and anticommunist Vietnamese against the National Liberation Front of South Vietnam and their comrades in the north. Johnson's successor, Richard M. Nixon, also found himself mired in a war that was becoming increasingly unpopular among Americans.

Protests against the war in the late 1960s and early 1970s highlighted an emerging youth culture. The baby boom generation, born in the two decades after World War II, embraced sexual freedom and new forms of music (such as rock 'n' roll) in an apparent attempt to defy their parents and "the Establishment" in general. Many Americans felt betrayed by both Johnson and Nixon, believing that tens of thousands of American soldiers had died in vain in Vietnam. The Watergate break-in at Democratic headquarters, leading eventually to Nixon's resignation, contributed to a growing, widespread disenchantment with government authority.

By the late 1970s, developments abroad had greatly complicated Cold War politics. Middle Eastern oil-producing nations imposed an oil embargo on the United States, highlighting U.S. dependence on fossil fuels. Islamic fundamentalists were beginning to retaliate violently against the spread of American influence and culture in Muslim countries. And at home, a conservative backlash emerged to counter the expansion of the welfare state, the heightened visibility of the feminist movement, and widening civil rights protests.

1968 Martin Luther King Jr. assassinated
Robert Kennedy assassinated
My Lai massacre
Wild and Scenic Rivers Act
Tet offensive

1969 Huge antiwar protests in Washington, D.C.
Indians occupy Alcatraz, San Francisco Bay
Stonewall raid, New York City
Astronauts Neil Armstrong and Buzz Aldrin walk on the moon

1970 United States invades Cambodia
National Guardsmen kill four students, Kent State University

1971 Pentagon Papers published
Nixon administration creates "plumbers" for illegal activities

1972 Watergate break-in
Nixon visits China
Founding of *Ms.* magazine

1973 *Roe v. Wade* legalizes abortion

American Indian Movement members occupy Wounded Knee
Endangered Species Act
OPEC oil embargo
American troops withdrawn from Vietnam

1974 Nixon resigns presidency; Gerald R. Ford becomes president

1975 *Mayaguez* incident
Vietnam reunified under communist rule
Congressional investigations of CIA covert operations

1976 Hyde Amendment prohibits use of Medicaid funds for abortions
Nation celebrates bicentennial

1977 President Jimmy Carter issues general amnesty for draft evaders
Trans-Alaska pipeline system completed
ABC airs miniseries *Roots*, based on book by Alex Haley

1978 *Bakke* Supreme Court decision
California Proposition 13

1979 Camp David peace accords
Partial meltdown of nuclear core at Three Mile Island nuclear plant
Iranian Revolution

CHAPTER 25

Domestic Dreams and Atomic Nightmares, 1953–1963

DR. TOM DOOLEY WAS KNOWN AS THE "JUNGLE DOCTOR." A NATIVE OF ST. LOUIS AND a devout Roman Catholic, Dooley joined the Navy medical corps during World War II and remained in the Navy reserves until 1950. After earning his medical degree, he moved to Southeast Asia, where he set up clinics to provide medical care for impoverished villagers. He quickly became a major celebrity. In a 1960 Gallup poll, Dooley was among the ten most admired Americans. President Dwight D. Eisenhower said of Dooley, "Few, if any, men have equaled [Dooley's] exhibition of courage, self-sacrifice, faith in his God and his readiness to serve his fellow man." When Dooley died of cancer in 1961 at the age of 34, he was honored by Congress and posthumously awarded the U.S. Navy's Legion of Merit. His legacy helped inspire John F. Kennedy's creation of the Peace Corps.

Although he was a practicing Catholic, Dooley rejected the role of the religious missionary—a role largely discredited in the anticolonial post–World War II years as tied to racist and imperialist designs. Rather, Dooley promoted modernization and development, embracing an internationalist vision that was grounded in respect and appreciation for the local culture and customs of the people with whom he lived.

Dooley's zeal to help the people of Southeast Asia went far beyond medical care. A passionate anticommunist, in 1956 he assisted the Central Intelligence Agency (CIA) and the U.S. Navy in leading the exodus of 900,000 Catholic refugees from newly created communist North Vietnam to South Vietnam, where the United States backed a noncommunist dictatorship under Ngo Dinh Diem. He recounted that experience in a best-selling book, *Deliver Us from Evil*, and wrote two other books that chronicled his activities at the clinics he founded in the villages and jungles of Laos. His books praised Diem's regime in South Vietnam and promoted the cause of anticommunism in Southeast Asia.

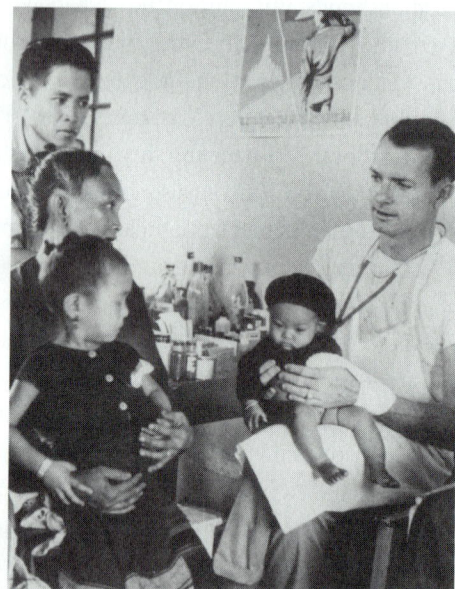

Dr. Tom Dooley is pictured here providing medical care to Laotian children. Known as the "jungle doctor," he represented American expertise and benevolence, as well as fervent anticommunism, during the early years of the Cold War.

CHAPTER OUTLINE

Cold War, Warm Hearth

The Civil Rights Movement

The Eisenhower Years

Outsiders and Opposition

The Kennedy Era

Conclusion

Sites to Visit

For Further Reading

Dooley's work in Southeast Asia provided essential medical care to people in need and also served American interests in the early years of the Cold War. But his decision to live and work in the remote villages of Laos was not based simply on self-sacrifice. As a homosexual, Dooley would have had a difficult life within the United States in the 1950s. Anticommunist crusaders purged homosexuals from government employment, and gay men and lesbians faced harassment, ostracism, and often the loss of their jobs. Dooley escaped the intense homophobia of his home country by creating communal living situations with other men in remote areas of Laos, far from public view. There he could keep his sexual orientation private. If he had remained in the United States, the anticommunists whose political passions he shared would have purged him from their ranks.

It is fitting that a doctor spreading the benefits of American medicine to Asia would become a Cold War hero. Science and expertise reigned supreme during the Cold War years. Parents turned to another famous physician, Dr. Benjamin Spock, whose 1946 guide to raising children, *Baby and Child Care,* became an instant best-seller. Unlike prewar child-rearing experts who encouraged discipline and discouraged coddling, Dr. Spock emphasized nurture and affection. Dr. Jonas Salk became a hero for developing a vaccine against polio in 1955. The oral contraceptive pill, which came on the market in 1960, provided relatively safe and effective birth control. Hailed initially as a boon to family planning, the pill also helped to usher in the sexual revolution of the 1960s. The National Aeronautics and Space Administration (NASA), established in 1958, sent the first American into space in 1961. But science also brought pesticides, smog, and other pollutants. Americans, at the time, rarely considered the environmental effects of consumer goods, cars, petrochemicals, or nuclear power.

The decade from 1953 to 1963, under the presidencies of Dwight Eisenhower and John Kennedy, was a time of expansive optimism about the future. Hawaii and Alaska became states in 1959. The **baby boom** demonstrated widespread faith in the future for American children. It was also a decade of growth for U.S. influence abroad, the domestic economy, consumer culture, and television. Suburbs, highways, and shopping malls expanded to meet the needs of increasing numbers of families with young children. Some teenagers and others rebelled against what they saw as conformity in American life. But African Americans organized in the civil rights movement to gain full access to the freedoms and comforts of this increasingly middle-class society.

It was also a decade of anxiety. Americans worried about the perils of the atomic age as the nuclear arsenals of both superpowers continued to grow. Science fiction films about alien invaders reflected concerns about foreign dangers. The Soviet Union's 1957 launching of *Sputnik,* the first artificial satellite to orbit the Earth, alarmed Americans and forced the nation to confront the possibility of Soviet technological superiority. The United States appeared to be at the height of its strength and power, yet at the same time, more vulnerable than ever before.

Cold War, Warm Hearth

The postwar era was a time of deep divisions in American society, yet in certain ways Americans behaved with remarkable conformity. This is nowhere more evident than in the overwhelming embrace of the nuclear family. The GI Bill, with its provisions for home mortgage loans, enabled veterans of modest means to purchase homes. Although residential segregation prevailed throughout the postwar era, limiting most suburban developments

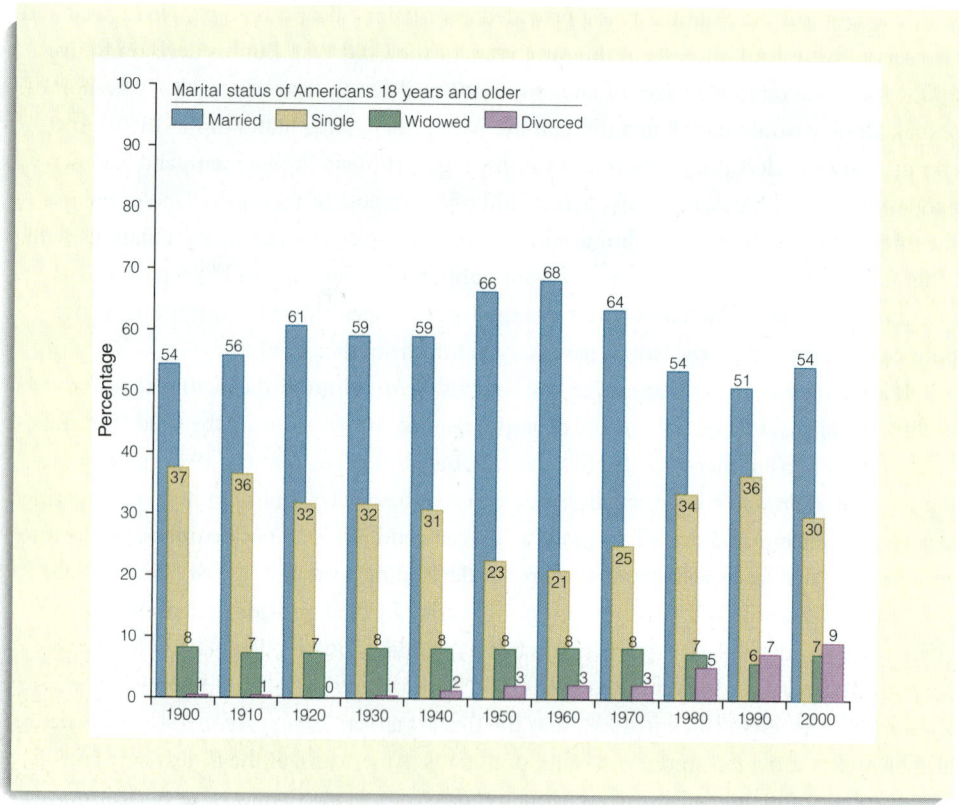

FIGURE 25.1
MARITAL STATUS OF THE U.S. ADULT POPULATION, 1900–2000 Following World War II, Americans married in record numbers. The high rate of marriage corresponded with a relatively low divorce rate. Beginning in the 1970s, the marriage rate plummeted and the divorce rate rose dramatically.

to prosperous white middle- and working-class families, many veterans of color were able to buy their first homes. Americans of all racial, ethnic, and religious groups, of all socioeconomic classes and educational levels, brought the marriage rate up and the divorce rate down. The "American way of life" embodied in the suburban nuclear family, as a cultural ideal if not a universal reality, motivated countless postwar Americans to strive for it, to live by its codes, and—for Americans of color—to demand it.

Consumer Spending and the Suburban Ideal

Between 1947 and 1961, national income increased more than 60 percent. Rather than putting this money aside for a rainy day, Americans were inclined to spend it. Investing in one's home, along with the trappings that would enhance family life, seemed the best way to plan for a secure future.

Between 1950 and 1970, the suburban population more than doubled, from 36 million to 74 million. Fully 20 percent of the population remained poor during this prosperous time. But most families of ample as well as modest means exhibited a great deal of conformity in their consumer behavior, reflecting widely shared beliefs about the good life. They poured their money into homes, domestic appliances, televisions, automobiles, and family vacations.

Nuclear families who settled in the suburbs provided the foundation for new types of community life and leisure pursuits, sometimes at the expense of older ones grounded in ethnic neighborhoods and kinship networks. Family-oriented amusement parks such as Disneyland in Anaheim, California, which opened in 1955, catered to middle-class tastes, in contrast to older venues such as Coney Island, known for their thrill rides, class and ethnic mixing, and romantic environments. Religious affiliation rose to an all-time high as Americans built and joined suburban churches and synagogues, complete with youth programs and summer camps. In 1949 fewer than 1 million American homes had a television. Within the next four years, the number soared to 20 million.

The Cold War made a profound contribution to suburban sprawl. Congress passed the Federal-Aid Highway Act of 1956, which provided $100 billion to cover 90 percent of the cost for 41,000 miles of national highways. When President Dwight D. Eisenhower signed the bill into law, he stated one of the major reasons for the new highway system: "[In] case of atomic attack on our key cities, the road net must permit quick evacuation of target areas."

The worst-case scenario was communist takeover and the defeat of the United States in the Cold War. Pentagon strategists and foreign policy experts feared that the Soviet Union might gain the military might to allow its territorial expansion and, eventually, world domination. But observers also worried that the real dangers to America were internal: racial strife, emancipated women, class conflict, and familial disruption. To alleviate these fears, Americans turned to the family as a bastion of safety in an insecure world. Most postwar Americans longed for security after years of economic depression and war, and they saw family stability as the best bulwark against the new dangers of the Cold War.

Race, Class, and Domesticity

After World War II, the nation faced a severe housing shortage. The federal government gave developers financial subsidies to build affordable single-family homes and offered Federal Housing Authority (FHA) loans and income tax deductions to homebuyers. These benefits enabled white working-class and middle-class families to purchase houses. Postwar prosperity, government subsidies, and the promise of assimilation made it possible for white-skinned Americans of immigrant background to blend into the suburbs.

■ Commuters, mostly men, left their suburban homes each morning to go to jobs in the cities, returning home at night. Suburbs served as "bedroom communities," inhabited mostly by women and children during the day.

Despite the expansion of the black and Latino middle class and the increase in home ownership among racial minorities, most suburban developments excluded nonwhites. The FHA and lending banks maintained policies known as **red lining**, which designated certain neighborhoods off limits to racial minorities. Although Americans of color remained concentrated in urban and rural areas, some did move to the suburbs, usually into segregated communities.

For Americans of color, suburban home ownership offered inclusion in the postwar American dream. In her powerful 1959 play *A Raisin In the Sun*, African American playwright Lorraine Hansberry articulated with great eloquence the importance of a home in the suburbs, not to assimilate into white America but to live as a black family with dignity and pride. Asian Americans also had good reason to celebrate home and family life. With the end of the exclusion of Chinese immigrants during World War II, wives and war brides began to enter the country, helping to build thriving family-oriented communities. After the disruptions and anguish of internment, Japanese Americans were eager

to put their families and lives back together. Mexican Americans and Mexican immigrants, including *braceros*, established flourishing communities in the Southwest. Puerto Ricans migrated to New York and other eastern cities, where they could earn four times the average wage on the island.

Racial segregation did not prevail everywhere. For example, in Shaker Heights, Ohio, a suburb of Cleveland, white residents made a conscious decision, as a community, to integrate their neighborhood. Drawing on postwar liberal ideals of civil rights and racial integration, they welcomed black homeowners. They succeeded in this effort by emphasizing class similarity over racial difference. White residents encouraged other white families to move into Shaker Heights, pointing out that their prosperous black neighbors were "just like us."

As residents and businesses migrated to the suburbs, slum housing and vacant factories remained in the central cities. The Housing Acts of 1949 and 1954 granted funds to municipalities for urban renewal. However, few of those federal dollars provided low-income housing. Mayors, bankers, and real estate interests used the money to bulldoze slums and build gleaming office towers, civic centers, and apartment complexes for affluent citizens, leaving the poor to fend for themselves in the remaining dilapidated corners of the cities.

Although intended to revitalize cities, urban renewal actually accelerated the decay of inner cities and worsened conditions for the urban poor. Federally funded projects often disrupted and destroyed ethnic communities. In St. Paul, Minnesota, the construction of U.S. Highway 94, while enabling suburbanites to commute to the city, obliterated the thriving urban African American neighborhood of Rondo. In Los Angeles, the Dodgers' stadium built in Chávez Ravine offered baseball fans and their families access to the national pastime, but it destroyed the historically rooted Mexican American neighborhood in its path. The $5 million project displaced 7,500 people and demolished 900 homes.

Along with the urban poor, rural Americans reaped few benefits of postwar affluence. The 1950s marked the greatest out-migration from the South as the mechanization of farms—particularly the mechanical cotton picker—reduced the number of workers on the land. More than one-fourth of the population left Kentucky and West Virginia, where unemployment in some areas reached 80 percent.

Women: Back to the Future

The nuclear family ideal of the 1950s included a full-time wife and mother and a breadwinner husband. This vision of domesticity marked a giant step backward for many women, whose opportunities and experiences had expanded dramatically during World War II. The elevation of the housewife as a major cultural icon contrasted sharply with the reality. The proportion of women who fit the mold of full-time homemaker was rapidly shrinking. Although most American women married, had children, and carried the lion's share of responsibility for housework and child-rearing, increasing numbers of married women also held jobs outside the home. The employment of married women began to rise during World War II and kept rising after the war, even though most of the well-paying and highly skilled jobs returned to men at the war's end.

Many women worked part-time while their children were at school, as they considered themselves homemakers not wage earners. With few other opportunities for creative work, women embraced their domestic roles and turned homemaking into a profession. Many fulfilled their role with pride and satisfaction and extended their energies and talents into their communities, where they made important contributions as volunteers in local parent-teacher associations (PTAs) and other civic organizations. Most postwar mothers finished childbearing by the time they were thirty and had many years ahead of them when their child-rearing responsibilities ended. Some expanded part-time employment into full-time occupations when their children left the nest. Others felt bored and frustrated and drowned their sorrow with

■ The Women's Council of St. Paul, Minnesota, was one of many service organizations in which black and white women joined in common projects. Volunteer activities enabled women to serve their communities as well as develop important political and leadership skills.

alcohol or tranquilizers. In 1963 author Betty Friedan described the constraints facing women as the "problem that has no name" in her feminist manifesto *The Feminine Mystique*.

Education was one avenue available to women, as students as well as teachers. But higher education did not open its doors fully to women. Because few women gained access to graduate and professional schools and most well-paying jobs were reserved for men, college degrees for white women did not necessarily open up career opportunities or greatly improve their job and earning prospects. By 1956 one-fourth of white female students married while still in college. Many of these women dropped out of school to take jobs in order to support their husbands through college. But the situation was quite different for black women. Like their mothers and grandmothers, most black women had to work to help support their families. Even in the prosperous postwar years, few black families could survive on the meager earnings of a single breadwinner. Job prospects for black women generally were limited to menial, low-paying occupations. Young black women knew that a college degree could mean the difference between working as a maid for a white family and working as a secretary, teacher, or nurse. Although few in number, more than 90 percent of black women who entered college completed their degrees.

Black women also aspired to the role of homemaker, but for very different reasons than white women. Although poverty still plagued large numbers of black citizens, the black middle class expanded during the 1950s. Postwar prosperity enabled some African Americans, for the first time, to strive for family life in which the earnings of men were adequate to allow women to stay home with their own children rather than tending to the houses and children of white families. For black women, domesticity meant "freedom and independence in her own home." It is no wonder that in the early 1960s, women of color bristled when white feminists such as Betty Friedan called upon women to break free from the "chains" of domesticity.

The Civil Rights Movement

As the civil rights movement gained momentum in the South, African American activists faced fierce opposition from local white authorities and contempt from national leaders. Persistent racial discrimination proved to be the nation's worst embarrassment throughout the Cold War. The Soviet Union and other communist countries pointed to American race relations as an indication of the hypocrisy and failure of the American promise of freedom for all. Yet national leaders paid only lip service to racial justice and failed to provide the strong support necessary to defeat the system of racial segregation in the South known as the "Jim Crow" system. Jim Crow was a legal, or *de jure*, set of institutions that prevailed throughout the South. Although the nation's leaders acknowledged the need to address Southern segregation, they did nothing to address the unofficial, or *de facto*, segregation that prevailed throughout the rest of the country.

Nevertheless, at the grassroots level, racial minorities continued to work for equal rights. For example, Mexican Americans in the Southwest continued to press for desegregation of schools, residential neighborhoods, and public facilities through organizations such as the middle-class League of United Latin American Citizens (LULAC) and the Asociación Nacional México-Americana (ANMA), a civil rights organization that emerged out of the labor movement. It was not until 1963 that the power of the civil rights movement—and the violence of southern white opposition—finally compelled the federal government to take action.

■ Children in segregated schools studied in wretched physical conditions but benefited from dedicated African American teachers. The Supreme Court struck down school segregation in the landmark 1954 case *Brown v. Board of Education*, arguing in its unanimous decision that separate facilities were inherently unequal.

Brown v. Board of Education

The first major success in the struggle to dismantle the Jim Crow system in the South came in the 1954 Supreme Court decision *Brown v. Board of Education*. Civil rights strategists decided to pursue their cause in the courts rather than through Congress. They knew that southern Democrats in Congress, who held disproportionate power through their seniority and control of major committees, would block any civil rights legislation that came before the House or Senate. They believed that they had a better chance of success through the courts.

NAACP lawyers filed suit against the Topeka, Kansas, Board of Education on behalf of Linda Brown, a black child in a segregated school. They were targeting the 1896 *Plessy v. Ferguson* decision, which had justified Jim Crow laws on the grounds that they provided "separate but equal" facilities. The case reached the U.S. Supreme Court, where NAACP general counsel Thurgood Marshall argued that separate facilities, by definition, denied African Americans their equal rights as citizens.

In 1953, during the three-year period that the Supreme Court had the *Brown* case before it, President Eisenhower appointed Earl Warren as chief justice. Warren had been state attorney general and then governor of California during World War II and had approved the internment of Japanese Americans—a decision he later deeply regretted. He now used his political and legal skills to strike a blow for justice. He knew that such a critical case needed a unanimous decision to win broad political support. One by one, he persuaded his Supreme Court colleagues of the importance of striking down segregation. On May 17, 1954, Warren delivered the historic unanimous ruling: "To separate [black children] from others of similar age and qualifications solely because of their race generates a feeling of inferiority as to their status in the community that may affect their hearts and minds in a way unlikely ever to be undone.... Separate educational facilities are inherently unequal."

Brown v. Board of Education of Topeka, Kansas

White Resistance, Black Persistence

Winning the *Brown* case was a great triumph, but it was only the first step. Desegregation would be meaningful only when it was enforced, and that was another matter entirely. At first, there seemed to be some cause for optimism. Although a few white officials in the South protested vehemently, many others seemed resigned to accept the decision. However, few were willing to initiate action to implement desegregation. Even the Supreme Court delayed its decision on implementation for a full year and then simply called for the process to begin "with all deliberate speed" but specified no timetable. Political leaders did not come forward to work on the task, leaving sympathetic educators and eager black Americans with no support.

The leader who could have done the most but in fact did the least was President Eisenhower. Expressing neither "approbation nor disapproval," Eisenhower said, "I don't think you can change the hearts of men with laws or decisions." Just before the Court's ruling, he told Chief Justice Warren that southern white segregationists simply wanted to make sure "that their sweet little girls are not required to sit in schools alongside some big overgrown Negroes." After the decision went against his wishes, Eisenhower remarked that his decision to appoint Warren to the court was the "biggest damn fool mistake" he ever made.

In 1955, the year after the *Brown* decision, white Mississippians murdered fourteen-year-old Emmett Till for allegedly whistling at a white woman. The boy had come from Chicago to Mississippi, where he was visiting relatives. His mutilated body was found in the Tallahatchie River. Although Till's killers later confessed to the murder, an all-white jury found them not guilty. Eisenhower remained silent about Till's murder and the travesty of justice, even when E. Frederick Morrow, his one black adviser, beseeched him to condemn the lynching.

Eisenhower's hands-off policy emboldened southern segregationists to resist the Supreme Court's desegregation decision. When it became clear that the federal government would do nothing to enforce the ruling, white resistance spread across the South. State legislatures passed resolutions vowing to protect segregation, and most southern congressmen signed the 1956 "Southern Manifesto," promising to oppose federal desegregation efforts.

A crisis at Central High School in Little Rock, Arkansas, finally forced Eisenhower to act. Under a federal district court's order to desegregate, school officials were prepared to comply and had carefully mobilized community support. But Arkansas Governor Orville Faubus, facing reelection, instructed National Guard troops to maintain "order" by blocking the entry of black students into the school. Eisenhower initially refused to intervene in the crisis. Hoping for a compromise, he met with Faubus, who agreed to allow the school to integrate peacefully. But Faubus broke his word, withdrew the National Guard troops, and left Little Rock, leaving the black students unprotected.

Executive Order 10730: Desegregation of Central High School

On September 23, 1957, as nine black students attempted to enter Central High, a huge angry crowd of whites surrounded them. With international news cameras broadcasting pictures of the shrieking and menacing mob, Eisenhower was forced to federalize the Arkansas National Guard and send 1,000 paratroopers to Little Rock. Eisenhower acted to maintain federal authority rather than to support integration.

> *Eisenhower acted to maintain federal authority rather than to support integration.*

Boycotts and Sit-Ins

Under Jim Crow laws in the South, black passengers were required to sit in the back section of buses, leaving the front of the bus for whites. If the "white" section at the front of the bus

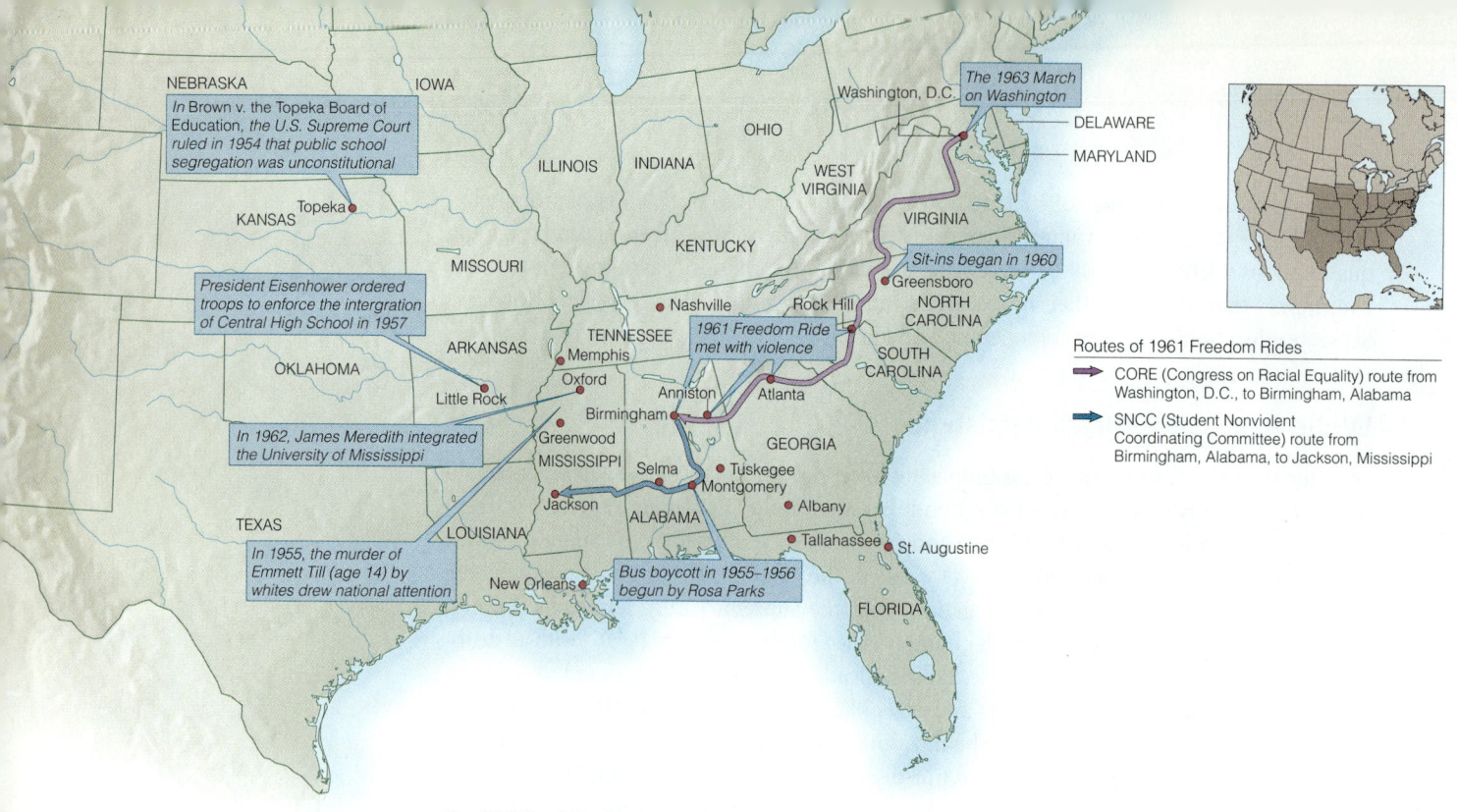

■ **MAP 25.1**
MAJOR EVENTS OF THE AFRICAN AMERICAN CIVIL RIGHTS MOVEMENT, 1953–1963 Most of the major events of the early stages of the black freedom struggle took place in the South. Black southerners formed the backbone of the movement, but the grassroots protest movement drew participants from all regions of the country, all racial and ethnic groups, cities and rural areas, churches and universities, old and young, lawyers and sharecroppers.

filled up, black passengers were required to give up their seats for white passengers. On December 1, 1955, Rosa Parks and the black community of Montgomery, Alabama, were ready to take on the system. Parks, who worked as a seamstress, was a widely respected leader in Montgomery's black community, active in her church, and secretary of the local NAACP. On her way home from work that day, sitting in the first row of the "colored" section of the bus when the front of the bus filled with passengers, she refused to move when a white man demanded her seat. Parks was arrested, and black Montgomery sprang into action.

Literally overnight, the Montgomery bus boycott was born. For 381 days, more than 90 percent of Montgomery's black citizens sacrificed their comfort and convenience for the sake of their rights and dignity. As one elderly black woman replied when a white reporter offered her a ride as she walked to work, "No, my feets is tired but my soul is rested."

Martin Luther King Jr., pastor of the Dexter Avenue Baptist Church, was a newcomer to Montgomery when the bus boycott began. He embraced the opportunity to become the leader of the boycott and, eventually, the most powerful spokesperson for the civil rights movement. His stirring and impassioned words inspired thousands of black citizens to join the cause. As he told the 5,000 listeners who gathered in his church on the first night of the boycott, "If you will protest courageously and yet with dignity and Christian love, in the history books that are written in future generations, historians will have to pause and say, 'there lived a great people—a black people—who injected a new meaning and dignity into the veins of civilization.' This is our challenge and our overwhelming responsibility."

The bus boycott ended a year later when the Supreme Court ruled that Montgomery's buses must integrate, but the momentum generated by the boycott galvanized the civil rights movement. King and other leaders formed the Southern Christian Leadership Conference (SCLC), which united black ministers across the South in the cause of civil rights. The boycott tactic spread to other southern cities. As boycotts continued, a new strategy emerged: the **sit-in**.

On February 1, 1960, four African American students at North Carolina Agricultural and Technical College in Greensboro, inspired by the example of the bus boycott, entered the local Woolworth store and sat down at the lunch counter. When they were told "We do not serve Negroes," they refused to leave, forcing the staff at Woolworth's to physically remove the nonviolent protesters. Undaunted, they returned to the lunch counter the next day with twenty-three classmates. By the end of the week, more than a thousand students joined the protest. By this time, white gangs had gathered, waving Confederate flags and menacing the black undergraduates. But the students responded by waving American flags.

In May 1961, members of the Congress of Racial Equality (CORE) organized the Freedom Rides, in which black and white civil rights workers attempted to ride two interstate buses from Washington, D.C., to New Orleans in an effort to challenge segregation at facilities used in interstate travel. Their journey began peacefully, but when they reached Rock Hill, South Carolina, a group of whites beat John Lewis, one of the young black riders, for entering a whites-only rest room. In Anniston, Alabama, a mob slashed the tires of one of the buses, threw a fire bomb through a window, and pummeled the riders with fists and pipes. After the brutal beatings, reinforcements from the Student Nonviolent Coordinating Committee (SNCC) arrived to continue the Freedom Rides. They persevered, facing beatings along the way until they reached Jackson, Mississippi, where they were immediately arrested and jailed. The spirit and strength of the civil rights workers inspired many others to join them in the movement.

The Eisenhower Years

The presidency of Dwight D. Eisenhower was notable largely for moderation and maintaining the status quo, with very few major new initiatives and a style of leadership that rested more on his personal stature than his actions. Ike, as he was known, presided over the nation during a time of great prosperity, and his policies encouraged business expansion. However, the former general did try to stem the defense buildup. In his farewell address at the end of his second term as president, Eisenhower warned the nation against the growing power of the "military-industrial complex," the term he coined to describe the armed forces and the politically powerful defense industries that supplied arms and equipment to them. Eisenhower tried to fight the Cold War in a fiscally responsible manner.

TABLE 25-1

The Election of 1956

Candidate	Political Party	Popular Vote (%)	Electoral Vote
Dwight D. Eisenhower	Republican	57.6	457
Adlai E. Stevenson	Democratic	42.1	73

The Middle of the Road

As president, the Kansas-bred Eisenhower pursued a path down the middle of the road. His probusiness legislative agenda and appointments pleased conservatives, and he placated liberals by extending many of the policies of the welfare state enacted during the New Deal. He agreed to the expansion of Social Security and unemployment compensation and an increase in the minimum wage. He also made concerted efforts to reduce defense spending, believing that continued massive military expenditures would hinder the nation's economic growth. In December 1953, Eisenhower announced the New Look, a streamlined military that relied less on expensive conventional ground forces and more on air power and advanced nuclear capabilities.

Eisenhower's plans to reduce defense spending derailed on October 4, 1957, when the Soviet Union launched *Sputnik*, the first artificial Earth satellite. Although *Sputnik* could not be seen with the naked eye—it was only 22 inches in diameter and weighed only 184 pounds—

it emitted a beeping noise that was broadcast by commercial radio stations in the United States, making its presence very real and causing near hysteria among the public. The Soviet's launching of *Sputnik II* a month later seemed to confirm widespread fears that the United States was behind in the space race and, more significantly, in the arms race. Eisenhower's popularity in the polls suddenly dropped 22 points.

Acquiescing to his critics, the president allotted increased funds for military, scientific, and educational spending. NASA, which developed the program of space exploration, was one result of this increase. But Eisenhower believed that "the most critical problem of all" was the lack of American scientists and engineers. He led the federal government to subsidize additional science and math training for both teachers and students.

"What's Good for General Motors . . ."

Eisenhower's secretary of defense, former head of General Motors Charles Wilson, made the memorable comment that "what's good for General Motors business is good for America." But not everyone agreed. Eisenhower's probusiness policies had a deleterious impact on the nation's environment. He promoted the passage of the Submerged Land Act, which removed from federal jurisdiction more than $40 billion worth of oil-rich offshore lands. Under the control of state governments, oil companies could—and did—gain access to them. The *New York Times* called the act "one of the greatest and surely the most unjustified give-away programs" in the nation's history. The administration's willingness to allow businesses to expand with little regulation, and with virtually no concern for the environment, contributed to increasing pollution of the air, water, and land during the 1950s and helped spark the environmental movement of the 1960s and 1970s.

National Defense Education Act

Eisenhower also supported the Federal-Aid Highway Act of 1956. As the largest public works project the nation had ever mounted, this centrally planned transportation system was a boon to the auto, trucking, oil, concrete, and tire industries. In addition, it contributed to the national pastime of family road vacations and tourism. Cheap gas also fueled America's car culture. Cars gave Americans increased mobility and enabled suburban dwellers to drive to work in the cities. But reliance on the automobile doomed the nation's passenger train system and led to the decline of public transportation. Cars also contributed to suburban sprawl, air pollution, and traffic jams.

Eisenhower's Foreign Policy

The New Look, while containing military spending, also shifted American military priorities from reliance on conventional weapons to nuclear deterrence and covert operations. During Eisenhower's presidency, the United States and the Soviet Union both solidified their separate alliances. The twelve original NATO nations agreed that an attack on any one of them would be considered an attack on all, and they maintained a force to defend the West against a possible Soviet invasion. NATO expanded in 1952 to include Greece and Turkey, and West Germany joined in 1955. The Soviet Union formed a similar alliance, the Warsaw Pact, with the countries of eastern Europe. Confrontations between the United States and the Soviet Union over the fate of Europe gave way to more subtle maneuvers regarding the Third World—a term originally referring to nonaligned nations in the Middle East, Africa, Asia, and Latin America.

After Joseph Stalin died in 1953, Nikita Khrushchev became the new leader of the Soviet Union and called for peaceful coexistence with the United States. To limit military expenditures and improve relations, the superpowers arranged high-level summit meetings. In 1955 delegates from the United States, the Soviet Union, Britain, and France met in Geneva. Although the meeting achieved little of substance, it set a tone of cooperation. In 1959 Khrushchev came to the United States, met with Eisenhower, and toured the country. Despite the Soviet downing of an American U-2 spy plane in 1960 and the capture of American pilot Gary Powers, the superpowers began to discuss arms limitation. Both countries agreed to limit aboveground testing of nuclear weapons in light of the health and environmental risks such tests posed. Soviet negotiations with the United States did not, however, mean greater liberty in eastern Europe, where Soviet forces crushed a 1956 uprising in Hungary.

The Eisenhower administration continued to distrust countries that maintained neutrality in the Cold War, fearing that those not aligned with the United States might turn to communism and become allies of the Soviet Union. Through covert operations in 1953, the Central Intelligence Agency (CIA) helped to overthrow the elected government in Iran—which had seized control of Western-owned oil fields in the country—and to restore the dictatorship of Shah Reza Pahlavi, whose unpopular Western-leaning regime would be overthrown by Muslim fundamentalists in 1979. In 1954 the CIA helped overthrow the elected government of Jacobo Arbenz in Guatemala. U.S. officials considered Arbenz a communist because he sought to nationalize and redistribute large tracts of land, much of it owned by the Boston-based United Fruit Company.

> *Anticommunism became the guiding principle behind nearly all U.S. foreign policy, taking precedence over other American ideals.*

In 1959 revolutionary leader Fidel Castro overthrew Cuba's U.S.-friendly dictator Fulgencio Batista. Castro established a regime in Cuba based on socialist principles. His government took control of foreign-owned companies, including many owned by Americans. Castro's socialist policies alarmed U.S. officials and investors in Cuba. Eisenhower's hostility encouraged Castro to forge an alliance with the Soviet Union. The CIA then launched a plot to overthrow Castro. In 1960–1961, the CIA also helped orchestrate the overthrow and assassination of the charismatic left-leaning Patrice Lumumba, the first minister of the Republic of the Congo in Africa, soon after its independence from Belgium.

U.S. policymakers, with their anticommunist preoccupations, and people in Third World countries, with their campaigns against colonialism and racism, had little interest in each other's priorities. A case in point was Egypt, where in 1952 Gamal Abdul Nasser overthrew the corrupt monarchy of King Farouk and established a government neutral in the Cold War. In 1954 Nasser declared himself prime minister of the new government and accepted aid from both the United States and the Soviet Union. When Nasser engaged in trade with Soviet-bloc countries and extended diplomatic recognition to communist China, the United States canceled loans that were to support the building of the huge Aswan Dam, a major development project for the Egyptian economy. In response, Nasser nationalized the British-controlled Suez Canal in 1956, arguing that canal tolls would provide alternative funding for the dam. The British government, with the help of France and Israel, launched an attack against Egypt to regain control of the canal.

Although he distrusted Nasser, Eisenhower strongly criticized Britain for its effort to retain its imperial position in the Middle East. To avoid further antagonizing Nasser and other Third World leaders, Eisenhower denounced Britain's Suez attack and threatened economic sanctions, forcing the British to back down. Although leaders in Africa and Asia applauded Eisenhower's actions, the episode weakened U.S. relations with Nasser, who forged ties with the Soviet Union. Eisenhower now feared that "Nasserism" might spread throughout the Middle East.

In the spring of 1957, Congress approved the Eisenhower Doctrine, a pledge to defend Middle Eastern countries "against overt armed aggression from any nation controlled by international communism." However, U.S. policymakers rarely distinguished between nationalist movements and designs by "international communism," which they defined as Soviet aggression. Because American leaders believed that struggles for national self-determination in Third World countries were inspired and supported by the Soviet Union, they used the Eisenhower Doctrine to provide justification for U.S. military intervention to support pro-Western governments.

■ **MAP 25.2**
COLD WAR SPHERES OF INFLUENCE, 1953–1963 During the early years of the Cold War, the United States and the Soviet Union developed formal military alliances, most importantly NATO and the Warsaw Pact. The American and Soviet informal spheres of influence also included trading and cultural ties to several other countries. Many independent nations, especially those just emerging from colonialism, remained neutral in the Cold War.

Military alliances in the 1950s
- U.S. allies
- U.S. allies/NATO members
- USSR allies
- USSR allies/Warsaw Pact members
- Neutral nation

Outsiders and Opposition

The 1950s often are remembered as a time of political and cultural complacency among white Americans, with most of the opposition to the nation's institutions emanating from people of color. But some young whites, in the South as well as North, joined in the struggle for civil rights; their numbers increased in the 1960s. Others were drawn to the music and dance of black America, especially the fusion of rhythm-and-blues with country-and-western, which took the form of early rock 'n' roll. Distinct forms of protest also emerged from within the white middle class: the rebellion of the Beats who rejected staid conformity,

the stirrings of discontent among women, and the antinuclear and environmental movements. The arts also reflected a rejection of mainstream values, as Jackson Pollock and other abstract expressionist painters challenged the artistic conventions of the time and shifted the center of the art world from Paris to New York. Even the sexual revolution of the 1960s had its roots in widespread defiance of the rigid sexual codes of the 1950s.

Youth, Sex, and Rock 'n' Roll

One clue that all was not tranquil was the widespread panic that the nation's young were out of control. Adult authorities worried about an epidemic of juvenile delinquency, blaming everything from parents to comic books. New celebrities such as movie stars Marlon Brando and James Dean portrayed misunderstood youth in rebellion against a corrupt and uncaring adult world. In their films, and in J. D. Salinger's now-classic novel *Catcher in the Rye*, young women and men strain against the authority and expectations of their parents and the adult world, dreaming of freedom and personal fulfillment.

Sexual mores were rigid in the 1950s—and widely violated. Single young women who became pregnant faced disgrace and ostracism unless they married quickly, which many did. Abortion, which had been illegal since the late nineteenth century but tacitly accepted until after World War II, became increasingly difficult to obtain, with hospitals placing new restrictions on legal therapeutic abortions. A double standard encouraged men to pursue sexual conquest as a mark of manhood and virility but tarnished the reputation of women who engaged in sexual intercourse prior to marriage.

In many ways, the youth of the 1950s were already undermining the constraints that toppled in the next decade. Nowhere is this development more obvious than in the explosion of rock 'n' roll, with its roots in African American rhythm-and-blues, its raw sexuality, and its jubilant rebelliousness. Rock 'n' roll emerged out of the fusion of musical traditions. Artists from many ethnic backgrounds experimented with a variety of forms. Jewish songwriters Jerry Leiber and Mike Stoller wrote songs such as "Hound Dog" for black artists such as Willie Mae Thornton that were later recorded by white Southerner Elvis Presley. The first Mexican American rock 'n' roll star, Ritchie Valens, sang such romantic ballads as "Donna" along with jazzed-up versions of Mexican folk songs such as "La Bamba."

■ Since sex was rarely discussed in most middle-class families, many parents relied on schools to provide elementary sex education, and a generation of suburban children learned the facts of life from nervous teachers and a variety of simplified texts.

Rebellious Men

Men, too, were in revolt. According to widely read sociological tracts of the time, such as William Whyte's *The Organization Man* and David Reisman's *The Lonely Crowd*, middle-class men were forced into boring, routinized jobs, groomed to be "outer-directed" at the expense of their inner lives, and saddled with the overwhelming burden of providing for ever-growing families with insatiable consumer desires.

A few highly visible American men provided alternative visions. Hugh Hefner built his Playboy empire by offering men the trappings of the "good life" without its burdensome responsibilities. The Playboy ethic encouraged men to enjoy the sexual pleasures of attractive women without the chains of marriage and to pursue the rewards of consumerism in well-appointed "bachelor flats" rather than appliance-laden homes. *Playboy* magazine celebrated this lifestyle.

Beat poets, writers, and artists offered a very different type of escape. In their literary works, such as Allen Ginsberg's poem *Howl* and Jack Kerouac's novel *On the Road*, and in their highly publicized lives, the Beats celebrated freedom from conformity, eccentric artistic expression, playful obscenity, experimentation with drugs, open homosexuality, and male bonding. While eschewing the sort of luxurious consumerism Hefner extolled, the Beats shared with the Playboy ethic a vision of male rebellion against conformity and responsibility. The mainstream men who indulged in these fantasies were more likely to enjoy them vicariously than to bolt from the breadwinner role. The dads who were honored on the new consumer holiday of Father's Day far outnumbered the freewheeling Beats and bachelors.

Mobilizing for Peace and the Environment

Some women did not wait for the new feminist movement to make their voices heard. Rachel Carson was one such woman. A marine biologist and a popular author, Carson became increasingly concerned about the impact of manufactured chemicals on the environment, especially the insecticide DDT, which had been poisoning the earth since World War II. Her last book, *Silent Spring*, published in 1962, brought attention to the worldwide problem of pesticide poisoning and helped launch the environmental movement that has flourished ever since.

Women also led the movement to stop the testing and proliferation of nuclear weapons. On November 1, 1961, 50,000 suburban women in more than sixty communities staged a protest, Women Strike for Peace (WSP). Participants lobbied government officials to "End the Arms Race—Not the Human Race." Within a year their numbers grew to several hundred thousand. Despite FBI surveillance, these women carried the banner of motherhood into political activism, much as their nineteenth-century predecessors had done.

The Kennedy Era

John Fitzgerald Kennedy was the first American president born in the twentieth century and the first Roman Catholic president. In his inaugural address, he claimed that "the torch has been passed to a new generation." It was a fitting metaphor for a young man who had been reared to compete and to win, whether the contest was athletic, intellectual, or political. But at the time of his election, it was not clear that a new generation had grabbed the torch. The young candidate was largely the creation of his father, Joseph, whose forebears had emigrated from Ireland during the 1840s. Joseph Kennedy rose to power and wealth as a financier, Hollywood executive, and ambassador to England. Ambitious and demanding, the elder Kennedy was known for his ruthlessness in business and politics and for his blatant philandering. He groomed his oldest son, Joseph P. Kennedy Jr., for greatness, specifically for the presidency. But when young Joe was killed in World War II, the father's ambitions settled on the next in line, John.

John (Jack) Kennedy became a hero during World War II, winning military honors for rescuing his crewmates on his patrol boat, PT-109, when it was rammed by a Japanese destroyer. The rescue left him with a painful back impairment and exacerbated the symptoms of Addison's disease, which plagued him all his life and necessitated daily cortisone injections. His father coached him to bear up under the pain, hide his infirmity, and project

■ On November 1, 1961, 50,000 women in communities across the country took to the streets to protest nuclear testing. Under the sponsorship of Women Strike for Peace, these demonstrators used their authority as mothers, and brought along their children, to highlight their stake in the future.

TABLE 25-2

The Election of 1960

Candidate	Political Party	Popular Vote (%)	Electoral Vote
John F. Kennedy	Democratic	49.9	303
Richard M. Nixon	Republican	49.6	219

INTERPRETING HISTORY

Rachel Carson, *Silent Spring*

In 1962, Silent Spring, *Rachel Carson's eloquent exposé of the chemical industry's deadly impact on the health of the planet, landed on the best-seller list, where it stayed for months. The book, which eventually sold 1.5 million copies and remains in print today, galvanized the environmental movement of the 1960s and 1970s. Carson called the chemical industry "a child of the Second World War" and creator of "elixirs of death." She reported that annual pesticide production increased from 124 million pounds in 1947 to 637 million pounds by 1960. Twenty years later it had reached 2.4 billion pounds. "In the course of developing agents of chemical warfare," she noted, "some of the chemicals created in the laboratory were found to be lethal to insects. The discovery did not come by chance: insects were widely used to test chemicals as agents of death for man."*

It took hundreds of millions of years to produce the life that now inhabits the earth—eons of time in which that developing and evolving and diversifying life reached a state of adjustment and balance with its surroundings. The environment, rigorously shaping and directing the life it supported, contained elements that were hostile as well as supporting. Certain rocks gave out dangerous radiation; even within the light of the sun, from which all life draws its energy, there were short-wave radiations with power to injure. Given time—time not in years but in millennia—life adjusts, and a balance has been reached. For time is the essen-

Environmentalist Rachel Carson, author of *Silent Spring*.

tial ingredient; but in the modern world there is no time.

The rapidity of change and the speed with which new situations are created follow the impetuous and heedless pace of man rather than the deliberate pace of nature. Radiation is no longer merely the background radiation of rocks, the bombardment of cosmic rays, the ultraviolet of the sun that have existed before there was any life on earth; radiation is now the unnatural creation of man's tampering with the atom. The chemicals to which life is asked to make its adjustment are no longer merely the calcium and silica and copper and all the rest of the minerals washed out of the rocks and carried in rivers to the sea; they are the synthetic creations of man's inventive mind, brewed in his laboratories, and having no counterparts in nature.

To adjust to these chemicals would require time on the scale that is nature's; it would require not merely the years of a man's life but the life of generations. And even this, were it by some miracle possible, would be futile, for the new chemicals come from our laboratories in an endless stream; almost five hundred annually find their way into actual use in the United States alone. The figure is staggering and its implications are not easily grasped—500 new chemicals to which the bodies of men and animals are required some-how to adapt each year, chemicals totally outside the limits of biologic experience.

Among them are many that are used in man's war against nature. Since the mid-1940s over 200 basic chemicals have been created for use in killing insects, weeds, rodents, and other organisms described in the modern vernacular as "pests"; and they are sold under several thousand different brand names.

These sprays, dusts, and aerosols are now applied almost universally to farms, gardens, forests, and homes—nonselective chemicals that have the power to kill every insect, the "good" and the "bad," to still the song of the birds and the leaping of fish in the streams, to coat the leaves with a deadly film, and to linger on in the soil—all this though the intended target may be only a few weeds or insects. Can anyone believe it is possible to lay down such a barrage of poisons on the surface of the earth without making it unfit for all life? They should not be called "insecticides" but "biocides."

Questions

1. What connection does Carson make between time and the environment?
2. Why does Carson believe insecticides should be called biocides?

---

an image of health and vitality. "Vigor" was a word Kennedy used often and an aura he projected, inspiring a national craze for physical fitness that survives to this day. Young JFK also emulated his father's brash sexual promiscuity, even after his marriage to Jacqueline Bouvier in 1953.

In 1946 Kennedy won election to the House of Representatives, and in 1952 he defeated incumbent Republican Henry Cabot Lodge to become the Democratic senator from Massachusetts. JFK's father financed all of his political campaigns, and in 1960 the elderly Kennedy bankrolled and masterminded JFK's narrowly successful run for the White House. Kennedy selected as his running mate the powerful Senate majority leader, Lyndon B. Johnson of Texas, whom he had battled for the nomination.

Kennedy-Nixon Debate

Domestic Policy

With such a thin margin of victory, Kennedy lacked a popular mandate for change. But he quickly established himself as an eloquent leader. In his inaugural address, the new president inspired the nation with his memorable words "And so, my fellow Americans, ask not what your country can do for you; ask what you can do for your country." Focusing his address on foreign policy, he declared, "Let every nation know . . . that we shall pay any price, bear any burden, meet any hardship, support any friend, oppose any foe to assure the survival and the success of liberty." In his first two years, he sought mainly to avoid division at home and to wage the Cold War forcefully abroad. He believed that prosperity was the best way to spread the fruits of affluence, rather than government programs that would promote a redistribution of wealth. Accordingly, he supported corporate tax cuts to stimulate the economy, which grew at a rate of 5 percent each year from 1961 to 1966.

Although Democrats held strong majorities in both houses, powerful southern conservatives often teamed up with Republicans to form a functional majority in Congress to defeat reform legislation. Kennedy knew that it would be futile to champion the cause of civil rights in the face of that alliance. But he did support issues important to his working-class constituents and proposed a number of legislative initiatives, including increasing the minimum wage, health care for the aged, larger Social Security benefits, and the creation of the Department of Housing and Urban Development (HUD).

Foreign Policy

Kennedy was the first U.S. president to understand and recognize the legitimacy of movements for national self-determination in the Third World. He endeavored to support movements to end colonial rule while at the same time containing the spread of communism. His efforts earned him a great deal of good will among Africans and other non-Europeans. But if nationalist movements appeared friendly to the Soviet Union, Kennedy worked against them. He sharply increased military spending and nuclear arms buildup as a show of strength and preparedness against possible Soviet aggression.

One of Kennedy's most popular initiatives was the creation of the Peace Corps, a program that sent Americans, especially young people, to nations around the world to work on development projects. In 1961 Kennedy signed the Charter of Punta del Este with several Latin American countries, establishing the Alliance for Progress, a program designed to prevent the spread of anti-Americanism and communist insurgencies in Latin America. The alliance offered $20 billion in loans to Latin American countries for democratic development initiatives.

Kennedy continued the strategies of Truman and Eisenhower to fight communism in South Vietnam by supporting the corrupt regime of Ngo Dinh Diem. But the National Liberation Front (NLF), founded in 1960 and supported by Ho Chi Minh's communist regime in North Vietnam, gained the upper hand in its struggle against Diem. In response, Kennedy increased the number of military advisers there from 800 to 17,000. By 1963 it was obvious that Diem's brutal regime was about to fall to the NLF, and Kennedy allowed U.S. military advisers and diplomats to encourage Diem's dissenting generals to depose Diem.

Kennedy also faced a crisis brewing in Cuba. Fidel Castro's revolution initially represented the sort of democratic insurgency that Kennedy wanted to support. But Castro's socialism turned the United States against him, and he established close ties with the Soviet Union. During the Eisenhower administration, the CIA began planning an invasion of Cuba with the help of Cuban exiles in Florida. Kennedy's national security advisers persuaded Kennedy to allow the invasion to proceed.

On April 17, 1961, U.S.-backed and -trained anticommunist forces, most of them Cuban exiles, landed at the Bahia de Cochinas (Bay of Pigs) on the southern coast of Cuba. Castro expected the invasion—his agents in Florida had infiltrated the Cuban exiles—so his well-prepared troops quickly surrounded and captured the invaders. No domestic uprising against Castro occurred to support the invasion. Kennedy pulled back in humiliating defeat. Nevertheless, the president continued to support covert efforts that tried but failed to destabilize Cuba and assassinate Castro.

Another crisis soon erupted in Berlin. Located 200 miles deep in East Germany, with only two highways connecting it to West Germany, West Berlin was a showcase of western material superiority and an espionage center for the western powers. In June 1961, Khrushchev threatened to end the western presence in Berlin and unite the city with the rest of East Germany. His plan was motivated in part to stop the steady stream of East Germans into West Berlin. Kennedy refused to relinquish West Berlin. On August 13, 1961, the East German government constructed a wall to separate East and West Berlin. Two years later, Kennedy stood in front of the wall and pledged to defend the West Berliners.

The most serious foreign policy crisis of Kennedy's presidency came in 1962, when the Soviet Union, at Castro's invitation, began to install intermediate-range nuclear missiles in Cuba. Kennedy's close advisers presented a series of options for actions that could be taken in response. The most dramatic and dangerous would be a full-scale military invasion of the island, which would topple Castro but would surely have prompted military retaliation by the Soviet Union. Another option was a more limited military intervention, an air strike to destroy the missiles before they became operational. Others proposed a blockade of Cuban ports to prevent the missiles from entering. Another possibility was to negotiate secretly with Castro, Soviet leaders, or both. Kennedy decided against behind-the-scenes negotiations as well as the drastic move of military intervention and instead established a "quarantine" around the island to block Soviet ships from reaching Cuba, hoping that the Soviet Union would back down and withdraw the missiles. A quarantine, unlike a blockade, was not considered an act of war; nevertheless, Kennedy put the Strategic Air Command on full alert for possible nuclear war.

Kennedy put the Strategic Air Command on full alert for possible nuclear war.

The Cuban Missile Crisis

Test Ban Treaty

It was a risky move. On national television, Kennedy warned the Soviet Union to remove the missiles or face the military might of the United States. For the next five days tensions mounted, as Russian ships hovered in the water beyond the quarantine zone. Finally Khrushchev proposed an agreement, offering to remove the missiles if the United States would agree not to invade Cuba. Kennedy also privately promised to remove Jupiter missiles in Turkey as soon as the crisis was over. The two leaders managed to diffuse the crisis, but they were both sobered by the experience of having come to the brink of nuclear war. In 1963 they signed a nuclear test ban treaty.

A Year of Turning Points

In 1963 the President's Commission on the Status of Women, which Kennedy had appointed under the leadership of Eleanor Roosevelt, published a report that documented widespread discrimination against women in jobs, pay, education, and the professions. In response, Kennedy issued a presidential order requiring the civil service to hire people "without regard to sex," and he supported passage of the Equal Pay Act of 1963.

Also in 1963, in Birmingham, Alabama, Martin Luther King Jr. led a silent and peaceful march through the city. Chief of Police Bull Connor unleashed the police, who blasted the demonstrators with fire hoses and attacked them with vicious police dogs. Four black children were later killed when segregationists bombed an African American church. The Kennedy administration responded by bringing the full force of its authority to bear on the officials in Birmingham. But the crisis intensified. Alabama's segregationist governor, George Wallace, refused to admit two black students to the University of Alabama, threatening to stand in the doorway to block their entrance.

Civil Rights March on Washington

Finally, on June 10, 1963, Kennedy federalized the Alabama National Guard and for the first time went before the American people to declare himself forcefully on the side of the civil rights protesters and to propose a civil rights bill. A few months later, on August 28, more than 250,000 people gathered at the nation's capital in front of the Lincoln Memorial for the culmination of the March on Washington, a huge demonstration for jobs as well as freedom, where Martin Luther King Jr. delivered his inspiring "I Have a Dream" speech.

In the fall of 1963, a confident Kennedy began planning his reelection campaign for the next year. To mobilize support, he visited Texas. "Here we are in Dallas," he said on November 22, 1963, "and it looks like everything in Texas is going to be fine for us." Within an hour of uttering those optimistic words, the president lay dying of an assassin's bullet.

As shock and grief spread across the nation, a bizarre series of events confounded efforts to bring the assassin to justice. Police arrested Lee Harvey Oswald, who had previously lived in the Soviet Union and who had loose ties to organized crime and to political groups interested in Cuba. Oswald claimed that he was innocent. But before he could be brought to trial, Oswald was murdered. Jack Ruby, a nightclub owner who also had links to organized crime, shot Oswald while he was in the custody of the Dallas police—an event witnessed by millions on live television. Ruby later died in prison. The newly sworn-in president, Lyndon B. Johnson, appointed a commission to investigate the assassination under the leadership of Supreme Court Chief Justice Earl Warren. The Warren Commission eventually issued a report concluding that Oswald and Ruby had both acted alone, although the report failed to end speculation about a possible conspiracy.

Conclusion

During the decade between the election of Dwight D. Eisenhower and the assassination of John F. Kennedy, the nation experienced unprecedented prosperity as increasing numbers of Americans moved into middle-class suburbs and enjoyed the fruits of a rapidly expanding consumer economy. Men and women rushed into marriage and childbearing, creating the baby boom and a powerful domestic ideology resting on distinct gender roles for women and men. At the same time, fears of nuclear war, intense anticommunism, and pressures to conform to mainstream political and cultural values contributed to anxieties and discontent.

Beneath the apparently tranquil surface, some Americans began to resist the limitations and exclusions of the widely touted "American way of life." African Americans in the South demanded their rightful place as full citizens, challenging the Jim Crow system and accelerating the civil rights movement through nonviolent protests, boycotts, and sit-ins. Young people created a vibrant youth culture to the pulsating rhythms of rock 'n' roll. Beatniks, peace activists, and environmentalists expressed incipient political and cultural dissent. The rumblings of vast social change had already begun and would explode in the years ahead, pushed along by a divisive war in Vietnam.

Sites to Visit

We Shall Overcome: Historic Places of the Civil Rights Movement
www.cr.nps.gov/nR/travel/civilrights/
This site of the National Register of Historic Places provides maps and information about the historic locations of the civil rights movement.

Dwight David Eisenhower
www.ipl.org/div/POTUS/ddeisenhower.html
This site contains basic information about Eisenhower's election and presidency, and online biography.

Literature and Culture of the American 1950s
www.writing.upenn.edu/~afilreis/50s/home.html
This site by University of Pennsylvania Professor Al Filreis contains a large array of 1950s documents, literature, and images.

Levittown: Documents of an Ideal American Suburb
tigger.uic.edu/~pbhales/Levittown/
Peter Bacon Hales of the Art History Department at the University of Illinois at Chicago developed this site, which includes images, articles, and information about the post–World War II Levittown suburb.

Hollywood and the Movies During the 1950s
lib.berkeley.edu/MRC/50sbib.html
This site from the University of California at Berkeley libraries includes information about Hollywood during the 1950s, and links to related sites, such as the Hollywood blacklist and film noir.

Rock and Roll
www.rockhall.com/home/default.asp
This Web site of the Rock and Roll Hall of Fame and Museum includes information about the history and major artists of rock and roll.

Little Rock 1957: Pages from History—The Central High Crisis
www.ardemgaz.com/prev/central/
This site documents the events surrounding the effort to desegregate Central High in Little Rock, Arkansas, in 1957.

From *Plessy v. Ferguson* to *Brown v. Board of Education*: The Supreme Court Rules on School Desegregation
www.yale.edu/ynhti/curriculum/units/1982/3/82.03.06.x.html
This site includes information about the landmark Supreme Court decisions compiled by the Yale-New Haven Teachers Institute.

Civil Rights Era
lcweb2.loc.gov/ammem/aaohtml/exhibit/aopart9.html
This Library of Congress site includes information about the people, events, and developments of the civil rights movement.

John F. Kennedy
www.ipl.org/div/potus/jfkennedy.html
This site contains basic information about Kennedy's election and presidency, and online biography.

For Further Reading

General

Taylor Branch, *Parting the Waters: America in the King Years, 1954–1963* (1988).
William H. Chafe, *The Unfinished Journey: America Since World War II*, 5th ed. (2006).
Pete Daniel, *Lost Revolutions: The South in the 1950s* (2000).
Eric Foner, *The Story of American Freedom* (1998).

Cold War, Warm Hearth

Barbara Ehrenreich, *The Hearts of Men: American Dreams and the Flight from Commitment* (1984).
Ruth Feldstein, *Motherhood in Black and White: Race and Sex in American Liberalism, 1930–1965* (2000).
Kenneth T. Jackson, *Crabgrass Frontier: The Suburbanization of the United States* (1985).
Elaine Tyler May, *Homeward Bound: American Families in the Cold War Era* (1999).

The Civil Rights Movement

Clayborne Carson, *In Struggle: SNCC and the Black Awakening of the 1960s* (1981).
Mary Dudziak, *Cold War Civil Rights: Equality as Cold War Policy, 1946–1968* (2000).
Steven F. Lawson, *Running for Freedom: Civil Rights and Black Politics in America Since 1941* (1990).

Harvard Sitkoff, *The Struggle for Black Equality, 1954–1992* (1993).

The Eisenhower Years

Stephen E. Ambrose, *Eisenhower* (1983–1984).
Thomas Borstelmann, *The Cold War and the Color Line: American Race Relations in the Global Arena* (2001).
Peter B. Dow, *Schoolhouse Politics: Lessons from the Sputnik Era* (1991).
Fred I. Greenstein, *The Hidden-Hand Presidency: Eisenhower as Leader* (1994).

Outsiders and Opposition

Rachel Carson, *Silent Spring* (1962).
Betty Friedan, *The Feminine Mystique* (1963).
James Gilbert, *A Cycle of Outrage: America's Reaction to the Juvenile Delinquent in the 1950s* (1986).
Joanne Meyerowitz, ed., *Not June Cleaver: Women and Gender in Postwar America, 1945–1960* (1994).
Rickie Solinger, *Wake Up Little Susie: Single Pregnancy and Race Before Roe v. Wade* (1992).

The Kennedy Era

Elizabeth Cobbs Hoffman, *All You Need Is Love: The Peace Corps and the Spirit of the 1960s* (1998).
James N. Giglio, *The Presidency of John F. Kennedy*, 2nd ed. (2006).
Herbert S. Parmet, *J.F.K.: The Presidency of John F. Kennedy* (1983).
Arthur M. Schlesinger Jr., *A Thousand Days: John F. Kennedy in the White House* (1965).

For quizzes and other resources on these topics, go to www.longmanamericanhistory.com.

The Nation Divides: The Vietnam War and Social Conflict, 1964–1971

CHAPTER

26

THE SOFT-SPOKEN BLACK MAN WITH THE STRANGE NORTHERN ACCENT FIRST SHOWED UP IN small-town McComb, Mississippi, in the summer of 1961. Robert Parris Moses had come on a mission of democracy. An organizer for the new Student Nonviolent Coordinating Committee (SNCC), he was there to encourage impoverished African Americans to register to vote. Over the next four years in the Deep South, Bob Moses paid a price for his commitments. Local police imprisoned him, and white supremacists beat him severely and murdered dozens of his fellow activists in the black freedom movement. But Moses remained committed to nonviolence and racial integration. His quiet courage became legendary in the movement. One summer night in 1962, he returned to a deserted SNCC office in Greenwood, Mississippi, that had just been ransacked by a white mob. Three other SNCC workers had barely escaped with their lives. Moses looked around, made up a bed in the corner of the devastated main room, and went to sleep. He refused to be intimidated.

During the 1960s, an extraordinary number of idealistic young people became involved in public life in an effort to make real their nation's promises of freedom, justice, and equality. The civil rights movement inspired the social movements that followed: for ending the war, for preserving the environment, and for liberating women, Latinos, Indians, and gay men and lesbians. But organizing for change inevitably brought activists up against fierce resistance from what they called "the establishment." Disillusionment and radicalization often followed. Public life became deeply contentious by 1968 as young radicals challenged more conservative citizens on issues of race, war, and gender.

The escalating American war in Southeast Asia loomed over all. Lyndon Johnson brought the nation to its apex of liberal reform with his extensive Great Society legislation. However, the

■ A native of New York City, Bob Moses graduated from Hamilton College in upstate New York and did graduate work at Harvard University. He was inspired by the sit-in movement that began in 1960 in the American South and soon moved south to join SNCC.

CHAPTER OUTLINE

Lyndon Johnson and the Apex of Liberalism

Into War in Vietnam

The Movement

The Conservative Response

Conclusion

Sites to Visit

For Further Reading

595

high-flying hopes of Democratic liberals crashed to earth with the destructive war that the Johnson administration waged against seasoned communist revolutionaries in far-off Vietnam. Out of the wreckage of 1968 emerged a Republican president, Richard Nixon, and a growing conservative backlash against the social changes advocated by people of color, the counterculture, the antiwar movement, and the rising tide of women's liberation.

Lyndon Johnson and the Apex of Liberalism

Wealth provided the foundation on which the Great Society was built. American economic expansion after World War II had created history's richest nation by 1960. From 1961 to 1966, the economy accelerated at an annual growth rate of more than 5 percent with very low inflation, stimulated by large tax cuts and extensive military spending. The 41 percent increase in per capita income during the 1960s was not evenly distributed, however. Economist Paul Samuelson explained in 1970, "If we made an income pyramid out of a child's blocks, with each layer portraying $1000 of income, the peak would be far higher than the Eiffel Tower, but almost all of us would be within a yard of the ground." And the distribution of wealth (stocks and real estate) was far more skewed than that of income. The president and the Congress believed that economic expansion would continue indefinitely and the nation could therefore afford government policies to improve the welfare of less affluent Americans. The Supreme Court expanded individual liberties.

The New President

Lyndon Baines Johnson was one of the most remarkable American characters of the twentieth century, both a giant among political leaders and a bully with those who worked for him. Johnson grew up in a family struggling to stay out of poverty in the Texas hill country west of Austin. He entered Democratic politics early as an avid supporter of Franklin Roosevelt and the New Deal, aided by the business savvy and loyalty of his wife, Lady Bird Johnson, who grew wealthy through ownership of TV and radio stations. As First Lady, she became

■ Lyndon Johnson took the presidential oath of office on board *Air Force One,* returning to Washington from Dallas, where John Kennedy had just been assassinated on November 22, 1963. Johnson's wife, Lady Bird, is on his right, and Jacqueline Kennedy, still in blood-stained clothes, stands on his left. Johnson adroitly channeled the public outpouring of grief for the murdered young president into support for their shared legislative goals.

widely known for her leadership in highway beautification. Lyndon Johnson rose like a rocket through Congress to become perhaps the most powerful Senate majority leader ever (1954–1960) and then vice president (1961–1963). Kennedy's assassination catapulted him into the Oval Office as the nation's first Texan president.

Johnson retained Kennedy's cabinet and advisers and used the memory of the fallen young president to rally support for his administration. Johnson turned out to be the more liberal of the two men, in part because his early years in Texas had given him a visceral understanding of poverty and discrimination that his predecessor lacked. Johnson's focus was different, too. He retained Kennedy's anticommunist commitments abroad, but his heart remained at home, where he wanted to perfect American society.

First he had to win reelection. Less than a year remained until voters went to the polls in 1964. The Republicans nominated right-wing Senator Barry Goldwater of Arizona, a sign of the party's sharp swing away from its moderate eastern elements toward its fiercely conservative western and southern constituencies. Goldwater believed in unrestricted markets and a minimal role for the federal government in every aspect of American life except the military. He spoke casually about using nuclear weapons against communists abroad. Goldwater declared that "extremism in the defense of liberty is no vice," but Johnson zeroed in on that extremism and swept to the largest electoral majority of any president (61 percent).

TABLE 26-1

The Election of 1964

Candidate	Political Party	Popular Vote (%)	Electoral Vote
Lyndon B. Johnson	Democratic	61.1	486
Barry M. Goldwater	Republican	38.5	52

The Great Society: Fighting Poverty and Discrimination

In pursuit of what he called the Great Society, Johnson first declared a "War on Poverty." No citizen in the richest nation on earth should live in squalor, he believed. More than one out of five Americans still lived below the conservatively estimated official poverty line ($3,022 for a nonfarm family of four in 1960), and 70 percent of these citizens were white.

Johnson, "The War on Poverty"

The president and a large congressional majority passed several measures to alleviate poverty. They sharply increased the availability of money and food stamps through the Aid to Families with Dependent Children ("welfare") program, and they raised Social Security payments to older Americans. Several programs focused on improving educational opportunities as an avenue out of poverty: Head Start offered preschool education and meals for youngsters, the Elementary and Secondary Education Act sent federal funds to the least affluent school districts, and an expanded system of student loans facilitated access to college. The Job Corps provided employment training, and Volunteers in Service to America (VISTA) served as a domestic Peace Corps, funneling people with education and skills into poor communities to serve as teachers and providers of other social services.

No barrier to opportunity in the early 1960s was higher than the color bar. Both opportunist and idealist, Johnson as president shed his segregationist voting record (necessary for election in Texas before 1960) and became the most vocal proponent of racial equality ever to occupy the Oval Office. Two factors facilitated his change in position. One, blatant inequalities for American citizens weakened the United States in its competition with the Soviets and Chinese for the loyalty of the nonwhite Third World majority. Two, the African American freedom struggle in the South had reached a boiling point. Black frustration was mounting over white brutality and the seeming indifference or even hostility of the national government.

The Civil Rights Act of 1964 fulfilled the implicit promise of the *Brown v. Board of Education* decision a decade earlier. The 1964 act made desegregation the law of the land as it outlawed discrimination in employment and in public facilities such as

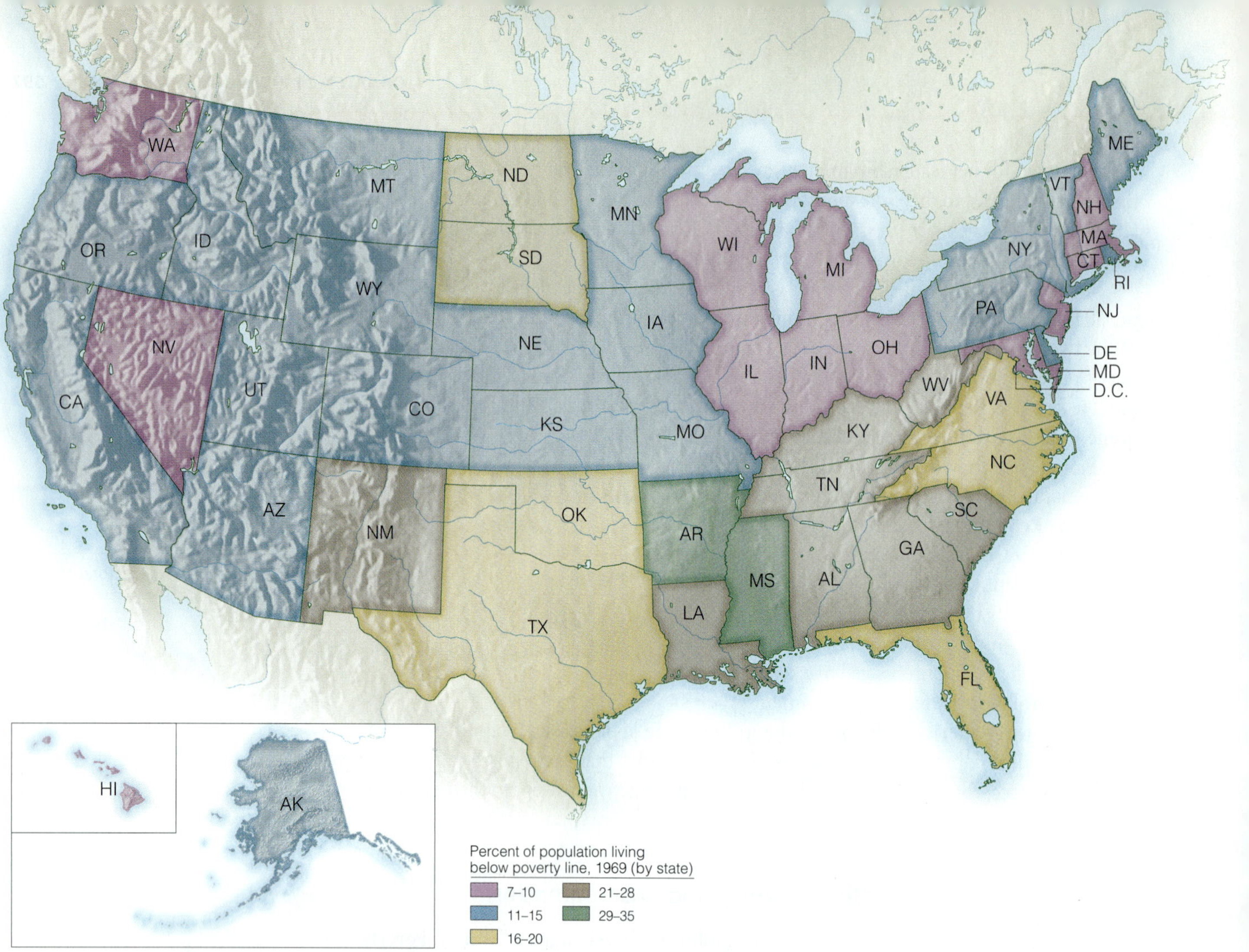

MAP 26.1
PERCENTAGE OF POPULATION LIVING BELOW THE POVERTY LINE, 1969 (BY STATE) The United States in the 1960s was a nation of unprecedented wealth and comfort. Yet millions of Americans still lived in poverty. Prodded by other reformers, President Johnson sought to reduce the number of impoverished citizens through the Great Society programs. The southeastern and south-central states had the highest poverty rates, a legacy of slavery and limited industrialization.

Impact of the Voting Rights Act of 1965

restaurants, theaters, and hotels. The Voting Rights Act of 1965 outlawed poll taxes and provided federal voting registrars in states that refused the ballot to African Americans. The single most important legislation of the twentieth century for bringing political democracy to the South, the Voting Rights Act increased the percentage of blacks voting in Mississippi from 7 percent to 60 percent in two years.

The Great Society: Improving the Quality of Life

Johnson's vision of the Great Society extended to the broader quality of life in the United States. Health care was perhaps the most fundamental issue for citizens' sense of personal security. After 1965, the new Medicare system paid for the medical needs of Americans age sixty-five and older, and Medicaid underwrote health care services for the poor. In 1964, when more than half of adults smoked tobacco, the surgeon-general issued the first government report linking smoking to cancer. Higher federal standards for automotive safety followed a year later. Public pressures also led to the establishment of new requirements for publishing the nutritional values of packaged food. The federally funded Public Broadcasting System (PBS) was established to provide television programs that were more educational than the fare tied to advertising on the three corporate networks (NBC, CBS, and ABC). In fact, most Great Society measures targeted all Americans rather than just the disadvantaged.

Nothing more directly threatened the quality of American life than the degradation of the natural environment. The costs of the unrestrained and much-heralded economic growth since World War II showed up in the nation's air, water, and land. The leaded gasoline that fueled products of the booming auto industry created smog; industrial effluents polluted lakes and rivers; and petrochemical wastes poisoned the ground. The products of science that had contributed so much to the creation of wealth were turning out to have hidden costs, and a new wave of citizen action to protect the environment began to build.

Growing public awareness prompted the Clean Air Act (1963) and the Clean Waters Act (1966), which set federal guidelines for reducing smog and preserving public drinking sources from bacterial pollution. Even the long dam-building tradition in the American West faced new questions, with the Wild and Scenic Rivers Act enacted in 1968. Meanwhile, Congress passed the Wilderness Act in 1964, setting aside 9 million acres of undeveloped public lands as a place "where man is a visitor who does not remain."

The Liberal Warren Court

The Supreme Court under the leadership of Earl Warren steadily expanded the constitutional definition of individual rights. This shift reached even those deemed to have lost many of their rights: prisoners. *Gideon v. Wainwright* (1963) established the right of indigent prisoners to legal counsel, and *Escobedo v. Illinois* (1964) confirmed the right to counsel during interrogation, a critical hindrance to the use of torture. After *Miranda v. Arizona* (1966), police were required to inform people they arrested of their rights to remain silent and to speak to a lawyer.

The Warren Court bolstered other rights of individuals against potentially coercive community pressures. Decisions in 1962 and 1963 strictly limited the practice of requiring prayers in public schools. In 1963 the Court narrowed standards for the definition of "obscenity," allowing freer expression in the arts but also in pornography. *Griswold v. Connecticut* (1965) established the use of contraceptive devices by married people as a matter of private choice protected by the Constitution. In 1967 the Court heard the case of Mildred Jeter, a black woman, and Richard Loving, a white man, Virginians who had evaded their state's ban on interracial marriage by traveling to Washington, D.C., for their wedding and then returned to Caroline County to live. In the aptly titled *Loving v. Virginia*, the Court declared marriage one of the "basic civil rights of men" and overturned the laws of the last sixteen states restricting interracial unions.

The Supreme Court's interpreting of the Constitution to expand individual rights disturbed many conservative Americans. They saw the Court as another arm of an intrusive national government that was extending its control over matters previously left to local communities. For them, the goal of integration did not justify the busing of school children. Rising crime rates troubled them more than police brutality. Many Roman Catholics were unhappy with the legalization of contraceptives. Incensed by the ban on requiring school prayer, Protestant fundamentalists sought redress through political involvement, which they had previously shunned, initiating a grassroots religious conservative movement that helped bring Ronald Reagan to power in 1980.

Into War in Vietnam

The 1960s also marked the culmination of the U.S. government's efforts to control revolutionary political and social change abroad. The Truman Doctrine's logic of containing communism spanned the entire globe, but few imagined that the United States would overreach itself, tragically, in Vietnam. Johnson's accomplishments at home were forever overshadowed by the war he sent Americans to fight in the quiet rice paddies and beautiful highland forests of Southeast Asia. An aggressive U.S. anticommunist policy abroad collided with leftist revolutionaries throughout the Third World, and it was ill fortune for the Vietnamese that this collision struck them hardest of all.

The Vietnamese Revolution and the United States

The conflict in Vietnam began as one of many efforts to end European colonialism. Vietnamese nationalists, varying in ideologies but led by Ho Chi Minh and the Indochinese Communist party, had sought since the 1930s to liberate their country from French colonial rule. Japanese advances during World War II put the Vietminh (Vietnamese nationalists) on the same side as the Americans, and Ho worked closely with the U.S. Office of Strategic Services (OSS), precursor to the Central Intelligence Agency (CIA).

After the defeat of Germany and Japan, however, the French wanted to regain control of their colonies in Africa and Asia, including Vietnam. The British provided troop transport ships for French soldiers, and the United States provided most of the funds to support France in its war against the Vietminh (1946–1954). Cold War priorities won out: a weakened France had to be bolstered as the linchpin of a reintegrated, anticommunist western Europe, while the Vietminh were led by Communist party members. But the Vietnamese defeated the much more heavily armed French at the battle of Dien Bien Phu in May 1954. Two months later, the Geneva Accords divided the country temporarily at the seventeenth parallel until national elections could be held within two years to reunify Vietnam. Ho's forces solidified their control of the north, the French pulled out entirely, and the Eisenhower administration made a fateful decision to intervene directly to preserve the southern part of Vietnam from communism. The United States created a new government led by the Roman Catholic, anticommunist Ngo Dinh Diem in a new country called "South Vietnam."

The Vietnamese Revolution was only half over, however. The French colonialists withdrew, but the Saigon regime did not hold elections. In the North, the sometimes brutal internal revolution for the creation of a socialist society proceeded with an extensive program of land redistribution. In the South, Diem ruled for eight years with increasing repression of communists and other dissenters. U.S. funding kept him in power. Southern members of the old Vietminh began a sabotage campaign against the Saigon government and formed the National Liberation Front (NLF) in 1960, with the support of North Vietnam. Diem and his American supporters called them Viet Cong or VC, roughly equivalent to the derogatory American term *Commies*. As the struggle to overthrow Diem intensified, several of his own generals assassinated him in November 1963 with the tacit support of U.S. officials in South Vietnam and Washington.

Johnson's War

Lyndon Johnson inherited his predecessors' commitment to preserving a noncommunist South Vietnam. Bolstered by Kennedy's hawkish advisers, he believed that American credibility was at stake. But Johnson faced a swiftly deteriorating military situation. The NLF, which the administration portrayed as merely a tool of North Vietnam, was winning the political war for the South, taking control of the countryside from the demoralized Army of the Republic of Vietnam (ARVN). Faced with the choice of escalating U.S. involvement to prevent an NLF victory or withdrawing entirely from the country, Johnson escalated.

How he did so was crucially important. There was neither a national debate nor a congressional vote to declare war. Johnson did not want to distract Congress from his Great Society agenda, nor did he want to provoke the Soviet Union or China. But he believed he had to preserve a noncommunist South Vietnam or else face a debilitating backlash from Republicans, who would skewer him as McCarthy had done to Truman over the "loss" of China fifteen years earlier. So the president used deception, describing offensive American actions as defensive and opening up a credibility gap between a committed government and a skeptical public.

In August 1964, North Vietnamese ships in the Gulf of Tonkin fired on the U.S. destroyer *Maddox*, which was aiding South Vietnamese sabotage operations against the North. The president portrayed the incident as one of unprovoked communist aggression, and Congress expressed almost unanimous support through its Gulf of Tonkin Resolution. With this substitute for a declaration of war, Johnson ordered American planes to begin bombing North Vietnam, and the first American combat troops splashed ashore at Da Nang in South Vietnam on March 8, 1965. In July the administration made the key decision to add 100,000 more soldiers, with more to follow as necessary.

Johnson, The Tonkin Gulf Resolution Message

American strategy had two goals: to limit the war so as not to draw in neighboring China (to avoid a repeat of the Korean War) and to force the NLF and North Vietnam to give up their struggle to reunify the country under Hanoi's control. The problem was the political nature of the guerrilla war in the South: a contest for the loyalty of the population, in which NLF operatives mingled easily with the citizenry. This kind of war made the enemy difficult to find, as had often been true for the British in fighting the American revolutionaries in the 1770s. The "strategic hamlet" program uprooted rural peasants and concentrated them in fortified towns, creating "free fire zones" in their wake where anything that moved was a target. The U.S. Air Force pounded the South as well as the North, dropping more bombs on this ancient land (smaller than either Germany or Japan) than had been used in all theaters on all sides in World War II. These tactics destabilized and traumatized society in South Vietnam as one-fourth of the population became refugees.

> American strategy had two goals: to limit the war so as not to draw in neighboring China (to avoid a repeat of the Korean War) and to force the NLF and North Vietnam to give up their struggle to reunify the country under Hanoi's control.

Americans in Southeast Asia

Given America's wealth, size, and superior weaponry, most U.S. soldiers who went to Vietnam in 1965–1966 had no doubt they would win the war. They typically looked down on Asians. Very few knew anything about Vietnamese history or culture, and almost none spoke the Vietnamese language. Although a small number of Americans worked closely with their South Vietnamese allies, most GIs encountered Vietnamese in subservient roles as laundry workers, prostitutes, waitresses, and bartenders. Blinkered by anticommunism and far removed from their own revolutionary roots, Americans from the top brass to the lowest "grunts" marched into a country they did not understand but assumed they could control.

The Vietnam War

President Johnson spoke of the conflict in Vietnam as a case of one sovereign nation—the North—invading another one—the South. However, few Vietnamese saw the war in those terms. The United States, dismissing the failure of the French before them, had intervened not so much in an international war as in an ongoing revolution that aimed to reunify the country. Few Vietnamese, whatever their opinions of communism, viewed the corrupt Saigon regime as legitimate or democratic. After all, it was kept in place by foreigners, whereas the North was ruled by people who had expelled the French foreigners.

Initial U.S. optimism reflected a grave underestimation of the NLF and the North Vietnamese. Ho Chi Minh was an extremely popular leader, and intervention from the other side of the world only strengthened his position. As the war expanded, NLF recruiting in the South snowballed, and the people of North Vietnam remained loyal to their authoritarian government. Communist forces proved willing to endure fantastic hardship and sacrifices to prevail. Their morale was much higher than that of the ARVN.

Who were the 3 million Americans who went to Vietnam? The initial forces contained experienced soldiers, but as the war escalated, this professional army was diluted with hundreds of thousands of young draftees. Student deferments protected more comfortable Americans, so GIs were predominantly those who lacked money and education. Although 70 percent were

■ A North Vietnamese militia fighter named Kim Lai escorts an American pilot whom she captured after his plane crashed over the North. American GIs often were struck by the diminutive size of the average Vietnamese in comparison to the average American. Bigger, better equipped, and much more well-armed than their opponents, most U.S. soldiers and officers before 1968 went into the field in Vietnam certain that they would be victorious.

white men, black, Hispanic, and Native American enlistees shipped out in disproportionate numbers. In sharp contrast to the motives of the NLF and the North Vietnamese army, few of these young men (along with 10,000 women who volunteered as nurses) were in Vietnam to win the war regardless of the cost or duration. They had only to survive twelve months before returning home to the safety of a peacetime society.

North Vietnamese regular army units came South to match the growing number of U.S. forces, and they occasionally engaged the Americans in large set battles, as at Ia Drang Valley in the fall of 1965. U.S. troops fought well in such firefights, making devastating use of their superior weapons and air power. However, the bulk of the fighting consisted of smaller engagements with deceptive enemies on their home turf who faded in and out of the civilian population with ease. Ambushes and unexpected death haunted Americans on patrol, and relentless heat and humidity wore them down.

American soldiers felt mounting frustration and rage over the nature of the war that they were ordered to fight. Lacking a clear battlefront and an understandable strategy for winning the war, they were commanded simply to kill the often mysterious enemy. Yet distinguishing civilians from combatants in a popular guerrilla war was not always easy, especially when so many civilians evidently supported the NLF and so few Americans spoke Vietnamese. Realizing that few of the people they were supposed to be defending actually wanted them there but under orders to produce enemy bodies, U.S. troops on the ground began to slide toward a racial war against all Vietnamese.

Many GIs resisted this logic, sometimes showing real kindness to Vietnamese civilians. But atrocities on both sides inevitably followed from this kind of war. The worst came in the village of My Lai on March 16, 1968, where 105 soldiers from Charlie Company—enraged by the recent deaths of several comrades in ambushes—slaughtered, often after torturing or raping, more than 400 Vietnamese women, children, and old men. The army covered up the massacre for a year and a half, and eventually found only Lieutenant William Calley, the leader of Charlie Company's First Platoon, guilty of murdering Vietnamese civilians.

1968: The Turning Point

In late 1967, the public face of the war effort remained upbeat, as General William Westmoreland declared that he could now see "some light at the end of the tunnel." But hopes of an imminent victory were crushed by the startling Tet Offensive (named for the Vietnamese New Year) that began on January 30, 1968. NLF insurgents and North Vietnamese troops attacked U.S. strongholds throughout South Vietnam. The blow to American public confidence in Johnson and his military commanders proved irreversible. Far from being on the verge of defeat, as the administration had been claiming, the communists had shown that they could mount simultaneous attacks around the country.

The Tet Offensive coincided with two other crises in early 1968 to convince American political and business elites that U.S. international commitments had become larger than the nation could afford. First, a week before Tet began, the North Korean navy seized the U.S. intelligence ship *Pueblo* in the Sea of Japan and temporarily imprisoned its crew. U.S. commanders

■ MAP 26.2
THE AMERICAN WAR IN VIETNAM Before U.S. combat troops entered Vietnam in 1965, few Americans knew where this Southeast Asian country was. Vietnam's geography and place names quickly became familiar in the United States as hundreds of thousands of young Americans served there and some 58,000 died there. Vietnam's elongated shape, its borders with Cambodia and Laos, and its proximity to China all affected the course of the fighting between 1965 and 1973.

were left scrambling to find enough forces to respond effectively without weakening American commitments in Europe and elsewhere. Second, a British financial collapse devalued the pound and caused the London government to announce its imminent withdrawal from its historic positions east of the Suez Canal, placing new military burdens on the United States in the Middle East. These events reduced international confidence in the U.S. economy, causing a currency crisis in March 1968 as holders of dollars traded them in for gold.

The political career of Lyndon Johnson was a final casualty of these events. His support on the left withered as the antiwar and **black power** movements expanded. Meanwhile, his more centrist supporters were joining the backlash against civil rights, urban violence, and antiwar protesters, peeling off to the Republican party. On March 12, antiwar challenger Senator Eugene McCarthy of Minnesota nearly defeated the incumbent president in the New

Hampshire Democratic primary. Johnson's vulnerability was clear. Senator Robert Kennedy of New York joined the race two weeks later. In a televised speech on March 31 that caught the divided nation by surprise, Johnson announced an end to U.S. escalations in the war, the start of negotiations in Paris with North Vietnam, and an end to his own political career. He would not seek reelection.

The Movement

While national leaders were defending what they called the "frontiers of freedom" abroad, young Americans in the mid- and late 1960s organized to expand what they considered the frontiers of freedom at home. Television for the first time tied the country together in a common culture whose shared images were transmitted simultaneously around the nation. The expanding war in Vietnam radicalized people who had initially been optimistic about reforming American society. Black power, the New Left, the counterculture, women's liberation, and other liberation movements often had quite divergent goals. But participants overlapped extensively and activists spoke of "the Movement" as if it were a unified phenomenon. At the heart of the youth movements of the decade lay a common quest for authenticity—a rejection of hypocrisy and a distrust of traditional authorities—that fused cultural and political protest.

From Civil Rights to Black Power

By 1966 the civil rights movement fractured as it confronted the limits of its success. It had achieved the goals of ending legal discrimination and putting southern African Americans in the voting booth, but it had not brought about a colorblind society. Racial prejudice among white conservatives remained virulent, and white liberals, such as those in the Kennedy and Johnson administrations, revealed themselves as not always trustworthy allies. Expecting only hostility from conservatives, civil rights workers were more disillusioned with what they saw as liberal betrayals.

The Justice Department and the Federal Bureau of Investigation (FBI) did little to restrain the violence of the Ku Klux Klan until the murders of white organizers Michael Schwerner and Andrew Goodman in the summer of 1964—along with black co-worker James Chaney. Two months later, at the national Democratic party convention in Atlantic City, New Jersey, Johnson crushed the effort of the biracial Mississippi Freedom Democratic party to replace the state's regular, all-white Democratic delegates. The president was determined to avoid further alienating white southern voters as he pursued a huge victory margin in the November elections.

The black freedom struggle for centuries had woven together elements of racial separatism with elements of integration into the larger American culture. For many younger African Americans, the pendulum now swung toward a need for greater independence from the white majority. They took inspiration from Malcolm X, the fiery and eloquent minister of the Nation of Islam (Black Muslims), who until his murder in 1965 captivated listeners with denunciations of white perfidy and demands for black self-respect. In 1966 SNCC members began to speak of the need for "black power" rather than for the integrated "beloved community" they had initially sought in 1960.

■ A leading spokesman for the Black Muslims, Malcolm X converted to orthodox Islam and softened his antiwhite rhetoric in the two years before his murder in 1965. Like SNCC's Bob Moses, Malcolm increasingly identified with the Third World. Here he is shown in Egypt on a 1964 pilgrimage to Mecca, Saudi Arabia.

The Black Panther party formed in Oakland, California, in response to police brutality. The heavily armed Panthers engaged in several shootouts with police and were eventually decimated by an FBI campaign against them. White Americans were shocked by the uprisings and riots that swept through black urban communities during the summers of 1964–1968. Triggered by the actions of white police, the riots expressed the fierce frustrations of impoverished people whose lives remained largely untouched by the achievements of the civil rights struggle. The most destructive outbreaks occurred in the Watts district of Los Angeles in 1965 and in Detroit and Newark in 1967.

Black power thrived primarily as a cultural movement that promoted pride in African American and African history and life. The slogan "black is beautiful" captured this spirit: long degraded by their white compatriots as inferior, black Americans in the late 1960s and 1970s reversed this equation to celebrate their cultural heritage. This could be as basic as a hairstyle, the natural Afro replacing hair straightened to look like Caucasian hair. At universities, new departments of African American studies fostered the exploration of black history. Unlearning habits of public deference to whites, most African Americans began referring to themselves as "black" rather than "Negro."

Cultural black power mixed with a different kind of political black power by the late 1960s: the election of black officials. Although militant black power advocates garnered the most media attention, most African Americans supported Lyndon Johnson and used the Voting Rights Act to pursue their goals in the realm of electoral politics. In 1966 Carl Stokes of Cleveland was elected the first black mayor of a major American city, and African Americans won local offices across the South.

The New Left and the Struggle Against the War

In 1962 a group of liberal college activists founded the Students for a Democratic Society (SDS). They called for a rejuvenation of American politics and society to replace the complacency that they saw pervading the country. Racial bigotry and poverty particularly troubled these optimistic young reformers, along with the overarching threat of nuclear destruction (highlighted anew by the missile crisis in Cuba). They hoped to become a kind of "white SNCC," promoting participatory democracy to redeem the promise of Cold War America.

SDS served as the central organization of the New Left. Communism was simply not important to these activists. Nor was conservatism, which was then at its lowest point. They focused instead on the behavior of the liberals who ran the U.S. government from 1961 to 1968. They developed a critique of "corporate liberalism" as promoting the interests of the wealthy and the business community far more than providing for the needs of the disadvantaged.

After 1965, SDS's initially broad reform agenda narrowed to stopping the Vietnam War. SDS members organized the first major antiwar protest outside the White House on April 17, 1965, bringing their organization into alliance with the small group of religious and secular pacifists already working against the war. Mainstream Democrats also began abandoning Johnson over the war as it grew. The president had alienated the powerful chair of the Senate Foreign Relations Committee, J. William Fulbright of Arkansas, with his misleading reports during the brief U.S. military intervention in the Dominican Republic in April 1965 to defeat a left-leaning but not communist coup attempt. Fulbright then held televised hearings on the American war in Southeast Asia in January 1966, raising grave doubts about its wisdom. Draft resistance increased: young men moved to Canada, as did SNCC's Bob Moses, or went to jail, as did champion boxer Muhammad Ali.

Antiwar protesters followed the same trajectory of radicalization as black power advocates. Their dismay turned to rage as the Johnson administration continued to expand a war that was destroying much of Vietnam while killing tens of thousands of American soldiers for no reason its opponents considered legitimate. In combination

"Protests Against the Vietnam War"

INTERPRETING HISTORY

Martin Luther King Jr. and the Vietnam War

Most Americans approved of the war in Vietnam until at least 1968. Appreciative of Lyndon Johnson's commitment to reduce poverty and end racial discrimination at home, African Americans generally supported the president's policies in Southeast Asia. However, younger, more radical civil rights workers were among those who opposed the first insertion of U.S. combat troops in 1965. Within two years, the nation's most prominent black leader, Martin Luther King Jr., decided that he could no longer keep quiet about his growing unease with the American war effort. A storm of criticism greeted his public denunciation of the war, most of it suggesting that he should limit himself to domestic civil rights work. But King no longer believed that events at home and abroad could be separated. The following excerpt is from his speech at Riverside Church, New York City, April 4, 1967.

A few years ago there was a shining moment in that struggle [against poverty and discrimination]. It seemed as if there was a real promise of hope for the poor—both black and white—through the Poverty Program. There were experiments, hopes, new beginnings. Then came the build-up in Vietnam and I watched the program broken and eviscerated as if it were some idle political plaything of a society gone mad on war. . . . I was increasingly compelled to see the war as an enemy of the poor and to attack it as such. . . .

We were taking the black young men who had been crippled by our society and sending them 8,000 miles away to guarantee liberties in Southeast Asia which they had not found in Southwest Georgia and East Harlem. So we have been repeatedly faced with the cruel irony of watching Negro and white boys on TV screens as they kill and die together for a nation that has been unable to seat them together in the same schools. . . .

As I have walked among the desperate, rejected and angry young men [in the ghettos of the North the last three summers] I have told them that Molotov cocktails and rifles would not solve their problems. I have tried to offer them my deepest compassion while maintaining my convictions that social change comes most meaningfully through non-violent action. But they asked—and rightly so— what about Vietnam? They asked if our own nation wasn't using massive doses of violence to solve its problems, to bring about the changes it wanted. Their questions hit home, and I knew that I would never again raise my voice against the violence of the oppressed in the ghettos without having first spoken clearly to the greatest purveyor of violence in the world today—my own government. . . .

[Our troops in Vietnam] must know after a short period there that none of the things we claim to be fighting for [such as freedom, justice, and peace] are really involved. Before long they must know that their government has sent them into a struggle among Vietnamese, and the more sophisticated surely realize that we are on the side of the wealthy and the secure while we create a hell for the poor.

His birthday now a national holiday, Martin Luther King Jr. has become widely accepted as a heroic figure in the American past. But in the last few years of his life, King's increasingly sharp criticisms of injustice in American society disturbed many fellow citizens.

Questions

1. How does King believe that the U.S. war in Vietnam is related to problems at home in American society?
2. What might have been the more negative and positive racial aspects of the Vietnam War?
3. What precisely does King believe to be wrong with the U.S. war in Vietnam?

Source: Bruce J. Schulman, *Lyndon B. Johnson and American Liberalism* (Boston: Bedford, 1995), pp. 208–212.

---

with or in support of black militants, white radicals took over buildings on university campuses in 1968–1969: Columbia, Cornell, Harvard, San Francisco State, and many others. SDS ultimately broke apart in the confusion and exhilaration of its growing demand for revolution against the larger systemic enemies, imperialism and capitalism, not just corporate liberalism. But radical rage could not be understood apart from the ongoing destruction of Vietnam by a government acting in the name of all Americans.

■ The search by many young people in the 1960s counterculture for greater consciousness led them to a spiritual path. These young evangelists held a Campus Crusade for Christ rally at the University of Texas at Austin in 1969. The emphasis of evangelical Christians on the person of Jesus rather than on a particular denominational tradition attracted many converts. The sandals, long hair, and gentleness associated with Jesus made a particularly good fit with the style and values of the "hippies," although most evangelicals appeared traditionally clean-cut and held conservative political views.

Cultural Rebellion and the Counterculture

While the New Left moved from wanting to reform American society to wanting to overthrow it, the counterculture sought to create an alternative society. Called "hippies" by those who disliked them, these young people were alienated by the materialism, competition, and conformity of American life in the Cold War. They tried to live out alternative values of gentleness, tolerance, and inclusivity. Sporting headbands, long hair, and beads, many identified with traditional Native Americans. In place of junk foods, they promoted health foods; in place of profit-seeking businesses, they established co-ops. "Do your own thing" was a common slogan.

In reaction against the conformity of mainstream society, members of the counterculture explored the limitations of consciousness to expand their self-knowledge. They went beyond the nicotine and alcohol that were the common stimulants of their parents' culture to experiment with such mind-altering drugs as marijuana, peyote, hashish, LSD, and cocaine. Spirituality was an important path into consciousness for many in the counterculture. Religious traditions associated with Asia, particularly Buddhism, gained numerous adherents, as did the spiritual customs and traditional practices of Native Americans. Others rediscovered the "authentic" Jesus obscured by the institutional structures of the formal Christian church (earning themselves the nickname "Jesus freaks"); Campus Crusade for Christ, InterVarsity, and other evangelical college groups spread across the country. Music served as the most common coin of the countercultural realm, from the political folk sound of Joan Baez and Bob Dylan to the broadly popular Beatles and the more distinctly countercultural rock 'n' roll of the Grateful Dead and Jefferson Airplane.

Older Americans experienced the counterculture largely as spectacle. The mainstream media emphasized the alternative aspects of the hippie lifestyle in its coverage. Viewers were varyingly disgusted by, attracted to, and titillated by the hair, clothing, nudity, and blurred gender distinctions. Meanwhile, entrepreneurs realized that they could market the antimaterialist counterculture profitably. Young Americans eagerly bought up records, clothing, jewelry, and natural foods—a revealing demonstration of how consumer values pervaded American life.

One of the most visible changes of the 1960s was often called the sexual revolution. Changes in Americans' sexual behavior in the 1960s reflected in part the counterculture's goal of living an authentic, honest life in which words matched actions. The sexual revolution removed some of the penalties for the premarital and extramarital sex that had previously been fairly common but unacknowledged. The appearance of the birth control pill in 1960 underpinned the shift to more open sexual relationships by freeing women from the fear of pregnancy. Attitudes toward abortion also became more tolerant. New York passed the first state law legalizing some abortions in 1970, and three years later the Supreme Court established a woman's constitutional right to abortion in the landmark case of *Roe v. Wade*.

■ The new wave of organizing for women's rights that emerged in the late 1960s had many faces. Some protests against sex discrimination and disrespect for women were angry and others were gentle, as in this 1970 scene. "Raising consciousness" was a central strategy of the movement, as women and men became more aware of the gendered assumptions that had long governed—and channeled—their lives and their thoughts.

Women's Liberation

The movement for women's liberation built on developments earlier in the decade, including Betty Friedan's *The Feminine Mystique* (1963), a widely read book that captured the frustrations of many women who had accepted the role of suburban homemaker after World War II. Friedan and other liberal feminists founded the National Organization for Women (NOW) in 1966 to lobby against sexual discrimination in the public sphere in such areas as employment, wages, education, and jury duty. These challenges had radical implications for women's and men's earnings and thus for responsibilities within families, but NOW did not yet focus on issues inside the private sphere of the home.

The shift to the view that "the personal is political" came from younger, mostly white women who had been active in the civil rights and antiwar struggles. Inspired by the courage and successes of the protest movements in which they figured prominently, these female activists had also learned that traditional gender roles restricted them even in organizations dedicated to participatory democracy. Ironically, radical men could be as patronizing and disrespectful of women's abilities as mainstream men. Younger feminists in 1967 and 1968 agreed with NOW's challenge to discrimination in the public sphere, but they focused even more on the personal politics of women's daily lives, on critical issues such as parenting, child care, housework, and abortion.

The new wave of **feminism** that washed through American culture at the end of the 1960s triggered fierce debates about the nature of gender. Was there a uniquely feminine way of knowing, seeing, and acting, or were women in essence the same as men, distinguishable ultimately by their individuality? Was womanhood biologically or only culturally constructed? Feminists disagreed sharply in their answers.

However, diversity within the feminist movement did not hide a common commitment to expanding women's possibilities. The women's movement that emerged out of the 1960s permanently transformed women's lives and gender relations in American society, in areas ranging from job and educational opportunities, sexual harassment, and gender-neutral language to family roles, sexual relations, reproductive rights, and athletic facilities.

National Organization of Women, Statement of Purpose

The Many Fronts of Liberation

Like the women's movement, the Chicano, pan-Indian, and gay liberation movements of the late 1960s were grounded in older organizing efforts within those communities. The struggles for "brown power," "red power," and "gay power" also reflected the newer influence of black power and its determination to take pride in what the dominant American society had denigrated for so long. Activists on college campuses successfully pressured administrations to establish interdisciplinary ethnic studies programs, such as the first Chicano studies program at California State University at Los Angeles in 1968. Ethnic cultural identity went hand in hand with the pursuit of political and economic integration into mainstream American life.

The most prominent push to organize Latinos was the effort led by Cesar Chávez to build a farm workers' union in California and the Southwest. These primarily Mexican American migrant workers harvested most of the hand-picked produce that Americans ate, but their hard work under severe conditions failed to lift them out of poverty. National consumer support for boycotts of table grapes and iceberg lettuce helped win recognition for the United Farm Workers (UFW) union and better pay by 1970. Younger Mexican Americans across the Southwest looked with pride on their Mexican heritage, even appropriating the formerly pejorative term *Chicano*.

Cesar Chavez, From "He Showed Us the Way," April 1978

Puerto Ricans, the largest Spanish-speaking ethnic group located primarily on the East Coast, experienced a similar growth in militancy and nationalist sentiment during the late 1960s. By the 1960s, more than a million islanders had moved to the East Coast, most to the New York City area. Despite being the only Latino immigrants already holding American citizenship when they arrived, Puerto Ricans experienced similar patterns of both discrimination and opportunity as Mexican Americans.

The most destitute of Americans, Indians also sought to reinvigorate their communities. On the Northwest Coast, they staged "fish-ins" in the mid-1960s to assert treaty rights, and in 1968 urban activists in Minneapolis formed the American Indian Movement (AIM). On November 20, 1969, just days after the largest antiwar march in Washington, seventy-eight Native Americans seized the island of Alcatraz in San Francisco Bay "in the name of all American Indians by right of discovery." For a year and a half, they used their occupation of the former federal prison site to publicize grievances about anti-Indian prejudice and to promote a new pan-Indian identity that reached across traditional tribal divisions. In 1973 armed members of AIM occupied buildings for two months at Wounded Knee, South Dakota, site of the infamous 1890 U.S. Army massacre of unarmed Sioux. Tribal governments sought "red power" in their own quieter way. They asserted greater tribal control of reservation schools across the country.

Although they lacked a unifying ethnic identity, gay men and lesbians also found opportunities to construct coalitions in the more open atmosphere of the late 1960s. Building on the earlier community organizing of older homosexuals in New York, San Francisco, and Los Angeles, more militant youth began to express openly their anger at the homophobic prejudice and violence prevalent in American society. This demand for tolerance and respect reached the headlines when gay patrons of the Stonewall Bar in New York fought back fiercely against a typically forceful police raid on June 27, 1969. Activists of the new Gay Liberation Front emphasized the importance of "coming out of the closet": proudly acknowledging one's sexual orientation as legitimate and decent.

The Conservative Response

The majority of Americans had mixed feelings about the protests that roiled the nation. They were impressed by the courage of many who stood up against discrimination, and by 1968 they wanted to find a way out of the war in Southeast Asia. But they were alienated by the style and values of others who loudly demanded change in American society. Moderate and conservative citizens and generations of recent European immigrants resented what they saw as a lack of appreciation for the nation's virtues and successes. The political and social upheavals of 1968 opened the door to a Republican return to the White House, and Richard Nixon slipped through.

Backlashes

A backlash developed in response to the increasing assertiveness of people of color. European Americans in every part of the United States had long been accustomed to deference from nonwhites and racial segregation, either by law in the South or by custom elsewhere. Conservatives resented what they considered blacks' ingratitude at the civil rights measures enacted by the federal government, including black power's condemnation of whites as "crackers" and "honkies." Urban riots and escalating rates of violent crime, along with the Supreme Court's expansion of the rights of the accused, deepened their anger. They associated crime with urban African Americans, for although whites were still the majority of criminals, blacks (like any other population with less money) were disproportionately represented in prisons. The rise of often angry nonwhite nationalism dismayed most European Americans. They were troubled by the militancy of Chicanos in the Southwest, Puerto Ricans in the Northeast, Indians on reservations and in cities, and African Americans almost everywhere.

Another backlash developed as a defense of traditional hierarchies against the cultural rebellions of the 1960s. Proud of their lives and values, conservatives rejected a whole array of challenges to American society. Raised to believe in respecting one's elders, they resented the disrespect of many youth, who warned, "Don't trust anyone over 30." A generation that had fought and sacrificed in the "good war" against the Nazis found the absence of patriotism among many protesters unfathomable. The United States remained one of the most religious

■ Cartoonist Jules Fieffer portrayed the generation gap that separated many younger Americans from many older ones by the early 1970s. Movements for black and Native American civil rights and against the U.S. war in Vietnam led to a profound shift in how many citizens, especially younger ones, understood their nation and its politics. A new generation of historians began to cast serious doubts on many long-accepted truisms about the American past.

of industrialized societies, and conservative churchgoers emphasized obedience to authorities. They feared the effects of illegal drugs on their children.

The backlash against the social changes of the 1960s contained elements of class antagonism as well. Working-class whites resented the often affluent campus rebels and the black and Latino poor targeted by some Great Society programs. They believed that their values of hard work, restraint, and respectability were increasingly unappreciated and even mocked. Republican leaders from Goldwater to Nixon to Reagan gave voice to these resentments and drew votes away from Democratic blue-collar strongholds. Democratic governor George Wallace of Alabama also became a spokesperson for the anger of many "forgotten" whites on both sides of the Mason-Dixon line.

The Turmoil of 1968 at Home

The traumas of 1968 brought the conservative backlash to the critical stage. First came the Tet Offensive in Vietnam, creating fears that the war might become an interminable quagmire. Then, on April 4, a gunman named James Earl Ray assassinated Martin Luther King Jr. in Memphis, where he had gone to support a strike by sanitation workers. King had become more openly radical in his final years, opposing the war and working on class-based organizing of poor people. But he remained the nation's leading apostle of nonviolence, and his murder evoked despair among millions of citizens, especially African Americans. Police battled rioters and arsonists in black neighborhoods of 130 cities across the nation, with forty-six people dying in the clashes.

Summer brought more shocking news. Charismatic senator Robert Kennedy's entry into the presidential campaign had inspired renewed hopes among Democratic liberals. But on the night of his victory in the June 5 California primary, Kennedy was killed by a deranged gunman. Vice President Hubert Humphrey seemed assured of the nomination at the Democratic convention in Chicago in August, despite his association with Johnson's war policies. Some 10,000 antiwar activists, including hundreds of FBI *agents provocateurs* (spies seeking to provoke violence), showed up to engage in protests outside the convention. Chicago's Democratic mayor Richard Daley unleashed thousands of police on protesters, bystanders, and photographers in an orgy of beatings that subsequent investigations called a police riot. Ninety million Americans watched on television as a deeply divided Democratic party appeared helpless before the violence.

Into the vacuum of public anger and alienation that accompanied the liberals' self-destruction in Chicago stepped two men. The spread of the conservative backlash from 1964 to 1968 gave George Wallace a wider constituency for his right-wing populist message of hostility to liberals, blacks, and federal officials. With the national Democratic party committed to racial integration, Wallace ran for president as an independent candidate and won 13.5 percent of the popular vote in November. Republican candidate Richard Nixon campaigned as the candidate of "law and order" and promised that he had a secret plan to end the war in Vietnam. Nixon won the popular vote by less than 1 percent.

TABLE 26-2

The Election of 1968

Candidate	Political Party	Popular Vote (%)	Electoral Vote
Richard M. Nixon	Republican	43.4	301
Hubert H. Humphrey	Democratic	42.7	191
George Wallace	American Independent	13.5	46

The Nixon Administration

A lonely, aloof man of great tenacity and ambition, Richard Nixon had worked hard to remake his public image for 1968. Widely viewed as a somewhat unscrupulous partisan since his early career in Congress, he had refashioned himself as a statesman with a broad vision for reducing international tensions between the great powers. He sounded like a conservative in the campaign against Humphrey, but once in the White House he governed as the most liberal Republican since Theodore Roosevelt, pressed by a Congress still controlled by Democrats.

Nowhere was this clearer than on issues related to natural resources. Much had happened to the environment since Republican Theodore Roosevelt's conservation efforts, little of it for the better. A powerful movement was building to protect natural resources and human health from the effects of air and water pollution. Biologist Paul Ehrlich's best-selling *The Population Bomb* (1968) warned of the dire consequences of the globe's runaway growth in human population. In 1969 the government banned the carcinogenic pesticide DDT. That same year, a huge oil spill off Santa Barbara fouled 200 miles of pristine California beaches, and the Cuyahoga River in Cleveland, its surface coated with waste and oil, caught fire and burned for days. Environmentalists around the country proclaimed April 22, 1970, as "Earth Day."

Congress responded with legislation that mandated the careful management of the nation's natural resources. The Environmental Protection Agency was established in 1970. Amendments to the Clean Air (1970) and Clean Water (1972) Acts tightened restrictions on harmful emissions from cars and factories. The Endangered Species Act (1973) created for the first time the legal right of nonhuman animals to survive, a major step toward viewing the quality of human life as inextricable from the earth's broader ecology.

What Nixon did care deeply about at home was politics, not policy. Antiwar demonstrations reached their height during Nixon's first two years in the White House (1969–1970). He and Vice President Spiro Agnew loathed the protesters, whom they saw as weakening the nation. The two men pursued what Agnew called "positive polarization": campaigning to further divide the respectable "silent majority," as the president labeled his supporters, from voluble liberal Democrats in Congress and radical activists on the streets, whom they associated with permissiveness and lawlessness. In this broad cultural battle for political supremacy, the president appealed to conservative white southern and northern ethnic Democrats.

> *Antiwar demonstrations reached their height during Nixon's first two years in the White House (1969–1970).*

Early in his administration, Nixon began wielding the power of the federal government to harass his political opponents. Johnson had used the FBI, the CIA, and military intelligence agencies to infiltrate and thin the ranks of antiwar demonstrators and nonwhite nationalists. Nixon continued those illegal operations, agreeing with his predecessor that radical activists constituted a threat to national security. Nixon went beyond other presidents in assembling an "Enemies List" that included prominent elements of the political mainstream, especially liberals, the press, and his Democratic opponents. The president was particularly concerned about controlling secret information. The Pentagon Papers were a classified Defense Department history of U.S. actions in Vietnam, revealing that the government had been deceiving the American public about the course of the war. When disillusioned former Pentagon official Daniel Ellsberg leaked the study to the *New York Times* for publication in 1971, Nixon was enraged. The White House created a team of covert operatives nicknamed the Plumbers to "plug leaks" by whatever means necessary.

Escalating and De-escalating in Vietnam

Nixon and his national security adviser, Henry Kissinger, had ambitious plans for shifting the relationships of the great powers to America's advantage. To deal with China and the Soviet Union, they first had to reduce the vast U.S. engagement in the small country of Vietnam, which had grown wildly out of proportion to actual U.S. interests there. Under the Nixon Doctrine, the United States would provide military hardware rather than U.S. soldiers to allied governments, which would have to do their own fighting against leftist insurgencies. In South Vietnam, this doctrine required "Vietnamization," or withdrawing American troops so ARVN could shoulder the bulk of the war.

The key to a successful withdrawal from Vietnam for Nixon was to preserve U.S. "credibility." The perception of power could be as important as its actual exercise, and the president wanted other nations, both friend and foe, to continue to respect and fear American military might. There was no immediate pullout but a gradual process that lasted for four years (1969–1973), during which almost half of the total U.S. casualties in Vietnam occurred. Nixon did his utmost to weaken the communist forces during the slow withdrawal. The president ordered the secret bombing and invasion of neighboring Cambodia and Laos, an intensified aerial assault on North Vietnam, and the mining of Haiphong Harbor near Hanoi. Enormous protests rocked the country after the announcement of the Cambodian invasion on April 30, 1970. National Guard troops killed four students at a demonstration at Kent State University in Ohio and two at Jackson State College in Mississippi, deepening the sense of national division.

Kent State Demonstrations

A majority of Americans now opposed the nation's war effort, a level of dissent unprecedented in U.S. history. Most telling of all was the criticism of some veterans returning from Vietnam. The morale of American soldiers still in Vietnam plummeted as the steady withdrawal of their comrades made clear that they were no longer expected to win the war. Drug abuse and racial conflict increased sharply among GIs. Even "fragging" (killing one's own officers) escalated before the peace accords were signed in Paris and the United States evacuated its last combat troops in 1973.

Richard Nixon, "Peace With Honor" (1973)

Conclusion

Between 1964 and 1971, young, nonwhite, and female Americans laid claim to greater equality. The ratification of the Twenty-Sixth Amendment in 1971 reduced the voting age from twenty-one to eighteen, in acknowledgment of the sacrifices of young people sent to fight in Vietnam. In large numbers, women challenged and overcame traditional limits on their personal and work lives. Racial discrimination and segregation were outlawed.

These years also witnessed striking disjunctures. The nation accomplished humanity's age-old dream of walking on the surface of the moon when Neil Armstrong stepped out of the *Apollo 11* spacecraft on July 20, 1969, while at home the country sometimes appeared to be coming apart at the seams. Poverty rates dropped to their lowest point ever, yet violence seemed to pervade the land. The slaughter of forty-three people (mostly African Americans) by white state police retaking the Attica prison in upstate New York after an inmate insurrection in 1971 was one of the single most deadly confrontations between Americans since the Civil War.

The deceptive manner in which Johnson and Nixon waged the war in Vietnam eroded Americans' faith in their public officials, a process that the Watergate scandal accelerated between 1972 and 1974. American life also grew more informal as the egalitarian style of the various social movements of the 1960s spread into the broader culture. But the removal of some of the most blatant distinctions of race and gender did not extend to differences of class. In the watershed cases of *San Antonio Independent School District v. Rodriguez* (1973) and *Milliken v. Bradley* (1974), the Supreme Court ruled that wealthier districts did not have to share financing with poorer ones, nor did they have to share students by means of busing. The Court found that there was no constitutional right to an education of equal quality. The ladder of social mobility remained slippery in a nation whose neighborhoods were still stratified between the affluent and the poor.

Sites to Visit

The Sixties Project
lists.village.virginia.edu/sixties/
 This University of Virginia site has extensive exhibits, primary documents, and personal narratives from the 1960s.

Lyndon B. Johnson Library and Museum
www.lbjlib.utexas.edu/
 This presidential library site has images and online exhibits.

The Wars for Vietnam: 1945 to 1975
http://vietnam.vassar.edu/
 Historian Robert Brigham's site offers an excellent overview of the U.S. war in Vietnam, along with critical documents and helpful links to other sites.

My Lai Courts-Martial (1970)
www.law.umkc.edu/faculty/projects/ftrials/mylai/mylai.htm
 This site contains images, chronology, and court and official documents maintained by Dr. Doug Linder at the University of Missouri–Kansas City Law School.

Digger Archives
www.diggers.org
 This site provides information about the San Francisco Diggers, a prominent countercultural group in the Haight-Asbury scene of 1966–1968.

U.S. Latino History and Culture
www.si.edu/resource/faq/nmah/latino.htm
 This Smithsonian Institution site offers exhibits, photos, resources, and links to other useful sites on the lives of Latino Americans.

Gay Rights Movement
www.columbia.edu/cu/lweb/eresources/exhibitions/sw25/
 This site includes articles from the New York City press as well as first-hand accounts of the 1969 Greenwich Village riots that are commemorated throughout the country during Gay Pride celebrations.

For Further Reading

General

William H. Chafe, *The Unfinished Journey: America Since World War II*, 5th ed. (2006).
David Farber, ed., *The Sixties: From Memory to History* (1994).
Maurice Isserman and Michael Kazin, *America Divided: The Civil War of the 1960s*, 2nd ed. (2004).
James T. Patterson, *Grand Expectations: The United States, 1945–1974* (1996).
Jeremi Suri, *Power and Protest: Global Revolution and the Rise of Détente* (2003).

Lyndon Johnson and the Apex of Liberalism

Robert Dallek, *Flawed Giant: Lyndon Johnson and His Times, 1961–1973* (1998).
Lucas A. Powe Jr., *The Warren Court and American Politics* (2000).
Bruce J. Schulman, *Lyndon B. Johnson and American Liberalism* (1995).

Into War in Vietnam

Michael Herr, *Dispatches* (1977).
George C. Herring, *America's Longest War: The United States and Vietnam, 1950–1975*, 4th ed. (2001).
Robert D. Schulzinger, *A Time for War: The United States and Vietnam, 1941–1975* (1997).
Marilyn B. Young, *The Vietnam Wars, 1945–1990* (1991).

The Movement

Terry H. Anderson, *The Movement and the Sixties: Protest in America from Greensboro to Wounded Knee* (1995).
Sara Evans, *Personal Politics: The Roots of Women's Liberation in the Civil Rights Movement and the New Left* (1979).
Malcolm X, *The Autobiography of Malcolm X* (1965).
Timothy Miller, *The '60s Communes: Hippies and Beyond* (1999).
William L. Van Deburg, *New Day in Babylon: The Black Power Movement and American Culture, 1965–1975* (1992).
Tom Wells, *The War Within: America's Battle over Vietnam* (1994).

The Conservative Response

Dan T. Carter, *The Politics of Rage: George Wallace, the Origins of the New Conservatism, and the Transformation of American Politics*, 2nd ed. (2000).
Lisa McGirr, *Suburban Warriors: The Origins of the New American Right* (2001).
Hal K. Rothman, *The Greening of a Nation? Environmentalism in the United States Since 1945* (1998).
Melvin Small, *The Presidency of Richard Nixon* (1999).

For quizzes and other resources on these topics, go to www.longmanamericanhistory.com.

Reconsidering National Priorities, 1972–1979

CHAPTER

27

ABC TELEVISION NEWS ANCHOR HOWARD K. SMITH BEGAN HIS COVERAGE OF A WOMEN'S RIGHTS march in New York City in 1970 by quoting with approval the words of Vice President Spiro Agnew: "Three things have been difficult to tame. The ocean, fools, and women. We may soon be able to tame the ocean, but fools and women will take a little longer." Condescension toward women still pervaded American society, and few men even noticed it. The political upheavals of the 1960s had barely touched the relationships between most women and men by the start of the new decade. But all this changed as the 1970s unfolded. The spread of ideas about women's liberation in the 1970s transformed the personal lives of almost every American, female and male alike. Feminism challenged the most basic and intimate assumptions about relationships, family, work, and power. It also sharply expanded women's opportunities. At the end of the decade, Dr. Martha Hurley of Kansas City recalled, "In the middle of an operation today, I looked around the room—to the first assistant, my scrub nurse, and circulating nurse, the anesthesia doctor, nurse anesthetist, and the patient—and suddenly realized that we were performing major surgery and there was not a man in the room!"

■ President Nixon met the premier of the People's Republic of China, Mao Zedong, in Beijing on February 29, 1972. The U.S. government had shunned China since its communist revolution in 1949. Richard Nixon's amiable visit there stunned observers and altered the dynamics of the Cold War.

Feminism joined with other developments of the decade to force Americans to reexamine much that they had taken for granted. Elected on the promise to end the war in Southeast Asia "with honor," President Nixon escalated the fighting before eventually withdrawing U.S. forces from Vietnam. At the same time, he repaired relations with both China and the Soviet Union as those two communist powers drew apart. Americans thus suffered their first clear defeat in war while also seeing the Cold War splinter. Scandal in the White House then forced the first resignation of a U.S. president and deepened public distrust of political authorities. American economic growth—the foundation of the country's power—stumbled

CHAPTER OUTLINE

Twin Shocks: Détente and Watergate

Discovering the Limits of the U.S. Economy

Reshuffling Politics

Diffusing the Women's Movement

Conclusion

Sites to Visit

For Further Reading

because of spending on the Vietnam War and oil shortages. High-paying manufacturing jobs declined as factories began to move overseas in pursuit of cheaper labor, and skilled blue-collar workers saw their status as middle-class Americans start to slip. Unemployment grew sharply. A growing environmental movement raised disturbing questions about whether an expanding economy and exploitation of natural resources should continue to top the country's list of priorities.

The nation celebrated its 200th birthday in 1976 amid these uncertainties. That year, one-term Georgia governor Jimmy Carter won election to the White House by promising to restore honesty and trust to the federal government. In his first two years in office, Carter shifted the nation's foreign policy focus away from fighting communism toward building warmer relations with the Third World. He saw Americans' dependence on imported oil as a primary national security problem and implored citizens to scale back their lavish consumption of fossil fuels. But his presidency eventually foundered on persistent economic stagnation and inflation at home, upheavals abroad, and Carter's own limitations as chief executive.

Journalist Tom Wolfe dubbed the 1970s the "Me Decade," a phrase that proved even more appropriate for the 1980s. The label did have some merit: many Americans turned away from the public sphere after the exhilarating but divisive politics of the 1960s and pursued self-exploration and self-fulfillment instead. Crime, divorce, premarital and extramarital sex, and drug use all increased while the nation's economic health and international status declined. But the 1970s also witnessed a rethinking of long-standing assumptions: about how democracy should work at home, what role the nation should play in international affairs, how people ought to treat the environment, and how men and women should relate to each other. The decade offered a window of opportunity for Americans to reimagine their values and priorities for the future.

Twin Shocks: Détente and Watergate

Richard Nixon had long been the nation's leading anticommunist. No one had more fiercely opposed leftists at home and communists in China and the Soviet Union. However, the president was more a savvy political opportunist than an ideologue. He and his national security adviser, Henry Kissinger, saw a chance to use mounting Chinese-Soviet tensions to the advantage of the United States as they withdrew American armed forces from Vietnam.

At the same time that Nixon manipulated the Cold War abroad, the Republican president initiated a campaign of illegal actions at home to destroy his political opponents in the Democratic party. This strategy backfired in a scandal that drove him from office in 1974. Having undercut the logic of anticommunism abroad by warming relations with communist leaders in Beijing and Moscow, Nixon eroded the bipartisan consensus at home that had long supported the Cold War.

Triangular Diplomacy

Nixon and Kissinger prided themselves on their "realpolitik" approach to foreign policy: their pragmatic assessment of other powers' security needs, regardless of ideology, and their collaboration with those powers on issues of common concern. In 1969 China and the USSR gave Nixon and Kissinger an ideal opportunity to exercise their realpolitik skills. That year, tensions that had been building between the two communist states erupted in brief skirmishing between Chinese and Soviet troops on their shared border. Nixon envisioned a "triangular diplomacy" that he hoped would divide the communist world.

The president and Kissinger, a former Harvard professor with an intriguing German accent, also shared a commitment to secrecy. Any fundamental revision of the nation's foreign policy, they believed, could happen only if they concentrated all decision-making in the White House. They set out to keep Congress, the press, and even their own State Department in the dark. Diplomatic innovation thus went hand in hand with an unprecedented extension of the secretive national security state.

Nixon's 1972 visit to China brought a host of benefits. Live television coverage showed Nixon toasting Mao Zedong, premier of the People's Republic of China, while a Chinese military band played "America the Beautiful" and "Home on the Range." Americans' impression of the People's Republic as a grim, forbidding land began to give way to a renewed interest in China as an exotic but intriguing place. Cultural exchanges soon proliferated: first ping-pong teams, eventually legions of students. U.S. businesses also cast a covetous eye at the immense China market. Trade between the two nations rose dramatically over the next three decades.

Nixon and Kissinger now constructed the other leg of their diplomatic triangle. As they anticipated, the Soviets had taken alarm at the warming of relations between their two greatest rivals. Nixon flew to Moscow for a summit meeting with Soviet leader Leonid Brezhnev in May 1972 that initiated a policy of **détente** (relaxation of tensions). A trade pact quickly followed. The two superpowers also agreed to limit offensive nuclear weapons (the Strategic Arms Limitations Treaty, or SALT I) and to ban antiballistic missile defense systems (the ABM treaty).

Like the Soviet leaders, Nixon and Kissinger sought to preserve the existing international balance of power. Deal-making with China and the USSR constituted one step in this process. In another, the two men sought to stifle socialist revolutions in Third World nations by bolstering pro-American allies there. For instance, the duo feared that the democratic election of socialist Salvador Allende in Chile in 1970 would lead to "another Cuba." A socialist leader might nationalize the investments of U.S. corporations in Chile and perhaps challenge Washington's capitalist hegemony in the Western Hemisphere. Determined to block these possibilities, the CIA secretly funded a right-wing military coup in Chile in September 1973. Allende died in the assault on the presidential palace, and the rebel forces murdered thousands of his supporters and established a brutal military dictatorship under General Augusto Pinochet. "I don't see why we need to stand by and watch a country go Communist because of the irresponsibility of its own people," Kissinger explained privately.

Scandal in the White House

Meanwhile, on the domestic front, Washington police caught agents of Nixon's reelection campaign breaking into the Democratic National Committee headquarters in the **Watergate** hotel and office complex on June 17, 1972. The burglars' goal was to put in place secret listening devices, or "bugs." Later, the White House tried to cover up its connections to the crime.

The Watergate break-in was only one step in Nixon's broader campaign of illegal warfare against his political opponents. An insecure and unhappy loner, Nixon harbored an almost paranoid suspicion when he took office in early 1969. The president and his aides regularly discussed "how we can use the available federal machinery to screw our political enemies," in the words of White House counsel John Dean. They persuaded the FBI and the CIA to monitor and harass antiwar activists and pushed the Internal Revenue Service to investigate prominent Democrats. They extorted large contributions to the Republican party from corporate executives by making it clear that federal agencies would otherwise impede the pursuit of their business interests. The *New York Times*'s publication of the classified Pentagon Papers in 1971 stiffened the resolve of the Committee to Reelect the President (CREEP) to stop any further leaks. The committee assembled a group of undercover operatives (the "plumbers") to stop leaks and to engineer "dirty tricks" against the Democrats.

After the "plumbers" bungled Watergate break-in, the president directed the cover-up from the beginning, then lied about it to the public. He also used the CIA to hinder the FBI's investigation into the matter. He approved payments of hush money to the burglars to keep them quiet about their ties to the White House. Nixon's abuse of power escalated as he pressured his subordinates to perjure themselves in court. For most of a year the cover-up held, and Nixon won reelection in 1972.

TABLE 27-1
The Election of 1972

Candidate	Political Party	Popular Vote (%)	Electoral Vote
Richard M. Nixon	Republican	60.7	520
George S. McGovern	Democratic	31.5	17

Richard Nixon, "I am not a crook"

But the persistent investigations by *Washington Post* journalists Bob Woodward and Carl Bernstein kept the heat on. In early 1973, the administration began to crack due to a grand jury probe in the federal court of Judge John Sirica. The president's men lost confidence that the cover-up would hold and began looking for ways to save their own skins. Congress initiated its own televised investigations that mesmerized a national audience. The Senate Watergate committee, chaired by eloquent conservative North Carolina Democrat Sam Ervin, methodically exposed the criminal actions in the White House, with growing bipartisan support. The key issue, as framed by Republican committee member Howard Baker of Tennessee, became, "What did the president know, and when did he know it?"

After the bungled Watergate break-in, the president directed the cover-up from the beginning, then lied about it to the public.

On July 16, 1973, White House aide Alexander Butterfield told the Senate committee that a built-in recorder taped all conversations in the Oval Office. Almost certainly, these tapes would provide answers to questions about the president's role. Both Congress and Justice Department special prosecutor Archibald Cox subpoenaed the White House tapes, but Nixon refused to hand them over. Instead, he fired Cox on October 20 in what became known as the Saturday Night Massacre. Outraged, Congress initiated impeachment proceedings against the president. In the spring of 1974, the House Judiciary Committee passed bills of impeachment for his specific abuses of power. Before the full House could vote to impeach him and the Senate decide on his guilt or innocence, the Supreme Court ruled that the White House had to turn over the subpoenaed tapes. The tapes revealed the extent of the president's involvement in the cover-up and his personal crudeness, vindictiveness, and ethnic and racial prejudices. Facing a certain guilty verdict, Nixon resigned on August 9, 1974, less than halfway through his second term.

DOCUMENT
Committee's Conclusion on Impeachment

The Nation After Watergate

Never before had a U.S. president resigned from office. Many citizens celebrated the outcome of the Watergate investigations as evidence of democracy's resilience and power to uncover criminal activity in the White House and bring down a corrupt president. But the affair also discredited political institutions Americans had long respected. Indeed, the Nixon administration proved quite corrupt. A whole raft of senior officials, including the president's closest aides, H. R. Haldeman and John Ehrlichman, went to prison. Even Vice President Spiro Agnew had been forced to resign amid the Watergate investigations when a Maryland jury found him guilty of tax evasion dating back to his years as governor there. Congress swung strongly to the Democrats in the 1974 elections, slowing the Republicans' rise to the status of majority party.

■ Many South Vietnamese fled the communist victory in their country in 1975, including this woman and her children crossing the Mekong River. Most of the refugees undertook extremely perilous journeys by boat to other Southeast Asian nations, and hundreds of thousands eventually made their way to the United States.

The man who replaced Nixon in the White House faced a daunting situation. Gerald Ford, longtime Republican congressman and House minority leader from Grand Rapids, Michigan, had been tapped by Nixon to replace Agnew as vice president. Well liked by members of both parties, Ford seemed to embody the antidote to the extreme styles of both Nixon and Agnew. To restore decency and trust in the government, Ford saw his role as healing what he called "the wounds of the past." Within a month, he granted a "full, free, and absolute pardon" to Nixon for any crimes he may have committed as president, precluding any trial and punishment within a court of law. However, most Americans believed that Nixon should have faced justice for his actions, just as the people did who carried out his orders. Ford's popularity plummeted overnight from 72 percent to 49 percent and never fully recovered.

If Ford inherited the fallout from Watergate at home, abroad he inherited the pending defeat in Vietnam. U.S. soldiers returned to a nation determined to ignore or demean their sacrifices, and they quickly learned to keep their combat-induced traumas to themselves. When Saigon finally fell to the combined invasion of National Liberation Front and North Vietnamese fighters on April 30, 1975, Americans watched the televised images with both bitterness and relief. Two weeks later, Cambodian communist forces briefly seized the U.S. container ship *Mayaguez*, provoking Ford to demonstrate that the United States was still ready and willing to flex its military muscle. But forty-one U.S. soldiers died in the rescue mission to save thirty-nine sailors whom, it turned out, Cambodia had already released. Ford and Kissinger, serving as the new president's secretary of state, continued to pursue détente with the Soviets at summit meetings in Vladivostock (1974) and Helsinki (1975). At the same time, they supported anticommunist forces in various Third World conflicts, such as the civil war that erupted in Angola after that country achieved its independence in 1975.

Discovering the Limits of the U.S. Economy

Defeat in Vietnam and corruption in the White House were soon joined by grim economic news. Generation after generation of Americans had watched their incomes rise, and most children expected to be wealthier than their parents had been. Since World War II had pulled the U.S. economy out of the Great Depression, median family income had doubled. But by 1973, the famous American standard of living began to decline. The three pillars of postwar prosperity—cheap energy, rising wages, and low inflation—simultaneously crumbled. The costs of the Vietnam War struck home at the same time that an oil embargo spawned by conflict in the Middle East gripped the country. Moreover, a widening environmental movement raised questions about the pursuit of endless economic growth on a planet that more and more people realized had limited natural resources.

The End of the Long Boom

During the 1970s, a new economic scourge dubbed "stagflation" hit the United States. For the first time, employment and wages stagnated while prices climbed. What explained this phenomenon? Spending on the Vietnam War and on Great Society programs had pulled prices upward. The government had never raised enough taxes to cover the expense of the war, so it paid the bills by simply printing more dollars. In 1971 annual inflation stood at 4.5 percent, more than twice the pre-Vietnam rate; two years later it reached 10 percent, and by 1980 it topped out at 18 percent.

These figures devastated Americans' sense of economic security. Average real wages (income adjusted for inflation) dropped by an average of 2 percent a year from 1973 to the 1990s. Unemployment rose to 9 percent in 1975. Only the continued flow of women into the workforce, seen by most families as an economic necessity, kept the majority of U.S. families afloat financially. The number of citizens living in poverty, which had dropped sharply through the 1960s to 11 percent in 1973, rose again, hitting 15 percent by 1982. The gap between rich and poor began widening, a process that has persisted into the new millennium.

Only the continued flow of women into the workforce, seen by most families as an economic necessity, kept the majority of U.S. families afloat financially.

Perhaps the most telling evidence of the weakening economy came with the drop in the growth of productivity: output per worker-hour had risen at an annual average of more than 3 percent during the postwar boom. From 1974 to 1992, it rose at less than half that rate.

This decline stemmed in part from competition from abroad, particularly West Germany and Japan. With U.S. assistance (and without the military expenditures that so burdened the United States), those countries had finally rebuilt their economies after World War II and boasted new, more efficient industrial facilities. The trade surplus that had long symbolized global U.S. economic superiority evaporated in 1971. That year, U.S. imports overtook exports for the first time in the twentieth century. Worried international investors traded in dollars for gold, forcing Nixon to end the twenty-seven-year-old monetary system formulated at the UN Monetary and Financial Conference at Bretton Woods, New Hampshire, in July 1944, that had linked all other currencies to the dollar at fixed exchange rates. Freed from the fixed rate of $35 per ounce of gold, the value of the dollar dropped like a stone; by the end of the decade, it took $800 to buy an ounce of gold.

In this competitive environment, the *Wall Street Journal* reported, American companies "seek places where labor, land, electricity, and taxes are cheap." Corporations found those places in the American South and Southwest, regions characterized by scarce unions, low wage rates, minimal taxes, and negligible local government regulations. Many more such places were in neighboring Mexico, where U.S. companies established *maquiladoras*. These assembly plants, often just a few hundred yards across the Mexican-U.S. border, allowed corporations to hire primarily female workers at low wages and avoid strict U.S. environmental, labor, and safety laws. The long-term decline of the Rustbelt—the series of urban industrial centers strung across the American Northeast and Midwest—accelerated in the 1970s.

High unemployment and shrinking real wages contributed to rising anti-immigrant sentiment. Two white autoworkers in Detroit in 1982 got into an altercation in a bar with Vincent Chin, a Chinese American (and son of a World War II veteran) whom they called a "Jap." Angered that Japanese auto sales were undercutting jobs in Detroit, they made Chin a scapegoat for their rage, chasing him down the street and beating him to death with a baseball bat.

Black Americans also faced an increasing backlash against hard-won civil rights gains. While court-ordered busing to integrate schools in segregated neighborhoods proceeded slowly but peacefully in the South, northern urban whites dug in their heels. In Boston, violence erupted in the school hallways and the streets from 1975 to 1978 as economically vulnerable working-class whites harassed African Americans attending schools in white ethnic neighborhoods of South Boston, and blacks defended themselves.

■ White resistance to school busing in Boston sometimes turned violent in the mid-1970s. On April 5, 1976, white high school students from South Boston and Charlestown met with a city councilwoman who supported their boycott of classes. Outside City Hall, they chanced upon lawyer Theodore Landsmark and assaulted him. Photographer Stanley J. Forman won the Pulitzer Prize for this photo.

The Oil Embargo

Nothing revealed Americans' newfound economic vulnerability more than the 1973–1974 boycott initiated by the Oil Producing and Exporting Countries (OPEC). The largest producers of oil were the Arab countries around the Persian Gulf, especially Saudi Arabia. These nations resented the creation of Israel in 1948 and the resulting displacement of the Palestinians.

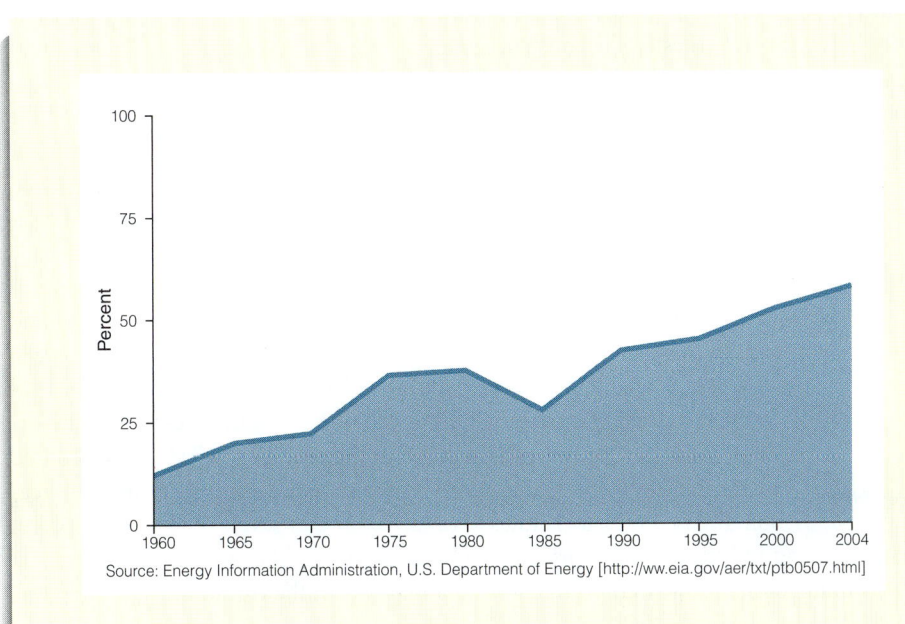

■ **FIGURE 27.1**
IMPORTED PETROLEUM AS SHARE OF U.S. PETROLEUM CONSUMPTION Abundant natural resources, especially coal and oil, encouraged Americans' long-standing feeling of national strength and autonomy. After World War II, however, the United States switched from exporting oil to importing oil. Conservation measures in the 1970s temporarily reversed America's growing dependence on oil from abroad.

Hostility intensified in 1967 when Israel seized control of the West Bank of the Jordan River and the Gaza Strip. Six years later, Egypt and Syria struck back, attacking and threatening to overrun Israel, but the United States gave the Israeli army a critical resupply of weapons that helped turn the tide of battle.

Henry Kissinger then shuttled between Tel Aviv and Cairo to negotiate a ceasefire. His diplomatic skills won him the Nobel peace prize and laid the groundwork for a warming of U.S. relations with Egypt (the most populous Arab nation though not an oil producer). However, the other Arab states expressed outrage at this demonstration of America's close links with the Israelis, and Arabs of all political persuasions were determined to voice their displeasure.

In October 1973, the OPEC nations initiated an embargo on selling oil to the United States and to western European nations that had supported Israel in the war. Oil supplies dwindled, and prices at gas pumps skyrocketed to four times their previous levels. Even when OPEC lifted the embargo after five months, it kept prices high by limiting production.

Steeper energy costs powerfully accelerated inflation. Decades of easy access to cheap gasoline came to a sudden halt. As American drivers formed long lines at the pump, President Ford urged them to drive at lower speeds to conserve gas. Americans confronted new and sobering limits on their mobility.

The Environmental Movement

The oil embargo encouraged many U.S. citizens to rethink the nation's cavalier use of natural resources. Environmental consciousness spread rapidly in the 1970s as evidence revealed the impact of industrial growth on the quality of life in the United States. Environmental organizations such as the Sierra Club, the National Wildlife Federation, and the Audubon Society saw their memberships soar. For the first time, the media began to examine the daunting range of environmental problems plaguing the United States and the rest of the world: acid rain, groundwater contamination, smog, rainforest destruction, oil spills, nuclear waste disposal, species extinction, ozone depletion, and global warming.

Environmentalists argued that the idea of unlimited consumption of natural resources was fundamentally irresponsible, both to future human generations and to other species. They urged Congress and the Environmental Protection Agency (EPA) to require fuel-efficient engines from carmakers and to promote renewable energy sources such as water, solar, and wind power. Citizen groups such as the Clamshell Alliance in New England and the Abalone Alliance in California protested the construction of new nuclear power plants. These operations, they pointed out, had no reliable method in place for disposing of nuclear waste.

A broad critique of the chemical industry's impact on public health also emerged in the 1970s. As it turned out, pesticides worked their way up the food chain into people's bodies. Some artificial sweeteners proved carcinogenic, and the lead that manufacturers had added to gasoline and house paint for generations caused brain damage. Long-standing industrial dumping of toxic chemicals made headlines.

Discovering the limits of the U.S. economy so soon after the Vietnam War and the Watergate scandal spawned a crisis of confidence.

The crisis at Love Canal in upstate New York helped bring the issue of toxic waste home to Americans. The Hooker Chemical Company had buried tons of poisonous waste in a dry canal in the town of Niagara Falls between 1947 and 1952 and then covered it over with dirt. The company gave the land to the town, which promptly built a school on it. A middle-class neighborhood soon grew up around the site. But the ground smelled odd and oozed mysterious substances. Sometimes it even caught on fire for no apparent reason. By the 1970s, local rates of cancer and other severe illnesses had soared. The chemical and industrial plant workers who lived in the neighborhood began to suspect that their quiet loyalty to their employers was no longer worth the risk to the health of their

■ Thousands of runners surge up the Hayes Street hill in San Francisco in the annual 7-mile Bay-to-Breakers race across the city. In the 1970s, regular exercise began to become a common part of daily life for many Americans. At the same time, fast food and higher-fat diets contributed to a growing pattern of Americans being overweight and even obese.

families. Persistent activism by community members finally overcame local, state, and company officials' efforts to keep the contents of the buried canal secret. In August 1978, New York Governor Hugh Carey at last agreed to buy out the entire neighborhood, seal it off, and move residents elsewhere.

Discovering the limits of the U.S. economy so soon after the Vietnam War and the Watergate scandal spawned a crisis of confidence. Many Americans resented the idea of limits. But others began to embrace the idea of creating a healthier lifestyle that focused less on material consumption. Exercise, especially running, began to become an increasingly common activity for middle-class adults. The wildly successful Nike athletic shoe company was founded in 1972, and entrants in the New York City Marathon ballooned from 126 in 1970 to 10,000 by 1978. Interest in outdoor recreation—hiking, camping, and bicycling—grew exponentially. Recycling also started its climb from a fringe activity to common practice in a few parts of the country.

Reshuffling Politics

The skepticism toward authority and tradition spawned by the counterculture, the Vietnam War, and the Watergate scandal spread through American culture in the 1970s. The use of illegal drugs, especially marijuana, was widespread. Casual sexual relationships proliferated in a decade when contraceptive pills had become widely available and the AIDS virus had not yet appeared. Popular and critically acclaimed films featured tales of malfeasance in high places. *All the President's Men* (1976) told the story of the Nixon administration's Watergate crimes. *Apocalypse Now* (1979) revealed the madness of the American war in Vietnam. *Three Days of the Condor* (1975) portrayed the CIA as a rogue agency beyond democratic

INTERPRETING HISTORY

The Church Committee and CIA Covert Operations

In 1975–1976 the U.S. Senate Select Committee to Study Governmental Operations with Respect to Intelligence Activities engaged in the first comprehensive review by Congress of the actions of the Central Intelligence Agency. Under the leadership of Frank Church (D-Idaho), the committee investigated both intelligence gathering ("spying") and covert operations, the secret side of American foreign policy during the Cold War. One of the most controversial issues that the Church committee examined was evidence of the CIA's attempted use of assassination as a means of dealing with key figures in Cuba, the Congo, the Dominican Republic, South Vietnam, and Chile.

Alleged Assassination Plots Involving Foreign Leaders (Interim Report, November 20, 1975)

The Committee has received evidence that ranking Government officials discussed, and may have authorized, the establishment with the CIA of a generalized assassination capability. . . .

The evidence establishes that the United States was implicated in several assassination plots. . . . Our inquiry also reveals serious problems with respect to United States involvement in coups directed against foreign governments. . . .

Once methods of coercion and violence are chosen, the probability of loss of life is always present. There is, however, a significant difference between a coldblooded, targeted, intentional killing of an individual foreign leader and other forms of intervening in the affairs of foreign nations. . . .

Non-attribution to the United States for covert operations was the original and principal purpose of the so-called doctrine of "plausible denial."

Evidence before the Committee clearly demonstrates that this concept, designed to protect the United States and its operatives from the consequences of disclosures, has been expanded to mask decisions of the President and his senior staff members. . . .

"Plausible denial" can also lead to the use of euphemism and circumlocution, which are designed to allow the President and other senior officials to deny knowledge of an operation should it be disclosed. . . .

It is possible that there was a failure of communication between policymakers and the agency personnel who were experienced in secret, and often violent, action. Although policymakers testified that assassination was not intended by such words as "get rid of Castro," some of their subordinates in the Agency testified that they perceived that assassination was desired and that they should proceed without troubling their superiors. . . .

Running throughout the cases considered in this report was the expectation of American officials that they could control the actions of dissident groups which they were supporting in foreign countries. Events demonstrated that the United States had no such power. This point is graphically demonstrated by cables exchanged shortly before the coup in Vietnam. Ambassador Lodge cabled Washington on October 30, 1963, that he was unable to halt a coup; a cable from William Bundy in response stated that "we cannot accept conclusion that we have no power to delay or discourage a coup." The coup took place three days later. . . .

Officials of the CIA made use of persons associated with the criminal underworld in attempting to achieve the assassination of Fidel Castro. These underworld figures were relied upon because it was believed that they had expertise and contacts that were not available to law-abiding citizens. . . .

It may well be ourselves that we injure most if we adopt tactics "more ruthless than the enemy."

A star baseball pitcher who once turned down an offer to sign with the New York Giants, Fidel Castro led a leftist, anti-American revolution in Cuba in 1959. U.S. hostility and Castro's evolving politics moved him to declare Cuba a communist state in 1961. The CIA tried unsuccessfully to arrange for Castro's assassination.

Questions

1. What are the dangers to the United States of using assassination as a tool of U.S. foreign policy? Is the use of assassination compatible with the practice of democracy? How might it affect American society at home, as well as the way other nations perceive the United States?

2. Did the attacks of September 11, 2001, change the way Americans view the possible use by their government of assassination and other covert operations abroad? Should the attacks have altered Americans' attitudes about these issues?

control. *Chinatown* (1974) suggested the vast corruption marring the early-twentieth-century growth of Los Angeles. *Blazing Saddles* (1974) hilariously spoofed the heroic Westerns that had long served as the staple of American moviegoers' diet. *One Flew over the Cuckoo's Nest* (1975) used novelist Ken Kesey's story of an insane asylum to imply that those in charge were more dangerous than the inmates. In this atmosphere Congress began to reassert its authority against the "imperial presidency," and in 1976 voters put an obscure, devout, Georgia peanut farmer and former one-term governor in the White House.

Congressional Power Reasserted

The double shock of defeat in Vietnam and the Watergate scandal reawakened a Congress that had grown accustomed to deferring to the White House in foreign affairs. Tellingly, Congress had never formally declared war on North Korea or North Vietnam, although such declaration is its constitutional duty. Angered by the illegalities and deception in both the Johnson and Nixon administrations, Congress passed the War Powers Act in 1973 to limit the president's capacity to wage undeclared wars. The bill required the chief executive to obtain explicit congressional approval for keeping U.S. troops in an overseas conflict longer than ninety days.

Defeat in Vietnam and the Watergate scandal reawakened a Congress that had grown accustomed to deferring to the White House in foreign affairs.

With encouragement from voters and journalists, Congress also uncovered its eyes and began to investigate the covert side of American foreign policy that had gathered momentum since 1945. After Watergate popped the cork on the bottled-up secret abuses of the executive branch, other troubling news spilled out about the nation's intelligence agencies, including CIA "dirty tricks" and the agency's Operation Chaos. The latter program of illegal domestic espionage against antiwar dissidents paralleled FBI abuses such as the COINTELPRO campaigns to defame Martin Luther King Jr. and destroy the Black Panthers and the American Indian Movement. Congressional investigators documented CIA involvement in assassination attempts against foreign leaders such as Fidel Castro of Cuba and Patrice Lumumba of the Congo.

These revelations stirred fierce controversy among those who took an interest in national and international politics. Many citizens decried what their government had done in their names and without their knowledge. However, officials claimed that the extreme conditions of the Cold War and the duplicity of the Soviets necessitated secrecy. At the core of this controversy were two burning questions. How transparent could a democratic society and its government afford to be when they also had global interests to protect? And when democratic openness and imperial self-interest conflicted, which should win out?

"I Will Never Lie to You"

In the backwash of Watergate, two presidential candidates—both outsiders to national politics—became advocates for opposing sides in the debate about power and openness in 1976. Former California governor Ronald Reagan made a strong run at the Republican nomination, falling just short at the Kansas City convention as incumbent Gerald Ford held on to head the GOP ticket. Reagan articulated conservative Americans' anger at seeing U.S. autonomy and power abroad hemmed in. He opposed détente with the Soviets, supported anticommunists everywhere, and warned against a treaty that would return control of the Panama Canal to the Panamanians. Ford found himself burdened by the faltering economy, weakened by Reagan's criticisms from the right, and hampered by widespread resentment of his pardon for Nixon.

TABLE 27-2

The Election of 1976

Candidate	Political Party	Popular Vote (%)	Electoral Vote
Jimmy Carter	Democratic	50.0	297
Gerald R. Ford	Republican	47.9	241

Jimmy Carter was the winner. The former Georgia governor based his candidacy on moral uplift. Contrasting himself to the Nixon administration, he told audiences, "I will never lie to you." Instead, Carter promised openness, accountability, and a government "as good and decent as the American people."

Carter was also a Naval Academy graduate, a former nuclear engineer, a successful peanut farmer and businessperson, and the first president from the Deep South in more than a century. A born-again Christian, he had supported civil rights during his governorship in Georgia. Carter kept his diminutive first name: Jimmy, not James nor even Jim. He wore denim, and he carried his own bags. At his inaugural parade, he and his wife Rosalynn chose to walk down Pennsylvania Avenue rather than ride in a limousine.

The new president entered the White House at a time of unusual resistance to executive authority. He encountered an assertive and suspicious Congress. He faced an economy still mired in stagflation as unemployment and prices kept rising and interest rates reached 21 percent.

Politics and ideology also hamstrung the new president, limiting his ability to lead his own party in governing the nation. The Georgian was the first Democratic president since the 1930s who did not fully subscribe to the New Deal principle of government regulation of the economy. As a social moderate but an economic conservative, Carter had a strong desire to balance the federal budget. This vision placed him closer to the Republicans than to many in his own party. A businessperson, he also considered fiscal responsibility a primary virtue. Powerful liberal Democrats in Congress, by contrast, remained committed to government spending on programs such as Social Security and welfare, which Carter supported with less enthusiasm.

Carter's tendency to take moralistic stands did not mesh well with the horse-trading style of compromise that characterized Congress. The president and his aides tried to govern as outsiders to the federal government. They viewed insiders as selfish and narrow-minded. They failed to cultivate relationships with Democratic leaders in Congress such as powerful House Speaker Thomas ("Tip") O'Neill of Massachusetts. Meanwhile, seasoned legislators of both parties looked down on the new administration as inexperienced and naive.

Rise of a Peacemaker

Carter's idealism proved more effective, at least during his first two years, in refashioning U.S. foreign policy. The president started the national healing process with his first official act in office: he granted a "full, complete, and unconditional pardon" to those who had evaded the draft during the Vietnam War. He also tried to replace indiscriminate anticommunism with the promotion of human rights as the main theme in international affairs. "We are now free of that inordinate fear of Communism which once led us to embrace any dictator who joined us in that fear," he told an audience at Notre Dame University.

All presidents since 1945 had loudly supported human rights in the Soviet bloc. Carter defended dissidents in authoritarian countries friendly to the United States as well. His commitment to ending racial discrimination at home and his promotion of human rights abroad led to his administration's strong support for an end to white minority rule in southern Africa, including the establishment of Zimbabwe out of the old white-ruled Rhodesia in 1980.

Carter encouraged Americans to shift their attention from the East-West Cold War to the burgeoning problems between industrialized nations of the North and mostly poor countries of the Southern Hemisphere. The president made control over the Panama Canal a test case for this reorientation. The huge canal symbolized U.S. dominance of the hemisphere and served as a focus of resentment among many Latin Americans. Since 1903, the United States had ruled the 10-mile-wide Canal Zone as its own colony. Acknowledging this colonialist past, Carter signed treaties on September 7, 1977, to return sovereignty of the canal to Panama.

The Carter administration's other great diplomatic achievement came with the Camp David accords, an agreement between Egypt's president Anwar Sadat and Israel's prime minister Menachem Begin. The Arab-Israeli conflict had remained one of the most intractable problems in modern diplomacy. Sadat created an opening for diplomacy in 1977 by becoming the first Arab leader to visit Israel. Carter then invited Sadat and Begin to Camp David, the presidential retreat in rural western Maryland. There his persistence, plus promises of American aid to all parties, kept the marathon negotiations on track. In March 1979, the Egyptian and Israeli leaders signed two accords: Egypt became the first Arab state to grant official recognition to Israel. In turn, Israel agreed to withdraw its troops from the Sinai peninsula and apparently to stop building additional settlements on the Palestinian West Bank of the Jordan River. The framework for peace implied eventual autonomy for the Palestinians in the West Bank and the Gaza Strip.

Though promising, the Camp David accords failed to bring peace to the Middle East. Israeli settlements in the West Bank continued to proliferate, and anti-Israeli terrorism by Palestinians persisted. But Carter had persuaded two major players in the region to take a big step back from open hostility. The world rightly proclaimed him a peacemaker.

■ After his inauguration as president, Jimmy Carter got down to work in the Oval Office. Serious, conscientious, and extremely hard-working, Carter immersed himself in many of the details of his administration's policies. The image of him sequestered and industrious at his desk came to symbolize, for many, both the strengths and weaknesses of his presidency.

The War on Waste

Within three months of taking office, Carter called for the "moral equivalent of war" to meet the deepening national energy crisis. He exhorted his fellow citizens to stop being "the most wasteful nation on Earth." Conserve energy, he implored them. Switch off lights and turn down thermostats.

The administration created the Department of Energy and granted tax incentives to promote development of alternative sources such as solar energy. The EPA required U.S. automakers to meet stricter fuel efficiency standards for their engines. High prices encouraged a renewed search for domestic sources of oil. In 1977 workers completed the 800-mile-long, 48-inch-wide Trans-Alaska Pipeline System. The system linked the state's northern oil fields at Prudhoe Bay on the Arctic Ocean with a tanker terminal in Valdez, on Alaska's southern coast on the Pacific Ocean. With new oil now flowing freely, Carter worked with Congress to pass the 1980 Alaska National Interest Lands Conservation Act. This legislation created the single largest addition ever to the nation's wilderness system, 47 million acres, and the new Wrangell–St. Elias National Park.

The most controversial power alternative came in the form of nuclear energy. Obtained by harnessing the force of splitting atoms, nuclear energy seemed to promise unlimited pollution-free power. But it entailed the use of a deadly radioactive fuel, uranium. In March 1979, a partial meltdown of the nuclear core of the Three Mile Island reactor near Harrisburg, Pennsylvania, leaked radiation and forced a major evacuation. Nevertheless, existing nuclear power plants continued to generate 11 percent of the nation's electricity in 1979, a figure that climbed to 22 percent by 1992 as other plants under construction came on line. However, because of negative public opinion and the high cost per unit of nuclear power, no new plants ordered by utility companies after 1974 were ever completed.

Mt. McKinley in Alaska's Denali National Park rises to 20,320 feet above sea level, the tallest peak in North America. Its scale and beauty inspired many supporters of the Alaska National Interest Lands Conservation Act of 1980, which dramatically expanded the nation's parklands and wilderness areas. The Alaska Lands Act and the new Trans-Alaska oil pipeline, completed three years earlier, helped residents of the lower forty-eight learn more about the nation's largest and most remote state.

Diffusing the Women's Movement

"Good morning, boys and girls!" This standard classroom greeting suggests the central place of gender in how Americans identify people from a young age. Few people consider the phrase offensive, even though they probably would protest if a teacher addressed class members as "blacks and whites" or "tall people and short people." Should one's sex (a biological characteristic) or gender (the social assumptions associated with sex) constitute the fundamental dividing line among human beings? The spread of feminism through U.S. society from the 1970s onward raised this question.

The Meanings of Women's Liberation

In a decade marked by hard rethinking of major issues, feminists provided one of the most profound challenges of all. Few American households avoided at least some reconsideration of the roles of men and women. Just as the nation reimagined its foreign policy in less assertive terms and with greater concern for human rights, feminists called for equality between the sexes while honoring their differences. The new title "Ms."—like Mr.—symbolized a desire not to have one's marital status revealed through the title of "Miss" or "Mrs." Thousands of consciousness-raising meetings also made women aware that their own experiences with discrimination were part of a broader pattern of injustice toward women.

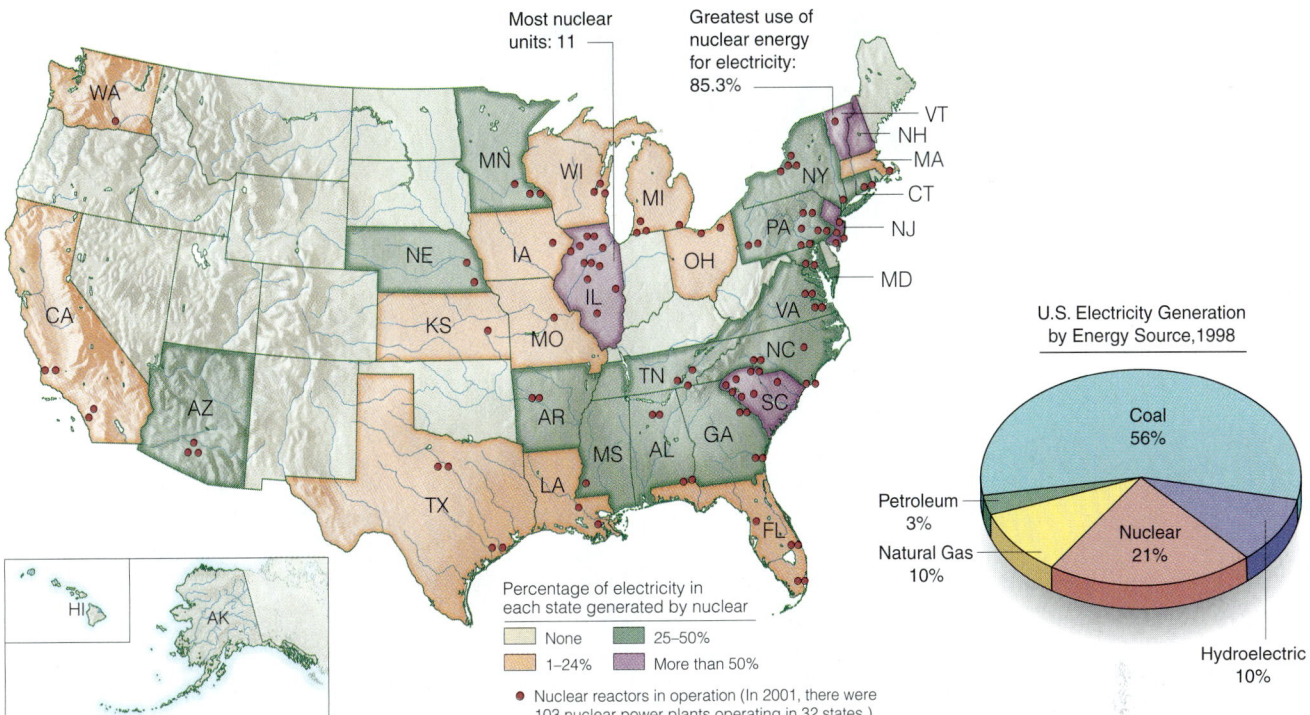

MAP 27.1
BUILDING NUCLEAR POWER PLANTS Between 1969 and 1980, all of the nation's 103 commercial nuclear power reactors either came on line (fifty-six) or were in the process of being planned or built (forty-seven). The United States has roughly one-quarter of the 434 commercial nuclear power reactors in the world. Despite nuclear energy's important role in U.S. electricity production, there is still no system in place for the permanent disposal of radioactive waste.

The millions of American women who found their lives changing in the 1970s did not agree on all issues. African American and Latino American women balanced identities as women with identities as people of color, which aligned them closely with men of their communities. Working-class women of all colors often focused on issues common to all workers, including wages, workplace conditions, and union representation. Community organizers such as Lois Gibbs of Love Canal zeroed in on neighborhoods and families. The educated white women who formed the most visible part of the movement for equality differed among themselves on such issues as pornography: some found it inherently exploitive of women, while others considered it primarily a matter of free expression.

However, all women shared certain concerns. Even as many female Americans remained wary of the label *feminist*—fearing associations with anger, militancy, and dislike of men—they nonetheless tended to side with feminist positions on issues from equal pay for equal work, to abortion rights, to more egalitarian distribution of household chores within families. Even women who still chose to wear makeup and dress in traditionally feminine fashion shared a desire for men to take women more seriously for their ideas and beliefs than for their appearance. The women's movement also sought to unmask the violence constraining all women's lives: sexual harassment, domestic abuse, and rape.

New Opportunities in Education, the Workplace, and Family Life

In the 1970s, educated women gained access to a host of new opportunities in the workplace. Young women in college, unlike their mothers, expected to choose and develop a career after

■ Gloria Steinem, kneeling, speaks at a meeting of a women's consciousness-raising group in the early 1970s. Similar groups gathered informally in homes around the country and helped women articulate their common struggles against discrimination.

graduation even more than they anticipated getting married. The number of women entering graduate and professional schools soared. The percentage of female students in law school shot up from 5 percent to 40 percent between 1970 and 1980. Most single-sex private colleges went coeducational. Many dormitories housed both men and women, allowing young people from the middle and upper classes to live in close physical proximity for the first time.

A similar process unfolded in the workplace. Employment in the United States, formerly divided into "men's" and "women's" work, saw a blurring of those lines. Help-wanted advertisements stopped categorizing jobs as male or female, and women joined the ranks of police officers and truck drivers. In 1980 more than half of women with children under six years old had paying jobs outside the home.

Not surprisingly, family life also changed shape in these years. In the 1950s, more than 70 percent of American families with children had a father who worked outside the home and a mother who stayed at home. By 1980, only 15 percent of families were configured that way. Yet society's growing acceptance of mothers in the workforce did not necessarily mean that these women enjoyed a lighter domestic load. Most working mothers still bore the brunt of the "second shift": child-rearing and housework in addition to a full-time paid job.

Changing roles brought new marital stresses, and divorce rates climbed in this decade. In 1970, one-third as many divorces as marriages occurred annually; in 1980, the figure was one-half. No-fault divorce laws, beginning with California's in 1970, eased the process and the stigma attached to divorce, although its emotional impact on adults and children remained difficult to measure. Men benefited financially when marriages split up. Their average living standard rose sharply, whereas that of women and their children plummeted.

Equality Under the Law

Paralleling the logic of the black civil rights movement, the modern women's movement pressured lawmakers to eliminate the legal underpinnings of sex-based discrimination. Title IX of the Educational Amendments of 1972 required schools to spend comparable amounts on women's and men's sports programs. This critical step symbolized women's shift away from spectatorship and cheerleading to the female athleticism that helped define American popular culture by the end of the twentieth century.

After languishing for decades among failed proposals in Congress, the proposed Equal Rights Amendment to the Constitution finally rode to an overwhelming victory among senators and representatives in 1972. The legislature then sent it to the states for possible ratification by 1980. Simple in its language, the ERA declared: "Equality of rights under law shall not be denied or abridged by the United States or by any State on account of sex."

Roe v. Wade

On January 22, 1973, in the landmark case of *Roe v. Wade*, the Supreme Court ruled (by a 7–2 vote) that constitutional privacy rights were "broad enough to encompass a woman's decision whether or not to terminate her pregnancy" in its first six months. This decision established women's constitutional right to determine the course of their own pregnancies.

Backlash

Even as the majority of Americans accepted the fundamental tenets of feminism, some fiercely defended existing gender roles. The mainstream media often painted women's rights activists as angry man-haters. Indeed, the media seized the opportunity to associate feminism with "bra-burning," a titillating way to blend women's rights with the sexual revolution and thus avoid the serious issues that women were raising. One Chicana worker involved in a strike against the Farah slacks company in Texas responded, "I don't believe in burning your bra, but I do believe in having our rights."

The women's movement posed a daunting challenge to traditional ideas about masculinity. Men wondered what equality for women really meant and how it might change their intimate and professional relationships with women. Should men still open doors for women? Should they begin to do half (or more) of housework and parenting? Should they not comment on a female colleague's appearance? Women's growing economic independence and educational opportunities often altered the dynamics of power in male-female relationships. Many men from all classes and ethnicities, feeling defensive about assumptions and behaviors that were increasingly labeled sexist, resisted these changes. Some found the increasingly open acknowledgment of lesbianism threatening because it implied their potential irrelevance to women.

> *Should men still open doors for women? Should they begin to do half (or more) of housework and parenting?*

That men would have mixed feelings about women's liberation surprised no one. But some of the stiffest resistance came from certain women. Those who had built their identities on motherhood and homemaking fiercely defended that tradition. They sought to uphold an established family structure that they believed divorce, gay rights, abortion, and day-care would destroy. In their view, femininity meant service to one's family. "Feminists praise self-centeredness," antifeminist Phyllis Schlafly declared, "and call it liberation." In addition to defending their own choices, female antifeminists worried about the impact of dual-career families on children.

Opponents of women's liberation made two major legislative gains in the late 1970s. First, Congress passed the Hyde Amendment in 1976, which forbade the use of Medicaid funds for abortions. In practice, the amendment limited access to abortion to those women who could afford to pay for it themselves. Second, Schlafly's Stop-ERA campaign helped defeat the Equal

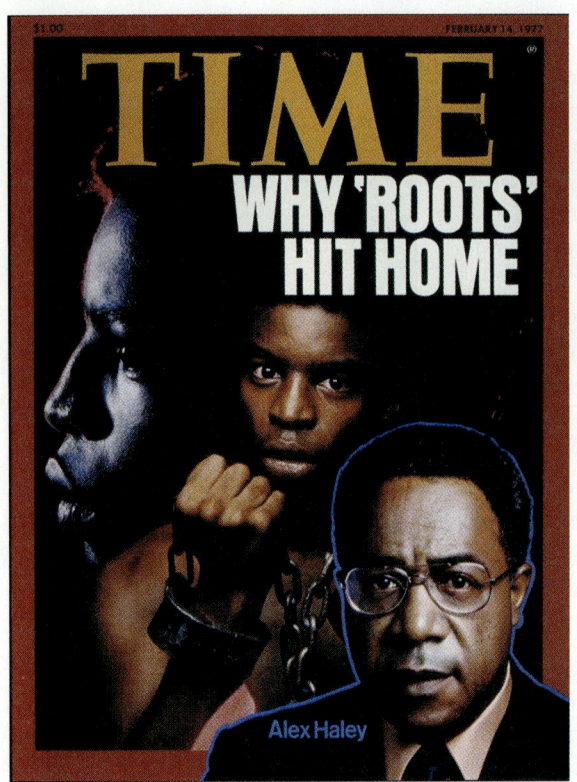

■ The 1977 miniseries version of Alex Haley's *Roots* captured the largest television audience ever to that time. The powerful drama about Haley's ancestors offered tens of millions of Americans an intimate and sympathetic understanding of the horrific story of black slavery and survival. *Roots* also represented the post-1960s emphasis on preserving and respecting group histories and identities rather than emphasizing only individual success and assimilation into the mainstream.

Rights Amendment by limiting its ratification to only thirty-five of the required thirty-eight states. Schlafly claimed that the amendment would "destroy the family, foster homosexuality, and hurt women." Opponents of the ERA argued that it would also draw out the worst in men, letting husbands opt out of supporting their wives and freeing divorced men from paying alimony. Antifeminists resented the disrespect for motherhood that they felt from some feminists. Still, they agreed with feminists that tens of millions of American women were just one man removed from welfare. The two sides differed on the best way to protect women's interests: should women be more economically independent, or should men be tied more tightly to their families?

Though discouraging for some, the narrow defeat of the ERA could not mask feminism's growing influence throughout American culture. The "first woman" stories that began showing up in the media during the 1970s marked the entrance of women into previously all-male roles. Like physicians, lawyers, and other figures of cultural authority, religious leaders now increasingly consisted of women, including the first Lutheran pastor (1970), the first Jewish rabbi (1972), and the first Episcopal priest (1974). In 1981 Sandra Day O'Connor became the first female Supreme Court justice. And mainstream organizations such as churches and municipalities ran feminist-created community institutions, including rape crisis centers, women's health clinics, and battered women's shelters.

Conclusion

In 1978 a divided U.S. Supreme Court handed down a ruling on the contentious policy of affirmative action. The justices decided by a 5–4 vote in the *Bakke* case that strict racial quotas were unconstitutional, but that universities could consider race as one of several factors in determining a candidate's qualifications for admission. The Court, like the American public, was wrestling with the broader 1970s problem of how to reform American society in ways that would preserve its historic strengths while removing the ills that the previous decade's political activism had laid bare. One specific problem was the tension between the ideal of colorblind integration and new expressions of pride in distinctive racial and ethnic identities. Many white ethnic Americans in these years leavened their long-standing cultural assimilation with renewed attention to their own roots in particular European countries, especially Ireland and Italy.

Americans' self-confidence and pride as a nation had been deeply shaken by the combination of the Vietnam War, the Watergate scandal, and the economic downturn after 1973. Disillusioned by the corruptions of public life, many citizens turned inward and heeded the advice of Robert J. Ringer in his 1977 bestseller, *Looking Out for Number One*. But others found motivation in the decade's events—especially the revelation that presidents, corporate executives, and other authorities had lied to them. They learned what earlier Americans had discovered in the 1760s and 1770s about imperious British officials and the corrupting effects of managing a global empire. Like the revolutionaries of George Washington's generation, they sought to strengthen democracy.

Sites to Visit

Divining America: Religion and the National Culture
www.nhc.rtp.nc.us/tserve/divam.htm
This site has essays by prominent historians on diverse aspects of the religious history of the United States.

Documents from the Women's Liberation Movement
scriptorium.lib.duke.edu/wlm/
Provocative and fascinating articles from feminists of the late 1960s and 1970s make this site worthy of a visit.

National Security Archive at George Washington University
www.gwu.edu/~nsarchiv/
This excellent site includes the most recent declassified documents on the making of U.S. foreign policy.

Natural Resources Defense Council
www.nrdc.org/
This site contains considerable information and links about environmental issues, particularly those that emerged into public consciousness in the 1970s.

Oyez Project of Northwestern University
http://www.oyez.org/oyez/frontpage
Arguments from important Supreme Court cases plus information about Supreme Court justices make this a most useful site for legal history.

Gerald R. Ford Library and Museum
www.ford.utexas.edu/
The Ford presidential library maintains this site, with documents and photographs from the mid-1970s.

The Watergate Story
www.washingtonpost.com/wp-srv/onpolitics/watergate/splash.html
The *Washington Post* created this informative site about the Watergate scandal twenty-five years after the event took place.

For Further Reading

General

Edward D. Berkowitz, *Something Happened: A Political and Cultural Overview of the Seventies* (2006).
Peter N. Carroll, *It Seemed Like Nothing Happened: America in the 1970s* (1990).
E. J. Dionne Jr., *Why Americans Hate Politics* (1991).
Bruce J. Schulman, *The Seventies: The Great Shift in American Culture, Society, and Politics* (2001).

Twin Shocks: Détente and Watergate

Walter Isaacson, *Kissinger* (1992).
Andreas Killen, *1973 Nervous Breakdown: Watergate, Warhol, and the Birth of Post-Sixties America* (2006).
Stanley I. Kutler, *The Wars of Watergate: The Last Crisis of Richard Nixon* (1992).
Melvin Small, *The Presidency of Richard M. Nixon* (1999).

Discovering the Limits of the U.S. Economy

Allen J. Matusow, *Nixon's Economy: Booms, Busts, Dollars, and Votes* (1998).
Thomas J. McCormick, *America's Half-Century: United States Foreign Policy in the Cold War and After*, 2nd ed. (1995).
Hal K. Rothman, *The Greening of a Nation? Environmentalism in the United States Since 1945* (1998).
Daniel Yergin, *The Prize: The Epic Quest for Oil, Money, and Power* (1991).

Reshuffling Politics

Samuel P. Hays, *Beauty, Health, and Permanence: Environmental Politics in the United States, 1955–1985* (1987).
Burton I. Kaufman, *The Presidency of James Earl Carter, Jr.* (1993).
John Ranelagh, *The Agency: The Rise and Decline of the CIA* (1986).
Gaddis Smith, *Morality, Reason, and Power: American Diplomacy in the Carter Years* (1986).

Diffusing the Women's Movement

Susan J. Douglas, *Where the Girls Are: Growing Up Female with the Mass Media* (1994).
Sara M. Evans, *Tidal Wave: How Women Changed America at Century's End* (2003).
Arlie Russell Hochschild, *The Second Shift: Working Parents and the Revolution at Home* (1997).
Ruth Rosen, *The World Split Open: How the Modern Women's Movement Changed America* (2000).

For quizzes and other resources on these topics, go to www.longmanamericanhistory.com.

PART TEN

Global Connections at Home and Abroad 1979–2006

1979 Iranian revolution; militants take American hostages
Soviet Union invades Afghanistan
Sandinista rebels seize control of Nicaragua

1980 Failed attempt to rescue American hostages in Iran
Ronald Reagan elected president

1981 Iran releases American hostages
U.S. funds "Contras" to try to overthrow Nicaraguan government

1982 Recession hits United States
Nuclear freeze movement holds large protests in the United States and western Europe

1983 HIV identified as virus that causes AIDS
First compact discs (CDs) marketed
241 U.S. Marines killed in bombing of Beirut barracks
Martin Luther King Jr.'s birthday designated a national holiday

1984 Russia boycotts summer Olympic Games in Los Angeles

1985 First Reagan-Gorbachev summit in Geneva

1986 Chernobyl nuclear power plant disaster (Ukraine)
Iran-Contra scandal revealed
Congress passes sanctions against South African apartheid government

1987 Intermediate Nuclear Force Treaty
Stock market crash

1988 Indian Gaming Regulatory Act
Libyan terrorist bomb downs Pan Am Flight 103 over Lockerbie, Scotland
United States invades Panama to seize Manuel Noriega

1989 Grounding of oil tanker *Exxon Valdez* off Alaska coast
Last Soviet troops withdraw from Afghanistan
Berlin Wall falls

1990 Nelson Mandela freed from prison in South Africa
Iraq invades and occupies Kuwait

1991 Clarence Thomas–Anita Hill congressional hearings
Persian Gulf War against Iraq
Los Angeles police beat, arrest Rodney King
Soviet Union dissolves into Russia and other component states

1992 South Central Los Angeles riots follow acquittal of police in Rodney King case
FBI shootout at Ruby Ridge, Idaho

AFTER THE UNCERTAINTIES AND REFORMS OF THE 1970s, many Americans sought reassurance about their country's direction. In the 1980s, President Ronald Reagan left his imprint on both domestic and foreign affairs. Reagan gave voice to conservatives, including those who favored a federal retreat from social welfare programs. Bolstered by the Moral Majority and other fundamentalist Christian groups, conservatives engaged in the so-called culture wars with liberals. Conservatives disapproved of feminists, black power advocates, gay rights activists, and environmentalists. Reagan and Congress implemented policies that shrank the federal government's commitment to social welfare programs. Reagan also reinvigorated Cold War rhetoric—he denounced the Soviet Union as an "evil empire"—and pushed military spending to unprecedented levels. Yet Reagan welcomed the initiatives of Soviet leader Mikhail Gorbachev, who sought to ease tensions with the West.

Unable to meet the basic needs of its own people and bogged down in an unwinnable war in Afghanistan, the Soviet Union disintegrated in 1991. Simultaneously, the United States embarked on a remarkable period of economic growth and expansion. President Bill Clinton favored free trade policies, such as the North American Free Trade Agreement (NAFTA), which he and others hoped would knit the world's nations together in pursuit of political and economic progress.

Nevertheless, domestic and foreign conflicts thwarted much of this hopeful vision. At home, the AIDS epidemic and drug addiction claimed many lives. Clashes among African Americans, Latinos, and Koreans in Los Angeles in 1992; the bombing of an Oklahoma City federal building by domestic antigovernment terrorists in 1995; attacks on abortion clinics; and a series of shootings by high school students revealed persistent faultlines in American society. Backed by the Supreme Court, a number of state and local governments passed anti-immigrant and anti–affirmative action laws. The culture wars were hot and, in some cases, deadly.

The most violent assault on the United States came from forces outside as well as within it. The Middle East had become a tinderbox of fears and resentments. In Iran, Islamic militants overthrew the U.S.-backed Shah in 1979. Throughout the region, many Islamic fundamentalists expressed their resentment over the military and political presence of the United States in Israel and Saudi Arabia. During the 1991 Persian Gulf War, the United States successfully reversed Iraq's seizure of oil fields in Kuwait. Yet U.S. attempts to protect its economic and political interests in the Middle East continued to outrage Islamic militants.

By the end of the 1990s, some Americans were able to focus inward and enjoy prosperity. The stock market was booming. Cheap gas prices encouraged affluent Americans to purchase huge sport utility vehicles with little regard for their environmental impact. However, ten years of high employment masked the hidden effects of a transformed economy, one characterized by a decline in labor union membership and the rise of an ill-paid service sector. A substantial proportion of Americans lived from paycheck to paycheck.

On September 11, 2001, Americans were forced to confront their own vulnerabilities. Anti-U.S. terrorists hijacked commercial airliners and flew them into the Twin Towers of the World Trade Center in New York City and into the Pentagon outside Washington, D.C. Some 3,000 people were killed. Within a month, anthrax-laced letters caused death and havoc in the offices where they were delivered and the postal centers that processed them, heightening pervasive fear and insecurity among Americans.

The events of September 11 highlighted a grim reality: certain foreign groups despised such cherished American values as democracy, liberalism, and consumerism. Moreover, U.S. foreign policies in the Middle East fanned the fires of anti-western extremism. Terrorists were becoming more successful in enlisting people who were willing to die in attacks on the United States and more resourceful in using modern technology in those attacks. These terrorists were stateless, freed from the political tasks of protecting their own citizens, monitoring national borders, or dealing with internal dissidents. In contrast to the cold warriors, fighters against terrorism faced an elusive, dispersed, and, in some cases, suicidal enemy. In 2002 these realities prompted the United States to invade Afghanistan and displace the ruling Taliban, hosts to Al Qaeda's training network. The following year the United States attacked Iraq, a preemptive attack on what the Bush administration called a dangerous, destabilizing regime—the dictatorship of Saddam Hussein. At home, issues related to war, terrorism, and civil liberties became increasingly divisive and bitter among Americans.

1993	FBI storms compound of the Branch Davidian cult in Waco, Texas Congress approves North American Free Trade Agreement (NAFTA) Arab-Israeli peace talks 18 American soldiers die in Somalia; United States withdraws
1994	House Republican leadership announces "Contract with America" Republicans win majority in House of Representatives O. J. Simpson murder trial Freedom of Access to Clinic Entrances Act
1995	Truck bomb destroys federal building in Oklahoma City Congress revokes 55-mph speed limit

	United States intervenes against Serbs in war in Bosnia Dayton peace accords signed
1996	Welfare Reform Act
1997	Dow Jones average passes 8,000
1998	Lewinsky-Clinton affair revealed Clinton impeached by House of Representatives
1999	Senate acquits Clinton Dow Jones passes 10,000 U.S. bombing campaign frees province of Kosovo from Serbian rule Elian Gonzales affair
2000	Supreme Court decides contested election; George W. Bush becomes president Scientists map human genome
2001	Democrats regain control of Senate after Sen. James Jeffords leaves Republican party Terrorists attack World Trade Center and Pentagon U.S. forces attack Afghanstan and overthrow Taliban regime
2003	Space shuttle Columbia destroyed during re-entry into earth's atmpshere U.S. and allied forces invade and occupy Iraq Supreme Court legalizes gay sexual conduct
2004	George W. Bush reelected president
2005	Hurrican Katrina devastates New Orleans
2006	130,000–160,000 U.S. troops in Iraq

CHAPTER 28

The Cold War Returns— and Ends, 1979–1991

On July 16, 1979, just west of Albuquerque, New Mexico, a dam holding wastewater and residue from a uranium mine broke. Some 94 million gallons of radioactive water flooded into the Rio Puerco. Nearby, the Anaconda Copper Company operated the nation's largest uranium mine, producing the fuel for nuclear power. The mine closed in the early 1980s. At public hearings in 1986 concerning the future of the mine and its small mountain of poisonous tailings, Anaconda's scientists argued that the mine did not threaten human health in the area. Thus, they said, the tailing piles and the polluted ponds did not need to be cleaned up. Herman Garcia, a Laguna Indian who lived in the adjoining village of Paguate, listened carefully but remained unconvinced. "We lost five people from cancer" last year in tiny Paguate alone, he explained. "I'm no expert," he concluded, but "I'd like for some of these experts to go out there and swim in those ponds. Then when I see them swim, then maybe I feel more secure."

The Native American West and the nuclear West have overlapped to a remarkable extent ever since participants in the Manhattan Project began building the first atomic bomb in 1942. Repeatedly, the U.S. government constructed major nuclear sites in the West on lands surrounded by Indian settlements. These included the laboratories of Los Alamos, New Mexico; the bomb factories and nuclear waste dumps of Hanford, Washington; the Nevada Test Site for atomic weapons north of Las Vegas; and uranium mines in the Black Hills of South Dakota. Some of this overlap resulted from geological coincidence: almost 90 percent of the nation's uranium lay on or adjacent to Indian lands. Some of it stemmed from politics. The sparse populations of Pueblo, Western Shoshone, and Yakima lacked the political clout to prevent their lands from becoming what the National Academy of Science called "national sacrifice areas."

In the 1980s, nuclear weapons and waste sparked controversy in the United States. President Ronald Reagan expanded the nation's nuclear arsenal, and his administration publicly

■ Ronald Reagan loved spending time outdoors at his ranch near Santa Barbara, California.

CHAPTER OUTLINE

Anticommunism Revived

Republican Rule at Home

Cultural Conflict

The End of the Cold War

Conclusion

Sites to Visit

For Further Reading

discussed fighting and winning a nuclear war against the Soviet Union. An accident in 1986 at the Chernobyl nuclear power plant outside the Soviet city of Kiev only heightened public concerns. The disaster killed more than 100 people and irradiated hundreds of thousands more. Frightened by rising U.S.-Soviet tensions, citizens in western Europe and the United States organized an international movement to freeze further development of nuclear weapons.

In 1979 two international incidents raised questions about U.S. military effectiveness. A revolution in Iran led to the taking of American hostages and a dramatic rejection of American cultural values, and the Soviet Union sent troops into Afghanistan to prop up a Soviet-allied but weakening government. Angered, Americans put tough-talking Republicans in the White House for twelve years. These leaders' emphasis on military power challenged the Soviet leadership, while changes in eastern Europe and the USSR brought an end to the Cold War and the breakup of the Soviet Union.

The Reagan administration also avidly promoted free markets. Its policies produced enormous wealth at the top of the socioeconomic ladder, increasing the distance between the daily experiences of the rich and the poor. These policies also catalyzed bitter struggles over natural resources, particularly those on western public lands.

Finally, the newly organized religious right clashed with liberal opponents over such issues as abortion and homosexuality. In these years, Christian fundamentalists and their allies sought to reverse cultural liberties that had emerged since the late 1960s.

Anticommunism Revived

"We're going down!" cried U.S. political officer Elizabeth Swift on the phone to the State Department. These were her last words as a crowd of young Iranians poured into the U.S. embassy in Teheran on the morning of November 4, 1979, and cut telephone lines. In a move that shocked Americans, Islamic militants seized fifty-two embassy personnel and held them hostage for over a year.

In the late 1970s, revolutionaries of a different political bent—that of socialism and the left—took the offensive against authoritarian regimes in Central America. Indeed, the Third World seemed to be turning away from U.S. leadership in the wake of the American defeat in Vietnam. To make matters worse, the Soviet Union stepped up its support for leftists abroad. In December 1979, the Red Army invaded Afghanistan. Fed up with these humiliating events overseas and with relentless inflation at home, American voters elected Ronald Reagan as president—the most conservative chief executive since Calvin Coolidge. Reagan promised to resurrect the Cold War, and he delivered.

Iran and Afghanistan

In January 1979, the Iranian people overthrew the longtime authoritarian government of Shah Reza Pahlavi. Under the shah's rule, the nation's enormous oil wealth had flowed into the hands of a small elite. Meanwhile, the impoverished majority of devout Shi'ite Muslims grew increasingly resentful of the shah's closeness with his American allies. His secret police had detained 50,000 political prisoners. The revolution found its leader in the austere religious figure Ruhollah Khomeini, who shouldered aside more moderate opposition groups. Returning from exile in Iraq and then Paris, Ayatollah Khomeini created a popular **theocracy**, state grounded in a strict interpretation of Islamic law.

■ Ruhollah Khomeini led the 1979 revolution in Iran that established the modern world's first Islamic theocratic state. The events in Iran encouraged Islamic revolutionaries across the Middle East, Asia, and North Africa. For Americans, the closest analogy was the Bolshevik revolution of 1917 in Russia, which provided a model for other communist revolutions abroad.

Hunted by the rebels, the shah took his money and fled Iran. Several months later, the Carter administration let him fly to New York to seek treatment for cancer. Enraged that the United States harbored their nation's most wanted criminal, Iranians demanded the shah's extradition to Teheran to stand trial. Washington refused. Within a month, militants stormed the U.S. embassy—"that nest of spies," Khomeini called it, referring to the CIA's considerable presence in Iran.

The hostages' captors paraded them before television cameras to force Washington to return the shah. Carter refused to give in. In April 1980, he finally approved a military rescue effort. But mechanical failures forced the mission to abort, and the collision of two helicopters during the attempt killed several U.S. soldiers. Secretary of State Cyrus Vance resigned in protest against the attempted use of force. Americans' resentment of anti-American radicals in the Third World intensified. Not until after the shah's death in 1980 did the two governments finally negotiate the hostages' release in January 1981.

Khomeini and his followers despised the values they associated with modern U.S. culture: secularism, materialism, gender equality, alcohol consumption, and sexual titillation. They sought to export the cleansing power of a puritanical Islamic faith throughout the Middle East and beyond. Indeed, the revolutionaries condemned the atheistic Soviets just as fiercely as they did the materialistic Americans.

> *Khomeini and his followers despised the values they associated with modern U.S. culture.*

Just seven weeks after the seizure of hostages in Teheran, the first of 110,000 Soviet troops rolled south across the USSR's border into neighboring Afghanistan. Their goal: to stabilize the pro-Soviet government there against anticommunist Islamic guerrilla fighters. Moscow had resolved to prevent the spread of Islamic revolution into the heavily Muslim southern regions of the USSR.

But few Americans saw this invasion as a defensive operation. Rather, they feared a push toward vulnerable Iran as Red Army troops marched beyond eastern Europe for the first time in more than thirty years. The Carter administration halted most trade with the Soviets and withdrew the nuclear Strategic Arms Limitation Treaty (SALT II) from Senate consideration. In addition, the president organized a western boycott of the 1980 Olympics in Moscow and increased military spending. The "Carter Doctrine" proclaimed the U.S. commitment to preserve the status quo in the Persian Gulf region, even if it meant the use of military force. And the CIA began funding Afghan guerrillas.

The Conservative Victory of 1980

By mid-1980, Carter's public approval rating had dropped to the lowest level of any modern president. Inflation reached 17 percent. Even the president acknowledged a "crisis stage." With their dollars no longer buying what they used to, Americans wondered what the future would bring. For many voters, Carter's inability to free the hostages in Teheran or reverse the Soviet occupation of Afghanistan symbolized the limitations of his presidency.

Onto this stage strode Ronald Reagan. Long considered too conservative to win the presidency, the former California governor projected the confidence and strength that many Americans wanted, even if they did not share all of his views. The sixty-nine-year-old one-time actor sailed through the Republican primaries. For his main tactic, he appealed to nostalgia, particularly among whites, for a rosier past—a time of rising wages and U.S. military might. While Carter spoke of learning to live within limits, Reagan insisted that "we are too great a nation to limit ourselves to small dreams."

The media loved Reagan. Indeed, his presidency fit with the new emphasis on constant entertainment, as cable television, VCRs (1976), MTV (1981), and CDs (1983) swept the culture. Daily newspaper readership plummeted from 73 percent to 50 percent during the 1980s. Equally telling, the average length of an uninterrupted "sound bite" on the evening news dropped from forty-two seconds in 1968 to fewer than ten seconds in 1988. Anything longer,

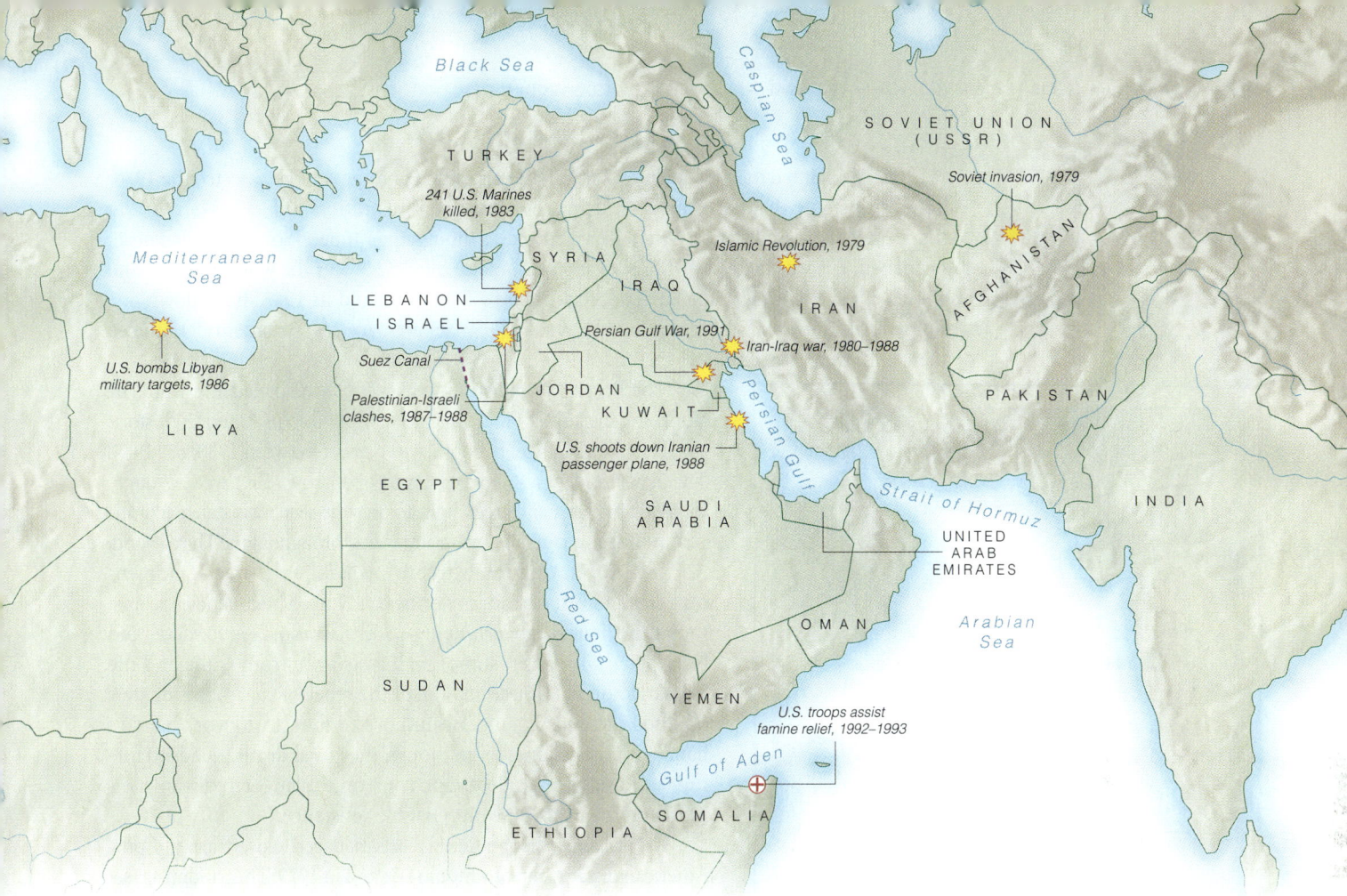

■ **MAP 28.1**
TROUBLE SPOTS IN THE MIDDLE EAST, 1979–1993 Oil production around the Persian Gulf and the close American relationship with Israel made political instability in the Middle East a central concern of the U.S. government. American leaders particularly feared the spread of either Soviet influence or Islamic revolution, both of which opposed American cultural values and U.S. strategic interests.

the networks believed, would bore viewers. And no one projected simplicity with greater warmth or sincerity than Reagan.

Yet the 1980 election was about more than just Reagan's likable personality. It revealed the nation's renewed interest in conservative ideas. Republicans won control of the Senate for the first time since 1952. Several basic values united the Republican party: an unhindered private sector and entrepreneurial initiative to create affluence, plus free markets and individual responsibility to solve the nation's social problems. Republicans, like most Democrats, also believed that the United States had a moral obligation to preserve world order and halt further expansion of communist influence. Reagan proclaimed that "government was the problem, not the solution."

Renewing the Cold War

"Sometimes in our administration," Reagan once joked, "the right hand doesn't know what the far-right hand is doing." But all hands in the White House agreed on the importance of restoring confidence in the nation's engagements abroad, particularly in the Third World. In the 1970s, leftist insurgencies in Asia, Africa, and Latin America—especially Vietnam, Cambodia, Angola, Ethiopia, El Salvador, and Nicaragua—had suggested the retreat of U.S. power.

TABLE 28-1

The Election of 1980

Candidate	Political Party	Popular Vote (%)	Electoral Vote
Ronald Reagan	Republican	50.7	489
Jimmy Carter	Democratic	41.0	49
John B. Anderson	Independent	6.6	—

DOCUMENT
Reagan, "Evil Empire" Speech

Reagan blamed the Soviet Union for "all the unrest that is going on." He rejected the 1970s policy of détente that had emerged during the Nixon administration and had taken further shape under Ford and Carter. Often, Reagan spoke as though the Chinese-Soviet split had never happened. His was "a kind of 1952 world," one aide recalled. "He sees the world in black and white terms." Pointing to the Soviet occupation of Afghanistan and its 1983 shoot-down of a Korean Air Lines civilian jet that had strayed into Soviet airspace, the president denounced the USSR as "an evil empire."

The Reagan administration backed up the president's words by launching the largest peacetime military buildup in American history. The Pentagon's budget ballooned 40 percent between 1980 and 1984. The new president also revived covert operations. He gave CIA director William Casey the green light to provide secret assistance to anticommunist governments and insurgencies throughout the Third World.

In Central America, extreme inequalities between landowning elites and vast peasant majorities had fueled insurgencies against the authoritarian governments of El Salvador, Guatemala, and Nicaragua. Moreover, some small assistance from Cuba and the Soviet Union had found its way to the rebels. Reagan passionately opposed these insurgents. He authorized the CIA to work hand in hand with the regimes, even though they used death squads to torture and murder dissidents and sometimes slaughtered whole villages and towns to wipe out possible resistance.

In Nicaragua, the Sandinista rebels managed to overthrow the pro-American dictatorship of Antonio Somoza in 1979. The Sandinistas set about building a more egalitarian and socialist state while still preserving 60 percent of the nation's wealth in private hands. Carter had adopted a wait-and-see attitude. But after Reagan took office in 1981, the CIA created the counterrevolutionary "Contras," recruited primarily from Somoza's murderous former National Guard. The Contras waged an undeclared war on the new government in the Nicaraguan capital of Managua. By 1987, 40,000 Nicaraguans had died in the fighting, most of them civilians. Reagan called the Contras "freedom fighters" and declared them "the moral equal of our Founding Fathers."

Nevertheless, several European and Latin American allies considered the Contras an illegitimate force of terrorists. A large coalition of church and university groups in the United States agreed. They organized fact-finding visits to Nicaragua and lobbying trips to Washington. Christian activists formed the "Sanctuary" movement to aid refugees from the right-wing dictatorships in Central America that sympathized with the Contras. The Pentagon, for its part, had no interest in sending troops to fight a popular government abroad. The opposition finally prevailed; Congress passed the Boland Amendments of 1982 and 1984 to restrict U.S. assistance to the Contras.

■ Critics of Reagan's policies toward Central America believed that he ignored the indigenous problems encouraging revolutions there, blaming instead the USSR and Cuba. The cartoon suggests that the Democratic party took a different view than the president. Many Democrats in Congress did, and they were responsible for limiting Reagan's promotion of the Nicaraguan Contras. But many others went along with the popular president in defending the Contras and supporting right-wing regimes in the region.

Republican Rule at Home

While reasserting U.S. power abroad, Reagan also aimed to reorient domestic policies toward the free market. Lori was what the president called a "welfare cheat." Writer Barbara Ehrenreich told the story of a young neighbor in New York City representative of welfare recipients: a single white mother with one child. Lori had been married for two years to a man who beat her and once chased her around the house with a gun.

Welfare had made it possible for her to leave him, a move she described as like being born again, "as a human being this time." Lori sometimes earned close to $100 a week from cleaning houses and waiting tables—not enough to support herself and her daughter, but a useful supplement to the small government payments. She chose not to report this to the welfare office, spending it instead on little things deemed inessential by welfare regulations: deodorant, hand lotion, and an occasional commercial haircut.

Lori's story helps illuminate some of the major trends of the 1980s. Inflation finally eased and the stock market perked up. Congress and the White House slashed taxes. However, annual budget deficits and the national debt soon soared as tax revenues declined and military spending increased. The administration shrank government programs for the poor and portrayed welfare recipients like Lori as lazy and irresponsible. Washington turned a cold shoulder to concerns over the environment and opened public lands in the West to new commercial uses. By the 1990s, the gap between rich and poor widened noticeably and the vaunted American middle class worried about its declining economic security.

"Reaganomics" and the Assault on Welfare

Taxes played a crucial role in the Reagan administration's efforts to reduce government involvement in the economy. In 1981 the president proposed a new tax law to lower federal income tax rates by 25 percent over three years. Congress passed the legislation, and the top individual rate—paid only by the wealthiest Americans—dropped from 70 percent to 28 percent. Congress also slashed taxes on corporations, capital gains, and inheritances, further benefiting the most affluent Americans.

As taxes shrank, federal spending on the military soared. The Pentagon bolstered its conventional and nuclear arsenals and gave service personnel a morale-boosting salary increase. After 1983, billions of dollars poured from the U.S. Treasury into the president's proposed Strategic Defense Initiative (SDI) for a missile defense system.

> *Congress slashed taxes on corporations, capital gains, and inheritances, further benefiting the most affluent Americans.*

The funds for the weapons buildup could come from only one source: social programs at home. However, most domestic spending went to popular programs, such as Social Security and Medicare, which primarily benefited the middle class. Leaving those in place, Reagan instead reduced funding for welfare programs, including food stamps, school lunches, job training, and low-income housing.

The Republican desire to transfer the responsibility for citizens' well-being from the national government to the states resonated with opponents of the civil rights movement. The Reagan administration opposed any form of affirmative action, calling instead for the "colorblind" application of law. The president and his supporters argued that prejudice no longer had any significant effect on the decisions that employers and others made. Ironically, Reagan's own Justice Department demonstrated the opposite: it sought unsuccessfully to win tax-free status for Bob Jones University in Greenville, South Carolina, and other schools and colleges that discriminated against people of color.

Reducing welfare spending did not close the budgetary gaps that lower taxes and higher military outlays had opened. To close these gaps, the government resorted to borrowing money. Formerly the world's largest creditor nation, the United States became its largest debtor nation. Between 1981 and 1989, the national debt ballooned to almost $3 trillion. Moreover, during twelve years of Republican rule ending in 1993, annual budget deficits jumped from $59 billion to $300 billion.

Despite these problems, "Reaganomics" did help the national economy recover somewhat from the traumas of the 1970s. The tight

TABLE 28-2
The Election of 1984

Candidate	Political Party	Popular Vote (%)	Electoral Vote
Ronald Reagan	Republican	59.0	525
Walter Mondale	Democratic	41.0	13

■ James Watt, Reagan's first secretary of the Interior Department, became one of the most polarizing figures in a polarized decade. He made clear that he considered environmentalists to be his opponents as he worked to promote the interests of mining and timbering companies as well as ranchers. The Interior Department manages the national parks, monuments, and wildlife refuges, as well as the Bureau of Land Management's extensive lands (national forests fall under the Department of Agriculture's jurisdiction).

money policies of the Federal Reserve Board after 1979 eventually tamed inflation, which dropped from 14 percent in 1980 to less than 2 percent in 1983. The Fed's high interest rates also choked off the nation's cash flow and provoked a severe recession in 1981–1982, with unemployment reaching above 10 percent. However, the economy revived again in 1983 and was growing at a robust annual rate of 6.8 percent by 1984. Rising confidence in the economy helped Reagan soar to reelection over his opponent, Carter's former vice president Walter Mondale.

An Embattled Environment

The 1980 election marked the sharpest turn ever in American environmental policy. The new administration reversed two decades of growing bipartisan consensus on the need for greater protection of the environment. Reagan instead supported corporations' demands for fewer environmental regulations and easier access to natural resources on public lands. The president ridiculed the idea of preserving wilderness for its own sake. He even claimed in 1980 that "trees cause more pollution than automobiles do."

The officials Reagan appointed to oversee these lands and assume responsibility for protecting them had little respect for the agencies they ran. Critics described the situation as "foxes guarding the chicken house." The officials openly disdained environmentalists, including those in the moderate wing of the Republican party. Anne Gorsuch at the Environmental Protection Agency (EPA), Robert Burford at the Bureau of Land Management (BLM), and John Crowell in charge of the Forest Service explicitly rewrote regulations to favor private enterprise. They sold grazing, logging, and mining rights on public lands at prices far below market value, despite their stated commitment to market economics.

Gorsuch, Burford, and Crowell were moderates, however, in comparison to James Watt, the new Secretary of the Interior who controlled national parks and wildlife refuges. A native of Wheatland, Wyoming, Watt declared that only two kinds of people lived in the United States: "liberals and Americans." Watt was also a Christian fundamentalist. In his Senate confirmation hearings, he suggested that the nation had little need for long-term public land management because Christ would soon be returning and the known world would pass away—an interpretation of stewardship that not even all fundamentalists shared, much less the broader American public. Watt's abrasive personal style eventually alienated even the White House, and he resigned in 1983.

The administration's reversal of federal environmental policies alarmed a wide range of citizens and stimulated a powerful backlash. Membership in environmental organizations soared, in such traditional groups as the Sierra Club and the Audubon Society, as well as in more radical ones, such as Greenpeace. Most Americans wanted to breathe cleaner air, drink safe water, and make recreational use of national parks, national forests, and BLM lands. In much of the rural West, jobs in the recreation industry outnumbered those in the logging, mining, and ranching businesses. In 1989 concern intensified when the oil tanker *Exxon Valdez* ran aground in Prince William Sound in Alaska, coating 1,000 miles of pristine coastline with crude oil.

A Society Divided

As the Reagan administration eased corporate access to the nation's natural resources, the disparity between rich and poor expanded further. Whereas most Americans' real wages (wages after inflation is factored in) declined, the professional classes fared well, and the wealthiest citizens gained enormously. For example, the salary of an average corporate chief executive officer was forty times greater than that of a typical factory worker in 1980; by 1989, it was ninety-three times greater. The top 1 percent of American families now possessed more assets than the bottom 90 percent—a ratio typical of Third World nations.

A series of corporate mergers and consolidations further enriched well-off Americans, as did financial speculation and manipulation on Wall Street. *Business Week* wrote of a "Casino Economy" in which insider trading and leveraged buyouts (business takeovers financed by debt) created paper wealth rather than actual products. This explosion of wealth at the top fueled an emerging culture of extravagance, reminiscent of similar trends in the late nineteenth century and in the 1920s. Newly identified "yuppies" (young urban professionals) embodied the drive for material acquisition, in contrast to the anticonsumerist inclinations of the late 1960s and early 1970s. Jerry Rubin, a member of the anarchist "yippies" in the 1960s, once dropped dollar bills onto the floor of the New York Stock Exchange—which traders scurried madly to grab—to dramatize the stock market's pursuit of profit. By the 1980s, however, Rubin was working as an investment banker. Ronald and Nancy Reagan were older but shared similar values. They relished lavish amenities like those made popular on the television shows *Dynasty*, *Dallas*, and *Lifestyles of the Rich and Famous*.

As the affluence gap widened, the broad middle class watched its job security slip. Early in the decade, the recession had prompted factory shutdowns and mass layoffs. More than a million industrial jobs disappeared in 1982 alone. Manufacturers' decisions to keep moving plants abroad for cheaper labor only worsened the situation. Although the 1980s saw the creation of 20 million new jobs, most of these were in the nonunionized service sector and offered low pay and few benefits.

The poorest Americans fared badly in the 1980s. The bottom tenth saw their already meager incomes decline by another 10 percent. In 1986 a full-time worker at minimum wage earned $6,700 per year—almost $4,000 short of the poverty level for a family of four. Homelessness worsened in cities as the government cut funding for welfare and institutional care for the mentally ill while housing costs rose. More than 1 million people lived on the streets, one-fifth of them still employed. One out of eight children went hungry and 20 percent lived in poverty, including 50 percent of black children. These Americans received minimal

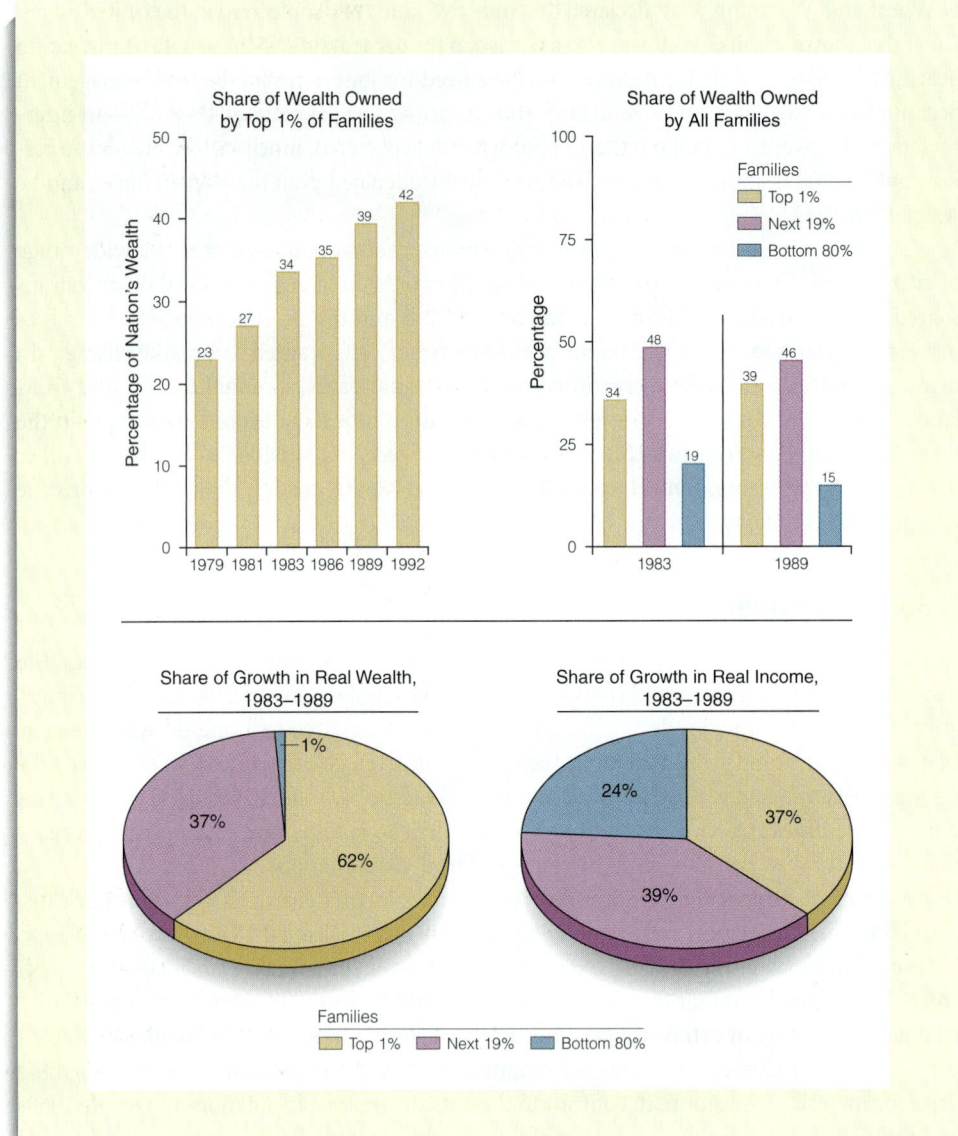

■ **FIGURE 28.1**
UNEQUAL DISTRIBUTION OF WEALTH AND INCOME The 1980s were excellent years for wealthy Americans. The "trickle-down" effect touted by some Reagan administration officials—predicting that greater wealth accumulation among the rich would trickle down to the less affluent—had little impact.

sympathy from the nation's political leaders. By contrast, Congress and the White House provided large federal subsidies to "needy" businesses such as the Chrysler Corporation and the savings and loan industry.

Despite Reagan's record, 40 percent of union household members and 50 percent of all blue-collar workers cast their ballots for this staunch opponent of unions. Why? Part of the explanation lies in the decline of working-class voting during the 1970s. Disillusioned with a political process they saw as corrupt, numerous workers neglected to go to the polls on voting day. Many of those who did vote decided that the Democratic party had become increasingly co-opted by cultural **liberalism** and no longer spoke for the working class. Reagan's charisma and appeal to patriotism also attracted many citizens who might once have voted for their economic interests instead. Finally, white Americans increasingly defined their political loyalties on the basis of social and cultural issues—such as opposition to abortion, homosexuality, and affirmative action—rather than economic interests. Conservative Christians, in particular, strongly supported the Republican cause.

Cultural Conflict

One of the nation's foremost religious figures, Reverend Pat Robertson, controlled the Christian Broadcasting Network and ran unsuccessfully for the 1988 Republican presidential nomination. Like other social conservatives of this era, he promoted "family values" and traditional gender roles. Robertson went so far as to declare that feminism "encourages women to leave their husbands, kill their children [and] practice witchcraft." In contrast, author Susan Faludi wrote the 1991 best-seller *Backlash* about opposition to the women's movement. She became an important critic of gender roles in American society and how they limit people's life experiences and possibilities. In contrast to Robertson, Faludi concluded, "All women are feminists. It's just a matter of time and encouragement."

> *Americans argued primarily about issues that had come to the fore during the social movements of the 1960s and 1970s.*

Throughout the 1980s, Americans embroiled themselves in a contentious debate about values. Their society had changed in the previous generation in ways that some citizens disdained but others applauded. Americans argued primarily about issues that had come to the fore during the social movements of the 1960s and 1970s: sexuality, gender roles, the place of religion in public life, and multiculturalism. These often bitter "culture wars" dominated talk shows and newspaper editorial pages throughout much of the last two decades of the twentieth century.

The Rise of the Religious Right

Some of the Americans most troubled by the state of American society were conservative white Protestants, disproportionately from the South. Along with conservative Catholics, they bemoaned the post-1960s shift in mainstream values away from respect for traditional authorities—the church, political leaders, and the military—and toward freer sexual expression and general self-indulgence. What the nation needed, they believed, was a return to reverence for God. The growth of Christian fundamentalism paralleled rising religious fundamentalism around the globe, whether among Jews in Israel, Hindus in India, or Muslims in Iran and the Arab Middle East. For all their differences, religious people in these cultures shared a common quest: preserving spiritual purity and cultural traditions in an increasingly secular, integrated world.

Conservative Christians were not a fringe group. As many as 45 million Americans—20 percent of the population—indentified themselves as fundamentalist Christians in 1980. In combination with a similar number of Catholics, they represented a vast potential force in American politics. And their ranks were growing, while membership in the more liberal mainline Protestant denominations, such as the Presbyterians and Episcopalians, declined steadily after the 1960s.

Conservative Christians mobilized in the 1980 campaign to support Reagan's candidacy. Critics noted that Reagan himself attended church only occasionally and seemed an indifferent father. They contrasted the divorced candidate with his born-again, Sunday-school–teaching opponent, Jimmy Carter. But Reagan's conservative views on abortion and gay rights and his support for school prayer resonated with fundamentalists. They flocked to the Republican party and to new right-wing religious organizations, such as the Moral Majority, founded in 1979 in Lynchburg, Virginia, by Reverend Jerry Falwell. More than 60 million people each week watched—and many sent money to—"televangelists," including Falwell, Robertson, and Jim Bakker.

Suffusing the GOP with a distinctly southern, grassroots flavor, the religious right also highlighted a major faultline in the modern Republican party: the tension between social conservatives, who emphasized community and tradition, and free marketeers, who promoted entrepreneurial capitalism. In its quest for profits, unrestrained capitalism had no inherent respect

INTERPRETING HISTORY

Religion and Politics in the 1980s

In 1979, Baptist minister Jerry Falwell founded the Moral Majority in Lynchburg, Virginia. The organization represented the growing engagement of conservative evangelical Christians in American politics, and Falwell emerged as the most prominent figure of the new religious right. However, not all Christians were conservative. Robert McAfee Brown, a Presbyterian minister and theologian, represented more liberal elements of the church that understood both the Bible and the problems of American society differently than Falwell.

Before he became involved in politics, Jerry Falwell had already made a name for himself as a prominent preacher in his hometown of Lynchburg, Virginia, as the senior minister of the large Thomas Road Baptist Church and the founder of Liberty University. His organization, the Moral Majority, became the most well-known conservative evangelical Christian organization of the 1980s.

The Goals of the Moral Majority (1980) by Jerry Falwell

We must reverse the trend America finds herself in today. Young people... have learned to disrespect the family as God established it. They have been educated in a public-school system that is permeated with secular humanism. They have been taught that the Bible is just another book of literature. They have been taught that there are no absolutes in our

---

for tradition. Indeed, it could bring unwelcome changes, as Rustbelt industrial workers had discovered when their employers moved south and overseas. Marrying Jesus to the market proved difficult: should the state play a minimal role in the economy and society, as free-market libertarians believed, or should it monitor personal behavior, as social conservatives implied?

Gender and sexuality issues particularly aroused the ire of religious conservatives. They blamed feminism for weakening male authority in the family and for increasing divorce rates. A growing antiabortion movement gained national visibility by 1980, and religious conservatives opposed Americans' slowly increasing acceptance of gays and lesbians. Dismayed by the prevalence of casual sexual relationships in the 1970s, church conservatives urged abstinence on young Americans.

The heyday of the sexual revolution ended in the early 1980s, when researchers identified the human immunodeficiency virus (HIV), which causes acquired immunodeficiency syndrome (AIDS). The deadly epidemic spread swiftly through the gay male communities of San Francisco and New York as a result of unprotected sex. AIDS continued to spread during the 1990s and beyond, among gays and heterosexuals, both in the United States and abroad—especially in such places as China, southern Africa, and Russia. New drugs slowed the onset of actual AIDS in many HIV-infected Americans while scientists continued the frustrating quest for a cure.

Yet another epidemic swept through the United States during the 1980s, striking impoverished urban neighborhoods especially hard. The culprit was crack cocaine. Powerfully addic-

world today. . . . These same young people have been reared under the influence of a government that has taught them socialism and welfarism. . . .

I personally feel that the home and the family are still held in reverence by the vast majority of the American public. I believe there is still a vast number of Americans who love their country, are patriotic, and are willing to sacrifice for her. I remember that time when it was positive to be patriotic. . . . I remember as a boy. . . when the band struck up "The Stars and Stripes Forever," we stood and goose pimples would run all over me. . . .

It is now time to take a stand on certain moral issues. . . . We must stand against the Equal Rights Amendment, the feminist revolution, and the homosexual revolution. . . .

Americans have been silent much too long. We have stood by and watched as American power and influence have been systematically weakened in every sphere of the world. . . .

The hope of reversing the trends of decay in our republic now lies with the Christian public in America. We cannot expect help from the liberals. They certainly are not going to call our nation back to righteousness and neither are the pornographers, the smut peddlers, and those who are corrupting our youth.

The Politics of the Bible (1982) by Robert McAfee Brown

In Christian terms, and I think in terms with which all Jews could also agree, my real complaint about the Moral Majority's intrusion of the Bible into American politics, is that they are not biblical enough. . . .

The Moral Majority's biblically inspired political agenda involves a very selective, very partial, and therefore very distorted use of the Bible. They have isolated a set of concerns that they say get to the heart of what is wrong with America—homosexuality, abortion, and pornography. . . .

Take the issue of homosexuality. If one turns to the scriptures as a whole, to try to come up with their central concerns, homosexuality is going to be very low on such a list even if indeed it makes the list at all. There are perhaps seven very ambiguous verses in the whole biblical canon that even allude to it. . . . [But there are] hundreds and hundreds of places where the scriptures are dealing over and over again with question of social justice, the tendency of the rich to exploit the poor, the need for all of us to have a commitment to the hungry, . . . [and] the dangers of national idolatry, that is to say, making the nation into God, accepting uncritically whatever we have to do as a nation against other nations. . . .

When one looks over the agenda of the Moral Majority there is absolutely no mention of such things. . . . We seem to be living in two different worlds, reading two different books.

Questions

1. Which specific issues in American society most trouble Jerry Falwell? What specifically about "liberals" does he seem most unhappy about?
2. What does Robert McAfee Brown find most unpersuasive about Jerry Falwell's use of the Bible to understand American society and its problems?
3. Which of these two interpretations do you find most persuasive, and why?

Source: Irwin Unger and Robert R. Tomes, *American Issues*, 2nd ed. (Prentice-Hall, 1999), vol. 2, pp. 362–364, 375–377.

---

tive, it contributed to gang violence and record homicide rates in several cities. Drug-related convictions skyrocketed, stimulating a boom in prison building, a doubling of the nation's inmate population, and new police special weapons and tactics (SWAT) teams to deal with heavily armed drug operators.

Dissenters Push Back

The liberal and radical reform energies that had percolated in the late 1960s and early 1970s did not evaporate entirely in the conservative 1980s. Nuclear threats engaged activists from both the peace and environmental movements. The accidents at Three Mile Island (1979) and Chernobyl (1986) intensified public anxieties about the dangers of nuclear energy and nuclear weapons. The sharp increases in both Soviet and U.S. nuclear arsenals alarmed residents in those countries and across Europe, where many of the missiles were located. The broad-based nuclear freeze movement that emerged in the United States and western Europe in the early 1980s encouraged arms control negotiations that would bear fruit a few years later.

Racial justice remained a primary concern for Americans of color and liberal and leftist activists, particularly in light of the Republican administration's opposition to affirmative action. Determined to honor the foremost leader of the civil rights movement, antiracists convinced Congress in 1983 to designate Martin Luther King Jr.'s birthday a national holiday. By 1985 a robust antiapartheid movement successfully campaigned to reduce U.S. investments in racially segregated South Africa. Perhaps the most prominent face of left-leaning politics in the decade was that of Reverend Jesse Jackson, a former aide to Martin Luther King Jr. Jackson sought the Democratic nomination for president in 1984 and 1988, winning a handful of primaries in 1988 with his multiracial Rainbow Coalition. Jackson's candidacy encouraged several million African Americans to register to vote for the first time.

> *Gays and lesbians remained the only Americans against whom tens of millions of their fellow citizens openly believed it acceptable to discriminate.*

Gay rights advocates also raised their voices in the 1980s. Faced with the twin scourge of AIDS and homophobic violence, homosexuals and their heterosexual supporters lobbied for the inclusion of sexual orientation as a category of discrimination in civil rights laws. Others took to the streets, organized by the militant organization AIDS Coalition to Unleash Power (ACT-UP). In October 1987, nearly half a million Americans marched in Washington in support of gay rights. A few widely admired figures, such as tennis champion Martina Navratilova, publicly acknowledged their homosexuality, helping others to view this sexual orientation as acceptable rather than deviant. By the end of the 1980s, the record was mixed. Gays and lesbians remained the only Americans against whom tens of millions of their fellow citizens openly believed it acceptable to discriminate, but the rights of homosexuals, nonetheless, had much wider support than ever before.

The New Immigration

For two decades after the restrictive immigration law of 1924, the flow of newcomers from abroad had slowed to a trickle. The trickle became a stream again after World War II, and then legislation in 1965 opened the gates even wider. As a result, a wave of new immigrants, 3.3 million in the 1960s and 4.5 million in the 1970s, hit the United States. In the 1980s 7.3 million people entered the country legally, along with a similar number without documentation.

These newcomers brought an unprecedented cultural and ethnic diversity. Only 10 percent of the most recent arrivals in the United States were Europeans. Forty percent came instead from Asia—particularly China, the Philippines, and South Korea—and 50 percent from Latin America and the Caribbean, particularly Mexico. From 1965 to 1995, 7 million Latinos and 5 million Asians moved to the United States.

The new immigrants came for the same reasons their predecessors had. Many were fleeing political and religious persecution in their home countries, but most sought new economic opportunity. A small number, primarily from South Korea and Hong Kong, arrived with some assets that helped them get started in business. However, most came with few resources and took what work they could find in garment sweatshops, on farms, as domestic servants and janitors, and as gardeners. These immigrants willingly endured profound hardship to build better lives for their families. They also rekindled the nation's long-standing cultural diversity, especially in Sunbelt cities from Miami, Florida, to San Diego, California. In 1981 citizens of San Antonio elected Henry Cisneros

■ While immigrants brought their own distinctive cultures to the United States, American popular culture spread abroad. The broadcast of National Basketball Association (NBA) games in dozens of other countries helped basketball climb to being the world's second most popular game (after soccer). Personable stars like Earvin "Magic" Johnson of the Los Angeles Lakers and particularly Michael Jordan of the Chicago Bulls became popular icons around the world.

as the first Mexican American mayor of a major city. In Los Angeles, one-third of residents were foreign born by 1990.

Most Americans had foreign-born ancestors who had come to the United States with the same dreams that motivated the newest arrivals. Still, the non-European origins of the latest immigrants troubled some white citizens. Conservatives, in particular, worried about the growing diversity of American society and feared a decline of the Eurocentric culture they had grown up with. They were also anxious that poor immigrants might drain taxpayers' dollars by winding up on welfare. The Immigration and Naturalization Service (INS) stepped up patrols of the 2,000-mile U.S. border with Mexico to limit the rising number of undocumented Mexican workers heading north. By the early 1990s, the INS was apprehending and expelling 1.7 million undocumented workers every year.

America' Move to the Sunbelt, 1970–1981

The End of the Cold War

For Americans, the greatest surprise of the 1980s was the warming of U.S.-Soviet relations after 1985. Few imagined such a scenario during Reagan's first two years in office, when his administration became the first in four decades not to collaborate on nuclear arms control with the USSR. But in the Soviet Union, the rise to power of Communist party reformer Mikhail Gorbachev permanently changed the face of international politics. The American president finally agreed to work toward the common goal of reducing tensions between the two superpowers. Reagan eventually traveled to Moscow, embraced Gorbachev in front of Lenin's tomb, and announced that the Soviets had changed.

At the same time, the Reagan administration stumbled badly at home when a scandal involving Iran and the Nicaraguan counterrevolutionaries (Contras) came to light in 1986. The disaster revealed a secret foreign policy apparatus and a president out of touch with the daily governance process. Dramatic events in Europe then unfolded with little input from the administrations of either Reagan or George H. W. Bush, his successor in the White House. In 1989 eastern Europeans tore down the Berlin Wall and ended Soviet rule in their countries. Two years later, the Soviet Union unraveled into its separate components, Russia being the largest. The end of the Cold War enabled Bush to focus on the Middle East, where an international force drove Iraq out of occupied Kuwait and reestablished the status quo in that oil-rich region.

From Cold War to Détente

By the 1980s, the USSR's state-run economy was creaking to a halt. It simply could not provide the consumer products that Soviet citizens had learned about from the world outside their borders. Events further weakened the authority of the Soviet government. The USSR's occupation of Afghanistan became a quagmire resembling the United States' disastrous involvement in Vietnam, and the last Soviet troops finally withdrew in 1989. Initial government efforts to cover up the nuclear accident at Chernobyl only worsened matters, revealing the costs of corrupt communist rule. Nationalist movements for independence in the Baltic states, the Caucasus region, and central Asia gathered momentum. In his six years in power (1985–1991), Gorbachev tried to preserve the Soviet system by reforming it through *glasnost* (greater political liberty) and *perestroika* (economic restructuring allowing some private enterprise). However, his government proved unable to control the forces for change that it had helped unleash.

Reagan's primary role in ending the Cold War was to support Gorbachev's quest for change within the Soviet Union. To that end, Reagan moved from confrontational rhetoric to pursuing a policy of détente. Gorbachev became head of the Soviet Communist party in 1985, at the start of Reagan's second term. The American president had already built up the U.S. military and was now thinking about his place in history. He wanted to leave office having earned a reputation as a peacemaker.

Beneath Reagan's strident rhetoric about national military strength ran a streak of radical idealism, including a desire to eliminate the threat of nuclear warfare. The Soviet downing of a Korean Air Lines civilian jet in 1983 reminded him and others of the tragic costs of making mistakes with weapons. Once he felt convinced of Gorbachev's seriousness about internal reform and rapprochement with the United States, Reagan took action. In 1987 the two leaders signed the Intermediate Nuclear Force (INF) treaty. The agreement removed short-range and intermediate-range missiles from Europe and enabled each side to conduct on-site verification of the other side's compliance. The INF treaty marked the first actual reduction in the total number of nuclear weapons stored in the two nations' arsenals.

The Iran-Contra Scandal

Failures elsewhere offset Reagan's success with the Russians. His administration suffered its worst damage when it tried through illegal means to solve two foreign policy challenges with one stroke. Its main strategy consisted of linking a problem in the Middle East with one in Central America.

Revolutionary fervor intensified in the Middle East after the 1979 Iranian revolution, and hostage-taking and terrorism—the "poor man's nuclear bomb"—proliferated. In 1986 Americans bombed the Libyan capital of Tripoli in retaliation for apparent Libyan involvement in the killing of two U.S. soldiers in Germany. In 1988 things took an even nastier turn when an American warship in the Persian Gulf killed 290 civilians by shooting down an Iranian airliner, apparently by mistake. In revenge, pro-Iranian agents exploded a bomb on Pan Am Flight 109 over Lockerbie, Scotland, before the end of the year, killing eleven on the ground and 259 aboard the plane, including thirty-five students from Syracuse University.

Islamic revolutionaries also threatened moderate Arab leaders and assassinated Egyptian president Anwar Sadat in 1981. Lebanon became the center of a radical anti-Israeli campaign to seize Americans as hostages, especially after the United States' 1983 engagement against Muslim forces in the civil war there. Despite his 1980 campaign promise never to negotiate with terrorists, Reagan approved the illegal sale of U.S. arms to Iran in return for the freeing of a handful of hostages held by pro-Iranian radicals in Lebanon.

Events were heating up in Central America as well. The CIA-created Contras failed to overturn the new Sandinista government in Nicaragua. Even though the Contras lacked public support in Nicaragua and the United States, the president and his advisers were determined to keep them afloat. But they had a problem: how to fund the effort. Most Americans did not share Reagan's enthusiasm for the Contras and feared greater U.S. military involvement in Central America. Congress passed the Boland Amendments, restricting aid to the Nicaraguan counterrevolutionaries. Faced with their chief's expressed desire to shore up the Contra cause, the president's men found an alternative solution.

The National Security Council (NSC) established a secret operation run by staff member Lieutenant Colonel Oliver North. Free from public or congressional oversight, North worked closely with CIA director William Casey. North and his colleagues solicited funds for the Contras from wealthy, conservative Americans and from sympathetic foreign governments, including Saudi Arabia and Taiwan. Then North hit on what he called the "neat idea" of "using the Ayatollah Khomeini's money to support the Nicaraguan freedom fighters." Iran desperately needed weapons for its war against neighboring Iraq (1980–1988), so North and his colleagues started diverting profits to the Contras from new sales of U.S. Army property to Teheran.

The NSC's action was illegal: it sold U.S. government property without authorization from the Pentagon, and it broke U.S. laws banning aid to the Contras. When news of the operation finally leaked out in November 1986, it shocked the nation. What did the president know, and when did he know it? The old Watergate question about Richard Nixon came to the fore again. Reagan called North a "national hero" but claimed ignorance of any illegal activities, including the diversion of funds from Iranian arms sales to the Nicaraguan rebels.

But in early 1987, 90 percent of Americans did not believe Reagan was telling all he knew. His job approval ratings dropped from 67 percent to 46 percent. The first round of memoirs by former aides also appeared in the final years of his administration, revealing an isolated president out of touch with the government he nominally headed. For example, the former actor breezily admitted that he was happiest when "each morning I get a piece of paper that tells me what I do all day long."

A Global Policeman?

Despite running a bruising presidential campaign in 1988, Reagan's vice president, George H. W. Bush, proved cautious once in office. Hemmed in by a Democratic-controlled Congress, he had what his chief of staff called a "limited agenda" at home. His most enduring domestic action came with his 1991 appointment of archconservative Clarence Thomas, an African American lawyer from Georgia, to fill the seat of retiring Supreme Court justice Thurgood Marshall. Only forty-three years old and with little experience as a judge, Thomas was chosen because of his conservative views and his race. The Senate narrowly confirmed him, 52–48, after contentious hearings in which a former aide, Anita Hill, accused Thomas of sexual harassment.

TABLE 28-3
The Election of 1988

Candidate	Political Party	Popular Vote (%)	Electoral Vote
George H. W. Bush	Republican	53.4	426
Michael S. Dukakis	Democratic	45.6	111

DOCUMENT

George H.W. Bush, Inaugural Address (January 1989)

"I much prefer foreign affairs," the president once confided in his diary. Some of the most dramatic events of the twentieth century unfolded during his presidency. Poles, Czechs, and Hungarians—encouraged by Gorbachev's promise not to intervene militarily in other Warsaw Pact nations—peacefully overthrew their communist rulers in 1989. East Germans did the same. The Berlin Wall—the twenty-eight-year-old symbol of Cold War tensions—finally toppled on November 8. Three months later, anti-apartheid leader Nelson Mandela walked out of the South African prison where he had been held for twenty-seven years. The white supremacist government there agreed to hold the first elections in which all South Africans could vote. The Baltic states of Lithuania, Latvia, and Estonia seceded from the USSR in 1990 and 1991. After a failed coup attempt by Communist hard-liners in August 1991, the Soviet Union broke into its sixteen constituent states. Russian president Boris Yeltsin replaced Gorbachev as the major figure in Moscow.

In Panama, under the brutal leadership of Manuel Noriega, tensions grew between the Panamanian Defense Forces (PDF) and U.S. soldiers based in the Canal Zone. Noriega deepened his lucrative role as an intermediary in smuggling Colombian cocaine into the United States. Meanwhile, the crack-cocaine epidemic tightened its grip in poor American neighborhoods. Rising popular concern about crack-related violence increased Americans' willingness to take action against Noriega. When the dictator overturned Panamanian election results that went against him and further confrontations erupted between American and Panamanian soldiers, Bush decided to step in.

In December 1989, 24,000 U.S. troops invaded the small Central American nation. They crushed the PDF, and thousands of civilians died in the crossfire. Noriega eventually surrendered and was brought to Miami, where he was convicted of drug trafficking and imprisoned.

Developments in the Middle East provoked the most important move of the George H. W. Bush administration: the initiation of the Persian Gulf War of 1991. In 1990 Iraq invaded tiny, neighboring, oil-rich Kuwait, annexing it as Iraq's "nineteenth province." With Americans and their Japanese and European allies dependent on Middle Eastern oil, Bush declared the invasion unacceptable. He rushed more than 200,000 troops to Saudi Arabia in "Operation Desert Shield" to discourage further aggression by Iraqi leader Saddam Hussein. At the same time, the United Nations slapped economic sanctions on Iraq.

Within three months, Bush shifted his attention to liberating Kuwait. He doubled the number of U.S. troops in the region to 430,000. He also gained the support of the UN, which demanded Iraqi withdrawal by January 15, 1991. The U.S. Congress backed him as well, voting to support any actions necessary to drive Iraq out of Kuwait. Bush went on the offensive because he faced a shrinking window of opportunity. He had wide international support, including troops from several Arab nations, but growing clashes in Jerusalem between Israelis and Palestinians threatened to break up this alliance by rekindling Arab anger at Israel.

VIDEO
Bush's Early Response in the Persian Gulf War

■ **MAP 28.2**
THE SOVIET BLOC DISSOLVES No change in world politics since World War II was greater than the collapse of the Soviet Union and its satellite states in eastern Europe. Eastern European countries soon sought membership in NATO and post-Communist Russia built closer relations with the United States and western Europe. The transition from socialist to capitalist economies was difficult, however, and many poorer citizens found daily life little easier than it had been before.

The Soviet Union and the Communist bloc in Eastern Europe dissolve
- Former Union of Soviet Socialist Republics (USSR), dissolved 1991
- Eastern European countries that overturned Communist rule, 1989–1990

On January 16, 1991, U.S.-led coalition forces began five and a half weeks of bombing against Iraq. Then, on February 25, coalition forces poured across the border from Saudi Arabia in "Operation Desert Storm." The offensive freed Kuwait and sent Iraqi troops in headlong retreat toward Baghdad. The Iraqis burned oil wells as they fell back, blanketing the battlefield in smoke. Four days later, Bush halted the U.S.-led advance, having restored Kuwaiti sovereignty. Saddam Hussein remained in power and later crushed uprisings by Iraqi dissidents. The politics of coalition warfare helped prohibit further U.S. action, for no Arabs wanted Americans ruling Iraq.

The Gulf War's outcome seemed to validate two strategic lessons that U.S. commanders had learned during the Vietnam War. The first was the importance of preserving absolute control of the media. During the Persian Gulf conflict, the Pentagon kept journalists away from most of the action to control the images that Americans saw of the fighting. The public viewed endless videos of "smart" bombs hitting their targets in Baghdad but none of the tens of thousands of Iraqi soldiers being slaughtered during their retreat from Kuwait. Second, General Colin Powell, the African American chair of the Joint Chiefs of Staff who emerged from the war as a national hero, insisted on marshaling overwhelmingly superior forces before going into battle, thus ensuring the success of the operation.

The Middle East in the 1980s and 1990s

The Gulf War seemed to demonstrate a U.S. willingness to act as a global police force in the post–Cold War era. Bush claimed at a 1992 international environmental conference that, when it came to oil, "the American lifestyle is not negotiable." But the war also stimulated the further growth of anti-Americanism among Islamic revolutionaries, including Saudi-born Osama bin Laden; they considered it sacrilege for non-Muslim American soldiers to operate bases in Saudi Arabia, home to Mecca, Islam's holiest site.

Conclusion

The Republican era of Ronald Reagan and George H. W. Bush reshaped American relations with the rest of the world, as well as politics and economics in the United States. Both sets of changes hinged on the elevation of individualism and market forces above communal values and government planning. The collective dreams represented by the Soviet experiment evaporated into history in these years, leaving capitalism unchallenged as a system of economic organization across most of the globe. U.S. military power stepped into the vacuum left by the Soviet demise, most visibly in the 1991 Persian Gulf War. But that military revival came at the cost of vast deficit spending and a sharp recession in 1991–1992, which paved the way for Bill Clinton's victory over Bush in the 1992 presidential campaign.

Sites to Visit

Digital Atlas of the United States, 1990
http://geogdata.csun.edu/USpage1.html
This site offers an overview of the geography and demography of the U.S. population in 1990.

Immigrant Fact Sheet, 1996
www.uscis.gov/graphics/shared/aboutus/statistics/110.htm
The U.S. Immigration and Naturalization Service posted this site with historical statistics about immigration into the United States, especially from 1981 to 1996.

Divining America: Religion and the National Culture
www.nhc.rtp.nc.us:8080/tserve/divam.htm
This site has essays by prominent historians on diverse aspects of the religious history of the United States.

Ronald Wilson Reagan
www.ipl.org/div/potus/rwreagan.html
The Internet Public Library maintains this site, which has essential information about Reagan and his presidential administration as well as his most important speeches.

National Security Archive at George Washington University
www.gwu.edu/~nsarchiv/

This excellent site includes the most recent declassified documents on the making of U.S. foreign policy.

Cold War International History Project
http://www.wilsoncenter.org/index.cfm?topic_id=1409&fuseaction=topics.home

The Woodrow Wilson International Center for Scholars maintains this site, which offers newly released documents and up-to-date interpretive essays on the American-Soviet struggle.

Persian Gulf War
www.pbs.org/wgbh/pages/frontline/gulf/

The Public Broadcasting System's *Frontline* series created this site with information about the Persian Gulf War, including oral histories of U.S. commanders and of Americans taken as prisoners of war.

For Further Reading

General

Frances FitzGerald, *Way Out There in the Blue: Reagan, Star Wars, and the End of the Cold War* (2000).

James Patterson, *Restless Giant: The United States from Watergate to Bush v. Gore* (2005).

Neil Postman, *Amusing Ourselves to Death: Public Discourse in the Age of Show Business* (1985).

Ronald Reagan, *Reagan, In His Own Hand: The Writings of Ronald Reagan That Reveal His Revolutionary Vision for America* (2001).

Michael Schaller, *Reckoning with Reagan: America and Its President in the 1980s* (1992).

Anticommunism Revived

James A. Bill, *The Eagle and the Lion: The Tragedy of American-Iranian Relations* (1988).

David Farber, *Taken Hostage: The Iran Hostage Crisis and America's First Encounter with Radical Islam* (2004).

Thomas Ferguson and Joel Rogers, eds., *The Hidden Election: Politics and Economics in the 1980 Presidential Campaign* (1981).

Walter LaFeber, *Inevitable Revolutions: The United States in Central America*, 2nd ed. (1993).

William E. Pemberton, *Exit with Honor: The Life and Presidency of Ronald Reagan* (1998).

Republican Rule at Home

Thomas Byrne Edsall and Mary D. Edsall, *Chain Reaction: The Impact of Race, Rights and Taxes on American Politics* (1991).

Barbara Ehrenreich, *The Worst Years of Our Lives: Irreverent Notes from a Decade of Greed* (1990).

J. R. McNeill, *Something New Under the Sun: An Environmental History of the Twentieth-Century World* (2000).

Kevin Phillips, *The Politics of Rich and Poor: Wealth and the American Electorate in the Reagan Aftermath* (1990).

Cultural Conflict

Todd Gitlin, *The Twilight of Common Dreams: Why America Is Wracked by Culture Wars* (1995).

Martin E. Marty and R. Scott Appleby, *The Glory and the Power: The Fundamentalist Challenge to the Modern World* (1992).

David M. Reimers, *Still the Golden Door: The Third World Comes to America*, 2nd ed. (1992).

Randy Shilts, *And the Band Played On: Politics, People and the AIDS Epidemic* (1987).

The End of the Cold War

Theodore Draper, *A Very Thin Line: The Iran-Contra Affairs* (1991).

John Robert Greene, *The Presidency of George Bush* (2000).

Dilip Hiro, *Desert Shield to Desert Storm: The Second Gulf War* (1992).

Michael J. Hogan, ed., *The End of the Cold War: Its Meanings and Implications* (1992).

For quizzes and other resources on these topics, go to www.longmanamericanhistory.com.

Post–Cold War America, 1991–2000

CHAPTER

29

O N A COLD DECEMBER NIGHT IN 1997, TWENTY-THREE-YEAR-OLD JULIA BUTTERFLY HILL climbed onto a small platform that had been constructed 180 feet above ground in a giant redwood tree in a forest in Humboldt County, California. She remained there for two years, trespassing in an act of civil disobedience on the property of the Pacific Lumber Company, which was threatening to cut down the 1,000-year-old tree as part of its logging operations. Julia Hill had not planned to become an internationally famous environmental activist. She grew up in Arkansas, the daughter of an itinerant preacher. When friends invited the restless young woman to join them on a drive to California, she eagerly went along. "I had been on a journey, searching for my purpose in life," she recalled. "I ended up finding it in the redwoods."

Hill's spiritual connection to the forest drew her to political activism, and she joined Earth First!, an environmental group that was working to save the redwoods from the logging industry. She discovered that 97 percent of the old-growth redwoods had already been destroyed and that the rest were threatened by clear-cutting, toxins, and diesel fuel. Tree sitting was a strategy the Earth First! activists developed to protest the destruction of the trees.

■ Julia Butterfly Hill in the giant redwood tree she named "Luna."

Those two years were rough. The young woman survived rain and hail storms, 90-mile-per-hour winds that tossed the tiny platform into the air, and bone-chilling cold that turned her feet black. Friends and supporters provided her with food and other supplies using a rope pulley. She ate mostly raw fruits and vegetables, slept in a hammock, took sponge baths, and used a bucket for a toilet. She faced harassment from the logging company and derision from some skeptics. But she also had a powerful network of supporters and celebrities who raised money, brought her food, and publicized her protest.

Hill's effort to save an ancient tree as old as the last millennium was conducted using the global technology of the new millennium. Critical to the success of her protest was her ability to

CHAPTER OUTLINE

The Economy: Global and Domestic

Tolerance and Its Limits

Violence and Danger

The Clinton Presidency

The Nation and the World

The Contested Election of 2000

Conclusion

Sites to Visit

For Further Reading

communicate with the entire world from her treetop perch. She set up an Internet Web site on the Internet visited by people from across the globe. She used a solar-powered cell phone to speak with radio stations, schools, rallies, religious groups, reporters, and talk-show hosts. The lumber company also used state-of-the-art technology in its efforts to stymie her protest, cutting down trees to make them fall in her direction, flying helicopters to hover noisily over her head, and using air horns to keep her awake at night.

The president of Pacific Lumber, John Campbell, eventually came to the tree to negotiate with Hill, and they made a deal. The company agreed never to cut down the tree or other trees in a 2.9-acre buffer zone. Hill agreed to come down. For her civil disobedience, she paid a $50,000 fine, contributed by supporters, which the court designated to Humboldt State University for forestry research.

Activists such as Julia Butterfly Hill addressed political concerns through personal beliefs and direct action. They were part of social movements that evolved out of a century of such protests. In the 1990s, the issues had reached a global scale. Internationally, Cold War power struggles gave way to other issues: regional and civil wars, ethnic strife, the environment and global warming, trade and labor relations, and terrorism.

In the United States, the economy expanded throughout the 1990s. Increasing numbers of Americans invested in the soaring stock market, many for the first time. The crime rate declined. Yet the strong economy also emboldened consumers to buy and use products and resources, such as huge gas-guzzling sport utility vehicles, with little concern for their environmental impact.

In national politics, the rifts between liberals and conservatives that had opened up in the 1960s persisted. Struggles over cultural issues such as abortion and gay rights polarized the political climate. In 1992 Democrats took back the White House, but in 1994 Republicans swept into control of Congress with a conservative agenda, hemming in President Bill Clinton, a Democrat of liberal social inclinations who, nonetheless, presided over the final destruction of the Aid to Families with Dependent Children (AFDC) program, the central feature of the national welfare system since the New Deal of the 1930s. In 2000 the Supreme Court decided one of the closest and most divisive elections in the nation's history, handing the White House to the Republican candidate, George W. Bush, son of the former president.

The post–Cold War era raised new questions about the role of the United States in the world. Americans no longer looked to Russia as a threat but to new international foes, especially terrorist networks operating outside the authority of particular countries. Within the nation, episodes of domestic terrorism, such as the bombing of a federal building in Oklahoma City and a series of school shootings by children, made Americans aware that dangers lurked within their previously safe havens.

The Economy: Global and Domestic

After the sharp recession of 1991–1992, by nearly all measures, the economy expanded in the 1990s. The stock market boomed, unemployment declined, and most Americans appeared to be better off financially at the end of the decade than at the beginning. But the overall growth of the economy did not benefit everyone, and many actually lost ground—especially those who lost jobs to mechanization, nonunionized workers who toiled for low wages under grim working conditions, and the nation's most vulnerable workers: poor single mothers, new immigrants, and unskilled people of color.

The Post–Cold War Economy

The end of the Cold War had a profound effect on the nation's economy. The demise of the Soviet Union put a final end to the arms race against a superpower foe and made cutting the defense budget politically acceptable. But the closing of defense-related plants in southern California, once the center of the nation's Cold War defense contracts that absorbed nearly a fifth of all federal defense dollars, devastated the regional economy. By the mid-1990s, half the workers in the southern California aerospace industry had been laid off.

While defense industries shrank, the technology sector of the economy expanded, opening up new opportunities for young computer experts and entrepreneurs and generating fortunes for corporate executives. At the same time, mergers of giant multinational companies concentrated wealth and power in an ever-smaller number of ever-larger corporations. In the last three years of the decade, mergers totaled $5 trillion. Media giants America Online and Time-Warner merged in 2000. In 2001 Nestlé bought Ralston-Purina for $10 billion. Many of the largest mergers crossed national boundaries, such as German automobile maker Daimler-Benz and U.S. Chrysler.

While corporations expanded, so did efforts to control their power. Microsoft initially lost an antitrust suit that ordered the computer software giant to be split into two companies. Microsoft appealed the ruling in 2001, and ultimately the Justice Department settled the suit with minor sanctions against the company. The controversial settlement generated opposition. Nine states that participated in the original suit refused to endorse the agreement, and calls for tougher penalties continued. In several states, civil suits against huge tobacco companies limited cigarette advertising and marketing and levied fines on tobacco companies totaling in the billions of dollars.

The nation's elite were not the only ones to capitalize on new entrepreneurial opportunities. The 1988 Indian Gaming Regulatory Act enabled Native Americans to build lucrative Las Vegas–style casinos on tribal lands, bringing new jobs and an estimated $4 billion a year to formerly impoverished communities. The Mashantucket Pequot east of Hartford, Connecticut, opened Foxwoods in 1992, and it quickly became the largest casino in the Western Hemisphere. The Oneida followed suit a few years later with the Turning Stone casino near Utica, New York. In Arizona casinos brought in $830 million a year. Some Indian casinos failed, however, and gambling always took a largely hidden toll in the losses of already poor local residents. Native Americans remained divided about the wisdom of trying to profit from America's growing inclination to take risks in hopes of winning big.

The Widening Gap Between Rich and Poor

In the last decade of the century, the bottom 60 percent of the population saw their real income decline, even as the economy boomed. Accumulated wealth—property and investments—was an even better measure of security and influence, and the top 1 percent of Americans owned more wealth than the bottom 90 percent combined. Microsoft chair Bill Gates alone was wealthier than the bottom 45 percent of all U.S. households together. Famed capitalist J. P. Morgan had maintained a century earlier that no corporate chieftain should earn more than twenty times what his workers were paid, but by 1980 a typical chief executive of a large U.S. company took home forty times the earnings of an average factory worker; by 1990 the ratio had grown to eighty-five times, and by 2004 it reached 431 times.

■ Casino Sandia on the Sandia Pueblo in New Mexico. Many Native American communities across the country built gambling facilities on tribal lands. Although casinos brought needed income, they remained controversial.

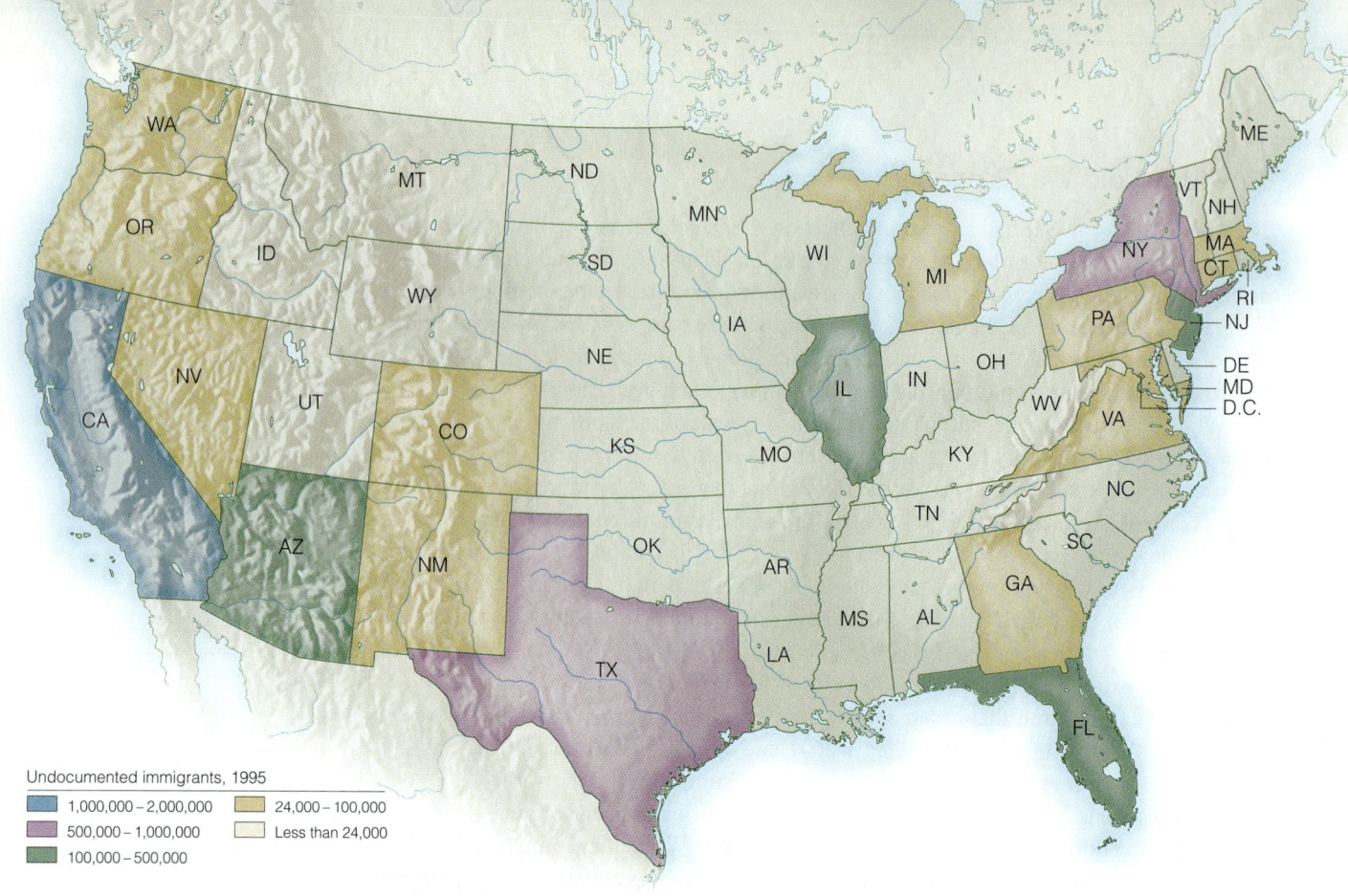

MAP 29.1
STATES WITH LARGE NUMBERS OF UNDOCUMENTED IMMIGRANTS, 1995 Fully 77 percent of all undocumented immigrants entered the country legally, with visas in hand. During the 1990s, the total proportion of the foreign born in the United States, including those with and without legal status, increased from 9 to 11 percent, still less than the 15 percent in 1900. Immigrants paid $133 billion dollars annually in local, state, and federal taxes, and generated an annual contribution to the American economy in the range of $25 to $30 billion.

Although one-third of the nation's African Americans were part of the middle class, black families had fewer assets and resources, making their hold on middle-class status more precarious than that of their white peers. The poorest African Americans were concentrated in low-paying jobs, lacking the quality health care and education that would make social and economic mobility possible. Full-time employment did not necessarily mean an escape from poverty. Among fully employed black heads of households without a high school education, 40 percent of the women and 25 percent of the men did not earn enough to achieve economic self-sufficiency. Almost 50 percent of all black children lived in households below the poverty line, compared to 16 percent of white children. The rate of unemployment was more than twice as high for blacks as for whites.

Recent immigrants from Asia, Africa, and Latin America joined African Americans in jobs at the bottom of the economy. Despite the controversy over illegal immigration, a quarter of a million undocumented workers toiled in the fields of agribusiness. At the same time, 2 percent of able-bodied citizens were in jail, nearly half of them black, because of the arrest and incarceration policies of the "war on drugs" that hit minority communities particularly hard. Prisoners were often required to work while incarcerated. Convicts provided data entry, packed golf balls, and filled a wide array of jobs for less than minimum wage, and most of their earnings went back to the government. These and other workers at the bottom of the labor force gained little or nothing from the economic boom of the 1990s.

Labor Unions

Low-wage workers in the service industries had one advantage over laborers working for multinational corporations: their jobs could not be exported. Many service workers organized successfully for better wages and working conditions. In 2000, for example, striking janitors of Service Employees International Union Local 1877 in Los Angeles achieved a wage increase of 26 percent, raising their hourly pay from less than $8 to more than $10. This was a tremendous triumph for a union whose membership was 98 percent immigrant: 80 percent Central Americans, more than half women, and all of them poor.

Other service workers also won improved contracts. Unionized hotel workers in San Francisco negotiated a five-year contract that increased pay for the lowest-paid workers, room cleaners and dishwashers, by 25 percent, from $12 to $15 an hour. In Las Vegas, African American hotel worker Hattie Canty helped organize 40,000 employees of large casino hotels. Yatta Staples went out on the picket line in front of the Minneapolis hotel where she worked as a waitress, telling reporters, "I'll stay here as long as it takes." In the summer of 1997, 185,000 Teamsters went on strike against the United Parcel Service and won an improved contract with higher wages and benefits for part-time as well as full-time workers.

■ Sweatshops like this one in the 1990s resemble those of a century earlier. Immigrant women labor in garment factories, working long hours in difficult conditions for meager wages.

Strikes did little to benefit nonunionized workers, especially undocumented immigrants, and sweatshop laborers both inside and outside the United States. There were some attempts to improve working conditions for those most exploited by the global economy. In April 1997, representatives from clothing manufacturers, human rights groups, and labor organizations drafted an agreement that tried to improve conditions for garment workers around the world. Companies that agreed to the voluntary pact would limit work weeks to sixty hours, with a maximum of twelve hours of overtime. The companies had to pay "at least the minimum wage required by local law or the prevailing industry wage, whichever is higher." The pact forbade children under fifteen to work and contained policies protecting workers from harassment and unsafe working environments.

Tolerance and Its Limits

Racial discrimination had eased over the course of the twentieth century, but persistent inequalities of power and economic opportunity continued to disadvantage Americans of color, who remained disproportionately poor, in prison, and on welfare. The economic downturn of the early 1990s widened the chasm between affluent white and poor nonwhite Americans. Highly publicized incidents of police brutality directed against Americans of color generated protests and, occasionally, violence. Nevertheless, there were signs that Americans were becoming more tolerant of one another and more willing to accept and even appreciate their diversity.

"We Can All Get Along"

Shortly after midnight on March 3, 1991, police pulled over Rodney King, an African American motorist, after a high-speed chase on a Los Angeles freeway. The four officers dragged the unarmed black man from his car and kicked and beat him with their batons for fifteen minutes. A bystander recorded the beating on videotape, which was broadcast repeatedly on national television, sparking outrage among Americans of all races.

At the highly publicized trial in April 1992, defense lawyers for the police officers argued that King, who was clearly cowering on the videotape, was resisting arrest and that the police responded appropriately. The jury of ten whites, one Asian, and one Latino acquitted the officers. The acquittal ignited five days of rioting in the African American community of South Central Los Angeles, leaving fifty-eight people dead and $1 billion in property destroyed. Community leaders called for calm; even Rodney King implored the public: "We can all get along. We've just got to." Months later, a federal court in Los Angeles convicted two of the officers involved in the beating of violating King's civil rights—too late to avert the violence that erupted after the initial verdict.

■ In the aftermath of the violent uprising that followed the acquittal of police officers in the beating of motorist Rodney King, Koreans and African Americans in Los Angeles express their solidarity, hoping to heal the wounds and divisions that had torn apart their city.

Of the fifty-eight people who died in the violence, eighteen were Latino, twenty-six were black, ten were white, and two were Asian. Of the 4,000 businesses that were destroyed, most belonged to Latinos and Koreans. Perpetrators of the violence, as well as the victims, came from all racial groups. Antonia Hernandez, president of the Mexican American Legal Defense and Educational Fund, noted, "The hardest part is rebuilding the spirit of the city—what holds us together as Angelinos. It's the rebuilding of trust.... It's connecting communities that have never been connected." Several community groups came together in an effort to ease tensions, including the Japanese American Citizens League, Chinese for Affirmative Action, and the League of United Latin American Citizens.

Values in Conflict

Many citizens worried that the bonds holding Americans together might be fraying. In 1991 former University of Colorado football coach Bill McCartney formed the Promise Keepers, a fundamentalist Christian group dedicated to restoring the traditional privileges and responsibilities of husbands and fathers in the home. The Promise Keepers held evangelical revivals that drew tens of thousands of mostly working-class white and some black men to rallies across the country. They believed that men should be good providers for their families, strong role models for their children, and committed spouses.

Although white men continued to control nearly all the major economic and political institutions in the nation, a 1993 poll found that a majority of white men believed that their advantage in terms of jobs and income, along with their influence over American culture, was declining. African American men also felt the need to bolster manhood and fatherhood. Efforts geared specifically toward African American men included the 1995 Million Man March, organized by Nation of Islam Reverend Louis Farrakhan, which drew hundreds of thousands of black men to demonstrate their solidarity at a rally in Washington, D.C.

At the same time, gay men and lesbians mobilized to gain acceptance and legitimacy for the families that they formed. Although a 1994 poll showed that 52 percent of respondents "claimed to consider gay lifestyle acceptable," 64 percent were opposed to legalizing gay marriage or allowing gay couples to adopt children. In 2000, Vermont became the first state to grant legal status to civil unions between same-sex couples, although a fierce backlash threatened to overturn the legislation.

Values also collided around the rights and traditions of Native Americans as tribal communities came into conflict with non-Native environmentalists, sports enthusiasts, and scientists. In the upper Midwest, treaties with the government in 1837 and 1842 granted the Chippewa hunting, fishing, and gathering rights in the territories ceded to the United States. Federal courts consistently upheld these treaties, which include rights to take up to half of the fish and game allowed by state conservation requirements and to use methods such as spear fishing that are illegal for non-Indians. In the 1980s and 1990s, non-Indians challenged these policies and accosted Native Americans in fishing boats with rocks and insults. Native American cultural practices also clashed with environmentalist sensibilities over religious practices involving the gathering and sacrificing of golden eaglets.

Courtroom Dramas

Two of the most controversial legal clashes of the decade centered on accusations against successful black men and exposed deep chasms along class and gender as well as racial lines. The first of these episodes was the Senate hearing of October 1991 to confirm the appointment of conservative Judge Clarence Thomas to the U.S. Supreme Court. Although President George H. W. Bush claimed that Thomas was the "best man for the job," the American Bar Association gave him the lowest rating of any justice confirmed in the previous three decades. When University of Oklahoma law professor Anita Hill accused Thomas of sexual harassment when she had worked for him at the Equal Opportunity Employment Commission in the early 1980s, the question of Thomas's professional qualifications faded to the background and the hearings focused exclusively on Hill's accusations.

In live televised hearings, the African American law professor testified that Thomas had made crude remarks to her as well as unwanted sexual overtures. Several of the all-white-male panel of senators questioned Hill's credibility, wondering why she continued to work for Thomas after the alleged harassment. Thomas drew on the long history of black men being falsely accused of sexual aggression to counter the charge of sexual harassment, accusing his Democratic opponents of conducting a "high-tech lynching." In the end, Thomas was confirmed. But Hill's testimony, and what appeared to her supporters as the insensitive behavior of the senators, brought the issue of sexual harassment to a high level of national consciousness. The hearings also highlighted the fact that Congress was overwhelmingly white and male, motivating female candidates and their supporters to alter that reality the following year. As a result of the 1992 elections, the number of female senators tripled from two to six, including the first black female senator, Carol Moseley Braun, Democrat from Illinois. The number of congresswomen rose from twenty-eight to forty-seven.

In 1994 television viewers were again riveted by a media spectacle, this time a sensational murder case in Los Angeles. The victims were the white ex-wife of black celebrity O. J. Simpson, former football star and film actor, and a male companion. Simpson's blood was found at the scene, hair and other forensic and DNA evidence linked him to the crime, he had no reliable alibi, and a motive was evident in his pattern of jealous rage and brutality against the murdered woman. No other suspects in the case were ever identified. But Simpson's

INTERPRETING HISTORY

Vermont Civil Union Law

On April 26, 2000, Vermont became the first state to grant legal recognition to same-sex couples, affording them all the legal protections, privileges, and responsibilities of married couples. The law unleashed a storm of controversy and raised questions about the legal status in other states of civil unions contracted in Vermont. Nevertheless, in the first year after its enactment, 2,479 same-sex couples forged civil unions in Vermont, 478 of them among Vermonters, and the rest from other states. Two-thirds were lesbian unions. Several states began to consider similar bills, but others moved to prohibit such unions. Nebraska amended its state constitution to outlaw same-sex marriage and civil unions. On the national level, conservative lawmakers endeavored to introduce a constitutional amendment that would ban civil unions and restrict marriage to heterosexual couples. Among other provisions, the Vermont Civil Union Law stipulated that

(1) Civil marriage under Vermont's marriage statutes consists of a union between a man and a woman. . . .

(2) Vermont's history as an independent republic and as a state is one of equal treatment and respect for all Vermonters. . . .

(3) The state's interest in civil marriage is to encourage close and caring families, and to protect all family members from the economic and social consequences of abandonment and divorce, focusing on those who have been especially at risk.

(4) Legal recognition of civil marriage by the state is the primary and, in a number of instances, the exclusive source of numerous benefits, responsibilities and protections under the laws of the state for married persons and their children.

(5) Based on the state's tradition of equality under the law and strong families, for at least 25 years, Vermont Probate Courts have qualified gay and lesbian individuals as adoptive parents.

Kathleen Peterson and Carolyn Conrad exchange vows in front of Justice of the Peace T. Hunter Wilson. The ceremony in Brattleboro, Vermont, on July 1, 2000, marked the first legal union under Vermont's Civil Union Law. Vermont was the first state to provide recognition and legal status to gay and lesbian couples.

(6) Vermont was one of the first states to adopt comprehensive legislation prohibiting discrimination on the basis of sexual orientation. . . .

(7) The state has a strong interest in promoting stable and lasting families, including families based upon a same-sex couple.

(8) Without the legal protections, benefits and responsibilities associated with civil marriage, same-sex couples suffer numerous obstacles and hardships.

(9) Despite long-standing social and economic discrimination, many gay and lesbian Vermonters have formed lasting, committed, caring and faithful relationships with persons of their same sex. These couples live together, participate in their communities together, and some raise children and care for family members together, just as do couples who are married under Vermont law.

(10) While a system of civil unions does not bestow the status of civil marriage, it does satisfy the requirements of the Common Benefits Clause. Changes in the way significant legal relationships are established under the constitution should be approached carefully, combining respect for the community and cultural institutions most affected with a commitment to the constitutional rights involved.

Granting benefits and protections to same-sex couples through a system of civil unions will provide due respect for tradition and long-standing social institutions, and will permit adjustment as unanticipated consequences or unmet needs arise.

(11) The constitutional principle of equality embodied in the Common Benefits Clause is compatible with the freedom of religious belief and worship guaranteed in Chapter I, Article 3rd of the state constitution. Extending the benefits and protections of marriage to same-sex couples through a system of civil unions preserves the fundamental constitutional right of each of the multitude of religious faiths in Vermont to choose freely and without state interference to whom to grant the religious status, sacrament or blessing of marriage under the rules, practices or traditions of such faith.

Questions

1. What political principles and values provided the foundation for Vermont's civil union law?
2. In what ways does the Vermont civil union law distinguish between civil marriages and civil unions?

team of lawyers unearthed evidence that, before the Simpson case, white police detective Mark Fuhrman had boasted of planting evidence and had made racist comments. The mostly black and female jury was sympathetic to the possibility that Fuhrman had framed Simpson. In Los Angeles, in the wake of the Rodney King beatings, African Americans had good reason to distrust the police.

Finally, in early October 1996, after a trial that lasted nearly a year, it took the jury only two hours to acquit Simpson of all charges. Pundits focused on the racial divide: blacks were more inclined to believe Simpson was innocent, and whites more likely to consider him guilty. Simpson was later convicted in a wrongful death civil suit (with lower standards for conviction than a criminal case), which found him responsible for the deaths, and he was ordered to pay damages.

The Changing Face of Diversity

These highly charged events illuminated racial tensions, but there was also evidence that Americans were accepting the nation's diversity and adopting a more inclusive vision. The number of immigrants represented 10 percent of the population, the highest proportion of foreign-born residents since the 1930s. The numbers of Asians and Pacific Islanders increased by 45.9 percent, with those of Chinese ancestry comprising the largest group, followed by those with origins in the Philippines. The Latino population grew by 39.7 percent. Among the nation's Latinos, nearly two-thirds were of Mexican ancestry.

Not everyone celebrated these developments. In California, with one-third of the nation's Latino population, voters responded with Proposition 187 to deny public education and most other public social services to undocumented immigrants, and Proposition 227 to end bilingual education. Large numbers of Latino voters opposed these measures. In subsequent elections, many young Latinos and new citizens marshaled their political power and voted for the first time. By 2000 whites no longer constituted a majority of California's multiethnic population, dropping from 57 percent in 1990 to 47 percent in 2000.

At the same time, politics and ideas based on distinct and rigid racial lines gave way to a growing recognition of intermixing. In the world of sports, young golfer Tiger Woods, son of a black Vietnam-veteran father and a Thai mother, became the reigning superstar of the sport most closely identified with the world of the white elite. Pop star Prince was one of many artists who crafted a persona that highlighted both racial and gender ambiguity. On job and college application forms, a growing number of mixed-race Americans refused to be identified as belonging to one particular racial group. Reflecting this development, the U.S. Census of 2000 allowed people to check more than one box to indicate their racial identity.

■ Golf superstar Tiger Woods celebrates his triumph at the U.S. Amateur Championships in North Plains, Oregon, August 25, 1996. Woods, the son of an African American father and a Thai mother, was one of several mixed-race celebrities in the 1990s.

Violence and Danger

Violence was nothing new in American society, but new types of mayhem in the 1990s—including domestic terrorism and school shootings–sparked national soul-searching and wide-ranging debate over the causes of violence and what to do about them. Meanwhile, ordinary Americans inflicted various harms on themselves, often in class-distinct ways. Eating disorders and obesity reached epidemic proportions, and Americans continued to turn to drugs, most of them legal, to make them feel better.

Watergate break-in. The independent counsel, former judge Kenneth Starr, with the help of the congressional Republicans, pursued Clinton throughout his two terms and nearly brought down his presidency.

Clinton's sexual behavior became an issue well before he entered the White House. During the 1992 campaign, Gennifer Flowers, a former nightclub singer, told a tabloid that she and Clinton had an affair when he was governor. Early in his presidency, Paula Jones, a former Arkansas state employee, filed a sexual harassment suit against Clinton, claiming that he had propositioned her when he was governor of Arkansas. Eventually, the case was dismissed, but it came back to haunt him later.

In 1998 Kenneth Starr reported to the House Judiciary Committee that he had evidence that Clinton had an extramarital affair with a young White House intern, Monica Lewinsky. Starr claimed that Clinton had broken the law in an effort to cover up the affair. Lewinsky and Clinton had both been called to testify in the Paula Jones case, and both denied having had a sexual relationship. Starr claimed that Clinton had lied under oath and had instructed his close adviser and friend, Vernon Jordan, to find Lewinsky a job to keep her quiet. Starr charged Clinton with perjury, witness tampering, and obstruction of justice. As proof of the affair, Starr produced twenty hours of taped phone conversations recorded by Lewinsky's co-worker and confidante, Linda Tripp. Clinton vehemently denied the charges, but Lewinsky had saved a dress with a stain containing the president's DNA, providing the investigation with the "smoking gun" it needed.

As Starr and congressional Republicans pressed the investigation with relentless determination, the media saturated the nation and the world with sordid and graphic details of the president's sexual encounters with the young intern. Polls showed that Americans disapproved of Clinton's personal behavior, but they did not want him removed from office. With the economy booming and the country running smoothly, Clinton garnered high job performance ratings, rising to 79 percent at the height of the scandal. Negative sentiment against Kenneth Starr and congressional Republicans mounted as the investigation dragged on for four years at a cost to taxpayers of $40 million.

Articles of Impeachment Against Clinton (1999)

Public opinion notwithstanding, the House of Representatives impeached—that is, brought charges against—Clinton on December 19, 1998, accusing him of perjury and obstruction of justice, based on Clinton's false testimony in the Paula Jones case. But the majority of senators determined that Clinton's misdeeds did not meet the standard for "high crimes and misdemeanors" required to remove a president from office, and acquitted him.

The Nation and the World

Stymied in Congress by Republican opposition, the president turned his attention increasingly to foreign policy. In foreign affairs, Clinton focused on peacekeeping and peacemaking while expanding trade and diplomatic relations, especially to countries that had been considered unfriendly during the Cold War. Clinton took on the role of peace broker by facilitating negotiations in long-standing conflicts in Northern Ireland and the Middle East. But hostilities in those areas proved too deep to be fully resolved. Military interventions in Somalia, Haiti, and Kosovo yielded mixed results, and trade agreements generated heated controversy. Episodes of international terrorism against U.S. embassies and military personnel killed hundreds of people and highlighted the strength of extremist groups whose members were deeply hostile to the United States and its interventions around the world.

Trade Agreements

In 1993, with the president's strong encouragement, Congress approved the North American Free Trade Agreement (NAFTA), eliminating tariffs and trade barriers among the United States,

Mexico, and Canada and thus creating the largest free trade zone in the world. In 1994 Congress approved the General Agreement on Tariffs and Trade (GATT), which reduced tariffs on thousands of goods and phased out import quotas imposed by the United States and other industrialized nations. Supporters argued that these measures would increase global competition and improve the U.S. economy. Businesses would benefit from the easing of trade barriers, and consumers would have access to lower-priced goods.

NAFTA and GATT barely passed Congress. Clinton faced strong opposition from liberal Democrats in industrial areas and from labor unions, who feared that these measures would result in jobs going abroad, declining American wages, and a relaxation of environmental controls over companies moving outside U.S. borders. In the first few years of NAFTA and GATT, these fears seemed justified. Some jobs went abroad, and threats of moving gave employers a negotiating edge over workers. In Mexico the impact of NAFTA was even worse. The peso collapsed as money and goods flowed across the border, and the average wages for workers fell from $1.45 to $.78 per hour.

Equally controversial were Clinton's efforts to grant China **most-favored-nation status,** which would designate China as a full trading partner with the United States. Human rights activists argued that China's dismal record of violent suppression and imprisonment of political dissenters should preclude favorable trading terms. But with an eye to China's huge potential market for American goods and favorable site for U.S.-owned factories, Congress approved Clinton's proposal.

■ Activists protest at the opening of the meeting of the World Trade Organization (WTO) in Seattle, Washington, on November 1, 1999. During the four days of the meeting, hundreds of demonstrators took to the streets in opposition to the organization's environmental and labor policies.

Efforts at Peacemaking

Less controversial than relations with China were Clinton's peacemaking efforts. Northern Ireland had been fraught with violent conflict for thirty years. Irish Catholic nationalists wanted to break ties with England and join the Republic of Ireland; Protestants loyal to Great Britain wanted to remain part of the United Kingdom. The United States, with political and diplomatic connections to London as well as strong ties to the Irish, wanted to help resolve the crisis. Clinton made several trips to Ireland to promote peace. He appointed former Senator George Mitchell of Maine as negotiator, who spent months working on a settlement. Despite dissent and violence by extremists on both sides, by the time Clinton left office, an agreement had been reached that established a shared coalition government.

In the Middle East, Clinton brought Yasser Arafat, leader of the Palestinian Liberation Organization (PLO), and Yitzak Rabin, Israeli prime minister, to Washington for talks that led to an historic 1993 handshake and pledges to pursue a peace agreement. As in Northern Ireland, those efforts were hampered by violent extremists on both sides. Rabin was assassinated by a fanatical right-wing Israeli, leading to the election of a hawkish new prime minister, Benjamin Netanyahu. The peace process fell apart for several years until negotiations finally resumed in the late 1990s. But just when an agreement seemed to be within reach, large-scale violence between Palestinians and Israelis erupted again in the summer of 2000. Clinton left office with no agreement in sight.

In the final weeks of Clinton's presidency in 2000, he made a historic visit to Vietnam— the first by an American president since the war. Because Clinton had protested against the war decades earlier, his visit held great symbolic power and his administration was the first to reopen formal relations with the Vietnamese government. Although the United States lost the war, westernization had taken hold in Vietnam, with investment beginning to flow in from Europe, the United States, and Japan, as well as American popular culture and technology. Cheering crowds welcomed the president of the superpower that had been vanquished twenty-five years earlier.

Military Interventions and International Terrorism

The end of the Cold War raised new questions about how and when to use American military force. Most of the overseas crises stemmed from problems of national disintegration, ethnic conflict, and humanitarian disasters resulting from political chaos and civil wars.

On the Caribbean island of Haiti, a military coup in 1991 had ousted the democratically elected President Jean Bertrand Aristide. In a striking departure from former Cold War policies, Clinton backed the black populist Aristide against the coup leaders, who had strong ties to the CIA. In 1994 the United States received UN support for an invasion to restore Aristide to power. To avert a large-scale military conflict, Clinton sent former President Jimmy Carter to Haiti to negotiate a settlement. The resulting agreement allowed the coup members to leave the country, and Aristide returned. Six years later, however, the United States criticized Aristide for corruption and fraud in his 2000 reelection.

In 1992 President George H. W. Bush had sent U.S. marines to Somalia in east Africa as part of a UN effort to provide famine relief and to restore peace in the war-torn nation. After Clinton took office, Somali warlord Mohammed Farah Aidid killed fifty Pakistani UN peacekeepers. The U.S. forces then mobilized against Aidid, shifting the peacekeeping mission to military engagement. As part of the effort to hunt down Aidid, U.S. soldiers killed hundreds of Somali citizens, creating intense anti-American sentiment among the population. Amid that hostile atmosphere, in September 1993, Aidid's forces killed eighteen American soldiers under the UN command in a firefight and dragged one of their bodies through the streets. The outraged American public viewed the grim spectacle on TV, and the experience left Clinton with no clear guidelines on **humanitarian intervention** abroad. Largely as a result of the disaster in Somalia, when ethnic conflict led to genocide in Rwanda in central Africa in 1994, the United States and other western nations refused to intervene.

The Balkan Proximity Peace Talks Agreement

Ethnic conflict was also the cause of trouble in the Balkans. From 1945 to 1980, Marshal Josip Broz Tito ruled over a unified communist Yugoslavia, maintaining stability by suppressing ethnic rivalries. But after Tito's death in 1980 and the end of the Cold War in 1989, ethnic nationalism pulled Yugoslavia apart, with Slovenia and Croatia breaking away in 1991–1992. The region erupted in bloody conflicts. After sustained Serbian attacks on Muslims in Bosnia between 1992 and 1995, Clinton reluctantly agreed to air strikes against the Serbs, leading to the 1995 Dayton Accords, which brought an end to the war. When Serbian president Slobodan Milosevic embarked on a murderous campaign to drive the majority Muslim ethnic Albanians out of Serbia's southern province of Kosovo, Clinton finally ordered airstrikes in 1999 that forced the Serbs to retreat.

In some regions of the world, resentment against the United States found expression in violence and terrorism. In June 1996, a truck bomb killed nineteen U.S. airmen in Dhahran, Saudi Arabia. Two years later, bombs exploded at two U.S. embassies in east Africa, killing 224 people in Nairobi, Kenya, and Dar es Salaam, Tanzania. Four men were convicted of conspiracy in the terrorist attacks. They were identified as followers of Islamic militant Osama bin Laden, who was also indicted in connection with the embassy bombings. Bin Laden, originally from Saudi Arabia, was living in Afghanistan under the protection of the fundamentalist Taliban regime and remained a fugitive. He was known to be the leader of Al Qaeda, a terrorist network operating in several countries throughout the Middle East. On October 12, 2000, a small boat pulled up next to the destroyer USS *Cole* in Yemen's port of Aden.

■ **MAP 29.2**
THE BREAKUP OF THE FORMER YUGOSLAVIA Created in 1919 as a multiethnic nation, Yugoslavia split apart in 1991–1992. After Slovenia and Croatia gained their independence swiftly, Bosnia deteriorated into fierce ethnic fighting dominated by Serb atrocities and encouraged by the Serbian government of Slobodan Milosevic. A brief U.S. bombing campaign in 1995 finally brought the Serbs to peace negotiations. Similar ethnic fighting in the province of Kosovo in 1999 led to another U.S. bombing campaign and Kosovo's current quasi-independence under NATO guidance. In 2006 Montenegro's citizens voted narrowly to establish their full independence from Serbia.

A bomb exploded and ripped a hole in the destroyer, killing seventeen Americans and wounding thirty-nine others.

Terrorists also struck at home. On February 26, 1993, a bomb exploded in the parking garage underneath the World Trade Center, the skyscrapers dominating the New York skyline in Lower Manhattan. Five people were killed and more than a thousand were injured. Eight years later, the same twin towers were attacked again, with far more devastating consequences.

The Contested Election of 2000

The first presidential election of the new millennium was the most bitterly contested in more than a century. The Democratic candidate won the national popular vote, but with ballot counts disputed in the key state of Florida, a Supreme Court decision ultimately made the Republican candidate the victor. The election exposed defects in the election process, from faulty ballots and voting machines to the role of the media, and raised serious questions about the value of the electoral college. The election also revealed that flaws in the system disfranchised large numbers of poor and minority voters. But in the end, the transfer of power took place smoothly, and the nation accepted the outcome.

The Campaign, the Vote, and the Courts

The Democrats nominated Vice President Al Gore, who hoped to benefit from Clinton's high approval rating and the healthy economy. The Republicans nominated George W. Bush, governor of Texas and son of the former president. Only half of the nation's eligible voters turned out to vote. Even before all the polls had closed, the national media began to report the results.

Early in the evening, they declared that Florida, a key state with twenty-five electoral votes, had gone to Gore. But soon after that announcement, they changed their projection and put Florida back into the "undecided" group of states. It became clear that whoever took Florida, where Bush's brother Jeb Bush was governor, would win the election. By the next day, Gore had won the national popular vote by half a million votes, but Bush was ahead in Florida. Bush's lead was so narrow that it triggered an automatic recount.

TABLE 29-3
The Election of 2000

Candidate	Political Party	Popular Vote (%)	Electoral Vote
George W. Bush	Republican	47.88	271
Al Gore	Democratic	48.39	266*
Ralph Nader	Green	2.72	—

*One District of Columbia Gore elector abstained.

With all eyes on Florida, a number of serious irregularities surfaced. Voters in Palm Beach County were given a confusing "butterfly" ballot, resulting in more than 20,000 mismarked ballots. In other counties, registered voters were turned away at the polls because of inaccurate and incomplete voter registration lists. Some voter lists inaccurately listed eligible voters as felons. Most of these disfranchised voters were African American, who usually voted Democratic. In several largely minority counties, old voting machines that used a punch-card ballot system failed to count thousands of ballots.

For weeks after the election, the outcome was still unknown. Democrats insisted that because Bush's lead had narrowed to a few hundred votes, tallied by inaccurate voting machines, ballots in four Florida counties should be recounted by hand. Republicans pointed out that it would be unfair to recount votes in only four heavily Democratic counties, especially with no standard way of determining voter intent on punch-card ballots with ambiguous marks on them. Florida's secretary of state, Katherine Harris, a Republican who headed Florida's campaign for George W. Bush, refused to extend the deadline to allow the recounts to take place and declared Bush the winner by 537 votes out of 6 million cast statewide.

Gore contested the results, and the Florida Supreme Court ordered that the recount proceed. Bush then appealed to the U.S. Supreme Court to reverse the decision of the Florida Supreme Court. After thirty-six days of partial vote counting and court battles, in a sharply divided 5–4 decision, the U.S. Supreme Court stopped any further vote counting, with the most conservative judges voting in support of the Bush request. The four dissenting judges issued a stinging rebuke of their five colleagues responsible for the decision. In his dissenting opinion, Justice Stephen Breyer wrote that the majority ruling "can only lend confidence to the most cynical appraisal of the work of judges throughout the land."

The Aftermath

What became clear in the months after the 2000 election were the widespread flaws in the election system in Florida and elsewhere. Across the country, outdated voting machines yielded inaccurate vote counts, and long lines at polling places prevented voters from casting ballots. Low-income and minority voters were more likely to be disfranchised because they lived in precincts with faulty voting machines or overcrowded polling places. The U.S. Civil Rights Commission estimated that in Florida, black voters were nine times more likely than white voters to have had their votes rejected.

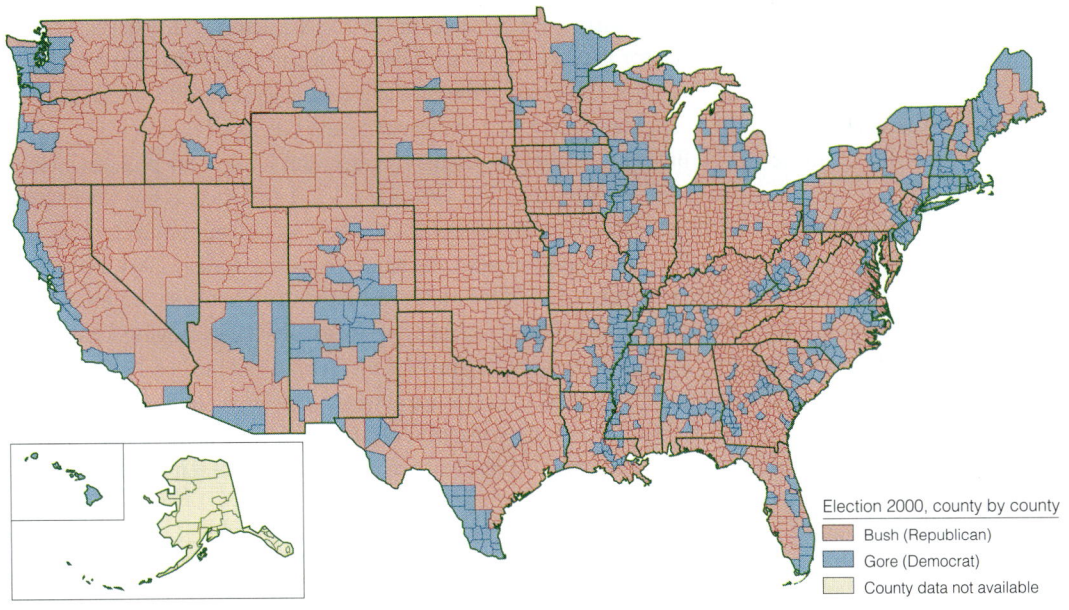

■ MAP 29.3
THE CONTESTED ELECTION OF 2000 The 2000 presidential election was so close, and so fraught with problems, that it was ultimately decided by a 5–4 vote of the U.S. Supreme Court. As this map shows, Democratic votes were concentrated in the densely populated urban areas and Republican votes in the sparsely populated rural areas.

In addition to those whose votes did not count, many others were prevented from voting altogether. In Florida, "suspected felons" were removed from voter registration lists without being informed and without the opportunity to demonstrate that they were law-abiding citizens eligible to vote. An estimated 15 percent of the list was inaccurate, and more than half of those voters were African American. According to the U.S. Civil Rights Commission, "Perhaps the most dramatic undercount in Florida's election was the nonexistent ballots of countless unknown eligible voters, who were turned away, or wrongfully purged from the voter registration rolls . . . and were prevented from exercising the franchise." As a result, hundreds of African American citizens with no criminal record arrived at the polls only to discover that they had been disfranchised.

Policymakers and media moguls debated the role of the media in reporting election returns. Some argued for a blackout on early returns until all polls across the country were closed, to avoid the possibility that early results might influence voters who had not yet voted. Others proposed that only official results be announced, to avoid the problem of erroneous reporting that occurred on election night 2000. But media representatives countered that a free press should be able to report the news as it happens, although they agreed on the need to ensure accuracy.

Legacies of Election 2000

In addition to the unprecedented Supreme Court decision, the 2000 election was remarkable in other ways. For the first time, a First Lady was elected to public office: Hillary Rodham Clinton became a Democratic senator from New York. Third-party politics also critically influenced the outcome of the presidential election. Several third-party candidates had achieved national visibility during the 1990s and won elections at the state and local levels, including professional wrestler Jesse Ventura, elected governor of Minnesota in 1998 on the Reform party ticket. In 2000 Ralph Nader wreaked havoc for the Democrats with his Green party candidacy for president. Although Nader gained fewer than 3 percent of the votes, his candidacy drew off some of the left-leaning elements of the Democratic party—enough votes to cost Al Gore the election.

President George W. Bush immediately began to reverse several Clinton-era policies, including a number of environmental protections. His first major legislative success was the passage of a major tax cut. During his first year in office, the economy went from boom to bust and headed into a recession. The robust stock market of the 1990s wilted in early 2001. Nevertheless, as the new millennium dawned, the United States remained the wealthiest and most powerful nation in the world. Bush retreated from international treaties on issues ranging from global warming to nuclear test ban agreements, and he revived the Reagan-era proposal for a nuclear missile shield. But the place of the nation in the global community was yet to be defined. Soon, monumental events shattered the nation's sense of security and forced Bush to abandon his retreat from international alliances and to engage in the world in unprecedented ways.

Conclusion

In the 1990s, the role of the nation in the world shifted and a half-century of political certainties evaporated. With the Cold War now over, conflicts around the globe, many of them grounded in ancient ethnic hostilities, posed challenges for the world's most powerful nation. The United States focused on markets and trade, the nation's supply of oil, the need for political order to maintain international stability, and the danger of "rogue nations" developing nuclear arms. President Clinton tried to be a peacemaker in hot spots around the world while attempting to respond to violent episodes of international terrorism.

At home, Americans demonstrated increasing tolerance for people who looked and acted differently from themselves. Polls showed declining levels of racial, ethnic, and religious hostility and greater acceptance of homosexuality, single parenthood, and family arrangements that deviated from the nuclear family model. But episodes of racial discrimination—by police, courts, and voting officials—continued. Politics remained an arena in which culture wars flared over abortion, gun control, and welfare reform. A Democratic president faced impeachment by his Republican foes in Congress while maintaining high approval ratings from the public.

At the dawn of the new century, several crises challenged Americans' sense of security. A deeply flawed presidential election revealed profound problems in the nation's voting system. A sharp and sudden downturn in the economy shattered the optimism many middle-class people felt during the booming Clinton years and forced many of the working poor into desperate circumstances. Already reeling from these disturbing developments, the nation was soon shaken to its core by a terrorist attack that forced a new reckoning at home and abroad.

Sites to Visit

William Jefferson Clinton
www.ipl.org/div/potus/wjclinton.html
This site contains basic information about Clinton's election and presidency and an online biography.

Distribution of Wealth and Income
www.inequality.org/facts.cfm
This site provides facts and figures about the distribution of wealth and income in the 1990s.

American Identities
xroads.virginia.edu/~YP/ethnic.html
This site of the American Studies program at the University of Virginia includes information and resources for studying America's multiple ethnic identities.

O. J. Simpson Trial
www.cnn.com/US/OJ/index.html
This CNN site provides basic facts and interpretive essays, plus additional links about the O. J. Simpson trial.

Investigating the President
www.cnn.com/ALLPOLITICS/resources/1998/lewinsky/
This CNN site provides information and documents about the scandals surrounding President Clinton's impeachment.

Focus on Kosovo
www.cnn.com/SPECIALS/1998/10/kosovo/
This in-depth CNN interactive site looks at the development of turmoil in Kosovo and its resolution.

Oklahoma City Bombing
www.cnn.com/US/OKC/
This CNN interactive site has information about the domestic terrorist bombing in Oklahoma City and the trial that followed.

Why Do Campaign Polls Zigzag So Much?
www2,psych.purdue.edu/~codelab/Invalid.Polls.html
This site, created by Gerald S. Wasserman of the Psychological Sciences Department at Purdue University, examines polling data from the 1996 presidential campaign.

For Further Reading

General
Stephanie Coontz, *The Way We Really Are: Coming to Terms with America's Changing Families* (1997).
Clara E. Rodriguez, *Changing Race: Latinos, the Census and the History of Ethnicity in the United States* (2000).
Leland T. Saito and Roger Daniels, *Race and Politics: Asian Americans, Latinos, and Whites in a Los Angeles Suburb* (1998).

The Economy: Global and Domestic
Sheldon Danziger and Peter Gottschalk, *America Unequal* (1995).
Jacqueline Jones, *American Work: Four Centuries of Black and White Labor* (1998).
William A. Orme, *Understanding NAFTA: Mexico, Free Trade, and the New North America* (1996).

Tolerance and Its Limits
Jane Mayer and Jill Abramson, *Strange Justice: The Selling of Clarence Thomas* (1994).
Michael Omi and Howard Winant, *Racial Formation in the United States: From the 1960s to the 1990s* (1994).
Alan Wolfe, *One Nation, After All: What Americans Really Think About God, Country, Family, Racism, Welfare, Immigration, Homosexuality, Work, the Right, the Left and Each Other* (1998).

Violence and Danger
Joan Jacobs Brumberg, *The Body Project: An Intimate History of American Girls* (2000).
Susan Faludi, *Stiffed: The Betrayal of the American Man* (1999).
Steven Wisotsky and Thomas Szasz, *Beyond the War on Drugs: Overcoming a Failed Public Policy* (1999).

The Clinton Presidency
William C. Berman, *From the Center to the Edge: The Politics and Policies of the Clinton Presidency* (2001).
James MacGregor Burns and Georgia J. Sorenson, *Dead Center: Clinton–Gore Leadership and the Perils of Moderation* (1999).
David Maraniss, *First in His Class: A Biography of Bill Clinton* (1995).
Steven E. Schier, ed., *The Postmodern Presidency: Bill Clinton's Legacy in U.S. Politics* (2000).

The Nation and the World
John Dumbrell and David M. Barrett, *The Making of U.S. Foreign Policy* (1998).
David Halberstam, *War in a Time of Peace: Bush, Clinton, and the Generals* (2002).
Thomas H. Henriksen, *Clinton's Foreign Policy in Somalia, Bosnia, Haiti, and North Korea* (1996).

The Contested Election of 2000
E. J. Dionne and William Kristol, eds., *Bush v. Gore: The Court Cases and the Commentary* (2001).
Alexander Keyssar, *The Right to Vote: The Contested History of Democracy in the United States* (2000).
Richard A. Posner, *Breaking the Deadlock: The 2000 Election, the Constitution, and the Courts* (2001).

For quizzes and other resources on these topics, go to www.longmanamericanhistory.com.

CHAPTER 30

A Global Nation for the New Millennium

AT THE BEGINNING OF THE THIRD MILLENNIUM, THE UNITED STATES WAS MORE closely connected than ever to the rest of the world. The processes of globalization—increasing trade, communication, travel, and migration—linked the nation to the rest of a world that often seemed to be torn by ethnic and religious strife. That strife from abroad impinged on Americans in a shocking new way on September 11, 2001. On a sunny Tuesday morning, 19 hijackers—four of them trained as pilots—seized control simultaneously of four large commercial jets and turned them into suicidal missiles. At 8:48 a.m., one flew into the 110-story north tower of New York City's World Trade Center, igniting an enormous fireball. Fifteen minutes later, the second plane flew into the south tower. In less than two hours, both towers collapsed, killing the thousands of people still inside. Among the dead were hundreds of firefighters, police officers, and other rescue workers who had raced into the towers to evacuate the occupants. The third plane flew into the Pentagon. The fourth was also being directed toward Washington, apparently to destroy the White House or the Capitol Building, until it crashed in a field 75 miles southeast of Pittsburgh.

■ Smoke rises from the crash of United Airlines Flight 93 near Shanksville, Pennsylvania. For almost all Americans, the hijackings and destruction of September 11, 2001, came indeed out of a clear blue sky. Anti-American actions of the previous decade by Islamic terrorists had created little anxiety in a powerful nation that had imagined itself safe from major attack.

The carefully coordinated assaults killed almost 3,000 people, destroyed the two tallest buildings in the country's largest city, and left a gaping hole in the headquarters of the nation's military command. Not since the Japanese assault on Pearl Harbor 60 years earlier had the United States experienced a devastating attack on its own soil. During the intervening half-century of the Cold War, the Soviet Union and other communist forces had never attempted direct aggression against the American homeland. Who was responsible for the most horrific act of terrorism against civilians in U.S. history?

The 19 perpetrators were self-styled holy warriors of a secretive, extremist Islamic organization known as Al Qaeda, organized by wealthy, charismatic Saudi Arabian expatriate Osama bin

CHAPTER OUTLINE

The George W. Bush Administration

The American Place in a Global Economy

The Stewardship of Natural Resources

The Expansion of American Popular Culture Abroad

Identity in Contemporary America

Conclusion

Sites to Visit

For Further Reading

Laden. Al Qaeda worked out of Afghanistan, hosted by the most repressive Islamic government on Earth, the Taliban, which rose to power in 1996 out of the chaos that followed the withdrawal of the Soviet army in 1989. The rage of bin Laden and other Islamic terrorists against the United States had been building throughout the 1990s, fueled by the presence of "infidel" American troops in Saudi Arabia since the 1991 Persian Gulf War, by American support for Israel, and by the rapid spread of secular American popular culture around the globe. At odds with moderate Islamic mainstream thought throughout the world, bin Laden announced in 1998: "To kill Americans and their allies is an individual duty of every Muslim who is able."

At the heart of American society remained a common assumption, that the United States is a democratic country. The events on United Airlines Flight 93, one of the four doomed planes on September 11, 2001, revealed the tenacity of the belief in majority rule. After the hijackers seized control and herded the passengers into the rear of the cabin, a dozen passengers and crew members were able to communicate by phone with people on the ground. They learned that two other planes had already crashed into the World Trade Center towers in New York City, and they realized that these hijackers—unlike previous ones who sought concrete gains and an escape—planned only destruction for them all. Face to face with imminent death and the certainty that many others would perish if they failed to act, the passengers discussed what to do. They made a plan to rush the hijackers, led by several large, athletic passengers, including Mark Bingham, a prominent gay businessperson and rugby player from San Francisco. Should they proceed? Quintessential Americans, they took a vote. GTE Airfone operator Lisa Jefferson heard the rest: "Are you guys ready?" asked Todd Beamer, a tall father of two from Cranbury, New Jersey. Screams and a sustained scuffle followed before the line went dead. The plane, headed for the heart of Washington, crashed in an unpopulated part of western Pennsylvania with no casualties on the ground.

The events on United Airlines Flight 93, one of the four doomed planes on September 11, 2001, revealed the tenacity of the belief in majority rule.

The George W. Bush Administration

The attacks of September 11, 2001, constituted perhaps the most significant event in American life since Japan's surrender in 1945. People remember where they were when they first learned what had happened, and they recall vividly the terrible televised images of destruction. As citizens of the sole remaining superpower after the collapse of the Soviet Union in 1991, Americans had grown accustomed to unprecedented global power and influence. They had no great power rival. For most of those ten years, they had experienced rapid economic growth as well. The nation, it seemed, was wealthy and secure.

The events on September 11 changed all that. The economy, already sliding into recession, accelerated its downward course. Just seven months in office, the administration of President George W. Bush responded by leading the nation into a "war on terrorism" abroad and at home. Within two years, U.S.-led efforts succeeded in overthrowing the governments of Afghanistan and Iraq. Complicated, long-term military occupations ensued, with U.S. forces continuing to engage in bloody battles against insurgents in both countries. In an effort to prevent further terrorist attacks at home, Congress passed the "USA Patriot Act," granting greater powers to the executive branch of the federal government. Authorities detained hundreds of immigrants, primarily young men of Middle Eastern descent. These policies then faced the test of public approval in the elections of November 2004.

The President and the War on Terrorism

George W. Bush did not have an auspicious record of achievement before his election as governor of Texas in 1994 and as president of the United States six years later. He grew up primarily in Midland, Texas, the grandson of a U.S. senator from Connecticut and the eldest son of a wealthy oilman, diplomat, and eventual U.S. president, George H. W. Bush. "W.," as he was sometimes called to distinguish him from his father, attended the elite Phillips Academy in Andover, Massachusetts, and he earned degrees from Yale and Harvard Business School, though his modest academic achievements hinted at the benefits of unofficial forms of affirmative action for the scions of wealthy and powerful families. His sociability and charisma earned him many friends. He avoided going to Vietnam when he was of draft age by serving in the Air National Guard, though he apparently failed to show up for much of a year of that service in 1972.

After a mixed career in business and a strong taste for the partying life, Bush gave up drinking at age 40 and became a devout, conservative Christian. This ambitious and now more serious man made his way up in Republican political circles, benefiting from family connections as well as a warm, "regular guy" personality that appealed to many working-class Americans. Despite his father's strongly international orientation, Bush himself before his presidency had left the United States only three times to go anywhere besides Mexico. "I'm not going to play like a person who has spent hours involved with foreign policy," he admitted during the 2000 campaign. Once president, he took a unilateralist and almost isolationist stance, to the dismay of close U.S. allies abroad. The United States rejected or withdrew from international agreements limiting global warming, weapons testing, and war crime prosecutions.

George W. Bush Address to Congress (September 20, 2001)

The events of September 11 stunned all Americans and gave the president a new focus. Finding and destroying Al Qaeda and its allies was now "the purpose of this administration," Bush told his cabinet. Four weeks after the attacks on New York and Washington, U.S. planes initiated the "war on terrorism" by bombing Taliban and Al Qaeda positions in Afghanistan. By October 19, U.S. special operations forces were working on the ground with anti-Taliban Afghan insurgents. Several European nations provided troops and other military assistance. By December, the Taliban had been driven from power throughout the country, and U.S. and allied forces had killed and captured hundreds of Taliban and Al Qaeda fighters. Many of the prisoners were transferred to the U.S. naval base at Guantanamo Bay, Cuba, to be held indefinitely and interrogated as enemy combatants. Despite continued pursuit and a reward offer of $25 million, the United States was not able to find Osama bin Laden, who was assumed to be hiding in the remote, snowy mountains of the Pakistan-Afghanistan border region.

Security and Politics at Home

George W. Bush, From "National Security Strategy of the United States of America" (September 2002)

The war on terrorism was not only a foreign affair. Just as the onset of the Cold War in the late 1940s had incorporated a hunt for domestic traitors, the war on terrorism in the early 2000s included a search for potential Al Qaeda sympathizers at home. Like the Cold War, the war on terrorism was framed as a long-term struggle against a maniacal, evil enemy who would not be easily defeated. Also as in the Cold War, American leaders announced that some civil liberties would have to be curtailed in order to protect the nation. The USA Patriot Act of October 2001 increased the U.S. Justice Department's range of options for spying on and detaining citizens and noncitizens suspected of pro-terrorist activities. Determined to prevent another major terrorist attack, Attorney General John Ashcroft oversaw the arrest of hundreds of illegal immigrants and their imprisonment in what the Justice Department later admitted were often unduly harsh conditions—not unlike Guantanamo, observers noted. Congress created the Department of Homeland Security (DHS) in an effort to better coordinate intelligence, police, and military authorities for defending the nation from future attacks.

Beyond terrorism, George W. Bush sought to move the nation in the direction of what he called "compassionate conservatism." One conservative activist noted that the new administration turned out to be "more Reaganite than the Reagan administration." In the economic realm, this meant promoting the private sector and reducing federal spending on social programs for the poor. It meant reducing the government's role in regulating health and safety issues in the workplace. And it meant pushing large tax cuts through Congress in 2001 and 2003 to the disproportionate benefit of the wealthiest 1 percent of Americans. The budget surpluses of Bill Clinton's last years disappeared, as the Bush administration ran enormous annual deficits by retaining the tax cuts while sharply increasing military spending. The nation's debt grew rapidly under Bush.

> *Like the Cold War, the war on terrorism was framed as a long-term struggle against a maniacal, evil enemy who would not be easily defeated.*

Bush's conservatism did not include conserving natural resources. Bush and Vice President Dick Cheney, both former oil executives, were closely allied with corporate interests, particularly in the energy business, that sought easier access to public resources. The administration promoted oil drilling offshore and in the Arctic National Wildlife Refuge, encouraged mining and timber clear-cutting across western federal lands, and refused to regulate carbon dioxide emissions despite powerful evidence of global warming. The administration also loosened federal regulations on industrial air pollution, on water pollution by the coal industry, and on arsenic levels in drinking water.

Sexual issues remained flashpoints of political controversy. Explicit and suggestive sexuality pervaded popular culture, including two-thirds of television shows, causing particular concern among parents of young children. At the same time, Americans were increasingly accepting of homosexual couples. In *Lawrence v. Texas* (2003), the U.S. Supreme Court overturned state laws banning private homosexual behavior between consenting adults. A year later, Massachusetts legalized gay marriage. One-third of the nation's largest companies now offered employees in same-sex marriages or committed relationships the same benefits and supports, such as health care insurance, that they offered employees with traditional families. Marriage and family remained social institutions in transition, for better or worse: only 56 percent of adults were now married, compared with 75 percent 30 years earlier. And only 26 percent of American households consisted of a married couple with children.

The War in Iraq

President Bush's most momentous decision was to invade and occupy Iraq in the spring of 2003. This was a very different proposition than the attack on Afghanistan. The effort to destroy Al Qaeda and its Taliban hosts in Afghanistan had widespread support in the United States and across much of the world. By contrast, invading a sovereign nation that had not attacked or even threatened the United States divided Americans and alienated most of the rest of the world. The United Nations refused to support the invasion. America's western European allies were dismayed. Among America's major allies, only the British government of Prime Minister Tony Blair provided enthusiastic political support and a significant number of troops. Given this lack of support, why did the Bush administration invade Iraq?

Some observers pointed to personal reasons. Bush would be "finishing" the Persian Gulf War of 1991, when his father oversaw the liberation of Kuwait from Saddam Hussein's invading Iraqi forces but did not send troops to Baghdad to overthrow Saddam. Bush would also be avenging Saddam's effort to assassinate the elder Bush on a visit to Kuwait. Other observers emphasized the centrality of Iraq's oil reserves, the largest in the world after those of Saudi Arabia and Canada. The president himself claimed two primary reasons for the invasion: that Saddam possessed "weapons of mass destruction"—chemical, biological, or nuclear—and could attack the United States or its allies "on any given day," and that Iraq had ties to Al Qaeda "and was equally as bad, equally as evil and equally as destructive." But after U.S. forces occupied Iraq, these two official reasons for the war were placed in doubt. U.S. troops found no weapons of mass destruction (though Saddam had indeed used chemical weapons on dissident Iraqi civilians 15 years earlier), and Secretary of State Colin Powell admitted there was no

■ Nothing undercut the U.S. effort to extend its influence in the Middle East more than the photographs that emerged in the spring of 2004 of U.S. troops abusing Iraqi detainees at Abu Ghraib prison outside Baghdad. Here, two of these photographs are displayed on a street in neighboring Iran. The Abu Ghraib scandal dismayed America's allies, enraged Muslims everywhere, and almost certainly enhanced Al Qaeda recruiting. One Iraqi-American observed that the Bush administration had "done a good job of occupying the land of Iraq, but a horrible job of occupying the hearts of the Iraqi people."

"smoking gun" proof of a link between Al Qaeda's religious zealots and Saddam's fiercely secular dictatorship. The bipartisan reports of both the 9/11 Commission and the Senate Intelligence Committee in 2004 found that the primary reasons the president gave for invading Iraq were not true.

A deeper reason for the U.S. invasion of Iraq appeared to be the administration's view of September 11 as an opportunity to preemptively reshape the Middle East into a region less hostile to the United States and Israel. A liberated Iraq, right in the center of the Middle East, might have a "demonstration effect" of pro-American capitalist democracy that would turn the rest of the region away from authoritarianism and Islamic revolution. Bush spoke of the overthrow of Saddam as "a watershed event in the global democratic revolution." This statement represented a highly optimistic view of how Americans might bring change to the Middle East, part of a new U.S. strategic doctrine emphasizing preemptive action against the nation's enemies. "We must take the battle to the enemy" in the war on terrorism, Bush declared in 2002, "and confront the worst threats before they emerge."

The U.S.-led offensive in Iraq that began on March 19, 2003, was a successful military action. Some 200,000 U.S. and British troops, with a few other allied forces, overran Saddam's defenses and occupied the entire nation of 25 million people within four weeks. The rapid military victory and the presence of so many U.S. troops initially stunned neighboring Iran and Syria into reducing aid to anti-Israeli terrorist groups. Most Iraqis celebrated their liberation from Saddam's brutal regime, and many seemed to welcome the American soldiers. Seven months later, U.S. soldiers captured Saddam himself.

But military occupations rarely age well, especially without sufficient troops for the task. Widespread looting ravaged Baghdad, and essential services and personal security deteriorated in the aftermath of the old government's defeat. "Baghdad," one gasoline station owner observed, "is like the Wild West now." Saddam loyalists, Iraqi nationalists of various stripes, and arriving foreign Islamic revolutionaries initiated a multi-sided insurgency against the American occupiers. The number of U.S. and Iraqi deaths shot upward, as did the number of American troops sent to Iraq. The U.S. invasion of Iraq seemed to be increasing rather than reducing the threat of terrorism to Americans and others. Indeed, some observers suggested that Osama bin Laden might be pleased to have so many U.S. troops trying to control an unhappy Muslim population for the stimulus it provided to recruiting anti-American jihadists. Sunnis and Shiites also faced off against each other in what began to look like civil war. Critics of U.S. postwar planning now included some prominent Republicans, and the commander of allied forces in Iraq, General Ricardo Sanchez, told Americans flatly "we're still at war."

The Bush administration turned over official sovereignty to a new Iraqi government on June 28, 2004, with 130,000 U.S. troops remaining in the country in an effort to provide security against insurgents. "We don't do empire," insisted Secretary of Defense Donald Rumsfeld. But two months earlier, photographs and eyewitness reports were made public of U.S. troops abusing, torturing, and sexually humiliating Iraqi detainees at the Abu Ghraib prison outside Baghdad. After a week's delay, the president finally apologized. For most Middle Easterners and for Muslims around the world, however, this was compelling evidence that Bush's rhetoric about liberating Iraq was merely a cover for what they saw as fundamental American disdain for Muslims.

The Election of 2004 and After

President Bush entered his campaign for reelection with solid support in his own party but mixed reviews from others. Many other nations considered the U.S. attack on Iraq to be unjustified and unwise. Western Europeans resented Bush's lack of interest in their concerns, making him probably the least-popular American president in Europe in 80 years. Less than three years after the attacks of September 11, 2001, Americans still tended to support him on foreign policy matters. But many voters were troubled by the growing insurgency in Iraq and by a still-weak economy, and the president's approval ratings remained below 50 percent.

The Democratic Party hoped to exploit Bush's vulnerability by nominating Senator John Kerry of Massachusetts, a decorated Vietnam War hero with a moderately liberal legislative record. Bush and Kerry had graduated from Yale within two years of each other, and both had very wealthy families. Democratic party activists hoped to blunt the appeal of the president's "war on terrorism" and emphasis on patriotism by nominating a man whose courage under fire in Vietnam contrasted with Bush's safe spot in the Texas National Guard during that war.

It did not quite work. The president prevailed in a narrow popular-vote victory. The Electoral College outcome of 2004 hinged on Ohio, where a difference of 136,000 votes put Bush over the top. Two issues predominated in the minds of the majority of voters. One was the war on terrorism, which they tended to see as the same as the war in Iraq (despite evidence to the contrary) and on which they trusted Bush's leadership more than Kerry's. The second was what voters described as "moral values," a sense that Bush—even if they sometimes did not agree with his specific policy choices—had personal integrity, a quality they were less sure of with Kerry's nuanced views of complicated policy issues. Christian conservatives were particularly important in getting Republican voters to the polls, passing initiatives in 11 states to ban gay marriage and winning four new seats in the Senate and four in the House to give the president a larger majority in Congress.

TABLE 30-1

The Election of 2004

Candidate	Political Party	Popular Vote (%)	Electoral Vote
George W. Bush	Republican	50.8	286
John Kerry	Democratic	48.3	251
Ralph Nader	Green	<1	—

The president's political fortunes declined swiftly after his reelection. The situation in Iraq continued to deteriorate in 2005, as deepening ethnic and religious divisions undermined efforts to reconstruct a stable and orderly society. At home, an ethics scandal brought down the once-powerful House majority leader, Tom DeLay of Texas, and dimmed public confidence in the Republican-run Congress. On August 29, 2005, Hurricane Katrina flooded New Orleans, causing hundreds of deaths and a massive evacuation of nearly the entire city. The Bush administration was criticized from all sides for what was widely seen as a slow and ineffectual response to an extraordinary human disaster. By May 2006 Bush's approval rating dropped to 31%, the third lowest figure (after Richard Nixon and Jimmy Carter) for any president in 50 years. In the November 2006 elections, the Republicans lost their majorities in both the House and the Senate.

The American Place in a Global Economy

While the president navigated difficult political waters, average Americans struggled to find and keep their place in a changing world economy. Mollie Brown James, for example, grew up in a small Virginia town west of Richmond. In 1950, at age nineteen, she moved to Paterson, New Jersey, joining the broad river of black Southerners who sought better economic opportunities and greater personal freedom in the North. She took a job in 1955 with the Universal Manufacturing Company in Paterson, with wages and decent treatment, unlike what had been available to her in Virginia. She stayed with Universal for thirty-four years. With union-negotiated wages, overtime work, and company-paid health insurance, she helped pull her family into the middle-class world of owning their own home and car and saving for retirement. But the peace of mind that came from a secure job vanished in 1989 when Universal closed the Paterson plant and moved its manufacturing operations to Matamoros, Mexico, just across the Rio Grande River from Brownsville, Texas.

James's job did not disappear. It moved and was inherited by twenty-year-old Balbina Duque Granados. She, too, had grown up in a small town located in an agricultural area, in the Mexican province of San Luis Potosí, and she, too, had moved 400 miles north to find better-paying work in a booming manufacturing city. She was thrilled to land the difficult, repetitive job—her "answered prayer"—at a *maquiladora*, one of the foreign-owned assembly plants along Mexico's border with the United States that wed First World engineering with Third World working conditions. Her employer was also satisfied, paying her $.65 an hour to do what James had been paid $7.91 an hour for. But Granados's job was no more secure than James's had been. The beginnings of successful worker organizing in Matamoros encouraged the company to shift many of its operations sixty miles upriver to Reynosa, where the union movement was weaker. A journalist asked whether she would move there if her job did. "And what if they were to move again?" she replied. "Maybe to Juarez or Tijuana? What then? Do I have to chase my job all over the world?"

The Logic and Technology of Globalization

Like many other workers in the United States and abroad, Mollie James and Balbina Duque Granados learned firsthand the relentlessly international logic of the economic system known as capitalism. Those who had capital—extra money—invested it in corporations, whose purpose was to produce a profit for their shareholders. A corporation's profitability depended on keeping costs—labor and materials—down and expanding into new markets. Just as the telegraph and telephone had helped create a nation unified by rapid communication in the late 1800s, the spread of personal computers and the Internet linked Americans even more closely to other nations in the late 1900s.

At the close of the twentieth century, engineering breakthroughs sped up the process of globalization. The integration of computers into every aspect of commerce and private life increased the efficiency with which businesses could operate. Computers boosted American productivity (the amount of work performed by a person in a given time period), which had declined between 1973 and 1996, and the U.S. economy enjoyed its longest-ever expansion during the presidency of Bill Clinton. Cable News Network (CNN) offered a standardized package of world news available twenty-four hours a day around the globe. CNN was so international in its aims that it banned the word *foreign* from its broadcasts.

Americans were also speeding up their daily routines as the new millennium approached. The desire for immediate gratification and efficiency that had nurtured fast food and microwave ovens encouraged the spread of cell phones, beepers, fax machines, overnight package delivery, and constant news headlines scrolling across TV screens. Computers processed more information faster on ever-smaller silicon chips. Cell phones proliferated among businesspeople, students, and drivers. As prices dropped, they even reached into poorer areas. International air travel for business and pleasure quadrupled between 1980 and 1998, and international tourism vied with oil as the world's largest industry. The spread of the Internet and the use of electronic mail (e-mail) and instant-messaging after the early 1990s epitomized the shift toward instant global communication.

Free Trade and the Global Assembly Line

The ideology of free trade underpinned the tighter meshing of Americans' lives with the world economy. Advocates of free trade argued that global markets unhindered by national tariffs benefited consumers everywhere by giving them access to the best goods at the lowest prices. America's NAFTA treaty with Canada and Mexico reflected this belief (see Chapter 29), as did the European Union with its newly unified currency, the euro. In the United States, by the start of the new millennium most leaders of both major political parties, corporate executives, bankers, and most other elites supported free trade.

But others objected to this internationalist economic ideology. Environmentalists and labor unions led the forces opposing unregulated globalization of the U.S. economy. Environmentalists warned of the pollution costs to the world's environment of U.S. factories relocating to poorer and less regulated nations, such as Mexico and China. Labor organizers decried the flight of American jobs as manufacturers sought less expensive and more compliant—often desperate—workers abroad. Human rights activists spotlighted the grim working conditions in many overseas plants, including the prevalence of child labor.

A "race to the bottom" for labor and environmental standards resulted from the development of a global assembly line. With capital able to move swiftly around the world and take its factories with it, nations and localities believed that they had little choice but to compete in offering multinational corporations the most advantageous terms possible. Such terms meant minimal government regulation, little protection for workers, nonexistent pollution standards, and local subsidies in place of corporate taxes. Corporate income taxes, which had been dropping since the 1950s, shrank by another third between 1986 and 2000. The *maquiladoras* on the Mexican border were part of a broader pattern of the corporate search for efficiency and profit, as companies, like Mollie James's Universal Manufacturing Company and RCA, took their production lines first to the American South and then abroad.

As a result, corporations and their products became less identifiable by nationality. Boeing Aircraft had long been the largest employer in the Seattle area, but was its new Boeing 777,

"On the Internet, nobody knows you're a dog."

■ The Internet provided both immediate connections with other people around the world and the safety of personal anonymity. Internet users could not be judged by their appearance or material possessions, only by the words they typed. Americans debated whether the popularity of the Internet represented a new kind of virtual community that would strengthen their connections to each other, or merely another way for citizens to remain isolated in their own homes rather than engaged with each other in civic organizations.

> *Was a Toyota made by American workers in Georgetown, Kentucky, a "foreign" car?*

manufactured piece by piece in twelve different countries, an "American" airplane? Japanese companies also moved many manufacturing plants overseas, including to the United States, to be closer to important markets. Was a Toyota made by American workers in Georgetown, Kentucky, a "foreign" car?

Who Benefits from Globalization?

The increasing globalization of the U.S. economy at the end of the twentieth century created enormous wealth while sharpening class inequalities. The stock market skyrocketed. The Dow Jones average of the value of thirty top companies' stocks rose steadily from 500 in 1956, to 1,000 in 1972, to 3,000 in 1991. Then it more than tripled in value in just eight years, surpassing 10,000 in 1999. Wealthy Americans who owned the bulk of corporate stock reaped the most gains, but middle- and even working-class Americans with retirement funds invested in the market also benefited handsomely. The process of globalization and the steady expansion of the U.S. economy after 1992 also encouraged a growing belief among Americans, especially affluent ones, that markets alone offered the best solution to social problems. But markets and their strict dependence on the profit motive proved unable to preserve the quality of the environment, to pull the 37 million officially poor Americans above the poverty line ($19,200 for a family of four in 2004), or to preserve the security of the vast middle class that had stabilized American politics since World War II. Inequalities within the United States reflected growing global inequality as 20 percent of the world's people (mostly in Europe and North America) consumed 86 percent of its goods and services.

American consumers enjoyed many of the fruits of the more integrated world economy. At least in industries not dominated by monopolies, the corporate quest for lower production costs, along with fierce international competition and technological innovation, reduced prices of many goods and services. Computers, airline travel, and gasoline were all significantly less expensive in real dollars (adjusted for inflation) than they had been a generation earlier. Competition abounded in the robust retail sector of the U.S. economy, including catalog and Internet shopping. Wal-Mart represented the epitome of how the globalized economy could benefit consumers. By 2000 the discount store surpassed General Motors as the largest American company, responsible for 6 percent of all U.S. retail sales. Wal-Mart's success resulted from relentlessly cutting costs through sharp management, using cheaper imported goods and employing a nonunion workforce, and passing some of its savings along to customers in the form of lower prices.

The benefits that Americans experienced as consumers in the global economy were offset by their declining status as workers. As manufacturers moved to the Sunbelt and then overseas, high-wage, unionized jobs providing health insurance and pension benefits disappeared. Average real wages declined for more than two decades after 1973, and union membership shrank from one-third of the workforce in the early 1950s to one-tenth in 2000. Family incomes were maintained only by the addition of second and third wage earners, especially women. Americans spent more than they earned. The average household had 13 credit cards and carried $8,500 in debt on them, in addition to owing car and home mortgage payments. In 2005, the average personal savings rate dropped below zero.

Already wider in the United States than in any other industrialized nation, the distance between rich and poor continued to grow, whittling away at Americans' self-image as a middle-class society. The share of the national income going to the richest 1 percent nearly doubled in the last quarter of the twentieth century, while the share going to the bottom 80 percent shrank. Three million Americans lived in gated communities in extremely affluent suburbs, while one of five American children grew up in poverty, and 21 million citizens sought emergency food assistance each year.

The political system, which helps determine how wealth and opportunity are distributed in a society, seemed to offer little respite from the widening gap between haves and have-nots. The fraction of eligible citizens who made the effort to vote in presidential elections declined to just half in 2000 and in off-year congressional elections to a mere third, with the likelihood of voting closely correlated to a person's affluence. The fierce partisanship, personal attacks, and culture of scandal that came to dominate American politics in the past two decades alienated many.

Citizens were also disillusioned by the blatant manner in which money came to dominate the political process. With the average cost of a successful Senate campaign at $7.5 million and a House campaign approaching $1 million, few but the wealthy could campaign for Congress, and elected members spent inordinate amounts of time raising money from wealthy donors. Republican Senator John McCain of Arizona called campaign financing "an elaborate influence-peddling scheme in which both parties conspire to stay in office by selling the country to the highest bidder." The ability of business to outspend labor fifteen to one in contributing to campaigns helped ensure minimal publicity to any discussions of the gulf between rich and poor.

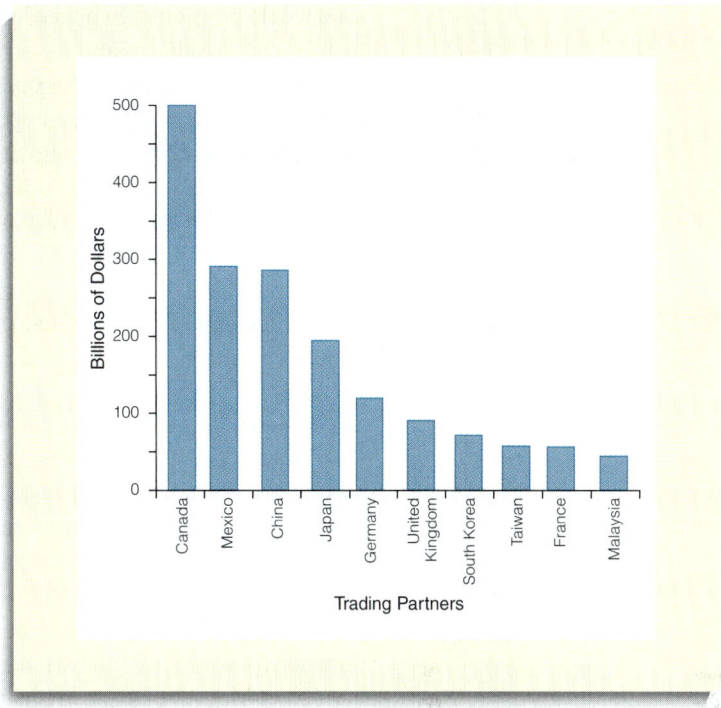

■ **FIGURE 30.1**
TOP TEN U.S. TRADING PARTNERS, 2005 (TOTAL VALUE OF IMPORTS AND EXPORTS IN BILLIONS OF DOLLARS) Americans do the most business with Canada and Mexico, followed by east Asia and then western Europe. U.S. economic vitality has always depended to some extent on foreign trade, but that dependence grew steadily in the past generation.

The Stewardship of Natural Resources

No issue was more global than the environment. Winds and waters did not respect political boundaries, nor did the materials borne on them. The condition of the natural environment affected all living creatures, yet the prevailing calculus of the market and private ownership did not apportion responsibility for its care. The free market system had no mechanism for offsetting, or even measuring, the costs of depleted natural resources. A generation ago, biologist Garrett Hardin had warned of "the tragedy of the commons": that individuals' incentives to preserve the quality of their own property did not carry over to resources held in common. Litter was an obvious example, and air, water, and ground pollution were the more serious cases. American culture had long celebrated human domination of the natural world and the benefits it brought, especially the growth in productivity that permitted living standards to rise dramatically across decades and centuries. At the same time, the rise of environmentalism and ecological understanding since 1960 offered a different way of imagining people's place on the earth.

Ecological Transformation in the Twentieth Century

Ecosystems are always dynamic, and changes in weather and Native American land use had reshaped the North American environment long before the followers of Christopher Columbus arrived on the continent. But European settlement and industrialization altered the face of the land in ways that would dumbfound a time traveler from the 1500s. Even a visitor from

1900 would be astonished by the intensity of human development of the land: vast cities with their sprawling suburbs and roads and highways everywhere. The key factor was population growth. Just as the number of people in the world quadrupled from 1.5 billion to 6 billion during the twentieth century, the population of the United States almost quadrupled from 75 million to 281 million, with the largest increase for a single decade (33 million) coming in the 1990s. Immigration and natural reproduction accounted for much of this, as did the much-longer average lifespan ushered in by antibiotics and antiviral vaccines.

The most dramatic changes in the land in the twentieth century resulted from the exploitation of wood, minerals, and water, particularly in the majority of the country lying west of the Mississippi River. Commercial logging destroyed all but 3 percent of the old-growth forests of the fifty states. The clearcuts scarring the mountainsides and hillsides of the Pacific Northwest and Alaska told the tale, as did the erosion caused by the overgrazing by cattle of public lands managed by the Interior Department's Bureau of Land Management in Utah, New Mexico, and other western states. The Mining Act of 1872 still granted to private corporations the rights to such valuable minerals as gold and copper on public land for the remarkable nineteenth-century price of $2.50 per acre. Mining companies took full advantage of the opportunity, resulting in rock and chemical wastes piled in vast slagheaps and dumped in toxic holding ponds from Arizona to Montana. In the arid but increasingly populated western states, water was the most critical resource for population growth. Increasing diversions of the Rio Grande left that now misnamed river so dry that, by 2001, it failed to reach the Gulf of Mexico, trickling to a halt 50 feet short. Groundwater pumping for agricultural irrigation in the Plains states and on the eastern slope of the Rocky Mountains was draining the vast underground Ogallala Aquifer at a rate that will empty it within a few more decades.

American prosperity came at a price. The prodigious growth of the U.S. economy in the twentieth century depended on the consumption of ever-increasing amounts of energy, most of it from coal, oil, and natural gas. Though making up less than 5 percent of the world's population, Americans accounted for a quarter of the globe's energy consumption. They depended on other countries to provide much of it for them: the United States imported 22 percent of its total energy needs and 69 percent of its oil, primarily from Saudi Arabia, Venezuela, Canada, and Mexico. Fossil fuels, such as coal and oil, could not be renewed; once burned, they were gone, and the world had a finite supply of such fuels. Americans were constructing a lifestyle that was unsustainable in the long run.

Pollution

The world's growing population was consuming five times as much fossil fuel in 2000 as in 1950, helping to stimulate a steady rise in the earth's average temperatures. Americans caused 36 percent of such carbon-based emissions, the largest contribution to the foremost environmental problem, global warming. In the summer of 2000, startled scientists found open water at the North Pole, a sight humans had never before seen. Greenhouse gases also contributed to a thinning of the ozone layer of the atmosphere, which enabled more of the sun's ultraviolet rays to reach the earth's surface and caused skin cancer rates to soar.

The internal combustion engine had long since surpassed coal burning as the leading cause of pollution. The United States produced and used more cars and trucks than any other nation. With minimal public transportation outside a handful of major cities, Americans were deeply committed to a car-dependent lifestyle. The highway infrastructure strained under the pressure of a 60 percent rise in the number of licensed drivers from 1970 to 2000 but only a 6 percent growth in total miles of roads. Negotiating traffic jams became a standard part of the daily lives of the majority of Americans who lived in the suburbs created by urban sprawl, especially around such cities as Los Angeles and Atlanta. Citizens spent three times as many hours stalled in traffic in 1999 as they had in 1982. Smog increasingly obscured such once-sublime vistas as that of Arizona's Grand Canyon.

Daily life in the United States came to depend in countless ways on the use of synthetic chemicals, production of which was 350 times greater in 1982 than in 1940. More than 50,000 known toxic waste dumps in the United States leached poisonous chemicals and heavy metals into the soil and water. Cancer rates among Americans grew sharply in the twentieth century, partly because people lived significantly longer lives (giving more time for cancers to appear) and partly because they were exposed to a much larger array of carcinogenic materials in the environment.

No synthetic product was more pervasive in the United States than plastic, a post-1945 product made from petroleum. But the most deadly and durable pollutants remained the radioactive wastes created by five decades of nuclear development. No one knew yet how to dispose safely of millions of tons of materials impregnated with plutonium and other human-made radioactive elements, 30 percent of it casually poured into dirt or stored in flimsy containers prone to leakage. The U.S. nuclear weapon complex of some 3,000 sites put its often fatal touch on the lives of millions of Americans: uranium miners, military workers, soldiers used to observe test explosions at close range, and citizens living downwind from the Nevada Test Site in Nevada and Utah. The National Academy of Sciences concluded in 2000 that many of these sites would be permanent national sacrifice zones, toxic to humans for at least tens of thousands of years.

> *No one knew yet how to dispose safely of millions of tons of materials impregnated with plutonium and other human-made radioactive elements.*

Environmentalism and Its Limitations

The ideas of most Americans about how to manage natural resources changed in the twentieth century. Environmental consciousness blossomed since the 1960s. Awareness of humans' connections with their broader ecological context led to significant reforms, such as the banning of carcinogenic pesticides and leaded gasoline, the cleaning up of polluted water in the Great Lakes, and the introduction of catalytic converters to reduce harmful emissions from automobile exhaust pipes and factory smokestacks. Recycling became common, and some dams were destroyed, freeing long-constricted rivers, such as the Penobscot in Maine. Yet issues of public land management and pollution control remained among the most controversial problems in American public life.

The relationship of Americans to their natural environment continued to be paradoxical. On the one hand, by large majorities in public opinion polls, Americans supported strong antipollution laws and the preservation of public lands from economic development. But on the other hand, in their daily lives, Americans consumed natural resources, especially gasoline, electricity, and water, at a rate unmatched by other societies. Measures that had reduced some of the nation's energy consumption since the 1970s were reversed by 2000: Congress revoked the national 55 mph speed limit in 1995, and ever-larger cars, trucks, and especially sport utility vehicles steadily reduced the average gas mileage of passenger vehicles.

■ The oil crises of the 1970s led automobile manufacturers to improve the efficiency of gas mileage in their cars. By the early 2000s, however, gasoline was once again inexpensive and growing numbers of Americans were buying large new sport utility vehicles (SUVs) such as the Chevrolet Suburban, despite their low gas mileage. A few environmentalists placed bumper stickers on other people's SUVs to highlight the key role of auto emissions in the accelerating process of global warming.

The Expansion of American Popular Culture Abroad

Just as the U.S. economy and American environmental problems could not be separated from the outside world, the nation's cultural life grew more closely tied to that of other nations at the dawn of the new millennium. During the Cold War, from the 1940s through the 1980s, American foreign relations hinged on problems of national security and the projection of military might abroad. The dissolution of the Soviet Union in 1991 and the retreat of communism ended the bipolar division of the world and left the United States the sole remaining superpower. By 2000 American popular culture rather than armed strength had emerged as the leading edge of U.S. influence around the world. American themes and products stood out in an increasingly global society, although they were resisted by some abroad who preferred more local identities and traditions, often rooted in ethnicity or religious conviction.

A Culture of Diversity and Entertainment

Known for its informality and diversity, American culture proved powerfully attractive to peoples all over the world, partly because racial and ethnic diversity was more pronounced in the United States than in any other major power. African Americans, Latino Americans, and Asian Americans all figured prominently in the popular realms of sports, music, and films. Television was the leading medium for this culture of entertainment, beaming CNN, MTV, and "reality" around the world. From jazz to rock 'n' roll to rap, American popular music spread across the globe, as did jeans and sneakers, symbols of informality and comfort. Hollywood's movies dominated cinemas and DVD players everywhere, providing 85 percent of films screened in Europe.

The idea of individual choice pervaded American culture, backed by constitutional guarantees of freedom of expression. Freedom to choose included matters of religion, politics, and other weighty areas, which had long made the United States a beacon of liberty to people oppressed for their beliefs. But freedom of choice came increasingly by the end of the twentieth century to refer to consumer goods. The United States was the largest market in the world, and its citizens had unparalleled choices of what to buy. The premium placed on acquiring material products seemed to many foreign observers the primary American value.

The premium placed on acquiring material products seemed to many foreign observers the primary American value.

Advertising grew in prominence as the central link between popular culture and the selling of goods. Sports became steadily more commercialized. Postseason college football games began in 1985 to include the names of their corporate sponsors, creating such events as the Chick-Fil-A Peach Bowl and the Weed Eater Independence Bowl. By 2000 newspapers ranked bowl games—once hallowed for their own distinctive traditions—by the simple criterion of how much money sponsors paid to participating teams. In the 1990s, "hoops" joined baseball as a popular U.S. export. National Basketball Association (NBA) games were telecast to more than 190 countries in forty-one languages. Sports also brought foreigners to the United States as professional baseball and basketball teams began recruiting Latin American, European, African, and Asian athletes.

U.S. Influence Abroad Since the Cold War

Cultural influences flowed both ways for Americans, with immigrants in particular bringing with them traditions and perspectives that refreshed the cultural mix of life in the United States. Japanese Pokémon trading cards, Thai cuisine, and Cuban salsa music helped shape daily routines for many Americans. But increased trade and communication since the end of the Cold War above all enabled the further spread of American popular culture. American-accented English straddled the globe, the language of international commerce and of 80 percent of listings on the World Wide Web. The informality and individualism of the Internet made it seem quintessentially American in style. The U.S. dollar remained the world's primary trading currency and became the de facto and even the de jure currency of many other nations.

America's most popular eatery served 20 million customers a day at its 23,000 franchises across the globe, earning half its revenues abroad. McDonald's Golden Arches appeared everywhere, from Japan and France to Russia and China. Even Mecca in Saudi Arabia, Islam's holiest site and the destination of millions of Muslim pilgrims, had a McDonald's.

Nor did only U.S. material interests spread abroad swiftly in recent years. American religious missionaries worked in poor countries around the world, combining their spiritual mission with a commitment to improving daily life in concrete ways involving health care, education, and agriculture. Pentecostalists gained millions of converts in Latin America since the 1970s, and mainstream denominations, such as Lutherans, Episcopalians, and Roman Catholics, saw their numbers rise sharply in Africa. The most fully homegrown American religion was especially active in proselytizing abroad. As a result, the Church of Jesus Christ of Latter Day Saints (Mormons), headquartered in Salt Lake City, had 5 million members in the United States and another 5 million worldwide.

The United States retained its military superiority, with a defense budget larger than that of the next ten biggest military powers combined. But the difficulties of unconventional warfare, from Vietnam in the 1960s to Somalia in 1993, combined with the apparent disappearance of a major threat to the nation's security after the demise of the Soviet Union, made U.S. policymakers and citizens reluctant to put American troops in harm's way abroad, at least until after the terrorist attacks of September 11, 2001. Instead, the expansion of American culture abroad seemed a safer and more effective way to influence other nations.

"Meritocracy worked for my grandfather, it worked for my father, and it's working for me."

■ An important tension in American history was the conflict between the ideal of equal opportunity for all and the reality of inherited wealth and privilege. The efforts of the George W. Bush administration to eliminate the federal estate tax, which affected the inheritances of less than 1 percent of U.S. citizens, represented the latest round in the debate about the relationship between political democracy and inherited economic inequality. In a pure meritocracy, all citizens would be rewarded for their personal achievements rather than those of their parents or ancestors.

Resistance to American Popular Culture

Like Christian, Jewish, and Hindu fundamentalists, all of whom grew prominent in the final decades of the twentieth century, Muslim fundamentalists rejected the radical egalitarianism and the unbridled pursuit of pleasure so prevalent in American popular culture. The relative equality of women and the lack of respect for traditional social and religious hierarchies seemed to them emblems of American decadence, as the Islamic rulers of Afghanistan—the Taliban—demonstrated in the 1990s in their brutal repression of women's rights. Osama bin Laden and his followers resented U.S. policies of supporting Israel and certain oil-producing Arab nations, but they also fiercely condemned the secular, egalitarian character of American society, which they considered anti-Islamic. During the 1991 Persian Gulf War, Saudi Arabian officials tried to isolate U.S. troops from Saudi citizens, fearing the effects of contact with such diverse forces as female soldiers, bawdiness, Christianity, and American music and television.

The demise of communist regimes in Russia and eastern Europe opened the gates to a flood of western influences and brought the opportunities and inequalities of a suddenly privatized economy. State-provided safety nets disappeared, class differences widened, women's economic status declined, and the old Communist parties regained some popularity among voters scared by the instabilities of American-style capitalism. Western Europeans also remained ambivalent about the spread of American values and lifestyles. Although many of them, especially among the young,

Roughly one-third of blacks were middle-class, and thousands won election to local, state, and national political offices. Black Americans became central in the nation's cultural life in music, literature, theater, and sports. By 2001 even a new president from the Republican party—known since 1964 for its lack of support from black voters—appointed two African Americans to direct the nation's foreign relations: Secretary of State Colin Powell and National Security Adviser Condoleezza Rice. Workplaces were racially integrated to an extent that would have been hard to imagine in 1950, and interracial marriages rose steeply in the final decades of the twentieth century.

The lives of women in the United States also changed dramatically during the last half of the twentieth century. Most worked outside the home, from jobs in the service and manufacturing sectors to careers in the professions and politics. In 2000 women made up one-third of the students in the nation's medical schools and one-half in law schools. Their presence in leading political positions ranged from local officials to more than a dozen U.S. senators, two U.S. Supreme Court justices, a U.S. attorney general, and a U.S. secretary of state. The passage of Title IX in 1972, prohibiting gender discrimination in school programs that received federal money, created a tidal wave of social change for American girls. In 1971 one in twenty-seven girls played high school sports; by 1998 the ratio was one in three. Sports programs and teams for girls comparable to those for boys nourished a new generation of American women for whom athletic competition and achievement were the norm rather than the exception.

These improvements for the majority of Americans who were not heterosexual white men jostled against abiding forms of discrimination and inequality. Violence and the threat of violence against homosexuals, people of color, and particularly women (primarily domestic violence at the hands of husbands and lovers) remained very real, but most prejudices found more subtle avenues of expression. Working women continued to average less than three-quarters the wages of working men. Many employers, police officers, store owners, bank loan officers, and others in positions of authority treated African Americans and Latino Americans with greater suspicion than they did other citizens, a practice that became known as racial profiling. Poverty and unemployment disproportionately affected black communities and families. Residential neighborhoods and public schools remained largely segregated by race, and the deeply symbolic Confederate flag still occupied a place of public honor in several southern states.

Native Americans shared this combination of improving status and continuing discrimination. Their numbers were reviving, from a mere 250,000 in 1900 to 2 million in 2000. A series of federal court decisions in the 1970s and 1980s strengthened Indians' "unique and limited" sovereignty over the tribal reservations, which constituted 2 percent of U.S. land. Starting with the Iroquois of upstate New York in 1970, several eastern Indian nations successfully sued state and federal governments for the return of parts of lands that had been illegally seized from them in the past, or for compensation. Casino revenues in the 1990s brought much-needed resources to a number of Indian nations. At the same time, the process of assimilation continued as a majority of Indians lived in urban areas and were married to non-Indians. Reservations suffered from severe unemployment rates and remained some of the poorest communities in the country, dependent on federal assistance for food and other basic necessities. Anti-Indian sentiments occasionally surfaced in states as diverse as Montana, Wisconsin, Arizona, and New York.

Still an Immigrant Society

Economic opportunity and individual liberty continued to lure millions of people from other nations to the United States at the start of the new millennium. About a million now came legally each year, and another 300,000 entered without official papers. For the first time since the 1930s, one in nine Americans had been born abroad; in New York City, the ratio was one in four. In 2004, 15 percent came from Europe, 33 percent from Asia, and 43 percent from Latin America and the Caribbean. Like Italy in 1900, Mexico in 2000 became the most important single source of new Americans. The demographic transition of California in 2000 from a white majority to a more diverse ethnic and racial mix like that of Hawaii symbolized the nation's turn to the South and West, even as the motives and work habits of the newcomers remained very much the same as those of their European predecessors.

Only the hardiest and most motivated people made the difficult, emotionally wrenching, and often dangerous move to the United States. Many fled political persecution in countries like Guatemala, Haiti, Vietnam, and Cuba. In contrast to the left-leaning and often socialist attitudes of immigrants in 1900, political refugees in 2000 were sometimes fierce anticommunists who helped pressure the U.S. government to take an even harder line toward regimes in Havana and Hanoi. Most immigrants came to stay, but some worked to save money and return home to their families, carrying with them not only money, but also bits of American culture.

> *Only the hardiest and most motivated people made the difficult, emotionally wrenching, and often dangerous move to the United States.*

Americans responded to the wave of newcomers with an ambivalence common in previous periods of high immigration. Many in the working class feared competition from highly motivated laborers accustomed to much lower wages. Many elites worried whether cultural diversity might weaken national unity. Conservative political leaders promoted new restrictions and stronger border patrols. Some U.S. Congressmen ridiculed the idea of there being value in traveling abroad by boasting that they did not even have passports. In 1998 Republican House Majority Leader Dick Armey of Texas announced, "I've been to Europe once; I don't have to go again." Such disdain for other cultures among some American political leaders dismayed U.S. allies overseas.

Most Americans simply got used to having more immigrants around. Americans cheered for the one in four major league baseball players who were born in Latin America or had parents from there, and they became accustomed to the high number of Asian Americans in college classrooms. Many churches worked to help new arrivals adjust to life in the United States. Above all, American employers depended on immigrant workers to keep the nation's powerful economy afloat—to pick its fruits and vegetables, tend its young children, and work in its factories.

Conclusion

What held Americans together as they set off into the twenty-first century was a common loyalty to a set of ideas about economic opportunities and individual liberties. Unlike such nations as Germany and Israel, where citizenship was extended automatically only to people of a certain ethnicity, the United States awarded citizenship to all those who were born within its borders, regardless of ethnicity or race. Those born elsewhere became citizens on the basis not of their past lineage but of their future commitments—of their newly sworn loyalty to the U.S. Constitution, with its guarantees of freedom and its responsibilities of citizenship. In a vast society of multiple political and cultural beliefs, the scope of specific freedoms and the nature of individual responsibilities inevitably remained matters of ongoing tension and conflict. Nonetheless, the United States continued to address most of its problems through an orderly legal system, in contrast to the ethnic and religious strife marking so many of the world's nations.

Americans will face some basic challenges in the near future, as suggested by the four main themes of this book. First, will the currently increasing inequality in American society—in terms of income, wealth, and power—weaken the bonds that hold the nation together? Policies regarding taxes, Social Security, health care, and welfare will help determine if most Americans will continue to see themselves as middle-class members of a mostly middle-class society. The process of globalization will not make this any easier. The tighter integration of the U.S. economy and the world economy has thus far helped create great wealth, but that wealth is distributed very unevenly among Americans. Who has how much wealth and influence will remain a crucial determinant of the nation's future.

Second, the use and distribution of natural resources will almost certainly become more contentious issues. As national and world populations continue to increase, so will the demand for oil, water, and timber. How will crowding and greater competition affect the quality of American life? How long can American society remain centered on the automobile and its emphasis on individual mobility? Behind all environmental issues looms perhaps the largest issue of all: global warming and how it may reshape societies around the globe, including the United States.

Third, the expansion of American influence abroad continues to create problems as well as benefits for Americans. U.S. military, economic, political, and cultural leadership is clear. But the enormous reservoir of goodwill toward the United States that was evident around the world through much of the twentieth century has been draining rapidly in recent years. Ongoing U.S. military operations in Afghanistan and Iraq have convinced millions of peoples in those regions and elsewhere, rightly or wrongly, that the United States is an aggressive nation bent on dominating the world in general and humbling Islamic nations in particular. Whether the United States will gain more than it loses by its military engagements abroad remains an open question.

Fourth and finally, American society has always been diverse and it continues to become more so. How well will Americans hold together as a people as their ranks come to include larger numbers of immigrants, non-Christians, people of color, open homosexuals, and people of other identities not previously considered mainstream? In comparison to most other cultures, American society has been unusually inclusive of people of diverse backgrounds and beliefs. Whether it will continue to be so will shape, as much as any other factor, the future of the United States.

Sites to Visit

Smithsonian Latino Center
latino.si.edu/
This site offers an array of links to information on Latino culture and history.

How Race Is Lived in America
www.nytimes.com/library/national/race/most-recent.html
This is a collection of revealing articles from the *New York Times* in 2000 on race relations and racial identities in contemporary America.

Muslim Life in America
usinfo.state.gov/products/pubs/muslimlife/
Here, researchers can find information on Muslims in modern America and links to other sources for research.

September 11 Digital Archive
911digitalarchive.org/
Created by the Center for History and New Media and George Mason University and the American Social History Project at City University of New York Graduate Center, this site offers a large collection of stories and images from September 11, 2001, when terrorists attacked New York City and Washington, D.C.

Native Americans
www.americanwest.com/pages/indians.htm
This site contains information about American Indian history and culture, along with links to the home pages of many Indian nations.

National Security Archive at George Washington University
www.gwu.edu/~nsarchiv/
This excellent site includes the most recent declassified documents on the making of U.S. foreign policy.

Natural Resources Defense Council
www.nrdc.org/
This site contains considerable information and links about an array of current environmental issues.

For Further Reading

General
Thomas Bender, ed., *Rethinking American History in a Global Age* (2002).
Godfrey Hodgson, *More Equal Than Others: America from Nixon to the New Century* (2004).
National Commission on Terrorist Attacks, *The 9/11 Commission Report* (2004).

The George W. Bush Administration
Ivo H. Daalder and James M. Lindsay, *America Unbound: The Bush Revolution in Foreign Policy* (2003).
Thomas Frank, *What's the Matter with Kansas? How Conservatives Won the Heart of America* (2004).
George Packer, *The Assassin's Gate: America in Iraq* (2005).
Kevin Phillips, *American Theocracy: The Peril and Politics of Radical Religion, Oil, and Borrowed Money in the Twentieth Century* (2006).

The American Place in a Global Economy
Jefferson Cowie, *Capital Moves: RCA's Seventy-Year Quest for Cheap Labor* (1999).
Thomas L. Friedman, *The Lexus and the Olive Tree: Understanding Globalization* (1999).
William Greider, *One World, Ready or Not: The Manic Logic of Global Capitalism* (1997).

The Stewardship of Natural Resources
David Goodstein, *Out of Gas: The End of the Age of Oil* (2004).
Al Gore, *An Inconvenient Truth: The Planetary Emergency of Global Warming and What We Can Do about It* (2006).
J. R. McNeill, *Something New Under the Sun: An Environmental History of the Twentieth-Century World* (2000).
Worldwatch Institute, *State of the World 2005: Global Security* (2005).

The Expansion of American Popular Culture Abroad
Benjamin R. Barber, *Jihad vs. McWorld: How the Planet Is Both Falling Apart and Coming Together and What This Means for Democracy* (1995).
Chalmers Johnson, *Blowback: The Costs and Consequences of American Empire* (2000).
Richard Pells, *Not Like Us: How Europeans Have Loved, Hated, and Transformed American Culture Since World War II* (1997).
Reinhold Wagnleitner and Elaine Tyler May, eds., *"Here, There and Everywhere": The Foreign Politics of American Popular Culture* (2000).

Identity in Contemporary America
David A. Hollinger, *Postethnic America: Beyond Multiculturalism*, rev. ed. (2006).
Gary Y. Okihiro, *Common Ground: Reimagining American History* (2001).
Robert D. Putnam, *Bowling Alone: The Collapse and Revival of American Community* (2000).
Ruth Rosen, *The World Split Open: How the Modern Women's Movement Changed America* (2000).

For quizzes and other resources on these topics, go to www.longmanamericanhistory.com.

Appendix

The Declaration of Independence

The Articles of Confederation

The Constitution of the
United States of America

Amendments to the Constitution

Presidential Elections

Present Day United States

Present Day World

The Declaration of Independence

In Congress, July 4, 1776

**The Unanimous Declaration
of the Thirteen United States of America**

When, in the course of human events, it becomes necessary for one people to dissolve the political bonds which have connected them with another, and to assume, among the powers of the earth, the separate and equal station to which the laws of nature and of nature's God entitle them, a decent respect to the opinions of mankind requires that they should declare the causes which impel them to the separation.

We hold these truths to be self-evident: That all men are created equal; that they are endowed by their Creator with certain unalienable rights; that among these are life, liberty, and the pursuit of happiness; that, to secure these rights, governments are instituted among men, deriving their just powers from the consent of the governed; that whenever any form of government becomes destructive of these ends, it is the right of the people to alter or to abolish it, and to institute new government, laying its foundation on such principles, and organizing its powers in such form, as to them shall seem most likely to effect their safety and happiness. Prudence, indeed, will dictate that governments long established should not be changed for light and transient causes; and accordingly all experience hath shown that mankind are more disposed to suffer, while evils are sufferable, than to right themselves by abolishing the forms to which they are accustomed. But when a long train of abuses and usurpations, pursuing invariably the same object, evinces a design to reduce them under absolute despotism, it is their right, it is their duty, to throw off such government, and to provide new guards for their future security. Such has been the patient sufferance of these colonies; and such is now the necessity which constrains them to alter their former systems of government. The history of the present King of Great Britain is a history of repeated injuries and usurpations, all having in direct object the establishment of an absolute tyranny over these states. To prove this, let facts be submitted to a candid world.

He has refused his assent to laws, the most wholesome and necessary for the public good.

He has forbidden his governors to pass laws of immediate and pressing importance, unless suspended in their operation till his assent should be obtained; and, when so suspended, he has utterly neglected to attend to them.

He has refused to pass other laws for the accommodation of large districts of people, unless those people would relinquish the right of representation in the legislature, a right inestimable to them, and formidable to tyrants only.

He has called together legislative bodies at places unusual, uncomfortable, and distant from the depository of their public records, for the sole purpose of fatiguing them into compliance with his measures.

He has dissolved representative houses repeatedly, for opposing, with manly firmness, his invasions on the rights of the people.

He has refused for a long time, after such dissolutions, to cause others to be elected; whereby the legislative powers, incapable of annihilation, have returned to the people at large for their exercise; the state remaining, in the mean time, exposed to all the dangers of invasions from without and convulsions within.

He has endeavored to prevent the population of these states; for that purpose obstructing the laws for naturalization of foreigners; refusing to pass others to encourage their migration hither, and raising the conditions of new appropriations of lands.

He has obstructed the administration of justice, by refusing his assent to laws for establishing judiciary powers.

He has made judges dependent on his will alone, for the tenure of their offices, and the amount and payment of their salaries.

He has erected a multitude of new offices, and sent hither swarms of officers to harass our people and eat out their substance.

He has kept among us, in times of peace, standing armies, without the consent of our legislatures.

He has affected to render the military independent of, and superior to, the civil power.

He has combined with others to subject us to a jurisdiction foreign to our constitution, and unacknowledged by our laws, giving his assent to their acts of pretended legislation:

For quartering large bodies of armed troops among us;

For protecting them, by a mock trial, from punishment for any murder which they should commit on the inhabitants of these states;

For cutting off our trade with all parts of the world;

For imposing taxes on us without our consent;

For depriving us, in many cases, of the benefits of trial by jury;

For transporting us beyond seas, to be tried for pretended offenses;

For abolishing the free system of English laws in a neighboring province, establishing therein an arbitrary government, and enlarging its boundaries, so as to render it at once an example and fit instrument for introducing the same absolute rule into these colonies;

For taking away our charters, abolishing our most valuable laws, and altering fundamentally the forms of our governments;

For suspending our own legislatures, and declaring themselves invested with power to legislate for us in all cases whatsoever.

He has abdicated government here, by declaring us out of his protection and waging war against us.

He has plundered our seas, ravaged our coasts, burned our towns, and destroyed the lives of our people.

He is at this time transporting large armies of foreign mercenaries to complete the works of death, desolation, and tyranny already begun with circumstances of cruelty and perfidy scarcely paralleled in the most barbarous ages, and totally unworthy the head of a civilized nation.

He has constrained our fellow-citizens, taken captive on the high seas, to bear arms against their country, to become the executioners of their friends and brethren, or to fall themselves by their hands.

He has excited domestic insurrection among us, and has endeavored to bring on the inhabitants of our frontiers the merciless Indian savages, whose known rule of warfare is an undistinguished destruction of all ages, sexes, and conditions.

In every stage of these oppressions we have petitioned for redress in the most humble terms; our repeated petitions have been answered only by repeated injury. A prince, whose character is thus marked by every act which may define a tyrant, is unfit to be the ruler of a free people.

Nor have we been wanting in our attentions to our British brethren. We have warned them, from time to time, of attempts by their legislature to extend an unwarrantable jurisdiction over us. We have reminded them of the circumstances of our emigration and settlement here. We have appealed to their native justice and magnanimity; and we have conjured them, by the ties of our common kindred, to disavow these usurpations, which would inevitably interrupt our connections and correspondence. They, too, have been deaf to the voice of justice and of consanguinity. We must, therefore, acquiesce in the necessity which denounces our separation, and hold them, as we hold the rest of mankind, enemies in war, in peace friends.

We, therefore, the representatives of the United States of America, in General Congress assembled, appealing to the Supreme Judge of the world for the rectitude of our intentions, do, in the name and by the authority of the good people of these colonies, solemnly publish and declare, that these United Colonies are, and of right ought to be, FREE AND INDEPENDENT STATES; that they are absolved from all allegiance to the British crown, and that all political connection between them and the state of Great Britain is, and ought to be, totally dissolved; and that, as free and independent states, they have full power to levy war, conclude peace, contract alliances, establish commerce, and do all other acts and things which independent states may of right do. And for the support of this declaration, with a firm reliance on the protection of Divine Providence, we mutually pledge to each other our lives, our fortunes, and our sacred honor.

JOHN HANCOCK

New Hampshire
Josiah Bartlett
William Whipple
Matthew Thornton

Massachusetts
John Adams
Samuel Adams
Robert Treat Paine
Elbridge Gerry

New York
William Floyd
Philip Livingston
Francis Lewis
Lewis Morris

Rhode Island
Stephen Hopkins
William Ellery

New Jersey
Richard Stockton
John Witherspoon
Francis Hopkinson
John Hart
Abraham Clark

Pennsylvania
Robert Morris
Benjamin Rush
Benjamin Franklin
John Morton
George Clymer
James Smith
George Taylor
James Wilson
George Ross

Delaware
Caeser Rodney
George Read
Thomas McKean

Maryland
Samuel Chase
William Paca
Thomas Stone
Charles Carroll of Carrollton

North Carolina
William Hooper
Joseph Hewes
John Penn

Virginia
George Wythe
Richard Henry Lee
Thomas Jefferson
Benjamin Harrison
Thomas Nelson Jr.
Francis Lightfoot Lee
Carter Braxton

South Carolina
Edward Rutledge
Thomas Heyward Jr.
Thomas Lynch Jr.
Arthur Middleton

Connecticut
Roger Sherman
Samuel Huntington
William Williams
Oliver Wolcott

Georgia
Button Gwinnett
Lyman Hall
George Walton

The Articles of Confederation

Between the States of New Hampshire, Massachusetts Bay, Rhode Island and Providence Plantations, Connecticut, New York, New Jersey, Pennsylvania, Delaware, Maryland, Virginia, North Carolina, South Carolina, Georgia

Article 1

The stile of this confederacy shall be "The United States of America."

Article 2

Each State retains its sovereignty, freedom and independence, and every power, jurisdiction, and right, which is not by this confederation expressly delegated to the United States, in Congress assembled.

Article 3

The said states hereby severally enter into a firm league of friendship with each other for their common defence, the security of their liberties and their mutual and general welfare; binding themselves to assist each other against all force offered to, or attacks made upon them, or any of them, on account of religion, sovereignty, trade, or any other pretence whatever.

Article 4

The better to secure and perpetuate mutual friendship and intercourse among the people of the different states in this union, the free inhabitants of each of these states, paupers, vagabonds, and fugitives from justice excepted, shall be entitled to all privileges and immunities of free citizens in the several states; and the people of each State shall have free ingress and regress to and from any other State, and shall enjoy therein all the privileges of trade and commerce, subject to the same duties, impositions, and restrictions, as the inhabitants thereof respectively; provided, that such restrictions shall not extend so far as to prevent the removal of property, imported into any State, to any other State of which the owner is an inhabitant; provided also, that no imposition, duties, or restriction, shall be laid by any State on the property of the United States, or either of them.

If any person guilty of, or charged with treason, felony, or other high misdemeanor in any State, shall flee from justice and be found in any of the United States, he shall, upon demand of the governor or executive power of the State from which he fled, be delivered up and removed to the State having jurisdiction of his offence.

Full faith and credit shall be given in each of these states to the records, acts, and judicial proceedings of the courts and magistrates of every other State.

Article 5

For the more convenient management of the general interests of the United States, delegates shall be annually appointed, in such manner as the legislature of each State shall direct, to meet in Congress, on the 1st Monday in November in every year, with a power reserved to each State to recall its delegates, or any of them, at any time within the year, and to send others in their stead for the remainder of the year.

No State shall be represented in Congress by less than two, nor by more than seven members; and no person shall be capable of being a delegate for more than three years in any term of six years; nor shall any person, being a delegate, be capable of holding any office under the United States, for which he, or any other for his benefit, receives any salary, fees, or emolument of any kind.

Each State shall maintain its own delegates in a meeting of the states, and while they act as members of the committee of the states.

In determining questions in the United States, in Congress assembled, each State shall have one vote.

Freedom of speech and debate in Congress shall not be impeached or questioned in any court or place out of Congress: and the members of Congress shall be protected in their persons from arrests and imprisonments, during the time of their going to and from, and attendance on Congress, except for treason, felony, or breach of the peace.

Article 6

No State, without the consent of the United States, in Congress assembled, shall send any embassy to, or receive any embassy from, or enter into any conference, agreement, alliance, or treaty with any king, prince, or state; nor shall any person, holding any office of profit or trust under the United States, or any of them, accept of any present, emolument, office or title, of any kind whatever, from any king, prince, or foreign state; nor shall the United States, in Congress assembled, or any of them, grant any title of nobility.

No two or more states shall enter into any treaty, confederation, or alliance, whatever, between them, without the consent of the United States, in Congress assembled, specifying accurately the purposes for which the same is to be entered into, and how long it shall continue.

No State shall lay any imposts or duties which may interfere with any stipulations in treaties entered into by the United States, in Congress assembled, with any king, prince, or state, in pursuance of any treaties already proposed by Congress to the courts of France and Spain.

No vessels of war shall be kept up in time of peace by any State, except such number only as shall be deemed necessary by the United States, in Congress assembled, for the defence of such State or its trade; nor shall any body of forces be kept up by any State, in time of peace, except such number only as, in the judgment of the United States, in Congress assembled, shall be deemed requisite to garrison the forts necessary for the defence of such State; but every State shall always keep up a well regulated and disciplined militia, sufficiently armed and accoutred, and shall provide, and constantly have ready for use, in public stores, a due number of field pieces and tents, and a proper quantity of arms, ammunition and camp equipage.

No State shall engage in any war without the consent of the United States, in Congress assembled, unless such State be actually invaded by enemies, or shall have received certain advice of a resolution being formed by some nation of Indians to invade such State, and the danger is so imminent as not to admit of a delay till the United States, in Congress assembled, can be consulted; nor shall any State grant commissions to any ships or vessels of war, nor letters of marque or reprisal, except it be after a declaration of war by the United States, in Congress assembled, and then only against the kingdom or state, and the subjects thereof, against which war has been so declared, and under such regulations as shall be established by the United States, in Congress assembled, unless such States be infested by pirates, in which case vessels of war may be fitted out for that occasion, and kept so long as the danger shall continue, or until the United States, in Congress assembled, shall determine otherwise.

Article 7

When land forces are raised by any State for the common defence, all officers of or under the rank of colonel, shall be appointed by the legislature of each State respectively, by whom such forces shall be raised, or in such manner as such State shall direct; and all vacancies shall be filled up by the State which first made the appointment.

Article 8

All charges of war and all other expences, that shall be incurred for the common defence or general welfare, and allowed by the United States, in Congress assembled, shall be defrayed out of a common treasury, which shall be supplied by the several states, in proportion to the value of all land within each State, granted to or surveyed for any person, as such land and the buildings and improvements thereon shall be estimated according to such mode as the United States, in Congress assembled, shall, from time to time, direct and appoint.

The taxes for paying that proportion shall be laid and levied by the authority and direction of the legislatures of the several states, within the time agreed upon by the United States, in Congress assembled.

Article 9

The United States, in Congress assembled, shall have the sole and exclusive right and power of determining on peace and war, except in the cases mentioned in the 6th article; of sending and receiving ambassadors; entering into treaties and alliances, provided that no treaty of commerce shall be made, whereby the legislative power of the respective states shall be restrained from imposing such imposts and duties on foreigners as their own people are subjected to, or from prohibiting the exportation or importation of any species of goods or commodities whatsoever; of establishing rules for deciding, in all cases, what captures on land or water shall be legal, and in what manner prizes, taken by land or naval forces in the service of the United States, shall be divided or appropriated; of granting letters of marque and reprisal in times of peace; appointing courts for the trial of piracies and felonies committed on the high seas, and establishing courts for receiving and determining, finally, appeals in all cases of captures; provided, that no member of Congress shall be appointed a judge of any of the said courts.

The United States, in Congress assembled, shall also be the last resort on appeal in all disputes and differences now subsisting, or that hereafter may arise between two or more states concerning boundary, jurisdiction or any other cause whatever; which authority shall always be exercised in the manner following: whenever the legislative or executive authority, or lawful agent of any State, in controversy with another, shall present a petition to Congress, stating the matter in question, and praying for a hearing, notice thereof shall be given, by order of Congress, to the legislative or executive authority of the other State in controversy, and a day assigned for the appearance of the parties by their lawful agents, who shall then be directed to appoint, by joint consent, commissioners or judges to constitute a court for hearing and determining the matter in question; but, if they cannot agree, Congress shall name three persons out of each of the United States, and from the list of such persons each party shall alternately strike out one, in the petitioners beginning, until the number shall be reduced to thirteen; and from that number not less than seven, nor more than nine names, as Congress shall direct, shall, in the presence of Congress, be drawn out by lot; and the persons whose names shall be drawn, or any five of them, shall be commissioners or judges to hear and finally determine the controversy, so always as a major part of the judges who shall hear the cause shall agree in the determination; and if either party shall neglect to attend at the day appointed, without shewing reasons which Congress shall judge sufficient, or, being present, shall refuse to strike, the Congress shall proceed to nominate three persons out of each State, and the secretary of Congress shall strike in behalf of such party absent or refusing; and the judgment and sentence of the court to be appointed, in the manner before prescribed, shall be final and conclusive; and if any of the parties shall refuse to submit to the authority of such court, or to appear or defend their claim or cause, the court shall nevertheless proceed to pronounce sentence or judgment, which shall, in like manner, be final and decisive, the judgment or sentence and other proceedings being, in either case, transmitted to Congress, and lodged among the acts of Congress for the security of the parties concerned: provided, that every commissioner, before he sits in judgment, shall take an oath, to be administered by one of the judges of the supreme or superior court of the State where the cause shall be tried, "well and truly to hear and determine the matter in question, according to the best of his judgment, without favour, affection, or hope of reward": provided, also, that no State shall be deprived of territory for the benefit of the United States.

All controversies concerning the private right of soil, claimed under different grants of two or more states, whose jurisdictions, as they may respect such lands and the states which passed such grants, are adjusted, the said grants, or either of them, being at the same time claimed to have originated antecedent to such settlement of jurisdiction, shall, on the petition of either party to the Congress of the United States, be finally determined, as near as may be, in the same manner as is before prescribed for deciding disputes respecting territorial jurisdiction between different states.

The United States, in Congress assembled, shall also have the sole and exclusive right and power of regulating the alloy and value of coin struck by their own authority, or by that of the respective states; fixing the standard of weights and measures throughout the United States; regulating the trade and managing all affairs with the Indians not members of any of the states; provided that the legislative right of any State within its own limits be not infringed or violated; establishing and regulating post offices from one State to another throughout all the United States, and exacting such postage on the papers passing through the same as may be requisite to defray the expences of the said office; appointing all officers of the land forces in the service of the United States, excepting regimental officers; appointing all the officers of the naval forces, and commissioning all officers whatever in the service of the United States; making rules for the government and regulation of the said land and naval forces, and directing their operations.

The United States, in Congress assembled, shall have authority to appoint a committee to sit in the recess of Congress, to be denominated "a Committee of the States," and to consist of one delegate from each State, and to appoint such other committees and civil officers as may be necessary for managing the general affairs of the United States, under their direction; to appoint one of their number to preside; provided that no person be allowed to serve in the office of president more than one year in any term of three years; to ascertain the necessary sums of money to be raised for the service of the United States, and to appropriate and apply the same for defraying the public expences; to borrow money or emit bills on the credit of the United States, transmitting, every half year, to the respective states, an account of the sums of money so borrowed or emitted; to build and equip a navy; to agree upon the number of land forces, and to make requisitions from each State for its quota, in proportion to the number of white inhabitants in such State; which requisitions shall be binding; and, thereupon, the legislature of each State shall appoint the regimental officers, raise the men, and cloathe, arm, and equip them in a soldier-like manner, at the expence of the United States; and the officers and men so cloathed, armed, and equipped, shall march to the place appointed and within the time agreed on by the United States, in Congress assembled; but if the United States, in Congress assembled, shall, on consideration of circumstances, judge proper that any State should not raise men, or should raise a smaller number than its quota, and that any other State should raise a greater number of men than the quota thereof, such extra number shall be raised, officered, cloathed, armed, and equipped in the same manner as the quota of such State, unless the legislature of such State shall judge that such extra number cannot be safely spared out of the same, in which case they shall raise, officer, cloathe, arm, and equip as many of such extra number as they judge can be safely spared. And the officers and men so cloathed, armed, and equipped, shall march to the place appointed and within the time agreed on by the United States, in Congress assembled.

The United States, in Congress assembled, shall never engage in a war, nor grant letters of marque and reprisal in time of peace, nor enter into any treaties or alliances, nor coin money, nor regulate the value thereof, nor ascertain the sums and expences necessary for the defence and welfare of the United States, or any of them: nor emit bills, nor borrow money on the credit of the United States, nor appropriate money, nor agree upon the number of vessels of war to be built or purchased, or the number of land or sea forces to be raised, nor appoint a commander in chief of the army or navy, unless nine states assent to the same; nor shall a question on any other point, except for adjourning from day to day, be determined, unless by the votes of a majority of the United States, in Congress assembled.

The Congress of the United States shall have power to adjourn to any time within the year, and to any place within the United States, so that no period of adjournment be for a longer duration than the space of six months, and shall publish the journal of their proceedings monthly, except such parts thereof, relating to treaties, alliances or military operations, as, in their judgment, require secrecy; and the yeas and nays of the delegates of each State on any question shall be entered on the journal, when it is desired by any delegate; and the delegates of a State, or any of them, at his, or their request, shall be furnished with a transcript of the said journal, except such parts as are above excepted, to lay before the legislatures of the several states.

Article 10

The committee of the states, or any nine of them, shall be authorized to execute, in the recess of Congress, such of the powers of Congress as the United States, in Congress assembled, by the consent of nine states, shall, from time to time, think expedient to vest them with; provided, that no power be delegated to the said committee for the exercise of which, by the articles of confederation, the voice of nine states, in the Congress of the United States assembled, is requisite.

Article 11

Canada acceding to this confederation, and joining in the measures of the United States, shall be admitted into and entitled to all the advantages of this union; but no other colony shall be admitted into the same, unless such admission be agreed to by nine states.

Article 12

All bills of credit emitted, monies borrowed and debts contracted by, or under the authority of Congress before the assembling of the United States, in pursuance of the present confederation, shall be deemed and considered as a charge against the United States, for payment and satisfaction whereof the said United States and the public faith are hereby solemnly pledged.

Article 13

Every State shall abide by the determinations of the United States, in Congress assembled, on all questions which, by this confederation, are submitted to them. And the articles of this confederation shall be inviolably observed by every State, and the union shall be perpetual; nor shall any alteration at any time hereafter be made in any of them, unless such alteration be agreed to in a Congress of the United States, and be afterwards confirmed by the legislatures of every State.

These articles shall be proposed to the legislatures of all the United States, to be considered, and if approved of by them, they are advised to authorize their delegates to ratify the same in the Congress of the United States; which being done, the same shall become conclusive.

The Constitution of the United States of America

Preamble

We the People of the United States, in Order to form a more perfect Union, establish Justice, insure domestic Tranquility, provide for the common defence, promote the general Welfare, and secure the Blessings of Liberty to ourselves and our Posterity, do ordain and establish this Constitution for the United States of America.

Article I

Section 1

All legislative Powers herein granted shall be vested in a Congress of the United States, which shall consist of a Senate and House of Representatives.

Section 2

The House of Representatives shall be composed of Members chosen every second Year by the People of the several States, and the Electors in each State shall have the Qualifications requisite for Electors of the most numerous Branch of the State Legislature.

No Person shall be a Representative who shall not have attained to the Age of twenty five Years, and been seven Years a Citizen of the United States, and who shall not, when elected, be an inhabitant of that State in which he shall be chosen.

Representatives and direct Taxes shall be apportioned among the several States which may be included within this Union, according to their respective Numbers, *which shall be determined by adding to the whole Number of free Persons, including those bound to Service for a Term of Years, and excluding Indians not taxed, three fifths of all other Persons.** The actual Enumeration shall be made within three Years after the first Meeting of the Congress of the United States, and within every subsequent Term of ten Years, in such Manner as they shall by Law direct. The Number of Representatives shall not exceed one for every thirty Thousand, but each State shall have at Least one Representative; *and until such enumeration shall be made, the State of New Hampshire shall be entitled to chuse three, Massachusetts eight, Rhode-Island and Providence Plantations one, Connecticut five, New York six, New Jersey four, Pennsylvania eight, Delaware one, Maryland six, Virginia ten, North Carolina five, South Carolina five, and Georgia three.*

When vacancies happen in the Representation from any State, the Executive Authority thereof shall issue Writs of Election to fill such Vacancies.

The House of Representatives shall chuse their Speaker and other Officers; and shall have the sole Power of Impeachment.

Section 3

The Senate of the United States shall be composed of two Senators from each State, *chosen by the Legislature thereof,* for six Years; and each Senator shall have one Vote.

Immediately after they shall be assembled in Consequence of the first Election, they shall be divided as equally as may be into three Classes. The Seats of the Senators of the first Class shall be vacated at the Expiration of the second Year, of the second Class at the Expiration of the fourth Year, and of the third Class at the Expiration of the sixth Year so that one third may be chosen every second Year; and if Vacancies happen by Resignation, or otherwise, during the Recess of the Legislature of any state, the Executive thereof may make temporary Appointments until the next Meeting of the Legislature, which shall then fill such Vacancies.

No Person shall be a Senator who shall not have attained to the Age of thirty Years, and been nine Years a Citizen of the United States, and who shall not, when elected, be an Inhabitant of that State for which he shall be chosen.

The Vice President of the United States shall be President of the Senate, but shall have no Vote, unless they be equally divided.

The Senate shall chuse their other Officers, and also a President *pro tempore*, in the Absence of the Vice President, or when he shall exercise the Office of President of the United States.

The Senate shall have the sole Power to try all Impeachments. When sitting for that Purpose, they shall be on Oath or Affirmation. When the President of the United States is tried the Chief Justice shall preside: And no Person shall be convicted without the Concurrence of two thirds of the Members present.

Judgment in Cases of Impeachment shall not extend further than to removal from Office, and disqualification to hold and enjoy any Office of honor, Trust or Profit under the United States: but the Party convicted shall nevertheless be liable and subject to Indictment, Trial, Judgment and Punishment, according to Law.

Section 4

The Times, Places and Manner of holding Elections for Senators and Representatives, shall be prescribed in each State by the Legislature thereof; but the Congress may at any time by Law make or alter such Regulations, except as to the Places of chusing Senators.

The Congress shall assemble at least once in every Year, *and such Meeting shall be on the first Monday in December, unless they shall by Law appoint a different Day.*

Section 5

Each House shall be the Judge of the Elections, Returns and Qualifications of its own Members, and a Majority of each shall constitute a Quorum to do Business; but a smaller Number may adjourn from day to day, and may be authorized to compel the Attendance of absent Members, in such Manner, and under such Penalties as each House may provide.

---

*Passages no longer in effect are printed in italic type.

Each House may determine the Rules of its Proceedings, punish its Members for disorderly Behaviour, and, with the Concurrence of two thirds, expel a Member.

Each House shall keep a Journal of its Proceedings, and from time to time publish the same, excepting such Parts as may in their Judgment require Secrecy; and the Yeas and Nays of the Members of either House on any question shall, at the Desire of one fifth of those Present, be entered on the Journal.

Neither House, during the Session of Congress, shall, without the Consent of the other, adjourn for more than three days, nor to any other Place than that in which the two Houses shall be sitting.

Section 6

The Senators and Representatives shall receive a Compensation for their Services, to be ascertained by Law, and paid out of the Treasury of the United States. They shall in all Cases, except Treason, Felony and Breach of the Peace, be privileged from Arrest during their Attendance at the Session of their respective Houses, and in going to and returning from the same; and for any Speech or Debate in either House, they shall not be questioned in any other Place.

No Senator or Representative shall, during the Time for which he was elected, be appointed to any civil Office under the Authority of the United States, which shall have been created, or the Emoluments whereof shall have been encreased during such time, and no Person holding any Office under the United States, shall be a Member of either House during his Continuance in Office.

Section 7

All Bills for raising Revenue shall originate in the House of Representatives; but the Senate may propose or concur with Amendments as on other Bills.

Every Bill which shall have passed the House of Representatives and the Senate, shall, before it become a Law, be presented to the President of the United States; If he approve he shall sign it, but if not he shall return it, with his Objections to the House in which it shall have originated, who shall enter the Objections at large on their Journal, and proceed to reconsider it. If after such Reconsideration two thirds of that House shall agree to pass the Bill, it shall be sent, together with the Objections, to the other House, by which it shall likewise be reconsidered, and if approved by two thirds of that House, it shall become a Law. But in all such Cases the Votes of both Houses shall be determined by yeas and Nays, and the Names of the Persons voting for and against the Bill shall be entered on the Journal of each House respectively. If any Bill shall not be returned by the President within ten Days (Sundays excepted) after it shall have been presented to him, the Same shall be a Law, in like Manner as if he had signed it, unless the Congress by their Adjournment prevent its Return, in which Case it shall not be a Law.

Every Order, Resolution, or Vote to which the Concurrence of the Senate and House of Representatives may be necessary (except on a question of Adjournment) shall be presented to the President of the United States; and before the Same shall take Effect, shall be approved by him, or being disapproved by him, shall be repassed by two thirds of the Senate and House of Representatives, according to the Rules and Limitations prescribed in the Case of a Bill.

Section 8

The Congress shall have Power To lay and collect Taxes, Duties, Imposts and Excises, to pay the Debts and provide for the common Defence and general Welfare of the United States; but all Duties, Imposts and Excises shall be uniform throughout the United States;

To borrow Money on the credit of the United States;

To regulate Commerce with foreign Nations, and among the several States, and with the Indian Tribes;

To establish an uniform Rule of Naturalization, and uniform Laws on the subject of Bankruptcies throughout the United States;

To coin Money, regulate the Value thereof, and of foreign Coin, and fix the Standard of Weights and Measures;

To provide for the Punishment of counterfeiting the Securities and current Coin of the United States;

To establish Post Offices and post Roads;

To promote the Progress of Science and useful Arts, by securing for limited Times to Authors and Inventors the exclusive Right to their respective Writings and Discoveries;

To constitute Tribunals inferior to the supreme Court;

To define and punish Piracies and Felonies committed on the high Seas, and Offences against the Law of Nations;

To declare War, grant Letters of Marque and Reprisal, and make Rules concerning Captures on Land and Water;

To raise and support Armies, but no Appropriation of Money to that Use shall be for a longer Term than two Years;

To provide and maintain a Navy;

To make Rules for the Government and Regulation of the land and naval Forces;

To provide for calling forth the Militia to execute the Laws of the Union, suppress Insurrections and repel Invasions;

To provide for organizing, arming, and disciplining, the Militia, and for governing such Part of them as may be employed in the Service of the United States, reserving to the States respectively, the Appointment of the Officers, and the Authority of training the Militia according to the discipline prescribed by Congress;

To exercise exclusive Legislation in all Cases whatsoever, over such District (not exceeding ten Miles square) as may, by Cession of particular States, and the Acceptance of Congress, become the Seat of the Government of the United States, and to exercise like Authority over all Places purchased by the Consent of the Legislature of the State in which the Same shall be, for the Erection of Forts, Magazines, Arsenals, dock-Yards, and other needful Buildings;—And

To make all Laws which shall be necessary and proper for carrying into Execution the foregoing Powers, and all other Powers vested by this Constitution in the Government of the United States, or in any Department of Officer thereof.

Section 9

The Migration or Importation of such Persons as any of the States now existing shall think proper to admit, shall not be prohibited by the Congress prior to the Year one thousand eight hundred and

eight, but a Tax or duty may be imposed on such Importation, not exceeding ten dollars for each Person.

The Privilege of the Writ of Habeas Corpus shall not be suspended, unless when in Cases of Rebellion or Invasion the public Safety may require it.

No Bill of Attainder or ex post facto Law shall be passed.

No Capitation, or other direct, Tax shall be laid, unless in Proportion to the Census or Enumeration herein before directed to be taken.

No Tax or Duty shall be laid on Articles exported from any State.

No Preference shall be given by any Regulation of Commerce or Revenue to the Ports of one State over those of another: nor shall Vessels bound to, or from, one State, be obliged to enter, clear, or pay Duties in another.

No Money shall be drawn from the Treasury, but in Consequence of Appropriations made by Law; and a regular Statement and Account of the Receipts and Expenditures of all public Money shall be published from time to time.

No Title of Nobility shall be granted by the United States: And no Person holding any Office of Profit or Trust under them, shall, without the Consent of the Congress, accept of any present, Emolument, Office, or Title, of any kind whatever, from any King, Prince, or foreign State.

Section 10

No State shall enter into any Treaty, Alliance, or Confederation; grant Letters of Marque and Reprisal; coin Money; emit Bills of Credit; make any Thing but gold and silver Coin a Tender in Payment of Debts; pass any Bill of Attainder, ex post facto Law, or Law impairing the obligation of Contracts, or grant any Title of Nobility.

No State shall, without the Consent of the Congress, lay any Imposts or Duties on Imports or Exports, except what may be absolutely necessary for executing its inspection Laws: and the net Produce of all Duties and Imposts, laid by any State on Imports or Exports, shall be for the Use of the Treasury of the United States; and all such Laws shall be subject to the Revision and Controul of the Congress.

No State shall, without the Consent of Congress, lay any Duty of Tonnage, keep Troops, or Ships of War in time of Peace, enter into any Agreement or Compact with another State, or with a foreign Power, or engage in War, unless actually invaded, or in such imminent Danger as will not admit of delay.

Article II

Section 1

The executive Power shall be vested in a President of the United States of America. He shall hold his Office during the Term of four Years, and, together with the Vice President, chosen for the same Term, be elected, as follows:

Each State shall appoint, in such Manner as the Legislature thereof may direct, a Number of Electors, equal to the whole Number of Senators and Representatives to which the State may be entitled in the Congress: but no Senator or Representative, or Person holding an Office of Trust or Profit under the United States, shall be appointed an Elector.

The Electors shall meet in their respective States, and vote by Ballot for two Persons, of whom one at least shall not be an Inhabitant of the same State with themselves. And they shall make a List of all the Persons voted for, and of the Number of Votes for each; which List they shall sign and certify, and transmit sealed to the Seat of the Government of the United States, directed to the President of the Senate. The President of the Senate shall, in the Presence of the Senate and House of Representatives, open all the Certificates, and the Votes shall then be counted. The Person having the greatest Number of Votes shall be the President, if such Number be a Majority of the whole number of Electors appointed; and if there be more than one who have such Majority, and have an equal Number of Votes, then the House of Representatives shall immediately chuse by Ballot one of them for President; and if no Person have a Majority, then from the five highest on the List the said House shall in like Manner chuse the President. But in chusing the President, the Votes shall be taken by States, the Representation from each State having one Vote; A quorum for this Purpose shall consist of a Member or Members from two thirds of the States, and a Majority of all the States shall be necessary to a Choice. In every Case, after the Choice of the President, the Person having the greatest Number of Votes of the Electors shall be the Vice President. But if there should remain two or more who have equal Votes, the Senate shall chuse from them by Ballot the Vice President.

The Congress may determine the time of chusing the Electors, and the Day on which they shall give their Votes; which Day shall be the same throughout the United States.

No person except a natural born Citizen, *or a Citizen of the United States, at the time of the Adoption of this Constitution,* shall be eligible to the Office of President; neither shall any Person be eligible to that Office who shall not have attained to the Age of thirty five Years, and been fourteen Years a Resident within the United States.

In Case of the Removal of the President from Office, or of his Death, Resignation, or Inability to discharge the Powers and Duties of the said Office, the Same shall devolve on the Vice President, and the Congress may by Law provide for the Case of Removal, Death, Resignation or Inability, both of the President and Vice President, declaring what Officer shall then act as President, and such Officer shall act accordingly, until the Disability be removed, or a President shall be elected.

The President shall, at stated Times, receive for his Services, a Compensation, which shall neither be encreased nor diminished during the Period for which he shall have been elected, and he shall not receive within that period any other Emolument from the United States, or any of them.

Before he enter on the Execution of his Office, he shall take the following Oath or Affirmation:—"I do solemnly swear (or affirm) that I will faithfully execute the Office of President of the United States, and will to the best of my Ability, preserve, protect and defend the Constitution of the United States."

Section 2

The President shall be Commander in Chief of the Army and Navy of the United States, and of the Militia of the several States, when called into the actual Service of the United States; he may require the Opinion, in writing, of the principal Officer in each of the executive Departments, upon any Subject relating to the Duties of their respective Offices, and he shall have Power to grant Reprieves and Pardons for Offences against the United States, except in Cases of Impeachment.

He shall have Power, by and with the Advice and Consent of the Senate, to make Treaties, provided two thirds of the Senators present concur; and he shall nominate, and by and with the Advice and Consent of the Senate, shall appoint Ambassadors, other public Ministers and Consuls, Judges of the supreme Court, and all other Officers of the United States, whose Appointments are not herein otherwise provided for, and which shall be established by Law: but the Congress may by Law vest the Appointment of such inferior Officers, as they think proper in the President alone, in the Courts of Law, or in the Heads of Departments.

The President shall have Power to fill up all Vacancies that may happen during the Recess of the Senate, by granting Commissions which shall expire at the End of their next Session.

Section 3

He shall from time to time give to the Congress Information of the State of the Union, and recommend to their Consideration such Measures as he shall judge necessary and expedient; he may, on extraordinary Occasions, convene both Houses, or either of them, and in Case of disagreement between them, with Respect to the Time of Adjournment, he may adjourn them to such Time as he shall think proper; he shall receive Ambassadors and other public Ministers; he shall take Care that the Laws be faithfully executed, and shall Commission all the officers of the United States.

Section 4

The President, Vice President and all civil Officers of the United States, shall be removed from Office on Impeachment for, and Conviction of, Treason, Bribery or other high Crimes and Misdemeanors.

Article III

Section 1

The judicial Power of the United States, shall be vested in one supreme Court, and in such inferior Courts as the Congress may from time to time ordain and establish. The Judges, both of the supreme and inferior Courts, shall hold their offices during good Behaviour, and shall, at stated Times, receive for their Services, a Compensation, which shall not be diminished during their Continuance in Office.

Section 2

The judicial Power shall extend to all Cases, in Law and Equity, arising under this Constitution, the Laws of the United States, and Treaties made, or which shall be made, under their Authority;—to all Cases affecting Ambassadors, other public Ministers and Consuls;—to all Cases of admiralty and maritime Jurisdiction;—to Controversies to which the United States shall be a Party;—to Controversies between two or more States;—between a State and Citizens of another State;—between Citizens of different States;—between Citizens of the same State claiming Lands under Grants of different States, and between a State, or the Citizens thereof, and foreign States, Citizens or Subjects.

In all Cases affecting Ambassadors, other public Ministers and Consuls, and those in which a State shall be Party, the supreme Court shall have original Jurisdiction. In all the other Cases before mentioned, the supreme Court shall have appellate Jurisdiction, both as to Law and Fact, with such Exceptions, and under such Regulations as the Congress shall make.

The Trial of all Crimes, except in Cases of Impeachment, shall be by Jury; and such Trial shall be held in the State where the said Crimes shall have been committed, but when not committed within any State, the Trial shall be at such Place or Places as the Congress may by Law have directed.

Section 3

Treason against the United States, shall consist only in levying War against them, or in adhering to their Enemies, giving them Aid and Comfort. No person shall be convicted of Treason unless on the Testimony of two Witnesses to the same overt Act, or on Confession in open Court.

The Congress shall have Power to declare the Punishment of Treason, but no Attainder of Treason shall work Corruption of Blood, or Forfeiture except during the Life of the Person attainted.

Article IV

Section 1

Full Faith and Credit shall be given in each State to the public Acts, Records, and judicial Proceedings of every other State. And the Congress may by general Laws prescribe the Manner in which such Acts, Records and Proceedings shall be proved, and the Effect thereof.

Section 2

The Citizens of each State shall be entitled to all Privileges and Immunities of Citizens in the several States.

A Person charged in any State with Treason, Felony, or other Crime, who shall flee from Justice, and be found in another State, shall on Demand of the executive Authority of the State from which he fled, be delivered up, to be removed to the State having Jurisdiction of the Crime.

No Person held to Service or Labour in one State, under the Laws thereof, escaping into another, shall, in Consequence of any Law or Regulation therein, be discharged from such Service or Labour, but shall be delivered up on Claim of the Party to whom such Service or Labour may be due.

Section 3

New States may be admitted by the Congress into this Union; but no new State shall be formed or erected within the Jurisdiction of any other State; nor any State be formed by the Junction of two or more States, or Parts of States, without the Consent of the Legislatures of the States concerned as well as of the Congress.

The Congress shall have Power to dispose of and make all needful Rules and Regulations respecting the Territory or other Property belonging to the United States; and nothing in this Constitution shall be so construed as to Prejudice any Claims of the United States, or of any particular States.

Section 4

The United States shall guarantee to every State in this Union a Republican Form of Government, and shall protect each of them against Invasion; and on Application of the Legislature, or of the Executive (when the Legislature cannot be convened) against domestic violence.

Article V

The Congress, whenever two thirds of both Houses shall deem it necessary, shall propose Amendments to this Constitution, or, on the Application of the Legislatures of two thirds of the several States, shall call a Convention for proposing Amendments, which, in either Case, shall be valid to all Intents and Purposes, as Part of this Constitution, when ratified by the Legislatures of three fourths of the several States, or by Conventions in three fourths thereof, as the one or the other Mode of Ratification may be proposed by the Congress; Provided *that no Amendment which may be made prior to the Year One thousand eight hundred and eight shall in any Manner affect the first and fourth Clauses in the Ninth Section of the first Article;* and that no State, without its Consent, shall be deprived of its equal Suffrage in the Senate.

Article VI

All Debts contracted and Engagements entered into, before the Adoption of this Constitution, shall be as valid against the United States under this Constitution, as under the Confederation.

This Constitution, and Laws of the United States which shall be made in Pursuance thereof; and all Treaties made, or which shall be made, under the Authority of the United States, shall be the supreme Law of the Land; and the Judges in every State shall be bound thereby, any Thing in the Constitution or Laws of any State to the Contrary notwithstanding.

The Senators and Representatives before mentioned, and the Members of the several State Legislatures, and all executive and Judicial Officers, both of the United States and of the several States, shall be bound by Oath or Affirmation, to support this Constitution; but no religious Test shall ever be required as a Qualification to any Office of public Trust under the United States.

Article VII

The Ratification of the Conventions of nine States, shall be sufficient for the Establishment of this Constitution between the States so ratifying the Same.

Done in Convention by the Unanimous Consent of the States present the Seventeenth Day of September in the Year of our Lord one thousand seven hundred and Eighty seven and of the Independence of the United States of America the Twelfth* IN WITNESS whereof We have hereunto subscribed our Names,

George Washington
President and Deputy from Virginia

Delaware
George Read
Gunning Bedford Jr.
John Dickinson
Richard Bassett
Jacob Broom

Maryland
James McHenry
Daniel of St. Thomas Jenifer
Daniel Carroll

Virginia
John Blair
James Madison Jr.

North Carolina
William Blount
Richard Dobbs Spraight
Hugh Williamson

South Carolina
John Rutledge
Charles Cotesworth Pinckney
Charles Pinckney
Pierce Butler

Georgia
William Few
Abraham Baldwin

New Hampshire
John Langdon
Nicholas Gilman

Massachusetts
Nathaniel Gorham
Rufus King

Connecticut
William Samuel Johnson
Roger Sherman

New York
Alexander Hamilton

New Jersey
William Livingston
David Brearley
William Paterson
Jonathan Dayton

Pennsylvania
Benjamin Franklin
Thomas Mifflin
Robert Morris
George Clymer
Thomas FitzSimons
Jared Ingersoll
James Wilson
Gouverneur Morris

---

*The Constitution was submitted on September 17, 1787, by the Constitutional Convention, was ratified by conventions of the several states at various dates up to May 29, 1790, and became effective on March 4, 1789.

Amendments to the Constitution

Amendment I

Congress shall make no law respecting an establishment of religion, or prohibiting the free exercise thereof; or abridging the freedom of speech, or of the press; or the right of the people peaceably to assemble, and to petition the Government for a redress of grievances.

Amendment II

A well regulated Militia being necessary to the security of a free State, the right of the people to keep and bear Arms, shall not be infringed.

Amendment III

No Soldier shall, in time of peace be quartered in any house, without the consent of the Owner, nor in time of war, but in a manner to be prescribed by law.

Amendment IV

The right of the people to be secure in their persons, houses, papers, and effects, against unreasonable searches and seizures, shall not be violated, and no Warrants shall issue, but upon probable cause, supported by Oath or affirmation, and particularly describing the place to be searched, and the persons or things to be seized.

Amendment V

No person shall be held to answer for a capital, or otherwise infamous crime, unless on a presentment or indictment of a Grand Jury, except in cases arising in the land or naval forces, or in the Militia, when in actual service in time of War or public danger; nor shall any person be subject for the same offense to be twice put in jeopardy of life or limb; nor shall be compelled in any criminal case to be a witness against himself, nor be deprived of life, liberty, or property, without due process of law; nor shall private property be taken for public use, without just compensation.

Amendment VI

In all criminal prosecutions, the accused shall enjoy the right to a speedy and public trial, by an impartial jury of the State and district wherein the crime shall have been committed, which district shall have been previously ascertained by law, and to be informed of the nature and cause of the accusation; to be confronted with the witnesses against him; to have compulsory process for obtaining witnesses in his favor, and to have the Assistance of Counsel for his defence.

Amendment VII

In Suits at common law, where the value in controversy shall exceed twenty dollars, the right of trial by jury shall be preserved, and no fact tried by a jury, shall be otherwise re-examined in any Court of the United States, than according to the rules of the common law.

Amendment VIII

Excessive bail shall not be required, nor excessive fines imposed, nor cruel and unusual punishments inflicted.

Amendment IX

The enumeration in the Constitution, of certain rights, shall not be construed to deny or disparage others retained by the people.

Amendment X*

The powers not delegated to the United States by the Constitution, nor prohibited by it to the States, are reserved to the States respectively, or to the people.

Amendment XI
[Adopted 1798]

The Judicial power of the United States shall not be construed to extend to any suit in law or equity, commenced or prosecuted against one of the United States by Citizens of another State, or by Citizens or Subjects of any Foreign State.

Amendment XII
[Adopted 1804]

The Electors shall meet in their respective states, and vote by ballot for President and Vice President, one of whom, at least, shall not be an inhabitant of the same state with themselves; they shall name in their ballots the person voted for as President, and in distinct ballots the person voted for as Vice President, and they shall make distinct lists of all persons voted for as President, and of all persons voted for as Vice President, and of the number of votes for each, which lists they shall sign and certify, and transmit sealed to the seat of the government of the United States, directed to the President of the Senate;—The President of the Senate shall, in the presence of the Senate and House of Representatives, open all the certificates and the votes shall then be counted;—The person having the greatest number of votes for President, shall be the President, if such number be a majority of the whole number of Electors appointed; and if no person have such majority, then from the persons having the highest numbers not exceeding three on the list of those voted for as President, the House of Representatives shall choose immediately, by ballot, the President. But in choosing the President, the votes shall be taken by states, the representation from each state having one vote; a quorum for this purpose shall consist of a member or members from two-thirds of the states, and a majority of all

---

*The first ten amendments (the Bill of Rights) were ratified and their adoption was certified on December 15, 1791.

the states shall be necessary to a choice. And if the House of Representatives shall not choose a President whenever the right of choice shall devolve upon them, before *the fourth day of March* next following, then the Vice President shall act as President, as in the case of the death or other constitutional disability of the President.—The person having the greatest number of votes as Vice President, shall be the Vice President, if such number be a majority of the whole number of Electors appointed, and if no person have a majority, then from the two highest numbers on the list, the Senate shall choose the Vice President; a quorum for the purpose shall consist of two-thirds of the whole number of Senators, and a majority of the whole number shall be necessary to a choice. But no person constitutionally ineligible to the office of President shall be eligible to that of Vice President of the United States.

Amendment XIII
[Adopted 1865]

Section 1

Neither slavery nor involuntary servitude, except as a punishment for crime whereof the party shall have been duly convicted, shall exist within the United States, or any place subject to their jurisdiction.

Section 2

Congress shall have power to enforce this article by appropriate legislation.

Amendment XIV
[Adopted 1868]

Section 1

All persons born or naturalized in the United States, and subject to the jurisdiction thereof, are citizens of the United States and of the State wherein they reside. No State shall make or enforce any law which shall abridge the privileges or immunities of citizens of the United States; nor shall any State deprive any person of life, liberty, or property, without due process of law; nor deny to any person within its jurisdiction the equal protection of the laws.

Section 2

Representatives shall be apportioned among the several States according to their respective numbers, counting the whole number of persons in each State, excluding Indians not taxed. But when the right to vote at any election for the choice of electors for President and Vice President of the United States, Representatives in Congress, the Executive and Judicial officers of a State, or the members of the Legislature thereof, is denied to any of the male inhabitants of such State, being twenty-one years of age, and citizens of the United States, or in any way abridged, except for participation in rebellion, or other crime, the basis of representation therein shall be reduced in the proportion which the number of such male citizens shall bear to the whole number of male citizens twenty-one years of age in such State.

Section 3

No person shall be a Senator or Representative in Congress, or elector of President and Vice President, or hold any office, civil or military, under the United States, or under any State, who, having previously taken an oath, as a member of Congress, or as an officer of the United States, or as a member of any State legislature, or as an executive or judicial officer of any State, to support the Constitution of the United States, shall have engaged in insurrection or rebellion against the same, or given aid or comfort to the enemies thereof. But Congress may by a vote of two-thirds of each House, remove such disability.

Section 4

The validity of the public debt of the United States, authorized by law, including debts incurred for payment of pensions and bounties for services in suppressing insurrection or rebellion, shall not be questioned. But neither the United States nor any State shall assume or pay any debt or obligation incurred in aid of insurrection or rebellion against the United States, or any claim for the loss or emancipation of any slave; but all such debts, obligations and claims shall be held illegal and void.

Section 5

The Congress shall have power to enforce, by appropriate legislation, the provisions of this article.

Amendment XV
[Adopted 1870]

Section 1

The right of citizens of the United States to vote shall not be denied or abridged by the United States or by any State on account of race, color, or previous condition of servitude.

Section 2

The Congress shall have power to enforce this article by appropriate legislation.

Amendment XVI
[Adopted 1913]

The Congress shall have power to lay and collect taxes on incomes, from whatever source derived, without apportionment among the several States, and without regard to any census or enumeration.

Amendment XVII
[Adopted 1913]

The Senate of the United States shall be composed of two Senators from each State, elected by the people thereof, for six years; and each Senator shall have one vote. The electors in each State shall have the qualifications requisite for electors of the most numerous branch of the State legislatures.

When vacancies happen in the representation of any State in the Senate, the executive authority of such State shall issue writs of election to fill such vacancies: *Provided,* That the legislature of any State may empower the executive thereof to make temporary appointments until the people fill the vacancies by election as the legislature may direct.

This amendment shall not be so construed as to affect the election or term of any Senator chosen before it becomes valid as part of the Constitution.

Amendment XVIII
[Adopted 1919, repealed 1933]

Section 1

After one year from the ratification of this article the manufacture, sale, or transportation of intoxicating liquors within, the importation thereof into, or the exportation thereof from the United States and all territory subject to the jurisdiction thereof for beverage purposes is hereby prohibited.

Section 2

The Congress and the several States shall have concurrent power to enforce this article by appropriate legislation.

Section 3

This article shall be inoperative unless it shall have been ratified as an amendment to the Constitution by the legislatures of the several States, as provided in the Constitution, within seven years from the date of the submission hereof to the States by the Congress.

Amendment XIX
[Adopted 1920]

The right of citizens of the United States to vote shall not be denied or abridged by the United States or by any State on account of sex.

Congress shall have power to enforce this article by appropriate legislation.

Amendment XX
[Adopted 1933]

Section 1

The terms of the President and Vice President shall end at noon on the 20th day of January, and the terms of Senators and Representatives at noon on the 3d day of January, of the years in which such terms would have ended if this article had not been ratified and the terms of their successors shall then begin.

Section 2

The Congress shall assemble at least once in every year, and such meeting shall begin at noon on the 3d day of January, unless they shall by law appoint a different day.

Section 3

If, at the time fixed for the beginning of the term of the President, the President elect shall have died, the Vice President elect shall become President. If a President shall not have been chosen before the time fixed for the beginning of his term, or if the President elect shall have failed to qualify, then the Vice President elect shall act as President until a President shall have qualified; and the Congress may by law provide for the case wherein neither a President elect nor a Vice President elect shall have qualified, declaring who shall then act as President, or the manner in which one who is to act shall be selected, and such person shall act accordingly until a President or Vice President shall have qualified.

Section 4

The Congress may by law provide for the case of the death of any of the persons from whom the House of Representatives may choose a President whenever the right of choice shall have devolved upon them, and for the case of the death of any of the persons from whom the Senate may choose a Vice President whenever the right of choice shall have devolved upon them.

Section 5

Sections 1 and 2 shall take effect on the 15th day of October following the ratification of this article.

Section 6

This article shall be inoperative unless it shall have been ratified as an amendment to the Constitution by the legislatures of three fourths of the several States within seven years from the date of its submission.

Amendment XXI
[Adopted 1933]

Section 1

The eighteenth article of amendment to the Constitution of the United States is hereby repealed.

Section 2

The transportation or importation into any State, Territory, or possession of the United States for delivery or use therein of intoxicating liquors in violation of the laws thereof, is hereby prohibited.

Section 3

This article shall be inoperative unless it shall have been ratified as an amendment to the Constitution by conventions in the several States, as provided in the Constitution, within seven years from the date of the submission hereof to the States by the Congress.

Amendment XXII
[Adopted 1951]

Section 1

No person shall be elected to the office of the President more than twice, and no person who has held the office of President, or acted as President, for more than two years of a term to which some other person was elected President shall be elected to the office of the President more than once. But this Article shall not apply to any person holding the office of President when this Article was proposed by the Congress, and shall not prevent any person who may be holding the office of President, or acting as President, during the term within which this Article becomes operative from holding the office of President or acting as President during the remainder of such term.

Section 2

This article shall be inoperative unless it shall have been ratified as an amendment to the Constitution by the legislatures of three-fourths of the several States within seven years from the date of its submission to the States by the Congress.

Amendment XXIII
[Adopted 1961]

Section 1

The District constituting the seat of Government of the United States shall appoint in such manner as the Congress shall direct:

A number of electors of President and Vice President equal to the whole number of Senators and Representatives in Congress to which the District would be entitled if it were a State, but in no event more than the least populous State; they shall be in addition to those appointed by the States, but they shall be considered, for the purposes of the election of President and Vice President, to be electors appointed by a State; and they shall meet in the District and perform such duties as provided by the twelfth article of amendment.

Section 2

The Congress shall have power to enforce this article by appropriate legislation.

Amendment XXIV
[Adopted 1964]

Section 1

The right of citizens of the United States to vote in any primary or other election for President or Vice President, for electors for President or Vice President, or for Senator or Representative in Congress, shall not be denied or abridged by the United States or any state by reason of failure to pay any poll tax or other tax.

Section 2

The Congress shall have the power to enforce this article by appropriate legislation.

Amendment XXV
[Adopted 1967]

Section 1

In case of the removal of the President from office or his death or resignation, the Vice President shall become President.

Section 2

Whenever there is a vacancy in the office of the Vice President, the President shall nominate a Vice President who shall take the office upon confirmation by a majority vote of both houses of Congress.

Section 3

Whenever the President transmits to the President pro tempore of the Senate and the Speaker of the House of Representatives his written declaration that he is unable to discharge the powers and duties of his office, and until he transmits to them a written declaration to the contrary, such powers and duties shall be discharged by the Vice President as Acting President.

Section 4

Whenever the Vice President and a majority of either the principal officers of the executive departments or of such other body as Congress may by law provide, transmit to the President pro tempore of the Senate and the Speaker of the House of Representatives their written declaration that the President is unable to discharge the powers and duties of his office, the Vice President shall immediately assume the powers and duties of the office as Acting President.

Thereafter, when the President transmits to the President pro tempore of the Senate and the Speaker of the House of Representatives his written declaration that no inability exists, he shall resume the powers and duties of his office unless the Vice President and a majority of either the principal officers of the executive department or of such other body as Congress may by law provide, transmit within four days to the President pro tempore of the Senate and the Speaker of the House of Representatives their written declaration that the President is unable to discharge the powers and duties of his office. Thereupon Congress shall decide the issue, assembling within 48 hours for that purpose if not in session. If the Congress, within 21 days after receipt of the latter written declaration, or, if Congress is not in session, within 21 days after Congress is required to assemble, determines by two-thirds vote of both houses that the President is unable to discharge the powers and duties of his office, the Vice President shall continue to discharge the same as Acting President; otherwise, the President shall resume the powers and duties of his office.

Amendment XXVI
[Adopted 1971]

Section 1

The right of citizens of the United States, who are 18 years of age or older, to vote shall not be denied or abridged by the United States or any state on account of age.

Section 2

The Congress shall have the power to enforce this article by appropriate legislation.

Amendment XXVII
[Adopted 1992]

No law, varying the compensation for the services of the Senators and Representatives shall take effect, until an election of Representatives shall have intervened.

Presidential Elections

Year	Candidates	Parties	Popular Vote	Electoral Vote	Voter Participation
1789	**George Washington**		a	69	
	John Adams			34	
	Others			35	
1792	**George Washington**		a	132	
	John Adams			77	
	George Clinton			50	
	Others			5	
1796	**John Adams**	Federalist	a	71	
	Thomas Jefferson	Democratic-Republican		68	
	Thomas Pinckney	Federalist		59	
	Aaron Burr	Dem.-Rep.		30	
	Others			48	
1800	**Thomas Jefferson**	Dem.-Rep.	a	73	
	Aaron Burr	Dem.-Rep.		73	
	John Adams	Federalist		65	
	C. C. Pinckney	Federalist		64	
	John Jay	Federalist		1	
1804	**Thomas Jefferson**	Dem.-Rep.	a	162	
	C. C. Pinckney	Federalist		14	
1808	**James Madison**	Dem.-Rep.	a	122	
	C. C. Pinckney	Federalist		47	
	George Clinton	Dem.-Rep.		6	
1812	**James Madison**	Dem.-Rep.	a	128	
	De Witt Clinton	Federalist		89	
1816	**James Monroe**	Dem.-Rep.	a	183	
	Rufus King	Federalist		34	
1820	**James Monroe**	Dem.-Rep.	a	231	
	John Quincy Adams	Dem.-Rep.		1	
1824	**John Quincy Adams**	Dem.-Rep.	108,740 (30.5%)	84	26.9%
	Andrew Jackson	Dem.-Rep.	153,544 (43.1%)	99	
	William H. Crawford	Dem.-Rep.	46,618 (13.1%)	41	
	Henry Clay	Dem.-Rep.	47,136 (13.2%)	37	
1828	**Andrew Jackson**	Democratic	647,286 (56.0%)	178	57.6%
	John Quincy Adams	National Republican	508,064 (44.0%)	83	
1832	**Andrew Jackson**	Democratic	687,502 (55.0%)	219	55.4%
	Henry Clay	National Republican	530,189 (42.4%)	49	
	John Floyd	Independent		11	
	William Wirt	Anti-Mason	33,108 (2.6%)	7	
1836	**Martin Van Buren**	Democratic	765,483 (50.9%)	170	57.8%
	William Henry Harrison	Whig		73	
	Hugh L. White	Whig	739,795 (49.1%)	26	
	Daniel Webster	Whig		14	
	W. P. Magnum	Independent		11	
1840	**William Henry Harrison**	Whig	1,274,624 (53.1%)	234	80.2%
	Martin Van Buren	Democratic	1,127,781 (46.9%)	60	
	J. G. Birney	Liberty	7,069	—	

[a] Electors selected by state legislatures.

Year	Candidates	Parties	Popular Vote	Electoral Vote	Voter Participation
1844	**James K. Polk**	Democratic	1,338,464 (49.6%)	170	78.9%
	Henry Clay	Whig	1,300,097 (48.1%)	105	
	J. G. Birney	Liberty	62,300 (2.3%)	—	
1848	**Zachary Taylor**	Whig	1,360,967 (47.4%)	163	72.7%
	Lewis Cass	Democratic	1,222,342 (42.5%)	127	
	Martin Van Buren	Free-Soil	291,263 (10.1%)	—	
1852	**Franklin Pierce**	Democratic	1,601,117 (50.9%)	254	69.6%
	Winfield Scott	Whig	1,385,453 (44.1%)	42	
	John P. Hale	Free-Soil	155,825 (5.0%)	—	
1856	**James Buchanan**	Democratic	1,832,955 (45.3%)	174	78.9%
	John C. Frémont	Republican	1,339,932 (33.1%)	114	
	Millard Fillmore	American	871,731 (21.6%)	8	
1860	**Abraham Lincoln**	Republican	1,865,593 (39.8%)	180	81.2%
	Stephen A. Douglas	Democratic	1,382,713 (29.5%)	12	
	John C. Breckinridge	Democratic	848,356 (18.1%)	72	
	John Bell	Union	592,906 (12.6%)	39	
1864	**Abraham Lincoln**	Republican	2,213,655 (55.0%)	212[b]	73.8%
	George B. McClellan	Democratic	1,805,237 (45.0%)	21	
1868	**Ulysses S. Grant**	Republican	3,012,833 (52.7%)	214	78.1%
	Horatio Seymour	Democratic	2,703,249 (47.3%)	80	
1872	**Ulysses S. Grant**	Republican	3,597,132 (55.6%)	286	71.3%
	Horace Greeley	Dem.; Liberal Republican	2,834,125 (43.9%)	66[c]	
1876	**Rutherford B. Hayes**[d]	Republican	4,036,298 (48.0%)	185	81.8%
	Samuel J. Tilden	Democratic	4,300,590 (51.0%)	184	
1880	**James A. Garfield**	Republican	4,454,416 (48.5%)	214	79.4%
	Winfield S. Hancock	Democratic	4,444,952 (48.1%)	155	
1884	**Grover Cleveland**	Democratic	4,874,986 (48.5%)	219	77.5%
	James G. Blaine	Republican	4,851,981 (48.2%)	182	
1888	**Benjamin Harrison**	Republican	5,439,853 (47.9%)	233	79.3%
	Grover Cleveland	Democratic	5,540,309 (48.6%)	168	
1892	**Grover Cleveland**	Democratic	5,556,918 (46.1%)	277	74.7%
	Benjamin Harrison	Republican	5,176,108 (43.0%)	145	
	James B. Weaver	People's	1,041,028 (8.5%)	22	
1896	**William McKinley**	Republican	7,104,779 (51.1%)	271	79.3%
	William Jennings Bryan	Democratic People's	6,502,925 (47.7%)	176	
1900	**William McKinley**	Republican	7,207,923 (51.7%)	292	73.2%
	William Jennings Bryan	Dem.-Populist	6,358,133 (45.5%)	155	
1904	**Theodore Roosevelt**	Republican	7,623,486 (57.9%)	336	65.2%
	Alton B. Parker	Democratic	5,077,911 (37.6%)	140	
	Eugene V. Debs	Socialist	402,283 (3.0%)	—	
1908	**William H. Taft**	Republican	7,678,908 (51.6%)	321	65.4%
	William Jennings Bryan	Democratic	6,409,104 (43.1%)	162	
	Eugene V. Debs	Socialist	420,793 (2.8%)	—	
1912	**Woodrow Wilson**	Democratic	6,293,454 (41.9%)	435	58.8%
	Theodore Roosevelt	Progressive	4,119,538 (27.4%)	88	
	William H. Taft	Republican	3,484,980 (23.2%)	8	
	Eugene V. Debs	Socialist	900,672 (6.0%)	—	
1916	**Woodrow Wilson**	Democratic	9,129,606 (49.4%)	277	61.6%
	Charles E. Hughes	Republican	8,538,221 (46.2%)	254	
	A. L. Benson	Socialist	585,113 (3.2%)	—	
1920	**Warren G. Harding**	Republican	16,152,200 (60.4%)	404	49.2%
	James M. Cox	Democratic	9,147,353 (34.2%)	127	
	Eugene V. Debs	Socialist	919,799 (3.4%)	—	
1924	**Calvin Coolidge**	Republican	15,725,016 (54.0%)	382	48.9%
	John W. Davis	Democratic	8,386,503 (28.8%)	136	
	Robert M. La Follette	Progressive	4,822,856 (16.6%)	13	

[b]Eleven secessionist states did not participate.
[c]Greeley died before the electoral college met. His electoral votes were divided among the four minor candidates.
[d]Contested result settled by special election.

Year	Candidates	Parties	Popular Vote	Electoral Vote	Voter Participation
1928	**Herbert Hoover**	Republican	21,391,381 (58.2%)	444	56.9%
	Alfred E. Smith	Democratic	15,016,443 (40.9%)	87	
	Norman Thomas	Socialist	267,835 (0.7%)	—	
1932	**Franklin D. Roosevelt**	Democratic	22,821,857 (57.4%)	472	56.9%
	Herbert Hoover	Republican	15,761,841 (39.7%)	59	
	Norman Thomas	Socialist	881,951 (2.2%)	—	
1936	**Franklin D. Roosevelt**	Democratic	27,751,597 (60.8%)	523	61.0%
	Alfred M. Landon	Republican	16,679,583 (36.5%)	8	
	William Lemke	Union	882,479 (1.9%)	—	
1940	**Franklin D. Roosevelt**	Democratic	27,244,160 (54.8%)	449	62.5%
	Wendell L. Willkie	Republican	22,305,198 (44.8%)	82	
1944	**Franklin D. Roosevelt**	Democratic	25,602,504 (53.5%)	432	55.9%
	Thomas E. Dewey	Republican	22,006,285 (46.0%)	99	
1948	**Harry S. Truman**	Democratic	24,105,695 (49.5%)	304	53.0%
	Thomas E. Dewey	Republican	21,969,170 (45.1%)	189	
	J. Strom Thurmond	State-Rights Democratic	1,169,021 (2.4%)	38	
	Henry A. Wallace	Progressive	1,156,103 (2.4%)	—	
1952	**Dwight D. Eisenhower**	Republican	33,936,252 (55.1%)	442	63.3%
	Adlai E. Stevenson	Democratic	27,314,992 (44.4%)	89	
1956	**Dwight D. Eisenhower**	Republican	35,575,420 (57.6%)	457	60.6%
	Adlai E. Stevenson	Democratic	26,033,066 (42.1%)	73	
	Other	—	—	1	
1960	**John F. Kennedy**	Democratic	34,227,096 (49.9%)	303	62.8%
	Richard M. Nixon	Republican	34,108,546 (49.6%)	219	
	Other	—	—	15	
1964	**Lyndon B. Johnson**	Democratic	43,126,506 (61.1%)	486	61.7%
	Barry M. Goldwater	Republican	27,176,799 (38.5%)	52	
1968	**Richard M. Nixon**	Republican	31,770,237 (43.4%)	301	60.6%
	Hubert H. Humphrey	Democratic	31,270,533 (42.7%)	191	
	George Wallace	American Indep.	9,906,141 (13.5%)	46	
1972	**Richard M. Nixon**	Republican	47,169,911 (60.7%)	520	55.2%
	George S. McGovern	Democratic	29,170,383 (37.5%)	17	
	Other	—	—	1	
1976	**Jimmy Carter**	Democratic	40,828,587 (50.0%)	297	53.5%
	Gerald R. Ford	Republican	39,147,613 (47.9%)	241	
	Other	—	1,575,459 (2.1%)	—	
1980	**Ronald Reagan**	Republican	43,901,812 (50.7%)	489	52.6%
	Jimmy Carter	Democratic	35,483,820 (41.0%)	49	
	John B. Anderson	Independent	5,719,722 (6.6%)	—	
	Ed Clark	Libertarian	921,188 (1.1%)	—	
1984	**Ronald Reagan**	Republican	54,455,075 (59.0%)	525	53.3%
	Walter Mondale	Democratic	37,577,185 (41.0%)	13	
1988	**George H. W. Bush**	Republican	48,886,000 (53.4%)	426	57.4%
	Michael S. Dukakis	Democratic	41,809,000 (45.6%)	111	
1992	**William J. Clinton**	Democratic	43,728,375 (43.0%)	370	55.0%
	George H. W. Bush	Republican	38,167,416 (38.0%)	168	
	H. Ross Perot	Independent	19,237,247 (19.0%)	—	
1996	**William J. Clinton**	Democratic	45,590,703 (50.0%)	379	48.8%
	Robert Dole	Republican	37,816,307 (41.0%)	159	
	H. Ross Perot	Reform	7,866,284		
2000	**George W. Bush**	Republican	50,456,167 (47.88%)	271	51.2%
	Al Gore	Democratic	50,996,064 (48.39%)	266[e]	
	Ralph Nader	Green	2,864,810 (2.72%)	—	
	Other	—	834,774 (<1%)	—	
2004	**George W. Bush**	Republican	61,873,000 (50.8%)	286	55.3%
	John Kerry	Democratic	58,895,000 (48.3%)	251	
	Ralph Nader	Green	463,653 (<1%)	—	

[e]One District of Columbia Gore elector abstained.

Glossary

Abdicate To give up a throne or high position, to renounce sovereign power. 73

Accommodationist A person who adapts or modifies a position to ease conflict rather than holding fast to convictions in the face of opposition. 427

Acculturate To change the behavior of a group to conform to the behavior of the larger society. 434

Adage A familiar saying that embodies a common observation or a wise idea. 165

Aliens Foreign-born residents of the United States who have not been naturalized as U.S. citizens. 491

Allies Members of an alliance, such as the military coalition led by the United States, the Soviet Union, and Great Britain during World War II. 544

Almshouse A privately financed home for the poor; a poorhouse. 124

Amphibious landing A military assault that begins on the water and ends on land. 305

Anarchists Persons who reject all forms of government as inherently oppressive and undesirable. 415

Annexation Addition of territory that had belonged to one nation into another nation. 302

Annulment An official pronouncement nullifying a marriage, or declaring it invalid. 24

Antebellum The extended period before a war; usually refers to the several decades immediately before the American Civil War. 257

Anthropology The study of the origin and development of humankind. 426

Anti-Federalists A diverse and unsuccessful coalition that opposed ratification of the Constitution and feared the increased power of the proposed central government. The Anti-Federalists were named by their opponents, the Federalists. 211

Antisemitism Prejudice against Jews. 389

Aqueduct An elevated conduit or channel built to transfer water flowing from a distant source, using gravity. 000

Archaic period The second long stage of North American habitation, covering about 7,000 years, from roughly 8,000 BCE to 1000 BCE (or from 10,000 to 3,000 years ago). During this period, inhabitants adapted to diverse local environments, gathering plants and hunting smaller animals than during the previous Paleo-Indian period. 6

Archipelago A group of islands, such as the Hawaiian archipelago. 12

Ardent Passionate, devoted, zealous, fiery. 41

Armistice A truce in a military conflict; a temporary halt in hostilities by agreement between the opposing sides. 439

Asiento A contract negotiated by the Spanish crown (between 1595 and 1789) with other European powers such as Portugal, France, England, and the Netherlands to provide a fixed number of slaves annually to Spain's American colonies for a set payment. 82

Assembly line A form of industrial production popularized by the Ford Motor Company in which workers perform one task repeatedly as the products they are jointly assembling move along a conveyor. 456

Atlatl A weighted, handheld device that enabled early Native Americans to throw spears with added power and velocity. 7

Avid Eager, greedy, enthusiastic. 169

Axis A political alignment or alliance, such as the military coalition between Germany, Italy, and Japan during World War II. 532

Babel A city described in the Old Testament where constructing a tower was made impossible by the confusion of varied languages. This term from the Book of Genesis is used to describe any scene of clamor and confusion. 110

Baby boom The period of increased U.S. childbirths from roughly the early 1940s to the early 1960s. 575

Baby boomers The generation of Americans born during the era from the early 1940s to the early 1960s. 665

Barracoon An enclosure or barrack used for the confinement of slaves before their forced deportation from the African coast. 92

Bill of Rights A set of amendments assuring basic rights, proposed by James Madison to help ensure acceptance of the newly drafted Constitution, and based on suggestions from the states. Ten of the twelve items passed by Congress were ratified by the states in 1791. Taken together, these first ten amendments to the Constitution became known as the Bill of Rights. 214

Black Codes Southern state laws passed after the Civil War to limit the rights and actions of newly liberated African Americans. 360

Blacklist A (figurative or real) list of persons to be denied jobs because of their alleged loyalty to a particular cause or institution. 414

Black power The slogan used by young black nationalists in the mid- and late 1960s. 603

"Bloody shirt" A partisan rallying cry used to stir up or revive sectional or party animosity after the American Civil War; for example, post–Civil War Republicans "waved the bloody shirt," associating some Democrats with a treasonous acceptance of secession during the war, while opponents had spilled their blood for the Union. 397

GLOSSARY G-1

Bolsheviks The Communist revolutionaries who overthrew the Russian czar in 1917 and established the Union of Soviet Socialist Republics (USSR). 480

Boston marriages Unions of two women based on long-term emotional bonds in which the women live together as if married to each other. 457

Braceros Mexican nationals working in the United States in low-wage jobs as part of a temporary work program between 1942 and 1964. (The *Bracero* program was established by an executive agreement between the presidents of Mexico and the United States, providing Mexican agricultural labor in the Southwest and the Pacific Northwest.) 578

Brunt The principal force, shock, or stress, especially of an attack. 203

Bull Moosers Supporters of Theodore Roosevelt in the 1912 presidential election when he broke from the Republican party and ran as a third-party candidate on the ticket of the Progressive (or Bull Moose) party. 464

Burgess A representative elected to the popular branch of the colonial legislature in either Virginia or Maryland. 44

Cajuns The Louisiana word for French-speaking people from Acadia (Nova Scotia) who were forced to move south in 1755 during the French and Indian War. Many of these refugees eventually moved to French Louisiana, where they have had a lasting impact on the culture. 119

Canal locks An enclosure on a canal or other waterway equipped with gates that can be closed so that boats can be raised or lowered by adjusting the water, in order to pass from one level to another. 265

Capitalism The now almost worldwide economic system of private ownership of property and profit-seeking corporations. 509

Capitulation The act of formal surrender, upon specified terms. 226

Carpetbaggers A negative term applied by Southerners to Northerners who moved to the South after the Civil War to pursue political or economic opportunities. 360

Causeway A raised roadway crossing above open water or wet ground. 10

Cede To surrender possession of. 312

Checks and balances The rules controlling interactions among the executive, legislative, and judicial branches of government, making up a novel system designed to prevent any single branch from overreaching its powers, as set forth in the Constitution in 1787. 208

Civic organizations Membership organizations that exist to further the public life and welfare of a community. 683

Coalition An alliance of parties, factions, or nations. 279

Coffle A procession or train of enslaved prisoners, bound together for travel (from the Arabic word for "caravan"). 92

Cold War The conflict and competition between the United States and the Soviet Union (and their respective allies) that emerged after 1945 and lasted until 1989. 550

Colonialism The centuries-old system of mostly European nations controlling and governing peoples and lands outside of Europe. 558

Columbian Exchange The significant two-way interchange of plants, animals, microbes, and people that occurred once Christopher Columbus established regular contact by sea between the eastern and western hemispheres. For thousands of years before 1492, despite occasional encounters, these two separate and different "worlds" had remained isolated from each other. 17

Comfort women Women, mostly Chinese and Korean, forced into sexual slavery by Japanese troops during World War II. 547

Commercial farming Agricultural system producing for markets and intended to yield a profit after crops are sold. 312

Common school system Tax-supported public education to provide elementary schooling free to young children. 297

Communism A totalitarian form of government, grounded in the theories of German philosopher Karl Marx and the practices of V. I. Lenin in Russia, that eliminated private ownership of property in supposed pursuit of complete human equality; the system of government also featured a centrally directed economy and the absolute rule of a small group of leaders. 550

Communitarian relating to communities practicing communitarianism, a form of cooperative living in small groups. 299

Conclave A private meeting, secret assembly, gathering, or convention. 211

Conservationists Advocates of conserving and protecting the natural world through the use of renewable natural resources. 462

Conspicuous consumption A term coined by the American social theorist Thorstein Veblen to describe the behavior of wealthy persons who flaunt their status through their purchase of fine clothes, large houses, fancy cars, and other highly visible material goods. 429

Consumer Economy An economic system in which most people work for wages, which they use to purchase manufactured goods and foodstuffs. 486

Containment The U.S. policy during the Cold War of trying to halt the expansion of Soviet and communist influences. 556

Contraband Goods (or, during the Civil War, slaves) seized from the enemy during war. 343

Cooperatives Organizations that produce or market goods and that are owned collectively by people who share in their profits or benefits. 376

Coverture French term for the dependent and legal status of a woman during marriage. Under English law, the male family head received legal rights, and his wife lost independent status, becoming, in legal terms, a *femme covert*. 68

Creoles People born in the United States but retaining a strong cultural identification with their forebears; especially persons of mixed Spanish or French and African descent speaking a dialect of Spanish or French. 258

Czar The monarch (king) of Russia before the 1917 revolution. 140

De facto government A government that is exercising power as if legally constituted. 156

Détente The lessening of military or diplomatic tensions, as between the United States and the Soviet Union. 617

Diaspora The dispersion of a population abroad, whether forced or voluntary. The term is often applied to Jewish settlement outside the eastern Mediterranean region, and to the spread of Africans across the Americas, due to the Atlantic slave trade. 108

Dispossession Act of taking land or other property from a group of people. 311

Don't ask, don't tell A policy established by the Clinton administration allowing gays and lesbians to serve in the military so long as they do not disclose their sexual orientation. 667

Double V The campaign by African Americans during the Second World War to fight simultaneously for victory against fascism abroad and racial discrimination at home. 543

Dust Bowl The plains regions of Oklahoma, Texas, Colorado, and New Mexico affected by severe drought in the 1930s. 512

Ecology The web of interconnections between organisms (particularly humans) and the natural environment. 265

Electoral College An intricate system in which each state appoints electors, equal in number to its representation in Congress, to elect the president and vice president. The electoral college is a provision of the Constitution (Article II, Section 1) because the framers were unwilling to approve the direct election of president and vice president. This group, or "college," of electors still makes the selection, voting according to prior party commitments rather than individual choice. 209

Emancipation National or state-sponsored program to free slaves. 345

Embargo A government order prohibiting the entry or departure of commercial ships from a port. 245

Emigrants People who leave one place and move to another. 286

Encomienda The Spanish encomienda system, imposed in Spain's American empire, requiring Indian communities to supply labor or pay tribute to a local colonial overlord (identified as an encomendero). 63

Enfranchised citizens Persons who are entitled to vote in government elections. 251

Entente The alliance of Britain, France, and Russia, later joined by the United States, during World War I. 467

Entrepreneur A person who organizes, manages, or assumes the risks in a business venture. 255

Evangelical Protestants Christians who emphasize the importance of personal faith, as well as seeking new converts. 292

Exposé A piece of investigative journalism that exposes corruption in government, business, or other institutions. 590

Extractive enterprises Businesses that harvest or extract natural products from the land or sea (fish, timber, minerals, crops). 387

Fall line The geographical division between the Piedmont and the Atlantic coastal plain where the land slopes sharply to the sea. 315

Family wage A level of income sufficient for an individual worker, usually a man, to support a spouse and family through a single salary. 524

Fascism A form of right-wing dictatorship exalting nation and race above the individual. 348

Fatigue work Unskilled manual labor. 000

Federalists A coalition of nationalist leaders who favored creating a stronger central government to replace the Articles of Confederation; they labeled their opponents as Anti-Federalists in the late 1780s. The strongest essays endorsing their proposed new Constitution were entitled *The Federalist Papers*. 211

Federation An alliance or compact between political units that agree to surrender certain powers to a central authority while still retaining other powers. 193

Feminism The belief that women and men are of equal value and that gender roles are, to a considerable degree, created by society rather than being simply natural. 608

Fireside chats The broadcasts by President Franklin Delano Roosevelt during which he spoke directly to American families, often gathered around a radio in their living room. 517

Flappers Young women in the 1910s and 1920s who rebelled against the gender conventions of the era with respect to fashion and behavior. 486

Flotilla Any sizeable fleet of ships, or, more specifically, a naval term for a unit consisting of two or more squadrons of small warships. 134

Foreclosure A legal process of seizing private property, such as a home or farm, in order to pay off a debtor's creditors. 203

Foundling home A residence for orphaned children. 449

Free trade International economic relations characterized by multinational investment and a reduction or elimination of tariffs. 534

Free labor ideology The ideas, represented most forcefully by the antebellum Republican party, that workers should profit from their own labor and that slavery is wrong. 315

Freighter Person, vehicle, or vessel that transports goods. 317

Fusion A combination, alliance. 432

Geographic mobility The phenomenon of people moving frequently from one place to another. 433

Glacier A large body of ice that endures for centuries, advancing or receding slowly as climactic conditions change. 5

Globalization The process of integration—economic, but also cultural—of different parts of the world into a more unified system of trade and communication. 13

Grassroots democracy A political system that relies on the active participation of people at the local level. 423

Great Awakening The title that was applied, in retrospect, to the interdenominational Christian revival that swept Britain's North American colonies between the 1730s and the 1750s, inspired at first by the preaching of Jonathan Edwards and George Whitefield. (A religious revival in the early nineteenth century became known as the Second Great Awakening.) 126

Great Migration The movement of African Americans out of the South to northern cities, particularly during World War I. 474

Guerrilla war A conflict fought not on the basis of conventional warfare, but rather by mobilizing small groups of fighters who attack and harass superior forces. 288

Gun control   The legal regulation of firearms. 665

Hard currency   Coins made of precious metals such as silver, gold, or nickel, as opposed to paper bills; also called hard money or specie. 219

Harry   To torment an enemy by destructive raids or repeated small attacks. 186

Hayseeds   A derogatory term applied to rural people deemed uneducated and naive (in contrast to self-proclaimed sophisticated city dwellers). 429

Headright   Under the headright system, English colonial governments granted a fixed amount of land, usually 50 acres, to any head of household for every family member or hired hand that person brought into the colony. Sometimes fewer acres were granted for women and children on the grounds that they would clear and plant less land. 44

Hinterland   A rural area that is linked to a nearby city through trade networks. 253

Hobo   Migrant worker or poor and homeless vagrant who traveled on trains from location to location, usually in search of employment. 512

Hoovervilles   Shantytowns, named for president Hoover and occupied largely by people who lost their homes and farms during the Great Depression. 452

Humanitarian intervention   Warfare undertaken ostensibly in furtherance of humanitarian objectives. 670

Iberian   Relating to Europe's Iberian Peninsula, the location of Spain and Portugal. 32

Impressment   A policy that authorizes the seizure of persons or private property in the service of a government. 219

Indenture   A document binding one person to work for another for a given period of time. Indentured servants received food, shelter, and clothing, plus "freedom dues" when their terms of service ended to help them get started independently. 86

Injunction   A court order prohibiting a party from certain kinds of behavior—for example, barring a labor union from striking. 431

Internal improvements   Turnpikes, canals, bridges, seaports, and other projects intended to facilitate trade and transportation within the country. 251

Iroquois League   A Native American confederacy, located in central New York, originally composed of the Cayuga, Mohawk, Oneida, Onondaga, and Seneca Indians, and later including the Tuscarora as well. 38

Isthmus   A narrow strip of land connecting two larger land areas (such as the isthmus of Panama). 18

Itinerant minister   A preacher who travels from place to place without invitation, or who visits a circuit of churches on a regular basis. 129

Jim Crow   The name given to the set of legal institutions that ensured the segregation of nonwhite people in the South. 408

Juke joint   A small, inexpensive establishment where patrons could eat and drink or dance to music from a jukebox. *Juke* is a word of West African origin popularized by African Americans in the Sea Islands of South Carolina. 486

Kachina   An Indian religious system, inspired by Mexican traditions, and present in the American Southwest for more than 800 years. The kachina cult used masks for group performances associated with rain, curing, fertility, warfare, and the ancestors. Among many Pueblo and Hopi Indians, this tradition was epitomized by kachina (or katsina) dolls. 64

Kayak   A highly maneuverable, decked-in canoe used by Native Alaskans for travel and hunting. The light frame is covered with skins, and the paddle has a blade at each end. Popular modern versions of this traditional boat are made with canvas or fiberglass. 140

Kickbacks   Money paid illegally in return for favors (for example, to a politician by a person or business that has received government contracts). 367

Laissez-Faire   a belief in little or no government interference in the economy. 000

Land speculation   The act of buying land in the hope of making a profit by selling it in the future. 228

Liberalism   Originally a nineteenth-century belief in free-market capitalism; in the twentieth century, a belief in using the power of the federal government to increase opportunity and provisions for the least affluent citizens; by the twenty-first century, increasingly a belief in multicultural tolerance and inclusion. 644

Litigation   A lawsuit or legal contest. 201

Longevity   Length of life, a long duration of life. 214

Manumission   A formal emancipation from slavery; the act (by an individual owner or government authority) of granting freedom to an enslaved person or persons. 101

Market Revolution   The combined effects of transportation innovation, technological change, and economic growth, especially during the first half of the nineteenth century. 254

McCarthyism   The political campaign led by Senator Joseph McCarthy (R-Wisconsin) to blame liberals at home for setbacks to U.S. interests abroad, due to what he considered liberals' sympathies with communism. 562

Meager   Thin, sparse, scanty; lacking fullness, richness, or strength. 38

Mercantilism   A commercial policy that sought to achieve economic self-sufficiency and a favorable balance of trade (often by planting colonies) in order to promote a country's prosperity, strength, and independence. Rival European imperial powers favored the strategy of mercantilism in the seventeenth and eighteenth centuries. 57

Merchant-capitalist   An entrepreneur who hires workers to perform piecework in the worker's home. 255

Mesoamerica   The transitional region between North and South America, composed of Mexico and Central America. 7

Mestizo   A person of mixed European and American Indian ancestry. 63

Middle ground   The geographical region occupied by diverse cultural groups engaged in trade. 426

Middle passage   For European slave ships, the middle passage was the second of three legs in the triangular round-trip voyage from Europe to Africa to America and back to Europe. For enslaved Africans, the middle passage came to mean not only the transatlantic journey itself, but the entire process of removal from an African homeland and ultimate sale to an American master. 91

Military-industrial complex The term given by President Dwight D. Eisenhower to the military arms industry nexus. 583

Monetary policy Government policies designed to affect the national economy through bank lending policies, interest rates, and control of the amount of money in circulation. 218

Most-favored-nation status A designation allowing countries to export their products to the United States with tariffs no greater than those levied against most other nations. 669

Muckrakers The name given to a group of investigative journalists in the early twentieth century whose exposés often challenged corporate and government power. 458

Mulatto A person of mixed European and African ancestry; the first-generation offspring of a Caucasian and a Negroid parent. 63

Muse In Greek mythology, one of the nine sister goddesses who preside over music, poetry, and the arts. 47

Mutual aid society An organization of people who voluntarily pool their resources in order to help members in times of illness or other personal crises. 284

NAACP National Association for the Advancement of Colored People, founded in 1909. 564

National security state The reorientation of the U.S. government and its budget after 1945 toward a primary focus on military and intelligence capabilities. 566

Nativists American citizens born in the United States who oppose further immigration, especially from anywhere outside northwestern Europe. 295

New Democrats Members of the Democratic party, many of them organized in the Democratic Leadership Council, who espouse center to center-right policies. 666

Nisei Japanese Americans born in the United States of Japanese immigrant parents. 535

NSC-68 The 1950 directive of the National Security Council that called for rolling back, rather than merely containing, Soviet and communist influences. 566

Nuclear family A basic family structure that has parents and their children at its center, or nucleus, but does not include grandparents, cousins, or other relatives. 284

Nullification The doctrine that a state has the right to ignore or nullify certain federal laws with which it disagrees. 272

Okies Migrants from Oklahoma who left the state during the Dust Bowl period in search of work. 513

Operative A machine tender. 624

Ordnance Cannons, artillery, and by extension general military supplies including weapons, ammunition, combat vehicles, and tools. 168

Overspeculation Buying stocks and land that turn out to be not as valuable as the investors had originally believed. 293

Pachucos Young Mexican American members of neighborhood gangs. 543

Paleo Indians The earliest human inhabitants of North America, who first migrated to the continent from Siberia more than 15,000 years ago. Faced with a warming climate and the disappearance of many large game animals roughly 10,000 years ago (8000 BCE), they learned to hunt smaller animals and adapted to varied local conditions during the Archaic Period (to c. 1000 BCE). 6

Parochial schools Schools sponsored by the Catholic Church or some other religious denomination (in contrast to public schools). 428

Patronage System that rewards political supporters with jobs and other favors. 335

Pest house In colonial times, a shelter to quarantine those possibly infected with contagious diseases (such as newcomers arriving in American ports from Africa or Europe) to prevent the spread of shipborne pestilence. 97

Placate To soothe or pacify, usually by granting concessions. 10

Planned obsolescence A concept whereby producers intend for their products to eventually become obsolete or outdated and require replacement, thus perpetuating a cycle of production and consumption. 436

Pocket veto An indirect veto of a legislative bill made when an executive (such as a president or governor) simply leaves the bill unsigned, so that it dies after the adjournment of the legislature. 358

Political machine A group that effectively exercises control over a political party, usually at the local level and organized around precincts and patronage. 490

Popular sovereignty The idea that residents of a state should be able to make decisions on crucial issues, such as whether or not to legalize slavery. 321

Postbellum Period after a war, especially after the Civil War, 1865–1877. 363

Precedent An earlier occurrence of something similar; something done or said setting an example or pattern that can justify later actions. 18

Preemptive attack A form of military aggression on the part of one country designed to thwart a perceived imminent attack from another. 438

Presidio A military garrison or fortified settlement in an area under Spanish control. 111

Privateers Ships (and their crew members) licensed to harass enemy shipping in wartime. 76

Producer economy An economic system dominated by individuals who are self-producers of manufactured goods and foodstuffs rather than employees working for wages. 486

Progressivism A notion of political reform central to the "Progressive Era" (the first two decades of the twentieth century), when urban reformers with a faith in progress sought to address local and national social problems through political and civic means. 458

Public domain Lands owned by the federal government. 424

Putting out System in which workers labor in their homes to produce goods for a merchant, who usually provides raw materials and pays them not by the hour but by each piece they finish. 255

Quitrent A fixed rent paid annually by a tenant to a proprietor or landowner. 69

Race suicide A fear articulated by Theodore Roosevelt and others that the low birthrate of Anglo-Saxon Americans, along with the high birthrate of immigrants from southern and eastern Europe, would result in a population in which "inferior" peoples would outnumber the "American racial stock". 454

Realignment Change in a coalition or alliance between political parties. 308

Reconstruction the U.S. government policies to rebuild the South after the Civil War and reintegrate it with the rest of the nation. 358

Redemption system An eighteenth-century arrangement in which potential migrants in Europe signed up with an agent who agreed to pay for their Atlantic passage. Reaching America, the newcomer signed a pact to work for several years for an employer. In exchange for much-needed labor, the employer agreed to pay back the shipper, "redeeming" the original loan that had been made to the immigrant "redemptioner." 117

Red lining A business practice in which lending institutions deny credit to racial or ethnic minorities who live in poor neighborhoods. 577

Redress A remedy for a wrong; a correction or reparation. As a verb, to redress means to correct, to set right, or to remove the cause of a grievance. 149

Red Scare Post–World War I repression of socialists, communists, and other left-wing radicals ("Reds"). 483

Regressive tax A tax that decreases in rate as the base increases, so that someone with a large holding pays a relatively small amount. A fixed tax of $100 is regressive, since persons with $1,000 or $1 million shoulder very different relative burdens. This is the opposite of a progressive tax, where those with less pay at a lower rate. 77

Rejuvenation To restore the youthful vigor or appearance of a thing or a person. 435

Republican mother A wife and mother whose primary role is caring for and socializing future citizens (her children); an ideal favored by some elites after the American Revolution. 232

Requisition To request, demand, or formally require something of someone. 36

Restitution Giving back to the rightful owner something that has been lost or taken away. 305

Restoration The political act of restoring monarchy to England in 1660 after the brief experiment of the Puritan Commonwealth, placing Charles II upon the throne once occupied by his Stuart father, Charles I. The following years, until the end of the Stuart family dynasty in 1688, are known in English culture and politics as the *Restoration Era*. 66

Rogue nations A label used by the U.S. government to refer to nations it considers hostile, unpredictable, and potentially dangerous. 674

Rosie the Riveter A heroic symbol of women workers on the homefront during World War II. 539

Sachem Algonquin Indian term for a Native American leader or chief. 70

Scalawag A negative term applied by southern Democrats after the Civil War to any white Southerner who allied with the Republican party. 360

Secession Withdrawal of a state from the authority of the federal government. 250

Second New Deal The agenda of policies and programs initiated by President Franklin Delano Roosevelt beginning in 1935 that was intended to strengthen the lot of American workers while simultaneously preserving the capitalist system. 518

Sedentary farming Activity that requires cultivators to live in one place for extended periods of time. 228

Sedition Acts that stir up rebellion against a government. 222

Separation of powers The novel idea that the powers of the three branches of government—legislative, executive, and judicial—should be kept separate from one another, so that each can check and balance the powers of the other two. 208

Sharecropping A system in which landless farmers grown crops on another person's land in exchange for a portion of the crops. 364

Sit-down strike A strategy employed by workers agitating for better wages and working conditions in which they stop working and simply sit down, thus ceasing production and preventing strikebreakers from entering a facility to assume their jobs. 526

Sit-in A form of civil disobedience in which activists sit down somewhere in violation of law or policy in order to challenge discriminatory practices or laws. The tactic originated during labor struggles in the 1930s and was used effectively in the civil rights movement in 1960. 581

Social Darwinism A late-nineteenth-century variation on the theories of British naturalist Charles Darwin, promoting the idea that only the "fittest" individuals will, or deserve to, survive (i.e., the idea that society operates on principles of evolutionary biology). 397

Speakeasies Establishments where alcohol was illegally sold during the Prohibition era. 490

Sphere of influence An area dominated by the military, economic, and cultural power of another country. 439

Squatters People who live on land that they do not own, without the landowner's permission. 226

Staples Important trade items or foodstuffs. 123

Steerage Section of a ship providing the cheapest accommodations for passengers. 000

Subsidies Government assistance in the form of tax breaks or cash bonuses given to a person or business. 256

Subsistence homesteading Farming to provide only for the necessities of one's family. 312

Substitute During war, a man paid to serve in combat in another man's place. 340

Suffrage The right to vote. 373

Sunbelt The band of states from the Southeast to the Southwest that experienced rapid economic and population growth during and after World War II. 561

Sweatshop A small factory where employees work long hours for low wages under poor conditions (especially in the garment industry). 659

Swords into plowshares Turning weapons of war into productive implements, such as plows, based on the biblical passage in Isaiah 2:4. 193

Tariff A government tax on imported goods. 218

Tejanos Spanish-speaking residents of the Mexican (and later, U.S.) state of Texas. 266

Temperance A social movement embracing either total opposition to alcohol consumption or support for its moderate use. 295

Tenant farmer A farmer who raises livestock and crops on land leased from wealthier owners. 150

Tenements Densely inhabited apartment buildings generally found in crowded and poor areas of cities where immigrants and ethnic minorities lived in unhealthy conditions. 310

Texians The name used by U.S.-born citizens who lived in the Mexican state of Texas. 266

Theocracy A government by officials who are regarded as divinely guided. 637

Tithe A levy or donation (generally a tenth part) given to provide support, usually for a church. 24

Total war The attacking of both military and civilian targets. 543

Townsend Plan A proposal by Dr. Francis Townsend in 1934 for a 2 percent national sales tax that would fund a guaranteed pension of $200 per month for Americans older than age 60. 521

Travois A French Canadian term for the A-frame device used by many traditional Native Americans to draw heavy loads over long distances. It consisted of two trailing poles attached to a dog or horse and supporting a platform to carry belongings. 113

Treaties Legally binding documents ratified by nations pledging them to engage or refrain from engaging in certain actions or policies. 410

Triangular trade The huge Atlantic slave trade that linked Europe, Africa, and the Americas from the sixteenth to the nineteenth century. Ships from Europe sailed to Africa to exchange trade goods for slaves. On their second leg (the infamous "middle passage"), these vessels transported the enslaved captives to ports in the Caribbean or on the American mainland. They completed their clockwise voyage by returning to Europe, usually carrying colonial staples produced by slaves, such as sugar, rice, or tobacco. 91

Trickle-down economics An economic concept whereby the government aids the wealthiest strata as well as large corporations in the belief that the benefits of this aid will "trickle down" to the middle and lower classes. 489

Truman Doctrine President Truman's March 1947 speech articulating the new policy of containment. 556

Trusts A combination of firms or corporations created for the purpose of reducing competition and controlling prices throughout an industry. 399

Tundra A cold and treeless plain typical of arctic and subarctic regions. 5

Two-party system A system of government characterized by two major political parties that compete against each other in "winner take all" elections. 218

Unicameral legislature A legislative body that has only one chamber, or house. 69

Utopian Relating to communities organized to strive for ideal social and political conditions. 299

Vagrancy The state of being unemployed and wandering from place to place. 311

Victorians Middle-class (chiefly Protestant) people living during the reign of Queen Victoria of England (1837–1901) who identified with British culture and who professed social values such as self-control, sexual restraint, and personal ambition. 427

Vigilantes People who seek to take the law into their own hands and punish or intimidate alleged criminals or persons who resist a certain social order (for example, white supremacy). 302

Wage slavery The idea that wage earners are exploited by employers as harshly as slaves are exploited by their owners. 316

War chest A fund accumulated to finance a war or earmarked to conduct some specific action or campaign. 195

War hawks Politicians who favor specific forms of military action as a tool of U.S. foreign policy. 245

War on drugs The global campaign spearheaded by the federal government to eliminate the production of illegal drugs and their importation into the United States, and its domestic counterpart in which drug violations are treated harshly by the legal and criminal justice system. 658

Watergate The Washington, D.C., hotel-office complex where agents of President Nixon's reelection campaign broke into Democratic Party headquarters in 1972. Nixon helped cover up the break-in, and the subsequent political scandal was called "Watergate." 617

Welfare reform The legislative campaign in the 1960s through the 1990s to abolish Aid to Families with Dependent Children in favor of a program that sets limits on the amount of time a poor family can receive government aid (culminating in the Temporary Aid to Needy Families Act of 1996). 635

Welfare state A nation in which the government provides a "safety net" of entitlements and benefits for citizens unable to economically provide for themselves. 510

Wildcat banks Small banks that make loans unsupervised by the state or other financial institutions. 267

Wobblies Members of the Industrial Workers of the World (IWW), a radical labor union formed in 1905. 460

Yellow journalism Newspaper articles, images, and editorials that exploit, distort, or exaggerate the news in order to inflame public opinion. 437

Yeoman A farmer who owns a modest amount of land (but no slaves). 123

Yiddish A language derived largely from German spoken mainly by Jews from eastern Europe. 509

Zoot suits Distinctive clothing in the 1940s worn largely by Mexican American and African American men, characterized by flared pants, long coats, and wide-brimmed hats. 543

Credits

Part One Opener
Page 2 (Top): Lee Boltin Picture Library; 2 (Bottom): Museum of the History of Science, Oxford, Oxfordshire, UK/Bridgeman Art Library; 3: The Granger Collection, New York

Chapter 1
Page 4: Courtesy Museum of New Mexico, Neg. No 50884; 6: Kenneth Garrett/National Geographic Image Collection; 7: Lee Boltin Picture Library; 8: Pair of keros with frog motifs in repoussé, Middle Sícán, Peru, North Coast, Batán Grande, A.D. 850-1050, 14.4 H x 10.4 Diam. centimeters. Collection of Duke University Museum of Art, museum purchase (1993.7.1–2).; 11: The Ohio Historical Society; 12: Richard A. Cooke/CORBIS; 13: Museum of the History of Science, Oxford, Oxfordshire, UK/Bridgeman Art Library; 14: Topkapi Serail Museum/akg-images; 15: Courtesy of Bancroft Library, University of California, Berkeley (SF309 G7 M25 1769 pl.20); 19: The Pierpont Morgan Library/Art Resource, NY; 20: Bibliothèque nationale de France; 20: Excerpt from "These gods that we worship. . ." in Kenneth Mills and William B. Taylor, *Colonial Spanish America: A Documentary History*. Wilmington, DE: Scholarly Resources, 1998.; 22: The Huntington Library, Art Collections, and Botanical Gardens, San Marino, California/SuperStock; 25: The New York Public Library; 28: © Copyright The Trustees of The British Museum

Chapter 2
Page 31: Leonard Harris/Stock, Boston, LLC; 35: Kevin Fleming/CORBIS; 36 (Top): Jerry Jacka Photography. All Rights Reserved; 36 (Bottom): Mission San Luis, Florida Division of Historical Resources; 38 (Top): Jomah Joseph, "Canoe Model, Passamoquoddy." Thaw Collection, Fenimore Art Museum, Cooperstown, New York. Photo by John Bigelow Taylor, N.Y.C.; 38 (Bottom): Harry Engels/Photo Researchers, Inc.; 40: Collection of The New-York Historical Society, Neg. #1049; 43: Steve Rawls/National Geographic Image Collection; 46: Worcester Art Museum, Worcester, Massachusetts. Gift of Mr. and Mrs. Albert W. Rice; 47: Courtesy of the Harvard University Archives; 47: Anne Bradstreet, "Verses Upon the Burning of Our House, July 18, 1666," 1666.; 50: Ashmolean Museum, Oxford

Chapter 3
Page 55: Courtesy, Peter Wood; 57: Réunion des Musées Nationaux/Art Resource, NY; 59 (Top): Museum Collections, Minnesota Historical Society; 59 (Bottom): The Granger Collection, New York; 61: William L. Clements Library, University of Michigan; 64: Harald Sund/The Image Bank/Getty Images; 67 (Top): The Granger Collection, New York; 67 (Bottom): The Pepys Library, Magdalenee College, Cambridge; 70: Courtesy, American Antiquarian Society; 72: Benjamin Henry Latrobe, "View of Greenspring House," 1796. The Maryland Historical Society, Baltimore, Maryland; 73: Jan Wyck, "William III Landing at Brixham,Torbay," 1688. © National Maritime Museum, London; 77: The New York Public Library; 78: © Copyright The Trustees of The British Museum

Part Two Opener
Page 82: Chicago History Museum, ICHi-x.1354; 83 (Top): Peabody Essex Museum. Photograph by Mark Sexton; 83 (Bottom): Library of Congress

Chapter 4
Page 84: Voyage Pittoresque dans le Bresil, Rugendas plate 10, 2nd part. The Newberry Library, Chicago; 86: © Copyright The Trustees of The British Museum, Museum of Mankind-The Ethnology Collection; 87: Anonymous, "Vue du Cap Francais et Du nvr La Marie Seraphique de Nantes," 1772–1773. Le jour de l'Ouverture de sa Vente, Troisieme Voyage d'Angole. Musée du Château des Ducs de Bretagne (950.4.3); 89: Alice Ravenel Huger Smith, "The Threshing Floor with a Winnowing-house," from the series, "A Carolina Rice Plantation of the Fifties, ca. 1935." Watercolor on paper, Gibbes Museum of Art/Carolina Art Association, 37.09.22; 93: Buttolph-Williams House, Antiquarian & Landmarks Society ; 94: Public Domain; 95 (Top): Werner Forman/Art Resource, NY; 95 (Bottom): The Library of Congress; 99: Chicago History Museum, ICHi-x.1354; 100: Courtesy Florida Museum of Natural History. Photo by James Quine. ; 103: George Morland, "Traite Des Negres," 1790–91. The Colonial Williamsburg Foundation; 103: "Releese Us Out of This Cruell Bondegg,." An appeal from a Virginia slave, 1723.; 105: William Hogarth, "The Gaols Committee of the House of Commons," ca. 1729. National Portrait Gallery, London.; 106: George Jones, "View of Savannah," 1734. The I.N. Phelps Stokes Collection, The New York Public Library/Art Resource, NY;

Chapter 5
Page 110: Theodore Gentilz, "San Francisco del Espada en 1844." Yanaguana Society Collection. Daughters of the Republic of Texas Library; 112: Harrison Begay (Navajo, b. 1917), "Night Chant Ceremonial Hunt," 1947. Watercolor on paper. Museum purchase, The Philbrook Museum of Art, Tulsa, Oklahoma (1947.40); 113: Charm, c. 1870. Potawatomi.The Detroit Institute of Arts, Founders Society Purchase (81.614). Photograph ©1992 The Detroit Institute of Arts.; 117 (Figure): Excerpted from "Gender and Age Structure of Population: British Mainland Colonies, 1760s and United States, 1980s" from Mark C. Carnes and John A. Garraty, *Mapping America's Past*, p. 73. © 1996 Arcadia Editions Ltd.;119 (Top): Courtesy, Dartmouth College Library; 119 (Bottom): Courtesy of Reading Public Museum, Reading, Pennsylvania (44-132-1); 120: John Wollaston, "Mary Spraat Provost Alexander," undated. Museum of the City of New York, Gift of William Hamilton Russell (50.215.4); 121: John Moale, engraving, 1752. The I.N. Phelps Stokes Collection, The New York Public Library/Art Resource, NY; 126: Paul Rocheleau Photography; 127: Courtesy, American Antiquarian Society; 128 (Top): Courtesy, Winterthur Museum (63.639); 128 (Bottom): Attributed to Mary Leverett Denison Rogers, "Harvard Hall," ca. early 18th-century. Silk, wool, and gilt-silver yarns on open plain-weave linen.Courtesy of the Massachusetts Historical Society, MHS image number 427); 130–131: Jean-Pierre Lassus, Early New Orleans; detail from "Vue perspective de la Nouvelle-Orleans," 1726. Centre des Archives d'Outre-Mer-France.; 132: Military History, Smithsonian Institution; 134: Thomas Johnson, engraving, 1759. Print Collection, Miriam and Ira D. Wallach Division, The New York Public Library/Art Resource, NY;

Chapter 6
Page 137: Edward Savage, "John Hancock and his Wife," n.d., (48.8). In the Corcoran Gallery of Art, Washington, D.C. Bequest of Woodbury Blair; 138: © Hunterian Museum and Art Gallery, University of Glasgow; 139: John Webber, "A View of Kealakekua Bay," c. 1781–83. Dixson Library, State Library of New South Wales; 140: Douglas W. Veltre, Anchorage, AK; 146: Library of Congress; 148: Peabody Essex Museum. Photograph by Mark Sexton; 151: Photo courtesy of Tryon Palace Historic Sites & Gardens; 151: Petition signed by 30 North Carolina Regulators, Oct 4, 1768.; 154: Library of Congress; 155: Library of Congress; 158: Amos Doolittle, "The Battle of Lexington, Plate I," 1775. The Connecticut Historical Society, Hartford, Connecticut (Acc. #1844.10.1)

Part Three Opener
Page 162 (Bottom): Collection of David J. and Janice L. Frent; 163 (Top): Courtesy, American Canal and Transportation Center; 163 (Bottom): Abby Aldrich Rockefeller Folk Art Museum, The Colonial Williamsburg Foundation, Williamsburg, VA

Chapter 7
Page 164: Henry Gray, "The Morning After the Attack on Sullivan's Island, 1776." Watercolor on paper, Gibbes Museum of Art/Carolina Art Association, 1907.02.01; 167: Charles Willson Peale, "George Washington in the Uniform of a British Colonial Colonel," c. 1772. Washington-Custis-Lee Collection, Washington and Lee University, Lexington, Virginia; 169: Library of Congress; 170: From Martha Ryan Cipher Book (#1940). Southern Historical Collection, Wilson Library, The University of North Carolina at Chapel Hill; 170: Cheraw District Grand Jury, "The Presentments of the Grand Jury of and for the Said District," South Carolina, May 20, 1776.; 172: Courtesy, American Antiquarian Society; 173 (Top): William Mercer, "Battle of Princeton," date unknown. Courtesy of The Historical Society of Pennsylvania Collection, Atwater Kent Museum of Philadelphia.; 173 (Bottom): Collection of the Museum of Early Southern Decorative Arts, Old Salem Museums & Gardens; 176: Courtesy of The Bostonian Society/Old State House; 177 (Figure): B.R. Mitchell, *British Historical Statistics*. New York: Cambridge University Press, 1988.; 181: Pennsylvania Capitol Preservation Committee & Brian Hunt; 184: ©1992 Angel Art Ltd.; 187: Réunion des Musées Nationaux/Art Resource, NY; 188: Benjamin West, "Signing of the Peace Treaty." Courtesy, Winterthur Museum (57.856)

Chapter 8
Page 191: CORBIS; 194: William Tylee Ranney, "Veterans of 1776 Returning from the War," 1848. Oil on canvas. Overall: 34 1/4 x 48 5/8 in. (86.99 x 123.51). Dallas Museum of Art, The Art Museum League Fund, Special Contributors and General Acquisitions Fund; 194: Joseph Plumb Martin, *A Narrative of Some of the Adventures, Dangers and Sufferings of a Revolutionary Soldier*, 1830.; 195 (Bottom): The American Numismatic Society, New York; 196 (Top): Abby Aldrich Rockefeller Folk Art Museum, The Colonial Williamsburg Foundation, Williamsburg, VA; 196 (Bottom): © Natural History Museum, London.; 197: © Natural History Museum, London.; 200: University of Michigan, WIlliam L. Clements Library; 202: Courtesy of Monroe County Historical Commission, Monroe, MI; 204: George Davidson, "Attacked at Juan de Fuca Straits," c.1792. Oregon Historical Society, OrHi 85076; 210: Susan Anne Livingston Ridley Sedgwick, "Elizabeth 'Mumbet' Freeman," 1811. Watercolor on ivory. Courtesy of the Massachusetts Historical Society (MHS image number 28); 212 (Both): Courtesy, American Antiquarian Society; 213: Collection of The New-York Historical Society, Accession #1903.12;

Chapter 9
Page 216: Gilbert Stuart, "Joseph Brant," 1786. Fenimore Art Museum, Cooperstown, New York. Photo by Richard Walker.; **217:** Collection of David J. and Janice L. Frent; **219:** Ralph Earl, "Elijah Boardman," 1789. The Metropolitan Museum of Art. Bequest of Susan W. Tyler, 1979. (1979.395). Photograph © The Metropolitan Museum of Art ; **220:** Courtesy, American Canal and Transportation Center; **221:** Frederick Kemmelmeyer, "General George Washington Reviewing the Western Army at Fort Cumberland the 18th of October," c. 1794. Courtesy, Winterthur Museum (58.2780); **223:** Courtesy of The New Bedford Whaling Museum (#803); **225:** "The Old Plantation," c. 1795. Abby Aldrich Rockefeller Folk Art Museum, The Colonial Williamsburg Foundation, Williamsburg, VA; **228:** Courtesy of Museo de America, Madrid. Photo by Iris Engstrand; **230:** Shaker Village of Pleasant Hill, Harrodsburg, KY; **231:** Paul Rocheleau Photography; **232:** George James Warner, "Means for the Preservation of Liberty," speech delivered July 4, 1797.; **233:** Courtesy of The General Society of Mechanics and Tradesmen of the City of New York; **234:** James Peale, "The Artist and His Family," 1795. Oil on canvas, 31 1/4 x 32 3/4 in. (79.4 x 83.2 cm). Courtesy of the Pennsylvania Academy of the Fine Arts, Philadelphia (Acc. no.: 1922.1.1). Gift of John Frederick Lewis.

Part Four Opener
Page 240 (Top): William Clark, "Eulachon (T. Pacificus)," 1806, Voorhis Journal #2. William Clark Papers, Missouri Historical Society Archives; **240 (Bottom):** The American Numismatic Society; **241 (Top):** Courtesy of the Massachusetts Historical Society(MHS image number 31); **241 (Bottom):** Samuel J. Miller, "Frederick Douglass," 1847–52. Major Acquisitions Centennial Endowment, 1996.433. Photograph ©The Art Institute of Chicago

Chapter 10
Page 242: Charles Balthazar Fevret de Saint Memin, "Captain Meriwether Lewis," 1807. Collection of The New-York Historical Society, Neg. #51322; **244:** William Clark, "Eulachon (Thaleichthys Pacificus)," Entry of 25 February 1806. Voorhis Journal #2. Clark Family Collections. William Clark Papers. Missouri Historical Society, St. Louis; **245:** Courtesy, JPMorgan Chase Archives; **246:** Library of Congress; **247:** Courtesy, Dartmouth College Library; **249:** Library of Congress; **252:** Peter Turnley/CORBIS; **252:** Cherokee Women to Cherokee Council, May 2, 1817, Andrew Jackson Presidential Papers.; **253:** Unidentified Artist, "Benjamin Hawkins and the Creek Indians," ca. 1805. Oil on canvas, 35 7/8 x 49 7/8 inches. Greenville County Museum of Art, Greenville, SC, Gift of The Museum Association, Inc., with funds donated by Corporate Partners: Ernst and Young; Fluor Daniel; Director's Circle Members: Mr. and Mrs. Alester G. Furman III; Mr. and Mrs. M. Dexter Hagy; Thomas P. Hartness; Mr. and Mrs. E. Erwin Maddrey II; Mary M. Pearce; Mr. and Mrs. John Pellett, Jr.; Mr. W. Thomas Smith; Mr. and Mrs. Edward H. Stall; Eleanor and Irvine Welling; Museum Antiques Show, 1989, 1990, 1991, Elliott, Davis and Company, CPAs, sponsor; Collector's Group 1990, 1991; **254:** Museum of Spanish Colonial Art, Collections of the Spanish Colonial Arts Society, Inc., Santa Fe, NM. Bequest of Alan and Ann Vedder. Photo by Jack Parsons; **257:** John Antrobus, "Plantation Burial," c.1860. The Historic New Orleans Collection, Accession no. 1960.46; **258:** Chicago History Museum, ICHi-22005;

Chapter 11
Page 261: John Gadsby Chapman, "Davy Crockett," date unknown. Harry Ransom Humanities Research Center, The University of Texas at Austin (neg. #65.349); **265 (Top):** William Henry Brown, "Hauling the Whole Weeks Picking," 1842. The Historic New Orleans Collection, Accession nos. 1975.93.1 & 2.; **265 (Bottom):** Collection of David J. and Janice L. Frent; **266 (Map):** Adapted from David J. Weber, *The Mexican Frontier, 1821–1846: The American Southwest Under Mexico.* Albuquerque: University of New Mexico Press, 1982. ; **269:** Library of Congress; **271 (Map):** Adapted from David J. Weber, *The Mexican Frontier, 1821-1846: The American Southwest Under Mexico.* Albuquerque: University of New Mexico Press, 1982.; **276:** From "José Agustin de Escudero Describes New Mexico as a Land of Opportunity, 1827" from *Three New Mexico Chronicles*, H. Bailey Carroll and Juan Villasana Haggard, trans. and ed. Albuquerque: Quivira Society, 1942.; **272:** Eric P. Newman Numismatic Education Society **273:** Richard T. Nowitz/CORBIS; **274 (Top):** The Newberry Library, Chicago; **274 (Bottom):** The American Numismatic Society, New York; **276:** © Kevin Fleming/CORBIS; **279:** Reproduced by permission of The Huntington Library, San Marino, California, RB 44872; **280:** Henry F. Darby, "The Reverend John Atwood and His Family," 1845. Oil on canvas, 183.2 x 244.47 cm (72 1/8 x 96 1/4 in.). Gift of Maxim Karolik for the M. and M. Karolik Collection of American Paintings, 1815–1865, 62.269. Museum of Fine Arts, Boston. Reproduced with permission. Photograph ©2008 Museum of Fine Arts, Boston.

Chapter 12
Page 283: Minnesota Historical Society; **288 (Map):** Adapted from "Indian Removal from the Old Southwest" in Carnes and Garraty, *Mapping America's Past*, p. 86. © 1996 Arcada Editions Ltd.; **290:** Scotts Bluff National Monument, Nebraska. United States Department of the Interior, National Park Service; **293 (Top):** Courtesy of the Massachusetts Historical Society (MHS image number 31); **293 (Bottom):** Samuel J. Miller, "Frederick Douglass," 1847/52.Cased half-plate daguerreotype, plate: 14 x 10.6 cm; plate in closed case: 15.2 x 12 x 1.4 cm; plate in open case: 15.2 x 24 x 2 cm. Major Acquisitions Centennial Endowment, 1996.433. Reproduction, The Art Institute of Chicago. Photography © The Art Institute of Chicago.; **294:** The Library Company of Philadelphia; **295:** Unknown Artist, "La Amistad," c.1839. The New Haven Museum & Historical Society, New Haven, CT (1972.1); **296 (Top):** Photo courtesy of the Milwaukee County Historical Society; **296 (Bottom):** The Library Company of Philadelphia; **297:** The Newberry Library, Chicago; **298:** Albertus del Orient Browere, "Mrs. McCormick's General Store," 1844. Fenimore Art Museum, Cooperstown, New York.; **304:** John C. Calhoun, speech delivered January, 1848.; **305:** Charles Bird King (attr.), "John Caldwell Calhoun," ca. 1818–25.National Portrait Gallery, Smithsonian Institution/Art Resource, NY; **306:** Joseph Vollmering, "The U.S. Naval Expedition Under Comore. M.C. Perry, Ascending the Tuspan River," 1848. Toned lithograph (hand-colored), 15 1/4 x 22 3/8 inches. Amon Carter Museum, Fort Worth, Texas (1976.33.2)

Part Five Opener
Page 308 (Top): Michael Freeman/CORBIS; **308 (Bottom):** Harriet Beecher Stowe Center, Hartford, CT; **309 (Top):** Antique Textile Resource, Bethesda MD; **309 (Bottom):** William T. Garrell Foundry, San Francisco, "The Last Spike." The Iris & B. Gerald Cantor Center for Visual Arts at Stanford University (1998.115). Gift of David Hewes

Chapter 13
Page 310: Courtesy of the California History Room, California State Library, Sacramento, California. Mines & Mining: Gold: Scenes from Dag. #3 "Head of Auburn Ravine," 1852 (Neg. #912).; **311:** Michael Freeman/CORBIS; **312:** © DLM - Ledermuseum Offenbach ; **315:** American Textile History Museum, Lowell, Massachusetts; **316:** George Caleb Bingham, "Raftsmen Playing Cards," 1847. The Saint Louis Art Museum. Bequest of Ezra H. Linley by exchange.; **318:** George Howe, "The Endowments, Position, and Education of Woman," an address delivered July 23, 1850.;**319:** Courtesy of the Georgia Historical Society, Savannah, Georgia. D.M. Wright Papers, #1277, Box 36, Folder 286; **320:** Bettmann/CORBIS; **321:** Collection of David J. and Janice L. Frent;**326:** Harriet Beecher Stowe Center, Hartford, CT; **329 (Both):** Library of Congress; **330:** The Ohio Historical Society

Chapter 14
Page 333: Chicago History Museum, ICHi-22172; **337:** The Museum of the Confederacy, Richmond, Virginia. Photography by Katherine Wetzel; **338:** Letter from John B. Spiece to Confederate Attorney General, December 4, 1861.; **339:** Library of Congress; **341 (Top):** Carl G. von Iwonski, "Block House, New Braunfels." Yanaguana Society Collection. Daughters of the Republic of Texas Library, CT96.8; **341 (Bottom):** Western History Collections, University of Oklahoma Library; **342 (Top):** Collection of The New-York Historical Society, Accession #41526; **342 (Bottom Left):** Library of Congress; **342 (Bottom Right):** Library of Congress; **343 (Left):** Library of Congress; **343 (Right):** Courtesy National Archives; **344:** Library of Congress; **345:** The Museum of the Confederacy, Richmond Virginia; **347:** Library of Congress; **351:** Image, Courtesy Colorado Historical Society (WPA-834; 10025492) All Rights Reserved; **353 (Map):** Adapted from *The Atlas of African-American History and Politics: From Slave Trade to Modern Times* by Arwin D. Smallwood with Jeffrey M. Elliot. © McGraw-Hill, 1998. By permission of The McGraw-Hill Companies.; **354:** The National Park Service

Chapter 15
Page 356: Courtesy of the Georgia Historical Society, William Wilson Collection; **359:** CORBIS; **360:** Antique Textile Resource, Bethesda MD; **361:** Library of Congress; **362:** Photo by H.P. Moore. Collection of The New-York Historical Society, Neg. #37497; **366:** Schomburg Center for Research in Black Culture, Art and Artifacts Division, The New York Public Library/Art Resource, NY; **368:** William T. Garrell Foundry, San Francisco, "The Last Spike." The Iris & B. Gerald Cantor Center for Visual Arts at Stanford University (1998.115). Gift of David Hewes; **369:** Robert Benecke, photographer. DeGolyer Library, Southern Methodist University, Dallas, Texas, Ag1982.86.60; **370:** Union Pacific Museum; **372 (Table):** From *Americans and Their Forests: A Historical Review* by; Michael Williams. Copyright © 1989 by Cambridge University Press. Reprinted by permission of Cambridge University Press.; **375:** Wisconsin Historical Society, WHi (D32) 821; **377:** *Harpers Weekly*, Sept. 16, 1871

Part Six Opener
Page 380 (Top): Michael Freeman Photography; **380 (Bottom):** Fair Street Pictures; **381 (Top):** Fair Street Pictures; **381 (Bottom):** Collection of David J. and Janice L. Frent

Chapter 16
Page 382: Hulton Archive/Getty Images; **383:** Carnegie Library of Pittsburgh (#P-1987); **385:** Michael Freeman Photography; **387:** Courtesy of the Burton Historical Collection, Detroit Public Library; **388 (Top):** Library of Congress; **388 (Bottom):** Oregon Historical Society, OrHi 92918; **390 (Map):** Adapted from Clifford Lord and Elizabeth Lord, *Lord & Lord Historical Atlas of the United States.* New York: Holt, 1953.; **392:** © Museum of the City of New York/CORBIS; **395 (Top):** Denver Public Library, Western History Collection, photograph by D. F. Barry (Call number #B-133); **395 (Bottom):** Collection of The New-York Historical Society, Liman Collection, Accession #2000.715.; **396:** Archives & Special Collections Department of the New Mexico State University Library, Las Cruces, NM; **400:** Public Domain; **400:** Andrew Carnegie, "Wealth," *North American Review*, June 1889.;

Chapter 17
Page 403: Photo by Ben Wittick, Courtesy Museum of New Mexico, Neg. Nos. 15821 & 58591; **405:** Courtesy of the California History Room, California State Library, Sacramento, California. (Neg. #23,239); **407:** San Diego Historical Society; **409:**

William Katz Collection; **410 (Map):** Adapted from Martin Gilbert, *American History Atlas*, revised edition. London: Weidenfeld & Nicolson, 1969.; **412:** Nebraska State Historical Society, Solomon D. Butcher Collection; **413:** Yale Collection of Western Americana, Beinecke Rare Book and Manuscript Library; **414:** Fair Street Pictures; **415:** Library of Congress; **415:** Albert Parson, "Parson's Plea for Anarchy," *The New York Herald*, August 30, 1886.; **416:** "Street Arabs at Night," c. 1890. Museum of the City of New York, The Jacob A. Riis Collection, #123; **418:** Courtesy of Hampton University Archives; **420:** May Wright Sewall Collection/Library of Congress;

Chapter 18
422 (Top): Reproduced by permission of The Huntington Library, San Marino, California, photCL11(52); **422 (Bottom):** Reproduced by permission of The Huntington Library, San Marino, California, photCL11(53) **424:** Courtesy National Archives; **425 (Map):** Paullin and Wright, *Atlas of the Historical Geography of the United States*. Washington DC and New York: Carnegie Institution of Washington and the American Geographical Society of New York, 1932.; **426:** National Anthropological Archives, Smithsonian Institution (neg. 008588); **433:** Virginia Historical Society, Richmond, Virginia; **434:** E. S. Frost & Son Photo (88-059-007), Mr. Pat Hathaway photo collection, Monterey, CA; **436:** Image #: 220545, American Museum of Natural History Library; **437 (Top):** Fair Street Pictures; **437 (Bottom):** The Granger Collection, New York; **438 (Map):** Maps, "Spanish-American War in the Pacific," *The Century Illustrated Monthly Magazine*, 1898 and "Spanish-American War in the Caribbean," *Harper's New Monthly Magazine*, 1898.; **440:** From "Proceedings of the Congressional Committee on the Philippines." Testimony of Robert P. Hughes and Charles S. Riley, 1902.; **441 (Top):** Keystone-Mast Collection, UCR/California Museum of Photography, University of California at Riverside. All Rights Reserved, University of California Regents; **441 (Bottom):** Collection of David J. and Janice L. Frent

Part Seven Opener
Page 444 (Top): From the Collections of The Henry Ford (T.31384); **444 (Bottom):** Hulton Archive/Getty Images; **445 (Top):** Fair Street Pictures; **445 (Center):** From the Collections of The Henry Ford (T.30044); **445 (Bottom):** Music B-946 Title: Old Man Jazz; on the Historic American Music web site of music in the Rare Book, Manuscript and Special Collections Library, Duke University. http://scriptorium.lib.duke.edu/sheetmusic/).

Chapter 19
Page 446: Brown Brothers; **447:** Library of Congress; **448 (Map):** Adapted from Clifford Lord and Elizabeth Lord, *Lord & Lord Historical Atlas of the United States*. New York: Holt, 1953.; **449:** Jessie Tarbox Beals, "Woman and Children in the Kitchen, "1915. Community Service Society, New York, NY. The Jewish Museum/Art Resource, NY; **450 (Figure):** From United States Immigration and Naturalization Service.; **451 (Map):** Adapted from Stephen A. Flanders, *Atlas of American Migration*. New York: Facts on File, 1998.; **452:** J. K. Oliver photo, Mr. Pat Hathaway photo collection, Monterey, CA; **453:** George Eastman House; **455:** S.R. Maki photo, Minnesota Historical Society; **456 (Top):** From the Collections of The Henry Ford (T.31384); **456 (Bottom):** Image courtesy of The Advertising Archives; **457:** George Luks, "The Cafe Francis" c. 1909. The Butler Institute of American Art, Youngstown, Ohio; **458:** Courtesy Lilly Library, Indiana University, Bloomington, IN.; **459:** George Eastman House; **460:** Collection of David J. and Janice L. Frent; **462:** Yale Collection of Western Americana, Beinecke Rare Book and Manuscript Library

Chapter 20
Page 466 (Top): Hulton Archive/Getty Images; **466 (Bottom):** Culver Pictures, Inc.; **467:** National Air and Space Museum, Smithsonian Institution (SI Neg. No. 79-759). Photo by Dane Penland; **470:** Denver Public Library, Western History Collection, photograph by Lewis Dodd (Call number X-60451); **473:** Hulton Archive/Getty Images; **474:** Historical Pictures/Stock Montage, Inc.; **475:** Fair Street Pictures; **477:** Courtesy, Hagley Museum and Library (Neg. #69.170.13,622); **478:** Courtesy National Archives; **478:** Addie Hunton and Kathryn Johnson, *Two Colored Women with the American Expeditionary Forces*, 1920.; **480 (Top):** Courtesy of Military Antiques & Museum, Petaluma, CA; **480 (Bottom):** From "Art of the October Revolution, Leningrad," Aurora Art Publishers, 1979; **483:** Museum of History & Industry, Seattle, WA/Pemco, Webster & Stevens Collection

Chapter 21
Page 486: AP Images; **487:** David J. & Janice L. Frent Collection/CORBIS; **490:** Bettmann/CORBIS; **491:** Bettmann/CORBIS; **492 (Figure):** From Unites States Immigration Service, 1891–1940.; **493:** Culver Pictures, Inc.; **494:** Photofest; **494:** Langston Hughes, "I, Too, Sing America" from *The Collected Poems of Langston Hughes*.; **495 (Top):** Photographs and Prints Division, Schomburg Center for Research in Black Culture, The New York Public Library, Astor, Lenox and Tilden Foundations; **495 (Bottom):** From the Collections of The Henry Ford (T.30044); **496:** © The New Yorker Collection 1956. Barney Tobey from cartoonbank.com. All Rights Reserved.; **499:** © The New Yorker Collection 1925 Rea Irvin from cartoonbank.com. All Rights Reserved.; **500:** Image courtesy of The Advertising Archives; **503:** Getty Images; **503:** Mario Puzo, *The Fortunate Pilgrim*. New York: Random House, 1997.;

Part Eight Opener
Page 506 (Top): Library of Congress; **506 (Center):** Nationalmuseet, Denmark/The Bridgeman Art Library; **506 (Bottom):** Gift of Mr. and Mrs. Jim Kawaminami, Japanese American National Museum (86.8.3). Photo by Norman Sugimoto; **507 (Top):** Fair Street Pictures; **507 (Center):** UN Photo; **507 (Bottom):** Cathy Crawford/CORBIS

Chapter 22
Page 508: Bettmann/CORBIS; **510:** Margaret Bourke-White/Time & Life Pictures/Getty Images; **514:** Arthur Rothstein, 1936. The Library of Congress; **516:** Bettmann/CORBIS; **517:** Franklin D. Roosevelt Library; **518:** Library of Congress; **520:** AP Images; **524:** Library of Congress; **525:** Ralph Stackpole, "Industries of California," 1934. Don Beatty Photo ©1981; **526:** Walter P. Reuther Library, Wayne State University; **528:** Air & Space Museum, Smithsonian Institution

Chapter 23
Page 530: U.S. Marine Corps/Courtesy National Archives; **532:** Nationalmuseet, Copenhagen, Denmark/The Bridgeman Art Library; **533:** Norman Rockwell, "Four Freedoms," War Bond Poster. Printed by permission of the Norman Rockwell Family Agency. Copyright © 1943 the Norman Rockwell Family Entities. Photo courtesy of the Norman Rockwell Museum at Stockbridge, Massachusetts; **534:** Fair Street Pictures; **535:** AP Images; **536:** Gift of Mr. and Mrs. Jim Kawaminami, Japanese American National Museum (86.8.3). Photo by Norman Sugimoto; **537:** Courtesy National Archives (210-CC-S-26C); **539 (Top Left):** Dwight D. Eisenhower Library; **539 (Top Center Left):** John F. Kennedy Presidentail Library and Museum, Boston.; **539 (Top Center Right):** LBJ Library Photo; **539 (Top Right):** The Richard Nixon Library & Birthplace Foundation, Album 43.6; **539 (Bottom Left):** Courtesy Gerald R. Ford Presidential Library; **539 (Bottom Center Left):** Jimmy Carter Library; **539 (Bottom Center Right):** Courtesy Ronald Reagan Library; **539 (Bottom Right):** George Bush Presidential Library ; **540 (Top):** Courtesy National Archives; **540 (Bottom):** Courtesy National Archives (NWDNS-44-PA-171); **542:** Courtesy, Zelda Webb Anderson and The University of Nevada Oral History Project; **542:** Interview with Zelda Anderson in R.T. King, ed., *War Stories: Veterans Remember World War II.*; **545:** Courtesy National Archives; **547:** Courtesy National Archives

Chapter 24
Page 550: Courtesy National Archives ; **551:** Ed Clark/Time & Life Pictures/Getty Images; **552:** UN Photo; **553:** John Vachon; **559 (Top):** Bettmann/CORBIS; **559 (Bottom):** Photofest; **561:** Collection of David J. and Janice L. Frent; **562:** Bettmann/CORBIS; **564:** Courtesy Los Mineros Photograph Collection, Chicano Research Collection, Arizona State University Libraries; **566:** ChinaStock; **567:** Bettmann/CORBIS; **567:** From NSC-68: United States Objectives and Programs for National Security, April 14, 1950.; **568:** Sfc. Al Chang/Defense Visual Information Center (Department of Defense), HD-SN-99-03118

Part Nine Opener
Page 572 (Top): Library of Congress; **572 (Bottom):** Roger Ressmeyer/CORBIS; **573 (Top):** Library of Congress; **573 (Bottom):** Courtesy, Inkworks Press

Chapter 25
Page 574: AP Images; **575:** Library of Congress; **577 (Top):** Photofest; **577 (Bottom):** "Chicago Commuters," 1953. Photo by Dan Weiner, Courtesy of Sandra Weiner.; **579:** Betty Engle photo, Minnesota Historical Society; **580:** Ed Clark/Time & Life Pictures/Getty Images; **583:** Collection of David J. and Janice L. Frent;**584:** Roger Ressmeyer/CORBIS; **588:** Social Welfare History Archives, University of Minnesota Libraries, American Social Health Association Records, box 179; **589:** Washington Post. Reprinted by permission of the D.C. Public Library; **590:** Alfred Eisenstaedt/Time & Life Pictures/Getty Images; **590:** Rachel Carson, *Silent Spring*. Boston: Houghton Mifflin, 1962.; **593:** Fair Street Pictures

Chapter 26
Page 595: © 1976 George Ballis/Take Stock; **596:** LBJ Library Photo by Cecil Stoughton;**597:** Collection of David J. and Janice L. Frent; **602:** Ngo Vinh Long Collection, University of Maine; **604:** John Launois/Black Star/Stockphoto.com; **605 (Top):** Collection of David J. and Janice L. Frent; **605 (Bottom):** Library of Congress; **606:** Getty Images; **606:** Martin Luther King Jr. Excerpt from "A Time to Break Silence" (Speech delivered April 4, 1967, New York, NY). Reprinted by arrangement with The Heirs to the Estate of Martin Luther King Jr., c/o Writers House as agent for the proprietor, New York, NY. Copyright 1967 Martin Luther King Jr., copyright renewed 1995 Coretta Scott King.; **607:** Courtesy of Campus Crusade for Christ; **608:** Bettmann/CORBIS; **610:** Jules Feiffer; **611:** Collection of David J. and Janice L. Frent; **612:** Collection of David J. and Janice L. Frent;

Chapter 27
Page 615: Courtesy National Archives (NLNP-WHPO-MPF-8649(01)); **617:** Collection of David J. and Janice L. Frent; **619:** Bettmann/CORBIS; **621:** Stanley J. Forman, "The Soiling of Old Glory," Pulitzer Prized 1977. ; **622:** Courtesy, Sharp Electronics Corporation; **623:** Peter Menzel/Stock, Boston, LLC; **624:** Bettmann/CORBIS; **624:** Interim Report of the U.S. Senate Select Committee to Study Government Operations, Nov. 20, 1975.; **626:** Collection of David J. and Janice L. Frent; **627:** Jimmy Carter Library; **628:** Danny Lehman/CORBIS; **630:** Sophia Smith Collection, Smith College, Gloria Steinem Papers; **631:** Courtesy, Inkworks Press; **632:** Photo by Jim Britt/Time Magazine, Copyright Time Inc./Time & Life Pictures/Getty Images

Part Ten Opener
Page 634: Collection of David J. and Janice L. Frent; **635:** AP Images/Justin Sullivan;

Chapter 28
Page 636: Courtesy Ronald Reagan Library; **637 (Top):** Vladimir Sichov/SIPA Press; **637 (Bottom):** Bettmann/CORBIS; **638:** Collection of David J. and Janice L. Frent; **640:** *The Sacramento Bee*; **642:** Oliphant © Universal Press Syndicate. Reprinted with permission. All rights reserved; **646:** William Sauro/The *New York* Times; **646:** From *Listen, America* by Jerry Falwell. Copyright © 1980 by Jerry Falwell. Used by permission of Doubleday, a division of Random House, Inc.; **647:** AFP/Getty Images; **647:** Excerpts from "The Need for a Moral Minority" by Robert McAfee Brown.; **648:** AP Images/Eric Draper;

Chapter 29
Page 655: Walker Shaun/SIPA Press; **657 (Top):** Courtesy, Casio Corporation; **657 (Bottom):** Miguel Gandert/CORBIS; **658 (Map):** Stephen A. Flanders, *Atlas of American Migration*. New York: Facts on File, 1998.; **659:** Michael Sofronski/SIPA Press; **660:** Lee Celano/SIPA Press; **661:** Tamiment/Wagner Poster and Broadside Collection, Tamiment Library, New York University; **662:** REUTERS/Jim Bourg; **662:** From The Vermont Civil Union Law, April 26, 2000.; **663:** AP Images/Jack Smith; **664:** AP Images/Joe Marquette; **665:** James Keyser/Time & Life Pictures/Getty Images; **669:** Reuters/CORBIS

Chapter 30
Page 676: Val McClatchey, "End of Serenity," 2001.; **680:** BEHROUZ MEHRI/AFP/Getty Images; **683 (Top):** Courtesy, Samsung Corporation; **683 (Bottom):** © The New Yorker Collection 1993 Peter Steiner from cartoonbank.com. All Rights Reserved.; **687:** AP Images/Justin Sullivan; **688 (Top):** Photofest; **688 (Bottom):** Courtesy, Newstream.com; **689:** © The New Yorker Collection 2000 Barbara Smaller from cartoonbank.com. All Rights Reserved.; **690:** AP Images/Hasan Hamali; **690:** The Slow Food manifesto, Nov. 9, 1989 of the Slow Food Movement, http://www.slowfood.com.

Index

Entries followed by *f, t, m,* and *i* refer to figures, tables, maps, and illustrations, respectively

A

AAA. *See* Agricultural Adjustment Act
Abalone Alliance, 622
Abenaki Indians, 39m, 78
ABM treaty, 617
Abolitionist movement
    in 18th century, 197, 241
    in 19th century, 293–294
    and Lincoln, criticism of, 342
    suppression of, 293–294, 294i
    on territorial expansion, 302
    Underground Railroad, 322, 326, 327m
    women and
        black, 320, 320i
        white, 293
    women's rights movement and, 300, 320, 320i
Abortion
    in 1940s, 561
    in 1950s, 588
    in 1960s, 608–609
    in 1970s, 631
    in 1980s, 644
    in 1990s
        anti-abortion violence, 664
        debate over, 664, 664i, 667
    Bolsheviks and, 482
    legalization of, 631
Abstract expressionism, 587
Abu Ghraib, 681
Acadia National Park, 474
Acadians, 119
Acheson, Dean, 555
Acoma pueblo, 33, 35i
Acquired immunodeficiency syndrome. *See* AIDS
ACT-UP. *See* AIDS Coalition to Unleash Power
Adamor, Refugio, 396i
Adams, John
    on Boston Massacre, 154
    constitutional model of, 179, 207
    Declaration of Independence and, 169
    election of 1796 and, 218, 222–223, 222t
    election of 1800 and, 235, 235t
    on political system in United States, 197
    as president, 222, 236
    on public unrest in Revolutionary era, 150
    on Stamp Act protests, 150
    Treaty of Paris and, 187, 188i
Adams, John Quincy
    Amistad case and, 295
    election of 1820 and, 267, 267t
    election of 1824 and, 268, 268t
    Monroe Doctrine and, 267, 268
    as president, 268–269
    slavery and, 263–264
    War of 1812 and, 250
Adams, Samuel
    attempt to arrest, 158–159
    Townshend duties and, 152
Adams, Will, 32

Adamson Act (1916), 474
Addams, Jane, 417, 457, 460
Administration of Justice Act (1774), 156
Advertising
    19th century
        exotic themes in, 435–436
        mass merchandising, 394, 395–396
        minorities and, 383–384
    in 1920s, 500, 500i
    popular culture and, 688
The Advocate, 312
AEF. *See* American Expeditionary Force
Affirmative action
    Reagan on, 641
    Supreme Court on, 632
Afghanistan
    Soviet invasion of, 637, 638, 648
    Taliban in, 677
    Taliban regime in, 670
    U.S. invasion of, 678
AFL. *See* American Federation of Labor
Africa
    African American return to, 165, 492
    AIDS and, 646
    Carter policy in, 626
    culture of, 84i
    English colonization in, 66
    European imperialism in, 435
    origin of life in, 2, 5
    slave trade and. *See* Atlantic slave trade
African American culture
    pre-Civil War, 255, 256–258, 257i, 319
    early 20th century, 458
    emergence of, 255
African American studies programs, 605, 606i
African American women
    19th century
        abolitionist movement and, 320, 320i
        employment and, 234–235
        reform movements and, 373–374, 435
    20th century
        activism of, 629
        employment and, 511
        first in Congress, 661
        New Deal and, 524
        role and status of, 579
        social life, 493i
        suffrage movement and, 459–460
        in World War II, 543
African Americans. *See also* Race; Slaves
    17th century, legal status of, 84–85
    18th century
        employment, 224, 225i
        population, 117, 217, 224
        status of, 102, 224–225
        white views on, 101–102
    and American Revolution
        British offers of freedom to, 164–165, 167
        British Southern strategy and, 182
        in Continental Army, 180
        disillusionment with, 163, 167, 167i
        impact of, 164–167
        suppression during, 167
        urge to freedom in, 146, 146i, 217–218

    pre-Civil War
        abolitionist movement and, 293, 320, 320i
        bias against, in Midwest, 314
        in California, 311
        culture of, 255, 256–258, 257i, 319
        diversity of, 315
        education, 298–299, 315
        efforts to control, 275–276
        employment, 234–235, 244, 254, 287, 293, 315, 316–317, 324, 328
        festivals and celebrations, 224, 225i
        Fugitive Slave Act and, 326
        integration-separation debate, 276
        migrations, 287–288
        in Republic of Texas, 301–302
        resistance to slavery, 315, 326
        restrictions on, 291
        rights of, 230
        slaveholders' myths about, 259
        status of, 275–276
        stereotypes of, 317
        voting rights of, 224, 275
        and War of 1812, 247i, 294–250
        in West, 230
        White fear of, 101–102
        worker resentment of, 287, 293, 324, 328
    and Civil War
        anti-black violence, 350
        Confederate brutality toward, 350–351
        Union employment of, 333i, 346–348, 350–351
    post-Civil War. *See also* Reconstruction
        aspirations of, 362–363
        citizenship of, 360
        class divisions among, 363
        education and, 356, 358, 360
        employment, 371, 391
        labor and, 361–362
        marriage and family, 363–364
        militancy of, 356, 358
        political organization, 363–364, 365
        religion of, 364
        rights of, 363, 367, 377–378
        self-help organizations, 356–357, 364–365
        sharecropping system, 364, 502
        status of, 357–358
        unions and, 376
        voting rights, 209, 359–361, 363–364, 365m, 367, 374
        white efforts to control, 356–357, 360
    late 19th century
        aspirations of, 427
        discrimination against, 404–405
        education, 427
        military service, 408–409, 408i
        population, 432
        resistance to discrimination, 427
        settlement houses, 434
        social class among, 407
        Social Darwinism and, 400
        in Spanish-American War, 439
        unions and, 376, 415
        violence against, 408, 426

I-1

African Americans, *continued*
    voting rights, 374, 426, 432
    in West, 408–409, 408i
    white efforts to control, 408–409, 426
    20th century
        in World War I
            migration to cities in, 445
            as soldiers, 478
            support for, 478
        in World War II
            in armed forces, 543
            employment, 536, 541
            racial tension and, 543
        2000 election, 672–673
        crime and, 610, 658
        cultural integration of, 509
        culture of, 458
        discrimination against, 470
        election of 1948, 562–563
        employment, 512
        Federal Theater Project, 524
        first black mayor, 605
        first major league baseball player, 554
        first public health nurse, 454
        first White House meeting, 462
        Great Migration, 445, 474, 474i, 477
        Harlem Renaissance, 493—495, 491i
        home ownership, 576, 578
        leaders of, 460–461
        middle class status, 579, 658
        Million Man March, 660–661
        music of, 486, 495
        party affiliation, 527
        political office, 605
        Red Scare and, 564
        riots, 604–605, 611
        role and status of, 466, 470
        Roosevelt policies and, 524
        Scottsboro Boys, 512
        service organizations and, 579i
        as sports celebrities, 527–528
        status of, 658, 659
        unions and, 460
        violence against, 460, 470, 483, 512, 522, 553, 581
        voter participation, 647
        voting rights, 553, 554, 595, 598, 605
        welfare state and, 524
        in West, 4, 4i
    back-to-Africa movement, 165, 492
    in contemporary America, 692
    population, 691
Afro hairstyle, 605
Agnew, Spiro, 612, 615, 618
Agricultural Adjustment Act (1933) [AAA], 518, 523t, 525
Agriculture. *See also* Drought; Plantation agriculture
    Native American
        Archaic period, 6–7
        500–1500, 8–11
    17th century, in Southwest, 36
    19th century
        agribusiness, 387i, 388
        economics of, 374–375, 375i, 412, 432
        labor unrest in, 412–413
        in Midwest, 314
        in New England, 315
        regions for, 386m
        sharecropping, 361–362
        technological advances in, 385, 385i
        transient labor in, 388i
    20th century
        economics of, 518
        mechanization of, 578
        sharecropping, 502
Aguinaldo, Emilio, 438
Ah Quin, 407i
Ah Sue, 407i
Aid to Families with Dependent Children, 597, 656, 667
Aidid, Mohammed Farah, 670
AIDS, 634, 646, 648
AIDS Coalition to Unleash Power (ACT-UP), 648
AIM. *See* American Indian Movement
Al Qaeda, 670
    Iraqi ties to, 679
    in September 11th attacks, 676–677
Alabama
    economy of, 19th century, 265
    readmission to Union, 365m, 368
    secession convention in, 335
Alabama (ship), 346
Alamo, 65, 301
Alaska
    European contact, 138
    natural resources in, 373
    Russia in, 140–141, 162, 193
    statehood, 575
    U.S. purchase of, 372–373
Alaska National Interest Lands Conservation Act (1980), 627, 628i
Alaska Native Brotherhood, 554
Albany Congress, 132
Albany Plan, 132
Alcan (Alaska-Canada) Highway, 561
Alcatraz, Indian seizure of (1969), 608
Alcohol. *See also* Temperance movement
    Georgia colony and, 104
    Native Americans and
        ill effects of, 275
        Indian resistance movement and, 247, 246i
        white manipulation and, 246
    New England distilleries, 123–124
    saloon proliferation, early 20th century, 456
    in West, ill effects of, 227
Aldrin, Edwin "Buzz," 573
Aleutian Islanders
    Russian fur trade and, 140
    World War II and, 71
Alexander, king of Wampanoags, 69
Alexander, Mary Spratt Provoost, 120i
Alfred P. Murrah Federal Building. *See* Oklahoma City Federal Building bombing
Algonquin Indians, 38, 39m, 216, 227. *See also* Ohio Confederacy
Ali, Muhammad, 605
Alien and Sedition Acts (1798), 223, 235
All the President's Men (film), 623
Allen, Ethan, 166–167
Allende, Salvador, 617
Alliance for Progress, 591
Alperovitz, Gar, 559
Alton Observer, 294
Amador, Martin, 396i
Amalgamated Clothing Workers of America, 526
America First Committee, 533
America Online, 657
American(s)
    characteristics of, 423
    as term, 138
American Anti-Slavery Society, 293
American Civil Liberties Union (ACLU), 498
"The American Crisis" (Paine), 171–173
An American Dictionary of the English Language (Webster), 196
American Duties Act (1764), 144
American exceptionalism, 423
American Expeditionary Force (AEF), 478
American Federation of Labor (AFL)
    19th century, emergence of, 416
    20th century
        activism of, 482
        anticapitalism and, 471
        and election of 1912, 471
        membership restrictions, 460, 526, 543
The American Geography (Morse), 197
American GI Forum, 564
American Glanzstoff plant, 502
American identity
    in 1930s, 527
American Independent party, 611t
American Indian Movement (AIM), 608–609
American League, 395
American Museum of Natural History, 435
American party, 323, 325, 325t
American Railway Union (ARU), 416, 431
American Republican party, 296
American Revolution. *See also* Revolutionary War
    African Americans and
        British offers of freedom to, 164–165, 167
        British Southern strategy and, 182
        in Continental Army, 180
        disillusionment of, 163, 167, 167i
        impact of, 164–167
        suppression during, 167
        urge to freedom, 146, 146i, 217–218
    challenges following, 192–196
    declaration of independence, 169
    economic impact of, 162–163, 189, 201–202
    events leading to
        Boston Massacre, 153–154, 154i
        Boston Tea Party, 155
        Gaspee Affair, 154
        oppressive measures, 144–156
        rural unrest, 150–151
    France and, 174, 176–177, 177f, 178, 187, 188
    social class and, 137–138, 146, 150, 159
    women and, 163, 181
American Spelling Book (Webster), 196
American System, 292, 385
American Telephone and Telegraph (AT&T), 495
American values, education reform and, 297–298
American Victorianism, 281, 373, 427
American Woman Suffrage Association (AWSA), 374, 432
Americas. *See also* North America; South America
    prehistory, Paleo-Indian era, 6
    European exploration and conquest of, 14–28. *See also individual nations*
    origin of name, 17
    prehistory, 2–14
        Paleo-Indian era, 6
        Archaic era, 6–7
        500-1500, 8–12
        European view of, 4–5
        peopling of, 2–3
        population in, 12
Amherst, Jeffery, 133, 142–143
Amistad case, 295i, 295
Amusement parks
    late 19th century, 394
    mid-20th century, 576
An Choi, 310
Anaconda Copper Co., 636

Anarchists
    late 19th century, 415, 434
    early 20th century, 488
    post-World War I, 483
Anasazi, 10–11, 9m
Anderson, John B., 639t
Anderson, Marian, 522
Anderson, Zelda Webb, 542, 542i
Andersonville Prison, 352
André, John, 184
Andros, Sir Edmond, 74
Angel Island, 448m, 451
Anglican Church. *See* Church of England
Anglo-Dutch Wars, 66
ANMA. *See* Associación Nacional México-Americana
Annapolis, Chesapeake trade summit in (1786), 207
Anne, Queen of England, 75
Anorexia nervosa, 665
Anthony, Susan B., 300, 374, 376
Anthrax letters, 635
Anthropology, establishment as discipline, 426
Anti-Federalists, 211–213, 218
Anti-Masonic party, 272t
Anti-Saloon League, 490
Antibiotics
    development of, 558
    impact of, 666
Anticommunism. *See also* Red scare(s)
    Reagan and, 625, 640, 640i
Antietam, Battle of, 344–345, 344i, 346
Antinomians, 48
Antisemitism. *See also* Holocaust
    early 20th century, Russia and Eastern Europe, 452
    mid-20th century, decline in, 563
    1930s, 521
    U.S., in World War II, 541
Antrobus, John, 257i
Anza, Juan Bautista de, 141, 142m
Apaches
    19th century, assimilation of, 422i
    alliances with whites, 113–114
    in Civil War, 344, 352
    Comanche raids on, 113
    horses and, 112, 114m
    raids on neighboring Indians by, 62
    reservation status, 344
    resistance to whites, 334, 368–369
    treaties, 110–111, 368
    war with whites, 368–369, 408
Apalachee revolt (1647), 37
Apartheid in South Africa
    activism against, 648
    ending of, 626, 651
Apex Mining Act (1872), 371–372
Apocalypse Now (film), 623
Apollo 11, 613
Appeasement, in World War II, 532
Appomattox Courthouse, 354
Arab oil embargo (1973–1974), 573, 621–622
Arabia, immigration from, 451m
Arafat, Yasser, 669
Arapahos
    19th century, land loss by, 323
    in Civil War, 351, 351i
    culture, 312
    Ghost Dance and, 409
    removal of, 288m
    treaties, 368
    war with whites, 351
Arbella (ship), 46
Arbenz, Jacobo, 585
Archaeology
    at Cactus Hill, Virginia, 6, 6i

    in Chile, 6
    at Fort Mose, Florida, 100i
    in Mississippi Valley, 11–12
    in New Mexico, 4, 5
Archaic era, 6–7
Architecture
    late 19th century, 391–392
    Greek Revival style, 273i
    skyscrapers, 392, 447, 453
Arctic National Wildlife Refuge, 679
Arikaras, 112, 114m, 242, 369
Aristide, Jean Bertrand, 670
Aristotle, 148
Arizona
    in Civil War, 344
    racial prejudice in, 449–450
    statehood, 467
    tourism and, 495
    U.S. acquisition of, 305, 312
    voting rights in, 554
Arkansas
    Black scare in, 483
    Little Rock school desegregation, 581
    readmission to Union, 365m, 367
    secession of, 336m, 337
Armed forces. *See also* Military budget
    desegregation of, 562
    segregation in, 408–409, 409i, 478, 543
    unification of command in, 567
    women in, 631
Armenia, immigration from, 19th century, 390
Arms race
    in Cold War, 572, 575
    under Kennedy, 591–592
    space exploration and, 583–584
Arms reduction treaties
    ABM treaty, 617
    Eisenhower and, 583–584
    Five-Power Treaty, 487–488
    Intermediate Nuclear Force (INF) treaty, 649
    Strategic Arms Limitations Treaties (SALT I and II), 617, 638
Armstrong, Neil, 613
Army-McCarthy hearings, 564
Army of the Republic of Vietnam (ARVN), 600
Arnold, Benedict
    in Revolutionary War, 166–167, 168, 173, 175, 175m
    treason of, 186
Art. *See* Literature and art
Arteaga, Ignacio de, 141
Arthur, Chester A., 397
Articles of Confederation. *See also* Confederation
    government structure under, 178
    ratification of, 178
    supplanting of, 211–214
Artisans, in Early Republic, 232
ARU. *See* American Railway Union
ARVN. *See* Army of the Republic of Vietnam
Ashcan School, 457, 457i
Ashcroft, John, 678
Ashley-Cooper, Anthony, Earl of Shaftsburg, 68, 78
Asia
    19th century, immigration from, 390–391
    20th century
        anticolonialism in, 552, 565
        immigration from, 450–452, 451m, 492, 577, 648, 663
    peopling of, 2, 5
Asian-Americans, 20th century
    citizenship and, 565
    family life, 577–558

Asiento, 85
Asociación Nacional México-Americana (ANMA), 580
Association(s)
    18th century, 197, 231
    as American characteristic, 217
    women's clubs, late 19th century, 435
Aswan Dam, 585
Atahualpa, 21
Atchison, Topeka, and Sante Fe Railroad, 403
Atlanta, Sherman's march to, 352, 353m
Atlanta Compromise, 427
Atlanta *Constitution* (newspaper), 406
Atlantic Charter, 533–534
Atlantic slave trade
    15th century, 14
    16th century, 18, 19i, 27
    17th century, 37, 41, 57, 67, 86–87
    18th century, 164
    African source regions, 91–94, 93m, 96m–97m
    British colonies in, 96m–97m
    Constitutional protections for, 210
    Denmark and, 96m–97m
    England and, 27, 67, 82–83, 91–95, 96m–97m
    France and, 57, 87i, 94, 96m–97m
    growth of, 79
    Holland and, 37, 41, 86–87
    importing regions, 96m–97m, 96–97
    loading and unloading, 87i, 94, 95
    Middle Passage, 91, 94–95
    Netherlands and, 96m–97m
    origins and expansion of, 85–91
    outlawed by U.S., 255
    Portugal in, 96m–97m
    post-Revolution, 202
    Revolutionary War and, 163
    size of, 91, 92, 96m–97m, 108
    slave experiences in, 94i, 94–96
    source regions, 96m–97m
    Spain and, 18, 19i
    trade items used in, 91, 92, 92f, 124
    volume of, 256
Atomic bomb. *See also* Nuclear arms
    bombing of Japan, 507, 547–548
    development of, 547
Atomic Energy Commission, 559
AT&T. *See* American Telephone and Telegraph
Attica prison riots (1971), 613
Attlee, Clement, 547
Attucks, Crispus, 153
Atwood, John, 280i
Audubon Society, 622, 643
Austerlitz, Battle of, 244
Austin, Moses, 266
Austin, Stephen, 266, 266m
Australia, peopling of, 5
Austria
    German annexation of (1938), 532
    post-World War II, 557m
Austria-Hungary
    immigration from, 427, 492f
    and World War I, 467, 481
Automobile industry, 1930s, unrest in, 526–527
Automobile pollution, 686
Automobiles
    in 1920s, 495–496
    federal safety standards for, 598
    fuel efficiency standards for, 627
    impact of, 491f
    mass manufacture of, 444
    pollution and, 584
    suburban culture and, 584
    and Western growth, 562

The Awakening (Chopin), 428
Axis alliance, 533
Axis Pact, 533
Ayllón, Lucas Vásquez de, 21, 26m
Aztecs, 9, 9m, 10, 19–20

B

Babbitt (Lewis), 501
Baby and Child Care (Spock), 560, 575
Baby boom, 507, 560, 573, 575, 665
Backlash (Faludi), 645
Bacon, Nathaniel, 71–73, 89–90
Bacon's Rebellion, 71–73, 89–90
Bad Axe River massacre, 274
Baez, Joan, 607
Baker, Howard, 618
Bakke case (1978), 632
Bakker, Jim, 645
Balboa, Vasco Núñez de, 18–19
Baldwin, F. L., 333i
Balkans, ethnic violence in, 670, 671m
Ballinger, Richard A., 463
Baltimore, Maryland, mid-18th century, 121i
Bambara, Sambra, 100
Bank(s), Great Depression and, 502, 517
Bank of United States
    first, 219, 247, 273
    second, 241, 266–267, 270, 272–273, 292
Banks, Nathaniel, 348, 358
Bannock Indians, white encroachment on, 372
Baranov, Alexander, 140–141
Barbary wars, 237
Barlow, Joel, 196
Barracoons, 92
Barry, Leonora, 414
Barton, Bruce, 500
Bartram, William, 197, 197i
Baseball
    in 19th century, 394
    Black Sox scandal, 483
    desegregation of, 554
    integration of, 554
Basketball
    as American popular culture, 648i
    invention of, 428–429
Bass, Morris, 452
Bataan Death March, 545
Bathtub gin, 490
Batista, Fulgencio, 585
Baumfree, Isabella. *See* Truth, Sojourner
Bay of Pigs invasion (1961), 591–592
Beamer, Todd, 677
The Beatles, 607
Beats, 587–588
Beauregard, P. T. G., 339
The Beautiful and the Damned (Fitzgerald), 501
Beaver Wars, 38–39
Beecher, Catherine, 278, 297, 320
Beecher, Eunice, 373
Beecher, Henry Ward, 373, 399
Begin, Menachem, 627
Belgium
    Communist Party rise in, 552
    immigration from, 314
    loss of colonies, 531
Bell, Alexander Graham, 385
Bell, John, 330, 330t
Bell Telephone, 388
Bellamy, Edward, 415
Belle (ship), 59i
Belleau Wood, Battle of, 480
Bemis Heights, 175
Benedict, Ruth, 540

Benezet, Anthony, 104
Benson, A. L., 473t
Bering, Vitus, 140, 140i
Bering Land Bridge, 5
Bering Straits, 5
Beringia, 5–6
Berkeley, Lord John, 69
Berkeley, Sir William, 71–73, 72i
Berlin
    siege of (World War II), 545
    Soviet blockade of, 557–558
Berlin Wall
    construction of, 592
    fall of, 558, 649
Bernstein, Carl, 618
Berry, Chuck, 554, 588
Bessemer process, 385
Bethabara, North Carolina, 121m
Bible
    Indian translation of, 50
Bicameral system, 208
Bicycle, modern, introduction of, 385
Biddle, Francis, 535
Biddle, Grace, 235
Bidwell, John, 431t
Bienville, 55, 60
Big Three, Versailles Treaty and, 481–482
Bight of Benin (slave coast), 93, 93m, 96m–97m
Bight of Biafra, 93, 93m, 96m–97m
Bigler, Henry William, 310
Bikini Islands, 560
Bilingual education, 663
Bill of Rights (England, 1689), 73
Bill of Rights (U.S.)
    debate over, 210–211
    passage of, 213–214, 218
    rights protected by, 214
Billboard (periodical), 554
Bin Laden, Osama, 653, 670, 676–677, 678
Bingham, Mark, 677
Birmingham, Alabama, civil rights march (1963), 593
Birney, James G., 295t, 302t
Birth control clinic, first, 471
Black Belt, 314
Black Codes, 360
Black Elk, 387
Black Hawk, 274, 279, 317
Black Hawk War, 274, 352
Black Hills, 368
"Black is beautiful" slogan, 605
Black Kettle, 351–352, 351i
Black Muslims, 595i, 604, 660
Black Panther party, 605, 625
Black Pioneers, 165
Black Power movement, 603, 604–605
Black Scare, 483
Black Sox scandal, 483
Black Star Line, 489–490
Black Tuesday, 502
Blackbeard, 77, 77i, 78
Blackfeet Indians, 112, 114m, 372
Blackstone Canal, 264m
Blackwell, Henry, 374
Bladensburg, Battle of, 248
Blaine, James G., 398, 398t, 436
Blair, Tony
    support for War in Iraq, 679
Blazing Saddles (film), 625
BLM. *See* Bureau of Land Management
Bloody Marsh, Battle of, 105, 107m
Bloody shirt, waving of, 396–397
Bloomer, Amelia, 300
Bloomers, 300
Blue Water raid, 323
Blues music, 495
Blunt, Maria, 345

Board of National Popular Education, 297
Boardman, Elijah, 219i
Boas, Franz, 470
Boatbuilding technology. *See* Navigation and boatbuilding technology
Boeing Aircraft, 683–684
Bohemia, late 19th century, immigration from, 393
Boland Amendments (1982, 1984), 640, 650
Bolshevism. *See also* Communism
    Russian revolution and, 445, 478–480, 480i, 482
    spread of, 480
    U.S. fear of, 482
Bonanza farms, 388
Bonsack, James, 406
Bontemps, Arna, 493–494
Bonus March, 515
Book of Mormon, 279–280
Boone, Daniel, 182, 183m, 199
Boonesboro, 182, 183m
Booth, John Wilkes, 354
Border Ruffians, 326
Bosnia, ethnic conflict in, 670, 671m
Bosque Redondo internment camp, 352
Bosque Redondo reservation, 344
Boston
    17th century, establishment of, 48
    18th century
        Boston Massacre, 153–154, 154i
        Boston Tea Party, 138, 155–156
        growth of, 119–120
        social class in, 137–138
        Stamp Act protest in, 145–146
        tax resistance in, 152
        vice-admiralty courts in, 152, 157m
        Washington's siege of, 168
    19th century
        Civil War draft riots, 349–350
        Irish in, 285
        runaway slaves in, 287
    20th century
        Boston Marathon, 82
        racial violence in, 621, 621i
        strikes in, 482
Boston Fruit Co., 388
Boston Marathon, 82
Boston marriages, 457
Boston Massacre, 153–154, 154i
Boston Port Act (1774), 156
Boston Tea Party, 138, 155–156
Boudinot, Elias, 289
Bourke-White, Margaret, 510i
Bow, Clara, 493
Bow and arrow, 11
Bowdoin, James, 206
Bowne, Eliza Southgate, 234
Boxer Uprising, 440
Boxing, 395, 527–528
Boycotts
    20th century, Taft-Hartley Act and, 554
    in American Revolution, 152, 156–158
Boyd, Belle, 349
Bozeman Trail, 286m
Bra burning, 631
Bracero program, 537, 577
Braddock, Edward, 132
Bradford, William, 45
Bradley, Aaron, 356
Bradstreet, Anne, 46
Bradstreet, Simon, 46
Brady, James, 665
Brady Bill, 665
Branch Davidian compound, FBI assault on, 664
Brando, Marlon, 588
Brandywine Creek, Battle of, 176
Brandywine Springs Amusement Park, 394

Brant, Chief Joseph, 182, 216i, 216, 227
Braun, Carol Moseley, 661
Bray, Thomas, 102
Brazil
    European control of, 40, 41, 86
    independence of, 268
    slavery in, 108
Breckinridge, John C., 330, 330t
Brest-Litovsk Treaty (1918), 480
Bretton Woods monetary system, 620
Breyer, Stephen, 667, 672
Brezhnev, Leonid, 617
Britain, Battle of, 532, 533
British and Foreign Anti-Slavery Society, 300
"The British Prison Ship" (Freneau), 196
Brock, Isaac, 247
Brooklyn Bridge, 391, 392i
Brooks, Preston S., 328
Brotherhood of Sleeping Car Porters, 541
Browere, Albertis, 298i
Brown, Ed, 502
Brown, John (of Ohio), 326, 329–330, 330i, 335
Brown, John (of Rhode Island), 154
Brown, Joseph, 334
Brown, Linda, 580
Brown, Moses, 220
Brown, William Henry, 265i
Brown, Willie Mae, 502
Brown family of Providence, 204
Brown v. *Board of Education* (1954), 580–581
Bryan, William Jennings
    and election of 1896, 432, 432t
    and election of 1900, 461t
    and election of 1908, 463t
    Scopes trial and, 496, 498–499
Bryant, William Cullen, 280–281
Bubonic plague, 17th century, 36–37
Buchanan, James
    and election of 1856, 325, 325t
    Lecompton Constitution and, 327
Buck, Carrie, 498
Buck, Doris, 498
Buffalo
    extermination of, 369i, 387, 387i
Buffalo Bill's Wild West show, 381, 395, 395i, 422–423
Buffalo soldiers, 408–409, 409i
Buford (ship), 483
Bulge, Battle of, 544m, 545
Bulimia, 665
Bull Moose party, 464
Bull Run, First Battle of, 338–339
Bully pulpit, 461
Bunker Hill, Battle of, 168
Bureau of Land Management (BLM), 642, 642i, 686
Bureau of Refugees, Freedmen, and Abandoned Lands. *See* Freedmen's Bureau
Burford, Robert, 642
Burgoyne, John, 174–176, 175m
Burlingame, Anson, 370
Burlingame Treaty (1868), 370
Burned-Over District, 279
Burnside, Ambrose E., 349
Burr, Aaron
    duel with Hamilton, 245
    and election of 1796, 222t, 223
    and election of 1800, 235, 235t
Burroughs, George, 76
Bush, George H. W.
    and Cold War, 648–649, 650, 651
    and election of 1992, 653, 666, 666t
    Panama intervention and, 651–652
    Persian Gulf War and, 651–653

and Soviet Union collapse, 649, 651
    Supreme Court appointments, 651, 662
    in World War II, 539i
Bush, George W.
    in 2004 election, 681–682
    approval rating, 682
    background of, 678
    compassionate conservatism of, 678–679
    domestic policies of, 674
    and election of 2000, 656, 672, 672t
    on same-sex marriage, 679
    War in Iraq and, 679–681
Bush, Jeb, 672
Business. *See also* Corporations; Industry
    18th century, enthusiasm for, 220
    late 19th century
        development of national markets, 388
        innovations in, 387–389
        mass merchandising, 394, 395–396
        mergers and integrations, 388–389
    20th century
        in 1920s, 495–496
        in 1980s and '90s, 643–644, 657
        Eisenhower administration and, 584
        flight overseas, 620, 646
        muckrakers' exposés of, 458
        regulation of, 472–473
        Roosevelt and, 527
        World War I earnings, 477–478
Business and industry
    internationalization of, 683–684
Busing, court-ordered, 599, 613, 621, 621i
Butler, Benjamin, 344, 348
Butler, Pierce, 208
Butler Act (Tennessee, 1925), 498
Butterfield, Alexander, 618
Butterfly ballot, 672

C

Cabarets, 456
Cabeza de Vaca, Álvar Núñez, 21, 22–23, 26m
Cable News Network (CNN), 683
Cabot[o], John, 17
Cactus Hill, Virginia, 6, 6i
Caddoan cultures, 112, 114, 114m
Cadillac, Monsieur, 60, 65
Cahokia, 9, 9m, 11–12, 60, 113
Cahokia, Illinois, 183m
Cajuns, origins of, 119
Calendar(s)
    Mesoamerican, 9–10
    in Mississippi Valley culture, 11
Calhoun, John C., 305i
    on Mexican conquest, 305–306
    nullification and, 272
    slavery and, 263–264
California. *See also* Los Angeles; San Francisco
    exploration and colonization of
        by England, 27
        by Spain, 32–34, 34m, 141–142, 142m, 228, 228i, 274
    18th century, smallpox epidemic, 191
    19th century
        African Americans in, 311
        China Exclusion Act and, 398
        Chinese immigrants in, 370
        discrimination against Chinese, 398, 405–406
        gold rush in, 310–311, 310i, 328
        immigration to, 452
        migration to, 310
        mining in, 386

        Native Americans in, 311, 370–371
        racial discrimination in, 316–317
        slavery and, 321–322
        statehood, 311
        U.S. acquisition of, 268, 305, 310
    20th century
        defense spending and, 657
        ethnicity in, 663
        immigration to, 474–475, 492
        migration to, 450, 513, 513m
        military spending and, 562
        politics in, 521
        Proposition 187, 663
        Proposition 227, 663
        tourism and, 495
        voting rights, 459–460
California Sanitary Canning Company, 539
California Supreme Court, on minority rights, 406
California Trail, 286m
Californios, rights of, 313
Calley, William, 602
Calvin, John, 23–24, 45
Calvinists, Puritanism and, 45
Cambodia
    USS *Mayaguez* incident, 619
    Vietnam War and, 613
Camden, South Carolina, Battle of, 185, 185m
Camp, Walter, 395
Camp Cedar Grove, 434
Camp David Accords, 627
Camp O'Donnell, 545
Camp Weld, 351, 351i
Camp Woods, 243m
Campaign financing
    cost of, 685
Campbell, Ben Nighthorse, 666
Campbell, John, 656
Campus Crusade for Christ, 606, 607i
Canada
    17th century, French in, 37–39, 57–58
    18th century
        African Americans in, 165
        American Revolution and, 162, 166, 166m, 167, 168, 170–171, 173–176, 188
        border with, 188
    19th century
        border with, 250, 251
        English in, 247
        Fugitive Slave Act and, 326, 327m
        War of 1812 and, 247–248, 248m
    20th century
        immigration from, 474, 492f
        NAFTA and, 668–669
    name, origin of, 21
    as trading partner, 685f
Canals
    construction of, 264m, 264–265
Candlefish, 244i
Caniba, 16–17
Canned food, introduction of, 385
Cannibals All! (Fitzhugh), 326
Canty, Hattie, 659
Cape Coast Castle, 67, 95i
Cape of Good Hope, 15
Cape Town, South Africa, founding of, 37
Capitalism
    cyclical nature of, 509–510
    globalization and, 682
    New Deal and, 519, 521, 528
    opposition to, 403–404, 413, 471, 521
    U.S. commitment to, 555
Capone, Al, 491
Caravels, 14, 16m

Caribbean
	20th century
		immigration from, 648
		U.S. interests in, 468, 469m
	British trade restrictions in, post-Revolution, 203, 205
	European arrival in, 15–16, 18–19
	French colonies in, 177
	slave revolts in, 216–217
	slavery and, 85–86, 96m–97m, 108
	U.S. interests in, 469m
Caribs, 15–16, 18
Carleton, James H., 343
Carlisle, Lord, 177
Carlisle Commission, 177
Carlisle Indian school, 418, 422, 422i, 427
Carlos II, King of Spain, 59–60
Carlos III, King of Spain, 141
Carnegie, Andrew, 383, 388–389, 400, 401, 429
Carnegie Steel Co., 429
Carolina colonies. *See also* North Carolina; South Carolina
	establishment of, 69–70
	growth of, 78
	slavery in, 69–70
	trade and, 65–66
	unrest in, 18th century, 78, 150–151
Carpetbaggers, 360, 366
Carson, Rachel, 589, 590, 590i
Carter, Jimmy, 627i
	Camp David Accords, 627
	domestic policies, 626
	and election of 1976, 616, 625t, 626
	and election of 1980, 638, 639t, 646
	as emissary, 670
	energy policy, 627
	foreign policy, 616, 626–627
	Iranian hostage crisis and, 637–638
	pardoning of draft evaders, 626
	political style of, 626, 627i
	in World War II, 539i
Carter, Robert, 226
Carter, Rosalynn, 626
Carter Doctrine, 638
Carteret, Sir George, 69
Cartier, Jacques, 21, 26m
Cary's Rebellion, 78
Casey, William, 640, 649
Casino Sandia, 657i
Casinos
	Native Americans and, 657, 657i
Cass, Lewis, 288, 321, 321t
Cassettari, Rosa, 389–390
Cassettari, Santino, 389
Castro, Fidel, 624i
	and Bay of Pigs invasion, 591–592
	Cold War and, 585
	U.S. assassination attempts, 624, 625
Catawba Indians, 182
Catcher in the Rye (Salinger), 588
Cathay, 13
Catholicism
	16th century
		emergence of nation state and, 24
		Index of prohibited books, 24
		new world exploration and, 16–17
		Reformation and, 23–24
	17th century
		Counter-Reformation and, 24, 38, 59
		English monarchy and, 46
		missions, 35–36
		in New France, 57
		Protestant fear of, 73–74, 75
		Pueblo Revolt and, 62
		slavery and, 86
	18th century
		in Africa, 94
		in Canada, British toleration of, 156
		missions, 58m, 62–64, 63m, 66, 141, 142m, 191, 191i
		Protestant fear of, 134i, 156
	19th century
		immigration and, 285–286, 296
		Protestant fear of, 296, 323, 449
		religious instruction in, 428
		Tammany Hall and, 376
		Texas settlement and, 266
	20th century
		conservative movement and, 645–646
		contraception and, 599
		Coughlin ministry and, 521–522
		eugenics and, 498
		first presidential candidate, 499
		Italian immigration and, 452
		Protestant fear of, 499, 563
		racial politics and, 449
	Pope
		emergence of nation state and, 24
		and new world exploration, 16–17
		Reformation and, 23
Cato, 149
Cato's Letters: Essays on Liberty (Trenchard and Gordon), 149
Catt, Carrie Chapman, 471
Cattle, introduction to New World, 36, 37, 65
Cattle drives, 371
Cattle ranching
	in colonial Florida, 65
	railroads and, 371
	resistance to, 403–404
Cayuga Indians, 184. *See also* Iroquois Confederacy
CCC. *See* Civilian Conservation Corps
Celebrities
	in 1920s, 487
	in 1930s, 527–528, 528i
Censorship, in World War II, 538
Census
	of 1790, 217
	of 2000
		ethnic identity in, 663
		reapportionment and, 209–210
		representation and, 208
Central America
	U.S. foreign policy in, 640, 640i
	U.S. intervention in, 468, 469m
Central Europe, Soviet domination of, 555–556
Central Intelligence Agency (CIA)
	abuses of power by, 625
	in Afghanistan, 638
	and Bay of Pigs invasion, 592
	Chilean coup and, 617
	Cold War operations, 585
	creation of, 566
	in Iran, 638
	Iran-Contra scandal and, 649
	political uses of, 612, 617, 618
	under Reagan, 640
Central Pacific Railroad, 341, 367, 370i
Central Park, 391
A Century of Dishonor (Jackson), 398
Chaco Canyon, 9m, 11
Champlain, Samuel de, 37–38
Chancellorsville, Battle of, 349
Chaney, James, 604
Chapman, John Gadsby, 261i
Character, American, origins of, 423
Charbonneau, Toussaint, 243
Charity
	19th century, Gospel of Wealth and, 400
	early 20th century, attitudes toward, 518–519
	in Great Depression, 515
Charles I, King of England
	beheading of, 49, 66
	Catholicism and, 46
	colonies and, 41–42, 45, 49
Charles II, King of England
	African trade and, 91
	colonial policy of, 66–67
	and Glorious Revolution, 73
	restoration of, 66
	slavery and, 88
Charles V, King of Spain, 21
Charleston, South Carolina
	epidemic in (1739), 100–101
	fire in (1740), 100
	founding of, 69–70
	tax resistance in, 146
	trade, 121
	vice-admiralty court, 152, 157m
Charleston (dance), 486
Charter of Privileges (Pennsylvania, 1701), 69
Charter of Punta del Este (1961), 591
Château-Thierry, Battle of, 480
Chávez, Cesar, 609
Cheney, Richard, 679
Cheraw District grand jury, 170
Chernobyl nuclear accident, 637, 649
Cherokee language, written form of, 274i
Cherokee Nation v. Georgia (1831), 270
Cherokee Outlet, opening to settlers, 424
Cherokee Phoenix, 289
Cherokees. *See also* Five Civilized Tribes
	18th century
		American Revolution and, 163, 165
		assimilation of, 227–228
		British chastening of, 142–143
		resistance, 199
		Revolutionary War and, 184–185
		trade, 123
		tribal lands, 198m
		white encroachment and, 182, 252
		Yamasee War and, 78
	19th century
		assimilation of, 251–252, 274, 273–277, 274i
		in Civil War, 341
		culture of, 234, 312
		leadership of, 251–252
		removal of, 271m, 271–272, 288m, 289
		and War of 1812, 247–249
	20th century, Will Rogers and, 508, 509
Cherry Valley slayings, 183
Chesapeake (ship), 244
Chesapeake and Delaware Canal, 264m
Chesapeake and Ohio Canal, 264m
Chesapeake Bay region. *See also* Maryland; Virginia
	colonization of, 26–27, 28, 42–44, 51–53, 52m
	economy of
		18th century, 120, 121–123, 122m
		19th century, 255–256
	overfishing in, 19th century, 386
	settlement of, 79m
	slavery in, 87, 88, 90–91
Chesnut, Mary Boykin, 337, 346
Cheyenne Indians
	culture of, 112i
	Ghost Dance and, 409
	land loss by, 323
	removal of, 288m
	resistance by, 334
	and Sand Creek massacre, 351, 351i
	treaties, 368
	war with whites, 352, 408

Chiang Kai-shek (Jiang Jieshi), 566
Chicago
    design and architecture of, 391–392, 393
    Great Migration and, 474, 475i
    Haymarket bombing, 415
    Hull House in, 417
    immigration to, 393
    organized crime, 488
    Sanitary and Ship Canal, 393
    segregation in, 460
    World War II and, 537
    World's Fair in (1893), 437
Chicamaugas, 198m, 199
Chicano, as term, 609
Chicano studies programs, 609
Chickasaws. *See also* Five Civilized Tribes
    as allies, 130
    assimilation of, 227–228, 274
    in Civil War, 341
    horses and, 112
    Oklahoma Territory and, 288m
    removal of, 289
    resistance by, 199
    trade with, 60
    tribal lands, 18th century, 198m
Child, Lydia Maria, 297
Child labor laws, 458, 459i, 474
Childhood
    18th century, 234i
    19th century, 298i
    20th century, 458, 459i, 561
        obesity and, 665, 665i
        violence and, 664–665
Chile
    U.S. intervention in, 617
Chin, Vincent, 621
China
    pre-1800
        European contact with, 13, 18
        ocean exploration by, 13–14
        trade, 13, 140, 193, 202
    19th century
        Boxer Uprising, 440
        immigration from, 310, 311, 370, 370i, 376, 390, 398
        Open Door policy and, 440
        trade, 440
        war with Japan (1894-1895), 440
    20th century
        AIDS and, 646
        Cold War and, 566, 566i
        communist revolution in, 558, 565–566
        immigration from, 450–451, 451m, 468, 492, 537, 648, 663
        Korean War and, 569
        Nationalist revolution in, 468
        trade, 669
        U.S. relations, 615, 615i
        war with Japan, 533
        World War II and, 530
    as trading partner, 685f
    U.S. special relation with, 565–566
Chinatown, San Francisco, 447i, 450
Chinatown (film), 625
Chinese-Americans
    19th century
        discrimination against, 370, 405–406
        employment, 405i, 405–406
        prostitution and, 419
        stereotypes of, 317
        women, 450–451
    early 20th century, population, 450
Chinese Communist Party (CCP), 565
Chinese Exclusion Act (1882), 398, 405, 450, 451m, 537
Chinese Exclusion Act (1902), 450

Chinese Mission Home, San Francisco, 407i, 435
Chinese Nationalists, 566
Chippewa, Battle of, 248, 248m
Chippewa Indians, 183, 183m, 661
Chiricahua, 368
Chivington, John M., 351, 351i
Choctaws. *See also* Five Civilized Tribes
    18th century, tribal lands, 198m
    alliances with whites, 100
    assimilation of, 227, 274
    in Civil War, 341
    Oklahoma Territory and, 288m
    removal of, 289
    resistance by, 199
    trade, 18th century, 60
    and War of 1812, 247
Cholera, late 19th century, 393
Chopin, Kate, 428
Christian Broadcasting Network, 645
Christian conservatives
    in 2004 presidential election outcome, 681
Christian Science, 429
Christianity. *See also* Catholicism; Fundamentalist Christians; Protestantism
    in 15th–16th centuries
        division of globe, 17
        Islamic conflicts, 13, 14, 15
        in Japan, 33
        Native Americans and, 19, 26
        Protestant Reformation, 23–24, 41
    in 17th–18th centuries
        African Americans and, 129
        Native Americans and, 33–36, 36i, 38–39, 50–51, 62, 125, 129, 143
    19th–20th centuries, 224–225
    in 1960s, 606, 607i
    missionaries, 565–566
    Native Americans and, 275, 418, 422
    slavery and, 86, 102, 125, 129, 258, 279
Chrysler Motors, 657
Chrysler's Farm, Battle of, 248m
Church Committee, 624
Church of Christ, Scientist, 429
Church of England
    in colonies, 127
    dissenters from, 45–46
    establishment of, 24
    Puritan movement and, 45–46
    slavery and, 102–103
Church of Jesus Christ of Latter-Day Saints. *See* Mormons
Churchill, Winston
    Atlantic Charter and, 533–534
    on iron curtain, 556
    loss of office, 552
    reconstruction planning, 507
    World War II and, 545, 547
CIA. *See* Central Intelligence Agency
Cibola, 23
Cigar Makers' International Union, 416
Cincinnati Daily Commercial, 328
Cincinnatus, 195
Cinqué, 295i, 295
CIO. *See* Congress of Industrial Organizations
Cipangu (Japan), 15–16, 16m
Circular Letter (1768), 152
Cisneros, Henry, 302, 648–649
Cities
    18th century, poverty in, 124
    19th century
        black migration to, 287, 407
        design and architecture in, 390–391, 391–393
        economic role of, 392–393

        government of, 393–394
        growth of, 391–393, 401
        internal migration to, 392
        machine politics in, 394
        poverty in, 416, 416i
        rural opinions on, 412
        water supplies, 393
    20th century
        first black mayor, 605
        growth of, 447, 491–492, 492f
        immigration and, 448, 449i
        migration to, 444
        poverty in, 578
        suburban growth and, 578
Citizenship
    19th century
        African Americans and, 360, 363
        Native Americans and, 417
        race and, 316–317
    20th century
        Asians and, 565
        for Puerto Ricans, 674
        race and, 454–455
Civil liberties
    Bill of Rights (England, 1689), 73
    Bill of Rights (U.S.)
        debate over, 210
        passage of, 213–214, 217
        rights protected by, 214
    in Northwest Ordinance of 1787, 201–202
    in Virginia Declaration of Rights, 177
    under Warren Court, 599
    in World War I, 478
Civil rights
    of African Americans. *See* Civil rights movement
    of disabled persons, 573
    of homosexuals, 573, 595, 609, 646, 647, 661, 662, 666–667
    of minorities, 19th century, 313, 371, 404–405
    of Native Americans
        17th century, 49, 70
        19th century, 273, 398, 417–419
        20th century, 554, 573
Civil Rights Act (1875), 378, 398, 406
Civil Rights Acts (1964, 1965), 573, 597–598
Civil Rights Bill (1866), 360
Civil rights movement
    early 20th century, 444
    in 1940s, World War II and, 543
    in 1950s–1960s, 582m, 593, 595, 604–605
        backlash against, 610–611
    in 1980s, 647–648
    backlash against, 610–611, 621, 621i
    Cold War and, 550–551, 554, 558, 580
    influence of, 595
    Johnson and, 597–598
    Kennedy and, 591, 592–593
    radicalization of, 604–605
    Reagan and, 641
    Truman and, 562
    voting rights and, 290
Civil Service
    desegregation of, 562
    reform, late 19th century, 398
Civil Service Commission, 398
Civil union for homosexuals, 661, 662
Civil War. *See also* Confederacy; Union
    African American employment in, 333i, 346–348, 351–352
    battles and skirmishes
        1861–1862, 337, 338–339
        1862–1864, 343–344, 344i, 349, 350
        1864–1865, 350–351, 352–353, 353m

Civil War, *continued*
    black soldiers in, 351–352
    blockade of South, 337, 345, 340–346
    casualties, 354
        at Antietam, 344i
        causes of, 344
        at Gettysburg, 349
    civil disorders in
        in North, 349–350
        in South, 348–349
    Confederate surrender, 354
    and disease, 345, 346, 348
    and emancipation, 341, 342
    events leading to, 321–331
    impact on South, 357
    mobilization for, 335–341
    prisoners of war in, 352
    profiteers in, 342
    secession, 335–337, 336m
    veterans' pensions, 429
    women and
        black, 347–348
        Confederate, 345, 345i, 346–347
        Union, 347–348
Civil Works Administration (CWA), 519, 523t
Civilian Conservation Corps (CCC), 519, 523t
Clamshell Alliance, 622
Clark, George Rogers, 183m, 184
Clark, William, 242–243, 243m, 244i
Clark Field, 534
Class. *See* Social class
Clay, Cassius. *See* Ali, Muhammad
Clay, Henry
    and election of 1824, 268, 268t
    and election of 1832, 272t, 274
    and election of 1836, 292
    and election of 1844, 302, 302t
    on Native Americans, 273
    North-South compromise and, 263, 272
    War of 1812 and, 250
Clay, Joseph, 203
Clayton Antitrust Act (1914), 473
Clayton-Bulwer-Treaty (1850), 322
Clean Air Act (1963), 599
Clean Air Act Amendments (1970), 612
Clean Waters Act (1966), 599
Clean Waters Act Amendments (1972), 612
Clear and present danger standard, 478
Clemenceau, Georges, 482
Clemens, Samuel. *See* Twain, Mark
Clermont (ship), 253
Cleveland, Grover
    and election of 1884, 398, 398t
    and election of 1888, 399, 399t
    and election of 1892, 431t, 432
    and election of 1896, 432
    Hawaiian annexation and, 438
    Monroe Doctrine and, 436
    as president, 398–399
    unions and, 433
Cleveland, Ohio, 474
Cliff Palace at Mesa Verde, 9m, 11
Climate change, Ice Age, 5–6
Clinton, George, 212, 244, 245, 245t
Clinton, Hilary Rodham, 666, 667, 673
Clinton, Sir Henry, 165, 170, 176, 182, 184, 185m
Clinton, William Jefferson "Bill"
    background and early career, 666
    cabinet of, 666
    domestic policies, 666–667
    and election of 1992, 653, 666, 666t
    and election of 1996, 667, 667t
    foreign policy, 668–671
    impeachment of, 667–668
    media and, 517i

    and Republican Revolution, 667
    scandals, 667–668
    Supreme Court appointments, 667
    trade policy, 634–635
    in Vietnam, 669–670
    welfare reform, 656
Cloning, 666
Cloverleafs, 561i
Clovis points, 5
CNN. *See* Cable News Network
Code talkers, 530, 530i
Cody, William "Buffalo Bill," 381, 395, 395i, 422–423
Coercive Acts (1774), 155–156
Coeur d'Alene, gold rush in, 384
Coffin, Levi, 327m
Coffles, 92, 94, 94i
Cohens v. *Virginia* (1821), 271
COINTELPRO, 625
Colbert, Jean-Baptiste, 57
Cold War
    in 1980s, 639–640
    arms race in, 572, 575, 591
    civil rights movement and, 550–551, 554, 558, 579
    colonialism and, 558
    covert operations in, 625. *See also* Central Intelligence Agency
    cultural struggle in, 574i
    culture in, 561–565, 572, 574–575
    Eisenhower and, 583–585
    end of, 634, 637, 649–659, 657
    Europe divided by, 557m
    family and, 575–576
    under Kennedy, 591
    McCarthyism in, 563–564
    and national security state, establishment of, 567
    Nixon and, 615, 615i
    origins of, 550, 559
    Reagan and, 637, 639–640, 649–651
    roots of, in World War I, 480
    space exploration and, 572, 575, 583–584
    spheres of influence in, 586m–587m
    in Third World, 584, 585
    U.S. covert operations in, 585
    U.S.-Soviet relations in, 615, 617, 619
USS Cole, 670–671
Colfax, Schuyler, 377
Collective bargaining rights
    late 19th century, 413–414
    early 20th century, 471, 478
    in 1930s, 521, 522
    post-World War II, 554
Collier, John, 520, 520i
Colonialism. *See also* individual nations
    mandate system, 482
    Monroe Doctrine and, 267–268
    opposition to
        American Revolution as, 138
        post-World War I, 480
        post-World War II, 531, 552, 555, 558, 572
Colonies, British
    in mid-18th century, 147m, 162
    Bacon's Rebellion, 71–73, 89–90
    disease in, 47, 100–101, 116
    diversity of population in, 115–116, 117–118
    economic regions, 121–125, 122m
    energy use in, 622
    growth of, 65–66, 115–119, 117f
        ethnic diversity and, 115–116, 117–118
        immigration, 83, 116–119
        natural increase, 116
        slave population, 117

    identification with North America, 138
    King William's War, 75–77
    and Native Americans, conflict with, 70–72, 142–143
    oppressive measures against, 144–159
    Pontiac's War and, 138, 142–143, 147m
    population, by age and gender, 117f
    ports, 119–120, 122m, 124–125
    printing and publishing in, 125, 148
    Queen Anne's War, 75, 76–78
    regional economies, 121–125, 122m
    religion. *See also* Puritans
        diversity in, 126–127
        Great Awakening, 127–131
    revolts in, 69–73, 78. *See also* American Revolution
    trade, 66–67
    view on European wars, 132
Colorado, women's voting rights and, 420
Colorado Cottage Home, 419
Colorado Fuel and Iron Co., 471
Colored Orphan Asylum, New York City, 350
Colt Tower (San Francisco), 525i
Columbia, as term, 196
Columbia (ship), 204, 204i
Columbia River, 204
Columbia University, 196
Columbian Exchange, 17
    Florida Indians and, 65–66
    and food, 17, 36, 65
Columbian Exposition (1893), 435
Columbine High School shootings, 665
Columbus, Christopher
    impact of, 2–3
    miscalculations of, 15–16, 16m
    post-Revolution lionizing of, 196
    view of Native Americans, 5
    voyages of, 13, 15–17, 16m–17m
Comanchería, 113, 114m
Comanches
    in Civil War, 341
    horses and, 64
    removal of, 288m
    rise to power of, 113
    treaties, 368
    war with whites, 408
Comfort women, 545
Comintern, 482
Command of the Army Act (1867), 366
Commissioners from Edisto Island, 363
Committee of Fifteen, 377–378
Committee of Public Safety, 156
Committee on Public Information (CPI), 477
Committee to Alleviate the Miseries of the Poor, 125
Committee to Reelect the President (CREEP), 618
Committees of Correspondence, 154
Common man. *See also* Workers
    post-Revolution
        and Constitution, design of, 207
        Constitution ratification celebration by, 213i
        debt and, 202, 203–206, 207
    19th century
        "age of the common man," 262
        economic plight of, 374–375
        fear of black competition, 287, 296, 325, 328
        fear of Chinese competition, 370–371
        Jackson as champion of, 269, 272, 281
    20th century, fear of black competition, 477
Common Sense (Paine), 168–169

Communication(s)
  19th century, 385
  20th century, 467
Communism. *See also* Containment policy; Red scare
  post–World War I
    Russian revolution and, 445, 479–480, 480i, 482
    spread of, 480
    U.S. fear of, 483
  in 1930s and '40s
    Chinese revolution, 565–566
    New Deal and, 527
    Scottsboro Boys and, 512
    spread of, 510–511, 521, 552, 555
  post–World War II
    expansionism of, 555–558
    U.S. fear of, 507
  in Cold War
    Cuban revolution, 585
    McCarthyism and, 563–564
    U.S. fear of, 551
Communitarian experiments, mid 19th century, 299–300
Community nurses, 453–454
Commuters, 577i
Company K (Michigan), 352
Compassionate conservatism, 678–679
Complex marriage, 299
Compromise of 1820, 328
Compromise of 1850, 311, 322
Compromise of 1877, 377–378
Computers
  impact of, 683i
Comstock, Anthony, 374
Comstock Law (1873), 374
Concord, Battle of, 82, 159
Conestoga Indians, 143
Coney Island, 558, 576
Confederacy
  black Union soldiers and, 351–352
  capital of, 337
  challenges faced by, 337, 338–339
  conscription in, 340
  currency of, 340
  diplomacy of, 345–346, 350
  economy of, 337, 340
  hardship in, 348–349
  internal opposition in
    from blacks, 309, 333–334, 346
    from whites, 309, 338, 342, 348–349
  secession, 335–337, 336m
  in Southwest, 340–341, 344
  and States' Rights, 339
  strategy of, 308–309, 337, 354
  support for, by region, 336m
  surrender of, 354
  taxation in, 349
  women in, 345, 345i
Confederate Army
  desertion from, 349
  enlistments in, 340
  Indians and, 341
  strategy of, 339
Confederate Territory of Arizona, 340
Confederation. *See also* Articles of Confederation
  challenges faced by, 192–196
  culture in, 195–197
  economy in, 201–206
    debt and, 201–202, 203–205
    trade and, 203–204
  war debt of, 193
    and political unrest, 203–206, 207
    speculators in, 204–206, 206f
  weaknesses of, 206, 207
  westward territories and, 197–202
Confiscation Act, Second (1862), 347

Congo, 20th century, U.S. involvement in, 625
Congo-Angola, slave trade and, 93m, 94, 96m–97m
Congo Square, 258
Congregationalism, 45
Congress
  pre–Civil War
    political division in, 245
    slave-free balance in, 329
    suppression of abolitionism, 293
  post–Civil War
    black members of, 356i
    Confederates in, 360
    Reconstruction policies, 363, 364–367, 365m
  20th century
    in 1980s, Republicans in, 639
    first black senator, 661
    first Native American senator, 666
    power of, 625–626
Congress of Industrial Organizations (CIO)
  activism of, 526–527
  communist influence in, 555–556
  establishment of, 526
Congress on Racial Equality (CORE), 582m, 583
Connecticut
  colonization of, 50
  Constitution ratification, 211
  free blacks in, voting rights, 275
  manufacturing in, 430m
  Metacom's War and, 70
  slave population, 98m
  voting rights, of African Americans, 275
  western land claims, 200, 201m, 229m
Connecticut Wits, 196
Conner, Howard, 530
Connor, Bull, 593
"The Conquest of Canaan" (Dwight), 196
Conquistadors, 19, 21–22
Conrad, Carolyn, 662
"Consciousness raising," 629, 630i
Conscription
  in Confederacy, 340
  in World War I, 477, 480
  in 1960s, 605, 626
  late 20th century, women and, 631
Conservationism. *See also* Environmentalism
  late 19th century, 424–425
  early 20th century, 463, 473–474, 519–520
Conservatives, late 20th century
  culture wars and, 634–635
  and election of 1980, 639
  factions in, 646
  on immigration, 648
  impact of, 653
  racism of, 604
  resentment of, 610–611
Conspicuous consumption, 429
Constitution, U.S.
  design of, 207–210
  implied powers in, 270
  loose construction of, 270
  ratification of, 211–214, 212i
  representation in, 208–210
  slavery and, 208–210
Constitution(s), state, creation of, 178–180
Constitutional Convention of 1787, 207–211
Constitutional Union party, 330, 330t
Consumer credit
  in 1920s, 500
  Great Depression and, 502–504, 511
  post–World War II, 560
Consumer culture

late 19th century, rise of, 380–381, 383–384, 394–396
  early 20th century, 445, 494, 500
  mid-20th century, 560, 575, 606
  late 20th century
    Cold War and, 574i
    and fall of Soviet Union, 648
    Islamic extremists and, 635
Consumer protection movement
  early 20th century, 458
  in 1960s, 598
Containment policy, 556–558
  China and, 568
  Korean War and, 567–569
  Truman and, 556
  Vietnam War and, 600
Continental Army
  African Americans in, 181
  demobilization of, 195
  discipline of, 172–173
  formation of, 166
  morale of, 171, 172, 181
  mutiny in, 186
  pay and pensions for, 193–195
  tensions in, 179–180
  training and provision of, 172–173, 181, 181i
  at Valley Forge, 176, 181, 181i
Continental Congress
  first, 157–158
    as misnomer, 138
  second
    Articles of Confederation and, 178–179
    call for, 158
    forces leading to, 138
    French alliance and, 176–177
    war preparations, 166–167, 180–181
Continental Navy, 191
Contraception
  early 20th century, activism for, 471
  in 1960s, 574–575, 608
  post–World War II, 561
  the Pill, 574–575, 608, 625
  Supreme Court on, 599
Contract with America, 667
Contras, Nicaraguan, 640, 649–650
Convention of 1800, 222
Convention of 1818, 251
Convict labor, 19th century, 407
Conway, Thomas, 180
Conway Cabal, 180
Coode, John, 75
Cook, James, 139i, 139–140
Cooke, Jay, 372
Coolidge, Calvin
  on business, 487
  as President, 488–489
Coolies, 311
Cooper, James Fenimore, 280–281
Copperheads, 345, 350
Copyright law, 18th century, 196
Coral Sea, Battle of, 545, 546m
CORE. *See* Congress on Racial Equality
Corn. *See* Maize
Corn belt, 386m
Corn Laws (Britain), 301
Cornell University, 384
Cornstalk, 182
Cornwallis, Charles, 173, 185–187, 185m
Coronado, Francisco Vásquez de, 23, 26m
Corporate liberalism, 605
Corporations. *See also* Business
  late 19th century, rise of, 380–381, 382–383, 387–389
  20th century
    antitrust suits, 657
    executive compensation, 657

Corporations, *continued*
    flight overseas, 620, 645
    globalization of, 679
    mergers and acquisitions, 657
    multinational expansion, 572
    trust busting and, 461, 463, 474, 657
    World War I earnings, 477–478
Correspondence schools, 428
Corruption
    in Reconstruction, 366–367
    late 19th century, in local government, 376–377, 377i, 393–394
    Civil Service reform, 398
    spoils system and, 270, 377, 398
Cortés, Hernán, 19, 20
Cortina, Juan, 313
Cortina's War, 313
Cotton, John, 48
Cotton economy
    Civil War and, 345
    impact of, 314
    industrialization and, 254
    Mississippi Delta and, 265i
    and Northeastern industry, 220
    production, 220, 301
        late 18th century, 255
        early 19th century, 255
    rise of, 255–256
    slavery and, 163, 229–230, 255–256, 314
    tariffs and, 271–272
    westward shift of, 265
Cotton gin, 219
Cotton plantations
    black life and labor on, 229–230, 256–258, 257i, 265i
    sharecropping system, 363–364, 502
    slavery and, 163
    soil depletion and, 321
Cotton States Exposition, 427
Coughlin, Charles E., 521–522
Councils for Trade and Plantations, 68
Counter-Reformation, 24, 38, 58
Counterculture, in 1960s and 1970s, 607, 625
Country Club Plaza, 500
Country marks, 84i
Court of Private Land Claims, 404, 424
Court packing plan, 525
Covert operations, in Cold War, 625
Coverture, 68
Cowboys
    African Americans as, 4, 4i, 371
    Mexicans as, 371
Cowpens, Battle of, 185m, 186
Cox, Archibald, 618
Cox, James M., 498t
Coxey, Jacob S., 431
Coxey's Army, 431
CPI. *See* Committee on Public Information
Crack cocaine, 646, 651
Craft, Ellen, 293
Craft, William, 293
Crafus, Richard, 247i
Crandall, Prudence, 293
Crane, Stephen, 428
Crawford, William H., 268, 268t
Credit cards. *See also* Consumer credit
    introduction of, 560
Crédit Mobilier, 377
Creek Indians. *See also* Five Civilized Tribes
    18th century, tribal lands, 198m
    assimilation of, 228, 274
    cession of lands, 250
    Oklahoma Territory and, 288m
    removal of, 289
    resistance, 78, 199
    Revolutionary War and, 185, 188–189
    trade, 121
    War of 1812 and, 249–250, 338–339

CREEP. *See* Committee to Reelect the President
Crèvecoeur, Hector St. John de, 197
Crews, Henry, 501–502
The Crisis, 461
Crittenden, John J., 335–336
Crittenden Compromise, 335–336
Crockett, David, 261i
    family history of, 267
    political career of, 261–262
    Texas independence and, 301
    on western expansion, 301
Crockett, Elizabeth, 267
Cromwell, Oliver, 66
Crook, George, 368
Cross of Gold speech, 432
Crow Indians, 369, 372
Crowell, John, 642
Crozat, Antoine, 60–61
Cuba
    Columbus and, 16
    Bay of Pigs invasion (1961), 592–593
    communist revolution in, 585
    constitution of 1901, 440
    Cuban Missile Crisis, 592
    immigration from, 390, 390m
    Platt Amendment, 339, 441
    revolution of 1895, 438
    Seven Years' War and, 134
    Spanish-American War and, 437–439, 439m
    U.S. designs on, 322–323
    U.S. interventions in, 469m
Cubism, 458
Cuffee, 101
Culpeper, John, 78
Culpeper's Rebellion, 78
Cultural imperialism, U.S.
    post-World War II, 560
    late 20th century, 687i
Culture
    early Republic, 195–197
    19th century, 380–381
        communitarian experiments, 299–300
        education reform, 297–299
        instilling in immigrants, 428
        literature and art, 280–281, 300, 317–318, 430
        migration and, 291–292
        psychology as discipline, 428
        shows and entertainments, 393–395
        Transcendentalism, 300
        Victorianism, 281, 373, 427
        violence in, 284–285
        westward migration and, 279
    20th century, 444–445
        pre-World War I
            entertainment, 456
            literature and art, 457i, 457–458
            sexual mores, 456–457
            in World War I, 478
        in 1920s, 486–487
            automobiles and, 495–496
            consumer culture, 500
            critiques of, 501
            entertainment, 486–487
            films, 492–493
            Harlem Renaissance, 493–495, 495i
            literature, 501
            radio, 495
            sexuality, 493
        in 1930s
            entertainment, 527–528
            WPA and, 524, 525i
        in World War II, 507, 540
        post-World War II
            entertainment, 554
            global spread of, 559

            racial integration and, 554
            sexuality, 561–562
        in 1950s, 561, 575–576, 586–590, 588i, 589i
        in 1960s and 1970s
            Cold War and, 574i
            counterculture, 607, 625
            films, 623–624
            literature, 632i
            music, 607–608
            sexuality, 574–575, 608, 625
        in Cold War, 561–565, 572
            as battleground, 574i
            impact of, 550–551
            McCarthyism, 563–564
        in 1980s and 1990s
            conflicts in, 645–648, 659–663, 666
            sexuality, 648
        late 20th
            music, 688
            overseas spread of, 688
            automobiles and, 584
    American, development of, 195–197
    Native American
        in prehistory, 7, 8–9, 9m, 11–12, 12i
        in 15th and 16th century, 28i
        in 19th century, 243, 312, 319, 369, 409–411, 499
        Columbian Exchange and, 17, 65–66
        dogs in, 113
        horses and, 82, 112i, 112–115, 114m
        individualism and, 319
        women in, 63, 64i, 115, 234, 243, 252, 278
Culture wars, late 20th century, 645–648, 666
Cumberland and Oxford Canal, 264m
Cumberland Gap, 182, 183m, 197, 199
Cumberland Road, 264m
Cumming, Kate, 345i
Currency, Confederate, 340
Currency, U.S., as global currency, 473
Currency Act (1764), 144
Custer, George, 357, 368–369, 408
Customs Act (1767), 152
Customs duties, colonies and, 144, 152–158
Cutler, Manasseh, 202
Cuzco, 8, 9m, 21–22
CWA. *See* Civil Works Administration
Czechoslovakia
    post-World War II, 557m
    creation of, 481m, 482, 532

D

D-Day, 544, 544m
Da Gama, Vasco, 15, 16m–17m
Dachau camp, 547
Dairy regions, in Midwest and Northeast, 386m
Daley, Richard, 611
Dalton, Mrs. L. L., 419–420
"The Danger of an Unconverted Ministry" (Tennent), 128
DAR. *See* Daughters of the American Revolution
Darrow, Clarence, 498–498
Dartmoor Prison, 247i
Darwin, Charles, 399
Daughters of Liberty, 153
Daughters of the American Revolution (DAR), 522
Davis, Bette, 527
Davis, Jefferson
    as Confederate president, 335
    day of prayer and, 350
    and fall of Richmond, 353
    Gadsden Purchase and, 312
Davis, John W., 488

Dawes, William, 159
Dawes General Allotment (Severalty) Act (1881), 398, 419, 449
Day care, in World War II, 539
"Day of infamy," 506
Dayton Accords (1995), 670
DDT, 589, 612
De Grasse, François, J. P., 185m, 187
de Kalb, Johann, 180
De Soto, Hernando, 21–23, 26m
Dean, James, 588
Dean, John, 617
Debs, Eugene V., 431, 460, 462t, 463t, 464t, 475, 488t
Declaration of Independence, 138, 162, 169, 170–171, 172i
"Declaration of Mental Independence" (Owen), 299
Declaration of Rights (Continental Congress), 158
Declaration of Rights (Virginia), 178, 210
"Declaration of Sentiments," 320, 374
Declaration of war, War Powers Act and, 625
Declaratory Act (1766), 148
Deere, John, 314
Deerskin trade, 18th century, 87m, 122m, 123
Defense Industry, post-World War II rise of, 506
Del Rio, Dolores, 493
Delaware
  in Civil War, 337
  Constitution ratification, 211
  economy, 18th century, 125
  slave population, 98m
Delaware and Hudson Canal, 264m
Delaware and Raritan Canal, 264m
Delaware Indians. *See also* Ohio Confederacy
  Gnadenhutten massacre, 183
  land sales by, 69
  Ohio Confederacy and, 216
  Oklahoma Territory and, 288m
  Quaker settlement and, 69
  relocation to Great Lakes region, 227
  Walking Purchase and, 125
Delaware Prophet, 143
Delaware River Valley, settlement of, 69
Democracy
  in Flight 93 resistance, 677
  Founding Fathers on, 207, 209
  Greek Revival style and, 273i
  Soviet view of, 480
  transparency and, late 20th century, 625
  Wilson on, 480–481
Democracy in America (de Tocqueville), 273
Democratic Leadership Council, 666
Democratic party
  in Civil War, 342
  post-Civil War policies, 357, 367
  19th century
    constituency of, 292–293
    Irish and, 286
    local political machines, 394
    origins of, 270
    platform, 396–397
    in South, 407
  20th century
    alliance with labor, 471
    constituency, 527, 563
    New Democrats, 666
  convention of 1964, 604
  convention of 1968, 611
  and election of 1828, 269, 269i, 269t
  and election of 1832, 272t
  and election of 1836, 292, 292t
  and election of 1840, 294–295, 295t
  and election of 1844, 302, 302t
  and election of 1848, 321, 321t
  and election of 1852, 322, 322t
  and election of 1860, 330, 330t
  and election of 1862, 345
  and election of 1864, 351–352, 352t
  and election of 1868, 367, 367t
  and election of 1872, 377, 377t
  and election of 1876, 377–378, 377t
  and election of 1880, 397, 397t
  and election of 1884, 398, 398t
  and election of 1888, 399, 399t
  and election of 1892, 431t, 432
  and election of 1896, 432t, 433
  and election of 1900, 461t
  and election of 1904, 462t
  and election of 1912, 463t
  and election of 1916, 473t
  and election of 1920, 498t
  and election of 1924, 488t
  and election of 1928, 489t
  and election of 1932, 516t
  and election of 1936, 525, 525t
  and election of 1944, 538t
  and election of 1948, 563, 563t
  and election of 1952, 568t, 569
  and election of 1956, 583t
  and election of 1960, 589t
  and election of 1964, 597, 597t
  and election of 1968, 611
  and election of 1972, 618t
  and election of 1974, 618
  and election of 1976, 625t, 626
  and election of 1980, 638, 639t
  and election of 1984, 641t, 642
  and election of 1992, 656
  and election of 1996, 667t
  and election of 2000, 672, 672t, 674
Democratic-Republicans
  Alien and Sedition Acts and, 222
  in Congress, early 19th century, 245
  and election of 1796, 222t, 223
  and election of 1800, 235, 235t
  and election of 1804, 244, 244t
  and election of 1808, 245, 245t
  and election of 1816, 251, 251t
  and election of 1820, 267, 267t
  and election of 1824, 268–269, 269t
  and election of 1828, 270
  Jay Treaty and, 221
  policies of, 218, 219
  support for France, 218
Denmark
  Atlantic slave trade and, 96m–97m
  Holocaust and, 541
  immigration from, 284
Department of Agriculture, 386, 424
Department of Defense, 566
Department of Energy, 627
Department of Homeland Security (DHS), 678
Department of Housing and Urban Development (HUD), 591
Department stores, rise of, 396
Depression of 1819, 272
Depression of 1870s-1880s, 376, 411–412
Depression of 1893, 431, 435
Depression of 1930s. *See* Great Depression
Desegregation
  backlash against, 610–611, 621, 621i
  black debate on, 275–276, 604
  Brown v. Board of Education and, 580–581
  of buses, 581–582
  Civil Rights Act (1964), 597–598
  and court-ordered busing, 599, 613, 621, 621i
  early efforts at, 554, 562
  of education, 554, 580, 580i, 580–581, 599, 613
  implementation of, 581
  white attitudes toward, 577–578
Desert Land Act (1877), 371
Détente
  development of, 617, 619
  Reagan on, 626, 640
Detroit. *See also* Fort Detroit
  in War of 1812, 247, 248m
  20th century, black riots in, 605
  British capture of, 18th century, 143
  establishment of, 60
The Devastation of the Indies (Las Casas), 18
Dewey, George, 438
Dewey, Thomas E.
  and election of 1944, 538t
  and election of 1948, 563, 563t
Dexter Avenue Baptist Church, 582
Diarrhea, in Civil War, 345
Dias, Bartolomeu, 15
Diaz, Jose, 543
Dickinson, John, 152–153, 172i
Didrikson, Mildred "Babe," 528
Dien Bien Phu, Battle of, 600
Dies, Martin, 527
diMaggio, Joe, 527
Diner's Club, 560
Diphtheria, late 19th century, 393
Disabled persons
  employment, in World War II, 538–539
  rights activism by, 573
Discrimination. *See also* Prejudice; Racism
  19th century, 316–317
    against African Americans, 287, 315, 324, 328, 406–409
    black resistance to, 407–408
    against Chinese, 370, 405–406
    employment and, 432, 434i
    against immigrants, 426–427
    motivations for, 423
    against Native Americans, 405
    racial categories and, 425–427
    in South, 432, 610
    in women's suffrage movement, 433
  20th century
    against African Americans, 470, 512
    in housing, 577–578
    against Latinos, 609
    remaining pockets of, 663
    resistance to, 483, 553–554, 564
    in North, 474
    in Southwest, 449–450
    against women, 592, 629–630
    post-World War II, 553–554
Disease
  Great Plague (England, 1665), 67, 67i, 87
  in colonies, 55–56, 116
  in Revolutionary War era, 168, 176, 191–192, 192m
  19th century
    in Civil War, 345, 346, 347
    Hawaiian Islands and, 436
    tuberculosis, 292
    urban water and, 393
    wildlife and, 387
  20th century
    AIDS epidemic, 634, 646
    drug-resistant bacteria, 666
    immigration and, 453i
    polio, 516, 575
    poverty and, 453
    public health measures, 453–454
    radioactive fallout and, 559i, 560
    in World War I, 472
    in World War II, 540
  Native Americans and
    15th and 16th century, 3, 17, 18, 19
    17th century, 31–32, 36–37, 38–39, 48, 50, 60, 62, 64, 70, 87

Disease, *continued*
    18th century, 55–56, 143, 191i, 191–192, 192m
    19th century, 291
Dismal Swamp Canal, 264m
Disneyland, opening of, 576
District of Columbia. *See* Washington, DC
Diversity. *See also* Ethnicity
    in colonies, 35, 115–116, 118–119
    18th century, 217
        challenges of, 111
        immigration and, 83
        in trans-Appalachian West, 227
    19th century
        advertising and, 383–384
        among African Americans, 315
        blending of cultures, 291–292
        cities and, 392
        impact of, 240, 384
        in Midwest, 313–314
        in New Orleans, 258
        Utah, 290
    20th century
        acceptance of, 663
        Great Depression and, 508–509
        immigration and, 648–649
Division of Forestry, 424
Divorce
    late 19th century, 434
    20th century, 576f
        early, 444
        in 1920s, 486, 490
        in 1950s, 576
        in 1970s, 630
Dix, Dorothea, 300, 343
Dixiecrats (State-Rights Democratic party), 562, 563t
DNA research, on Native Americans origins, 6
Doctors
    in Civil War, 345
    licensing of, 299
"Dog," 559i
Doheny, Edward L., 498
Dole, Robert, 667t
Dollar. *See* Currency
Dollar Diplomacy, 463
Dollinger, Genora Johnson, 526–527
Domestication of plants, in Americas, 7–8
Domínguez, Father, 141, 142m
Dominican Republic
    U.S. designs on, late 19th century, 373
    U.S. intervention in, 469m, 605
Dominion of New England, 74
"Don't ask, don't tell" policy, 667
Doolittle, Amos, 158i
"Double V," 543
Douglas, Stephen A., 329i
    debates with Lincoln, 328–329
    and election of 1860, 330, 330t
    slavery and, 322, 323, 324m
Douglass, Frederick
    abolitionist movement and, 293, 293i
    black rights and, 320
    unions and, 376
    women's rights and, 374
Draft. *See* Conscription
Drake, Sir Francis, 26m, 27, 28
Dred Scott v. Sanford (1857), 328
Dreiser, Theodore, 458
Drinker, Elizabeth, 235
Drought
    Anasazi culture and, 11
    16th century, in Eastern U.S., 43i
    17th century
        in Eastern U.S., 43, 43i
        in Southwest, 33
    late 19th century, 411, 412i
    in 1930s, 512–513, 513m, 514i
Drug use
    in 1960s, 607, 611
    in 1970s, 623
    in 1980s, 646–647
    in 1990s, 665
Du Bois, W. E. B., 427, 461, 477
Duke, James Buchanan, 406
Duniway, Abigail Scott, 419
Dunmore, Lord, 164, 167, 169
Dust Bowl, 512–513, 513m, 514i
Dutch Americans, 18th century, in New York, 217
Dutch East India Company, 37, 39
Dutch Reformed Church, 24, 28
Dutch West Indian Company, 40–41
Dylan, Bob, 607
Dysentery, in Civil War, 345

E

E-mail, 683
Earhart, Amelia, 528, 528i
Early Republic
    cultural tensions in, 217
    culture, 196–197
    economic policy, 218
    European influences in, 217, 222
    industry in, 219–220
    reform movements in, 230–231
    slavery in, 223–225
    social class in, 231, 232–235
    tariffs, 218
    taxation, 202, 203–204
        constitutional limitations proposed for, 214
        resistance to, 205—206, 217, 220–221
        war debt and, 193, 203–206, 219
    war debt and, 193, 203–206, 219
    women in
        education and, 232–233
        elite, 231–233
        nonelite, 234–235
        rights of, 231
Earth Day, establishment of, 612
Earth First!, 655
East Germany, post-World War II, 557m
East India Company, 154–155
Eastern Europe
    19th century immigration from, 426
    20th century immigration from, 445, 452
    post-World War I political order, 480, 481m
    post-World War II
        control of, 546–547, 552
        Soviet domination of, 552, 555, 584
        Warsaw Pact and, 584
    late 20th century
        Soviet Union collapse and, 649
Eating disorders, in 1990s, 665
Economic theory
    late 19th century, 397–398
    early 20th century, 472–473
Economy. *See also* Cotton economy
    18th century, 203–207
        debt and, 203–204, 206–207
        economic regions, 120–125, 122m
        trade and, 203–204
    19th century
        centralization of, 404
        cities' role in, 392–393
        depression of 1819, 273
        depression of 1870s-1880s, 376, 412–413
        depression of 1893, 432, 436
        guiding principles of, 384–385
        labor supply and, 389–391
        nationalization of, 316
        panic of 1819, 266–267, 271
        panic of 1837, 293
        post-Civil War, 374–375
        post-War of 1812, 252–254
        railroad's impact on, 371, 380, 382–383, 386m, 398
        regional economies, 311–316
        rise of consumer culture, 380–381, 383–384, 394–396
        in South, 255–256, 406
    20th century
        early, 444–445, 467–468
        in 1920s, 487, 500
        in 1930s. *See* Great Depression
        in 1950s, 561, 570
        in 1970s, 615–616, 620–621, 623, 626
        in 1980s, 641–642, 643–645
        in 1990s, 635, 656–657, 667
        government regulation and, 509–510
        oil and, 622–623
        post-World War I, 497–498
        recession of 1913-1914, 477i
        recession of 1991-1992, 653, 656, 666
        stock market crash of 1929, 487, 502–504
        World War I and, 472, 477i, 477–478
        World War II and, 539, 547, 553, 555
        post-World War II, 552
    in 2000s, 674
Eddy, Mary Baker, 429
Edenton Ladies' Tea Party, 158
Ederle, Gertrude, 486i, 487
Edgar Thomson Steelworks, 388
Edict of Nantes (1598), 37, 57, 73, 118
Edison, Thomas A., 385, 456
Edisto Island, 362i, 362–363
Edmunds Act (1882), 397
Education
    18th century, women and, 231–233
    19th century
        African Americans and, 298, 315, 356, 358, 360, 427
        discrimination in, 406
        engineering and, 384
        of immigrants, 427, 428
        middle class and, 428
        in Midwest, 313–314
        for mountain people, 435
        Native Americans and, 418i, 422, 422i, 427
        parochial schools, 428
        reform movements in, 297–299
        segregated, 406, 408, 426, 427, 428–429, 452
        of slaves, 428
        social settlement houses, 419
        state bureaucracy for, 428
        women and, 278
    20th century
        affirmative action and, 632, 692
        African American studies programs, 605
        bilingual, 663
        Chicano studies programs, 609
        desegregation of, 554, 580, 580i, 580–581, 599, 613
        GI Bill and, 553
        prayer in public schools, 599, 645
        segregated, 427, 461
        sex education, 588i
        standardization in, 428

women and, 579, 630
in United States, history of, 427–428
Educational Amendments of 1972, Title IX, 631
Edwards, Jonathan, 128
Efficiency, industrial labor and, 391
Efficiency experts, 391
Egalitarianism, early 19th century, 241
Egypt
    Camp David Accords, 627
    under Nasser, 585
    U.S. relations with, 622
Ehrenreich, Barbara, 640
Ehrlich, Paul, 612
Ehrlichman, John, 618
Eight hour day. *See* Work day
Eighteenth Amendment, 445, 477, 489
Eisenhower, Dwight D.
    civil rights movement and, 581
    and desegregation of schools, 581
    domestic policies, 583–584
    and election of 1952, 568t, 569
    and election of 1956, 583t
    foreign policy, 584–585
    Interstate Highway Act and, 577
    Sputnik and, 583–584
    Supreme Court appointments, 580
    Vietnam War and, 600
    in World War II, 539i, 545
Eisenhower Doctrine, 585
El Alamein, Battle of, 544m
El Caney, Battle of, 438, 439m
El Congreso de Pueblos de Habla Española, 527
El Paso, Texas, as Ellis Island of South, 469
El Salvador, 8, 639, 640
Eldrige, Eleanor, 235
Election(s)
    of 1788, 217
    of 1792, 218
    of 1796, 218, 222–223, 222t, 223
    of 1800, 235–236, 235t
    of 1804, 244, 244t
    of 1808, 245, 245t
    of 1816, 251, 251t
    of 1820, 267, 267t
    of 1824, 268–269, 268t
    of 1828, 262, 269t, 270
    of 1832, 272t
    of 1836, 292, 292t
    of 1840, 294–295, 295t
    of 1844, 302, 302t
    of 1848, 321, 321t
    of 1852, 322, 322t
    of 1856, 325, 325t
    of 1860, 330, 330t, 335
    of 1862, 345
    of 1864, 351–352, 352t, 359
    of 1866, 363
    of 1868, 367, 367t
    of 1872, 377, 377t
    of 1876, 377–378, 378t
    of 1880, 397, 397t
    of 1884, 398, 398t
    of 1888, 399, 399t
    of 1892, 431t, 432
    of 1896, 432t, 433
    of 1900, 461, 461t
    of 1904, 462t
    of 1908, 463, 463t
    of 1912, 463, 464t, 471
    of 1916, 473, 475–476
    of 1920, 483, 488, 488t
    of 1924, 488t
    of 1932, 514, 516, 516t
    of 1936, 524–525, 525t
    of 1944, 538t
    of 1946, 554
    of 1948, 562–563, 563, 563t
    of 1952, 569
    of 1956, 583t
    of 1964, 597, 597t
    of 1968, 603–604, 611, 611t
    of 1972, 618, 618t
    of 1974, 618
    of 1976, 616, 625t, 626
    of 1980, 638–639, 639t, 646
    of 1984, 641t, 642, 647
    of 1988, 645, 647
    of 1992, 653, 656, 661, 666, 666t
    of 1994, 656, 667
    of 1996, 667, 667t
    of 2000, 656, 671–674, 672, 672t, 673m
    campaigns, early 19th century, 261–262
    decided in House of Representatives, 269
    voter participation
        early 19th century, 262
        in 1980s, by African Americans, 647
Electoral College
    in 2004 election, 681
    debate over, 217
    and election of 2000, 671
    establishment of, 217
Elementary and Secondary Education Act, 597
Elevators, introduction of, 393
Eliot, John, 50
Elizabeth I, Queen of England, 24, 27, 28, 41
Elkhorn Tavern, Battle of, 341
Ellis Island, 448m, 453i
Ellsberg, Daniel, 612
Elmina Castle, 15
Emancipation, 309, 322, 343
Emancipation Proclamation, 345–347
Embargo Act (1807), 245
Embargo of 1807, 244–245
Emergency Banking Act (1933), 517, 523t
Emergency Relief Appropriation (1935), 523t, 524
Emerson, Ralph Waldo, 300, 317–318
Empire Zinc Mining Co., 564i
Employment
    18th century, of African Americans, 224
    19th century
        of African Americans
            pre-Civil War, 235, 254, 288, 294, 315, 316–317, 324, 328
            in Civil War, 333i, 346–348, 350–351
            post-Civil War, 371, 391
        competition for jobs, 414, 434
        minorities and, 316–317, 324, 434i
        women and, 233–235, 276–278, 280, 298, 315i, 315–316
    20th century
        of African Americans, 511, 512
        in Great Depression, 512
        in World War II, 536, 541
        early, 453
        for minorities, 511, 512, 539, 658
        women and, 458–459, 502, 511, 538–540, 553, 561, 578–579, 620, 630–631, 632, 659i
        in World War I, 478, 478i, 530, 541
        in World War II, 536, 538–542
Empress of China (ship), 203
Enclosure movement, 27
Encomienda system, 35, 63
Endangered Species Act (1973), 612
The Endowments, Position and Education of Woman (Howe), 318–319
Energy. *See also* Nuclear power; Oil
    consumption of
        20th century, 622–623, 684i, 686
    history of, 622–623
    sources of, 20th century, 623, 628
Engineers, 19th century
    growth and, 401
    training of, 384
England/Great Britain. *See also* Colonies, British
    16th century
        Atlantic slave trade, 27
        conquest of Ireland, 23, 27
        emergence as nation-state, 24
        emergence as naval power, 27
        exploration and colonization, 27–28
        population growth in, 27
    17th century
        Atlantic slave trade, 67, 82–83, 91–95
        Civil War, 42, 49, 66, 148
        colonization and, 60
        Glorious Revolution, 73–74, 148
        Great Plague (1665), 66, 67i, 87
        London fire, 66, 87–88
        Puritan Revolution, 66
        Restoration Era, 66
    17th century exploration and colonization, 56
        in Africa, 67
        on Atlantic Coast, 31–32, 34, 37, 41–45
        in Carolinas, 66
        in lower Mississippi, 60
    18th century
        Atlantic slave trade, 82–83, 96m–97m
        emigration to colonies, 164
        exploration and colonization in Pacific, 139–140
        French and Indian War, 131–134, 133m
        military spending, 177f, 179
        Native American trade and, 112
        as political model, 218
        population, 115
        seizure of Canada, 132–134, 133m
        Seven Years' War, cost of, 144
        Spanish cession of Florida, 134
        suppression of press in, 144
        union with Scotland, 78
        war with France, 131–134, 133m, 219
        war with Spain, 100, 105–106, 107m
    and Revolutionary War
        domestic opposition to, 177
        as global conflict, 166m, 175–176, 181–182, 184–185
        Indian allies, 182–184, 183m
        offers of freedom to slaves, 164–165, 167
        peace negotiations, 187–188
        strategy, 169–171, 176, 182
        surrender at Yorktown, 186–187, 187i
        troop distributions, 147m, 157m
    late 18th century
        impressment of U.S. sailors, 219
        new world ambitions of, 193
        in North America, 199, 217, 219, 227, 297–298
        Ohio Confederacy and, 219, 227
    19th century
        abolition of slavery, 293
        in Americas, 437
        Boxer Rebellion and, 440
        Corn Laws, 301
        immigration from, 389–390, 427
        impressment of U.S. sailors, 244
        Ireland, treatment of, 285
        in North America, 244–246

England/Great Britain, *continued*
    U.S. Civil War and, 345–346, 350
    20th century
        Five-Power Treaty, 487–488
        immigration from, 492f
        in Middle East, 585, 603
        retreat from Colonialism, 555
        Socialist Party rise in, 552
        World War I and, 467, 480–481
        World War II and, 531, 532, 533, 555, 558
English Channel, first woman to swim, 486i, 487
English East India Company, 37
English language
    20th century, global reach of, 688
    American form of, 196
    Cold War and, 559
    Dutch loan words in, 68
English Turn, 60
Enlightenment, 125–126
Entente. *See* Triple Entente
Entertainment
    late 19th century, 394–396
    20th century
        early, 456–458
        in 1920s, 486–487
        in 1930s, 527–528
        post-World War II, 554, 575–576
Entrepreneurial spirit, late 19th century, 388, 401
Environment and environmentalism
    20th-century transformations in, 685–686
    pollution, 686–687
    in resistance to globalization, 683
Environmental damage. *See also* Pollution
    19th century, 386–387, 387i
    20th century
        in 1930s, Dust Bowl, 512–513, 513m, 514i
        in 1960s, 575, 599
        nuclear weapons development and, 559i, 560
        uranium mining and, 636
Environmental Protection Agency (EPA), 612, 622, 642
Environmentalism. *See also* Conservationism
    late 19th century, 372
    20th century
        early, 462, 462i
        in 1950s, 584
        in 1960s, 575, 589, 590, 599, 612
        in 1970s, 623–625
        in 1980s, 642i, 642–643
        in 1990s, 655i, 655–656
EPA. *See* Environmental Protection Agency
Equal Pay Act (1963), 592
Equal Rights Amendment (ERA), 488, 631, 632
Equal Rights Association, 373
ERA. *See* Equal Rights Amendment
Era of Good Feelings, 251–254
Erie Canal, 264m
Erik the Red, 13
Eriksson, Leif, 13
Ervin, Sam, 618
Escalante, Father, 141, 142m
Escobar, Carmen Bernal, 512
Escobedo v. Illinois (1964), 599
Escudero, José Agustin de, 276–277
"The Establishment," 595
Estate tax, early 20th century, 472
Esteban, 21, 23, 26m
Estonia, creation of, 481m
Ethiopia, Italian invasion of (1935), 509, 532
Ethiopian Regiment, 167

Ethnic liberation movements, in 1960s, 609
Ethnicity. *See also* Diversity; *specific groups*
    late 18th century, 217
    19th century
        employment and, 316–317, 324
        in Midwest, 313–314
Etowah, Georgia, Native American culture at, 9m, 11
Eugenics movement, 454–455, 497–499
Eulachon, 244i
Europe. *See also* Eastern Europe; Southern Europe
    Protestant Reformation in, 23–24
    Communism in, 552
    immigration from, 452
    imperialism of, 436
    peopling of, 2, 5
    peopling of America, 2–3
European Recovery Program, 557
Exceptionalism, 423
Executive Order 8802, 541
Executive Order 9066, 535
Executive power, Founding Fathers' fear of, 178–179
Exercise, in 1970s, interest in, 623, 623i
Exodusters, 409
Exxon Valdez oil spill, 643

F

Fair Employment Practices Commission (FEPC), 541
Fair Labor Standards Act (1938), 523t
Fairbanks, Douglas, 493
Fairmont Waterworks (Philadelphia), 273i
Falconbridge, Alexander, 95
Fall, Albert, 488
Fallen Timbers, Battle of, 220, 226m, 227, 229m
Faludi, Susan, 645
Falwell, Jerry, 646–647, 646i
Family
    19th century, 281, 320, 373
    20th century
        early, immigrants and, 503
        post-World War II, 560–561
        in 1950s, 577–579
        in 1970s, 630–631, 632
        in 1990s, 660
        Cold War and, 572, 574, 574i, 575, 576
        Victorianism and, 281, 373, 427
Family and Medical Leave Act, 667
Farm Mortgage Act (1933), 523t
Farm Security Administration (FSA), 518i
Farmers
    18th century
        in Democratic-Republican ideology, 218
        unrest, 150–151, 203–206, 217
    19th century
        government services for, 424
        and Panic of 1819, 267
        plight of, 432
    20th century
        subsidies for, 488, 518
        World War II and, 538
Farmers' Alliance, 412, 431
Farouk, King of Egypt, 585
Farragut, David, 344, 352
Farrakhan, Louis, 661
Fascism
    discrediting of, 552
    rise of, 531–532
Fast food stores
    cultural resistance to, 690
Faubus, Orville, 581
FBI. *See* Federal Bureau of Investigation
FDIC. *See* Federal Deposit Insurance

Corporation
Federal Aid Highway Act (1956), 577, 584
Federal Bureau of Investigation (FBI)
    abuses of power by, 612, 617, 625, 664
    Black Panther party and, 605
    at Chicago Democratic Convention (1968), 611
    Ku Klux Klan and, 604
Federal courts, establishment of, 236
Federal Deposit Insurance Corporation (FDIC), 518, 523t
Federal Emergency Relief Act (1933) [FERA], 523t
Federal Emergency Relief Administration (FERA), 519
Federal government
    20th century
        in 1960s, public disenchantment with, 573
        in 1980s and 1990s, Republican view of, 639
        growth of, 461, 463, 464, 472–473, 477, 518, 528
        national security state, establishment of, 567
Federal Highways Act (1916), 495
Federal Housing Administration (FHA), 523t, 560, 577
Federal lands
    in 1810, 246i
    20th century
        exploitation of, 584, 642–643
Federal One program, 523t, 524
Federal Radio Commission, 495
Federal Reserve, Great Depression and, 504
Federal Reserve Act (1913), 472
Federal Reserve Banks, establishment of, 472
Federal Theater Project, 524
Federal Trade Commission, 473
The Federalist, 211–213
Federalists
    in Congress, early 19th century, 245
    Constitution ratification and, 211–213
    and election of 1796, 222t, 223
    and election of 1800, 235, 235t
    and election of 1804, 244, 244t
    and election of 1808, 245, 245t
    and election of 1816, 251, 251t
    ideology of, 211–213, 218
    as political party, 218, 219
    rural resistance to, 220
    support for Britain, 218
Feebleminded persons, sterilization of, 498
Feme covert, 68
The Feminine Mystique (Friedan), 579, 607
Feminism. *See also* Women's liberation movement; Women's rights movement
    19th century, 300
    1970s, 628–632
    1980s, opponents of, 645, 646
    FEPC. *See* Fair Employment Practices Commission
FERA. *See* Federal Emergency Relief Act; Federal Emergency Relief Administration
Ferdinand, King of Spain, 15
Ferguson, Patrick, 185m, 186
Fern, Fanny, 320
FHA. *See* Federal Housing Administration
Fieffer, Jules, 610i
Fifteenth Amendment, 367, 374
"Fifty-four forty or fight," 302
54th Massachusetts Infantry, 346
Figgins, Jesse, 4
Fillmore, Millard, 321, 325, 325t
Final Solution, 541, 547
Financing, late 19th century, innovations in, 387–389

Finland
    20th century, immigration from, 454–455
    creation of, 481m, 482
Finney, Charles Grandison, 279
Firearms. *See* Guns
Fireside chats, 515i, 517, 520, 527
First Amendment
    Alien and Sedition Acts and, 222
    in Cold War, 563
    Supreme Court on, 599
First lady, first elected to public office, 673
First South Carolina Volunteers, 348
Fiscal policy, late 19th century, 376
Fishing Creek, Battle of, 185, 185m
Fishing industry, 18th century, 124
Fisk, Clinton B., 399t
Fitzgerald, F. Scott, 501
Fitzgerald, Zelda, 501
Fitzhugh, George, 326
Five Civilized Tribes
    assimilation of, 228, 274
    in Civil War, 341
    culture, mid 19th century, 312
    removal of, 241, 265i, 288m, 288–289
Five Nations. *See* Iroquois Confederacy
Five-Power Treaty, 487–488
Flanagan, Hallie, 524
Flappers, 486, 493
Flathead Indians, 520i
Flight 93, 676i, 677
Florida
    16th century, Europeans' contest for, 18, 21–22, 22i, 25–27
    17th century
        exploration and colonization of, 36–37, 64–65
        Native American exploitation in, 64
    18th century
        American Revolution and, 162, 184, 188
        conflict with Georgia, 100, 105–106, 107m
        slave population, 98m
        Spanish cession to Britain, 134
        Spanish regaining of, 198, 198m
    19th century
        economy of, 265
        readmission to Union, 365m, 367
        U.S. acquisition of, 267
    20th century
        hurricane of 1928, 445
        land boom of 1920s, 500
        tourism and, 494
    2000 election and, 672
Florida (ship), 346
Florida Supreme Court, and election of 2000, 672
Flowers, Gennifer, 668
Floyd, John, 272t
Folsom points, 4–5
Food, Columbian exchange and, 17, 36, 64
Food labels, introduction of, 598
Football
    as college sport, 428
    history of, 395
Forbes, Charles R., 488
Ford, Gerald R.
    Arab oil embargo and, 622
    assumption of presidency, 619
    and election of 1976, 625, 625t, 626
    Nixon pardon, 619
    Vietnam and, 619
    in World War II, 539i
Ford, Henry, 456, 495
Ford Motor Co., 456
Ford's Theater, 354
Foreign Miners Tax (California, 1852), 311
Foreign policy. *See* Containment policy; *individual presidents*

Forest Reserve Act (1891), 424
Forests
    19th century
        destruction of, 386
        management of, 424–425
        railroad construction and, 372t
        Timber Culture Act (1873), 371
    20th century
        management of, 462, 462i
Forman, Stanley J., 621i
Forrest, Nathan Bedford, 351
Fort Ancient peoples, 12i
Fort Buford, 409
Fort Caroline, 26
Fort Christina, 40, 52m
Fort Clatsop, 243m
Fort Concho, 409
Fort de Chartres, 60
Fort Dearborn, 226m
Fort Defiance, 248m
Fort Detroit, 183m, 226m
Fort Donelson, 343
Fort Duquesne, 132, 133m, 143
Fort Frontenac, 58m, 133, 133m
Fort Henry, 343
Fort Laramie Treaty (1851), 312, 317
Fort Lee, 172
Fort Louis, 60
Fort Loyal, 59
Fort Mandan, 242–243, 243m
Fort McHenry, 249, 249i
Fort Meigs, 248m
Fort Michilimackinac, 58m, 143, 147m, 157m 226m
Fort Mims, 249
Fort Molden, 248m
Fort Mose, 100, 100i, 105, 107m
Fort Necessity, 132, 133m
Fort Niagara, 133, 133m, 147m, 183, 184i, 226m, 248, 248m
Fort Orange, 39, 39m, 40, 68
Fort Oswego, 133m, 226m
Fort Pillow, Battle of, 352
Fort Pitt, 133, 143, 147m
Fort Rosalie, 58m, 61
Fort Stanwix, 174
Fort Stephenson, 248m
Fort Sumter, 336
Fort Ticonderoga, 133, 133m
Fort Toulouse, 58m, 61, 78
Fort Wagner, Battle of, 346
Fort Washington, 167, 172
Fort William Henry, 132
Fort Wilson Riot, 180
The Fortunate Pilgrim (Puzo), 503
Forty-Niners, 310, 316
Fossil fuel depletion, 686
Fossil fuels
    consumption, 573, 616, 686
    supply of, 686
Founding Fathers, on democracy, 223
Four Freedoms, 533, 533i
The Four Horsemen of the Apocalypse (film), 494i
Fourteen Points, 480
Fourteenth Amendment, 360–361, 362, 366
"40 acres and a mule," 363
Fox Indians
    home region of, 227
    Oklahoma Territory and, 288m
    resistance by, 279
    Revolutionary War and, 184
Foxwoods casino, 657
France
    16th century exploration and conquest, 25i, 25–27
    17th century
        Atlantic slave trade and, 57, 87i
        exploration and conquest, 3, 34,
        37–39, 55–65, 58m
        King William's War, 59–60
        Louis XIV and, 56–57
        trade with Native Americans, 37–39, 55
    18th century
        American Revolution and, 174, 175m, 176, 177f, 182, 186–187, 187i, 188
        Atlantic slave trade and, 87i, 94, 96m–97m
        cession of Louisiana, 162, 198
        colonies, 82, 100, 133m
        loss of, 132–134
        emigration to colonies, 119
        exploration and colonization, 130–132
        French and Indian War, 131–134, 133m
        new world ambitions of, 193
        as political model, 217
        population in America, 130–131
        Quasi War, 222
        and Revolution of 1789, 218, 219
        slavery and, 236
        trade with Native Americans, 112, 113–114, 130
        war with Britain, 219
    19th century
        Boxer Rebellion and, 440, 462
        U.S. Civil War and, 346, 350
    20th century
        post-World War II, 557m
        Aswan Dam controversy, 585
        Communist Party rise in, 552
        Five-Power Treaty, 487–488
        in Vietnam, 558, 600
        World War I and, 467, 479–481
        World War II and, 531
    as trading partner, 685f
Franciscans
    in California, 141
    in Florida, 36
    in Southwest, 33–36
Franco, Francisco, 532
Franklin, Benjamin
    accomplishments of, 125
    Albany Congress and, 132
    at Constitutional Convention, 209
    and Declaration of Independence, 169
    on emigration from Pennsylvania, 123
    as Enlightenment figure, 125
    family of, 116
    in France, 176
    replacement as minister to France, 200
    Revolution and, 155, 180
    on Six Nations, 216
    Treaty of Paris and, 187–188, 188i
    on Whitefield, 126
Franklin, state of, 198m, 199
Franklin Tree, 197i
Free fire zones (Vietnam War), 601
Free market conservatives, 646
Free market economy
    Great Depression and, 509–510
Free-Soil party, 321, 324
    and election of 1848, 321, 321t
    and election of 1852, 322t
    Kansas-Nebraska Act and, 323
Free speech
    Alien and Sedition Acts and, 222
    in Cold War, communists and, 563
    Supreme Court on, 599
Free State of Jones (County), 349
Free trade. *See also* Tariff(s)
    post-World War II, U.S. commitment to, 555
    late 20th century
        agreements on, 667–669
        globalization and, 683–684

Freed, Alan, 554
Freedmen's Bureau, 356–357, 358, 359i, 360–363
Freedom of Access to Clinic Entrances Act (1994), 664
Freedom rides, 582m, 583
Freeman, Elizabeth, 210i
Freeman's Farm, Battles of, 176
Frémont, John Charles, 290, 325, 325t, 342
French and Indian War, 131–134, 133m
French Revolution, American reaction to, 216–219
Freneau, Philip, 196
Freud, Sigmund, 428
Frick, Henry Clay, 429, 430
Friedan, Betty, 579, 608
Frobisher, Martin, 27–28
Frontier. *See also* Settlers; West
   as America's defining concept, 423, 424i
   as cultural battleground, 227
   disappearance of, 423, 424i
   exploration of, water travel and, 243m
   land speculators and, 128, 143, 201, 229
   slavery in, 228–230
FSA. *See* Farm Security Administration
Fuchs, Klaus, 563
Fugitive Slave Act (1850), 308, 322, 324, 326, 330i
Fugitive Slave Law (California, 1852), 311
Fuhrman, Mark, 663
Fulbright, J. William, 605
Fuller, Margaret, 300
Fulton, Robert, 253
Fundamental Constitutions (Ashley-Cooper), 69
Fundamentalist Christians, late 20th century
   cultural impact of, 634, 660
   culture wars and, 637
   opinions of, 643
   rise of, 645–647
   sexuality and, 646
Fur trade
   17th century
      Dutch and, 39
      England and, 48
      French and, 37–39, 39m, 55
      trade routes, 39m
      in Virginia, 71
   18th century
      England and, 140
      firearms spread and, 112
      French and, 113–114
      in Georgia and South Carolina, 121
      in Pacific, 140–141, 202–203
      Pacific northwest, 140
      Russians and, 140–141
   19th century
      in Rocky Mountains, 291–292
      U.S. desire to capture, 242–243

G

Gabriel rebellion, 216–217
Gadsden, James, 288, 312, 313m
Gadsden Purchase, 312, 323
Gage, Thomas, 144, 156, 158–159, 167, 168
Galleons, 21, 32
Galloway, Joseph, 158–159
Galloway Plan, 158
Gálvez, Bernardo de, 184
Gang system, 229, 257
Gangsters, in 1920s, 490
Garbo, Greta, 493
Garcés, Father, 141, 142m
Garcia, Herman, 636
Garcia, John, 534
Garfield, James A., 397, 397t, 398
Garnet, Henry Highland, 293

Garrison, William Lloyd, 293–294
Garvey, Marcus, 492
Gasoline
   importance of, 622
   leaded, 599
   pollution and, 635
Gaspee Affair, 154
Gates, Bill, 657
Gates, Horatio, 175, 175m, 180, 185, 185m, 186
GATT. *See* General Agreement on Tariffs and Trade
Gay Liberation Front, 609
Gay marriage, 661, 662
Gay rights movement
   in 1960s and 1970s, 573, 595, 609
   in 1980s, 644, 646
   in 1990s, 661, 662, 666
Gays. *See* Homosexuality
Gays and lesbians
   same-sex marriage and, 671, 679
Gender roles
   late 19th century, challenges to, 433–435
   in 1930s, 511, 528, 528i
   post-World War II, 560–561
   in 1960s, 608–609
   in 1980s, debate over, 645
General Agreement on Tariffs and Trade (GATT), 669
General Federation of Women's Clubs (GFWC), 433
General Motors, 496, 526–527n 560, 584, 684
General Society of Mechanics and Tradesmen, 231, 233i
General Trades Union, 293
Genet, Citizen Edmund, 219
Geneva Accords (1954), 600
Genome, human, mapping of, 666
Gentlemen's Agreement (1907), 451i, 452
Geography Made Easy (Morse), 197
George, Henry, 414
George, Presley, Sr., 364
George III, King of England
   on Colonial revolt, 156
   in Declaration of Independence, 169
   and Grenville administration, 144
Georgia
   18th century
      conflict with Spanish Florida, 105–106, 107m
      Constitution ratification, 211
      economy, 121, 122m
      establishment of, 104–107
      Revolutionary War in, 185
      Savannah, establishment of, 106i
      slave codes, 107
      slave population, 98m
      slavery in, 105–107, 107m
      western land claims of, 229m
      Yazoo claim, 199m, 228
   19th century
      economy of, 265
      Native Americans in, 270–271, 271m
      readmission to Union, 365m, 367
      Savannah, post-Civil War, 356, 356i
Germain, Lord George, 170, 188
German Americans, 18th century
   in Pennsylvania, 217
   religion and, 126
German pietists, 126
Germantown, Battle of, 176
Germany
   18th century, immigration from, 119, 120, 125
   19th century
      Boxer Rebellion and, 440
      immigration from, 284, 285, 287, 295, 312, 313, 314, 389, 393, 427

   20th century
      World War I and
         anti-German activities in U.S., 477
         causes of, 465
         peace settlement, 480–482, 481m
         U-boat warfare, 475–476
         Zimmerman telegram, 476
      post-World War I
         fascism in, 531–532
         imperialism of, 532
         U.S. loans to, 511
         Weimar Republic, 484
      World War II and
         imperialism of, 532, 533
         Jews in, 532, 540–541, 547
         nonaggression pact with Soviet Union, 532, 533, 544
      post-World War II, 557m
         occupation of, 557–558
         reconstruction, 558
         immigration from, 492, 492f
   as trading partner, 685f
Geronimo, 368–369
Gerry, Elbridge, 208, 210, 222
Gettysburg, Battle of, 349
Gettysburg Address, 350
GFWC. *See* General Federation of Women's Clubs
Ghost dance, 409–410
GI Bill. *See* Servicemen's Readjustment Act of 1944
Gibbs, Lois, 629
Gideon v. Wainright (1963), 599
Gilbert, Sir Humphrey, 27–28
Gilded Age, 397
The Gilded Age (Twain), 397
Gilliam, Eliza, 291
Gilliam, Frances, 291
Gilliam, George, 291
Gilman, Charlotte Perkins, 434
Gingrich, Newt, 667
Ginsberg, Allen, 588
Ginsburg, Ruth Bader, 667
Glacier National Park, 425, 473
Global assembly line, 683–684
Global warming, 622, 656, 674, 679, 686, 687i, 694
Globalization
   beginnings of, 13–14
   free trade and, 683–684
   pros and cons of, 684–685
   technology of, 682–683
Glorious Revolution
   in America, 73–74
   in England, 73, 148
Gnadenhutten massacre, 183
GNP. *See* Gross National Product
Godey's Lady's Book, 280
The Godfather (Puzo), 503
Gold Coast, 15, 27, 67, 93, 93m, 95i, 96m–97m
Gold rush
   Black Hills, 368
   in California, 308, 310, 310i, 311, 328
   Coeur d'Alene, 384
Gold standard, 432
Goldman, Emma, 434, 460, 483
Goldwater, Barry M., 597, 597t
Gompers, Samuel, 416, 471
Goodman, Andrew, 604
Gookin, Daniel, 70
Gorbachev, Mikhail, 648–649
Gordon, Thomas, 149
Gore, Al, and election of 2000, 672, 672t, 674
Gorée Island, 93, 93m
Las Gorras Blancas, 403–404
Gorsuch, Anne, 642
Gospel of Wealth, 400

"Government for the Western Territory" (Jefferson), 200
Governors, restrictions on powers of, 177–178
Grady, Henry, 406
Graff, Frederick C., 273i
Graham, Sylvester, 299, 300
Graham crackers, 299
Granados, Balbina Duque, 682
Grand Army of the Republic, 397
Grandy, Moses, 287
The Grange, 375–376, 396, 398
Grant, James, 142
Grant, Ulysses S.
   in Civil War, 342i, 343, 350, 353, 354
   and election of 1868, 367, 367t
   and election of 1872, 377, 377t
Grantham, Thomas, 90
The Grapes of Wrath (Steinbeck), 513
Grateful Dead, 608
Gravier, Jaques, 61
Gray, Robert, 204–205, 204i
Great American Desert, 312
Great Awakening, 125–129
   consequences of, 128–129
   second, 279
Great Britain. *See* England/Great Britain
Great Depression. *See also* New Deal
   causes of, 502–504, 509–511
   charity in, 515
   culture in, 513
   employment in, 511–512
   end of, 506, 548
   government economic intervention in, 509–510
   Hoover policies and, 514–515
   minorities in, 508–509, 512
   political impact of, 506
   poverty in, 510i, 511–512, 518i
   Weimar Republic and, 484
Great Flood of 1927, 496–497, 497m
The Great Gatsby (Fitzgerald), 501
Great Intrusion, 270
Great Labor Uprising of 1877, 383i
Great Migration, 444, 474, 474i
Great Migration of 1843, 291
Great Plague (1665), 67, 67i, 87
Great Society, 573, 595, 596–599
Great Swamp Fight, 71
Great Wagon Road, 120, 121, 122m
Greece
   19th century, immigration from, 389
   20th century
      Cold War and, 555, 556
      immigration from, 492
      NATO and, 584
Greek Revival style, 273i
Greeley, Horace, 377, 377t
Green Mountain Boys, 166–167
Green party, late 20th century, 674
Green Spring faction, 71, 72i
Green Spring Plantation, 71–73, 72i
Greenback Labor party, 376, 397t
Greenbacks, 376
Greene, Nathaniel, 186
Greenhouse gases, 686
Greenland
   Peary expedition to, 435–436, 436i
   Viking settlements in, 13
Greenpeace, 643
Greensted, William, 84
Greenwood riots, 466–467
Grenville, Robert, 144
Grimké, Angelina, 293, 299
Grimké, Sarah, 293, 299
Griswold v. *Connecticut* (1965), 599
Gross National Product, post-World War I, 487
Guadalcanal, Battle of, 545, 546m

Guadeloupe, 134
Guam, Spanish cession of, 439–440
Guantanamo, U.S. base at, 469m
Guatemala, 585, 640
Guggenheim, David, 463
Guilford Courthouse, Battle of, 186
Guinan, Mary Louise, 489i
Guiteau, Charles J., 397, 398
Gulf of Tonkin Resolution, 601
Gulf War. *See* Persian Gulf War (1991)
Gullah, 258
Guns
   gun control debate, 665
   Native Americans and, 113–115, 114m
   in West, impact of, 219
Guthrie, Woody, 513, 516–517
Gypsies, Nazi Germany and, 531

H

Habeas corpus, suspension of, 342
Haiphong Harbor, mining of, 603m, 613
Haiti
   slave revolt in, 217–218
   U.S. intervention in, 469m, 670
Hakluyt, Richard, 28, 42
Haldeman, H. R., 618
Hale, John P., 322t
Hale, Sarah, 280
Haley, Alex, 632i
Haley, Bill, 554
Half Moon (ship), 39
Halifax, Nova Scotia, vice-admiralty court, 144, 157m
Hamar, Josiah, 226m
Hamer, Fanny Lou, 604
Hamilton, Alexander
   antislavery activities, 197
   Bank of United States and, 218
   Confederation finances and, 193
   Constitutional Convention and, 207
   death of, 245
   economic policies of, 218, 219–220
   The Federalist and, 211
   as Treasury secretary, 218, 220
   and two-party system, 218
Hamilton, Henry, 182–184, 183m
Hampton Institute, 418i
Hampton Normal and Agricultural Institute, 427
Hancock, John, 137, 137i
   Boston Tea Party and, 156
   British attempt to arrest, 159
   Continental Congress and, 138
   and Declaration of Independence, 169
   social class and, 138
   Townshend Duties and, 152
   wealth of, 137
Hancock, Winfield S., 397, 397t
Hanford, Washington, nuclear waste dumps, 636
Hanna, Marcus "Mark," 433
Hannah's Cowpens, 186
Hansberry, Lorraine, 577
Hard money policy, 220, 272
Hardin, Garrett, 685
Harding, Warren G., 487–488, 488t
Harlem, in 1920s, 493
Harlem Renaissance, 493–494, 495i
Harper, Frances Ellen Watkins, 408
Harper's, 377i, 396
Harpers Ferry, Brown's attack on, 327m, 329–330, 335
Harrington, James, 69
Harris, Katherine, 672
Harrison, Benjamin
   and election of 1888, 399, 399t
   and election of 1892, 430, 431t
Harrison, Benjamin (of Virginia), 212

Harrison, William Henry
   and election of 1836, 292, 292t
   and election of 1840, 294–295, 295t
   as governor, 246
   and War of 1812, 248, 251
Hartford Female Seminary, 278
Harvard College, 47i, 49, 127, 515
Harvard Indian College, 51, 69
Hawaiian Islands
   peopling of, 13, 139
   European contact, 138, 139i, 139–140, 162
   19th century
      annexation of, 436
      immigration to, 390, 436
      planter revolt in (1893), 436
      U.S. interests in, 436
   20th century
      public interest in, 561
      statehood, 575
      World War II and, 506, 534, 535i
Hawkins, John, 27
Hawley-Smoot Tariff (1930), 504
Hay, John, 439, 440
Hayes, Rutherford B., 397
Haymarket bombing, 414–415
Hays, Mary, 181
Head Start, 597
Headright system, slavery and, 90–91
Health
   pollution effect on, 687
Health and health care
   18th century, improvements in, 116
   20th century
      early 20th, 453–454
      in 1940s, 559, 562
      in 1950s, 574, 585, 591
      in 1960s, 598
      in 1970s, 622–623, 632
      in 1990s, 658, 665–666
      Clinton reform efforts, 667
      Medicaid, 598, 631
      Medicare, 598, 641
Healy, Dorothy Ray, 539
Hearing, history of, 128–129
Hearst, William R., 437
Hefner, Hugh, 588
Hemings, Sally, 235
Henrietta Maria, Queen of England, 46
Henry, Patrick
   Constitutional ratification and, 212
   Continental Congress and, 158
   Stamp Act and, 145
Henry, Prince of Portugal, 14, 16m
Henry IV, King of France, 37
Henry VII, King of England, 17, 24
Henry VIII, King of England, 24, 27
Henry the Navigator. *See* Henry, Prince of Portugal
Henson, Matthew, 466, 466i
Hepburn, Katharine, 527
Hernandez, Antonia, 660
Heroes of America, 349
Herrera, Juan Jose, 403
Herrera, Nicanor, 403
Herrera, Pablo, 403
Hewes, George, 137–138, 156
Hidatsas, 112, 114m, 242
Higginson, Humphrey, 84–85
Highway beautification program, 597
Highway construction
   early 19th century, 253
   in 1920s, 495
   post–World War II, 560, 561, 561i, 577
Hill, Anita, 651, 661
Hill, Julia Butterfly, 655i, 655–656
Hillman, Sidney, 526
Hillsborough, Lord, 152, 153, 154
Hindman Settlement School, 434

Hine, Lewis, 458, 459i
Hippies, 607, 607i
Hirano family, 537i
Hiroshima, atomic bombing of, 507, 548
Hispanic Americans
    in contemporary America, 692
    population, 691
Hispanics. *See also* Latinos; Mexican Americans
    19th century
        in Civil War, 344
        culture of, 381
        land rights of, 371, 403–404
        Protestant view of, 295, 304–305
    20th century
        civil rights activism, 580–581
        liberation movement, 609
        New Deal coalition and, 527
History textbooks, on early Americans, 4
Hitler, Adolf
    death of, 545
    domestic policies, 532
    Final Solution of, 541, 547
    rise of, 532
Ho Chi Minh, 552, 565, 591, 600, 601
Hobos, in 1930s, 512
Hogarth, William, 105i
Hohokams, 9m, 10
Holland
    17th century
        exploration and colonization, 31, 32, 37–41, 40i, 56
        loss of New Netherlands, 67
        slave trade and, 37, 41, 86–87
    18th century
        American Revolution and, 182
        immigration from, 119
        slave trade and, 96m–97m
    20th century, loss of colonies, 531
Hollywood
    early 20th century, 456, 486, 493–495
    Cold War and, 563
Holmes, Oliver Wendell, 498
Holocaust, 530–531, 540–541, 547, 563
Home Insurance Building, 392
Home Owners' Loan Corporation, 520, 523t
Homeland security, 678
Homelessness, in 1980s, 643
Homemaking, as profession, 578–579
Homosexuality
    early 20th century, 457
    AIDS epidemic and, 646, 647
    feminism and, 631
    gay marriage and civil unions, 661, 662
    military service and, 666–667
    Nazis and, 531
    reaction against, 563
    religious right and, 645
    rights activism, 573, 595, 609, 646, 647, 661, 662, 666
    World War II and, 538, 540
    post-World War II, 563
Hooker, Joseph, 349
Hooker Chemical Co., 624
Hoover, Herbert
    background and career of, 489
    as Commerce secretary, 495, 497
    and election of 1928, 489, 489t
    and election of 1932, 516t
    Great Depression and, 514–515
    and stock market crash of 1929, 502
Hoover, J. Edgar, 535
Hoovervilles, 502
Hope, John, 427
Hope (ship), 435
Hopewell Indians, 9m, 11
Hopkins, Elizabeth, 31–32
Hopkins, Harry, 519
Hopkins, Stephen, 31–32

Horizontal integration, 389
Hormone replacement therapy, 665
Horses
    and Comanche rise to power, 113
    introduction and spread of, 17i
        cultural impact, 82, 112i, 112–115, 312
        in Southwest, 36, 64, 64i, 112i, 112–113, 114m
        trade and, 114m
Horseshoe Bend, Battle of, 250
Horticultural societies, rise of, 7–8
House Committee on Indian Affairs, 273
House of Burgesses, in Colonial Virginia, 44
House of Representatives, elections decided in, 268
House Un-American Activities Committee (HUAC), 527, 563
Housing, post-World War II
    segregation in, 560, 577
    shortages in, 576–577
Housing Acts (1949, 1954), 578
Houston, Sam, 301
How the Other Half Lives (Riis), 416, 416i
Howard, Oliver O., 357, 362i
Howe, George, 318–319
Howe, Richard, 171, 175m
Howe, William, 168, 172, 173, 175m, 176
Howl (Ginsberg), 588
HUAC. *See* House Un-American Activities Committee
HUD. *See* Department of Housing and Urban Development
Hudson, Henry, 39, 42
Hudson Valley revolt, 150–151
Hudson's Bay Company, 68, 135
Hughes, Charles E., 473t, 498
Hughes, Langston, 494–495, 495i
Hughes, Robert P., 440–441
Hughson, John and Sarah, 101
Huguenots
    Calvinism and, 24
    colonization and, 25i, 25–26, 38, 41, 60, 118
    and Edict of Nantes, 37, 118
    suppression of, 57
Hull House, 417
Human genome mapping, 666
Human rights
    UN Human Rights Charter and, 553
    in U.S. foreign policy, 20th century, 626–627
Humans, early history of, 2, 5
Humphrey, Hubert, 611
Hungary
    post-World War II, 557m
    19th century, immigration from, 384
    in 1950s, uprising in, 585
    creation of, 481m
Hunting and gathering societies, 5–7
Hunton, Addie W., 478
Hurley, Martha, 615
Huron Indians
    17th century
        alliances with Europeans, 38–39
        territory of, 39m
    18th century
        in French and Indian War, 132
        resistance, 143
Hussein, Saddam, 651–652, 679
Huston, John, 538
Hutchinson, Anne, 48–49
Hutchinson, Thomas, 146, 155, 156
Hyde Amendment (1976), 632
Hydrogen bomb, development of, 560, 572

I

"I Have a Dream" speech, 593
Iberville, Pierre le Moyne d', 55, 58m, 60

Ice Age, 5–6
Ickes, Harold L., 520i
Idaho
    statehood for, 384
    women's voting rights and, 420
Ideology of Americans, late 20th century, 692
Illinois. *See also* Chicago
    manufacturing in, 430m
    migration to, 313
Illinois and Michigan Canal, 264m
Illinois Anti-Slavery Society, 294
Illinois Indians, 227
Imamura, Ichiro, 547
Immigration. *See also individual source nations and regions*
    18th century
        to colonies, 83, 164
        culture clash and, 111
        dangers of, 117
        religion and, 125–126
        Revolutionary War command and, 178
    19th century
        city growth and, 393
        and competition for jobs, 414, 435
        discrimination and, 426–427
        diversity and, 240, 384
        education and, 427, 428
        labor supply and, 389–391
        opponents of, 296, 323
        pull factors in, 380
        by region, 390m
        to South, 314
        volume of, 285, 427, 450f
        from Western Europe, 285–286
    20th century
        backlash against, 454, 478, 491, 621
        cultural impact of, 456
        destinations for, 448m
        diversity and, 663
        employment and, 658, 659
        illegal, 648, 658, 658m
        to Midwest, 448m, 449
        poverty and, 448, 449i
        restrictions on, 450–452, 451m, 565
        return, 448
        settlement houses and, 420, 434
        source regions, 492f, 648
        to Southwest, 448m, 449–450
        volume of, 445, 447, 450f, 648
        westward, 501m
    in contemporary America, 692–693
Immigration and Naturalization Service (INS), 649
Imminent Dangers to the Free Institutions of the United States (Morse), 296
Imperialism
    late 19th century, 436–441
        critics of, 441
        justifications of, 435
        in Pacific, 437
        Spanish-American War, 437–440, 438–439m
    20th century, 462, 467
        collapse of, 534
        Taft and, 463
        U.S. opinion on, 468
    cultural, of U.S., 559, 687i
Implied powers, 271
Impressment, British
    late 18th century, 219
    early 19th century, 244
Inca empire
    characteristics of, 8, 9m
    Spanish Conquest of, 21
Inchon landing, 568, 569m
Income
    mid-20th century, 575

in 1970s, 620
in 1980s, 643–644, 644f
in 1990s, 657
Income distribution
in global economy, 684–685
Income tax
early 20th century, 514
in 1980s, 641
introduction of, 472
Supreme Court on, 431
Indentured servants
characteristics of, 117
disadvantages *vs.* slaves, 88
Independent Counsel, in Clinton administration, 667–668
Independent party
and election of 1832, 272t
and election of 1836, 292t
and election of 1980, 639t
Index of prohibited books, 24
India
anticolonialism in, 552
immigration from, 451m
independence, 558
Indian(s). *See* Native Americans
Indian boarding school movement, 418
Indian Brigade, 340
Indian Claims Commission, 564–565
Indian Removal Act (1830), 271
Indian Reorganization Act (1934), 521, 523t
Indian Territory
in Civil War, 341
removals to, 288m, 288–289
Indiana
black law, 230
eugenics laws, 454
Indian cession of, 227
manufacturing in, 430m
migration to, 313
state constitution, anti-black bias in, 314
Indigo, as crop, 99, 122
Individualism
in 19th century, 316–318, 401
challenges to, 319–320
in 20th century, unions and, 483i
Indonesia
anticolonialism in, 552
immigration from, 451m
Industrial Revolution
in early Republic, 219
energy needs and, 622
impact of, 254–255
warfare and, 472, 473i
women and, 278
Industrial Workers of the World (IWW), 460, 471
Industry
in Early Republic, 219
19th century
and American system of manufacturing, 385
centers of, 430m
in Civil War, 342
growth of, 253–254
imperialism and, 436
Lowell model of production, 254
mass production and, 384
Rhode Island system of production, 254
in South, 406–407
technological innovation and, 385–386, 391
textiles, 253–254, 278, 391, 430m
urban growth and, 392–393
worker unrest, 413–415
20th century
early, 430m
flight overseas, 620, 645, 681

mass production and, 444, 455–456
scientific management and, 455
World War II and, 536–538, 543
INF Treaty. *See* Intermediate Nuclear Force (INF) treaty
The Influence of Sea-Power in History, 1660-1763 (Mahan), 436
Influenza
Native Americans and, 36–37
in World War I, 472
Infrastructure construction
early 19th century, 253, 264
post-World War II, 561i, 576
Inquisition, 24
INS. *See* Immigration and Naturalization Service
Installment buying, in 1920s, 500
Integration. *See* Desegregation
Inter Caetera, 16
Intermediate Nuclear Force (INF) treaty, 650
Internal Revenue Service (IRS), political uses of, 617
International Typographic Union, 415
Internet, 683, 683i
The Interpretation of Dreams (Freud), 428
Interstate Commerce Act (1887), 398–399
Interstate Commerce Commission, establishment of, 399
Interstate Highway Act (1956), 577
InterVarsity, 607
Intolerable Acts (1774), 156, 158
Iran
Cold War and, 555, 556
hostage crisis in, 637–638
Islamic revolution in, 635, 637, 649
U.S. involvement in, 585
Iraq. *See* Persian Gulf War
Iraq, U.S. involvement in
Abu Ghraib, 681
as "demonstration effect," 680
justification for, 679–680
occupation in, 680–681
Ireland
English conquest of, 23, 27
immigration from, 285–286, 296, 389–390, 393, 427
Irish Americans
Civil War and, 334
World War I and, 472
Irish confetti, 294
Irish potato famine, 285
Iron Curtain, 556, 557m
Iron range, 449
Iron Teeth, 312
Iroquois Confederacy
17th century
disease and, 38–39
fur trade and, 38–39
King William's War and, 59–60
territory of, 39m
war with Europeans, 38–39, 39m
18th century
American Revolution and, 163, 165, 182, 184i, 216
Christianity and, 125
in French and Indian War, 131–132, 132–133
neutrality of, 59–60
relocation to Great Lakes region, 216
Tuscarora in, 78
Irrigation, late 19th century, innovations in, 385
IRS. *See* Internal Revenue Service
Irving, Washington, 280–281
Isabella, Queen of Spain, 15
Islam
fundamentalism

anti-Americanism, 638, 689
Gulf War and, 653
Iran and, 585, 635, 637–638, 650
rise of, 635
terrorism by, 650, 670–671
September 11th terrorist attacks, 635, 676, 677, 680
in Middle Ages, 13, 14, 15
Islamic fundamentalism
September 11th attacks and, 676–677
Israel
Arab conflicts, 621–622, 627, 639m, 650
Aswan Dam controversy and, 585
Camp David Accords, 627
creation of, 573
Gulf War and, 651–652
peace negotiations, 669
Italian Americans, in World War II, 536, 547i
Italy
19th century, immigration from, 389, 426, 427
20th century
Communist Party rise in, 552
fascism in, 531–532
Five-Power Treaty, 487–488
immigration from, 452, 492, 492f, 503
imperialism of, 532
World War I and, 467, 479m, 481, 481m
World War II and, 533–535, 544, 545
Iwo Jima, Battle of, 530, 546, 546m
IWW. *See* Industrial Workers of the World

J

Jackson, Andrew
background of, 262
as champion of common man, 262, 267, 270, 281
character of, 262
and election of 1824, 268, 268t
and election of 1828, 262, 269, 269t
and election of 1832, 272, 272t
and election of 1836, 292
as governor of Florida territory, 267
inauguration of, 269i
as Indian fighter, 267
on Native Americans, 249–250, 262, 267, 270, 271m, 271–272
popular support for, 262
as president
and Bank of United States, 272
federal power and, 269–273
Native Americans and, 271m, 271–272
policies of, 241
and Tariff of Abominations, 271–272
rise to power, 268–269
and spoils system, 269
War of 1812 and, 249–250, 251, 252
Jackson, Graham, 551i
Jackson, Helen Hunt, 398
Jackson, Jesse, 648
Jackson, Thomas "Stonewall," 338, 339, 343i, 349, 354
James, Duke of York, 68, 69
James, Henry, 417
James, Mollie, 682
James, William, 428
James Fort, 67, 93, 93m
James I, King of England, 41–42, 43, 51
James II, King of England, 70, 73–74
James River and Kanawha Canal, 264m
Jamestown colony, 3, 4, 31, 42–44, 51–52, 52m

Japan
  early efforts to reach, 15–16, 16m
  early isolationism of, 33
  European contact, 18, 32–33
  19th century
    Boxer Rebellion and, 440
    immigration from, 389–390
    trade, 323
    war with China (1894-1895), 439
  20th century
    pre World War II
      Five-Power Treaty, 487–488
      immigration from, 451m, 451–452, 492
      imperialism of, 468, 532–533, 534
    World War II and
      brutality of, 545
      Pearl Harbor attack, 506, 534, 535i
      surrender, 547
      U.S. atomic bombing of, 507, 547
    post-World War II
      economy of, 570, 620
      political vacuum left by, 565, 567
      reconstruction, 558
      U.S. occupation, 558
  as trading partner, 685f
Japanese American Citizen League, 564
Japanese Americans
  World War II and
    internment of, 507, 535–536, 536m, 537i
    in U.S. Army, 530, 535–536, 537i, 547
  post-World War II
    employment, 553i
    family life of, 577
Jay, John
  anti-slavery activities, 197
  Jay Treaty and, 220–221
  Treaty of Paris and, 188i
Jay Treaty (1795), 221–222
Jazz
  origins of, 258, 458, 486
Jazz Age, 490, 493, 495, 499, 201, 504
Jefferson, Lisa, 677
Jefferson, Thomas
  Alien and Sedition Acts and, 222, 235
  Bill of Rights and, 213
  character of, 235–236
  cultural interests of, 197
  Declaration of Independence and, 162, 169
  and election of 1796, 222t
  and election of 1800, 235, 235t
  and election of 1804, 244, 244t
  and election of 1808, 245
  on government role, 236
  inaugural address, first, 237
  on Intolerable Acts, 156
  Lewis and Clark Expedition and, 242–243
  Louisiana Purchase and, 237, 242–243
  on Native Americans, 235–236
  as president, 235, 236–237, 242–243
    economic policies, 219
    embargo of, 1807, 245
  Sally Hemings and, 235
  on slavery, 235–236, 262
  and two-party system, 218
  as vice president, 221
  Virginia constitution and, 178
  on Washington, 195
  western lands and, 143, 199–200
Jefferson Airplane, 608
Jenney, William LeBaron, 392
Jeremiah, Thomas, 167, 169
Jerome, Chauncey, 253
Jesuits
  in Chesapeake region, 26–27

Counter-Reformation and, 24, 38
expulsion from Spanish territory, 141
in French Canada, 38–39
in Southwest, 63m
Jeter, Mildred, 599
Jews. See also Antisemitism; Israel
  15th century, in Spain, 15
  17th-18th century, immigration by, 41, 125–126
  19th century
    immigration by, 389, 426
    in South, 427
  20th century
    film industry and, 456, 486
    immigration by, 446, 452, 492
    in World War II
      Holocaust, 530–531, 541, 547, 564
      immigration by, 541
      in Nazi Germany, 532
      U.S. antisemitism and, 541
Jiang Jieshi (Chiang Kai-shek), 565
Jim Crow system. See also Segregation
  dismantling of, 580–583
  in South, 407–408
  Supreme Court on, 426
  in West, 408–409
Johnson, Andrew
  background of, 359
  and election of 1864, 351–352, 352t
  impeachment of, 367
  political career of, 358–359
  Reconstruction policy, 358, 359–361, 362i, 365m
Johnson, Earvin "Magic," 648i
Johnson, Kathryn M., 478
Johnson, Lady Bird, 596, 596i
Johnson, Lyndon B.
  African American support for, 605
  antiwar protests and, 605
  assumption of presidency, 593, 596i
  character and background, 596–597
  civil rights and, 597–598
  and election of 1960, 589t
  and election of 1964, 597, 597t
  and election of 1968, 603–604
  environmentalism, 599
  Great Society and, 573, 595, 597–599
  health care and, 598
  Vietnam War and, 573, 595–596, 599–600, 603–604, 605
  and War on Poverty, 596
  in World War II, 539i
Johnson, Sir William, 133, 133m
Johnson, Thomas, 134i
Johnson-Reid Act (1924), 491, 492
Johnston, Joseph, 339
Joliet, Louis, 57–58, 58m
Jones, John Paul, 182
Jones, Paula, 668
Jordan, Michael, 648i
Jordan, Vernon, 668
Joseph, Chief, 357
Journalism, early 20th century, 458
Juarez, Benito, 345
Judicial activism, Warren Court and, 599
Judiciary Act (1789), 217
Judiciary Act (1801), 236
The Jungle (Sinclair), 458
Justice Department, 604

K

Kachina dances, 35, 64
Kaiser, Henry, 536
Kansas
  19th century
    black migration to, 409
    in Civil War, 350
    Lecompton Constitution, 327–328

population of, 368
slavery conflict in, 326–327
20th century, education in, 499
Kansas-Nebraska Act (1854), 323, 324m
Kansas Pacific Railroad, 369i
Kansas Territory, 324m
Kaskaskia, Illinois, 55, 58m, 61, 113, 114m
Kaskaskia Indians, 274, 288m
Kaskaskia mission, 60
Kearny, Stephen Watts, 305
Keller, Helen, 459
Kellogg, Noah S., 384
Kelly, Oliver H., 375–376
Kennan, George, 556, 567
Kennedy, Jacqueline Bouvier, 590, 596i
Kennedy, John F.
  assassination of, 593
  background and early career, 589
  and Berlin Wall, 592
  civil rights movement and, 591, 593
  and Cuba
    Bay of Pigs invasion (1961), 591–592
    Cuban Missile Crisis, 592
  on discrimination against women, 592
  domestic policy, 591
  and election of 1960, 589t, 590
  foreign policy, 591–592
  inaugural address, 589
  Vietnam War and, 591
  in World War II, 539i
Kennedy, Joseph, 589
Kennedy, Joseph P., Jr., 589
Kennedy, Robert, 604, 611
Kent State shootings, 613
Kentucky
  18th century
    Alien and Sedition Acts and, 222
    slave population, 228
  in Civil War, 337
Kentucky Federation of Women's Clubs, 434
Kenya, bombing of U.S. embassy in, 670
Kerouac, Jack, 588
Kerry, John
  in 2004 election, 681, 681t
Kesey, Ken, 625
Kettle Hill, 438m, 439
Key, Elizabeth, 84–85, 86–87
Key, Francis Scott, 249, 249i
Key, Thomas, 84–85,
Khomeini, Ruhollah, 637i, 637–638
Khrushchev, Nikita, 584, 592
Kickapoo Indians, 227, 274, 279, 288m
Kim Il-Sung, 568
Kim Lai, 602i
King, Charles Bird, 274i, 305i
King, Martin Luther, Jr., 606i
  assassination of, 611
  Birmingham civil rights march (1963), 593
  birthday holiday for, 647
  "I Have a Dream" speech, 593
  March on Washington, 582m 593
  Montgomery bus boycott, 582
  radicalization of, 611
  Vietnam, 606
King, Rodney, 660, 663
King, Rufus, 244, 251t, 263
King Dick, 247i
King George's War, 131
King Philip, 69–71
King Philip's War. See Metacom's War
King William's War, 59, 75–77
King's Mountain, Battle of, 185m, 186
Kinji Ushijima, 390–391
Kino, Eusebio, 63, 63m, 65
Kinsey, Alfred, 561
Kinsey Reports (1948,1953), 561

Kiowas
 in Civil War, 341
 culture, 312
 removal of, 288m
 war with whites, 408
Kissinger, Henry, 612, 616–617, 619, 622
Kivas, 11
Knights of Labor
 activism of, 376, 403–404, 431
 decline of, 414–415, 415–416
 minorities and, 380, 405, 415
Know-Nothing party
 and election of 1856, 325, 325t
 and election of 1860, 330
 platform of, 296, 323
Knox, Henry, 168, 175m, 196, 207
Knoxville, Tennessee, 196
Kocherthal, Joshua von, 118
Korea
 20th century, immigration from, 451m
 Japanese annexation of, 468
Korean Air Lines jet, Soviet downing of, 640, 650
Korean War, 567i, 566–569, 569m
 casualties in, 569
 as Cold War outbreak, 550
 cultural impact of, 560
 McCarthyism and, 562, 563
 political impact of, 568–569
Koresh, David, 664
Kosciusko, Thaddeus, 180
Kosovo, ethnic conflict in, 670, 671m
Kroger grocery stores, 388
Ku Klux Klan
 in 20th century, 604
 founding of, 362–363
 violence by, 367
Ku Klux Klan Act (1871), 367
Kublai Khan, 13
Kuwait, Iraqi invasion of, 651–652

L

La Follette, Robert M., 488, 488t
La Purisima Concepción mission, 274
La Salle, René-Robert Cavelier, Sieur de, 58, 58m, 59, 59i, 60
Labor supply, late 19th century, 389–391
LaCole Mill, Battle of, 248m
Ladies Magazine, 262, 280
Lafayette, Marquis de, 187, 187i
LaFlesche, Susan, 418i
Laguna Indians, 636
Laissez-faire economics
 19th century, 397–398
 early 20th century, 472–473
Lake Mohonk conferences, 419
Lancaster Turnpike, 253
Land Act of 1820, 264
Land management
 19th century, 424–425
 20th century, 462, 462i
Land Ordinance of 1785, 201–202
Land ownership, 19th century, as conflict source, 312–313
Land redistribution, post-Civil War, 362i, 362–363
Land speculators, western frontier and, 130, 143, 199, 201, 226, 226m, 229, 229m
Land warrants, post-War of 1812, 246m
Landon, Alfred, 525t
Landsmark, Theodore, 621i
Lane, Ralph, 28
Lange, Dorothea, 513, 518i
Lansing, John, 208
Lansing, Robert, 476, 482
Laos, Vietnam War and, 603m, 613
Las Casas, Bartholomé de, 18, 27
Las Vegas
 nuclear testing near, 559i, 560, 636
Lasselle, Marie-Thérèse, 202i
Lassen Volcanic National Park, 474
The Last of the Mohicans (Cooper), 132
Lateen sail, 14, 14i, 16m
Latimer, George, 287
Latin America, 20th century
 immigration from, 647
 U.S. in, 468, 469m, 585
 U.S. relations, 626
Latinos. *See also* Hispanics; Mexican Americans
 immigration by, 692
 party affiliation, 527
 political power of, 663
 population, 663
 women, activism of, 629
Latvia, creation of, 481m
Laud, William, 46
Laurens, Henry, 146, 165, 188i
Law enforcement, Prohibition and, 488, 489, 490i
Lawrence, Kansas, Confederate destruction of, 350
Lawrence v. Texas, 679
Lawson, John, 78, 79m
Lazarus, Emma, 389
Le Sueur, Pierre-Charles, 55
League of Nations, 480, 481–482
League of United Latin American Citizens (LULAC), 554, 580
League of Women Voters, 490
Leaves of Grass (Whitman), 318
Lecompton Constitution, 326–327
Lee, Charles, 180
Lee, Richard Henry, 212
Lee, Robert E., 343i
 and Brown's Harpers Ferry attack, 329–330
 in Civil War, 349, 353–354
 and Cortina's War, 313
 on secession, 336
Legal counsel, right to, 599
Leiber, Jerry, 588
Leisler, Jacob, 74
Leisler's Rebellion, 74
Lemlich, Clara, 446
Lend-Lease program, 533, 552
Lenin, Vladimir, 480, 480i
Lenni-Lanape. *See* Delaware Indians
Let There Be Light (film), 538
"Letters from a Farmer in Pennsylvania" (Dickinson), 152
Letters from an American Farmer (Crèvecoeur), 197
Levine, William, 525t
Levittown, 560
Lewinsky, Monica, 668
Lewis, John, 583
Lewis, John L., 526
Lewis, Meriwether, 242i, 242–243, 243m
Lewis, Sinclair, 500–501
Lewis and Clark Expedition, 242–243, 243m, 244i
Lexington, Battle of, 157m, 158i, 159
Liberalism
 late 20th century, culture wars and, 634–635
 corporate, 605
Liberation movements. *See also* Women's liberation movement
 backlash against, late 20th century, 610–611
 ethnic, in 1960s, 608–609
 gay rights movement, 573, 595, 609, 646, 648, 661, 662, 666
The Liberator, 293
Liberty (ship), 153, 154
Liberty party, 321, 324
 and election of 1840, 295t
 and election of 1844, 302, 302t
Libya, U.S. conflict with, 650
Licensing of professionals, introduction of, 299
Life expectancy, 20th century
 of Native Americans, 543
Light bulb, invention of, 385, 391
Liliuokalani, Queen, 439
Lincoln, Abraham, 329i
 assassination of, 354
 background of, 325
 Douglas debates, 328–329
 and election of 1856, 325, 325t
 and election of 1860, 330, 330t, 335
 and election of 1864, 351–352, 352t
 and Emancipation Proclamation, 345
 and fall of Richmond, 352–353
 on free blacks, fate of, 345
 Gettysburg Address of, 350
 on goals of Civil War, 341
 inaugural address, first, 336
 military experience of, 352
 political support for, 335
 on readmission of Confederate states, 358, 365m
 Reconstruction policy, 358
 on slavery, 328–329
 strategic sense of, 352
 and *Trent* affair, 345
 troops' loyalty to, 352
 and Union Army command, 349
 writ of habeas corpus and, 342
Lindbergh, Charles, 487, 533
Ling Sing, 405–406
Ling Sing v. *Washburn* (California, 1862), 406
Linganfield, Lorimer, 486
Linganfield, Marsha, 486
Literature and art
 early 19th century, 280–281
 mid 19th century, 300, 317–318
 late 19th century, 430
 in 1900s, 457i, 457–458
 in 1920s, 501
 in 1960s and 1970s, 632i
Lithuania, creation of, 481m
Little, Keith, 530
Little Richard, 554
Little Rock, Arkansas, school desegregation in, 581
Little Turtle, 227
Livingston, Robert, 68, 237
Lloyd George, David, 482
Local government, late 19th century
 corruption in, 376–377, 377i, 394
 growth of, 393–394
Locke, John, 69, 78, 169
Lodge, Henry Cabot, 440–441, 482
"Log College," 128
Logan, Greenbury, 302
Logging
 19th century, 384, 424
Lôme, Dupuy de, 439
London fire (1666), 67, 87–88
Lone Star Republic, 301
The Lonely Crowd (Reisman), 588
Long, Huey P., 521, 522
Long Island
 Battle of, 172
 settlement of, 41
Long Walk, 344
Looking Backward (Bellamy), 414
Looking Out for Number One (Ringer), 632
Lookout Mountain, Battle of, 350
Lord & Taylor department store, 396
Lorenzana, Apolonaria, 278
Los Alamos, New Mexico, 636

INDEX

Los Angeles
  in 1960s, black riots in, 605
  founding of, 141
  immigration to, 475
  Mexican-American population, 475
  racial unrest in, 543, 635, 660, 660i
  urban renewal in, 578
Lost Batallion (World War II), 535
Lost Colony at Roanoke Island, 27–28
Louis XIV, King of France, 56, 57, 57i
  death of, 61
  and Edict of Nantes, 57, 73, 119
  reign of, 56–57
  and War of Spanish Succession, 60
Louis XVI, King of France, 218
Louisburg, English assault on, 131, 133m
Louisiana. *See also* New Orleans
  establishment of, 55–56, 59–61
  18th century
    Cajuns, origins of, 119
    Louisiana Purchase, 162, 237, 246m
    slavery in, 100
    struggle over, 196–198
    trade, 113–114
  19th century
    cotton plantations in, 265i
    economy of, 265
    readmission to Union, 365m, 367
    slave revolts, 258
  20th century, politics in, 522
Louisiana Purchase, 162, 237, 246m
Louisiana Territory
  exploration of, 242–243, 243m
  French ceding to Spain of, 134
  Spanish administration of, 138–139
Louisville and Portland Canal, 264m
Love Canal, 624
Lovejoy, Elijah P., 293–294
Loving, Richard, 599
Loving v. *Virginia* (1967), 599
Lowell mill girls, 278
Loyal Nine, 145–146
Loyalists
  in American Revolution, 137
  compensation for seized property, 188
Loyola, Ignatius, 24
Ludlow massacre, 471, 471i
Luks, George, 457i
LULAC. *See* League of United Latin American Citizens
Lumumba, Patrice, 585, 625
Lunas, 436
Lundy's Lane, Battle of, 248m
Lusitania (ship), 476
Luther, Martin, 23
Lyceums, 298
Lynchings
  late 19th century, 408, 426
  early 20th century, 460, 470, 483
  mid-20th century, 512, 522, 553, 581
  in 1990s, 661
Lyon, Matthew, 222

M

MacArthur, Douglas
  Bonus March and, 515
  in Korea, 569
  in occupied Japan, 558
  in Philippines, 545
Machine politics, 394
Macy's department store, 396
USS Maddox, 601
Madison, James
  Alien and Sedition Acts and, 235
  Bill of Rights and, 213
  and Constitutional Convention, 207–208
  and election of 1808, 245, 245t
  The Federalist and, 211
  War of 1812 and, 247
Magellan, Ferdinand, 16m–17m, 19
Magic code, 530
Magnum, W. P., 292t
Mahan, Alfred Thayer, 436
Mahicans, 39m
Mail order catalogs, 383, 396
Maine, statehood of, 263, 263m
Maize, cultivation of
  in prehistory, 7–8, 11, 20
  in 17th century, 64
Malaria, 17, 37, 345
Malaysia
  as trading partner, 685f
Malcolm X, 604, 604i
Malcontents, 106
La Malinche, 19
Mallet, Paul, 129, 130
Mallet, Pierre, 129, 130
The Man That Nobody Knows (Barton), 500
Mandans, 319
Mandate system, 482
Mandela, Nelson, 651
Manhattan Island, purchase of, 40
Manhattan Project, 547
Mankiller, Wilma, 252i
Manifest destiny, 300–301, 440
Mann, Horace, 297–298
Mann Act (1910), 459
Manufacturing. *See* Industry
Manumission
  18th century, 225
  19th century, 274
  restrictions on, 101–102
  Society for the Promotion of the Manumission of Slaves, 197
Mao Zedong, 565, 566i, 615i, 617
Maquiladora, 682, 683
Maquiladoras, 620
Marbury v. *Madison* (1803), 236
March on Washington (1963), 582m, 593
Marina, Doña, 19
Marine Corps, establishment of, 222
Marion, Francis, 185
Marketing. *See* Advertising
Marquette, Jacques, 58, 58m
Marriage
  19th century
    experimental forms of, 300
    of freed slaves, 362–363
    late, status of, 434
  20th century, 457, 486, 561, 575, 576f
    in 1950s, 588
    in 1970s, 631
    communism and, 482
    immigrant picture brides, 451–452, 452i
    interracial, 599
    same-sex, 661, 662
    in World War II, 540
  interracial, 91, 599
Married Women's Property Law (Mississippi, 1839), 300
Marshall, George C., 557, 558
Marshall, John, 222, 236, 270–271
Marshall, Thurgood, 580
Marshall Fields department store, 388, 396
Marshall Plan, 557
Marti, José, 437
Martin, Joseph Plumb, 194
Martin, Luther, 212
Martinique, 134, 135
Maryland
  17th century
    slave population, 90, 97–98
    slavery in, 88
  18th century
    Constitutional ratification by, 213
    slave population, 97–98, 98m
    tobacco economy in, 122–123, 122m
  19th century
    in Civil War, 337
    economy of, 265
    McCulloch v. *Maryland* (1819), 270
Masculinity, late 20th century, 631–632
Maslov-Bering, Aleksandr, 140i
Mason, Biddy, 310
Mason, George, 178, 210, 212
Mason, James, 346
Mass marketing, rise of, 384, 385
Mass production, development of, 384, 455–456
Massachusetts
  18th century
    Constitution ratification, 212i, 213
    post-Revolution unrest in, 204–206
    Provincial Congress, 156, 158
    slave population, 98m
    state constitution of, 178, 207
    tax resistance in, 145–146, 152
    war debt and, 204
    western land claims, 200, 229m
  19th century
    education in, 298
    textile industry in, 278
  early 20th century, manufacturing in, 430m
Massachusetts Bay colony
  chartering of, 46
  dissenters in, 48–49
  establishment of, 74
  slave trade and, 86
Massachusetts Bay Company, 45–49, 52
Massachusetts Charter (1691), British modification of, 156
Massachusetts Government Act (1774), 156
Massachusetts Institute of Technology (MIT), 384
Massachusetts Regulation, 206–207
Massasoit, 31, 45, 70
Materialism, critiques of, 19th century, 318
Mather, Cotton, 71, 76, 102
USS Mayaguez, 619
Mayans, 8, 9m
Mayflower (ship), 31i, 31–32, 44
Mayflower Compact, 31, 44
Mayhew, Jonathan, 127
McAdoo, William G., 488
McCain, John
  on campaign financing, 685
McCarran-Walter Act (1952), 564
McCarthy, Eugene, 603–604
McCarthy, Joseph, 551, 563, 569
McCarthyism, 562–563
McCartney, Bill, 660
McClellan, George, 344, 349, 352, 352t
McCord, Louisa, 319i, 326
McCormick, Cyrus, 314
McCulloch v. *Maryland* (1819), 270
McDonald's, 689, 690
McDonough, Thomas, 249
McGillivray, Alexander, 199
McGovern, George S., 618t
McGuffey, William H., 297
McGuffey's Reader, 297
McJunkin, George, 4, 4i
McKinley, William
  assassination of, 461
  and election of 1896, 432, 432t
  and election of 1900, 441, 461, 461t
  Spanish-American War and, 437–438
  tariffs and, 429
McKinley Tariff (1890), 429, 437
McNary-Haugen bills (1926, 1928), 499
McVeigh, Timothy, 664
Me decade, 616
Meade, George G., 349

Measles
- 15th-16th century, 3, 17
- 17th century, 36
- 19th century, 291

Meat Inspection Act (1906), 458

Media. *See also* Printing and publishing; Television
- and election of 2000, 673
- Gulf War and, 653
- presidents' use of, 515–517
- Reagan and, 638
- Roosevelt (F.D.) and, 515, 517–518, 527
- late 20th century mergers in, 657

Medicaid
- abortion and, 631
- introduction of, 598

Medicare
- in 1980s, 641
- introduction of, 598

Medicine. *See* Health and health care

Medicine Lodge Creek Treaty (1867), 368

Melting pot, 462

Melville, Herman, 317–318

Men, feminism and, 631–632

Mendez v. *Westminster* (1946), 554

Menéndez de Avilés, Pedro, 26

Mennonites, 127

Menominees, 227

Mercantilism, 57

Mercer, Erminia Pablita Ruiz, 511–512

Mercer, Hugh, 173i

Mercer, William, 173i

Meredith, James, 582m

Merrimack (ship), 346

Mesa Verde, 9m, 10, 11

Mesoamerica
- agriculture in, 7–8
- cultures of, 8, 9m, 9–10
- definition of, 7

Mesoamerican calendar, 8–9

Messier, Marguerite, 55–56, 60

Mestizos, in Southwest, 63

Metacom, 70–71

Metacom's War, 70–71, 75

Métis, 291

Mexica. *See* Aztecs

Mexican-American War, 302–306, 303m, 306i

Mexican Americans
- 19th century
  - employment, 371
  - rights of, 311, 313
  - stereotypes of, 317
- 20th century
  - civil rights activism, 554, 580
  - deportation of, 512
  - discrimination against, 554
  - employment, 512
  - family life, 577
  - first mayor of major city, 648
  - first rock 'n' roll star, 588
  - hostility toward, 543
  - unions and, 564i, 608

Mexican Cession, 310–311, 313m

Mexicas. *See* Aztecs

Mexico
- 19th century
  - American migration to, 265–266
  - border violence, 426
  - Mexican-American War, 302–306, 303m, 306i
  - northern frontier, 266m
  - Protestant view of Catholics in, 296, 304–305
  - and Texas annexation, 302
  - and Texas independence, 301–302
  - and U.S.-Mexican War, 302–306, 303m, 306i
- 20th century
  - immigration from, 445, 450, 468–469, 474, 492, 492f, 537, 647–648
  - industry flight to, 620
  - NAFTA and, 668–669
  - nationalist revolution in, 445, 468
  - Revolution of 1911, 450, 468–470
  - U.S. intervention in, 469m, 469–470
  - World War I and, 476
- *maquiladora*, 682, 683
- as trading partner, 685f

Miami and Erie Canal, 264m

Miami Indians. *See also* Ohio Confederacy
- home region of, 227
- Oklahoma Territory and, 288m
- resistance by, 227
- Revolutionary War and, 184

Michigan Carlson Works, 387i

Micmac Indians, 21

Microsoft Corp., 657

Middle class
- 19th century
  - education and, 428
  - growth of, 373, 383, 399, 401
  - values of, 281
- 20th century
  - African Americans and, 579, 658
  - decline of, 616, 644–645

Middle colonies, economy, 18th century, 122m, 123, 124–125

Middle East
- 9/11 as pretext for intervention in, 680

Middle East, 20th century
- British withdrawal from, 603
- instability in, 637–638
- trouble spots in, 639m
- U.S. policy in, 635, 649, 651–652, 669

Middle Passage, 84i, 91, 94–95, 96m

Middlesex Canal, 264m

Midnight judges (1801), 236

Midvale Steel Plant, 391

Midway Island, Battle of, 545, 546m

Midwest
- 19th century
  - economy, 313–314
  - ethnic groups in, 313–314
  - rural unrest in, 412–413
  - settlement of, 283–284, 367
- 20th century, migration to, 448m, 449, 474, 474i

Migration(s). *See also* Immigration; *specific regions and groups*
- 19th century, 283–292
  - to cities, 287, 392, 407
  - and education standardization, 297–298
  - westward, 252–253
- 1870-1930, 501m
- 20th century
  - early, 501m, 501–502
  - in 1930s, 513, 518i
  - in World War II, 536–537
  - to cities, 444, 448, 449i
  - to Midwest, 448m, 449, 474, 474i

Military budget
- in 1950s, 568, 583–584
- in 1960s, 596
- in 1980s, 641
- in 1990s, 657, 667

Military districts, post-Civil War, 365m

Militias, state, tensions in, 179–180

Milliken v. *Bradley* (1974), 613

Million Man March, 660

Mineral Act (1866), 371

Minik, 437i

Minimum wage
- under Eisenhower, 583
- under Kennedy, 591

Mining
- late 19th century, 371, 384, 387
- Chinese and, 405i
- environmental impact of, 386
- hazards of, 413i

Mining Act of 1872, 686

Mining operations, 686

Minkins, Shadrach, 326

Minnesota, statehood, 329

Minnesota territory, 324m

Minorities. *See also specific groups*
- American Revolution and, 146, 146i, 159, 163
- 19th century
  - advertising and, 384
  - employment, 316–317, 324, 434i
  - Populist party and, 423
  - resistance to white dominance, 403–411
  - rights of, 313, 371, 405–406
  - role and status of, 311
  - unions and, 415
- 20th century
  - education and, 608
  - employment, 511, 512, 539, 658
  - Great Depression and, 508–509, 512
  - motion picture industry and, 527
  - New Deal and, 524, 527, 528
  - resentment against, 621
  - as sports celebrities, 527–528
  - suffrage movement and, 459–460
  - unions and, 521, 527, 608
  - World War II and, 530–531
  - employment, 539
  - GI Bill, 575
  - unions and, 539
- 2000 election and, 671–673

Minuit, Peter, 40

Minutemen, 156, 159

Miranda rights, 599

Miranda v. *Arizona* (1964), 599

Mission homes, late 19th century, 432

Mission San Diego, 278

Mission San Francisco de la Espada, 110i

Missionary Ridge, Battle of, 350

Missions, Catholic
- 17th century, 35–36
- 18th century, 58m, 62–64, 63m, 66, 141, 142m, 191

Mississippi
- 19th century
  - Black Codes, 360, 426
  - economy of, 265
  - Married Women's Property Law, 300
  - readmission to Union, 365m, 367
- 20th century, voting rights in, 598

Mississippi Freedom Democratic Party, 604

Mississippi River Commission, 496

Mississippi River/Valley
- Native American cultures, 500-1500, 8–9, 9m, 11–12, 12i
- 17th century, French colonization and exploration, 55–56, 57–58, 58m, 59–60, 61
- 18th century, struggle for control of, 196–201, 222
- 19th century
  - in Civil War, 342
  - cotton economy and, 265i
  - culture of, 256
  - economy of, 256
  - Great Flood of 1927, 445, 496–497, 497m
  - levee construction on, 496

Missouri
- in Civil War, 336, 337
- statehood of, 262, 263, 263m, 264

Missouri Compromise (1820), 240, 263, 263m, 264, 323, 324

MIT. *See* Massachusetts Institute of Technology
Mitchell, George, 669
Mitchell, John (UMW president), 461
Mittelberger, Gottlieb, 117
Mobile, Alabama
    18th century, in Revolutionary War, 183m, 184
    colony at, 55–56
Moche people, 9m
Moctezuma, 19
Model T Ford, 502
Mogollons, 9m, 10
Mohawks. *See also* Iroquois Confederacy
    Metacom's War and, 70
    Revolutionary War and, 182, 216
    war with whites, 120, 132, 182, 216
Mohegans, 50
Molano, Elvira, 564i
Mondale, Walter, 641t, 642
Monetary policy
    post-Revolution, 203–206, 206f, 219
    late 19th century, 376, 430–431, 431, 432
    early 20th century, 473, 504
    in 1970s, 620
    in 1980s, 641–642
Monmouth, Battle of, 175m, 180, 181
Monroe, James
    and Constitutional Convention, 222
    and election of 1816, 251, 251t
    and election of 1820, 267, 267t
    Indian policy, 267
    Louisiana Purchase and, 237
    on Native Americans, 251
    policies, 251
    on territorial government, 201
Monroe, Marilyn, 539
Monroe Doctrine, 240–241, 267–268, 323, 471
    in late 19th century, 436–437
    Roosevelt Corollary to, 463
Montana, statehood for, 384
Montcalm, Marquis de, 132, 134, 133m
Monte Verde, Chile, archaeological sites, 6, 7, 11, 29
Montgomery, Richard, 167, 168, 175m
Montgomery bus boycott, 581, 582, 582m
Montgomery Ward catalog, 396
Montreal
    American seizure of, 168
    British seizure of, 134, 142
    establishment of, 38
    in War of 1812, 248
Moon, U.S. landing on, 613
Moore, James, 66
Moors. *See* Islam
Moral Majority, 634, 645
Moravians, 82, 123, 127, 135, 183
Moreno, Luisa, 539
Morgan, Daniel, 186, 189
Morgan, John Pierpont, 382, 388, 400, 463, 657
Morgan v. Virginia (1946), 554
Mormon Corridor, 392
Mormon Tabernacle, 391
Mormon Trail, 286m
Mormons, 279, 289, 290, 299, 300, 397, 689
Moroni, 279
Morrill Act (1862), 343
Morris, Gouverneur, 211
Morris, Robert, 203, 208, 211
Morrow, E. Frederick, 581
Morse, Jedidiah, 197
Morse, Samuel F. B., 296
Mosby, John Singleton, 350
Moses, Robert Parris, 595, 605
Moslems. *See* Islam
Mothers' Magazine, 290, 291

Motion picture camera, invention of, 456
Motion picture industry. *See also* Hollywood
    early 20th century, 423, 456, 465, 527
    in 1950s, 548, 588, 588i
    Cold War and, 527, 588
    science fiction films, 559, 575
    in World War II, 464, 527
Mott, Lucretia, 300, 320
Mottrom, John, 84–85
Mound-building societies, 8, 11, 12i
Moundville, 2, 9m, 11, 29
Mount, Julia Luna, 512
Mount Holyoke College, 298
Mount McKinley, 628i
Mount Ranier National Park, 425
Mourning wars, 38
"The Movement," 595, 604, 608, 614, 629, 690
Mozambique, and slave trade, 93m, 96m–97m
Ms. (title), 628
Muckraking, 458
Mugwumps, 398
Muhammad (prophet), 13
Muir, John, 372, 424–425, 462
Mulattos
    legal status of, 17th century, 84–85
    in Southwest, 63
Muller v. Oregon (1908), 444, 459
Mumbet, 210i
Munich agreement (1938), 532
Murphy, Frank, 526
Murrieta, Joaquin, 313
Muscovy Company, 27
Music
    early 20th century, 458
    in 1920s, 493
    African Americans and, 486, 493
    blues, 493
    jazz, 458, 493, 559
    rock 'n' roll, 554, 559, 588, 606, 686, 687i
Muslims. *See* Islam
Mussolini, Benito, 522, 532, 545
My Lai massacre, 573, 602
Myer, Dillon S., 564

N

NAACP. *See* National Association for the Advancement of Colored People
NACW. *See* National Association of Colored Women
Nader, Ralph, 672t, 674
    in 2004 presidential election, 681t
NAFTA. *See* North American Free Trade Agreement
Nagasaki, atomic bombing of, 507, 548
Napoleon, 62, 236, 237, 244, 248
Narragansett Indians, 48, 50, 71, 78
Narváez, Pánfilo, 21, 26m
NASA. *See* National Aeronautics and Space Administration
Nash, Francis, 196
Nashville, Tennessee, 327m, 353m, 427, 519m, 582m
Nasser, Gamal Abdul, 585
Nast, Thomas, 366, 377i
Natchez, Louisiana, 113
Natchez Indians, 100
Natchitoches, Louisiana, 58m, 61, 114
The Nation, 429, 513
Nation of Islam. *See* Black Muslims
Nation state, modern, emergence of, 24
National Aeronautics and Space Administration (NASA), 575, 584
National American Woman Suffrage Association (NAWSA), 433

National Association for the Advancement of Colored People (NAACP)
    anti-lynching campaign, 470
    anti-segregation activism, 543, 554, 580, 582
    establishment of, 461
    Red Scare and, 564
National Association of Colored Women (NACW), 433
National Baseball League, 395
National Basketball Association (NBA), 648i, 688
National Broadcasting Company (NBC), 495
National Child Labor Committee, 459i
National culture, development of, 604
National debt
    in 1990s, 666
    federal assumption of, 218
The National Era, 326
National Farmers' Alliance, 380
National Grange of the Patrons of Husbandry. *See* The Grange
National Industrial Recovery Act (1933) [NIRA], 520, 523t
National Labor Relations Act (1935), 522, 523t
National Labor Union (NLU), 309, 376, 403
National Liberation Front (Viet Cong; NLF), 591, 600, 573, 619
National Organization for Women (NOW), 572, 608
National Park Service, 473
National park system, 372, 424–425, 462, 462i, 474
National Recovery Administration (NRA), 520, 523
National Republican party
    and election of 1828, 269t, 270
    and election of 1832, 272t, 274
National Rifle Association, 665
National Road, 240, 241, 254, 264
National sacrifice areas, 636
National security, post-World War II redefinition of, 555
National Security Act (1947, 1949), 566
National Security Council (NSC)
    document 68 (NCS-68), 567
    Iran-Contra scandal and, 649–650
    role of, 567
National security state, establishment of, 565, 566
National Socialist (Nazi) party
    eugenics program, 498
    Nuremberg trials for, 558
    rise to power, 532
    sports and, 527–528
    in World War II, Holocaust death camps, 541
National Trades Union (NTU), 282, 292
National Wildlife Federation, 622
National Woman Suffrage Association (NWSA), 374
National Women's Party (NWP), 471
Native American women
    in 16th century, 28i
    first physician, 418i
    in Navajo culture, 63, 63i
    role and status of, 63, 63i, 115, 234, 243, 252, 278
    in World War II, 543
Native Americans. *See also specific tribes*
    prehistory, 2–14
        Paleo-Indian era, 6
        Archaic era, 6–8
        500-1500, 8–12, 9m
        European view of, 4–5
        origins of, 2–6
    15th and 16th century

Christianity and, 19, 26
culture, 28i
disease, 3, 17, 19
early contact with Europeans, 15–23
European conquest of, 17–28
European cruelty toward, 18, 27, 28, 33
17th century
   aid to European settlers, 3
   assimilation of, 50–51, 69
   Christianity and, 33–36, 36i, 38–39, 50–51, 62
   culture, 64–65
   disease, 31–32, 36–37, 38–39, 48, 50, 60, 62, 64, 70, 87
   displacement of, 50–51
   education of, 36
   enslavement of, 33, 35, 61, 65, 72, 87
   European cruelty toward, 33, 50, 51
   land rights of, 49, 69
   and Metacom's War, 70–71, 75
   religion, 35–36
   revolts, 36i, 62, 63m, 64–65
   settlers' view of, 76
   trade, 36i, 37–39, 55, 64–65. *See also* Fur trade
   uprisings, 37, 63, 63m
   wars with whites, 49–51, 69–71
   women in, 63, 63i
18th century
   American Revolution and, 163, 164, 182–184, 183m, 188, 216–217
   assimilation of, 227–229
   and Christianity, 125, 129, 143
   culture, 82, 112i, 112–115
   dependent status of, 199–200
   disease, 55–56, 143, 191i, 191–192, 192m
   displacement of, 163, 182, 199–200, 227, 290
   firearms and, 113–115, 114m
   Jefferson on, 235–236
   Proclamation Line of 1763, 143, 182
   removals, 216
   resistance, 78, 138, 141, 199, 220, 227, 229m
   Seven Years' War and, 137, 142–143
   in Southeast, 198m
   trade, 112–115, 114m, 130, 143. *See also* Fur trade
   treaties, 110–111
   uprisings, 138, 141, 143, 147m
   war hawks on, 245
   wars with whites, 226m, 227
   white views of, 142
   women, 115, 234
19th century
   alcohol and, 246, 246i, 275
   allotment of land to, 398
   assimilation of, 251–252, 274–275, 357, 417–418, 422i, 422–423
   in California, 311, 370–371
   and Christianity, 275, 418, 422
   in Civil War
      alliances, 339–341
      internment of, 352
      Union brutality toward, 343, 351, 351i
   culture, 243, 312, 319, 369, 400, 409–411
   discrimination against, 405
   disease, 291
   education, 418, 418i, 422, 422i, 427
   land losses, 410m
   land rights of, 272, 398
   railroad and, 368–369, 381
   religion, 409–411
   removals, 241, 288m, 288–289, 424
   reservation system, 368, 417, 423, 425m
   resistance by, 243–244, 246, 246i, 279, 289, 316, 357, 381, 409–411
   rights of, 417
   roles and status of, 275
   Social Darwinism and, 400
   subduing of, 410–411
   Tocqueville on, 274
   uprisings, 274–275
   U.S. policy on, 398, 417–418
   wars with whites, 367–369
   white views on, 275, 395
   women, 243, 278
20th century
   activism, 423, 661
   assimilation of, 564–565
   casinos and, 657, 657i
   civil rights activism of, 554
   discrimination against, 554
   federal policy on, 520, 520i, 564–565
   life expectancy, 543
   militancy of, 608–609
   nuclear contamination and, 636
   religious influence of, 606
   rights activism, 573
   role and status of, 494i
   in World War II, 530, 530i, 543
in contemporary America, 692
Nativists
   mid-19th century, 241, 292, 296
   U.S.-Mexico War and, 304
Natural resources
   19th century, exploitation of, 384, 386–387, 387i
   20th century
      energy needs and, 616, 620–622
Naturalists, 244i
Nauvoo Legion, 289
Navajos
   in Civil War, 334, 343, 352, 427
   culture, 63, 63i, 112i
   Pueblo Indians and, 62, 63, 63i
   reservation, 63m
   in Southwest, 63m
   uranium mining and, 560
   World War II and, 530, 530i
Naval Stores Act (1705), 78
Navarro, Jose Antonio, 301
Navarro, Ramon, 493
Navigation Acts (1660; 1663), 67, 74, 144
Navigation and boatbuilding technology
   15th-16th century, 13–16, 16m, 17m, 18
   17th century, 34, 58
   18th century, first U.S. circumnavigation of globe, 203
   19th century, clipper ships, 301
Navratilova, Martina, 648
Navy, British, in Revolutionary War, 181–182
Navy, U.S.
   late 19th century, growth of, 437
   in War of 1812, 247
NAWSA. *See* National American Woman Suffrage Association
Nazis. *See* National Socialist (Nazi) party
NBA. *See* National Basketball Association
NBC. *See* National Broadcasting Company
NCS-68, 567
Nebraska and Nebraska Territory, 324m, 327m, 336m
   agriculture in, 412i
   settlement of, 367
Negro Acts (South Carolina), 99
Negro Acts (Virginia, 1705), 101
The Negro Christianized (Mather), 102
Neighborhood Union, 434
Nelson, Lord, 244
Neolin, 143
Netanyahu, Benjamin, 669
Neugin, Rebecca, 289
Neutrality Acts (1935, 1936, 1937), 533
Neutrality Proclamation (1793), 219
Nevada. *See also* Las Vegas
   nuclear testing in, 559i, 560, 636
   U.S. acquisition of, 312
New Amsterdam
   culture and population of, 40–41
   English seizure of, 67, 68
   establishment of, 40i, 40–41
New Archangel, 140–141
"The New Colossus" (Lazarus), 389
New Deal, 506, 508, 509, 517–525
   advocates of, 508
   capitalism and, 519, 521, 528
   effects of, 506, 509
   Eisenhower and, 583
   and election of 1932, 516
   goals of, 506
   Indian policies, 520, 520i
   legislation, 518–520, 523t
   minorities and, 524, 527, 528
   opposition to, 521–522, 527
   second, 518, 522–524
   and welfare state, 528
New Deal coalition, 527
New Democracy, 268
New Democrats, 666
New England
   17th century
      colonization of, 44–51
      religion in, 75–76
   18th century
      economy, 122m, 123–124
      religion in, 126
      shipbuilding in, 123
      unrest in, 203–206
   19th century
      economy, 315–316
      industry in, 253–254
New England Society of New York, 406
New France
   17th century, French policy in, 57
   founding of, 37–38
New Freedom (Wilson), 463, 470
New Hampshire
   17th century, settlement of, 50
   18th century
      Constitutional ratification, 212i, 213
      economy, 204–206, 206f
      population, 206f
      slave population, 98m
      war debt and, 204
New Harmony community, 300
New Haven and Northampton Canal, 264m
New Jersey
   17th century, settlement of, 68, 69
   18th century
      abolition of slavery, 224
      Constitution ratification, 211
      economy, 124
      slave population, 98m
      slavery in, 315
      voting rights, 224, 276
      women's rights in, 163, 217
   20th century
      manufacturing in, 430m
      race riots in, 605
New Jersey Plan, 208
New Lebanon community, 230i
New Left, in 1960s, 604, 605, 607
New Lights, 128–129
New Look, 583, 584
New Mexico/New Mexico Territory
   17th century
      Pueblo Revolt of 1680, 36i, 61–62, 63m, 64, 112
      Spanish colonization, 33–36, 34m, 35i
   19th century, 324m

New Mexico/New Mexico Territory, *continued*
    in Civil War, 343
    cultural strife in, 403–404
    Hispanic land rights in, 371
    slavery and, 322
    U.S. acquisition of, 305, 312
    20th century
        nuclear contamination in, 636
        statehood, 467
        voting rights in, 554
    Santa Fe, 34, 35, 36i, 62, 63, 227, 403i
New Nationalism, 464
New Netherlands, 24, 85, 97
New Northwest, 420
New Orleans
    18th century, 82, 100, 111, 113
        French cession to Spain, 134
        rebellion of French inhabitants, 141
    19th century
        economy of, 256
        post–Civil War, African Americans in, 363
        racial violence in, 426
        slave life in, 258
        Union capture of, 358
New Orleans, Battle of, 240, 250
New South, 406, 412
New Sweden, 40, 52m
New York
    17th century, unrest in, 74
    18th century
        abolition of slavery, 224
        Constitutional ratification by, 213
        economy, 124
        Hudson Valley revolt, 150
        in Revolutionary War, 172
        slave population in, 96–97, 98m
        western land claims, 200
    19th century, African American voting rights, 276
    20th century, manufacturing in, 430m
New York City
    17th century, government of, 68
    18th century
        ethnic diversity, 118–119
        growth of, 119–120, 124
        slave uprisings, 100, 101
    19th century
        anti-black riots, 294
        architecture of, 391, 392i
        Civil War draft riots, 349–350
        corruption in, 376, 377i, 394
        immigration to, 393
        Irish in, 285
        Peary exhibit in, 436–437
        poverty in, 416, 416i
    20th century
        African American community in, 474
        gay and lesbian culture in, 457
        Marathon in, 624–625
        strikes in, 446–447
        Triangle Shirtwaist Company fire, 446i, 446–447
New York Morning News, 300
New York Slave Plot, 101
New York Sun, 377
New York Times, 376, 400, 584, 612, 618
New York Tribune, 300, 377, 416
Newark, New Jersey, 478, 605
Newburgh Conspiracy, 162, 193–195
Nez Perce Indians, 112, 114m, 290, 357
Ngo Dinh Diem, 591, 600
Niagara Movement, 460–461
Nicaragua
    U.S. foreign policy in, 640, 649–650
    U.S. intervention in, 323, 469m
Nichols, Terry, 664

Nimitz, Chester, 545
Nineteenth Amendment, 444, 445, 459, 460, 471, 483
NIRA. *See* National Industrial Recovery Act
Nisei, 535, 547
Nixon, Richard M.
    antiwar protests and, 612
    background and character of, 611, 617
    in China, 615i, 617
    Cold War and, 615, 615i
    debates with Kennedy, 516
    domestic policies, 611–612
    economic policy, 620
    and election of 1960, 589t
    and election of 1968, 610, 611, 611t
    and election of 1972, 618, 618t
    enemies list of, 612
    foreign policy, 612–613, 615–617
    impeachment of, 618
    pardon of, 619
    political dirty tricks, 612, 617–618
    resignation of, 618
    in Soviet Union, 617
    as vice president, 574
    Vietnam War and, 573, 612–613
    Watergate scandal, 573, 613, 618, 622, 623, 625, 632
        historians' view of Cold War and, 559
        impact of, 625
    White House tapes and, 618
    in World War II, 539i
Nixon Doctrine, 612–613
NLF. *See* National Liberation Front
NLU. *See* National Labor Union
Noise pollution, history of, 128–129
Non-Intercourse Act (1809), 245
Nootka Indians, 204
Noriega, Manuel, 634, 651
North
    abolition of slavery in, 224–225
    in Civil War. *See* Union
    economy, 315–316
    free blacks in, 224–225
    slavery in, 315
North, Lord
    American Revolution and, 171, 173, 176, 187
    policies of, 153–154, 156, 187
North, Oliver, 650
North America. *See also* Americas
    prehistory, 2–14
        Paleo-Indian era, 6
        Archaic era, 6–8
        cultures, 8–9, 9m, 10–12
        European view of, 4–5
        peopling of, 2–6
        population in, 12
        rise of agriculture, 7–8
    European exploration of, 14–28, 16m–17m, 26m. *See also individual nations*
North American Free Trade Agreement (NAFTA), 634, 635, 668
North Atlantic Treaty Organization (NATO), 507, 550, 558
North Briton (periodical), 144
North Carolina
    settlement of, 78, 79m
    18th century
        Constitutional ratification by, 213
        economy, 121, 122m, 220
        establishment of, 78
        Revolutionary War in, 186
        slave population in, 98m
        unrest in, 150–151
        western land claims of, 229m
        westward expansion, 199
    19th century
        economy of, 265

        readmission to Union, 365m, 367
        secession of, 337
North Dakota, statehood for, 384
North Korea, 556–569, 587, 602, 625. *See also* Korean War
North Pole
    Peary expedition to, 466, 466i
North Vietnam. *See also* Vietnam War
    establishment of, 600
    morale of, 601
    U.S. bombing of, 601, 613
    U.S. underestimation of, 601–602
Northeast
    early 20th century, manufacturing in, 430m
    free blacks in, 102
    slave population in, 96–97, 98m
Northern Alliance, 411
Northern Ireland, Clinton in, 668, 669
Northern Pacific Railroad, 368, 372, 425
Northern Securities Co., 461
Northrup, Solomon, 293
Northwest, 18th century, U.S. trade in, 202–203, 204i
Northwest Ordinance of 1787, 202, 226, 227
    impact of, 227
    Indian resistance and, 226m
    slavery in, 210
Northwest Territory
    culture of, 226, 227, 230, 259
    English in, 220
    migration to, 290–291
    Native American resistance in, 216, 226m, 227, 229m
    trade, 202–203, 204i
    white settlement in, 217
Norway, immigration from, 283i, 283–284, 375i
Notes on the State of Virginia (Jefferson), 197
"Nothing to fear but fear itself," 516–517
NOW. *See* National Organization for Women
Noyes, John Humphrey, 299
NRA. *See* National Recovery Administration
NSC. *See* National Security Council
NTU. *See* National Trades Union
Nuclear arms. *See also* Arms race
    in 1990s, rogue nations and, 674
    atomic bomb
        bombing of Japan, 507, 547
        development of, 547
    environmental damage from, 559i, 560, 636
    hydrogen bomb, development of, 560, 572
    production and test sites, 636
    protests against, 589, 589i, 637, 647
    Soviet acquisition of, 566–567
    testing of, environmental damage from, 559i
Nuclear deterrence, 584
Nuclear freeze movement, 647
Nuclear power
    controversy over, 628
    as percent of total, 628
    plant locations, 629m
Nugent, Polly, 235
Nullification, 241, 272
Nullification Proclamation (1832), 272
Nuremberg trials, 558
NWP. *See* National Women's Party
NWSA. *See* National Woman Suffrage Association

O

Oakley, Annie, 395
Oberlin College, 298

Obscenity, Supreme Court on, 599
Occaneechi Indians, 71
Ocean travel. *See also* Navigation and boatbuilding technology
    pre-1400, 12
    15th-16th century, 13–28, 16m, 17m
    18th century, 117
    late 19th century, 417
    circumnavigation of globe, 16
Oceana (Harrington), 69
O'Connor, Sandra Day, 632
O'Donnell, Edward, 413
Office of the Independent Counsel, 667–668
Office of War Information (OWI), 538
Oglethorpe, James, 104–107, 105i
Ohio
    Indian cession of, 227
    manufacturing in, 430m
    migration to, 313
    population, 252
    settlement of, 201m
Ohio and Erie Canal, 264m
Ohio Company, 131, 133, 228
Ohio Company of Associates, 229–230
Ohio Company of Virginia, 128
Ohio Confederacy
    British support for, 217, 219, 227
    establishment of, 216–217
    resistance by, 227
Oil (petroleum)
    Arab oil embargo (1973–1974), 573, 621–623
    U.S. economy and, 622–623
    U.S. importation of, 621f
Oil industry
    Bush administration's alignment with, 679
Oil Producing and Exporting Countries (OPEC), 621–623
Ojibways, 227
Okies, 513
Okinawa, Battle of, 545, 546m
Oklahoma, 20th century
    oil boom in, 466
    racial violence in, 467
    statehood for, 424
Oklahoma City Federal Building bombing (1995), 635, 664
Oklahoma Territory
    establishment of, 424
    removals to, 288m, 288–289
Old Lights, 129
Old Northwest
    division of, 198–201, 200i, 201m
    government in, 201, 274
    Native Americans in, 216
    veteran's land grants in, 274
    white expansion into, 197, 198–201
Old Southwest, struggle for control of, 196–201, 198m
Old Spanish Trail, 286m
Oliver, Andrew, 145–146
Olmecs, 7–9
Olney, Richard, 268
Olympic Games of 1980, 638
Omaha Indians, 114, 130
On the Road (Kerouac), 588
Oñate, Juan de, 33, 34, 34m
One Flew over the Cuckoo's Nest (Kesey), 625
Oneida Community, 299
Oneidas, 184, 657. *See also* Iroquois Confederacy
O'Neill, Thomas "Tip," 626
Onondagas, 182. *See also* Iroquois Confederacy
Opechancanough, 50, 51
Open Door policy, 440
Operation Chaos, 625

Operation Desert Shield, 652
Operation Desert Storm, 653
Order of the Star-Spangled Banner. *See* Know-Nothing Party
Orders in Council (England, 1806), 244, 250
Oregon, statehood, 329
Oregon Territory, 251, 263m, 284, 303m, 324m
    Russia in, 267
    settlement of, 290–291
    Spanish cession of, 267
    U.S. acquisition of, 267
    U.S. claim on, 302
Oregon Trail, 286m, 290, 343
The Origin of Species (Darwin), 399
Osage Indians, 114, 291, 425m
Osceola, 288
Ostend Manifesto, 323
Oswald, Lee Harvey, 593
Ottawas, 143, 160, 183, 227
Ottoman Empire, World War I and, 467, 481m
Our Country (Strong), 400
Our Nig, or, Sketches from the Life of a Free Black (Wilson), 320
Outsourcing
    maquiladoras and, 620, 682, 683
Owen, Robert, 300
OWI. *See* Office of War Information

P

Pachucos, 543
Pacific Islands, 20th century immigration from, 663
Pacific Ocean
    European efforts to dominate, 21, 32
    European exploration in, 21, 139i, 139–140
    18th century, U.S. trade in, 202–203
    19th century
        balance of power in, 162
        trade, 240, 323
Pacific Railroad Act (1862), 308, 343
Pahlavi, Reza, 585, 637, 638
Paine, Thomas, 162, 168, 169, 171, 173, 179, 190
Paiute Indians, 290, 409
Paleo-Indians, 6
Paleo-Indian era, 6
Palestine, British withdrawal from, 558
Palestinian Liberation Organization (PLO), 669
Palestinians, 558, 621, 627, 652, 669
Palmer, A. Mitchell, 483
Palmer raids, 483
Pamunkeys, 51, 52, 71
Pan Am Flight 109, 650
Pan-American Conference (1890), 436
Panama, U.S. intervention in, 650, 651
Panama Canal, 467, 469m, 625–627
Panic of 1819, 266–267
Panic of 1837, 292, 293
Parades, Early Republic, 231, 232
Pardo, Juan, 26, 26m
Pareja, Francisco de, 36
Parker, Alton B., 462t
Parks, Rosa, 582
Parochial schools, late 19th century, 428
Parsons, Albert, 414, 415, 415i
Parsons, Lucia Gonzalez, 415
Parties, political
    19th century, 241, 279, 281, 292, 294, 322, 325, 330, 357, 420, 432
    in Confederacy, 341
    Washington on, 218
Parton, Sarah Willis (Fanny Fern), 320

Paterson, William, 209
Patriot Act, 677, 678
Patriotism, late 19th century, 427
Patriots, in American Revolution, 137, 158, 165, 218, 233
Patronage system. *See also* Spoils system
    late 19th century, 377, 397
    British, critiques of, 149
    reform of, 398
Paul, Alice, 471
Pawnees
    19th century, land loss by, 323, 424
    culture, 319
    horses and, 112, 114m
    reservation, opening of, 424
    trade, 114, 115
Paxton Boys, 143
Payne-Aldrich Tariff (1909), 463
PBS. *See* Public Broadcasting System
Pea Ridge, Battle of, 341
Peace Corps, 574, 591, 597
Peace of Westminster (1674), 67
Peale, Charles Willson, 197
Peale, James, 234i
Pearl Harbor
    Japanese attack on, 506, 530, 534, 535i, 536m, 544, 545, 676
Peary, Robert, 435, 436i, 466, 466i
Pelican (ship), 55–56
Pendleton Act (1883), 398
Penn, Thomas, 125
Penn, William, 69
Pennsylvania. *See also* Philadelphia
    abolition of slavery, 224
    African American voting rights, 276
    Constitution ratification, 211
    economy, 123, 125
    manufacturing in, 430m
    religious tolerance in, 126
    settlement of, 69
    slave population in, 98m
    state constitution of, 178
Pennsylvania Dutch, 121
Pennsylvania Hospital for the Sick Poor, 125
Pennsylvania Journal, 173
Pennsylvania Main Line Canal, 264m
Pennsylvania Railroad, 382, 383
Pensacola, American Revolution and, 183m, 184
Pension Act (1890), 429
Pentagon, terrorist attack on. *See* September 11th terrorist attacks
Pentagon Papers, 612, 618
People's party. *See* Populist Party
People's Republic of China (PRC), establishment of, 565
Peoria Indians, 61, 143, 227, 274, 275, 288m
Pequot Indians, 50, 657
Pequot War, 49, 50, 71
Pérez, Eulalia, 278
Perkins, Carter, 311
Perkins, Robert, 311
Perkins, Sandy, 311
Perot, H. Ross, 666, 666i, 667t
Perry, Matthew C., 306i, 323
Perry, Oliver H., 247, 248
Perryville, Battle of, 346
Pershing, John J., 469, 470, 480
Persian Gulf War (1991), 635, 651–653, 677, 689
    causes of, 622, 623
    women in, 631
Peru, prehistory cultures in, 8
Pesticides, 589, 590, 622, 687
Peters, Sally, 164, 165
Peters, Thomas, 164i, 164, 165, 166m
Petersburg, siege of, 353
Peterson, Kathleen, 662

Petroleum. *See* Oil
Philadelphia
  17th century, establishment of, 69
  18th century
    British assault on, 176
    Constitutional Convention in, 206–208
    First Continental Congress, 158
    growth of, 119, 120, 124, 125
    unrest in, 143
    vice-admiralty court in, 152, 157m
  19th century
    anti-black riots, 294
    Bettering House for poor in, 235
    Fairmont Waterworks, 273i
    Irish in, 285
    union unrest, 293
  20th century, African American community in, 474
Philadelphia Turnpike, 253
Philanthropy, Gospel of Wealth and, 400
Philip, King of Wampanoags, 70, 75
Philip II, King of Spain, 24, 26, 27, 32
Philip V, King of Spain, 62
Philip of Anjou, 60
Philippines
  immigration from, 648, 663
  independence, 468, 558
  Seven Years' War and, 134
  Spanish-American War and, 439m, 439, 440
  U.S. pacification of, 440, 462, 463
  U.S. purchase of, 440
  World War II and, 545, 546m
Phonograph, invention of, 385
Photography, early 20th century, 453, 458, 459
Phyllis Wheatley Settlement, 434
Physicians. *See* Doctors
Piankashaw Indians, 288m
Pickens, Andrew, 185
Pickett, George, 349
Pickett, John T., 345
Pickett's Charge, 349
Picture brides, 451., 452, 452i
Pierce, Franklin, 322, 322t
Pietism, 127
Pike, Albert, 340
Pill, the, 574, 575, 608, 625
Pinchot, Gifford, 424, 463
Pinckney, Charles C., 235, 235t, 244, 245, 245t
Pinckney, Thomas, 222t
Pinckney, William, 263
Pinckney Treaty (1795), 221
Pine Ridge Reservation, 409, 422, 425m
Pinkerton, Allan, 414
Pinkerton National Detective Agency, 414, 429
Pinochet, Augusto, 617
Pinups, in World War II, 538, 539
Pirates, 18th century, 77, 77i, 78, 163, 222
Pitcher, Molly, 181
Pitt, William, 132, 134, 148
Pizarro, Francisco, 21
Plains Indians
  assimilation, resistance to, 357
  culture, 312
  Ghost Dance and, 409, 410
  Kansas-Nebraska Act and, 323, 324m
  resistance by, 357, 381
  treaties, 312
  war with whites, 367–369, 410, 411
Planned obsolescence, invention of, 496
Plantation agriculture. *See also* Cotton plantations; Rice plantations; Sugar plantations
  mid-19th century, 314
  early 20th century, 502
  in Chesapeake region, 18th century, 121–123
  on Hawaiian Islands, 438
  industrialization and, 254
  slavery and, 85–87, 88, 91, 89i, 229, 230
  and wealth per capita, 123
Plantation Duty Act (1673), 67
Platt Amendment (1901), 439, 442
Playboy culture, 588
Pledge of Allegiance, 427, 563
Plenty Kill, 422
Plessy v. *Ferguson* (1896), 381, 426, 580
PLO. *See* Palestinian Liberation Organization
Plumbers, 612, 618
Plymouth colony, 31, 32, 44–48
Pneumonia, in Civil War, 345
Pocahontas, 42, 50
Pogroms, 389, 452
Poland
  creation of, 481m
  German invasion of (1939), 532
  immigration from, 390, 393, 426, 492
  World War II and, 530, 556
Police brutality, late 20th century, 599, 605, 659, 660
Police power, international, Roosevelt Corollary and, 462, 463
Polio
  FDR and, 516
  vaccine development, 572, 575
Politics
  19th century
    corruption in, 270, 376, 377, 377i
    pre-Civil War, 292–296
    in West, 261, 262
  20th century
    muckrakers' exposés of, 458
    in 1920s, 487–490, 497, 498
    post-World War II rise of left, 552
Polk, James K.
  and election of 1844, 302, 302t
  Mexican American War and, 302–306
Poll taxes, 426, 598
Pollock, Jackson, 587
Pollock v. *Farmers' Loan and Trust Company* (1895), 431
Pollution, 387, 462, 464, 562, 584, 599, 612, 627, 642, 643, 679, 683, 685, 686, 687. *See also* Environmental damage; Environmentalism
  19th century, urban water supplies, 392, 393
  20th century
    radioactive waste, 559, 629m, 687
Polo, Marco, 13, 15, 16m–17m
Polowsky, Joseph, 550
Polygamy, 289, 397, 419
Polynesians, early ocean voyages, 12, 139
Ponca Indians, land loss by, 323
Ponce de León, Juan, 18, 26m
Pontiac, 138, 143, 160
Pontiac's War, 143, 147m
Popé, 62–64
Pope, John, 344
Pope, Roman Catholic
  emergence of nation state and, 24
  and new world exploration, 16
  Reformation and, 23
Popular culture
  early 20th century, 456
  in 1990s, international spread of, 670
  exportation of, 677, 687–688
  influence of, 384, 688–689
  international resistance to, 689–691
  slow food movement as counter to, 690
Population
  of prehistoric Americas, 11, 12
  18th century
    1790, 217
    African American, 116, 217, 224
    British mainland colonies. 115, 117, 117f, 118
    of New Hampshire, 206f
    slave, 90, 96–98, 98m, 102, 117, 118, 255
  19th century, 240
    African American, 334m, 432
    of Kansas, 368
    late, 384, 390m
    of Ohio, 253
    slave, 2256, 256, 334m
  20th century
    Chinese-American, 450, 663
    Latino, 663
    urban *vs.* rural, 493f
  21st century
    2000, by age and gender, 117f
  in environmental transformation, 686
The Population Bomb (Ehrlich), 612
Populist party
  demise of, 432
  and election of 1892, 431, 431t, 432
  and election of 1896, 432
  and election of 1900, 461t
  impact of, 429
  rise of, 381, 411, 412, 423, 431
Pornography, Supreme Court on, 599
Port Royal Sound colony, 25, 25i
Portolá, Gaspar de, 141, 142m
Ports, major, 18th century, 120–121, 122m, 124
Portugal
  consolidation with Spain, 32
  New World exploration by, 13–14, 16m–17m
  slavery and, 85–86, 96m–97m
Potato famine, 285
Potawatomi Indians, 143, 227, 274, 279
Potsdam Conference (1945), 547
Pottowatamie Creek massacre, 326
Poverty
  18th century, urban, 125
  late 19th century
    reform movements and, 414, 416–417, 419
    urban, 416, 416i
  20th century
    early, 453
    in 1920s, 487, 501–502
    in 1960s, 597, 597m, 598m
    in 1980s, 643
    disease and, 453
    urban renewal and, 578
Poverty Point culture, 8
Powderly, Terence V., 414
Powell, Colin, 653, 679, 692
Powers, Gary, 585
Powhatan, 42–43, 51
Powhatan Confederacy, 43, 51, 52m
Powhatan Indians, 42–43, 50, 51
Prayer in public schools, 599, 645
Praying towns, 70–71
PRC. *See* People's Republic of China
Prejudice. *See also* Discrimination; Racism
  early 20th century, 478
  in 1960s, 604, 609
Presbyterians, Calvinism and, 24
Presidency, late 20th century, power of, 625
Presidential elections
  of 2004, 681
President's Commission on the Status of Women, 592
Presley, Elvis, 554, 588

Prester John, 14, 14i
Priber, Christian, 102, 111
Prince (pop star), 663
Princeton, Battle of, 173, 173i
Princeton University, 128
Principles of Psychology (James), 428
The Principles of Scientific Management (Taylor), 455
Printing and publishing
   18th century
      in colonies, 126, 148
      in England, 144
   19th century
      by abolitionists, 293, 294i, 326
      investigative journalism, 376–377, 377i
      by Native Americans, 289, 312
      newspapers, proliferation of, 281
Prisons, war on drugs and, 658
Privateers, 76, 182, 345
Proclamation Line of 1763, 143, 147m, 182
Productivity, 683, 685
Productivity, Early Republic ,219–220
Professional licensing, establishment of, 299
Progress and Poverty (George), 414
Progressive Era
   conservationism and, 462, 473
   evaluation of, 510
   reform impetus in, 447, 461
Progressive party
   and election of 1912, 464t, 666
   and election of 1924, 488, 488t, 499
   and election of 1948, 563t
   formation of, 464
   in Wisconsin, 522
Progressivism, 447, 458–464
   decline of, 484
   education and, 427
   environmentalism and, 462, 462i
   impulses behind, 458
   labor movement and, 460
   Roosevelt and, 461
   in Taft administration, 463
   women's suffrage movement and, 459–460
   World War I and, 475
Prohibition, 460, 587, 490–491, 491i
   and election of 1928, 489
   Harding and, 488
   repeal of, 518
Prohibition party
   and election of 1888, 399t
   and election of 1892, 431t
Promise Keepers, 660
The Prophet, 246, 246i, 249
Prophet's Town, 246
Proposition 187 (California), 663
Proposition 227 (California), 663
Protect the Emperor Society, 450
Protest movements. See also Reform movements
   in 1950s, 582–583, 582m
   in 1960s and 1970s, 586–587, 589, 589i, 604–609
      antiwar protests, Vietnam War, 573, 605–606, 612, 613
      backlash against, 610–611
   in 1980s, 647–648
Protestant fundamentalists, school prayer and, 599
Protestant Reformation, 23–24
Protestantism. *See also* Fundamentalist Christians; Huguenots; Puritans
   17th century
      fear of Catholics, 73–74, 75
      in New England, 75–76
      slavery and, 86
   18th century

      emigration to America, 118–119
      fear of Catholics, 156
   19th century
      Catholic immigrants and, 295–296
      fear of Catholics, 295–296, 323
      Indian assimilation and, 418–419
      Irish immigrants and, 285
      mission homes, 418–419
   20th century
      fear of Catholics, 499, 564
      religious right, 645
      values, 493
   21st century
      affiliation, 691f
Providence, Rhode Island, establishment of, 48
Prozac, 665
Psychology, introduction as discipline, 428
PT-109, 589
Ptolemy, 15
Public Broadcasting System (PBS), 598–599
Public health measures, early 20th century, 453–455
Public institutions, 19th century, as social bond, 428, 429
Public schools, rise of, 297–299, 427–428
Public Works Administration (PWA), 523t
Publius, 211
Pueblo(s), Anasazi, 10
Pueblo Bonito, 10
USS *Pueblo* incident, 602–603
Pueblo Indians
   Anasazi, 8, 9m, 10–11
   religion of, 35–36, 61–62
   revolt of 1680, 36i, 62–64, 63m
   revolt of 1696, 63i, 64
   Spanish contact with, 23, 33–36
Pueblo revolt of 1680, 36i, 62–64, 63m
Pueblo revolt of 1696, 63i, 64
Puerto Rico
   citizenship rights for, 468
   militancy of, 609
   Spanish cession of, 439
Puget, Peter, 192
Pulaski, Casimir, 180
Pulitzer, Joseph, 437
Pullman Palace Car Co., 431
Pullman strike, 432–433
Punch, John, 87
Pure Food and Drug Act (1906), 458
Puritan Revolution, 48, 66
Puritans
   Calvinism and, 24
   dissenters, 48–49
   Massachusetts Bay colony, 45–48, 86
   missionaries to Native Americans, 50
   persecution of, 41, 45
   Plymouth colony, 31–32, 44–48
   Salem witch hunts and, 75
   theology of, 46
Purvis, Robert, 295
Puzo, Mario, 503, 503i
PWA. *See* Public Works Administration
Pyle, Ernie, 547
Pyramid of the Sun, 9

Q

Qisuk, 436i
Quakers
   in New Amsterdam, 40–41
   in Pennsylvania and Delaware, 69
   services to poor, 125
   and slavery, 102–104
Quantrill, William Clarke, 350
Quapaws, 288m
Quartering Act (1765), 144, 152
Quartering Act (1774), 156

Quasi War, 222
Quebec
   in 18th century, 134i
   American assault on (1775), 167
   British capture of, 133–134, 134m
   establishment of, 21, 26m, 38
   expansion of (1774), 156, 157m
Quebec Act (1774), 156, 157m, 188
Queen Anne's War, 75, 76–78
Quetzalcoatl, 10, 19
Quivira, 23

R

Rabin, Yitzak, 669
RAC. *See* Royal African Company
Race
   18th century, as classification, 85–91
   19th century
      as classification, 426–427, 429
      and employment
         pre-Civil War, 254–258, 315, 316–317, 325, 328
         post-Civil War, 369–370, 390– 391
      as justification for exploitation, 404–405, 426–427
      regional definitions of, 291
      and social class, 316–317
      worker conflict and, 429
   20th century
      definition of whiteness, 454–455
      interracial marriage, 599
      mixing of, 663
      interracial marriage, 91, 599
The Races of Mankind (Benedict), 540
Racial discrimination. *See* Discrimination
Racial minorities
   in contemporary America, 691–692
Racial quotas, Supreme Court on, 632
Racism. *See also* Discrimination; Lynchings; Prejudice
   19th century
      growth of, 317
      imperialism and, 435
      Social Darwinism and, 400
   20th century
      in 1960s, anti-Asian, 601–602
      challenges to, 541–543
      eugenics and, 454–455
      of Japanese, 536–537
      race riots, 477, 483
      Tulsa race riot (1921), 467, 483
      in World War II, 540–542, 546–547
Radical politics. *See also* Protest movements; Reform movements
   early 20th century, 458–460, 483
   in 1960s, 605–607, 607i
   civil rights movement and, 604–605
Radio
   in 1920s, 493, 495
   fireside chats on, 515i, 517, 527
   first trial broadcast on, 499
   Roosevelt (F.D.) and, 527
Radioactive fallout, 559–560, 559i
Radioactive waste, 559–560, 627, 629m, 636
Railroad(s)
   19th century
      big business and, 382–383
      and buffalo, 387, 387i
      consolidation of, 387–388
      impact of, 371, 382–383, 386m, 398
      Indians and, 368–369, 381
      and national integration, 368
      refrigerated cars, 383
      regulation of, 399
      resource exploitation and, 384–387
      strikes, 412
      tourism and, 369i, 372, 425

Railroad(s), *continued*
    transcontinental line, 368, 369–370, 370i
    trees used in building, 372t
    urban growth and, 392
    worker unrest, 382, 383i
    workers for, 369–370, 370i
    20th century, Trans-Siberian line, 467
Railroad Administration, U.S., 476
Rainbow Coalition, 648
Rainey, Ma, 493
A Raisin in the Sun (Hansberry), 577
Raker Act (1913), 462
Raleigh, Sir Walter, 28
Randolph, A. Philip, 541
Randolph, Edmund, 210
Ray, Dorothy, 539
Ray, James Earl, 611
Reagan, Nancy, 643
Reagan, Ronald W., 636i
    anticommunism of, 640
    assassination attempt against, 665
    budget deficits and, 641
    Cold War and, 636, 639–640, 649–650
    domestic policies, 640–644
    economic policies, 637, 641–642, 643–644, 644f
    and election of 1976, 625
    and election of 1980, 638–639, 639t, 645
    and election of 1984, 641t, 642
    environmental policies, 642–643
    foreign policy, 639–640
    on government, 639
    impact of, 634
    Iran-Contra scandal and, 648, 649–650
    media and, 638
    nuclear arsenal and, 641
    Panama Canal and, 625
    Soviet Union and, 640
    Strategic Defense Initiative and, 641
    support for, 643, 644
    unions and, 644
    World War II and, 539i
Real Whigs
    political theory of, 148–149, 152
    on standing armies, 153
Realism, in art, 457i, 458
Reason, Charlie, 346
Recession of 1913–1914, 472, 477i
Recession of 1991–1992, 653, 656, 666
Reconstruction
    close of, 377–378
    corruption in, 366–367
    debate over, 357–367
    under Johnson, 358–363
    land redistribution and, 362i, 362–363
    radical, 360, 363, 365m, 366–367
    readmission of states, 365m, 367
    Republican policy on, 358
    white unrest under, 362–363, 365, 367
Reconstruction Act (1867), 366, 365m
Reconstruction Finance Corporation, 514
Red Army socialism, 552
The Red Badge of Courage (Crane), 428
Red Cloud, 368
Red lining policies, 577
Red scare(s)
    Korean War and, 569
    post-World War I, 483, 491, 502
    post-World War II, 551, 554, 563
Red Sticks, 249–250, 251
Redemption contracts, 117
Reform movements. *See also* Protest movements
    Early Republic, 230–231
    19th century, 416–420
        in education, 297–299
        rise of, 297
        trans-Atlantic networks, 417
        women and, 297, 419–420, 420i
    20th century, 446
        in 1960s, 604–606
        in 1980s, 647
        backlash against, 603, 610–611
        consumer protection, 598
        Progressivism, 447, 458–464
        World War I and, 475
Reform party, 666, 674
Regulator Movement, 150–151
Reign of Terror, 218
Re'is, Piri, 14i
Relation (Cabeza de Vaca), 21
Religion. *See also specific religions and denominations*
    in prehistory
        Archaic period, 7
        Aztec, 8, 9, 10
        Mayan, 8, 9
        Olmec, 8
        Pueblo, 35–36, 62–64
    in colonies
        diversity in, 126–127
        Great Awakening, 127–129
    19th century
        African American, post-Civil War, 365
        Christian Science, 429
        missionaries to freed slaves, 356
        proliferation of, 278–279
        schools and, 427
    20th century
        in 1960s, 606, 607–608, 607i,
        business and, 500
        communism and, 482
        prayer in public schools, 599, 645
        proselytizing abroad, 689
        Scopes trial and, 498–499
        in suburbs, 576
Religious right. *See* Fundamentalist Christians
Remond, Charles Lenox, 293
Remond, Sarah Parker, 293
Renaissance, European, 18
Representation
    Colonial dissatisfaction with, 145, 150–153
    and Old Northwest, division of, 200–202
    slave population and, 209
    in U.S. Constitution, 208–210
Republic of Texas, 301–302
    African Americans in, 301–302
    slavery in, 301–302
Republic of the Congo, U.S. intervention in, 585
Republican Mothers, 231–233
Republican party
    pre-Civil War
        emergence of, 308, 324–325
        platform, 325
        Southern fear of, 335
    Civil War policies, 342–343
        and election of 1860, 335
        Native Americans and, 344
        resistance to, 345
    post-Civil War
        opposition to, 373, 375, 377
        policies, 357–362, 366–367, 365m, 372, 373, 375, 376, 377
    late 19th century, platform, 396–397
    20th century
        constituency, 527
        factions in, 645
        impact of, 653
        platform in 1990s, 666
        Red Scare and, 554, 563
        religious right and, 645–646
        Republican Revolution (1994), 666–667
        Versailles Treaty and, 482
        as voice of resentment in 1960s, 611
    and election of 1860, 330, 330t
    and election of 1864, 352, 352t
    and election of 1866, 363
    and election of 1868, 367, 367t
    and election of 1872, 377, 377t
    and election of 1876, 377–378, 377t
    and election of 1880, 397, 397t
    and election of 1884, 398, 398t
    and election of 1888, 399, 399t
    and election of 1892, 430–431, 431t
    and election of 1896, 432, 432t
    and election of 1900, 441, 461, 461t
    and election of 1904, 462t
    and election of 1908, 463, 463t
    and election of 1912, 464t
    and election of 1916, 473t
    and election of 1920, 487, 488t
    and election of 1924, 488t, 488
    and election of 1928, 489, 489t
    and election of 1932, 515, 516, 516t
    and election of 1936, 518, 524–525, 525t
    and election of 1940, 533t
    and election of 1944, 538t
    and election of 1946, 554
    and election of 1948, 562, 563t
    and election of 1952, 568t
    and election of 1956, 583t
    and election of 1960, 589t
    and election of 1964, 597, 597t
    and election of 1968, 611, 611t
    and election of 1972, 617–618, 618t
    and election of 1976, 625–626, 625t
    and election of 1980, 638–639, 639t
    and election of 1984, 641t, 642
    and election of 1988, 645, 651t
    and election of 1992, 666t
    and election of 1994, 667
    and election of 1996, 667t
    and election of 2000, 671–672, 672t
    and election of 2004, 681, 681t
Reservation system, 425m
    creation of, 417
    critics of, 423
    expansion of, 368
Reisman, David, 588
Restoration Era, 66
Resumption Act (1875), 376
Revenue Act (1766), 152
Revenue Act (1916), 472
Revere, Paul, 154i, 159
Revolutionary War, 164–189. *See also* American Revolution
    Boston, siege of, 168
    British strategy, 169–171, 176, 182
    British surrender at Yorktown, 186–187
    campaigns, 175m
        1775, 166–167, 168
        1776-1777, 169–175
        1778-1781, 182, 184–187
        final, 186–187
        in Northeast, 175m
        in South, 185m
        in West, 183m
    casualties, 189, 354
    coalitions within, 162
    Continental Navy in, 182
    debt from, 193
        federal assumption of, 219
        and political unrest, 203–207
    disease and, 168, 191–192, 192m
    as global conflict, 166m, 175–176, 181–182
    Hudson Valley campaign (Burgoyne), 174–175, 175m
    ideological foundations of, 148–149, 169
    mercenaries in, 171

minorities and, 159
Native Americans and, 163, 182–184, 183m, 188, 216–217
New Jersey, Washington's retreat through, 171–173
New York, British assault on, 173
North-South politics in, 167
peace negotiations, 187–188, 188i
Philadelphia, British assault on, 176
at sea, 181–182, 187
in South, 184–187, 185m
start of, 82
tactics of, 152–153, 156–158
war preparations, 166–167
Western frontier and, 182–184, 183m
Reynolds, E. B., 409
Rhode Island
  17th century
    establishment of, 49, 50
    Metacom's War, 70
    slavery in, 87
  18th century
    Constitution ratification, 211, 213
    religious tolerance in, 126
    in Revolutionary War, 180
    slave population, 98m
    unrest in, 154, 204
  20th century, manufacturing in, 430m
Rhode Island system of production, 254
Rica de Oro, 32
Rica de Plata, 32
Rice, Condoleezza, 692
Rice plantations
  black life and labor on, 257
  in Georgia, 122
  post-Revolution, 202
  and slavery, 88, 89i, 99
  in South Carolina, 122
    early 19th century, 256
    and slavery, 88, 89i, 99
Richelieu, Cardinal, 38
Richmond, Virginia, in Civil War, 343, 349
  as Confederate capital, 337
  Union capture of, 352–353
The Ridge, 251–252
Ridge, John, 289
Ridge, Major, 289
Rights. *See* Civil liberties; Civil rights; Human rights; Voting rights; Women's rights movement
Riis, Jacob, 416, 416i
Ringer, Robert J., 632
Rio Puerco valley, nuclear contamination, 636
Roads. *See* Highway construction
Roanoke Island colony, 3, 28
Roaring twenties, 487
Robertson, Pat, 645, 646
Roberval, 21, 22m
Robinson, Jackie, 554
Rock 'n' roll, 554, 588
Rock Springs massacre, 405
Rockefeller, John D., 388–389, 401, 458, 471
Rockford (Illinois) Female Seminary, 419
Rockingham, Lord, 148
Rockwell, Norman, 533i
Rocky Mountain National Park, 474
Roe v. *Wade* (1973), 608, 631
Rogers, Ginger, 538
Rogers, Will, 508i, 508–509, 527
Rolfe, John, 43
Roller coasters, 394
Romani, Nazi Germany and, 531
Romania, creation of, 481m
Roosevelt, Eleanor
  activism of, 522, 524, 527
  background of, 515
  flying lessons by, 528i
  letters to, 518

  marriage of, 515
  and President's Commission on the Status of Women, 592
Roosevelt, Franklin D., 508i, 515i
  African Americans and, 522, 527
  background of, 515
  conservationism and, 519
  death of, 507, 545, 551, 551i
  early career of, 515
  and election of 1932, 516, 516t
  and election of 1936, 524–525, 525t
  and election of 1944, 538t
  fireside chats, 516, 517, 527
  first hundred days, 518–520
  inaugural address, first, 516–517
  Manhattan Project and, 547
  marriage of, 515
  media and, 516, 517, 527
  and New Deal, 518–525
    legislation, 518–520, 523t
    opposition to, 521–522, 527
    second, 518, 522–524
  policies, 506, 509, 517
  polio, 515–516
  Rogers (Will) and, 508, 508i
  second term, 524–525
  Supreme Court packing scheme, 525
  World War II and
    Atlantic Charter and, 533–534
    discrimination in defense industry, 541
    Four Freedoms, 533, 533i
    Japanese aggression and, 534
    Japanese internment, 535–536
    Lend-Lease program, 533
    peace settlement, 547
    reconstruction planning, 507
    strategy for, 531, 543
Roosevelt, Theodore
  death of, 483
  domestic policies of, 461
  and election of 1900, 441
  and election of 1904, 462t
  and election of 1908, 463
  and election of 1912, 463, 464t
  environmentalism and, 462, 462i
  eugenics movement and, 454
  foreign policy, 462
  ideology of, 436, 441
  on immigration, 461–462
  media and, 516
  Progressivism and, 461
  Roosevelt Corollary, 463
  Rough Riders and, 438
  on segregation, 452
  World War I and, 475
Roosevelt Corollary, 463
Root, Elihu, 475
Roots (Haley), 632i
Rosebud Reservation, 425m
Rosenberg, Ethel, 562
Rosenberg, Julius, 562
Rosenwald, Julius, 427
Rosewood, Florida, riots (1923), 483
Rosie the Riveter, 539
Ross, John, 289, 341
Rough Riders, 441
Route 66, 513m
Royal Adventurers into Africa, 67
Royal African Company (RAC), 67, 73, 91, 95i, 98, 104
Rubin, Jerry, 643
Ruby, Jack, 593
Ruiz, Francisco, 301
Ruiz de Burton, Maria Amparo, 371
Rumsfeld, Donald, 681
Rural areas
  18th century
    resistance to Federalists, 220–221

    unrest in, 150–151
  late 19th century
    unrest in, 412–413
  20th century, population, 491–492, 492f
Rush-Bagot Treaty (1817), 251
Russell, Osborne, 290
Russell, Rosalind, 527
Russia. *See also* Soviet Union
  18th century
    in Alaska, 140–141, 162, 193
    fur trade and, 82, 140–141
    U.S. trade with, 202
  19th century
    immigration from, 390, 412, 426, 427
    in Oregon, 267, 268
    sale of Alaska, 372
  20th century
    AIDS and, 646
    Allied intervention in, 482
    anti-Americanism in, 482
    Bolshevik revolution in, 479–480, 480i, 482
    deportations to, 482
    immigration from, 452, 468, 492f
    nationalist revolution in, 468
    World War I and, 467, 478, 479–480
Russian-American Company, 140
Russo-American Treaty (1824), 268
Rustbelt, decline of, 20th century, 562, 620–621
Rusticating, 425
Ruth, Babe, 487
Rwanda, genocide in, 670

S

Sacajawea, 243
Sacco, Nicola, 491, 491i
Sadat, Anwar, 627, 650
Saehle, Jannicke, 283–284
Sagadahoc settlement, 42
Sagres, Portugal, 14, 14m
St Augustine, Florida
  in 16th century, settlement at, 3, 26m, 26–27
  in 17th century, 36–37
St. Clair, Arthur, 227
St. Mihiel, Battle of, 480
St. Paul, Minnesota, urban renewal in, 578
Sahagén, Bendicto de, 20
Saint-Denis, Louis, 58m
Saint-Mémin, C. B. J. Févret de, 242i
St Thomas Protestant Episcopal Church, 224
Salem witch hunts, 75–76
Sales, Luis, 190i
Salinger, J. D., 588
Salk, Dr. Jonas, 575
SALT. *See* Strategic Arms Limitations Treaties
Salt Lake City, 290, 391
Salt of the Earth (film), 564i
Saltwater slaves, 95
Same-sex marriage, 679
Samoa, late 19th century, 436
Sampson, Deborah, 181
Samuelson, Paul, 596
San Antonio, Texas
  Mission San Francisco de Latin America Espada, 110i
  peace treaty with Apaches, 110–111
San Antonio de Valero, 65
San Antonio Independent School District v. *Rodriguez* (1973), 613
San Francisco
  19th century, 393
  20th century
    Bay-to-Breakers race, 623i
    earthquake (1906), 445, 447, 447i
    immigration to, 452

San Francisco Chronicle, 450
San Francisco Presbyterian Chinese Mission Home, 407i
San Francisco Workingmen's Party, 398
San Gabriel mission, 141, 142m, 191, 278
San Jacinto, Battle of, 301, 302
San Juan Hill, 438
San Marcos, Fortress of, 64–65
San Miguel, church of, 36i
San Xavier del Bac mission, 63m
Sanchez, Jose Maria, 291
Sanctuary movement, 640
Sand Creek massacre, 351i, 352
Sandia Pueblo, 657i
Sandinistas, 640, 649
Sanitation, early 20th century, 453–454
Santa Ana, Father, 110–111
Santa Anna, Antonio Lopez de, 301
Santa Fe
   late 19th century, 403i
   Pueblo revolt of 1680 and, 36i, 62–63
Santa Fe Ring, 371
Santa Fe Trail, 286m
Saratoga, British surrender at, 173–175, 175m
Saturday Evening Post, 533i, 543
Saturday Night Massacre, 618
Sauk Indians
   American Revolution and, 183m
   home region of, 227
   Oklahoma Territory and, 288m
   resistance by, 274
   Revolutionary War and, 184
Saukamappee, 115
Savannah, Georgia
   in Civil War, 353, 353m
   Civil War damage to, 356i
   establishment of, 106i
Savannah Education Association (SEA), 356–357
Scalawags, 360, 367
Scales, Jesse Sleet, 453–454
Scandinavia. *See also* Vikings
   in prehistory, explorations by, 436
   Communist Party rise in, 552
   immigration from, 283–284, 314, 412
Scanlon, Emily, 394
Scarification, ornamental, 84i
Schenck v. *United States* (1919), 478
Schenectady, founding of, 41
Schlafly, Phyllis, 631–632
Schmeling, Max, 527–528
School shootings, 656, 664–665
Schuyler, Philip, 166–167, 200
Schwerner, Michael, 604
Science. *See also* Medicine
   early 20th century
      eugenics and, 454–455
      public health and, 453–454
Scientific management, 391, 455
Scioto Company, 201, 201m
SCLC. *See* Southern Christian Leadership Conference
Scopes trial, 496–497
Scotland
   18th century, emigration from, 119
   union with England, 78
Scots-Irish immigration, 119
Scott, Dred, 328
Scott, Thomas A., 382–383
Scott, Winfield
   in Civil War, 342
   and election of 1852, 322, 322t
   in Mexican-American War, 305
   and Trail of Tears, 289
   in War of 1812, 248
Scottsboro Boys, 512
Scribner's, 396

SDI. *See* Strategic Defense Initiative
SDS. *See* Students for a Democratic Society
Sea Islands
   land redistribution on, 362i, 362–363
   Union free labor experiments on, 358
Sears Roebuck catalog, 396
Seasoning of slaves, 95
Seattle, general strike in, 483, 483i
Seattle General Strike Committee, 483i
SEC. *See* Securities and Exchange Commission
Secession
   Confederate, 335–337, 336m
   right of, 273
Second Amendment
   debate over, 665
Second Confiscation Act (1862), 347
Second Party system, 284, 292, 308
Second Seminole War, 288
Securities and Exchange Act (1934), 523t
Securities and Exchange Commission (SEC), 518
Segregation
   19th century
      in armed forces, 408, 408i
      in education, 406, 408, 426, 427, 428–429, 434
      unions and, 415
      in West, 408–409
      in women's movements, 434–435
   20th century
      in armed forces, 478, 543
      Asians and, 452
      in education, 428, 460
      in federal government, 470
      in Great Flood refugee camps, 497
      in housing, 560, 577–578
      opposition to, 460, 573
      psychological effects of, 580–581
      resistance to, 554. *See also* Civil rights movement
      in World War I, 478
      post-World War II dismantling of, 579–583
   Supreme Court on, 426, 554
Seguin, Juan, 302
Selective Service Act (1915), 476
Selective Service Act (1980), 631
Self-determination, post-World War I, 480
The Selling of Joseph (Sewell), 102
Seminole War, Second, 288
Seminoles. *See also* Five Civilized Tribes
   assimilation of, 228, 275
   as buffalo soldiers, 408i
   establishment of, 250
   homeland, late 18th century, 198m
   Oklahoma Territory and, 288m
   removal of, 288–289
   U.S. war on, 267
Seneca Falls Convention, 300, 320, 374
Senecas, 182, 288m. *See also* Iroquois Confederacy
Senegambia, 93, 93m, 96m–97m
Separation of church and state, early proponents of, 49
Separation of powers, in state constitutions, 178
Separatists, 45
September 11th terrorist attacks, 676–677
   impact of, 635
   president's response to, 677–681
Sequoyah, 275i
Serpent Mound, 9m, 12i
Serra, Junípero, 141, 142m
Service organizations, mid-20th century, race and, 579i
Servicemen's Readjustment Act of 1944 (GI Bill), 553, 575

Settlement houses, 419, 434
Settlers
   anti-elitism of, 262
   challenges facing, 252
   debt and, 226, 266–267
   economic challenges of, 226
   Indian resistance and, 246
Seven Years' War, 82–83, 131
   cost of, 144
   impact of, 137, 141, 142
Seventeenth Amendment, 473
Severalty Act (1881), 398, 419
Seward, William H., 354
Sewell, Samuel, 102
Sexual harassment, in 1990s, 661
Sexuality
   18th century, 116
   19th century, 299–300
   20th century
      early, 456–457
      contraceptive rights activism, 471
      eugenics movement and, 455
      vice crusaders and, 459
      in 1920s, 496
      in World War II, 540
      post-World War II, 560–561
      in 1950s, 587, 588, 588i
      in 1960s, 574–575, 606
      in 1970s, 625
      in 1980s, 646
Seymour, Horatio, 367t
Shaftsburg, Earl of. *See* Ashley-Cooper, Anthony
Shaker Heights, Ohio, 578
Shakers, 230i
Share-Our-Wealth Plan, 522
Sharecropping system
   19th century, 363–364
   20th century, 502
Shawnee Indians. *See also* Ohio Confederacy
   home region of, 227
   Ohio Confederacy and, 216
   Oklahoma Territory and, 288m
   resistance, 246, 246i
   Revolutionary War and, 182, 183m
Shawnee Mission, Kansas, 326
Shays, Daniel, 206
Shays's Rebellion, 206
Sheep, introduction of, 36, 64, 64i
Shelburne, Earl of, 188
Shelikov, Grigorii, 140
Shelley v. *Kraemer* (1948), 554
Sheridan, Philip, 352, 357
Sherman, Roger, 169
Sherman, William T., 342i, 352, 353m, 356, 357, 362–363
Sherman Anti-Trust Act (1890), 399, 461
   in early 20th century, 473
   in 1990s, 657
   Supreme Court on, 431
Sherman Silver Purchase Act (1890), 430–431
Shi'ite Muslims, 637
Shima, George, 390–391
Shipbuilding. *See also* Navigation and boatbuilding technology
   Naval Stores Act (1705) and, 78
   in New England, 123, 220
Shopping centers, first, 500
Short, Mercy, 76
Shoshones, 112, 114m, 372
Sieh King King, 450–451
Sierra Club, 424–425, 462, 643
Sierra Leone, Back to Africa movement and, 165
Silent Spring (Carson), 589, 590
Simpson, O.J., 661–663

Sinclair, Upton, 458
Sioux
    18th century
        culture, 113
        migrations, 114, 114m
        Revolutionary War and, 182, 183m
        trade, 114
    19th century
        assimilation of, 422
        Black Hills and, 368
        culture, 312, 400
        Ghost Dance and, 409
        resistance, 316, 334, 411
        war with whites, 323, 343, 351, 357, 408
        wealth of, 369
        in Wild West show, 395, 395i
Sirica, John, 618
Sister Carrie (Dreiser), 458
Sisters of Mercy, 285
Sit-down strikes, in 1930s, 526i, 526–527
Sit-ins, in 1960s, 582
Sitting Bull, 368, 381, 395, 395i, 410
Sixteenth Amendment, 472
Sky City, 35i
Skyscrapers, 392, 447, 453
Slater, Samuel, 219
Slave Coast (Bight of Benin), 93, 93m, 96m–97m
Slave Power Conspiracy, 323
Slave trade
    domestic, 19th century, 287
    international. *See* Atlantic slave trade
Slavery
    in prehistoric Native American cultures, 7
    17th century
        in Carolina colonies, 69
        of Native Americans, 33, 35, 61, 65, 72, 87
        in Virginia, 44, 87, 88, 89–91
    18th century
        Declaration of Independence and, 169
        in Early Republic, 224–226
        France and, 236
        on frontier, 229
        Georgia prohibition of, 104–107
        Jefferson on, 235–236
        manumissions, 225–226
        in U.S. Constitution, 208–210
        in Virginia, 91, 98m
        white views on, 101–104
    19th century
        challenges faced by, 321
        Dred Scott decision, 328
        emancipation, 309, 341, 342
        Emancipation Proclamation, 345, 346
        English abolition of, 293
        expansionism of, 321, 322–323
        hardening of attitudes toward, 277
        manumissions, 275
        plantation economies and, 255–256
        as political issue, 294, 302, 321–325
        Republic of Texas and, 301–302
        slave states, 324m
        Wilmot Proviso and, 304
    abolition of
        emancipation, 309, 341, 342
        Emancipation Proclamation, 345, 346
        by England, 293
        in North, 224
        Northern opinion on, 309
    advantages over free labor, 88
    and Christianity, 86, 102, 279
    Declaration of Independence and, 169
    effect on whites, 264
    on frontier, 226–227
    headright system and, 90–91
    as hereditary condition, 84–85, 88
    importation of slaves. *See* Atlantic slave trade
    justifications of, 86, 87, 90, 259, 337
    Middle Passage, 91, 94–95
    and miscegenation, 91
    of Native Americans, 33, 35, 61, 66, 72, 87
    in Northeast, 102
    origins and expansion of, 82–83, 85–91
    and plantation agriculture, 85–87, 88–91, 89i, 229–230
        cotton, 163, 230, 255–256, 314
        rice, 88, 89i, 99
        tobacco, 88
    regional variations in, 255–256
    in Virginia, 88
        17th century, 44, 87, 89–90
        18th century, 91, 98m
    and wealth per capita, North *vs.* South, 123
    in western territories
        Compromise of 1850, 311, 322
        Crittenden Compromise, 335–336
        Kansas-Nebraska Act (1854), 323, 324m
        Missouri Compromise, 263–264, 263m
        Northwest Ordinance (1787), 200–201, 210, 227, 229m
        spread of, 226–227, 229–230, 265
Slaves
    17th century, in New Amsterdam, 41
    and American Revolution
        British offers of freedom to, 164–165, 167
        British Southern strategy and, 182
        manumission following, 225–226
        resistance during, 146
        suppression during, 167
    19th century
        diversity of, 315
        Dred Scott decision, 328
        education and, 428
        population, 334m
    and Civil War
        Confederate employment of, 337, 339
        perception of War, 346
        resistance by, 309, 333–334, 346
        runaway, 343, 346–348, 347i
        Union employment of, 346–348
    conversion to Christianity, 102, 125, 129, 258
    culture of, 125
    emancipation of, 309, 341, 342
        Emancipation Proclamation, 345, 346
        by England, 293
        Northern opinion of, 309
    families of
        benefits to slaveholder from, 99, 256
        breakup of, 287
    manumission
        18th century, 225–226
        19th century, 274
        restrictions on, 101–102
        Society for the Promotion of the Manumission of Slaves, 197
    Middle Passage and, 91, 94–95
    ornamental scarification, 84i
    on plantations, life and labor of, 256–258, 257i
    population
        18th century, 96–98, 98m
        in Kentucky, 228
        in South, 225
        19th century, 226, 256, 334m
    punishment of, 91, 99
    religion of, 257
    and representation, 208
    resistance by, 99–101
        in American Revolution, 146
        19th century, 258–259, 315
        in Civil War, 309, 333–334, 346
    restrictions on, 99
    runaway, 287
        advertisements for, 258i
        in Civil War, 343, 346–348, 347i
        in Constitution, 210
        and Fugitive Slave Act (1850), 308
        as resistance technique, 99
        Seminoles and, 267, 289
    sale of, 95, 287
    saltwater, 95
    seasoning of, 95
    theft by, 258
    uprisings
        18th century, 100–101
        19th century, 258–259, 275–277
        Bacon's Rebellion and, 71–72, 89–90
        Virginia (1800), 217
    white fear of, 99, 259, 275–277, 347
Slavs, 20th century, immigration by, 492
Slidell, John, 303, 346
Sloan, Alfred P., Jr., 496
Slovakia, late 19th century, immigration from, 393
Slow Food Movement, 690
Smallpox, 191i
    15th-16th century, Native Americans and, 3, 17
    17th century
        Native Americans and, 36–37, 39, 48, 50
    18th century
        epidemic, 191–192, 192m
        in Revolutionary War, 168, 176
        use against Indians, 143
Smith, Alfred E., 489t
Smith, Bessie, 493
Smith, Howard K., 615
Smith, Hyram, 289
Smith, John, 42–43, 45
Smith, Joseph, 279
Smith, Joseph, Jr., 289–290
Smith, Mary Rozet, 457
Smith v. *Albright* (1944), 554
Smog, 575, 599
SNCC. *See* Student Nonviolent Coordinating Committee
Social class
    in pre-history, emergence of, 7
    18th century
        American Revolution and, 137–138, 146, 150, 159
        in Early Republic, 231, 232–235
        military service and, 179–180
    19th century
        among African Americans, 363, 407
        class struggle and, 415, 417, 423, 430–434
        education and, 299
        race and, 316–317
        Social Darwinism and, 399–400
        in South, 314
        Tocqueville on, 273
        wide difference in, 262, 397
    20th century
        class struggle and, 538, 554, 611
        eating disorders and, 665, 665i
        Great Depression and, 504, 511
        wide difference in, 596, 637, 641, 643–644, 644f, 657–658, 659
        women's movement and, 444
        World War II and, 531

Social conservatives, 646
Social Darwinism
　imperialism and, 441
　theory of, 381, 399–400, 496–499
Social engineering, late 19th century, 397
Social Gospel, 417
Social Security
　in 1980s, 641
　Eisenhower and, 583
　Kennedy and, 591
Social Security Act (1935), 521, 522–524, 523t
Social Security Administration, establishment of, 523–524
Social settlement houses, 434
Socialism
　19th century, limited appeal in, 434
　20th century
　　advocates of, 459, 460, 522
　　fear of, 446, 471
　　increased interest in, 510–511, 521, 552, 555
　　New Deal and, 527
Socialist party
　early 20th century, 460
　and election of 1904, 462t
　and election of 1908, 463t
　and election of 1912, 464t
　and election of 1916, 473t
　and election of 1920, 488t
　and election of 1928, 489t
　and election of 1932, 516t
　World War I and, 478
Society for the Promotion of the Manumission of Slaves, 197
Society for the Propagation of the Gospel in Foreign Parts (SPG), 102
Society of Jesus. *See* Jesuits
Society of the Cincinnati, 195, 208
Sod houses, 412
Somalia, U.S. intervention in, 670
Some Considerations on the Keeping of Negros (Woolman), 104
Somoza, Antonio, 640
Song of Myself (Whitman), 318
Sons of Liberty
　and Boston Massacre, 154
　and Boston Tea Party, 155
　British view of, 155i
　and social class, 150
　Stamp Act and, 146, 146i, 148
Sooners, 424
Sound, in 18th century, 128–129
South. *See also* Civil War; Confederacy
　18th century
　　American Revolution in, 167
　　economy of, 220
　　Indian groups in, 198m
　　manumissions, 225–226
　　religion in, 126
　　Revolutionary War in, 184–187, 185m
　　slave population, 98m, 226
　pre–Civil War
　　abolitionist movement in, 293–294, 294i
　　economy of, 254, 314–315
　　education in, 299
　　election of 1860, 330, 330t
　　free blacks in, 275–276
　　industrialization in, 254
　　manumissions, 275
　　regional economies, 256
　　religious institutions, 279
　　slave population, 334m
　　social class in, 314
　　voting rights in, 209
　post–Civil War
　　African Americans in, 406–408
　　black flight from, 409
　　discrimination in, 426, 434
　　economy, 371, 406
　　impact of War, 357
　　Jews in, 427
　　labor issues in, 361–362, 391
　　sharecropping in, 362–363
　　white supremacy doctrine in, 426, 434
　20th century
　　anti-Catholic sentiment in, 499
　　economy, 562
　　migration from, 578
　　New Deal and, 506
　　sharecropping system in, 502
　　voting rights in, 595
South Africa, apartheid in, ending of, 626
South America. *See also* Americas
　in prehistory
　　agriculture, 7
　　Incan empire, 8, 9m
　　slave trade and, 86–87, 96m–97m, 108
South Carolina
　16th century, Spanish colonization of, 25, 25i
　18th century
　　Constitutional ratification by, 213
　　economy, 121, 122m, 220
　　Negro Acts, 99
　　in Revolutionary War, 167, 170, 184–185, 185m
　　slave population, 97–99, 98m
　　slave revolts in, 167
　　slavery in, 100–101, 202
　　tax resistance in, 146
　　western land claims of, 229m
　　westward expansion, 199
　19th century
　　economy, 256, 265, 314
　　nullification and, 273
　　readmission to Union, 365m, 367
　　rice plantations in, 121, 256
　　and slavery, 88, 89i, 99
　　secession, 335, 336m, 337
　　slave revolts in, 275–276
South Dakota, statehood for, 384
South Korea
　immigration from, 648
　as trading partner, 685f
South Vietnam. *See also* Vietnam War
　Army of, 600
　establishment of, 600
　fall of, 619, 619i
　morale of, 601
Southern Alliance, 414
Southern Christian Leadership Conference (SCLC), 582
Southern Cultivator, 342
Southern Europe, early 20th century, immigration from, 452
Southern Manifesto, 581
Southern Overland Trail, 286m
Southern Tenant Farmers Union (STFU), 521
Southwest. *See also* Old Southwest
　16th century, Spanish in, 22–23
　17th century, Spanish in, 33–36, 34m, 35i
　18th century, resistance to Spanish rule, 141
　19th century, 266m
　　cultural conflict in, 403–404
　　land conflict in, 312–313
　　Native Americans in, wars with whites, 368–369
　　property rights in, 371
　20th century, immigration to, 448m, 449–450

Native Americans in
　500-1500, 10–11
　assimilation, 229
　wars with whites, 368–369
Soviet Union
　World War II and, 533, 543–544, 545
　　casualties, 530
　　nonaggression pact with Germany, 532, 533, 543
　　U.S. relations, 543, 545, 550, 550i
　post–World War II
　　economy of, 555–556
　　expansionism of, 555–558
　　fear of, 507
　　policy goals, 555–556
　　power of, 548, 556
　　U.S. relations, 552, 554, 555–558
　in Cold War
　　atomic arms acquisition, 566–567
　　Berlin Wall construction, 592
　　Cuban Missile Crisis, 592
　　mutual defense treaty with China, 566, 566i
　　Reagan on, 640
　　space programs, 572, 575, 583
　　Spanish civil war and, 532
　　sphere of influence, 586m–587m
　　spies, 563
　　U.S. relations, 615, 617, 619
　late 20th century
　　in Afghanistan, 637, 638
　　Chernobyl nuclear accident, 637, 647, 648
　　collapse of, 634, 648–649, 650, 652m
　　economy of, 648
　　historians' view of, 559
Sozodont dentifrice, 396
Space exploration
　Cold War and, 572, 575, 583
　moon landing, 613
Spain
　15th-16th century
　　Atlantic slave trade and, 18, 19i
　　explorations and colonization, 15–21, 16m–17m, 25–27, 26m
　　Inquisition in, 24
　　slavery and, 85–86
　　Spanish Armada, 24, 27
　17th century
　　consolidation with Portugal, 32
　　explorations and colonization, 32–37, 34m, 63, 63m
　　Indians, slave raids on, 62
　　Pueblo Revolt and, 62, 63m
　　slavery and, 86
　18th century
　　American Revolution and, 174, 181, 184
　　explorations and colonization, 58m, 63–65, 113, 138–139, 141–142, 142m, 229i
　　loss of Florida, 82–83
　　Louisiana and, 162, 197
　　Native American policies, 112
　　new world ambitions of, 193
　　in Old Southwest, 196–197, 198m
　　Treaty of Paris (1763) and, 134
　　war with England, 100, 105–106, 107m
　19th century
　　colonial losses, 237, 267, 268
　　explorations and colonization, 162, 275, 278
　　Spanish-American War, 381, 438–440, 439m
　　U.S. wariness of, 267
　　and U.S. migration to Texas, 265
　　women's role and status, 277–278

20th century
post-World War II, 557m
civil war in, 532
fascism in, 531–532
Spanish-American-Cuban-Filipino War (1898), 381, 438–440, 439m, 468
Spanish Armada, 24, 27
Speakeasies, 490i, 491
Spectacles, late 19th century, 395–396
Speert, Edith, 540
Spelling, American, origin of, 197
SPG. *See* Society for the Propagation of the Gospel in Foreign Parts
Spice trade, and search for route to Asia, 13–17
Spiece, John B., 338–339
Spirit of St. Louis, 487
Spiro, Oklahoma, mound-builders in, 9m, 11
Spock, Benjamin, 560, 575
Spoils system, 270, 377, 398. *See also* Patronage system
Sport Utility Vehicles (SUVs), 635, 656
Sports
late 19th century, 394, 395
20th century
in 1920s and 1930s, 486i, 487, 527–528
desegregation of baseball, 554
women and, 486i, 487, 528, 631, 691i
commercialization of, 688
Title IX and, 692
Spotted Tail, 368
Sputnik, 575, 583
Sputnik II, 583
Squanto, 31–32
Stackpole, Ralph, 525i
Stagflation, 620, 626
Stalin, Joseph
communist bloc and, 566i
death of, 584
fear of U.S. power, 552
reconstruction planning, 507
World War II and, 543, 546–547, 556
Stalingrad, Battle of, 544, 544m
Stamp Act (1765), 145
repeal of, 148
resistance to, 145–148, 147m
Stamp Act Congress, 145, 146
Standard Oil Trust, 389, 458
Standardization
in education, 429
railroads and, 383
Standing armies
in colonies, 1763-1766, 147m
fear of, 73, 195
in Real Whig ideology, 153
World War I and, 475
Standing Bear, 418, 422
Standing Bear, Luther, 422–423
Standing Rock Reservation, 409, 425m
Stands-in-Timber, John, 112i
Stanton, Edwin, 366, 367
Stanton, Elizabeth Cady, 278, 300, 320, 374, 434
Stanton, Henry B, 278
Staples, Yatta, 659
"Star Spangled Banner," 249i
Star Wars. *See* Strategic Defense Initiative
Starr, Kenneth, 668
State(s)
constitutions, creation of, 176–178
government of, in Anti-Federalist theory, 212–213
governors, restrictions on powers of, 177–178
legislatures, under Reconstruction, 367

western land claims of, 199–200, 201m, 229m
State militias, tensions in, 180
State-Rights Democratic party (Dixiecrats), and election of 1948, 563, 563t
States' rights
Confederate union and, 341
in Jacksonian era, 270
nullification principle, 223, 272
Statue of Liberty, 389, 391
Steam Cotton Manufacturing Company, 219
Steamboats
19th century, expanded use of, 265
introduction of, 253
Steel production, late 19th century, 385, 388
Steffens, Lincoln, 458
Steichen, Edward, 458
Steinbeck, John, 513
Steinem, Gloria, 630i
Stephens, Alexander H., 360
Stephens, Uriah, 376
Sterilization, compulsory, 454–455, 497
Steuben, Friedrich von, 180, 181i
Stevens, Thaddeus, 366
Stevenson, Adlai E.
and election of 1952, 568t, 569
and election of 1956, 583t
Stewart, Maria, 275, 293, 319
STFU. *See* Southern Tenant Farmers Union
Stieglitz, Alfred, 458
Stille, Wilhelm, 286
Stock market
1929 collapse of, 487, 502–504
late 20th century, 634, 656
in 2000s, 674
Stokes, Carl, 605
Stoller, Mike, 588
Stone, Lucy, 373
Stone age hunter-gatherers, 5–6, 6i
Stonewall Brigade, 354
Stonewall riots, 609
Stoney Creek, Battle of, 248m
Stono Rebellion, 100–101, 105, 107m
Stop-ERA campaign, 631–632
Stowe, Harriet Beecher, 326
Straits of Gibraltar, 13–14, 14m
Strategic Arms Limitations Treaties (SALT I and II), 617, 638
Strategic Defense Initiative (Star Wars; SDI), 641
Strategic hamlet program, 601
Streetcars, electric, introduction of, 393
Streeter, Anson J., 399t
Strong, Josiah, 400
Stuart, Gilbert, 216i
Stuart dynasty, 66
Student Nonviolent Coordinating Committee (SNCC), 582m, 583, 595, 604
Student radicals, in 1960s, 605–606, 606i
Students for a Democratic Society (SDS), 605–606, 606i
Stuyvesant, Peter, 40–41, 68
Submarine warfare, in World War I, 475–476
Submerged Land Act, 584
Suburbs
commuters, 578i
growth of, 393, 561, 575, 577
minorities and, 577–578
Sudetenland, 532
Suez Canal, 467, 585
Suffolk Resolves, 158
Sugar Act (1764), 144
Sugar plantations
in Caribbean, 85–86
in Cuba, 437

on Hawaiian Islands, 436
Sullivan, Ann, 459
Sullivan, John, 182–183, 184i, 205, 206, 207
Sullivan's Island, 97, 107m
A Summary View of the Rights of British America (Jefferson), 156
Sumner, Charles, 327–328, 366, 373
Sumner, William Graham, 399–400
Sumter, Thomas, 185, 186
Sun Yat-sen, 468
Sunbelt, 20th century growth of, 562
Supreme Court
on abortion, 608, 631
on affirmative action, 632
on African American rights, 308
Alien and Sedition Acts and, 222
Amistad case and, 295
on Anti-Trust law, 431
chief justices of, 236
on Civil Rights Act of 1875, 377, 398
Civil War and, 335
on compulsory sterilization, 496
on desegregation of schools, 580–581
Dred Scott decision, 328
and election of 2000, 656, 671–672, 673m
establishment of, 217
first female Justice, 632
on free speech, 599
on income tax, 431
on interracial marriage, 599
on interstate regulation, 398
on Japanese internment, 536
on local school autonomy, 613
on minority rights, 406
on Native American legal status, 272
on Nixon White House tapes, 618
on prayer in public schools, 599
on racial discrimination, 454–455
on racial quotas, 632
on right to legal counsel, 599
Roosevelt court packing plan, 525
on Scottsboro Boys, 512
on segregation, 426, 554
settlers' view of, 262
on state power, 271
on teaching of evolution, 496
Warren Court, 599
on worker protection legislation, 459
Susquehannock, 39m, 71
Sutter, John, 310
SUVs. *See* Sport Utility Vehicles
Svan, John, 454–455
Sweatshops, 20th century, 659, 659i
Sweatt v. *Painter* (1950), 554
Sweden
17th century colonies, 40
19th century immigration, 284
Swift, Elizabeth, 637
Swiss Reformation, 23–24
Switzerland, immigration from, 314
Symmes purchase, 201m
Syngman Rhee, 568

T

Taft, William Howard
career of, 463, 464
and election of 1908, 463, 463t
and election of 1912, 464t
as president, 463
Taft-Hartley Act (1947), 554
Taiwan
Chinese Nationalists on, 565
as trading partner, 685f
U.S. defense of, 568–569
Taliban, 677, 678
Taliban regime in Afghanistan, 670

Talleyrand, Charles, 222
Tammany Hall, 376, 377i, 394
Taney, Roger B., 328
Tanzania, bombing of U.S. embassy in, 670
Taos Trail, 286m
Tape, Joseph, 406
Tape, Mamie, 406
Tape, Mary, 406
Tape v. *Hurley* (1885), 406
Tappan, Arthur, 294i
Tappan, Lewis, 294i
Tarbell, Ida, 458
Tariff(s)
    18th century, 218
    19th century, 396–397, 399, 429–430, 432, 436
    20th century, 463, 472, 504, 511, 668–669
    Corn Laws (Britain), 301
Tariff Act of 1930, 504
Task system, 257
Taxation. *See also* Income tax; Tariff(s)
    pre-Revolution, 144–145
        representation and, 145, 150–152
        resistance to, 152–153, 154–158
    early Republic, 202, 203–204, 219
        constitutional limitations proposed for, 213
        resistance to, 207, 217, 220–221
        war debt and, 193, 203–206
    19th century
        of Chinese workers, 406
        city growth and, 394
        in Confederacy, 348
        policies, 388
        in Union, resistance to, 345
    20th century
        early, 473, 504
        in 1960s, 591, 596
        in 1980s, 641
        in 1990s, 667
        in 2000s, 674
Taylor, Frederick Winslow, 391
Taylor, Susie King, 348
Taylor, Zachary, 303, 321, 321t
Tea Act (1773), 155–156
Tea trade, 18th century, 202–203, 204
Teach, Edward (Blackbeard), 77, 77i, 78
Teamsters Union, 659
Teapot Dome scandal, 488
Technology. *See also* Railroad(s)
    19th century
        agriculture, 314, 412
        communications, 296, 385
        education and training in, 382
        and growth of cities, 391–393
        innovations, 240, 385–386, 391
        mining, 387
        navigation and boatbuilding, 301
        transportation, 253
        urban design and architecture, 391–393
    20th century
        early, 445, 467
        mid, 574–575
        late
            economy and, 657
    communications
        19th century, 296, 385
        early 20th century, 467
    in globalization, 682–683
    Native American
        Archaic period, 6, 7
        bow and arrow, 11
    navigation and boatbuilding
        15th century, 13–16, 14m, 16m
        17th century, 34, 58
        18th century, 203

    19th century, 301
transportation
    19th century, 253
    early 20th century, 467
Tecumseh, 246, 247, 248, 249
Teheran Conference (1943), 547
Tejanos, 291, 301, 313
Telegraph, invention of, 296
Telephone
    invention of, 385
    service to Europe, 467
Television
    in 1950s and 1960s, 576
    national culture and, 604
    Public Broadcasting System (PBS), 598–599
Teller Amendment (1898), 438
Temperance movement
    18th century, 197
    19th century, 296, 297, 417, 420i
        African American women and, 435
        nativists and, 295
        women's rights movement, 299, 300
    20th century, Prohibition, 490i, 490–491
Ten Percent Plan, 358–359, 365m
Tenements, early 20th century, 448, 449i
Tennent, Gilbert, 128
Tennent, William, 128
Tennessee
    18th century, establishment of, 199
    19th century
        economy of, 265
        election campaigns in, 261
        readmission to Union, 365m, 367
        Reconstruction and, 364–365
        secession, 335m, 336
Tennessee Coal, Iron, and Railway Company, 406
Tennessee Supreme Court, Scopes trial and, 498
Tennessee Valley Authority (TVA), 519m, 519–520, 523t
Tenochtitlán, 9m, 10, 19, 20, 22
Tenskwatawa (the Prophet), 246, 246i, 249
Tenure of Office Act (1867), 366, 367
Teotihuacan, 9m, 10
Territories. *See also* Frontier; *specific territories*
    government of, 201
    slavery in
        Compromise of 1850, 311, 322
        Crittenden Compromise, 335
        Kansas-Nebraska Act (1854), 323, 324m
        Missouri Compromise, 263–264, 263m
        Northwest Ordinance (1787), 200–202–203, 226m, 227, 229m
        spread of, 226, 229–230, 265
Terrorism
    September 11th attacks, 676–677
Terrorism, late 20th century, 634, 635
    domestic, 664
    as elusive target, 635
    by Islamic fundamentalists, 670–671
        September 11th attacks, 635, 676i, 677-678, 693i
Tet Offensive, 602, 603m, 611
Texas
    17th century, Spanish settlements in, 62–64
    19th century
        American settlement in, 266, 266m
        annexation of, 302
        diversity in, 291
        independence of, 301–302
        migration to, 312–313
        racial discrimination in, 317

        readmission to Union, 365m, 367
        secession of, 336m, 337
        U.S. conquest of, 268
    20th century, immigration to, 492
Texas Rangers, 301, 313, 409
Textile industry
    in North, 253–254, 278, 430m
    in South, 253i, 254, 391
Thames, Battle of, 248, 248m
Thanksgiving, 45
Thayendanegea, 216, 216i
Third World
    early 20th century, anticolonialism in, 480
    Carter foreign policy and, 616
    Cold War in, 575, 584, 585, 640
Thirteenth Amendment, 359, 360
33rd United States Colored Cavalry, 348
This Side of Paradise (Fitzgerald), 501
Thomas, Clarence, 661
Thomas, Gertrude, 349
Thomas, Norman, 489t, 516t
Thoreau, Henry David, 300
Thornton, Willie Mae, 588
Thoughts on Government (Adams), 179
Three Days of the Condor (film), 623
Three-fifths rule, 210
Three Mile Island nuclear accident, 627, 647
Thurmond, J. Strom, 563t
Tiffany and Co., 435
Tilden, Samuel J., 377–378, 378t
Till, Emmett, 581, 582m
Timber Culture Act (1873), 371
Time-Warner Corp., 657
Tippecanoe, Battle of, 226m, 246i, 246
"Tippecanoe and Tyler Too," 294
Title IX, 692
Title IX, Educational Amendments of 1972, 631
Tito, Josip Broz, 670
Tobacco
    Chesapeake Bay economy and 18th century, 121–123, 121i, 122m
    19th century, 256
    cigarette-rolling machine, 406
    civil suits against, 657
    Jamestown colony and, 42–43
    marketing of, 435, 500
    slavery and, 88
    soil depletion and, 228
    surgeon-general's warnings on, 598
    women and, 500
Tocqueville, Alexis de, 273
Tojo, Hideki, 534
Tokugawa dynasty, 32–33
Toltecs, 9m, 10
Tonkawa, reservation, opening of, 424
Tories, in American Revolution, 137–138
Torjersen family, 283
Tourism
    late 19th century, 369i, 386–387, 425
    in 1920s, 496i
Townsend, Francis, 521
Townsend Plan, 521
Townshend, Charles, 152
Townshend Duties, 152–153, 154
Toynbee Hall, 417
Trade. *See also* Atlantic slave trade; Free trade
    in pre-history
        Mississippian cultures and, 11
        Vikings and, 13
    15th century, search for Indies, 13–17
    17th century
        with Native Americans, 36i, 37–39, 64–65
        Navigation Acts and (1660; 1663), 67

18th century, 119–121, 253–254
   Mississippi River and, 196–197, 198m
   with Native Americans, 112–115, 114m, 130, 143
   post-Revolution, 203–204
19th century, 301
   in Pacific, 323
   transportation and, 264–265
20th century
   in 1930s, 511
   with Native Americans. *See also* Fur trade
   17th century, 36i, 37–39, 55, 64–65
   18th century, 113–115, 114m, 130, 143
   top ten trading partners, 685f
Trade unions. *See* Union(s)
Trafalgar, Battle of, 244
Trail of Tears, 288m, 288–289
Trans-Alaska Pipeline System, 627
Trans-Siberian railroad, 467
Transcendentalism, 300, 304
Transcontinental railroad, 491f
   construction of, 367, 369–370, 370i
   impact of, 398
Transcontinental Treaty (1819), 266m, 267
Transparency, democratic society and, 625
Transportation. *See also* Automobiles; Railroad(s)
   19th century
      infrastructure growth, 253
      innovations in, 253
      westward migration and, 264–265
   20th century, innovations in, 467
Travels of Marco Polo (Polo), 13
Treaty(ies), with Native Americans. *See also individual treaties and tribes*
   U.S. policy on, 368
   as white manipulation, 246
Treaty of Fort Atkinson (1854), 312
Treaty of Fort Laramie (1868), 369
Treaty of Ghent (1815), 250
Treaty of Guadalupe Hidalgo (1848), 305, 310, 311, 312
Treaty of Horseshoe Bend, 250
Treaty of Medicine Lodge Creek, 368
Treaty of Paris (1763), 131, 134
Treaty of Paris (1783), 188, 188i, 198
Treaty of Payne's Landing (1832), 288
Treaty of Tordesillas (1494), 16m
Treaty of Utrecht (1713), 77-78
Treaty Party, 289
Tredegar Iron Works, 337, 349
Trench warfare, 472, 473i
Trenchard, John, 149
Trent (ship), 346
Trenton, Battle of, 173
Trial by jury
   Gaspee affair and, 154
   vice-admiralty courts and, 144
Triangle Shirtwaist Company fire, 446i, 446–447
Trickle-down economics, 644f
Triple Alliance, 467
Triple Entente, 467, 472, 475, 479m
Tripoli, war against, 237
Tripp, Linda, 668
Troy Female Seminary, 278
Truman, Harry S
   assumption of presidency, 507, 551
   atomic bomb and, 547
   civil rights movement and, 562
   containment and, 556
   decolonization and, 558
   and election of 1946, 554
   and election of 1948, 562–563, 563t
   Israel and, 558

Korean War and, 567–569
McCarthyism and, 562-563
policies of, on Native Americans, 564–565
post-War vision of, 555, 556
and Soviet atomic bomb, 565–566
Soviet relations and, 552
Truman Doctrine, 556
unions and, 554
World War II peace and, 547
Truman Doctrine, 556
Trusts
   late 19th century, rise of, 388–389
   busting of, 461, 463, 474, 657. *See also* Sherman Anti-Trust Act
Truth, Sojourner, 320, 320i, 374
Tryon, William, 150–151
Tryon Palace, 150–151, 151i
Tubman, Harriet, 322
Tudor dynasty, 24
Tulsa race riots (1921), 466–467, 483
Tumulty, Joseph, 483
Tunica Indians, 114
Turkey
   Cold War and, 555, 556, 558
   NATO and, 584
Turner, Frederick Jackson, 423, 424i, 428
Turner, Nat, 275– 277
Turning Stone casino, 657
Tuscarora Indians, 78, 182
Tuskegee Institute, 427
Tuxpan, Mexico, 306i
TVA. *See* Tennessee Valley Authority
Twain, Mark, 397, 440
Tweed, William M. "Boss," 376, 377i, 394
25th Infantry, 408
Twenty-First Amendment, 518
24th Infantry, 408
Twenty-One Demands, 468
Twenty-Negro Law, 334
Twenty-Sixth Amendment, 613
Two party system
   collapse of, 321–323
   emergence of, 218
Tyler, John
   and annexation of Texas, 302
   and election of 1840, 294–295, 295t
   Monroe doctrine and, 268
   as president, 295
Typhoid
   in Civil War, 345
   early 20th century, 454
Typhus, Native Americans and, 37

U
U-2 spy plane incident, 585
U-boats, in World War I, 476–477
UAW. *See* United Auto Workers
UMW. *See* United Mine Workers
Uncle Tom's Cabin (Stowe), 326
Underground Railroad, 322, 326, 327m
Underwood-Simmons Tariff (1913), 472
Unemployment
   in Great Depression, 510, 511–512
   New Deal and, 518
   in 1970s, 616, 621
   in 1990s, 658, 666
Unemployment Councils, 506
Unemployment insurance, 583
UNIA. *See* Universal Negro Improvement Association
Union(s). *See also* Collective bargaining rights; Workers movements
   19th century
      African Americans and, 376, 415
      efforts to suppress, 415, 431, 432–433

militancy of, 412–415
minorities and, 415, 434
and politics, 292–293
rise of, 375–376, 380
Social Darwinism and, 399
socialism and, 415
strikes, 382, 383i, 413–414, 415, 431, 432–433
violence by, 415–416
women and, 315i, 376, 413–414
worker resistance to, 434
   early 20th century
      alliance with Democratic party, 471
      fear of, 482
      legitimization of, 518
      radicals and, 460, 482
      recognition efforts, 482
      resistance to, 482
      rise of, 460
      strikes, 446–447, 461, 471, 482
      suppression of, 461, 471, 471i, 502
      women and, 460, 502
      World War I and, 478
   in 1920s and 1930s
      activism of, 506, 507, 521, 526–527, 526i
      hostility toward, 502
      legitimization of, 518
      minorities and, 521
      strikes, 521, 526–527
      women and, 526–527
   World War II and, 539, 541
   post-World War II, 554
   in 1950s and 1960s
      for farm workers, 608
      minorities and, 564i, 608, 608i
   in 1970s and 1980s, Reagan and, 644
   late 20th century, 659
      decline of, 635
      free trade and, 669
      globalization and, 679
Union (Civil War)
   anti-black violence in, 350
   civil disorder in, 349–350
   conscription in, 349–350
   consolidation of power in, 341–342
   industrial base, 342
   rise of, 19th century, 292–293
   strategy of, 342, 348, 350
   women in, black, 347–348
Union Army
   African American soldiers in, 333i
   brutality toward Native Americans, 351, 351i
Union Labor party, 399t
Union Navy, 345
Union Pacific Railroad, 343, 368, 377, 405
Union party, 525t
United Airlines Flight 93, 676i
United Auto Workers (UAW), 527
United Fruit Co., 585
United Kingdom
   as trading partner, 685f
United Mine Workers (UMW), 416, 461, 483
United Nations
   establishment of, 552–553
   General Assembly, 552–553
   Human Rights Charter, 553
   Persian Gulf War and, 652
   Security Council, 553
United Nations of Indians, 341
United Parcel Service, 659
United Society of Believers in Christ's Second Appearance, 230i
United States
   challenges facing, post-World War II, 551, 552

United States, *continued*
　　Cold War sphere of influence, 586m–587m
　　as global policeman, 462, 653
　　policy goals, post-World War II, 555
　　power of
　　　global, emergence of, 467–468
　　　post-World War II, 543, 556
　　Soviet relations. *See also* Cold War
　　　in World War II, 543, 545, 550, 550i
　　　post-World War II, 552, 554, 555–558
　　　in Cold War, 615, 617, 619
United States v. *E. C. Knight* (1895), 431
Universal Negro Improvement Association (UNIA), 492
Upper South
　　secession, 336m, 337
　　slavery in, 225
Uprising of twenty thousand, 447
Uranium, mining of, 636
Urban mob violence
　　19th century, 284, 286
　　　anti-abolitionist, 293–294, 294i
　　　anti-black, 294
　　　anti-draft, 350
　　　in Civil War, 349, 350
　　20th century
　　　gay riots, 609
　　　race riots, 466–467, 478, 483, 604–605, 611
Urban renewal, mid-20th century, 578
Urrutia, Turibio de, 110
U.S. Forest Service, 642
U.S. Geological Survey (USGS), establishment of, 385
U.S.-Mexican War, 302–306, 303m, 306i, 310–311
U.S. Sanitary Commission, 342
U.S. Steel, 527
USDA. *See* Department of Agriculture
Utah and Utah Territory, 324m
　　in late 19th century, 391
　　nuclear testing in, 559
　　settlement of, 289–290
　　statehood and, 322
　　U.S. acquisition of, 312
　　women's voting rights and, 420
Utes, 64, 112, 114m, 408
Utopias, 19th century, 299–300

V

V-E (Victory in Europe) Day, 545
V-J (Victory in Japan) Day, 547i, 548
Valens, Ritchie, 588
Valentino, Rudolph, 493, 494i
Vallandigham, Clement, 350
Valley Forge, Continental Army at, 176, 181, 181i
Van Buren, Martin
　　Amistad case and, 294, 295t
　　and election of 1836, 292, 292t
　　and election of 1840, 294, 295t
　　and election of 1844, 302, 302t
　　and election of 1848, 321, 321t
Vance, Cyrus, 638
Vance, Zebulon, 341
Vancouver, George, 191–192
Vanzetti, Bartolomeo, 491, 491i
Vargas, Diego de, 64
Vatican Index of prohibited books, 24
Veblen, Thorstein, 429
Velez, Lupe, 493
Venereal disease, in World War II, 540
Ventura, Jesse, 674

Vera Cruz, U.S. landing at, 305, 306i, 469, 469m
Vergennes, Comte de, 177
Vermont
　　in 1990s, same-sex marriage in, 661, 662
　　civil union law in, 661, 662
Verrazzano, Giovanni da, 21, 26m
Versailles, 57
Versailles Treaty (1919), 467, 481, 482, 484
Vertical integration, 388–389
Vesey, Denmark, 274–275
Vespucci, Amerigo, 17
Veterans Administration, 553, 560
Viagra, 665
Vice-admiralty courts, 144, 152, 157m
Vice crusaders, early 20th century, 459
Vicksburg, siege of, 350
Victorianism, 281, 373, 427
Victory gardens, 539
Victory girls, 538–539
Viet Cong. *See* National Liberation Front
Vietminh, 600
Vietnam
　　Clinton visit to, 669–670
　　post-World War II
　　　French in, 558, 600
　　　independence of, 552, 600
Vietnam War, 573, 599–604, 603m
　　antiwar movement, 573, 605–606, 611, 612, 613
　　atrocities in, 602
　　bombing of North Vietnam, 601, 613
　　casualties in, 354
　　containment and, 599, 600
　　costs of, 620
　　draft resistance in, 605, 626
　　under Eisenhower, 600
　　escalation of, 600–601
　　events leading to, 600
　　fall of South Vietnam, 619, 619i
　　Ford and, 619
　　Gulf of Tonkin Resolution, 601
　　historians' view of, 559
　　impact of, 625
　　Johnson and, 573, 595–596, 599–600, 602–603,
　　Kennedy and, 591
　　Laos and Cambodia in, 613
　　lessons learned from, 653
　　My Lai massacre, 602
　　Nixon and, 573, 612–613
　　resistance to, 603
　　Tet Offensive, 602, 603m, 611
　　U.S. reasons for fighting, 600
　　U.S. soldiers in, 601–602, 602i, 613, 619
　　U.S. view of, 601–602
　　veterans' antiwar activism, 613
　　Vietnamese view of, 601
　　Vietnamization of, 613
　　women in, 602, 602i
Vietnamese, U.S. view of, 601–602, 602i
Vietnamization, 613
Vigilantes
　　19th century
　　　in California, 405
　　　post-Civil War, 362–363, 364, 367
　　　in South, 408, 426
　　　in Southwest, 403–404
　　20th century
　　　anti-black, 483
　　　lynchings, 460, 470, 483, 512, 522, 553, 581
　　　in Southwest, 449–450
　　　Tulsa race riots (1921), 466–467
　　　in World War I, anti-German, 478
Vikings, new world explorations, 2, 13
Villa, Francisco "Pancho," 468m, 469

Vindication of the Rights of Woman (Wollstonecraft), 231
Vinland settlement, 13
Violence. *See also* Urban mob violence
　　19th century, in dispute resolution, 284–285
　　20th century
　　　against African Americans, 460, 470, 483, 512, 522, 553, 581
　　　school shootings, 656, 664–665
Virgin Islands, 469m
Virginia. *See also* Richmond, Virginia
　　17th century
　　　Bacon's Rebellion, 71–73
　　　colonial government in, 44
　　　colonization of, 42–45
　　　slavery in, 44, 87, 88, 89–91
　　　tobacco economy in, 43–44
　　18th century
　　　Alien and Sedition Acts and, 222
　　　Constitutional ratification by, 212i, 213
　　　Declaration of Rights, 178, 210
　　　economy of, 121–123, 220
　　　free blacks in, 101–102
　　　Gaspee affair and, 154
　　　manumission in, 225–226
　　　slave population in, 97–98, 98m
　　　state constitution of, 178–179
　　　tax resistance in, 145
　　　tobacco economy in, 121–123
　　　western land claims, 201, 229m
　　　westward expansion, 199
　　19th century
　　　economy of, 265
　　　free blacks in, 291
　　　infrastructure development, 253
　　　military district, 201, 201m
　　　readmission to Union, 365m, 367
　　　secession, 336m, 337
　　　slave revolts in, 275–276
　　20th century, eugenics laws, 497
Virginia Company, 42–44, 51
Virginia Plan, 210
Virginia Resolves, 145
"The Vision of Columbus" (Barlow), 196
VISTA. *See* Volunteers in Service to America
Vizcaíno, Sebastián, 32–33, 34m
Voluntary associations. *See* Association(s)
Volunteers in Service to America (VISTA), 597
Voter(s)
　　participation by
　　　19th century, 262
　　　20th century, 647
Voting age, Twenty-Sixth Amendment and, 613
Voting rights. *See also* Women's suffrage movement
　　18th century
　　　of African Americans, 224, 276
　　　in Constitution, 207–208, 209
　　　property requirements, 201
　　　of women, 163, 217
　　19th century, 241, 262, 274
　　　of African Americans, 276, 374, 426, 434
　　　of Native Americans, 209
　　　post-Civil War
　　　　of African Americans, 210, 358–361, 363–364, 365m, 367, 374
　　　　of Confederates, 364
　　　in Western states, 261
　　　of women, 209, 373–374, 419–420
　　20th century
　　　of African Americans, 553, 554, 595, 598, 605

and election of 2000, 672–673
women and, 459–460, 471
Voting Rights Act (1965), 598, 605

W

Wabash and Erie Canal, 264m
Wabash v. *Illinois* (1886), 398
Wachovia, North Carolina, 123
WACs. *See* Women's Army Corps
Wade-Davis Bill (1864), 358
Wage slavery, 316
Wagner Act (1935), 522, 523t
Wal-Mart, 684
Walden (Thoreau), 318
Walker, David, 275, 293
Walker, William, 323
Walker's Appeal to the Coloured Citizens of the World (Walker), 275
Walking Purchase, 125
Wall Street Journal, 620
Wallace, George, 592, 611, 611t
Wallace, Henry A., 563t
Walton, George, 199
Wampanoags, 69–71, 78
Wanamakers stores, 396, 422
War Bonds, World War II, 533i
War hawks, in Congress, early 18th century, 245–247
War Industries Board, 477
War Labor Board, 477
War of 1812, 247–250, 248m
   African Americans and, 247i, 250
   British prisoners in, 247i
   events leading to, 244–245
   impact of, 240, 244, 251–252, 253
   Native Americans in, 249–250
   northern front, 247–248, 248m
   peace agreement, 250
   veteran's land grants, 275
War of Spanish Succession, 60, 75, 77
War of the League of Augsburg, 75
War on Drugs
   in 1980s, 647
   in 1990s, 658
War on Poverty, 597
War on Terrorism. *See also* September 11th terrorist attacks
   homeland security in, 678–679
   Patriot Act and, 678
   as president's defining focus, 678
War Powers Act (1973), 625
Ward, Nancy, 252
Warfare, mechanization of, 472, 473i
Warner, George James, 232–233
Warren, Adelina Otero, 460
Warren, Earl
   Japanese internment and, 535
   Supreme Court under, 581, 599
   Warren Commission and, 593
Warren Commission, 593
Warsaw Pact, 557m, 584
Washington, Booker T., 427, 462
Washington, DC
   British burning of (1814), 248–249
   slavery and, 311, 322
Washington, George, 167i
   as commander of Continental Army, 175m, 185m
      on Army discipline and supply, 173, 181
      crossing the Delaware, 173, 175m
      defense of New York City, 174
      defense of Philadelphia, 174
      disease prevention efforts, 174
      and Newburgh Conspiracy, 195
      opponents of, 180
      public reaction to, 167, 167i
      retreat through New Jersey, 171–173
      siege of Yorktown, 186–187
      Southern command and, 186
      troop morale and, 173
      at Valley Forge, 180–181
   and Constitutional Convention, 4207
   and election of 1788, 217
   and election of 1792, 218
   and election of 1796, 220
   in French and Indian War, 131–132, 133m
   Indian wars and, 227
   on political parties, 218
   as president
      on entangling alliances, 2223
      farewell address, 222
      Neutrality Proclamation (1793), 219
      support for, 218
      Whiskey Rebellion and, 220–221, 221i
   in Revolutionary War, siege of Boston, 168
   and Society of the Cincinnati, 195
   western lands and, 143
Washington Post, 618
Washington Society, 297
Washington State and Territory, 324m
   statehood for, 384
   voting rights in, 420, 459–460
Water
   19th century, and disease, 393
   20th century
      and disease, 453
      and pollution, 599
Watergate scandal, 573, 613, 617–618, 625
Waters, Ethel, 495
Watie, Stand, 341
Watt, James, 642i, 642–643
Watts, in 1960s, riots in, 605
WAVES (Women Accepted for Voluntary Emergency Service), 540
Wayne, Anthony, 227
WCTU. *See* Women's Christian Temperance Union
Wealth
   in 18th century, North vs. South, 123
   in 1980s, 643–644, 644f
"Wealth" (Carnegie), 400
Weapons of mass destruction (WMD)
   in Iraq, as justification for U.S. invasion, 679–680
Weas, 288m. *See also* Ohio Confederacy
Weaver, James B., 397t, 431t
Weaver, Randy, 664
Webster, Daniel, 292, 292t
Webster, Noah, 196, 297
Weimar Republic, 484
Welfare Reform Act (1996), 667
Welfare state
   in 1930s, 522–524
      Great Depression and, 510
      New Deal and, 528
      two-track system of, 523–524
   in 1940s and 1950s, 552, 583
   in 1980s, 634, 640–641, 641
   in 1990s, reform of, 656, 667
Wells, Ida B., 426, 460
Wells-Barnett, Ida B. *See* Wells, Ida B.
Wesley, John, 126
West. *See also* Settlers; Territories
   18th century
      control of, under Articles of Confederation, 176
      division of, 199–201, 201m
      expansion into, 216–217
      Northwest Ordinance of 1787, 202–203, 210, 227, 229m
      Revolutionary War in, 183m
   19th century
      African Americans in, 230, 408–409, 408i
      economy of, 371
      Indian land losses in, 410m
      labor shortage in, 369–370
      land management in, 424–425
      manifest destiny, 300–301
      migration to, 252–253, 264–266, 279, 286m, 289–291
      opening of, Native Americans and, 357
      property rights in, 371
      railroads and, 372t
      routes to, 264–265
      segregation in, 408–409
      slavery in, 210, 226–227, 229–230, 256, 262–264, 263m, 265
      women's rights and, 419–420
   20th century
      growth of, 562
      nuclear sites in, 636
West, Benjamin, 188i
West, Mae, 527
West Central Africa. *See* Congo-Angola
West Coast. *See also* Alaska; California
   16th century, English exploration of, 27
   18th century
      British exploration of, 139–140
      Spanish exploration and colonization of, 141–142, 142m, 229i
   20th century, immigration to, 501m
West Germany, economy, in 1970s, 620
West Indies
   16th century, Spanish exploitation of, 18–19
   17th century, English colonization of, 46
   post-Revolution, British trade restrictions in, 202, 204
   slavery and, 90, 108, 293
West Virginia, formation of, 337
Western Federation of Miners, 430
Westmoreland, William, 602
Whaling industry, 124, 223i
What the Social Classes Owe to Each Other (Sumner), 399
Wheat belt, 386m
Whig(s)
   in American Revolution, 137–138
   political theory of, 148–149
Whig party
   19th century, 273, 295
   and election of 1836, 292, 292t
   and election of 1840, 294–295, 295t
   and election of 1844, 302, 302t
   and election of 1848, 321, 321t
   and election of 1852, 322, 322t
   and election of 1856, 325, 325t
Whiskey Rebellion, 220–221, 221i
White(s)
   in 1960s, anger of, 610–611
   in 1980s, religious right and, 645–646
   in 1990s
      as minority in California, 663
      status of, 660
   definition of, 454–455, 470
White, Hugh, 292, 292t
White, John, 28, 28i
White Antelope, 351, 351i
White Cloud, 279
White House plumbers, 612, 618
White House tapes, subpoena of, 618
White Indians, 292
White Sticks, 249–250

White supremacy doctrine. *See also*
    Apartheid
  in 19th century, 426, 434
  early 20th century, 492–495
  eugenics movement and, 454
  post-World War II, discrediting of, 552
Whitecaps, 403–404
Whitefield, George, 128i, 126–128
Whitewater scandal, 667
Whitman, Marcus, 290–291
Whitman, Narcissa, 290–291
Whitman, Walt, 318, 368
Whitman mission, 290i, 290–291
Whitney, Eli, 219
Whyte, William, 560, 588
Wichita Indians, 113, 114
Wickett, Susanna, 251–252
Wild and Scenic Rivers Act (1968), 599
Wild West show, 381, 395, 395i, 423
Wilderness Act (1964), 599
Wildlife, extinctions in Archaic era, 6–7
Wilkes, John, 144
Willard, Emma, 278
Willard, Frances, 420i
William and Mary, 73–74
William III, King of England, 59, 73–74
William of Orange, 74
Williams, John D., 361
Williams, Roger, 48–49
Williams, William Sherley, 291–292
Wills, Helen, 528
Wilmot, David, 304
Wilmot Proviso, 304, 306, 321
Wilson, Charles, 584
Wilson, Edith, 483
Wilson, Harriet, 320
Wilson, Woodrow
  antitrust activities, 473
  conservationism and, 473–474
  domestic policies, 473–474
  and election of 1912, 464, 464t
  and election of 1916, 473t, 475
  eugenics and, 497
  and League of Nations, 480, 482
  on Mexico, 469
  minorities and, 470
  monetary policy, 473
  stroke suffered by, 482, 483
  on unions, 471
  on women's suffrage, 470–471
  World War I and
    Fourteen Points, 480
    peace settlement and, 480–482
    purpose of fighting, 467
    sympathy for Entente, 475
    U.S. entry into, 476
    U.S. neutrality and, 472, 475, 476
Windmills, 412i
Windward Coast, Africa, 93, 93m, 96m–97m
Winnebagos, 57, 227, 274
The Winning of the West (Roosevelt), 435
Winthrop, John, 46–48, 49, 50
Wirt, William, 272t
Wirz, Henry, 352
Wisconsin, migration to, 283–284, 313–314
Wise, Stephen S., 541
Wobblies, 460
Wolfe, James, 133m
Wolfe, Payson, 352
Wolfe, Tom, 616
Wollstonecraft, Mary, 231
Woman in the Nineteenth Century (Fuller), 300
Women. *See also* African American women
  17th century
    Antinomian Crisis and, 49
    right of, in New York, 68
    and Salem witch hunts, 75–76

18th century
  education and, 233–234
  elite, 232–234
  in New England, 124
  nonelite, 234–235
  Republican Mothers, 232–234
  in Revolutionary War, 163, 179–180
  rights of, 163, 234
  voting rights, 163, 217
19th century
  abolitionism and, 293, 300, 320, 320i
  in Civil War
    black, 347–348
    Confederate, 344, 344i, 348–349
    Union, 347–348
  clubs and organizations, 434–436
  education and, 278, 298
  employment, 234–235, 277–278, 280, 298, 315i, 315–316
  individualism and, 320
  industrialization and, 254
  literature and, 300
  property rights, 300
  reform movements and, 297, 419–420, 419i–420i
  role and status of, 252, 277–278, 280, 281, 299, 318–319, 319i
  unions and, 315i, 376, 413–414
  urban migration and, 392
  voting rights, 373–374, 419–420
  working conditions of, 413
20th century
  activism of, 589, 589i
  Chinese-American, 450–451
  in Congress, 666
  discrimination against, 592, 629
  education and, 579, 630
  employment, 458–459, 502, 511, 538–540, 553, 578–579, 630–631, 632, 659i
  eugenics and, 497
  first to swim English Channel, 486i, 487
  first trans-Atlantic solo flight, 528, 528i
  gender roles and, 560
  as heroes, 528, 528i
  role and status of, 470, 486, 486i, 487, 493, 578–579, 615, 630–631, 661
  sports and, 486i, 487, 528, 631, 691i
  unions and, 446–447, 460, 502, 526–527
  voting rights, 459–460, 471
  welfare state and, 524
  in World War I, 477i, 478
  in World War II
    in armed forces, 540
    child care and, 540
    employment, 538–540
    minorities, 543
    unions and, 539
  in contemporary America, 692
Native American
  in 16th century, 28i
  first physician, 418i
  in Navajo culture, 64, 64i
  role and status of, 64, 64i, 115, 234, 243, 252, 278
  in World War II, 543
Title IX and, 692
Women Strike for Peace (WSP), 589, 589i
Women's Army Corps (WACs), 540, 542, 543
Women's Christian Temperance Union (WCTU), 419, 420i
Women's Council, 576i

Women's Emergency Brigade, 526
Women's Foreign Missionary Society, 419
Women's liberation movement
  in 1960s, 607–608, 608i
  in 1970s, 615, 628–632, 631–632
  in 1980s, opposition to, 645, 646
Women's rights movement
  18th century, 234
  19th century, 278, 320, 434–435, 436
    abolitionist movement and, 300, 320, 320i
    temperance movement and, 300
  20th century, 458–459, 470–471, 478–488, 573
Women's suffrage movement
  19th century, 373–374, 419–420, 434–435
  20th century, 459–460, 470i, 471
Wood Lake rebellion, 343
Woodhenge, 11
Woodhull, Victoria, 374
Woods, Tiger, 663, 663i
Woodward, Bob, 618
Woolman, John, 102–104
Woolworth lunch counter sit-ins, 583
Worcester v. Georgia (1832), 270
Work day
  eight hour
    activism for, 413, 415, 432, 461
    federal promotion of, 476
  ten-hour, introduction of, 459
Workers. *See also* Common man
  in Early Republic, plight of, 232
  19th century
    anarchist movement and, 415
    dangers faced by, 413, 413i
    industrial unrest, 413–415
    mechanization and, 385–386, 391
    plight of, 374–375, 430
    resentment of black workers, 288, 292, 322, 323
    and rise of corporations, 380
    unrest, 380, 412–416, 431
  early 20th century
    in 1920s, 501–502
    in 1930s, 511–512
    unrest, 471, 471i, 478, 482
  late 20th century
    in 1970s, 620
    in 1980s, voting tendencies of, 645
  plight of, 656–657, 658
Workers movements. *See also* Union(s)
  Early Republic, 231
  19th century, 375–376, 432–433
  20th century, 446–447, 460, 526–527
Workingmen's Party of California, 405
Workplace, early 19th century, transformation of, 253–254
Works Progress Administration (WPA), 523t, 524, 525i
World Anti-Slavery Convention (1840), 300
World Trade Center
  1993 bombing of, 671
  2001 attacks on. *See* September 11th terrorist attacks
World Trade Organization (WTO), protests against, 669i
World War I
  African Americans in, 478
  causes of, 467
  context of, 467–468
  disease in, 472
  Eastern and Western fronts, 478–480, 479m
  horrors of, 472, 473i
  impact of, 445
  peace settlement for, 480–482, 481m
  repression of dissent in, 477

U.S. economy and, 476, 477i
U.S. neutrality in, 471, 472, 475–476
U.S. preparation for, 469–470, 475, 476, 477
women in, 478, 478i
World War II
African Americans in, as soldiers, 542
casualties in, 530–531
cultural impact of, 507
destructiveness of, 552
employment in, 538–542
in Europe, 543–545, 544m
events leading to, 531–534
Japanese Americans in
internment of, 507, 534–536, 536m, 537i
in U.S. Army, 530, 535–536, 537i, 547
Japanese brutality, 546
Jews in
Holocaust, 530–531, 540–541, 547, 563
immigration by, 541
in Nazi Germany, 532
U.S. antisemitism and, 540
minorities and, 530–531, 539, 575
Native Americans in, 530, 543
in North Africa, 544m, 545
in Pacific, 545–547, 546m
peace settlement, 547–548
Pearl Harbor attack, 506, 534, 535i
post-War occupations, 556–558, 557m
racist attitudes and, 540–543, 546
reconstruction planning, 507
segregation in, 542
U.S. censorship in, 538
U.S. domestic impact, 531
U.S. entry into, resistance to, 533–544

U.S. home front, 537–540
morale in, 538
racial tension in, 541, 543
women workers, 538–540
U.S. migrations in, 536–537
U.S. power following, 543
U.S.-Soviet relations in, 544–545, 550, 550i
U.S. strategy in, 531
veterans, and GI Bill, 553, 575
war crimes trials, 558
women in
in armed forces, 540
child care and, 539
employment, 538–540
minorities, 542
unions and, 539
Wounded Knee, AIM occupation at (1973), 609
Wounded Knee massacre, 410, 422
Wovoka, 409–410
WPA. *See* Works Progress Administration
Wrangell-St. Elias National Park, 627
Writ of habeas corpus, suspension of, 341
WSP. *See* Women Strike for Peace
Wyandot Indians, 227, 288m
Wyoming
statehood for, 384
women's voting rights and, 420

X
XYZ affair, 222

Y
Yalta Conference (1945), 547
Yamasee Indians, 78, 104

Yamasee War, 78
Yank, 539
Yankee Strip, 313–314
Yates, Robert, 208
Yazoo Act (1795), 228
Yazoo claim, 199
Yellow fever, 55
Yellow journalism, 437
Yellowstone National Park, 372
Yeltsin, Boris, 651
Yick Wo, 406
Yick Wo v. *Hopkins* (1886), 406
Yorktown, siege of, 185m, 186–187, 187i
Yosemite Indians, 424
Yosemite National Park, 425, 462
Young, Brigham, 289
Yucca Flat, 559i
Yugoslavia
post-World War II, 557m
collapse of, 670, 671m
creation of, 481m
Yuma Indians, 141
Yuma Revolt, 141, 142m

Z
Zavala, Lorenzo de, 301
Zheng He, 13, 16m–17m
Zimbabwe, establishment of, 626
Zimmerman, Arthur, 476
Zimmerman telegram, 476
Zoning, late 19th century, 393
Zoot suits, 543
Zuni Indians, 11, 23